STICKY WRISTS

By Dan Melynden
(Daniel Duckfield)

Chapter 1	So Beginneth the Lesson	Page 8
Chapter 2	A New Beginning	Page 30
Chapter 3	The Golden Eagle	Page 43
Chapter 4	A Sting in the Tail	Page 60
Chapter 5	All Change	Page 83
Chapter 6	Follow the Rules	Page 106
Chapter 7	A Trip to the Land Of Song	Page 122
Chapter 8	A Jolly Xmas	Page 135
Chapter 9	Pints & Poems	Page 147
Chapter 10	A Chinese Every Night	Page 191
Chapter 11	Trains & Pains	Page 233
Chapter 12	The Hardest Time Of All	Page 278
Chapter 13	In Sickness & In Health	Page 326
Chapter 14	A Will to Win	Page 359
Chapter 15	Another Life Begins	Page 414
Chapter 16	Life Begins Again	Page 461
Chapter 17	The beginning of the end	Page 490
Chapter 18	Is this the end	Page 505

This book was written by a totally blind man and without any help from any seeing person. It took 7 years to complete and was even proof read letter by letter over the last 13 months by him as any seeing person wanted over 2 thousand to do this another rip off for any blind person as always. I only learned by the use of a speech system named J.A.W.S to learn to do this since I went blind and rever used a computer until I went blind, and so it shows in this book as punctuation is as it was written and over the 7 years you can see the improvementas the book goes along as it would be seen by any blind man. So please excuse any imperfection as it has been written as it would be conceived by any blind man and if I could see it it would be perfect.

FORWARD

Black, black it is all black, like a coal miner underground turning his cap lamp off sheer blackness. I was in Singleton hospital on the top floor watching the tide go out that took it seemed forever and little did I know that was going to be the very last thing my eyes would see, the following morning I had an operation on my eyes and I would be living the rest of my life in darkness.
My life had now changed and my mind started to run away with itself I wanted to die and nothing else would do, panic was now a part of my life from that day on and there was no way I could cope with this, it's the worst thing that could happen to anyone this was deaths brother. There is nothing I could now possibly do for myself, I can't let others do things for me I am my own man I do not want help I want to do this for myself but I can't so please somebody stand me on a train track and let the train end it for me for good. I am no good to anyone and life is over for me as from that awful day forward, I am finished.

Danny has had an adventure he never wanted and his life had been split into two halves, The seeing man who stood arrow straight and tall with not much of a care in the world and the blind man stopped in his tracks like a car hitting a brick wall and his life turned tragically around, so he felt small and unimportant to the human race and many people he had known all his life. Danny only wanted death to come as fast as it could so he could escape, a life with no future of no sense, more a existence than a life, he felt he was invisible as he remembered when he could see he never noticed a blind person on the street but they were there. His friends made him feel as if he was a joke now he was blind and not to be taken seriously, an incompetent person who knows nothing about life anymore, even believing he was a man who was using the system to live off as if there was nothing wrong with him. People started talking for him, making decisions for him, pulling him around like you would pull a dog on a lead, even shouting at him and talking amongst themselves with other people as if he was not there. He was someone to laugh at, even being spat at because of his blindness, to an eventual time when the thought of going out on the street was not for him and better to stay indoors and let other people do the shopping and other things for him and never go out ever again unless picked up from the door and be brought back to his door, nothing in between, as many of the blind people do this time in the twenty first century, rather than be jeered at or made fun of. A sad existence if you could only Imagine or is this the way to be? You will if you looked see thousands of people like this living as hermits out of society's way so as not to be a nuisance. Danny thought not he has

battled against the people who would rather be like this and got on his high horse and fought back and said we must be counted as normal people who have got as much to offer as anyone else on this planet, in fact he feels now that blind people are more loving than any seeing person he knows , they see things as they are, they tell sport things like football as they hear it, politicians as they tell their ~~ the noint in question, because a blind man's ears are so well trainec s are easier to define, because they cannot see th  who talk to them like little kids always want some with them or have your insurances etc. with them idiot. People think how the world is to blind pe int to understand and it's them that have the prob

Well that is the serious bit over now; let us start as I mean to go on. My name is Daniel Duckfield and this book is a bit of a biography, after I went blind through no fault of my own. This is not a book about poor old blind people it is about adjustment after a person went blind through no fault of his own and the trauma he went through and will not except he is any different now, he is the same man full of fun and Jokes, but will not be bullied into thinking he has not got a place in this world. He can't be as good as Joe Blogs because he cannot see and after you start reading this book you will forget it is about a blind man. All characters in this book are real and some names have been changed for fear of their reaction, ha, ha, and the 3 main characters Niel, Danny and Jeff are very real and loved to have fun although some of the events are slightly exaggerated so as to get the full Impact of their adventures together. The fun was a way of getting into a new way of living and not worrying about making fools of themselves and helping the younger students along the way to realise their potential and what they are able to understand as I once was asked by a young totally blind girl who had never seen, "what is water like? It's funny to touch. What colour is it? And why does it slide through my hands? Please tell me what it looks like." As a onetime seeing person we had the answers although it was hard to explain the water question. It was possible to get them closer to the answers and if people who can see and who can do things blind people can't had the same temperament, life on this planet would be a much happier experience for all.

It was 1997 when I realised something was going wrong, I was working as a self-employed builder and Conservatory erector and I was having lots of trouble with my whole body, I was losing weight rapidly and having trouble with my nervous system. I eventually came down to just under 9 stone in weight and became very ill indeed and the whole of my nervous system collapsed. I was on many pills by this Time and I felt as if I was dying, then one day whilst driving to work I could see what appeared to be cobwebs floating in my vision, another day driving back from France one dark night I recall pain from the headlights coming towards me was incredible and I had to pull over and wait until it was light. This panicked me and as soon as I was back in Wales I went straight to the hospital, I told them what had happened and they did some tests and said I had conjunctivitis and there was no need to worry, this continued for some months, it gradually got worse as the days went by, my eyesight was disappearing and I was very concerned. Well it was now January 1998 and things were serious I had given up work and was very ill indeed and didn't know where to turn so I was speaking to my sister in law and she suggested I went to see a man in London and he was a homeopathic doctor and he could help me as the medical profession had let me down, I was not sure about this but did as she said. I gave it a go and went to London, I saw the doctor who gave me medication which cost me £60, this treatment was to treat the symptoms from which I was suffering and it was cheap as he dropped the consultancy charge because I had travelled so far. I thought this was going to be a waste of time so I took the tablets and medicines he gave me as prescribed, at first it appeared that the medication was not doing anything. My next appointment came around quickly and I travelled again to London, by this time I had given up smoking and drinking and had been in hospital a few times in agony. I got to see the homeopathic Doctor who examined me and changed some of my medication which he had previously prescribed. I then decided that the medicine I was taking from my Dr at home was doing some damage as I was taking pills for a certain problem and they were having an effect on something else in my body, so I was taking pills to stop this reaction and these tablets were causing another problem and so on and so on. I then decided to start from scratch and do away with my chemical tablets from the national health as I got to the point where I had nothing to lose. I collected them all together removing them from their packaging and put them in a bucket, There were a lot of tablet's, 26 daily', I dumped the tablet's in the toilet, I then went to put the bucket away by the time I got back to flush the toilet the tablet's had all infused together and were foaming up like an acid in the water. The toilet was about to overflow so I flushed quickly, Imagine what damage they were doing to my stomach if that's what they were doing in the water; I have never taken chemical medicine since. Since this day I have continued to take the homeopathic medicines, it amazed me how much better I was getting I put weight on and my nervous system Improved in a few years, however my eyesight was getting worse and worse, this was due to laser treatment, I was having at the hospital. I felt I didn't want to take a chance with my eyes. How wrong could I be? I wished I had let my Homeopathic Dr treat this also, his name was Dr Jan-De-Vries and he was brilliant, I am under no illusion that it is because of him I am alive to write this book.

It was now 1999 and I had given up driving, depression had set in and I was in a downward spiral, my eyesight was so bad I was in the hospital. I attended an appointment this one week as usual there I was greeted with panic, my consultant was desperately trying to get hold of a chief consultant in Swansea to see me Immediately as a Matter of urgency, at this point I became worried, I was rushed down to the chief consultant Immediately in Singleton Hospital in Swansea, I met this man who had travelled the world and was a expert in ophthalmology. He saw me Immediately it was so urgent I was seen in the evening when the department was closed and the news was not good I remember his words to this day, he said "The last Time I seen eyes this bad was in the outback in Australia on an aborigine who had never even seen a white man in his life, it is really bad, I don't know what I am going to do about this, I wished you had seen me earlier, my god."

I knew from that day on I was going to go totally blind and nothing could stop it, I just felt it. I was given some powerful laser treatment Immediately and was taken in the hospital within a few days. The surgeon would be the consultant who would operate on my left eye straight away, without delay. He told me that the right eye had, had it but he will do his best with my left one, he also told me he then proceeded to tell me that the operation would be carried out under local anaesthetic because of my diabetes it was too much of a risk to knock me out. This really frightened me and he was not happy doing it this way but it was the only option I had left at this point. I only had 3 days to prepare myself for surgery, knowing that I would be awake. I remember going into Singleton Hospital in Swansea, It was on the top floor and I was on a ward of 8 beds on my own and the view was beautiful

looking out on Swansea Bay, I could see the sea going out, I watched this for about 3 hours and went to bed to rest before my operation. I had difficulty sleeping and a kind nurse popped home to fetch a radio for me to keep me company, I thought that was very kind or did she know something I didn't? the next morning I was awoken and taken down to the theatre on a trolley, there I was prepped and although I was used to needles I was not used to needles being used to freeze my eyes, it was horrible first the needle would be pushed into one corner of my eye, it went in about one inch to the back of my eye and then the same in the other corner. My whole forehead went numb; All the while I was totally conscious and could see everything going on. I remember laying there and he cut the top of my eye off like taking the top off a boiled egg for breakfast, exactly like that. He then started work on my eye and he put music on which was comforting and something I liked it was Simon and Garfunkel's Greatest Hit's. The operation lasted for four hours and ten minutes, towards the end the operation became very excruciating indeed, the pain was seriously bad and it left me suffering all day. I had an aluminium plate placed over my eye and I don't remember anything much for the rest of the day, I just lay there feeling as if I was going to die, then I fell asleep after many injections for the pain, little did I know that the day before when I was watching the tide going out was the last thing I would ever see. From that day on I have never seen and I totally lost control of my life from then on.

It was December 1999 just before the millennium, what a time for this to happen. The world was ready to celebrate the millennium, while I was to celebrate the rest of my life in darkness as a blind person, how cruel was that? I was devastated and just wanted to die, I tried to end my life using my diabetic insulin and ended up in hospital a few times, without effect. I got really angry and hated everyone and in turn they all began to hate me. I needed anger management. Why me? What had I ever done to deserve this? Then as if by magic all my friends disappeared and no one came to see me, or try to help me get over it. Everyone had changed the way they were around me, even close family acted the same way.

I was now all alone, trying to get to grips with this awful affliction, I felt like I just wanted to roll up in a ball and die; I went to bed hoping to die as soon as possible. Later I was told that I had, had a nervous breakdown, which came as no surprise as the shock of losing my eyesight so quickly set in. Could you Imagine it, one day you are looking at a nice girl in a mini skirt walking by, driving your car, off on holidays and going out on nice sunny days and then all that is gone, not even in the blink of an eye. I was unfortunate enough to miss out on seeing any of my grandchildren, I missed the little things like sitting down watching television and playing with your children and then it hits you again with nothing to look forward to, nothing but blackness. People never realise the trauma that I went through, I can honestly say that it's the worst thing that could possibly happen to anyone. If you go deaf, you can at least get on with your life, if you lose a leg you can still get on with your life, but when a seeing person goes blind there are a lot of adjustments to make and get used to before you can regain any sense of normality. To make a simple cup of tea is very difficult when you can't see the cup and where to pour boiling hot water. I used to love to watch a few sports, but now I can't even watch Wales's vs England in a simple rugby match, or watch formula 1 racing. I can't even take the dog for a walk up the road, or even go up the shop for a paper, even if I could, I would not be able to read the paper. In the beginning I missed not being able to go down the club or pub for a pint by myself. I got fed up of having to rely on everyone else to help me do almost everything. Sex with your partner is hopeless as you can't see her to get excited, as you are blind, half the women in the county could be standing in front of you naked and you would not know. , As the joke goes 'How do you spot a blind man on a nudist beach?' It's not that hard. I bet as you are reading, you are thinking I went blind because of my diabetes, well you would be wrong, it was smoking that caused this trauma.

So it was Time for all the nonsense of the do gooders coming along to make me feel good about myself. I was so depressed I needed death and nothing else would do! Well after a few months I began to get myself together as best as I could and tried to think what my future was going to be all about. I started to think that maybe I could do this and i set my mind to giving it a go, as I could see my children getting upset and I felt I was not being fair to them, because I love them very much. I soon realised the do gooders were the ones who would help me more than I thought. I met two people who changed my life forever, one such person was a patient lady who was formerly a nun and I thought here we go, but actually she was a wonderful person, her name was Margaret Monkhouse and was worth her weight in gold. Many times she came along and sorted out my problems with a positive effect, she was easy to talk to and made it easy to ask anything, nothing was ever a problem. She was truly an angel in disguise to me, I eventually began to see my life having some purpose and problems of everyday life through being blind get a little easier but still very hard, with some flashes of normality coming back to me. Margaret worked tirelessly and nothing was too big or much of a problem for her.
The other lady who made my life worth living was a wonderful woman named Catherine Greenwood, she had plenty of time for me, she was so patient and taught me to read brail, she also taught me how to cope with going out and about, that believe me was nerve wrecking indeed. I felt safe with Catherine and she had a great sense of humour with it, this really helped me to relax and feel at home. Eventually I began to see light at the end of the tunnel with the help these ladies were giving me; it was possible to do many things in my condition. I remember a time with Catherine when I had trouble with my now ex-wife not having patience taking me to town and she said to Catherine "Well he is a pain, he goes so slowly and there is nothing for him to worry about." Catherine said to her "Ok I should have done this with you when I suggested you leading Danny through town, have you got a scarf and we will go for a walk Angie." Angie got the scarf and went outside, she used the scarf to cover her eyes and so as she could not see where she was going. Catherine then lead Angie in a walk around familiar territory which took about 15 minutes, to help her understand how it felt. After their little adventure Catherine and Angie sat in the lounge and Angie said "Oh my god, I never realised it was that bad, I am a nervous wreck!" she sat there shaking and needed a fag and a cup of strong tea to settle her down, Catherine said chuckling "Now you can see what he is going through Angie, it's a terrible affliction and you take your eyesight for granted and it's not until you lose it does it almost destroy you." Angie "Yes I see what you mean, that was awful and I will take my time from now on." From that day I started to make sense of a lot of things and was thankful for those ladies I so called do gooders, I would never have got on with my life if it wasn't for them.
The year 2000 was the slowest year of my life, but I decided to pull my socks up and try and see what this blindness was all about. I remember a little thought went through my mind, I was 44, I had seen for most of those years, but there was so many who had never seen at all. What's more, I thought of those poor people much worse off than me who never even see their second birthday in many countries, so what have I got to complain about. I was so weak now with everything that had happened I felt so ill I needed to get in the gym and try

6

to regain some strength, it was agony but I got on with it. I was told I could learn to use a computer with a system called Jaws a speech programme that is for blind people. I visited my local college to try to find out more, they enrolled me and I had a few good months there with a partially sighted man called Steve Jones, he remembered me from my D.J years and we had some fun during my time in the college. It was at Bridgend college that I found my sense of humour, it just came flooding back, it is here my story begins and I believe my life took a U-turn and an incredible Journey of tears, pain, love, determination and courage started, to bring me to here where I am now, and most of all the fun that I had learning to be blind. I am going to tell this story from the outside looking in.

CHAPTER 1
SO BEGINNETH THE LESSON.

How am I going to find my way around the college? How am I going to be able to eat? If I can't see how am I going to be able to use the computer? I have never even known how to turn one on, it's going to be Impossible, I realised it was going to be nerve racking for me and I was about to realise just how difficult it was going to be and the most frustrating thing I would ever experience. I knew I was going to make a complete fool of myself without question. My first day as a blind fool, this was going to be something else. A taxi picked me up and I was led out by my wife who was glad to see the back of me because of the way I had become. It was like going to infant's school all over again I was almost in tears getting into that taxi and I remember I was trembling so bad I thought I was going to collapse. I sat by the taxi driver and thought now what was I going to do? But it was amazing Danny said "Allright drive, you know where I am going I hope? " He replied "Yes I do so sit back and relax." This Danny did but he found himself talking away like an old man, as if he had not talked to anyone for years. When they got to the college he thought here we go. He was in a real state, he thought he was going to have a heart attack, the driver led him into the building and then another person took him into the lecture room. He was shocked how easy it was to get into the access centre. They were greeted by a Lady lecturer named Annette and Danny was introduced to everyone. Danny had it in his mind these people were all normal and had nothing wrong with them, how wrong Danny was they had Bob who was an ex speedboat racing champion, he had lost his arm, part of his head and had severe damage to his legs through a racing accident. Another man named Jim was in a wheelchair and Rhys he was totally unable to use his body and was learning to use a computer that was speech activated. Tracy she had multiple sclerosis and was in a wheelchair and a lovely lady Yvette she was 18 and had a brain tumour, a delightful young Lady. Danny was going to get on well with these people for the next couple of months. The building he studied in was all kitted out for all different disabilities and even had residential flats across the road, for the colleges disabled students to stay. Danny soon began to settle in and was introduced to a man named Jonathan Warren, Danny called him bunny, he was the man who would teach Danny about J.A.W.S. and it was some time before Danny realised he was disabled too. Jonathan was an epileptic and it was not mild in him. Next in walked another man with S.P. an eye problem that takes years to affect you before you become totally blind. This was Steve Jones, Danny hit it off straight away with Steve, he was to be his guide for the first part of his stay, they even shared taxis for a week or two and Danny had a cane but had no clue how to use it properly.

Danny first sat in front of this Computer at the age of 44, having never used a computer before, he was about to learn how to with great difficulty, he thought. When he turned it on it spoke to him, Danny was amazed by this and he started to play with the keys and he was hooked. Jonathan then started telling Danny to use some of the keys showing him how it worked. He just went off giving Danny orders, as if Danny knew how to use a computer, but Danny soon stopped him and said "I can't see the keys so I must learn where they are." He was lost as to how he was going to learn this so Danny took over and taught himself by trial and error, Danny learnt this in less than a week he was determined he just sat there A BBB CCC DDD EEE FFF..... Right the way through the alphabet every day for a week, until he knew them off by heart. Danny soon became quicker than those who had been using the computer for a coup e of years. Lessons began but with great difficulty, little did Danny know that Jonathan was also learning how to use the J.A.W.S. programme to be able to teach Danny. So much for Danny's learning shouldn't the teacher know what they are teaching, what a shambles it was a nightmare but not Jonathans fault. Danny suddenly realised this course was a bit of a joke, sometimes Jonathan was ill and he never turned up. If he wasn't there, there was no one else to teach Danny, so Danny found himself going to college and going home a lot of the time to. This place was run by a shoestring, non-effective for a blind man, this made Danny furious, but Danny let them know what he thought. Great Danny thought, more frustration to go with his already mixed up head, the college soon became a place to clown around and Danny took full advantage of this opportunity and he quickly became the joker, creating a lot of fun.

It was a few weeks later and his luck had changed, he met a man who would be one of his life savers, a man who he gave a Job to some years earlier when no one would employ him and his name was Gareth Garfield (Gaffo) Gareth was a man who was a great friend to Danny's family and his younger brother who had also given him a Job. Gareth was a man who found it seriously hard to learn as he had severe dyslexia and found it virtually hard to understand anything, but this man had a heart of gold indeed, Immediately he took Danny under his wing and he led him everywhere and would run to beat anyone else to lead Danny to breakfast and dinner. He would pick him up in the morning and take him home in the night and Danny was so pleased to have someone so kind to guide him. They formed a little posse, consisting of Danny, Steve and Gaffo the 3 stooges look out college. There are some stories they can still laugh about, One day Gaffo, Danny and Steve were sitting in the canteen having dinner and Danny had chips and pasty, well they sat and ate and Danny said after finishing his meal "Well there were not many chips were there?" Gaffo and Steve started laughing out loud and Danny said "What's the Matter?" Gaffo said "You have eaten all the chips in the middle of the plate and left loads all around the edge of the plate." There were many such occasions and Danny recalls a time when he was eating and he pressed the fork into a piece of fish and it flew off the plate and landed in a person's lap opposite, Danny realised eating was hard and embarrassing. Danny soon started to buy dark clothes as they didn't show the stains.

Danny also found difficulties with the toilet division, on many occasions he found after relieving himself that the toilet lid was down, and by damn it doesn't half make a mess on your shoes and jeans when it splashes and bounces off the lid. It's very embarrassing walking around smelling of urine. However nothing was to beat the day he trod in dog dung and he didn't realise it, trampling it all through the college, until one day he arrived with his jumper inside out, how much more embarrassing could it get, he soon learnt humility and was able to laugh at himself.

Soon Danny started to pick up certain things on the computer after many attempts, as poor young Jonathan did not fully understand the programme himself. It was a farce and the management knew it and it was not Jonathan's fault. Soon Jonathan was to become the only person able to teach the J.A.W.S. programme, but he was paid a pittance, but eventually he became very good at teaching it. Danny was getting on with his life and had started to get fed up of people walking all over him and was about to stand up for himself. He came across this woman who was really snobby and thought she was better than everyone else, she was attending the same class as Danny, so Danny and Steve set out to play a practical joke on her. Steve had a gadget which was a farting machine and he showed it to Danny and Danny thought excellent this is something we can really have some fun with. Steve and Danny decided to put the speaker behind her computer out of sight, it had a radio remote control which could be hidden in your hand, when pressed the switch would let out a series of different fart sounds. So Steve and Danny sat down at their stations and put on their headphones, it was dead quiet and Steve pressed the button and it sounded as if she had farted, she looked up but Steve and Danny kept straight faces, they just looked up as if to say what was that? Steve left it a little while and he pressed it again, the fart sound that came out and made it look as if she had done it again, so Danny looked towards her and apparently she was as red as a tomato and Danny gave a little grin, they found it very hard not to burst out laughing. She carried on but was visibly embarrassed, well Steve pressed the button again this time it was a rasper of a fart and the whole class looked at her and laughed, but she was insistent and kept saying "It's not me, it's not me." After a bit of laughter the class all got down to it again and were just waiting for another fart, but Steve held on for about 3 minutes and pressed the button twice an what a set of fart sounds came out, she jumped up in horror and started shouting. The whole class were in stitches and rolling around laughing, even the tutors were laughing but the miserable woman stormed out and never returned. They really did have some fun with that gadget for some time.

Danny however was not a 100% happy at the college as it felt like a home for stupid people and he felt as if he was inadequate which made him want to get out of there as soon as possible. The reason for feeling like this started when ordinary people in the college showed lack of thought for any of the people Danny had become friends with, all because they were disabled in some way or another. It all started one day when a fire alarm went off in his access centre, they had never done a fire drill and it caused a bad accident. Many people were laughing at them because it was funny I mean what if it had been a real fire. How embarrassing for them. This fire alarm went off one morning when everyone was working on the computers quietly and fair play there was no panicking, everyone was all told what to do. Danny grabbed hold of the handles of Jim's wheelchair and pushed him outside. Jim would guide his wheel's with his hands and Danny powered him along, they all learned how to help each other out. The fire door was opened and down the ramp they all went, all of a sudden they came to a sudden halt as the wheelchair rolled into gravel, the front wheels had dug in, The next thing Danny knew he was in a heap on the floor, poor Jim had been tipped out of the wheelchair onto the floor and Danny had gone tumbling over the top injuring both of them. So who's brilliant idea was it to put down loose chippings outside of a fire door of a wheel chair ramp from a disabled users access centre and all the others behind were stuck behind Danny and some still in the building. After this incident there were people back and forth for the next few days, trying to find out what had happened. There was never any explanation for why the chippings were ever laid there, nor was there any apology for their accident ever happening. Danny would often sit in his bedroom reflecting on this incicent, even bursting into tears, how let down they all really were, Luckily they never had serious injuries, but would often hear the other kids heckling them in the cafeteria, which left Danny feeling even lower, feeling like a no body, even Danny's wife and some of his neighbours ignored him, Danny was sinking fast and heading back into that deep dark depression that clouded his life before was hovering over him again.

Then one day at college two new students started, they made Danny feel completely normal. The first woman was named Caroline Wilkinson. Caroline was totally blind from birth and Danny assumed she was in her early thirties; she Impressed Danny, but why? Because here is a blind woman living by herself, self-sufficient holding down a full time job with the Police Force. How can this be? Danny asked himself. Danny spoke to her, "Hello Caroline my name is Daniel but people call me Danny." She replied "Well hello I thought you were blind as I could hear the Jaws on your computer , so how long have you been blind?" "Only recently I am having a go with this J.A.W.S. programme as I need to get some sort of normality back in my life." Caroline replied "Yes I know what you mean but it is easy when you get used to it, believe me." Danny then said "Do you think so I hope you are right but it's fun, tell me is it true you work for the Police?" "Yes I do, I sit in the court and take all the notes of many cases, I was taught to do this and have never looked back." Danny "And I believe you live in a bungalow by yourself, is that true?" Caroline replied "Yes it is, why do you ask?" Danny says "How do you manage by yourself? How can you do this being blind? Are you totally blind?" It was like Danny was asking her a quick fire round of questions on a game show and Caroline sighed and answered "I don't understand, yes I am totally blind and that does not mean I can't look after myself. I know where everything is and I have all the gadgets I need to assist me." Danny "Please don't think I'm nosey, but I can't see how you can do this, am I missing something?" She chuckled back "I see now what you mean; I have been blind all my life so it was easier for me, as I had to do it or I would starve. But it's not the end of the world when you go blind, you will learn to do all this by yourself I assure you, you will be cooking for yourself and going out on your own and many other things. It all just takes time you will see." With a puzzled look on Danny's face he replied "I don't think so it's Impossible I think." "You will think that now, but you will do something one day and only because you have to and you will think to yourself, that was easier than I could have Imagined. You will do it again and again, until you get braver and braver, you wait and see." She said to him with her soothing voice. Danny then said "I hope you are right I really do, I can't see me walking through Bridgend by myself and how does it work? A guide dog I bet." "No I have not got a guide dog, I use a simple white cane that's all and if you do it all the time it's like washing your face, after a while it is natural, you'll see." With sincerity Danny replied "I suppose if you keep on doing it long enough it will stick, well I can't wait for that day." Caroline and Danny talked for a long time and a few days later someone else surprised Danny a Dr, who made an Impact on him, whether it was because she was a Dr, and they were not supposed to go blind as far as Danny was concerned. He met her in his class one morning and he introduced himself to her "Hello my name is Danny and you are?" She replied "I am Christine and I am from Porthcawl, it is nice to meet you." "So have you been blind for long Christine?" She briskly replied "I have not been visually Impaired for long and this is a refresher course for me on the super nova and you?" Danny replied "I went blind in December last year a cock up by some bloody doctors in the Princess of Wales hospital, they are idiots some of these doctors" Christine sat up when Danny said this and said "Do you think so and do you feel like that about all doctors or just them?" So Danny continued with his story "No just them I was miss-diagnosed over a period of 14 months and when they realised it, it was too late and I lost everything almost my Job my car and my wife by the looks of it, so you can understand why I feel like that." "I was just asking because I am a Doctor myself and so even doctors are not Immune you see." Laughing Danny replied "Right I have put my foot in it again I see, sorry, me and my big mouth." Christine smiled and said "It's ok I can understand it Danny, I would feel the same myself." Danny was happy she was so nice and said "I never pictured a doctor having an eye problem." "Well there we go then, I am like a fish out of water since it happened mind, how about you? How do you feel?" Danny thought and replies "Exactly the same and a bit embarrassed sometimes." "Yes I know, so you said your wife is getting a divorce because you have gone blind or what?" Danny "Yes, I don't know I just think she is going to divorce me as we have gone through a seriously bad patch with me going blind and everything else. I really think she will

11

in time and what about you? Are you married?" "Yes and my husband is also a doctor he is well known his last name is Dr. Cobbledick that's a mouthful." She laughed. Jokingly Danny said "If you think that's bad my last name is Duckfield ha, I hope you are staying here for a while and we can compare notes as we go along." "Good idea, do you use Supa nova then or Jaws?" "I used to use Supa nova but I find the voice is too robotic and I like the jaws as the voices are more human and you can change them to suit yourself." Danny said quietly "Yes I've heard that myself, can I try it sometime?" Danny replied "Of course you can and you can try my Jaws also ha, ha." Christine smiled and said "I see a practical joker, that's good I like someone with a sense of humour, let's all get together for dinner with Caroline for a good chat."

At this dinner some days later and Danny, Christine and Caroline were comparing notes, Danny says "It's nice to be in the middle of 2 such lovely women but I fear not for much longer, as I am not happy with the tutoring here it's terrible." Caroline feeling sorry for Jonathan snaps at Danny. "Oh, poor Jonathan he tries his very best he really does, don't be nasty about him he is a lovely man too. " Christine backs her up and says "Oh Danny she is right, he is such a tryer, and he has epilepsy too." Danny interrupted and said "I am not referring to bunny he is the only one here that has any clue what he is doing with the blind, I am referring to the staff in the higher element they don't give a stuff. If Jonathan left here they would be stuffed and so would I, I mean it's, like they just want to get the unemployment figures down and as long as we don't ruffle their feathers that's ok, it's a Joke here. I am just about fed up with it, because every time I want something I have to make a fuss." Caroline agreed with Danny and replied "Yes I know it can be frustrating, but there is not much we can do is there?" Danny replies "Not really, and if you cause a fuss you are always in danger in getting yourself black balled as they say in the lodge, but I agree it's not fair and I hope you will stay it's nice the three of us comparing notes and being very helpful to one another." Christine chirped in. "Yes and we have Caroline to help us as she is a veteran now." Danny said "She has excited my mind at some of the possibilities." Christine smirking says "Oh yes Caroline, so what is this all about then?" Caroline blushing giggles out loud and says "He is talking about being able to get around with a cane and other things that are possible even when you are blind." Danny said "I just sit in the house listening to my music; I don't go anywhere except around my garden." Caroline said "I am also a pianist and have been on the television and the radio. I have done a solo for the orchestra of Wales. Have you heard it?" Christine was Impressed by this and said "Never, I have not heard about this have you got any recordings, if you have you must bring it in for us to hear please." Danny replied "Yes you must and I am in the company of class then, I am getting more and more excited about this blindness as the days go on."

The girls and Danny got to be very good friends and so did many of the other people within their class. One day Danny spoke to a delightful girl named Yvette although she was a very shy girl, he took a liking to her, Danny was helped by her one day, she had a limp and used a stick for walking and for a 18 year old girl this was not good, she guided Danny back to his desk, they both struck up a conversation and Danny said "Well thank you Yvette I do really appreciate it, i feel really it now being escorted by a lovely pretty teenager, I will be bragging about this forever." Yvette chuckled and replied "Don't be silly, I am not special, anyone would have given you a helping hand." Danny says "I don't think so. I'm Impressed with you; most teenagers would run a mile instead of helping an old blind man, but not you a true princess. I am Impressed with a lovely pair of boobs helping me, I think you are so special to be so caring and where are you from then?" Yvette went red and says "I am from

Gilfach Goch." Danny replied "I used to do a lot of work up there, I am from Bettws." Yvette got excited when Danny said this and replies "I have an uncle living up there, Derek Williams, do you know him?" Danny looked shocked and replied with shock in his voice "Well bloody hell, big D, he is married to Denise Hodges of course I know him, he is a brickie isn't he?" "Yes that's right. So you know him well then? He's a hell of a boy and a good laugh but he likes his drink." Danny was laughing and said "You can say that again. He worked for me from time to time and I had to go and find him many a time in a pub, but what a brilliant brickie and a lovely chap, He gives his wife the run around sometimes mind, he goes out with the boys on Friday night and she don't see him for the weekend ha, ha." They both chuckled. Danny continues "I am the reason he married Denise and the reason that most of the people in Bettws got married in the seventies and early eighties." "How do you make that out then?" Danny smiled and says "Because early in the 70's I was working with a man and his disco was called Sam's Incredible Wax Collection' and I got the club to start disco's there, it was such a success that the club became the sixth richest club in Britain. People came from all over the valleys to dance there and they used to queue up for hours just to get in, it was here everyone ended up getting together and many got married. Ask your uncle he will back me up on this and if it wasn't for the committee of Bettws Social club and me getting together and doing this he would have never have met Denise, So there, something new you learned." Yvette "Yes I remember him saying something well, well I never so it's your fault ha, ha." She laughed. Danny says "You really do have a great sense of humour; I only wish I was a lot younger, no one else would stand a chance. Ok. See you later Yvette and thanks, remember me to your uncle if you see him." Yvette went back to the other side of the room and the lecture started.

A few days later and they met up again, the same thing she helped Danny to his desk and she said "I was talking to big D; he said you were a nice man and he loved doing work for you, He told me about the day you both went to work only to end up drinking all day, so funny, but he has fond memories and said to say hello." Danny said "I bet he told you to give me a kiss too didn't he?" Yvette blushed and said "No he didn't, I once kissed a boy in a cupboard you know it was nice mind ha, ha." Danny teased her and one or two others were listening, Danny said "I want a kiss before you leave me on my own as I think you are so lovely even if I am too old, I can't understand why you haven't got a boyfriend I really can't, your so nice. I want a kiss on the cheek please or I will kiss you on the lips! "She giggled and said "I can't people are watching." So Danny put his arm around her and give her a smacker of a kiss on the cheeks and said "There you go, I am in love with you and I want to marry you." Someone said "You are already married." Danny looked down and said "Oh yes, I forgot, never mind I can't win an argument lately, sorry Yvette I only needed a kiss off such a lovely girl it will keep me smiling for a fortnight thanks." She said "Your welcome." Danny teasing said "And don't tell your uncle I don't want to get beat up, ha, ha." She replied "I won't and he will never hurt you he likes you too much and I will beat him up anyway ha, ha." Danny and Yvette always talked a lot and Danny always teased her but he really loved her in his own way. He often said he wished he was a lot younger, but he became like a father to her or at least a loving uncle and Danny still thinks about her to this very day hoping she met a nice young lad and is living happily ever after."

Jonathan one day was trying his best to teach Danny and it all went pear shaped and poor Jonathan showed Danny how serious it was with his health. He was teaching Danny and then all of a sudden he disappeared and Danny was still talking to him as if he was still there. He had only gone and had a serious Epileptic fit and fell to the floor, well of course

Danny did not realise until Annette rushed over to tend to him. The next thing the paramedics were there and tending to him, he had by now come around and was a little stunned as to what was happening and said Immediately. "I am not going to hospital so don't mention it, it is ok now." But the paramedics were insisting he did go, but Jonathan was not having any of it. After a while he got back on his seat by Danny and Danny broke the ice and said to Jonathan "Your an ignorant bugger, I was talking to you and you go and have a fit on me, no consideration at all, thanks mate." The whole class started laughing especially Jonathan and he said "Oh, sorry Danny." And laughed himself, that broke the tension there. Jonathan never went to hospital because he was frightened of losing his Job. Danny got so frustrated and said to him "I wanted to see the person in charge of my computer division." An appointment was made, Danny had to go and see the woman mind, she was too Important to come to him, although she had nothing wrong with her, so off Danny went.

Danny went into her office and she in a sergeant major voice snarled "So what can I do for you then?" Danny replied "Well I am not happy by the teaching service I am getting, as a blind man I am trying to get my life back on track by learning to use a speech activated computer, so as I can write letters receive letters and scan them so the computer can read them to me. This would enable me to live life to the full, but no one here knows how to teach it. Poor Jonathan is learning as we go along and he is very good, but it's not fair for him neither. Although he will be very good in time, it's hopeless now." She replied "Well it's how this college is run, it's not easy you know it is all different for many people here. We have different disabilities not just yours you know, you must be patient." Gob smacked at her comment Danny replied "I at this rate will be an old aged pensioner by the time I finish this course but I am only allowed two terms here, That's all they will pay for me to learn with someone who can't teach me because he knows nothing about it himself. How would you like it if you were deprived from your computer and the internet? How would you feel?" In a bit of a tizzy, she replied "I can't use a computer so it would not make a blind bit of difference to me." Laughing in anger Danny said "Your kidding aren't you? The head of the computer section in our department." "Yes I am not being able to use a computer has nothing to do with it." She snapped. Danny then said "Well I was told about a college in Hereford for the blind who can teach me, but I have a family but I should go there it's quicker and easier." She then said "Why don't you then?" "I cannot believe what you just said, it's all about getting the unemployed numbers down, It's nothing to do with all the fuss and caring offered to us poor disabled people, none of you give a stuff do you I am amazed. A case of Jobs for the boys and it's just a salary for you and nothing else isn't it?" Danny growled across the table, she replied "I think your exaggerating now." Danny butted in "I don't want another word from your mouth as your just a wolf in lambs clothing, I have heard enough of your crap, I am off goodbye." She then said "Goodbye Mr Duckfield." Off Danny went red in the face and totally dumfounded and angry, to think he believed he was being looked after by the state to rehabilitate him to get his life back on track.

After thinking a lot about the system Danny began to realise he was sold the idea of using jaws by blind people who could use the computers with jaws brilliantly and did so to be able to get a Job but none of them had a Job. So why were these people in colleges teaching jaws to someone who knows It but none of the blind have been offered the Job and a few had applied for them and here we have a woman in charge of a department who cannot use a computer let alone a sophisticated system like Jaws and all the blind people who can use them still unemployed, why? It beggars belief and it probably cost more for that woman than it would for a blind person from the other end of the country and from that day Danny was getting madder and madder and started taking it out on everyone.

Well it all came to a head a few weeks later, outside the access centre were several disabled parking bays all around the building to enable Jim and bob etc. to be able to get into the access centre otherwise they would have to walk or wheelchair from a very long distance and by the Time they got there it would be Time to go home, so these were provided especially for their access centre only and strictly their access centre only. At this Time of the year the whole college was open for about 30 governors to come to the college for some 2-3 weeks to watch classes being taught and take notes a long and daunting task for them I suppose. Well the lads turned up the first day and lo and behold they could not get near the access building as there were cars parked everywhere and it was just Impossible for them to get in their access centre and bob, Jim, Rhys and a few who come in and drive in and use the parking bays could now just not and why? It's for them to use not anyone else. The lads were shocked indeed, well after a hour or so and some help from tutors they finally started their lessons, it was a Joke and they were all mad about this, well lessons were cut short in the afternoon so as they could all be helped to their vehicles. The next day Danny, Gaffo and Steve were standing outside and waiting for the others knowing they were going to be late as these cars were still parked there and all of a sudden Bob came into the car park area and could not find a parking space so Danny shouted to him "Is the principles parking space empty there ?" Bob shouted back "Yes." Danny said "Well park your car there and stuff him he don't care so why should we?" Bob replied "I can't park there I will be chucked out of the college, I can't." Danny stormed "Do it bob, I will back you up and I will bloody tell them stuff them." Well a few hours later and the principles secretary came to the access centre and found Bob and asked why he has parked there and would he please move it Immediately. Danny shouted across to Bob "You leave it there Bob if he has not thought about why Bob is parked there then he is an idiot." The secretary says "What do you mean?" Danny snapped "I am the blind one here not you, don't tell me you haven't noticed the governors cars parked over all the disabled parking bays so he can't park there so tell the principle to come over and tell Bob himself and then we can all have a go at him." Secretary replies "Fine I will pass your message on." And she stormed off and that was the last they heard from either of them that day, no one came over to listen to their complaints with all of this.

Danny went home and thought about this and he started to cry because he felt sorry for the others and thought we are nobodies, no one cares, he was really finding out the hard way that most people don't care about them and they were a nuisance to them and they can't do anything about this. Danny was crying now more than anytime than when he was a normal person.

The next day he sat behind his computer and told Jonathan to leave him get on with what he was going to do today as he was about to write a letter to the local Gazette about all of what was happening and this was his first of many battles with bullies. It read like this .

To the Glamorgan Gazette

Dear Sir\Madam

I am a disabled person attending the Access Centre at the Bridgend technical college and also there are many people who have other disabilities such as people who are wheelchair bound and most have to use a car for them to be able to attend this centre and outside there are disabled parking bays provided for these people and only these people to enable them to park outside the ramps etc. provided, well to our horror last Monday we arrived at the access centre and lo and behold all the bays were covered by cars not only that all the ramps were parked in front of, these cars were large cars such as BMW'S, Rovers and many more, who do these cars belong to you maybe asking? Well they belong to the Governors of the college and it's one person to a car and these people were told to park there by our principle of the college, stuff the disabled people. The governors are more Important, is this the way to treat the disabled students? and is it much more easier to let the governors park in a car park in town and ship them in by bus and show them how well the college is as regards being able to accommodate the disabled people and students there, it's a Joke how dare they treat us like this and how have the principle and other staff got their positions that they have if they can do this type of thing. I think heads should roll after this, it's disgusting.

Danny asked the Gazette to keep this letter anonymous as he wants the principle to come and look for him as he has not done so so far and we want to confront him, well there was a huge stink about this article and the vice principle and the principle would not confront them until one day after sending his secretary and others to see them to try and find out who it was that sent the letter to the gazette. The vice principle had to come to try and find out, no one knew who it was not even Danny's class mates and he was not speaking until someone came and spoke to them. Well it was early one morning the principle came and they were all asked to stop work. Principle spoke "Can you all stop what you are doing for a minute please and all turn to me so as I can speak to you." They all turned and the principle continued "I think you all know why I am here, I can't understand why whoever wrote this article in the local paper did not come and speak to us first before doing this, so is anyone going to own up to writing this?" It all went silent and then Danny said "Well now you have finally had the guts to come over and confront us, it was me I did it." He then said "Why did you not own up earlier? And why didn't you come and see me instead of writing this article?" Danny smiling says "Am I a child you can treat like a naughty boy? I have owned up now you have come over to speak to us, why didn't you come over earlier? And why didn't you come over to us before you decided to let the governor's park outside this complex on disabled bays? Instead of just letting them do it? Why didn't you have any consideration for the disabled here?" Next thing all the class started clapping, the principle was dumfounded and embarrassed by this and he said "So where was I supposed to put the cars?" Danny replied "Down in a car park in town and ship them in by bus instead of letting the disabled suffer for them, are they more Important than us? Is this Germany in World War 2? Do you really think that it was the right thing to do? Did you think we would just sit here and do nothing about it? Well you thought wrong and are we going to hear an apology from you?" He muttered "I suppose we could have done it a little better, I shall return." He walked out and there was a deadly silence and after about a minute as if to make sure he had gone, the tutor spoke up and said "Well done, I think it is about Time someone spoke up." Next thing everyone spoke up and was very cheerful about the outcome and Danny felt so good after. Well the vice principle must have been the person who had decided to let the cars be parked there as he was dismissed the following week and a formal apology was read out to the whole building. It was a victory.

It was around this Time Danny had met a man who he got to be very friendly with and was going to make a mark on his life and Danny on his, his name was Niel David, he was a large man as bald as a fish and a man who had gone blind because he was diabetic and was afraid of needles and so did not inject himself as he should have, so lost his sight, a lovely man indeed with many stories to tell and many stories was told to Danny about this man, they became good friends, they met many Times while convalescing or out for meals etc. They became the best of friends, he teased Danny's wife and Danny teased his but that was it, he was a family man through and through, he was very much in love with his wife and his 2 sons and that came first in his life. He also had a guide dog named Abby and was always talking about them all the time, he told Danny of a place he had gone to in Torquay and how it had changed his life because of his blindness, Danny was told however that it was about to close though and if he wanted to learn how to be blind he would have to go to Hereford college for the blind and Danny spoke to him about this as he had already been there he was not Impressed about the place but Danny had decided this is the place he had to go to and told Niel so. Although it meant he had to live up there as it was too far away to travel every day, it was 2 weeks up there and a weekend home which they paid for. It was difficult for Danny as he had children and one was only 8 but he needed to get his life back together the best he could and little was he to know this is where his life really began, a real life changer for the best for him.

Danny finished his Time in the Bridgend college and they all went out for a meal to say goodbye to each other and Danny arranged to visit the Hereford College for the blind for a 2 day Assessment visit to decide which subjects to take as well as the Braile, J A W S and computer course that's if he passed the assessment in those 2 days. Danny was very nervous about all of this, Danny's friend Gaffo offered to take him up to arrange everything and they had a lovely day up there and all was set up for a month later. It was a beautiful place and Gaffo described it to Danny, it was set in the outskirts of Hereford and in surrounding country side with orchards surrounding it, the old college building had the exact look to Hogwarts in the Harry Potter books. Danny was taken around this place and seen everything in a few hours, it was a lot to take in but he was beginning to get excited about this place, it was Danny's future after all we were talking about, or should he sit in the house and fester? I don't think so, that was not Danny but how was he going to look after himself? What about his medical meads? How was he going to get around without Gaffo, being blind? How was he going to manage this? So many worries to consider, should he forget it? He was so confused he thought it was because he was going to a place he never knew and he knew nobody or anything about this place. It was frightening.

The day arrived and off Danny went to see how he would cope with all that was about to happen to him and it was his good fortune that Gaffo took him up to the college to help him settle in, they arrived and Danny was taken in and Danny said goodbye to Gaffo and he was taken over to his room in the grounds of the college for the 2days, he was surprised when he was walked over by Anna a German student support worker (S.S.W.) as he held onto her arm she told him if there was any obstacles and described the way "We are going out of the rear of the college now across the main road to the dorm's, we are now walking on a narrow flat path to the dorm you are staying in, past the orchard and here we are." Danny was surprised it was so easy. Danny said "Well that didn't hurt at all and it smells so fresh around here, thanks again Anna." Anna said "No problem, this is your support lady Hazel." Danny smiled and said "Hello Hazel I am all yours." Hazel replied "Hello do I call you Daniel or Dan or what?" Danny "I don't mind most people call me Dan or Danny up to you." Hazel smiling says "I'll call you Dan then, grab my arm and I will show you around." She proceeds to walk Danny through the building and tells him everything "This is the Common room where we all meet for breakfast and watch TV etc. now go left up this corridor and the door at the end on the left is your room for the next 2days, so feel the wall as we go along and there is 2 doors and the third one is yours and if you need anything just shout, I am here all evening and night and you have a telephone that connects you to anywhere in the college if you hit 55 you will get me if I am not already seeing to someone, patience is the key here, this is your single bed and a wardrobe and set of draws for anything you want to put in. Showers and toilet's next." She leads him off to the shower room and explains it is shared by males and females and that there are locks on all doors and she would help him to understand the shower system when he needs to use them.

Next thing Danny realised he was sitting alone on his bed and it was so quiet and he was alone all of a sudden and then it hit home, Danny was all alone from here on, he felt no one cared anymore, Danny had gone blind and he was not wanted anymore, he was far away from his family and they were happy he was out of the way. Danny was an embarrassment so it was a good thing just stay here out of the way and everyone would be very happy, all these things went through his mind and it got all too much for him and he started to cry uncontrollably for a long Time, or so it seemed. He had never felt so alone in all his life and he felt it was the end for him, he thought to himself the very same thing that hurt him so much, why me? Why me? Why did I go blind? anything but go blind, I have got nothing now I can't see anything, I am no good to anyone, I will be looked on as a degenerate, a fool because I cannot see, if there is a god please, please, please give me my eyesight back, please, I am not alive without my eyes, I can't do nothing anymore without them, just let me see again my grandchildren, my children, and my friends and maybe they will talk to me again, please. Well he sat there for an hour and a half but it seemed like 24 hours. Danny got so down and wondered what was going to become of him, he thought of his wife and how happy she was when he told her he maybe coming to this college for a few years and he would be staying here, she seemed very happy about it and on the radio came the song your baby doesn't love you anymore by Roy Orbison. Danny really felt his life was not going to be the same anymore and that she really didn't love or want him anymore. Danny was pretty sure about this, he then from that day started to think about his future in a different way, everyone he knew rejected him after he went blind, boys that used to work for him avoided him on the street. Family stayed out of his way and many pitied him which is not what Danny needed, why was this happening to him? Danny hadn't done anything to deserve this. He is now on his own now so that's it he had to pull himself together and if the future does not work out he would end it that's how he felt, that is how down Danny felt. Well as these thoughts were running through his mind he heard a little tap on the door, Danny called out "Come in." It was Anna and she said "Hello Daniel, I have come over to walk you over for you to have some tea, are you ready?" "Yes of course I will swill my face and I am ready." "Ok " Danny swilled his face with some water and off they went back through the orchard and back across the road and into the rear of the college and into the refectory. All the way over Danny was wondering how is he going to choose his food and Get it to the table? And eat it, more reasons to worry. Well he got in and into a queue, he was still holding Anna's arm tightly, he then arrived at the counter and he was asked what he would like, the lady serving the food told him what was there and it was easy, he selected what he wanted and just slid the tray along the track and the food was placed onto the tray. When he got to the end Anna said "Right would you like to sit amongst the rest of the students or somewhere quieter?" "I would like to sit alone if I can." Danny felt too down to be chatty so she carried his tray to a secluded place and he sat down, she put the tray in front of him and grabbed his hand and proceeded to tell him where everything was on his tray. Brilliant but simple, he took his Time and ate, he sat there and listened to everything that was going on around him, it was like a Normal school feeling, lots of laughing and gossiping and blind lads talking about football, some girls talking about music and boys etc. it sounded very normal and plenty of Joking and laughter, Danny was amazed, all this relaxed him a bit and he finished with his tea and someone came up to him and said "Have you finished?" Danny replied "Yes thank you." She proceeded to take his tray and clean the table and she said to him "Your new here aren't you?" "Yes I arrived here today for an assessment, my name is Danny, hi." "Oh hello my name is Christine I work here, I am not a student." "It's nice to meet you I am hoping to start here in a few months, will I like it here?" Christine replied "Yes I don't see why not, everyone is nice and lots of them are always having lots of fun, your Welsh aren't you?" Danny says "Yes I am as you can tell by my accent, do you like Welshmen?" "I like Tom Jones, would you like another cup of tea?" Danny's face lit up and he says "I would love one please, thank you." Off she trots and returns with his tea "There you go Danny let me put your hand on it." "That's very nice of you, I am going to enjoy coming over here for food, you must talk to me when you see me." "I will no problem, I must get on with my Job now as I am being watched by my boss, see you tomorrow bye." "So long Chris, I will see you." Danny sat there and enjoyed his tea and felt a little better after meeting Christine. Next Anna walked him back over to his room and Danny decided to stay in there for the evening, he found it hard to sleep that night but finally did and all sorts of things were running through his head and more tears came as well, he thought he actually cried himself to sleep.

Danny awoke early that day, he could remember it was a nice day as he could hear the birds singing very early and somehow he knew it was sunny, he wanted to get out of his room and have a cup of tea but he couldn't as he forgot the way and felt unsafe to try and find out so he decided to stay put, this was another bad feeling that went over him and he began to get depressed again, he thought if he was at home he at least would be able to roam around his house as he knew where everything was. Danny could make himself a cup of tea use the bathroom, put the TV on and listen to the news or his music and stroll out into the garden he knew where he was there, how the hell is he going to manage here? or anywhere else for that Matter, he felt he was finished, he can't manage with this blindness it was not going to work out, he thought he just as well kill himself and have done with it and save everybody the problem of doing things for him as he can't look after himself. What's the point in carrying on? well he just sat there and felt totally down and useless again, the other thing he needed his diabetic injection before his breakfast and this had been arranged he hoped, they will remember he did not want to be ill as he was on an ordinary needle injection and he could not do it himself as he could not see if there is the right amount and if there was any air in the needle, he thought, oh god this is not going to work out is it? I cannot see any future for me here either just then a knock on the door and a little voice say "Are you decent?" It was Anna Danny replies "I am indeed, come in." "Good morning have you slept well?" "Half and half, so what's happening?" "I have come to take you over to the nurse's surgery to have your injection, are you ready?" Danny says "Yes I am thank you, do I need a coat?" "No it's beautiful out there." Off they trotted and it was indeed lovely, Danny felt happier that she was there early and he need not worry at all. They arrived outside the nurse's surgery and there was a few people there waiting for their treatment. Next thing the surgery door opened and Danny was called in before the people who was already there, Danny said "But there are people before me." The nurse says "I am afraid your situation is more Important than theirs, so you get priority." Danny says "Ok I understand." Danny entered the surgery and sat down "Hello my name is Rosemary I am one of the nurses here who will be looking after your medical needs while you are here, I need to know everything about you when you start here properly and if you are not well in your dorm then phone me and I will attend." "Well that's great I was very concerned about this but you have already set my mind at rest." Rosemary says "Your welcome , it will not take you long to learn the use of your cane while here and you will be running over here by yourself I can assure you of this, we endeavour to get everyone independent here that's what this college is all about so don't worry about a thing and why are you using a normal needle? Haven't anyone suggested a pen so as you can do your own injection without worry and I will sort this out also when you return as a full Time student." "Do you think so? I can't see that far ahead, I feel it is hopeless." Rosemary smiles and says "Oh yes many people come through this college and they will be taught everything trust me." This made Danny feel much better and the thought of getting around again on his own was a great feeling." Well Anna took him over to the refectory and back to his room after for a short break before his day of seeing a lot of people who were going to seek out his needs and what he was going to do there.

Later Anna came and took Danny to meet his main tutor to introduce him to some others who will be hoping to start here, his name was Rory, was Danny in Haven holidays or what? a funny name for a man, well he was a very nice man. Danny was introduced to him "Daniel this is Rory he is going to sort u out." "Hello Daniel take a seat." "Thank you Rory, it's a lovely day isn't it?" "Yes it is, there are 2 more people sitting here and I will introduce you, next to you on the right is someone named Chris, he is from Birmingham and by his side is Jamie, he is from Bolton . " We all said our hello's . Rory "I am your tutor for this week so as your introduction to this college is made simple I will be arranging for you to have a tour of the facilities and meet other tutors and look into what you will be learning to make your life much simpler and also get an insight into any course you would like to take up as a Job if it is suitable for you, any?." Danny said "What do you mean a Job? Who would give me a Job being blind? What sort of thing can I possibly offer anyone?" Rory continues "You would be surprised, look at David Blunket, he came through this college and look at him now a member of parliament " Danny "Exactly, look at him now." We all laughed and Rory said "Yes I see what you mean, but many people here go on to work for banks, solicitors and many for themselves like doing Massage, teaching J A W S in other colleges etc. it's not something that is Impossible, so Jamie what do you want to get out of this college? And how long have you been blind?" Jamie answers "Well I want too just learn to be an adviser etc. and I have always been blind from birth." "So what about braile and using a computer can you do these?" Jamie "Yes I can use both, I learnt them in school." "What about you Chris?" Chris replied "I want to be a singer, I have been blind from birth and can use a computer and do Braile and play video games. " Rory said "That's very good so you are going into music tech as a student here?" Chris excitedly said "Yes and I want to record my songs and make a mint." Rory "Well good luck there are some lovely studios here and some good tutors there. So what about you Daniel?" Danny in sarcastic mood answered "I just want to learn to be blind, I have only been blind for a short period of Time and have had enough of it already." There was a minute of silence. Rory then said "What do you mean you want to learn to be blind? You are blind." Danny then said "Well as the lads just said they have been blind since birth they know nothing else, I have just gone blind and don't see a way to survive unless I get my finger out and find out if it is possible, I at this Time can't see how I can survive." Rory "I see what you mean but I can assure you it is possible to get on with your life as normal as a seeing person." "Oh so I will be able to drive again, walk down the road and see a nice girl in a mini skirt and whistle at her, go and see a performance with Eric Clapton, go into the pub with my friends and have a game of cards?" Rory interrupted Danny "Ok, ok I understand what you are saying I am sorry I should be more understanding and realise that as a new comer to blindness it is very hard for you to understand what I am trying to say and I bet you are thinking what does he know he can see and you are right I wish to explain myself better. Well I should have said that life is not over just because you have gone blind and In Time you will know what I am on about and I really mean that, life has given you a bad blow and it seems as if there is no way out now but I have seen lads come through here and when I first seen them they were sore at the world and never smiled with heads bowed and they couldn't see any way out and after a period of Time I have seen them in the Student bar having a laugh with some mates singing on the Karaoke getting their post in the mornings scanning it on a computer and typing out a letter in reply , spell checking it, printing it out and printing out an envelope and sending it off, getting a girlfriend, going out in taxi's to the local pubs, Joining in the pub quiz, going to the train station and going off on a train to anywhere they like, learnt to cook themselves a meal and they all held their heads up high." Danny butted in "Ok, I get the message but is that everyone?" Rory in positive voice "Yes we have champion rifle marksmen and one of them is a world champion, writers, actors, singers and sportsman and more things, nothing is Impossible and I will prove it to you when you have finished in this college in a few years' time you just wait and see." Danny said "Ok I get the message, god you are passionate about this aren't you?" Rory "Yes I bloody well am, I hate to see anyone giving up before they start, don't be a defeatist and give it a damn good go, pick yourself up, dust yourself off and start all over again, that's what they say isn't it? Ha, ha, ha." Danny replies "Ok, I won't be so negative from now on until I try it." Rory now smiling says "That's better, I'm sending you off with one of our students to see a few places here and ask any questions you like to get a feel at what it is all about, this is Mandy she will look after you until lunchtime and I will see you after lunch back here, don't worry about getting back, someone is assigned to look after you and will know where you are at all Times, see you later." Danny smiled and grabbed Mandy's arm and off they went .

Danny spoke "Hello Mandy have you been here long?" Mandy answers "Yes I have been here 5 years and I am like a fixture here now and I help out as a way of training as I am doing a customer relations course at the moment." "So what's it like here really like?" "It's brilliant here and the tutors are brilliant, you will like it here and it's so easy going and that makes it easier to get on with life and learn so easy." "Your a good advert for this place aren't you? I hope to learn braile and get my life back on track, I have not long gone blind and the local college was useless for learning to use the J A W S on the computer, can you use it?" "Oh yes I can and so can everyone else here, it is a thing that is expected of everyone to learn and so many good tutors who patiently teach you, I am very good now and I could not use it at all when I first got here, I do e-mails, use the internet and it is now part of my life." Danny said "I hope I can learn it I really do" "Oh you will, I am taking you over to where all the computers are now for a little taster, here we are and on queue, this is Jude, take a seat." Jude sat next to Danny and Danny had a lesson with her for about 15 minutes and was shocked how easy it was, nothing like in the college at home, he was so pleased how much he was at ease also, well he finished there and Mandy took him off to the gym and he was shown all around the equipment and shown how he could use it, this was shown to him by someone who was a blind man learning to do this for a living and he was fabulous, that Impressed Danny . So it was off to lunch and Danny was amazed by what happened next, they stopped just inside the refectory and Mandy said "This is how you find out what is for lunch and tea." She grabbed Danny's hand and put it on a large speaker and found the button and told him to press it then a voice started to speak and told him everything that was on offer to eat firstly for dinner and then what was for tea that day, it was brilliant and Danny krew exactly what he was going to order, he sat down with his meal and was told by Mandy that she has told Anna where he was and she was going to take him back to his dorm when he finished. Next thing a voice spoke to Danny "Hello Daniel it's Chris, I spoke to you last evening at tea Time, do you remember?" Danny replied "Hi Chris how are you? I have been running around this college so much I am confused, nice to see a pretty face." "Oh you are settling down I can see that, so what do you think of it here then?" "Well so far I am Impressed but it's early days yet how things work out in the next few days will determine if I return." "Oh I hope so, you seem like a nice person not like some of them here, little buggers some of them, I really hope you come back that would be nice, I will see you later." "I will come back just for you it will be worth it, see you bye Chris." She smiled and off to work, Danny then went back to his dorm and met up with some of the students there who were only there for a few days , they were called telly tutors or telly tubbies for a nick name, they use a computer at home and learn on the internet from home and come in every few months to qualify on the subjects done, amazingly they were all girls except one, 5 girls and one boy and they sounded a lot of fun. Danny wondered. Danny went off and spent some Time in the college that afternoon and after tea he was back in his dorm and sitting in the common room and some of the girls were there. Danny was asked if he wanted to go to the pub with them but he was not going to embarrass himself, so Danny said no he made up excuses but they didn't give up so he made them promise to get him back and not to leave him alone in the pub and they promised. Well it was later in the pub and they were all sitting and having a good laugh. Danny was enjoying the beer and was feeling tipsy so he slowed down and he began to tell Jokes and was by the end of the night propositioned by one of the girls "So Daniel are you going to attend the college soon?" "I don't know yet but it is looking promising, I do like it there." " Totally tubby "Are you married or single ?" Danny thought and said "Yes I am married but I don't know for how long, I think she is going to divorce me now, because I am blind, I don't blame her really it's difficult for her." "Well if you need company I don't think you will have much trouble in the college it's a den of iniquity there, they are all shagging themselves stupid there." Danny sat up quickly and said "Really I am not surprised in a normal college but how do they manage being blind?" She laughs and said "What do you mean they are normal just because they are blind don't stop them shagging, they are worse than most, you will find out, I had a boyfriend and he finished with me a few weeks ago so I am on my own now and I haven't had a good shagging for a while now." Danny gulped in surprise and said "Oh I am sorry to hear that, if I can be of any help ha, ha." "We will see I am a lot younger than you, I am only 20 and I bet you are early forties, a bit of experience I suppose." Danny agreed his age and said "Well you don't have to ask me twice it's a messy Job but somebody's got to do it and it's a lovely night for it." Well it was later that night they were all sitting outside swigging a couple of cans of lager and she went and sat on Danny's lap, they were all around the side of the building and Danny was enjoying all the attention, she said that she was leaving in 2 days as if to say we don't have much Time and this was the Time Danny was going to find out that blind girls are not shy. She lifted her little skirt and placed his hand on her thighs, she was not wearing anything underneath and with the others sitting around she said "Don't worry none of them can see a thing." So they carried on Danny was amazed, so there is an advantage to being blind, Danny was getting to really like it there.

Next morning Danny awoke with a hangover and wondered where he was for a minute, then it hit him it was 8.15 and any minute Anna was coming to take him to the nurses for his injection and he was not washed or anything, he rushed around and got ready feeling awful, he sorted himself out. That morning he visited many more classrooms and everyone was laughing at him with his hangover. Well after lunch there was a fun cricket match with students versus staff which was going to be attended by all. Danny couldn't wait, he was picked up by Mandy and they went along. She explained the idea of the game as Danny asked her to do this as he could not understand how they could play this as it was a blind college. She explains "Well the students that are playing are partially sighted and they are using a larger ball with a small bell in it. it has a bell so as the partially sighted can hear where the ball is at all Times and that's how they play they also are all blind folded, that's all of them and after many Times of playing they get used to it and get very good at it, only today they are playing the staff who are all much too old to win but usually they only play other blind or partially sides in other countries all over the world." Danny says "That's amazing and they just get on with it no problems." "Yes and they are helped only by some shouting on the side-lines by sighted people, do you fancy a couple of scones and strawberries? They are free and for everyone, I will go and get some if you like." "Yes please if you don't mind." Mandy replies "No don't be silly, I will sit you down on the grass embankment for you to listen to the match and I will go and fetch them, won't be a minute." "Ok see you in a minute." Well Danny sat there and soaked up the sun and listened to all these students slagging off the tutors and all of them joking with each other and it felt and sounded good to him listening to them having so much fun together, can this be true? Blind people enjoying a good cricket match and loving every minute of it, he started to feel at home. Next thing Mandy came and sat by his side and said "Here we are Daniel I will put them in your hand and here are some napkins for you ok?" Danny smiling replies "Yes that's great thank you and please call me Dan or Danny, tell me how much can you see?" "I can see a good bit although it is getting worse all the Time, I can still read writing on a piece of paper and my long vision is not brilliant." Danny bit into his food it was so fresh and tasty he then said "Have you got a boyfriend here?" "Yes I have, his name is Lee he is a student here and he is totally blind and has a guide dog, I just left him earlier as I must not let him interfere in my work." "I am going up the student bar tonight, I am being taken up there by Anna and am a bit nervous about it. What is it like there?" "Oh it's ok up there and me and Lee will be up there if you feel better about it you can sit by us if you like." Danny said "Do you mind? Won't Lee be Annoyed about it?" "No he is always drinking too much so he won't notice after a while as long as I am there to go up to the bar for him he is happy." "Oh you don't seem very happy about him." "No he is ok, I am just fed up with him getting pissed all of the Time that's all, you come up and sit by us and if I can do anything for you I will ok?" "Mandy that's great I am feeling better now you will be there and I will try not to take advantage of your generosity I promise." "Don't be silly I don't mind at all honestly. " They sat there in the lovely sunshine for a good hour and Danny was given the rest of the afternoon off.

So back to his dorm for a nap and a shower, Danny has been dreading the shower so he however must have one today as he hadn't had one for 2 days. So this is going to be fun I expect.

It was 6PM and he asked the warden to help him to have a shower and show him how it works. Hazel was a woman with incredible large breasts and Danny was aware of this and tried to miss them as much as he could, this was going to be an experience trying to do this as it proved later. Hazel finds Danny and says "Right Daniel this is how it works there are 2 doors one for getting off your clothes and the inner door for showering in, it's very difficult to explain, however it is easier as you are blind to undress here and put a dressing gown on or a towel securely around your waist, I will step into the first cubicle with you and show you how to use the shower controls and I will then step out, is that clear." Danny with huge smile on his face said "I think so, so I will come out with my towel wrapped around me and my shower gel and get into the cubicle with you, I can gladly do that." They both started laughing and Hazel says "Behave yourself now, this is serious I will be back in a minute so get ready before anyone else gets in there, there are only 2 showers altogether, I will be back." "Ok I will get ready." Both of them still smiling, Danny started to get ready but was a little apprehensive unaware how this was going to go. Heading to the shower, gel in one hand holding Hazels arm with the other and hoping that the towel around his waist was going to stay there, he was panicking, they entered the first cubicle and Hazel explain "Right I have the first door open you have to step up." He stepped up and the towel nearly went but he was up and Hazel says "Very good Dan I will shut the door so no one can see you." "Hmm this is my lucky day I think." "Behave yourself now and pay attention." Danny felt her blushes and she was laughing, she opened the door to the shower cubicle grabbed his hand and put it on the controls and said "This shower does not get too hot but can be very cold if you use the controls wrongly so try and keep it in the middle." Next thing she pulled his hand over further to see where the soap dish was and yes you guessed it, his towel fell down to the floor and everything was out for all to see, she started laughing and Danny whipped his hands down to get the towel but grabbed her breast instead by accident, they were huge he started to stutter "Oh, oh I am awful sorry I didn't mean it, I feel such an idiot now." Hazel said "Don't worry about it I will get out for you to sort yourself out." Still laughing she leaves as Danny picks up his towel no urgency now it was too late she had seen it all, Danny wondered if she had done it on purpose, they became really good friends after that day and Danny does not embarrass easily anymore, he just let's it go over his head.

Later that evening Anna came and got Danny and she took him to the bar and got him a pint and he sat with Mandy and her boyfriend Lee, he was introduced to him by Mandy "Dan this is Lee my boyfriend." Danny said "Hello Lee nice to meet you." He shook Danny's hand and said "Allright mate another Welsh man ay, never mind fancy a pint or what?" "I'm fine thanks I have one." "Ok matey, Mandy will you get me one and get one for yourself if you want one, so Dan are you starting here?" Danny replies "Yes I am coming back in a couple of months if they will have me." Lee says "They will have you that's all they think about is money and the more students the more money, it's all about money here." Danny shocked says "Do you think so? I have found it a nice place here and the tutors are nice enough." "Wankers most of them, don't give a shit about no one as long as the money is coming in, most of them have houses that are rented to the college for big money and the rest are screwing the system here, you will realise this when you have been here for a few months. Tell me have you got a fag?" Danny says "No mate I don't smoke sorry, I gave it up." He then shouts at another student "Oy Davis have you got that fag you owe me? You twat." Davis answered him "No man I got no money to buy any." Lee then said "Well I better have it soon or god help you, wankers, scroungers all of them cadging fags and never give them back. God where is that girl she is so slow honestly, can't get a decent woman here man." Danny looking serious says "Don't be horrible, Mandy is lovely she is doing her best." "If that's her best god help us, huh." Danny shut up before Danny said anything wrong or smacked him around the ear. He was the most arrogant man he has ever met and he took a instant disliking to him. Well Mandy came back and put his beer on the table and grabbed his hand and put it on his pint, what was this lovely girl doing with an asshole like him? Danny could not understand it, next thing Mandy sat between them "Hi Danny everything allright with you?" Danny smiled and says "Yes thank you Mandy I am fine, what about you?" "Yes fine thank you, when you want a drink just say and I will get one for you." "Thank you Mandy that is very kind of you." "No problem, do you like it here?" Danny answers "Yes I really do, however there are some negative people here I think I will like it here, but I will be back in a few months. Will you still be here?" "Yes I expect so, I am part of the fixtures here. I have been here for a few years now but I will still be here." "Well there will be one lovely person here to greet me." All this Time Lee was talking to a load of his pals on the next table. Danny said to Mandy "Do you fancy a drink with me?" "Yes please I will if you don't mind." Danny then said "What about lee." He chirped up "Oh yes please matey, I will have a bitter please." Then carried on talking to his mates as Mandy gets up to fetch them "What is your drink Dan I will go and get them for you." Aa pint of lager please Mandy, thank you." Danny handed her the money and off she went. Danny sat there still wondering what she was doing with this man and what she saw in him, such a pig, she returned and put the beer on the table and gave Danny the change "There you are give me your hand." She put it around the pint of lager and sat down and said to Danny "It's packed in here tonight, most of you are going home tomorrow so they always come up here for a few beers to see what it's like here." Lee chirped in "Yes and good riddance to most of them sitting there drinking coke, what a waste of Time, they can drink that in their rooms not a decent drinker amongst them, huh." Mandy said to him in a snappy voice "Not everyone is like you, a piss head, you don't have to drink to have a good Time you know." Lee replies "You are a bright one to talk." Mandy says "I don't hardly touch the stuff so leave it there, or go home if you are drunk, I am having another one after this." Lee "Good it's your round then." Danny interrupted to stop the squabbling "Are the wardens here punctual? As one of them is coming over at 11o'clock to fetch me." Mandy assures Danny "Yes they are pretty good ... he gets on my nerves sometimes I am sorry about him." Danny says "No problems I understand its ok?" Well she was having a small argument with him and Danny sat there not getting involved, next thing she got up and went to the bar and came back with a round, they drunk them and Danny expected him to go and get the next round but instead he got up and went over and sat by his friends. Mandy said " see what I mean he is pissed again and gone over there with his mates, I am fed up sometimes ." "I don't know why you put up with him he is an asshole but he is your asshole, I suppose there's no accounting for taste, I suppose you are too nice for him and if I was not married....well." "That's very nice of you to say that." "I am trying to cheer you up, have I succeeded?" "Yes you have , I am off now shall I get you one in before I go?" "Oh yes please Mandy here I will pay for my own are you having one ?" "No thanks, I have to go I am up early but I will fetch you one before I go." Off she went and gave Danny a pint and left.

The warden came over later and took Danny back to his room.

Danny got up the next morning for a 1 hour talk with his chief tutor and then here comes Gaffo to pick Danny up, Danny then began to go through his mind what he had seen and heard and what he was going to do when he returned. At last it seemed as if life was on the turn and all Danny's problems were working out for him, or were they?.

Well Danny arrived back in Bettws and there was his youngest son Josh to greet him he was 8 now and growing up fast, he was so glad to see his dad and asked loads of questions. Josh said "Where have you been dad?" Danny smiling said "I had to go to school and I had to stay there because I was a naughty boy and my teacher kept me in." Josh looked at Danny with a little smile on his little face as if to say you don't go to school "Why dad what did you do?" "Well I was cheeky and wouldn't listen." "We have to sit in the naughty chair, did you?" "Yes I did and I had to write lines and it said I must not cheek my teacher and know that silence is golden 600 times." "Oh we don't have to do them, I got a girlfriend have you got one?" "no not yet but I know one of the dinner ladies and she gives me extra custard and one day I forgot my dinner money and she let me off and said don't tell anyone." "My dinner lady don't ask me for my dinner money, mummy gives it to my teacher." "Josh, we done sums singing in assembly and at playtime we had a game of cards and some of them go out the back of the bike sheds for a fag." "Oh dad that's naughty, they will catch on fire if they are not careful, I am going out to play now see you." "Bye, I will see you later." Angie was hinting to Danny and was hinting about when he was going back as if she couldn't wait to get rid of him "So when can you start there? Have they decided if you are acceptable? Will you be resident there if so?" Danny with serious look on his face "For god's sake I have only been here for 20 minutes and you want me to go back already." "I'm only asking, can't I ask?" "Oh hello Dan nice to see you Josh has missed you so and so was asking about you how have you been? It's really nice to have you home." "Oh allright Dan I was going to ask." "Yes I bet you was, so what's been happening here anything?" "Not really it's been quiet here haven't seen no one much, your brother Mel phoned to see how you are, Clare called this morning to see if you were home as Lauren wanted to speak to you, that's it really." "Right I will give her a ring to see how my granddaughter is after she has got home from school, I will probably go back up in about 4 weeks as a resident as I passed everything with flying colours, no problem and the medical care is very good there, I will be coming home every fortnight on a Friday and going back on the Sunday or Monday if that's ok with you?" "I only asked no need to be like that." "Well, you can't wait to get rid of me can you?" "Well it's much easier here if you are not sitting in that bloody chair every day of the week waiting to be waited on hand and foot, it will do you good that's all I am saying." "Well that should cheer you up then, I am going to phone my granddaughter she will be happy to speak to me." Danny picked up the phone and his daughter in law spoke and he could hear his granddaughter crying in the background "Hi Clare it's me Danny, how are you?" "Yes I am fine, did everything go allright up the blind college? Did it go allright for you?" "Yes I am going back for a few years to study and learn how to be blind, is that Lauren crying in the background?" "Yes it bloody well is." "What's the Matter with her then?" Clare replies "Well you wouldn't believe it, I will put her on the phone to let her explain herself." She puts his granddaughter Lauren on the phone, she is 4 and she says "Hello babe what's the Matter? Why are you crying? C'mon tell bampi." She was in tears and she started to tell Danny as she was sobbing "It's mummy she is spiteful I don't like her." "Why? What has she done babe, don't cry." Sobbing still she explains "Well bampi my friend Alison in school has got nit's and mammy won't let me have any." Danny burst out laughing and she started laughing at him laughing at her and Danny said "No babe you don't want any of those, they are dirty." At that she started crying again so Danny consoled her and after coming off the phone he was so cheered up by what she said. Danny felt better and began to think that things are getting better at last. Danny was coming out the other side and was accepting the fact he was blind and that the college was going to be his saviour, he just had to wait for a few weeks and it will all begin and life was going to get better and better.

Well Times were slow and Danny spent most of his Time on his own as his wife was always over her fathers any Time she could or up her sisters or down her other sister's anywhere but in the house with Danny, so most of the Time he was playing music, he had always loved music and found a lot of enjoyment in it. Well he was happy as there was nothing he could do about it anyway but the worst was over or so he thought. Danny was preparing for his return to college and had everything he wanted ready to take up with him, it was about a week before he was about to return to college and just as he thought nothing else could go wrong anymore and then the next thing would hit him like a hurricane. He was sitting down watching television and the telephone rung it was his oldest brother Melvyn from Milford Haven. Danny spoke to him "Hi Mel how are you mate, I haven't heard from you for a while?" there was a deadly silence and he said "I am sorry Dan but I have some bad news for you, I am afraid that Dennis dropped dead this morning." Before he had any Time to say anymore Danny lost it "Oh no, oh no, oh no, I don't believe it your wrong, please don't tell me, I don't know, I don't know, oh no, oh no." Danny started crying uncontrollably and his wife came over to comfort him and was very concerned, Mel was on the other end of the phone silent while Danny composed himself, his wife said "What's wrong? Tell me." In tears Danny said "It's Dennis my brother, he dropped dead a little while ago." Danny's wife put her hand over her mouth and said "Oh no that lovely man, I don't believe it, are you allright?" Still crying Danny said "I am ok." Danny proceeded to speak to his brother and asked "I am sorry Mel I just don't believe it he was only 54 and it's not fair, so what happened to him?" Mel answered "Well apparently he got up for breakfast with all the others, he sat on the sofa and he was dozing and after a while his carer was worried as he had been like it for a good while, she tried to wake him but he gave no response so she called a colleague and they put him on the floor and gave him cpr and tried to restart his heart, then the doctor arrived and he tried but nothing, he was dead from a massive heart attack." It went silent as both of them let it sink in, Danny was devastated and crying uncontrollably. Danny said to Mel "Just as life was getting back to some sort of normality , this happened, it will set me back years, I can't believe it, he was such a lovely man and his life was all set for him he had Janet his girlfriend there and was so happy, he lived in a beautiful place and so young, why? Why? It's not fair." Mel said "Yes Dan he had a good life there and began to enjoy it, I am so upset, I went along to see him and I was so staggered by it all, he was lying on the floor and his eyes were open, I put my hand over them and closed them, he looked so peaceful, I sat there with him for it seemed forever and had a good cry, he will always be in our hearts we must remember him as he always was and he was talking about getting married soon as well and I was all for it, he was so in love with Janet. I will do all of the arrangements if it's allright with you, I want him to be cremated in Narberth Crematorium if it's allright with you and Lyndon and we must decide where his ashes go." Danny said "Yes of course Narberth is a beautiful place and it's ideal as that is where our family came from originally and I would like him to be put down in Pencoed with mum in her grave, he would be happier there and what about Lyndon have you told him yet?" "No I am just about to phone him after speaking to you, he will be devastated but I think he would also like him to be buried with mum, I will also tell all the rest of the family." "Yes ok, I could not face it, I will tell my children and make arrangements for us to drive down there, can you order some flowers at the same place as you and I will pick them up on my way there." "Yes of course, you try and relax now as I am worried about you now, I will sort out everything at this end and I will give you a ring to keep you up to date with everything, are you ok now?" "Yes I am ok but I feel sick to my stomach, this has destroyed me it really has, I will miss him so much." "Yes we all will but he had a good life in the end and remember he was not expected to live past his first birthday with all that he had wrong with him, so we must think he was very lucky and loved life and bless him he is out of his suffering now." "Yes you are right I know, I just can't believe it I will never see him and hear his voice again, it's a very sad day for us all, I will speak to you later Mel, bye mate." "Yes I will phone you Dan, look after yourself, bye." Danny put the phone down and just sat there and broke his heart, he was in such a state for many days to come, Danny spoke to many people who knew and loved Dennis and they were all very shocked and upset. Danny always remembered him when he heard the song , He's not heavy he's my brother by THE HOLLIES as the words always said what Danny thought of his loving brother. Dennis was Danny's older brother who had been born mentally retarded and had a speech defect because he was born with no roof to his mouth, a cleft pallet and he had a hair lip to go with it and his mind was that of a person 20 years younger, he was teased and was never understood by many, he was so gentle and a incredible human being, Danny had to fight his battles all his life and he had about five years earlier moved down to Neyland Pembrokeshire to live in a beautiful home overlooking the haven with palm trees in the gardens and their own rooms and he had a girlfriend Janet who he thought the world of. He worked in the local Co-Operative stores stacking shelves, he loved it there, no one made fun of him and he was at peace there, bless him. It was a difficult Time in Danny's life, he phoned the college and cancelled until further notice but to be honest Danny did not have the interest he had a few weeks earlier and forgot all about it, who cares now Danny certainly didn't, he was heartbroken and so was his little brother Lyndon, he was in a hell of a state as he looked after Dennis for many years after their mum died and before as he nursed his mother and looked after Dennis. Danny and Melvyn got Dennis in the home to give Lyndon a chance with his new wife as he had looked after Dennis most of his life, he must have been devastated much more than anyone of them .

Dennis loved Lyndon's daughter Wendy and was always asking about her and always wanted to go home for a while to see her and missed Lyndon and his family so much but when he got home to see them after about six hours he was asking to go back to see Janet and seemed to be in the middle all of the time. Danny had informed his children and they were all very upset and they all arranged to go down to the funeral in Milford Haven about 80 miles away and good old Gaffo offered to take some of them as he was a good friend of the family, it was going to be one of the worst days of Danny's life and very difficult to cope with.

Well they all arrived down in Milford Haven and Danny decided to take them all to the sea front in the café overlooking the haven on the Rath , it was a beautiful day the sun was beaming down and the whole day was going to be nice and considering it was winter it was a real beautiful day just for Dennis, they all entered the kingdom hall where he had his funeral and all the family and friends were there and Mel Danny's brother was there and they embraced and shed a tear or 2 and it must have been hard for him as Mel was the minister doing the funeral talk etc. and this was very touching as it was all straight from the heart not too much religion so very personnel. After the service it was on to Narberth crematorium, it was beautiful and a pleasure for den, he deserved it such a wonderful day especially for him, god bless him. Danny went back for something to eat and his brothers carers were there and so was Dennis's girlfriend Janet, she was also slightly retarded and she came up to see Danny and said "Dennis is gone, I want to see him but he won't be coming back." Danny just cried and so did Janet and many others there when they heard these words, this was so honest, so genuine, Danny expected to see him or hear him all of a sudden. He was always playing little pranks and always laughing never had, a real credit to the human race. Danny struggled all day and so did his brothers but life had to go on, Danny went outside at one point and Mel his brother was across the road looking over the haven and stood there silent Danny's son took him across to see him and they spoke embraced and Danny said "Hi Mel are you alright? I can't believe he has gone and I have been expecting him to sneak up behind me as he used to do all the time, it's not fair." Mel replied "Yeh, I know this is so very hard Dan and it is such a beautiful day just for him, it's perfect." "I don't think anything can go wrong now it's all happened for me this last 2 years and this has topped it all off and it's going to be so hard to get used to the fact I will never hear him again and poor little Janet she is devastated and her carer said to me that she was not told for a few days after he died because they didn't know how she would react, it's so sad." The boys bowed their heads in sadness they were devastated, Mel then said "I will have the ashes home with me and bring them down after we arrange with aunty Mabel and all the rest of the family and just put them in the grave with mum, he would have liked that,, so another sad day before this is all over and Dan I will just say a few words and a prayer ok?" "Of course Mel that will be nice, I am not going to get over this ever. I am so sad about this, poor old Den he was such a lovely man, a great loss to this cruel world." Mel said "Yes I agree, he was such a gentle mannered man and never experienced the world like the rest of us, he was constricted by everyone for most of his life especially those who thought he was not supposed to be here and should be hidden from society, it's sad Dan it really is, well we had better get back in there before they start fighting ha, ha, ha." "Yes you know what these Bridgend people are like ha, ha, ha." The day was lovely and Dennis was gone and Danny realised this now and another setback for him and he still had not put his brother to rest with his mother yet.

Danny stayed home for a week and after lots of row's with his wife he decided it was time to go back and he phoned up the college but not with the same enthusiasm as he had before, he just couldn't give a damn what happened, he lost interest in everything.

A few weeks later it was the day he had to go with his brothers and family to put Dennis's ashes into their mums grave in her beloved village of Pencoed where she grew up and this was harder than the funeral, it was like as if their mum was waiting for him. Mum was a quiet woman and she was so protective of Dennis and it felt as if she was waiting with her arms open wide to embrace him again and finally look after him again. Danny and many of the family cried that day, you could not write a book with so much sentiment in it, the whole place was embraced in love. Danny however was thinking he was now one of the people who in this world that were forgotten about and Dennis was gone another person disabled and misunderstood and someone who didn't stand a chance in this world and had decided to show the world that disabilities did not mean they were not able to contribute and that those people were just narrow minded and only think of this when something happens to them besides that sod them.

Well a few months later and the day came around and Danny was ready for the adventure of his life, it was exactly like being born again he had to start from the very beginning, learn to walk, learn to read, learn to write and communicate and most of all learn how to love again

CHAPTER 2
A NEW BEGINNING

It is early on a warm September morning and Danny and Angie gets off a train at Hereford in a strange place and entered the unknown for the first time since he lost his eyesight, he looked as if he was walking the plank to who knows what, his face told it all. They both walked to the outside of the train station and stood very quietly waiting for a taxi, it was deadly silent you could hear a pin drop. Then suddenly there was a lot of commotion and grumbling coming from the entrance of the train station, cursing, moaning, calling his Alsatian guide dog everything. It was Danny's friend Niel. In his Welsh accent looking all hot and bothered and looking down at his dog Abby in disgust "Well thank you Abby you done it to me again." The dog looks pleased with herself and wagged her tail. "You could have waited to go busy, you didn't have to crap on platform 1, you could have at least done it on platform 3 there was no one on platform 3, you deliberately waited until you got to platform 1 didn't you? Because i would not share my sausage roll with you, i am the one in charge you know not you. You see Abby you are a big dog and when you do one of them on a narrow platform it looks like a sleeping police man because you are like a horse not a dog." Angie and Danny were trying not to laugh but could not; Danny says "What a load of crap he talks." Niel with a little smile "Who is that? I know that voice that's it, hi is that Danny i can hear?" "Yes it is Niel" "Well were you on that train? And is your lovely wife with you?" Angie says "Hello, how are you" "I am great and i see you are looking as gorgeous as ever" "You always say that and you have glass eyes, so how the hell do you know?" "I know" Danny says "Have you got that donkey with you that you call a guide dog?" "You leave my guide dog alone just because she is a German Sheppard you leave my Abby alone" "I thought her name was Pedro the donkey" Niel looking stern "I'll give you Pedro, she has got feelings you know" "What was you shouting at that poor dog again for? She has a lot to put up with, with you, haven't you Pedro?" "She as you know will do what she wants too to wind me up, first i thought she was asleep by my feet on the train but she was in under my seat and under the next table behind me being fed by a load of pensioners and kids, then she decided to spite me for telling her off by crapping in the most busiest part of the train station, somebody could have tripped on it and killed themselves, if that is not winding me up i give up. I am sure that dog knows exactly what she is doing i am sure she is my mother-in-law come up to haunt me." "Get out of it your mother-in-law would have crapped on your bed." Niel replies "Don't say that about my mother-in-law we are the greatest of friends. Well are you looking forward to starting in this college? I have been here before and it is ok." Danny looking unsure "I have to give it a try as i need to learn how to be blind and this is the only way, i am a bit nervous but it's a messy job but somebody's got to do it." "You will fit in well as you are very outgoing and it will be messy but if anyone can, you can. I was so sorry to hear about your brother Dennis, he was such a nice man and he loved you and your other brothers and you boys did everything for him he is with your mum now and happy still, is that the taxi?" All of them laugh as taxi's start to turn up Danny says "Well you and that dog will not fit in the taxi with us so we will see you at the college" " OK i will see you there" They jump in the cab and off to the college.
They arrive at the college and almost Immediately behind them Niel pulls up in another cab with the dog Abby with her head sticking out of the sun roof. They go into the reception and were greeted by the head tutor and after a chat and a cup of tea each and reassured

they would not be left to fend for themselves until they could, then they are shown to their different rooms.

Danny and Angie are looking around the room Danny will be spending a few years in, it is more like a cupboard than a bedroom, but has a rooftop veranda which is nice. Angie with a smirk on her face "Well it is not that bad is it?" Danny's face all crumpled up and a look of amazement. "Well if you like sleeping in a coffin it's not that bad, i will never ever criticize the council in Wales again, the toilet's in our house wasn't as small as i used to say." Angie smiling "You knew what you were letting yourself in for, it is not Oxford or Cambridge what did you expect?" Danny shrugged his shoulders and just made a little whimpering sound Angie just smiled and coughed. Danny said "If i stretch my arms out i can feel the walls each side of the room every time it's so small, no fear of me getting lost in here" "Well there we are then Danny it's time for me to get my train, i will see you soon when you come home ok?" Danny now looking worried replied "Yes i suppose so i bet you can't wait to leave can you?" "Oh don't start, it was your decision to do this not mine, i am off." Angie left in a taxi and Danny was on his own from then on and looked sad and frightened, he started to unpack and looked really sorry for himself. Just then there was a knock on the door, he opened the door, there stood a young man who looked like a lost animal, dark skinned and with a piece of paper in his hand he then spoke. Speaking in a broken Spanish type of accent looking very lost and sorry for himself "I am Hose i am from Brazil" "Good god man your a long way from home and if you want directions to get home i can't help you, i do not even know where i am myself." Waving his hands in the air and head deep in his shoulders "I no understand, my name is Hose" "Where is Hose B?" "I no understand" Patting Hose on the back in a friendly manner Danny continues "Never mind, what can i do for you?" Hose relaxed and chuckling to himself. "I come take you dinner." "Well that's very nice of you but i am not that way inclined." Waving his hands about again "I no understand, i no understand" With an i give up expression on Danny's face "Oh never mind, what do you exactly want?" "I take you reflectory,eat." "Oh i understand at least one of us does." Off the two men go Hose walking like an Urangutange and Danny holding his elbow.

In the refectory they go and they get some dinner on a tray, Hose helps Danny to the table and there are some mature students, John and Lisa his girlfriend and a man named Percy is with them and Danny says "Hello who's on this table with me?" John replies "I am John, this is Lisa and Percy " "I am Danny i am a new student starting today" Lisa says "Are you Welsh?" Looking confused Danny says "No i am Danish….. Only kidding." With a wry smile on her face Lisa says "Are you married?" Making eyes at her Danny replies "Yes at the moment but we are about to get a divorce but i will keep you in mind when i do." Blushing and not knowing what to do with herself she says "No i didn't mean that way." John started getting a bit concerned that Danny was trying to chat his bird up and decided to make an exit with Lisa. John trying to look macho "Well Lisa and i have to go to my room and swot up on our next lecture, see you around." Lisa was smiling straight at Danny and said "It was nice meeting you hope to see more of you." Dan with a cunning look on his face "Exactly what i was thinking, i look forward to it." John tugs Lisa's arm and off they run, Lisa with a big smile on her face,. giving a little chuckle. Percy said to Danny "That put him in his place, he treats her like a dog, that's the first time i seen her with a smile on her face" Danny replied "Yes, if i had someone like him next to me i could not smile much either." "I think she was very interested in you by the look on her face." "Oh, do you think so? Why is she good looking or what?" "Nothing special but a cracking body" "That will do me" Percy stood up and said "Well i have a lecture in 10 minutes i will see you around."

"You can depend on it" As Percy was leaving someone was taking his place this person sounded like a dotty cockney that was very nervous. Danny says "Hello out there, who is there?" With a heavy cockney accent "Hi my name is Jeff but people call me slim." With a big grin on his face, Danny says "Is that because you are a fat pig?" Looking a bit shocked "So.... you can't see very well either and you can call me Widget if you prefer." "No i can see light and dark and some shadows but that's it and i do prefer Widget but why Widget?" "I used to like them until Cliff left them; they call me Widget because i have always got my head in a can of lager." "Ah ha....someone else with a sense of humour, at last, there are some miserable people here aren't there." Jeff "There was until now, i just met a nice Scottish lass and she is a cracker." "You do have a sense of humour nice Scottish lass, now you are having a laugh." They had a good chuckle, Danny says "I started today and i have a cupboard in Gardner number b11." Jeff "I am in Gardner in b16 we are neighbours, what a coincidence" "What course are you doing here? I am doing the music technology, and what are you doing?" "Intercourse and advice and guidance" "No serious now. " Jeff looking even more serious "Yes i am." With a puzzled look and rubbing his chin. Danny says "Well i never." Jeff concerned "Well what's wrong with that?" Danny trying to pass it off "No, no, nothing" " Ha, ha, ha, your winding me up aren't you?" "Am i?" "This place needs cheering up time to party " "I could not agree more" "Up the bar it is tonight it is then?" Dan with a smile "Well if you can help me get there it is on" "Consider it done" "It's a messy job but somebody's got to do it" They both laugh and in comes Hose to take them both back to their hall of residence.

Danny and Jeff sitting in the student bar that evening on their own Jeff says "I suggested to the Scottish girl to meet me at this bar tonight, hope you do not mind?" "Of course not, i like someone who has no sense of humour, is tight with money and talks as if she has a bunch of grapes in her mouth" "Now, now play nice she is quite nice you wait and see" "Yes ok, i will be nice, i am a nice guy and i will be pleasant" "Why do i not believe you?" "No i mean it I will......well tell me Jeff how did all your troubles with your eyes start?" "I have RP it is something that just happened to me and no one else in the family has it, it is just one of those things, i can see ok until it gets dark then it is a bit more difficult ....What about yours?" "Oh i am diabetic and the hospital never picked up on this when I had problems they said it was conjunctivitis and it got worse and by the time it was sorted out it was too late and i was rushed in for an op and it was too far gone and i went totally blind in my right eye and i can see light and dark in my left and some shapes but not enough to get me a pilot's licence." " God man, you should sue them" "I am, it has been going on now for 2 years and i will make them pay" "You should get a fortune if you win" "And i would give it all back if they could give my sight back, i would rather see than be rich" "Yes of course you must be devastated" In serious mood Danny continues "I felt like killing myself when it first happened but now i have decided to give it a go, it has even ruined my marriage, she is thinking of leaving me because i went blind although she will not admit it" Jeff looking stern "The bitch it is for death do us part,, in sickness and in health" "I cannot blame her I married her when i could see and provided for the family and all of a sudden i go blind, it is not fair for her neither, it is a bit of a shock for her too, i understand how she must feel" "Well you are very forgiving, i could not forgive her just like that" "Well that's how it is, i took a long time to forgive but what else can you do i still love her but if she does not love me there is nothing i can do is there? I cannot make her love me .... What about you Jeff are you married?" "I am divorced she left me for another man and that was it, i have 3 children one of each, (they both laugh) no they are all boys" "Do you still get on with her?" "No i

32

tolerate her, she is nasty to me but she has got me by the short and curlies with the children, if i give her any bother she stops me seeing the boys, i have her in my telephone under evil and one of my boys dropped me in it by telling her, she was under the heading evil, and she asked me why, i just made a run for it" Both men roared with laughter" "What about you any children?" "Yes I have 6 3boys and 3girls and i have a granddaughter who is 3 years old." "You have been a busy boy haven't you? No television?" "Well i am irresistible so we could not help it." Next in walks a loud speaking Scottish lass"" Uncle Jeffrey is that you?" Danny looked up and said "Oh my god who the hell is that?" Jeff says "That's Carol the Scottish girl i told you about, sh sh she is coming over you said you would be nice...Hello gorgeous, hows you then?" Carol replies "I'm fine hows my little friend Uncle Jeffrey then?" Danny sarcastically says " Oh my god " Jeff coughed "Ah, this is a friend who also started today this is Danny, he is Welsh" Carol with a feel sorry look on her face replies "Oh, never mind" Danny smiling says "Very funny it's nice to meet you" Carol "Likewise I'm sure ...my god it's cold out there feel my ears" Both men take turns to feel her ears and both admit they were cold, Danny says "My god you do have big ears don't you? they are more like wing nuts than ears" Carol says "What is a wing nut?" Danny "Well it is like a nut that has pretty ears" Carol "Well that's nice being called a pretty nut, thank you i have been called some things before but not a pretty anything before" Danny said under his breath "I can see why...Well that's it then i shall call you lady wing nut then...I was just going to get a pint in, anyone for any more?" Jeff "Yes a pint of lager please" Carol says "Oh, i just got one in but i will have another, just a half please" Danny asks "I believe the bar is straight ahead isn't it Jeff?" "Yes it is only about 10 foot straight ahead take your time though... that's it your nearly there and follow my voice when coming back" Danny goes off and finds the bar easily and this pleased him so much just finding the bar and Jeff continues with Carol. He cuddles up to Carol and says "So tell me again what is a beautiful girl like you doing in a place like this on her own?" "Well i am doing the massage courses" "Well if you ever need a body to practise on i am always available, you really have taste will you come to my room tonight and tell me what colour you think i should paint my bedroom ceiling." "I will keep that in mind " ignoring his last comment "You do that ...What is your room number in Gardner in case i cannot sleep tonight and you need some company" Carol acting all coy. "Uncle Jeffrey, you are a naughty boy aren't you?" "Oh we must look after each other as we are a long way from home, if you need coffee in the morning let me know i will fetch them both into your room, or i can keep you warm tonight and cook breakfast in the morning for us." "Uncle Jeffrey, behave yourself" Danny had been listening to all of this and he put the beers on the table and said "Well Jeff i worked out that you must be here for the guide dog training" Jeff replies "Why do you think that?" "Well you are like a randy old dog there, down boy, down boy" Just then another voice came out of nowhere and it sounded like a nervous wreck talking, there sat a woman in black looking straight ahead with no expression on her face and she never even looked up when replying. With a deep eerie voice which stayed at the same deep tone.   "I would not mind a massage if you got some time and coffee in the morning, sounds nice too." Jeff says "If you are in Gardner you are in luck" Danny "Oh my god, take your time man you will be shagged out in the first week" Maxine gives out a silly laugh, Carol thinking she was trying to muscle in on Jeff "Who are you? I have not met you yet." Maxine replies "I am Maxine, i am here for some training" Danny murmurs "I bet you are" Maxine "Pardon" Danny "Nothing, i was talking to myself" Maxine "I must go to the bar for some coke" Danny said quietly "So she could not hear him "I was wondering what you were on." Off she goes to the bar for a drink. Jeff looking worried says "She is not the full shilling is she? and i tried to get off with her" Danny says "She would make you a lovely bride i think, she fancies you" Jeff with nasty look on his face "Please, don't say that, i just had a shiver right down my spine" Next in walks Niel and Abby the dog you could hear him shuffling in. Danny shouted to him "Niel, over here there are plenty of seats here." Niel shouts back "I will be over now i just want to get a pint in" Jeff says to Danny "Who's that?" Danny said "I will introduce him now, he lives about 8 miles from me in Wales" Jeff rolls his eyes and says "Oh, no not another Welshman" "Yes and he is bigger than me, he is about three times the size of you" Niel sits down and he is introduced to everyone "Well what's happening man? Any nice talent about?" Danny says "Yes one just went up to the bar and she is a cracker" Niel "If she is that nice why are you not after her yourself?" Bluffing Niel "Well she is a bit talkative for me, i know you like them talkative and on the chatty side so she is yours even your guide dog is a German shepherd" Jeff says "God they even have their own dogs to round up the sheep in Wales and i thought it was only a rumour, what they do to sheep" Danny says with a smile "Well we might shag them but you eat them for Sunday dinner and you leave Pedro alone" Niel says "Stop calling my dog Pedro her name is Abby" Carol says "Why do you call her Pedro?" Danny "Have you seen the size of her? She is as big as a donkey" Niel chirps up to Danny "And your remark about me liking chopsy women is incorrect my wife is quiet and slim so watch it" Back comes Maxine and sits down right next to Niel. Niel says to Maxine sarcastically "Hi i am tiny." Maxine in a serious voice said "Well you do not look that tiny to me" Niel replies "No my name is tiny" "Why do you call yourself tiny" Danny said "You have not stood by the side of him in the toilet have you?" Niel smiling says "Get stuffed Danny, don't listen to him he talks a load of ballucks .....No my name is Niel and what course are you doing here, i am doing the advice and guidance course" Maxine "I am doing the computer course" Niel says "I could not do that one i am dyslexic" Danny "Yes he is, Niel sing old McDonald had a farm" Niel sings with a smile "Old McDonald had a farm k m f c i g " Everyone started laughing loudly except Carol. with puzzled look " I don't get that" Danny says "He is dyslexic, he gets his letters mixed up, oh never mind" Danny egging Niel on "i think you are in there" Niel "I think you are right should i tell her about my operation." Danny "No i would keep that under your helmet until you get to know her, it might be a bit of a shock and you do not want to frighten her away" "Yes you might be right" Danny "Well when i meet a few new mates i like to give them nicknames, so i will say them and see what you think Tiny speaks for itself, Widget says it all, Carol i name you lady wing nut" Carol looking pleased " Yes i like the sound of that" Danny continues "Maxine i name you mad Max." Maxine gives a silly grin and says "Drink up my round, let's party ...Danny what's yours lager for you and Jeff half for lady wing nut" Niel chirps up "And a pint of bitter for me too please" Maxine goes off to the bar with that silly grin on her face Niel says teasingly "I think i am going to be lucky there" Jeff says "Not if you keep on drinking like you are, you will get drinkers droop" Niel "No chance of that, i never get drinkers anything" Jeff "Oh i suppose it's because you are Welsh i bet" Danny nudging Niel as if to say let me sort this out says "Yes us Welshmen are renowned for it" Jeff "What a load of crap" Danny "I will bet you that she will be well satisfied by tomorrow a tenner maybe?" Jeff "No way she will tell me yes or no " Danny "Well we will get lady wing nut to find out for us" Jeff "How many more pints are you going to have Niel?" "I expect i will have another 4 pints" Jeff "Danny your on a tenner it is" Jeff goes off to the toilet and Niel says quietly to Danny so as none of the others could hear "Danny what are you on about, I am not going to get involved with no other woman, i love my Ceri so no way matey" Danny "It's ok, i need to win this bet so just play along with me on this you won't have to do anything, just follow my lead, i don't think Maxine knows what it is for anyway, look out Jeff is on his way back, act normal now" They enjoy a few more pints and they convince Jeff this was actually going to happen.

It is 8am in the morning in the common room and Zarrine is in there making tea and toast for everyone coming in, the television is on but there is not a very good picture on it and it is making a fuzzy noise. In strolls Danny followed by Jeff and Carol, Danny had a bit of a hangover and said to Jeff and Carol "Good morning guys, have you been to bed together? Because you went up the stairs together and now your coming down together." Zarrine stamps her foot on the floor and speaking in her Indian accent "You must not say this and what is wrong with this television? I can't get a good photo at all" She bangs the top of the television. Carol says "For your information Jeff brought me a cup of tea to my bedroom, bless him he is my own uncle Jeffrey, aren't you my little uncle Jeffrey." Zarrine "Well that is very nice isn't it Danny." Jeff looking a little embarrassed "I went to warm her wing nuts up" Danny said "You went there to warm more than her wing nuts up." Carol in a warning stern voice "Daniel" Danny "Sorry, well what happened did you find out anything?" Carol said "You did not have to ask them you should have heard the noise she was making in his room even i am afraid to ask what went on." Danny fisted the air and said "Yes my son, a real Welshman, that's a tenner you owe me" Jeff looking coy "Wait he might have been beating her up the noise she was making." Danny "That was screams of ecstasy and pleasure being with a real man." Jeff "Well i want proof " next thing the door opens and there stood Niel barely able to stand and looked as if he had not slept all night, he staggered up to a sofa and just flopped down on it, next to the television and the screen on the television all of a sudden went crystal clear and had a perfect picture, everyone stopped everything and just stared at the television in amazement. Jeff said "My god man is you allright what happened?" Danny said "So how did it go?" Niel looking at Danny in said disbelief "How did it go?..... he asks me how it went, never mind how are you Niel, she nearly killed me, she is a maniac, she has only just left and skipped off to see someone in the college about the gym, probably to get fit for another round tonight" Danny Then said "So things are going well then? So what is she like did you ... you know?" Niel "Of course i did you know i can never fail" Danny "See i told you Jeff, a real Welshman, we never fail real men, right let's have it " Danny slapped his hands together and Carol jumps. Jeff hands him the £10 reluctantly and Danny had a beaming smile on his face "Thank you, easy money." Jeff "Huh, real men indeed, i think i was conned at least it felt like it, perhaps it is because your Welsh" Zarrine says "You two behave and get ready for lessons." Danny said "Yes i am off, see you at lunch, i might go out for a pint tonight on my winnings." Jeff replies "I hope you choke on your pint, see you later." "See you." Danny left the room and Jeff starts to talk seriously with Niel as Zarrine goes off to clean some bedrooms. "Well how did you do it? You drank six pints last night and she was going most of the night, it's Impossible." Carol chirps up "I was amazed myself and very Impressed but i do not believe it is because your Welsh that's a load of crap" Niel "I can't say, i promised Danny i would not say anything about how i do it." Jeff "I feel i have been conned, i do not know how or why but i got a feeling you are going to tell us." Niel looking nervous "If i tell you he will think i am a grass and if i don't i will feel awful." Carol says "I think i will just tell all the girls and get them up outside your room that should sort you out, so you better tell us." Niel "Ok, ok, i will tell you, i am a diabetic and i lost the use of my old boy as a result it was what you call dysfunctional, so i had an operation and i had a silicone rod Implanted in my penis and so now it is permanently erect, it is the worst thing i have ever had done, i only did it for my marriage to be kept alive." Carol spoke in amazement "I don't believe it are you kidding? I have never heard of something so ridiculous in all my life, so why don't it stick out all the time." Niel replies "Well it is like a bendy toy i can bend it into any position and it will stay there in that position, it is handy when i go to the toilet, i can't miss the pan." They all have a good laugh and Niel gets up and goes off to his room and all of a sudden the television goes back to a bad picture and all fuzzy as Niel leaves and Carol and Jeff start laughing even more. Jeff still laughing says "I am going to kill that dodgy Welshman he has done me up like a kipper but ten out of ten he had me brilliantly, my turn next." Carol "I am amazed, i can't believe that these things happen to people, i wonder if i can get one, ha, ha" Jeff looking excited "Do you want me to enquire about one for you? i know you can get similar things In Anne Summer's shops and i have one under my pillow" Carol eyes wide open says "What do you mean? In your room?" Jeff "haven't you got one in your room." Carol "One what? I don't know what you are talking about, where in my room? Come and show me" Jeff "It's a fire alarm for the deaf, it vibrates under your pillow if a fire starts it's like a little space ship just ideal as a vibrator for you women" Carol's eyes lit up and she said "Let's go to your room and you can show me yours "Jeff chuckling said "No problem, i have been trying to show you mine for a few days and does that mean you will show me yours too?" Carol sternly replies "Uncle Jeffrey i mend the vibrating disc you naughty little Uncle Jeffrey you" Off they trot to their rooms to investigate.

Later that afternoon sitting outside enjoying the sunshine is Danny, Jeff and Carol. They are enjoying the afternoon off and getting ready for the next day when they start their lectures. Danny spoke up and said "Well this is glorious weather, i can sit here all day." Jeff replied "Hope you get sunburnt." Danny "Your not still holding a grudge about that are you?" Jeff "Yes you stitched me up and you know it you pig." Carol got her ten penneth worth in "I think you should put that tenner behind the bar for you and Uncle Jeffrey to enjoy or Niel your so called friend will start to get very ill." Danny "How do you make that out? He enjoyed it and no harm was done to him so how will it be any different from now on?" Carol "Well when i tell all the other girls in this college he will not have a single minute's peace, his life will be hell, unless of course you see things my way." Danny "Yes ok, i get the message, i was going to do that anyway." Jeff replied "Of course you were and you think i believe that." Danny "Yes i was but you didn't give me a chance to prove it." Just then a taxi pulled up and out got Niel and his dog Abby. Carol said to him "Hello Niel. Niel says "Hello who is that?" Carol replies "It's me Carol and Danny and Jeff." "Oh Carol how are you, i have been to the doctors." Carol "What is the Matter?" Niel " I suffer with my nerves and needed some tablet's because i am having trouble trying to get rid of Maxine, i can't move she is there where ever i go, i am knackered." Jeff speaks up "Well you can thank your so called mate for that and he profited out of it at the same time." Danny said "Now wait a minute, i did not twist his arm you know." Carol said "No but now look at the mess he is in." Danny said "Niel you just have got to ignore her and she will get fed up." Niel "I have tried but without success, she is up for it any time of the day and i can't hide, i can't see her coming." Jeff "Danny you have got to think of a way to get him out of this mess." Danny said "You mean we, have got to think of a way to get him out of it." Jeff "Well we better get our story right and do it quickly." Danny "Yes i agree, what about Carol." Carol sits up and says "Yes count me in, but i am a bit concerned about Maxine, she is a bit nutty." Danny "Oh don't worry about her we shall sort her out, one way or another." Niel said "I am starting to worry now if the dodgy Welshman is involved, i usually get into deeper problems." Danny says "Niel it's a messy job but somebody's got to do it."

36

Later Niel and Maxine sitting in the bar Maxine is cuddling up tight to Niel and looking like a lovesick dog. Maxine says "I fancy an early night, how about you?" Niel answering her quick as if to dismiss the idea. "Well i told Danny and Jeff i would meet them up here tonight." "Ok it does not Matter, i got all night." In walks Danny, Jeff and Carol, Danny shouts across the room to Niel "Hello Niel are you in here?" Niel replies with relief on his face "Yes, i am over here." Danny "Ok, i will be over now." Danny and Jeff stand by the bar to get a drink, Carol sits down near Niel and Maxine. Danny shouts across to Niel. "Well Niel what did the doctor say about the rash?" Niel looking embarrassed says "What do you mean?" Danny "Oh, i am sorry i didn't mean to shout it out." Maxine with concerned look "Niel what is he talking about?" "He is kidding I am sure. " Danny and Jeff sit down across from Niel and Maxine "So everything ok at the doctors? "Niel "Yes everything is fine "Danny says "Are you going to take my advice and have a word with Max? " Niel "Yes when the time is right i will." Maxine looks a bit concerned and worried said. "Well what is it? i am worried now?" Niel "Well it's a bit personnel and i do not like talking about it so let it drop." Jeff says "Well the weather has been terrific today hasn't it and my little Carol gave me a nice thrill today, didn't you babe?" Carol blushing replies "Yes i did but it was an accident, i will never wear that blouse again and i thought your eyesight was not that good." Jeff grinning from ear to ear "I do not tell you everything." Niel going to take his dog out says "Well, i am going to take Abby to the pen for her to do her business, i won't be long." Niel puts Abby's harness on and trotted off. Maxine speaks to Danny with urgency "So why did Niel go to the doctors?" "I don't know if i should be telling you anything if Niel finds out i will lose a good friend." Maxine in a very serious mood "I will not say a thing i promise." "Well i think you should really know because it will affect you in time." Maxine looking concerned "What do you mean?" "If i tell you it must not go any further." "I promise you i will not say a word." "Ok let's go over there in private, Jeff, Carol sorry i must speak to Maxine in private,, be back soon." Both of them agree and Danny and Maxine go and sit in a private corner. Danny starts to tell her "Well it's like this, you know Niel has a what i call a metal Mickey, well it is more than that, he had an operation and things went a bit wrong and he was blasted with some gamma rays by accident and got a large dose of radiation in his metal Mickey. and he used to be known as the incredible bulk although he never turned green thank god as he would look like a cabbage, he went to the doctors today to get plugged in to release some of that radiation because he does not want to affect you too much." Maxine still looking worried "How can he affect me? What do you mean?" "As you can see he is as bald as a fish not a hair on his body hardly, well if he didn't get plugged in today well by next week you, you would not need to pluck your eyebrows again or shave your legs and you will never need a French wax it would all fall out in time and you wouldn't need to charge your phone batteries again, but if you are good friends it will never be a problem will it." Maxine looking even more worried "Your not serious" "Would i lie about my friend? It is a shame really i think in years to come things will start to fall off, he will be like Mr Potato head but I am glad you are a good friend to him. " now she is really panicking and rambling " I do not know what to do i only become good friends with him for some company, i feel sorry for him but I do not want to make it a permanent thing, Danny what shall i do? I do not want to hurt him but i do not want to end up looking like Mrs Potato head I will look ridiculous as a bald woman, what can i do?" "Well it's a messy job but someone's got to do it, i could have a word or you could just let him down lightly an i will help him get over it by having a few drinks with him until he finds someone to replace you as a good mate." Maxine "Do you think that would be the best thing to do? I do not want to hurt him." "I think he will be gutted but i will stick by him for you, that is the least i can do." "What is his metal mickey?" Danny looking flustered lied and said "Oh, oh, it is the metal bit that sticks out under his belly that they plug him into, nothing to worry about, leave it all to me" "Danny i think you are a wonderful man and i have always had a soft spot for you since i first seen you" Danny interrupts her by coughing out loud. "I am sorry but i am spoken for, i am a married man sorry, mind you Jeff is looking for a girl, but i would not try with him for a few days until this thing about Niel cools off, look why don't you head off home and get some rest and i will have a word with Niel tonight for you in private." "Yes i do feel a bit tired, i will just get a double Scotch for Niel as it was my round, do you want a drink? That's the least i can do for you for all you are doing for me." "OK, i will have a Scotch as well please, thanks" Maxine goes off gets the two glasses of Scotch and gives them to him, she then puts her coat on and rushes off. Danny smiling to himself picked up the two glasses of Scotch and poured them into one glass and returns to sit by Jeff and Carol. Danny says to them "Hi guys, i think i have got rid of her at last, so you can all get off my back." Jeff replies "Well you sort of caused it all, that poor old Niel, i feel sorry for him." Danny looking serious "You do not want to feel sorry for him, he is a clever man and if i had not got rid of her he would have in the end, but he would not mess with her he would have told her straight." Carol butts in "Do you think so? He seems so quiet." Danny "I do not think so i know so, he can look after himself but rather somebody else sort it out for him as he does not like confrontation as he will make them look a fool and later regret it." Jeff "We are all sitting here we should have phoned him on his mobile when we had got rid of her." Danny gulping said "Oh shit, your right i forgot about that, i will do it now." Danny pulled out his mobile phone and calls Niel. "I just called him and he is on his way up." Jeff says "He will be pleased that things are going to be ok."

Next in walks Niel with Abby both shivering, he sits down by them all and said "What took you so long? I was freezing my cockles off out there." Danny said "That's the gratitude i get for getting you out of the shit, well you have got rid of her for good, she is going just to be your distant friend." Niel with huge smile on his face "Thanks mate, i owe you one, i can get a good night's sleep now." Niel feels around for his whiskey but there is nothing there. "Well would you believe it, she got out of her round, she said she was going up to the bar to get me a drink , mad cow, i thought she was a genuine person well that just goes to show." Danny looking innocent replied "The cow, well you just never can tell." Niel "Well what did you tell her to make her change her mind about me? because she was besotted with me" Danny "Well i told her that you have a problem that could do her damage but it was not anything that was catching, nothing serious and she said well she thinks it would be better if she gave you some space to sort out your health." Niel gets a bit annoyed "Oh no, you didn't spin her load of crap did you? Because i know you never worry what damage you cause." Danny "Who me? How dare you, after all i have done for you in the past." Niel "Sorry mate, i do not mean to be unkind or ungrateful but you do tend to drop me in it from time to time. Look don't take it to heart let me buy you a drink to show you my appreciation." Danny looking as if all his birthdays had come at once said "I understand i do not mean to and as for the drink, thank you, i will have a double Scotch the same as you." Niel "Ok i will go up to the bar now in a minute.... How do you know i am drinking Scotch?" Danny looking flustered "A lucky guess i suppose." Jeff says to Niel "I do wonder why you bother with that dodgy Welshman after all he does to you." Niel "No he is a good friend really, just a bit stupid for his own good." Niel goes off to the bar. Jeff says to Danny "What did you really tell her?" Carol "I can't wait to hear this" Danny said "Oh don't be like that, i am just trying to help out a friend and i have not benefited out of it, i shared my tenner between us on drinks didn't i?" Jeff "Yes we had a single drink out of it, thanks, so what did you really tell her to make her run off so fast?" Danny answer's "Nothing just said he was not interested in a relationship and asked if she knew he was a happily married man? Then off she went" Carol "I don't think so, she is as mad as a hatter and she would not let a wife stop her in her tracks, it must have been something else" She chuckles. "You have wound her up with some sort of tall tale" Danny "Don't be silly, watch it Niel is coming back" Niel sit's by Danny and hands him his double Scotch as Jeff and Carol looked on with amazement and he says "There you go mate, that's for saving my bacon" Jeff says out loud "What do you mean? he was the one who put you in that position in the first place, it was his fault" Niel says in a tender voice "You would not understand we are Welsh" Carol "Oh god" Danny "So keep your nose out you Cockney git" Jeff "I give up, Carol fancy going and sounding out the fire alarm?" Carol looking at Jeff seriously "Uncle Jeffrey" Niel "What's this about then?" Carol snaps "Nothing, nothing at all, is it Jeff?" Jeff looking sheepish "I don't know what you mean, i am off."

Next day in the morning it's coffee break and in the bar is Niel sitting down talking to a young girl who he has never met before but sat by him to speak to him about Abby. She is about 20 years old shaven head punk style with Goth style makeup rings in her eyebrows and 1 in her nose with a chain from the ring in her nose to the rings in her eyebrows. Her belly is bare showing a bar pierced through her belly button.

Niel speaks to the girl "So your mother breeds German shepherds, how many have she got?" "She has 4 she keeps as pets and for breeding." "I love Abby and i would not be without her as she is a good friend as well as a guide dog, what are you doing in this college?" Young girl says "Well I am resitting some a levels and i am doing some performing arts as well." "That's good and have you any eye problems?" "No, i have no problems but i admire how you all cope with your blindness etc." "Well it's no good giving up you have got to get on with it." "What are you studying here?" "Well i am doing the advice and guidance course and some computer work with the JAWS system." Meantime on another table are Danny and Jeff and behind that table is Maxine watching Niel with this new girl and it sets her wondering. Just then she gets up and sits between Danny and Jeff. She stairs at Jeff then gives him a lovely smile and Jeff does not know which way to look. Maxine speaks to the lads "Hi guys, have you seen Niel and who he is sitting with?" Jeff speaks "Yes, so what? He can sit with who he likes." "No, i am not saying that, but i think he has been seeing that girl all the time." Danny said "Why do you say that?" Maxine "Because she has no hair and she looks disfigured, just like you said." Jeff looks daggers at Danny and says "What has he said now?" Maxine "Danny you know is it allright to say it in front of Jeff?" Danny looking down said "Yes, as you know myself, Niel and Jeff are the best of friends." Maxine "I don't bother much from now on with Niel as you know because i was worried about ending up like that girl he is talking to, bald and disfigured with pins and chains etc. to hold her together and i didn't want to go mad with all the radiation coming from Niel." Jeff says with serious face "What the hell is she talking about?" Danny coughing nervously "Yes i see what you mean, you see i told her all about Niel's operation now i better bring you up to speed. Well when he had his metal mickey operation they accidentally shot some gamma rays into him by accident and that's why he is as bald as a fish and if she stays with him the same will happen to her." A long period of silence and Jeff looked at Danny as if he was a rat. "What a load of crap." Danny's face had a very guilty look "It's true, i know, Niel he told me about it and i felt it only fair to tell Maxine." Maxine said "Yes and i am grateful, look at the state on that poor girl, i bet he has been with her for many years for her to get into that state. Especially those chains holding her face together." Danny said "And not only that, look at that bar in her belly button, do you know what that is for." Maxine said "No, what is it for, i thought it was for decoration or is it to plug her in to drain the radiation?" Danny continues "Well do you know what will happen if she took that bar out?" Maxine "No, what would happen." Danny "Well her ass would fall off in time." Maxine looking sad "That's awful i guess i am lucky." Maxine got up and walked out. Jeff was just sitting there looking at Danny with disbelief and laughing and Jeff says "What a load of crap you have spun to that girl." Danny smiling ever more "I was trying not to laugh, it's true i am not joking." Both of them burst out laughing and the tears were rolling down their faces, Jeff says "I do not believe you sometimes, i can see we are going to have some great fun me, you and Niel the 3 musketeers." Danny says "You don't believe me do you?" "What do you take me for my name is not Maxine, i don't believe you just did that, i thought she was a bit weird but that takes the biscuit." Danny says "I can see i am going to like it here" "That's if you survive it, i can see the size on Niel i hope he can take a joke." "Yes he can that i can rely on and if he had the chance he would do it to me and you and not bat an eyelid." "I think we had better keep this one to ourselves for your sake." "Oh yes please, i could not think of a way of letting her down and it just flowed out of me until it was too late to turn back." Jeff picks up his folder and says "Well i am off, i will see you later, chow." "Yes i will see you"

Later that evening sitting in the common room was Carol, Danny and Jeff and Jeff was sitting by Carol and acting like a lovesick teenager while Danny was trying to watch the TV, but the TV had a terrible picture and was making a terrible crackling noise.

Danny said "This bloody television is awful, i wish they would fix the flaming Ariel." Not a word came from the love birds speaking to himself again "No Dan it is awful isn't it?" still no answer came from the love birds. Again Danny was sarcastic. "Yes i agree, anyone fancy a pint?" Jeff sprung up and said "Yes when do you fancy going?.... now? " "You heard that no problem didn't you?" Jeff "Sorry mate, i never heard you." Danny "I was commenting on this bloody television it's awful." Jeff "I know i can't watch it." Carol says "I can't get over that TV, it is like that and no one can do anything with it, but as soon as Niel walks into the room it has a perfect picture, strange." Jeff replies "Now you come to mention it i noticed that the other morning." Danny said "Yes so did i, i wonder if it has got something to do with his metal mickey, or it might be radiation." They had a good chuckle and Jeff said "Well serious now, what time are we going out?" Danny "I don't know i am fed up of having to get Hose over here when we have to go anywhere." Jeff "No problem , i know the way now so i can take you over." Carol speaks sarcastically to Jeff "Thanks desert me would you?" Jeff says "No i can take you as well, no problem." Carol "No i am going to stay in and have a shower." Jeff "Well i can stay in if you like and scrub your back if you want." Carol "No, that's allright i can manage." Jeff "I don't mind, as long as i get a pint later." Carol "Forget it i am not that sort of girl and i have never come second to a pint of beer." Danny spoke up "What sort are you then?" Carol "Daniel, that's enough of that." Danny "No one calls me Daniel unless i do something wrong, my father never called me Daniel unless i did something wrong." Jeff butts in "And i bet you were a little angel when you were little." Danny "No i was a little horror." Carol again says "I could believe that." Jeff says "Well back to the question what time are we going out?" Danny "Well i was thinking of having a night off the beer tonight but stuff it i feel like a couple and i want to see Niel and see if that nutter has said anything to him." Carol says "Who's that? Maxine?" Jeff "Who else is nutty here?" Danny said "I would say most of them here have something missing that's why i fit in so well... Oh let's go over now i am fed up with this bloody television." Jeff "Ok i am ready, let's go."

In the bar and Niel sitting having a nice cool glass of cider with Abby stretched out in front of him relaxing after a busy day. Next in walks Maxine she makes a b line for Niel. Maxine speaks to Niel "Hello Niel, i was hoping to catch up with you." Niel almost drops his drink and stammering with fear. "Oh hello i want to explain." "I should think so, i am not very happy with you, you could have caused me a lot of problems if Danny had not told me about the problems you are having with radiation and your gamma rays, i could have gone bald and sexless." Niel's face turns serious "What the hell are you talking about? I am radioactive?" "Well i do not think you should have kept it to yourself." Niel "Wait a minute, i do not know what the hell you are talking about, don't tell me, Danny has been talking to you and i bet he missed out the truth, So tell me what he has said to you." Maxine "Well he told me about your metal Mickey operation and how you got a accidental overdose of gamma rays and how you have radiation poisoning and that's why your hair has fallen out and he said i could catch it, but he did tell me not to say anything to anyone and i have only told my tutor and she said to come and tell you and to talk it over with you." Niel looking up at the ceiling and annoyed "The bastard, i never learn do i know he would try and make a joke of it and make me look like a fool and he has. Let me tell you how it really is" Niel starts telling her most of the truth or at least as much as he wanted her to know and in the meantime in walks Danny and Jeff, they get a drink and sit away from Niel and Maxine. Jeff speaks to Danny "Why are we sitting here? Niel is over there and we normally sit over there." Danny "I thought we would have a change and besides Maxine is with him and they might be having a private conversation and it is nothing to do with us, i hope." Jeff "Are you sure that's the real reason? Or have you said something wrong to Maxine." "Don't be silly would i do a thing like that? I expect trouble mind, i do not like the look of how things are going over there." Maxine leaves and after she has left the room Niel shouts out Danny if you are here get here i want to have a word with you." Danny and Jeff get up and change tables and sit by Niel Danny with worried look on his face "Hello Niel, hows things then? I hope you and Maxine are going to remain good friends." Niel still looking evil "You bastard how could you do this to me? I never learn as far as you are concerned do i? Why did you spill out all that crap about me having radiation poisoning? And that's why i have no body hair etc." Jeff starts to laugh and soon stops when Niel looks at him with a look that could kill. "Sorry, i shouldn't laugh it's not funny." Danny said gulping "Oh come on Niel i got rid of her didn't I, it worked didn't it?" Niel "I thought you promised me you would tell her that i could not have children and i am a lazy pig." Danny "Well that was my intension but it went all pair shaped when i was watching the incredible hulk on television and you walked past the common room and every time you did the picture on the TV became clear as a bell AND WHEN YOU LEFT THE picture became bad again, how do you do that? And so my brain got mixed up" Niel "You have made me a laughing stock here now." Danny "No i haven't no one can make you look a fool, you have got a brain and your Welsh." Niel " Don't try and soft soap me I know you and I will not fall for that one " Jeff says " I don't blame you NIEL I am learning a lot about this dodgy Welshman. " Niel "I am fed up i have got a good mind to pack it in and go home, i enjoy a practical joke but this is not funny." Danny "Oh don't be like that now, you will make me feel awful." Niel "And so you should." Danny sat there looking very concerned "Look i am sorry, i won't do it again." Niel "No i think i will go home tomorrow as she is going to play around with me again now i have had to tell her the truth." Danny "No she won't i know a way to get her off your back, i will take her out i know she fancies me." Niel "You would do that for me? You wouldn't would you?" Danny "Yes of course you are one of my bestest friends." Niel "No i do not believe you, i am going home." Danny " I swear i will ask her out as soon as possible, in fact i will ask her out the very next time i see her." Niel "Oh i do not know whether to believe you, i think i will pack up and go home all the same." Jeff says "I would not believe you neither, you are a bit of a tosser." Danny "I swear cross my heart the very next time i set eyes on her i will ask her out." Jeff chirps up with a smile "Well it's your lucky day she is standing right behind you, now's your chance." Danny "Yeh, Yeh, right she is" He turned around and she was there, he looked very sheepish and lookec as if his world had come to an end. "Hi Maxine, fancy seeing you here i thought you had gone home." Maxine smiling says "Yes, i went home to change my shoes." Jeff says "Well Niel and i are waiting." He turned around to Maxine and said in front of Niel and Jeff sitting there waiting for him to ask tapping their fingers on the table. "I was wondering if you fancied a date with me." Maxine still smiling "Yes thanks for finally coming around and forgetting your shyness, i would love to go out with you." Danny gulping "That's great." Sne snuggles up to Danny and looked at Niel as if he was responsible for this and says "I really think you are a great bloke Niel, i hope you are not too upset me with Danny, i mean and thanks for fixing us up, i will never forget this you said you would and you were right he must have been shy when i tried to ask him before and i am glad you told me he was mad about me, i am so happy, anyone for a drink?" Everyone gave her their drinks orders and she went up to the bar to get them. Danny said with angry face and looked as if he had just lost money you bastard, you set me up i am going home, what a sucker i am listening to you, you set me up now i am stuck with her." Jeff says with a big grin on his face "Well i never the dodgy Welshman has been silenced and had a good smack around the ear." Niel joined with a few chuckles "You are my bestest friend, i would not do that to my bestest friend, now would i, you are messing with the king of spin and you remember it and when she buys me a double scotch next time do not drink it you give it to me. Well i am off, i will see you in our common room in the morning." Jeff still smiling "Good, so you are not going home?" Niel smiling "No, i was never going to go home I just had to sucker Danny in." Danny in a temper said "You rat, i will never forgive you for this unless you help me get out of this." Niel " Sorry mate you are on your own as you say, it's a messy job but somebody's got to do it, have a nice kip."

CHAPTER 3

THE GOLDEN EAGLE.

2 weeks later in the common room in Dowdell is Zarrine sipping a cup of tea when in walks Niel followed by Danny with his head in one hand and looking as if he had been on the beer all night.

Zarrine "Good morning you two." Niel says "Good morning." Danny in a gruff voice. "Good morning, i think." Zarrine spoke "Oh dear Danny, what you do yourself? It's not good." Danny "I drunk too much last night in the Pretty Pigs pub, there was a karaoke in there and Jeff and i had a great night but i am sorry now as i have to start my lectures properly today." Zarrine says "And Jeff has no lectures" Danny said in urgent voice "Yes he should have gone by now as he starts very early." Zarrine in a panic "I not think so he in bed i think." Danny snaps "Well we had better get him out of bed quickly." Zarrine rushes off to wake Jeff up. Niel looking at Danny and grinning says "Well good morning mate, hows things? We have got somebody named Lennox after 11 o'clock today and it should be fun, i wonder what problem solving is?" Danny with hand on forehead "I am not sure but i could do with a few problems solved including my drinking." Niel "Yes you are hitting it a bit hard lately, is it Maxine causing it?" Danny "No i managed to blow her out last night, i hope, i introduced her to another nutter in the pub and then went off with Jeff to help him chat up the barmaids and she left with the nutter to a night club, i told her i think my rash was getting worse since i took up with her and would you believe it? She took offence at what i said." Niel laughing with a chuckle "I am so pleased you have had so much trouble with her she is really nuts and i think you should tell all concerned that i never had sex with her in case my missus comes in to see me, because you won the bet." Danny "Let's just let it go for a few more days" Niel "Well did you get off with the barmaids?" Danny "Are you kidding, i had Jeff with me and i had no chance especially when he started with his corny chat up lines, that finished off any chance we had." Next in walks Zarrine followed by Jeff rubbing his eyes and looked as if he did not know where he was and what he was doing there. Danny said "Last time i seen something like that it had a shell on it's back." Jeff with head hanging and looking lost "Oh leave me alone, i am dying, too much drink last night, it's your fault." Zarrine standing there with arms folded "I am going to be sorry with you two, stop drinking." Danny said "We have not got a drink problem, we drink, we get drunk, we fall down, no problem." Zarrine sit's Jeff down and gives him a drink of orange juice. Jeff looks sick and says "What's this" Face all screwed up says "I don't do healthy and i only drink tea in the mornings and a fag." Zarrine takes the juice off him and hands him a cup of tea and pats him on the head and says. "Is that better?" Jeff "Now we are getting somewhere, i will come alive after this." Niel says "I heard off a little bird that you had no luck with the barmaids last night." Jeff replies "That was no little bird it was an old crow you heard that off and if i hadn't had that old codja with me i would have had a girlie dressed in pink on my arm last night." Danny said "You had no chance mate, let me tell you." Jeff with surprised look. "I just had a thought, what the hell am i doing up this time in the morning, i have not got anything until 11 o'clock this morning, so why did you get me up so urgently?" Zarrine said "Danny tell me get you up, you 3 lots of trouble for me." Zarrine goes into the kitchen and Danny and Niel laugh while Jeff looks at Danny as if he wanted to kill him. Danny said with a smile. "Well you should be up by now anyway, you really do not need any beauty sleep it is too late for you, you need handsome lessons." Niel chuckling out loud "Handsome lessons indeed." Jeff looking annoyed "Never mind every dog has his day." Danny says "Yes and you must stop wearing that bone aftershave it always attracts the old dogs." Next in walks Hose and looks at Jeff and has a little giggle and says "Ha, ha, ha, hello what happened him?" Danny said "He is having a no bad hair day, you have come to take me over for my mobility lesson." Hose in his broken English "Yes you ready go?" Danny says "Yes ready go, see you all later." Niel "God man you must have drunk them dry last night Jeff by the sound of you." Jeff looking grey and ill "I don't remember, i do not know who i am this morning but i must pull it together i have lectures at 11." Niel says "Well Danny has blown Maxine out, it was fun while it lasted." Jeff replies "Let's just hope she leaves you alone" "No fear about that I like my sleep too much" "I thought you would like a bit of nookie now and again." Niel "You don't really think i was having sex with that nutter do you?" "You were i heard you and so did Carol" "No you heard what Danny and i wanted you to believe, what happened" Jeff looking puzzled "Don't be stupid i heard her going nuts in your room." Niel looking very serious answers "What you heard was Maxine enjoying my television and playing with Abby her television has a seriously bad reception so she just wanted to see her programmes like gladiators and WWF wrestling but she liked to get into the action with Abby and the dog loved it, it was like a war zone in there and you and lady wing nut believed we were having sex which also suited Danny, me i love my wife and would not do anything like that." Jeff with a look of disgust "Well that scheming git, i thought i was being caught why didn't you tell me you rat." "I couldn't Danny is my mate and i would do the same for him, we are Welsh and if we can get one over on an Englishman we will." Jeff with a look of anger on his face and Niel with a smile on his face , Jeff says "You pair of pigs, I'm off see you and that rat later."

Later Danny and Ann his mobility trainer who teaches you to use a white cane for the blind properly are in the grounds and this is the first time he has used one ever and Ann is a bit of a ditherer and gets it a little wrong from time to time. Anne speaking to Danny "Well this first lesson is to do any routes you need to learn urgently, are there any you need Immediately?" Danny said "Yes now you come to mention it, i need to get to the social bar." "Anywhere else?" Danny blows his lips and paused to think. "No i can't think of anything more Important." "What about the refectory and student services?" "Yes of course but the bar first aye." "Right we are outside your hall of residence, so we will start from here, just let out the cane and it will click together in a straight piece of steel and it has as you know a nylon ball on the end to allow you to swing it in front of you covering the whole of the width of your body, this ball will take a bit of a bashing and is replaceable." Danny was on the side of the road and Ann is still instructing him, he was on a pavement and is swinging his cane from side to side and at the same time keeping his ball of the cane tapping on the inside of the kerb of the shoreline. He was looking so pleased with himself. Danny said "Well this is a doddle i can get used to this, it's brilliant." Ann snapped at him "Do not get too cocky, this part is easy, keep swinging the cane in front of you so as to cover the width of your body." "Like this" Just then he came to a hedge on the side of the path and the ball of the care got caught in the bush, the ball got jammed and he was pulling but the ball stayed there but the elastic in the cane let him pull it back and forth and he looked as if he was on the end of a bungee rope. Danny said "Oh my god, i am stuck, i will get it out now." Danny bent down and as he did he went head first into the bush, there he was head in the bush and ass up in the air, Ann had her hand over her mouth and laughing, she tried

To pull him out in between bursts of laughter. Danny said "My god, what happened? I thought i was a gonna." Ann turned him around and was just about to brush him down when she seen his face all scratched, she started laughing again and tried to talk to him. "What are you doing? (She could not stop laughing) I have never seen anything so funny in my life, you must take your time when you bend down that bush was there and you weren't aware of it so take your time." "That will teach me to drink too much before i have mobility the next morning, i knew it as soon as i bent down i lost my balance because of the drink last night, that will teach me." He started pulling out some twigs from his hair as Ann was still laughing. Ann said "I think we should go inside the building and go from the door going in and up to the bar." Danny "Yes ok it might be safer am sorry about this it will not happen again." "No problem, if it is as entertaining as this every week you keep on doing what you are doing." Ann continues "Right you are about to go into the building and the stairs to go up to the bar are to your left opposite the phone box, so go ahead" Danny looked as if he had been to war set off with Ann following closely behind. Danny says "Now i am getting it together." Danny sticks out his hand to open the doors and enters, you see him going up the stairs holding the continuous banister rail, he stops after the first flight of steps and he is red in the face and puffing like an old man, he gets to the top of the next set of stairs and he is bent over leaning on the bannister coughing and still red in the face and puffing Ann is chuckling still thinking about the incident with the bush. Next Danny gets to the top of the stairs and he is bent over coughing and puffing even more holding on to the bannister. Danny said gasping for air "Oh my god, i am knackered is there a pub on the ground floor nearby? I am not doing this every night, i will lose too much weight" "Well we can use the lift if it is easier." Danny looked at her as if to say you idiot and said sarcastically and eyebrows raised "Never that's a good idea isn't it" They turn and go back down the stairs again and at the bottom they stop and Ann revised the day's work "Well that is enough for today, i will arrange the next session and let your tutor know when, so you can go off for your coffee break now which is now up in the bar from today on" "Well can you show me where the lift is please? I am not taking those bloody stairs again." Ann was muttering "Oh, oh " Danny said "What's the Matter?" Ann looking down to the ground "I am afraid the lift is out of order and you will have to take the stairs, sorry, bye." Danny looked as if the world is about to end.

It was later in the first lecture of the day and Danny, Niel, Gupta, Maxine and Tim sitting in a classroom waiting for the tutor Lennox.

A new person Danny had never met spoke first his name was Tim "Hello who is in this room today?" Danny said "I am Danny this is Niel and Maxine, i don't know the other person." A voice came out of the blue in a Pakistani voice "I am Gupta i started today, i am originally from Pakistan." Tim said "I'm Timothy but people call me Tim and my dogs name is Laddie." They all greet each other and talk about the lecture. Tim again "Does anybody have any idea what problem solving is all about?" Niel chirps up "I suppose it is something deep and meaningful." Danny said "I hope it is not one of those boring lectures." Gupta "I think it's all about helping you work out any problems in your life" Tim sarcastically "Do you think so?" Next in walks a short Caribbean man with some books in his hand. Lennox with a broad smile on his face and with a spring in his voice "Hello and welcome and i hope you are all well let's introduce ourselves. Start from left to right." Maxine went first "I am Maxine " "I am TIM" "I am GUPTA, i am from Pakistan." "I am NIEL" "I am known as Danny." Next he spoke "My name is Lennox, i am originally from Jamaica but have been in this country for 30 years and today we are going to start your term with problem solving, i hope you are going to learn a lot from this lecture and you will relax and enjoy it. First has anybody had any problems difficult to solve in the past?" There was a lot of nodding and tutting but no one said anything. He spoke again "Well here's one, if you were on a desert island and there was no fresh water but it had been raining and on the pebbled beach there was some water in a deep hole in a rock but you could not get your hand in to scoop up the water and you had nothing to use such as a spoon or ladle etc. How would you get that water to stop you from dying of thirst?" They all looked at each other and you could see them thinking really hard. Tim spoke first "Get your tongue in and lap it out." Lennox smiling replies "No the water is down too deep and your tongue will not reach." Then it was Maxine "You take off your shirt and drop the end in and soak up the water and squeeze it in your mouth." Lennox still smiling "Very good answer but no you are totally naked and so it is Impossible." Maxine has a little giggle. Danny decided to join in "That's true she would not get near the water with those big beauties on her chest." Maxine gives another little giggle. Lennox says "Gupta what about you? What do you think?" Gupta says "I do not know." Lennox "Well keep thinking, i will come back to you, how about you um sorry what is your name? I forgot." Niel realising it was him he was talking to said "It's Niel, um, um, what's yours?" Lennox looking embarrassed says "Lennox, i am Lennox, well Niel what do you think?" Niel with serious look "Well i think you catch an eel and stick his head down there then stick your finger up his ass and the eel will suck in with fear, pull him out and squeeze him and catch the water in your mouth." They all started laughing except Lennox. Lennox in serious voice "Very inventive but no unlikely, Brian how about you?" There was a silence as there was no one there named Brian. Lennox was looking at Danny "yes i am asking you." Danny said "Well my name is not Brian, my name is Danny, Bob." Lennox rolls his eyes feeling silly "Sorry, i thought it was, it's because you probably look like a Brian to me, Daniel well what do you think?" Danny replies "Give me a minute to think." Lennox "Well i will come back to you Gupta, what about you? Have you any thoughts yet?" Gupta just shrugged his shoulders. "Anybody else?" Danny then had a sudden brainwave "I think i have it." Lennox looking excited says " Right Brian let us hear what you think." Danny continues "Danny or Dan but not Brian, you grab the small pebbles and you drop them in the hole until the water rises to the top and then you lap it up." Lennox "Correct." Everyone starts to agree with each other. Lennox says "As you can see there is always a way of working these things out, always, right has anybody got anything of their own we can solve?" Danny said "Yes i have one." Lennox "Ok let's have it." Danny proceeded "I heard this in a quiz once and had me thinking for a long time and there is an answer that can be worked out logically." Lennox "Ok let's hear it" Danny continues "If a Golden Eagle was gliding through the sky at a height of 14 foot from the surface of a perfectly flat desert, at exactly 5 minutes to twelve before midday and the shadow on the ground was 14 feet from wingtip to wingtip whilst flying away from the sun. At exactly midday to the second the Golden Eagle turned and started flying towards the sun at exactly the same height what would be the size of the shadow on the ground from wingtip to wingtip?" Lennox with lots of hand gestures "So let's get this right the Golden Eagle was flying over a flat desert at 11.55am and was flying with his back to the sun and his shadow on the desert measured 14 foot from wingtip to wingtip, at a height of 14 foot. Then at exactly midday when the sun is at its highest, the Golden Eagle turned and started flying towards the sun, facing the sun at the same height what would be the measurement of the shadow from wingtip to wingtip?" Danny says "Yes that's right." Danny said "Right let's throw it open for answers, anybody got an answer?" Maxine spoke up first "Well it would be exactly the same measurement." Danny said "No" Tim "Well at

46

midday the sun is at its highest isn't it so when something goes nearer the shadow will get longer, so i will say about 14 foot one inch." Danny smiling says "No but you have got the right idea." Next in jumps Lennox "Anybody else how about you Niel." "That's a good question, i will say 10 foot." Danny speaks "We need a reason as well." "I don't know it has got me but i will keep on trying to work it out." Danny said "Sorry mate that's not the answer but you are too low." Lennox turned to Gupta "Gupta what about you?" "What is this Golden Eagle?" Lennox with surprised look on his face "You do not know? Well it is a bird of prey." Gupta smiling "Like my next door neighbours daughter she is praying at all times and she is a nice bird, ha, ha." Danny said "Well come on it's a problem to solve and there is an answer." Lennox walked up to the blackboard and spun it round until he had a white board in front of him and started to do some equations. As he was doing this he was muttering. "So the Golden Eagle was 14 foot up in the air at 5 minutes to midday and the shadow was 14 foot wingtip to wingtip. (Lennox writes some figures on the board.) 5 minutes later at midday when the sun is at its highest he turns and flies towards the sun at 14 foot off the ground the same, (He then continues to write some more numbers on the board.) So what is the shadow from wingtip to wingtip?" Lennox done a lot more calculations and after about fifteen minutes stopped and turned to his class. Lennox smiling broadly "I have your answer, he looked so pleased with himself and thought he was so brainy proclaimed. "The answer is 13 foot9and a half inches." There was a long pause and then Danny looked up and said. "I am sorry you are wrong." Lennox looked straight at Danny and stood in amazement and his face went all serious and he became Jittery. He then said "I just calculated it out, i am right or at least within a 100th of an inch." Lennox then went back to his calculations and looked them over again muttering all the time. "Yes i came up with the same result again, are you sure your answer is right?" Danny says "Positive." Lennox now very agitated "I do not want to question you but i feel i am right and i feel you are wrong." Danny replies "Well you are not right this time." Everyone was talking amongst themselves and arguing about what it could be. Lennox said "Well this will have to be continued this afternoon in the last lecture of the day and before then i have a class of A level maths students and they can join me and i can tell them this riddle and we can make a lesson of it, see you all then." They all went off to the refectory to dinner.

In the refectory Danny and Tim meet Jeff and sit together for dinner. Danny said "Well if it isn't that cockney man from outer space,, i want you to meet Tim, this is Jeff or Widget so called because he is always with his head stuck in a can of lager just like the widget." Tim puts his hand out for Jeff to shake and says "Hi nice to meet you Jeff." Jeff replies "Likewise, i am just glad you are not Welsh i could not take another flaming Welshman." Tim "No, i am from Tamworth near Birmingham." Danny said "Jeff, i bet you never could tell could you?" Jeff "Well the accent did stick out a bit." Tim "Do you think so? I don't think i have a brummy accent." Jeff "Yes you definitely have, but at least it is not Welsh, thank god." Danny said "Now, now be good for us Welsh will have to sort you out again." Jeff smiling "Yeh, yeh, so what are you doing here Tim?" Tim "God knows, i am doing the E C D L in computers." Jeff "HUH, That's intelligent so how did you meet him then?" Tim "We have the same tutor and we have Lennox for English etc." Jeff "You mean the super intelligent Lennox who will baffle rocket scientists, he really thinks he is clever don't he?" Danny said "Well be fair he is a very clever man, i take my hat off to him he gets me excited with his work and keeps your mind ticking over and thinking." Tim "Yes i enjoyed his first lecture it was fascinating wasn't it?" Danny replied with cunning look "Can't wait to see him after and his clever little students as he calls them and see if they worked out my little puzzle." Tim

"Yes that is a difficult one you set him and he will not give in will he?" Danny "No he is a determined man, i will give him that and he will not let me tell him how to get to the facts of the answer." Jeff said "Come on then tell me and see if I can work it out." Danny started to laugh "You, you have got no chance this is for very intelligent people and you do not fit into that category I'm sorry." Jeff looking annoyed said "No come on tell me, it can't be that hard if you are the one asking the questions. " Tim said "Well i think it's a stinker." Danny then said "Well are we going to that pub in a taxi tonight?" Jeff "Yes if you like, what about you Tim do you drink?" Tim answers "Yes i like a few pints most nights, where are you going?" Danny replied "We thought we would have a change from the student bar as the lager is awful there and try this pub we were told about they say it is a popular pub but you get a few druggies there sometime but they are allright and if you like we can all meet outside gardener hall at 7.30 this evening and the taxi rank is right outside the pub so it will be easy for us all, i hope as this is the first time we are trying it but we think what can go wrong?" Tim "What about my dog?" Danny replied "No problem we will have a mini bus as my mate Niel and his guide dog Abby always comes with us where ever we go." Tim "Count me in then it will be great." Jeff "Well come on then tell me this problem of yours and i will solve it easy." Danny "Ok then and if you get the answer the beer is on me all night but if you don't i want you to buy my round once instead ok?" Jeff "Oh here we go again it has got a catch again." Danny "No, no catch." Jeff "Just like you taking that tenner off me under false pretence,, Niel told me the truth about what happened, Ok your on so tell me." Danny started to explain the puzzle to him and Jeff listens to him intently.

It was back in with Lennox later that afternoon and he has several students with him and they all sit down and he explains to them again the problem to be solved and introduces them to Danny, Tim and the others. Lennox continues speaking "Well this is Maxine, Gupta, Niel, Tim and Brian." Danny said "No, my name is Danny." Lennox tutting "Yes of course, i can't get it out of my head Daniel not Brian, i will get it right in time. Anyway we have come to the conclusion Daniel that you are wrong so can you tell these students again what you told us as we come to the same answer every time." Danny speaks up "Well Lennox i can tell you that i am absolutely correct and you will come to the same conclusion as me for definite." Lennox "Ok well please tell my first year students the problem and see if i have told them as you told me." Danny "Yes ok here we go again. If a Golden Eagle was gliding through the sky at a height of 14 foot from the surface of a perfectly flat desert, at exactly 5 minutes to twelve before midday and the shadow on the ground was 14 feet from wingtip to wingtip whilst flying away from the sun. At exactly midday the Golden Eagle turned and started flying towards the sun at exactly the same height, what would be the size of the shadow on the ground from wingtip to wingtip?" Lennox chirped up "Is that the same way i told you students? (The students nodded to Lennox that it was the same.) And we still say the answer is thirteen feet9 and half inches." All the students agreed with Lennox. Danny then dropped the bombshell "Well i am sorry to tell you that you are all wrong and the answer is ten feet and 6 inches, now you tell me why?" There was a deadly silence and everyone was looking at each other and all looked as if they had lost a thousand pounds each. Lennox Looking serious and nasty says "No you are wrong, you must be, i cannot be that far out and all the students agree with me, how the hell do you come to that answer? Are you 100% sure that the answer is right?" Danny smirking says "I am absolutely sure, i would bet my life on it." Lennox "Well i will get the reason why if it kills me and the other students will want to stay and help me when do i have you all again?" Tim says "We are all with you again tomorrow last lecture." Lennox says "We will definitely know by then." Niel says "Excuse me can i just say i was the closest, so do i get a prize?" Danny said "Yes your right you said ten foot you were only six inches out closer than all the brainiacs here, i think you deserve something." Niel excited "Yeah,yeah." Lennox says "I will let you have extra lessons here at no extra cost" Niel speaks in a hurry "No that's allright" Lennox "Right see you all tomorrow"

Well it was later that evening out to the pub and in the entrance of the pub and the pub is over flowing with youngsters all looked like hippies etc. and Jeff, Niel, Tim and Danny were sorry they had gone there. Danny said "Well it looks like a big mistake coming here." Jeff agreed "Yes it was, i wished we had hung on to that taxi now and we had gone somewhere else." Niel said "You give up too easily when i want a drink somewhere i get a drink there." Tim "Well they are right there is nowhere to sit and we have our dogs with us, we are even having trouble getting to the bar." Danny said "We will need a miracle to get a seat and the smell in here, i think someone is smoking them Jamaican old holbourne reefers i am getting high myself." Jeff "Well here is a case of problem solving as Lennox would say so let's solve it." They all stood around all thinking and just then Niel got an idea his face lit up "Right i have an idea Danny give me your phone" Danny says "Why do you want my phone?" Niel "Because you have one of those special phones that talk." Tim said "All phones talk, that is what they do." Niel says "No i know that but Danny's phone is one of the special ones designed for the blind it speaks out loud when you use a function and speaks your text messages and you can turn up the volume." Jeff "So what does that have to do with getting a seat?" Niel said "You just wait and see." Niel whispered in Danny's ear and he started tapping out a text message on his phone Jeff speaks to Tim with worried look on his face. "Oh god time to panic if Danny and Niel are doing something together it is going to end up in tears" Tim looking concerned "No they can't be that bad surely." Jeff continues "You don't know these pair they make bonnie and Clyde look like Jehovah's witnesses, i live in fear with these two, if i don't end up with a criminal record at the end of this course it will be a miracle." Tim "Are they that bad? I think they are a lot of fun and there is no sign of madness." Jeff "No sign of madness, your kidding they are bloody Welsh and there two of them the Welsh Kray twins." Tim laughs at Jeff and Jeff gives a wry smile and then Danny gives the phone to Niel. Pointing to his phone and putting Niel's finger on a large button on his phone, Danny says "Just press this button when you want it to speak, i have set the loudspeaker to high." Niel says "Right Tim you come in by my side and do as i do look straight ahead as if you can see and say as i say to your dog and we will be sitting down soon." Jeff "What the hell is he up to now?" Danny said "Just follow them, listen and learn and put a hard look on." Jeff looking terrified "Are you kidding i am like a matchstick and about 7 stone, they will laugh, we are not going to end up fighting are we? They will kill us." Danny smiling says "Just do as i say and follow close to Niel, and put your canes out of sight." Niel and Tim started walking in the doors and on one side was about 15 lads standing by a fruit machine looking hard and smoking. Next thing Niel put the phone near his ear but a bit away so as all could hear what was being said from the text they had sent to Danny's phone voice was heard clear from Danny's mobile phone, it was perfect. "Ok we are nearly in position outside get ready to start operation blow." The lads heard what was happening and thought it was a police raid and all run off to their mates, next thing Niel and Tim started walking through the pub with Danny and Jeff close up behind them. Niel and Tim speaking to their 2 large dogs "Right dog, find the drugs, find the drugs, find the drugs." Tim, Jeff and Danny kept walking in and everyone just disappeared they sat down as there were plenty of tables and all started laughing. Jeff said "Well i will give it to you Niel that was brilliant." Tim "You can say that again, they were like rats leaving a burning ship." Danny said "Right what is everyone having to drink?" Jeff "I will have a lager." Niel "I will have cider." Tim "I will have a beer as well." Danny said "I will have a beer too, Jeff." Jeff with shocked face "What do you mean? You asked what we wanted." Danny replied "Yes and you could not give me the answer about the Golden Eagle, so you can get my round in, go on take your time and hurry up." Jeff looking sheepish "I cannot win an argument lately." Tim said "Well are you going to tell us how you got to the answer you done about that Golden Eagle?" Danny smiling "No, i want you all to think about it, it is logical and it smacks you in the face and that's all i am going to say about the Matter." Tim "That's fair enough but what about Jeff are you going to keep him to that bet?" Niel says "Danny will keep anyone to a bet, i know, i have been caught by him so many times." Danny said "If you want to play with the big boys then you must learn to pay your debts, or go and play with the children, don't worry he will get it back out of me one way or another." Jeff comes back from the bar and hands out the pints and says "Guess what i have just been asked by a barmaid if we want any sauces with our burger and chips. Then she said is that your table over there where those guide dogs are? So i said yes and she said well it is table 23 and you are the only 4 people on one table and you ordered 4 burger and chips, didn't you? I said well i came in after my mates did, so did they pay for them all? She said of course they paid at the bar when ordering, i told her not to say anything to you guys as i think you forgot to ask me for my money." Tim said "Your kidding, it must have been those boys who run out of here thinking we were the drug squad, ha, ha." Danny said "Well keep your mouths shut and we will get a free meal as well." Tim "I don't believe it, i am enjoying it with you guys, it's great." Danny said "It's a messy job but somebody's got to do it." All of them laughed and the food was delivered. Niel said "God this is nice, i am glad we came here now we have had a bit of fun and been fed." Jeff jumps to his feet and stares at a girl in amazement "Shit look at that girl she is wearing a belt not a skirt, bloody hell i will have to give her the eye." Niel with a giggle "Here i can give her 2 as long as she gives them back after or sit's on my lap for a cuddle." Jeff excited "No, don't Niel, i can't handle it I have not had a girlfriend for 2 years and i have forgotten what it is like to have a bit, so keep it to yourself." Danny said "He will not get a chance with all the good looking men here." Jeff "I think you under estimate me Danny, you wait and see." Danny replies "I bet you." Jeff interrupts "No more bets with you, i can't afford it anymore, i will just have her my way you will see." Danny "Yes you may be right, i think you are due some luck and it's a messy job but somebody's got to do it, isn't it." Niel "Will you do me a favour Jeff? Will you go and get the pints if i give you the money?" Jeff smiling "No problem i can make some eyes at that bird at the same time, see you tomorrow." Tim "How long have you 2 been friends?" Niel says "Who? Danny, i have known him about 3 years now and believe me that is long enough." Danny says "You love me really and i think we have hit it off pretty well, he tries to chat up my missus and i try to chat up his." Niel "And you do not stand a chance with my missus and i do not stand a chance with yours." Tim "Oh your both married, i didn't realise." Danny says "Yes but not for long, i fear, she is going to divorce me soon i feel." Tim "Sorry mate why is she doing that?" Danny says "It's a long story mate." Niel "Me i am very much in love with my woman and she loves me and i do miss her very much." Tim "So you don't see her much?" Niel says "Yes i do to be honest." Tim "And what about Jeff is he married?" Danny said "No he is divorced but he has a few children and what about you?" Tim "I am single and i think i will stay that way, it's difficult to fancy anyone when you can't see them, i mean how can you eye someone up across a bar or let them know you fancy them and i had a woman once i thought she was lovely but when i finally put my arms around her she was flat breasted twice my size just like a man and it put me off, i am afraid of making that mistake again and hurting someone's feelings, you know what i mean?" Niel "Yes i am lucky i got a great woman and we met many years ago before i went blind and she has stuck with me through thick and thin. But i know what you mean." Danny said "I can understand what you mean but look at Jeff he is a hell of a nice fella and is inoffensive and if it works out it does if it does not, well no harm done and i think that's the way to be, even if he does make an ass of himself with his corny chat up lines and i feel a couple coming up again tonight the way he is looking at that girl with the mini skirt on, Tim if he does you are in for a real treat he is so funny." Niel "Yes i will back you up, look out i can hear him coming he is on his way back." Jeff puts the drinks on the table and gives Niel the change and says "Well i think i have cracked the case she is all mine, she is coming over to see the dogs and me in a minute." Danny says "Oh she is only interested in dogs then?" Jeff with grin on his face says "Ha, ha, very funny." Over she comes and she strokes the dogs and is a bit tipsy. The young girl says "What are the dog's names?" Niel says "This is Abby that is Laddie and that is Jeff." The girl laughs and Jeff gives Niel a stern look and Jeff hands the girl a drink and says "Here is your drink and do not pay much attention to what they say they are all foreigners." She replies "Thanks for the drink, god i can't believe it in here tonight it is usually packed in here." Niel "Is it? Perhaps it is because we are here." She continues "No they are not like that they are no problem but it is nice to be able to sit down for a change. You are all in the college are you?" Jeff butts in "Yes and what about you?" Looking calm she says "I am a student in the art college and what is your name again?" Jeff "My name is big Jeff and i am mighty tall as well." The lads all started tutting Jeff continues "Oh do you know the difference between sex and a burger?" The young girl looks stunned at Jeff and giggles and says "No." Jeff with punchline "Fancy something for supper?" The young girl laughs louder and the others grin and look embarrassed. Jeff continues "Have you got 20p? I told my mother i would give her a ring when i fall in love. Bet you ten quid you will turn me down. Do you sleep on your stomach? If not can i?" The young girl was now really laughing and Danny, Tim and Niel were wishing the floor would open and swallow them up. Danny couldn't stand it anymore and said "Please no more, no more, i can't take anymore." Jeff "Just ignore these old fogies they are only jealous." The young girl by this time was getting very drunk and decided to go to the toilet and so left, Jeff wondering. She returned and said "Well i am off now, i must get home to bed as i have college tomorrow, nice meeting you all especially you Jeff, see you again sometime, by now." Jeff in sorrowful mood "Oh no don't go i was just getting warmed up." Girl "I must, i will see you again, can you guys keep a secret? I am really with the drug squad and i have let them down tonight, i have been staking this place out for about 6 weeks now and there have been a lot of drugs here and tonight i set up a raid to take place here about 45 minutes ago and look at it it's bloody empty, i had to cancel it and i will be in trouble tomorrow as a lot of manpower was wasted tonight, never mind i can always get a job somewhere else, it's only my career down the drain." Jeff was about to spill the beans "Oh dear, i am sorry but…." Niel quickly interrupts "But there is a concert in one of the colleges and perhaps they have gone there." Young girl "Oh, i never heard about that, well such is life." Danny said "Such is life without a wife and a damn sight worse when you got one and when you meet them you could eat them and when you have married them you wish you bloody had." The young girl said "I beg your pardon?" Danny says "Oh nothing, sorry you just reminded me of a few sayings, sorry." Young girl "Well i must go home and worry about tomorrow, see you all about." Everyone bids her goodnight and Jeff is looking sorry for her. Niel says "You bloody idiot Jeff, you were about to tell her what happened she is a police woman she would have thrown the book at us." Tim "This is unreal, i am going to get into trouble that's for sure with you lot, brilliant, bloody brilliant." Jeff looking very sorry for himself. "Ah well, crashed and burned again, the story of my life." Danny said "Hey mate there are plenty more fish in the sea, don't worry there must be an old squid out there somewhere for you." Jeff in lonesome mood "Yes, i guess your right, and besides she was a bit young for me...what do you mean old squid?" Tim speaks up "What are the girlies like in the college?" Niel "I hear there a few more starting next week, some from abroad like China and South America etc." Jeff cheers up and pays attention "I feel better already, so when do they start?" Danny says "Don't you think you should give yourself time to get over this one tonight?" Jeff "I don't think you should dwell on relationships if they don't work out then move on and besides she was from the drug squid ha, ha." Niel "Yes you have mourned over her for long enough." Danny says "Well it's bloody dead in here isn't it?" They all laughed. Niel "Yes we done a really good job and now we are lonely." Tim "Never mind it was brilliant pretending to be the drug squad and i thought that being blind was boring." Danny says "Which goes to show never mind what disability you have it's not the end of the world, i will never be sombre and miserable it's happened to me but life goes on and you must grab it with two hands and give it your best shot." Jeff said "That's what i admire about us we just get on with it, it's the people who can see that keeps reminding us we are blind, it's like being in another world." Niel "What do you mean, you are in another world." Tim says "Yes you may be right but it changes from time to time when i am home, i get a bloody nudge to remind me i am blind, it's the loneliness and then you can't just get up and jump in your car and go for a drive, or go off on holidays on your own it is then i feel down." Danny says "I know what you mean, i do get very down at home as i live in the middle of nowhere and i can't do what i have always done it kills me all the time then, but now i feel i must change my life and move to somewhere where i can get about and do my own thing and use the bus and train to do this, i must think positive, i don't know how this is going to work out but somehow i will solve it to my benefit, i got to, that's why i am here to learn how to be blind." Jeff says "What do you mean learn to be blind? You already know you have gone blind." Danny replies "No you dick head, i mean i have gone blind but i now need to learn the tricks of how to be as normal as i can with a disability or in other words learn to be blind properly." Tim frowns and says "I hate the word disability it is not me but people use it Willy nilly, i hate it, i feel normal as i did before i went blind and i don't want to be referred to as disabled." Niel joins in " Yes I agree but they have to call it something but it is very rarely heard spoken to us is it? but it's up to us to either let them think we are disabled or not they can only tell by the way we act about it" Danny "I suppose your right, i don't feel disabled neither, i can still tell a good joke, drink like i have always done, have sex the same but slower, i just need to be able to use the JAWS system so as i can put a letter i receive through the door, scan it, read it, write a reply on the same computer, print it, get an envelope out type the address in my computer put an envelope in the printer and print the address and then put the letter in the envelope and post it. Once i can do that i am halfway to my goal of learning to be blind, do you see what i am saying?" Tim "Well put, i see now what you mean." Danny says "And then there is only one thing left, i need to get some brains into that cockney git over there." All the lads laughed and Jeff said "I won't learn anything off any stupid Welshman like you or Mr. Potato head over there, because between you both there is no brains what so ever." Niel chirps up "You cheeky little git, i will sit on you if you are not careful." Jeff "Pervert."

Niel chuckles and says "I'll give you pervert, you little primp." Tim laughing says "Now be good you two be good." Jeff "Well it's had it here now, let's get some taxi's and head for the student bar for one or two so as we know where we are, what do you think?" Tim "Yes it might be a good idea and we can have a couple of shorts." Danny says laughing "Jeff can't wear shorts they drag on the floor, he is so short." The boys went off back to the college.

It was the next day and Danny is in the main building with Anne again for another lesson on mobility with a cane, they are at the bottom of the stairs at the entrance below the bar stairs near the lift. Ann says "Well how are you getting on after the last lesson?" "Fine except i am about 2 stone lighter because of the lift going up to the bar it never seems to be working." "Yes i know, i will get onto the company after this lesson and get them to do it Immediately." "Good, so what is on the agenda today?" "Well i thought i would take you up to the shopping precinct for a lesson as it is a lovely day, are you ok with that?" "Your the boss but do you think i am ready for that after what happened outdoors last time?" "I think you will be ok but if you feel unsure at any time let me know and watch out for any nasty bushes, ha, ha." "Ok if you say so i am ready." They both go outside and off they toddle to College Green, Danny in front of Ann with his White cane going back and forth feeling his way and Ann a few steps behind. "You are doing well are you confident enough to cross some roads at some traffic lights?" Danny starting to look very nervous says "Bring it on, i have got to learn, haven't i?" At the traffic lights Ann shows Danny how to tell when they change as there were some cones that spin under the light controls that will only spin when it is safe to cross and also they beep. They cross at some traffic lights and start heading down a narrow path and onto another road that is much quieter and stop to talk about what they are about to do next. Ann says "Right that was very good, now i want you to remember everything you do today as this precinct is easy to get to and is handy for students to get money out of a hole in the wall or the post office and there is a chip shop and a mini-market and also a hairdressers, and if you want to get into town the bus stops here as well." "I don't think i will go to town, it is too risky." "Why do you say that? Most students say that but within six months they are all doing it, you must have confidence in yourself, it will happen you cannot live the rest of your life in doors." "Do you think so? I hope your right, i soon will be alone again and will have to do all this myself as i soon will be divorced, i think." "Oh, i am sorry to hear that, but i assure you that it will be a doddle soon and you will do it without thinking." "I hope so, i really do, i need to get some money out today if i can." "No problem, i will show you how it is done, right let's go on up to the shops." "OK let's do it, it's a messy job but somebody's got to do it." Off they go walking up the road but suddenly there was a car parked half on the pavement, Ann did not say anything to Danny just to see what he does. He walks up to the car and his cane hit's the car. Danny looking annoyed and starts talking to himself. "What the hell is this car doing on the pavement? I don't believe it, i don't sit on the road and expect the cars to go around me." Next thing Danny folds his cane in half and uses the jagged edge of the cane and scraped it along the length of the car, Ann looks on in amazement and puts her hands over her mouth in shock, Danny stood there with smug look. "Take that you bastard, that will teach him to park on the pavement, he has no consideration for us so why should we have any for him." Ann says looking very shocked "Oh my god, did i just see what i seen? Fair enough he deserved that, i understand what you are saying, you don't mess around do you?" Danny looking serious says "Well, he must be an idiot, he must know blind people use this pavement regularly and if he doesn't care, why should we?" "I agree, i have told the very person several times and he just ignores me, so good on you, I must say but i will deny it if you tell anyone i said that." "Is it a nice car?" "Yes it is almost new." "I wondered, because if he keeps on parking like that it will be in a hell of a mess by the time i leave the college as i am here for 3 years." They both laugh Ann with her hands over her mouth "Quick let's move on before he comes out, carry on i will follow." They head off again and around the corner and into the shops, Danny and Ann use the hole in the wall with the shopkeeper helping they both find the hair dressers and the chip shop and were there for a while learning this and they come out again and as they come around the corner Ann sees the owner of the car bending down feeling the scratch on his car. Anne panicking says with a whisper "Oh my goodness Danny, the man who owns the car is looking at the scratch on his car and he looks as if he is going to cry, please don't say nothing to him, let's just ignore him." "Ok, i will not say anything but do not avoid going past his car or he might suspect it was me." They carry on walking Ann looking really worried, they come up to the car with man besides it and Danny hit's the front of the car with his cane. The man looks up to see Danny coming straight at him banging his car as he goes with his cane as if to find his way, the man says loudly to Danny "Wow, wow, wow, gently that's my car." Danny says "It can't be i am on the pavement, cars are on the road, pedestrians walk on the pavement." The man replies "I beg your pardon, do you know anything about this scratch on my car?" Danny sarcastically says "What scratch? What car?." Man "Very funny, i bet you know something about this." Danny "Why do you think i had anything to do with it? I can't see your bloody car? And why would i scratch it? What reason could there be to do that?" The man snaps at Danny "Because it is half parked on the pavement." Danny "So you know the reason why it might be scratched by somebody do you? Because it is half parked on the pavement, so why the hell don't you park it on the road? Instead then, the road is wide enough." Man "It was you i know it was your a menace, i ought to smack you in the gob." Danny in serious voice "Go ahead mate, take your best shot, I only need to get a hold of you and i will kick the shit out of you, i have met your sort before, no consideration for anyone else." Man in argumentative mood "Your lucky your blind." Danny quick as a flash answered "No mate, your lucky i am blind believe me you are the lucky one, i warn you if you keep on parking on the pavement it will happen again every time i come up these shops and i am going to make it my business to come up to these shops every day for the next 3 years, i am at this college, good morning to you." Danny walks on Ann following closely behind, the man with is mouth wide open and standing there puzzled and Ann passed him she spoke to him "I asked you several times not to park on the pavement.." They head on back to the college and outside the lift going to the bar and the sign has gone and it looks as if the lift is now working again. Ann says "You promised you would not say anything to that man." Danny says "Well, he started on me and i don't take fools lightly and besides i like a challenge." "Yeh, i hope he will just leave it at that as people like him mostly don't." "Don't worry i will take a walk up there and take Niel and his dog Abby with me, he won't do much to me but Niel and me together look a formidable pair and i wouldn't take on anyone like him and me, right where are we?" Ann "Looks as if the lift is working now, well i am having a funny day things seem to be sorting themselves out." "Yes i am sorry about that incident with that man and his car, i just can't stand a bully and a person like him who don't give a damn about anyone else." Ann "Please don't, i thought you were correct and i think he has got the message, i thought you were brilliant the way you handled him, well i think that was enough for today, we are a little bit early but never mind go and have a early coffee break, here is the lift, it only stops at the top and the bottom it's easy." She puts his hand on the controls inside and tells him. "Only two buttons up and down, i will see you tomorrow."

"Yes see you and thanks." Danny gets into the lift and the music in there is a bit loud. In the lift and Danny presses the button the lift gets to the top the lift stops but the lift doors do not open he only finds 2 buttons so presses the down button and down the lift goes down again it reaches the bottom and the doors open again, so he presses the up button and up it goes, it stops again and nothing, the door stays shut so he in temper presses the down button again, down it goes again and stops at the bottom and the doors open again. This time 2 young girls get in and Danny presses the button up, it goes again and stops at the top, the door does not open again he presses the up button to try and get the door open, nothing so he turns and says to the girls "Sorry i don't know what's wrong, these doors won't open and this bloody music is driving me nuts." But there is no one there he looks with total fright on his face so down he goes, at the bottom and the doors open again, he mutters to himself "Right last time." Up the lift goes again it reaches the top and nothing the doors stay shut but he could hear a load of giggling and someone says behind him. "Why are you going up and down in that lift?" Danny turns and realises it's the 2 girls who were in the lift with him earlier standing outside behind him on the landing. Danny had not realised the lift had 2 sets of doors on both ends of the lift but never heard them opening because of the loud music and looked on with a stupid idiot i am look. "I was testing it for Ann and it is working ok now." He gets out of the lift and rushes past the girls feeling stupid. Danny went straight into the bar for coffee and sat alone muttering to himself and having a little chuckle and in walks Niel and Abby. Danny said "What an idiot, what an idiot, ha, ha, ha, ha, ha, ha." Niel sat down and looking at Danny and he started to laugh as well. "Ha, ha, what's the Matter with you? I have heard you laughing since i got in here." "I have had a weird day so far mate, i don't believe what just happened to me, i have been going up and down in that lift for about ten minutes and looked a right fool as it has two doors and i never knew until i heard 2 girls laughing at me outside when i had my back to them." Niel "Never, ha, ha, ha, I use it all the time and i knew it had two sets of doors on it ha, ha, I bet you felt a right idiot? Ha, ha," "Too bloody right, i felt a fool i have never seen a lift before with two sets of doors, one either end, ha, ha," Niel now laughing out loud "Well that has cheered you up anyway i bet you will remember next time, i have just been sitting outside the front entrance of the college, it is a lovely day isn't it? We could have sat there all day it was nice." "Yes it is gorgeous, i have been up the shops at college green and had my first lesson getting up to the shops it was good but i had a bit of a problem with one of the natives here, he had parked his car half on the pavement and i walked into it so i scratched it with my cane. Ann was shocked and he came out when i was on my way back and he confronted me and threatened me so i threatened him back and he was then the shocked one." "I bloody hate that and lots of people do that, my neighbour at home used to do it until i sorted him out, i used to wait until Abby had a crap then i used to pick it up and instead of putting it in the bin in a bag, i used to lay it out right by his driver's door, i think he took the hint and stopped doing it." Danny smiling says "He probably tripped over it and broke his nose." Both of them laughed" Niel tells a funny story "Do you know the funniest thing i had with him was when i was coming back from the paper shop early one morning after getting the milk and his wife was on the pavement shouting at him to stop, he was in his car going past his house and his wife was waving at him to get his attention trying to give him a message but he never even looked over and as he passed she was turning as he passed following the car going down the road until she came face to face with me and she shouted "You blind bastard." Just as she came face to face with me, i said, i know, she was calling her husband a blind bastard not me but she rushed off as fast as her feet could carry her, a few days later she approached my missus and she was all apologetic to her saying . "I was not calling your husband a blind bastard, i was referring to my husband, he did not see me trying to stop him and i give him what for after that, but i felt awful after that and hope Niel didn't think i was referring to him. " Danny says "Never, what did you think?" "I thought that was the case and i had a real good laugh about it, she though goes very quiet when i am around, but now i tease her about it." "Isn't it funny how easy these things happen, i always find it funny when things like that happen. I was in a pub a few weeks ago and i was standing there with my friend and he went to the toilet and a man came up to me and said "Mate you had better stop staring at my wife's boobs." I said "I was not" But he insisted i was. I said "I wish i could see her boobs but... and as I said that he grabbed me and threw me against the bar so i was trying to tell him but he would not listen, he was a big lad too, next thing my mate came back from the toilet and shouted to him "What the hell is going on? What the hell do you think you are doing?" he said " he is staring at my missus boobs" my mate said "I don't think so." The man holding me said "Look if i said he is staring at my missus boobs, then he is." My friend said "I don't think so, he is blind." All of a sudden you could hear a pin drop and i started smiling, he said "No he is not." and the bar man said "He is mate." He did not believe it, he said to me "But your eyes are perfect." I said to him, don't try that on with me, i am not that way, i am straight." He said "Look mate, i didn't know sorry." As he brushed me down and bought a few pints all night, he was lucky as some people wanted to give him a good kicking." Niel said "I should think so too, he would have deserved it, i bet his missus was embarrassed?" "Only a bit, she tried to make up for it at the end of the night, she came up and kissed me and grabbed my hand and placed it on her boob and said "It's yours anytime." and i was grateful she did, but it just goes to show there are some benefit's in being blind and lots of things you can get away with." "Yes i know what you mean, many times i have had a boob in my hand by accident." Next in walks Jeff he sat down next to the lads and spoke "Hi guys everything allright? I have been busy this morning god there is a lot of work with this advice and guidance, i don't think i will be out for a pint for a couple of weeks with all this work." Danny said "Ok, mate." Jeff looking dejected "Is that all you can say mate, won't you miss me?" Danny smiling "No." Jeff "Great mate, thanks don't beat around the bush mate why don't you tell me straight." Niel said "He did, leave him alone he has had a trying day, especially with that lift out there, he has been going up and down it for the last half hour and he has jet lag." Jeff "Ha, ha, ha, I bet he didn't realise that there was two sets of doors did he? What a dick head." Niel "Correct and he made himself look a right idiot in front of two young girlies." Danny said to Jeff "And you do that every day of your life, never mind i will have the last laugh by the end of the day." Jeff "What do you mean?" Danny said "Never mind, so what have you got next, i have more cd's to play and go and see if i have any mail in student services. You two have advice and guidance don't you?" Danny looking heaven would says "God help us if one day you two get to give anyone advice for anything, this country will be in a mess and as regards advice, well, i shudder to think." Niel joins in "Yes i agree i will have anybody doing criminal acts hanged and i will make Melinda Messenger queen." Next Jeff starts "Yes good idea and i would ban trousers and jeans on women and bring back the mini skirt as law and ban the bra and bring back stockings and crutchless knickers and ban bikini waxing and..." Both Danny and Niel look up at the ceiling and both at the same time said "Shut up."

It was later that day they all gathered again in Lennox's lecture there they were and Lennox and the A level students were ready for a showdown with Danny. Lennox with a smug grin on his face "Hello everyone, well we have all got different ideas on your problem you set us

56

Brian, so we will open the discussion and i must ask you first. Are you sticking to your answer?" Danny said "Daniel, not Brian, Bob and yes i stick to my answer and i know for a fact it is right without a shadow of a doubt." Lennox with broad smile "Yes Daniel sorry not Brian, right who wants to start." Niel starts the discussion "I think it has a lot to do with the fact it is midday and the sand myself." A young student says "I think the sand is a lot to do with it like the heat when it creates mirages it also affects the shadow, it distorts it." Danny said "Good thinking, but that's not the reason." Another student says "I think it is to do with the intense heat and how it affects the feathers." Danny said "No." Another student "Is it anything to do with the equator?" Danny replied "I don't think so to be honest." Maxine "Is it anything to do with the position of the moon that affects it?" Danny said with a smile still "No does it affect you?" Maxine with a nasty look "What do you mean?" Danny said "Nothing only kidding." Some of the students huddled around each other and started to argue out the reasons and getting irritated by it while others had their head in their hands thinking hard. Next in walked Jeff with a few other students who wanted to know what the answer was. Jeff said "Excuse me Lennox we have been standing outside listening, so can we Join in this lecture as we are curious as to what the answer is?" Lennox with a look of amazement said "My god i have never had so many students in this room at one time, i am glad that my lecture is becoming so popular. Have you any ideas?" Jeff said "Well we have been listening at the door and we are stumped." Jeff and friends join the other students to discuss more. Lennox "Is it anything to do with winds?" Danny "No." Lennox "Atmospheric pressure at that time of the day or moisture etc. "Danny says "No." A student then spoke up "I think it has something to do with the colour of gold, the feathers on the Golden Eagle is gold and the sun shines right through them and so reduces the shadow in size." Danny said "That's a really good answer." He looked happy and said "So i am right?" Danny said "But your wrong." He flops his shoulders and makes a groaning sound says "Shit i thought i had it then, was i near?" Danny answers "No." Jeff says "Has the eagle bowed his wings instead of keeping them straight?" Danny says "No, do you want a clue?" All of them got a bit excited and said "Yes." at the same time. Danny said "Just think of the sun it has a lot to do with the answer." The students all went back into their different huddles and continued to haggle and even started arguing. Lennox thinking out loud. "It's to do with the sun, it's to do with the sun, what the hell could it be the sun, the sun." Danny also starts to mutter, "And i thought these students were supposed to be intelligent." Lennox said "Well I am stumped anyone else got anything to add?" they wanted to wait a minute as they started to argue about the subject and calling each other idiots etc. Jeff said "Ok now we will never hear the end of this, the big Welshman has the floor." Danny said "Now don't be like that or I will not tell you." Lennox "Ok Brian, i mean Daniel you must tell us or give us another clue." Danny in deep thought said "I tell you what, i will do all the actions of the golden Eagle and if you get it as i do it shout out." Lennox "Yes that is fair enough, how would you like to do this Daniel?" Danny "Have you got a football or a globe in here?" Lennox "Yes i have got a globe here." Danny making lots of gestures with his hands says "We can use that there as the sun and put it on top of those shelves near the ceiling and clear a pathway from the back of the room to the blackboard." Everybody helped and done as Danny asked and all went to the side of the room, some sat on chairs and some on the window cills. Danny then proceeded "Now pretend that globe is the sun and i will be the Golden Eagle interrupt at any time with the answer." Danny stood up with his back to the globe and spread his arms out as the Golden Eagle would and started to walk forward to the blackboard and talking his problem out as he went along. "I am flying away from the sun at this height and the shadow is 14 foot on the ground, (Danny was moving very slow almost standing still he was going so slow.) Now it is just striking midday (he reaches the blackboard and turns.) I am turning, I am turning and now i am facing the sun and the shadow is now going to reduce to ten foot six inches, why?" Everyone just stared and looked like expectant fathers and some were biting their nails. Danny stopped and waited for a minute or two with his hands on his hips. Maxine looking as if she was about to have a nervous breakdown said "For Christ's sake, tell us, please tell us, i am going mad." Niel said "Calm down Maxine, calm down, you will have a coronary in a minute." Danny said "Right, i will tell you, or at least i will show you. (Danny went back to the globe and put his back to the sun and started to show them again.) I am flying away from the sun, i am flying away from the sun, (Danny reaches the blackboard again , his arms acting like 2 big wings sticking out either side of him like a aeroplane and begins to turn arms still outstretched like a flying Golden Eagle.) I am now turning towards the sun, i am turning towards the sun." He turned and faced the sun and his arms were outstretched then he bent his right arm and put it over his forehead and shaded his eyes from the sun and the other arm wing stayed out straight, he used his other arm (wing) to shade his eyes from the sun and started to fly towards the sun. There was a pause for a second and then the place erupted with incredible laughter, people were falling all over the place and even Lennox was stunned for a second then threw his felt pen across the room and burst out laughing it was just a crazy scene of total laughter and Danny was still doing the actions keeping them laughing, tears were flooding out of their eyes. After a few minutes everyone calmed down and started to compose themselves. Jeff said "That is the funniest thing i have ever seen." Lennox was still laughing and said "Daniel, very good, very good, i have never heard or seen anything so funny in all my life, brilliant." Maxine "So why was he shading his eyes? I have never seen a bird do that before." Niel said "Oh Maxine, have a day off."

Later on and Danny Niel and Jeff in the bar having a good laugh at the day's proceedings. Niel said "Well that was what i call a cracker you certainly put him in his place, he thinks he knows everything but he was a picture to see, it was brilliant, just brilliant." They all laughed again Danny said "I love it when you have a lot of swats in one room and you make them look as dopey as everyone else and i have come to really like Lennox, he is not so stuck up as everyone thinks." Jeff "Yes he is a good sport, did you hear about David Blunket he was in the houses of parliament and the prime minister went up to him and said "David you don't work here anymore" David said "I wish you would tell my bloody guide dog that." They all fell about laughing. Next in walks one of the young swats from Lennox's lectures bragging as usual. They come and stand by the boys. The one student says "Well look who it is the Eagle man, that was a cracker but i should have known it was a trick and there was nothing intelligent about it." Danny said "Well i thought it was very intelligent as it took a hell of a lot of you 2 days not to work out it was possible to work out something like this if you suspected it was a hoax." Next in walks another swot bragging. Next student "Hi guys, guess what i just did, i beat my tutor in a game of golf easy, easy, that oldie is past it as most of these oldies are." Danny and the boys hearing this looked very mad Jeff and Niel were just about to say something when Danny gestured to them not to say anything. Danny said "I will give you a game." The student replied "You got no chance, your blind your joking." Danny "Huh, i can beat you with one arm behind my back" Student "Oh no we are talking about golf not boxing." Danny "Yes i can beat you in that too." The swots laughed out loud which made Jeff, Niel and Danny go red with temper Niel was just about to start on them when Danny interrupted him again. Danny said "Yes you have a good laugh i am serious, i will bet you fifty quid." The student replied "You can't be serious, with a head start i could still beat you." Danny "You think your so great i will up the odds, i bet you fifty quid Niel will bet you fifty quid and Jeff will bet you fifty quid as well that i will beat you." Niel and Jeff started to choke on their beer and looked at Danny in a horrified manner as if to say, you got to be kidding. Jeff said quickly "We will? ..." Danny speaks very quietly to Niel and Jeff "Now just back me up i am on a certainty." Niel whispering "I can't afford that neither can Jeff, what do you think you are doing?" Danny says "Just trust me have i ever let you down? Sh, sh, sh, leave it to me." Jeff and Niel looked terrified. Danny says to the students "Well are you going to put your money where your mouth is." The student in an arrogant way said "You are telling me your betting me £150 that you can beat me in a game of golf." Danny looking serious says "Easy, easy as you say." Student "Ok when? I could do with earning some easy money." Danny replies "Tonight at midnight." From a dim silence came a deafening roar of laughter and Niel and Jeff laughing with their hands on their foreheads as if to seem totally relieved. Student "We should have known there would be a catch to it and i will not go ahead with it, because your too dodgy and will win somehow or another with your tricks." Danny said "So let that be a lesson to you, don't be too quick to judge as you never know when the cards are stacked against you. I'm older than you and have more experience to use that makes me far more intelligent than you and there is always more than 1 way to catch a mackerel." The swots move off moaning as they went. Jeff in cocky voice "yeh, yeh, go on off with you and don't come back you can't make fools of us, i was totally confident you was in charge of the situation." Niel said "You lying sod you were crapping yourself and referring to Danny as an idiot to me." Danny said "I could see you were on my side and full of confidence." Jeff looking sheepish "I was, i was just giving those idiots a false sense of security " Danny smiling "Yeh, yeh, bloody foreigner, i think you should get the beer in and stop crawling." Jeff "But it's Niel's round." Niel whispers to Jeff "I think you should get them in or i will tell him what you really said." Jeff stalls for a minute and then decides. "So same again is it?"

CHAPTER 4
A STING IN THE TAIL.

It was a few days later and things in the college was going well for Danny and his new found mates but hell was about to break out there and this hell was going to cause a little hell for Danny. It was in the name of a man who was away for a few weeks before Danny, Jeff, Carol and Niel started and they had heard about this person but did not pay any mind about him as he was in his 40's and Danny didn't take him serious as he had never met him but he soon found out life in the college was not as it seemed. It was one lunch time he and Jeff was sitting on the bench outside Gardner and this man appeared and said cockily to them "Allright move over for me to sit and give me a light mate." He pushed himself onto the bench and grabbed the lighter Jeff had offered him and threw it back on Jeff's lap so ignorantly and continued speaking "The bastards here are making my life a misery, god, i feel like going over there and giving someone a good slap, i do." Danny "Who are you talking about?" Bobby replied "Oh those bloody do-gooders on the staff, they give me the hump they really do." Jeff said sarcastically "My name is Jeff and this is Danny, i call him dodgy." Bobby "Right, i expect you have heard of me, i am Bobby Maclean, i bet they are all talking about me here." Danny said "No i can't say i have ever heard of you, what is it again Bobby Mac what?" He replied "Bobby Maclean as in the toothpaste, i am the hardest man ever to come here so i am told and some of these kids here are assholes so stupid they really are and so what are you both doing here? Jeff looking serious" I am doing the advice and guidance here." Bobby laughed out loud "Jeff you don't stand a chance in hell in getting a job doing that, it's Impossible to get a job after the way they teach you here ha, ha, do you really think anyone will give you a job in a CAB office looking as weak as you do? The public will rip you apart, forget it man and just ride the system it's a good crack and what about you mate?" Looking at Danny, and Danny didn't answer him on purpose as he didn't like his attitude so Bobby said again after whistling at Danny "Yes you, Jeff what's his name again?" Danny looking nasty at him " My name is Danny not what's his name, so what was the question again thingamy." Bobby laughed out loud as if to say it don't bother me "Ok Danny so what are you supposed to be doing here?" Danny said "I am here to learn to be blind and i am also doing some work in the music tech." Bobby "So you are into music then, i love all the heavy groups Deep Purple, Led Zeppelin, the heavier the better man, you know." Danny tried to be civil to see where it got him and said "Yes i am into all types of music so at least we have something in common then, i like to blast it a little bit in my room." Bobby "So what is your room number then?" Danny "B 11 on the balcony." Bobby "Well be prepared to be blasted out, i am in B14 and don't take any prisoners with my music." Jeff moaned "Oh great i am almost next door to you, i hope you are not the type to blast it in the night." Bobby "I certainly do matey, so look out, well until the warden threatens me to fetch in the gestapo then i turn it down a bit and i only do it when i am drunk." Jeff "Most weekends then." Bobby showing off "Oh no i am pissed every night so look out but you will love my music." Jeff says with a worried face "Oh dear,, i knew it was going too well here." Danny said "So what are you supposed to be doing here?" Bobby "Shagging, chasing all the little girls and getting pissed and having the odd joint, do anyone of you take a spliff at all?" Both lads say no and Bobby says "Squares ay, i thought so, so you are boring then, well get it on man don't be so boring." Danny replied "So what course are you doing here?" Bobby "Intercourse and shagging and wanking now and again, they try to get me to do the braile and i would love to give 2 of them girls one and i am supposed to be doing the massage course and turn up sometimes when i feel like it, i am my own boss and they are afraid of me and leave me alone." Danny "So why were you calling them bastards and why have you not been here for the last 3months?" Bobby looked very coy and replied "Because i was suspended for throwing a glass at a youngster in the bar and i had to have some time off anyway as my bitch of a daughter owed me money and i had to get it and go on a bender for 2 weeks, i don't let the soil stand still beneath my feet. You know i have so many friends i need time for them and i had to see my man in the police station there as i have to attend once a month as i have not long got out of prison, i am considered dangerous and the pricks here took me out of a nice room over the road with en-suite and put me here in this hole, what a shit house it is too and i can't find my way around over here at all." Jeff says "So how bad is your eyesight then?" Bobby "Oh, i can't see at all in my left eye and only a little tiny in the other I, i went blind in prison and so they let me out early because of it and sent me here to be taught to use braile and computers etc. and if you ask me this place is ok for idiots and degenerates and that's all." Danny said in a snappy voice "So you are calling us degenerates then, i don't think i like that description mate." Bobby replied "Take it easy man, we are all fucking degenerates here, we don't stand a chance without our eyesight man and you know it, it's the end as the doors say, this is the end my friend, the end ha, ha, ha, and fuck um all, sex and drugs and rock and roll ay man." Jeff "Ha, ha, ha, what a way to express it, i don't think it is the end or at least i didn't until i met you, you are depressing Bobby." Bobby "It's a fact man, it's a fact, i live for sex and booze and the occasional bit of dope and what do you think Dan?" Danny sat there silent for a minute and then said "I was ok until i met you, i was just excepting the fact i am blind and getting to grips with it and you make it sound like a disease that is very defeatist and i wonder if you are really covering up your hurt because you have gone blind or have no outlook on life or just a sad person." Bobby laughed and said in a cocky way "I don't care what you think of me man as long as i don't get hurt by you because i will not put up with being judged as i am my own person and will never bow down to anyone or anything, i am Bobby Maclean and am untouchable a free person, so are you both blind too? i bet Danny can see allright or he would not be saying things like that to me, because if you seen me i would put the fear of god into anyone man." Jeff sees Danny getting uptight and tried to cool things down he said "I have got R P and can see with both eyes but on the outer side of my eyes and not my centre of my eyes and Danny is totally blind in his right eye and can see shapes and light and dark like you really." Danny butts in "And i am Welsh and six foot tall and built like a brick shithouse and am also not afraid of anyone, so we are very much alike in that way only." Bobby dismisses Danny and says "Whatever, whatever, i am not too worried, where is that bitch that is supposed to be taking me up the shop and to see the ayatollah, you know the principle, these foreign girls are useless they can't tell the time and can't even speak the Queen's English, what a waste of time, but a good shag i expect, i must try them all out before i go." Danny says smiling "You don't have much respect for anyone have you? These girls and boys are here to learn English and they get a pittance for what they do you know." Bobby "Yeah, i know and i wonder if i can get their knickers off if i offer them some extra money, hey Jeff, what do you think? I bet you like the girls you look a bit pervy.." Jeff "Funny enough Danny says that too, but i respect the females as long as they are female from birth, ha, ha." Bobby "Yes that's right, here she comes is it and about time too." But it was Carol walking back to have a sit on the bench with her uncle Jeffrey, she said "Hello is that you Uncle Jeffrey? And who else is there?" Jeff "Danny and a man named Bobby." She said "Oh hello guys, nice to meet you Bobby, can i sit down by you Jeff? I am knackered." Bobby "Here come and sit besides us both and a lass from Scotland then, i like the girls from up there keep you warm in bed and they like it up trap 2. they nearly have all got big nice asses to cuddle up to man, you know what i mean?" Carol with serious face said "I don't know how to take that mate." Bobby "No malice intended, it's a compliment and if you get fed up with this man and want a real man my room is b 14 just walk in no need to knock." Carol "You are cock sure of yourself aren't you? For one thing Uncle Jeffrey and me are the best of friends and for the second i only go to bed with real men, sorry." Danny said "Right let's keep it nice and easy and here is your S. S.W. and she is a he, it's my old friend Hose, allright matey?" Hose "Yes, i am fine Danny and how are you?" Danny smiling to Hose says "I am fine thank you mate, have you come to take old Bobby to the shops then? "Hose now smiling "Yes, are you ready Bobby if we go now? As i must be back soon." Bobby "Hello Hose that bloody dago is pathetic, i thought Katalina was taking me, i don't like going with you holding a stupid dago's arm, i feel like a poofta so why is she not taking me then?" Hose looking worried said "Because i am the only left, the others are busy somewhere else so are you ready?" Bobby "Ok wait a minute i tell you what, i am not going up the shop with you, you take me to principal's office to see her and you get up the shop and get me a pouch of Virginia tobacco and some papers ok?" Hose "Yes Bobby i understand, ok." Hose leads him off and Bobby said "See you all later man and Carol keep it warm for me." They go off and Carol says "Who the hell was he? I don't like him at all." Danny looking a bit nervous said "That was Mr Bobby Maclean the hardest man in this college, according to himself." Carol looking amazed "So that's Bobby Maclean he is a right asshole, he is a nasty bit of stuff, he threw a glass at a young lad here because he would not give him a light because the lad didn't smoke that's all and another lad was beaten up by him in the toilet's here in Gardner but would not say to the staff here that it was him and is he in our dorm then?" Jeff "He certainly is and he is next door but one to me, which makes it worse he plays his heavy rock music loud at night." Carol "And i am the room above you so it will affect me to, ok, i tell you what i will complain if he does and he is creepy, he is so suggestive like you, i suppose uncle Jeffrey." Danny said "Carol, Jeff is nothing like that creep he is a horrible man he really is he has given me a different outlook on this college now it's the end i know it i will kick his teeth down his throat if his attitude doesn't change." Jeff "Not a good idea mate, he is not worth getting expelled from here, he is not worth it." Carol "And besides by what I have heard about him he will be the one kicking your teeth down your throat, he went to prison for grievous bodily harm, i was told and it's not the first time so be careful Dan, Jeff is right he is not worth it let's just stay out of his way and enjoy our time here and keep ourselves to ourselves." Danny looking fed up said "Yes you may be right, but in my experience he is the type that just makes th ngs worse and worse until someone cracks, he is so arrogant, i need a pint and it's too early let's go for a cuppa is it?" Jeff "Yes let's go and see Polly in the bar for one she will cheer you up." Off they go.

In the Student bar for coffee and standing in the queue and it was just their luck they were listening to Bobby Maclean getting served and he was saying to Polly "A cup of coffee and a smile and get those lovely jugs out for me again." Polly said "Ha, ha, ha, Bobby don't say things like that i have never got my jugs out for you or anyone else here, thank you very much so behave." Bobby "I bet you are dying too though and take me over in the corner to sit in my seat so as i can have a smoke and give your pussy a stroke ha, ha, " Polly "I will take you over but you behave or this coffee will cool you down when i chuck it over you." She takes him over to the corner but there was some young lads sitting there and she said to him "You can't sit in the corner, there are people sitting there." Bobby said to the lads "Who is there then? C'mon tell me who are you?" They said "We are from the I.T. class." Bobby "Well piss off, before i put my foot up your ass now go on." They scuttle off and Polly put his coffee down on the table and said to him "That wasn't nice was it?" Bobby "They are only little wankers who shouldn't be here at this time of day, c'mon Polly let me have a little feel." Bobby tries to pull her over and she pulls free and says "Right that's enough or you will be on report again mate." Bobby replied "Yeh, right, you love it really, if these people weren't here you would be begging me for it and you know it ha, ha." Polly shrugged it off and went back to serving and as she did muttered "Asshole, i got to serve all these people and he is giving me trouble." Bobby shouts across the room "Who has got a fag to give me until that stupid dago comes back from the shops." Nobody answered and he says Andrew you were behind me in the queue, so give me a fag and i will give it back in cancer corner later." Andrew said "Oh Bobby, you always say that you owe me about 7 fags now." Bobby snaps "Give me a fag before i get nasty, c'mon." Andrew goes over and gives him a cigarette and a light and Danny was about to say something to Bobby and Jeff and Carol grabs his arm and says "No matey it's not worth it, that boy is as big as Bobby and he can see so it is his own fault if he does not stand up to him, leave it, leave it now, ok." Danny biting his lip let's it go and they get their coffee and sit down and stay far away from Bobby and have a chat, Carol "So lads what have you got next? I am doing my biology test for the first time and i will pass it it's the easiest of the lot." Jeff said "I have got to go and see someone about some folders and other things, i have not yet picked up and then go up to b 14 and on with my advice and guidance even though it's a waste of time according to Bobby." Carol "Awe, uncle Jeffrey, don't listen to that idiot, he has not got a clue, he probably can't even spell his name, people like him have no outlook on anything in life, so carry on doing what you are good at. Danny you are quiet, don't tell me that you are bothered about what he says also?" Danny looking down to his feet says "It makes you think Carol, i wonder if this is a waste of time, i felt like this before i came here and this place gave me some real hope and meeting him has brought it all back and i feel depressed now, god, he is really a pitiful person but he might be right you know. Who knows." Jeff "Yes he brought me back to earth too, i was in cloud nine until i spoke to him, i feel a little down now too." Carol chirped up "Ok, i have had enough of this, you 2 are what keeps me going and that daft Niel, so please don't give up on us now, we have a lot of fun together, so Danny what have you got next?" Danny answers "I had I.T. but stuff it now, i am off to my room and play some sounds. I can't be asked, i will be allright though i will snap out of it he will not beat me." In the background he could hear Bobby complaining about Hose being a long time getting his tobacco and Hose walked in on cue and Danny calls him over and said "Give me his tobacco and you go off to your next job, i will give it to him." Jeff said excitedly "Dan what are you doing? Please don't start nothing now." Carol said "I am going, i don't want to be here when it blows up." Danny smiling says "Sit down Carol, i am not going to do anything just a bit of a mind game that's all." Bobby listening to his watch "It's late now, where is that bloody dago." Danny shouts out "Oh Bobby is that you? i didn't know you were over there or i would have come and found you and given you your tobacco, Hose give it to me as he had a rush job on so come and get it then." Bobby in a right strop said "He is a dickhead, i can't see to come and get it mate and i need a fag so fetch it over here." Danny "I beg your pardon?" Bobby "I said fetch it over here." Danny "What, no please?" Bobby sat there wondering what to say next "Please. " Danny "Sorry mate i am blind and can't see neither, so i will wait until i leave in a minute and i will pass it to you when i pass you to go, ok." Bobby getting irritated said "But i need a fag now mate." The room by now was silent and you could hear a pin drop and Danny said "Well come and get it i said, as i cannot see." Bobby "Are you taking the piss or what?" Danny with sarcastic voice "No, i am deadly serious, i will get Jeff to guide me past you when i leave, in a minute." Jeff says "Oh, give me the tobacco and i will pass it over." He goes over to Danny and goes to snatch the tobacco off him and Danny pulled his hand back and said to Bobby sarcastically "Is that ok with you Bobby?." Bobby in a deadly serious voice said "Why wouldn't it be ok?" Danny replied "Because Hose said to make sure i give this to you and no one else, he is a sensible man is Hose." Bobby coughed and said "Yes that is ok, i understand now." Jeff snatched the bundle off Danny and gave it over to Bobby and said to Danny in a little voice "You really are an idiot." Then off they went, round 1 to Danny.

It was later in the bar and Danny and Jeff were sitting together having a pint and Jeff was still going on about earlier "Danny you were trying to get a rise out of Bobby, he is dangerous by the sounds of him and you are almost blind now and can't take the chance he sounds demented and in my opinion he would stab you and just walk away as if nothing happened, look at what he has done to all the youngsters here, they are petrified of him, he is a nutter and i don't want anything to happen to any of us so cut it out ok?" Danny "You don't half talk a load of crap, he is a man who lives on putting the shits up everyday people and likes to be the man and as you say he frightens the shit out of vulnerable kids and people like Clamper etc. I am a person who won't be bullied and he is thinking about that, he did not go over the line with me as he is unsure in case i give him what he gives the youngsters here and i promise you Jeff he will go over the line one day to test me and he will have the biggest shock of his life, i promise you, because if you let someone like him get under your skin he has won." Jeff "Yes i agree but do you want to take that chance? In case you are wrong he looks as if he can handle himself you know." Danny smiling "And so can i mate, you don't really know me as yet but i am not a person who will shy away from bullies and anyway he will probably leave rather than confront someone who sticks up for themselves, so don't worry. Look out it's the crazy haggis, hi Carol" Carol said "Hello Daniel and hows my uncle Jeff, i was overhearing your conversation and he is weird isn't he? I was just coming out of Gardner and he was waiting for a taxi to go to town, he said to me, "Fancy coming out to town with me and we will take the town apart and i can have you proudly on my arm." I told him no thank you i am fussy who i drink with, he said "suit yourself you don't know what you are missing girl and I have a cock like a donkey and can use it but you probably wouldn't know how to use it anyway." I replied, whatever ha, ha, he is really up himself, i can't stand him." Jeff "I know what you mean he is a pig and the way he speaks to women is awful and this dickhead wants to have it out with him." Carol "Good, the man wants to be put in his place, i would love to witness that. Well at least he is banned from here thank god, so hows things going then?" Danny "Who me?" Carol laughs and says "I don't care anyone of you, i am just asking." Danny "Sorry, yes, things are fine now i have had a good blast of music this afternoon, he made me feel inadequate earlier and i really needed that like a hole in the head, i began to feel like i did when i first lost my eyesight and that was awful it almost made me commit suicide and i don't want to feel like that again, phew it was close." Carol "I could feel you were losing it and was a little worried for you as it is very traumatic losing your eyesight, i know many who have ended up in a mental hospital and hope you are ok now." Danny "Yes i am ok now, i must keep focused and life does not end just because you have gone blind so time to party again." Jeff chirps up "Carol i have not felt good about that this morning either, i have felt lost and lonely since and hope i can cope with it." Carol smiling "Ha, ha, Uncle Jeffrey stop it, i know you and i won't fall for that one." Jeff "What? I have got feelings too you know and i get depressed too, so what about a bit of sympathy for me too then?" Carol puts her arms around his neck and says "There is nothing wrong with my uncle Jeffrey, you are just trying it on and it is not working Uncle Jeffrey it isn't." Jeff "Well it's worth a try isn't it ha, ha, and this bloody dodgy Welshman is capable of looking after himself so stop it." Danny "What's the Matter Jeff? Jealous matey? Ha, ha." Jeff "Yes i seen her first." Niel had come in in the meanwhile and sat on Carol's lap by accident and said "Oh sorry Carol, i didn't realise you were sitting there, ha, ha." Niel sat down next to Danny and said "I was busting for a pint i have had a hell of a day. The computers wouldn't work properly, the lift in the Queens building wasn't working properly the dog is pouting and took me the wrong way and look at her now she made me sit on Carol's lap, she is in a mood today, she missus Ceri and the kids i think, so i heard Hose coming in to get you pair tonight, he was laughing his head off he sounds funny when he does that what was he laughing about?" Danny laughing "Oh Jeff he had his slippers on and didn't realise it, it don't take much to make him laugh and did you know that Mickey Mouse has got a Jeff Maxam wrist watch, ha, ha, I didn't expect to see you this early, i thought you would be listening to the Archers tonight." Niel "I did it was on early tonight because of some political thing on there and i was fed up with your music tonight so decided to come over early." Danny "Sorry mate, i didn't think you minded some Phil Collins and it was not that loud." Niel looking puzzled said "Oh right, i am the one is sorry, it was not you then, it was somebody playing the real old Black Sabbath and Deep Purple, mind you it brought back memories but it was too loud." Jeff said "Oh you know who that would be don't you?" "Yes, that bloody Bobby Maclean that horrible bastard." Niel "Who?" Jeff "Oh, a man who is the curse of the college is name is Bobby Maclean, he is a right bastard" Niel "Him, i have heard a little about him but never met him." Carol "You are not missing nothing Niel, i assure you he is the man from hell and a male chauvinist pig, he makes my skin crawl." Niel "That bad ay, someone said he bullies the youngsters here and is a bit of a pisshead, ha, ha." Jeff "So it seems him and Danny had a bit of banter in the coffee room this morning and i have been trying to warn him he is a dangerous man." Niel said smiling "No Danny is not dangerous he is a pussy cat, don't let Jeff talk about you like that Dan." Danny laughed and Jeff snapped "Not Danny you dickhead, i am talking about Bobby, he is the dangerous one and Danny will be the one getting his head kicked in." Danny said "He will have to bring his gang with him Jeff." Carol said "Ha, ha, hee, hee, bring his gang with him, i have not heard that said since I was an infant in school ha, ha." Niel "This Bobby must be big then to sort you out mate." Danny "I don't know-how big he is but like i said i don't put up with bullies and if he wants to tangle with me i will not run away, that's all I am saying, he is an asshole and deserves anything he gets and I am surprised the lads here haven't ganged up on him and kicked his head in themselves." Niel "They won't do that will they? they weren't brought up like you and i was, they were mostly blind from birth and don't get much opportunity to mix with adults who have been to prison, the government are funny like that." Danny replies "Yes your right at least in Wales we had to fight our own battles." Jeff butts in "Oh here we go, the hard Welshmen and the stories, at 11 years of age i left school and went straight in pit lad and crawled on my chest for the years leading up to my 18 birthday and i was up to my chin in water and watched the rats doing the breaststroke, i had to put my sandwiches in my helmet, but the camaraderie was next to none and all for ten bob a week and we used to go to the pictures and have a chip dinner and a return on bus and still have change out of a shilling, yeah, yeah, ha, ha." They all laughed out loud and

Danny said "I don't think i like your attitude and they used to talk like that in Yorkshire not Wales, you ignorant git but it was funny the way you put it over." Niel still laughing said "Very good Jeff, so do you think he will be trouble then Dan?" Danny in serious mood said "Maybe not to us but he will always pick on the youngsters until someone expels him i bet." Niel "Well mate, i agree with Jeff he is probably dangerous and it might be a good idea to give him a wide birth unless he insists on bugging you." Danny "I have decided to do just that mate so don't worry, right Jeff leave that Scottish girl alone and get the beer in for goodness sake, he is like a dog on heat." Jeff "Oh shut up, i am on my way." Niel said "Nothing for me Jeff, i am off to get some sleep." Jeff "Ok mate see you, Carol a glass of cider or what?" Carol "Yes please Jeff, see you Niel, can i walk back with you two later, i don't feel safe with that creep now and i don't mean Jeff ha, ha,ha." Danny replies "Of course you can but maybe you would be safer with Bobby than Jeff, ha,ha, no i am only kidding, i am wondering if Katie and Lulu are ok with that pervert there as you know they love their miniskirts and he is not going to leave them alone them being so young and all." Carol "I was speaking to them earlier he has already made a few passes at them and they don't care at all they are not worried especially Lulu she just gave him a mouthful." Danny " Ha, ha, that's lulu, as long as he keeps his hands to himself i can't see any problems, i hope he does something so as we can get rid." Carol "I think he will eventually cut his own throat and i don't think it will be long neither, i can hear that uncle Jeffrey with my drink." Jeff "Yes hear it is."

After the bar had shut they went back over the dorm in Gardner for a cup of coffee and sat in the communal lounge for a chat and Jeff was making Carol laugh about things he done when he was a kid. Jeff "I used to have all the hand me downs from my sisters and i thought i was a girl until i was 15 ha, ha, only kidding, i am one of 7 children and only one sister." Danny "It is nearly time for a can Jeff, have you got any?" Jeff "Do worms live underground, i will pop up and get some now." Danny "I will wash up these mugs while you get some, have you finished Carol?" Carol "Yes, here we are, i bet you would make someone a lovely wife, i have never seen a man offer to do the washing up before." Danny smirking "Don't get used to it, i don't make a habit of it so is there anything happening with you and Jeff?" Carol replies "No, no, i love him dearly and he makes me smile all the time but he is too nice for me, i would ruin him he is too nice for that, better off as he is i need a man who has more grit if you know what I mean, but Jeffrey is lovely." Danny sarcastically said "Grit, like Bobby you mean?" Carol snapped "I said grit, not shit, he is a prat, i don't know how anyone could go to bed with someone like him." Jeff returned with 8 cans in his arm and said "Eight cans, is that enough? Do you want one Carol?" Carol "Oh, no thanks, i have had enough for one night thank you" Danny "And if you think i am drinking 4 of those before i go to bed your wrong mate, maybe 2 and that's it." They sat down and opened a can and after chatting for a while they could hear someone singing and a little worse for wear it was that Bobby returning home drunk and being led in by the taxi driver. He slurred to the taxi driver "Great man, i thank you, i thank you, now piss off." Taxi driver replies "It's a pleasure to see the back of you and in future call someone else, i will never pick you up again." Bobby "Ha, ha, you dick head, piss off, wanker, you are lucky i am blind and drunk, bog off, right who is in this room then?" He found the settee and fell onto it and Jeff said "It's me and Danny here, i see you have had a good night by the looks of you." Bobby could not sit straight and said "Oh you pair, i remember now the man who had my tobacco and his skinny friend, so how are they hanging lads? I am pissed for a change and is the lass with the nice ass with you?" Jeff "No she has just gone to bed, i think she could hear you coming and run ha, ha." He replied "Right she is afraid of me and she is lucky i wanted to empty my sack tonight and she was going to be the lucky girl, never mind i will have a wank when i wake up ha, ha, i need a fag." He put a rolly in his mouth and was searching for a lighter and Danny said "Sorry bobby there is no smoking in the common room, you will have to go outside for it." Bobby "Fuck that, i will open the window as i always do and sit on the cill and have it it's too cold outside, stuff it, got a light Jeff?" Jeff said "Yes but I will not give it to you until you are in the window with the window open." Bobby replied "I see just because i am pissed don't take the Mick out of me and i can see you have a can, any spare ones for me mate?" Jeff "I could spare one maybe after you have had a fag." Bobby said "Hey man i will do what i like, i can get a light off the cooker you know and don't think i won't remember you tomorrow mate, so give that lighter and i will give it back don't worry, you 2 are like Laurel and Hardy there ha, ha, right which way to the window." Jeff replied "Straight ahead and a little to your left, that's it put your arm up and you will feel the curtains." Danny says "Be careful in case you fall through it by accident, ha, ha." Bobby "Yes very funny and here comes your lighter Jeff." He threw the lighter straight at Jeff. Jeff put his hand over his face and said "Awe, take it easy that hit me in the face then, god." Bobby sniggering "Right Jeff, sorry pass me a can mate, i am comfortable now sitting on the window cill, thanks mate and you would never know that there is 35 people living here would you? when i first started here this room used to be full of people at this time of night, but no more i think they are all afraid of me you know ha, ha, i can't understand that." Danny said sarcastically "Well i can understand that boy ." Jeff "He means there is not a great deal of room in here." Danny snapped "No i don't, i mean it exactly the way i said it, he is enough to put anybody off Jeff, so don't make me out to be an idiot." Jeff "Oh sorry." Bobby laughing said "So you are a hard man also are you Dan? Dan, Dan the dirty old man, ha, ha,ha." Danny said "No, i am not saying anything of the sort i just say exactly what i think and if people don't like it tuff." Bobby "That's my man, i like it, not like these pussies here, afraid of their own shadows another man like me full of grit and no fear at all, well done." Jeff "Yes guys very macho indeed ha, ha." Next thing in shuffled a little woman so quiet and only said "Excuse me please." You could tell she was a foreign student by her accent and Jeff sat up and his eyes lit up and he said "Well hello, who are you then? I am Jeff." She replied "Oh hello i am Dina, i am not so new i never come down very often but i need some hot water for my drink and i will be off." Jeff "Well hello Dina this is Danny by my side and he is Bobby." She says "Hello." Danny said hello and Bobby said "Hello babe, and so where are you from then?" Dina replies "I am from Iran thank you." Bobby "A trainee suicide bomber ay, well hello girl i got a new blow up doll the other day from Iran it blows itself up and are you promised to anyone? If not i will take you on ha, ha." She finished pouring her hot water and rushed off. Danny shouted after her "Please don't take any notice of him we are not like him, sorry for him." But it was too late she was gone as fast as her legs could carry her and Jeff said to Bobby "Yes, well done, no wonder this room is so empty i can see why now." Bobby "Well, if these bloody foreigners can't take a joke then they should stay where they came from, ha, ha." Danny biting his lip said "I didn't think that was very nice, she was so frightened if it was your daughter and someone did that to her you wouldn't like it." Bobby replied "Ha, ha, my daughter would have grabbed me by the neck and bit my nose off and then we would have laughed, don't be so soft man, she is only on this earth for one thing and that's shagging, women are not good for anything else mark my words, she is probably up there playing with herself by now, i excited her so much." Danny looking shocked said "Well Jeff i am off to bed i can't finish this can, i feel sick now sorry mate, i am off." Jeff "Yes i am off too." Bobby "Well don't waste them cans leave them on the table i will finish them off." Danny "Ok mate." And proceeded to spit in it and the lads went off to bed.

It was the next morning and Danny went into the breakfast room an in there was Alun Young a lad from Scotland and another man named Mathew a farmer's son from up north of England, Mat was a strange lad but nice and very quiet indeed. He however was obsessed about mad cows disease for some reason and kept on about it, he said to Danny "Hello mate how are you settling in now?" Danny with big smile on his face says "Hi Matt i am fine thank you, i am glad however that bloody Bobby is not here this morning, he got on my bloody nerves last night." Alun said "Oh you won't see him much before 11 o'clock he is out for the count until then thank god, he gets on my nerves to, he is very annoying isn't he?" Danny "Isn't he just, that's why i haven't seen you lads here in the night since he arrived back pay." Mat "Too right, he will only pick on us, he never fails to so, it's best if we don't hang around here in the evenings ha, ha, i have enough with my own worries as i am sure i have got mad cows disease you know." Danny laughs and says "That's the second time you have said this to me so why do you think that Matt?" Matt "Well ha, ha, i am a farmer's son and have had close contact with a large herd of cows most of my life and i think i have contracted it from them, i have not been checked out for it mind, but i really think it's a possibility ha, ha." Danny "Don't be so soft mat i don't think you have got it mate, it's just your Imagination mate, don't let it worry you." Next thing in walks Jeff and Danny said to him "Hello Jeff, did you know Matt here thinks he has mad cows disease, ha, ha." Jeff says "Ha, ha, you play it and i will sing it ha, ha, did you hear what one cow said to the other cow?" Matt said "Ha, no." Jeff continued "The vet is around this afternoon so act sensible ok, he is checking for mad cows disease." The other cow replied "It will not affect me i am a donkey." The men laughed and Matt said "You wait i think i am right ha, ha." Alun said "Awe Matt, you keep on saying that, change the bloody record." Jeff said "Well i was dropping off last night and that dickhead came up to his room and started playing his music a bloody nuisance and the warden came up pretty quick to tell him to shut it off. I think he was waiting for Bobby to put his music on and nipped it in the bud Immediately." Danny "That's the way stop it Immediately. Did he say anything to the warden?" Jeff "Oh he moaned and groaned but he sounded as if he was drugged up to me and shut it off and was snoring in about ten minutes flat." Alun said "He really is a nerd, i moved from him because of the noise, he is driving people away from this college, i wish they would chuck him out he is no use to anyone and he insults all the girls here and threatens everyone, he will have a go at you 2 soon enough, you wait and see." Jeff snaps "Well he better be aware we will not put up with it, i myself will report him Immediately if he bothers me, i mean it." Alun "They won't do anything about it he gets away with murder, it's as if they are afraid of him too, he is untouchable here." Danny speaks seriously "Well if he gets under my skin i will smack him one and i don't care if i get chucked out i will not put up with his nonsense ever. I mean it." Matt "Well be careful he is a nasty one, he does not play fair, he is an animal, i heard him beat up a lad in the toilet and i was so frightened i would not tell the staff what happened, I just couldn't he would kill me easy." Jeff "That's awful he is a real bully then, i would not trust him especially with all the knives hanging around this kitchen." Mary the housekeeper speaks up "He wouldn't dare try anything like that he would be gone Immediately, his feet would not touch the ground i can promise you that. Right lads it's time you learnt to change your bed clothes and i mean today, don't wait for us to do it all the time and we are short staffed to do it this week, so make sure you do it, i mean you Danny and Jeff ok?" Danny "Yes i will, i have never changed a duvet cover before and being blind is hard but i will give it a try after breakfast." Jeff "Sorry, i didn't know we had to change it, i actually thought you were supposed to do it. Ok i will do it now in a minute." Danny "Right Jeff, take your time and hurry up ha, ha,." Mary "I will be about and will be checking later this morning and look out if you haven't done it mind." Danny "I will, it can't be that hard surely." Jeff "I hate changing those duvet covers i get into a spin with them, i have to hold the corners and get inside the cover to get the quilt to the corners and it gets bloody hot doing them, so matey make sure you get the corners right or it will be so uncomfortable on your bed." Danny "Yes ok and thanks for the advice and i will play some loud music for Bobby while i am at it." Matt "Good thinking Dan ha, ha." Mary "Another shit stirrer ay, he needs some of his own medicine and play some Roxy music you played yesterday, i like Brian Ferry." Danny "No problem Mary, i will do that for you."

Up in Danny's bedroom and Danny was in his boxer shorts waiting to attack his duvet and had it spread across the bed and tried to put the cover on that way but failed and then he rolled the quilt up and tried to get the cover on that way and failed. All the time he was losing his patience and was visibly sweating heavily and tried a few ways and failed with them all and then he remembered what Jeff said, get inside the cover with the quilt holding it by it's corners and get them in the duvet cover to its corners. So Danny stood there with the quilt holding it by its corners and the cover at the beginning of the top 2 corners and he was like the x man holding it up so high and then he pulled the duvet cover down over himself and the quilt itself until he was in it almost completely and as soon as he had it on he tried to get out of it and couldn't, he had been sweating so much the cover had stuck to his whole body and would not slide off him and so he panicked after a while and as he was waving his hands around he snapped the light bulb out of its socket and it hit the floor with a huge pop and Mary was walking around the corridor outside and could hear this pop and Danny saying "Hello, hello, help me, help me, i am stuck, i am going to die, please someone help me, help, help, help." Mary barged the door open in panic and was confronted by a huge duvet standing on end with someone inside it, it looked frightening and she screamed "Hello it's me Mary, what are you bloody doing Danny?" Danny in a panicky voice "I am stuck in here and can't get out and i am going to have a heart attack soon, help me get out of it." Mary said "Right calm down and bend over and i will pull it off you, don't panic." Danny bent over and she peeled it off him and he appeared and his hair was sticking up and he was red in the face and sweating very badly and he pulled out and gasped for air and ran an opened the French doors going out onto the veranda and staggered outside and was gasping for air and the rooks in the tower started crowing at Danny as if to say idiot and Danny said to them "And you can bloody shut up too, making that silly noise at me, your all a pain in the ass." Danny carried on giving the Rooks and Crows verbal and Mary came out onto the veranda and was laughing her head off and Danny then broke into laughter as he was dripping and said "Ha, ha, ha, i thought i was going to die and i nearly suffocated and these birds were the last straw ha, ha, ha." Mary still laughing said "Ha, ha, ha, that was the funniest thing i have seen for ages and it was like a hammer horror film when i seen you in that duvet and then you was giving the birds what for ha, ha, that was so funny, are you allright now?" Danny looking more relaxed said "Yes i am now, i have got my breath back thank you, you saved my life, i think. I would have died with a heart attack honestly I would have." Mary with concerned look "Yes it seemed funny but i think i will leave a message for one of us to change your duvet every week, so just do the rest ok, i don't want to take a chance ok Dan." Danny says "Yes ok i think it will be a good idea after all, i think i will lose it so thanks." Mary left and Danny put some music on and blasted it for a hour before his lecture and went down to the common room to meet Hose.

In there was Mary and Bobby complaining to her he said "It's only ten o'clock and if it was me there would be a fuss like last night. " Danny walked in and said "Hello it's a lovely day and i will make a cup of tea if i can before i go." Mary said "Sit down and i will make it, i am listening to Bobby's complaint a minute and so Bobby what music was it then." Bobby "Bloody Roxy music and was very loud and it woke me up." Danny said on hearing this "Oh that was me i am afraid, don't you like Roxy music Bobby?" Bobby replies "Not this early in the morning mate, it's only ten now and you were playing it at about 8. 30, i was sleeping you know." Danny "Right and it's not illegal to play music that early but it is at midnight like you were last night." Bobby just sat there wondering what to say "I see, trying to be funny are you? well i can play that game too mate." Mary said "Right wait a minute he has a point Bobby it's in the book for last night that you were playing heavy music late last night so what's good for one is good for the other, but i am knocking this on the head now. If there are grudge fights in here i will move you again to an outside house Bobby i promise you and i mean it ok?" Bobby "Ok, ok, i see what is happening here I will bide my time and be sensible about it, i have got a good music system there my Amstrad will win in the end." Danny laughed and said "Amstrad your joking, i have a powerful Panasonic that will make yours sound like a car radio mate but you have your little game i didn't do it to annoy anyone and if you had asked me to turn it down i would have, so don't be petty about it ok?" Bobby smirking says "Right, i will let it go this time but don't cross me too often or." Mary butts in and said "And what Bobby? go on, give me an excuse to send you to an outside house please." Bobby stormed off to his room and Danny said to Mary "Sorry about that, i will keep it down next time." Mary "He should be up at that time anyway so don't be sorry, he has had his life disturbed for a change and he don't like it but be careful he is a man with a great temper and will remember this so please be careful." Danny "Don't worry i will, he has got a large chip on his shoulders hasn't he?" "Yes he has and so did you i bet when you first went blind, so i can understand him being a little fed up with his situation can't you?" "Well no, i was suicidal when i first went blind but you have to get on with it it's not anyone else's fault here, we are all in the same boat and if we all turned like him there would be chaos here and we would all kill each other, i can't understand why they let him come here in the first place." "I don't know either perhaps they needed the money, perhaps they think he deserves a chance, or they had to by law I don't know" "Well after the trouble he has caused here, why don't they get rid of him now? are they afraid of him too?" "Maybe they are, but it can't go on much longer that's a fact." "No your right there and here's my mate Hose, i am ready mate, just let me finish my tea." Hose smiling "Yes ok Danny, i don't want to see Bobby today he is a bad man i just heard him shouting at someone outside, i sneaked past him ha, ha." Mary "He is outside is he? i bet that is the first time he has been outside this early in the morning since he left prison." Danny "Yes i bet it is, so Hose we will sneak past him and if he asks who it is don't say anything, ok?" Hose "Yes ok." Mary smiles and says "Danny you are a bad bugger, ha, ha." Danny "It's a messy job but somebody's got to do it, ha,ha, ha, i will see you tomorrow." Mary "Yes and be careful, bye."

Danny and Hose left the building and as Hose said Bobby was sitting on the bench and heard them pass and they kept quiet and he said "Ok, who is that? Hello, hello, i see silly buggers ay, come on who is it then? ok piss off then." Danny and Hose were laughing after and Bobby was mumbling away long after they left.

70

It was in the bar for coffee and Danny and Niel were sitting in there having a cup of coffee and talking and Niel said "I heard about your duvet difficulties this morning, it was funny when Mary was telling me and Jeff about it, you idiot, mind you i would have had the same trouble so they change mine as well, i am a shower of sweat to and it's not easy if you can't see i know mate and i met Bobby as i was leaving he is not Impressed with you either. He asked me if i knew you well and if you were hard or what, i told him you are a pussy and was afraid of his own shadow so don't worry mate." Danny looking annoyed said "Oh thanks mate, he will think he can do me in now and if it kicks off it will be your fault." "Calm down i am only kidding, he was fishing about you and i told him you were not a man to mess with and let it go at that as i don't want to get involved and that's what i told him, ok? and nothing else." "Ok, i am getting fed up with him and I really am he is a pain." Jeff sat down by Danny and said "Who is a pain in the rear? or need i ask, does his name begin with Bob? good guess ay." Niel "Good guess mate but i think he will not be here for much longer the staff are all talking about him and nothing good is being said." Danny "I am not surprised at all." In walks Katie and Lulu and sat by Jeff. Jeff said "Oh Look out the sexy girls are here it's Katie and Lulu, have you got your miniskirts on then?" Lulu "No only at nights out do we wear them uncle Jeffrey." Danny "Well there's a shame i have never been around when you have got them on, have you Niel?" Niel says "No i bloody haven't i miss all the fun here." Katie "Well lads you might be in luck if Jeff says yes to this next question, are you coming up here for the Karaoke tonight? as we have never come up for a drink before and we need someone's arm to latch onto to get here tonight." Jeff all excited and a huge smile says "No problem girls, i am your man no problem and will both of you be wearing these miniskirts tonight?" Lulu "We most certainly will and Carol is coming to with her mini on as well, she suggested asking you." Jeff "No problem, 3 young girlies with miniskirts on, it's my lucky night and i am not singing mind." Katie "Ok and i will get us girls to make sure we let you have a feel of our legs to make sure we are not telling lies, but behave Danny and Niel or that will be the last ha, ha, ha." Danny "Your on, i will wash my hands especially for the occasion." Niel "And me i will wash everything, i will, ha, ha." Next thing they could hear Bobby sitting down near them and he said "It's the northern slappers who are wearing those miniskirts is it tonight?" Lulu snaps at him "Mind your own business Bobby you will never find out what we are wearing if you were the last man on this earth." Bobby replies "I won't be up here, so you will have to just put up with the crap that's left, but i am sure you will get someone to hump you by the end of the night, no problem." Lulu "Why don't you crawl back under the stone you came out of and stay there, it would be good for everyone here so piss off." Bobby "A nice mouth for a little girl, i am sure, you have Impressed the lads here by now and the only bloke you will attract is one with a guide dog, ha, ha, and i will wait for you to come begging for a real man ha." Katie replies "Be prepared for a long wait then." Jeff butted in "Ok that's enough we are not animals, let's behave ourselves and act like adults." Lulu "Yes your right, he is not worth it." Danny "I fancy another coffee Niel what about you? i was going but i will stay for a while." Niel said "Yes please Dan I will, it will help my nerves thinking about those miniskirts." Danny goes off for the coffee and Niel said "He was funny this morning, he got stuck in a duvet and Mary had to get him out he then went out onto the veranda and started swearing at the rooks and crows, ha, ha." Lulu "Yes i heard about that, he is funny at times." Jeff "I was the one who suggested to get inside the duvet cover to put it on, ask him about the joke about the royal family when he gets back, it's a cracker. Here he is now." Niel "What's this joke about the royal family then Danny?" Danny started laughing and said "Well it goes like this. The Royale family, Jim,

Barbara and Denise the daughter sitting in the living room and Jim said to his wife "fancy making a cup of tea Barb?" she replied "no Jim, i am fed up of making tea, you make your own, it's your turn" Jim then said to Denise "go on Denise, you make one" she replied "no dad i am always making it, it's someone else's turn" Jim said in a temper "right, then i tell you what, the first one to speak a word makes the tea ok" Denise and Barbara agreed and so they sat there for an hour and no one said a word. Next in walks Dave, Denise's boyfriend. He sat there by Denise and said "Anyone making tea then?" to which there was no reply as no one wanted to make the tea and Dave thought this was funny no one talking at all so he sat by Denise and pulled her jumper off her and proceeded to play with her boobs in front of Jim and Barbara her parents, well they never said a word for fear of having to make the tea and so Dave thought well no one is awake they are just sitting there with their eyes open so he then started pulling off Denise's knickers and proceeded to give her a good seeing to and still no one took any notice. Well he finished off and sat there for a moment and decided to pull Barbara's blouse off and bra and started playing with her boobs and nothing again was said so he pulled her knickers off and gave her a good seeing to in front of Denise and Jim and still nothing was said for fear of having to make the tea. Next thing Dave thought to himself i must go to the toilet and he went in and pulled his dick out and had a pea and he had a sore dick after all the shagging and so shouted "where is the Vaseline?" and Jim shouted out in temper "allright, allright, I'll make the bloody tea" They all roared with laughter as it had gone so quiet and all were listening and Bobby said "Very good mate, very good, my type of joke." They all ignored him and Jeff said "I will have to remember that one for my brothers, ha, ha, right i am off, i will see you girls in the common room at 7.30 tonight for the Karaoke." They all dispersed to their classes.

Later on that evening and in the common room was Carol, Lulu, Katie, Danny, Niel, Bobby and Jeff having a glass of wine and a couple of tins of lager, Bobby said "Any chance of a tin Jeff? i will get some tomorrow." Jeff pondering said "Yes ok, but i will expect one back tomorrow mind." Bobby snapped "I said i would didn't I." Danny chirped up "Like that lad you owe 7 fags to Andrew, i believe." Bobby "I was asking Jeff not you, i will make sure i give it back tomorrow ok?" Danny "Yeh right, Niel what are you doing with Abby? are you taking her to the Karacke with you?" Niel "No i am going to take her back up to my room and she can have a rest tonight and guard my room." Bobby "Is she a German shepherd then Niel? as i don't like those dogs, one of them bit me on the leg once and i have a scar there now, bloody mad dogs." Niel said "Yes she is and very protective too so look out, she can smell a criminal a mile away." Bobby "I will watch i don't poison her by mistake then, ha, ha, ha." Niel in nasty voice "I hope your joking mate, that's not funny at all." Bobby "She will be ok, she is not a pigs dog so don't worry unless it bites me of course." Jeff seeing Niel getting angry said "Leave it now Niel and let's have a nice night ok?" Niel "Yes ok, let me take her up and i am ready." Niel goes off to take Abby to his room and Bobby laughs and says "God he is touchy isn't he? you would swear it was his daughter not a mutt." Danny said "Well it's as good as, it's his eyes also, so don't tease him, he is a nice man." Bobby "Yeah, yeah, whatever." Lulu said "So how are we going to do this then? i will hang onto Danny and guide him and Carol can grab Jeff and Niel can grab Katie until we get there ok? and Jeff can lead as it is difficult when it is dark, and Jeff you must keep on telling us how to get over there step by step as i don't like that dark path going over there at all." Danny "Well that will work out ok then let's go, we can meet Niel outside the dorm."

Off they went and all got over the bar successfully and in they went, the girls all grabbed Jeff when they got there and the lads went up to the bar to get the drinks and all the other lads stopped and looked at Jeff looking so proud with 3 cracking birds with miniskirts on all on his arms as if he was Paul Raymond the porn millionaire . They all sat around Jeff and the lads came and sat with them and smiled all night being with these girls. Danny said "God they are like dogs on heat these young lads, look at them." Jeff "Yes, i know, i can feel their eyes on the back of my neck." Niel "Well Jeff, you are their protector here tonight, good luck, i am not fighting anyone tonight i am going to enjoy the disco and Karaoke, anyone singing?" Jeff "No bloody fear." Danny "No chance unless i get plastered." Katie said "It's just us girls then, as usual, you men are boring in Karaoke nights." Niel "I am going to ask if he has got that song the wind beneath my wings, Bet Middler, i absolutely love that song, i won't be long now." Off Niel goes and finds his way over to the D J and as he went the music seemed to change all of a sudden and the police control came over the speakers of the dj and Danny spit his beer out and started laughing again and he said to Jeff "It's Niel causing that every time he goes near any amplifiers he changes the frequency, isn't that something?" Jeff "I know, i wonder how he does it?" Carol explains to Lulu and Katie "Every time Niel goes near the telly it stops hissing and the picture goes clear and when he goes it goes back to the same as before and now he has changed the dj's equipment and he has a what we call a metal micky and we think it is that what causes it." Lulu "What the hell is his metal micky?" Carol "I will explain quickly before he comes back. Well he had a operation to have his cock permanently erect to keep his love life going as he cannot get it hard because of his diabetes, it is a silicon rod inserted inside it and when he gets it out he can bend it to any shape and it will stay like that until he moves it again ha, ha, ha." The 2 girls sat there with their mouths open and started to laugh and Katie said "Your kidding right?" Niel had sat down and was listening to the conversation and smiling said "No it's true." They giggled and Carol said "Oh Niel you have been sitting there listening to me all this time, i was just trying to explain to them ha, ha." Niel "Ha, ha, i can say what Carol is saying is true all of it, shall i pull it out to show you?" Lulu "Ha, ha, yeah." Katie snapped at Lulu "No , we believe you Niel ha, ha, ha." Niel "Oh that's good as i have bent it into 2 so as i can have a dance later if any one of you fancy it." There was a deadly silence and then Danny said "Ok Niel i will dance with you." They all laughed and Niel said "No thanks sweetie, I am not that way inclined, I was asking the girls, so what about it then?" Lulu jumped at the offer "I will Niel no problem and Katie will I expect." Katie "Of course I will. " Carol "And it goes without saying I will Niel but don't take your handbags out with you girls as it sometimes pops out looking for sweets in them ha, ha, ha." Niel "Ha, ha, she's not kidding ha, ha, I was once in a dinner and there was bread rolls on the table and it got out of my trousers and grabbed one of the rolls and disappeared back in my trousers and a woman said, I seen that, that was fantastic, can you do it again? I said in reply, yes probably but there is no way it will get another roll up my ass, ha, ha,ha." The girls burst out laughing and Lulu asked him "So is it permanently erect then?" Katie "Lulu, don't be so personel." Niel "No that's allright, I don't mind, yes it is permanently erect and do you know I went in for this operation and the surgeon was horrible, he gave me one the same size as the one I had before, a small one, ha, ha." Carol "Listen girls just leave it to your Imagination, ok? I bet Lulu is in a horny state as it is so try and think of something else ok?" Lulu giggled and Danny said "That reminds me my neck is stiff tonight, I swallowed a Viagra earlier and it got stuck in my throat, ha, ha." they laughed and Jeff said "I am taking Viagra eye drops now, it makes me look hard, ha, ha."

Next thing a man came to the table with a very feminine voice and said "I am taking any names that want to sing and what they are going to sing." Niel said "Bend me shape me by

Dave Dee." Carol said "Don't listen to him, he is only kidding and I will sing with these 2 sex mad maidens so ask them." The girls told him a few songs they wanted to sing and he left, all of a sudden there was a lovely voice coming from the stage and it was a very young girl and it was a cracking singing voice and as she finished the dj said "Right that was Kez, wasn't she good?" There was a lot of clapping and Danny screamed "Yes, brilliant girl, a cracking voice, she was bloody good, mind I hope you 3 can sing like that?" Next thing Kez was passing bye and Danny said to her "Hello miss Kez, I thought you were great singing." She giggled and said "Eek, eek, I thank you, I thank you, it is a banging song to mind not as good as Miesha Paris mind, ha, ha, what is your names? Mine is Kerry Marshal but they call me Kez " Danny said "I am Danny and this is Carol, Katie, Lulu, Jeff and Niel. Are you sitting by anyone special Kez?" Kez replied "No, can I sit by you lot?" Carol "Of course you can." She sits down and Jeff said to her "Haven't you got a drink Kez?" She replies "Oh no, I am skint, I don't get my money unti Wednesday and I go to 2 different Karaoke's on the weekend but that's ok." Niel gives Jeff some money and said "Here Jeff will you please get them in and get one for the lovely Kez as well?" Jeff "No problem Niel, so what are you drinking Kez?" Kez "Awe, I will have a pint of cider please, thank you Niel." Danny "So Kez you are a Karaoke diva then? I suppose you don't miss many do you?." Kezz says "Not one, I just love singing but it is better in the other pubs I go in no trouble there it was banned here for a few months because of the fighting here it was a bummer all because of that old wanker Bobby." Danny "There's that name again, you mean Bobby Mclean do you?" Kez "Oh, is he your friend? I didn't mean it if he is." Niel "He is no mate of ours I can safely say that unless one of you girls has got a crush on him." The girls recoiled and nodded no and shivered . Kezz "Good, I was worried then, he is a bully and threatens us all he threw a glass at one of the young boys here, he is a nutter and I am glad he is barred from here. He spoiled the karaoke here for everyone and this time it is empty as he frightened most of the younger students here, he is a tosser." Niel "I hate him, he thinks he is it, I feel threatened by him all the time." Danny looking shocked said to Niel "You don't, you don't think he will tangle with you, you are huge and you only have to sit on him and he is finished." Niel "If he wanted to do anything to me he is the sort to have me from behind with a chair or a bottle, I wouldn't see it coming mate so you need to be careful or he will be waiting for you one night and do the same to you as you are getting to nasty with him." Danny "I see what you mean, I shall play it cool and he will slip up and I won't give him a chance to do anything like that to me. " Jeff was back and said "Yes dodgy you wind him up and he will store all of it up in his head and look out one day, I will be visiting you in hospital mark my words." Danny "You pair talk as if I am incapable of looking after myself or something." Niel "Just be careful that's all we are saying." Kez "He is a nutter he hurt a guide dog here one day, he trod on his leg and he was limping for ages, he said it was an accident but the day before he was arguing with the man who owns the guide dog." Niel "Well let me tell you if he ever touched Abby he is dead, I mean it." Jeff "I don't think Abby will sit there and let him do anything to her, she is very protective to you and herself and he would probably run a mile now, he knows she is a German shepherd." Danny "I wouldn't worry about Abby she has got an old head on her shoulders she is more intelligent than he will ever be, come to think of it she is more intelligent than most of us ha,." Katie "He is a creep mind I wish he would leave he is like a fish out of water, I blame this college I do." Danny "Well they have to give everyone a chance and he is just not worth giving a chance to but this college is very good at looking after most of their students and a very caring college, I must say it is turning my life around what do you think Kez?" Kez "Well I have been here a few years now and I love it here, I am dreading the day I have to leave here I don't know what I am going to do with myself. They keep me here just for the fun of it as I am not good at anything." Danny "Oh don't say that Kezz I just heard you singing like an angel so don't be silly" Kez laughs out loud and made everyone jump and said "Eek, eek, give me an eek Dan." Danny "What do you mean?" Kez "Shout eek as loud as you can it's good for you." Danny looking silly said "Don't be silly I can't do that." Kez "Awe, go on for me do an eek, go on." The rest of them tell Danny to do it and he shouts "Eek." Out loud and she laughs out loud again and made everyone jump. Next she says to Jeff "Your turn Jeff c'mon let's hear it out loud." Jeff was nagged by everyone to do it also and he says "Eeeeeek." Kez all excited asked them all one by one to do this and they did at the end,, she said "Banging, banging, bloody banging guys I am going to sing again now." Danny asked her if she wanted a drink again and she said "Oh yes please, I would a dry cider please that sweet cider is too weak for me." Danny goes off to get the drinks and she goes off to sing, the others speak about Bobby again and Jeff said "I am worried about that dodgy Welshman, he will not let it go, he is begging for Bobby to start something and it will go off like an atom bomb, so I will stick to him like glue for a few weeks until it cools down a little." Carol "Well I hope it doesn't go off in front of me they will probably kill each other, but I don't ever see it cooling down Bobby is too much of an idiot and loves confrontation it's in his nature." Katie "Yes it is he is nothing but trouble I think he has not got used to going blind and has a big chip on his shoulders about it." Jeff "Yes I agree, so look out then and talk of the devil he brings the drinks at last." Danny looking flustered said "Shit, I put the drinks on the wrong table at first and sat down and there was no one there so I was talking to myself for a while." Jeff "Nothing new there then." Danny hands out the drinks and Kez came back from singing and Danny said "Another good song, sung just right, here is your cider Kez." Next thing the girls were called out to sing and Kez said "Awe, that's better, I love dry cider it quenches my thirst and helps my voice for singing eek, eek, these 3 sing allright don't they?" Jeff said "Yes, if you like cats ha, ha, I am only joking I would never go out there to sing." Well the night went off well and all enjoyed their selves very much and off they went to the lounge of their digs.

In the lounge was a swaying Bobby the girls went in and turned on their heels and said goodnight as he was there and Bobby said "Don't go girls I will sort you out if you could not find anyone ha, ha, these 2 should have done that for you ha, ha." Danny said "Don't speak about us like that mate we are nothing like you we respect other people." Bobby "That's why they have gone to bed then is it?" Danny "No because they can't stand the sight of you and listening to your fowl mouth, that's why they went up to bed mate, allright, nothing to do with us " Bobby "Touchy aren't we? calm down man I am only joking chill man, any cans Jeff.." Jeff said looking disgusted said "I thought you were sorting out the cans tonight mate not me, you said I will have some cans you have been having off me back." Bobby "I had some and drank them sorry, I will give them back mate honestly I will ha, ha, honest mate." Danny "And we are supposed to believe you, I don't think so." Bobby "Don't call me a liar mate if I said I will give them back I will, ok." Danny " you keep saying this but he has never seen any not even the ones you drink." Bobby "It's nothing to do with you so butt out " Jeff tries to cool things off." Jeff snaps at Danny "Right forget it, I can have them back another day for god's sake it's only a few cans, forget it." Bobby "Right, Jeff have you got a few more to lend me or what?." Jeff answers in snappy voice "Or what, I am off to bed, I can't stand the macho smell in here, sorry Bobby no cans, I'm off." Jeff leaves and Bobby shouts out after him "Ok mate, stick them where the sun don't shine ha, ha." Danny "And you wonder why no one will give you anything." Bobby " well I don't care man, I am my own man and can't be bothered with whimps, I got a can in my room I am off to drink it." He goes and Danny sits alone until he nods off in the chair and after a long while he felt someone prodding him and trying to wake him up. It was Matt, he awoke and said "Oh, hello Matt, I fell off to sleep." Matt said "Would you like a cup of coffee? Me and Alan are having one." Danny "So what time is it then?" Alan said "It's 1.15 in the morning." Danny shakes his head and says "Right, I will have a cup of coffee please, no sugar thank you, so why have you come down this time of night? you should be sleeping now." Allen said "Well we heard Bobby big head go off to bed and waited a while and came down for a cuppa as we were waiting ages for him to go to bed, we don't want to speak to him or be in the same room as him he is always bragging and threatening and poking fun at people that's why." Danny "Well that's not on is it, he is putting the frighteners up everyone here making their lives a misery." Matt "Yes he is before he came here this lounge would be full until about 1.30 every night and all having a good laugh, now no one comes in here, there is 2 new girls on the top floor and we have never met them at all, he is a nuisance, he really is." Allen "Matt is telling the truth that man has got a lot to answer for." Danny "Yes he has, I don't know why you all don't stick up for yourselves as a gang he might think twice then, I will be with you and he might leave you all alone if he thinks that you will all have him." Matt "Ha, I hope you are not including me in that statement? and no one else will stand up here, forget it ha, ha." Allan "See what I mean he will have us all one at a time." Danny "I see and don't blame you it's not in your nature to fight so I respect that, so what are we going to do?" Matt smiling said "Ha, ha, who's we forget it." Danny "Well it will never get better then will it." Alan said "We will put up with it until it gets too much then leave I suppose." Danny looking shocked said "You would leave because of that asshole?" Matt "Yes we would, no problem, better than being beat up ay." Danny "Fair enough, have you said anything to the staff or the principle here?" Alan "Yes we have with no affect, I think they are afraid of him as well." Danny looking thoughtful said "Well will you both do me a favour and leave him to me after?" Matt "What is it? I don't like the sound of this one bit ha, ha." Danny said "Look don't walk away from him if you want to watch telly and I will come in here last thing at night after the bar is closed and if he gives you any problems I will sort him out, ok?" Alan "Huh, do you think you can sort him out then?" Danny "Yes I can at least I am almost sure I can and if he gives me a good hiding then he will be expelled from here, so you don't have to worry about anything, promise me and we might get something out of this and I think he will not hassle you if I am about, he knows I am not afraid of him at all and if it kicks off just go to your room I will not expect you to get involved at all, what do you think?" Alan "We'll see Dan ok?" Danny "Yeah I understand lads I don't want to see you 2 hurt so just think about it and we can get rid of him or at least let him know I will sort him out if he don't behave." They sat there and drank their coffee and went to bed.

It was a few days later in the evening and Danny and Jeff were in the bar late evening and having a laugh about Kez and Niel said to Danny "That Kez is a hell of a girl isn't she? she is only a youngster but she is like she has been here before, I mean in an earlier life." Jeff "Yes she was teasing you Niel and you was having a good laugh she is cute and a lovely girl and don't she drink a lot for a youngster?" Danny replied "Yeah, it is as if she has hollow legs and the things she comes out with ha, ha, and she is an inspiration the way she gets around with no help at all and she is totally blind, it's amazing it is, a credit to her." Jeff "Yes she is, no one's fool and did you hear Niel laughing he was chuckling like a jelly. He was enjoying her humour. Well I am knackered I am off straight to bed when I get back I need my beauty sleep. So are you ready to go?" Danny said "Yes I am having a cup of tea and then off to

76

bed for me to, I am knackered." The lads go off and Jeff and Niel goes straight to bed and Danny went to have a cup of tea and was amazed to see a few in there. There was Matt Alan and Bobby in there and they were having a nice conversation. Danny said "Hello everyone, allright then?" Alan said "Yes" Matt agreed m, Bobby said "Why? are you a doctor, ha, ha, we have been watching that crap called the Eurovision song contest, what a load of crap, but Alan is into that, he has no taste for good music and he can't sing neither but he is Scottish a old haggis so what do you expect." Alan said "Awe, I was not that bad." Bobby "You sounded like a cat being strangled. But there you are Scottish and I can't understand a bloody word you are singing, it's a good thing we own Scotland as the English are perfect, ay Matt." Matt "Yes Bobby, my singing was not that bad." Bobby "I would not go that far but at least you are English not any Gallic waste of space, ay." Bobby hurled a empty can of beer into the bin and made everyone jump and he growled and tried getting a light off the electric cooker ring and you could smell his dark glasses burning on the hot ring so Danny grabbed him off the ring and said "God Bobby you will have the place on fire if you are not careful, god what a smell those glasses are smouldering mate, be careful." Bobby "Don't be stupid they won't hurt I can't feel them being hot dickhead, I am having my fag by the window, so where is the skinny one? has he gone to bed with that large assed Carol? she is a foreigner to. I can't understand why we English put up with the Celts like Scotland the bloody Irish and the Welsh, when we beat them we should have put them all together in Scotland out of the way." Danny looking very annoyed said "The English never beat the Welsh and the proof is that our colours are not on the union jack flag, so stick that up your ass." Bobby in a temper said "Don't be silly." Alan said "He is right the Welsh colours are not represented on the English flag at all, however the Irish and the Scottish are. " Bobby snapped at Alan and said "You asshole, what do you know about it? you bloody Scottish eat their young until we told them it was wrong, so piss off you prick before I give you a dig, you idiot." Danny "Why Bobby, because he is right the English have never beat us Welsh that's why offers dyke is near here to keep the Welsh from massacring the English, you could never beat us." Bobby getting more irritated said "There we are then, if you say so, Matt got any beer in your room?" Matt looking nervous said quietly "No I haven't I don't drink, sorry." Bobby "You whimp a waste of space not a real man and you should be ashamed as an Englishman, another prick." Danny "Don't ask me I have had enough in the bar and if I had a can in my room I would not give it to an Englishman." Bobby " I am sure we beat the hell out of the Welsh many times, I think you are on our flag because you were all sheep shaggers until we educated you, ha, ha." Danny "Wrong, do you know why we have so many mountains in Wales? ...because we won so much land off the English we had to pile it up and make mountains out of it, ha, ha, ha." By now Bobby was red in the face and he lost it. Matt went to say something and Bobby said "Matt why don't you shut up you asshole, you do talk a load of shit, we are talking, shut up before I smack you a bastard and that goes for you Alan too. So shut up, I am having a conversation with a very brave Welshman whose mother was probably an old ewe, we taught you everything, we own Wales now so forget it mate without us you are sunk nothing." Danny just as mad said "You talk so much crap, you do you even smell of shit and this is one Welshman who has never been beaten by no Englishman and I think the Englishmen I know would be ashamed you call yourself English your disgusting and not worthy to hold any union Jack flag, you are a disgrace to your nation." Bobby "Oh you think so do you, well let me tell you now and you can ask these 2 the last person to answer me back got beaten up in the toilet out there, so be careful Taff." Danny just blew and said "Ok you big brave pom, let's go to the bog and let's see you do this to me then shall we?" Bobby "Don't push me mate you won't like me when I am mad so be very careful, I am getting mad." Danny grabbed the arm of Bobby and said "I tell you what, let's go outside the fire door into the field behind and we can sort this out now ok?" Bobby was trying to pull away from Danny and was growling and saying "If I go out there with you I will kill you mate." Danny dragging him out of the door and kicking the fire doors open said "I am shaking in my boots, get out here and we can settle this for good, you excuse for a man." Meanwhile Matt and Alan stood at the entrance listening and Matt was telling Allen what was happening. Danny had Bobby outside in the garden and they were hitting seven bells out of each other until Danny hit him to the ground and the warden came running out to stand between them but Bobby had, had enough and Danny was marched into the warden's office and told to sit down and he went out to pick up Bobby and also brought him into the office and sat them down and called a manager over to sort things out. Allen and Matt made a fast exit to bed.

Manager said "You again Bobby I see and Danny, I am surprised at you, I am and look at the state on you both, I am sorry I will have to get a full report made out and both of you stay away from lectures tomorrow until the principle and other college members have seen you and decided what is to be done with you both. But in my opinion I think you can both start packing your bags, warden please do your report tonight for the meeting thank you, now get to bed the both of you " Danny went to bed while Bobby was kept back to keep them apart until Danny was in his room, there was no sign of Matt or Alan and they would not help Danny either in his defence and Danny knew this later after cleaning himself up. Bobby was walked to his room, tomorrow was going to be very eventful.

It was the next morning and there was Danny sitting alone on the settee in the community lounge and in walked Mary and said to him "Hello scrapper how are you this morning? you look sick, fancy a cup of tea?" Danny "Yes please, yes I am feeling sick because I am about to be thrown out of the college and I was getting on so well my life was being sorted out and now I am back to square one again." Next in walks Jeff and he said "Good morning." Mary said "Good morning Jeff, but it is not so good for Danny and Bobby I am afraid and your mate here is worrying about the fact he may be expelled from here today so things are not good at all." Jeff stunned shouts "What, so what happened then? I have not heard anything at all." Danny said "Well, I had it out with Bobby last night I am afraid I snapped, he was slagging off Alun and Matt and then had a go at me and said a few nasty things about my mother and so I cracked and dragged him outside and gave him a good pasting and the warden split us up and sent for the night manager of Gardner and she has had to report it and now I am waiting to get expelled this morning." Jeff "I knew it, I warned you he was a dick head now you had to snap and do it your way, well matey I am going to miss you ha, ha, ha." Danny "Oh, thanks mate, I love you to." Jeff "Sorry matey I was only kidding, they won't throw you out, he deserved it, you will have a slap on the wrist and that will be that, i bet you." Danny "Well the manager said to start packing my bags, I am not kidding so it is not looking good is it?" Jeff "Serious? na, na, Mary what do you think?" Mary shrugs her shoulders and said "I don't know, I only experienced this once and they were both expelled, they take a dim view of fighting here." Jeff "Well matey it's not looking good, I must get over the main building early now then." Mary "I can't see how you can help him." Jeff "I know, I want to ask for his room it's bigger than mine." Danny looked at Jeff sarcastically and said "I wish you would piss off as you are only making me feel worse than I feel now Jeff." Jeff "Sorry mate I am only kidding I hope they use their heads and realise it's Bobby's fault not yours and Alun and Matt will stick up for you do you want me to have a lecture off and I can come with you to support you? surely they won't expel you, I hope not I need my drinking partner." Danny "Thanks mate I appreciate it but I will be allright and I will hang about to say goodbye don't worry." Mary "Oh Danny, don't say that, it will not be the same without you here." Next in walks Niel and he said "Is the dick head here?" Jeff "Bobby, no he is still in bed I expect. Danny is here though." Niel "Danny I mean, I just heard from the warden, you idiot we told you didn't we? why didn't you listen? we are going to miss you as the warden said you have not got a chance in hell of staying now this has happened." Danny "Did he? well there you go then, it's official if he said it it's what is going to happen, well lads I will hang around until 2 o'clock to say goodbye ok? it's my fault." Jeff "Oh dear, I will miss you matey, it was fun while it lasted, anyway good luck I am off to lectures." Niel "Yes Dan good luck I am off too, I will see you before you go, what time is your meting then?" Mary said "It will be 11 o'clock it usually is." Danny "There we are then, I will see you both at dinner ok?" The lads agree and off they went, next in walks Bobby in a stupid mood and says "Any chance of a cup of tea then Mary? I see Danny is here then?" Mary in stern manner said "Yes Bobby I will make you tea and no-nonsense now ok? you are in enough trouble as it is." Bobby "I didn't start it last night and I will be allright they will never get rid of me, they never do I will have a few weeks out of here again that's all ha, ha, and I could do with the break." Danny said "I would not bet on it mate this time it is more serious as I will tell the truth, I am not Matt or Alan or some little student afraid of you, the truth will come out this time mate and about time to." Bobby smirking said "Yeh whatever, they are afraid of me and won't go that far I bet." Mary snapped "I think you will be out of here today Bobby in fact I am sure of it and I will be sorry that you have taken a good student with you it's a pity, you deserve to go, Danny does not." Bobby "What do you mean? he started it, he was the one who dragged me outside and threw the first punch, not me." Danny was holding his temper back and then stormed out of the room before he lost it again.

11 o'clock came around and in the meeting were about seven main people from the college residing over the meeting and they had Bobby in first and questioned him for about forty five minutes and next thing in went Danny and was asked to sit on his own in front of the committee to explain himself and to answer their questions.

The principle spoke first and said "Your name is Daniel Duckfield am I correct?" Danny said he was, she then said "Ok you know why you are here and we are not happy about the events that occurred in Gardner last evening so we will now let you explain your version of events leading up to the disturbance last night." Danny sat back and proceeded to explain and it went like this "I only met Bobby Mclean a few weeks ago and he was a total fool, that was my first Impression and I tried to get on with him as much as I could, I found out he was a bully and had attacked younger students here and got away with it." Danny was interrupted by the principle and she said "I am afraid Daniel that was not proved as there were no witnesses but carry on." Danny continued "Fair enough but he is nothing but trouble I can assure you and I was told by the boys involved they were much too afraid to come forward as witnesses as he would only put the fear of god into them, but anyway he was always in my and other people's faces who were with me and was clearly controlling younger students with his fear tactics and I am afraid I am not one of those people, I was listening to him bully everyone in my building every night and last night he went too far, he was calling Alun young as Scottish this and that and believe me it was not nice and Alun was petrified of him and so was the quiet Matt who would not harm a fly, he was threatened and I told them I was not going to get them here today to witness the problems to stop them worrying it's not fair on them so don't ask me about witnesses as I will not be calling any at all. Then Bobby said something about my mother that hit the nerve as my mother has not been dead many years and she was such a lovely human being, she was so quiet and a loving person. He had no right to say nasty things about her, then he was calling me a sheep shagger and other things and threatening me because I am Welsh and warning me what he would do to me and I just cracked and dragged him outside and gave him what every student wanted to give him since they very first met him, a damn good hiding. You see it's like this, I came here after a very bad trauma of losing my eyesight and nearly took my life a couple of times and if I hadn't had any children I would have done so, I could not see no life for me and could have given up but decided to diversify and get my life together now I am blind and I tried a normal every day local college and it didn't work and so I tried it here and it was working fantastically, until I met him I was getting my head around the fact I can use a computer to run most of my life, braile that would help me with other parts of my life mobility that his Improved my life Immensely good friends in the same difficulty as me working it all out together living my life independently as I was being taught to do here and many other things here that I could never get anywhere else and dare I say it not because it sounds like a load of flannel to get you to let me stay but because it's true you people who are so caring and devoted to making our lives better every day it has been noticed here by every student coming here, I will stand by what I have done and recognise it was not the best way of sorting things out but it was my way if not for the benefit of the rest of the students here as Bobby only stands for doubt dismay and screwing the system and as far as I can see he is the only one here that don't give a damn and he will hold back others who must learn or die and if I am the person who has to be sacrificed for that purpose then let it be done, I stand by what I have done. I am sorry enough is enough ." Danny looking serious sat back and there was a long silence and the principle asked him to wait outside in another room for their decision. He went out and could hear bobby in another room moaning as usual, he was led into another room to keep them apart and sat there for about ten minutes and then heard Bobby being called back into the room. Danny was getting hot and bothered and got very nervous as he waited, it seemed like hours before bobby was finished and he came out of the meeting room raving saying to a warden "They must be kidding it was that bloody Danny dickhead who caused all the problems, now I am on my way home the bastard as he is, never mind at least I know now he is going to get the same as me ha, ha, right mate get me to my room I can get into Manchester for a few pints with my mates and be rid of these wankers here, huh that Welshman was lucky mind." Bobby and the warden went off and Danny by now knew what the outcome was going to be and got resigned to the fact he was going home and bowed his head and looked absolutely upset as anyone could be, he sat there for a while and wondered why it was taking so long then it happened he was called back in and asked to sit down in front of them again. There was a long pause and the principle said "Right Daniel we have listened to all the facts presented in this Matter from you and Bobby and the warden and staff in your dorm and other tutors who have dealings with you and Bobby and I will tell you our decision about the both of you." There was a long pause again and she continued "Bobby Mclean has returned to this room and our decision was that he was expelled from this college with effect Immediately for his part in the Matter, he has already been escorted off the premises .... We now come to your part in this nasty event... we have listened to you and what you have had to say to this committee and listened to the warden and manager of Gardner hall and to other tutors on your behalf and this is our decision... we have decided to place you on probation here in this college for a year and keep an intensive eye on your progress and if at any time we have a reoccurrence of this problem again we will have no choice other than to expel you, do you understand?" Danny just stood there and he was white in complexion and his face fell with relief but was shaking profusely and he said "So I am not expelled then?" "No but you will be on a probational period of 1 year and if you do anything like this again you will be gone." Danny's face lit up and he smiled broadly and said "Yes I understand and I agree, and I want to thank you all for believing me." Principle said "We feel you have a great deal to offer this college and that you are genuine in your goal here please prove us all right, good day Daniel you can get back to your lectures and don't let me see you in front of us again." Danny "Yes of course and thank you." Danny left and sat outside in the sun for a few moments in a state of relief after a while someone sat by him it was one of the committee who made the decisions about his case, he leant over to Danny and said to him in a calm quiet voice "Are you ok?" Danny replied "Yes I am now, thank you." stranger "No thank you." Danny looking shocked said "Why do you thank me?" Stranger replies "Because you got rid of that man, we had a real bad time trying to do that because no one would stand up to him and give us the ammunition to get rid, you did and you have done a huge favour for your fellow students the college and everyone's sanity here, well done it's a huge lot of pressure let out today but if you ever say I said this I will deny it." The man grabbed Danny's hand and shook it and said "Well done and I hope you can carry on as before this little glitch in your promising student years here." "Well thank you I will and it's nice of you to say so, goodbye." "Goodbye Daniel." The man went and Danny felt relieved and a little proud of himself for ousting Bobby Mclean out of the college.

It was later in the refectory and he was sitting waiting for Niel and Jeff to come in for dinner and thinking how they are both thinking Danny was leaving the college. They both arrived and sat down by Danny who had finished eating by now and Jeff said "Alright matey and why are you not eating then?" Danny replies seriously "I don't feel like eating mate." Niel "Awe dear, things went bad then mate?" Danny still with serious face "Yes Niel I am afraid so, I have to get out of here by the end of the day, so it's goodbye I am afraid." Jeff went silent for a while and then said "Oh never, I am so sorry mate, never mind we can still keep in touch ay and we can call each other on the mobiles and they might give you another chance in a few months when things cool down." Danny "I don't think so mate it sounded final to me, sorry but it was fun while it lasted wasn't it?" Niel said "Awe shit, that bastard has got a lot to answer for, it has spoilt it here now it's not going to be the same is it? well if it goes downhill I might pack it in also." Jeff "Yeah right, all leave me here alone lads, I don't know now awe, this has made my bloody day worse than it could have been, shit." The table fell into silence for a while and Danny could take no more and started laughing and said "Ha, ha, ha, I never thought of it I am not going to be pestered by you pair anymore am I, bloody great." Jeff "Don't sound so happy about it matey, I don't think it's funny." Niel chirped up and said "Your not going are you, are you?" Jeff "What are you on about Niel?" Danny "I am sorry lads but I am not going, I have been put on probation for a year." Jeff "Your joking, honest?" Danny "Honest they think I will have to stay to look after you pair I am definitely staying." Niel "Fantastic a pint it is tonight to celebrate, yes." Jeff "So I am not going to get your room then? ha, ha, only kidding." Danny "No but you can have Bobby's room he has already gone, they were glad I gave them the bullet's to get rid of him so his room is now empty." Jeff "Oh no thanks mate, I don't know what he has been doing in there, so it's the 3 Amigos still then." Niel lifted his cup of tea up and said "Here's to the next few years, who said there is no god?" Danny "It's a messy job but somebody's got to do it. "

Things soon changed in the college after that day Immediately people were gossiping about Bobby going and there was an easy love like feeling in the air and even the staff were much happier and Danny became very popular there for a good while and that very evening after the lads went home from the bar and the lounge in Gardner was packed with students of all nationalities and creeds. It was back to being a fantastic place that all the blind partially sighted and seeing people could get together like a huge melting pot and show that world how people from different cultures should be together.

It was a few days later the warden pointed out that there was a dart stuck in Danny's door a little memento left by Bobby for Danny, was he telling him something.

In the common room for breakfast and in there was Danny, Jeff, Niel, and Zarrine the house carer, they are discussing the move to another hall of residence. This is a move that Zarrine is making along with Danny, Jeff and Niel.

Zarrine speaks with an Indian accent "Well I hope you have all packed your things ready for the move today?" Danny said "I don't know why we are moving I like it here, yes it is old but it's lived in." She replied with a big sigh "You know why, I have told you so many times they want to renovate this building and so we have got to go to another already renovated building which I have been told is very nice, it has en-suite facilities in every room." Jeff "And there is three new girlies coming in today to the same floor as us, that's reason enough for me." Niel "We know why you want to move you only need a sniff of a skirt and your gone, you were packed four days ago ready to move. They could be three dogs." Jeff "As long as they are female from birth who cares." Zarrine in stern voice "Do you mind I am still here you know. Now there are three S.S.W's (student support workers.) coming over to move your things to your new digs and if there are any things you have not packed, then get on with it and I will be into check in about 30 minutes." Danny said "Yes boss, she is like a little Hitler isn't she? very masterful. So Zarrine do you know who these new students are? I bet you do." Zarrine replies "No I do not, but I know one of them is from China and she is a doctor, the other is from Stoke on Trent and I have heard the other is a 17 year old already in the college and there maybe another one coming in to but it's not definite yet." Jeff sitting there with his ears pricked up. "A 17 year old ay, that' sounds interesting hmmm." Niel "You don't stand a chance, your old enough to be her old father." Jeff "Say you don't know the Adonis of Swindon has plans." Danny said "You need a healthy bank balance mate, that's the only chance you got mate." Jeff "Ah you haven't seen me in action yet matey." Niel "God help us, I can't wait it will be amusing if not silly." Jeff "As Danny say's it's a messy job but somebody's got to do it." Zarrine with hands on her hips "You three had better behave yourselves, I wonder what I done to deserve to have you three in my hall. I must have done something real bad in my last life, perhaps I killed somebody, it must have been serious." Jeff "You love us really." Zarrine claps her hands and said "Right get on with it, you have five minutes." They all go off to their rooms.

It was sometime later and Danny, Niel, Jeff and Zarrine sitting in the new common room lounge called Dowdell. Danny said "This is nice I love my room it's huge and en-suite to boot and this lounge is like a football pitch it's huge." Jeff "Mine is smaller than I expected." Zarrine "Yes that's because you smoke and the other bedroom in your wing will be used by a smoker she is coming next week." Jeff "She, another female now your speaking my language, I will not complain then." Zarrine "And she is Caribbean, from Jamaica originally, I believe." Jeff "It's getting better all the time." Zarrine "I think her name is Rhoda." Jeff "Oh dear, I know her from Torquay we were there together a couple of months ago." Danny smiled and said "You sound as if you crashed and burned with her too, mate." Jeff "No we were just friends, she is not my type but she is a very nice lady." Niel "Well lads I am very happy with my room it has a bath and that will suit me fine."

Next in walks Hose with bags galore and he is red in the face and panting. Hose said with broken Spanish accent "Hello Zarrine, i have key for somebody Lilly, Lolly or something." Zarrine pulls out a piece of paper from her pocket. "You mean Lola." Jeff shouted very loudly with a shocked look. "What." Niel "Shit, I jumped then, why did you shout?" Danny said shaking "Yes, I bloody jumped then too." Jeff "Sorry, Zarrine did you say Lola?" Zarrine looking shocked said "Yes, Lola." Jeff "From Stoke on Trent?" Zarrine "Yes that's right, why?" Jeff starts to shake and looked as if the world is about to end striding back and forwards. "Oh no, oh no, i want my room back in Gardener, i am not staying here with her here, oh no, oh no." Danny said with a look of concern "Calm down man, what is the Matter with her?" Jeff looking all done in says "We just as well go home the fun stops here man, she is the devil herself, she will make our lives a misery and she will take over, we are doomed." Zarrine "She can't be that bad." Jeff "My mate Dan from South Africa who is 6 foot 4 and built like a brick shed was dragged down to a shrivelling wreck by her just because one day he turned the television over by accident." Danny said in stern voice "Oh that kind of woman is she? well she better not start on me because I will not put up with any crap at all." Zarrine "Now this is a different place and she might not be so bad, give her a chance." Niel "She is probably very nice and you are making a fuss over nothing as usual, didn't she fancy you either then Jeff?" Jeff "I was too afraid of her to even think about anything like that, she does have a cracking body mind and a nice pair of boobs and I think she is half German, because she has only got hair growing under one arm pit." Niel "There you go, she has excited my Imagination already, she sounds lovely." Next in walks Lola like the Queen. She speaks in masterful voice "Hello i am Lola, (she then spots Jeff in the corner) Oh hello Jeff, fancy meeting you here, what are you doing here? and who are all of your friends?" Jeff "I am here for some education, what about you?" Lola "Well that makes a change Jeff, I am training to be a teacher's assistant." Niel "Hi, I am Niel, pleased to meet you." Lola looked Niel over and replied "Well your not very slim are you Niel? you want to watch your cholesterol with all that fat your carrying." Zarrine says "I am Zarrine and I am your support worker." Lola "Hello Zarrine is it? I can look after myself but I will certainly help you to look after the others if I can." Danny said "I am Danny and I can be your worst nightmare" Lola seeming unconcerned "Yes I'm sure, i don't know what the college done by sending me that weakling of a boy to do a man's job, look at him pathetic, i hope there are some men here with some muscle for me. Well have i got the biggest room, as you can see i need one, never mind i will complain if not. And i like to use the kitchen between 5.30 and 7.30 to do my dinner etc. i hope that will be ok with everyone." Zarrine in sharp voice "We all share here and that goes for everyone." Danny said "And as for a man there's always Jeff." Lola laughing "I said a man with a bit of muscle, no offence Jeff. Yes, yes ok, well must unpack see you all later I'm sure." She walks out of the room and there was a deadly silence and everyone looked stunned. Niel was the first to speak "The cheeky bitch, she called me fat, the cheeky bitch." Danny said "Niel, you are fat and Jeff you are right she has a lovely body" Niel smiling says "Yes I know but she is horrible, I don't like her already." Jeff "Now we should give her a chance Niel that's what you said." Niel "She has got to go, I hate her already." Zarrine "Maybe it's nerves she will settle down you'll see, I would be a bag of nerves if I was confronted by you 3 for the first time." Jeff "I wouldn't bet on it if it's anything like Torquay, it will get worse and she always gets her own way." Danny said "Well I hope your right Zarrine or I will have to sort her out." Zarrine looking worried "Oh no, i hope we are not going to have trouble." Danny replied "Not from me as long as she behaves, no problems, if she wants trouble she has come to the right place. There is more than one way to skin a cat." Zarrine "Remember you are on a years' probation, so if you fight you are gone so be quiet Danny." Next in walks Lennox and behind him was a Chinese Lady about 30 years old and looked very lost. Lennox in posh English perfect voice said "Oh good, i am glad to find so many of you here as this is your new neighbour miss Winnie Woo from China, Lan Chow Province and i will introduce you to these new neighbours, right first this is Zarrine, your support worker if you want anything she is the person to see." Winnie in broken Chinese voice "Hello, pleased to meet you." Zarrine "Hello I hope you will like it here." Lennox continues "This is Jeff." Jeff with broad smile "Hi it's very nice to meet you and if you need anything I want you to ask me and I will sort it for you and my Knick name is Adonis." Winnie speaks "That is very kind of you, I am sure." Lennox "And this is Brian, I mean Daniel beware of him he likes to tease and he is a practical joker." Danny smiling "Hi they call me Danny and I promise I will not do anything to offend such a lovely lady from China, because I am from Wales and our national emblem is also a Dragon." Winnie with huge smile says "That is fascinating, I hope we can be good friends." Danny with cunning smile "You can bet on it." Niel "And I am Niel but I am very large in size so some people call me Tiny the very opposite, I am also from Wales the land of the Dragon." Winnie "Yes but our land of the Dragon is very large compared to yours I believe." Lennox "Well can I leave you here with your new neighbours to get to know them?" Winnie looking panicky and unsure says "Well i don't know, oh well yes i suppose i will see you tomorrow for my induction." Lennox "Yes I will come over personally to get you, see you tomorrow." Zarrine "Would you like a coffee or a tea Winnie Woo." Winnie replies "No thank you ,I would however like a glass of water please." Zarrine "Ok would you like to sit by Danny and I will fetch it." Winnie "Yes ok thank you." Danny said "Well when did you arrive in Great Britain?" Winnie "I landed in London on Saturday and stayed in a hotel until today." Jeff "Is this the first time in Britain for you?" Winnie looking panicky with all the questions said "Yes I have never been outside of China before, this is the first time." Jeff "And are you a married Lady? Have you a husband in China?" Winnie getting more irritable says "No I am a professional Lady and I have worked for my doctrine in herbal medicine and Chinese massage, no time for men." Jeff "And your not on the other bus?" Winnie looking rattled with all the questions "I do not understand what this other bus is and you ask a lot of questions." Danny said "Oh ignore him he was asking if you preferred women instead?" Winnie grinning nervously "Oh no, no, no." Jeff "Oh good." Niel joined in "Tell me Winnie Woo is it as beautiful in China as they say? I always wanted to come to China when I could see." Winnie looking more relaxed "Yes it is very beautiful as you say, we have lots of wild life and this time of the year we have honey melons growing on the side of the road they are sweet and thirst quenching and very pretty." Jeff "Yes we have some large melons in this place too and they are also very beautiful." Winnie "You do, you will have to show me sometime." Jeff being rude "No problem, you show us yours and we will show you ours and compare." Zarrine stamps her foot at Jeff as if to say behave or else and says "Here is some fresh bottled water from the fridge." Winnie "You are very kind, thank you, can I go to my room now? Thank you." Zarrine "Yes of course I will take you there." Winnie "I must say sayonara now as I must get a bit of rest ready for tomorrow, goodbye." They all said goodbye and she toddles off to bed. Niel "Well she is better than the poke from Stoke, much more polite." Danny said "Yes but I wonder what Lola will do to that poor girl in the future." Jeff "Yes I agree with you, we must look out for her." Niel "So, anybody going for a pint tonight?" Danny said sarcastically "Do squirrels chew their nuts? I will be going up but I will come back here for an early night and watch some telly." Jeff "I am meeting Carol up there so it will be a good thing if you leave early to give me some prime time with her." Danny said "You got it and Niel what about you?" Niel "I am going to bed about 9 o'clock tonight but will have a pint with you."

Later on back in the lounge and in the common room was Lola she was facing the window with the lights off and the TV on and trying to make a phone call on her mobile and the television was on. Next in walks Jeff and stands there for a second listening to the television then Lola speaks "Oh hello everything ok?" Jeff "Oh hello." "So what do you fancy tonight?" Jeff "Tonight, when?" Lola "About 9.30 in my room" Jeff's face lit up and a smile came over it as he said. "Yeh no problem." Lola "What about a 69?" Jeff swallowed hard then answered "Yeh, yeh." Lola "I love a sixty nine" Jeff smiling from ear to ear. Lola continues to speak "Then we can have a couple of glasses of wine and we can have a shower and jump into bed." Jeff's little face now beaming and very excited said "Great, i am up for it; you know you are quite a nice person, i don't believe anything they say about you." Lola "We could do this every week if you fancy it and I can come to your room another time and we can do something different." Jeff by now is bouncing "Yes I am up for that and I will provide the wine and the entertainment." Just then Lola turned around and with her phone still by her ear said . "Hang on Jeff I am talking to my friend on my mobile a minute." Jeff went all red and realised she was talking to someone on the phone and not to him and felt a real idiot and his face just dropped and he flopped down on the settee. Just then Lola switched off her phone and said to Jeff. "Right what were you talking about, I could not hear you ,I was on the phone to my friend Jean." Jeff "I was just wondering what you were talking about a 69, I got very hot under the collar." "Jeffrey don't be so disgusting, I was after a house special curry as there is enough in one portion for two of us to share and Jean and I were planning a night for a while and she has come to this college today as well so what did you think was happening?" Jeff feeling stupid said "Nothing, nothing, as bloody usual" Lola "What is up with your friend Danny? He did not seem to like me, have you said anything to him bad about me?" Jeff being defensive said "Who me? No I do not know what you mean." Lola "I do not like anybody spreading rumours about me." Jeff "Well I am not like that." Next in walks Danny and Niel. Jeff said "Talk about the devil and he appears." Danny said "So what have you been saying about me?" Lola "Don't flatter yourself I have better things to talk about." Danny replied "Have you finished with your cauldron in the kitchen?" Lola smiling "Ha, ha very funny, my sides are splitting." Jeff "Now, now, play nice." Niel "Oh come on I want a pint, I can't be bothered with all this crap." Jeff "Yes let's go, I could murder a pint." Danny said "Yes I could murder something too." Niel "Right let's go." Lola "Tatty bye, be good." Off the boys go with Danny muttering.
In the social bar Danny, Niel and Jeff sitting down sipping a pint. Jeff said "I just had a thrill of a lifetime." Danny said "You have got a hole in your pocket." Jeff "No." Niel "He would have to have a pocket missing to find what he got." Jeff "Oh shut up a minute, I thought Lola was making a pass at me, she was asking me if I fancied some fun in her bedroom but she was talking to a friend on her mobile phone, I felt a right idiot." Danny said "You thought she wanted some sex in her bedroom but she was not speaking to you but someone on the phone, I bet you thought your luck was in." Jeff smiling "Yes I did and I would have had no problem with it with her neither, she is very sexy if she could only keep her big gob shut." Danny "So tell us exactly what happened " Jeff still smiling "Well I entered the lounge and she was on her hands and knees with just the telly on and I could not see hardly anything but recognised her voice and she asked me if I fancied a 69 and a bottle of wine then an early night in bed, I was so excited and jumped at the chance as I was agreeing with everything she said. Then she said "Hang on Jeff I am talking to my girlfriend on the phone." I was devastated and felt a right idiot at the same time and went red in the face ha, ha, ha." Niel said "What do you think about our little China girl though?" Jeff "An

even nicer body and very pretty with it, I would, no problem." Danny said "Well I think she sounds a very intelligent Lady, but I think she is a bit of a, I don't know how do you explain it, she is more interested in work than anything and that's how they are in China, very focused, you know what I mean?" Niel "Yes I think I know what you mean." Jeff "Still very nice though." Danny said "Yes, she is." Next a little voice broke the silence Carol in a broad Scottish accent "Uncle Jeffrey." Jeff "hello Carol, I wish you would call me Jeff." Carol with huge smile said "Ok Uncle Jeffrey, have you been here long?" Jeff "No we only just got here." Carol "Who's we?" Jeff "I am with those 2 dodgy Welshmen, I can't get rid of them they are like lost dogs they follow me everywhere." Carol "So is Abby with you Niel?" Niel "No she is in my room having an early night, she is knackered." Danny said "She is guarding his room from a beast of a woman named Lola." Carol looking puzzled "I can't say I have met her." Niel "Your lucky, your not missing much she is horrible." Jeff "Never mind my woman is here now, here come and sit by me." Danny said "Oh god here we go again." Jeff in serious face "Oh shut up, that's all you have done today is moan." His face changes to a broad smile as he looks at Carol. "I am looking for treasure can i have a look at your chest?" Carol looking embarrassed says "Uncle Jeffrey." Jeff continues "You know you look like my next girlfriend. I'm like vitamin c I do your body good." Danny said "Stop, or I am going home, I feel sick, I have never met someone with such corny chat up lines in my entire life." Carol "Awe Uncle Jeffrey you are so romantic but Danny is right they are corny." Jeff smiling "Ten out of ten for trying though." Danny said "Yes you are very trying." Niel "Well I am in the chair who wants a pint?" Danny said "Bottle of pils please mate." Jeff "Pint of lager please." Carol "I will have a glass of cider please Niel." Niel "Yes I think I will have a pint of cider too, be back in a minute." Jeff "I see that that seventeen year old didn't turn up, I thought Zarrine said she was coming to our hall today." Danny said "Perhaps we have frightened her off after all what the hell is she coming to our hall for? It is full of 40 year olds. Why is she coming there?" Jeff "Yes it seems a bit silly when there are lots of residences with teenagers in them, perhaps she prefers the older man." Danny "Maybe, or she prefers Welshmen." Jeff smirking now "Ha, ha, mate the only good Welshman is a dead one." Danny pretending to be hurt said "Well thanks mate, I love you too." Jeff "That's ok, anytime." Carol "Now stop it, I have never seen someone like you two, if someone else said that to Danny or vice a versa you two would gang up on them." Danny said "Yes you maybe right." Niel arrives back with the drinks and says "I have just been talking to Tim at the bar he is coming over in a minute." Tim sits alongside Niel. Tim says "Hello everyone." Everyone greets him Jeff says "Your late aren't you? I expected you in earlier." Tim "I went to the extreme sports meeting tonight. I want to do something like parachute jumping and we talked all about it and the man said that after the 5 weeks training even if you are blind you will be able to do a jump on your own." Danny said "You mean even Jeff can have a jump on his own, that would be a first for him." Tim "Yes I have heard that too, but how do you know when you are about to land? I mean you cannot see the ground coming up so if you are totally blind how can you tell?" Niel "That's simple just think about it." Tim "Well I have been trying to think how all evening." Niel says "It's simple just as your feet are about to touch the ground the guide dog's harness goes slack." Everyone burst out laughing. Niel "I always wanted to do some hand gliding, do they do that?" Danny said "Only indoor hand gliding." Niel "Do they." They all laughed again. Niel chuckling to himself said "I once had a flying lesson in a biplane but I was a nervous wreck and the trainer had to land as I was in such a state" Danny said "I would have thought it would have been your thing what went wrong" Jeff "It's all that loos skin his forehead slipped down over his eyes with the wind and he could not see where he was going." Niel "Your not far out there, I was in the seat behind him and he panicked when he turned around and looked at me." Tim still laughing "Why did he panic what was the Matter?" Niel "Ha, ha, well I had the full force of the wind in my face and my false eyes were spinning around and around in their sockets and it frightened the hell out of him, ha, ha, ha, ha." Everyone started laughing out loud uncontrollably then Jeff said "Your Joking" Niel wiping the tears from his eyes "Do you think i would joke about something like that. Well i am having this pint and I am off to bed." Danny said "I won't be long behind you." Tim "Hey darling, I did not know you were like that." Danny said "No way Hose I am definitely normal I have not got any male admirers thank you very much, as long as they keep it to themselves that's ok by me." Tim "Well there are one or two of them in this place." Niel "Well like Danny said, as long as they keep themselves to themselves that's ok." Tim "I see Jeff is up to his old tricks again, he loves the attention of a nice girlie don't he?" Danny "He does that, and as long as she is a she, we will be friends, and besides she is not interested in him she thinks he is her uncle for real" Niel "Yes I think he tries too hard and his chat up lines don't do him any favours." Danny said "I find them very amusing; where he gets them all from I would like to know." Tim "Yes he is funny especially when he has had a few." Niel "Well I must love and leave you all, I am knackered, goodnight all." All wish him a goodnight. Tim "He is a nice fella too isn't he?" Danny said "Who Niel, yes he is the salt of the earth he will give you his last pound if you needed it and he is always there when you need someone to listen, a real good mate." Tim smiling says "I never thought of you as a man who cares much." Danny "Me I am just a fool sometimes but I think a lot of good friends, they are worth more than gold even that stupid cockney git over there and as I always say I would rather see someone laughing than crying about me." Tim "Yes I agree, fancy a pint?" Danny "No thank you anyway but I am in a round and I am only having another two tonight, but thanks." Tim "I will be back now." Danny "Ok see you in a minute. (Danny turns and looks at Jeff and says.) "God it's very dry in here." Jeff said "Well get them in then." Danny "Lager for Jeff and cider for you Carol?" Carol "Yes please."

Later Danny went back to his hall of residence and in the common room was the new seventeen year old girl and another male teenager were in there, the girl was cooking something and the young lad was sitting down watching television. Danny said "Oh hello alright, I am Danny I live here, who are you?" Patsy replied "Hello I am Patsy I was in Armitage hall but they have decided to move me here because I didn't like the childish students there." Danny replies "Pleased to meet you Patsy and is this your boyfriend?" Patsy in a stern voice "No bloody way, i am a lesbian mate." Danny with surprised look on his face said "Never and what part of lesbania do you come from?" The young lad had a big smirk on his face and Patsy was a bit agitated by Danny's comments and then proceeded to try and shock Danny even more. Patsy "No he is my friend I prefer women and their bodies, I like to play with their bodies and seduce them naked with some of my toys." Danny said "Shit, I think I am a lesbian too." This angered her more and the young lad put his hand over his face to cover his laughter not to annoy his friend Patsy and he said "No I am solo my name is William." They shook hands. Danny said "Well Patsy, your a lesbian and you have your own willy, what a combination. And I hope you are not a nuffta William? I mean I hope you are not on the other bus?" William "No way I am straight so your safe with me." Patsy "I don't see what is so funny, I am proud of to be what I am and I have still got men as friends, I just don't find them as good in bed." Danny said "God girl you are only seventeen and you talk as if you have been having relationships for years your only a kid, so get off your high horse and enjoy life, don't take it so serious as I am not the only person here in this building who likes to enjoy life, there are a lot of us. For god's sake lighten up." Patsy "Well don't try to take the piss because I am Gaye, I can be whatever I want to be ok?" William "Oh come on Patsy he is not trying to upset you, he is having a little bit of banter with you it is harmless." Patsy in a huff. "Well thank you William, i will see you tomorrow, i can manage with the rest of my bags now thank you, i will see you tomorrow." William "Oh dear she is throwing her toys out of her pram now, I'm off now, see you again Danny." Danny "Yes see you mate, I am sorry mate I didn't realise she couldn't take a Joke." Patsy "I am still here you know, I can hear what you are saying you know." William "I will see you all bye." Danny said "Bye mate." Patsy "Bye William thanks for your help, I will see you tomorrow. I don't want to sound ignorant but I must do my cooking." Danny "Yes of course, I am just going to watch some telly just ignore me." "Yes I will."

Next in walks Jeff muttering to himself, he just slumped down across from Danny, looking down and feeling sorry for himself he said "I just cannot figure out what is wrong with Carol, I tried again and with no response, crashed and burned again." Danny said "She is a teaser mate you will never get anywhere with her as long as you have got a hole in your ass." Jeff "No I think she is cracking mate." Danny "So let me ask you how many drinks did you buy her?" Jeff looking uncomfortable "3, what has that got to do with the price of milk?" Danny "And how many pints did she buy you?" Jeff "That has nothing to do with it." Danny "How many?" Jeff looking annoyed "You don't buy someone drinks to get one back." Danny smiling "How many?" Jeff "NONE." Danny "I rest my case, she is just using you mark my words, I am right." Jeff "Yeh whatever." Suddenly out in the kitchen there was a loud clang of dishes. Jeff "What the hell was that?" Danny replies "Oh that was the sound of our teenager making some food for herself." Jeff speaking in a soft voice. "You mean she has arrived at last? What is she like? A cracker i bet." Danny "And what about Carol?" Jeff interrupts him "Oh never mind about her, what's she like this young girlie?" Danny "Yes you fretted over Carol long enough, well I think this one is much more your type she is absolutely charming and very chatty and has a great sense of humour but has a little hang up and that's why she left her last hall of residence. So be careful what you say." Jeff still whispering "What do you mean? What's the Matter with her?" Danny answers "Well she left her last place because she didn't like some of the girls there." Jeff looking concerned "What do you mean?" Danny in shifty manner says "Well there were some girls there who were Gaye and she just don't like that sort of thing." Jeff with surprised look. "Lesbians you mean?" Danny "Sh, sh, keep it down." Jeff "I didn't know we had lesbians." Danny "You make them sound like a dose of head lice, she left because she can't stand that kind of thing so be careful what you say to her, in fact it's best if you do not even mention it." Jeff replies "No worries mate I am not that fussed on them either." Danny "You lying git." Next in walks Patsy and sits down and starts to gather her things together and she was in a skimpy little nightie which leaves nothing to the Imagination and Jeff's eyes were hanging out on his cheeks and his face told you how pleased he was. Danny said pretending to be nice and caring. "Did you enjoy your supper Patsy? i would like to introduce you to Jeff he is in a room in the wing near to you and if you need anything he is very nice and very helpful too, you and him will get on like a house on fire." Jeff smiling "Hello it's a pleasure to meet you, Danny is a bit forward but he is right i am about if you need anything." Patsy "Well thank you, that is very nice of you it's nice to see there some gentlemen in this college at last." Jeff replies "Yes there are not many of us left, I see you have met the dodgy Welshman, beware of him." Patsy "Don't worry I will I don't like his views but he is entitled to them." Danny said "Leave it now that is water under the bridge, let's start again." Patsy "Ok, I will be back now I must put these things in my room." Patsy toddles off to her room. Jeff "I see you have been your usual idiot self, what did you say to her to upset her?" Danny "I made the mistake of defending lesbians and she took offence at it, but I have promised not to bring up that subject again." Jeff looking surprised "I always thought you hated what homosexuality stood for?" Danny smiling says "I am a lesbian myself and I don't mind them as long as they don't push it in my face, I think she fancies you." Jeff "What do you mean? How do you know?" Danny "Well she was in a big hurry to go to bed until she met you, I think she fancies you a bit and if you don't use any of your silly chat up lines you could end up with a lovely girlie." Jeff looking suspiciously at Danny "What are you up to? You are never this nice to me, what's the catch?" Danny "Oh grow up I am only trying to tell you how I see it but that's up to you." Jeff "Hang on mate don't get nasty I was only asking, ok I will see how the land lies with her." Danny "You may be shocked how she will respond to you, as I say there is someone out there for everyone and it's a messy job but somebody's got to do it." Jeff now smiling says "She is a bit young though." Danny "Well that has never bothered you before and besides she is very old for her age, I mean she acts about 35 and has a bit of a neck on her." Jeff "I thought then you were being serious for a change." Danny "Yes your right I think when she comes back I will go to bed and then I will not cramp your style." Jeff "Well thanks mate that's very nice of you but you will never cramp my style." Danny replies "That's what friends are for, in fact I am off she is on her way back, I can hear her." In walks Patsy and sits near Jeff with a bar of chocolate. She says "I'm back anyone for a piece of chocolate?" Jeff "I will try a piece please." Danny "Not for me thanks, I will say goodnight then I am knackered see you both in the morning." Patsy and Jeff "Goodnight." Jeff "Are you from London?" "No I am from near Swindon." "Well, I am from Swindon and all, what a coincidence." Patsy smiles and replies "Well, well and Danny is Welsh you can tell." "He's a hell of a man." Patsy "I don't like his attitude about some things." Jeff says "I know, he told me what happened and I agree with you so I think it's best forgotten we do not really want to discuss that do we?" Patsy "No your right, so you are going to be my guardian angel are you?" Jeff's eyes lit up and he got closer to Patsy and said. "Oh yes it will be my pleasure, I am good at most things if you know what I mean." Patsy looking eager "MMM I think I do, are you any good with your hands?" Jeff gulped and his face changed with that hopeful look. "As Danny said i am very good with everything you like." Teasing Jeff thinking he knew she was a lesbian, played his little game for fun. "Good, I will definitely keep it in mind and what about washing and ironing everything i wear? Including the small bit's, as i am hopeless and ruin everything." Jeff now looking very eager "Anything you like, I am a man of many means." Patsy "I have a basket full of washing and if you are doing any tomorrow I will be ever so grateful and I have a few toys I would like you to put new batteries in if you wouldn't mind and if I have any bad dreams in the night will you come in and comfort me? " Jeff with huge smile on his face "Absolutely no problem." Patsy keeping up the taunting of Jeff says "I Think you and I are going to hit it off very well especially in my room. Well i am knackered I will see you in the morning or whatever." Jeff "Yes whatever, shall I tuck you in?" Patsy "Not tonight babe, I am so very tired, goodnight babe." Jeff "Yes goodnight doll." Patsy goes off to her room and Jeff is a bit agitated. Jeff toddles off to Danny's room.

Danny in his room watching his badly focused television on his bed when a knock comes on his door, it was Jeff. Danny said "Who the hell is it?" Jeff "It's me Jeff" Danny gets up and goes to his door and opened it and in comes Jeff. Danny said "What the hell time is this to visit?" Jeff looking so excited "Got a can in here or what? I am in love." Danny hands Jeff a can and takes one for himself. They both sit down. Danny looking shocked said "What did you say as if i didn't hear it?" Jeff replies "No I am serious this time I am in love and I think she fancies me." Danny says "There I told you she fancied you but why are you here and not in her room." Jeff "Well I respect her and do not want to look like a perve." Danny chuckling "Yes I can understand that, so how as it progressed?" Jeff now trying to be serious "Well I am doing her washing tomorrow and she wants me in her room to fix some of her toys and I think it is a plot to get me into bed but I think she is a bit shy really." Danny tries to reassure Jeff says "You think she is shy ok, you will get that shyness out of her won't you? And washing her clothes is the same as getting engage, or as good as." Jeff swooning says "It's a start she has the real hots for me mate this is it, we were meant to be together." Danny replies "If you say so mate, so where is she from?" Jeff replies excitedly "That's another thing, she doesn't live far from me." Danny with surprised look says "So when will you be going to meet her parents? Have you discussed this?" Jeff's face changed "Oh it's early days mate give us time." Danny said in sarcastic mood "Perhaps you know her father, maybe you went to school together ha, ha, ha and you are probably the same age." Jeff looking daggers at Danny replies "Very funny, I should have known you would make fun." Danny "Sorry matey I was only Joshing with you I hope you are happy together." "Thanks mate so how many beers have you got left?" "I have only 2 slabs left." Just then a perfect picture came on the television and they just looked at each other in amazement. Danny Shouts "Goodnight Niel." Niel shouts back "Goodnight guys." Jeff "How did you know he was out there?" Danny replies "Because the television went so clear." The two men just looked at each other for a second. Danny said "don't ask because i don't know." Jeff says "It's funny isn't it? I wonder what it is never mind, how many cans did you say you have?" Danny "Only 2 slabs and that's all why?" Jeff looking as if he was counting says "That's 48 cans things are looking up." Danny says "What do you mean? You are not having a party here tonight matey, I am going to bed it's late so get your butt ready to go." Jeff "Aw matey, I am your mate and I would give you my last Rollo you know what I mean, I am wide awake now I will not be able to sleep and ..." Danny hands Jeff 4 cans and said "Here now bugger off before I change my mind, goodnight." Jeff smiling "Thanks matey I won't stay, I have some washing to do in the morning, see you goodnight."

The boys went to bed and the next morning in the common room is Zarrine and Jeff. Zarrine says to Jeff "How are you up so early? I have never seen you up this early before." Jeff looking hurt says "You cheeky so and so, I have some things to do today and I have only the morning to do them." "Like what?" "Well I have about two loads of washing to do." "Oh that reminds me thank you Jeff, I must get the engineers over to fix one of the washing machines and only 1 of them is working so you will have to do two separate loads." Zarrine is on the mobile college phone "Oh hello, is that the college repair people? ok i want you to fix the washing machine on c floor Dowdell as soon as possible, yes i will hold, Jeff will you need me to show you how to use the washing machine? Oh hang on Jeff, (speaking on the phone again.) Right you will be here this morning to fix it, thanks." Jeff says "Zarrine I will not need any help, I can manage." "Ok please yourself, you usually want me to do it all, but I am glad you are doing it yourself." Jeff sighs with relief as he is doing Patsy's washing and does not want anybody knowing. "Have you seen Danny? has he had breakfast?" Zarrine "Yes he has breakfast and he will be back for Hose to take him to lectures, in fact talk of the devil and he appears." In walks Danny and says "Good god Jeff, what the hell are you doing up this early on a Tuesday? You don't have any lectures until this afternoon." Jeff replies "I have a lot to do this morning." Danny said "Have you seen your little darling this morning?"

Jeff smiling says "Yes she has gone to lectures, thank you." Zarrine "Do you mean Patsy? I didn't think she was your type Jeff." Jeff looking puzzled says "What do you mean?" Zarrine says "Well" (Danny interrupts and winks at Zarrine as if to say I will tell you later.) "You must not interfere Zarrine with anybody's love life even if she is young enough to be his daughter, it is none of our business, so leave the poor lad alone and he will do what he wants anyway." Zarrine "Ok, if you say so don't get me involved." Danny said "Well I'm off here comes Hose i can hear that silly whistle of his, I will meet him half way." Jeff "Thanks mate, I wish people would keep their opinions to themselves and stop making other peoples life a misery." Danny replies "We must look out for each other mate, you know what I mean? Sometimes it is best to keep things to yourself. See you later." Jeff "Ok man, see you."

A little later in the laundry room was Jeff with a cup of coffee and two bags full of washing he decides to save time he would put Patsy's and his washing in the same washing machine and dryer. He then sets about getting the dry washing out and sorting them out and singing "Happy talk, keep talking happy talk, talk about things we used to do, deed a, Dee, Dee, Dee, Dee, Dee. (out comes a skimpy pair of knickers) MMMMMM (next out comes a mini skirt) that's more like a belt, I can't wait to see her in this. (Next a large cupped bra)I hope she fills this too, Jeff your a lucky so and so, well I have to put them in for a bit longer as they are still a bit damp." Jeff goes off to his room and listens to some radio until the washing is done. it's 1 hour later and Jeff returns to the laundry room and starts to unload the drying machine and folds them on top of the machines neatly and half way through in walks the engineers not 1 but 2 and the knickers bras etc. were over Jeff's shoulders in front of him for all to see. One of the engineers said "Oh hello we have come to fix the washing machine ....." The both engineers looked at Jeff with a bra slung over his shoulders and he is holding a pair of knickers in front of him and they both start to smile. Jeff was stunned and didn't know what to do with himself so he slapped the knickers on the pile of washing quickly and started to stammer. Jeff "Um, um, um, no, no, no, it isn't what it looks like these don't belong to me I." The second engineer smirking "It's ok mate, we see a lot of things in this college, don't worry we won't say a word." Jeff tries to make it out to be normal says "No you don't understand, these are not mine." The first engineer interrupts Jeff and says "Don't worry mate we have witnessed worse we have only come to fix the machine, so when you have finished we will get on with our job ha, ha, ha, ha." Both engineers were laughing and Jeff went red and was so embarrassed and scampered out of the laundry room into his room with the underwear draped all over his arms etc. but in his room was Zarrine tidying his room up. She just stood there with a shocked look on her face. Jeff tried to explain "Zarrine No, no it is not what you think; honestly this is not what you think." Zarrine "I do not want to know, Danny said something about your habit's once, now I wished I had listened to him, I am leaving now, we shall not say any more about this ok?" Jeff pleading with Zarrine "Zarrine this is not what you think, please come back, let me explain." Zarrine stormed out of the room without finishing off what she was doing.

Later that evening and in the common room are Jeff and Danny and Jeff looks as if the world had come to an end. Jeff "I just don't know what to do now, I feel a right perve." Danny said "You are a perve." Jeff not very happy said "Oh thanks that's all I need, you are just going to make it worse." Danny laughing said "Sorry mate where's your sense of humour?" Jeff "It went home with those engineers, I bet they think I am kinky." "And they would be right." "I'll throw something at you in a minute, can't you take anything serious?" Danny smiling "Yes sorry mate, don't worry about it Zarrine will come around, she is a woman of the world." "She reckons you said something about me being a bit odd." "Well you are a bit odd to me, I am always telling her you are not normal and you tell her the same about me so don't take it to heart, I bet no one will mention it at all." Jeff looking sorry for himself says "I hope you are right being a sex symbol I must put up with this type of thing and having a nice young chick on my arm I must put up with these people, jealousy is a funny thing." Danny with a big Smile on his face. "Yes…. are you meeting her tonight?" "Yes I hope so as she has not had her washing back yet, I am expecting her any moment." And in she walks right on time. Jeff "Hello I was just saying you were due to come in" Patsy "Was you? And how are you? And did you manage to do my washing?" Danny said "Well hello Danny, how are you?" Jeff "Yes all done and ready for you to slip into and would you like to join me for a drink in the bar later?" Patsy replies "Um, um, yes why not but first I would like to visit your room for my clothes" Jeff's eyes lit up and he says "Well if you would prefer we could stay in my room instead" Patsy making excuses "No I have had a hard day and a drink would be nice, but that's later." (spoken in a suggestive manner.) Jeff rushes her into his room and they both ignored Danny as they went. Danny talks out loud to himself being sarcastic. "Yes tat ta i will see you both again don't worry about me i am invisible." Next in walks Winnie Woo the lovely China girl "Hello is there anyone here?" Danny perks up and says "Yes I am here it's Danny." "Oh hello Danny I just seen all the college and met some of the tutors it's nice here" Danny says "Not a bad place at all, I like it here, have you seen the college bar? It is where we all get together in the night" Winnie looking unsure says "I have heard of this place but i have never been to a bar in my life" Danny replies "Well it's your lucky day we are all going to the bar tonight, would you like to come up with us?" Winnie with a worried look "Oh no i do not think so" "Oh go on you are in my country now and you must try out our customs and see how we spend our time" Winnie still looking unsure says "Well I do not know…. oh allright I will." Danny looks delighted and says "Ok I will meet you here in 1 hour and take you up" "Yes ok see you later" Danny was left looking very pleased with himself.

Later in the bar was Patsy and Lola sitting together with no sign of Jeff, next in walks Danny and Winnie Woo and Danny with a look on his face as if to say he is with Winnie Woo. They walk up to Patsy and Lola and Winnie Woo sits next to Patsy. Danny said "Hello and where's Jeff?" Patsy with stern look "I don't know and i don't care." Danny replied "Oh dear what has he done now?" Patsy says "He is no different to you in his stupidity about people who are different, (her face changes to a smile) and who is this Chinese lovely Lady?" Patsy shows a great interest in Winnie Woo. Winnie says "I am Winnie Woo I arrived here last week from China." Patsy "I am Patsy and this is Lola." Lola says "Hi nice to meet you, so do you fancy a drink? I am going to the bar" Winnie replies "Yes please I will have a glass of water." Patsy "Oh have vodka or something, I am it will help you to relax I do" Winnie "Yes I will try one thank you." Danny said "No I am fine thanks for asking" Lola said in a sarcastic mood "Ok that's allright then." Lola goes up to the bar and the other two girls started chatting and giggling, Danny felt left out so went in search of Jeff, next thing he found Jeff by the bar with his head down and looking very miserable. Danny said "Oh there you are, what are you doing here? Why aren't you sitting by your little girl?" Jeff in nasty voice says "Don't you dare talk to me i am not speaking to you, you knew she was a lesbian and tricked me, very good I fell for it and if it was me I would have done it to, so you don't have to say sorry just go away." Danny looking concerned says "So what is the problem then? Why do you look so sad?" "Well that bitch Lola helped to spoil things, the engineers have put it around that I am a cross dresser and I tried to tell someone who was picking on Patsy to stick her lesbianism where the sun don't shine and then Patsy let the cat out of the bag by saying she was a lesbian and I could go to hell and then Lola joined in and I have now crashed and burned again thanks." Danny looking sorry for Jeff said "Come on man I would have thought you of all people would have seen the funny side of it, she is too young for you anyway and be honest she has a lot of growing up to do anyway, that's why she was put in our hall because she does not get on with anybody and we were elected to look after her. And anyway she has stolen my date off me the Chinese girl Winnie Woo so I am also pissed off." Jeff burst out laughing and said "Ha, ha, ha, about time you had a bit of your own medicine ha, ha, ha. Well man we have got to do something about that Lola she is going to spoil things for us and everyone else." Danny replies "Don't you worry about her, she and the Patsy will ruin things for themselves you wait and see with a little help from us." "Yes I think your right and we must not let them think we are beaten so let's have a smile on our faces." Danny said "I agree, do you want a pint mate?" Jeff's face lights up says "Ok go on then, I will have a pint of lager." Danny says to the barman "I will have a pint of lager for Danny- La- Rue and a bottle of Newcastle brown please " Jeff says "I'll give you Danny-La-Rue, I didn't know you liked Newcastle brown." Danny "Yes I love it it's the best pint around matey, but no good for you and the youngsters mind it's too strong for boys you stick to your boys piss (the barman hands over the drinks and Danny says to him) I am a bit concerned that you serve underage drinkers here." The barman says "We don't, who is under age here and is drinking?" Danny replies "The young girl between the Chinese girl and the battle axe over in the corner, she is being plied with vodka bought for her by the same battle axe next to her but don't tell her I told you, it will only cause a fight as she is only 17, but the Chinese girl is nothing to do with it. " The barman says "Thanks mate, I will sort it out now I will get in trouble if anyone finds out, we take it serious here." Danny smiling says "No problems mate, I have teenage daughters myself we must look out for them." The barman moved away and Jeff says to Danny "You are a bad bastard mate, I like it I really do, I could not do anything like that." Danny says "There is more than one way to skin a rabbit mate without starting a fight but I think they might suspect it's us so keep your mouth shut if they come onto you. If you say it wasn't you, you won't be lying." Next thing the barman was throwing Patsy and Lola out and Winnie went with them patsy and Lola arguing with the barman . Jeff says "Oh my god they are not very happy are they?" Danny "Sorted."

Next in walks one of the tutors with two young girls and walks straight up to Jeff and Danny. Pat "Here he is, Jeff these girls said they know you from Torquay." Jeff "Well I'll be blown, how are you girls? I haven't seen you for a long Time how are you?" Jane "We are fine we are staying for a few days to see what it's like here." Jeff "Great...Danny this is my friends from Swansea Jane and Paula Bird friends I met in Torquay, girls this is Danny he is also Welsh from Bridgend near you." Danny said "Well hello pleased to meet you, especially as you are from Wales." Jeff "You have cheered me up no end, what do you want to drink?" Jane "We both drink cider please." Danny said "Well you wouldn't believe things have looked up and now I believe in Chinese proverbs." Jeff "What do you mean?" Danny smiles and says "Well a bird in the hand is worth two in the bush." Both men laughed, Pat left them with their new conquests and Jeff came back to himself. Jeff says "So where are you staying here?" Jane replied "We are staying in a outside house not far from here." Jeff "Well if you don't want to walk after a few drinks you can stay in my room." Jane says laughing "God you never give up trying do you? and please don't start up with the chat up lines or we are off." Danny says "I know aren't they awful, it drives me mad but they are funny, but useless." Paula says "That was the only thing I can remember about him in Torquay and the cans of lager." Danny "Yes he is still the same he hasn't changed at all." Jeff laughing says "I am here you know, I think they are very inventive chat up lines unless you are on the other bus." Paula "What do you mean?" Jeff says "I am in the dog house with my house carer she thinks I am a cross dresser and so does half the college, I done some washing for my neighbour to help her out, she is a lesbian and the engineers came to fix the washing machine and I had all her smalls over my shoulders and then I went into my room in a hurry and there was Zarrine our house keeper, she hasn't spoke to me since, I am in a mess, I really am." Danny "Don't worry mate it will sort itself out, you wait and see, Zarrine will come around she is lovely and don't hold a grudge." Paula "Ha, ha, I can see how she got the wrong end of the stick, but Jeff it's not like you to worry about things like that, c'mon let's get pissed we don't start our lectures until after lunch tomorrow." All of a sudden in walks Niel and shouts out "Hello Danny, is Lilly Savage with you? ha, ha,." Jeff holds his head and says "Not the other Welshman, I am surrounded by them, I'll give you Lilly Savage, it's not true I tell you and look who is here the girls from Swansea." Niel stopped gave them a hug and the night was set, they have a good drink and a good laugh.

It's the next morning and Patsy and Lola was waiting for Danny and Jeff in the lounge and in they walk Lola says "Here they are, we have been waiting for you 2, so what have you got to say about last night?" Jeff says "It was a good night, we had a good drink and a good laugh with some good company, 2 lovely girls from Swansea and the music was good up there." Patsy "No we didn't mean that, I mean why we got thrown out." Jeff "I don't know what you mean." Lola "I think you know what it is all about, Patsy got chucked out for drinking under age and I got thrown out for buying the drinks for her and you told the barman." Jeff "I think you had better be sure before you accuse me of grassing, I would never grass on anyone, so I want an apology." Danny butts in "So what your telling me is Patsy got thrown out for drinking under age, Patsy are you 17 and was you drinking vodka?" Patsy "Yes you know that." Danny "and Lola was you going up to the bar and getting her drinks because they would not serve her?" Lola "God well done, he has worked it out." Danny "Well there you are then the barman was right to throw you out, he is no idiot he watches the youngsters like a hawk and you was caught out, you only have yourselves to blame, don't look for anyone else. So how was your night last night? we told you about ours." Patsy and Lola looking really nasty and Lola says "I can't prove it but I know it was you and we still had a good night, we went to my room and had a good drink there thanks for asking." Danny "I am so happy for you." Patsy with a cunning leer says "Yes I had a good time with Winnie, I think you have lost her, I am more to her liking now and we are seeing each other again tonight, you are not man enough so get another life." Danny in reply said "I can't see Winnie picking up with a chubby little tart like you, she is too much of a lady for even you and I can't see her lowering her standards that low, I'm sure once she gets to know you she will give you a big berth, especially with that big ass you got, I can see why you are a lesbian now as no man has ever wanted you." Patsy now fuming "What do you mean? Jeff was trying to get into my knickers and he is a man." Danny smiling says "Well that's debatable." Jeff says in a snappy voice "Hey matey wait a minute, what do you mean that's debatable?" Danny "Only trying to rub her up the wrong way matey, I don't know who she thinks she is." Patsy "At least I am not an old man who has fun trying to get off with young girls half his age and gets knocked back on his first attempt and probably has a little pecker that takes all day to work, go away little man." Lola laughing joined in "She has a point you 2 are just bitter and no fun this is a college not the houses of parliament, it's for fun and plenty of sex to go with it and that's what is the Matter with you 2, you have not got it in you, but there is an old aged pensioners place around the corner, I am sure you will score there if you can find one who is deaf and dumb and incontinent." Just then a almighty row erupted and Zarrine walks in shouting "Right quiet, stop this shouting and arguing now, this minute before I bang your heads together." The noise calmed down and Zarrine says "Right get off to your separate lectures and let things cool down now, I mean it, go." Off they all go without saying a word, all fuming.

It was 11's and Jeff came back to see Zarrine to try to explain about the woman's underwear. He walks in and Zarrine sitting with a cup of coffee in her hand said nothing, he goes into the kitchen and puts on the kettle, he then comes into the lounge again and sit's opposite her and says "Hello Zarrine." Zarrine looks up from reading a magazine and says " hello." She looks back down at her magazine. Jeff tries again to speak to her "Look Zarrine about yesterday morning, it was not what you think it really wasn't I assure you." Zarrine butts in "Look Jeff don't worry about it your secrets safe with me, I will not say anything." Jeff looking flustered says "No, no, you don't understand I am not a cross dresser I am not it was a favour I did for someone honest." Zarrine looks up again and says "Ok so why did the engineers even say the same as me? and Danny says you have strange habit's." Jeff "Oh god, don't listen to that dodgy Welshman, you know what he is like and those engineers like to believe only what they want, I have known you now for a while c'mon you don't really think I am like that do you?" Zarrine with serious face says "Jeff I see lots of things here and I am not one to judge so don't panic, I will leave it at that." Jeff "So you believe me? Phew, I was worried all night about that." Zarrine says "No, I didn't say I believed you at all, I just think these things should be kept in your room and not paraded around the college, just keep it to yourself." Jeff head in hand says "Oh no, I don't know, what have I got to do to prove it? come in my room and check my draws there is nothing belonging to any woman in there ,c'mon I will show you." Zarrine with fear on her face says "No thanks, I am not coming to your room no way mate, it is not safe and you probably thrown out all the woman's clothes because you have been found out." Jeff replies "No, no, I haven't they were belonging to Patsy she asked me to do her washing honest." Zarrine pricked up her eyebrows and said "So that's what that almighty argument was all about was it? she caught you with her undies ay, it's all coming to light now and that Danny has been hiding from me this morning, he has stayed in his room all morning, he usually comes out for a cup of tea with me." Jeff tries to explain more "No that argument was all about Patsy getting caught underage drinking she thought it was me and Dan who told the barman, please believe me I am telling the truth, I wouldn't lie to you." "I don't know you do look like a pervert sometimes especially when you and Carol are on that settee together and those dirty chat up lines, I think I will keep myself to myself as regards you from now on." Jeff looking upset said "Oh don't be like that Zarrine, I am harmless I would not hurt you for the world and I am having a lot of trouble over that event in the wash room please believe me, I will never help anyone with their washing again i..." Jeff was rabbiting on and Zarrine was being serious then all of a sudden a laughing sound came from behind the settee Zarrine was sitting on. It was Danny crouching down behind it. Next thing Zarrine started laughing and Danny stood up. Jeff said "What the hell?" Danny started mocking Jeff "Honest, Zarrine I am not a cross dresser honest now." Zarrine and Danny had cooked this up in the morning and Zarrine carried it out perfectly, she was sitting there with tears running down her cheeks. Then Jeff started laughing and said "You buggers, you done me up like a kipper, you sods you and I was almost on my hands and knees begging for forgiveness, I am surprised at

96

you Zarrine, I really am and as for that stupid dodgy Welshman I can expect it from him so don't pick up his bad habits." Zarrine said "You should not say that about Danny he was the one who told me the whole story that got you off the hook." Jeff "Yes and I bet he told you every little detail." Danny "Well how could I get you off the hook if I didn't?" Jeff sighing "Well I am glad that's sorted out now, we only have to sort out those pair after this morning." Zarrine says "Oh no you don't, I want peace and quiet , or heads will roll just let it rest I will speak to those pair myself, so cut it out."

Later in the lounge and Danny and Jeff were sitting there having a can of beer each and it was late and next in walks Patsy and a strange girl. Her girlfriend had come to stay for a few days with Patsy. She was about 25 years of age, Patsy spots Danny and Jeff and said "Well look what we have here, it's the dickheads from our floor, this is my girlfriend Susan, this is the miserable pair here I won't tell you their names as they are not worth talking to, so sit here Sue and I will make you a drink." Susan giggled and they were a little worse for wear and were falling all over the place and they were acting very raunchy. Jeff was loving it, Jeff says "Are you a student here as well?" Susan "No you got to be kidding, I am Patsy's partner, I have come to visit her for a day or two and for plenty of action." Jeff looking all excited "What do you mean by that? it sounds inviting to me." Susan says "Well don't get to excited I wouldn't have sex with any man and I am a one woman, woman and that's it I hate men." Danny says "You are a dyke you mean?" Susan gets annoyed and says "How dare you, take that word back I am a lesbian and not a dyke you tosser." Hearing this Patsy comes back in and starts on the boys "How dare you speak to my guest like that, you pig." Danny smiling "What's the Matter Patsy the truth hurts as I can remember lesbians are referred to as dykes aren't they?" Patsy "Bastard say what you like your only jealous I and Susan don't like men, we love each other and sticks and stone, whatever." Next thing Patsy sit's on Susan's lap and starts snogging and pushes her hand down her blouse and starts playing with her breasts and Susan starts moaning in pleasure, Jeff was enjoying this but Danny realised this was to annoy him only because of Patsy he said "Oh god do we have to listen to you perverts?" No reply came from the girls and Danny was getting a little more annoyed, then Susan put her hands up Patsy's skirt and Patsy pulls her skirt down so as the boys could not see and said "Steady Susan I don't want these paedophiles to see my pussy." Danny said "I can't see a thing I am blind and I don't want to see anything of yours, you give the gay community a bad name girls." Jeff chirps up "Speak for yourself matey." Danny says "Typical of you mate, listen why don't you 2 take it to your bedroom, your disgusting." This made them even worse and they were really into it by now and get up and says "Let's go to my room and get that new double ended dildoe out and give it a whirl." Susan "Mmm let's go." Well Patsy's room was next to the lounge and the walls are very thin and you could hear everything clearly. Danny says "Bloody hell have we got to listen to this, it's awful." Jeff "I like it." Danny now red in the face said "She is doing this for my benefit to annoy me, I have daughters her age and I would go nuts if I thought they were doing this in public, I am going to bang on her door now and tell her." Jeff butts in and shoves a can in Danny's hand "Now shut up, if you let her know it is annoying you they will just make it worse, calm down, I will turn the TV up a little." Danny "Well, it's disgusting and Patsy is only just turned 17 and is not showing her elders any respect at all, she is sticking her finger up to me virtually." Well Jeff turned the television up and the girls just made louder noises and Danny cracked and stood up and banged the wall and said "Keep it down in there for goodness sake." Then the sex noises just got louder and then there was a loud sound of them both climaxing and then followed a sound of heavy breathing which got lower and

lower. Jeff said "There we are it's all over, it's made me a little stiff." Danny laughed and said "They sound so close I feel I need a pregnancy test myself tomorrow, at least they have finished the dirty little cows." Next in walks Patsy all sweating and went into the kitchen for a drink of water and from the kitchen said "I need this, I have a pubic hair stuck in the back of my throat." She returns to the lounge and said "Have I got any shit on my nose?" Jeff laughs but Danny sat there stony faced, she continues "Did you like that boys? do you want a sniff of my fingers?" Danny said "You are really a dirty little dyke aren't you? and if you think this shocks me think again, it's just the tarty way you are, does your mother know about this, I wonder." Patsy "I couldn't care less what my mother thinks so fuck off, I will leave the door ajar if you want to peak, because I know all you older men are just dirty old men, any requests for which position I can do for you? I tell you what I will put the vibrator up my ass and sit on Susan's face for her to lick my fanny for you to see." Patsy goes off to her room and Danny still stony faced said "This is just to shock me but I think if she was a real woman I might get excited, but her abuse for men is really not funny, she tries to make us feel inferior and I don't like it and if I said these things about gay people in general then I would be called homophobic and put in jail but it's allright for them to say these things." Jeff had walked over to the door going into Patsy's room and Danny said "Jeff get back here you prick you are doing exactly what she wanted." Jeff toddles back into the lounge and says "Huh the door was shut anyway I thought she was serious." Danny "You donkey, you believed her she just wanted to hear you outside her door and now you have. She is making us look fools and enjoying it and it's really getting to me, but I will have the last laugh." Next all the sex sounds and laughing started again but this time even worse so much that Niel walked into the room wiping his eyes and said "What the bloody hell is all that noise? turn that bloody television down a bit will you?" Jeff turned the television off and Niel said "Oh sorry boys I thought the loud noise was the television, so what is it then? I thought it was a sex film." Danny said "It's pervy Patsy and her girlfriend saucy Susan having full blown sex in her room." Niel "Bloody hell, she is not shy is she?" Jeff "Mmmmmmmmmm." Niel "Trust you, how long have they been at it? and why so loud? you would think they would keep it to themselves being in a dormitory wouldn't you?" Niel goes and knocks on Patsy's door, she shouts from behind the door "Hello who is it? and what do you want?" Niel "It's me Niel can you keep the noise down in there." Patsy replies "Sorry Niel I will shortly... aw, aw, aw oh, oh, oh." And she just continues. Niel comes back into the lounge and says "This is ridiculous isn't it? what are they doing to each other?" Danny says "Use your head Niel it's just to piss us off as we are only men, no good to the likes of them and they enjoy trying to make us feel inadequate." Niel "I hope this is not going to happen every night, I need my sleep." Danny "Don't worry mate I will put a stop to this tomorrow first thing." Jeff "Spoil sport."
The next morning and in the lounge was Danny on the telephone and in walks Zarrine. Danny finishes on the phone and said to Zarrine in an up tempo voice "Good morning Zarrine, how are you? and it's a lovely day isn't it?" Zarrine "Are you allright? you look as if you found £20 or something." "No I have just set up a meeting with Anthea to get some problems sorted out that are getting on my nerves." Zarrine looking nervous says "You mean like Patsy and Lola?" "Not necessary just Patsy for now, Lola will just have to wait." "Oh dear, what's happened now?" Danny smiles and says "Well she was in her room with her girlfriend and they were having sex with their toys out as loud as possible and woke up Niel and half the dorm and it was disgusting. if you were here you would have put a stop to it, but we could not and it must stop." Zarrine looking shocked said "Do you really think Anthea will do anything about it? because I don't." Danny "well I have a meeting with her

and my tutor at 10am this morning, I will not let this lie I assure you." Jeff by now had come into the room and said "spoil sport isn't he?" Zarrine slaps Jeff on the shoulder and says "She must be in the same gang as you Jeff." Jeff "What do you mean? I thought that was all over and done with." Zarrine said "I am only joking Jeff." Jeff said "That's ok then, but I agree I don't think Anthea will do much about this from what I have seen in the past." Danny looking concerned said "She will bloody do something about this I promise you, I am not putting up with this, I can see why now she was moved from her other dorm and we have been made her protectors but not for very much longer." Jeff "We will see but I don't hold out much hope for you." Danny "You are just hoping I fail you dirty little man." Jeff "Woo, nasty, now who is throwing his toys out of the pram." Danny smiling "Sorry mate it's not your fault, I know, right I am off, see you later." Zarrine and Jeff say goodbye and Zarrine says to Jeff "Was it that bad last night with them?" Jeff "Well it was a bit loud but I don't think it was that bad although it woke up Niel, but I don't think much will be done about it and Anthea is off on holiday this lunchtime as I have to see Mark her stand in this afternoon instead." "Why, what have you done ?." "Oh nothing, I just want him to have a word with those engineers about them spreading rumours about me as it is affecting my street cred." "Oh ok good luck look out here is Patsy." In walks patsy and Immediately Zarrine started on her and said "Well hello Patsy I heard some complaints about you this morning." Patsy replies "I know who that was Danny and Jeff I bet, well I don't know why, they are just party poopers and miserable old farts, we were not doing any harm they are just miserable." Jeff spoke up "Now wait a minute I have not complained about nothing have I Zarrine?" Zarrine says "No you haven't Jeff." Patsy continued "Oh sorry then, but I am not allowed friends in my room now am i? it's not often I get my partner up for a visit and she is lovely and would not hurt a fly so what's the problem?" Zarrine "Well apparently the noise of a sexual nature upset Danny and woke up Niel who was furious." Patsy "I can't see what the fuss is about, I can't help it that the walls are like cardboard and I can hear Niel snoring plainly sometimes, so what can I do?" Zarrine looking understandingly "Yes the walls are thin I know it surprises me just how thin they are, well I think you will be getting a visit from Anthea sometime this morning." Patsy looking annoyed says "Oh the creep has gone to her has he, well I can sort it out with her no problem, I am going to have a coffee and take one in to Sue so is that it, can I go now." Zarrine "Of course you can." Jeff speaking after patsy has gone says to Zarrine "I feel world war 3 coming on I don't think Danny will leave it just drop and I am not getting involved with it at all." Zarrine "Neither can I, but if he has a problem then he must work it out and I am not getting involved either, Jeff you had better make a move it's five to nine." Jeff stammered and said "Oh shit, I will see you later." Zarrine goes into see Patsy "So how long is your partner staying? as I don't think it is legal for her to be here in the week, it is a college rule that students cannot have visitors in the week." Patsy says "Oh it's ok as I have no lectures for 2 days as my tutor for these 2 days is ill and I had permission from the college." Zarrine "Well I am surprised, who give you permission?" Patsy nervously replies "Um, um, um, I don't know his name but I know what he sounds like, right I am off to my room to give this coffee to my partner, see you later." Patsy rushes off to her room and wakes up Susan and says "You won't bloody believe it but that Welsh prat has gone to see a woman named Anthea and she is going to be looking for me this morning so we must get the hell out of here this morning, I suggest we go into town shopping for the day." Susan wiping her eyes says "I thought we were staying in bed all day today, that's what you said." "I know what I said but Anthea has been on my case all this year and she will not be happy with me this time and you are not supposed to be here so get up and get showered and dressed and let's get out of here ha, ha, ha." "OK let me get my coffee down me first, I can't do anything until I have had my coffee fix and my head is banging, how much did we drink last night?" Patsy looking panicked says "Oh god that reminds me I had better hide that bottle of vodka and that gin, if she finds that we will be in the shit, we might as well have a shower together and don't look at me like that Zarrine is next door and she will not put up with the noise we make like last night so forget it till later, I will book a taxi for ten o'clock."

Over at the college and Danny was in a room with his tutor Alison a lovely woman very well spoken a real lady and one you cannot swear in front of and a caring person indeed. Alison speaking to Danny explaining the procedure "Well Danny this is what happens in this situation, when a student has a complaint of a serious nature it is conducted in front of their own tutor who takes notes and witnesses everything said and so when Anthea comes in I will sit here and do this, so speak slowly and clearly and please watch your language and your temper if you don't mind." Danny says "Of course Alison that goes without saying, I just want a problem solved, but where is Anthea? she is late." "She is on her way up she phoned me a moment before you came in and she has a lot to do this morning as she is off on holidays this afternoon, ah here she is, come in Anthea." Anthea enters the room and says "Oh hello Danny, (she shook hands with Danny) so I am sorry for being a few minutes late but I have a lot to do this morning as I am off on holidays this afternoon." Danny says "Yes Alison just told me." Anthea sits down and starts the ball rolling "Right you have a serious complaint to be resolved as I am told and I will just let you know Alison will be taking notes is that ok with you?" Danny says "Yes that's ok with me." Anthea says "Right what is it I can do for you?" Danny starts his complaint "I have been having trouble with a young girl who arrived at our dorm Dowdell recently, since she arrived she is claiming to be a lesbian named Patsy and she has a hatred towards men in general." Anthea interrupts "What do you mean a hatred against men?" Danny continues "Well she just keeps putting us down and says we are dirty old men and says things like she would never go to bed with a man she prefers women, that type of thing and she is constantly being suggestive about her sexuality like she refers to her personal parts of her body and her sex toys and what she does with them in her bedroom in detail and this week she has her girlfriend as she refers to her staying with her and last night she was having sex with her out loud in her room and waking up everyone with the noise, it's disgusting and the things she says to me is terrible, my daughters are her age and if they spoke to anyone like that I would wash their mouths out with soapy water, it's not on." Anthea replies "I know the girl you are referring to I have had problems with her before and that is why I moved her into your dorm to put a stop to this and I can't see what the problem is, she is just a little bit of a handful and I thought that being with adults would be a good thing for her, just let her have some time to sort herself out and I think things will settle down, I know she can be a handful." Danny looking surprised says "Is that all you got to say?" Anthea looking cocky says "I can't see what I can do, this is the 21st century we have to put up with these things since the political correctness has been established, this is how life is now I am sorry we have to embrace it. Is there anything else?" Danny looking dumb founded "Am I hearing what I am hearing? I don't believe what you just said I must except a young seventeen year old girl speaking to me a forty five year old man old enough to be her father, speak to me like that with a stinking mouth with no respect for her elders, is that what you are saying? If she spoke to you like that you would not say anything at all? you would just ignore it? is that what you are saying?" Anthea with a I don't give a damn expression says "Yes I can except it, it's how

100

life is now and not much can be done about it, but I will have a little word with her as she should not have anyone visiting her in the middle of the week any way but that's all I can do." There was a few minutes silence Danny then spoke up "So that's it is it? you are just going to let this go and just tell her off for having a visitor in the middle of the week? and that's it?" Anthea with a little smile on her face says "That's it I am afraid there is nothing else to be said, I am sorry and if that's it I will have a little word with her and then I am off on holidays." Danny says "well I am afraid it's not good enough, you seem more interested in your holiday than the big mouth of a teenager who is uncouth and a total embarrassment to the gay community." Anthea now getting annoyed says " Now look Danny you must except it and get on with your life please you have old fashioned ideas and I am afraid the world has moved on and we must except these things." Danny with a real nasty look says "So you have put her in there for us to baby sit and we must hurry up this meeting as you keep saying you are off on holiday, well I tell you what Anthea, what are you doing after lunch?" Anthea replies flippantly "I just told you I am off on holidays why?" Danny smiling says "Well I am going to come and see you in your office." Anthea looking annoyed snaps "Why? what for? we have sorted this out now, no need for a second meeting it's over, it's sorted and that's it." Danny says "No not that, I just wanted to come and see you." Anthea now getting mad says "Why? it's sorted." Danny "Well I wanted to come and see you and pull your trousers down and then your knickers spread your legs apart shave your pussy and get my head between your legs and lick your pussy and to finish off give you a good shagging doggy fashion over your desk, then stick my finger up your ass and ask you to fart, whilst playing with your tit's, what do you think." Anthea said Immediately in a snappy voice "Don't you speak…." and she stopped speaking Immediately and Danny finished her sentence off as Anthea looked severely shocked by what Danny said "What was you saying, don't you speak to me like that? but I am expected to except Patsy saying it to me? but I must not say it to you, why not? It's politically correct isn't it? now how do you feel about me speaking to you like that? and that is mild compared to what she has said to me, Jeff and Niel." There was a deadly silence and next thing Anthea said in a snappy voice "Right I will have a word with her Immediately about all of this, is that it?" Danny sarcastically says "yes for now." Anthea bids them goodbye and left.

There was a deadly silence in the room as Alison was finishing off her notes and Danny was feeling awful about what he had said in front of Alison. He waits for her to finish and said in a soft voice "Look Alison I am so very sorry for my comments, I really am please forgive me, pleas I am sorry but she was not listening to me and I had to get my point over." After a long pause she said "Danny that was brilliant, I thought you were spot on in what you said. I have never seen that woman so speechless and put in her place before, ever, it was a pleasure to see and I think you put the point over in the best way you could, a bit unconventional mind but affective, brilliant just brilliant, but if you ever say I said any of that, I will deny it, ha, ha, ha, ha." Danny said "I won't say you said that, I just hope this won't have any effect on our friendship in any way?" Alison smiling says "You don't have to worry about that, I have great respect for you, you have a knack of getting things solved to everyone's satisfaction in a way everyone understands."

Sometime later in the day in the common room in Dowdell and there was no one around, it was so dead in there and Jeff walked in and he sat down with a cup of coffee and next in a mood came Anthea. She said to Jeff "Hello Jeff have you seen Patsy around at all? as she is not in her room and I can't find her anywhere." Jeff replies "No sorry, I haven't I guess Danny has been talking to you by the look on your face." Anthea snaps "I am not able to talk about it to anyone except those involved and I need to see her but she must have been forewarned I was coming." Jeff gulped as he realised he might have said something or Zarrine. Anthea says "Well I will have to leave her a note in her room and see her when I get back from holidays. Are you a mate of Danny's?" Jeff ponders on the question and says "I don't know weather to say yes or no as I know he has been to see you so I will say yes sometimes." "What sort of answer is that?" "The best one you are going to get." "I see you are as strange as him, never mind I am off bye." "bye." In comes Zarrine about five minutes later and says to Jeff "Has she gone?" Jeff jumps as she was so silent coming in "God you made me jump then, yes she has gone and before you ask I don't know what has happened but she was not very happy and she has left a note in Patsy's room as she has disappeared off the face of the earth and she is not sure if someone has informed her she was coming." Zarrine looking worried "Oh dear, I might have let the cat out of the bag, oh dear." Jeff "Don't tell Danny it was you, but as long as Patsy gets the note things will be ok." Zarrine looking worried says "Do you think so?" "Yes I am sure." "Right I am off I am late today as I have been hiding from Anthea as I don't want to get involved, see you tomorrow."

Later that evening in the student bar is Danny, Jeff and Niel and in walks Patsy, Susan and Lola singing sex on the beach, they spot Danny and Patsy said "Ready for a session tonight Susan?" Danny said "You have obviously not seen Anthea then have you? I certainly have and I hope Susan is not planning to stay tonight as she has found out about your nonsense and she is not supposed to be here." Patsy "Well I knew I was warned you were going to see Anthea but I went shopping so I never seen her, so I don't know nothing so get stuffed." Danny "Well I am telling you that she has said she will sort you out and sorry Sue you will not be staying there tonight as I will go and see the warden and Jeff tells me there is a note in your bedroom saying words to that effect." Patsy goes off her head and starts swearing and cursing. "So you think I am bothered she has gone on holiday and you have lost this round mate, I am sure." Danny " I don't think so dick van dyke I am sure of my facts, but I see you are not." Patsy was about to start shouting again and Lola stopped her and said "Don't bother we will go and sort it out with the warden and sort out a room for sue somewhere else." Off they went and Niel says "That told them mate perhaps we will get some sleep now." Then Jeff says "Yes it's going to be a quiet night by the looks of it." Danny says "Well it's a messy job but somebody's got to do it and I don't think I am going to have peace tonight as she will go mad when she reads that note."

Later in the lounge in Dowdell and Danny was waiting for trouble and the boys went over with him as they didn't want to miss anything, they walked in to the lounge and it was deadly silent and not a soul in sight , Danny said "Well lads they are not here " Niel said "Oh as soon as they hear us they will be out mark my words, fancy a slug of whiskey lads?" Jeff "Oh yes please mate, I have got some lemonade in my room I will go and get it." Danny said "Us Welshmen don't want to spoil the whisky mate not at all." The lads sitting down each with a whisky and Niel said "Still no sign of them, good, we can have a nice quiet drink now as it should be." Jeff "Yeh, I am a bit disappointed now it was nice last night ,I could not sleep after that but never mind the dodgy Welshman has sorted it out ay?" Danny said "Look mate I didn't like doing it but I won't let some teenager talk to me like that, it's not on, what if it was one of your daughters ay?" Jeff "I suppose your right I would not like it." Niel chirps up "It's a shame she is like she is mind I think she could have been a lovely girl and that Lola eggs her on." Danny says "I think it's more bravado with her if she was on her own she probably would not say those things and I think her mother has not disciplined her enough because she is a poor little semi blind girl and as for Lola I can't understand that girl, she has a cracking body and a good looking girl but her mouth let's her down and she tries to run everyone's life and if you don't listen in the end she will make your life hell, shame." Jeff says excitedly "Oh yes, I agree she is and I would give her one." Niel "Jeff you would give a frog one if you could stop it hopping." Danny feeling a little tipsy "God I have dreamed about giving Lola one, (Danny shakes his head furiously) c'mon Dan pull yourself out of it, phew." The lads laughing had another whisky and Niel says "Danny it's about time you bought a bottle of whisky, you are always drinking mine." Danny "I'll get one next time." Niel "No, I am only kidding mate, well I am finishing this one and I am off to bed." Jeff says "And me, there don't seem to be any fireworks tonight and I don't want to be having a hangover tomorrow." The lads go off to bed.

Next morning in the lounge and Danny walked in and Zarrine was making a cup of tea and made Danny one and they sat down. Zarrine says "Everything ok with you? how did your meeting go with Anthea?" Danny replies "Well I think it did the trick, it was very quiet here last night, I was not going to let that Susan stay at any cost." "There we are then, but I am surprised Anthea sorted it out, she is too laid back most of the time." "Well I put it in a way that she had to do something I didn't mince my words." Zarrine looking intrigued sais "Why what did you say to her?" "Oh I can't say and besides you are a lady I can't, no." "Go on I am street wise living here, nothing can shock me." "No Zarrine, I can't honestly, I haven't even told the lads, sorry." Zarrine looking disappointed says "Fair enough, well she will be here now so please keep your temper please." "No problem, I am cool as the youngsters say, even my generation were the first to use those phrases back in the sixties." Next in walks Jeff and Niel with Abby chuckling to themselves. Danny says "Morning guys, everything ok?." Niel says "We are ok but I don't think you will be happy in about, I would say now." In behind Niel and Jeff came in Patsy, Susan and Lola laughing out loud just for Danny's sake. Danny was furious and tried not to show it. Patsy says "Good morning everyone." Susan says "Good morning, I am off in a few minutes home for a rest, I am knackered after last night." Lola smiling says "Yes I bet you are, I found your bedroom very comfortable last night Patsy and some interesting toys too." Danny sat there saying nothing, he just let it sink in and realised that Patsy and Susan could not be heard because they slept in Lola's room at the other end of the building and Lola slept in Patsy's room and he tried to not let it affect him. He spoke calmly "Well we had a silent night at least ay lads?" Patsy said "Yes I knew I would only have a slapped wrist at most, I can't even remember what the note said I just threw it down the toilet where it belongs, no problem." They went into the kitchen with Lola and there was a deadly silence in the lounge then Danny spoke up as if nothing had happened "Well I see what you all mean now about Anthea nothing done, nothing at all, what a dick head I am but I tried my best, what a dick head, what a dick head. Right I am off now before I say something I will regret, see you ." Danny stood up and left the room as the girls in the kitchen laughed out loud, after he had left. Niel said "I feel sorry for him now, he was sure he had sorted out the problem and it is not as if he was trying to get Patsy kicked out, he just wanted her to show some respect . I wouldn't like to be in their shoes soon, I really wouldn't." Jeff said "No he will forget it now surely." Niel "Do you want to bet? he might if they forget it but do you think they will now they have got one over on him. I don't." Zarrine speaks up "This is my fault, if I had not said anything to her that Danny was going to see Anthea she would not have that smile on her face now." Niel in calm voice "I don't think that would have made a difference Zarrine, don't worry about it, right see you later." Jeff says "Well I think it will all blow over myself." Zarrine "I hope so." Patsy steps back into the lounge and says "Run away has he? is he an idiot? he will learn though I will not put up with any homophobia, I will drive him out if I have to, what do you think girls?" The girls laugh and agree with her and Jeff says "I think you underestimate him, it will take more than a silly thing like this to put him off and it is silly." Patsy says "I don't think so it will still be the same in a week or two when Susan comes to see me on the weekend." Jeff " You had better hope Danny has gone home for the weekend then." Patsy "From what I heard his wife and his family don't want him there either, huh, right I am off to see my girl off, bye, bye." Susan says Goodbye and Lola speaks up "As Danny says it's a messy job but somebody's got to do it, ha, ha and it's about time he realised he is not the only person in this place and we would like some fun to." Jeff says "He is not trying to …" Lola butts in "Whatever, whatever." And she walks off and leaves them both there in the lounge. Zarrine "Oh dear." Jeff replies "You can say that again, I think Danny's met his match and they will make his life a misery and he said if it got worse he was going to a outside house, maybe for the best ay." "This place would be dead without him here so don't be silly and if they push him out you would be pushed out next by them and then Niel, oh dear."

later that evening the lads had arranged to go to the Pretty Pigs pub and Tim and Laddie had decided to join them. Danny was sitting there very silent indeed and Tim said to him "Don't worry about her mate she is a dick head, don't let her get to you." Danny says unconvinced "Yeh." Niel says "Oh c'mon mate it's not that bad, you can't win every fight." Jeff joins in "Ha, ha, the dodgy Welshman has been sacrificed and by a little girl, I heard her telling everyone in the college how she tamed you and she couldn't stop bragging, you have lost your touch mate so forget about it and let's have a good drink." Danny "Yeh, yeh." Tim feeling sorry for Danny says "Oh Dan snap out of it, I have never seen you like this, what is it mate? tell us." Danny says "I can't tell you as it is something I done in the meeting and thought it would help to sort things out and I am not proud of, but I can't tell you, anyone fancy a whisky? I am in the chair." All excepted and Jeff went up for Danny to get them. Danny continues "Look guys I have had a smack in the mouth but not by Patsy or her bitch but by Anthea herself, that's what's pissing me off, I really thought I was on a winner." Jeff said "Funny she was in the dorm yesterday looking for Patsy in a real temper but could not find her and just left a note for her instead, but she was really not happy." Tim "Well I can't understand it." Niel looking puzzled "I think Patsy is putting on a face and the note really was to the point and has scared her, but she is not going to tell us what was in it is she? she is going to cover up what it really said and her mate Lola has told her not to let her feelings out of the bag and let you think nothing has been said." Danny's face lit up and a smile appeared and he said "Of course, that's probably it, Patsy is not wise enough to think of that, of course well done Niel don't ever listen to what other people say about you, you are not thick just round." Niel "You cheeky git, I'll give you thick." Danny "Sorry matey I am only kidding here Jeff here is a tenner will you go up for another 4 whiskies please. "A bit later all of them were well oiled and slurring a little and laughing as you do when drunk and Niel says "Right Danny, so what did you really say to Anthea? c'mon tell us." Danny "No I shouldn't I really shouldn't . Ok I will tell you if you promise not to say anything to anyone else , promise me." All the men promised and Danny tells the story as it really was. "Well I was in with Alison my tutor and before Anthea came in she told me she was going to take notes and I was to watch my language, I agreed as I would not swear in front of Alison anyway. We started the meeting and I told her about Patsy speaking to me in a stinking manner and she said she cannot do anything about it as it was all about political correctness and I was old fashioned and the only thing was not ok was Patsy having her lesbian friend to stay in the middle of the week and she would have a word with her about it. Well I was dumbfounded. I couldn't believe it I said so you are going to ignore my complaint and I was a forty five year old man being talked to in a foul mouthed manner by a teenager and if it was one of my daughters I would wash their mouths out and does she think that was allright, she said I am sorry I don't see the need to do anything just get on with your life and at the end of the meeting as she was off on holiday's after lunch. I sat there and said so what are you doing after lunch I need to see her in her office. She snapped at me I am off on holidays and the problem had been sorted out as far as she was concerned, I then said I don't want to see you about that I want something else. She said what is it? I sat back and said I want to come into your office pull down your trousers then pull down your knickers, then spread your legs, shave your pussy, stick my head in between them and lick your fanny, then after I will bend you over the desk and give you one doggy fashion, then stick my finger up your ass and ask you to fart whilst playing with your tit's." All the boys laughed their heads off and Jeff said "Bugger off you didn't, your lying." Danny said "I am not I swear it on my granddaughter's life I did, then she looked at me really shocked and said in a nasty voice don't you speak … then she stopped talking all of a sudden and I butted in what did you say don't speak to me in that disgusting way, but Patsy can speak to me like it. Well she said leave it to me is that it and she stormed out of Alison's office and there was a deadly silence." The lads were laughing their heads off and tears were coming out of their eyes and Niel said " that's the funniest thing I have ever heard ha, ha,ha, ha" Tim said " bloody hell, and what did Alison say? I bet she was not happy " Danny said " that is exactly what I was thinking at the time but I was surprised I said to her I am so sorry I really am but she was not listening to me at all I had to get my point over I did, I am sorry there was a deadly silence and I felt awful and Alison said Danny that was brilliant really brilliant, I have never seen that woman speechless in my lifetime, I thought you were right, a bit unconventional mind and if you ever say I said that to you I will deny it. Well I was shocked I really was and felt a bit macho." By this time the lads were killing themselves laughing and so was Danny.

CHAPTER 6
FOLLOW THE RULES

It was a few weeks later and on the bench outside of Dowdell was Jeff, Danny, Niel and Abby the guide dog all nursing hangovers from the night before. Niel holding his head and looking very ill and speaking with south Wales accent "I have the hangover from hell, my head is thumping, and it's your entire fault Danny." Jeff with both hands over his face and speaking with a cockney accent "Yes i agree, i am still pissed because of that dodgy Welshman." Danny sitting with legs apart and head hanging down and speaking with a south Wales accent "Blame me why don't you, i never had your arms behind your backs forcing you to drink." Jeff "I hardly used to drink until I met you." Danny said "It's a messy job but somebody's got to do it and you had better lighten up if you want to drink with me, I don't want you embarrassing me, act like a man." Niel "What can you expect from a heathen from England?" Jeff "I am still here aren't I? I kept up with you pair and I had a tinny before I went out. Well what do you think of that stupid Patsy? and how she treated Winnie Woo?" Danny "Yes what was all that about? I heard something but I didn't get it all" Jeff "Neither did Patsy, she tried it on with Winnie and she thought that's how girls acted here in this country, until Patsy tried to kiss her and she went berzerk and threatened Patsy and Patsy started crying and then Lola picked on Winnie and Winnie thought she would be sent home and she was really upset." Niel "I tell you if she had been left to sort it out she would have killed the pair of them as she is a black belt in almost every marshal art in China." Danny "Well there is a turn up for the books, I was wondering if Winnie was on the other bus, but she's normal, well I think it is a Matter of time before those two will get into big trouble here." Niel "Well what's everyone doing today? I am going to town to change my mobile phone, I sat on it last night and I think it's knackered." Danny "That will do it every time, I am surprised you found your phone the size on your ass, do you mind if I tag along with you to town.? as I have things to pick up and the S.S.W's are off this weekend." Niel "After what you just said to me … Yes no problem, you cheeky git, we will manage I know the town very we l, what about you JEFF what are you doing?" "I am not doing a thing I am sitting here for most of the day doing absolutely nothing, I am knackered sitting up listening to Patsy and her partner getting it on in her room until late and they were still at it this morning." Danny "I think she does it just to annoy us, I think it's awful, they should be a bit more private about it and that meeting I had with Anthea has not changed anything has it? like you all said." Jeff "Oh I am not complaining so give it a rest." Niel with meaningful tone to his voice "Danny i am telling you now, i am not going into any pubs in town." Danny "Your kidding? it's Saturday, everyone goes to the pub on a Saturday afternoon if their in town." Niel "Well I am not and I mean it, I am off to have a late breakfast anyone coming?" Danny "Yes I feel a bit peckish." Jeff "Awe I could not eat anything." Danny "C'mon it will do you good bacon, sausage, runny eggs, fried bread and some fried soggy potatoes and" Jeff interrupted Danny quickly and said "That's enough, I will be sick you carry on, I am staying here and having a fag and a good cough. See you both later, go away." The lads go off for food.

Danny and Niel in the refectory, Danny still in the queue and Lola is talking to Niel at his table, one of the dinner ladies carried Danny's tray and put him to sit by Niel. Niel said "Well you just missed that, I just had Lola asking me to Sunday dinner tomorrow in our hall, that was nice wasn't it?" "You two faced sod, the other day you was running her down calling her everything and besides you seen what they did to Winnie Woo, because she would not play their little game, you must be mad if you except it, it will end in tears." Niel "Ok, ok, I know where you are coming from but she might have had a change of heart and have come around to our way of thinking, she is not as bad as I thought and I expect they will invite you as far as I can see, she is inviting everyone." Danny with stern look on his face "Well as far as I am concerned she can stick it." "Grow up, it is no good holding a grudge, we all have to live together." "I would agree but that woman is not going to be happy until she has everyone where she wants them, you mark my words." Niel looking calm says "Well we shall see who is right."

Later back at the same bench as before and Jeff was laid out the length of one of the benches and Niel, Danny and Abby approached. Danny "I think we had better phone the council, someone has left a load of crap on the bench, oh sorry Niel I forgot your phone is knackered." Niel "Crap oh yes, it's Jeff same thing." Jeff "You two can't upset me today, I am not paying attention, I have just been accosted by a lovely." Danny "Who was that? I hope you didn't give her guide dog any sweets." Jeff "Ha, ha, very funny it was Lola and she has invited me to Sunday dinner, I think I am falling in love again." Niel "Well that doesn't make you anyone special, I have had an invite off her to in the refectory." Danny "Oh dear this is going to end in tragedy, I can see it now." Jeff "What the hell is the Matter with you?" Niel "Oh he hasn't had his invite yet so he thinks she has an ulterior motive, I keep telling him he is paranoid." Danny "Well you wait and see I know what people like her are like, if you don't do what she wants and she can't control you she will make your life hell as she is doing to Winnie Woo and I for one will not be her puppet." Jeff "For god's sake DANNY give it a rest." Next here comes Rhoda, she arrived last night at the college she is also staying at Dowdell. She is a larger than life well-spoken lady originating from Jamaica. Rhoda speaks to the lads "Hello who is that?" Jeff "Rhoda how are you settling in?" Rhoda " Hello Jeff I am fine thanks, I got through the night I could not get over the noise in that Patsy's room, I think there was an orgy in there last night. Did I hear Niel here?" Niel "Yes, how are you my darling? I have been looking forward to seeing you again and I have Abby with me." Rhoda "Oh can I stroke her?" Niel "Of course you can." Jeff says to Rhoda "And this is Danny another bloody Welshman." Danny "Pleased to meet you, I hope you are not another English person." Rhoda "Well I am from Redding but I am originally from Jamaica." Danny "Oh that's ok then, tell me have you had a invite to Sunday dinner from Lola?" Rhoda looking puzzled says "Yes I have I knew her from Torquay (then she put her hand to her mouth and started to whisper.) Really don't trust that girl so i don't know what to think as she was a lot of trouble up there." Danny "I have told these two the same but they think I am stupid." Jeff says "Don't be stupid, stupid ." Danny smiling says "See what I mean." Rhoda "I will go but I hope she is genuine and not using me like she has in the past, she is very domineering." Jeff "Perhaps she is feeling guilty and is trying to make up for it, I mean I would not make dinner for anyone else, I don't even make any dinner for me." Rhoda "No change there then." Niel "Oh god I am going to phone a taxi, are you ready Dan?" Danny "Yes let's go before I get an invite." Jeff and Rhoda "See you later." Danny and Niel go off to town.

Later in town Danny, Niel and Abby walking through town looking for the shop Niel bought his phone from and Danny was holding onto Niel's elbow Danny "Well it's a nice day for shopping." Niel "Yes and not too many people so I can find my way to this shop easily, it's just along here, right here it is" They try to get into the shop but Abby cannot find the entrance and then they realise it is boarded up and has scaffolding around it so it must be shut. Niel looking very worried said "I don't understand it, it was here i know it was."

Danny "Are you sure we have come the right way?" "I think so I will ask somebody." Just then an elderly man was passing and Niel stopped him. Niel "Excuse me sir, is this the mobile phone shop?" The elderly man replied "Well it was but they have moved, this shop is being renovated after a little subsidence. You have a beautiful guide dog, what's her name?" Niel replied "Her name is Abby; do you know where they have moved to?" Elderly man "Yes if you come a few yards up the road I can show you easier." They move up the road about 10 yards. The elderly man stands right up close and starts giving directions but with lots of gestures with his hands. Waving his hands around "You go up this road and at the police station you go right and past the third lamppost near the phone box, down the second alley and the shop you want is the second green one." The man finished and there was a deadly silence and Niel looked bemused and totally confused. Niel said "I do not wish to be funny but I have a guide dog I thought she would have been a good clue that we was totally blind" Elderly man "Oh I am sorry (he then got down on his hands and knees with his head alongside Abby and started to do the same gestures but telling the dog as if he should have been giving her the instructions. waving his hands around) you go up this road and at the police station you go right and past the third lamppost near the phone box, down the second alley and the shop is the second green one." There was another deadly silence and you could see Niel's face going red thinking the man must be an idiot then the silence was broken by Danny silently laughing in disbelief. Niel "No, no, I don't believe you just did that, I give up, I just give up, Danny get me out of here" Danny stopped a woman and said to her. "Excuse me my darling is there a pub nearby?" The woman said "Yes you are right opposite one, shall I guide you to the door." Danny "Thanks c'mon Niel we are going for a pint" Niel "It's a double whisky for me and a slab of vallium" The both men go into the pub Niel shaking his head and muttering to himself. Danny and Niel sitting in the pub and Abby was lying down by their side. Niel "I didn't believe that man, how dull can you be? I could not believe him." Danny "Never mind your in the pub now relax." "Yes and I said I was not going to come in the pub today, I am only having 2 pints and I am off" "Yeah, yeah, I won't hold my breath." "No I mean it, I am off and I will leave you here if you don't believe me." "Ok. I agree I was only kidding and I do not want to miss anything in the college this weekend." Niel says "Tell me do you really believe Lola and Patsy are up to something?" "Yes definitely, she and the Pasty are not concerned about no one but themselves but I am not sure what they are up to, but mark my words somebody is going to get hurt. And as for Patsy's fancy woman is staying here in her room and all the sex that goes on in her room it is for my benefit alone just because it pissess me off, but I will put a stop to it somehow." "Well I hope your wrong about somebody getting hurt, but I worry about Jeff he falls for it every time." "I think he can handle them, he pretends to be hurt but I think he is a man of the world I don't think we have to worry about him. And what about you? how are you? I know you always seem to be happy but what's the truth are you happy? as I know you are missing your misses and the boys." Niel replies "Yes I am coping with things, I sometimes have lots of trouble with my diabetes and I have not got much patience with computers etc. but otherwise ok." Danny "I start full time in the braile class very soon, I bet you would enjoy that as they are a nice set of ladies, I think it would suit you." "I have not much feeling in my fingers." "I have the same problem as you I am diabetic also, just give it a try it might give you some ideas like cheese graters or back scratchers ha, ha, ha." Niel seeming eager says "When are you going up there next?" "I am up there on Tuesday, I will ask them to see you, they will love you and you will love them" "Ok I will." Danny says "In the meantime get the beer in." Niel smiling says "Here's a tenner you go I will look after my Abby." Next the elderly man came in and spoke to Niel. Elderly man said "Hello I don't suppose you remember me?" Niel "I certainly do." "Well I am sorry about earlier, I made a right ass of myself,. Are you still looking for that shop? I can take you up there if you like." "Well we are just having a pint first but thanks anyway." "That's ok this is my regular, I will have a pint by the bar and when I can see you are ready I will pop you up there on my way home." Niel with huge smile says "Thanks very much that's very kind of you." "See you in a minute." Danny sat back down and give Niel his pint. Niel "I think our luck has just changed, when we have finished our pint we will be shown where the phone shop is by the elderly chap as it is on his way home." Danny "That's very nice of him isn't it?"

Later Danny and Niel are being led to the shop by the elderly man. Elderly man speaks "Well here we are I will leave you now you are right outside the shop door." Niel "Thanks mate I hope I did not offend you, I am sorry." Elderly man "No I was a bit stupid and you put me right." Danny "No worries mate, I will see you around." The elderly man went off and Danny and Niel went into the shop. They started to feel their way around and Niel picked up what he thought was a phone. Niel "What the hell is this? (He picks up two round things with a wire going to a control) god what will they think of next." "Why, what have you got?" "It seems like a new type of mobile phone it's like two round things and a control panel; you have a feel of this." Danny and Niel have a good feel of the gadget. Danny "I think it's a new hands free phone, it's amazing what technology can do now, I wonder how it works it must be a hands free phone." Next a male shop assistant asks Niel and Danny in a very feminine voice. "Oh hello, can I help you dears." Niel "Tell me is this a hands free model." Assistant "Yes if you like, are you sure you are looking for one of these?" Danny "Yes just because we are blind it does not mean we are unable to use one of these, you don't have to have a car do you?" Assistant looking puzzled but not wanting to make things worse "No i suppose not, but these are mostly used by women but i suppose they can do the same for a man, so yes i will agree with you." Niel "When you are blind you do not worry about colour or size, I think they are a bit small though, do you do any bigger ones? as I think they would be more comfortable." Assistant "They do them all sizes." Niel "Well I sat on my last one and it broke not very strong and can you get the talks with them?" Assistant "What the hell are talks?" Niel "The ones for the blind that talk to you and tell you what you are doing and will also tell you when you need to charge it up again." Assistant "I have never heard of them but I will certainly look into it, it sounds very exciting, you may have started a new trend." Niel "Oh the blind have had this type for some time now and they even tell you how to use the functions and they will also choose different voices when they speak to you." Assistant "God you people are very fortunate to have these toys that tell you what they are doing it must add to the excitement." Danny "Excuse me, exciting; we are in the phone shop aren't we?" Assistant now looking very flushed and excited says "No you are in the Anne Summers shop and you have been looking at the female vibrating eggs and you lovely pair are getting me all excited what are you both doing later? I get off at about 5." Danny "Don't go there mate, we were thinking this was the phone shop, so can you tell me where it is?" Assistant "And I thought my luck was in, the shop you want is next door, do you want me to show you?" Danny "No thanks I would feel safer if you stayed here." Assistant in snappy voice "Don't flatter yourself sweetie you are not my type, (face turns to a broad smile) but this one with the dog speaks my language." Niel looking nervous "I am a married man and my dog is trained to kill." The both men leave the shop as fast as their legs could carry them. Niel in snappy voice "That bloody old man he had his revenge." Danny "Yes I think that was brilliant. " Both men started laughing uncontrollably.

It was the next day and in the common room were Lola, Patsy and her fancy woman Susan, Rhoda, Jeff, Niel and about 7 students not from their hall invited by Lola and Patsy, Lola and patsy were in the adjoining kitchen cooking everyone's Sunday dinner. In walks Danny as they were all about to go into the kitchen, Danny "Good god what's happening? are we being raided? " Jeff "No it's like a party there are loads for dinner I have never seen so many for dinner, well I am going in the kitchen so as to get a decent seat." Danny "Yes see you later." They all go into the kitchen and leave Danny in the lounge watching telly on his own, he turns it over to watch formula 1 racing , as he did Lola closed the kitchen door as if to say to Danny i have mates and you haven't. They all have a good time in the kitchen, lots of laughing and jollity coming from Lola and Patsy. Danny talking to himself. "I am not worried if she has a thousand for dinner and i am the one left out as long as no one gets hurt, they are very childish." Just then in walks Winnie Woo. She says "Who is in here?" Danny "Hello Winnie, how are you?" "Ok I think, what is going on in the kitchen?" "Oh that stupid Lola has invited half the college in for dinner and all of this hall, why didn't you have dinner with them?" "I was not invited." "Your kidding they asked everyone except you, that's awful didn't they mention it to you at all?" "No I was just going in for a bite to eat but I will wait until after as she and Patsy will only make me look a fool." Danny shocked said "I can't believe anyone could be so pig ignorant, this is not the way to treat a visitor to our country. And if you want something to eat I will come in with you and if they say anything we do not like I will sort them out, I will not put up with their nonsense, I will throw all the people who are not from this hall out." "No I will have something later, but why are you not in there having dinner?" Danny says "Because like you I will not bow down to them and play their little games, so I was not invited" "But your friends are in there didn't they stand by you?" "No they think I am making trouble for Lola and Patsy, but Lola and Patsy will soon cut their own throats mark my words. anyway who cares about them?" "I see you are not afraid of them unlike half of those in there they are weak and deserve each other." "Yes I suppose you are right, how did you manage to fall out with them then?" "Well Patsy was getting too friendly, she was putting her arms around me and trying to kiss me, then I knew what she wanted and I am not like that, so she made Lola dislike me but I will not lose sleep over them." "Good for you...so what are you doing now? do you fancy coming to my room to play Chinese checkers or something?" Winnie snapped at Danny "Now you are trying to do things to me." "Yes but that is natural I am a male and you are a female that's what they do." "No thanks I have some letters to write but if I am invited up the bar again I would like that, are you going up tonight?" "Are Easter eggs made of chocolate? of course we go up the bar every night and I would be honoured if you would join me, in fact I am going for a walk in the orchard behind this building, fancy a half hour walk? no tricks I promise I will be a good boy." "Yes I think I will can I hold your elbow I do not know the way?" "Absolutely no problem, but I am only sure of the way down to the seats, as that is all I have learnt from Ann so far."

After their walk Danny and Winnie enters the common room and they were all sitting in there lots of people who were not from the hall of residence and there was a very feminine man talking to Jeff and Patsy and Susan in the corner. Niel was sitting on his own in another corner, so Danny went and talked to Niel. Niel says "Danny how are you? why didn't you join us for dinner? as if i didn't know, you should have joined us it was nice." Danny replied "I am very happy it went allright, i however was not invited, they probably knew i would have refused." "See you just made life harder for yourself you might have enjoyed it." "if I had gone along with it I would have been ashamed after what they done to Winnie Woo."

Niel "What do you mean?" "They didn't even invite her and we should make foreign students welcome, it is bad enough them being homesick." "I bet they didn't invite her as they knew she would refuse." "That's beside the point, I think it's disgusting." "God your a stubborn man aren't you? just forget it don't let it get to you?" Danny smiling says "Yes everything rosy in the garden at the moment but you wait and see." Niel interrupts Danny "Oh change the record it's all you keep saying, give it a rest." Danny gets up and goes into the kitchen to make himself a cup of coffee. Over to Jeff and his friend River who is talking very camp about Danny to him. River "Who is that large good looker who just went into the kitchen?" Jeff "That was my mate Danny, he is from Wales." "He is very butch and he has lovely muscles and nice legs. if you know him you must introduce me to him." Jeff with serious face "No I don't think you want to go there I assure you, you don't want to go there." Just then Patsy butted into the conversation and trying to make trouble for Danny says "Yes he seems to be your sort of man River, I would go for it if I were you, he is always on his own." Jeff "I don't think that is a good idea, Danny is not that way, you really don't want to go there." River "How do you know what he likes and does not like? you haven't known him long." Jeff "Danny would probably take you out for a curry, ten pints of Guinness and a bowl of prunes and rhubarb tart to finish off" River "Why would he do that?" Jeff "To teach you what your ass is really for." River "Don't be stupid, he would not do that." Jeff "o your right, he would probably rip your head off and pour chili pepper down your neck, if I was you I would wipe him out of your mind as you will only suffer if you mess with that dodgy Welshman." River "Well we will see." Back over to Niel and Lola talking and behind them listening was Danny. Niel "Well I got to say that was a lovely dinner, thanks." Lola "We will do this regular, we must all put money in and we can all eat together, it will be like a big family and Abby liked it she had the left over so you don't need to feed her tonight, I have already done it." Niel his face became very serious "I hope your kidding she is a guide dog, i am the only one to feed her, or she will not react to my commands, please don't do that again please, she may have the runs etc. if you change her diet, i wish you had asked me first." Lola snapped at Niel "Oh shut up, she looked as if she could do with something to eat she is thin and your so fat she looks ridiculous walking besides you, so stop making such a fuss." Niel GETS even more serious "You don't understand she is not a pet, she is a working dog, without her I am lost, so don't do it again." Lola snubbingly "Yeah whatever." Niel "No I mean it." Lola says "Well why don't you join her on a diet, such a fuss over nothing, go away Niel." Lola stands up and walks away. Niel is now really mad and talking to himself "The bitch she thinks she knows it all, the bitch." Danny sarcastically calm "What? Talking to yourself Niel." Niel tells Danny "Did you hear what she just did to Abby?" Danny "Yes she fed her without your permission, your getting like me making a big fuss over nothing." Niel "Am I the only one with intelligence?" Niel storms off to his room. Lola says after Niel leaves "And good riddance to the fat pig." Danny says "That's charming." Lola "Mind your own business." Danny "Oh excuse me." Next in walks Winnie Woo looking for Danny to go up the bar. Lola gets the first word in "Oh look what the cat has dragged in." Patsy joins in "Yes I thought I could smell something." Winnie hearing this said "I wish for you to tell me what you mean by that?" Patsy feeling brave because Lola was there said "I do not have to explain myself to the likes of you." Winnie "Who do you think you are you pig?" Danny said "Winnie Woo please, please, don't you drag yourself down to their level, you stay a lady not the garbage who tries to get your back up, they are not worth it, let's get the hell out of here." Lola "Yes go, it is nicer here when you are not here, we know how to have fun." Danny "I never try to stop anybody having fun but you and that fat Pat are vindictive and use people to get what you want and if it ever affects me I will show you the other side of me that even I don't like, you just try me." Patsy "Oh we are shaking in our boots, c'mon Susan let's go to my room and have some fun, Danny gets off on listening to us in my room." Jeff try's to calm things down "Now stop it let's not let this get out of control, play nicely now. Where are you off Danny?" Danny "We are going up for a few pints, are you coming up?" Jeff "A silly question if ever I heard one." Lola says "Aren't you going to help us drink this wine?" Jeff "Oh yes of course, I will see you later mate." Danny sarcastically "Yeh whatever." Lola has a big smirk on her face and Jeff looked pretty timid. Danny and Winnie Woo leave the room.

It was 2 hours later and in the bar and Danny and Winnie Woo were having a good giggle and Jeff, Lola, Rhoda Patsy and River sit on the next table. Jeff sounding worse for drinking wine says "Hello you two having a nice time? I see." Winnie says "Yes I am happy to talk to someone who is a gentleman and a credit to his country." Jeff "OOOOOOOOOOOW that was bitchy, I was hoping that it was all going to be forgotten and it was water under the bridge." Danny "Yes it is for tonight, but things will never be like it was before they arrived in our hall. And what about Niel why is he not here?" Jeff in serious face "Well he has got a huff on, he stayed in his room." Danny "Yes and did you hear the way she spoke to him? who the hell does she think she is?" Lola hearing this said "I hear everything you are saying, I can do what I like so get a life." Danny with raised voice "Not if it effects other people you can't." Lola "Just keep your nose out and get on with Hong Kong phooey." Winnie replied "I will come over there in a minute and give you something to make you respect me." Lola and Patsy "Yeah whatever." All this time River was making eyes at Danny and making suggestive sounds. Danny with serious face "And what is the Matter with fruit and fibre? has he got a problem to." Lola "Who the hell is fruit and fibre?" Danny "The poofta with the wig making all those silly noises and smiling all the time." Jeff laughed and River said "I am just fascinated with you, I am starting to fancy you, your so butch mmmmmmmmmm." Danny said "I hope your kidding for your sake." Jeff looking at River. "I warned you, best leave it alone now while your still able to walk." River says "Oh he would not hurt me, he likes me really." Lola butts in "If he does your the only person he does." Danny "I'm off before it all gets out of hand, goodnight." Jeff "Don't be like that matey, stay and have another." Danny and Winnie Woo get up and leave without saying another word. Lola smiling says "Good riddance to bad rubbish let's forget about them stuck up dick heads." Patsy "Yes he won't beat me, I think he will go from our hall and share a house with that other fat Welshman with a bit of luck." River "He can always share with me no problem." Lola "No accounting for taste River." Jeff with serious look of sadness "Why are you being like that? he is allright really." Lola snaps at him "Well go on then run to your little friend."

Next morning and in the common room is Zarrine muttering to herself not sounding very happy. In walks Danny, Zarrine says to him "I work hard enough without all this extra mess, the kitchen is a mess, flowers everywhere, personel stuff everywhere. I am fed up." Danny says "Good morning my darling, what are you muttering about and who in your mind are you going to kill?" Zarrine rambling on and waving her arms about "Good morning, are you anything to do with this mess? the kitchen has food everywhere, dishes everywhere in here, clothes, make up, shoes and to top it all someone has put flower vases around with flowers in them. This is no good for blind and partially sighted people here, they will knock them over and there will be water everywhere, i don't know, I." Danny butts in "Hold it Zarrine sit down here for a minute. it is no good being like this you will make yourself ill, calm down, now is that better?" Zarrine with hand over her forehead "I am sorry, i wish i knew what went on here this weekend? this is ridiculous." "Right, you know who is responsible for all of this as well as I do, it is that idiot from Stoke on Trent, and the two lesbians who have a show in Patsy's room every weekend that keeps everyone awake every night over the weekend. But don't worry we can sort it out." "I should not let it get to me but where do I start?" Next in walks Niel he knocks over a vase and the flowers and water goes everywhere. Niel in a frustrated state "I am sorry, I didn't see them, I am blind you know." Zarrine says "See what I mean? they should not be here." Niel in raised voice "Well i didn't put them there." Niel turns on his heels and storms out to his room again. Zarrine shouting after Niel. "No i didn't mean you Niel, i know it's not your fault, please come back, see i have upset him now." Danny says "No it's not your fault Zarrine, it happened last night when Lola fed Abby and Niel went mad, so they have fallen out big time now. Don't worry he will come around, what if you take him a nice cup of tea to his room and have a little chat with him." Zarrine almost crying says "Yes that's a good idea I will, do you want one?" "Yes please, I shall pick up the flowers and get a cloth and wipe up the water." They both get up and do the tea and Danny gets a cloth and wipes up the water. Zarrine takes Niel his tea, next thing Danny is coming back from taking the cloth to the washing room and he puts his foot on a high heel shoe and does the split's, he is on the floor holding his leg when in walks Zarrine. Zarrine hand over her mouth "oh my god, are you alright?" Danny said "It is ridiculous someone is going to break something, I don't think so, open the window Zarrine." Zarrine "Why? what are you going to do?" "Just open the window and get out of the way I will sort this problem out, if you do not want to see it go out of the room for about five minutes." "I will take Niel his biscuit's." Zarrine opens the window and leaves the common room, next Danny grabs the shoes the clothes the makeup and throws them out of the window. He shuts the window grabs all the flowers and throws them in the bin and tips the water out and puts the vases in a empty cupboard, he then sits down and drinks his tea. Next in walks Zarrine very silently. Zarrine speaks in a calm voice "Oh my god, i don't believe you just did that." She starts laughing and said "She is going to go mad." "Ask me if I care?" "Do you care?" "I don't give a shit. now what is it you were complaining about?" Zarrine with a big smile on her face. "Just the dirty dishes now." "Well you put up a sign and make it apply to everyone saying that this kitchen will be shut by the management if the kitchen is left in a mess again and I guarantee she will get them clean next time. If she thinks that it will stop her entertaining her friends." "Good idea." Danny "Right I will wash you can wipe and put them away and we will between us sort this awful mess out." "I cannot understand why that wife of yours is trying to divorce you." "Neither can I and as regards this mess it's a messy job but somebody's got to do it." Next in walks Jeff holding his head and looking very ill. He says "Oh my god, I am sick and I am still drunk." Danny "There is one of the culprit's and I think he's a rat and a traitor." Zarrine looking at Jeff with a nasty look "Yes i think he would be like that if a woman was involved, he is a traitor." Jeff with a look of shock and looking sick "Oh don't be like that, i only had a drink and Sunday dinner, that's all." Danny "So why am I and Zarrine doing all the washing up? I never had Sunday dinner, the mess in this building was a total mess and you were one of them." Jeff "I told you what she was like, she is smothering once she has got you she makes it Impossible for you, I can't say no, I don't like upsetting people." Danny "Well as long as you have a clear conscience that is ok." Jeff "I am sorry, I am really sorry I never meant any harm here, let me give you a hand." Danny snaps "No don't bother mate we can manage you just get your priorities right and stuff everyone else." Next they finish the dishes and Danny goes off to lectures without saying a word , Jeff speaks out loud "Oh be like that mate I don't care."

Zarrine says "I don't believe you mean that, do you?" Jeff looking sorry for himself "Well, he can be so damn righteous sometimes, why doesn't he just go with the flow? like everyone else." Zarrine says "Because he will not put up with a bully and he will fight even if no one else does because he thinks that freedom anywhere is Important for all and he will not sit back and let anyone get bullied and I think you are the same deep down. I hope this is not the end of a good friendship, because it will be a shame." Jeff looking sheepish says "No that will not happen he will forget about it by the time I see him next Time and I will do the same because that's how we both are. I have it said to me sometimes "are you and Danny speaking now after that hell of a row last night?" and I and Danny always say "That was last night" the next time we meet it is as if it never happened." Zarrine smiles "That is good people like that always remain friends and I for one am pleased."

Later that day sitting in the Dowdell lounge is Danny and Jeff Danny is waiting for Lola to come in and ask what happened in the morning with her shoes make up etc. Jeff says "I haven't seen Niel since the incident with him and Lola." Danny "No he is in his room pouting, he will be out as soon as he is ready or he wants something." "I thought he went over the top a bit." "I think Lola went over the top by interfering with his dog, she had no right at all, would you feed his dog without asking him?" Jeff pondered and says "Well no I suppose not." "Well there you are then so stop trying to defend her she is wrong as usual and you will stick up for her because she is female so shut up because you just drop yourself in it more and more." Next in walks Lola and Patsy and she caught sight of Danny and went like a mad dog. Lola in a nasty tone "So you have come out of hiding have you? suppose you had something to do with all my stuff being thrown out of the window and my flowers being chucked in the bin? now don't deny it, i know it was you even if there are no witnesses." Danny calm y with smile "Yes." Lola looking shocked says "So you admit it?" Danny "Yes." Lola "Who do you think you are? they are nothing to do with you so when I replace them you leave them alone." Danny replies "I promise you if you put these items back the same thing will happen again, I will throw anything personel things cluttering this place up out of the window and flowers are a really nice fixture here but not if most people are blind and knock them over all the time so don't think of it, I nearly broke my leg doing the split's on your high heels, so it's up to you if you want to go outside to put your shoes on each day that's up to you." Patsy joining in and nasty "My god, who do you think you are? I think you should leave and go and live with another old age pensioner in an outside house." Danny "Excuse me what has this got to do with you?" Patsy retaliates "I live here to and I have got a say." Lola says "And when you threw my shoes out the heel broke off." Danny "Well put them away you two are not the only people living here, there are twelve on this floor, it is not just your place we must learn to share and think of the other people in here, because if it does not change I will be getting Anthea over for a meeting to get all of this mess sorted out and the culprit's thrown out." Lola "Yes why not let's do it, bring her on and I shall win and what do you think Jeff? you have not said anything there or you sucking up to him?" Jeff says in a serious mood "Time for a ciggy, I do not want to get involved I just want a quiet life." Danny "You just sit on the fence or are you still worrying about getting into their knickers? mind you, you probably stand a chance with these two; they will do anything to get their own way." Lola "You cheeky pig." Danny "Well I am off to my room,, it is getting a bit smelly in here, see you, (Danny looks over to Jeff and said.) and you, you big shithouse." Jeff looking stunned "What have I done?" Danny "You just shit out."

Danny was walking past Niel's room and the door was open and in there was the college nurse. Danny went in after knocking the door. He said "Well hello Gloria, what are you doing here? is Niel not well?" Gloria "No I had a phone call to say that Niel had a diabetic fit." Danny looking concerned said "Oh dear, he has not had any of them for so long, is he alright?" Niel looked at Danny as if he was invisible says "Yes I am, I am here you know I do live here, it is my room." Danny "Sorry mate, I didn't know if you were up to talking, so why has this happened?" Niel answers "It might be something to do with the fact that I am diabetic." Danny smiling says "Well done, I should have thought of that, silly me." Gloria "The reason is that Niel has not been eating his meals at regular times and you must if you are diabetic, as you know Danny because you are diabetic too." Danny "Well of course, so why have you not been eating regular?" Niel "There is always someone in the kitchen when I want to cook they are using the cooker." Gloria "Well why don't you eat in the refectory?" Niel "Have you tasted the food in there, they cater for the youngsters here not us older ones, like chicken nuggets, pizzas, burgers and chips. I don't like them." Gloria "That's fair enough but you must eat never mind what." Niel snaps "Yes ok, I will." Danny "If there is a problem I will cook something for you just let me know." Niel "I don't like toast, boiled egg or beans on toast." Danny with huge smile says "You cheeky git, I will have you know I am a ninth darn in cookery." Niel now smiling "Yeah, yeah." Gloria "Well you must insist on eating when your ready." Niel "Yes I will, but I don't eat the same time all the time." Gloria "Well I am off if you need me do not hesitate to call any time." Niel "Ok Gloria I will, thanks my darling your one in a million." Gloria "Bye." Danny "Goodbye Gloria nice to see you again. Right so what is going on mate? I know you and there is more to this than meets the eye." "I don't know what you mean." "Come on you big dopey lump, I have known you long enough now and I know when something is wrong, now stop messing around and tell me the truth." Niel being coy says "Oh it's nothing I am just being silly, I will sort it out." "No, I know you, you will bottle it up until it gets too much and go home for a while, Niel it's no good doing that you have a lot of friends here and I know something is wrong and I shall get to the bottom of it come hell or high water." Niel opens up and says "Well I am having a tough time with Lola and that little faggot Patsy." Danny reasons with him "I knew it had to do with those two, they are taking over here." "Listen, listen, I don't want a big fuss as you go in like a bull at a gate, I can sort this out myself, ok? you promise me not to." Danny says "I can't promise anything just tell me what they are doing to you?" "If you embarrass me I will never talk to you again so promise me." A long pause "Ok I promise I will not embarrass you, now tell me and we can if possible sort this out properly." Niel "Well I as you know am self-catering and I eat in the evening any time between 5 and 7 in the evening, well the kitchen and common room has been full of strangers being fed by Lola and her butty never mind what time I get in there, they are all partying or eating, I can never get to the cooker or I won't because I just cannot eat with strangers there, so I am not eating or I am buying crisps or biscuit's and as you know they are no good for diabetics." Danny says "Have you asked Lola to let you have the kitchen for a few minutes just to make yourself something to eat?" "You must be kidding, you know what she is like she just ignores you as it is, she starts giggling out loud whenever I go in there, she is the bitch from hell, no wonder she can't keep a boyfriend they are all afraid of her. No I think I shall ask for a transfer to an outside house." Danny in serious voice "Over my dead body mate, you and I have been here together with that cockney git a while now and it is going to stay that way, I mean it." "How? there is nothing we can do about it, she has got us licked." Danny says "You just hang fire mate, I will sort it out you leave it to me, anyway do you fancy eating out until I have sorted things out, I know a nice pub called the Pretty Pigs, the manager there is a good mate, we will eat like kings for next to nothing for just a few days and I promise things will come back to normal." "Oh dear, I am now starting to panic don't do anything silly will you?" "Who me? it's a messy job but somebody's got to do it and I will not involve you at all." Both men started to laugh.

A few days later in the evening and in the kitchen was Lola, Patsy, Jeff, Rhoda and a load of students from all over the college having a meal and partying and in the lounge was Winnie Woo watching TV. Next in walks Danny, he walks straight into a settee that had been moved to the centre of the lounge. Lola and Patsy had decided to rearrange the room and Danny flipped over the settee and rolled over it and ended up on his backside in front of the television , Danny with huge look of surprise "Shit what the hell happened? that wasn't there before, i could have broken my neck" Winnie was laughing about what just happened and said "Good evening Danny, that was clever, did you used to work in a circus? I didn't see what happened but just know what did although I am blind, ha, ha, ha." "Oh hello Winnie Woo, no but I was lucky I didn't, what has happened here?" Winnie replied "Well it seems that Lola has rearranged the room to suit her, I came in here and now I do not know where to go as I fell back on this settee and stayed here until the kitchen is empty, but I just as well go back to my room for 1or 2 hours until the party is over again in there. There is even Rivers huge suitcase by the kitchen door I nearly fell over it." Danny got up in a nasty mood and said "Right I have had enough of this and I am going to put a stop to it." Danny pushed the settee back to the wall and moved everything back to where they were, then opened the door to the kitchen loudly and there was a deadly silences, he burst in. "Ok I have had enough of this every night so those who do not live here please get your belongings and get the hell out of here and do not come back here unless you are invited by every person on this floor, we have to live here and we can't get in our own kitchen because it is always full of outsiders and strangers. So move it now." There was a deadly silence for a minute then Lola spoke up. "Who the hell do you think you are? you can't just come in here and talk to my friends like that, get out and shut the door after you." Danny looking determined sais "I am sorry that is not going to happen I warned you this could happen, you have got on the wrong side of me once too often and you and your friends have alienated certain people on this floor and it is their hall and these people are invading their space, so get out before I throw you out." Lola "You all stay put." Danny said in a firm voice "Well it is Lola or me and I have just hurt myself in there because she decided to move furniture around without informing any of us, so I am in a very bad and violent mood, so move it." everyone started getting out very quickly except River who carried on eating. Danny continued speaking "Thanks and please don't come back and by the way fruit and fibre I mean you to, so move your ass." River said "You don't mean me, I am always here and you love me really." Danny "Now you listen to me you little poofta, get your suitcase and get the hell out of here and if you visit again go to Lola's room and not in our common room, unless invited by the rest of us." River in serious mood says "I am not leaving, I must support my friends." Danny said "Now listen to me Eric Lewis, that's your real name isn't it? if you don't hurry up I shall send your suitcase out the window like Lola's rubbish." River laughs and says "Ha, ha, my suitcase won't fit through the opening ha, ha." Danny answers him "Who said anything about opening it I will just throw it through the glass, and then Eric that is your real name, isn't it? I shall proceed to put my size 9 boot in your ass and kick you down those stairs and out the door." There was a long pause and very silent. River "Right I will see you all later in the bar, bye, bye." Off he trotted and Lola was looking daggers at Danny then stood up and started wailing and crying and stamping her feet, leaving all the dishes and ran out of the kitchen through the common room and into her bedroom. The only one left was Patsy it is

116

her turn to have a go at Danny. Danny walks back in the common room where Winnie Woo is still sitting down. Patsy's turn to have a go "Oh well done you think your so big don't you? it will not make any difference, we will get our own way in the end, you can't do nothing to me I am a 17 year old woman and untouchable." Winnie said "I think your wrong there, because if you cause any more trouble I shall sort you out and I am not kidding." Patsy looking smug said to Winnie "And what are you going to do?" Winnie "I am a visitor to your country and you and Lola have made my stay a misery so far but I tell you now I am a martial arts expert and before I leave here I shall teach you and that Lola a lesson and I do not make idle threats." At that Patsy looking worried storms off to her bedroom. Danny "I didn't know you are a martial arts expert, I thought you looked fit." "Yes I am a black belt in all martial arts." "Do you have a black belt in dish washing? as I had better clean up all that mess I caused the trouble and I can't leave them to Zarrine." Winnie smiling says "I only wash up my dishes I am sorry, shall see you later."

The next morning in the common room and there is Zarrine with her hands on her head. Next in walks Danny. Zarrine "Ah Danny so what the hell happened here last night?" "What do you mean? the kitchen is clean and no one is dead." Zarrine smirking says "You know what I mean, I have had a phone call this morning from Anthea she is coming over here tea time at 5 o'clock for a hall meeting and I have to come back to work, what have you done?" Danny with bemused look says "Why has it got to be me? you always blame me." "Well who is it then?" Danny "Me, I had a big run in with hinge and bracket." Zarrine looking confused says "Who the hell is hinge and bracket?" "Oh Lola and Patsy, it all blew up last night so they have probably called a meeting before I had the chance to, well you know what it's like here and she has made everyone's life a misery." "So it's her and her friends against you, I don't fancy your chances." Danny with smile "Well the others will have their say." Zarrine says with poker face "In my experience in this place they will just sit there and keep quiet, your On your own mate." Danny says "We will see, i can't let this carry on, there used to be lots of people in here for breakfast, now it is like a ghost town all because of them two, someone has got to stand up to them." "But what if you lose the argument tonight?" Danny "Then I will leave because if this is how it is going to be I don't want to be a part of it." Zarrine looking concerned "Oh now don't be silly you can't leave please." "Rest assured if I can't sort this out to suit everyone I will leave tomorrow." Zarrine looking sad said "Oh don't say that." "I mean it."

Later that night and in the common room and there is Winnie Woo, Mark, Lola, Jeff, Patsy, Gupta, Rhoda, Zarrine, River and Anthea. Next in walks Danny he is 30 minutes late but Lola and Patsy are sticking the knife in for Danny, it goes silent when he walks in for a second. Danny smiling speaks up "Oh hello everyone, i am sorry i am late, i was busy in the recording studio and the time just run away with me." Lola says "We are surprised you had the nerve to turn up." Danny "I have never been afraid of anything like this in my life, so would anyone like to bring me up to date." Anthea "Well we have started and so far it seems to be all about you and some of the things you have done." Danny says "And has anyone come to my defence?" Anthea "Well no nobody has I am afraid." Danny "Well I am here now so I can defend myself and anything that has gone on, so fire away, I for one am not afraid of the Gestapo." Anthea starts referring to her notes on her lap. "Right, as far as the common room and some flowers destroyed." Danny starts to defend himself by saying "Surely you can see how Impractical it is, within seconds Niel knocked a vase of flowers and water all over the place and got very upset about it, am I right Zarrine?" Zarrine answers "Well yes it's true." Anthea "Well I agree it is a bit inconvenient, so no more flowers in vases." Lola slaps her hand on her knee and said "Oh my god, unreal." Anthea continues "Next you threw Lola's clothes and personel belongings out of the window and rearranged the furniture after students put them in a nicer homely way." Danny answers "The belongings are only personel things of one person and I did the split's on them and nearly broke my ankle and the furniture was arranged by the same person and I went head over tip and could have broken my neck, you can't move furniture around when there are blind persons here and neither can you leave stuff in here for the blind to fall over. what if we all decided to leave our shoes and personel things in here it's a stupid thing to do and shows the mentality of that person." Anthea "Yes I agree with you on that point also sorry Lola." Lola mouths off that it was not fair and put her head in her hands and Patsy looked daggers at Anthea. Anthea continues "Right this is one thing that has annoyed me, yesterday you came in here and abused and threw out several students out who had been invited here for dinner and threatened one of them that you would throw their suitcase out of the window and kick him down the stairs, what have you got to say about that? I for one do not condone violence in this college." Danny speaks "Yes well, I went in there in a rage after just falling over the settee, but the real reason is that Lola and Patsy have been having these dinner parties every night and never asked anyone in this place if it is ok and I found out that some of our students have not eaten until 9pm at night because of this, also some have diabetes and one of them has been having diabetic fit's, namely Niel as the nurse will bear me out. Also some of our foreign students have to wait for half of the college to come over here to eat before them and they live here and after the meal they stay and have wine till god knows what time." Lola chirps in "I never stop anyone having food here." Danny "Niel has told me he will not eat in front of strangers and you take the piss as soon as he comes into the room that's why he is not in the room now and Winnie Woo has been treated by you and Patsy very badly since she will not join in your vindictiveness." Winnie comes to Danny's rescue "Yes he is right, I would not let Patsy kiss me so they have been very horrible to me." Anthea "Will anyone back this up besides Danny and Winnie Woo?" There was total silence. Danny said "Oh for god's sake say what you all think. For instance, Jeff you nearly went home when Lola first arrived, you said and Zarrine will back me up, she is a nightmare there will be trouble here now she is here all the fun stops here, she is the bitch from hell and you remember her from Torquay, she was hell there. Rhoda you said the same she was a horrible bitch in Torquay and most of you stay in your rooms since she arrived. She only wants her friends here and the rest of you are intimidated by her." Lola says "I don't believe you said that about me Jeff or you Rhoda, did you really say that?" Danny continues "Tell the truth you two, I have witnesses." Jeff with his head bowed "Well I did say that because you were loads of trouble there and you were warned there and I am sorry but what Danny has said is the truth." Rhoda "I only said you were trouble in Torquay, but you were." Lola had a face that said it all and said "This is not fair they are just saying that ." Danny "What all of us?" Anthea and most of them were silent thinking then Anthea says "I am afraid I have to say as from now on you will refrain from dinner parties in here it is not a place for that type of thing anyway and we have to think of other students here and it is obvious none of them want it here." Lola said "You must be joking I live here to and if I want friends here it is up to me." Anthea "That's where you are wrong it is a place you all have to share if you want anyone of your friends that is up to you but if the other students do not want them in here you do not fetch them in that is the rules and you should not be bringing drink onto the premises neither." Lola started wailing and stamped on the floor takes her cup in the kitchen and started crying out loud and stormed off to her room.

118

Danny said "What's the Matter? didn't get your own way, told you, you can't walk over people." Anthea "We have not finished yet, you are still in trouble Danny and this meeting isn't over yet. What about the trouble you are giving to Patsy? I have a complaint from her you are homophobic and I am aware about you making remarks about her friend who comes to stay, this is the year two thousand and two you must put up with things like that these days." Patsy "Yes if I want my friend here on a weekend it's up to me nothing to do with you and what I do in my room is up to me, I think you should leave this hall for all our sakes." Zarrine "Please don't say that we have never had this trouble until recently." Anthea "Well what have you to say on the Matter?" Danny sighed and said "You keep on addressing the fact it is politically correct, I have never taken much in what the government say and I can make my own mind up as regards if it is right or wrong, some people believe in god some don't and neither will change their mind because the other one said they have to. I am entitled to my opinion and that is the prerogative of all humans. She calls me straight, I don't agree with that and would like to be known as normal and that is what people like me are if they have sex with a woman it is natural and the other is not at all, it teaches it in the bible when god destroyed Sodom and Gomorrah because it was being abused by lesbians and homosexuals and I didn't have nothing to do with that did I? I am not the only one who finds it disgusting, I think if you ask the majority are of the same belief and they don't keep on about homosexuality like the gays of this world, I will respect them if they show the same courtesy as I would, I am married but do not keep on about it every minute of the day what I do to my wife in explicit fashion , even the gay community would be ashamed of Patsy ." Patsy speaks up "See what I mean, he is homophobic and he should be thrown out." Danny said "Shut up you have had your say wait until I have finished, Jeff if I am wrong in what I am going to say now please correct me. She came in out of her room a few weeks ago just before I complained to you Anthea and she was pretty pissed and had just had a rampant session of sex with her friend and came in the kitchen and said to me I am having a cup of water I have a pubic hair stuck in my throat and then came back in the lounge and said to myself and Jeff have I got shit on my nose (everyone said agh that's disgusting) then proceeded to ask if I wanted to smell her fingers? Isn't that shoving it in my face or what?" Anthea said "I must agree there is no need for that Patsy it is disgusting and you must show a bit more respect I want you to apologise ." Patsy smiling said "Ok fair enough I shouldn't have said that but I had a drink down the pub in town and not in this college ha, sorry." Anthea I hope that is to your satisfaction? she is only a teenager after all." Danny snaps "And that makes it right? do you let your children get away with things like that? because I certainly don't." Patsy still smiling and Anthea says "Right that's it I think we have covered it all I will see you in my office tomorrow Patsy and give you a formal warning about your behaviour, so I will call this meeting to an end if no one has any more to say?" Danny said "I have not finished yet... so well let's look at the situation we have a 17 year old girl put into this hall because of all the trouble she has caused in other halls with students of her own age, so we are babysitting her because she is claiming to be a lesbian she thinks." Patsy "See what I mean." Danny "Wait a minute you have had your say now it's my turn, I am not homophobic I will however not put up with it pushed in my face and Anthea as we had this meeting a few weeks ago and you have done nothing about it surprise, surprise. On weekends she has a 22 year old woman staying in her room with her, they spend all weekend in bed next to this room and they don't hide the fact they are having lesbian sex, the noise is awful it makes me sick, I have daughters in their teens I hope they do not get off on having sex so that anyone living around them have to endure the noise." Anthea "Well I can't do anything about that, I would just hope Patsy will in future keep the noise down." Patsy with a big smile on her face as if to say i got you beat. "I will try to control it a bit." Anthea with a smile saying "We are all agreed then? So that's it." Danny had other ideas and said "Not quite, I was wondering what the papers and the governors would have to say on the Matter?" Anthea "What do you mean? there is not much they can say on the Matter." Danny "Are you sure? because the way I look at it the college is breaking the law and I want her moved out as I do not want to share the hall with her." Patsy still smiling "You have lost it mate, grow up and get on with your life there is nothing you can do to me." Danny "You keep on saying that to me and I warned you not to be so cocky, well she is under the age of consent." Anthea looking shocked "The age of consent is sixteen." Danny in certain voice "Yes for a heterosexual person but not for any gay person, it is eighteen and she is seventeen and the other person is a twenty two year old mature woman. Now I wonder what the principle and the governors and the papers would think If they found out that this college are letting a seventeen year old have homosexual activity with a twenty two year old mature woman who is allowed into her room every weekend to have sex with this minor and this mature woman comes down from Manchester just for the privilege." There was a deadly silence for a minute and Patsy's face dropped and Anthea was looking very nervous. Anthea with sheer panicky look on her face "Well i never thought of it that way, i suppose you have a point I, am sorry Patsy i must insist you stop having anyone staying in your room while you are a student here." Patsy with agitated look on her face "You can't do that, i won't allow you." Anthea "I am sorry that Is the law and we have to abide by it and I think I had better split you and Lola up so I shall be transferring you to an outside house this weekend for everyone's sake." Patsy started crying and wailing. Danny looking straight at Patsy "I warned you both not to mess with me I will not put up with your nonsense, even if this lot will, it was nice meeting you bye, bye." Patsy stormed off to her room and Anthea went after her. Jeff said "Well that's that, I knew it would not last long before there was trouble." Danny "And if you all had the guts to stand up to them this might never have happened." Jeff "Well we were all waiting for you to sort it out, we knew you would." Danny "Your so full of it mate." Next in walks Anthea and said "It was like a court of law, I hope things are sorted out now." Danny "Yes I think it was a result, I hope you stick to your word about a certain person leaving this weekend?" "Yes you can be assured, I could not leave her here now this has all happened and this is for your ears to, I don't think you are squeaky clean in all this I know you but can't figure you out yet. Let's hope things get better and no trying to get back at Lola, please let's have peace as I expected you to be nailed to the door, maybe next time." Danny replies "It's a messy job but somebody's got to do it, I am a good boy, I just do not like verbal bullies or otherwise." Jeff "What happened to Niel? where was he? why was he not in the meeting?" Danny "He could not put up with it all he is going to be ok now, I think he thought I would embarrass him. Why don't you go and tell him what has happened." Jeff "I am on my way as we speak." Danny "Well Rhoda I am sorry I had to bring you and Jeff into it all but if people don't speak up it will never change to what they really want." Rhoda "I just feel sorry for Lola and Patsy, you really did not hold back." Danny says "I expect they are already planning their next move, I have not heard the end of it yet." Next in walks Jeff and Niel, Niel with huge smile on his face . Niel "Good god man, what have you done? I just heard from Jeff you sorted her out." Danny now smiling "Yes with a little help from that dopey cockney, I sorted the worst of the problem with his help." Niel "How did he do that?" Danny "Well he was the one who reminded me about the fact that consent for lesbian or gays is eighteen

120

and that she is seventeen, I and no one else ever twigged." Jeff looking too smart for his boots "Yes and why didn't you say this in the meeting?" Danny still smiling says "Because they already hated me why should I put you in the same position? and so anyone for something to eat." Niel with huge smile on his face that has never been seen for a few weeks said "Danny tell me do you like duck in orange sauce?" Danny "Yes why?" Niel "I have a pack of two and you can have one because you are a true friend." Danny "Well thank you Niel that is very nice of you." Niel smiles even more and says "That's no problem, you start cooking them I will go and wash and dress for dinner." Danny "I might have known there was a catch in it, ok then it's worth it to see that smile on your face, but I am not washing bloody dishes again, I am fed up with washing dishes."

CHAPTER 7
A TRIP TO THE LAND OF SONG

A Few months later in the summer and in the kitchen Niel is all alone having breakfast when in comes Jeff and says" Good morning." with his head resting in hand as if he had a headache Jeff replies "Hows you then?" Niel "Very good but you sound as if you had a good few last night." Jeff "Yes I was out with that dodgy Welshman and we put a few away, then we got back and had a couple of cans, so I am taking my pillow to lectures with me." Niel "Where is Danny?" Jeff still head in hand "He has not got any lectures until after dinner so he can sleep in; i swear I will never drink with that dodgy Welshman again." Niel laughing at Jeff says "You always say that, but you are with him in the bar every night, it's like you are both attached at the hip." "I know, I will never learn." In walks Zarrine clutching bread and milk. She says "Good morning you two?" she sees Jeff and takes a step back "Oh my god, you and that Danny have been drinking again, you look awful." Jeff "Thanks." Niel "Good morning Zarrine." Zarrine with eyebrows raised and pointing at the empty cans "What are these empty cans here Jeff?" Jeff shrugging his shoulders "Nothing to do with me, it's that dodgy Welshman." Zarrine hands on hips as if she is fed up with this every morning says "Jeff you always blame Danny and he always blames you all the time, but i counted 9 cans in your waste bin in your room yesterday morning." Jeff "Yes he came to my room the night before last and as you know I put my initials on the bottom of my cans I drink and none of them had my initials on them, did they?" "I don't know what I am going to do with you pair and where is Danny? this morning? hasn't he got lectures?" Jeff says in urgency "Yes he has but he is probably still drunk and can't get up." Zarrine in panic says "Well we shall see about that, I will give him a knock and get him up." She toddles off to call Danny, Niel says "Jeff, you have done him up like a kipper again, Danny is not going to be very happy when Zarrine calls him and he has no lectures." Jeff smiling says "Hasn't he? well I must have forgotten." The both men roar with laughter then in walks Zarrine in her strict mode and says "Jeff, you told me he had lectures and I knocked his door he was expecting me and he said he had no lectures until after lunch and to tell Jeffrey he will see him later if he can keep up with me." Jeff looking innocent "Oh did he? I thought he said he did, oh well never mind." Zarrine chases him into the lounge and pretends to slap him across the back. Next in walks Winnie Woo the Chinese Lady, Zarrine said to her "Good morning Winnie Woo, how are you?" Winnie looking all hot and bothered "I am fine thanking you, but i must rush to my lectures. That silly Jeff and that velshman made lots of noise last night, silly people." She then storms off to her lectures. Niel "She's as happy as a death-watch beetle."

Its elevenses and all were sitting down having coffee in the student bar. Danny with nasty look on his face "Well Jeff you had me again this morning but never mind every dog has his day. Niel i thought you was my mate?" Niel "I am, but you know what these English men are like and you just can't educate pork, he thinks that diabetes is a Welsh flyweight boxer." Jeff "What do you call two sheep tied to a fence in Wales?" Rhoda "I don't know." Jeff "A leisure centre." Rhoda looking puzzled "I don't get that." Danny "Well Niel I am taking Jeff down to Wales this weekend to show him our beautiful land and women and let him spoil himself and bring him back a man." Niel "Well keep him away from my valley they have only just cleaned up the foot and mouth and we don't want any more problems." Jeff "If I catch anything I'll blame you dodgy Welshmen." Niel "What time are you going? because I can't go until later this afternoon as I have lectures?" Danny "We are catching the midday train as I have to get down there as soon as, but we will see you on the early train Sunday coming back." Niel "Yes I will be on it" In walks Gupta and Lola,, Lola giving Danny and Jeff a talking to "What the hell was all that noise last night? laughing and loud talking it kept me awake and I have to fly to Glasgow today from Birmingham and I am shattered with you pair keeping me awake." Danny "Well you should try some laughter sometime, it's not hard but there again the only thing that makes you smile has to be hard." Lola storms off and mumbles to herself. Danny "Hello Gupta how are they hanging?" Gupta blushing and in his Pakistan accent "Good, good, very well thank you, i am going to Birmingham to visit my brother. He works at Birmingham airport and he let's me drive the buses on the tarmac, it is fun." Jeff "You could take Lola with you she could kick start the Jumbo's for your brother." Gupta "That's a very good idea but she will never stop talking." Niel "You must take Jeff out for a real pint while he is in Wales, not this crap they drink up here." Jeff "I can handle any drink you can throw at me in your land, we taught you heathens all about the world anyway." Niel "Oh yeh,, I bet you won't be shooting your mouth off down there, go and see our national stadium while your there and ponder and one day we will be back on top in the rugby world to and wait until you see some of those valley girls, you will not know which way to turn." Danny "As long as he doesn't turn the other way that will be ok." Jeff "So they got them down there to have they?" Niel "God they are everywhere now and some of the women down there are so big and lumpy they could make a real man of you and to look at you, you need a good woman from Wales." Jeff "Bring them on I will get the weight off them and they will be wondering if they should move to Swindon to be with real men, I just hope they don't start talking Welsh to me as all that spitting can put me off, do you think I got a chance with your wild and woolly women then?" Danny "Well Niel was just 7 stone when he met his missus and look at him now, with all that loving from her and all the cider and beer he has drunk over the years it's no wonder he is so cuddly." Jeff " I don't want to end up looking like him, I am a slim Adonis and want to stay like that." Niel "You cheeky git, I spent a lot of money to get to look like this you know and they would rather a hunk like me than a skinny little runt like you, what do you think Dan?" "Yes I think your right he will be taking his life into his own hands with all those valley women this weekend but it's a messy job but somebody's got to do it." Niel "As I say keep him from my valley, I could not forgive myself if I saw something like that running around the streets in the near future." Danny "Well it's time to go, Jeff I will meet you at the train station as I have a mobility lesson in town, you all be careful out there and don't let anyone spoil the day for you." Jeff "You have already spoilt mine."

In town centre for mobility lessons with Ann standing outside a shop and Ann explaining about mobility in a busy town. Ann "Tell me, were you out last night?" Danny "Yes, why?" "Oh dear some more fun then, I have been dreading this if you have had a drink the night before." "It can't be that hard, I am feeling good about this, don't worry it's a messy job but somebody's got to do it." Ann with a worried look "Ok we must consider other pedestrians in a busy town and take care at all times and listen for different clues you may be able to use as we get around, we will be using the shops as the shore line and i will explain as we go along. I need to go to the bank at the other end of town, is that allright with you?" Danny replies "No problem, I will do as I am told, let's go." Off they went and it looked as if Danny was to confident and starts making mistakes Immediately, he had a man walk into him and the man bounced off Danny and almost sat down on the pavement, Danny said to him "Do you want to borrow my white cane? watch where you are going, I am the one who is blind." The man says " Sorry mate your right, I must get my eyes checked." Danny starts again and made loads of mistakes then he walks along knocking people on the ankle with his cane and they were dancing out of his way Danny hitting everyone "Oh sorry, sorry i am sorry, oops sorry, bloody hell i am knocking everyone." Ann snarls at Danny "Take your time and not so hard with the cane, it's not a game of golf." A woman jumped over his cane, 2 dogs coming toward him barked turned around and dragged their owner the other way, then he knocked an old man right on the ball of his ankle and the old man's face all crumpled up "Oh shit that hurt." Danny "Sorry mate are you allright? I'm new at this you know." Ann grabs the old man's arm "Are you allright? i am so sorry." She turns to Danny and with serious face "Take your time you nearly broke that man's ankle then, swing the cane slowly and not so aggressive and wider so as to cover the width of your body. That's better, now take your time, you are coming to a bench and you will have to go around it, feel it with your cane." There was a Lady sitting on the bench with her handbag over her knee and Danny's cane went through the strap of the bag and took the bag off her knee and it was off with Danny wrapped around his cane snaking down the road with him, the woman screamed out at Danny as she thought he was a bag snatcher. "Stop thief, that's my handbag, somebody stop him, thief, thief." Ann sees this and with hand over her mouth runs up to Danny, takes her hand away and screams at Danny "Stop, Danny stop." She grabs the bag from around his cane and hands it back to the woman. "I am so sorry it was not on purpose he is new and i am the poor sod who has to teach him." The woman her face brightens up "Oh that's ok it just made me jump." Danny "What do you mean poor sod?" "Well I am, every time you have had a pint the night before things go wrong for us, although her face was a picture ha, ha, you are a big man and like a tank, you must learn to slow down as there is no hurry to learn." Danny "I understand I will slow down a bit, it makes you tense the first time with so many people around, are you allright?" Ann smiling "Yes she has gone and that old man is sitting on that bench now rubbing his ankle, it looks as if the s.a.s has just gone through here, never mind we will grab a take away cup of tea off this stall here and i will go in the bank and i will leave you outside against the wall and you can drink your tea there." Danny says "That sounds good to me, I fancy a cup of tea now." They get a cup of tea and Danny is standing outside the bank leaning against the building, with plastic cup of tea in one hand and leaning on his white cane with his left hand looking as if he was a beggar from many years ago, just then two lads came past and dropped some coins into his cup with a plop, plop sound as it hit his tea and the boys laughed out loud , the 2 boys said "Ha, ha, ha, ha." Danny with a serious look on his face but realising what happened, his face turns to a huge smile and mutters to himself (The little buggers, well i never (voice gets louder and still smiling) "Come here you little buggers, that was my tea in don't believe what you just done." One of the boys said "We thought you wanted some money mister and so we put some in your cup." Danny now smiling from ear to ear says "You little sods, that was so funny so I can go out for a drink tonight now." The other boy said "Can we have our money back now? we were only kidding." Danny "Oh I don't know about that, well so long as you were only kidding I suppose so." Danny gets the money out and gives it back to them. Danny continues "What twenty p is that all you give me? god your tight." Danny gives them the money and said "There you go you little sods, off you go and be good." The boys said "Thanks mister, bye." Danny "Bye." Next Ann comes out of the bank and says "Right, done, everything ok?" Danny replies "Yes I just had a bit of fun with two lads, they chucked some money in my tea for a bit of fun." Ann looking concerned "Are you allright? the little horrors, where are they now? I will speak to them." "No need they were only two lads having a little fun with me, no harm intended we had a good laugh over it, it's nice to have young lads with a good harmless sense of humour. Did you get everything you wanted?"

Ann replies "Yes thanks, so what is the time of your train?" "Yes I was going to say it's at twelve, we had better be off." "Right I will get the car, you wait here and I will pick you up." Ann goes off to get the car.

Off to Wales on the train. Danny and Jeff sitting on the train each side of a table seat with canes folded up on the table in front of them and they were sitting as if to be looking out of the window. A young boy say's to them "Are you blind?" Jeff replies in a joyful manner "No sonny, we just can't see, but we are just amazed how good this train driver is, his driving has kept this train on the tracks perfectly, it has not come off once." a young boy said "Yeh he is good." His young brother speaks to Jeff with a heavy Welsh accent "I have been on holidays to Spain, do you want to see my four doors?" Jeff "Your floors?" The young lad "Yes my four doors from holidays." Jeff "What are your four doo Danny butts in "He wants to know if you want to see his photos from his holidays, you amus." Jeff "Oh I see." Jeff proceeds to look at his photos and says to Danny in lower voice so as it is just Danny who can hear him. "I think he is feeling sick." Danny "Why you say that?" Jeff "Because he keeps going buthere, buthere." Danny smiles and says is not being sick when you asked him where his parents are he is saying by thereby Jeff looking confused "Oh i see, we seem to be going through a lot of tunnels since into Wales, it's all mole hills." Danny "Do you know why we have so many moun Wales?" Jeff with a lot of thought says "No why?" Danny now smiling broadly say e we won so much land off the English in previous wars we had to pile it up and mountains out of it." Jeff now laughing "I might have known there would be some sill so how far is it now to your place." "It's not far now about an hour and when we please try and talk sensibly as the women down here are not all that fond of Eng "Oh they will love me as my mum is Welsh, she is from a place called Tradegar lly where are they." "Penally let me think, Penally, oh I know it is near Tenby." enby." Danny smiles and says "A mile up the road from nine b...... no it is in P re, it is a very pretty area, and Tredegar is in the heads of the valleys.. My fam near Penally a place called Narberth and I will retire down there one day, it is ve so you have a fair bit of Welsh in you, so your not that ignorant after all." Jef s "I will never admit that I have any Welsh in me, if you say it to anyone i Danny says "Looking at you noone would believe you are Welsh anyway should not be ashamed of your roots, I'm not, I have Dutch in me as my an m Holland so I suppose that makes me half Dutch and half Welsh and you the other half ignorant, I don't think anyone today can say they are pure Scottish, Irish, Pakistani or anything for that Matter." Jeff "No I suppose t Winnie Woo, maybe she is Chinese." Danny "Well your wrong there to, s of things about herself It is fascinating, she is half Chinese and half Russian, an and her dad is Chinese and they are both English professors and once w hina because of the cultural revolution and it's something like that, that m lucky we are." "Good grief ,I didn't know that, so she has had it ruff to." Yes she told me how she lost her sight, it was heart breaking, she played was narrated by her father and was very touching, it made the hairs stan went something like this, Winnie was born to us and at the age of just 2 spital found she had eye cancer but she was such a pretty and excitabl ays dancing and they wondered what would become of her. She had an of nearly 3 and had her eyes taken out to stop the cancer spreading, b dering what she was going to be like when she had come around, but d up on her bed

125

and her mun was crying and Winnie said don't cry mummy, look, I can still dance and started dancing on her bed." Jeff looking very sad "Oh my god how sad, i never knew, that's awful it just goes to show we don't see what other people have had to put up with, Winnie wo must be very special to her parents, after all they have had to go through." Danny said that's not all, she told me she lives on her own in China as her mother and father have ne to Australia to live to escape the past troubles in China but could not take her with th because the Australian government will not grant her Australian citizenship because of blindness and because she cannot make a contribution or support herself." "That's bloawful, how horrible can you get? I feel sorry for her." "I don't think she is doing so b she has her cwn flat near her college and just gets on with life and fears no one or not and she says one day it will happen and she will end up down in Australia with her p , I think that would be nice." Jeff says "Oh I don't know she has a thing for you, I think becoming very fond of you, anyone could tell as she does not bother with any other "Well I can understand that, I don't talk a load of crap to any women." Jeff smirking " t are you trying to say?" Danny also smiling "If the cap fit's..... Well we are the next s ve better get ready."

In Danny's nd there was Danny, Angie and Jeff having a cup of tea, Angie says "Well what do y of Wales?" Jeff "It's nice, I find it pretty as well but it is a bit quiet isn't it?" Angie are a village on top of a mountain and when the kids are in school it is dead arou so what are you two doing this weekend?" Danny "Well I thought I would take r the Odd-ellows arms for a pint and take the dog with me for his walk and hope otices he is English, Jeff I mean." Jeff "Oh do we have to go to the pub again? I ng all the time." Angie "Yeh, if you are a good friend of Danny's you know the very pub in Hereford, as you will only find most Welshmen in a pub if they are home and I know you would not come down to Wales just for sightseei es I know what you mean, I suppose I will have to go with him to look after him Welsh beer out he claims it is much stronger than it is up in god's country, an." Danny "Yes it is real beer here not that gnats piss from up there, you had I with care as it will knock you out." Angie "And I am warning you two if any on o it in the garden and not in here or you will be going back with a broken s I got that loud and clear, I will make sure he does not have too many to drink u need the toilet before we go?" Jeff "Yes please where is it? up the garden? eeky bugger, you have a strange idea of how we live here in Wales" Jeff "So elp it, me and him are like this all the Time" Angie "Well you are insulting be careful because I have 3 huge brothers and they eat Englishmen for breah only kidding, I am looking forward to this." Danny "Don't worry I will sort any trouble with you, I will get you drunk and dress you up as a sheep a side the farmers arms tied to the fence ." Jeff "Yes I have heard some st it sheep and Welshmen in wellies."

Danny g out to the pub in the afternoon on a nice sunny summers day but Dan his pet dog Murphy with him. The dog is a small Staffordshire bull ter bout 14 inches off the ground and Danny loves Murphy as he taught Murphy goes crazy with love for Danny as soon as he sees him, a real b Danny has the dog lead in one hand while guiding himself with his Whi hand. Jeff and Danny approach the pub and as they enter there are a fe he bar and the landlord behind the bar cleaning glasses with a tea to ter the room , the landlord said to Danny and Jeff "Sorry mate

126

you can't come in here with that dog, no dogs allowed in here." Danny with surprised look on his face says "It's my guide dog." The landlord replies "Yeh, Yeh." Danny "Well it is, honestly it is, I'm not Joking." Landlord smiling says "Oh yeah, well most guide dogs i have ever seen are either Labradors or German shepherds." Danny looks down at the dog pathetically and say's "Oh shit what have they given me?" With that everyone at the bar started roaring with laughter and one person swigging a pint spat all his beer all over the bar. Landlord finishes laughing and says "Brilliant, brilliant, well because of your cheek you can sit in the corner by the door with your guide dog. What are you drinking?" Danny chuckling Two pints of lager please, but nothing for the dog never mind what he says he is under age." Danny turns to Jeff "Well Jeff I have been invited to a friend's party tonight his daughter is getting engaged and I asked him if I could bring a friend and he said yes. Now I must find someone to ask, I'm only joking, so put on your best Welsh accent." "Well what a nice pub they are very friendly here." Danny "Yes and they are new here as I knew the people who had it before and they were nice to but the landlord went off with the barmaid and he had a beautiful wife, I don't understand it." Jeff says "Perhaps he wasn't getting it from his wife and fancied a change." "Yes I don't know what is happening today, you can just cast off your partner as if you are changing a jumper or something." Jeff says "I thought you said Angie was going to divorce you?" "Yes she is going too; believe me I know the signs are there." "Do you really think so? I felt she really cared for you earlier when we were talking, you both seem happy." Danny looking serious says "It's hard to explain, I changed when I became blind and that made everything change in our lives and it was no fault of ours, I can't expect her to stay with me because we had a different life before I lost my eyes and a hell of a lot different to now, she didn't marry this person she married the person I was then and that made her happy, now it is different and I lost my patience with life when this happened and she seen a side of me that we both never knew existed, so everything has changed and is nothing like it was before, so I can't blame her for what she is about to do with our marriage. This has damaged her just as much as it has me and I have nothing to forgive her for, it is life and that is that, I must get on with my life because there are many more people worse off than me, many die before they are 5 years old in Africa etc. I have very little to complain about compared to them." Jeff looking as if he was about to cry said "Yes I can see what you mean now if you put it like that, I suppose I expected too much from evil but I never thought of it like that, well put together mate." Danny "The world changes mate and we have to change with it, so what do you think of this beer here?" "I see what you mean it is a cracker of a pint, I had better watch how many I drink or I will end up making sounds like a sheep." Danny shook his head and said "Yes this is affecting me to, I am not used to this good beer now after drinking that dishwater up there, I will buy you a nice drink tonight up this club, it is a pure Welsh pint of beer it's called S.A. short for skull attack it is a cracking pint and you won't need many of them and it puts lead in your pencil." "I have plenty of lead in my pencil matey, I don't need it." Danny "Right let's have another for the road." Jeff replies with huge smile "I shall go and get one." Jeff gets up an off to the bar but the beer has made him a bit wobbly and makes him feel brave and on the way to the bar a man got up and bumped into Jeff buy accident and Jeff took offence at it and says to the man "Hey watch what you are doing, you nearly hit the glasses out of my hand then." The man said "Dim problem mate." Jeff not happy said "I beg your pardon?" Man "Dim problem." Jeff "Well that's charming there is no need for that, i can't help it being partially sighted, it is not something I chose and to say that to me I think is ignorant." The man replied "I don't know what you are talking about, I am not ignorant and I think you should apologise." Jeff feeling brave said "I will not, I am not in the wrong here." The two men just set off in a hot argument and Danny could hear this and rushed down to see what was happening with Jeff, Danny said "Hey, hey, what the hell is the Matter here I can hear you from the other end of the pub." Jeff "He insulted me by making comments about my bad eyesight." The man said "You lying little shit, I never, that's all I said was dim problem, I would never say anything like that." Jeff "There see I told you, he said I had a dim problem, I know my eyes are dim and I struggle getting around he does not have to remind me." Danny with a smile said "No you don't know what he means." The man said "He is a nutter and I ought to smack him in the gob." Jeff "Ok I will put these glasses down and sort you out." The two men squared up to each other and Danny had to stand in between them. Danny said "Right shut up the pair of you, shut up." The two men went silent and Danny started to laugh. Jeff "I don't understand you why are you laughing?" Danny "This gentleman said to you dim problem am I right?" Jeff "Yes he bloody well did." Danny "Well you are in Wales and here dim means the word no so he was saying no problem." Jeff just stood there for a minute and realised what had happened and looked stupid after he realised I.T Jeff with silly I am look "Oh, oh, I owe you an apology mate, I am so sorry I have made a right idiot of myself." The man said "Dim problem man, dim problem." With a little smile on his face Jeff also had a little smile said "i am sorry would you like a pint mate?" Man "Dim problem, I will have a pint of lager please." Everything settled down and Danny sat down and Jeff re-joined him Jeff "Well I feel a bit of an idiot now, never mind, he was lucky mind, I could have done him some damage if he had started on me." Danny "Yes I could see that, it's a good thing for him I came along when I did, I could see you were getting the better of the situation." Jeff smirking at the situation says "Yes a couple of seconds and I would have blown and nothing would have stopped me except a pint, dim problem." They both laughed and Danny said "Well things have cooled down up the college at last." Jeff "You mean hinge and bracket, I don't think it will last, especially Lola she will not let it drop, I think Patsy mind will not bother as you sorted her out and she is keeping a low profile, as she is afraid of getting thrown out, so we won't see much of her anymore and Niel is so much more settled now they have been sorted out. I am surprised he didn't take the afternoon off and come home with us." Danny "Yes I was surprised he stayed but I know he loves his braile with Ginny and Christine, if you notice he has not got any male tutors now as he don't like being taught by them. All his lecturers are female because he likes a good gossip with them and if he is happy then we can all be happy when he is around." "Yes that's true and Tim is a nice guy too." Danny with a smile says "Yes he is a nice lad and loves it with us and all the tom foolery when I leave the college we will all have to get together for some fun." Jeff "If we are still alive with all this drink we have up there." "Yes it's like poison not like here." Jeff "Yes it's strong here I didn't believe you but I can feel it hitting in the back of my brain." Danny laughing says "Well there is nothing to stop it in the front of your brain, but it is nice mate isn't it? Phew." "God you can say that again." Danny "I think if you are feeling like that we will finish this and go, I don't want you making an idiot of me tonight." Jeff says in a urgent voice "Oh no I didn't mean that, we could have another if you like." Danny "Ok I am off to the bar then." Jeff talks to the dog while Danny went to the bar and a nice girl comes and collects some glasses and says to Jeff "He is a lovely dog isn't he? Is he yours?" Jeff replies "No he is belonging to my mate; he has gone up to the bar for some drinks." She replies "So you are from up England then?" Jeff "Yes I am." She said "Never mind ay." Jeff smiling "What do you mean by that? there's nothing wrong with us English at all." Smiling she says "No I am only kidding I like a bit of banter sometimes so where are you from?" Jeff "Swindon." "Oh dear huh, who are you staying with here." Jeff "Danny up by the bar, do you know him?" She said surprised "Danny, yes I went to school with him many years ago, he is a bit of a nutter isn't he? a good laugh, it was awful when he went blind mind wasn't it?" Jeff in silent voice "I have not known him for long we met in the college for the blind." "I remember him and his brother Lyndon they were inseparable, they went everywhere together and had some great times, a good laugh but look out when they were pissed, they would fight often and the next day covered in bruises and black eyes they would be drinking together again as if nothing had happened and they have a brother named Dennis he lives down west Wales now, he is lovely, he is mentally retarded and all the villagers love him." Jeff in a sad mood said to her "Danny said he has passed away last year, he had a massive heart attack and died Immediately." The woman looked visibly shocked and with her hand over her mouth said "Oh my god, I am shocked now, the poor man and he was not very old, oh dear, Danny has had so much heartache he must be devastated, I won't speak to him now I am in shock, tell him Jan said hello." Jeff "I will." A few minutes later Danny returned to sit by Jeff. Jeff said "I was just talking to a lady named Jan, she was shocked when I told her about your brother Dennis and she sends her condolences and said she will see you later." "Oh right, I know who you mean, yes he was dearly loved here and we all loved him deeply, I still have trouble getting my head around it, I miss him very much, especially with the fact he was so settled down in Neyland and his life was so Improved and he was talking about getting married to Janet his long-time girlfriend, such a bloody shame he never had much luck, I really miss him, let's change the subject I get emotional about it when I am drinking, what else did she say?" Jeff "Oh she was referring to your other brother Lyndon and said about you 2 fighting yet always being together, why not anymore?" Danny "Well he is married to a right cow now and his mother-in-law is the mother-in-law from hell, she is always in his house and she is the type of woman if you have had an illness, she has had it but worse, a real hypochondriac a woman who is a total waste of time and his wife is ok as long as she is spending lots of money and I am afraid my brother does not know when to leave the drink alone and he has a daughter who is only very young and I don't see him anymore I love him he is my little brother and I miss him, but he won't listen to me about his drinking and it worries me, you think I am bad you want to see him drinking but he drinks because things don't seem so bad if you are pissed every night and if I was married into that family I think I would be the same, but you never know we might see him tonight, I hope so." Jeff says "I know what you mean but you can't live their lives for them can you?" "No your right, I just hope things Improve for him, he has gone to pieces lately, if I was religious I would be doing a lot of praying for him." Jeff "What no religion at all?" Danny "Absolutely none mate, my father was a Jehovah's witness and he made me and my brothers and my mother's life a living hell and most of this world are fighting why? Over religion and nothing and let's be fair the bible is just a good story book and nothing else but I am not going to debate this as I will not argue about religion, so change the subject." Jeff looking stunned said "Fancy another beer." Danny laughing " Are you sure I am ok, but I am used to it you are not." Jeff slurring says "I know what you are saying but one more won't kill us and then off." "Ok matey on your head be it." Later the lads leave the pub and head for home to get ready for the night.

At the party that evening they get into the foyer of the club the party was at and Danny slips off to find which room the party is in, he leaves Jeff standing by a coat and umbrella stand. He is swaying after drinking all day and he is looking pleased with himself. Jeff mistakes the stand as being a young girlie and starts speaking to it. Jeff speaking to himself "Hi what's a nice girl like you doing in a place like this? I bet you are wondering what me the Adonis of Swindon is doing in this part of the woods, well I heard that heaven was missing an angel and it looks like I have found her, what would you like on your toast in the morning?" Danny quietly walks back in after listening to the last couple of sentences Jeff had spoken and realising he was talking to a hat stand and said. "Jeff I think you have already scored with the hat stand you have been chatting up for the last 10 minutes, but it might be too fat for you and a lot better looking than your usual birds." Danny starts to laugh while Jeff shakes his head with embarrassment.

They arrive in the party room and are greeted by Danny's friends standing by the bar waiting to get served. The barman said "What can I get for you?" Danny replies "Two pints of brains s a please" The barman starts to pull two pints Danny has some small talk with the barman while Jeff is as usual trying to chat up one of the barmaids. Jeff acting smooth "I am staying at Danny's house where are you staying tonight and how do you like your eggs in the morning? Poached, boiled, scrambled or fertilised." She smiles but does not answer. Jeff "Oh well never mind." Danny says to the barman with a smile "If you knew what i had you would not be serving me those beers.." The barman with a concerned look "OH I'm sorry to hear that, what is it you have got?" Danny quick as a flash "About forty seven pence." The barman and Danny both laugh. Jeff steps back by Danny and starts to talk to him. "God these Welsh girls are all dogs" Danny "My uncle thought he was a dog" Jeff "What happened to him?" Danny replies with huge smile "He went to the doctors and said to the doc, I think I am a dog all the time, the doc says come in and get on the couch, uncle said I can't, I am not allowed on the furniture." Jeff and Danny laughed Jeff "No I am not Joking I have not seen a nice girl here yet and none of them are paying any attention to me considering I am the new man in town." "Well down here in Wales you do not try to chat up our women, they do not respond" "Oh Yeh what should I do then?" "Well you do nothing, it's better if another Welsh person fixes you up, as Welsh women are brought up not to trust strangers even more so if they are English." Jeff looking worried "Yeh, yeh, i feel another wind up coming up here." Danny smirking "Well I am telling you the truth, but if you want to spend the weekend without any nookie well that's up to you." "No, no, I am listening and if it makes sense I might go for it." Danny says "We'll look around and as I know most of the women here and I know you very well, I know what you like and so I can fix you up and vouch for you to them as a friend and that's all I can do." "And no funny business." Danny with surprised look says "How can I these people are my friends and neighbours and they would crucify me as I am too close to them all." "Ok I believe you." "Leave it to me if someone comes in I will sort it out for you, I am not promising." They stand by the bar and all of a sudden Danny is approached by a old friend named Clare Fairy, they shake hands and Danny thinks this is the perfect person, very tall, big boned, beautiful shoulder length hair, nice boobs, a bit too much make up, short leather mini skirt, leather boots, the makeup is the only turn off but Danny thinks Jeff's eyesight is not very good either so he won't notice anything, but he will try to fix them up. He chats to Clare first quietly. "How are things? I have not seen you for some time now." Clare "Well as you know I have had a lot of operations but I am ok now." "Yes I know, are you with anyone now?" "No I have not had a relationship since I was living in Brighton." Danny continues "Well I have a friend with me and he is at a loose end this weekend and I told him about you and as he is very shy he has asked me to have a word and see if you fancy a date tonight?" Clare reluctant look "Well i don't know, I remember you as a bit of a prankster and this might be a bit of a wind up." Danny "No I have changed since I lost my eyesight, I am a different person now and I am trying to help my friend out as he is new at this type of dating, as he likes not to talk about himself or others until he gains his confidence with them. So he likes to get on with the job without making any fuss, just have fun." Clare unsure look "Well ok he is quite sweet, i will go for it, it might be fun." Danny look of victory but shifty with it "He is always looking for fun and you will not be disappointed with him in the bedroom." Claire laughs in a dirty fashion and looks flushed. Danny Approaches Jeff And tells him about how much of a stunner Clare is and Jeff can't believe how lovely she is and starts asking questions. Jeff "Why is such a good looking bird not courting?" Danny "Well she was but it did not work out and she is a bit upset but accepts it is all over, but you must not say I told you it will only upset her." "Why would such a girl want to go out with me?" "God knows, ha, ha, no I am only joking Because I told her you are a nice guy not after anything, does not ask questions as she does not like men who try to pry into her private life and keep asking lots of questions, as she has had a lot of operations and it's behind her almost and she asked me not to say anything, so I haven't. She is a nice quiet girl and if you go in like a bull at a gate you will put her off and besides I do not mind lying for a friend." Jeff looking excited said "Ok matey I will be the gentleman and I owe you one, you are a true mate. Let's go and sit by them." They move over to the table and sit and start chatting. Danny "Clare I would like you to meet my mate Jeff." Jeff "Hi it's a pleasure to meet you, what would you like to drink?" Clare "Oh I will have a pint of lager please." Jeff whispering to Danny "A pint of lager." Danny says to Jeff "Well most women in Wales drink pints and while your up you can get me a pint for fixing you up." Jeff heads for the bar. Danny to Clare "I hope you are going to be gentle with my mate, as he is not very backward in coming forward, if you know what i mean, let him do all the work as he is learning to gain his confidence. All his chat up lines and fast talk is a nervous thing." Clare "Yes I understand, I will let him be the master, is that the best thing?" "Exactly." Jeff returns with the drinks and sets about chatting up Clare. Jeff "I have a word for every day and today's word is legs and I hope you are going to spread the word?" Clare starts to laugh in a dirty manner and Jeff continues chatting up Clare. In the meantime Danny goes off to mix with his mates; he is standing by the end of the bar with three mates. Danny said to his friends "Well how's things lads?" Shane "Not bad but I see you have brought a mate back with you and he's chatting up Clare, somebody should tell him about Clare, she would kill him in the bedroom if she has her wicked way." Danny looking clever "You leave him alone, he can handle anything, so he keeps telling me, so please don't say anything, it's a messy job but somebody's got to do it." All four men start laughing especially when they see Jeff dancing on the dance floor.

End of the night and Danny, Jeff and everyone at the party are quite drunk, and slurring. Back at the table Clare, Jeff and Danny are talking. Jeff slurring through drink "Well you are quite a mate, she is gorgeous i might even go all the way with her if her luck holds out and as i always say what i lost in height, i gained in length. You know what i mean? She's in for a treat and a bit of a shock." Danny say's quietly "She's not the only one." Jeff "Pardon?" "Nothing, I never said anything." Clare speaks "Jeff are you coming back to my place for coffee or what?" Jeff "Or what... see you when I see you dodgy. Maybe when you come home next time if I am lucky, better give me a key in case I get to exhausted and want to come back and crash for a breather." Danny coughs and splutters and in a shaky voice "Um, um, i only got one key and Angie will be in work and i won't be able to get in." Jeff "Well I don't expect I will need it, just think what I will be doing while you are laying in your bed doing nothing." Danny "Don't you worry I will be thinking about you and Clare." Jeff leaves being quite cocky and very show offish in front of the crowd as if to say look at me and my girl. With a stupid lovesick smile on his face.

It's 2 o'clock in the morning Danny is dozing on the sofa and there is a knock on the door and some very loud mumbling in a nasty tone. Danny presses the intercom system. Danny "Hello who is it?" Jeff in a bad mood "I'll give you who is it you git" Danny in a childish voice "Jeff   is that you? your back early, is there something wrong?" jeff now raging says "Is there something wrong? you wait till I get my hands on you?" Danny "Now calm down or I will not let you in until you calm down" "Let me in its brass monkey whether out here, I will be calm until tomorrow then I'll kill you." Danny let's Jeff in and they go down to his garage and open some cans of lager. They sit on some boxes and light a caller gas fire. Danny trying to sound concerned "Now calm down and tell me all about it." Jeff upset "You know what i am talking about." Danny shrugging shoulders "No i don't." "You are a liar, how long have you known Clare?" Danny with a shifty innocent look on his face "Oh well not long." (There was a short pause) "now tell me all about it." Jeff "Your extracting the Michael." "Honestly I have no clue what you are talking about, what happened?" Jeff continues "Well I took her home we had a can of beer each, I started cuddling up to her and was trying to change the channels inside her bra, I was playing with them for ages and fell in love with them. Then we decided to go upstairs and so I fell up every step and we got into bed and I continued massaging her, she was really enjoying it I was good, too good... then I slipped my hand down her knickers and guess what I found?" Danny with laughter "A pint of lager and forty fags." Jeff "No meat and two veg, she is a he or at least half of one." Danny trying to look really shocked "Never, your joking, well i never." Jeff "Dim problem, yes as I am sitting here on this box she is a he and a good-looking one, I am a broken man." Danny "So when are you seeing each other again? funny thing it's Clare's birthday week after next, you could buy her a bra and a month's supply of condoms to be on the safe side." Jeff gets annoyed with Danny and Danny has to calm him down. Jeff "You said she had a lot of operations and that she was living in Brighton for a long time, so you must have known for a long time, I think your lying, you knew all along." Danny looking serious says "Who me? you can't believe that." Next in walks Danny's wife Angie. Angie "Hello again Jeff, had a good night?" "Yes you could say that we went to a party and I met Clare." Angie "I was going to come to that party but I had to work tonight and you met Clare ay, I do not agree with that type of thing, it's not normal in my view." Jeff "What do you mean?" Danny trying to cover up "Oh she just has different friends to me." Angie "To right, I do none of my friends are transvestites or had operations to change their sexuality, although Clare Danny's cousin is quite attractive as a woman, his name used to be Clive but I would not go through all those operations for no one, well I am going to bed I will see you in the morning." All this time Jeff was looking at Danny with a view to kill. Danny "Now calm down, calm down, it was only a bit of fun I know you like a laugh." Jeff "A laugh, that's funny I am going to kill you the first chance I get, the first chance I get to trip you up in front of a car or nudge you into the path of a train, I will." Danny looking sheepish "You know you used to be able to take a joke but not anymore." Jeff "You have stitched me up once too often and I will never forgive you, you git." "Well I can't wait to tell them back at the college on Sunday." Jeff with panic on his face says "You wouldn't dare? I think I will kill you now not tomorrow, you must look left and right when crossing the road, accidents do happen right when crossing the road, hold tight to any banister when going down any stairs and above all watch what you are eating."

On the train were Jeff, Danny and Niel heading back up to the college. Niel "Well did you have a good time here in Wales Jeff?" Jeff "Yes it was great and Angie was a doll and we had a nice cooked breakfast this morning." Danny "Yes it was nice and we had a very interesting weekend didn't we Jeff?" Jeff looked at Danny as if to say if you say anything i will kill you says "It was nice and that is all it was." Danny "Yes, well how was your weekend mate?" Niel "I have been in the doghouse this weekend, everything that could go wrong went wrong. Ceri was glad to see me leaving I bet." Jeff "Ceri is that your wife's name?" Niel "Yes I ruined her jumper and next doors new greenhouse." Danny "How in the hell did you do that?" Niel continues "Well I done the washing while she went to bingo as I wanted all my stuff washed and ready to come back to college and I put everything in the washing machine and she put in the powder and so I just kept an eye on it so to speak. Well it finished just as she came back from bingo and lo and behold there was water on the floor, she went nuts after getting her jumper out as one of the sleeves was jammed in the door, well she unscrewed the sleeve and it was about 15 foot long and the other was it's normal size, well I couldn't keep a straight face and burst out laughing and she went mad, so I was in the doghouse all day Saturday. But it was so funny." Danny and Jeff were having a good laugh and Niel had a big smile on his face. Danny "So what happened to the greenhouse next door then?" Niel "Oh dear I felt sorry about her jumper so I decided on Saturday morning to put up her new line post which she had been waiting for me to do for ages, so I stood it up in place in the hole and my boy was mixing some concrete to put around the post and Abby was laying out in the sun. I went to go in to the toilet and tripped over Abby and knocked the post over and it went straight through next doors greenhouse, oops not a good weekend, it cost me £45, an expensive line post" Jeff "Never mind you get days like that, I remember doing the washing once and everything came out of the washing machine pink in colour, us men are useless when it comes to that type of thing." Danny "I don't touch washing machines as I can knacker a plough when it comes to that type of thing. I wonder how things have been up the college while we have been away, has Winnie killed anyone? she must get fed up being in that college all the time." Niel "Well why don't you take her off for a dirty weekend? she fancies you something awful." Danny "Get out of it she don't." Jeff "Yes I said that over the weekend she does, I noticed that to, she never says anything bad about him." Niel "Get in there my son, she might be waiting for the word off you and might be after a ticket to Britain, you could do worse a cracking little body." Danny "How do you know? you can't see her." Niel "Everyone is saying how pretty she is and what a cracking body she has." Jeff "Well I can see her and Niel is right, she has got a lovely body and she was doing a bit of modelling in China, I have seen the photos." Danny "I must wait and see how the land lies first, I have had enough trouble with women up there to last me a lifetime." Jeff "You can't compare her with those pair hinge and bracket, she is a Lady compared to them, if you ain't going for it I will." Danny "Oh I don't know, I am confused, how old would you think she is?" Jeff "She is 30 I asked her one day." Danny "Well there you go then, much to young." Niel "Don't be silly could you see her going out with anyone her age? she has a very grown up brain, now your talking rubbish." Danny "Well we'll wait and see."

Back at the college and everyone meets as usual on a Sunday afternoon in the lounge at Dowdell and speaks about all what they got up to over the weekend. Winnie "Well I went to town and bought some fruit, yoghurt, and some herbal things." Jeff "Very well what else." Winnie "That's it." Jeff "Right." Lola "I had an argument with my boyfriend and the weekend was awful without him." Rhoda "Why?" Lola "He went off with another woman and I have no one to go out with tonight." Rhoda "We can go out to the art evening class." Lola with worried look "Well i think i should wash my hair, but thanks anyway, i have been upset about all the trouble with my flights today, because i was seven hours delayed because of all the trouble at Birmingham. Birmingham had some sort of scare and diverted some of their planes to Heathrow and we were delayed. I would love to get my hands on whoever caused this to happen it ruined my day." Rhoda "I have made some punch to drink for my birthday party and I put them in milk bottles to fool the wardens." Danny "Well that's a good idea you must tell me where they are in the fridge in case I mix the bottles up and drink the wrong thing, we wouldn't want that would we?" Rhoda "Ok." Danny "I think you better show Jeff as well in case I get mixed up" Saying it with a big grin on his face and Jeff was also grinning. Rhoda said " Well how did the trip to Wales go? did you educate Jeff?" Danny "Yes I taught him a lot, he now knows what the difference is between a male and a female." Jeff stares at Danny in a very nasty way. Gupta smiling says "What do you mean?" Jeff trying to cover up "Oh it's nothing, it's Danny being stupid as per usual." Niel "Oh do you mean he has met your cousin Clare?" Jeff in temper "You told me you would not say a word, how much have you told them?" Danny shrugs his shoulders and said nothing. Then Jeff starts to shout and rave. "I suppose you told them everything? how I ended up in bed with a man and how I was kissing him on the dance floor and cuddling and canoodling in the bed, everything?" Danny "I have not said a word." Jeff "You liar, so how did they know?" Danny "I have not said a word." Jeff "Niel just said, how would he know if you had not opened your mouth?" Niel "Danny caught my mate out with her two years ago and told everyone, because he was lonely, but he sorted him out he always says if you have got a problem tell him and he will tell everybody else and no more problem, but he never said a word this time." Everyone roars with laughter and Jeff put his head in his hands, all of a sudden in runs Rhoda and is very excited and starts to shout Rhoda. "Quick turn up the TV it's the news and about Birmingham airport." Jeff turns up the TV and the news tells all what happened . Newscaster "In Birmingham airport today, there was a suspected terrorist scare when a airport bus seemed to career across 2 landing runways and planes had to take evasive action. It lasted for about 15 minutes, airport security was called into action and the bus came to a halt at the boundary fence. It was Immediately surrounded but the terrorists must have scaled the fence and escaped. One hostage was found in the bus but was not hurt, he was a blind gentleman named Gupta Malix. He was unable to identify any of the terrorists because of his blindness. His brother who was in charge of the airport bus said "One second I was on the bus then I left my brother on the bus and it drove away, I seen nothing. The airport was Immediately closed and all air traffic was diverted to other airports and delays of up to 10 hours were reported." Gupta went very red and looked very guilty. Jeff "You said your brother let's you drive that bus ...was you driving that bus?" Gupta "No, no." Jeff "Were you?" Gupta " No, no " Danny "You were driving it weren't you?" Gupta looking very sheepish said " Yes I was, but my brother I thought was on the bus also and he gives me directions only if I go wrong, he never said nothing, so I assumed I was getting better with my driving until I heard all that skidding of those damn planes and I panicked and drove into the fence, I then jumped off the driving seat and hid in amongst the luggage and they did not think it was me because I am blind and were very concerned, they gave me lots of free gifts etc." Lola shouting "So it was you, it was you." Gupta put his hands above his head and run to his room and locked himself in. Lola sat there with a face like thunder and Jeff and Danny just burst out laughing. Danny said "Well Jeff do you remember Gupta saying that his father was an Elephant trainer, well I think it has rubbed off on Gupta." Jeff "What do you mean?" Danny "Well he sorted out a couple of Jumbos today and redirected them ." Lots of laughter was heard all over the building.

CHAPTER 8
A JOLLY CHRISTMAS

Early morning in the kitchen and in there is Danny, Niel, Gupta and Zarrine talking amongst themselves. Zarrine "And what did you and Jeff get up to last night?" Danny "Well I stayed in most of the night and studied, and at eleven o'clock I went over the bar to carry that dopey English cockney non-understandable when sober git, never mind when he is drunk home and put him to bed and as I dragged him from the bar you could hear all the girls sigh with relief to see him go." Zarrine "Danny don't say things like this about Jeffrey, he is lovely." Danny "You don't know him and what he gets up to, last night alone I had to get him off the floor, he was looking up Winnie Woo's mini skirt through two empty Newcastle brown bottles." Zarrine with shocked look "I don't believe it, You should not say things like that about Jeffrey, he is lovely." Danny "You keep on saying he is lovely but it is going to be in the student magazine, as the photographer took some photos and said it was the funniest thing he has seen for a long time." Niel in a gossipy manner. "And Jeff said that Winnie Woo was only wearing a G-string, so it must have been true, because she is the only one who wears a G-string in this building." Zarrine "Niel how do you know that?" Niel with a smile "Because Danny bought them for her and told her they were the fashion here, that's why Winnie gets so many colds and we get so many thrills." They all laugh and Zarrine chases Niel around and slaps him on the bum. Next in walks Jeff looking as if he had been on the drink all night. Jeff with a big sigh said "Good morning all." Everyone says "Good morning." Zarrine "So is this true what I hear about you looking up Winnie Woo's mini skirt last night?" Jeff "More gossip about me. I am shocked that you listen to what other people say, especially that dodgy Welshman..... Yes, it's true, but only in the interest of science." Zarrine puzzled look "What do you mean?" Jeff "Well I was always told that oriental women were different to our European women and I was investigating." Zarrine "Well, is it true? whatever it is?" Jeff with his head in his hands. "I don't know, I was too pissed to tell." Pointing at Danny. "That dodgy Welshman dragged me out of there like a rag doll and everyone was laughing, it was humiliating, I think Winnie Woo was falling in love with me, she could not resist me and I think that dodgy Welshman was jealous." Danny "Well that's the last time I stop you making a fool of yourself, But there again you are always making a fool of yourself, you dopey cockney git." Zarrine in stern voice says "Now stop it you pair, you are always at each other's throats and then end up drinking together after, i do not know what we are going to do with you pair." Danny "Well you could marry me and chuck him out." Jeff "I'll be glad when they start sending you Welshmen back to your own country." Danny "Jeff, I am shocked that you talk to your superiors like this. Winnie Woo says you remind her of China, your eyes are always like little piss holes in the snow through all the drink you put away...I'm off to lectures see you all later."
Later and up the coffee bar and Danny, Jeff, Niel, Winnie Woo, Clamper and Mark sitting around a table talking and drinking coffee. Jeff with nervous voice "Hello Winnie Woo is you talking to me now? I said i was sorry." Winnie in snappy mood "No i will never talk to you again and never will i wear a mini skirt again." Danny "It's not the skirt, it's the beer bottles you must stop Jeff getting his hands on, that's something I would never do." Winnie "Yes I know you would not, you are a gentleman you are not like that dirty old Vidget." Danny "I know." Jeff "You got to be joking, that dodgy Welshman is worse than me." Winnie "I have never had any trouble with Danny like this." Niel all smiles and looking very excited "Guess what? I got a chance to make some money over Xmas." Mark "Da, Da, Da Doing what?"

Mark Is a tall lad around 22 years of age from Cardiff and has got a prominent stammer. Niel continues "I have been asked to be a Father Christmas in a toy shop in town for little children to get to meet and understand blind people while they are young and I and Clamper have been asked to put our genius inventions together and come up with something novel." (Clamper real name Andrew Blatchley is a 20 year old lad who gets most things he does wrong, shoes on the wrong feet, T shirt inside out and back to front etc. a well-spoken lad very lord snooty type who gets very excited and has a lot of changes to his voice sometimes high pitched and sometimes very bass sounding and always laughing) Clamper "I will think of the best idea for Niel, which the children will love." Danny "What is it?" Clamper trying to look very Important. "I cannot say it will be kept under wraps until the big opening day of Santa's grotto at the toy shop." Jeff "Niel you will tell us won't you?" Niel shrugging his shoulders "I do not know what it is as he won't tell me either." Clamper "It's a work of art and the children will fall over laughing and I think it will be made into a doll for next Christmas and will outsell everything before it." Jeff "Clamper do you know you have got your shoes on the wrong feet?" Clamper "If you hum it I'll sing it, ha, ha, ha, ha." Jeff "No I am not kidding, they are on the wrong feet." Niel "And he is an inventor, no wonder I am a bag of nerves." Jeff "What are you doing tonight Danny? I fancy going down the Pretty Pigs for a couple of sherbets." Danny replies "I can't make it tonight as I have to finish an assignment to hand in tomorrow or I will be in deep trouble." Jeff "I will be thinking of you as I am swigging back some lovely pints of lovely lager, are you sure you won't change your mind?" Danny "No absolutely not." Jeff "Ok, on your head be it." In walks Lola moaning as usual, she sees Clamper and makes a B line for him. Lola in bossy voice "Clamper when are you going to grow up? and stop playing with those silly toys and give up trying to invent things? they never work but you make a lot of noise in your bedroom trying and i am kept awake with it all night." Clamper in a very nervous voice "i am sorry i will try to keep it down in future." Lola "I will not tell you again next time I will shove one of your inventions where the sun don't shine." Danny "In that case you should know exactly what to do you had enough practises, your head is always stuck up somebody's arse, usually somebody Important." Lola "Was I talking to you? and Clamper do you know you have got your shoes on the wrong feet?" Lola storms off and everyone goes off to their lectures.

Danny and Jeff sitting in the lounge having a cup of coffee and chatting, and Danny says "Well what did you have for tea in the refectory? I had something foreign, I could not tell what it was." Jeff "Well I had this round thing I think they call it a pizza, although I thought it was a squashed mince pie." "I saw a cockroach coming out of the kitchen earlier chewing a rennie." They both have a good laugh. Danny "I wonder what that Clamper is up to, I hope he does not do too much damage to that poor old Niel, his inventions never seem to work very well." Jeff "Well I think he is onto something this time as he seems to be very confident about this invention whatever it is." Danny not looking convinced says "Well I hope your right or Niel will end up in bed for a long time again and Clamper will be hiding again for weeks and we will be running around after Niel again." Jeff "You will, I won't." Danny smiling says "Did you hear what happened to Jeff and his guide dog Bernie ?" Jeff answers "No, what happened?" Danny explains "Well he was waiting to cross by the lights and Bernie cocked his leg up and pissed all down Jeff's leg and Jeff put his hand in his pocket and pulled out a dog treat and gave it to Bernie , standing by them was Alison the tutor and she said to Jeff, "Well that's the kindest thing I have ever seen your dog piddled down your leg and you gave him a treat." Jeff continued "I gave him a treat to know which end to put my toe up." Danny and Jeff laugh Jeff "so you are still determined to stay in and do your assignment are you?" "Yes I have to and it would not hurt You to have a night in and study." Jeff wide eyed says "I am going out to study that lovely barmaid that always dresses in pink with the large shop fronts." Danny "Well I will see you later." They both go off in different directions.

Jeff is in the pretty pig's public house and Gupta is already in there having a sly glass of Guinness. Jeff with shocked look. "What are you doing in here? I have never seen you in a bar before." Gupta "Well I am going back to Pakistan for Christmas to meet and marry my new bride and I am nervous about being able to perform, you know." Jeff looking puzzled says "No, what are you on about?" Gupta "Well I was talking to Danny and I told him I have never had women before. This will be the first." Jeff "Good god man, you are 39 and never been grappled with by the enemy? have never had an evil one?" Gupta looking coy sais "No, that's the problem, I do not know if it will work." "If what will work?" Gupta in embarrassed mood "You know, my little chapatti, you know as you English call it your pecker." Jeff seems to finally understand says "Oh I see what you mean what's that got to do with being in a bar?" Gupta says "As I was telling you I mentioned it to Danny and he said to go to a pub and drink some Guinness, it will put lead in your pencil and it will help my complexion and if it works I said he could have her sister." Jeff sat up straight and said "How many sisters do she have?" Gupta smiling says "She has six sisters." Jeff all excited. "Drink up the next pint is on me if you fetch me a sister back." Gupta replies "Yes that's very nice, but I must be going after that as I have got to find my prayer mat and use it." Jeff goes up to the bar and the pink beauty is not there but a rather large lady who resembles a rugby prop forward. Jeff looking very disappointed says to her "Hi, two pints of Guinness please (she tries to make eyes at Jeff but he just nervously smiles and as he picks his pints up he says as he is leaving the bar) you look a million dollars tonight." and as soon as he is far enough from the bar Jeff says to himself "all in loose change." He gives himself a Wry smile . Gupta "Jeff, what are you chuckling about?" Jeff still smiling "I just met the woman of Danny's dreams, she would sort out that dodgy Welshman and I must introduce them." Just then a pretty young girl in a short skirt started to clean their table. Jeff acting all suave and sophisticated. "Oh my god i have died and gone to heaven, hello your new, my mum said if i didn't find a girlfriend tonight i will be up for adoption in the morning." The young girl said "I hope you like your new home." Jeff continues "I think I am falling madly in bed with you." Young girl "Well sleep well in your captain bed." The young girl walks away blushing and smiling. Jeff "Yes I think she fancies me."

Later on that night and Jeff is walking home swaying just a little, using his white cane to guide himself, it is very dark and he is singing quietly as he approaches his digs at Dowdell. Someone is lurking and pounces out on Jeff pushing him against the wall quiet roughly. The man has some sort of bottle in his hand with bleach in it which he waves in front of Jeff's face, the mugger being very nervous and shifty. "Hand over any money or I will let you have it, I will throw this bleach in your eyes, give me all your money." Jeff calmly stands still and says in a quiet voice. "Your new at this aren't you?" The mugger with a shocked look says "What do you mean? give me all your money." Jeff "Yes your definitely new at this, I don't think you will do anything." The mugger looking unsure says "Why do you say I am new at this?" Jeff explains with lots of hand gestures. "Because I have not got any bloody money coming home from the pub. The best time to rob someone is when they are going to the pub, they have money going to the pub and they spend all the money in the pub and then go home pissed because they are skint and totally pissed." The mugger looking relieved and after a short pause. "Oh yes i suppose your right, thanks mate." Jeff smiling. "Your welcome." The mugger turns tail and makes a run for it. Jeff shakes himself off and walks up to the building, opens the main door with his key, gets in shuts the door quickly and let's out a big sigh and puts his hands over his face and starts to shake with fright. The shock has hit him and he looks ill with fear, he heads upstairs.

In the common room lounge is Danny, Niel, Winnie and Mark . In walks Jeff, they see that he is very shaky and traumatised and all start to talk to him. Danny "What's the Matter mate? had to pay for your own beer for a change? some pretty barmaid said yes to you and your in shock?" Niel joins in "No I don't think so all the barmaids in there have good eyesight except for the old boiler and she would fancy a frog if she could stop it hopping." Jeff visibly shaking "No this is not a joke, I have just been mugged outside here." Winnie looking very concerned says "What, are you kidding?" Jeff still shaking "No this is serious I was threatened for money by a young lad with a bottle of bleach in his hand." Danny seriously concerned "Are you allright? sit here and I will get you a whisky to calm your nerves." Mark "D, D, D, Did you recognise him by his voice? was he a college l,l,l,lad?" Jeff "No, I think he was not from the college, I would have known him if he was." Mark "I am g g g glad I did not go out tonight." Jeff "If it had been you he would run a mile with fright, as you are six foot four and built like a brick shit house." Danny hands Jeff a glass of whisky. Jeff "Thanks." Mark pretending to be in shock "I, I, I, feel a bit nervous myself now." Danny "I suppose you want one too, here you are give anyone else who wants one a glass, (Danny hands the bottle to Mark .) so Jeff what did you do?" Jeff looking a little better said "I told him that I thought he was not all there, who robs me coming home from the pub when I had no money then he just ran off and that was it." Winnie "Well you had better phone the police and soon." Jeff "No I do not think they will catch him, I will go and have a fag and then see how I feel." Jeff has a fag and the police come out to see him. They arrive and they all sit in the lounge and Jeff tells them all about it. After finishing the statement they chat Jeff "So you have been chasing him for a while?" The police man replied "Yes he has been at this for several weeks' probably needs the money for Christmas." Jeff "Why the bottle of bleach?" Police man "Well he tells people that if they do not pay up he will throw the bleach in their eyes, we in the force have named him the germinator." Danny sarcastically says "So he robs them and then cleans up after himself." Police man with grin on his face "Yes, you could say that sir, well we will keep in touch and let you know as soon as something happens, goodnight all." Everyone bids them goodnight and all continue talking. Next in walks Clamper with his fingers covered in plasters and his t shirt on inside out looking like a surgeon, just behind him was Lola . Lola in serious mood. "Is it true that you have been mugged?" Jeff "Yes it's true." Lola "Are you allright? they should catch him and lock him up and throw the key away, just think it could have been me, I just came in before you." Danny "He probably seen you coming and thought well I am not that brave and give you a miss, he was probably afraid of you." Lola "Very funny you have to make a joke about everything." Danny "Sorry, you are right, this is not a very funny thing and we should take it a bit more serious." Lola "Yes I should think so." Winnie "I think Danny should accompany me in the nights from now on until he is caught." She gave a hopeful look. Danny "Yes I think that is a good idea." Winnie smiling "Do you really think so?" Danny "Well of course I do." Jeff "Danny your all heart, if you had come out for a drink tonight it may not have happened." Danny "I came here to learn how to be blind and not sit in a pub, there is more to life." Niel "That's telling you if he did not have those papers he has to hand in tomorrow he would have been there, dim problem." Winnie says "Well I am going to bed." Danny starts to get up from his chair. "Ok let's go." Winnie in snappy tone. "What do you mean?" Danny smiling replies "You said I should accompany you in the night times." Winnie "Danny stop it, don't be silly." Danny "Goodnight Winnie Woo." Winnie "Goodnight silly man." Jeff "Clamper what have you done to your hands? they are all covered in plasters and did you know you have got your T-shirt on inside out?" Clamper "I have been working on my invention for Christmas and I have been having some glitches." Jeff "Your not kidding and have you anything to do with these fairy lights missing off the college Christmas tree?" Clamper looking worried says "Who me? no, would I ?" Lola "I expect it has something to do with this new invention for Christmas, I know it will end in tears, I just know it, he is a walking disaster." Danny "Don't beat about the bush Lola just tell him straight. Well Clamper how is it going? the new invention I mean, will it be finished in time?" Clamper "Yes it will be finished in time, I need to get some new watch batteries and it will work." Jeff "Come on tell us what it is." Clamper answers "No I want it to be a surprise, the kids will think it's a scream, they will love it and Niel will be the most successful Santa ever, he will make us a fortune." Danny "When is the big day?" Clamper "Tomorrow evening and you are all welcome to see him on the day, it will be a day that will never be forgotten." Danny "We will look forward to it" Lola "Well I won't be there, I will have better things to do, goodnight I am off." Jeff "I thought I could smell something, only kidding Lola." Mark "God she is a happy one isn't sh, sh, sh, she." Niel is sitting next to Clamper looking sorry for himself. Jeff "God Niel you are quiet, what's the Matter? I hope you are not having a change of mind, think of all those little children's faces." Niel with worried look. "Yes i suppose you are right, Clamper if you do any damage to me again i will never speak to you again, is it safe?" Clamper "Of course it is safe, you know I would not let anything happen to you, you are my mate, well back to the grind, goodnight." All bid him a goodnight. Niel "I have been back on the sleeping tablet's since I consented to do this with him, I never learn do I?" Jeff "Well you love kids so there's no backing out." Niel "I know, your right, I am off to bed." off they all go to bed leaving only Danny and Jeff . Danny "Are you sure your allright?" Jeff "Yes I am now but at the time I thought my heart was going to explode, I was so frightened." Danny "Do you want another drop of whisky?" "Do bears crap in the woods?" Danny smiling says "Silly question I suppose, well I think I better keep you company." Danny pours out two drinks. Jeff "I think that Winnie Woo has a bit of a crush on you, she never says anything bad about you." Danny says "You keep saying that to me, I can't help it if I am irresistible to women. Last month it was that little one from Ireland, now my little China girl, you either got it or you haven't." Jeff "That reminds me, I saw Gupta in the pub and he tells me you have conned him into introducing you to his sister in law from Pakistan." "Yes that's true and I have arranged to meet Zarrine's sister from India next month, because if I do not have a Chinese I can always have an Indian." Jeff says "Yes that's very good I never thought of that." Danny "Well as regards Winnie I am not sure as I am still married and maybe it would be different if I wasn't." Jeff says "But you said she is going to divorce you so what is the problem?" Danny "We have been together for sixteen years now it is not something you can just switch off never mind what she thinks of me and there is Josh my son, I just don't know and what if I am wrong and she still loves me, I don't know what to think." Jeff says with sympathy "I know what you are saying but as you said life goes on and I think it is going to be hard from now on with your problem to find someone else, this is your opportunity to find someone who thinks a lot of you, because Angie won't be there for much longer." Danny looking sad says "Yes your probably right, I must start thinking about my future. I will just see how things pan out, I mean I will play it by ear and see what happens. I do fancy WINNIE but I must get to know her first and I am still trying to get used to being blind and keeping me from killing myself first." Jeff "Well do that, no hurry, and if you don't get on with her you can always try Lola." Danny smirking "I would rather have pins stuck in my eyes, but there again she has a lovely body and is attractive, but she is too much trouble." Both men laughed and went off to bed.

It's breakfast the next morning and Zarrine is washing up dishes and in walks Niel looking worried and seems to be looking for something. Niel feeling around "Hi Zarrine." Zarrine replies "Good morning Niel you look as if you lost a £1 and found 20pence." Niel still searching says "Well I think I am going mad, I have 4 pairs of eyes and I can only find 3 pair and the two are odd ones one is light blue and the other is dark brown." Zarrine "They should have called you spider not Niel, your lucky most people only have one pair, you should be in the book of Guinness's, do not worry I expect a couple have rolled off the dressing table and under your bed, I will find them and put them back on your table, I do not think anyone would pinch your false eyes do you? and tell me why have you got dark brown eyes? when you were originally a blue eyed boy." Niel smiling says "Well they are for funerals and what is the book of Guinness's?" Zarrine laughing says "You know the two brothers on the TV (Zarrine starts singing) dedication, dedication that's what you need...." Niel starts laughing "Ha, ha, the Guinness book of records you soppy bugger, the programme record breakers." Next in walks Jeff. Niel and Zarrine says "Good morning Jeff." Zarrine continues talking to him "How are you feeling today? have you got over your episode last night? I was shocked to hear about it and I was worried about you." Jeff answers her "Yes I am allright and after a lot of thought I feel sorry for the lad." Niel "How can you feel sorry for vermin like him? I wonder if he had my eyes." Jeff "we do not know what he might be going through, he must be desperate to have to do something like that, he probably has a young family and does not know where his next penny is coming from." Zarrine "Yes it's possible I come from a poor country and it is awful in this day and age to have this poverty problem" Niel "I suppose if you put it like that I must agree" "Well I hope someone helps him before it is too late, anyway what is for breakfast? " Zarrine Tea and toast." Jeff smiles "yes thank you... Niel what's the Matter?" Niel still feeling around for something. "i can't find two of my eyes" Jeff "You haven't swallowed them in your sleep have you? as you are taking tablet's all the time and might have made a mistake. That happened to my mate, he swallowed one of his glass eyes once and had to go to the doctors" Zarrine "What happened to him?" Jeff "Well the doctor told him that it would come out naturally in his motions and told him to keep an eye out for it and if it did not appear in the next week to go back and see him. Well it did not come out naturally so back he went, well said the doctor no sign of it, well drop your trousers and bend over the desk and I will have a look up there for it with my torch. Well the doctor looked up his backside and said I cannot see anything at all, and my friend chirped up and said well that's funny doc, I can see you." They all enjoyed the joke. Next in walks Danny he says "Good morning everyone, how is Jeff this morning?" Jeff "I am much better this morning." Niel "He is thinking of not pressing charges against this fella as he feels sorry for him." Jeff "I never said I was going to drop the charges, I just think he needs help." Danny "Well I think he should have helped himself when he was younger and paid attention in school and got himself a proper education and a better job would have followed." Jeff "Yes why don't we put them in boot camps and whip them." Niel "Not a bad idea." Danny "I am not saying that but most of these problems are brought on by themselves, they should sort out the parents they think the government should sort out their children for them, why should they? they brought them into the world not the government. So who's fault is it?" Niel "I agree parents don't give a damn these days and the children have no respect. In my day my father would put a slipper to my backside and if the local bobby caught me doing something he would give you a clip around the ear and you would never go back and tell your mother or father or they would give you a clip around the ear to go with it, today parents always think their children are the perfect ones and if anything goes wrong it is always somebody else's fault and" Next thing Danny interrupts Niel "Wow calm down I will find you a soap box, he is right though discipline Is missing these days." Zarrine "Yes I get some cheeky ones here with the youngsters but not the older ones, except Lola." Jeff "I'm just saying we don't know the circumstances that's all, he must be desperate." Next in walks Winnie Woo and Rhoda. Rhoda says "Good morning, I am going to church later and I will say a prayer for that lad from last night." Niel "Not another one? give him to me he will never do it again." Winnie "In my country he would be severely punished indeed, this place is a joke." Danny "To bloody right, bring back the Burch I agree. Winnie." Winnie with huge smile says. "Do you really, that's nice." Off they all go to their lectures.

It's early evening and at the student bar and all were sitting around the table. Danny, Jeff, Winnie woo, Clamper, Mark and Gupta. Danny says first "Well do you want a pint? Everyone says "Yes please." Danny looking stunned says "I was asking Jeff, I know I can maybe get him to buy one back." Jeff "Oh yes please, I will have a pint of lager." Danny "How can you drink that excuse for a pint? it's awful." Jeff "It's not that bad." Danny "Oh I forgot I am in England and they will drink anything here and you English only need a sniff of the beer mat and you are anyone's. There is not even a head on it, I have tasted better dish water." Winnie asks "Danny will you get me a drink? and I will get you one back after." Danny "What do you want? Whisky?" Winnie replies "No I get too drunk and do not know what I am doing on that stuff, you British people drink too much." Danny says quietly "Whisky it is then." Jeff "Yes you watch him Winnie Woo, Gin makes you sing, brandy makes you randy, whisky makes you frisky and cider makes you wider." Winnie says "I will have a Wodka and coke." Danny goes up to the bar and the barman says "Danny what can I get you?" "I will have a double whiskey in a tall glass and top it up with coke please, a pint of lager and a bottle of pills lager and can you carry them over for me I will take the whisky." barman says "Ok you go and I will fetch them over." Danny "Thanks." Danny arrives back at the table and the barman brings the beer Danny "Here we are Winnie your wodka I mean vodka and coke." Winnie smiling at Danny says "Thank you Danny." Danny "Your velcome." Winnie "You are very good to me." Danny under his breath says "i will be after …hopefully." Jeff says "Have you seen Niel today?" Danny rubbing his chin says "Oh I think he is fast asleep as he is back on his sleeping tablet's for his nerves, since Clamper has started inventing again for his father Christmas job." Clamper ears pricked up and says "I do not know what he is worrying about it is a cracking invention and he will be made up over it and it will make him famous and you should come and see it for yourself and you can say I knew the man who invented this and made him a million and Niel a household name with the children." Danny "We will be there, we would not miss it for the world and when you make it you must think of your friends." Clamper "Of course I will you are my mates." Jeff "Gupta is looking worried about something, what is the Matter Gupta?" Gupta answers "Well I am getting nervous about my marriage it Is less than three weeks out in Pakistan." Jeff says "You will be allright once you have cracked the case, it's like riding a bike after that." Gupta "What is a bike?" Jeff "Well it is like riding an elephant." Gupta "Oh yes I understand now I am having my honeymoon over here is there any way you can help me?"

Jeff smiling "We will think of something, just let me and Danny think and we will get back to you ." Mark says "I I, I, I would not let them pair think of anything it will be a disaster If they are involved." Gupta "Oh dear, oh dear." Danny snaps "Don't listen to that Welsh Moose he knows nothing, if there is anything we can do we will... tell me is she fully sighted?" Gupta "No she can see a little bit not much after dark or in a room lit with light bulbs and she is pretty deaf with it." Danny "Sounds like the type of girl that would fancy Jeff, leave it to us we will help ewe, we will talk tomorrow." Gupta looking a little happier says "Yes ok." In comes Lola, she breezes in like as if she was carried in without moving her feet, looking pleased with herself and says. "Hi everyone, i have just sorted out that Niel he was like a bag of nerves now he feels much better, now i have had a word with him." Jeff "Hello Lola, that's nice deodorant you are wearing, have you been jogging?" A few chuckles and Lola shrugs her shoulders. Jeff "We were wondering where he was and if you were giving him a good seeing to" Lola "Well somebody had to do something for ....What do you mean seeing to?" Jeff "Never mind. It's a messy job but somebody's got to do it." Lola "I think that Clamper has something to do with Niel's problem." Danny "You leave Clamper alone, he is only trying to help him out, that's more than some do." Jeff "Right, bottle or what?" Danny "Is a sand crab's ass waterproof? Winnie Woo are you allright?" Winnie replies "Yes I am allright I will get myself one now and a bottle for you." Danny "Thank you.... when is the grand opening for Niel?" Clamper "It is tomorrow afternoon at four o'clock after school, the mayors grandchildren and other dignitaries are coming first, then it will be opened the next day and the money will start to roll in." Danny "OK we will be there at about three forty five, that's when the big hand is on the 9 and the little hand is on the 4 and make sure your shoes are on the right feet." Clamper "Cool." Jeff "Here you dodgy Welshman, your pills." Danny "Thanks mate, Clamper said the father Christmas starts tomorrow afternoon and I said we would be there." Jeff "Yes of course we will all be there." Several drinks later and Winnie Woo was drunk and Danny and Jeff were not far off being drunk . Jeff "I wonder if they have caught the boy who mugged me yet?" Danny "I would not put any money on it mate." Jeff "Well if he is out there tonight he must be freezing, I wish I could get to talk to him again and try to make him see sense." Danny "You could try and I dare say you could do it, your good at keeping your cool with the youngsters." Jeff "I wish I had tried that night." Danny "Well take Lola with you for protection." Jeff "I will." Danny " In the meantime I had better walk Winnie Woo home, she is a little bit worse with drink." Jeff "God your a gentleman and good luck." Danny "Luck doesn't come into it see you in the morning if I am lucky or had I better walk you home first? I wouldn't want you mugged twice in two days, your my mate and it does not look good for my reputation." Jeff with smile says "No you go I can look after myself, besides Linda the barmaid is looking good tonight so I will try my luck." Danny says "You have more chance of winning the lottery mate." "We shall see, see you tomorrow."

It's breakfast again and Jeff and Zarrine are sipping tea. Zarrine says "Have you seen Niel? he is a bag of nerves, he has lost two of his glass eyes and he thinks he is going off his head, what is that Clamper doing to him?" Jeff "I would not worry about that oversized Welshman he can look after himself, Clamper is half his size and that's why he has been asked to be father Xmas and because he adores kids, he is still one himself." Next in walks Danny but he is walking as if he just got off a horse in lots of pain and barely able to bend and sit down. Jeff and Zarrine are just staring at him in disbelief. Zarrine has her hands over her mouth and Jeff gets a smile on his face . Danny moaning as he is sitting down says "Oh my god, oh dear my back, my legs, oh, oh." Zarrine looking worried says "Oh my goodness, what happened to you?" In a whimpering voice Danny replies "Winnie , Winnie ." Jeff says "Bloody hell man, is she that good? your in a hell of a mess, you must have been at it all night as you are still in the same clothes, or did she show a few moves with her Marshal arts? ha, ha." Danny holding his ribs says "Just don't make me laugh please don't make me laugh, I have been in agony for a long time now." Jeff "Flipping eck, she is good in fact she must be fantastic to disable you like that." Zarrine says "Don't be silly, what are you talking about?" Jeff "He took Winnie Woo home last night and he was going to score and by the looks of him he scored allright, she has killed him in bed." Zarrine scorns Jeff "Jeff behave yourself, I knew she is fit with all of her Marshal arts but I didn't think she would reduce him to this, should I get a doctor?" Danny struggling to speak "No, no, i will be alright in a minute." Jeff "Is she that good? tell me mate what happened?" Danny struggles to explain "Well we came back from the bar and I thought here we go but all she was interested in was giving me a Chinese massage and I excepted and 2 hours later she was helping me into my room as I could hardly walk let alone do anything else. My god, I am aching all over, she is an animal, I am glad we never had sex because I don't think I would be here now." Zarrine smiling says "Massage, Hmm, that's interesting I could do with some for my bad back." Danny "Well thanks Zarrine don't worry about me just think how you can benefit out of it." Zarrine said "Sorry Danny." Jeff "Your kidding a massage, I thought you had been on the nest all night no nookie then?" Danny smiling says "No mate sorry to disappoint you but that's how it was." Jeff "I Wonder if she will give me a massage?" Danny "Take my advice mate leave it there, she will make you into a bag of firewood as there is nothing of you now and after she finishes with you you'll never walk again." Zarrine "I am still worried about Niel." Danny "Well what can go wrong? he is in a grotto and he has only to sit the children on his knee and say a few words and give them a little gift. What scope is there for anything to go wrong? even with Clamper." Zarrine still looking concerned says "Nothing I suppose, what time is the grotto opening?" Jeff "About four this afternoon with the mayor's two little grandchildren going first, I think there are twenty five children going in together first." Danny "Perhaps that's what is the Matter with Niel he is nervous about the opening or the amount of children they are letting in at once.... that's what it is I bet it is." Zarrine "Yes you maybe right." In walks Niel looking like death warmed up everyone says "Good morning Niel how are you?" Niel head bowed, eyes hardly opened, shoulders drooped says. "I am knackered, I have not slept a wink I have been worrying myself stupid over everything that is happening today." Danny "Don't worry it will work out allright and we are all coming down to support you, mind you, ...you are looking like death warmed up your as white as a bottle of milk and being as bald as a fish does not help." Niel "I do not feel very well at all and I have taken enough sleeping tablet's to put an elephant to sleep but still have not slept." Jeff says "You worry too much." Niel "Well sod the lectures I am having two sleeping tablet's and going back to bed. Zarrine will you give me a shout at 1 o'clock please?" Zarrine replies "Yes of course I will." Off Niel goes to his bed and all the others go to their lectures.

One hour later Zarrine is answering the telephone in the lounge. Zarrine "Hello Dowdell third floor." Caller replies "Yes this is Niel David's tutor, can you tell him he has an Important appointment with the vice principle first thing this morning and he had better not miss this one or he will be on his way home." Zarrine "Is it that Important? he is not very well." Caller "Yes it's a Matter of life or death for Niel." Zarrine looking worried replies "Ok I shall send him over there as soon as he can, good bye." Zarrine goes off to get Niel out of bed, she knocks the door but gets no answer so goes in and tries to wake him but has great difficulty but finally succeeds. Niel is very drowsy and not with it at all. Zarrine speaks loudly to him "I am sorry Niel but you have to go and see the vice principle straight away it is a Matter of life or death." Niel eyes closed and head still hanging. "Yes ok I am going but I must get some sleep or I will die of tiredness." Zarrine says "Yes you do not have time now before you do your father Christmas bit this afternoon, you will have to go to bed as soon as you return from that." Niel "Ok" Zarrine has to walk over to the vice principals office with Niel as he can hardly stand.

It was a lot later that day and Niel and Clamper are in Santa's grotto and Clamper is getting Niel ready dressed and setting the scene for the children. Meanwhile outside Jeff, Danny, Zarrine, Winnie, Mark, Gupta and all the children are waiting to see Santa with excitement. They are all around the age of between 5 and 7. Then all of a sudden Clamper comes out and announces to the gang that everything is ready as the mayor is waiting to cut the ribbon but there is a delay as her grandchildren have not arrived. Danny says "Clamper is everything allright?" Clamper replies "Yes it's brilliant you will be proud of me when you get to see how good things have worked out in the grotto, it is perfect." Danny "And Niel how is he now?" Clamper "He is happy and very relaxed, in fact I have never seen him so cool calm and relaxed you would think he has had a sedative." Danny "That's good I have been worried about him lately." Jeff smiling says "You wait he will be a big hit with these little ones, he loves doing things with children, they have the same I,Q as him, ha, ha, ha." Everyone laughs. Zarrine says "Well he will be relieved to be here after the day he has had, he never got his sleep after all, never mind he can go home after this and get as much sleep as he likes." Jeff "He will want to go for a few pints tonight to celebrate I expect, here we go at last she is about to cut the ribbon." The mayor says a little speech "It is my great pleasure to be here today to open this grotto and I wish to thank the College for all the effort put into this venture and I am told we are in for a lovely surprise in there. So without further to do I declare this grotto open" The ribbon is cut and all the children are let into Santa's grotto. They all sit and stand in rows in the dimly lit grotto and wait for the curtain to open to reveal Santa, then all of a sudden the curtain goes up and all hell was let loose and all the children started screaming crying and running away and you could see the terror in their little faces and as they ran away the grotto tend just fell down all around Niel. The curtain had come up and there was Niel dressed as father Christmas with only his beard on and his hood had slipped down to reveal his bald head, he is fast asleep and snoring but for all the world he looks dead and his eyes are flashing on and off one brown one light blue. He looks like something from the exorcist in the darkness it looked evil. The invention of the flashing eyes were terrifying and even frightened the adults. Then in walks the shop owner wakes up Niel and fires him, Clamper takes flight waving his arms in the air and all the students are in fits of laughter.

Back at the common room for supper Danny, Jeff, Winnie, Mark, Gupta and Lola were sitting talking about the events that afternoon. Jeff spoke first "Has anybody seen Clamper yet?" Everyone says "No, he has fled." Next Lola said "He should be expelled for what he did to poor old Niel." Danny "Well I thought it was brilliant, brilliant, just what the doctor ordered, so funny. Niel looked like a geriatric ZZ Top member with the bald head and those flashing eyeballs were so funny, I think Clamper done a cracking job. I have not laughed so much since I kissed my mother in law with a lighted cigar in my mouth." Mark "Ha, ha, ha, ha, ha, the t, t, t, tears have been rolling down my face ever since. Even Z, Z, Z, Z, Zarrine was in hysterics and I was crying at her laughing at N, N, N, N, Niel." Jeff "And the funniest thing about it was that Niel slept all the way through it and even the mayor could not stop laughing and I have never seen her laugh. Niel looked like Mr Potato head with his head and those eyes and those ears sticking out." Just then Jeff's mobile phone rang and he answers. He takes the call and afterwards speaks to everyone. Jeff says In serious mode. "Well that was the police, they have caught that lad who mugged me, they cornered him in an alley and he threw the bottle of bleach at the police and it burned their uniforms. So he was not afraid to use it. I was asked to go down to the police station to identify him and I told them I was not pressing charges." Lola looking nasty said "Why not? he deserves to be put down after what terror he has caused." Jeff looking sad said "Well I think he needs help not incarceration and it is Christmas, a time to forgive and forget, I think he will learn his lesson." Danny with wry smile says "Are you sure you can forget?" Jeff smiling "Yes I am sure." Danny "Well he will not get off Scott free." Lola ponders and says "What do you mean?" Danny with huge smile "Well it's the problem of throwing the bottle of bleach at the police." Jeff "Well that's not much is it?" Danny still smiling "Yes it is, that's called the bleach of the police." (The breach of the peace) Everyone roars with laughter except Lola and Winnie woo who do not get the Joke. Lola says "Goodnight, I am off to bed, see you all tomorrow." All say goodnight and sat there still chuckling to themselves. Winnie was hanging around to try and get Danny on his own next Mark and Gupta goes off to bed and it was just Danny, Jeff and Winnie left, Jeff says "I wonder what happened to Clamper, he has just disappeared out of sight. He is an absolute nutcase but you have to laugh ." Danny "He is probably in one of the younger students places waiting for it to cool down, why I don't know it was brilliant, brilliant, you couldn't make it up." Jeff "Yes it was brilliant, so what are you doing for xmas dodgy?" "I am off to see my sons and daughters and my grandchildren and that miserable woman I am married to." Next thing Winnie got up and went off to her room without saying anything. Jeff remarks "I wonder what that was all about, I think you upset her talking about your misses." "I don't think so I have told her that she is going to divorce me at least I think so, so she knows the crack, I think she is not getting my undivided attention, she is strange like that ." Jeff "Do you think so? well, well, I am going up to Swindon to see my boys and daughters and hope they don't want nothing heavy for xmas but I am planning to stay in the pub as much as I can and mum is doing xmas dinner so I am not going to do any hard work." Danny smiles "So you have still got your mum around your little finger ay, handy, it's going to be strange being home for a fortnight, I am getting used to this place now it's worrying, god." Next thing there was a loud sound like snoring. Jeff jumps and says "What the hell was that? did you hear that?" Danny answered "Yes I did, what the hell was it." They stayed silent and heard it again and it came from the area behind the settee. Danny said "It's coming from behind the settee, let's pull it out and if it is an intruder jump on him and I will call the police." Jeff looking worried says "What do you mean jump on him? you jump on him and I will call the police, if it is a female then I will jump on her and you leave the police where they are." They both crept up to the settee and pulled it out slowly without making a sound and as the person appeared they could tell it was Clamper. Danny and Jeff let out a sigh and slumped onto the settee. Jeff said "So that's where he got to, I wondered what the hell the sound was, so what do we do with him now?" "I know what I should do with him but we could never wake up Niel and he did it with all good intentions so let's just wake him up and get him to bed." They shook him and he woke up with a start and said "Oh hello, it was not my fault he fell asleep, he had had so many sleeping tablet's it was his fault.." Danny "Yes we know it's all over and done with, I thought it was brilliant and so does Jeff." The lads had a good laugh about it all and Clamper got up and sat on a chair. Jeff said "So is that why you were hiding?" Clamper starts to explain "Well I was back here before all of you and next I heard Lola coming in and hid behind the settee and I was there for ages and I finally fell asleep, that's how boring you all were." Danny "Steady mate or I will hand you over to Lola myself." Clamper begs "No I was only joking honest, so what about Niel? is he ok about it all?" Jeff smiling from ear to ear "We don't know he never really woke up he went straight to bed and never uttered a word." Danny "I think you are safe Niel never gets nasty about things like that anyway, after the holidays he will be laughing about it, anyway I am off to bed, see you all in the morning." They all wished each other a goodnight and went to bed.

CHAPTER 9
PINTS AND POEMS

Well not much happened up to Xmas and they all went off to their different parts of the land and Danny went back down to be back with his family hoping things had Improved in many ways. He had got his life back in a lot of ways and had a new batch of friends that he had never dreamed of before, are things changing for the better? time would tell. He got back home and was greeted by his son Josh, he was now nearly 10 years old and Danny had one of the best greetings he had ever had for a long time, but as soon as he sat in his old chair he felt like a fish out of water, he was back stuck in his own house a prisoner again because he could not walk around like in Hereford as people would stare and whisper and some of the kids would make fun and so many dogs roaming around would attack him because he had a cane and would think he was going to hurt them with it, so he was back in prison the only time he could go out was if his wife would take him and she could not stand to be near him. She had changed with the outcome of his blindness, so he started to get that old feeling back the only Time he had someone to speak to is if his lovely neighbours were out in their garden that was Jane and Leighton others just ignored him as if to say he was not normal anymore.

 Well Danny and Angie had arranged to visit a club down the valley where Danny had some friends left and some of Angie's friends moved to. Danny was not sure what would happen that evening but he was going to find out. The night went off great and they enjoyed themselves and met people Danny had not seen for a long time, but Danny sat there like a tailors dummy and still felt like a fish out of water. Danny then realised he could not wait to get back to the college in Hereford. Had Danny become institutionalised? or what was happening? he was feeling nervous about everything he did and took some time to settle down again but he had that niggling feeling he was not wanted there anymore, not by his son but his wife, what was Danny going to do about it? His mind was working overtime and he could not sleep thinking about it all the time. Then Danny had another problem to think about and it was something he could not do much about.

Danny has a younger brother, his name is Lyndon and he loves him dearly and Lyndon loves Danny, he has decided at an early life he would follow Danny's footsteps he loved to have a pint or two of beer, not like Danny he loved to drink but never knew when to leave it alone. Danny can take it or leave it and he has always drunk good beer never rubbish or cheap stuff. Lyndon will drink anything now, he had a very sheltered upbringing as their dad was a staunch Jehovah's Witness and they had to do as he wanted to the letter or there was punishment dealt out at all times. Their father was a verbal bully and was good with his hands if you crossed him. You were not allowed to make up your own mind you had to follow his beliefs, you were not allowed your own and until Danny was 15 and a half Danny lived as their dad insisted with a lot of punishments to Danny and his mother, they never celebrated birthdays, xmas, parties were taboo and girlfriends were out unless they were of his faith.

Danny's younger brother was born into this religion and witnessed many upsetting things and Danny was sure that this made him a resigned, nervous and withdrawn person and always seemed uneasy, so he never seen the outside world as it really was until he left school and he turned from being a very quiet little boy to a drinking machine. From an early age he would drink when he had money. Danny never seen much of him from time to time as Danny would work away a lot but Danny was aware he was drinking much too much and his best friend Alwyn Jenkins had died when he was about 13 and he could not understand why and Danny felt he turned after that and got in with friends who egged him on to drink and many were not good for him at all and Danny realised how much he had really missed Alwyn. He was lost without him.

Well as Danny said he adored him and was concerned about him for a few years as he had started drinking in the early mornings as soon as he got up, he would not even venture far from the marital home now and was getting worse. Danny tried to talk to him many, many, times but he always insisted he was ok, nothing to worry about, his marriage was something he never really wanted, Danny could tell the responsibility was just too much for him and when he had a child and became a father he was just not a person who could handle it. She would walk all over him at all times and you could tell his nerves was shattered and Danny was worried so he asked him over to do some little jobs for him and Danny was shocked when he appeared, it was just after xmas he obviously needed money for drink probably and when Danny put his arms around him he was so huge and he hardly knew what to say. Danny asked him if he would do some little jobs for him, he said ok. They had a good couple of days together, Danny felt it was a good time to talk to Lyndon about this problem but Danny was going to get a real shock, Lyndon had a car and Danny asked him to take him to pick up something about 20 miles away and he refused. Danny asked him why? He said his car wouldn't make it, Danny said o problem he could borrow a car, but he still made an excuse.

Danny asked their friend one day if he knew why? this man was Gaffo and he replied "I can't figure it out myself Dan, he don't go nowhere now only around the estate where he lives. I have a idea why but you may laugh." Danny said "I think I know what you are going to say, his nerves have gone." Gaffo replies "Yes he went on a holiday with Debbie, his mother in law and step father in law, they took them up with them for a holiday in north Wales, so he didn't have to drive. After 2 days up there he phoned me to go back up to pick him up as he wanted to come home and he was panicking on the phone, so I went up half way and brought him back and as soon as he was home he was ok again but his wife and his daughter stayed up there. He is in a mess, I tell you and he has always got alcohol on him from morning to night." Danny looking down to the ground says "Oh my god, it's got that bad, I am worried now, what's going on?" Gaffo "Dan I am worried to he won't listen to noone, I think he should never have moved from his family home in Glannant, he was happy there, that was her doing, he was ok until then and his bloody mother in law is always in his house, she never leaves him alone. She is a nosey cow, he has no family life, she is always there." Danny "Yes I know I have spoke to him about it and he is fed up with it and I think he regrets marrying her daughter, I must get him to talk about it to me and try and get him some help." Gaffo "Yeh I agree it's going to be hard for you now you can't see but if I can do anything I will don't be afraid to ask ok?" Danny with wry smile says "Thanks Gaffo I will, right thanks for helping me figure what's going on I am really worried now. He is coming over tomorrow to do some little jobs for me so I will try then and I will not mention that I have spoke to you ok?" "Ok good luck, I am off Dan, bye."

Danny went off and forgot all about his problems and started to worry about his little brother praying he could do something quickly.

Well he turned up the following day and Danny greeted him and he asked Danny how he was doing up the college, Danny said "I am doing fine, I feel like a real novice though, but I will get the hang of it ." Lyndon then said "How are your eyes now? any chance they will

Improve?" Danny looking serious says "No I don't hold out any hopes of that but you never know, many cures are possible, we must just wait and see." Lyndon with concern on his face. "I hope so, things are not going well for our family lately are they? I don't believe it." Danny said "And how are you? I have heard from a little birdie you are drinking worse now than ever before, in fact I have heard from a lot of birdies." Lyndon looking mad said "That's a load of crap I don't drink more now than any time in the past so ignore them." Danny "So how did the holiday go?" Lyndon "I didn't like it up there, I came home early it wasn't for me." Danny says "I heard you was having panic attacks up there and demanded for someone to pick you up and when you got home you was ok and you have refused to drive out of the village, what's going on then?" Lyndon straight faced says "So why did you ask me about my holidays then? if you know and I won't drive far if I have been drinking the day before, surely there is someone who can run you there." Danny in serious voice "Lyn I absolutely believe you are an alcoholic and you must get some help, so why don't you?" "Don't talk crap, I am not an alcoholic at all, you always dramatize things, just get off my back and give me the things you want me to do." Danny "So you are in denial that's how all alcoholics are, you won't admit it will you?" Lyndon says in snappy voice. "No because you are taking it all out of proportion again as usual." Danny looking sad says "Well I have been talking to some people and they agree with me and we are all worried about you, it's 2001 now it can be sorted out easily, let's do it together." Lyndon loses his temper and snaps at Danny. "Right I am not sitting here listening to this crap, do you want me to sort a couple of things out or not? if not I am off." Danny looking sympathetic says "Yes ok, fair enough I won't keep on but please have a think about it." Lyndon nodded and got on with putting some things up such as shelves a house sign and so on. Danny even tried to speak to him again and he made an excuse to get home. Danny felt betrayed he could tell by him he was an alcoholic and Danny could definitely smell a strong dose of alcohol on him. Danny had only lost a brother Dennis a year before and that tore him apart, now he has another brother to worry about he was fragile, Lyndon looked after their mother after their dad had died with no help from Danny and he felt bad about this. Danny had wished he had pulled his head out of his ass and helped, Lyndon did not cope with it at all when his mum died and even worse when Dennis died, now Danny had gone blind and Danny felt he thought he was next and they have all left him one after the other and his mind couldn't take it and if he died first or was always in a drunken stupor it would all go away, he needed help and Danny can't force him but he will try to do something. But when he has a lot to cope with himself and Danny is blind what can he do? this was frustrating and made Danny feel useless. Well Danny was now feeling so bad he wanted to curl up and die, he could not think of anything to cheer himself up, he was getting more depressed, it was so lucky his youngest son was there to cheer him up from time to time as most of the time Danny was on his own as his wife was always somewhere else, in her sisters or walking the streets anything than being in the house with him and Danny just wanted to get back with his own type and out of the way of everyone else.

Well the time came to get back to the college and Danny was up at about 4am in the morning that's how excited he was, Danny kissed his youngest son Josh and realised he would not see him growing up, not only because of his blindness but because he was sure his wife was waiting to divorce him and with everything else Danny was a wreck and just felt like crying all the time. It was a very hard time for him.

It was as Danny got on the train he changed and the reason was that Danny heard a voice he had not heard for a while, yes his good mate and a person who would cheer anyone up just by his laugh. Niel said "Hello mate, how's things mate? I was hoping we would meet up on this train, how did Xmas go then?" Danny looking solemn "Not too good I had more worries piled on me as if I didn't have enough to worry about. My young brother is a alcoholic and it is serious, he won't get help and I don't know what to do." Niel looking concerned for Danny says "So he is following your footstep then, no I am only joking, but Dan you must not punish yourself as he must make the move to put it right, he is not going to listen to you and nagging him to do something won't do it. Try and get his wife and you to get together with him and talk it out, then you may get somewhere." Danny "Yes your right, I will phone the old cow tomorrow and see what we can come up with, so how was your xmas?" Niel smiling "It was just what the doctor ordered, I had loads of cuddles with Ceri and the boys, it was a good xmas and I am ready to rock now, I am well rested after the father xmas thing, never again, I mean it." Danny chuckling says "Oh my god it was so funny, I laughed for days after that, did you know Jeff and I found Clamper sleeping behind the settee in the common room, it was so funny, he didn't mean anything with it." Niel also smiling says "No I know he didn't, I was to blame I was so drugged up with sleeping tablet's I didn't know where I was, I couldn't keep my eyes open at all, it was Impossible and as regards Clamper I must buy him a pint to apologise ha, ha." Danny "Well I wonder what that dopey cockney has been up to and who is the lucky girl this month. He can't wait to get back to college. He told me on the phone he will be back before us and I expect Winnie is going to be waiting on the door for me." Niel "Yes I know she is, I don't know why you don't take her out a few times and don't tell me because you are married because you and I know your wife is going to leave you and I think if she was asked out she would do it behind your back." Danny looking agitated snaps at Niel "Why what have you heard? tell me." Niel looking shocked says "I haven't heard anything, I am just saying after what you have told me we don't know what is going on, do we?" Danny looking sad "No I suppose not, I slept in a bed on my own when I was home, she said it was because of my snoring but I hardly went out and I only snore bad when I have had a drink, I also believe she is carrying on behind my back mate and my life has just stopped." Niel looking nervous said "Now wait mate I never accused her of carrying on, I just think it is possible, so don't listen to me I sometimes talk crap." Danny now smiling says "What do you mean sometimes? no I just as well face reality it is just about all over and find some happiness somehow and I might take Winnie out, she is a cracker mind." Niel says "From what I hear I don't blame you, she is described as a cracker, a great body and very pretty." Danny "And very strong, she gave me a total all over massage and nearly killed me, I have not long got over it. But matey it done me the world of good, honest." Niel smiling and happy for Danny says "There we go then, enjoy, fancy a cup of tea? the trolley is here." Danny "Oh yes why not." Niel ordered tea for them both and continued. "So have you heard anything to make you believe that Angie is carrying on?" Danny looking down "Well it's a combination of things. Craig my stepson came home for a visit from Wolverhampton and he told a man to get out of the house so I am told by my neighbours and it's a man who lives down the road, but it maybe just me thinking the worst, I don't know." Niel "Your just being suspicious Dan, your mind is working overtime I think, everything is making you suspicious, you need to calm down I fear you will have a nervous breakdown if your not careful, so calm down mate." Danny "Yes you maybe right, I am jumping to conclusions, I must chill out a little. Do you know I felt like a fish out of water down there over xmas, I just didn't feel I belonged there since being up this college and not having to worry about people who can see, I am with mostly blind people and feel right at home, it's funny." "Yes I know what you mean Dan, I feel normal in the college, not that I feel lost at home but when I go out and things like that happen, but it's Impossible to live in the blind world all of the time, some day you will have to get back in the real world as you know." Danny realises this and says "Yes I know what you mean, oh well we must just get on with life and hope for the best, I have been blind now for 2 years and still can't get used to it. I suppose it will take many years and sometimes I dream it's all a dream and I will wake up and be able to see and get into my car and go out for the day as normal persons do and then I wake up for real and realise I am still blind and will never see again." Niel sounding worried says "Now calm down Dan it's getting to you, you never know Dan it may happen for you one day so let's wait and see, I am a pessimist and never rule anything out." Danny being serious says "Well we will see mate."

Back at the college and it is just after tea and they are all in the common room chatting Danny said "Anyone up for a drink up the student bar tonight?" Jeff "Is Jordan a female? I will be there." Winnie" I will come up with you if you like." Danny "I like." She gives him a big smile. Niel "I will come up for a couple, anything for a bit of peace." Carol Agrees to so off they went.

In the bar and Jeff was cuddled up to Carol and he started to charm her "Hi I can make more money than you can spend, there's a gap in your life, do you mind if I fill it? I am like vitamin C I do your body good, I have a twelve inch tongue and I can breathe through my ears." Carol stops him "Uncle Jeffrey now be good I warn you." Jeff "Your so gorgeous I want every bone in your body including mine." They all started laughing and Carol went red, Carol slaps Jeff and he shuts up, he is pushed out of his chair and moves over by Danny to escape. Danny says "Don't sit by me, I don't want to hear your chat up lines." Jeff "I wouldn't chat you up if I was queer, so don't worry matey." Niel joins in "I don't think he would want you to chat him up if he was gaye mate, us Welsh people are fussy you know." Jeff "I am just glad I am not a sheep shagger." Danny "Steady mate don't go there." Jeff says to Danny "God matey, you are dull tonight, smile for goodness sakes, what's the Matter with you? get some beer down you and cheer up." Danny "Sorry mate I can't get my brother off my mind I wish he would get some help with the alcohol problem, I just can't get him out of my head." Jeff "Well it might be a good idea if you phone him regularly and speak to him, because he might open up a bit on the phone because he cannot see you face to face it might be easier for him, what do you think?" Danny yes that might be a good idea I never thought of that, I'll try it tomorrow." Next thing Winnie speaks up and says "I cannot understand people who drink all day and night, it makes me ill if I only drink a few in the evening, why do the British do it?" Danny "I think he does it and many others to escape from their problems and it makes everything seem better than it really is." Winnie "But the problem is still there when you wake up the next morning, they should ban alcohol all together." Danny "I agree it's true we drink too much and I wonder how they used to manage before alcohol was invented? what did they do for instance I wonder." Jeff say "I couldn't Imagine it without beer, there would be nothing to do but stay in bed, I say ban beer and we can all go to bed and find something to do." He looks straight at Carol and she senses it and said "Don't go there uncle Jeffrey." Danny smiling says "Now that makes sense, well Niel how are things going in the braile class?" Niel "Brilliant I love it and I can braile up to J in the alphabet now, not bad and I can even feel the dots better now, how are you doing? Dan." Danny answers "I am getting there and am having extra classes now from this week on and the girls are wonderful aren't they?" Niel "Yes I love them all. Margaret is leaving soon she is retiring and I will miss her and bubbly Chris and Ginny they are lovely aren't they?" Danny "Yes and they are so funny and like a joke or two, I have named them the Braile Babes and they love me calling them that." Niel says "Yes I think it's apt they do a good job in there." Danny "Don't they? they are so dedicated to their job and take it serious and so organised they are brilliant, I have them tomorrow and I am in there with Tim, we have a good laugh." Niel "Oh god yes he loves the braile girls too and talking about Tim have you seen him? I wonder where he is." Danny wondering says "Yes I wonder to, he has not come back yet, I hope he is allright." Jeff butts in "Yes I haven't seen him either he will turn up." Danny "Right time for a pint, get them in Jeff." Jeff gets up and goes to the bar. Winnie moves closer to Danny and says to him "I am a braile reader and can give you help if you like with it." Danny with a huge smile "Well thank you, I will probably take you up on your offer, thanks." Winnie "We can do it any time you like, just let me know." Danny with a devilish smile says "Yes but what about the braile?" Winnie looking flustered "What do you mean? I am not talking about anything else but braile." Danny "Of course I will help you with your English as I know you are looking for someone to help you with your spelling and vocabulary, so I am at your disposal." Winnie looking confused says "What does disposal mean?" Danny "In other words I am always ready to help at any time, I don't think we will get any peace though in the common room, so I suggest we do it in our rooms." Winnie looking nervous says "Oh I don't think it is a good idea, in my country it is not permitted so let me think about this." Danny says "Ok I will wait for you to think about this." Winnie smiles in a way that she has already made her mind up. Winnie then says "Do you want a massage tonight?" Danny "I will have the head massage if you like and I will have the all over massage on the weekend if you don't mind, as I want to be able to walk for my lectures tomorrow." Winnie laughs and says "Yes you maybe right after last time, but it is your fault for being so unfit, you must exercise more." Niel speaks up "You can give me a massage if you like." Winnie says "I asked Danny not anyone else." Niel "Oh fair enough, don't bother." Jeff says "I am giving Carol a massage." Carol "Are you hell, I wouldn't trust you to give me a massage, thank you." Jeff "Damn crashed and burned again, I will have to get Geraldine to let me give her one instead." Carol looking serious says "Who the hell is Geraldine?" Jeff "She is a lovely girl who is in my advice and guidance class and she is gorgeous and I am in love with her." Everyone looks at him and Carol says "Ah, so I am not your number 1 girl anymore am i?" Jeff "Of course, but I have to keep my options open as I need as much love as I can get." Niel says "I don't think you have got much chance with Geraldine mate but you certainly try with her every day don't you?" Jeff "She is coming around to the idea, in time she will not be able to resist me." Danny says "Do I know her?" Jeff "Yes you know her she is always with Rhoda, she lives in Hereford, she is divorced with 2 lovely children always laughing in cancer corner with Rhoda." Danny "That's Geraldine? I never knew her name but I know she is always jolly and sounds a bit of a laugh." Jeff "Yes that's her and you are right she is a good laugh and she drinks in a pub named the Rose and Crown and she wants us all to go over there one Saturday or Sunday for a few pints." Niel says "That sounds like a good idea and they do meals there too I am up for it." Danny "Yes why not you set it up Jeff and let us know." Jeff "Yes ok matey I will." Carol in a mood says "I will not bother I like to go out with the girls on the weekend." Danny says "What's the Matter? Carol it's nice to have a rival." Carol in bad mood "Now Daniel don't be silly I love my uncle Jeffrey and no girl is good enough for him ha, ha." Jeff smiling says "God I will have them tripping over me now." Danny smirking at Jeff "i can't see you having that problem mate." Jeff "Say you don't know matey."

It's the next day in the braile class and Danny and Tim are already in there and the braile babes were setting things up for the boy's lesson and Danny says to Tim "So where were you yesterday evening? we were all up the student bar and we never seen you at all, have you taken up religion or something?" Tim smiling as he explains "No, no chance, I had a date here with a lovely young lady I have met here, we went down the Rose and Crown for a quiet drink and get to know each other." Ginny chirps up hearing this "There's nice Tim, who is she? do I know her?" Tim "Yes you all know her, I was introduced to her by my tutor Rory, apparently she was fancying me for a while and I liked her to a lot but she was going out with someone else, but now she has got rid of him, and now I am it." Danny "Yes, well come on tell us who it is." Tim "Oh yes of course, it's Mandy the one who has been taking us around the college when we first came here." Ginny "Well that's lovely, is it serious or just a fling?" Tim "Well I hope it is serious I like her a lot." Danny "Well you old dog you, I never, It's nice for you and Mandy is a lovely girl I am glad to see her away from the idiot she was with, I didn't like him at all he was ignorant and right up himself, Lee was his name I remember now and so she is with you now, never mind aye." Tim snaps "What do you mean never mind? you cheeky git." Danny laughs "I am only kidding mate, I am so pleased for you, I remember you saying to me you found it hard to chat up a girl and you found it hopeless to find a girlfriend, so how did it happen?" Tim sounding excited says "Well I can blame Rory he was the match maker or it might never have happened, he was great with the both of us." Ginny Well that's nice for you, I am so glad and when are you seeing her next?" Tim "Lunch time we are together now all the Time." Ginny looking very happy said "Oh good I am so pleased for you I really am." Christine looking all gooi "Well that's a lovely story Tim I feel like crying, it's so nice, I hope it all works out for you." Tim "Thanks I am sure it will." Ginny said "Right it's time to do some work at last, so let's have a go at brailing some exercises. Put your name on the top of the paper first and we will continue." They had done as she asked and then continued until they had filled the page with narrated braile. Well Danny had a problem with some of the braile as it was something Danny just could not remember, if you can Imagine the number six on a dice that's how brail is formed all from the six dots as you see them. Well if you Imagine using the dots from top left and the top dot is dot number 1 the middle one underneath is 2 the one under that is no 3 and back up to the top on the right is no4 under is no 5 and the last one under that's no 6, then that's how you work out the brail letters to match with our alphabet. But Danny used to get his letter F which is dots number 1 2 4 and letter D which is dots 1 4 5 the opposite, well Danny had made the same mistake with this paper and this was to be one of the funniest things Danny had ever done. Well they finished the exercise and handed the papers to Ginny and Ginny is also blind and can read brail very fast and accurate and this is what happened . Ginny starts reading their papers and suddenly burst out laughing hysterically and they could not get a word out of her at all and everybody started laughing and they didn't know why but it sounded funny then she stopped laughing long enough to explain and said "I am afraid Danny you will have to do it all again." And started laughing uncontrollably again. Danny said "Why? what is wrong with it?" Ginny sat back and explained "What is your name?" Danny replied "It's Danny Duckfield why?" Ginny said "Well you have put Fanny Fuckdielf as you have got the F and your D's mixed up again." As Ginny finished the whole room erupted in laughter. After the laughter died down Danny said "I don't believe I did that, I never knew my name would come out like that so funny, so funny." Tim wiping the tears from his cheek says "Brilliant, brilliant, I thought that was classic, only you could do that." Christine "Ha, ha, ha, ha, that was so funny, I don't believe it, so funny, this is something we can't hold back and must tell everyone it's so funny, Danny only you could do this ha, ha, ha." Danny started telling a story "My next door neighbour is partially deaf and one day we were talking in the garden over the wall between us and I began to tell him a long drawn out story about when we were children, I was talking for about 15 minutes and then my wife stood behind me and said "Who are you talking to?" I said "Leighton next door." She said "He has gone in about 10 minutes ago." People had been passing back and forth and must have thought he has finally gone mad, he's talking to himself now. My neighbour thought I had finished talking because I was talking quiet and he could not hear me so went in to do some work. I felt a right fool and wonder if that's why a lot of people have started to ignore me." Christine said in amazement "What do you mean ignore? your kidding aren't you?" Danny "No I am serious, since I have gone blind many of my so called friends have stopped talking to me for no reason other than I have gone blind, honest." Tim "Yes I can vouch for that, I have had similar things happen to me but my real friends have stuck with me but many have not, I think it is because they see you differently and really don't know what to say." Ginny "Yes I have had similar things, it's strange." Danny "I felt hurt by it all and it made me uneasy with people even my wife changed and some family that's why I am sure I am going to be divorced by her, but in a way I can understand it, it's hard to explain but I am prepared for it, it's just the wait for it to happen is the hard bit." Tim "You can't tell for definite, perhaps when she gets used to it, it will change." Danny "No I don't think so it's funny I know for definite because if she had the choice in the beginning as to weather to marry a blind man or someone who is not, she would not hesitate and take the seeing person, you don't see many seeing persons marrying blind people out of choice do you?" Christine says "No you might be right." Tim "And if you were blind it's a case that you tend to hang around with your own kind, like Danny said once he felt like a fish out of water when he went home for a weekend, I have that feeling over xmas." Danny "There you go, I said exactly the same thing to Niel on the train coming back from home the last time." Tim starts to smile again says "Talking about Niel how is he? he is a character isn't he?" Danny "He certainly is, I can't help having a good laugh when he is around." Ginny with wry smile says "Yes since he has started the braile course here it's been a delight with him he don't do much work but can talk a donkey to sleep, but is a very interesting man he really is, he told me about his horse Tommy and how he used to ride it up to his home town Maesteg and leave it outside the shop or pub then ride it home again and when he sold it to someone, the next day the horse had come back and was in the field outside and he lent Tommy to someone who was building a pub up there to pull in the bricks and other materials as you could not get in a lorry. The stories he tells are great I don't know if they are true or not." Danny butts in and says "Oh yes they are true allright, he gets up to lots of things and he is a very stubborn man, when he makes his mind up there is no changing it. A man in a D.I.Y. store once seen him riding his sons motorbike up the lane behind Niel's house as Niel was fixing it and tried it out, he told his mate he didn't think Niel is blind and is claiming money off the government for nothing, so Niel went up to see the man. He went in the D.I.Y. Store and said "So you say I can see and I am lying do you?" Niel then took out his false eyeballs and shook them in his hand, the men gasped and stood there speechless and their customers were horrified, then Niel turned on his heels and walked out, a true character." Christine looking lovingly says "Well we love him in here, he is a breath of fresh air." Tim laughs out loud and says "Remember when we went into that bar in town it was full and we could smell drugs and Niel and Jeff had the idea of using the dogs as sniffer dogs and walked in saying find the drugs, find the drugs and the room emptied." They all started to laugh. Danny "I have had so much fun since going blind with things that happen to me, it wasn't funny when I first went blind mind, I was a right misery

154

but now I could write a book about this place alone." Ginny "You ought to write a book, why not?" Danny "Me write a book, I wouldn't know where to start, and I can't write my name in braile right so what chance do I have." Tim "Well you could start with Niel." Danny "That would be a book on its own, my family met him once when we were on a campsite in Carmarthen and it was the first time my young son Josh met him. He was only 8 and we were sitting outside his caravan on a few plastic chairs and my son was balancing back on the back 2 legs and Niel took his eyes out and shook them in his hand, my son said "Yeh, yeh they are marbles not your eyes" then Niel put his eyes in his pocket and using his both hands he opened up his eye sockets and there were just big holes, my son fell backwards off his chair with the shock and my son was horrified and Niel said his sons have friends come up to his caravan to see him and says to him will you take out your eyes and show my brother and this happens regular, he is a damn good laugh but there is a sad side to him also he gets very emotional, he remembers his dads death and his mums like it is printed in his mind and always has a little tear in his eyes for every day of their deaths and he hates his brother because he reckons he fiddled him out of his share of the pub his parents built up and will not speak to him and he is very nasty about the situation and it tends to eat him away sometimes, but he wears his heart on his sleeve and it can be worrying sometimes. I don't think it's good for him and I try and get him off the subject, then again he is a good listener and very good with advice, a really nice man and don't give him a computer he hates them and really gets nasty with them when they go wrong but it's never his fault." Tim "Yes he is a pleasant man to talk to I get on with him really well and when you 2 are together it's manic and I love it and I hear we are all going to the Barrels for a quiz night on Thursdays." Danny "Well do you fancy it? it will be great, it's a fun quiz not a master mind thing, it will be fun and all proceeds go to charity and at the end they feed us." Tim "Really." Danny "Honest, they do and it is next to a nice Indian restaurant if you fancy a sit down." Tim "Count me in and I will ask Mandy." Danny "Done, right what about this paper of mine Ginny? have I got to do it again now?" Ginny "No I have checked and you both need to do them again, it might be a good idea if we keep you together for the first few lessons if Tim don't mind and the time has already gone." Tim "Yes that's ok by me, until this Welshman starts falling behind ha, ha." Danny "He's getting cheeky now he has a new woman in his life, right I am off for my lunch, coming Tim I will escort you to your Lady friend." The lads went off to dinner.

They met up with Mandy outside the refectory and Danny said to her "Well hello Mandy how are you? I was so happy to hear you and Tim are together it's lovely for you both." Tim says "Thanks mate very nice of you to say. Danny said there is a quiz at the barrels in town on Thursday, a fun one for charity, do you fancy it?" Mandy says "I am not fussed on quizzes but you go and have a night out with the boys, you will enjoy it." Tim "Well I will see how I feel Dan." Danny." Danny replies "Ok mate, no problem, I won't hold my breath as you are both madly in love." Tim "Well I will see you later man, I am off to dinner."

Later that night Danny has trouble sleeping and gets very irritable by it and so he thought of putting on some music but he is afraid of waking up the others as the walls are paper thin, so he starts to think about what Ginny said about writing a book while lying there and his mind wanders until he grabs his little hand Sony tape machine. He speaks it on to his machine, he only takes about 20 minutes to think of a poem that would change his life in a way with a strange twist of fate. The next day he has a lesson in his computer class and decides to copy this poem onto paper and made some copies of this and entered it into his documents for safe keeping. Later in a lecture with the very intelligent Lennox, he found he was the only one there and they both could not understand where all the others were, but Lennox asks Danny "Well I don't know what has happened to the others and I don't think it is a good idea for us to do anything if they will miss out on it, so is there anything I can help you with?" Danny replied "No I can't think of nothing, oh wait a minute I have written a little poem do you fancy looking it over? just to see what you think." Lennox "Yes of course I will." Danny hands the paper over to him. Lennox reads it and says "This is very good, when did you write this? when you went blind?" Danny "No I wrote it last night in only 20 minutes, I could not sleep so wrote this as I was bored." Lennox "Well it's very good but needs a few little changes to make it better slightly like the sentences being around the same size." Danny "Do you think so? I thought it was a good first time effort." Lennox "Oh yes it is but there is a little something missing and I can't put my finger on it, but leave it with me if you want and I will look it over before the next lesson if you like and we can make a lesson of it." Danny "Yes ok thanks, I will see you tomorrow." Danny leaves and you could hear Lennox speaking out the words of the poem.

Later Danny was in his room and showed the poem to Zarrine and asked her for her view of this poem. She read it and to Danny's horror she started crying and stood there with her hand on her face. Danny said " Zarrine what's the Matter are you allright? Why are you crying?" Zarrine after a few seconds replied "It's so sad, it really is and it's beautiful Danny, it really is." Danny looking puzzled "Oh come on it's not bad for a first attempt but nothing special." Zarrine wiping tears from her eyes said "I am not joking it is a lovely poem, I have not read nothing like it before, you must show someone, it deserves to be published somewhere." Danny "No I don't think it's good enough, I have got Lennox running his eye over it and he is doing some final adjustments, I will show you it again when he has finished looking over it." Zarrine "Yes please, let me have a look when it is finished please, but can I have a copy of this now to show a couple of people?" Danny "Of course you can." Zarrine "Thank you I will show my husband tonight and tell you what he thinks tomorrow, see you tomorrow." "Goodbye."

Well it was the next day and in with Lennox they went through the poem and had changed it but Danny was not too sure about this and showed it to Zarrine later and Zarrine did not like all the changes just 2 small changes , so Danny decided to make only 2 little changes and put it on his computer and came up with the final finished poem and it read as follows.

You have to be blind to see.
By Daniel Duckfield

The sky was blue, the sea was green
At least it was when last I seen.
The moon was round white-faced with sheen
But that's the way it's always been.
Young children screamed, they laughed they played.
And they would show me what they had made.
All my friends have gone somehow,
I wonder what they are doing now.
My life my love just went that day,
When they took my eyes away.
I felt the devil had struck me down,
And opened hell's doors to let me down.

I wandered in a hopeless fear,
Because my mind was not that clear.
And should there have been a chance that day,
I would have given my life away.
Just then I started to realise,
There was more to life than just my eyes.
The love I had was far too much,
And I would use it as a crutch.
I went to a place with people like me,
Who have their eyes but cannot see.
All the worlds blind children are here,
Who learn to cope with every fear.
They learn to read, to dance, to sing,
And they can do most anything.
Now life and love are back to stay,
Who cares about that awful day.
Because With all the love from you and me,
You would have to be blind to see.

Well Danny had hit the jackpot but was not going to know how much for a few weeks and quite by accident.

Well it's the night of the quiz and none of the students had ever been to the barrels pub and they had heard some disturbing rumours about it, like it was rough and there were huge men in there covered from head to toe in tattoos and they were wondering what they had let themselves in for. Well in the mini bus was Jeff, Danny, Niel and the student president a man named Jimmy, he was a man who had just put his name down and invited a few others who live in Hereford. A man named Mark a lovely man so quiet a true gentleman. So it was in the pub and they all got their drinks and sat down around a table. Danny said "Well it is nice here a bit like a saloon with wooden floors and some very rough people in here." John the president said "Yes it's a little rough, I hope there is no trouble, if there is I am off." Mark says in gentle voice "I don't think there will be any trouble will there?." Jeff "I am ready to go now if you fancy it." Niel says "God, give it a chance it's only 7 o'clock, if it kicks off it will be later when they are all drunk." Danny agrees "I can't see any trouble if there is a quiz for charity they will hardly fight will they?" John "Well the beer is nice indeed I am on the real ale here on the pull it's gorgeous, so I will love this." Danny says "Yes your right and I am going to enjoy myself never mind what, so who is going to do the writing on the paper for the quiz? because I cannot see to do it." Niel "Well I can't obviously " Jeff "I am a hopeless speller so I think John should do it." John " no problem I have it in my hand we must put a name for our team, what shall we put?" All the men started to think and no one could think of anything and the question master turns up and said "Right our subject tonight is horses and horse racing, so I want your team to be something to do with horses as a theme." The lads started to think and Niel suggested "We could be the rear enders." They all said together "No." Danny said "The blind jumpers." Altogether they said "No." Jeff then said "What about the blinkies?" John "No it's blinkers not blinkies." Danny said "No, he is right it is perfect well done Jeff a good play with words, well done, I think it's perfect." Niel "Ha, ha, it is good and I thought he was stupid." Jeff "Well thanks mate." Danny said smiling "The blinkies it is then." The quiz master continued with some questions and the boys were doing well and it was a good night and lots of silly answers were shouted out one question was what is the rarest stamp in the world? and Danny shouted out "Jeff's national insurance stamp." It got a good laugh but all of the quiz was so much fun and at the end the pub sent to all the teams a selection of food that was very nice indeed. After feeding them all the winners were decided but points were deducted from some teams for showing off and points added to teams with poor points because they were accused of having a poor captain and at the end of it all , all the teams were all winners because they all had the exact same final score. Danny "Well I enjoyed that it was very entertaining , a lot of fun." Next the quiz master came up for a chat with the boys. "Hello my name is Steve I am the landlord, it was nice to see you all here tonight, did you enjoy it?" Danny replied first "Yes I was just saying to the lads how much fun it was, a good quiz and the food too was a good gesture, my name is Danny and we also have Jeff, Niel, John and Mark." Steve said hello to everyone and continued "Well we have a good turn out here most weeks and the money goes to charity and some even goes to your college to help pay for foreign visitors to be able to come over here to your college and it works out great." John "Well that's nice to know and we will be sure to come here often ourselves to support it." Steve "That's great I will look forward to seeing you soon then, have a good night, see you later," All the lads wish him goodnight and Danny says "Jeff do you fancy the loo? I am busting." Jeff said "Yes but where is it?" John says "it is down the step over there and on the left." Jeff "C'mon then let's go grab my elbow." The 2 men approached the steps and just before there sat a man who was huge about six foot four and about eighteen stone but it was all muscle and he was covered in tattoos and looked as if he could kill you with just his fingers, as Danny got to the steps he was swinging his cane and the large man thought he was going to fall down the steps and dropped his pint and put his hands out to stop him falling and the pint just shattered on the floor, the man was more concerned about Danny and Jeff hurting themselves more than saving his pint. The man then realised that Danny would have stopped as soon as his white cane touched the edge of the step and the man said "Are you allright mate? I thought you were going to go ass over tip down those steps." Danny said "No I would have realised the step was there, but thanks very much for your concern, I am just sorry you dropped your pint because of me." He replied "Oh stuff the pint, as long as you are ok I can always get another pint, you just take care and I will be happy." Danny said "Well let me get you a pint to say thank you." Man replies "No don't be silly I am ok, you carry on and take care." In the toilet and Jeff said "Well that shocked me that man looked like an animal but he was such a gentleman, he would rather drop his pint than let you fall down the steps, if it was me stuff you I would rather guard my pint." Danny "Well thanks man I love you to, but your right he amazed me how kind he was and that just goes to show how people can be deceiving and we can be wrong about them, I like it here and will not hesitate to come back." The boys finished and Danny went to grab Jeff's elbow and he first rubbed his fingers across his shoulders as if he had a drop of pee on them and Jeff went nuts. "Urgh, you dirty pig, I don't believe you just did that." Danny laughing said "There's nothing on my hands, I was doing it to find out your reaction, my hands are clean." Back at the table and it's nearly time for the mini bus to pick them up and they stand up to go out for it and here comes Steve with a woman, he says " ready for home lads? this is my partner Francine we will come out to the street to see you off." All the lads said hello to Francine and they stand together outside of the pub waiting for the mini bus. Steve and Francine stay there until the mini bus arrived and seen the lads onto the bus .

It was early the next morning and in there for breakfast was Niel, Danny, Jeff and Zarrine. Danny spoke and said "Great night last night, I enjoyed it very much, we went to the Barrels pub for a quiz night and we couldn't believe how nice the people are there but they look like a load of killers but how wrong we were a man even dropped his pint because he thought I was going to fall down the steps and he was like a skyscraper he was huge and covered in tattoos." Zarrine "Good grief, I know there are some tuff nuts drink in there, I would not go in there. Did you enjoy it Jeff?" Jeff replies "Yes I did, as a Matter of fact, the quiz was good I had a few answers." Niel chirped up "And helped us get some wrong, he is like a doubting Thomas he really is." Danny agreed and Jeff says "What do you mean?" Danny takes over "I will tell you what he means, a few times we had the answers and was sure they were right, then Jeff would say are you sure it could be this mind and it is probably a trick question and then we would think the same and change the answer and when the answers were given out we were right the first time but we had changed it because of your doubts, so we shall not be listening to you from now on." Jeff "That's right blame me as usual, ha, ha, ha." Niel "See you are laughing because we are right and John was just as bad sometimes." Danny "Yes he was but what a nice man that Mark was, he was so placid a real nice lad, he just sat there and ate all night and enjoyed the company and a few pints, a nice person." Jeff "Yes he was, well I am off early to see my darling Geraldine." Zarrine says smiling "And who is this Geraldine? I have not met her so you have a new girlfriend." Jeff "I am working on it and she will come around to my way of thinking." Danny says "You have more chance of getting a quiz answer right mate." Jeff "We'll see, I am off see you later." All said goodbye and Zarrine says "I showed that finished poem to Peter my husband and he thinks it is marvellous and very touching." Niel says "Danny has written a poem, I don't believe it, what is it all about? no don't tell me it's about being blind." Danny "Yes it is, it's all about what I felt when I went blind." Niel "Oh I haven't got time for blind stories and people feeling sorry for themselves especially bloody blind and deaf people, they go on and on about it, it's crap." Zarrine says looking shocked "I don't believe you just said that, your blind and there is nothing wrong with someone writing about their blindness." Niel "Maybe not but if you have heard so many as I have you would be sick of it." Danny looking serious said "That's fair enough mate, your entitled to your opinion and I respect it but that does not go for all of us, we are entitled to our opinion also and I didn't write this for pleasure or because I feel sorry for myself, I just tried to capture how I felt and what was going on around me because I went blind." Niel "Whatever mate, I am not interested at all, Zarrine can I ask you to look after Abby for me for half an hour later? as I have someone coming to see me in my room later please." She replies "Yes no problem I can, I will be in here all morning." Niel "Thanks, I will see you all." Niel gets up and goes to his room. Zarrine says to Danny "I wonder what that was all about, he seemed uncaring about blindness." Danny "He is entitled to his view and I mine and if they clash no problem, just get on with your life, that's what I say." Next in trots Lola, she says "Good morning." Danny and Zarrine wished her a good morning and Lola continues "I see last night that Hong Kong fuey was waiting up for you." Zarrine butts in "Who is Hong Kong Fuey?" Danny says "She is being sarcastic, she is talking about Winnie." Lola "Yes and she was looking mad I think, she was waiting for you and I think she stayed up most of the night the poor girl." Danny "I don't think she was waiting for me at all." Lola "Who else was she waiting for then? I think she was a bit pissed off because you went to the quiz and didn't ask her." Danny "I don't think so, you are just stirring it and I am not going to bite." Lola "Ok on your head be it, I am just telling it as it is ta, ta." And off she went. Zarrine says "Why would Winnie be waiting up for you?" Danny

"I think she is after my body as I offered to help her with her English and she offered to help me with my braile, I hope I have not made a mistake." Zarrine "I don't know what to think about that girl at all I can't get close to her, she switches off when I try to talk to her, if I was you I would be careful." "I will but I don't think there is much to worry about I will see you later." Danny goes off to his lectures.

Later that morning and Danny was sitting on the bench outside his dorm and it was very peaceful and all of a sudden someone sat there next to him and Danny said "Hello who is that?" All of a sudden someone jumped and almost choked and said "It's me Winnie." Danny feeling a bit nervous said "Oh hello Winnie I was just having a sit here for a while listening to the birds and resting." Winnie said "I think you need rest after getting drunk last night." Danny smirking says "What do you mean? I wasn't drunk last night." She replies "Well why did you go to bed as soon as you came in?" Danny then says "Because it was 12 30 and I had a early lecture this morning." "You usually come in to the lounge for a few tins of lager, are you trying to avoid me?" Danny "No, no I am not at all, I was just tired, what are you doing now?" Winnie looking suspicious "Why do you want to know this?" Danny "I was just asking if your not doing anything we can go for a walk in the orchard if you like." Winnie looking pleased says "Yes ok I will grab your elbow if that is ok with you?" Danny answers "Yes no problem, i will find the path opposite and there is a few benches down there somewhere, we will find one as there is markers on the path." Off they go and find a bench and sat down, it was so lovely there and the birds were singing their hearts out and Winnie said "This reminds me of the parks in my home town and the sun is nice today, but I am missing home a lot and I am feeling lonely without my friends." Danny looking sad for Winnie said "Oh don't be sad you will get used to it here don't worry." Winnie then pours her troubles out to Danny "I am having a lot of trouble here with a few things and don't know what to do, I just want to go home." Winnie started to cry and Danny felt very sorry for her and said "Oh don't cry, what's the Matter? surely things aren't that bad are they?" He comforts her and she pulled herself together and Danny continued speaking to her "Are you allright now? please tell me what the Matter, is it Lola and Patsy? are they bothering you again?" Winnie says "No, no I can handle them, it's all the promises I had before I came here from this college and they lied to me and you said you would help me with my English and even you told me lies." Danny looking guilty said "Well I have been waiting for you to come and say when you need help and you haven't yet." "You are stupid I was waiting for you last night and today I went to a lecture and an English test and I failed it badly and I wanted some things from town and I have not got any money." At that she started crying again and Danny felt bad, he comforted her and said "Right we will spend some of our free time working out the English and I will get you speaking English like me pretty fast ok and what do you mean you have not got any money? How has that happened then?" Winnie speaking quietly "The college said they would give me money every week when I am here and they have not given me nothing." Danny "Have you spoken to anyone about this?" Winnie looking confused says "I do not know how to do this." Danny snaps "Right let's go and sort this out with whomever Immediately." Winnie "What do you mean?" Danny jumps up and says "Just as I say find out who is the one who is responsible for this cock up and sort them out fast." Off they go Danny in a stinking mood, he goes off with Winnie to student services. On the way Winnie seeming concerned says "Where are we going?" Danny "We are going off to see the main man in this college, he gets things done, Barry Morris he is brilliant." Winnie starts to panic and says "I have a lecture in 15 minutes I must go to it or I will get into trouble." Danny snaps "No you won't I will sort them out, you must sort this money out now not later or tomorrow, now and we will do it together I will not leave you for anyone to say that it will be sorted out in a few days, you have been here for months now and you have not had a penny to live on, it's ridiculous, even I am unhappy about this." Winnie smiles and they go into student services and Barry was there and he said "Mr Duckfield what can I do for you? and it's nice to see you both, my wife has been shouting your praises lately but I don't know why ha, ha." Danny replies "Oh thank you Mr Morris what about?" Barry says "It's about a poem she found while on her cleaning rounds, you must have dropped it and she read it and she was crying for a long while overcome by passion." Barry smiles Danny shocked said "Oh right I must have dropped one in my room, the poem I mean." Barry says "Well I read it and it is very good, she is showing everyone you have become famous." Danny "See I am not a waste of time at all ha, ha." Barry "Well we have only got your word for that, so what is it I can do you for?" Danny stood back and said "Well it's not for me but I have taken it on my back because nothing is getting done about it, you see Barry Winnie has just told me she has not received any money since arriving at this college and that is ridiculous, who do I see about it?" Barry looking shocked says "Oh dear that is unusual you will have to go to the bursary and speak to them and they will tell you what to do, this is stupid but they will sort it out straight away. To get there go to the main doors and turn right follow it all the way to the next set of double doors go through them and it's the first door on the right and the girls will sort you out." Danny says "Thanks Barry I will see you later." Barry "Yes I am missing you already ha, ha, ha."

Danny and Winnie went off to the bursary and spoke to them Danny says "Hello this is Winnie Woo and she has been a student here for a long time now and she is from China and she has not received a penny from this college at all and she needs money urgent now as she needs personel stuff as soon as." The woman replied "Hello my name is Sheila and I don't know what has happened I will look it up now." She sat at her computer and tapped in some things and said to Winnie "Right what is the name again?" Winnie replied "Winnie Woo." Sheila then said "And your tutors name?" Winnie "Lennox Adams." She taps it out on the computer and she says "Oh here we are I have found you but I am afraid an acquisition form has not been received for us to proceed with it and until I receive one my hands are tied I'm afraid." Danny said "I hope your joking this poor girl has not had a penny for months and she still cannot get any?" Sheila "This is unusual I have never seen this happen before, tell me Winnie have you spoken to anyone about this besides Danny like your tutor or Anthea." Winnie says "No I haven't." Sheila "Well that is why and until I get the nod I cannot do anything." Danny looking nasty said "Surely someone should have sorted this out for her she is a foreigner here and if she went to a hotel they would not forget to put towels in her room or give her a key for the room they would make sure it was done, not wait for her to ask this is criminal, can't you give her a bit of money to let her carry on and sort it out Immediately?" Sheila looking uneasy "No I am afraid I cannot you will have to go to Anthea she is the one who has to arrange for her to get some money, she is in her office go and see her now." Danny says "I am on my way this is ridiculous I will sort her out now, thanks Sheila." Back to student services and there was Barry holding his head when he seen Danny coming back he said "Oh dear no luck." Danny "Yes all bad, I need to see Anthea as soon as possible it's urgent and we are not leaving here until I have seen her, it's serious please Barry." Barry "I will go into her office now and speak to her." Danny and Winnie sit down next Barry comes back and told Danny "She has someone with her and if it's not urgent you will have to come back tomorrow, I told her that steam was coming out of your ears and she said oh dear I had better see him in a minute, I hope no one has upset him I have no rooms left to move anyone. So have a minute and she will call you." Danny says "Thank you Barry I owe you one." A few minutes later and Anthea called him and Winnie in to her room. Danny and Winnie sat down and Anthea said in a jolly mood "Right what can I do for you." Danny said "We have been all over the college trying to sort out a problem for Winnie here, she has been here for a long time now and no one here has the decency to arrange for her to get her money from the bursary and she has not had a penny for her personel stuff or anything can you tell me why?" Anthea "And so what has this got to do with you Danny?" Danny said "I found her crying uncontrollably she wants to go home as she does not like the way she is being treated here, she is homesick and not a care in the world has been given to her and I am here to sort it out for her with her permission." Anthea replies "Is this true Winnie?" Winnie nods yes. Anthea continues "Right let me get your personnel things up on the computer " Danny snaps "You don't need a computer to tell you she has not had a penny" Anthea "Here it is yes you should have been having forty seven pounds a week, I don't know what has happened here but I will get it sorted as soon as I can, come back and see me on Friday it should be sorted out by then." Danny said "Oh no we will sort it now and she will have some money now as I think it's bullying and I am going straight to the principle if you don't, let me think know you owe her over three hundred pounds, how would you like it if you had no money for over six months." Next thing Winnie spoke up and said "And you must give me my air fare back you promised." Danny looked at Anthea and said "And she has not had her air fare back yet I think someone is not doing their job I wonder how the governors will take it when I tell them and how much is her airfare?" Winnie says quickly "In English money it's nine hundred and eighty one pounds and I have to send half of the money back to my father " Danny "What, so what can be done today? not Friday, she needs some money to get on with as she is owed over a thousand pounds and I know that she has been awarded the air fare by a charity organisation but it is in the college bank gaining interest while she is going stony broke." Anthea said "I will give you a note Winnie for a hundred pounds to tie you over until I sort it out." Danny "I think four hundred will be better as she needs a lot of things for her to get sorted out Immediately don't you?" Anthea thinks and says "But I will have to go to the bursary and sanction this myself and I am busy. Danny sarcastically says "I think this is too Important to your future don't you?" Next thing Anthea storms off to the bursary and a few minutes comes back with a bundle of notes five hundred pounds in total and gives it to Winnie and Winnie's face just lit up and Anthea said "And I will sort the rest out by Friday for you." Danny then said "I hope so or I will be back with her and thank you for sorting this out for her and now can she have a S.S.W. to take her into town to pick up a lot of things and take her to the bank to put some of it in safe keeping, it will have to be a female one she will only embarrass a male one is that ok." Anthea looking beaten said "I suppose we can arrange that I will send one in a car in a hour is that ok? Winnie." Winnie all excited said "OH yes I will have a shower and I will wait outside on the bench for her, thank you." Danny and Winnie left and Danny walked her back to her room and she said outside her room to him "You are a clever velshman I am more happy now thank you, see you again." She unlocked her door and was just about to disappear and Danny said "That's ok anytime if you have any problems just come and see me." Winnie "Yes I will, you are good to me bye."

Later Danny finds Jeff in the lounge and he asks him "Where have you been? I was out on the bench for a while but you did not turn up." Danny said "I have been helping Winnie to get some of her money due to her, do you know she has not had a penny since she has got here? not even her air fare refunded, I just sorted it out as I found her crying about it, she was eventually owed over a thousand pounds." Jeff shocked says "Bloody hell, matey how did she manage?" "She has had no money at all but I sorted it out and she has just had almost half of it to go shopping and I arranged a S.S.W. to take her in a college car and she was smiling from ear to ear, it was nice to witness that as she has not had much to smile about at all, so she is in town spend, spend, spend." Jeff says "Oh you are a nice man aren't you? I bet she will be all over you now." Danny looking smug says "Yes I think so, she wants me to help her with her English and I said I would, it's a messy job but somebody's got to do it." "And I bet your dreading it aren't you? so it looks as if you will be having a Chinese every night now ha, ha, ha. " Danny still being smug says "Looks like it, as long as I get my pints in i won't mind helping her. So how is it going with Geraldine then?" Jeff smiling says "She is in Rhoda's room a minute, she is looking at something for Rhoda, I think I could settle down there with her, she is nice and very giggly and likes a drink to go with it, my type of girl, I will introduce her when she comes in now." "Ok mate I am having a coffee do you want anything?" Jeff "No thanks I have got a tinny here and I have finished for the day now, what about you?" "I have a lecture but I am not going I am knackered after that fight for justice for Winnie, I am bushed." Jeff said "I should go over and do some paperwork in the Queens building but I can't be bothered." Danny "Only because Gerry is here, look at you, you are like a cat on hot bricks, calm down man you try too hard, let her do the chasing." Jeff acting confident says "I can't take that chance she might not chase me, she thinks I am kidding, so I will do it my way as the song says so please don't louse this up for me will you?" Danny says "I will keep myself to myself, don't panic I had a phone call from my aunty this morning telling me my uncle had a few falls night before last." Jeff looking concerned says "Oh dear, is he allright now?" Danny replies "I think so, he was in the pub in his condition and he was a bit stupid, he got absolutely pissed he could not stand to save his life and my aunt his sister who looks after him said the landlord of the pub got pissed with him and told my uncle it was too late and he had better go home after the last drink. Well my uncle apparently got up off the bar stool and fell flat on his face, he then dragged himself to the front door of the pub and pulled himself up on the door frame and started to walk up the road to his house a few doors away and fell down again well he crawled to his house pulled himself up on his front door frame opened the door and got in closed his door, fell again and pulled himself up the stairs and got into bed safely." Jeff said "My god he must have been really pissed to be in that state and lucky he didn't kill himself but at least he is allright." Danny continued "Yes and my aunty went around there the following morning and found him in bed almost unconscious and she woke him and said to him "You were pissed last night then was you?" He opened his eyes and said "How did you know?" She said to him "Because Vick the landlord phoned me and said you left your bloody wheelchair there again." Jeff and Danny laughed profusely and Jeff said "You dick head I believed you for a minute, that's a cracker, I can't wait to tell that one."

Next in walked Geraldine and Rhoda and Jeff introduced Danny to Geraldine "Geraldine this is Danny." Danny still smiling says "Hello pleased to meet you, I started to panic and shake there for a minute I thought it was my first wife and I had gone to hell, although I have seen or rather heard you about here." In a giggly manner Geraldine says "Hi pleased to meet you, I have seen you about also and i know you are Jeff's best friend here and I know Niel he often speaks about you and when he does he is always laughing." Danny "Yes we all have a good laugh here and even Rhoda of the god squad enjoys a good laugh." Jeff speaks "Yes we are always having fun here, do you want a drink of anything Geraldine?" Ger. replies

"Oh yes please I will have a coffee strong with milk and 2 sugar's thanks." Danny looking shocked "Good grief, I have never seen him making anyone a drink before not even himself, he must be in love or something." Jeff smiles and says nothing but Rhoda says "Yes I suspect he has a thing for our Ger." Geraldine says "Don't be silly Rhoda he is just being nice." Danny says "I'm not saying nothing, so you are in the same course as Jeff, Rhoda and Niel are you?" Ger. "Yes I am I have a good laugh with Niel he is so funny but no patience at all." Danny "No your right he sometimes has his moods but a person you can rely on for a good laugh, I give him a different name every month and he has to guess why I call him that last month it was Mr Potato head and he got it straight away, this month is Dolls eyes and he so far has not guessed it right." Ger. "Is it because he has plastic eyes?." Danny "No." Rhoda "Is it because his eyes stay open when he lies down or something like that?" Danny "No." Ger. "Well tell us we won't split." Danny "No if I tell you I will have to kill you both, it is top secret and it will spoil it for Niel as he has a bit of fun with it, sorry," Jeff says "He won't tell anyone especially me and I am his bestest friend." Danny replies "Especially you as you would tell him straight away, I notice things about people and I just Imagine them as it is." Ger. "So can you see at all Danny?" Danny "I can see light with my left eye a very little but nothing with my right and I can sometimes see shapes but I cannot see you at all." Ger. says giggling "Well I am almost six foot big bust an hour glass shaped body and very good looking and nice legs." Jeff "Yes I agree at least about the boobs and the legs." Danny "And his eyes are not that good I will wait until you are drunk and I usually squeeze the girls asses and that tells me everything I want to know and besides it's personality that counts I believe." Jeff "No, you are just a pervert that's all." Danny "Listen to the kettle calling the pot black, and I think perverts do things to children and people of the same sex in my opinion." Ger. "So you are homophobic are you?" Danny "Oh no, I hope you are not a lesbian or something I meant I think a heterosexual is the real Rolls Royce of the human race and as long as the other don't push it in my face I don't care what they are." Ger. "No I am not a lesbian and never will be, I like my men even if they are sometimes a load of pigs." Jeff "Well I am not a pig." Danny "Yes I stood up for him last week, someone said he was not fit to live in a pig sty and I said he was." Ger. and Rhoda laughed next thing Rhoda spoke up "I went to the cathedral in Hereford on the weekend it was lovely and I joined in the prayers there it was nice." Jeff "Oh Rhoda don't start that dodgy Welshman up on religion again please." Rhoda "Sorry, you might be right pretend I said nothing, you see Ger. he has tried to make me swear since I got here and he will lose, I love my god and I live as I want to." Danny butts in "Just because I am a atheist I don't try and run your god down I just have my beliefs and you have yours I just think I will need proof to believe anything, I cannot live on faith but I do not condemn you at all it's a pity more people are not like you and there would be less trouble in this world." Rhoda " these things happened in the bible what about Noah's ark? they found the remains of it on Mount Ararat there's proof." Danny " Yes and how big was it? it was no bigger than a large yaught and there was then 270 million different species of animals and others etc. on earth and they in pairs got onto that ark did they? that ark would have to be larger than Africa to get them all in it's Impossible and think about all that crap they would produce and just eight people to see to them all it would take them 3 years to feed them all and longer to shovel the shit over the side." Ger. laughing said "And Imagine all that shit floating on the water, god." Danny "Well that's right and do you know what happened to all that shit Ger.." Ger? "No." Danny "Well a few thousand years later Columbus discovered it and named it America." They all started laughing then Rhoda said "What about the walls of Jericho?" Danny "Earthquake." Rhoda "Daniel in the lions den." Danny smiling "He was too tough to eat." Rhoda "The plague, the plague." Danny "He was on fantasy island wasn't he." More laughter and Rhoda said "You celebrate xmas don't you? the birth of Jesus." Danny "No I don't and many other religions don't as he if he existed was not born in December as it has been proved as the shepherds would not be in the fields at that time of the year because it would be to cold and it was put on new year's day originally until someone decided to move it back a few days   so as to celebrate the new year and xmas separately and that's the truth and can be proved everything is not provable at all and that's why all wars are started because of religion and Rhoda yours is no different." Rhoda now looking nasty said "Your just a heathen and I cannot understand why people are like you are." Jeff "Steady Rhoda you nearly used bad language and Danny nearly beat you." Rhoda slapping her legs said "Well he is enough to make a vicar swear." Ger. having a good laugh said "Well, well is it like this all the time here? it is a funny thing to witness, I love it, you will all have to come down to the Rose and Crown by me and we must have a good drink and a good laugh." Danny "Yes I am up for it let Jeff know an I will come down with them, I must be off now my son is due home from school and I want to have a good chat to him on the phone in my room, see you all later I am going up the bar with that daft cockney tonight see you all. " Danny went off to his room and the others continued chatting. Jeff "He don't half go on don't he?" Ger. "I think he is lovely and very tall and a great sense of humour and he has a son so he is married is he?" Jeff looking worried said Immediately " Yes he is and he loves his wife very much as far as I know and very happy as I said." Rhoda "I thought you told me he is getting a divorce and his wife is divorcing him you fibber you." Jeff "Oh yes that's right but I meant to say he is chasing Winnie Woo the Chinese girl sorry." Rhoda "Is he, I never knew that, he is always on his own or with you and he said he was going up the bar with you tonight." Jeff "He never sees her every night that's why, so are you coming up the bar tonight? I heard there is a disco up there tonight it should be good." Ger. "If I can find a baby sitter I will be there." Rhoda "I am going up it should be good." Ger. "I will phone a baby sitter when I go home, I can't see no problem at all, so what time are you going up?" Jeff about eight o'clock I expect." Ger. "No Jeff I meant Rhoda." Rhoda smiling says "Oh I am going up about eight to eight thirty." Ger. "I will get a taxi to here and go over with you then." Rhoda "Ok I will be ready and I have got some Bacardi in my room, we will have a few before we go over." Ger. "Good thinking Batman, I am up for that and Jeff get your dancing boots on I want a dance tonight matey and I will try and get the dodgy Welshman out for one too." Rhoda "Oh yes, one what?. " Ger. "Mmm a dance, what do you think." Jeff looking worried says "Him dance, I don't think so, huh, I only dance mind when I have had a good drink and then I can dance all night, I am like John Travolta, no problems." Next in walks Niel and Abby Ger. calls Abby and she starts to wag her tail wildly and Ger. Says "Hello girl how are you then? your lovely girl aren't you." She pats Abby and Niel says "Hello Geraldine lost your way? ay, but it's nice to see you out of lectures for a change. " Ger. "Yes Niel I thought to come and see how the other half lives and I met your dodgy Welshman as Jeff calls him, he seems nice enough." Niel "Oh dear you have, have you, he is a nutter and so funny him and Jeff are like cabbage patch dolls and always pissed together it's so funny never a dull moment, I get on brilliantly with him and his wife is lovely it's a pity she is going to divorce him, I always thought they were well suited, but there you go." Ger. "So he is getting divorced is he? he is very nice." Niel "Nice he maybe but beware he has a ruthless side to him too, he won't suffer fools lightly, so I can't understand him hanging around with Jeff, only kidding mate and he misses his sons and daughters a lot and is having trouble with is younger brother who is a alcoholic and

Danny is worrying about a lot, he has his hands full at the moment, but I know that man and he will get through it. He is made of stern stuff, nothing will phase him." Rhoda "Oh I didn't know about his brother, there's a pity isn't it." Niel "Yes it is he is very, very close to him, they did everything together and he is pulling his hair out about it all." Ger. "How many children has he got then?" Niel "He has 3 girls and 3 sons, mind one of his sons is adopted and he lost his first son, a cot death, he was nearly seven months old and he has not been the same man since it happened, I know his ex-brother in law and he told me he turned after the death of his son, he has had a terrible time since he was about eight his father was a Jehovah's witness and was not a nice man then he was secretly courting a lovely girl for several years and when she was nearly fifteen she got run down by a car and killed and only 2 years ago his other brother Dennis who was a lovely chap and he was mentally retarded died of a massive heart attack." Rhoda "Oh my god just a list of tragedies no wonder he don't believe in god, the poor man." Ger. "Well he seems a strong man considering, I don't know what I would do if I lost a child to cot death especially if it was six months old, how sad. Well I will cheer him up tonight and get him dancing with me and that Jeff." Niel "Of course the disco tonight I will probably come up tonight but I am not drinking with you and Danny mate and please don't tell him I told you all I did, he don't need to be reminded about tragedy ok?" All of them agreed and Jeff was looking so sad and thought he had no chance with Ger. now but took it in his stride. Ger said to him "What's the Matter Jeff? you look sad and that's not like you." Jeff starts to smile and says "Oh I am ok I was thinking about Dan and all the trouble he has and Niel didn't even mention that his mother and his father also are dead, I don't know what I would do if all that happened to me, I wouldn't know if I could take it all." Rhoda said "My god he must be the only one left of his Immediate family except his younger brother of course, how much bad luck can one person take, he must be very strong minded and yet he is always cracking jokes it must be his escape I suppose." Jeff says "Maybe your right we are lucky, so I feel like getting a few sherbets down me now, I feel depressed like his young brother I hope he gets himself together for Danny's sake and do you know probably that is what is wrong with his brother he is on the verge of cracking and has turned to the booze for comfort, what a pity." Ger. "Yes you can say that again, I would crack up to, well we must keep our chins up for Danny's sake I am off, I must get a bus home and get sorted for tonight, see you all, I will see myself out, bye all." They all say goodbye and Rhoda looking so sad said "It's a funny old world isn't it ? I think you are very fond of our Ger, and I think you are worried she fancies Danny I could see it in your face earlier." Jeff "Yes I am very fond of her indeed but I can't stop her if she fancies someone else can I? but I am used to it I suppose." Rhoda tries to comfort Jeff "I don't think Danny is the type to step on his mates toes, I think he would turn her down for you as he is your friend so don't worry."

It was later on that evening and up the bar and Danny and Jeff were propping up the bar and Jeff was half drunk and Danny says "I think that Geraldine is a very nice person when I met her I can see why you fancy her now, very nice indeed." Jeff says "Do you really think so?" Danny replies "Yes a nice personality and very chatty and likes a joke, very rare in a woman." "I really like her indeed , I can't stand here much longer let's find a seat before I fall down." The lads go and find a large table and sit down. Danny says "I think you should slow down with the drink or you will be on your ass before she gets here." Jeff now wobbling a little says "Awe I am allright I can drink for England you know." Danny looking stern "Well I don't think Geraldine will be very Impressed if you are pissed do you?" Jeff looking sorry for himself "Yes your probably right, I really like her you know." Danny smiling says "Yes I know and I think I can see a little glint in her eyes for you." Jeff eyes lit up and he said "Yes, you maybe right, I am going to have a coke want one?" "Get out of here, I have only had one drink I am not half cut I will have a Newcastle brown please." Next thing Rhoda and Ger. came in and sat by Danny and Geraldine sat next to Danny as tight up to him as she could get and Rhoda went up to the bar and got themselves some drinks and Immediately returned and said "Jeff has offered to get them in, have you and Jeff been here long? Jeff looks drunk." Danny "This is going to be my second drink but you are right, Jeff has been on it all afternoon I think to pluck up courage to chat up you Ger." Geraldine looked shocked "Oh right, I see but I don't think so we are just mates don't be silly." Danny "Ok if you say so." Rhoda "Well he definitely has a crush on you I know it." Ger. "Oh, right well he is coming back now so drop the subject." Jeff arrived with the drinks and he saw Ger sat close to Danny and looked a little upset and sat opposite her and said "Ok are you allright Geraldine? I am drinking coke as I drunk a little too much this afternoon so that's why the coke." Ger. "Yes I was wondering if it was all coke but I can see you are a responsible drinker that's good." Jeff "Yes that's me, well it's a good disco and some good dancing music." Danny "To early for me to dance I will have a few more before I have a dance." up to the table came Niel and said "Hello guys, having a good night, I left Abby over my room as she will dance all night, I'm not Joking she loves music, Ceri my wife always dances with her in the house and she loves it, not a bad pint of cider in here tonight and Danny where is your little China girl?" Danny replies "I don't know in her room I expect ,I haven't seen her since I packed her off to town this afternoon, I am not seeing her you know." Niel "Not yet but I will give it a fortnight she is nuts over you I can tell." Jeff loving this conversation butts in "Yes she definitely fancies you and she Is gorgeous and a cracking body to go with it and there is a lot of guys chasing her so don't leave it to long." Danny smiling "What are you on about I am not seeing her or courting her and nothing is happening with us 2, I am just helping her with her English and that's all, so give it a rest." Geraldine says "I have seen her, yes she is beautiful and very cute and a models body, I heard she used to model in China, some people get all the luck ay." Danny "Give it a rest I helped her out with a problem and now everyone is taking it the wrong way and she is only 28 I am nearly old enough to be her father." Jeff said "You are nearly old enough to be her grandfather." Everyone laughed and Danny said "Very funny, I am splitting my sides, so Rhoda do you want to join in and have a go at me maybe one from the bible for good measure." Rhoda "Daniel I will not bite and neither will I curse but I will have a dance with you later, I am hopeless and will love it when I step on your toes ha, ha. I look forward to the experience with great pleasure." Rhoda "Well thank you Daniel." Niel chuckling "And if you don't tell me why dolls eyes this month I am going to crack up, I cannot think why for the life of me." Geraldine says "Yes I have been racking my brain about that one also and can't think why." Niel "God everyone knows and is trying to think why he calls me that and it is driving me mad ha, ha, ha." Danny says "I am going off for a wazz I must have one." Off he went and Jeff jumps into his seat Immediately and starts up with his chat up lines to Geraldine "I am looking for treasure can I have a look at your chest? If you take me home I will do breakfast, how do you like your eggs, poached, scrambled, fried or fertilised? (Geraldine was now laughing and Jeff was smiling lovingly) I am going to name one of your legs xmas day and the other new year's eve, can I visit between the holidays? I ain't no Fred Flintstone but I can make your bedrock." They by now were all laughing their heads off and Jeff was pulling faces at Geraldine and Jeff loved it . Niel said "Bloody brilliant and so funny never a dull moment is there?" Danny returned and sat where Jeff was sitting and asked

"What's so funny then?" Niel " that daft bugger and his chat up lines, so funny." Danny "Oh god, he is at it again is he? yes they are funny and the way you do them." Ger. "Yes I get them all the time in the lectures, he never stops." Jeff "Would you have sex with strangers?" Ger. "No way." Jeff "Well let me introduce myself." Everyone laughed again. Ger and Jeff went out and had a few dances and Jeff was having a great time with Geraldine and Danny, Niel and Rhoda were laughing. Danny to Niel "Well you are a little happier now compared to this morning." Niel "Yes I am sorry about that I was just a bit miserable and having a lot of trouble with my I T lectures, I just can't get it right and want to pack it in and they said if I do I will not have enough subjects on my agenda to let me stay here and I will have to leave and that is what the lecturer said to me this morning in my room, so I might be leaving soon." Danny "And why can't you do another subject then?" Niel "There are no places they are all taken and I don't know what to do." Danny "And who is taking you at the moment in I T?" Niel stern faced said "Oh a Mr Marsh and I just can't seem to grasp the subject at all with my dyslexia no way and I don't want to leave." Danny "Can I ask you in all your lectures how many male lecturers have you got?" Niel "Only him all the others are women, why?" Danny "Well you used to have I think about 4 didn't you, if I remember right, yes I'm sure you did." Niel "Yeh, so." Danny "And you have got rid of them one at a time and replaced them with women, doesn't that tell you something?" Niel "No, what does it tell you then? because I bet you are dying to tell me." Danny "Oh if you are going to get nasty I am not going on with this conversation." Danny turns away and sips his drink and Niel says "Fair enough, you seem to think you know everything and you don't so come on tell me if it is not the case I will tell you what I think, come on." Danny said "Why are you getting nasty I am only trying to help, forget it your on your own mate, I have enough problems of my own see you." Danny drunk up and left and Niel sat there fuming next thing Rhoda spoke up " Are you allright Niel?" Niel "Aye, I wish people would keep their opinions to themselves, I don't tell them what I think they should do, do I?" Rhoda "Actually Niel , you do all the time and if you want my advice I think you were wrong the way you spoke to Danny, he was only trying to help." Niel still fuming says "Oh there we are then." Jeff sat down and Ger. was behind him Ger said Danny gone for another wazz then?" Niel "No he has gone back to Dowdell, I just put him in his place and he has gone off pouting, good riddance." They all went quiet for a moment and Ger said again "Pity I was going to have a dance or two with him, never mind." Rhoda says "Yes I was looking forward to treading on his toes, I will have to tread on Jeff's and Niel's instead, fancy a dance anyone?" Jeff "Not me I am knackered dancing with this lovely one, Niel is still only on his first pint and he won't have a dance until he has a few more." Niel snapped "Yes my darling I would love to dance with you." Rhoda and Niel got up and went out to dance and Ger says to Jeff "What was that all about I wonder." Jeff replies "Probably that dodgy Welshman said something to Niel and Niel put him in his place, he had a go at Danny this morning about something or other, but I don't know what is going on." Ger "I am staying out of it, so fancy a drink or what?" Jeff "Or what? only joking I will have a pint of lager please, thank you." Jeff was left there sat on his own and all of a sudden a voice says. "Uncle Jeffrey is that you?" Jeff kept quiet and hoped she was not coming to sit by him and spoil the chances for him with Geraldine, so he kept silent but Carol was persistent and spoke again "Uncle Jeffrey is that you? I know you are there, uncle Jeffrey what are you playing at, I heard you." Jeff looking annoyed says "Oh hello gorgeous hows you then?" Carol says "Is there a seat by you for little old me?" Before he could say anything he was being pushed and she sat in Geraldine's seat and Jeff looked dejected and said "I was wondering where you were tonight I have been with my mates from the advice and guidance classes you know Rhoda from our block and I will introduce you to my other friend she is coming back with the drinks." Geraldine came back and sat on the opposite seat and never commented about the loss of her seat but Jeff looked as if he had lost a thousand pounds. Jeff introduced Ger "Geraldine this is Carol, Carol this is Geraldine." Both women said hello and then Ger said "So how do you know Jeff then?" Carol said in a childish voice "Oh he is my little uncle Jeffrey and I am his very bestest girl aren't I uncle Jeffrey?" Jeff just sat there with a dumb smile on his face and Geraldine rolled her eyes and said "Are you her little uncle Jeffrey then?" Jeff looked heaven would and chuckled "Looks like I am, don't it?" Jeff said no more as he did not want to stuff his chances up with Carol in case Ger did not want to know, then Carol said "If I give you the money uncle Jeffrey will you go up to the bar and get me a drink sweetie? thank you darling." Jeff said "Yes I will get it don't worry about it." Carol never even made an attempt to get any money out of her purse and Jeff went off to the bar for her drink. On the dance floor and Niel and Rhoda was dancing and they went near to the kiosk of the disco and all of a sudden the speakers went funny and it was picking up the local police control centre and a woman was saying car " s22 please go along to the rose and crown and tend to a drunken disturbance " Rhoda just looked at Niel and wondered what was happening and Niel moved away from the speakers and it stopped and Rhoda looked even more puzzled. Meanwhile back at the table Carol said to Ger "So have you been here long in the college?" Geraldine not really wanting to speak to her said "Four years off and on, I live in the town with my 2 children." Carol "So you are married then?" "No divorced and happy on my own to." Carol replies "Oh it suit's some people, I am trying to get Jeff off the fags it's awful, I am trying to find his tobacco on the table, he must have it in his pocket but I will get it later." Ger looking surprised said "Why do you need to make his life difficult?" Carol replied "He should not be smoking it's bad for you, and it's fun, he laughs about it." Ger "As long as you don't touch my fags that's ok, I am surprised he puts up with it, so are you and Jeff a couple?" "He would love to think we are but just really, really good friends, he tries hard mind to get me into bed and once accidentally got his hand in my bra and it's harmless fun really, but I won't let anyone hurt him mind." Ger "Oh there we are then, he must be a little horny man then as he is trying to get me in bed also and he has no conscience, but he is lovely." Jeff turns up with Carol's drink and sit's back in a seat by Ger and Carol said "Uncle Jeffrey why are you sitting over there? am I smelling or what?" Jeff looking annoyed says " no I am off to the loo now and I will sit by you when I get back." He gets up and leaves Ger says to Carol "You sound like a girl who likes to get her own way never mind what?" Carol "No, not really, I just didn't understand why he went over there as he always sit's by me and gives me a load of silly chat up lines." Ger "Funny you should say that I was getting a lot of chat up lines off him before you came in, so I think we have a man who wants every woman he can get, aye." Carol smiling says "Yes, that's our uncle Jeffrey and if another gorgeous woman sat here he would be all over them as well, he is always the same." Ger "Well I am not interested in a man at the moment, I have got enough trouble with my course to keep me going, so you can have him." Carol "I love him to bit's but in my own way and love him as a real good friend, so where is his side kick the dodgy Welshman?" Ger replies "He has fallen out with Niel and has gone home and Niel is dancing with Rhoda and here is Jeff, hi mate." Jeff says "Hello I am back and sitting by you Carol, I know how lonely you get so I am here, so what have you girls been saying about me?" There was a silence and then Ger spoke "Nothing why do you think we are talking about you? we were talking about Danny and what has happened to him tonight." Carol "Uncle Jeffrey this world does not revolve

169

around you, so what happened with Danny and Niel?" Jeff "We don't know we were out dancing but I can tell you Niel is not in a good mood at all, so there we go." Niel returning from the dance floor heard Jeff saying this and said "What did you say? i am in a bad mood, I don't think so I am just pissed off with people talking behind my back." Jeff tries to explain "No mate I was asked where Danny was and I said you and him fell out and he has gone back to his room and yes I said it put you in a bad mood." Niel "Yes, right, Danny wants to keep is nose out of my business and get on with his own life." Carol "Oh dear I hope this is not going to spoil the night, I came out for a relaxing night after this week's lectures, c'mon let's have a good drink up." Ger says "Well I am half pissed now, that's that, Bacardi Rhoda? God." Rhoda "Well you did hit it hard you should have taken your time, like me."

It was later that night back at the lounge in Dowdell and Danny and Winnie was watching TV and Ger, Rhoda, Jeff and Niel came in a little worse for wear and Danny was sipping a whisky and said "Hello, have a good night?" Jeff "Yes, what happened to you then?" "I came back for a quiet night and have a head massage off Winnie." Jeff "Oh hello Winnie, I didn't hear you over there, I hope things are ok now Danny told me about this college, what a load of plonkers they are." Winnie said "Yes but my Danny sorted them out, I went to town and bought some things I needed and I am happy now, thank you." Ger says "Hi Winnie I am Geraldine nice to meet you." Winnie says "Yes nice to meet you also." Niel says to Winnie "Hello I am Niel nice to meet you Winnie." Winnie says harshly "Niel, don't be silly, I know who you are silly man." Niel smiled. Ger "Rhoda go and get that Bacardi and we can have a drink and I will get the next bottle." Jeff "I am going to get some tinnies." They both went off and came back with the goods and Rhoda poured out a drink for Ger and asked Winnie "Winnie do you want a Bacardi? if you like vodka you will like this." Winnie "Yes please." Rhoda "Niel do you want one? " Niel "No thanks I don't like Bacardi thanks." Danny said "There's whisky here Niel if you want one." Niel answers sarcastically "No, not for me thanks." Danny "Anyone else want one help yourselves." Jeff was clowning around and having a good laugh, he then said "I am going for a ciggy, anyone else coming?" Rhoda and Ger went with him to his room for a fag and next thing Niel says "I will see you all in the morning, I am off." and off he went and left just Danny and Winnie there. Winnie said "What is the Matter with Niel? he is not very nice man tonight." Danny says "I don't know, he has been funny all day and he is very touchy with me, I don't know what I have done but he can please himself, just because he can't get his own way in this college he picks on everyone and it's never his fault." Winnie "So he is nasty?" Danny "He is like a little child if he can't get his own way." Next thing a voice came from behind Danny "Oh I am, am I?" It was Niel, he had said he was going to bed but he just opened the door and closed it as if he had gone to bed, but he had not left the room and just stood in the corner out of sight and kept silent and listened to them and what they were saying behind his back, he continued. "Childish am I? And like to get my own way do I?" Danny said "Well I'm right aren't I? and to add to it a snooper to, I don't understand you." Niel now fuming said "Your not happy unless you are poking your nose into somebody's business that's your problem, I ought to smack you in the nose." Danny "Yeh, you and who's army mate? I tried to help you out and that's all I done and you got nasty and you did the same this morning, what's the Matter mate? no one paying enough attention to you, if not go and pick on someone else." Niel "Not enough attention is it, well let's pay some attention to you outside, c'mon I will sort you out, don't think I am afraid of you." Next thing Danny stood up and they were toe to toe and shouting threats at each other Danny said "I won't come outside with you as I don't want to hurt you." Niel "Do you think so? and whose army are you going to bring with you?

I am not afraid of you mate c'mon let's go." Next thing Winnie was running down to Jeff's room. She found them and said whilst puffing "Please quickly come and stop them, they are going to kill each other." Ger said "Who?" Winnie "Danny and Niel they are shouting and going to fight." At that Jeff and the girls ran back into the lounge and Danny and Niel were still toe to toe and getting very nasty and still shouting loudly. Jeff ran up to them and got between them and it looked so funny as Jeff was so tiny compared to them and he shouts "Right that's enough you two, stop it you are frightening the girls now, sit down, Danny back in your seat and Niel please cool down and have a breather." Danny and Niel sat down but were still arguing Niel shouts "I am not afraid of you Danny, you may bully the others and be the big man, but I am not afraid of you." Danny replies "This is all down to you mate and I am glad it's you or I would knock your head off." Niel "Yeh c'mon then let's go outside then and sort it out man to man." Danny shaking his head "No Niel I don't want to hurt you, we are friends and I will be sorry if I beat you up." Niel "You think so? I am not afraid of you mate or you just a shit house, c'mon let's do it I will go down and wait for you." Danny "Leave it Niel I don't want to hurt you so let it drop." Jeff shouts "Shut up, shut , just shut up, I don't know what this is all about but it must stop now, look at you, you are mates and trying to kill each other." Next in comes the warden and says "Right what's all the noise here? people are trying to sleep." Jeff "It's allright now Richard it's all over, a misunderstanding." Richard "Are you sure? I hope so, this is going in the report book and will be dealt with by Anthea tomorrow." Jeff "Yes ok mate it's all over now." Richard leaves and Geraldine says "Danny and Niel leave it go now until we are sober and sort it out then, please will you do that?" No reply came from the boys and then Niel said "Right I am off to bed, see you all tomorrow." And as he passed Danny he whispered "Bastard." And off he went next thing Winnie said "That was nasty, Danny are you allright?" Danny replies "Yes I am ok, a bit shaken but ok." Rhoda "What started it off again Dan?" Danny "I am not saying nothing as he might still be in the room and I have had enough for one night." Winnie spoke up "Niel said he was going to bed opened the door and closed it but never went through it and listened to our conversation and went mad saying we were talking about him and we were." Ger "I see." Danny let it go now, I don't want to know any more, he is on his own." Next Jeff said "Mind it was lucky I was here to sort them out, did you see me separate them?" Ger said "Yes you disappeared between them for a while and I thought you were going to get crushed there for a minute." Jeff "That did not worry me, I have four brothers and I was often separating them." Ger said "Well is it like this every night? As I don't know if I want to be involved with thugs and men who try to chat up every woman he sets eyes on." Danny says "Oh Jeff you mean, I know I love his chat up lines, I bet he tried some on you tonight." Ger "Yes he did and Carol came in and said he does the same to her and I think if a Scotsman in a skirt came in he would chat him up with the same chat up lines, Jeff your awful." Jeff sniggering said "I only use them lines on girls I am in love with like you." Ger sat back as she did not expect it and said "And Carol and whoever and you are pissed you need to sleep it off Jeff and don't get embarrassed in lectures tomorrow." Jeff "Aw Ger, I do though, I told Danny didn't I matey?" Danny "I am not saying anything, I don't want any more trouble, sorry." Rhoda "You never know Ger, he might be serious and he has said it to me a few times." Ger "Right I am off I need to get home to my bed." Jeff head wobbling just like a dog in the back of a car slurred "Don't go home, I am enjoying myself now and I want to talk to you some more." Ger "Right Rhoda I am off, I need my beauty sleep, goodnight Jeff I will see you when you are sober and Danny don't worry things will work out and Winnie nice to meet you, Rhoda I am going to phone a taxi from your room if you don't mind and use your loo, good night all." They all wish her good night and left, Jeff then said to Danny sadly "Ballucks, crashed and burned again matey, story of my life and things were going well until Carol came in and sat by me, damn." Danny "I knew she would get in your way sooner or later, I warned you, but it's your problem now." Jeff "Don't be like that matey, but what do you think of her she is lovely isn't she? I am in love with her and won't stop trying, well I am off outside to see her off, see you both." He goes off and Winnie said "You British are silly, you always worry about everything and fight when you have been drinking all the time, are you allright Danny? you are very quiet, I will give you another head massage if you like." "That's very nice of you I am having another whisky and off to bed, unless you want me into cuddle you up in your room." Looking shocked she said "Don't say things like that, you must not say these things Danny, I have finished my drink and I am off." "Goodnight Winnie, I will see you in the morning." Winnie said goodnight and did not look happy when she left, Danny sat there in deep thought and was almost crying and things were really getting to him and the drink was not helping a lot. Next in comes Rhoda and Jeff laughing and Rhoda said "Danny you should have seen him outside with Geraldine, he was like a lovesick dog and Geraldine was laughing her head off and he fell all the way up the stairs." Jeff "God I am drunk matey, so don't listen to Rhoda, but Ger is nice isn't she?" Danny replied quietly "Yes Jeff she is lovely." Rhoda looked at Danny and remembered what she was told about all the death attached to him and felt sorry for him and said "Jeff sit down and shut up for five minutes. Danny don't take what happened tonight to heart, I think Niel was out of order and he will realise it tomorrow and I think he will feel awful about it, so don't worry about it." Danny "I have a lot more to worry about than that idiot and he maybe right I should mind my own business and let everyone look after their own problems, then that would not have happened tonight." Jeff said "I would be happier if you did and it would not cost me so much ha,ha." Danny said a stern goodnight and just walked out then Rhoda set upon Jeff and said "You ungrateful pig you, he sorted out a lot of trouble here a few weeks ago for us all as we were having a horrible time here and he was the only one who had the guts to do so and you and bloody Niel have forgotten that already. Some friends you are, I don't know why he bothers with the both of you. And remember he is going through hell with a future divorce and his brother killing himself with alcoholism and even you said a few hours ago that you would not be able to cope if some of these things happened to you, you make me sick I am off to bed." She stands up and storms off and Jeff was trying to explain "Rhoda wait a minute, I was not being serious, I am sorry." But it was too late and she had gone to bed and did not answer and Jeff felt awful and so went off to Danny's room to say sorry. He knocked Danny's door and Danny shouts "Who is it?" Jeff "It's me Jeff, I want to see you and say sorry, let me in." Danny replied "Leave it there and go to bed, I am not letting you in, go away." Jeff says "Oh don't be like that matey, I am not serious I really am sorry matey." No answer was heard and Jeff went off to bed.

Well it was the next morning and Zarrine was sitting sipping a cup of coffee and Winnie came in and said "Hello is that you Zarrine? I am early as I could not sleep last night." Zarrine says "Yes it's me and it's just you and I in here, so why couldn't you sleep last night?" Winnie replies "Because of all the trouble with Danny and that stupid Niel fighting last night after they came in and even Richard came up and told them off and if it was not for Jeff they would have killed each other." "Why were they fighting?" "Niel pretended to leave this room and opened the door and then shut it and stayed in the corner in here and heard Danny talking about him and they started fighting or shouting rather and Jeff stopped them." Zarrine said "I wonder what that was all about, I will find out off the management here I expect sometime today and Jeff will be hurrying to tell me now as soon as he comes in." Winnie said "It was that silly Niel's fault not Danny's, I heard him he was nasty to Danny." In came Jeff and he was looking like death warmed up. Winnie excited said "Here he is ask him." Jeff said holding his head "Ask me what?" Zarrine "What happened last night with Danny and Niel?" Jeff smiled and said "Oh yes I forgot about that, I was sure something happened to. Well I was in my room and Geraldine and Rhoda were with me and we were having a ciggy and next thing Winnie came running in and said they were both fighting and I ran in and got between them and sorted them out, mind they were very nasty, but I sorted them out and the warden came in and it all went quiet but I don't think we have heard the last of it." Zarrine looking worried says "No, I hope it is all over, I seen Niel earlier and he never said nothing, they will get over it, they are good mates, it will all blow over." Jeff "I don't know they were at it all yesterday and I have no clue what it is all about and I don't think Danny is speaking to me either, I think I said something to upset him and I can't remember what I said." Zarrine "Aw he is ok he will not hold a grudge and you are hopeless, you drink too much that's your problem. And who is this Geraldine do I know her?" Jeff "Maybe you do I expect so as she has been coming here for a few years now and she is the girl of my dreams and I am in love, I really am and wish I didn't drink so much last night as I can't remember what I said to her neither." Winnie spoke up "I remember, you said to her that you loved her and she was the girl for you and kept on about it to her and in the end she went home as you were so drunk." Jeff looking depressed said "Oh dear did i? oh dear, I am stupid and I have a lecture with her in about 15 minutes oh dear, Zarrine will you tell Danny I am not going home this weekend and I will see him lunchtime in the refectory at 1 o'clock, thanks I am off, see you." He leaves and Winnie says "British men are stupid, why do they drink so much? it makes them forget things and act silly all the time." Zarrine says "Yes your right and some of them die very young because of alcohol and some of the girls here are just as bad mind. Do you drink in China?" "No I don't drink in China but I have tried some of the drinks here, but I don't drink more than 2 as it makes me go funny in my head." In comes Danny and says "Good morning, both of my favourite girls." With a beaming smile. Winnie with big smile says "Hello I was waiting for you to ask you if you will help me with my English this weekend?" Danny "Yes of course I was going home this weekend, but changed my mind as I must go home next Thursday to go with my brother somewhere. So yes not a problem, where and when?" Winnie I "In the lounge if you like tomorrow afternoon at about 2 o'clock." Danny "Yes ok." Zarrine asks Danny "So what went on here last night with you and Niel?" Danny "That, it was nothing just a silly thing Niel done and it got a little out of hand." Zarrine "Not according to Jeff and Winnie it was like world war 3 in here, are you and Niel allright now?" Danny "I don't know, I have not seen him since and he can please himself, he was just so miserable yesterday and said some nasty things to me and it's up to him, I am going to leave it there now." Zarrine "Well he has already left for his lectures and he is going home this weekend so let him think about it if I was you, I don't know what is wrong with him, he has been off a bit with everyone." Danny "Tell me about it, I am getting it worse than anyone and don't know why me." Winnie says "Oh don't worry about that silly man he is childish." Zarrine "Jeff said to tell you he is not going home either this weekend, he has already gone to his lectures and he will see you later." Danny "Right, I am off to lectures, are you going over Winnie? If so we can walk together if you like." Winnie with smile "Oh yes ok, I will see you down stairs as I must get my things in my room." Off they both went.

Danny out with his white cane training with Ann again and for a change sober and they were doing the route around town again Ann said to him "Well Danny I am going to help you find the bank and anything you need to find, by using some things that give you a clue as to where you are ok? right, we just got off the bus at Maylord Orchard and we are entering the maul, the doors open automatically this end, so walk from the bus about ten steps to the left and listen for the doors opening, can you hear them?" "Yes I heard them and I will walk through them and see you inside." he did this and inside Ann said "Right, stay to the left of the maul and follow the shop fronts all the way around and remember the doors and count them, there are six altogether then you come to the doors going out the other side and they are not electric." Danny does this and at the other end are 3 sets of doors to get back out to the shopping centre. He stops and Ann continues "Right now you have 3 sets of double doors that are manual and if you find them with your stick and I will meet you outside ok? go ahead." As Danny went forward a lady held the door open for him and Danny put his hand out to open it also and he put his hand right on the woman's breast and was pushing it and then grabbed it and tried to pull it, as he thought it was the door pad and kept on fiddling with it for a while and the woman had gone red by now and said "When you have quite finished sir I will have my breast back." Danny jumped back and said "Oh I am awfully sorry I didn't realise I am so sorry, I really am, it was an accident." The woman answered "I realised that and don't worry about it, I am still holding the door if you want to go through it." Danny went through and Ann who was pretending not to be with Danny waited until the woman had gone and then went and joined Danny and said "Oh my god that was funny and easily done mind ha, ha, ha." "Well it is a good excuse only a blind man could get away with it and nice too." "Danny, stop it, I don't know why all these things happen with you, I really don't, I am keeping my distance." Danny "Spoil sport, was she young?" "She was in her 30's maybe early 40's I think." "Oh dear, I am surprised she didn't smack me across the face." "She looked as if she enjoyed it, she probably never gets much excitement at home and it's made her day." Danny smiling said "Yes I didn't mind making her day." "I bet you didn't. Now let's get on with it, now we have a wide open space here and as you come out of the door you need to go straight ahead at about twelve o'clock, avoiding the benches, if you hit them move to one side and keep walking straight until you reach the shops on the other side, then turn left and follow the shops ok?" "Ok." Danny did this and he had to carry on until Ann says differently. She was waiting for Danny to come to a ramp and at the bottom of it she would give him more instructions. Danny came to the ramp and of course he could not see it coming up and went hurling down it so fast and he nearly took off and Ann run up to him to see if he was allright. Ann said in panic "Are you allright? I thought you were not going to stop, slow down there is no hurry at all as a blind person now you must slow down as it is too dangerous and you will have a nasty accident if you don't ok?" Danny sweating says "Yes I am over the shock now, so what now?" "I will guide you back to the bottom of the ramp and we will go from there , at the bottom of this ramp there is a music shop. At the bottom you must take five or six paces and then drift along to the other side to the left until you find the shops and shoreline ok?" Danny "Yes ok, that's handy the record and cd shop there, I will remember that ok, let's go." They reached the other side and Ann said "Very good now you will come to the end of the shops and you will realise it is more open as the sound will change. Then you need to turn left Immediately on to the next road and the bank is the fifth open doorway you come to on the left ok?" Danny looking excited says "No problem, this is going to be easier than I thought, I am so pleased." Danny and Ann went on through to town and got to the bank and got through that ok and it went brilliant until they got to the bus station when Danny went to get on the bus and his White cane with its roller ball went down a drain and it got stuck and Danny got on his hands and knees and tried to release it, but couldn't and so Ann got on her knees and she tried but failed and so Danny lifted the drain and got it out that way while all the people getting on the bus had to wait for them, yet another disaster.

Danny arrived back in the refectory for dinner and Niel, Jeff and Geraldine were sitting down eating and Danny was helped by a new S.S.W. worker and she was a Spanish speaking woman Danny said to her "Hello, who are you then? you are new aren't you?" She replied "So sorry, English is not good, I am Lidia." "Well hello Lidia and where do you come from?" Lidia "I am from Peru, do you know this place?" "Yes it's the same place as Paddington bear comes from, do you know Paddington bear?" Lidia looking confused said "No I not know this." Danny said "Paddington bear he comes from darkest Peru, have you never heard of him at all?" "No I not know of this person." Danny said "I will get a video for you to see who he is, it's for little children and is on the television here. I will get it for you and you can see him ok? My name is Danny." Lidia "Yes ok, I will see it for you, thank you, see you." Danny "Yes Lidia I will see you soon, bye." Danny sits down and says "Hello Jeff how are things mate?" Jeff replies "Oh you are speaking to me then?" Danny says "Of course I am." Jeff "Well I had a little go at you last night I was told, so I was wondering." Danny says "Don't worry there was a lot of things said in the heat of the moment, I think we should drop it now." Niel got up and said "Bye." Danny did not realise he was on the table and they all said goodbye to Niel and then Geraldine said "Hello Daniel, are you allright On this lovely day then?" Danny "Yes I am fine and am afraid to say anything today, but are you allright my dear?" Ger smiling said "Yes a little headache earlier but ok now." Danny "Yes Jeff is a little headache isn't he? never mind." Jeff smiles and says "It's ok now Niel has gone and I see you are still not speaking." Danny said "I didn't know he was on the table or I would have spoken to him, it's all over as far as I am concerned." Ger "Good he is not repentant mind, he has hardly said a word in the lectures this morning, he is still in a mood, I think." Jeff said "And if I hurt you or Niel last night when I separated you both I am sorry , ha, ha." Danny laughing said "I had a sore rib this morning as if I had walked into a tooth pick or something and have you forgiven him after last night Geraldine?" Ger "No not yet he was disgusting, I try and keep my distance from him now." Jeff concerned said "Why? I didn't do anything wrong did I?" Danny "Mate some of the things you said to Geraldine was disgusting and if you spoke to my daughter or my wife like that I would have knocked you out. I have never said anything like that to any woman, you should be ashamed of yourself." Ger "Yes it was lucky it was me and not someone else, I can take your crap talk, but you will never share my soap ever after that." Jeff looking worried says "I never said anything or you would have told me earlier." Ger "I am polite and wanted for someone else to say it as you would never have believed me and I have heard some stories about you and women's clothes so let's leave it at that now ok?" Jeff "What do you mean? I never done anything and those clothes were not mine, I was just doing someone a favour and if I was out of order last night I am sorry." Ger "I am sorry Jeff I will let it go this time but I will be watching you from now on." Danny said "Ger I don't think he meant it, it was the booze talking, I am sure but it was rude mind, I would not say that to someone." Ger "It's lucky I am a woman of the world, but I will never get in the situation of being in the same room as him on my own if he has had a drink, but let's just leave it there now ok? let's not hear no more about it." Jeff "Oh no, we can't leave it at that as I need to redeem myself." Ger said "No Jeff I mean it, it was embarrassing, so please leave it there, I don't want to know any more ok?"

175

Jeff looked unhappy and Danny said "I have just met a lovely S.S.W. she is from Peru and has a bad English speaking voice and she has never heard of Paddington bear, so I am going to get her the video of it. She is really a lovely girl and looks and sounds so lost far from home, bless her." Jeff did not answer and Ger said "Yes she is nice and is standing there wondering what is happening. Danny are you coming up the Rose and Crown for a few bevies tonight? If so I will see you there ok? I am off now see you both later." The lads said goodbye and Jeff says to Danny "What did I say last night mate? was it bad or what?" Danny answered "It was not nice at all and I can't remember all of it, but you referred to her large bust and how lucky her children were having to be breast fed and I recall you saying something about her large bum and how it turns you on, in fact I think you referred to most of her body sometime in the evening." Jeff looking totally dejected says "Oh god, I wish I could remember, I will never drink again if that is what it does to me. What am I going to do now? I have blown it, I think." Danny "Yep." "I am an idiot." Danny "Yep." "Just when I was getting close to her." Danny smiling says "Yep." Jeff snapped "Will you stop saying yep?" Danny "Yep." Jeff "So are you coming up the Rose and Crown tonight? it's going to be fun." Danny "Oh I don't know, I don't want another fight with Niel." Jeff "He won't be there he has a meeting with his tutor now as we speak and he is off to his home for the weekend, so are you coming or what? you, me, Rhoda, Ger, and whoever wants to come." Danny "What about Carol? have you asked her?" Jeff rubbing his chin says "No I haven't, so don't you mention it to her please, so are you coming?" Danny says pondering "Yes it will be a nice change I am going to sort out some things now and I will see you tea time at 5 o'clock in here mate."

Danny and Jeff went onto their different destinations and Danny later went to see Anthea as he had been summoned to her office like a naughty schoolboy.

In the office and Anthea says to him "Trouble last night then again." Danny replied "I didn't start it, I was a victim." Anthea looked at Danny and said "A victim aye, I don't think you will ever be a victim, so what happened with you and Niel has to stop and I will be putting you on report so let's not have a repeat of this again and I have had a word with Niel and he is not a happy bunny at the moment, so it might be a good idea if you 2 stay away from each other for a bit." Danny "Oh you do, do you? I never have hidden from any trouble that comes my way and neither has Niel and the best way in my experience is to let it go and act as if it never happened and then people forget all about the argument Immediately, as I am sure Nièl will. But thanks for your advice, but we will sort it out our way and I feel Niel is having problems here that is unnecessary pressure here , as he needs help not threats as he told me they will get rid of him if he packs in the I.T. and it is only because he is dyslexic and if he was put in a class with a woman teaching him with a bit of tolerance and patience he will be ok." "Is that what the trouble is then? how do you know?" Danny "Because that is why he is not talking to me, as the pressure is something he does not need. if you check he had 4 male lecturers here when he started and he has whittled them down to one and if you changed it to a woman he will be happy and you won't hear a word from him." Anthea looking serious said "Yes you may have a point there, I will put it to his tutor after as she is coming to see me later and if it is so I will suggest it to her as we have a lady here who teaches people with them sort of problems you just spoke about thank you Danny, I hope I will not see you again this term please." Danny smiling says "I hope not I am fed up with Niel's moods."

Well Danny finishes his lectures for the day and heads off to meet Jeff in the refectory and he meets up with Lidia again and says "Well hello my lovely Lidia, are you ok? and settling in alright? I haven't forgotten about Paddington bear." Lidia smiles and said "Paddington bear and what is your name please?" Danny said "What a cracking accent you have and my name is Daniel, or Danny, I don't mind." Lidia "Oh Daniel I have a friend his name is same." Danny "Do you like it here so far?" With difficulty she replies "Oh how you say freezing here, i am shaking all the time, yes." Danny smiles "Yes it is cold in this country but the summer is just around the corner." Lidia "Ah yes cold that is the word I am going to sit on heat later." "Well you be careful you don't burn your butt." Lidia looking puzzled says "What is my butt?" Danny smiling says "Your bum like what you sit on." "I no understand you." Danny pats his bum and said "This is your butt or bum yes?" Lidia now smiling says "Oh yes I know I will take you to sit, yes?" "Ok my darling I need to sit by my friend I will call him now, Jeff, Jeff." Jeff shouts back "Over here mate." Lidia takes him to find Jeff and he says to Jeff "Right mate this lovely charming lady is Lidia and she is from Peru, Lidia this is Jeff." Lidia "Hello Jeff nice meet." Jeff says "Yes Lidia nice to meet and a nice piece of meat you are too." Lidia "Sorry." Jeff "Nothing never mind, I am being silly, I will see you soon." Lidia goes off and Jeff says "What a cracker she is, I would, no problem." Danny rolls his eyes and says "You would give anything one you would, what time are we going tonight?" "Well Rhoda is having a taxi with us so I told her 7 o'clock." "That's a bit early mate." Jeff "Well I said that because I remember her from Torquay she is so slow so she will be ready for about 8 o'clock. You see there's method in my madness." Danny said "Yes there's something there and Ger is sorted out is she?" "Yes she will be there and she only lives just around the corner, so it might be a drink over her house after I hope." Danny "You are hoping are you? I think you have burned your bridges there mate." "Na I am a stud she will forget all about last night after a few chat up lines and it will be nice to have a drink in peace for a change." "Yes, you might be right, I could do with a peaceful one, I will see you later then." "Ok matey."

Danny and Jeff in the lounge in Dowdell and sitting there is Winnie and Danny was not saying where he is going and told Jeff to do the same Danny says "Well Winnie are you ready for your first lesson tomorrow?" Winnie replies "Yes and I hope you don't get too drunk tonight for me." Danny answers quick "No I will be ok and we will have a lot of fun together." Winnie snaps "What do you mean?" Danny "I mean you will be smiling at some of the funny English words there are that's all." "I see I will have it on a tape and we can do it on the table." Jeff in a rude way says "On the table ay, then on the work surface and then on the telly and I want to watch." Winnie snaps at Jeff "What do you mean by this Jeff? you are being nasty and dirty, I will not stand for this." Danny says "Oh Winnie don't listen to that idiot he is nutty." Winnie "He is, I know, I will tell Carol about him and Geraldine." Danny "They already know, at last Rhoda, we have been waiting long enough for you, are you ready now?" Rhoda "Yes I am, have you booked a taxi yet?" Danny "I am doing it as we speak, let's go outside and wait for it."

Later in the pub and they were getting tipsy and laughing and Danny was telling lots of jokes and the tears were running down their faces. Danny "I am in the chair anyone for a drink?" Rhoda " A Bacardi for me and a vodka for Ger." Danny "And a lager for you Jeff? and a drink for me, I will be back." Ger "He is so funny isn't he, I bet he is always a good laugh and he is quite good looking too, I bet he is something when he gets started." Jeff listening to this says "Any chance of coming back to your digs for a night cap? then darling." Ger "I don't see why not as long as it is not too late as my children will not go to bed if anyone is there but no problem." Rhoda "Not so noisy as last night is it, I hope they get back to normal after the weekend it is not good having an atmosphere in there." Jeff "No your right it is off-putting, it's that dodgy Welshman's fault." Danny was putting the drinks on the table and said "What's my fault now?" Jeff "Nothing mate." Geraldine says "We can go back to my home if we want as long as it is not too late." Danny "Great I am up for it." Ger suggestively says "You are, are you? that's nice to hear." Rhoda "Steady Geraldine, steady." Danny "Rhoda you are pissed aren't you? What would god say?" She replies "Nothing at all as long as I am good no problem." Jeff "dim problem, dim problem." Ger "What the hell are you on about?" Jeff "That is no problem in Welsh and without the spitting." Danny "Well done matey, we can't make a Welshman out of you as you haven't got it in you." Jeff "Thank god for that."

Later they are walking down the road Jeff was holding Geraldine's arm and smiling from ear to ear and Danny was holding Rhoda's arm and they were walking and Geraldine was telling them "Keep on going and cross the zebra crossing up ahead." Danny stops at the road edge and Jeff said "Why have you stopped dodgy?" Danny replies with a smile on his face "It's a one way road it's too dangerous crossing with Rhoda I must go on the other side of her so as the cars can see me, sorry Rhoda I must switch arms." Rhoda "I don't understand why?" Danny "Well a zebra crossing is black and white and it's dark." Geraldine looking puzzled says "So, what's that Matter?" Danny "Well it's Rhoda crossing, now you see me now you don't, now you see me now you don't." Rhoda and the others burst out laughing and Rhoda said "I don't believe you just said that and I am not going to swear." She laughs aloud and Danny said "I hope you didn't take offence at what I just said, it was a joke." Jeff "It is not politically correct dodgy." Danny "Stuff political correctness, it is a load of shit I was having a little joke with my friend from Jamaica and she has not taken offence and it was not meant to be offensive and if she said something about my Welshness or the colour of my skin I would laugh as much as she did a minute a go." Rhoda "Well said Daniel I am not offended at all it was the funniest thing tonight and I want more Bacardi." Ger "Here we are I will open the door." They went into Geraldine's house and was greeted by her young son and daughter and off they went to bed and the 4 adults were left drinking. Jeff said "This is homely, I could get used to this." Ger sarcastically said "Well don't" She started flirting with Danny and you could see Jeff didn't like it and Danny was not getting involved, by now Rhoda was slurring her words "Goodness I haven't been this drunk for a long time but I have enjoyed myself especially at the zebra crossing that was funny." They all had a good chuckle and Danny said "They have a new machine in tesco's now and a man who had a bad arm read the notice on it and it said put your urine sample in the draw and a £1 coin in and we can tell you if an what is wrong with you. So he thought I wonder if it can tell me what is wrong with my elbow, so he put a urine sample in and a £1 coin in and a slip of paper came out and it said, you have tennis elbow go home and soak it in warm water regularly and rest it as much as you can for a week. The man was fascinated by this and decided he would try and fool the machine. So at home that night he took a bit of his pet dogs pooh an put it in the cup and a urine sample from his daughter and his wife then he put some of his seamen in it and stirred it altogether and thought he would confuse the machine. Well he went back next day to Tesco's and put it in the machine and put his £1 coin in and stood back and he took the slip of paper and it read.

1 your dog has ring worm get him to the vets Immediately

2 your daughter is on cocaine take her to rehab.

3 your wife is having twins and they are not yours go and see a solicitor Immediately.

4 And if you don't stop wanking your elbow will never get better.

Thank you for shopping at Tesco's." They all were in fits of laughter and falling all over the place. Jeff "That was so funny and I haven't heard you tell that one before." Danny "Mark Mathews told me it, a good joke." Jeff tried to cuddle up to Geraldine and she was smiling all over her face and Jeff was just about to start his chat up lines "Have you got a boyfriend? it's about time you got an upgrade." Danny "Oh no Jeff please." Jeff "Hi I have lost my virginity can I have yours? you could do with putting on 8 stone and i am 8 stone, do you have any English in you? Would you like some?" Geraldine was killing herself laughing and Rhoda was now blotto and out of it and she said I must go to the toilet. She was sitting on a low couch and she tried to shuffle to the edge of the couch and she went and dropped her cigarette lighter and bent over to pick it up and done a rolly polley on the carpet and stopped facing the wall they cracked up laughing and decided to get a taxi home after that. They were on the road and waiting for the taxi and Jeff was doing anything to keep Geraldine away from Danny and Danny was holding up Rhoda and Jeff got lucky with Geraldine and had a smacker of a kiss from her and he was bouncing all the rest of the night. They get back to the college and went into the lounge quietly and Danny and Jeff was sitting there having a tin of lager before they went to bed and Jeff said to Danny "I think I am in love as she gave me a huge kiss before I left, I am in love mate this is it." Danny smiling said "Yes I am happy for you mate, good luck but take it easy don't go at it like a bat out of hell." "I know mate and thank you for not trying to get off with her, I won't forget it matey." Danny replies "What are you on about? I never would do that anyway, god you and Niel don't think much of me? both of you think I am a bastard or you wouldn't say these things in the first place, I don't do things to my mates like that so no need to thank me as you are showing weakness, you are capable of getting a girl without worrying about other people taking them off you, think positive." "I know I should not have said that, forget I said it ok?" Danny then snaps at Jeff "Right I will never chase any woman you are interested in but let me tell you now, if my wife divorces me while I am here I will only allow you to have one woman as you fancy everything in a skirt, understand?" Jeff looking resigned to this said "Fair enough but I thought you are going after Winnie? well are you yes or no?" "I don't know mate I wish I knew what my wife has in mind and I wish she would tell me it's murder wondering all the time so I have to play it by ear." "Yes I see what you mean at least I know where I am, divorced,, I am off to bed mate see you in the morning." Danny replies "Yes, goodnight mate and good luck with Ger." "Goodnight." Danny was sitting there all alone and next as Jeff closed his bedroom door another one opened and it was Winnie and she pretended to get a cup of water and spoke to Danny "Oh hello, are you drunk?" Danny says in response "Why do you want to take advantage of me?" Winnie snaps at Danny "Danny don't be silly, why do you say this?" "Winnie it was a joke, don't they have jokes in China?" Winnie replies "Yes they have funny stories." "Well you could have fooled me, so why are you up so late? can't you sleep?" Winnie "I have not had much sleep since I arrived to England, it's so different to my country." "I am cream crackered." "What is this cream thing?" Danny smiling says "It's just a saying instead of tired the English say cream crackered." "That is stupid, why not say it properly?" "This is why the English language is naughty, it is made up from many, many languages from all over the world, like taxi it comes from France and bungalow it comes from India and many more and I think English is the hardest language to learn, but I think you are intelligent enough to learn it quickly as you seem nice and sensible to me." Winnie smiled and was enjoying his compliments and asked him "Would you like a head massage to settle you down?" Danny smiles from ear to ear on hearing this and said "Oh yes please, I love you doing that, it makes me sleep and so relaxing and you have such nice hands, thank you Winnie." "It's my pleasure in China it is very much a good way to unwind is that what you say here?" "Yes, see you are learning already I will help you I am good at the English and will get you through your exams." Winnie "I believe you, my father is a teacher of the English language, a professor." Danny shocked says "Well I don't understand why did he not teach you?" "Because he spent many of my years in prison, he was a prisoner of the cultural revolution and my mother was and after they were released they were forbidden to teach this and then went to Australia and I was never allowed to learn this off my father but they cannot stop me here." "How sad I cannot understand why some countries are like this and yet again this country has gone to the dogs no discipline with youngsters at all." Winnie now looking sad said "In my country this will not be tolerated and I was in school and I was made to clean the windows and some of them were up on the second and third floor and I was made to stand on the outside ledge and clean them. We had no cleaners in the school we had to keep the place clean ourselves without question." Danny looked amazed and said "Good gracious, I don't believe it but I think a good idea and more of this we need here for our kids. This is a nice massage Winnie, thank you again and I am off to bed if you have finished or have you something in mind?" Winnie stamps her foot and says "Danny be good." "I am sorry I can but try, goodnight." "Goodnight."

It was the following evening and Danny and Jeff in the Rose and Crown as Jeff wanted to go there to see if Geraldine was in there. Jeff said to Danny "Not a bad pint here is it matey?" "Not bad considering it is in an English bar, I suppose, if Geraldine is not here by 9.30 I am off to the barrels for a pint of real ale." Jeff "Ok I agree, how did it go this afternoon with Winnie and her English lesson?" Danny rolls his eyes and says "Don't ask it was difficult at first as she was criticizing everything, I said as you know English is a stupid language and the other thing was all of you were back and forth and asking questions and we took three times longer to get through one lesson but she got It all in the end." Jeff said "Well it is the community lounge and you can't expect everyone to stay quiet for her." "I know I was not saying that but every time I say to her to do it in her room or mine, she thinks I am trying to get my wicked way and it would be easier for us to get it done more quickly, but I will put up with it for a while and she can get someone else to teach her and that's it." Jeff "She needs to catch up with the 21st century, she is 29 and is still a virgin and when she goes back to China she will notice the difference then and wish she was still here or another western country, mind you she is very pretty mind and I think most men here would be too shy to ask her out." Danny says "Yes I think that to but she is like a old fashioned headmaster but today she was actually touching as she sat by me as you know she is usually far away from anyone even if you are both sitting on the same couch but she is starting to relax now so you never know, it's a messy job but somebody's got to do it." Jeff looking around for Ger says "Well no sign of her I really thought she would be here tonight, I might go to her house and see if she fancies a drink." Danny says "See there you go again and you will get on her nerves if you keep on at her all the time and besides she has children and not a lot of money because of that and can't waste money on drink all the time." Jeff says "Well I will get her drinks no problem." "See what I mean trying to buy the girl again, no good mate, give her a ring on your mobile and tell her we are here and wondered if she fancies a drink if not we will go to the Barrels." Jeff's eyes lit up and said "Right I will get a pint in and I will give her a ring." Danny "Give me the money and I will get them in for you while you phone." Jeff phoned and she answered Jeff says "Hello gorgeous hows you then? I am up the Rose and Crown with that dodgy Welshman and wondered if you fancy one or two…. Oh ok babes I understand some other time then bye." Danny says "Your change mate, don't tell me she can't afford it?" Jeff "No she is knackered, she has been shopping with the kids but she says she will see me on Monday in lectures, well that's it then I offered to get her a drink, she does not fancy me." "Don't be silly give her a chance and phone a taxi, let's go to the Barrels there must be some women there and some nice music on the jukebox."

Later in the barrels it was very busy and Danny and Jeff were standing by the bar talking Jeff "God it's lively here isn't it? and plenty of totty here." Danny "Yes and a nice pint of real beer so I wonder how that bloody Niel is enjoying his weekend." Jeff "Dunno, I think I will ask Geraldine out for a meal sometime." Danny "Hello earth to Jeff, I think there is more to this weekend than Geraldine, so I am off if you don't shut up about her." "Sorry mate, I just can't get her out of my mind, right fancy a pint?" Danny looking relieved says "Yes we have been here over half an hour and just one pint." "Yes sorry mate, god you should see these barmaids, their skirts up to their boobs and gorgeous with it and a lot of girlies on the pool table. So what are you doing tomorrow night? fancy the student bar as I am a little skint." Danny "And you was going to buy her beer all night and you are skint, see what I mean? and yes I don't mind the student bar, I like to sit there and listen to some crap some of them young students talk to Impress the younger students, it's so funny." Danny has a sip of his beer and says "What a lovely pint of ale you can't beat the real ale especially this Malvern ale." Next thing a young girl who was from Belgium who was a S.S.W. in the college not so long ago came up to speak to Danny "Hello Dan it's Catalina, I seen you through the window as I passed, I live in a flat across the road and funny enough I was at the college this afternoon and someone was talking about you, Lidia, do you know her?" Danny said "Oh yes she is from Peru, she is lovely and so natural just like yourself. So how are you then? I heard you had split up with your fella the lecturer then." She replies "Yes he went back to his wife after all but we keep in touch from time to time." Danny "And so how do you know Lidia?" "Well I only met her today as I still use the library in the college and I was sitting in the sun on the bench outside Gardener and she was there, she is nice and we are having a drink in my place tomorrow evening. I am trying to get her settled in and do you know Joanna? she is from Poland, well they have become good friends also, you know Joanna? she speaks very slowly." Danny said "Oh yes a lovely girl too, as a Matter of fact all you S.S.W's are lovely and have you ever met Jeff? this is him." Danny and Catalina turned to Jeff and she said "I have seen you around but never spoke to you." Jeff smiling from ear to ear said "Hello Catalina I am pleased to meet you, I am sure, would you like a drink?" She replied "Well i shouldn't really." Jeff jumped in "Go on please it gives us a chance to get to know you better." She agrees and Jeff gets her a red wine, Catalina sips it and says "Thank you Jeff so the last people I thought I would see in here was you two." Danny "Well we come here on a Thursday for the quiz and they do a good job of it, it is a charity one and they use some of the money to pay for foreign students to attend the college and it's a good laugh and they feed us also." Catalina "Well that's allright isn't it? I will come over one Thursday and Join in with you, mind you I am not very good at quizzes, but it will save money on food." Jeff says "Oh it doesn't Matter it's only for fun no one wins at the end of it that's why it is so good no one is embarrassed and you would enjoy it." She replies "Good then I will come over then." Jeff "And you could bring Lidia over to, she might enjoy the company." Catalina "Yes I will ask her and she could get a taxi back with you or stay the night if she wants." Jeff "Great idea I look forward to it." Danny "Yes it would be fun and it will help to relax Lidia more, she seems nervous and tense as she is new." Catalina "Yes she is I think and It will do her some good, I can only ask." Danny "And how are you? ok and when if ever are you going back to Belgium?" "I am enjoying it here at the moment and still at the local college and I went home a few months ago for xmas and after being away for so long it didn't seem the same, so I was glad to get back here, I love it here and I am just waiting to see what happens as regards him." Danny "Yes I didn't have a good xmas either and was glad to get back but I am off home next Thursday, so I won't be here for the quiz as my brother is an alcoholic and I said I was going home as he promised to go to alcoholics anonymous and I told him I would go along with him, as it was worrying me a great deal so I must do that at all costs." Catalina said "Ok I see I will leave it until a week Thursday then and I am sorry to hear about your brother, I hope it all works out for him." Jeff "Do you go over the college much? it is a good night in the bar there sometimes." Catalina replies "I will be going over there a lot more now I have met Lidia and Joanna, I suppose and I will keep a look out for you." Danny says "We will do the same, another wine Catalina?" Catalina replies "No I shouldn't I only popped in to say hello honestly." Danny "I will get you one in as you are nicer and more pretty than Jeff, more pleasing on the eye." She says "I wish you didn't I cannot afford to buy you one back and I feel awful." Jeff says "Don't be silly it's nice to have female company for a change, I am fed up at looking at that awful Welsh face also." Danny "And we won't hear of it we don't expect to have a drink back at all and if we didn't like you or didn't want your company we would not buy you a drink, it's our pleasure, honestly." Catalina "That's very nice of you, I will remember this if I ever get rich." Danny sorts out a couple of drinks and Jeff says "So you are single then? a good looking girlie like you, I don't understand it at all." Catalina replies "Yes I am now, I was living with a tutor from the college but he was missing his children and went back to his wife, but never mind I am happy at the moment and what about you? are you with someone?" Jeff excited says "Oh no I am single and waiting for the right girl to come along, no one on the cards at the moment and if you fancy a night out sometime, I will give you my mobile number." Catalina making excuses says "That is not necessary, I am always in the college and I don't use a mobile much, so have you ever been married?" Jeff "Yes I was but she got rid of me for another fella and I have 3 children all boys and 2 step daughters, but I don't see the daughters much and have you got any children?" She laughs and says "Me, I can't look after house plants let alone children, but one day I suppose." Danny hands out the drinks and he sees Jeff all over Catalina and says "I hope you are not going to start those stupid chat up lines or I am leaving and you will drive her away." Jeff in mood "Oh shut up, I will keep my chat up lines to myself until I get to know this lovely girl a bit better." Catalina "You will, will you? I can see I will have to watch this one." Lots of laughter was heard from them for most of the night and it was closing time, time for a last pint and Catalina was leaving and said goodnight to the boys and next they were on their own and Jeff said "Are we having another pint or what? I am going home sober and this will not do." Danny "Well it's your round get them in before they ring the last bell." Jeff looking down to the floor says "I can't I am skint, I have no money left, you will have to get this last one in or lend me a fiver please." Danny "See I told you if you had, had Geraldine out and bought her drinks you would be borrowing a twenty note off me, so it's lucky she did not take up your offer." Jeff smirking says "Yes, ok, I thought I had more money than I did, just lend me a fiver and another thing we have only had 4 pints all night, that's amazing isn't it. " Danny look of amazement says "What are you talking about? only 4 pints." Jeff "Yes that's right 4, I have only been up to the bar four times that's all, I can count you know." Danny "Yes so can I, listen Jeff we have had more than four pints." Jeff in argumentative mood says "Only four I went up for a pint only four times, don't argue." Danny "You dick head yes I agree you only went up to the bar four times but." Jeff butts in "Right, so why are you trying to say different then?" Danny "I'm not I said you went up four times... and so did I, I went up four times also for four pints and so we have had eight pints altogether ok?" Jeff stood there and pondered for a minute and said looking stupid "Aah, yes, right, I am not with it mate, I didn't think of that, sorry." Danny looking up to the ceiling says "God why me lord, why me." Danny was looking heavenward, as Jeff gets the pints and returns and says "Danny I think I am in love." Danny rolls his eyes and says "I know with Geraldine and Carol and probably Catalina and anyone in a skirt." Jeff "No listen, I was getting the come on with Catalina, did you see her smiling at me all the time?" "She wasn't smiling at you, she was laughing at you." Jeff's face told it all he said "Right, forget it, just forget it." "Sorry mate I could not resist that, so what do you mean?" "Well she was very chatty to me and got very close to me all the time." Danny replies "So she is like that, she is a very warm person, she got very close to me also, it is just her way and she is from Belgium that's how they are." Jeff continues "I wonder if she comes from Amsterdam, they have some lovelies who sit in the window out there and I could give her one in the wink of an eye, I bet she wants it too." Danny chuckles and says "Steady man, Belgium is a large place and Amsterdam is just the capital city of Holland dick head and not all of Holland is like that, look at Soho in London it's the same but it don't mean all of England is the same." "I love Dutch people and she ticks my box." "Jeff anyone ticks your box and yes she is a cracker and thank you for the compliment." Jeff says in amazement "What do you mean thanks for the compliment? I meant her." Danny "Well I am Dutch, or half Dutch, my fore fathers are from Arnhem, so that makes me Dutch." Jeff looking amazed says "Oh forget it then, I will phone a taxi let's go."

Later the lads arrive home and into the lounge for a tinny and in there waiting was Winnie, Danny sees her and says "Hello Winnie, are you waiting for me?" She looks daggers at him and says "No, I was watching television." Danny then says "But it's not on." Looking nervous Winnie says "I know I just turned it off, that is why, you silly man ha, ha." Next Jeff walks in with a couple of tins and hands one to Danny and says to Winnie "Hello Winnie, do you want one?" Winnie declines and says "Have you both had a good night?" Danny "Yes we went to a couple of pubs and enjoyed it." Jeff says "And we met a Dutch cracking woman last going off and she was gorgeous." Danny said "Yes she is lovely and not from Amsterdam, pity mate." Jeff "Yes I agree." Winnie says "Amsterdam why does she have to be from Amsterdam? it's not special." Jeff excited says "Well out in Amsterdam they have women half naked in the shop windows and very sexy and if you give them money they will have mad passionate sex with you." Winnie stamping her foot on the floor then she snaps at Jeff "Why do you like these things? it is disgusting, we do not have any in my country." Jeff continues "No all your lot are in London doing it." She says "What do you mean?" Jeff replies "Well they all come over to Soho and make a lot of money with us English male hunks and they love it and earn lots of money " Winnie looked astonished and says "Jeff you must not say this, Danny he is a pig, tell him off." Danny laughs and says "Why Winnie? He is right except about English hunks there, all the Asians there from Japan, Thailand, Malaysia and whether you like it or not, China, they are all there and If you do not like sex, you are in the minority." Winnie says to Danny "You must not say this, take it back, that is horrible." Jeff stands up and says "Oh dear, time for a ciggy ha, ha." Danny "Yes that's right, start her off then piss off and leave me to pick the pieces up." Jeff ran off to his room and Winnie continued "What do you mean by this?." Danny smiling says "Well it happens all over the world Winnie, in London, Paris, Washington and anywhere else you want to mention and there is nothing wrong with it, most women love to have sex with men, it is normal like dogs do it and horses and all creatures on this planet, except you ha, ha." Winnie is now going mad and says "You must not laugh at me, I am not liking sex as you say I will keep it for my husband and no one else, you are a pig." "No Winnie, I am not it's human nature and when you have sex with your husband that is ok but you are entitled to do what you want but you are nearly 30 now and most girls are having it from the age of 14 and that is up to them, it does not make it wrong, they are also entitled to do what they choose and besides if you don't get married for another ten years and then have sex at 40 and you discover you love it, what a lot of time you have wasted and you maybe off it by the time you are 47, as most women are and it is too late your life is over." There was a deadly silence and in walks Jeff and he says "Is it safe now to come in? ha, ha." Winnie starts shouting at Danny "You must not say this, I am a decent girl not like these dirty girls who have it with all men, I will have only one man not like you." Jeff says "Oop's, I am off for another ciggy, ha, ha." Danny shouts after him "Hey you, get back here, you started this and then leave it to me, get back here, ha, ha." Next thing Winnie comes over to wrestle with Danny and sits on his lap and wrestles his arms above his head and says "You are a horrible man and I don't like you anymore, I am going to beat you up." She was very strong and had Danny pinned in the chair and Jeff walked back in and seen them and said "Ha, ha, right, I am off for another ciggy this is too violent for me." Winnie said to Danny "Do you give up? Do you? I am going to teach you a lesson then I am going to bed happy." Next Danny got her arms down and wrapped them around her body and she was now tied up and could not move and she started laughing "I don't think you are funny Danny ha, ha and I am getting mad now so you had better let me go or else." She got up on her feet and fell to the floor and Danny was pulled onto his knees and she got her legs around his waist and got him in a scissors hold and squeezed hard, he was in agony, so she let him go but he was hurt and she just got up and sat back on her chair." Winnie smiling said "Danny I hope you have learnt a lesson now and don't say these things again." Danny holding his stomach says after groaning a lot "Very good Winnie I was only playing with you and you got serious and you have hurt me now." Winnie smiling "Ha, ha, ha, that will teach you not to mess with me next time." Danny got up and sat back on the chair and said in a nasty voice "Ok, that's fair enough I hope you realise if you was a man who just done that I would have head butted him and kicked his head in for doing that, you are lucky." Winnie "No you are lucky Danny don't mess with me." Danny said "No problem about that I will keep myself to myself from now on, I am finished with you, your on your own, don't ask me for a thing ok?" Winnie replied "Fine, I am off." She storms out and Jeff was the other side of the door and Winnie walked into him and she said "Silly man, out of the way." Jeff said "Sorry Winnie my fault sorry." "Yes it is Jeff you are a fool." Jeff says "Yes goodnight." Danny holding his side says to Jeff "Thanks mate, stir up the shit and leave it to me I should have took her to your room and you should have explained the whole thing." Jeff tries to explain "Please do next time I nearly ran out of bacco, and if it only takes a little girly like her to Immobilize you like that, well I don't know a big man like you." Danny looks nasty at Jeff and says "Mate you don't know how bloody strong she is, she really hurt me, she wrapped her legs around me and squeezed and I felt the life draining out of me, I am certainly not having sex with her if she does not like it, she will squeeze you to death, forget it." They both burst out laughing and Jeff said "Never mind I will see to her, she will be Impressed with what I got, what I lost in height I made up for in length and it's a messy job but somebody's got to do it, ha, ha, shall I help you to bed mate?" Danny "Piss off Jeff, I have her on my back now and Niel is back tomorrow afternoon, I think I will bugger off for the day, or you could take on Winnie for me and I will let Niel pick on me." Jeff "Oh I hope he is in a good mood now, or I am coming with you, right I am off to bed."

Next day and Jeff and Danny head into the refectory for dinner and they bump into Lidia Danny says "Hello Lidia, how are you?" Lidia "I am fine, you ok?" Danny "Yes I am fine, I was talking to Catalina last night in a local taverna, she says you and her are good friends and we are getting together you me Jeff and Catalina and a few others for a quiz and some food in a taverna near to Catalina's flat." Lidia not knowing what he was on about says "Oh ok I am not understanding you much, I leave it to Catalina ok? You want to sit please?" Jeff "Hello Lidia I am Jeffrey it's nice to meet you again." Lidia "That is ok please sit and eat." She sat down for a minute with the boys as it was quiet there and she said "I am not good at English and will get understand one day, I want to go student bar this ok for me?" Danny "Yes it is ok, I will meet you tonight if you want up there and you and Joanna can sit by us." Jeff says "Yes Lidia it will be ok for you." Lidia "I want to dance is it up there for me?" Danny "Yes it is but no salsa, but if you have some it will be ok to play it up there." Lidia "Yes ok for me." Danny smiling says "Yes it is my dear and we have Jeff as a body guard." Jeff looking hard says "Dim problemo, I will make you safe, dim problemo." Danny laughs and said "Jeff what's this dim problemo? Ha, ha." Jeff Laughing says "Ha, ha, I am saying it in Spanish for her." Danny "Ha, ha, well don't, we are trying to help them with their English and you sound ridiculous talking like that." Jeff "Ha, ha, do you think so? Ha, ha." Lidia was laughing at the boys laughing and said "I meet you with Joanna, Catalina and the other ones ok? And bring Paddington bear." Danny looked at her strangely and said "Ok, I don't think she knows who Paddington bear is, she thinks he is real." Lidia sits there and smiles very cutely and said "I go now and work, I see you after." Danny "Yes, see after." She goes off and Jeff said "She has a nice body and very dark skin phew, I would." Danny rolls his eyes and says "For god's sake Jeff is that all you think of?" "What else is there at our age?" Danny "You think there just for playing with ,you want to try it with Winnie mate, she would curb your love life pal, I am still hurting from last night." Jeff said "Because she has had the best of you then, I am a different kettle of fish she will have to try and keep up with me, I will leave her for dead and she will not be looking for another man mate, I guarantee it." "I hope your right so shall I set you up with her or what?" Jeff looks worried and says "Or what, I am not that desperate, I don't want to end up in hospital do I? But you can set me up with Catalina if you like." Danny smiling says "I can't see you having much luck there mate, she is still getting over her last love and I think if he turned up she would be gone with him without question." "Do you think so? I am in love with Geraldine anyway but I cannot seem to get through to her but time will tell, I won't give up." Danny looking a little bit worried said "Well Niel is due back in an hour, here we go again." "I think he has forgotten about it now mate." Danny "I hope so." Lidia said as she was passing "Danny, what is napkin?" Jeff says "It is something you put on a babies ass ha, ha." Danny says "Shut up Jeff, she is confused enough now if you can't help just shut up ....Lidia on the end of the counter there is some paper in a pile they are napkins, can you see them?" Lidia scans around and says "I think these yes." Danny felt one and said "Yes Lidia that's right, see you have learnt something today already." Lidia "Yes good, yes." She rushes off and hands them to a lad in the corner and he just grunts. Danny shouts "That's thank you was it? Hope so." The lad quickly says "Thank you Lidia." Danny "I should think so, manners doesn't cost nothing well done." Lidia came back with a huge smile on her face and you could see her gaining confidence, Danny said to Jeff "I think you could be a bit more help to her it's difficult enough you know." Jeff replies "Sorry I was having a bit of fun with her that's all matey." Danny "Well you can't until they can understand what the hell you are talking about." "Ah, I never thought of that, so what shall we do this afternoon then?" "How much money have you got?" Jeff ponders "I can always get some money out of the hole in the wall if you fancy a pint or two, what do you think?" Danny "Where?" Jeff says "The Rose and Crown." Danny "Why did I know what you were going to say?" "Allright then, the Barrels." Danny thinking said "Oh dear, the beer in there is very strong, we will get pissed though, I don't know what to do?" Jeff looking excited "We might as well and I can give Catalina a knock and see if she fancies a drink." "Funny enough I thought you were going to say that too huh, the trouble is if I drink too much and come home and meet Niel and he is still in a foul mood I will only end up arguing with him again and I don't want that." Jeff "Ok, let's try another pub we haven't been to then like the rose gardens outside of town, they have a lot of real ales there and it is a nice pub, a country one, what do you think?" Danny says "Well done mate, I fancy that so we will have to go up college green first then for you to get some money, right let's go."

Later that night the boys Danny Jeff arrived back at the lounge in Dowdell and there was only Winnie in there and Danny said "Hello Winnie where is everyone?" Winnie replies "Why should I know? I am sitting here alone and Niel is not talking to me and he has gone somewhere and Lola has gone up to the student bar and you and Jeff are nearly drunk again so go away." Jeff says sternly "Winnie, that is not the way to talk to someone because he helped you out the other day, you are horrible you are." She said "Good , he and you were nasty to me last night so go away ok?" Danny "C'mon Jeff let's go up the student bar in case Niel comes in, I just want to have a nice night up the student bar."

The lads are in the student bar and sitting in the corner was the S.S.W'S all sitting in a group and Danny said "Hello all, are you enjoying yourselves?" All in a glum mood said yes but seemed pre-occupied and Jeff said to Danny "God it's like a funeral over there, they all look like lost animals." Danny went over and said "Why are you not drinking? And smiling?" Lidia said "We don't want nothing." Danny "Jeff stand by the bar and I will shout out what drinks to get, right Jeff? a red wine for Catalina." Catalina said "Oh no Danny I am allright." Danny interrupts and said "Look I am not asking for anyone's permission for me to buy my friends a drink so be quiet, Jeff a red wine for Catalina and Lidia what about you do you like wine?" Lidia replies "Yes please." Danny "Anyone else want a wine?" No answer was heard. Danny continues "Another red wine for Lidia and I think 2 lagers for Hose and Jacob (they both nodded yes) and a vodka for Joanna I think." Joanna in very slow speech says "Yes please with coke cola please Danny thank you very much." Danny "And a double vodka for Joanna and whatever she wants in it, right let's liven this show up is it?" They all started smiling and got very chatty and Danny was Impersonating them and making them laugh and later Jeff went up and got them another drink each and by the end of the night they were very merry and next in walks Carol and Jeff got up and went and sat by her and started chatting her up and cuddling up and laughing and then Jeff had a big shock someone said to him "Hello Jeff can I sit by my girl please?" Jeff dumfounded said "Ah, ah, of course you can." Jeff stood up and went to the other side of the table and sat down and Carol introduced them "Jeff this is Adi he is my new boyfriend." Jeff stunned said "Oh hello Adi I think I know you don't I?" Adi replies "Yes Jeff I am a trainer student in the gym and we have never really had anything to do with each other." Jeff sarcastically said "I go in the gym at least 5 times a week." Adi looking shocked "Do you? I have never seen you in there what days?" Jeff "Oh different days I can go in whenever I like." Adi "So what do you do in there?" Jeff says with a smirk on his face "I go in there for a drink of water ha, ha, ha." Adi smiled but did not like Jeff's attitude at all and said "There we are then, by looking at you it might be too hard for you in there ay?" Jeff "Do you think so? I don't see the need to walk around looking all macho at all, I can't be bothered a good fag does the same for me and a good pint." Adi said "Tell me Jeff , have I done anything to upset you?" Jeff answers "No not at all, it's just the way you talk I think but don't worry about it." Adi was about to tell Jeff what he thinks and Carol butts in "Now c'mon lads play nicely now lads, please." Adi says "He does not like it because I am going out with you, he was all over you until I came here, now he is upset about it." Jeff "Ha, ha, don't be stupid it's allright by me just don't act like I am a dick head because I don't work out and act macho." Adi "I never said nothing of the sort, I never opened my mouth, so don't go there mate." Jeff "I am not your mate, I am choosy but I respect Carol's decision and I am happy for you ok?" Carol says "Well thank you Uncle Jeffrey." Adi "Uncle Jeffrey, who is Uncle Jeffrey? Ha, ha, yes thank you Uncle Jeffrey ha, ha." Jeff "Ha, ha, ha, right it's ok I am going to get a drink see you later." Adi mutters "Have we got too?" Carol tugs his arm and said "Don't be awful Adi he is my friend." Adi "Your friend he was all over you like a rash and he is jealous I could tell he took a instant dislike to me because I am with you are you blind? Sorry I didn't realise what I was saying." Carol "That's ok, but don't have a go at him he is a good friend ok?" "Ay allright." Jeff had gone to sit by Danny and Danny was still taking the Mickey out of the S.S.W's and they were enjoying every minute of it. Jeff says to Danny "Well I have seen it all now, Carol is going out with that bloody Welsh Adrian who is in the gym do you know him?" Danny answers "Yes I do he takes me in the gym, he is very good so what has he done? Besides going out with Carol?" "Well he acts so macho and he is ignorant and he made me move so as he could sit by Carol." Danny "I see what is wrong here." Jeff "Allright what is it then?" "He has pushed your nose out, you don't like it because he is going out with Carol, another woman spoken for and now you have to behave and not try and get into her knickers." Jeff "Huh, he won't stop me talking to her and I will try and chat her up as usual ." "Well good luck I will see you in the hospital as he won't take any messing with you and it will be your fault mate and I will not stick up for you, it's on your head be it." Jeff looking startled says "Oh thanks mate, thanks a bunch." Danny "Well it will be your fault not his if you mess with someone's girlfriend then you must except the consequences mate, it is only what you deserve, so don't go there." "Right but I still don't like him though." Danny smiles and says "Don't worry you don't have to like him, that's Carol's Job, so let it drop in case Geraldine finds out about this, because she will never bother with you if she does." Jeff says "I am running out of options lately, god, I give up it's always happening to me." Next up comes the girl in charge behind the bar Linda and she said to Jeff "I had a call earlier behind the bar for you I didn't know who you were at first now I do a girl named Geraldine and at first it was funny as I don't ever remember your name and myself and my colleague said who is Jeff? And it was said to me oh it's Danny and Barbara, did you know that is what we call you here?" Jeff smiling says "Danny and Barbara, why do you call me Barbara then?" Linda "Because we can never remember your name as there are so many Jeff's here, but you look like a Barbara to me ha, ha, sorry." Jeff still smiling "I look like a Barbara so that's it I am going to be known as Barbara up here from now on." Linda "Ha, ha, ha, I am sorry but that is how we have always known and I know who people are talking about then sorry mate, anyway she said she is going to be late in tomorrow and can you inform her tutor as you are in the same place tomorrow." "Of course, does she know you refer to me as Barbara?."

187

Linda replies "Yes, see you later." Jeff "Yes ok, I will see you, Danny did you hear what she just said about referring to me and you as Danny and Barbara?" Danny "Yes I did and I knew I had something to tell you last week, but it slipped my mind she referred to us as Danny and Barbara as she can never remember your last name, nothing wrong with that is there?" Jeff looking dejected said "Well not for you it is your name but Barbara, I am a man why Barbara? It's silly." Danny smirking says "Don't worry about it I am not, it is nice I think and you need to cheer up mate forget about Carol and Adrian she was never on the cards anyway, she just likes the attention and now she has Adi, so get over it." Jeff "Yeh, just like that I am still going to speak and be big friends I don't care what you all say and that's it." Danny "Ok Barbara I understand but don't go out of your way to be obnoxious as you will lose her to if she has to decide between you, don't forget that, go and get the pints in mate for me." Jeff "Do you want any for the S.S.W's or what?" "No I think they have had enough tonight, they are merry and happy so I don't want to get them too drunk or I will get the blame as per usual, just one for me and you then." Jeff goes off for the beer and after he returns he looks at Adrian and Carol and says to Danny "Yes, another dodgy Welshman got under my craw, I heard that it is still legal to shoot a Welshman in the square in Hereford on a Sunday with a bow and arrow, I must get a long bow and plenty of arrows." Danny laughing says "Hey Barbara, I don't like your attitude mate, I have not done anything have I?" "No but you are Welsh and I need the practice don't I?" "But you are so short you would only be able to shoot up in the air ha, ha." Jeff says "Ha, ha, ha, you are probably right I am having this beer and going over Dowdell for a couple of tinnies, what about you?" Danny looking puzzled says "Yes, why not? It is going to get empty here before long so I will join you."

They walk into Dowdell and in the lounge was Winnie and Danny and Jeff walked in and sat down and Jeff handed the tins to Danny and said "God it's quiet here too, has there been anyone in Winnie?" Winnie in calm voice said "Only Niel and he has gone to bed early, he said he was tired and had a meeting early tomorrow with Anthea about him and Danny fighting, but that is all." Danny said "I think everyone is a little fed up and skint this time of the year as it is a case of saving money to pay for xmas, never mind it will get better now summer is just about here." Jeff "Yes I think you are right, so Niel is in front of Anthea is he? I would like to be a fly on the wall, I wonder what will happen? What did she say to you Dan?" Danny smiling says "Oh nothing really, she give me the rights and wrongs and gave me a formal warning and that's it and Niel will probably charm his way out of anything, because she is a woman and we can all get back to normal again." Winnie "Ha, ha, so does that mean you will help me again with my English?" Danny coughs and says "You got to be joking, after the way you treated me I don't think so." Winnie "Your a horrible man." Jeff "Time for a ciggy." And off he went. Danny says to Winnie "I told you I was finished with you once and for all after what you done to me, because it was nasty and besides it is too much like hard work in this lounge with everyone back and forth, it takes bloody ages so the answer is no thank you very much." She looks at Danny and acted like a little girl the way she spoke to him "Aw, please, I am sorry but you started it not me, you were horrible to me it was not my fault." Danny "I am sorry Winnie I don't need that problem, I want to just mind my own business and get on with my life and that's it sorry but that's how it is." Winnie "Right then we can do it in my room then if you like and I will be nice to you and not shout or complain." Danny sat there and his face lit up and he had a good think and said "I will think about it." Winnie's face lit up and a huge smile appeared and she said "And I will give you a massage every night if you want one Danny." Danny snapped "Ok, your on I will do it starting tomorrow night at 10.30 after I have had my pint." Winnie complained "That is too late, It is better if we do it earlier." Danny "Take it or leave it." She moaned "Oh ok , do you want a head massage now?" Danny "No thanks I will save it for tomorrow." Jeff entered and said "Is it safe now?" Winnie with a spring in her voice said "Yes things are good and I am happy again." Jeff "So what has happened to make you so happy then?" Winnie said "Nothing at all it is mine and Danny's and nothing to do with you ok? I am off to bed, goodnight both." They said goodnight to her and Jeff was curious to know everything and said "So are you going to tell me or what?" Danny thought for a while and thought this will give him the hump but he was not going to say it was just to help her with her English he was going to make him jealous, he said "I think I am on to a winner mate with Winnie but I cannot tell you, as you will tell everyone if I do, I know you." Jeff looking hurt "Don't be silly mate, I won't say a word I promise, on my kids lives, tell me." Danny smiling from ear to ear said "If I tell you it better be between me and you and that's all, I mean it." "Yes I promise I won't tell anyone else, tell me." Danny says "Well I am going to her room tomorrow night for some fun, but I must be in there before you all get back here or the deal is off." "Shut up, your lying, I don't believe it your making this up." "Think what you like mate but that's how it is, she has the hots for me and don't say anything to her neither." Jeff "Why? Don't she know?" "No you idiot, she gets wind I have told you and she will kill me and then I will kill you, got it?" "So it's the truth, you are really going there are you? I don't believe it, you lucky git you, well bloody hell I never I wish something would happen like that to me, ah dear, well, well." "You must know how I must feel now I am stunned I really am." Jeff "You jammy git you." Danny grinning behind Jeff's back says "I bet it is going to be fantastic and she is a virgin, I will have to take it easy on her for the first night, I suppose and after tomorrow she will never look at another man again, she is in for a treat matey." Jeff looking sick and wishing he could be there instead of Danny says "Aw, shut up you make me sick, you make me sick and a jealous man piss off please." Danny says "Right man I am off to bed, I must save my energy for tomorrow night, you must understand mate see you tomorrow."

The next day and Niel was in with Anthea and she said "I think you probably know why you are here, I have seen Danny and he has had a formal warning from me and I want to know your version before I decide what to do." Niel said "I have been home for the weekend and have had plenty of time to think and I think it was probably my fault I was all tensed up with what is happening in my I.T. classes and I have been told if I pack it in with Mr Marsh, for that subject I will have to leave, I was very angry about this and took it out on everyone and as you know Danny will not take any nonsense and we got into a bit of a silly scrap but I am feeling a lot better now and I am sorry and I didn't have to say that as I am probably not going to be here anymore but I am sorry." Anthea says "And are you and Danny ok now?" "I have not seen him as yet I have been dodging him until I seen you but I will sort it out before I leave." Andrea "What does that mean?" "I will apologise to him as I was a misery and should not have taken it out on him at all and I can't leave unless I do as we have been friends now for a long while." Anthea sat there silent for a while and then said "You keep on saying you are leaving, are you sure you are? Or have you decided you want to? Because of the problems with I.T." Niel says "Well I can't get on with the man who teaches me so I will have to won't I?" "No not really, I have had a suggestion put to me and discussed it with your tutor, it was suggested because of your dyslexia that you go to a person who understands this problem and teaches I.T. also and she has been approached and she is happy to do this and so if this suit's you we can go forward with it." Niel's face was a picture and he said "Well if that's ok I am all for it thank you, thank you, thank you, there is a god, I don't want to go, that was a good idea." Anthea said "Right I am going to overlook this problem with you and Danny and just give you a formal warning and I hope you speak to Danny and make friends again as Danny is good at making suggestions that is good for you and his friends to help them overcome problems." Niel just sat there stunned when he realised that it was Danny who had suggested to Anthea about him having a different tutor for I.T. and was so pleased he got a tear in his eye and choking back the tears said "Maybe I should listen to my friends next time instead of starting a fight with them." Anthea replied "It might be a good idea, it sometimes is the answer to your prayers, as they know you better than anyone." "Thank you Anthea this is brilliant I can't wait to phone my wife so can I go now?" "Yes of course, bye."

Niel left Anthea's office almost skipping now to meet up with Danny and sort things out but it will have to wait until coffee break, that soon came around. Danny was sitting with Jeff and having a laugh about a joke and Niel sat next to the lads. Niel said Allright lads?" Jeff replied "Yes hi Niel have a good weekend?" As he was telling Jeff all about the weekend Danny got up to get his coffee Niel says "I have had a funny weekend I was all uptight about the trouble with Danny and have felt awful, has he said anything?" Jeff "No, not much he just commented he was fed up with everything that had happened that's all, you have been in front of Anthea haven't you?" Niel looking sad "Yes and I have made a real plonker of myself I have, but I will put it right now and I have just had a written warning that's all." Jeff "That's all Danny had to." Danny sat down with his coffee and said "Allright Niel have a good weekend?" Niel replies "Not bad Dan Ceri sends her love and you were lucky you stayed this weekend with the trains I was a hour and a half delayed by them, but that's the bloody trains for you, what about you?" "I can't complain and we had some fun with the S.S.W's and got them tipsy on Saturday night and Carol has a new boyfriend that has upset Jeff." Niel said "I thought he was after Geraldine and who is Carol with now?" Jeff jumped into the conversation and said "I love Geraldine and Carol is going out with another dodgy Welshman Adrian in the gym." Niel "Oh he is ok I like him he is allright but I bet you don't like him do you?" Jeff "No I bloody don't." Niel "Just because he is going out with Carol that's why." Danny "Exactly what I said." Jeff "Right I have had enough of bloody dodgy Welshmen to last me forever I am going, I can't get any sense out of you lot, bye, bye." Niel "See you Jeff." Danny said "Yes I had better be off too I have to go to my room for some stuff." Niel said "Hang on Dan, I want to say something mate, look I am sorry mate I." Danny butted in "Awe, don't worry about it mate it happens." "No mate I was out of order and I am sorry, I should have listened to you it might have saved me a miserable weekend, Anthea told me in so many words you suggested someone to sort out problems with students who has dyslexia problems, meaning me really, and get a tutor who understands it and also teaches I.T. and now I am staying because it has been sorted out with a lady named funny enough Geraldine and I am so happy and I have you to thank, so thanks mate." Danny "Oh god, you are staying, oh no." Niel "Piss off you tosser." The both men laughed and Niel grabbed Danny's arm and shook his hand and hugged him and said "You really are a true mate and next time I tell you to keep your nose out, smack me in mine." Danny said "Don't be silly mate as I say it's a messy job but somebody's got to do it, see you later." Niel sat there and was feeling so happy now things were sorted out.

CHAPTER 10
A CHINESE EVERY NIGHT

It was a fine day and in the morning in the lounge was Niel and Zarrine sitting eating some toast and tea. Zarrine said to Niel "So tell me again what Anthea said?" "She has given me a warning the same as Danny and I am not leaving now I have Geraldine the tutor as my new I.T. tutor and everything is hunky dory,." "You said Danny did something and did you know Geraldine is Mandy the warden's mother?" Niel said "Is she? I hope she is as nice as her daughter then, are you listening now I said Danny was the one who suggested to Anthea I had a tutor who understands dyslexia and I gave Danny hell last week and I feel awful now but we have made friends now, so life is good." Zarrine says "Oh right, I understand now, Danny is going home this Thursday to see his brother and try and get him sorted out, I hope he is as good as that at sorting things out for him, he is in a state, I was told by Danny, there's a shame." Niel said in a calm voice "Yes, I feel for Danny it must be hell for him and he didn't need me giving him trouble, but let me say if his brother is as bad as Danny says then Danny will not give up easily and I think he has a good chance." Jeff walks in half way through the conversation and says "I agree Danny will sort him out because it is crushing him and I think it will destroy Danny if anything happens to his little brother." Niel " yes I agree he is so close to him and being his younger brother is hard to except, if it does not work out, I feel for them both" Zarrine looking sad said "Well whatever happens I think we must support him without question, all of us." Niel "That goes without saying." Jeff says "Yes we will I am sure." Carol walks in and said "Good morning all." They all said good morning and she said "Uncle Jeffrey how are you?" Jeff smiling said "Ha, ha, I am fine and you?" Carol replies "Yes I am fine and I hope you and Adrian get on a little better soon." Jeff "Well I will tolerate him I suppose but I don't have to like him." Carol "Uncle Jeffrey, what is the Matter with you? Adrian is lovely. "Niel butts in and says "He is jealous and don't want you with any other man, never mind who you went out with, he will not like them, am I right Jeff?" Jeff "No, it's not that at all, I just don't like the man." Zarrine "What has he done to you Jeffrey?" Jeff "Nothing, I just can't take to him." Carol says "Last night was the first time you spoke to him uncle Jeffrey, he told me he has never had anything to do with you before last night and has never even spoke to you, so I don't understand it." Niel says "Exactly, he does not want him with you, he was hoping to have you to himself and many other girls too." Jeff "Leave me alone I just can't get on with him and that's it, huh, he said he was in the gym and I said I go to the gym a few times a week." Zarrine says "You go to the gym, I don't think so." Jeff "I could tell by his face he thought that also and I said I do, I go in there for a drink of water when I am passing it ha, ha." Carol "Uncle Jeffrey." Jeff says "I am off, coming Niel?" Niel replies "Yes wait for me I tell you what meet me by the front door." Off the lads went and passed Danny on the way out. Danny sat down by Zarrine for a cup of tea." Zarrine said "I was proud of you this morning." Danny "Who me, why?" Zarrine says "I know what you done for Niel, he is over the moon now he is not going." Danny says "God, if he had brains he could have done the same thing for himself, it's not nuclear science." Carol says "Still Daniel, you did it for him and he is glowing now, so you are going home on Thursday then? Good luck with your brother I hope he sorts himself out I really do." Danny "Thanks Carol I appreciate it and Adrian ay, how are things going with you two?" Carol replies "Oh, it's early days yet, I will wait and see." Danny "Good thinking, but he seems nice enough to me." Carol says "Yes I hope so, I am off see you all." She goes off and in walks Winnie and says to Danny "I can't get my tape machine to work and all what we done is on it, oh dear." Danny says "Ok don't panic, I will have a look at it." Danny fiddles with it and says "I think it might be the battery." Winnie says "No I put new batteries in it a moment ago." Danny replies "I can't think what it could be then, you will have to manage." Winnie goes into a panic and says "Oh dear, I can't I must get it fixed, they won't give me another chance." Danny said "Right I will lend you my tape machine and sort it out later, you leave me your machine and I will hand it into technical support and get them to fix it." Winnie says "Thank you, I am sorry but I must get it right today, I am lucky you have one." Danny "No problem I am off now so come to my room and I will give you my tape machine." Winnie looking worried says "Can't you bring it in here to me please?" Danny says "Why, do you think I am going to jump on you or what?" Winnie said "Danny don't be silly, I am not going into your room in the morning and please will you bring it to me?" Danny in a huff says "Right wait there and I will go and fetch it, give me your tape machine, bloody hell." Danny goes off to get the machine and Zarrine speaks up "Winnie, it was allright to go to get it from his room, he is not a sex maniac, it's ok in this country." Winnie snaps "Zarrine I will ask you to mind your own business please, I was talking to Danny." Zarrine says "Ok sorry, I am out of here." Zarrine storms off and Danny comes back and says "There it is, it's in my machine and it is working ok now, what is the difference in you coming to my room and me coming to your room tonight?" Winnie say's, sh, "Sh, sh, sh, someone will hear you, the reason is you asked in front of someone that's why... I am off." She storms off and Danny had another cup of tea.

It was later in the student bar and Danny Niel and Jeff were having a pint or 2 and Jeff says "I have got to say it's nice here now that the 3 amigos are together again without all the arguing, you pair, honestly." Niel says "Jeff you don't understand us Welsh do you? we don't keep on about it we have a scrap and the next day forget about it, not like you English, you go on and on about it forever." Jeff says "Oh there we are then, ah look who just come in Tim and Mandy, I will tell them where we are sitting." Jeff toddles off and Danny said "Perhaps they don't want to sit by us, maybe they want to be on their own." Niel "I would think they have had enough of being alone and run out of things to say." Danny says "You might be right, it's like being married and they say women can multi task, so why can't they have sex when they have a headache." Niel "Ha, ha, yes I wonder, they say the best thing to kill your sex life is a wedding ring ha, ha." Danny says "I have been married 4 times because I love wedding cake ha, ha." Niel said "Now you are diabetic all the women are safe, do you think anything will come of Tim and Mandy?" "Oh yes, anyone can tell they are very much in love and they are suited together and will have a wonderful life I think." Niel replies "I think you are right, we just need to get Jeff sorted out with a woman now." "That is going to be hard I think, it would be easier to kick start a jumbo jet, but there is someone out there for everyone I think even him." Tim, Mandy and Jeff sit down and Tim says "Hi guys, hows things?" Danny says "Good Tim and hows the lovely Mandy then?" Mandy says "I'm fine, thank you Danny, and you?" Danny smiling says "Yes I am ok thank you it's nice of you both to surface out of your rooms isn't it lads?" Niel "Yes we were worried about you, wondering if you have eaten lately and Tim as not had a pint for a while." Tim "So you call this dishwater a pint Niel?" Niel "Yes you maybe right, I only drink the cider up here." Danny says "I only drink anything out of a bottle the tap beer is so bad." Jeff says "When is the wedding then Mandy?" Mandy acting coy says "Oh you had better ask Tim not me." Tim says "Well you will be surprised to hear we have been discussing it and we will be announcing it shortly." Niel smiling says "That's nice Tim and Mandy I am so pleased for you both." Jeff "Yes if anyone is a perfect match you two are, I am pleased for you." Danny says very much the same and Tim says "Well thank you lads and you will be the first to know I shall make sure." Danny "I think it is a good reason for a toast, to Tim and Mandy." They all toast them and sit down again.

Next in walks Carol and Jeff spots her and rushes off to see her, he sits down beside her and is all over her again as Adrian is not there. Back at the table and Danny says "Oh he is off with Carol again, he is taking a risk, if Adrian sees him there will be trouble and I have warned Jeff he is silly." Tim "Yes I agree he is not a small man and fit to go with it, he is dicing with death. Niel I thought you were leaving?" Niel replies "No I am staying now it has been sorted, I am with a woman tutor named Geraldine, she is taking me as she is trained to cope with dyslexia and I am happy now." Mandy says "Oh, that's good Niel do you know Geraldine, she is lovely and you will get on like a house on fire with her, she is so patient, she took me as she did it for me." Niel "Well I hope she does it for me too ha, ha." As they were talking about Niel's new tutor Geraldine you could see Jeff pricking his ears up as he heard Geraldine's name mentioned and Danny said "Every time we mention Geraldine Jeff listens intently he is dying to know what we are saying. he thinks we are referring to Geraldine the student he fancies madly, but he does not know we are referring to Geraldine the tutor and I am going to wind him up. Listen lads I will have to say this quiet as he will hear, I am going early tonight and Niel is going at 9. 3o and I am off at 10 o'clock and Tim when we have gone say to Jeff when he comes back that Geraldine is seeing Niel now then and I will back you up in the morning as he is bound to ask me and don't panic Niel as Geraldine is back in 2 days so he will find out the truth then and laugh his head off and Tim if he asks if you know Geraldine say you don't but all you know is that Niel is with her from now on ha, ha." Mandy says "Danny, don't be cruel to him that is not nice." Niel says "Mandy he would do it to us no problem." Mandy feeling sorry for Jeff says "Tim are you going to do it to him?" Tim with a smile says "To bloody right I am just to see his face ha, ha." Danny says to Mandy "It is only a bit of fun he will laugh after and will say himself he would have done it if the tables were turned. Right my round Tim pint of beer Mandy half of lager and Niel cider and Jeff what about you lager." Jeff shouts back "Yes please matey, I will be over now when her wolf gets here." Carol said "Oh, he is not coming up until half past ten, he is moving his mate to a different hall." Jeff smiling says "Right, so I can chat you up in that case and we have time to jump into bed and get back here for a pint after." Carol "Uncle Jeffrey behave yourself."

Back at the table with Danny Tim and the others Danny "We had a good time in the barrels last night, what a good pint of real ale in there Tim, it's Malvern ale and it's gorgeous it really is and you said you would come and try it." Tim "Well when you get back after the weekend I will come over there one night for a couple what do you think?" Danny "Yes, good idea and it will be nice to have a real ale drinker with me for a change and Mandy what about you are you coming too." Mandy says "No I will catch up with my course work and leave the drinking to Tim and you lot." Tim "Have you been up with the braile girls yet since the trouble with your name?" Danny "No we had it cancelled last week and they said we will stay together until I bollocks it up again remember." Tim says laughing "I told Mandy about it and we killed ourselves laughing all the time." Niel chuckling said "What was that Tim? ha, ha." Tim could not talk for laughing then said "Tell him Danny it was the funniest thing." Danny said "Well in the braile I cannot get the hang of the difference of a D or a F and get them mixed up and put a D's an F and an F as a D and I done an exercise and after it was all done Ginny went over the paper and Immediately started laughing uncontrollably and we could not get out of her why and it lasted for a long time and she composed herself and said what I had done, she said what is your name I said Danny Duckfield well she said you have written Fanny Fuckdielf." Everyone roared laughing and the whole place laughed as they had all been listening and laughter was heard for several minutes. Danny said "God that was so funny and we did nothing for the rest of the lesson. We were weak and every time she says now to put my name on the top of the paper I know I will burst out laughing." Tim said "Funny that's what I have been thinking I won't be able to hold it I just won't I know it." The laughter settled down and Danny told a joke that reminded him of it "A woman who was besotted by her new boyfriend said to him one day so why do you love Bridgett Bardot so much, the boyfriend said I just love her to bit's I really do, so she decided to have a tattoo on her ass and put the initials of her on her bottom and so had a large B on one cheek and a B on the other cheek and one night she said do you fancy some sex? He said oh yeah, she said fancy it doggy fashioned? the boyfriend said brilliant and she thought he will see the 2 B's on her bum and be so happy, so she bent over and kneeled on the bed and he looked at her ass and said who the hell is BOB? " At that everyone started laughing and Niel says "Ha, ha, ha, that was brilliant, bloody brilliant, I am off before I pea myself, see you guys." They said goodnight and Niel was laughing so much he sounded as if he was crying and Mandy was having a fit she was laughing so much. Tim says "Brilliant Daniel very good, I must say, so you are off on Thursday then?" Danny "Yes, I am off to try and help my little brother get over a serious problem and to get hold of my older brother and see if we can do something to help him, it is breaking my heart." Tim "I can't Imagine what it is like but I hope it all works out for you and I didn't know you had a older brother. I thought there was only 2 of you." Danny said "No I never see much of him he lives down the west in Milford Haven, he is a lovely bloke and likes a good joke like me however he is a Jehovah's witness and don't like them so crude but I get on with him very well and a very trustworthy man, if he says something is right it is right you can take it to the bank and he will do anything for you, he is ok and has a heart of a lion and I love him very much." Tim "That's nice to know and your little brother do you think he will listen to you and sort himself out?" Danny "God I hope so he is worrying me and his missus don't really give a shit, she is only interested in her mother and I think uses Lyndon for his money and he hasn't got a lot of that, with her In debt all the time, I think that is what is wrong with him, she has dragged him down he should never have married her, he is not the marrying kind, it has ruined his life." Mandy "Awe, there's awful he sounds nice too the way you described him before, I hope he listens to you and gets himself sorted out." Danny "And me, right I am off I am having a Chinese so I am going, nice to see you both, I will see you tomorrow night if you are coming up." Tim "Yes but we are coming up late and I will see you in braile tomorrow." Danny "Yes, of course, I hope I can remember my name ha, ha."

Jeff shouts "Danny are you leaving already?" Danny replies "Yes I am off for a Chinese as you know I told you." Jeff "Oh yes, see you in the morning and enjoy your Chinese." Danny "Don't worry I will." Carol says "I fancy a Chinese now too, but it is too late now, never mind." Jeff smiling "Yes I wish I was having the same Chinese as him and I think the wolf is due so I will slip off when he arrives." Carol "Don't be silly he is alright and what Chinese is Danny having then? as you fancy it so much?" Jeff "Oh I think he is trying a traditional Chinese, so I might like it so I don't know." Next thing he starts up his chat up lines "Hey baby I must be a light switch, because every time I see you, you turn me on and that is just for starters. Wouldn't we look good on a wedding cake together? I am going to have sex with you tonight, you just as well be there to enjoy it, ha, ha, ha, my beds broken can I sleep in yours?" Carol says "Uncle Jeffrey, Where do you get all these chat up lines from?" "I have gathered them up over the years ha, look out I think the gym boy just came in, I will be off then." Adi heard him and said "No, don't run away mate, I am not complaining at all " Jeff replies "Oh I don't want to cramp your style mate." Adi replies "Oh you will never do that mate, so you haven't anything to worry about." Jeff says "I need some peace and quiet from the sexy Carol anyway."

He sit's by Mandy and Tim and says "Hi guys, everything allright?" Tim says "Yes thanks Jeff, we have enjoyed it tonight and I am just about ready for bed, I caught up with all the gossip now so I am happy." Jeff looking confused said "Ok, what did they say about me then?" Tim says "Nothing about you, I heard about Danny going home to see is brother and help sort him out, he must be pulling his hair out and Niel's new woman Geraldine." Jeff's eyes lit up and he snapped "What about Geraldine and Niel?" "His new woman is a woman named Geraldine and he is going to meet with her day after tomorrow and he can't wait." Jeff says "No Tim you must have got it wrong, he is married." Tim "No mate he definitely did say Geraldine I know it was and he is so excited about it all." Jeff's face dropped and he muttered "No, no, he can't go out with Geraldine, it's not fair I can't see that and it must have been going on beneath my very nose, well, well, and what did he actually say?" Tim says "He is very happy and I asked him why? And he said he was so pleased he has a new woman and her name is Geraldine and he is in her class I don't know this Geraldine but he is thrilled about it, he was like a child with a new toy, fancy a pint mate? it's my last one." Jeff says looking dejected "Yes please mate I just as well get pissed now, I am feeling so sick." Tim goes off to the bar and Mandy says "So is this Geraldine and you a couple then?" "Oh no we wasn't but I was trying to get off with her and now look everyone has a girlfriend, even bloody Niel and me, I am not even in a relationship, in fact he has 2 and me nothing it's not fair." Mandy says "Awe, never mind Jeff it will happen soon don't worry." Tim comes back from the bar and he is trying not to laugh and says "So who is this Geraldine then Jeff? a girl belonging to your troop?" Jeff replies "What do you mean troop?" Tim says "Well you have Carol there and Geraldine there and is it Catalina and who else have I missed and now Geraldine is with Niel, Carol is with Adrian and the only one left is Catalina, perhaps they think the same as me that you are going out with the other bird, it's hard to keep up, you need to make up your mind." Jeff looks very sad and says "Maybe you are right mate it's all going bad for me, I wish I still had Geraldine's telephone number, I have lost it somewhere, well crashed and burned again." Tim "Well Jeff I think you should stick to getting one girl and stick to her and that's it." Jeff "I think your right." Carol says out loud "Uncle Jeffrey are you still here? I am ha, ha, I will be off now in a minute as we are going for a Chinese to, see you tomorrow and behave yourself with all these women." Jeff "I don't have much choice." Tim says "Never mind mate I wouldn't lose no sleep over it be like Danny get a Chinese and have a good night's sleep, things will look different in the morning." Jeff says "I wish I could have a Chinese like Danny, I really do." Mandy says "Well phone and get one Jeff." Jeff smiling says "Oh it's shut now and I want to have Danny's Chinese it's nicer." Mandy "Well go and knock his door and he might share his with you." Jeff smiling says "No I don't think so he wants this Chinese for himself, I know him, never mind I will go and get a packet of crisps and go home and pout, I will see you both tomorrow, goodnight." Tim and Mandy says goodnight to Jeff and Mandy says to Tim "Awe I feel sorry for him and I hope he finds someone soon, he is really nice."

It was the next morning and Jeff, Danny and Zarrine were in the lounge having breakfast and Jeff says to Danny " so how long have you known about Niel and Geraldine?" Danny "Since Monday why?" Jeff "So why didn't you tell me then? " "I thought you knew." Jeff "No I bloody didn't and you knew I was chasing her myself." Danny replies "So I don't keep an eye on your love life, one minute you are chasing Geraldine and then it's Carol and then Catalina then someone else, I can't keep up with you mate and if she is seeing Niel I can understand it as they are thinking the same, ask anyone you are like a hungry wolf about the place so don't blame me it's your own fault." Zarrine was chuckling and she said "Jeff he is right, I don't know who is your latest girlfriend or who is going to be next weeks." Jeff "I see I will have to slow down, I suppose, but I will see Niel and ask him why he didn't tell me." Danny "Why? he does not have to explain it to you, it's his business and nothing to do with you." Jeff "Well he must have known I was after her I said it enough times." Zarrine "And the same about Carol, Catalina and so on and so on." Danny " and if he waited for you to make up your mind he will never get somebody ha, ha." Jeff "Still." Zarrine says to Danny "So you had a Chinese last night, I hope you have not made a mess in your room with it?" Danny says "No I have already put it in the main bin so no mess." Next in walks Niel and says "Good morning all it's a lovely day, I am late again." Jeff says to him "I hear you are seeing Geraldine tomorrow then, a bit sudden wasn't it?" Niel "Yes I suppose it was, I am surprised to, some of us have it and some of us haven't sorry mate." Jeff "I am surprised you didn't go away with her." Niel "No I was too busy but I will see Geraldine tomorrow, I can't wait." Jeff "Well good luck matey, I am happy for you, tell me have you got her mobile number?" Niel replies "No I haven't sorry." Jeff "Oh, not that close then." Niel says "Oh no it's only a college thing, nothing else, I don't need problems after I leave here thanks, see you all I am late." Niel leaves and Jeff says to Danny "He's flippant about it isn't he? I think it is just for sex and that's all." Danny "I expect so, most relationships here are a college thing and after they leave it fizzles out." Jeff "I think she deserves more than that myself, I could not do that to her." Danny "Perhaps she is feeling the same, Waite and see you can ask her tomorrow." Jeff "I bloody will." Zarrine "That's the second time you have sworn, I will put you in the naughty corner mind." Jeff "Sorry Zarrine, I am just gutted." Jeff goes off to his lectures without saying much more and Zarrine says to Danny "What is going on? I thought Niel was madly in love with his wife? I am surprised." Danny replies "He is and he is not seeing Geraldine in his class he is having Mandy's mother Geraldine teaching him I.T. and we have let Jeff believe it is his Geraldine if you know what I mean." "Oh, oh, I see, you will push Jeff too far one day Danny, he will take it to heart one day and you will lose a good friend." Danny says "No he loves a joke as much as I do and will laugh about it and he will know the truth tomorrow so don't worry." Zarrine says "Well I think you go too far sometimes, I know I would be unhappy if you did it to me, so be careful." Danny smiling says "Oh, don't worry he is ok I can never have as much fun if he was not around, he is a good laugh, I will see you later."

Danny did not see Jeff much that day until he went up the student bar later on that night and Jeff was there leaning on the bar looking sorry for himself. Danny said to him "Allright matey?" Jeff "Yeh, I am allright why shouldn't I be? I am all alone and being laughed at by you lot and sit on my own all the time here, like a spare prick in a Bangkok brothel and I am waiting for you now to say something to make me worse." "Oh dear, we are feeling sorry for our self-tonight, how many pints have you had?" "What has that got to do with the price of eggs?" No serious, how many? As you sound half cut." Jeff replies "Why should you be worried? I am nearly 40 now and I can look after myself." "C'mon, don't be like that mate, I am only concerned." "Well you don't have to be, just leave me alone for once." Danny looking a little worried says "Sorry mate I can't I am your mate and I am worried so how many have you had?" "5 I think and I am having another now and don't tell me it's only 8 o'clock because I already know and have a pint with me a Newcastle is it?" "Yes please mate I will get them now." Jeff snarls at Danny "No you bloody won't I asked you are you stupid, listen to me for a change will you?" "Ok, ok, I am happy to have a drink off you, so what is this all really about Jeff?" Jeff in a temper replies "You don't know, where have you been?" Danny looking confused says "I think you are going to tell me whether I want to know or not but I suspect it is something to do with Geraldine and Niel." "Good guess and Carol and all the other girls who never take me serious." "I am sure you are exaggerating you just let them think you are a man who is out for a laugh and don't take girls serious and that is your fault, you chase all the women here and don't think the other women don't notice but Jeff they do, so how can you expect them to take you serious? Be honest." Jeff says "Yes you might be right, I must stop it I know, but even Niel has a girlfriend now even him and he tells everyone he is a happily married man and he still gets a girl, I don't believe it." "Don't say that out loud mate he might hear and it is not his fault he is a hunk of a Welshman, but we can't help it, but serious you need to pick on one girl and stick to it with her until it fizzles out or you both become close, don't chase everything." "Yeh, yeh, drink up your round." Danny looked in amazement and says "God you only just bought that last pint and you have drunk it already? Slow down man." Jeff "Right, barman another 2 pints here please and charge the dodgy Welshman." Danny says "You will be pissed before 9 the way you are going, slow down Jeff please." "If you can't keep up don't worry mate drop out." "Hey don't go there, I am only worried you have lectures tomorrow." Jeff "So I will take my pillow with me, oh sorry mate I am down tonight, I can't help it I must have a girl soon or I am going to burst." "Hang on in there mate, I think things are going to change for you sooner or later, I'm sure." Next in walks Carol and says "Uncle Jeffrey how are you my uncle Jeffrey?" Jeff says "Hello Carol, and where is macho man?" She replies "If you mean Adrian he is in the gym and will be up later and what is wrong with my uncle Jeffrey then?" Danny says "He hasn't had a shag for a while and he is depressed and I can't help him out what about you?" Carol snaps "Daniel, you mustn't say that." Danny smiling says "Well your a girl he needs a girl so I will not do and I was just asking." Carol "Well don't." Jeff then says "See what i mean, I am just a plaything and that's all." Danny says smiling "Well Jeff if I was a girl and a good friend I would help out my bestest mate." Jeff plays along and says "Yes I know you would mate, I know." Carol not knowing what to say says "That's not fair, you buggers are taking advantage of me and I am not biting I am sorry." Jeff "See crashed and burned again, the story of my life." Carol "Sorry Jeff I think you are drunk aren't you?" Jeff "Not yet but I will soon be but that's ok don't worry about me I am ok." Carol "Uncle Jeffrey, now stop it or I am off." Danny "He is a bit tiddled he has had 8 pints already, but I will see him home no worries." Carol says "Ok then, as long as he can get home I will see you later, bye." Jeff "Yes bye, at least I know who my friends are and what about your Chinese?" "I will have a Chinese tomorrow night before I go home Thursday no problem." Jeff says "I am going to miss the quiz on Thursday as no one will go now, but there is always Pam." Danny "Yes I suppose so, ah look who it is Lidia." Jeff shouts "Hello Lidia how are you?" Lidia says "Hello Jeff nice to see you, are you ok?" Jeff "I think so, I am a little drunk though." Lidia "What is this" ? Danny tells her "He is falling after tequila too much." Lidia laughing says " Sorry understand, pissed." Danny "Correct, he is unhappy with his girls, he has none." Lidia "Ah, ah, ah, I think too, my Catalina is not happy with boyfriend also." Danny "Never mind Jeff will be better tomorrow when he is sober, I am getting drinks in, would you like one Lidia? Maybe a red wine, yes." Lidia "Please, thank you." Jeff "Yes about time matey I am empty and I am in love with Catalina." Lidia not understanding says "Yes her to." Jeff "Yes, never mind I will not bore you with my problems."

Later on in the evening and Jeff by now was paralytic and falling about and laughing and Danny got hold of him and took him to his room and put him to bed and went into the lounge and in there was Winnie waiting for him and looking annoyed. She said "Oh hello, I have been waiting for you, what happened to you?" Danny now slurring his words said "I am sorry but Jeff was not well he was drunk and I had to get him to his room as he could not stand, I am sorry." Winnie in bad mood said "Oh good, I have to wait for drunk man and not have my English lesson because he was drunk and I think you are also drunk to, this is not good you promised." "Yes I know but I will do it for you tomorrow ok?" "You are a silly man and I am not speaking to you." Winnie storms off to bed.

The next morning in the lounge for breakfast and Zarrine and Winnie were having breakfast and in walks Danny holding his head and he said "Good morning." Zarrine says "Good morning Danny." Winnie says "Huh, the drunk velshman, I am off." Danny says "Winnie I said I am sorry." Winnie storms off and Zarrine says "Oh, you have upset her, what have you done?" "Jeff was drunk in the bar last night and I didn't get here in time to help her with her English and ended up getting a little drunk with Jeff, but he was pissed the worst I have ever seen him." "Why did he do that?" "Well it's all about his let down with the women here, but it is his fault not anyone else's, so don't get him out of bed this morning, he will still be drunk and they will not be Impressed over there and the mood he is in he might say something he will regret and I don't want to see him get expelled, so leave him sleep it off." Zarrine looking concerned says "Ok I think you maybe right if he is that bad, is this to do with Geraldine or what?" "I think it is to do with all his women and he does not help himself, he wants every woman he sets his eyes on but he will be happier when the truth comes out about Geraldine, don't worry." "I hope you and him don't have a fight tonight please or are you staying out of his way until you get back from Bridgend? I hope not, you must tell him because he will never forgive you, so please do this." Danny replies "Yes ok, I can't wait to see his face, I will get Niel to tell him, I think for my sake ha, ha." "I think you have a horrible side to you sometimes I do." Jeff walks in looking like death warmed up and said "Oh my god, I am dying, what did I do last night? God awe." Zarrine looking shocked says "Oh Jeffrey, you look awful please sit down I make you a cup of tea." Danny says "You were very drunk last night." Jeff says "I certainly was and still am, I feel like I have been hit by a train and I am going back to bed now, I am missing lectures today, I don't feel good at all how many did I drink last night?" Danny says "I lost count man I remember you on 9 and I was only on 3 and I am not too bright today neither but not half as bad as you, I reckon you were well into 2 figures and I bet you are feeling bad as I had to carry you home and I got into trouble with Hong Kong fuey, but never mind." Jeff "I am going back to bed as I am terrible and I am sorry about last night man, I really am." Danny "Think nothing of it mate we all get like it from time to time," Zarrine gives Jeff a cup of tea and says "There you are Jeff, get that down you, do you want some toast? I will make you some if you like." Jeff "Yes I will try a round or 2 please, I never ate last night and I am starving now thank you Zarrine, Dan can you give room b14 a ring and tell them I am not well mate? So as I get my mark please " Danny." Danny "certainly mate I wouldn't go like that today, you will get expelled and I will tell Niel before he goes so as he is aware of it so he don't drop you in the shit." Jeff "Thank you mate, Zarrine no jam on my toast please I can't stand it this morning thank you." Carol sneaks in behind Jeff and says " Uncle Jeffrey, I don't know whether to speak to you after last night." Jeff replies "Hello Carol, so I suppose I had a go at you too did i? I don't know what I said but I am sorry." Carol "You wanted to have sex with me as you have not had it for a while and tried to make me feel awful about it ha, ha." Zarrine says "Aw, Carol don't pick on him this morning, he is not well at all, look at him he looks as if he was dumped on a doorstep after he was born." Jeff chuckles and says "It's not that bad Zarrine and this toast is lovely thanks and Carol I am sorry but I was drunk and it won't happen again." Carol "I'm only joking Uncle Jeffrey it was really funny ask Danny, it was him that suggested it." Danny had come in and said "Suggested what?" Carol said "You suggested I had sex with Jeff as you are a man and can't and as I was one of his bestest friends and female I should oblige." Jeff smiling says "Dan thank you mate, a true friend." They all laughed and Jeff said "I am off to bed and don't want to be disturbed unless it is Carol deciding to oblige me after all." Carol slaps him on the back and they all laughed again and all went off.

Later that afternoon and in the common room was Jeff sitting watching television and in walks Niel and sit's by him, at first Jeff didn't say a word then Niel spoke up and said "Hello Jeff I have had a great day and you missed it this afternoon it was funny as Rhoda had put on 2 different shoes one brown and one black it was funny, Rhoda and Geraldine are in Rhoda's room they will be in now, she was asking about you as you were ill, I told her." Jeff says "Did you, thank you Niel how has your day been in general?" Niel replied "Great it was fantastic with Geraldine today, we had a good start and hit it off Immediately, she is very nice indeed, we have a whole day planned on Friday, it is looking like it will be a marriage made in heaven until I leave here next year. She said we will do everything by then as there is so little time to get it all in and she wishes we were going to be together for longer." Jeff sarcastically says "There we are then, don't rush it mate enjoy it while it lasts." Niel plays among and says "Yes I think the same, I will give it all I got I think and my missus will appreciate it at the end of it all as I will get used to helping myself instead of her doing it all aye." In walks Danny and says "Hello lads how are you Jeff? And how did it go with Geraldine for your first time Niel." Niel answers first "Oh man it was fantastic nice and easy just right you would have enjoyed it mate if it was you." Jeff said "I am fine but not as fine as Niel though, I need a tinny I am going to get one." He goes off and returns with 4 cans and Danny says "Oh c'mon Jeff don't start again mate, not again." Jeff says as Geraldine walks in "I am not matey, I would not get drunk over a woman like her anyway." Niel says "Who do you mean Jeff?" Jeff "If the cap fit's mate." Geraldine says "Hello Jeff how are you feeling now? I was worried about you." Jeff snaps "Ok thank you, I can look after myself don't worry." Geraldine says "I was only asking, no need to be like that." Jeff "Whatever." Ger. says "Who has stood on your toes, I won't bother asking again." Jeff said nothing and carried on drinking out of his can. Next in walks Rhoda and Mandy the warden and they said "Hello all working hard again I see." Rhoda says "Jeff skiving again today hey, we had a hard day today and you are sitting here drinking " Jeff "Hi Rhoda, yes I have as my friends keep stabbing me in the back." Geraldine says "Don't listen to him Rhoda he is in a funny mood." Rhoda says "I can see that, someone upset you Jeff?" He answers sarcastically "No, noone." Mandy speaks up "Cheer up Jeff, last week it was Niel and Danny now you and by the way Niel my mum was talking about you a minute ago, she says what a charming man you are but I will put her right ha, ha." Niel says "Oh Geraldine you mean, I forgot she was your mum, she was brilliant, I was just saying to Jeff about her, yes Geraldine, she is a good teacher, I am glad to be in her classes as she is a good patient teacher and I would give up computers if it wasn't for her and another Geraldine, it's easy to get confused, isn't it?" Jeff had a face on him as if he had just been kissed by a camel realising that Niel was referring to another Geraldine and he had made a fuss about nothing but Danny and Niel had made out it was his Geraldine. Jeff then said "Ha, ha, ha, I have been stuffed by you bloody Welshmen again, I am stupid, I really am, I thought it was this Geraldine you were seeing Niel and you both led me to believe it too, you bastards." Mandy says "Jeffrey language please, not in front of ladies." Jeff looking sick said "Geraldine I was thinking you were going out with Niel, these 2 made me believe he was and I am sorry for earlier, I listened to these 2." Ger "I am confused but don't speak to me Jeff not after the way you just spoke to me, I am not interested until you apologise to me properly." Jeff "I just did, I am sorry I really am." Ger "Accepted this time but don't you talk to me like that again." Jeff said to Danny and Niel "Very funny lads you had me again and I fall for it all the time, Ger, let me tell you Danny and Niel played a name game, I thought you and Niel were seeing each other and they were talking about Mandy's mother he is having lessons with." Mandy "What about my mother? She is not having anything with Niel, so don't Imply that." Jeff "No I know I do now but never mind I have been made a fool of ." Rhoda "Right Jeff, Geraldine has not gone out with anyone and Niel has had lessons with another Geraldine, so forget all about it and get on with your life ok? Let's forget it now ok?" Jeff was feeling stupid and was very happy also but had not finished with Danny and Niel you can be assured, life was back to normal for him for now and Geraldine forgave him after he explained to her what the other pair had done to him.

Later in the student bar and Danny, Niel, Geraldine, Jeff, Rhoda, Tim and Mandy were having a drink and having a laugh about Jeff and the mistakes etc. Jeff "Tim I am not going to forgive you for Joining in with these bloody Welshmen against me, but it was good, I can now laugh about it ha, ha, and Mandy I am surprised at you, I didn't think you would help them." Mandy said "I am sorry Jeff, I was forced into it and it hurt me to do it, I was dying to tell you, honest." Jeff "Don't worry I forgive you, I know it was all up to those Welshmen, I will get my own back, it's my turn." Danny said "Well you will have to get up early to catch me matey." Niel added "It was Danny not us, so don't have a go at me." Jeff "I know I guessed he was behind it all and it nearly ruined my love life with Geraldine." Geraldine's ears picked up and she said "I heard that, there is no love life to ruin and the way you spoke to me I will not even think about it now, so forget it mate." Jeff pleaded "It was this lot winding me up, I really didn't think you could go out with Niel." Niel snapped "Oy, who are you talking about? What's the Matter with me? You cheeky git." Jeff "No I didn't mean that, I am going to shut up, I keep on dropping myself in it." Danny smiling said "Good idea mate you are making things worse even Rhoda is waiting for an insult. Right I am off." Tim says "Hey it's only 9. 30 mate it's too early for you." Danny said "Oh I am off for a Chinese in my room and I have my lectures and dinner time I am off home." Tim says "Right I hope things go well for you and your brother, all the best." They all say very much the same to him, he replies "Thanks guys I really appreciate it, see you all Sunday when I get back." Niel says "God, he will be like a tank with all these Chinese meals all the time." Jeff smirked and says "I think he will be the opposite myself." Niel says "Don't be so daft, how do you work that out?" Jeff "I just got a feeling he is on the good stuff and he is not using chop sticks with it, so no quiz tomorrow then is there? Anyone fancy going?." No reply came and Jeff gave up asking, next thing a little girl came bounding through the door and shouts "Banging, that was banging, bloody banging." Niel says "Kezz is that you?." She replied "Who's that?." Niel "It's me Niel, come here and say hello." Kezz says "I am listening to my tape machine and there is my favourite singer on there, do you know Miesha Paris?" Niel says "You hum it and I will sing it." She laughs ha,ha,ha, banging, I am going to get a drink and sit by you."

Off she goes and Geraldine says "Who the bloody hell is that Niel? Ha, ha, ha." Niel replies chuckling to himself "Don't you know Kezz? She is a character and a good laugh, she is only about 18 and loves music and especially Miesha Paris, that's all she keeps on about, she is a good friend of Clamper and his age." Geraldine "She sounded funny when she came through that door, I was wondering what it was ha, ha." Kezz approaches the table and says "Eek, eek, hello tickle, tickle, Miesha Paris is banging mate and she is on the radio tomorrow." Niel says "Kezz this is Geraldine." Geraldine says "Well hello Kezz, how are you?" Kezz "Eek, eek, do you like Miesha Paris? I love her, she is banging." Jeff laughing says "I will have to, is she a singer then?" Kezz "She is banging, eek, can you do an eek? Go on try it." Jeff still laughing says "Eek." Kezz "Louder." Jeff does it again "Eek." Kezz "See how loud you can do it go on try hard." Jeff feeling silly said "Oh I can't ha, ha." Kezz "Try, eek loud." Jeff screams out a loud eek and she doubles up laughing and silence fell all around, Kezz still laughing "Oh that was a good eek Jeff I am going to see Amanda my friend bye." And off she went and Jeff says "What the hell was that all about?" They were all laughing at Jeff and Jeff said to Geraldine "Now you have met Kezz real name Kerry she is funny and so innocent ha, ha. I know now I am not the only nutter here and of course Clamper and the dodgy Welshman, who has gone for a Chinese." From a distance Kezz heard him and said "Eek, eek, eek, ha, ha." They all cracked up laughing and you could hear Kezz and Amanda laughing with them and then she said out loud "Banging man." This made them laugh louder.

Thursday in Bridgend with Danny and he meets his brother and his wife and Angie was helping him from the train station to the place he was going to with Lyndon his brother, it was a small corner shop type property and nothing special at all and they spoke to each other outside before going in. Danny said to his brother with a big smile "Hi Lynd, how are you then? I am pleased to see you, good man." He Hugs his brother and continues "How are you feeling mate? I had a great journey down and how is Debbie?." Debbie replies "Aw, I am allright thanks, I managed to coax him down here." Danny "No he didn't take any coaxing did you mate?" Lyndon "I did, I didn't want to come here at all, this is your idea, not mine, so there and I can't wait to go home." Danny "Well Lynd I know what you mean but it is for your own good and I will be happier for us both if you get help, I care Lyn and I am so worried." Angie spoke up "Lyndon you must realise things are really bad now and you must trust Danny and us to help you it's for your own good and if it goes well it will make you feel a lot better to." Lyndon "Well we will see, right let's get on with it." They head for the door and went in and Danny said "Debbie if you don't mind I will go in with him first, as they will not fob me off with anything, I won't put up with it." Debbie "Yes ok, I will have a fag outside with Angie." The boys go into the room when they were called and sat opposite the woman councillor in charge she said "Hello Mr. Duckfield I am Jane." They shook hands and she said "Firstly have you had a drink today Mr Duckfield?" Lyndon answers " Only 2 cans this morning that's all." Jane says "Oh well, we can't do anything for you today if that's the case." Danny hearing this went mad "What the hell do you mean? He is an alcoholic that's why we came to you because he has a drink problem." Jane "I am afraid he has to come to us sober to get the treatment he needs, sorry that is the rules." Danny "You must be kidding he is an alcoholic and needs help it's like saying to a smoker I can't give you patches if you have had a fag this morning, that's ridiculous for god's sake." Jane "I'm sorry that's the rules, can you bring him back next week, without any drink in him?" Lyndon said "I am here you know, this is a waste of time, I will not be back anytime." Danny in nasty mood said "Please, this is stupid he needs help, he has only had 2 drinks, he is not pissed is he?

You can't turn him away please, if you know the trouble we had getting him here then you would realise how stupid this is." Jane "Sorry I really am, but I can't do nothing." Danny "Not as sorry as I am, I didn't realise that alcoholic anonymous was so petty and a total waste of time, I really didn't." Jane replies "I am sorry you feel like that and wish you a good day." Danny and Lyndon left the room and Danny was furious and got outside and said out loud "What a stupid lot of idiots they really are there, I have never seen such idiots in all my life." Lyndon "Calm down Dan, you will have a coronary, let's just go please." Debbie said "What happened in there?." Danny said in a real temper "They won't do anything because Lyndon has been drinking, because he has had 2 cans he cannot be seen by them, it's ridiculous it really is." Angie "Your joking, did they say that to you?" Danny "Yeh, it's ridiculous isn't it.? I can't believe it." Debbie said "Well so they can't help him at all?" Danny "Yes if we bring him back here sober next time and they don't open until half past ten in the morning, it's a pathetic arrangement and a waste of time." Lyndon "Good, at last, I told you that before we came here I am off, this is stupid see you later up the house, I will come over for a cup of tea." Danny looking sick said "Ok mate, but please try and come over sober ok?" Lyndon with smile on his face says "I am not promising but I will try and be sensible ha, ha,ha." Danny "Lynd it is not funny really it is not." Lyndon "I think it is, alcoholic anonymous that wants only people who are sober to cure ha, ha." Danny "Yes I see what you mean, it's a joke isn't it? Sorry mate, we will have to try something else." Lyndon smirking says "I don't think so, this has been enough for me, forget it Dan this is how things are and there is nothing else." Danny "Oh, don't be like that Lynd we must try everything." Lyndon "We have tried everything that's it, what else is there ay?" Danny." I will think of something, I will." Lyndon "Think Dan, there is nothing else is there? Give it up I am off see you later, see you." He and his wife left and Danny stood there in bewilderment and looking so sad and Angie said to Danny "C'mon Dan you can't do much else today, so don't worry now, we will think of something, let's go." Danny "He might be right who else is there to help, I don't know anyone, I will give Mel a ring when I get home." Angie "What can he do? He lives miles away, he can't just drop everything and come down here all the time, can he?." Danny screams "Well he will bloody well have to won't he, I can't do much with him can i?." Angie shouts back at him "Allright, it's not my fault and besides Lyndon is a grown man and he will do what he wants and there is nothing you can do about it is there?" It went silent and Danny realises she is right and says in a calm voice "Yes I know, but I must try something, you know me I will not be beaten and he is my little brother and this is eating me up it really is, I have only just began to get over losing Dennis and I can't take losing anyone else especially my little brother." Angie "Oh it won't come to that, he will be ok you'll see, let's go and have lunch somewhere." "Yes you might be right but I must try and do something." Angie "If you keep on at him he will stop talking to you, just take it easy with him and play it by ear." They go off to lunch.

Later on Danny is on the phone to his older brother who lives miles away and says to him "Well Mel I managed to get him to alcoholics anonymous and they said they could do nothing because he had, had 2 cans before his appointment and so would not do anything at all, isn't that ridiculous?" Melvyn on the phone said "Well that is stupid are they real or what? And so what is Lyndon going to do now then?." "Oh, he was happy about it all and smiling as if to say I told you so." "That's Lyndon for you, so how bad is he now then? I didn't think he was that bad." "Yes he is worse and getting worse by the day, Debbie left him for a few days and stayed with her sister because of his drinking, but I don't think she is much help to him and I think she is some of the cause of his drinking." "Do you think so? I

202

was wondering if she might not be much use and she seems to turn her back on trouble as long as she is ok." "Yes she is bloody useless and don't give a damn, when Dennis was there she kept him in rags and used his money for drinking, he walked around like a tramp and Lyndon daren't say a word to her. She made them move from our family home and he changed soon after, but he sits back and takes it all and his mother-in-law makes his life a misery, she is in his house all the time, he never has a break from her, I seen a video taken in his house and Debbie and her mother kept on talking and never stopped and totally ignored Lyndon all the way through the video and he showed me it one day and said the same thing, he is fed up too. He calls her the black widow the amount of men she has had and all have died after meeting her." "Really, I didn't think it was that bad, I will have to get myself down there as soon as I can. When are you going back to Hereford then?." "I don't know, I am having my own problems with Angie, she is never here when I come home and things are getting worse here also, if I can sort out something for Lyndon I will go back as soon as possible, I am bored out of my skull, I don't know what the hell is wrong with Angie, I feel like a fish out of water, I am sitting here all day alone." "Do you still think something is going on behind your back then? Because I can't see Angie doing anything like that, I don't know, everything is going mad isn't it." "You can say that again but there you go I feel like everything is getting out of control, so what do you think about Lyndon what can we do?" "Well there's not much we can do other than keep on to him to get off the drink, there is no one else to ask at the moment, he is old enough to make his own mind up about what he does, we can only support him and try and help but he needs to want to give it up. I will get down there on Tuesday to see him I promise, he will listen to me more than you as he knows I mean what I say and he seems to take notice, I will try my best." "Shall I stay home and meet you or what?" "No I think I will have a good word with him and try and get through to him on my own and don't tell him I am coming." "Ok I won't, I will probably go back up on Saturday if things don't Improve here as Josh is off school tomorrow as the teachers have a training day, so I will phone you on Wednesday from college ok?" "Ok Dan, I will do my best and speak to you then and keep our fingers crossed, ok?" "Ok Mel and before you go I need to find an answer to a crossword question, it's the only one I need so can you tell me the clue is, flightless bird from Iceland, any ideas?" "A flightless bird from Iceland an any clues at all?" "Yes, there are six letters and seven so it's six and seven letters both words ending in the letter N , any idea?" Mel thought hard on the end of the ;phone and then said "I don't know of any birds in Iceland I can't think, leave it with me to think about it and I will get back to you if I get it, what will you win then?" "A large sum of money I got all the other answers but need that one and I will give you a couple of bob if you get it." "Right let me think about it speak later bye." "Yes ok, see you Mel." Danny puts the phone down and sighs and chuckles to himself. Well Lyndon didn't turn up as he said he would but Debbie came over to have a cup of tea and was speaking to Danny. She said "Well Dan I don't know what to do I really don't, he drinks from morning to night, he hides drink all over the house, it's like a off licence over there and it is not good for Wendy, she is seeing all this, I can't put up with much more, I will be leaving again if he don't change, I mean it." Danny says "Steady on Debbie, we must try and help him, don't give up on him yet please, he can't help it." "Danny he is not helping himself, he goes up stairs and stays up there if I am down stairs and down stairs if am up stairs drinking, he does not stop and my mother stopped coming over now." "Well that might be a good thing for the moment, I think and I have talked to Mel he is coming down on Tuesday to see him and have a good talk to him but you must not tell him as he will disappear ok?" "Ok, maybe he will listen to

Mel he usually does but after he has gone he goes back to himself as you know, I think the only way is to have him sectioned into a hospital I really do, as he is getting worse." "Well, I think you might be right, but let's wait a little longer and see what happens first, then if he is still the same in a month I will do this myself, I will go and see the doctor myself ok?" "Ok, I agree and he said he was coming over here behind me that was an hour ago now, he is not coming I know he won't." "No I think your right, so how is Wendy then?" "She is ok and doing well in school she loves it but she is being teased sometimes about her dad and that is pissing me off." "Yes I bet it is, never mind we must keep on trying, do you think he has got worse since you moved from 51 Heol Glannant?" "No not really, I think it has got worse and worse since just before Dennis died, I do." "Maybe he still thinks about Dennis and it has affected him more than we think and he looked after mam for years on his own and In the later days of course you were there, I never did a thing but I was working far away most of the time and was always knackered, I wish I had done more I do, but I wish I could get through to him and the way we used to drink when we were younger has not helped things I don't suppose." "No I think your right there, I remember you 2 only a few years ago out every night and coming home pissed every night, god I was amazed and that did not help Lyndon at all." Danny looking sad said "No, it didn't, I wish I could turn the clock back and I would have done things differently and that mate of his ginger made him worse trying to be big about how much he could drink, but ginger only went out once a week Lyndon was on it every night so ginger could not handle it really, that made him worse and I also think he had a very bad shock in his teens too." Debbie looking puzzled says "How do you mean? Danny." "Well I remember him in junior school and starting in Ynysawdre comp school, he was a happy little fella and he and his best friend Alwyn Jenkins who lived just down the road from us were inseparable and real good friends, they did everything together and this lasted for years and in their teens I think Alwyn was about 13 or 14, he died all of a sudden and that destroyed Lyndon, I remember his face it was a terrible time in his life and I feel he never got used to not having Alwyn about. It was as if someone had taken a chunk out of him." Debbie said "What happened to Alwyn, I remember Lyndon saying one day but he never wants to speak about it." "Alwyn was a lovely lad I liked him and his family a great deal and Alwyn had a hole in the heart, he was born with it and he died because of it and it was awful and Lyndon cried and cried for a long, long time and was never the lad he was before Alwyn died it was a tragedy, it really was and I know that Alwyn's mother and father loved Lyndon and often speak about how Lyndon and Alwyn were so close, it's so sad and I know Lyndon still misses him to this day and I sometimes wonder if he is in a hurry to be with him again, as things have never been the same since for him.." Debbie now looking as if she is about to cry said "Isn't that a sad thing to happen to anyone, bless him, I hope you were wrong about Lyndon wanting to be with Alwyn." "Well we don't know what he is going through in his head do we? And he has never had a friend like Alwyn since, has he?" "What about Alan?" "No I can't see anyone replacing Alwyn and if you asked him he would say the same and Alan blows hot and cold, Lyndon did definitely change for the worse since Alwyn left him on this planet on his own and the world is a worse place without Alwyn it really is, he was a gentleman, but we must do something for Lyndon now, so remember don't tell him about Mel coming down." "I won't, well I must push off now and pick up Wendy I am late, see you." "Yep, I will see you and tell Lyndon to pop over as I am probably going back Saturday ok? Bye." "So long, I will see you, bye."

Danny sat on his chair on his own again and looked really sad, he wiped a small tear away and got deep in thought.

It was later that day and Joshua his youngest son came home from school, this put a smile on Dan's face Immediately, Josh ran to Danny wrapped his arms around him and said "Dad, hello where have you been? I have missed you." Danny said to him with a huge smile on his face "Hello Josh my boy, I have missed you lots, I really have, I am in a special school now for the blind and I am mitching today and tomorrow, so if the phone rings don't say I am here ha, ha." Josh asks him "Why dad? What have you done?" "I am supposed to be in lessons and I am down here instead, I am in trouble now with my teacher." "Oh no, I bet they will tell you off when you go back won't they? I know don't go back, we will hide you here ok?" Danny smiles and says "No I must go back as Niel knows I am here and he will tell them where I am, I will just have to have lines and stay in after school that's all." Josh in serious voice says "Never mind I was told off yesterday for talking and I had to write some lines it said silence is golden, so will your teacher be nasty with you?" "I expect I will have to say sorry and promise not to do it again, and they will stop my pocket money for a week and then I will not be able to have a pint." "I got some money in my bank I will lend you some if you want." "No it's allright mate, I have some stashed away and how is school then?" "I am in sports day when I go back next week, I think it's next week anyway but I am the best in my class with my sums because you told me how to do them didn't you? And I have got a girlfriend I have." Danny looked surprised and said "Well what is her name then?" "She is Melanie and she is in my class in school and some of my class mates are not happy because they wanted to go out with her ha, ha, can I put the telly on to see my cartoons please dad?" "Yes of course you can here is the T V controls." Next Angie said "So what did Mel say then?" Danny replies "He is coming down on Tuesday to see him but don't tell him he is coming as he will go out to avoid him ok? He does not know what else to do either so we are back to square one." Angie said "I can't see what he can do either, so I can expect him to call here to can I?" "I don't think he will as he has not much time and I told him I was going back to Hereford anyway. I am staying until Sunday I was going back on Saturday but it will be nice to see Josh for a change." Angie screws up her face and says "Well I was going to take him out with my sister to Folly Farm on Saturday and I have arranged it now" Danny looking dumbstruck said "Oh great, I come home to see my son and you have arranged to take him away, why? You know I was coming home and I don't see much of him now, so you will have to cancel it." Angie said anxiously "I have sorted It out now and he knows about it so he will be disappointed and I am not telling him, you can" "Well, well, you just don't care about me seeing him as far as you are concerned I am not wanted here and if I am not here you are much happier, great." Angie says "No it's not, I only knew it was this week yesterday and life does not stop just because you are home, so are you going to tell him or what?" Danny looking annoyed said "No, I can't and you know it and I hope he is about tomorrow for me to see something of him." "Yes he is but I am going out to Bridgend with my other sister to sort some things for the boys club and then I am working down there tomorrow night, so I won't be here." "Tell me something new you are never here so what's new then? Maybe you want me to go back up tonight do you?" "If you are going to have that attitude you might as well, I am not staying here tonight if you are going to be in that mood" Danny says "Maybe you would be happier with a divorce, what do you think?" Angie "At this moment in time that don't seem a bad idea and if you are going to cause a row every time you come home I will insist on it, so shut up for god's sake." "Yes you would like that wouldn't you?" Josh says "Sh, sh, I can't hear the telly" Danny says "Sorry mate, I fancy a cuddle mind." Josh got up and give him a cuddle and Angie said "So what are you doing for tea?" Danny teasing Josh says "I suppose we might have to have a Chinese, that's

205

all I am having lately" Josh says "Oh yes please dad." Danny gave Angie the money and settled back to listen to the cartoons and she went off again .

Well the next day Josh and Danny were in the garden playing football and Murphy the pet dog was playing with them also, they had a fun day and hardly seen Angie and so on the Saturday Danny went back to the college early, he sat on the train and looked as if his world had come to an end. Even though it was a lovely sunny day he felt dejected by his family. Later he arrived back in the college and was shocked to find Jeff in the lounge trying to chat up Winnie. Danny walked in and Winnie jumped up and attacked Danny playfully and Jeff said "What are you doing back so early? It's Saturday." Danny replied "Oh things were a bit sordid in Bridgend so I decided to come back and so it's time to party." Winnie said "I had full marks for my English I was very good the tutor said, but it has been very silent here in the college. Jeff and I are the only ones here all weekend and we had lots to drink last night and Jeff's room is too small, not like mine and it smells of cigarettes, phew." Danny said "Does it really? Is that right Jeff?" Jeff sniggering says "Ha, ha, ha, I kept her company as we were both at loose ends ha, ha." Winnie "He tried to be rude with me so I beat him up ha, ha, I don't like tins of lager now, so can you help me do more English sometime?" Danny "Of course I can and why won't you come in my room and yet you went to Jeff's then?" Winnie replies "Oh because he made me a little drunk and I could not stop laughing, we watched a film on his DVD player and I went to bed then and if you like I will come to your room and watch a film on your Television too." Danny "I will see and I might be able to help you with your English sometime tomorrow ok " Winnie " yes please, I will have a shower now and see you later as I am going to go out to the Cadbury place in one hour, see you." Danny said "Yes I will see you later." She went off and Jeff looked sheepish and said "Dan it was not what you think mate, I would not do that to my friend." Danny "You lying git, I bet you wouldn't, so she was not on for it then was she?" Jeff said "No, she has only eyes for you I think, I was afraid she was going to kill me so I let it go, so don't worry." "I am not worried matey, I knew she wouldn't I know her culture won't allow her to throw it around, she is a reliable girl no problem, anything else happened here?" "Not a lot, I met Kezz and she is so funny, Geraldine and Rhoda have gone off for the weekend with the children, it's been dead here, I should have gone home this weekend if I thought it was going to be so quiet, so how did it go with Lyndon?" "It didn't it was all a waste of time, they would not see him as he had, had 2 tins of lager before he went and I told them he is alcoholic that's the reason but no luck so my older brother is going to see him on Tuesday and try and get some sense into him and my youngest son has gone to Folly Farm for the day, that's my wife's excuse for me to get lost, so I am back here again, I give up I really felt unwanted there at all times, it was awful but I had some fun with my youngest Josh, it was great but he knackered me out in the end, so I am ready for a few pints now." Jeff said "Oh you think she really is going to divorce you do you?" "I am more sure now than ever, it's just a Matter of when, not if, I think she is seeing someone to, absolutely nothing has gone right mate it is a crappy end to it all, I feel like getting pissed now." "God man you are down, I am sorry it did not work out but it can only get better matey, chin up, you still got me." Danny looking horrified says "Oh dear, haven't I just and you are trying to donk my bird, a good mate you are." "Ha, ha, but I didn't did I? And you could see the look on her face, she was so happy to see you, if I hadn't been here she would have jumped all over you, so what are we doing then?" Danny looking cunningly at Jeff said "I am going to have a shower and fancy going to the barrels for a pint or two it's a nice day and I can't have a Chinese tonight so we can party what do you think?" "I was hoping you were going to say that, I am up for it." "Right then I will have one of your tins please as I have none left and I will get the first drink in tonight." "In the fridge in the kitchen mate." "I know they were I bet they were in there for you and to help Winnie to settle down this evening ha, ha, I know you mate and don't forget it." "Who me? I don't think so, I am just her plaything matey ha, ha." "I think I will go and have a shower and have a bit of food over the refectory and see if the S.S.W's are feeling like a drink down here what do you think?" Jeff's eyes lit up and he says "Good idea matey, Catalina might be up for it I bet and Lidia will be with her, she was yesterday, let's go."

They went over for something to eat but Lidia or Catalina were not there and so they decided to go to the barrels anyway and Jeff looked unhappy. They were standing by the bar in there and Jeff said to Danny "Well it's busy in here again but not enough totty for my liking, I was hoping Catalina and Lidia were here, I wonder where they are? I might go over and give her a knock and see if they fancy a beer, what do you think?" Danny looking unsure said "I don't know, I think they might think we are trying to get a leg over or something." "Well we are aren't we?" "Speak for yourself mate, I am not like you, but they are nice company I like the accents and the mistakes they make and they make me happy when they are around so if you want to go and give them a knock I think it is a good idea, go on then." "Right take your time I am going to finish my pint and I will go over and give her a knock." "Well take your time and hurry up, ha, ha, I think we should find a table first as it is not good to stand up all night, is that a empty table over there by the window? I think it is." Jeff looks and says "Yes it is and it's in a quiet spot, c'mon let's grab it." The lads sit down and Jeff then says "I will get a fresh one in and go over and see if they are there." "Ok matey I will have the Malvern ale please, I can't drink that bloody cheap lager it's awful." Jeff "Ok matey I will stay on the lager I will, be back now." As Jeff left Peter the landlord came up to talk to Danny "Well hello there, how are you? I seen you come in it is going to be a quiet night here tonight as there is a band playing in the Victory tonight, but I can recommend the Malvern ale it's on offer." Danny says in reply "I am already on it peter it's gorgeous isn't it? But why so cheap?" "There are a lot of heathens here this weekend who are lager louts, they don't drink a good pint, I really don't think they can handle it really." "You could be right mate it's too strong for them, and I will take advantage of the drop in price don't worry about that, it's a messy job but somebody's got to do it." "Well thank you sir, I see Jeff is with you he is funny isn't he? he always makes me laugh and his eyes can't get enough of the girls in here, I can see him now by the bar he is posing and chatting up one of the barmaids, ten out of ten for his efforts, where were you on Thursday for the quiz?" "My little brother in Bridgend is having trouble with his drinking he has become an alcoholic and I took him to alcoholics anonymous but they were useless, they told me they won't help him if he has a drink before he attends the appointment, that's ridiculous but I will keep on trying don't worry." "I sympathise with you mate, I have seen them here and so many of them go on and on and there is nothing you or anyone else can do, it's an Impossible scenario I really feel for you but keep on trying and don't let him give up, it's these supermarkets and cheap beers and lagers and ciders that are to blame not the pubs, I think I can buy beers in those places cheaper than I can get them trade, it's stupid." Jeff comes back and says "Hello Pete how are you?" Peter replies "Fine Jeff and you?" "Oh can't grumble only that dodgy Welshman is always on my case all the time, but I have found out you can shoot a Welshman with a bow and arrow in the square here on a Sunday morning legally, so I am practising." Peter laughed and said "That's not very nice is it?" Danny laughing says "No it's not is it, but he would be bored without me, he is a little bore sometimes and he is always trying to bonk all the girls you know." Peter "That makes a change these days as most of them these days are gay you know." Jeff says "Oh don't go there mate, I couldn't stand the pain sorry, I will stay as I am thanks." Danny "Yes you got a point, you don't know who is who these days I dropped a wallet in a gay bar one night I went there by accident and I kicked that wallet back to my car before I picked it up, ha, ha." Peter was laughing and Jeff went off to give the girls a knock Peter said to Danny "Where is he off to now?" Danny replies "He is off to give a few friends a shout to come and have a drink one is Peruvian and the other is from Belgium and of course both women are heterosexual or so they said." "Well I am glad you are bringing some trade in for me, I will see you Thursday mate, have a good night, see you."

Meanwhile Jeff is outside Catalina's door and rings the bell and wait's but no one answered so he is just about to leave and all of a sudden there was Catalina standing there with nothing but a towel around her as she has just got out of the shower and this towel was more like a handkerchief than a towel and Jeff's eyes just lit up and he stammered "A, a, ah, hello um, Catalina." Catalina smiling says "Oh hello Jeff I thought you were Lidia she is due to get here, so what can I do for you?" Jeff "Quite a lot dressed like that, mmm." Catalina smiles even more and says "Right." Jeff tongue hanging out "Really, sorry, me and Danny was wondering if you fancy a drink in the barrels as it is a nice night? That is you and Lidia." "Well, why not I must finish my shower first though." "Ok I will come in and wash your back and that." Catalina smiling even more now said "No it's allright I can manage thank you, we will see you over there later ok Jeff?" "Spoil sport, I will see you later then." Catalina said "Ok" and as she turned Jeff got a peak at her lovely shaped bum and couldn't wait to tell Danny. Back in the pub and Danny was sitting there waiting for Jeff and was talking to one of the lads in there who was also Welsh and a bit of a rogue, Taffy says to Danny "So Danny if you can get your hands on a cheap hi-fi I will buy it off you ok man?" Danny replies "No problem Taffy I will keep my eye out for one so to speak." Taffy "Yes very good, look out here comes a fireman it's Jeff, hello man." Jeff run in and said "Hello Taffy, I am thirsty sorry." Taffy "You must be man." Jeff panting said to Danny "I just had the thrill of my life, I was ringing the doorbell in Catalina's flat and there was no answer and I was just about to leave and all of a sudden, she appeared at the door with just a tea towel covering her bit's and her bare legs were right in front of me, it was gorgeous it really was, one little move and I would have seen everything, I mean it." Danny interrupts and says "So are they coming over or what?" "Yes she is waiting for Lidia to arrive and they will be over, listen now, I haven't finished, after she finished she turned before she had shut the door and I seen her lovely ass ,it was beautiful it was perfect man it was gorgeous." Danny was just sitting there wondering what it must be like he said "Oh don't Jeff, I can Imagine it mate is that all? I can't take anymore." Jeff laughed out loud and said "You idiot you, I will never forget that moment as long as I live, I very rarely get that lucky, I could really sort her out, if you know what I mean, I could no problem." "Jeff tell me again please it is like poetry mate." Jeff starts telling him again and Danny stops him and says "No mate, I can't take anymore I will get a pint in instead to cool me off, I need it, here give me your glass." Danny orders some beer and Jeff is glowing. Danny said to him "Here mate your pint and did she say what time they are coming over?" Jeff daydreaming says "Who me, sorry, they won't be long I hope, I fancy it with her mate, god I feel horny as hell now, she is a cracker, I might try it tonight see how the land lies." Danny sniggering says "Yes mate if she was flashing it at you I would not have a problem but don't charge at it like a bull at a gate as you usually do, ok?" "Yeh, yeh, I will play it easy and hope I am on top of the case later." Danny "On top of the case, very good mate, this beer is lovely here isn't it? and a good atmosphere and good music on the juke box, I wonder what Niel is up to this weekend, he is a nutter and the stories he tells ha, ha." "I thought he was staying this weekend as he usually goes home the same as you." Danny "Yes but I jumped a week to go home and see my brother so I will maybe go home next weekend , hello look out here comes Catalina and Lidia." The girls went up to the bar and got their drinks in and a pint for Danny and Jeff, they were dressed up and looking very sexy and the other lads in the bar stood and stared in amazement when they arrived, they sat down on the table with the boys. Catalina says "Hello Danny and I have already seen you Jeff ha, ha." Jeff replied "I have seen more of you than you have seen of me." Catalina "And if I had realised it was not Lidia I would have put more around me." Jeff said "It was more like a handkerchief than a towel but I am not complaining." Catalina smiled and said "At least I made your day." Jeff "You can say that again." Then Danny said "He described it to me and it made my day to." Lidia was just sitting there smiling and said "Hello guys is that right? You are guys as I am learning my English, I will be good soon." Jeff "Lidia you speak better English than most English men ha, ha." Danny says "Hello Lidia how are you enjoying it here in the college?" Lidia "Good yes it is good, thank you and I have had some money this week so we have a drink tonight but I cannot drink much yes?" Danny "Yes, we must enjoy the night no work tomorrow." Lidia "No just Joanna, I sleep all day." Jeff "Yes the way me and Danny are going we will be sleeping all day too and what about you Catalina?" she replies "Yes a day off for me also, but I must just phone my mum and dad in the afternoon then we are going into town for a walk to see the Cathedral as Lidia has never seen one so I will show her." Danny "Oh it's beautiful Lidia and I bet you are a catholic aren't you?" Lidia "Yes, how you know this?" Danny answers "Because you are from Peru and Spanish as most Spanish people are Catholics." Lidia "Ah, I see, I like this music it is good." Jeff "If I have a little more to drink I will have a dance with you ok?" Lidia said with a gleaming smile "Oh, yes please I like dancing." Danny "And Catalina do you like to dance?" Catalina "Yes only if I have had a drink though and I will never go on a karaoke neither." Lidia "Catalina what is that." Catalina "It is a machine that plays the music and not the words and you see the words of the song on the screen and sing the words." Jeff "I used to be a professional on the karaoke in my pub then one day someone came that could really sing ha, ha." Catalina "And what about you Danny? They say the Welsh can really sing" Danny "I don't think I am that bad a singer but I would rather leave it to the others, I am like you Catalina I need a few drinks inside me before I will sing or dance." Lidia says "Is there somewhere we can do this Danny?" Danny thinks and says "Yes there are a few here one is my bedroom, ha, ha, I will ask Kezz where she goes and I will sort out a night out there for a load of us, I know a few people who would like that ok?" Lidia "Oh, yes I would like this, thank you, I will show some salsa and teach you how to dance to this." Jeff "We will look forward to it I love Latin music." Danny "I love the Latino music also it is very happy music." Lidia "Yes it is and the tango and I like some English music too." Catalina "Well it's getting busy here it's time for me to get a round in so are you all ready?" Danny "Oh Catalina you don't have to I will get them in." Catalina "No, no, I insist it's my turn I have never bought you a drink so let me get this one I, insist." Danny "Ok just this once and it's my turn next." Catalina "Don't be silly I don't buy you a drink to get one back." Jeff "It feels like a party and I am up for it." Lidia "I know party it's good, yes." Jeff "Yes it is Lidia." They all party until late in the pub and it the end of the night and Danny said "Right Jeff it's time to book a taxi before it is too late as it is busy tonight." Jeff "Awe, I was enjoying myself and it's time to party I think so Catalina what about it?" Catalina smiling says "What about what?" Jeff "A party in your digs, I will get a few bottles and Danny will and we can party all night, what do you think?" Catalina "Why not Jeff, let's do it." Lidia looks confused and says "What is this?" Catalina " carry on drinking in the flat Danny and Jeff will come over for a few drinks and a laugh." Lidia smiling says "Yes this is good." Danny and Jeff gets some bottles in and went with Catalina and Lidia to Catalina's flat.

In the flat and Danny and Jeff laughing at some of Danny's Jokes and all enjoying the drink and laughter, Danny said "Well Catalina this is cosy isn't it?" She replies "Yes it was until he left me here and now it is like living in a vacuum, it is dead here most of the time, I think you are the only ones who have come here since he left and this is nice, but that is the past and this is the future and I must roll along with it." Danny said "Yes girl, life changes right before your very eyes and there's nothing you can do about it and then one day you think why worry about stupid things and get on with your life, I know I have been there, so many times disappointment is a phase of life and if you dwell on it, it will never get better." Catalina "Yes, you are probably right Danny but it is hard and as long as you have got your health it is the main thing." Jeff "Right let's cheer up is it? It's like a morgue in here all of a sudden, so Catalina you know men buy big cars to make up for shortages on their bodies, well I don't own a car. And if I said you have a beautiful body would you hold it against me ?" Catalina was laughing and Danny said "Oh no, here we go again." Jeff "Ha, ha, ha, I've got a condom with your name on it, I wonder what our children are going to look like, Catalina do you know the difference with conversation and sex?" Catalina "No." Jeff "Shall we go up to your bedroom and talk about it?" Danny "ha, ha, that was funny and he can go on all night and I can't take this all night." Lidia "I understand some of this ha, ha." Catalina " very good Jeff very good mate I think you are so very funny." Danny says "Yes he can be very funny but never knows when to stop, he wears the Joke out ha, ha." Catalina says "Is he like this all the time? And how much have you 2 had to drink?" Danny "Yes he is and yes we have had about 8 pints now and drinking wine makes it worse, I have had enough now and Lidia is sober I don't get it." Lidia "I not drink much, I get bad if I drink much." Jeff says slurring his words "I thought she was not drinking much but I have almost had enough, I must take it easy now as I will not remember jumping into bed with Catalina, I can't miss that." Catalina "Jeff cut it out mate, I am not jumping into bed with anyone, so don't go there." Jeff said "Don't jump to conclusions yet take a while to think about it for a minute Catalina." Catalina giggling says "Right I have thought about it and I have decided not to go ahead with it Jeff." Jeff looking sad said "Have another drink before you decide don't rush a decision you might regret ha, ha." Danny laughing said "He will keep on now so you might as well give up Catalina and I think you will be safe as he couldn't get a belch up let alone anything else, he is knackered." Jeff said "Hey what I lost in height I gained in length, if you know what I mean and she will be in for a treat." Catalina snapped "Right Jeff give it up now, I am not sleeping with anyone so shut up and it's nearly 4 o'clock in the morning and I am going to bed so shall I get you a taxi lads?" Danny says "No it's alright Catalina I have a number for one in my phone, I will do it." Jeff says "Well crashed and burned again."

The lads got into a taxi and went back to their digs, the driver said to them "You were lucky to get a taxi at this time in the morning lads I was just going home and I am the last one out, so where are you going to?" Danny said "Dowdell hall in the college please driver, I can't wait for my bed I am worse for wear now." Jeff says "I nearly got her into bed mate, never mind, I will do it next time." Danny "Yeh, yeh, I don't think anyone stands a chance with her mate except the tutor she was with, I can see she is hurting because of him leaving her." The lads arrive home or so they thought, they pay the driver and head towards what they think is the entrance to Dowdell, as they approach the entrance they find a steel bench and

Jeff says to Danny "Oh no, the taxi has dropped us in the wrong place this is not Dowdell, I don't know where we are, but it's not Dowdell mate, here is a steel table so we are not home." Danny looking concerned said "Oh dear, what the hell are we going to do it's 4 o'clock in the morning and no one around to ask and the taxi drivers are in bed, we are stuck, any suggestions Jeff?" The lads sat down on the steel bench and Jeff says "No I have no idea what we are going to do, let's think for a minute." They both started to think. Danny said "I think we will just have to sit here until the morning and wait for someone to tell us where we are, I can't think of nothing else to do." "And I am to pissed to do much, I wish I had not had that much now we are what we commonly called stuffed well and truly, it's lucky it's not too cold." "That bloody driver is an idiot, he knows we are blind and even worse in the dark, what was he thinking about? a true idiot I could be in my bed now if it wasn't for him the ass hole as what he is." Jeff says "Calm down Dan it could be worse, this could be the middle of Manchester or Birmingham, so what are we going to do for 2-3 hours then?" Danny sarcastically remarked "A game of eye spy or a game of touch maybe." Jeff "Ha, ha, I was only asking, don't be like that and there is no drink neither and Sunday today, we might be in for a long wait." Then all of a sudden a voice came from nowhere and said "Hello lads can you jump off and let me go? I need to deliver the rest of my milk" Next thing Danny and Jeff stood up and this steel bench they were sitting on moved off into the distance, it was only a milk float and it was parked in front of the entrance of Dowdell, they had been home all along and thought the milk float was a permanent fixture and felt fools. Danny says "What a pair of plonkers we really are, we were home all along ha, ha, ha." Jeff laughed and said "Ha, ha, I don't believe it I really don't, I could have sworn we had been dropped into the wrong place, that was funny ha, ha."

It was the next morning at 11o'clock and Danny was having a bit of extra sleep and he was exhausted and the next thing a knock on the door and Danny said out loud "Yes who is it?" The answer came "It's me, Winnie I am ready for my lesson now please." Danny got up in his boxer's and rubbing his head opened the door and said "What is the time then?" she replied "It's 11 o'clock now and I have been waiting for you to come in to help me " Danny looking a bit miffed said "I am still pissed I can't do any lesson in this state I need time to wake up and I am not even dressed you know." Winnie in strict mood said "Danny you mustn't say this and if you have not got any clothes on then you must do this now." "I am not kidding I only got back at 4 this morning I went to a party with Jeff and got very drunk and I just want to sleep, I tell you what you come in and get undressed and jump in beside me in my bed and read what the exercise is and I will help with it ok?" "Do not be silly, we must not do this." "Right then I will see you later if that's the case ok? Bye." Winnie put her foot in the door and said "I will sit on a chair and speak to you and don't try to do rude things to me ok?" Danny sniggering and Winnie said "Why do you laugh?" "I do something rude to you that's a laugh, I can't pea through it let alone do anything else with it I am cream crackered." "This word again I understand it so get in bed and we will do the lesson." Danny jumps back into bed after showing Winnie the chair and she says "I have a problem with 3 words the same, these are they , to, too, two." "First of all you say these are the words not these are they and tell me the words one at a time and spell them ok?" Winnie mimicked Danny and spoke very slowly and said " T, this is spelled to. " Danny giggled and said "This word means to go to or he was talking to it means several things and so it is to someone to somewhere etc. and used in many sentences." Winnie says the same into a recorder and continues "Then you have a too again spelled t o o ." "This means also and the sentence that sums this word up is, I am coming with you too, or Jeff had one of them too, you got it?" "Right, I see now and the last one is two spelled t w o." "Ok, this refers to the number 2 like there two of them or there are two cakes for me. " Winnie speaks this into her tape machine again and says "Right now these ones site and sight, the first one spelled s I t e." "Right, this means on site or at a specific place like if you were meeting someone at a certain regular place you frequent, like Dowdell and you would say I will see you on site, or like a village of houses I will see you at the site, a group of houses I think ha." Winnie in snappy voice "Oh Danny, I must be right or I will give you some of my martial arts mind and the last word is sight spelled s I g h t now get right or else ha, ha." Danny laughing said "Sight is like your eyes, you have sight through your eyes or I will keep you in sight." "I see." "Yes that's see you have got it already." The lesson went on and on and Danny was by now fed up and wide awake and said to WINNIE after an hour. "How much more is there? I am not a tutor you know and it's Sunday a day of rest so give me a break please." "What is this break Danny?" "It means let me have a rest from all the questions, I can come to your room and finish this off tonight." Winnie got off her chair and started to bash Danny and Danny went under the bed clothes, but Winnie was play fighting with him but didn't realise she was doing it a little hard and Danny grabbed her wrists and she was laughing and said "You can't hold me for long I am too strong for you Danny." Danny let's her go and said "Why don't you just lay down and have a rest then with me?" "I must not do this thing, it must be for my husband only, so please don't say this to me, I am off now and will see you tonight for the rest of the lesson, don't forget now or I will beat you up ha, ha." "Yes ok Winnie I will be in for my Chinese tonight, bye." Winnie stopped and said abruptly "Are you making humour of me?" Danny laughing said "No I am not, I use it as a code for Jeff to let him know I am off to give you another English lesson, that's all, don't get your knickers in a twist." She said in a snappy voice "I don't twist my knickers and don't talk about my knickers to anyone, you leave my knickers out of conversations ok?" Winnie slaps him across the back and Danny protests "It's a saying meaning don't get nasty about it, it is not serious so just chill, I mean calm down that's all." Winnie storms out of Danny's room and Danny gets up as he is not tired anymore, he goes off to Jeff's room and knocks his door, it was now 12.30pm and decided he needed company and Jeff answer's shouting "Go away I am dying whoever it is, go away." "Jeff it's me Danny come over for dinner I am starving mate." Jeff answers "Oh, give me five minutes and I will meet you on the bench outside, ok?" "Right."

Later in the refectory they sit heads bowed and looking sick as dogs. Danny said "I had a Chinese earlier and it was as nice as usual." Jeff "That will teach you for getting up so early matey." "Get up, I didn't she came to my room this time and woke me up and wouldn't let me sleep until I helped her with her English lesson and I felt sick as a dog." Jeff's eyes lit up and he said "She came to your room, there's a turn up for the book, so did you give her a good seeing to then?" Danny smiling "I did try but she could see I was still pissed and could not raise a smile let alone anything else, but I tried to get her to get into bed for a cuddle but no chance she just beat me up and I have to finish the lesson tonight." "Just as well mate the look on you, so I can't eat this food my stomach feels as if I have been poisoned, too much wine and not enough sex, I nearly had her last night, she is so sexy, she has a lovely ass and lovely boobs to go with it, god and that stupid taxi driver, he made us look fools didn't he? I am glad there was no one around." Next thing on the table behind a voice, Lola said "Are you sure there was no one around, as I was awake and seen you from my room and was wondering what you were doing sitting on the back of that milk float and you were both like nodding dogs on the back of it ha, ha." Jeff sarcastically "Hi Lola I was going to tell you a joke that would make your tit's fall off but I can see you have already heard it."

Danny says "Ha, ha, hello Lola do you always listen to someone else's conversation then?" Lola answers "There is no need for sarcasm Jeff, I could not help listening you are so loud you two." Jeff said "I would like to screw your brains out Lola but I can see someone has beaten me to it, ha, ha." Danny "God Jeff you are in a foul mood this morning, Lola excuse him he hasn't had a bit of sex for so long it's making him crazy." Lola smiling "Can I be of any help then Jeff?" Jeff turned to Lola and had a huge smile on his face said "Yeh, I would give you one no problem Lola, you have a lovely body and you wouldn't regret it, I will satisfy you no problem." Jeff was almost panting and Lola said "Jeff my vibrating rabbit is a lot bigger than your whole body so I don't think you can satisfy me and besides I wouldn't touch you with his so piss off" Jeff's face went serious and she was leaving and he said to her "I may not be the best looking guy here but I am the only one talking to you." Danny in amazement said "Nice one mate that was good for you this early and in a stupor." Jeff "Well she is a funny girl, I love her body but she has no character at all, let's go for a drink is it I can't take anymore, the swan is not far let's go and sit in the garden for a couple, I will guide you there. What do you think?" Danny ponders "I don't know, allright then only for a hour mind and just 3 pints max mate, I mean it." "Ok, let's go then."

The lads walked down the road chatting as they went and Jeff said "It's nice to have a bit of fresh air, I am feeling a little better now." "Well you could have fooled me, you have been making a lot of spewing noises for a while now, I see the Scottish girl from Gardner has another boyfriend, she don't half go through the men there, I am surprised she has not had you yet." Jeff said enthusiastically "I don't know her, who are you talking about." "You do mun, she is Scottish and has a black Labrador, I can't think of the dog's name but she is Kay, you must have seen her Jeff for goodness sake ." Jeff ponders "A Scottish girl with black Labrador dog in Gardner mmm, mmm, no I can't replace her." Danny said "Yes you do, she is always with a gang of boys in the student bar, she is never with girls and I said about her when we were in Gardner as she was having sex with 2 men in her room right above my room and her guide dog was howling and she was howling because Kay was making so much noise enjoying it all and I said it sounded so close I was going for a pregnancy test in case as they were that close and my light was swinging on the ceiling" Jeff rubbing his chin said "No I can't remember you saying about that and you say there was 2 men giving her one, god she sound so absolutely delightful but I can't place her at all." Danny now getting frustrated said "Jeff you do bloody know her, remember we came home to Gardner one night and past the public telephone kiosk in the entrance and she was up on the shelf and had her legs wide open and someone was giving her a portion, do you remember now." "You mean the one inside Gardner near the nurses room?" "Yes that's right and you and I walked past and laughed." Jeff still unsure "No I can't remember that and the only Scottish girl I know is Carol." "No not her you idiot, she has long hair and sometimes wears miniskirts, she is very silly with that guide dog of hers, what's the dog's name now? I can't remember it see, she was talking to me one day near cancer corner and complained about smokers and sat on the table and her legs were on the seat and everyone was looking at her legs, big boobs, you must have noticed them surely?" Jeff still thinking hard "Sorry man I can't remember anyone like that and I would have remembered her boobs if nothing else, you know me." "Let me think what else will make you remember, right I know she had a pair of hot pants on in the bar on Tuesday last, now do you remember?" "No sorry mate." Danny stands still for a minute and said "She shaves her pussy." Jeff Immediately said "Oh, her…. why didn't you say, I know who you are talking about now ha, ha, ha." The both lads laugh a lot and someone behind them listening laughed also and this made them laugh again. Jeff then said "So what about her anyway?" Danny said "Bloody hell I forgot now ha, ha." "You dipstick you, I wonder if Catalina shaves it as the foreign women often do that, that reminds me it's pancakes for lunch today and doughnuts ha, ha." "Really I can't wait to get my teeth in them, here goes I am having a pint of bitter and a packet of crisps, I will get them in first, go and find a table and come back to help me." Later the lads sit in the garden and a dog is playing with Danny and asking Danny to throw a stick so Danny does this for a few times and Jeff says to Danny "Throw it harder he is back before it lands and he is not even out of breath, go on throw it harder." Danny threw it harder and the dog came back with it and he kept on throwing it until he threw it and It landed on someone's table and the dog jumped up and nearly hit all the pints over and the man on the table shouted at Danny "Hey do you mind mate he nearly hit all the drinks over then." Danny said "Oh, sorry mate, I won't throw it again , Jeff you told me to do that because I can't see them sitting there, thanks, the dog is nuts." Jeff says "So what shall we do tonight then down the barrels or what?" "The way I feel now I won't be going out at all, I am going up the student bar and then a Chinese for me and off to bed." "Yes, you might be right I will Join you and we can see Kezz and see where she goes to Karaoke and take Catalina and Lidia out again." "Oh yes I forgot about that, I think Kezz goes off with a load of kids her age mind so just find out and we will go on our own." "Yeh, I was expecting that anyway, I am not hanging around with those boys they are not all there sometimes." Danny said "God I know and they have never got any money and try and bum a drink off you, I feel better now I have had the hair of the dog so to speak and nearly got into trouble because of you."

It was later on that night and Danny and Jeff sat down and next to them was Kezz and Danny started to speak to her and she was very troubled about something and Danny said "Eek, eek." Her little face lit up and she said "Eek, eek, is that Danny? I think it is eek, eek." Danny says "Yes Kezz it is, you know my voice now don't you?" She replied "Eek, eek, I know Jeff too eek, eek, Jeff done a eek for me last week didn't you Jeff?" Jeff replied "Yes I did, didn't I?" Kezz "Do a loud one for me Jeff, go on." Jeff feeling silly said "Oh I can't tonight Kezz, you do it." Kezz said out as loud as she can "Eek, eeeeeek, what do you think?" Jeff "Very good, that was banging Kezz." Kezz "Yes it was banging." Danny said "So where do you go for your karaoke in the week Kezz?" Kezz replies "There are 2, on Tuesday it's In O'Neil's and on the Friday it's in the pretty Pigs, I am not going this week because that bastard owes me money and he won't give it back to me, so I can't go and I want to go so I won't be eeking for a week now." She bowed her head and Danny could tell she was very upset and Danny said "Who owes you money Kezz?" Almost crying she replies "Chris my old boyfriend, he is not my boyfriend now I have finished with him, he always borrows money but never gives it back, now I am stuck in my room all week and my dad won't send me any money." Danny says "Do you mean Chris Jones?" Kezz "Yes he won't give it back to me and no one here will help me get it back, Anthea told me it's my fault for giving it to him, so I have had it now." Danny "Maybe not, I might be able to help you, have you got a drink?" Kezz snaps "No, I told you I have no money." Jeff says "I will get you a drink Kezz what do you want?" She says "A pint of lager please, thank you Jeff, how can you help me get my money back, if you can I will be a happy person and will eek for the rest of the week." Danny said "How much money does he owe you?? She replied "£60 now." Danny looking shocked said "Kezz how did you let it get that bad?" "Because he kept saying he can give it back to me if I lend him another £10 but he never did, he asked me last night but I have none left." Kezz starts to cry and Danny says "No don't cry now, let's see what we can do, have you stopped crying yet?" She snivels a little and says "Ok I have stopped now, sorry."

214

Danny then took a wad of notes out of his wallet and said "Here is your £60, now he owes me the money and when you see him tell him I have bought his debt off you and now he owes me the money and put it away and don't give any of it to anyone or that will be the last ok?" Kezz face lit up and she didn't believe it at first, she said "I don't understand, I lent him the money and you are giving it back to me and now he owes you the money is that right?" Danny smiling says "Yes tell him from me he now owes it to me and I want it back by next Friday or I will be looking for him and I won't take any excuses allright Kezz?" Kezz was all excited and was smiling from ear to ear and said "Brilliant eek, eek, I will tell him and he will shit himself when I do ha, ha, I can go to the karaoke now hooray." Danny said again "Keep it down Kezz if any of the youngsters hear know you have money they will all be asking for a loan and I am not doing it again, so stick it down your knickers or somewhere out of sight and don't get pissed tonight while you have that money on you." Jeff said "I hope you are listening Kezz because it will be your fault if you lend it out again and can't go anywhere and your pint is in front of you." Kezz giggles and says "Thanks lads you are true friends eek, eek, I am going to tell his friend to tell him, see you later,, thanks again." Danny "Your welcome Kezz, it's nice to see a happy face isn't it?" Jeff said "God you are a softie ay, that was £60 not a few quid and how do you know you will get it back?" "I will get it back don't worry he will shit himself when he finds out he now owes me the money, I am looking for him and I will get it back, he will be seeking me out to give it back you wait and see, do you want a bet on it?." Jeff nods his head no "Not me mate, I have learned not to bet with you so forget it." Next in walks Carol followed closely by Niel, they sit by the lads. Jeff sit's up on seeing Carol and says to her "Hello gorgeous, hows you then?" Carol answers "I am fine Uncle Jeffrey, hello, how are you then, I have just got back, I have been home to see mum and I am knackered now and need a pint or two." Jeff "So what do you want to drink then?" Carol "Thank you Uncle Jeffrey I will have a glass of cider please." Niel chirps up "Jeff if I give you the money will you get me a pint of cider please?" Jeff said "I will get it Niel and you can get me one next time." Niel says "No I am going home sober mate, I am not drinking with you 2 thank you." Jeff laughs and takes the money from him, Niel continues "And how have things gone with your brother Dan? If you don't mind me asking?" Danny said "No problem mate, I will tell you what happened and you tell me what you think, I went to Bridgend and met my brother and his wife and we went into the Alcoholic anonymous and we sat down at about 11.30 in the morning and the woman there said she could not see him as he had, had 2 cans of lager and dismissed us there and then." Niel said "Your kidding, you must be, they would not see him because he had 2 cans of lager, that's ridiculous mate so what are you going to do?" Danny says "Well my brother rubbed it in because he had already said it was a waste of time and he was not bothering anymore and said he would come over to see me and discuss it but I never seen him again that day and his wife said she will not stand much more and she would be off if it got much worse, so I am stumped now." Carol spoke up and said "I know how you feel Danny I had the same experience with my friend's father, he would not try and find help and alcoholics anonymous were a Joke and not even any doctor could help and he was found dead in bed one morning, he was only 38 it was awful." Jeff said "Well done Carol that's all Danny needs to hear." Carol "I am just telling him how difficult it is to get any help at all and if I knew where to get it I would tell him that's all." Niel says "I am afraid she is right it is Impossible to get much help at all, but the dole people will subsidise alcoholics and give them money to drink in their money each week, it's bloody awful, I don't know what to suggest mate." Danny "Well my older brother is going to see him this week and try and drum some sense into him, I hope he can but I think after he has gone he will go back to the same ways, but I am not going to give up mate, I won't." Jeff "That's right you got to keep on trying never mind how much he does not want it and if it makes him mad keep on trying that's all you can do." Danny "So Niel how did your weekend go?" Jeff says "Yes did you take Geraldine with you? Ha, ha." Niel "No I didn't and you have not got over that yet have you? No I had a good weekend with the boys and Ceri sends her love and she was wonderful as usual and we had a good night out in the club on Saturday and I didn't want to come back really, but here I am. I expected to see you on the train mate what happened?." Danny replies "The usual mate she was never there and I seen Josh all day Friday as he was off school because of teacher training and she had arranged a trip for him on Saturday to Folly Farm and I could not stop him really could I? he was looking forward to it and that was down to Angie again, so I came back and went on the drink with that idiotic English cockney git over there." Jeff took over the conversation and told them about the milk float incident and they all laughed out loud and Jeff was showing everyone how him and Danny were sitting on the back of the float nodding . He said to Carol "So where is the Adrian then? Tell me you and him have finished and that will make my day." Carol said "Uncle Jeffrey, don't be nasty he is lovely and for your information he is not coming back until tomorrow, so I am yours tonight Uncle Jeffrey." Jeff sits up excitedly and says "Carol that's a nice top you are wearing can I talk you out of it? Ha, ha." Carol said "Uncle Jeffrey." Jeff "If I follow you home will you keep me? Ha, ha, all those curves and me with no brakes, ok cheer up its ok it's personality I look for." Carol "Uncle Jeffrey, you cheeky man you, watch it mate." Jeff chuckling says "Sorry Carol I was only joking." Danny said after he finished laughing "He has not been the same since Saturday night when he saw most of Catalina when she opened the door with just a handkerchief covering a small part of her body and he saw her ass the lucky git, he hasn't been the same since." Carol "Is that true Uncle Jeffrey?" Jeff smiling "Oh yes, oh yes, it was gorgeous it was perfect, a lovely bum and what a body, god I am never going to be the same man, Niel it was a dream thing to see it really was." Niel said "So how did you see her then?" Jeff excited says "It was when she went to shut the door after speaking to me she thought I was Lidia knocking the door and only grabbed a hand towel and covered her front and when she turned to shut the door there was nothing covering her rear and a cracking rear it was too, god you should have seen it." Carol with a bit of jealousy in her voice "Right calm down Uncle Jeffrey, so you don't love me anymore ay?" Jeff "Oh yes, of course I do but you are spoken for now, so I am out in the cold." She says "But you are still my uncle Jeffrey." Danny says "Yes and he needs a good bonk not a friend who is spoken for unless you are offering." Carol sternly says "Daniel." Danny "So Jeff you know where you stand now and it's home to Pam tonight again." Niel says "A good night was had by all last night then by the sounds of it." Danny "Oh yes and I am having one more then I am off." Danny gets up and get the beer in and Jeff says to Niel "He is a silly sod he just sorted out a problem for Kezz, her ex-boyfriend owes her £60 and she has had trouble getting it off him, so Danny went and gave her the £60 because she was so upset and told her to tell him he now owes Danny the money and he wants it by next Friday or else." Carol says "Who is her boyfriend?" Jeff "Chris Jones." Niel says "Oh that little wanker I hate him he is so ignorant, good he won't mess with Danny and vice a versa." Carol says "Yes he is a horrible little git he really is no good for Kezz." Jeff "Well she is well happy about it because she can go to the karaoke now and I agree I suppose as a lot of the younger students here are bullied and can do nothing about it." Niel "Yes and Danny can't stand a bully verbal one or one who uses his fists, I am not going to be late tonight as I have the lovely Geraldine tomorrow all morning and I hope you won't get jealous again mate." Jeff "Ha, ha, no problem I will be with the other Geraldine all morning, so no problem or as you bloody Welsh say dim problem mate, dim problem." Danny is back and says "Flipping heck have you seen Linda behind the bar, she is wearing a neck tie around her waist, it's not worth wearing and you can see the sump there easy." Niel laughs and says "The sump, what a thing to call it ha, ha, ha, ha." Carol looking puzzled "What is her sump? I don't get it." Jeff laughs and says "Carol, think about it the sump it hangs down or the dolphins nose is another word." Jeff whispers in her ear and she laughs and says "What a thing to call it ha, ha, ha." Danny "Jeff have you seen her? I have never seen a shorter one and by the way she said to say hello to Barbara." Carol "Who is Barbara?" Danny says "It's Jeff they call me and Jeff Danny and Barbara because there are so many Jeff's in this college they call him Barbara." They all have a laugh and Niel says "Well that's the limit I have heard some names that is the best Barbara." Jeff chuckling says "Ok it's funny but please don't you lot start calling me it." Next thing Kezz comes up and says hello "Eek, eek, hello Niel where is Abby tonight?" Niel "She is knackered babe, so she is sleeping in my room." Kezz then says "Well give her a hug for me and say eek ok? I am going home now to see Miesha Paris on the TV, I hope I will see you in the karaoke Danny and Barbara ha, ha." Jeff says "Kezz don't you start or I will not buy you a drink again." Kezz "ha, ha, sorry but it is funny I am off now and thank you Danny eek, eek I love you all goodnight." They all say goodnight to her and Niel says "I heard you have become a money lender now Dan?" Danny says "Oh no mate, it's a one off to sort out a lad who has taken advantage of a lovely little girl and I will teach him a lesson he will never forget, that's all and I will." Carol says "Danny that's a lovely thing to do it's a shame there aren't more of you about, I am owed £120 and I can't get it back either and it is a bully of a man too," Danny "Ha, ha, don't go there girl I am not stupid." Carol laughing says "No honest now I am not joking." Danny "yeh right ha, ha, I am off now for a Chinese." They all wish Danny goodnight and Carol looking puzzled says "God another Chinese, he must have a lot of money, he has one every night and his figure is ok, if I had one that often I would be like a tank." Niel says "And me I only have to look at food and I am putting on weight." Jeff "Yes I wonder how he can handle it so many times a week too, he was telling me about you and some of the things you used to get up to and your horse Tommy, very funny." Niel said "He is no better he has been a little devil too, he once had 2 mates and one of them was a little slow, you know what I mean and him and his other friend were sitting outside his house because he had been kept in by his mother and told he had to stay in his bedroom and Danny and his friend Wyndham looking up at him in his window told him to open the window and speaking to him said "have you got any spinach in your pocket" the boy took a handful of grass out of his pocket and said "Yes" they used to pretend grass was spinach as Popeye ate spinach and was so strong, well anyway Danny and his mate said to him "take some of the spinach and chew some and pretend your Popeye and jump out of your bedroom window" he started to chew the grass and down in the garden was a lot of huge boulders as a rockery his father had just put in, well he finished chewing the spinach and stood on the window cill inside his bedroom and Danny and Wyndham said "now you are Popeye and you can't hurt yourself so jump and we can go and play" well Danny and Wyndham never thought he would jump at all but he did and as he did Danny and Wyndham shouted "no, no, no I was only kidding" but it was too late he landed on the rockery and broke his leg ha, ha,." Carol said with hand over mouth "Oh my god, what happened to Danny?" Niel tears running from his eyes said "Him and his mate legged it over to the other side of the village but his dad had him and he stayed in for a fortnight ha, ha, ha." Jeff "I bet his father was not happy at all either." Niel continued "Another time he had bought a motorbike with his friend Alan Burfitt and Alan was something like six foot 3 and they were too young to ride this bike on the road so they took the back lanes home, well they came up a huge hill called Shwt hill and at the top was a junior school and the wall going around it in a perfect circle was around about 14 foot high and you had to bank the bike down to get it around the corner quickly, well they came around that corner like a bat out of hell and his mate was on the back of the bike and was like a lightning rod sticking up and as they went around the corner all Danny could hear was ratat at tat ratat atat ratat atat ratat atat ratat atat, so Danny stopped and thought the bike had something wrong with it and as the bike stopped his mate just fell off the back and slumped to the floor. The noise was his crash helmet rubbing on the wall and had almost knocked him out, the wall was made of rock not brick and his mates helmet was all scratched to hell it was so funny ha, ha, and another time the same thing and his tall mate was on the back of another bike and going down a footpath in the dark and it had kissing gates to stop the cars driving up it and the actual gates were missing and they decided to go that way to avoid the main roads and the coppers well he sped through the kissing gates and his mate on the back was with him after a while Danny stopped and turned to speak to Alan and found he was not there and so went back to see where he was, well he got back to the kissing gates and saw Alan rolling around in pain behind the gates well Danny said "what happened to you?" Alan said " you idiot I was sitting there one minute and the next thing I was on my ass in agony on the floor, my knees hit the posts either side of the kissing gates and propelled me off the bike and my knees are busted ha, ha, " Jeff and Carol were in tears and Niel could not speak for laughing, well they finally stopped laughing and Niel then said "Did you know he had a beautiful custom car a Ford Capri the old one with the huge bonnet and it had general grabber wide tyres, silver side exhausts a lotus engine and nothing could catch it and one day he had the local vicar, it all went back when Danny was younger and him and his friend pinched some biscuit's from a farm shop store and the vicar caught him and handed him over to the police and Danny never forgot it and he hated that vicar and this vicar had a steel hand as he lost his hand for some reason or another, anyway the weather had had rain for a week or so and outside the vicarage was always a huge collection of water on the road and the vicarage was a mansion really and had huge steel gates and this vicar thought he was somebody, well the vicar was outside his gates alongside the water on the side of the road but it was not raining and the vicar had his umbrella in his hand but was not up, well Danny was coming through the village and from a distance could see the vicar standing by this vast amount of water and Danny put his foot on the gas and the vicar seen him coming at speed and realising he could not get out of the way in time and he was trying to open his umbrella quickly as possible to stop getting soaked well Danny hit the water fast and hard and the vicar didn't make it with his umbrella and whoosh the vicar was soaked through to the skin, it was like a tidal wave hitting him. Danny told me he looked in his rear mirror and he could see the vicar standing there soaked to the skin and his fists were in the air waving them at Danny ha, ha, and that's not all a few weeks later Danny went to a christening to his church and as the baby was being christened and the same vicar sprinkled the water over the baby's head, in all the silence Danny just burst out laughing and had to go outside and some of his friends laughed too in the church and after the christening he apologised to the father of the baby, but before he could do so the father burst out laughing too, it was so funny." Carol said "He must have been a little sod then." Niel said "Yes he was, one day he was coming home from somewhere late about midnight and the local copper was walking from the village about 3 miles away and Danny stopped and picked him up, he said to the copper " hello Alf where have you been until this time of night then? Up to no good I bet." Alfie the copper said "Ha, no I have been for a pint in the Fox and Hounds for a couple and missed the last bus so had to walk." well Danny got outside the police house and let the copper out and said to him " "goodnight Alf." the copper replied "Goodnight Dan, thanks for the lift home very good of you and the next time I see this car I hope you have got a valid tax disc mate, goodnight" Danny laughed and so did Alf. Jeff "Well there seems a lot of camaraderie in Wales villages." Niel "I think that yes Danny and me are little rogues and did things a little below the law but we never hurt anyone and never made anyone cry and that is rare today." Carol "I know what you mean as it is the same in Scotland, lots of little sods but no offence to anyone, I like that in a man." Jeff said "I found that when I went to Wales they like a good laugh as long as it does not hurt anyone, right I am off are you coming we can walk together and I hope Carol takes me home with her" They all leave and return to the dorm.

It was the Tuesday Danny's brother Mel was visiting Lyndon and that night Danny was on the phone to Mel "So how did it go Mel?" Mel replied "I don't know what to say, he has a problem allright, I went in and had a good welcome but he was on pins as soon as he seen me as if he wanted to hide something, well he went to take the car back over to his mother in law and Debbie showed me all the booze he has stashed all over the house, it's incredible and I think he has a real problem Dan, he really has." "Oh dear, I was hoping you were going to give me some good news." "No sorry it's not good, the way Debbie was telling me he is at it all day and she has had enough, she is going back for a week to stay with her sister and see if it shakes him out of it. After Debbie went out I had a good talk to Lyndon and asked him why he was doing it, he denied it and said it was not any different from before and kept on trying to change the subject and Dan he looks yellow his skin is yellow, that's not good." "Mel I wonder what we can do, he is doing himself no good and I am so worried, any ideas?" "I have tried to get some advice on the Matter and there is none to be had, I think the only way is to keep on to him." "Oh well I can't do much from up here can I? we will just have to keep on phoning him, there's nothing we can do, ok Mel I will give you a ring next week, see you." Mel said "Hang on Dan did you get that answer about the flightless bird from Iceland, I think it is a penguin but can't get the first six letters." Danny said "Oh I got it Mel so that makes me more intelligent than you ay." "Oh yeh, so what was it then ?" Danny "It is obvious really and you have not got a clue then?" Mel says "Ha, ha, ok big head what is it then? C'mon tell me." "A flightless bird from Iceland, well it's obvious, it's a frozen chicken isn't it?" There was a short delay and you could hear Mel laughing his head off.

Danny put the phone down and looked frustrated and went into see if Jeff was in the lounge. He got there and Jeff, Carol , Lola and Winnie were there, he said "Hi Jeff are you going to the bar? Or what?" Jeff says "Do trains run on tracks? Of course I am." Winnie chirps up "Velshman always in pub ha, ha." Danny said to her "Hey don't be cheeky or I will not help you anymore, have you done all your homework yet? Or are you a naughty girl." She laughs and says "Yes I have, have you? And I will give you a head massage later if you are good." Danny said "Ok I look forward to it." Lola "So you are giving head later, can we watch?" Winnie "Lola don't be rude, I think." Carol said "Adrian is coming over and we are having a night in for a change and if he is good he can buy me a curry later ha, and if he is not I will bring him over to see my uncle Jeffrey." Jeff "Don't threaten me Carol, I am not afraid ha, ha." Danny said "It's mother's day next weekend isn't it?" Lola "Oh god it is isn't it? I forgot, I will have to go into town for a present for her." Carol said "I got mine a nice pack of stuff from the body shop." Danny said laughing "No what I meant, it's the England and Irish game of rugby on the telly and am wondering where to go to see it, I thought we can go for dinner somewhere and watch the match there." Jeff "Good idea where? Rose and crown I will book a table for us ok?" Danny replies "Right and we can have a quiet drink after." Winnie "You and Danny have a quiet drink, I don't think you know what it is." Danny "It will be a slow drink for me that day, I am getting used to drinking heavy again and it's no good for me." Winnie grabs Danny's shoulder and shakes him and says "You tell lies, you always drink too much." Danny "I drink because of all you women who take advantage of me." Winnie "You are getting too cheeky now." Lola added "I will not take advantage of you don't worry." Danny "Oh crashed and burned then." Winnie looking jealous said "You must not play with all these women it's not good, stop it." She proceeds to punch Danny on the arm and Jeff says "Oop's, time for a ciggy ha, ha." Jeff goes off for one and Carol says "So Lola where is your boyfriend? I haven't seen him for a while now." Lola replies "He won't come up here now because a certain person won't let him watch the telly here, don't you remember he turned it over for you once to watch the EastEnders omnibus when he was watching formula 1." Danny said "Yes that's right, he can't take over our telly while all of our women etc. want to watch the other side and for your information I am a fanatic for formula 1 so it was not for my own ends, ask Jeff what my favourite sport is on telly." Lola "Whatever." Jeff walks in and Danny said "Jeff what is my favourite sport programme on telly?" Jeff thought about it for a moment and said "Rugby." Lola laughed and so did Carol, Danny then said "Right, and what else?" Jeff said Immediately "More rugby ha, ha." Danny looked at him seriously and smiled and said again "Right stop messing about I also watches what else through this summer in my room, even Winnie knows this as I have refused to give her English lessons when it's on." Winnie was just about to say what it was and Danny said "No Winnie, this is for Jeff and only for Jeff, think Jeff, but today would be nice." Jeff then said "Formula 1 racing." "Very good Jeffrey, I will give you a blue peter badge for that correct answer."

It was mother's day and Jeff and Danny were unable to get a table for dinner anywhere and were a bit miffed and settled for a few sandwiches and were not in a very good mood and were so fed up they decided to go out on a Sunday for a drink at noon and went to the Barrels public house for a couple to try and get themselves out of the blues that had set in. Well it was also the day of the Rugby international between Ireland and England in Ireland, well the pub was packed and it was a nice day lots of sunshine so the lads went in and got a pint and sat just outside in the beer garden in the sun. Danny said to Jeff "At bloody last, somewhere to sit and enjoy a pint, the people in this country have gone wild over mother's day you can't get a meal anywhere and just to get in for a pint anywhere was stupid." Jeff replied in a huff "You can say that again, I didn't think I was going to get a pint today at all and having the bloody rugby on does not help, but it's nice here in the garden and a damn good pint phew, it's a lovely place to sit especially in this sun and can you hear the water fall over there? It sounds really nice and nerve settling." "Yes it feels like I was in the country not in a city it's lovely and what a gorgeous pint I have nearly finished mine already and this sun is beautiful on my back, I only wish we had been able to get more to eat, what do they have here behind the bar Jeff?" "Only crisps, nuts and that's it and the Indian restaurant don't open until 7 tonight, so we have had it matey." "Great, at least the beer is good, I must stop moaning and enjoy the day, what have you sent your mother for mother's day then Jeff?" Jeff looking shifty says "Um, um, I ah, think I sent her flowers or chocolates I will have to think." "What is there to think about it's your mother and you don't remember what you sent, you only have one mother and there is not much to remember huh." "I am phoning her later and I will tell you then ha, ha." "I think you had better stop drinking with me as you are like someone with althziema, surely you can remember what you got your mother for mother's day, c'mon pull yourself together man." "I don't know because my sister has got something for me and I just pay her for it when I go home that's why." "Well you should be ashamed of yourself it's your mother and you only get one mother, make an effort don't be so lazy." "I know I should make an effort I sent her a mother's day card and signed it in Braile, what more do you want?" Danny looking serious said "I really wish my mum was still alive, I would make such a fuss over her today, I really would, she was a fantastic woman and I miss her so much, a very loving woman and so quiet and she didn't have much of a life with my father at all, I used to be like you and now I wish I had been more of a son to her but it's too late now, do you know what I mean?" "Yes I should be more of a caring son, but we are very close mind, we love each other's company and I never go long without seeing her. I bet your mum was a lovely lady." Danny with head bowed says "Yes she was an angel and never asked for much out of life and today is the right day to remember her and she has my brother Dennis buried with her who was very much like my mum and they are probably happier now than when they were alive. My mum had long black hair and was so cuddly, she was a cracking cook and loved anything to do with Hawaii and the hula skirts, the music and she often said she was a gypsy and loved their life style, a real loving and caring woman, but suffered because of the war, she was poisoned by sulphur and many chemicals after making many bombs and it ate her away inside, so Jeff I want to give a toast to our lovely mums." They toasted their mums and a little tear came to their eyes and Jeff said "Right give me some money mate time for a pint." Jeff gets the beer in and sat back down and said "What happened to the sun then?" Danny said "I don't know it's cold when it goes isn't it?" Jeff looked around and said "Oh the sun has gone behind the roof of the pub, if we move down the garden to the next table we will be back in the sun, c'mon." They moved down a table or 2 and sat down. Danny said "Oh that's better, I was a little cold for a minute there but it's good here." Jeff said "I must go to the toilet, I think that bloody water feature over there makes me want to go for a pee all the time, I won't be long." "Wait for me, I need a pee too." Off the lads went and returned again and sat down sipping their beer, Jeff said "That's better I wish they would turn that water feature off, look out here comes that lovely barmaid in her pink dress, god, I would." She approached the lads and said "Hi lads, it's the Irish and England international and when a game is on we make the food to match the country who is hosting the game and today it's Ireland so we have Irish stew, would you like some and some rolls? Peter told me to ask." Danny with a big smile said "Oh yes please, we are starving we didn't have a meal as everywhere was booked up, brilliant, we love you, thank you." Jeff said "Yes please I will have some to, thanks, my name is Jeff by the way." The barmaid says "Ok Jeff and sorry, what is your name?" Danny replied "Sorry, it's Danny and yours is." The barmaid replies "Rita, I will go and fetch a bowl each and some rolls, won't be long." Off she trots and Jeff said "Well, that is very nice of them and she is gorgeous mate, a cracking pair of legs and I hope she bends over for me to get a good look at her boobs, they might even fall out for me and trust me I will try and catch them ha, ha." Danny laughing said "Ha, ha and when you catch them pass them over to me after you finished as it is international day and we can pretend it's Wales vs. England ha, ha, but all Jokes aside what a lovely pub not only a damn good pint and good service and they feed you to, you think about it, we hardly ever go home from here without being fed, that's the best thing here." "Yes your right and the sun has gone further behind the roof, we will have to move again to the next table." The lads move and Rita returns with a tray full of food and put it on the table and said "Have you moved? I could swear you were sitting on this table." Danny "Yes the sun keeps going behind the roof of the pub and so every so often we have to move." She puts 2 big bowls of stew and some rolls and said to them "Shall I get you a couple of pints save you struggling to the bar?" Jeff said "Do you mind? That will be fantastic if you don't mind, here and have a drink yourself." Rita replies "Don't be so soft, I don't mind and it gets me in the sun for a bit, I won't be long lads." Off she goes and Danny said "Well isn't that just brilliant, we are being looked after hand and mouth, I feel like a lord here fantastic mate and a beautiful girlie too, can't beat it." "Too right and getting the drinks in also for us that is what is missing today courtesy and good care in the public sector, It gets my vote, I won't hesitate to come back here and what a pair of knockers mate and a great cleavage ha, ha." "This stew is absolutely beautiful isn't it? And I am glad now we did not have much to eat this is lovely." The lads finished the stew just as Rita returned and she put the pints on the table and said "Did you enjoy that, looks as if you did as you seemed to have licked the bowls and here is your change Jeff." Jeff "Thank you lovely Rita you are spoiling us and we like it that was gorgeous stew thanks." Danny "Yes it was absolutely beautiful, compliments to the chef." Rita said "Would you like some more if there is any left later?" Danny said "Oh yes please, thank you." Jeff "Oh yes please Rita but not a full one for me thanks." Rita said "Ok, I will bring you some in about half an hour ok?" Danny said "I tell you what Rita if I give you some money can you bring some more pints out for us at the same time? If you don't mind, or am I being too cheeky." Rita "No not a problem at all, see you in half an hour bye." The boys said goodbye to her and Jeff said "God, I must go to the toilet again I am busting, that bloody water feature is causing it, do you want to go mate?" "Yes I do mate, your right that water feature makes me want to go all the time, listening to that water trickling all the time." Off to the loo again and they come back and a few pints later they were at the edge of the garden because the sun kept on going behind the roof until they were totally in the shade and decided to go in the bar for a couple and by this time they were a little tipsy. At the bar and the match was coming to an end and the men in the bar by now were worse for wear and still drinking and next thing a load of women come in and sat alongside the lads and were also a little worse for wear and Danny struck up a conversation with them and said "You girls enjoying the rugby then?" A woman replied "Not really we have just been out for a boozy day out as our husbands are here watching the rugby and so we get together and have our own fun, because we are fed up with them on the beer all day then coming home pissed out of their minds, as far as we are concerned what's good for the goose is good for the gander." Danny "Fair enough and how many of you are there? As this pub has been boring until you lot came in." She replies "There are 7 of us and we love a bit of fun if you know what I mean? " Jeff's eyes lit up on hearing this and he was brave due to the drink and said "Yes it's about time we had a bunch of sexy girlies here, it was boring earlier but now we have some gorgeous girlies in we may stay now, do you believe in love at first sight or do I have to walk past again?" Danny said "Oh no, here we go again, you have got to hear this girls." They all listened intently and Jeff continued "If I told you, you reminded me of my mam, would you tuck me in tonight? Ha, ha, hi my name is big Jeff and I am mighty tall as well, do you know the difference between a burger and sex?" She said "No I don't." Jeff continues "Fancy something for lunch ha, ha." The girls by now were laughing their heads off and Jeff finished off by saying "What has a thousand teeth and holds back a monster?" She said "I have no idea." Jeff "My fly ha,ha." The afternoon was by this time getting wild and very much full of

Jokes and laughter Danny said "A sailor goes on leave in Egypt and he went to his room with a lady of the night and in the morning he awoke and found all his clothes had been pinched except his pants he had on and lucky he had put his wallet down them, he started to panic as he had to be back on his ship before 2 o'clock. He opened the curtains and seen a bizarre outside and a man selling clothes on his stall, he rushed out and said to the Arab behind the table "Have you got any clothes to fit me? I need them urgent." The Arab said in his broken English "Yes sir, do you want a nice jacket? a nice shirt? a nice tie? a nice pair of trousers? And a nice pair of shoes?" The sailor said "That's brilliant I will take them all." The Arab then said "Sir you have spent a lot of money with me, I will make you an offer that is special, I have a pair of magic slippers." The sailor looked at him and said "Ok so what's magic about them?" The Arab said "Sir, when you put these magic slippers on, your cock goes like a rod of iron and you can shag any woman any time anywhere they never will say no." The sailor said "I'll have a pair of them." He took the slippers off the Arab and put them on and all of a sudden he run around behind the counter lifted up the Arab and laid him over the table pulled his trousers down and started to roger him from behind, the Arab with a frightened look on his face said to the sailor "Sir, you have got them on the wrong feet." The whole room of women Jeff and Danny were in hysterics laughing and one of the women said "I got to go for a pee, I will pee myself if I don't." Jeff said "It's that bloody water feature again." The women by now was holding their self and the tears were streaming down their face. Jeff then slurred and swaying "I am going for a pee Dan do you want to go or what ?" Danny slurred "No thanks mate I don't, see you in a minute." Jeff wobbled off to the toilet and tried to walk sensibly as he was trying to Impress the women. The women were waiting for another Joke or 2 but Danny was getting so pissed he just carried on drinking. Next thing in walks Jeff from the toilet and he was by now staggering along, well he approached the bar and the women were watching him as if to say will he make it to the bar before he falls, but what happened next was so funny, he went to put his foot on the foot rest at the bottom of the bar just like the cowboys used to do but he missed it and the momentum made him nod and head butt the bar and it was a big bang sound that came from his head hitting the bar, he staggered even more after he did this and he just said "Phew, phew, what happened then?" He Immediately held his fore head and everyone started laughing uncontrollably and Danny was on his hands and knees as he did not see what happened he just knew what had happened by the banging sound and the footsteps, the place was full of laughter and after they settled down again it was like a delay because of shock and then Jeff started laughing out loud and they all started laughing again. After a few minutes Jeff said "Oh, my god my head has swollen up and I have an ostrich egg on my fore head." This brought on the laughter again, Danny felt Jeff's fore head and said "Oh dear, that is what I call a lump and you will have a headache in the morning after that." The girls by now was feeling sorry for Jeff and gathered around him like concerned mothers and Jeff was lapping this up for a long time, but by now the husbands were also gathering like wolves to see what the wives were up to and soon they all dwindled off home. Danny and Jeff by now were absolutely legless and were down to their last £1 and Danny said to Jeff "How much money have you got mate? I only have a £1 left, I came in here with £40 and it's all gone and it only went on beer." Jeff staggering still looked in his pocket and said "Shit me to, I have gone through a whole £40 but I have got a £5 note tucked away in my back pocket for an emergency for a taxi just in case." "And I fancied another pint, looks like we have had it ha, ha." Jeff said slurring "Me too." Peter said from behind the bar after hearing this "My god lads you have put some beer away today, I have never seen anyone drink like that before and if you want to spend your last bit of money here for a pint go ahead and do It, I will sort a taxi out for you don't worry about it." Jeff said "Oh I don't know, allright then ha, ha, ha." Peter said "You took a lot of convincing didn't you ha, ha, ha." Danny said "Well Peter it's a messy Job but somebody's got to do it   ." Peter said "My goodness it's been a damn good day and you pair have been the centre of attention here with the Jokes and those women loved it and went home pissed and still laughing that's unusual and I think you put the frighteners up their husbands too ha, ha." Jeff said "What, what, what, I'll get it out now in a minute, god I'm pissed, woops I nearly hit this box off the bar then, what is it Pete?" Peter said "Steady Jeff or you will be on your hands and knees picking up a lot of coins, it's full and it's funny enough it's the blind box ha, ha, ha." Jeff replied in a slur "Right Dan drink up there is enough in there for a few more pints I'm sure, fill them up Peter." Peter said "What do you mean?" Jeff "Take the money out of the blind box and cut out the middle man ha, ha, ha." They all laugh and Danny said "Good thinking Jeff I never would have thought of that ." Peter said "Well I wonder if you are right because it says money for the blind ha, ha." Jeff "Yes why not? I have been thinking we have spent forty quid each and have not bought anything to eat, it's all gone on beer so how many pints have we had then at £2. 30 a pint?" Danny said "A good point I wonder let me see I reckon about 14 pints or more mate, god no wonder we are in such a mess and it's time for me to go home and have my injection, so how are we going to do this then?" Peter said "I will order a taxi and pay for it so don't worry about it, are you ready for it now?" Danny and Jeff said the same time "Yes please Peter, thanks mate." The lads waddle out to the entrance of the pub to wait for the taxi and it pulls up and they fall into it and said to the driver "Dowdell hall please driver and don't spare the horses." The lads fall out of the taxi at Dowdell. At the college and they stagger up to the lounge.

They walk into the lounge and it seemed everyone was there and as they fell through the door Lola said "Oh my god, look at the state on them, Jeff your pissed aren't you?" Jeff replied "I don't know I am too drunk to tell and it's that dodgy Welshman's fault." Danny slurred "Of course it is, is there any where to sit before we fall down." Winnie grabbed Danny and let him to a sofa and giggled "Huh, a drunk velshman again and that silly Jeff both very drunk again ha, ha, ha." Rhoda laughed and said "Oh Jeff and Danny what a state and it's only seven o'clock." Niel said " Look at these pair." Jeff went to sit by Danny and missed the settee and sat on the floor and said "Oops, missed, Danny have your insulin before you forget please then I can go to bed." Danny mumbled "Ay ok, I will do it now Immediately." Niel commented "Yes Dan do it now before you forget or you will be ill." Rhoda took Danny off to let him have his injection and brings him back and Jeff was telling them all about the day and Danny sat on the settee and fell asleep. Niel said to Jeff "Has he had anything to eat Jeff?" Jeff "Oh yes, we had lots of Irish stew and £80 of beer between us." Niel said "Your Joking I have seen you pair drink but never that much." Jeff said with serious face and head bobbling about like a nodding dog in the back of a car said "That's true we didn't believe it at first but I have not got a penny on me and I went out with forty five quid and Danny had forty and we are skint and the food was free and we can't play pool or anything." Lola said "That's disgusting I would be ashamed." Winnie said "Yes it's stupid." Niel laughed and said "That's 20 pints each, well no harm done I hope as Danny could be very ill with his diabetes if he is not careful, I had better wake him up and make sure he is allright." Niel shook Danny but no reply was had he was snoring and did not react to the shaking and so they all got a bit concerned and went and got the warden Mandy. She came in and seen Jeff and Danny and put her hands on her hips and said "Oh my god, look at the state on these 2, I give up with you two I really do, look at the lump on your forehead Jeff, how did you do that?" Jeff says "I walked into something I think ha, ha, ha." Mandy "Well it is going to be like a gooses egg by the morning and what is wrong did you say ?" Rhoda said "Danny won't wake up and he had a lot to drink, we have shaken him but he just keeps on snoring." Mandy "How much have you two had to drink Jeff?" "About 15- 18 pints, we lost count ha, ha, and I am off to bed." Mandy said "What, that much, it's a wonder you two aren't dead, right I will have to wake Danny up, out of the way Jeff." Jeff stood up and said "Ha, ha, good luck he has drunk enough to sink a battle ship, I will see if he is allright and then I am off to bed." Mandy shook Danny violently and shouted at him "Danny c'mon, c'mon time for lectures ha, ha, ha." Danny finally mumbled "Oh leave me alone I am sleeping." Jeff said "Right goodnight, I am off." He went to move and went flat on his face and Lola picked him up and laughed and Mandy shook Danny again and said "C'mon mate get to bed and sleep it off." Danny looking bleary eyed said "Ok I am off." He stood up and fell back on the settee and so Mandy got one side and Niel the other side and frogmarched him into his bedroom and Danny got onto his bed fully clothed and pulled the divan over him and went to sleep. Back in the lounge they were all laughing at Danny and Jeff and Niel told them a story about Danny he had heard "He once got drunk and he is petrified of spiders and he at the time was going blind and he went for a crap on the toilet and was sitting there with his trousers down to his ankles and a spider fell from the ceiling and it was a large one and it landed on his leg, he screamed got up and ran straight into his open door and knocked himself out all because of this spider and when he came too he had a huge lump on his fore head and it was split , ha, ha, ha, and when his wife told me about it I killed myself laughing for days. He had left the door open and had run into the front edge of it ha, ha." Rhoda said "Ouch, I bet that hurt, why does he drink so much Niel?" Niel "I was like him once, that's how they drink in the valleys, like fish no reason except that's all there is to do and lots of clubs that serve many affordable beers and better than that crap they serve up here, it's a way of life down there." Winnie said "Well it's silly he can kill himself doing that and he has a brother who does the same, I think he needs help too." Niel "No, he is not a alcoholic he knows when to stop and he drinks and gets drunk and goes to bed, he will not get into bother, he just goes to bed and that is the way to be and he will be suffering tomorrow and in the night he will have a pint or 2 and he will be fine. It's Jeff I am more worried about, he is like a stick insect and about less than 4 times the size of Danny and drinks with Danny and there's nothing of him, so he will feel it tomorrow, I just hope he will be alright." Rhoda says "I just passed his room and he is snoring so loud the door is vibrating and I will keep an ear out for him, but your right he will be very sorry tomorrow ha, ha, ha." Lola "I think they are stupid doing all that drinking, there is more to life." Winnie "Yes I think so too and I needed my lesson in English tonight but not now, huh." Niel laughed and said "I can't wait to see that cockney git in the morning ha, ha, ha."

It was a little later and the lounge was empty and in crashes Danny and said "Hello, hello, is there anyone about, shit I am pissed and if they had left me sleep on that settee I would be sleeping now and I feel like a drink and no money." Danny staggered to Jeff's room and banged the door "Hello Jeff, hello Jeff, wake up I need some money have you got any until tomorrow?" But Danny could not wake him up and that was that, no one around and he knew Winnie would not let him have any money and so went back to bed and finally fell asleep.

It was the next day and sitting in the kitchen was Zarrine, Lola and Rhoda and Rhoda said "Well Zarrine you missed it here last night, Danny and Jeff were in the worst state I have ever seen them in, falling about and you could not understand a word they were saying ha, ha, ha." Lola said "It was so funny the both of them had, had it and Mandy had to come up and see if Danny was alive, he would not wake up and she really had to shake him to get him awake, he and Jeff had about 18 pints and this was 7 o'clock ha, ha." Zarrine looking concerned said "Did Mandy check on them in the night do you know?" Rhoda said "I never heard her and I know Jeff is allright he is still snoring like a dragon so he is ok." Zarrine said "I had better go and check on Danny Immediately." She got up and went off. Lola said "Yes go and look in on your man, she thinks the world of that man and that Jeff." Rhoda "Are you jealous then?" "No it's always them 2 she runs about after, I don't know why especially that Danny he can be Impossible, but there we are." Next in walks Niel and says "Hello all, anyone seen Jeff and Danny this morning?" Lola "Oh, not another one, the world doesn't revolve around them 2 you know, I'm off see you." Off she goes and Niel says to Rhoda "Oh dear, someone trod on her foot ay, so have you seen them at all Rhoda?" "No but Jeff is still snoring loudly so he is allright and Zarrine has gone off to check on Danny." "I expect he is ok but he takes some chances with his diabetes." Zarrine walks in "He is ok, a bit fed up because there was no one around apparently to lend him some money last night." Niel "What did he need money for? I would have lent him some, he knows that, but I had gone for a pint in the student bar." Zarrine said "You wouldn't believe what he wanted the money for?" Niel "Let me guess, he wanted a pint." Rhoda "Never, he was too drunk for a pint." Zarrine "Yes, your right he said Mandy woke him up and he could not get back to sleep and so banged Jeff's door your door and finally went back to bed, he will be in now in a while." Niel said "I thought that is what he wanted the money for, he is a lad." Rhoda says "Flipping heck he is an animal." Danny walks in rubbing his eyes and said good morning to all and Niel said to him "Well hello there, how are you this lovely morning then? Huge hangover I reckon." Danny laughed "Ha, ha, no not really, I think I drunk myself sober and Mandy woke me up and I was ready to go again, but had no money, so I had a can or 2 and finally fell asleep and here I am." Niel "My god mate, you have a problem and Jeff is dead to the world and snoring for England, I would have given you some money if I was here but I didn't expect to see you until today." Danny "Oh, that's very nice of you, can you lend me a fiver? Until I can walk straight to get some money out of the hole in the wall up college green?" Niel digs in his pocket and says "Here it's a tenner, I have only got tenner's on me." Danny "Oh, thank you man, I will give it back later this afternoon ok?" Niel "Oh don't worry about it mate, give it back when you have got it, is that enough?" Danny "Yes thanks I won't be drinking many tonight that's for sure." Zarrine walks back in and says "Well Jeff is ok, he is just groaning and said to go away and don't come back, so he is allright ha, ha, ha." They all laugh and Rhoda says "Well we will have peace and quiet from him today and I think Danny is going back to bed too." Danny "Who me? I am going over for my Braile lecture no problem and that's it I am not going back to bed no way, I think a cup of tea and some toast will sort me out." Zarrine "Ha, ha, a hint to me I think I bet it is." Danny "Oh if you insist then Zarrine I know you love me, so I will let you." Zarrine grabs Danny's hand and sit's him down and says "You sit there and don't move, I will get you some toast and tea ha, ha, you lazy person." Danny smiles and Niel says "Lola is right he gets his own way with you." Danny "It's a messy Job but some body's got to do it ha, ha, and you can talk Niel, she runs about after you enough and baby sit's Abby for you so steady man." Niel replies "Yes she is wonderful isn't she? We would be lost without her." Danny smiling said "Yes, I would be lost without her and she can be so funny when she tries to describe something ha, ha, and she really does look after us and that bloody cockney git will have her running around later when he wakes up." Rhoda says "Yes he loves it too, he will be dying later when he gets up and I can visualise him now holding his head and moaning." Niel "I can't see him getting out of bed today the state he was in last night, but there again I didn't expect to see you neither mind so perhaps he has drunk himself sober too." Danny says "I can't believe we drunk so much, we each went through £40, only on beer alone, we ate for free so at £2.30 a pint that is a lot of drink each and look at the size of Jeff he has to be congratulated he put the same away as me and I am 3 times his size, most men would be dead drinking that much so he deserves a sleep in and if anyone of the lecturers asks for him tell them he is ill and that isn't a lie, he is suffering with the biggest hangover in his life, I will never do that again, I tell you." Niel said "My god, did you really drink that much?" Danny "Honest, we did and I can say that is the most beer I have ever drunk in my life in one go and in a way I was lucky no one was about last night to lend me money, just think what I would be like now, I might be in hospital, time to grow up now I think." Rhoda "Yes I agree, you are dicing with death with your diabetes mate and Jeff will not be able to keep up with you and he will be getting ill soon at that rate, so cut it down Dan." Danny "Yes I know I will just have a pint or two from now on." Niel chuckling said "Yeah, yeah, I have heard that one before Dan, sure I am going to believe that too." Danny "No I mean it this time and my guts is churning up, ah my toast thank you Zarrine but faster next time please." Zarrine slaps him on the shoulder and said "Behave now and don't be cheeky to me or I will report you for drinking too much." Danny "It's too late for that, Mandy had to put it in the book I expect, as it is her Job so all will hear about it later." Niel "You had better tell the braile babes for them to have a laugh, they are so funny and will have to know to take the piss out of Jeff." Zarrine "He is snoring like a bear and he said to me to go away sweetie and don't come back and my room doesn't need hoovering as most of the dust are up my nose, see you next week my darling ha, ha, ha." Niel said "Ha, he is so funny, he will be a great laugh when he gets up, I wish I was here." Rhoda "If he does not drink tonight I will get some sleep as he won't snore so much." Zarrine "I am going to tell Carol she will go and see him and her loud screeching voice will go through his head like a giant bell ringing, that will teach him." Danny "Oh dear, he will love you for that, she would make me suicidal in my state now so god help him ha, ha, I am off for a bath before my cheese grater making class." Rhoda looking confused said "What is cheese grater making ?" Danny says "Braile, because after you have brailed on that hard paper you could grate cheese with it after, or it will make a good back scratcher, get it?" Rhoda "Oh right, I see now." Danny goes off to have a bath and get ready.

Later in the braile class Danny is just finishing telling them about the night before and said "So when you see Jeff ask him about him head butting the bar in front of all those women, I was killing myself laughing and he was standing there stunned ha, ha, it was so funny." They all laughed and Tim said "See, I missed it again, so how the hell are you here if you drunk all that beer, I would be in bed for a fortnight if it was me." Danny said "Tim I really don't know, I was woken up by Mandy and I just sobered up it's crazy, it really is, I have a rough stomach but otherwise I am allright just one of those things but I will rub it in to Jeff and make out he is a light weight ha, ha." Ginny said "Poor Jeff, I hope he is allright, besides his headache I mean, I will tease hymn tomorrow mind." Tim "And I will be here to see it, I can't wait, so Dan are you going out for a pint tonight?" Danny "Oh, I don't know yet, at the moment I would be sick but I will probably have the hair of the dog, but not many more. Time to put my name and lesson number on my paper, ay." Ginny "Well you have got it right for a while now and everyone is talking about the time you got it mixed up and they all ask me if it is true and when I tell them it is they all laugh." Danny "I bet and I can't wait to see how Jane and Jimmy get on in the next lesson, it is so gripping." (Jane and Jimmy are the characters in the braile training books and are used to teach them braile terms etc. and they are so boring as characters) Ginny "Now Daniel don't be awful, just think about us we have been learning about Jane and Jimmy for a couple of years now, so think about what we feel." Tim laughing says "Oh dear I bet it's murder but we could change the story as we go along." Christine chirps up "I don't think so not with Danny here it will be classified as a cert x, we will stick to the book because you 2 will be getting us all to do the actions too, so leave it now ha, ha, ha." Ginny "Good thinking I like my Job so don't go there ha, ha." Tim "Yes we don't want to end up fighting do we, it would be like shadow boxing." Danny said "My father was a boxer you know." Ginny replies "Really, was he?" Danny smiling says "Oh yes and my mother was a cocker spaniel ha, ha, ha." Ginny stops laughing after a while and says "You silly sod, I believed you then for a while, I should have known better shouldn't I?" Tim "Very good Daniel, I never believe him anymore, I have set the date for my wedding by the way, it's the end of April and it's in Drayton Manner theme park and you are welcome, I will give you the invitations soon ok?" Ginny "Aw, that's nice, some good news at last." Danny "Does Mandy know yet?" Tim looks at Danny and said "Of course she knows you idiot, you don't think I would say it if she didn't know, she would kill me." Christine "That's lovely Tim, I am pleased for you." Margaret said "Yes congratulations Tim and good luck for the future, I am so pleased, I know you will be happy together." Tim "Thank you all, I am dreading the stag night though." Margaret "Why is that Tim?" Tim "I am inviting Danny." They all say together "Oh dear." Danny looks puzzled and says "What do you mean? Oh dear, I am not that bad." Ginny "I hope Tim you are having it a month before the wedding for your sake, he will get you as drunk as he got Jeff last night and I don't fancy your chances much." Tim says "I have already thought of that and my best man is going to keep an eye on the evening and I will have a damn good drink as Danny and I drink the same and it's going to be a long night around Tamworth in all the pubs with a lot of my friends and for a Chinese at the end of the night. I think we will have to pace it matey." Danny looking rejected says "I don't know if I want to come now, after all the insults, I am only Joking, I wouldn't miss it for the world and will your dad be there?" Tim "Oh yes he will be there, he never misses a good piss up but he will not be there all night, it would be too much for him with his problems." Ginny "Yes I understand it, he must look after himself." Danny "I can't wait to meet him, he sounds like a nice man, nothing like his son ha, ha, ha." Tim said "Cheeky git, what do you mean? Ha, ha." Danny "I am only Joking mate, I hope your mates like a good laugh." Tim "Oh yes, I have warned them about you already and they can't wait, it's going to be a good night, you wait and see." Ginny slaps the desk and says "Right time to work. We are going to do something different this morning, I have got some leaflet's in braile we received this morning nothing special but it is just any normal mail, so try and read some of it just for the experience. Danny first, just pick a random sentence." Danny reads very slow with his fingers rubbing the braile trying to work out what it says "The, that's easy singer is, right I am getting there, looking good, the next word is tin, tin, a, tin a tu, tun tuna tin a tuna." Ginny "I don't think so, I have read that it's not tin a tuna, try it again." Danny concentrating hard "Tin a tuna, it is as I have said it ." Ginny starts laughing uncontrollably "No it's not tin a tuna, it's Tina Turner the singer." They all laugh for a long time at Danny yet again.

Later Danny goes into student services to pick up his mail and takes them back to get Zarrine to read them. He sat on his bed waiting for Zarrine, she arrives and starts to read the letters and then stopped speaking and says "Oh, my goodness look at this." Danny says in urgent voice "What? What is it Zarrine?" She continues to read it to herself and drops her hands onto her lap and says "I don't believe it, it's amazing it really is." Danny says "What? Please tell me before I die, am I in trouble again? Am I getting expelled? Have I got a terminal illness?" Zarrine continues "It's from a publishing company about that poem you wrote." Danny "What about it?" "Well it's being published in a book and it says it's been selected from many hundreds of poems and will be published next month and it asks if you need any copies and for you to give them permission to publish it and you have to sign this form to allow publication, it's incredible, it really is, I told you it was good didn't I?" Danny was beaming from ear to ear and said "Well I never, I have been told by everyone it is good but never in my life did I think it was good enough for a book, I should have listened to you and Sarah Barry's missus, well, well, well." "Well done Danny I am so pleased for you, I really am, it's fantastic, I bet you are pleased aren't you?" "Oh yes, I think it's incredible for just 20 minutes to write it and look now it's published in a book at my first attempt, this has come as a shock to me it really has." "You will have to sign a copy for the college and put it in the library now and you are now officially a poet, we will be able to tell everyone about you now." "It's amazing, I didn't think this type of thing happens to people like me, fancy that." Danny stopped talking and there was a pause and then he said "But I never sent it into anywhere to be looked at by any publishing company, so how the hell did they get it?" "You didn't, so how did they get it then." Danny shrugs his shoulder and said "It's a mystery to me isn't it, aw well whoever it was it worked and I am so thrilled about it, I must take it over to see Janet in the library in the queens building and she can read it, she will be pleased about this and I will tell everyone now and I might do a little more writing, flipping heck it's amazing it is Zarrine and if I didn't have such a hangover I would go out and celebrate and this will shut up Niel who says it is rubbish writing about blind and deaf people, he knows nothing does he?" "No he will eat his words now, well done Danny, take it over to see Janet, I am off now, I have finished my shift 15 minutes ago, see you Danny, bye." Danny grabbed Zarrine and give her a big kiss on the cheek and said "I am so happy, goodbye Zarrine see you tomorrow, bye."

Danny Immediately set off to see Janet and was by the crossing lights on the main road and a voice said in a deep voice "Hello." Danny said "Jeff is that you?" Jeff "I don't know is it?" Danny "My god you sound awful and I thought you would still be in bed, are you going to lectures then?" "Yes, and I am not pleased about it as the lecturer who is taking us who we call fluffy will make my life hell if I do not attend, so I am on my way and when I get in there I am going to go to sleep." "Really." Jeff said holding a pillow under his arm "Yes I have a pillow in my hand and as soon as she has marked us present I will lay on my pillow and go to sleep as she is boring and she will send me to sleep Immediately, see you later, so long." Jeff marches off like a zombie and Danny carries on to see Janet.

Janet says "Well that is a turn up for a nice change, you should be proud of yourself, it's fantastic and what a nice name for the book Awakening Spirit, you must order a book for the library here and the college will pay for it, so do you want to sign the contract and I will get it posted back for you, it's only to give your permission for them to use it in their book and all rights to your poem stay yours and no one can use it without your permission ok?" Danny with a beaming smile says "Yes no problem, give me the pen and I will sign it, it's exciting isn't it, it's a shame my mum and dad was not alive they would be proud especially my mother, but maybe they are looking down as long as they are not together ha, ha, ha." "I think they probably are, you should keep on writing Dan it's good and I heard you wrote this in 20 minutes didn't you?" "Yes I did but that is not what is confusing me, I didn't send this in to the publishers mentioned I never sent it off to anyone so how they got it I don't know, it's a mystery." "Honestly, well, well, you must find out who did then, well I will post this off for you if you like and well done again and when the book comes back bring it in and sign it for us ok?" "No problem Janet thanks and don't forget to send for 3 books as I want 2 for myself, thanks again." Danny left with a huge smile on his face and continued with his lectures.

Later he phoned his son to tell him and was puffed up with pride all the rest of that day.

Later at about 7 pm he went into the lounge only to find everyone in there and as soon as he walked through the door everyone said "Here he is." Danny shocked said "What have I done now?" Jeff looking sick said "Your famous now then, we had trouble with you before and now we won't be able to live with you." Danny said "What the dickens are you on about?" Rhoda said "You are all over the e-mail system here in the college, we all had an e-mail telling that congratulations is in order about the poem you have had published, that's fantastic Dan, we are all proud of you." Lola says "I wouldn't go that far." Danny "Honestly, is it? well, well, it's all a shock to me I didn't send it in someone else did, so I only wrote it someone else is to blame for it being published, but it is nice to have it published and it was my first attempt too, you could blow me down with a feather." Niel added "Well done mate it takes some doing, well done." Danny replies "Well thanks mate, I am surprised as blind and deaf poetry is boring as far as you are concerned ay." Niel "Well it shows how wrong I can be, we must go over the bar for a pint to celebrate." Danny says "Yes, I might get one or two and that's it and what about you Jeff are you up to it?" Jeff nodding in his chair said "What, what, sorry, what, I am dying leave me alone and look at my head did you do this?" Jeff had a large bump on his head and half a black eye. Danny said "No, you done that and you can't remember it can you?" Jeff "No I bloody can't remember it, I can't remember my name because of you." Danny "Me, you did not say once I have had enough I am off, you loved it and the reason for the lump is that you went to put your foot on the foot bar and missed it completely and head butted the bar in front of all the women in there and we all laughed our heads off, that's why you have a lump nothing to do with me." Everyone was laughing and Jeff started laughing and said "It's still your fault, I have never been so drunk as this in all my life and this lot said we had about 18 pints, that's Impossible tell me." Danny said "Well Jeff you work it out I had forty pounds and you had forty five pounds, work it out for yourself and we didn't pay for anything else that night and peter paid for the taxi, in my books it's more than 17 pints Jeff and by the sound of you it's bad." Jeff "It is, I had 17 text messages on my phone mostly from Geraldine, she wanted us all to meet for a drink and I missed all the messages and her just my luck." Rhoda started laughing and Niel said "Ha, ha, what are you laughing about Rhoda ha, ha." Rhoda said laughing at the same time "This afternoon Jeff came into the lecture room and got his mark and pulled his pillow out and put it behind his head and went to sleep and fluffy said to him what are you doing Jeff with that pillow? he said I am going to do what I always do in your lecture and this time I am going to do it comfortably on a pillow and he fell asleep but this time he was snoring and we had to wake him up a few times and we were all laughing it was so funny." Jeff sniggering said "Ha, ha, ha, she didn't like it but it saved me from missing my mark but my neck is so stiff now and before you ask you dodgy Welshman I am not going for a pint, I just can't, one pint and I will be pissed again ha, ha, ha." Danny said "Fair enough mate we will celebrate without you ok? Let's go then." Jeff chirped up "You could have tried harder than that mate to get me up the bar, ok I give up I am coming up but I am not drinking much."

Niel "Yeah, yeah, another one who tells porkies like Danny." They all went off and Danny and Jeff were dragging behind them looking like 2 old men waddling along.

Up in the bar and Danny and Jeff sitting there looking so rough and Niel put a pint in front of the both of them and said "Here we go lads, a nice pint each ha, ha, ha." The lads looked sick as parrots and Jeff had the first sip and screwed his face up and said "Argh, the smell makes me feel ill." Danny said screwing his face up "Argh, your right and I could feel it go down all the way, I think we should get the first one down as quick as we can and we will feel better right?" Jeff "If you want to you go ahead I am not." Danny picked his drink up and drunk it down and shook his head made a lot of noises and said to Jeff "That's better mate, I am ready for another and feel much better now and I just farted to, go with it Jeff." Jeff started heaving at the smell Danny made, he was making a choking sound and Danny moved as he thought he was really going to be sick. Jeff then said "You smelly sod, I can't breathe you pig that's it." He picked his pint up and drank it all up and he also made a lot of horrible sounds, slammed his empty pint on the table and said "Right mate whose round is it?" They all started cheering Jeff and Jeff stood up and promptly fell back in his seat and said "Oh shit, my head went funny then." Danny said "I will get them in mate don't worry." Next in comes Carol and shouted "Uncle Jeffrey is that you my darling." She shuffled over and sat by Jeff and Jeff was holding his head and she was giving him the sorry I am treatment and she kept asking him if he was allright until Adrian came in and she went off to sit by him. A few pints later and in walks Tim and Mandy and Tim said after settling down "I hear we have a poet here in our midst Dan." Danny said "Yes you could say that, it's all over the college now, so I can't deny it, it's a nice feeling really." Mandy says "Yes well done Danny, it's a fantastic poem and made me cry it was so close to the heart." Jeff said "Yes it tells my life story especially when it says about the devil dragging me down to hell it's exactly how it felt, perfectly told." Tim said "I hear Jeff you and Danny had a session last night or yesterday afternoon is that true?" Jeff "Yes it's true enough I have been dying since, I expect he told you everything and especially about my head injury." Tim "Yes he did, that was so funny ha, ha, ha." Jeff "I am feeling better now I have had a pint and here comes my next one, thanks Dan and thanks for telling everyone about my accident." Danny "No problem, have I told you Mandy?" Mandy said "Tim told me all about it, poor Jeff." Danny "Well it's water under the bridge now and by the way everyone the reason he missed the bar with his foot is because there is no foot rest in that bar." They all laughed again Danny continues "And congratulations both, I am so happy for you both." Jeff "Congratulations, what's this Dan?" Danny stood up and said to everyone "Can I ask you all to raise your glasses to Tim and Mandy who are now engaged to marry and have announced their wedding day …. To Tim and Mandy congratulations." They all toast them and sit down and Jeff said "You kept that quiet Tim, when did you decide this?" Mandy "Just over the weekend, I am so happy." Danny "Why did you get something else too? Only kidding Tim ha, ha, ha." Jeff "Congratulations both, I hope you are both happy, well done." Tim "Yes thanks Jeff and I hear I am going to be calling Danny and WINNIE John and Yoko, is that true Dan?" Jeff said "Oh dear, the cat is out of the bag ha, ha, John and Yoko be buggered ha, ha, ha." Danny smirking said "Very good Tim, what makes you think I am with Yoko I mean Hong Kong fuey ha, I am solo mate I am just teaching her English." Tim said smiling "Yeah, of course you are and we all believe that don't we? Right." Danny looking worried as if Winnie hears this it will infuriate her and it will be over between them. Danny insists "I am on my own, honest now, ask her if you dare." Jeff butts in "Are you telling us you are not giving her one? Yeah." Danny didn't know what to do so he said "Ok so as long as she is a woman from birth that's ok then, so." Mandy laughs and says "John and Yoko indeed, there's a thing to call them and if he is going out with Winnie what's it to do with anyone else, she is a beautiful woman, I wish them good luck they make a fine pair." Jeff "I agree Mandy the lucky git, she deserves a real man like me, I wouldn't settle for second best." Danny "You, I don't think so and I know you have had a go at getting her in your bed but she has got taste, so give it a rest you don't stand a chance matey." Tim "Yes Jeff I thought you were after Geraldine mate?" Jeff "I hope I have not knackered that up as I had 17 missed calls last night as she wanted my body and I hope I have not messed that up." Danny says "Well I am going home for a Chinese lads and ladies see you all tomorrow." Danny left and Jeff said to Tim "I like Chinese too you know and I feel like one now too, he won't be much good after what he drank last night, I know, sorry, I am just jealous time for a pint." Tim "I heard he has another girl back and forth to his room, Lidia I think." Jeff "Yes that's another beauty and he helps her with her English 3 or 4 times a week, she is a Spanish girl from Peru, cor, I would." Mandy said "Well he is only teaching her English or is there more to it?" Tim "I expect he is giving her one too." Jeff chirps up "no I can definitely say it is a Matter of good friends, she is a Catholic and she will not put up with any nonsense and Danny treats her like is daughters, he really helps her and she is picking it up with Danny, she is really good at her English now fair do's to him." Tim "That surprises me with Danny mind." Jeff "Yes I have heard him teaching WINNIE and he knows what he is talking about and he only teaches them English so as he can stop speaking to them ha, ha, ha." Tim laughs and Mandy said "You are looking a little better now Jeff, you looked like death warmed up earlier, you have a bit of colour to you now." Jeff says in reply "I am surprised I am still here and I vow I will slow down from now on and avoid that bloody Welshman a little more."

CHAPTER 11
TRAINS AND PAINS.

It was a few months later in late summer when things had sorted themselves out and Danny was by now getting used to getting around and using his cane and Danny and Jeff were closer than ever. Jeff was still swooning with all the women he could and Niel was enjoying his lessons in braile but was still losing his temper with computers, although he loved the classes with Geraldine and was spending more time drinking with the lads. Tim and Mandy were very much in love and spent more time with each other, the summer was terrific and everyone seemed happy. Danny was still teaching Lidia and Winnie English in his spare time and all were enjoying the help that is until jealousy set in from Winnie, this happened one evening when WINNIE came into the lounge only to find Danny helping Lidia with some homework.

Danny said to Lidia "Lidia if you slowed down a little you would not make so many mistakes, for instance in the book it says Paddington saw Mr. brown from the top of the bus, not too fast and it makes sense so slow down, you don't read English the same way as you speak Spanish, as you Spanish speakers speak very fast so slow down and it also makes enjoyable reading." Lidia "I see, ok, I shall go slow now, I am however having fun made of me at college." Danny looking concerned "Why is that?" "Because the other students say that this Paddington bear book is for 8 year old little people, is that right?" "Well yes it is but it is the best way to learn English as it does not have words that are very long and so you will understand it easier and then you can read more harder books sooner than them, so don't listen to them, Lidia I know what is best, has your tutor said anything to you about it?" Lidia "What is this person? a what you say, tutor?" "The person in your class the teacher who is in charge." "Oh yes, I see he has never said nothing so it is ok then?" "Yes it is ok and you are getting better all the time, you are very good now, you will be a teacher before long." Next thing in walks Winnie and tuts as she realises Danny was helping Lidia. Lidia says "Hello Winnie how are you." Winnie snaps "I am fine, why are you here?" Lidia says "Danny is so kind to help with my work." Winnie "Stupid velshman, he is always helping girls, he is a dirty old man and you should stay away from him." Danny looking nasty said to Winnie "Excuse me, I want you to say sorry to me for that remark and don't be so horrible to my visitor, she is a friend to me." Winnie said "She must find someone else to help her and you should stay away from her." Lidia looking shocked said "Winnie why say these things? I am a friend of Danny's he helps me that's all." Danny sensing Lidia was a little upset said to Winnie "I don't like what you have said to me and Lidia and if you are not going to apology's I shall not help you anymore sorry." Winnie in a temper said "I don't want to speak to her she is a pig and I am not happy with you Danny, I think you should not bring her here again, so go away." Winnie storms out of the room and Danny and Lidia sat there stunned. Danny speaking with calm voice said "Lidia I am so sorry, she is a very jealous person but she has never done that before, well I lie I went to town with her once and she tried to stop me talking to a barmaid as she claimed me as hers and in China the relationship between a woman and man stops a man talking to other women. So I say sorry for her." "I am sorry for that Danny, I did not know she was your as they say girlfriend." "Oh no, you are wrong, she was for a short time so she thinks, but we are not together but she thinks we are and I keep telling her but she won't listen to me and she thinks you and I are having sex and she won't listen, sorry." "I must make her listen to me then and I will tell her what is true, I am sorry if I have made life worse for you." Danny with concerned look says "No Lidia she is the one that is wrong not you and don't worry about me, she is wrong and that is it." Lidia puts her books in her bag and said "She is not a very nice person then, so I will tell her not to speak like this again, I am not afraid of her and she must stop being nasty. So Danny don't worry she is wrong not us, I will see you at lunch tomorrow." She gives Danny a kiss on the cheek and left. Danny was sitting down looking disgusted.

Later in walks Jeff and Carol and they were cuddling and laughing together and they both sat down on the settee and were all over each other. Jeff said to Danny "Ok matey? I just seen Lidia leaving and she was talking to herself as if someone had upset her, you I suppose ay?" Danny said "No not me, Hong Kong fuey, she came in here and was not happy that I was helping Lidia and she insulted her and me, I was furious, I could have killed her." Carol said "Yes she is mad about you, she told Zarrine off last week because she was talking to you, she is getting a bit much, she wants your body all for herself ha, ha, ha." Danny "Well she has had that now, I wouldn't touch her with Jeff's ha, ha, I am happy on my own. Women are too much trouble and that's a fact, as the saying goes, when you meet them you could eat them and when you have married them you wish you bloody had." Jeff laughs and Carol sniggled and said "Daniel that's not very nice." Jeff "But true though." Carol slaps him and puts her legs over Jeff's and snuggles up to him.

Next in walks Rhoda "Danny what have you done to Winnie? She is raving in her room, she is calling you everything in their ha, ha, ha." Danny smiling "She came in and I was helping Lidia wither homework and Winnie went mad and said some nasty things to me and Lidia and I put her right so she can go to hell now." Rhoda said "Yes she upset Zarrine yesterday morning because she helped you." Danny "What do you mean ?" Rhoda "Well Zarrine was talking to you over breakfast and made you tea and was asking you about anything you need help with and then after you had gone Winnie snapped at her and said "Why do you not leave Danny alone and mind your own business and stay away from Danny please and Zarrine replied, don't you talk to me like that Winnie, I do the same for everyone and what is it to do with you anyway? Winnie said something to her that sounded very nasty and then stormed off to her room, she is getting a bit neurotic and will be stalking you next so be careful." Danny looking shocked said "Looks like I had better put some distance between us, she is getting paranoid now and we are not together but she will not except it, I tell her we are not boyfriend and girlfriend and she thinks I am kidding." Jeff "Oh dear, no more Chinese from now on." Carol looking shocked said "So that is what it was, I thought he was actually having a Chinese meal every night, but he was having her, the Chinese girl ha, ha, ha, uncle Jeffrey why didn't you explain? Ha, ha, ha." Jeff laughing said "I couldn't tell you could I that dodgy Welshman would have sat on me or something, but serves his right now he has a real problem with her as she will never let him go ha, ha, ha." Danny said "Don't say that mate, I will tell her straight she will listen before I finish, this is stupid I am having a can, anyone else?" Jeff "Oh yes please, I will get some out of my room later." Rhoda said "I hope she settles down before I go to bed, she makes quite a noise in her room when she is in a temper." Danny "She will settle down now I expect, well I wonder where Niel is I haven't seen him for a day or two now." Jeff said "He is down Wales he had an appointment in the hospital in Bridgend, he will be back tomorrow. Oh Carol watch where you are putting your feet I may need that sometime you know and I have only got one." Carol "Oh sorry Uncle Jeffrey, my feet are cold, let me put them under your arm so as to keep them warm." Jeff "Carol, you are getting me excited now, stop it or I will have to sort you out in my room." Rhoda said smiling "Hey you two take it easy you will be ripping your clothes off next in here." Jeff said "Not a bad idea Rhoda, what do you think Carol?" She replies teasing him "Mmmmmm, mmm." Carol and Jeff go into a huddle and forget Danny and Rhoda are there. Danny said to Rhoda "Aw their off, just ignore them I do, he is stupid and will never learn." Rhoda "I can see that, I should get a bucket of cold water just in case." Next in walks Adrian Carol's boyfriend and caught them canoodling and Immediately got annoyed with Jeff and said to them "Ah, everything allright then?" Carol didn't move neither did Jeff and Danny said "Allright Adi, I am nothing to do with this and don't want anything to do with it it's none of my business so I am staying out of it." Next thing Jeff and Carol parted as Carol could sense Adrian was upset and Jeff moved over to the other end of the settee and Adrian said sarcastically "Oh don't worry about me Jeff, you just carry on with my girl mate." Jeff being cocky said "Yeah ok, we have always been like this long before you appeared on the scene ,it's harmless enough, so don't get your knickers in a twist ,we will always be close and no one will get between us, so let's leave it at that." Adrian said in a huff feeling a little uncomfortable "So if it was your girlfriend and I was doing that you would sit back and say nothing would you?" Jeff "I wouldn't care I am not a jealous person." Adrian "Of course not, I bet you would be up in arms, I heard what you were like when you thought Geraldine was trying to get off with a friend of yours, you were writhing with jealousy, don't deny it ." Jeff snapped "I don't think so mate, ha, ha." Jeff's laughing made Adrian nasty and Danny said "I think Adrian is right and Jeff I have warned you if this happened I would not get involved so you are on your own mate, because I would not like it done to me and neither would you." Carol said "Oh god, be good boys this is ridiculous." Adrian said "Yes you are loving this, 2 men having a disagreement about you ay and if I was going to do what I wanted I would smack you in the gob Jeff." Jeff got up and went into the kitchen for a fag and Adrian followed him and they were arguing and next thing you could hear them Jeff said "Oh get over it Adi I am just good friends and there is nothing you can do about it matey" Adrian in a temper said "What if I kick your teeth down your throat then? What are you going to do about it mate?" Jeff still smoking said "Listen mate I have 4 big brothers and if you lay one finger on me I guarantee they will be up in a Iffy and they will sort you out." Adrian "Ha, ha, ha, is that the best you can do then as I am afraid if they are anything like you I am a winner, whimp." Next thing Carol got up and took away the doorstop and shut the door so as Danny and Rhoda could not hear them and she said "There we are then boys you fight it out ha, ha." She sat by Rhoda and Rhoda said to her "Aren't you afraid they will fight Carol? And Adrian will kill Jeff he is twice the size of Jeff." Carol "Oh good for them, let them sort it out" Danny snapped "My god you are loving this aren't you? 2 men fighting over you, you know you have dumped Jeff in it as you were all over him and leading him on as you do all the time, why don't you leave him alone and he can get on with getting a girl for himself? You really are self-centred." Carol said "It's them, not me." Danny "Yes but you are encouraging it and don't say otherwise." Rhoda said "He is right Carol Jeff is a lovely guy and you do take advantage of the fact he is infatuated by you, so don't deny it." Carol "There we are then." Danny got up and opened the door and put the doorstop back and said to the boys "Right that is enough then, I am not interfering, but it's obvious that Carol is causing all this and I am not going to let you 2 beat the shit out of each other because of her. She is not worth it." Carol said out loud "I heard that." Jeff said "I am not afraid of him." Adrian said "I would snap you like a match mate" Danny said "Ok that's enough Jeff you are wrong messing with Carol get your own girl and Adrian it's Carol you needed to sort out not so much Jeff but I agree if it continues he deserves a clip or 2 and I am not going to interfere so let it go for now." Danny left the kitchen and Carol got up and stormed off to her room and Adrian went after her, it all

235

settled down and Jeff sat on the settee and said "He was lucky matey, he was." Danny sniggering said "Yes I could see he was in trouble mate." Rhoda giggling said "Ha, ha, I was worried about you Jeff, he only had to sit on you and I heard you say to him, I have 5 big brothers and they will sort you out ha, ha, it was like being in school in the infants the way you said it." They all chuckle and Jeff "Well he is stupid ha, ha, ha." Danny "You are the stupid one Jeff, I told you what would happen many a time didn't I? It's you are the one to blame not Adrian and Carol loved every minute of it." Rhoda said "He is right Jeff, Carol loved every minute of it, she didn't give a shit if he beat you up, sorry but it is true." Jeff looking sad said "Yes I realised that tonight, I am going for a couple of pints over the bar, coming Dodgy?" Danny "It's a bit late to go over there isn't it Jeff?" Jeff snapped "Are you coming, yes or no? That's all I am asking." Danny "Ok don't get your knickers in a twist, Rhoda are you coming?" Rhoda replies "No I am off to bed if Winnie has shut up, see you lads tomorrow."

The lads went up the bar and in there was just a few people and they got some pints and sat down by Kezz, in a dark corner in the bar as there was a disco there.

Kezz said "Eek, eek, who is that sitting down? Is that Danny and Barbara? Ha,ha." Jeff had a wry smile and said "Eek, Kezz yes it's Danny and Barbara if you like, I can't be bothered to argue, ha, ha." Danny said "Eek, hello little Kezz you sound a little drunk." Kezz replies "Eek, I am happy as I have been watching my programme on TV with Miesha Paris, she is banging isn't she? and I am going home and listening to a new music programme later to see what it is like ha, ha." A voice next to Kezz said in a very posh English voice "Kezz is always talking about music aren't you? I like it mind but not as much as Kezz." Jeff's eyes lit up and he said "Hello, who is that beautiful voice I can hear? And where have you been all my life?" Danny rolls his eyes and said "Here we go again." Jeff said "Aw shut up, I am not talking to you, sorry for my idiot of a friend, so what is your name then?" She replied "My name is Jo Lloyd, I am from Oxford and a last year student here, I have heard you talking to Geraldine before you are Jeff, aren't you?" Jeff smiling from ear to ear said "Yes that's right I have never seen you before have I, because I would have remembered it for definite." Jo said "I have been here for 3 years now and I am leaving next xmas, but I don't come up here very often only when there is nothing on the television and this is my dog she is sleeping under the table so don't disturb her, so what are you doing here? I am doing customer service." Jeff "I am doing mainly advice and guidance, it's lovely to meet you, you are lovely I think, god is missing an angel and I have found you for him, or maybe me." Danny interrupted and said "Jeff it's nearly ten o'clock no time for your stupid chat up lines, so Jo Lloyd that is a Welsh name isn't it?" She said "Yes my grandfather was Welsh so that makes me half Welsh." Danny said "Jeff don't like anyone with any Welsh in them so your safe ha, ha, ha." Jeff said quickly "Don't listen to him he is Welsh and I drink with him every night of the week and he loves my chat up lines really." Kezz said "Eek, eek, they are so funny he really makes us laugh when he tells them to the women here, he even said them to mad max once ha, ha." Jeff said "Don't listen to these, they talk a load of crap sometimes, so what hall are you in then? I am in Dowdell." Jo said "I am in Gardener top floor as they didn't have to do anything up there so I stayed." Jeff "I was there and they moved me from there to Dowdell, shit just my luck, do you have a boyfriend Jo?." Jo "No I am single and still happy, what about you Jeff? I bet you are married ay and trying to chat up a bit on the side." Jeff snapped quickly "Oh no, no, no, I am single no ties at all, I am waiting for the right one." Danny laughed and Jeff kicked him on the ankle, Danny let out a loud cry "Argh, argh, Jeff that bloody hurt you know." Jeff said "Oh sorry mate, ha, ha, I didn't mean it, do you want a drink Jo and Kezz? What do you think?" They both said yes and Danny looking concerned said "What about me then?" Jeff said "There is no need to ask you, you never say no." Danny said as he was leaving for the bar "Cheeky git, so Jo he is taken with you, his eyes lit up when he seen you, I think you may have the starts of a boyfriend." Kezz said "He is lovely is Jeff, I like him as a friend, I mean." Danny said "And what about me then Kezz?" Kezz said "And you eek, you are my favourite man here as you look after me when I get trouble don't you? Did you get the money back off Chris after eek?" Danny replied "Yes he was looking for me by the Thursday and I had it all back every penny." Kezz laughed out loud and everyone turned to see what is happening and Danny continued "So Jo Jeff is a lovely fella and I think he is going to ask you if he can walk you back to gardener and I am just going to say he is a nice bloke and he will protect you above himself, he is not a run of the mill man he is gentle and a good laugh and." Next thing Kezz butted in and said "Danny stop telling her a load of crap, ha, ha, ha." Danny laughed and said "Sorry Jo I like Jeff and he is a nice guy but I am going to shut up now he is coming back." Jeff returns and sit's by Jo and hands out the pints and said "There we are then Jo your coke, I bet you don't drink at all." Jo "Oh, yes I sometimes do but you will never see me drunk, I don't like getting drunk at all, I know you and Danny do very regular and Kezz." Kezz "Yes I bloody do eek, eek, I get pissed when I can afford it especially in karaoke it's banging eek and Danny and Jeff ha, ha, ha." Jeff tries to protect his honour and says with lying eyes "Oh, I only get drunk because I am bored and that dodgy Welshman gets me drunk every night, otherwise I don't bother." Danny coughed and said "Yeah, yeah, I have got his arm behind his back ha, ha." Jeff continues "Have you got a map Jo?" Jo answered "No why?" Jeff "Because I have got lost in your eyes, if a thousand poet's wrote a thousand poems they would still not describe your beauty, I've lost that loving feeling, please help me find it." Jo with soppy eyes said "Awe, that's lovely Jeff how nice." Jeff continues "Roses are red violets are blue, if I had a wish I would wish for you ." Danny said "Look out here comes the dirty ones Kezz." Kezz laughs out loud again and everyone turns to see and Jeff said "Ha, ha, no I am not , I don't care if I go to hell now because I have just saw heaven. Have you got a boyfriend? It's about time you got an upgrade." Danny said after Jo stopped laughing "Well Kezz I think he is in love again and eek, eek, she is loving his Jokes so they are well suited." Kezz and Jo laughs and Jeff continues "So Jo did you say you are leaving at Xmas?" Jo replied "Yes I am afraid so, I have enjoyed it here mind." Jeff "So there is no time to waste then, can I walk you home later and make sure you get home ok?" Jo "Oh that's lovely Jeff, thank you that is very nice of you, I except." Kezz "So it's now Jo and Barbara not Danny and Barbara, Danny you can walk me home if you like so you don't feel left out eek, eek, ha, ha, ha." Danny "Well eek, eek, thank you Kezz I except ha, ha, ha." Jo said "Am I missing anything?" Jeff "Oh don't listen to them they are always taking the Mick out of me." Jo says sympathetically "Aw, poor Jeff, stop it you 2 ha, ha, ha." Jeff "Yes you 2 leave me alone ha, ha, I am not going to have another one dodgy but I will get you one and what about you girls." They both said no and Jeff got Danny one in and grabbed Jo when he got back and they went off and so did Kezz and Danny.

Back in the lounge in Dowdell and in walks Danny to find Winnie sitting there waiting for him and he ignored her and made himself a cup of coffee and sat down and she said to him "I see, all by yourself now then hey? Your girlfriend gone home then." Danny ignored her and she continued getting nastier and nastier "And Jeff is not speaking to you neither, I don't like silly velshman like you." Danny said "Good, so you don't have to talk to me now then." "So he speaks now, why do you chase other women then?" "I can do what I like I am not married to you and never will be, so give it a rest ok?" "Don't be silly, you don't mean this." "Oh yes I bloody do, I am not your boyfriend and you are not my girlfriend, so get that into your head I am a free person and will do what I like, got it?" "But we are together most of the time and we are good too." "After tonight we are not doing anything together like English anymore, so forget it, no more, understand this because I mean it." She smiles to herself and says "You are being silly now." Next in walks Jeff and says Immediately "Time for a ciggy." Danny snaps "No Jeff you stay here and tell me about your date as I have nothing to say to her now or tomorrow." Jeff stood his ground and Winnie looking serious said "Silly velshman." Then she storms out. Jeff sat down and said "Sorry mate, I came in at the wrong time." Danny replied "There is nothing to apology's for, so how did it go?" Jeff beaming said "I don't believe it matey, she is gorgeous matey and I think she likes me too, she was getting up early this morning so I didn't push my luck so that's why I am back so soon but she is lovely isn't she?" "Too right mate, she is a cracker but she is only about 23 , very young don't you think? And a very posh voice ay." "I don't care how old she is it makes no difference to me, I am in love matey, I think this is it. I am meeting her for lunch tomorrow and who knows ay?" "Well done mate I hope it works out for you, it's about time you had a bit of luck." "Yes and we can make a foursome, me Jo you and Winnie after you have made up." Danny looks at Jeff seriously and says "No chance of that mate, it's not going to happen, she is not my type of girl, so it's just you and Jo, unless you get together with Carol and Adrian." "No chance mate, absolutely no chance ever, fancy a can mate?" "No thanks mate I am going to bed and I suggest you do the same, get up fresh for her and things will go off swell ok?" "You might be right, see you in the morning."

It was first thing the next morning about 7 am. And Zarrine walks into the lounge and was shocked to see Jeff sitting in the lounge watching TV with some toast and tea. This has never been seen before as Jeff is normally in bed with a hangover. Zarrine with shocked look said to him "Jeffrey, what is wrong? Are you ill? Has something happened at home? Have you been expelled? What's the Matter? I am worried now." Jeff laughing said "Ha, ha, ha, calm down Zarrine there is nothing wrong at all, why do you think something is wrong?" "I don't know, I have never seen you in here before anyone else before and you have had a shower and you are neat and tidy for a change and you are eating and you have not got a hangover, have you found god Jeff?" Jeff smiling replies "You cheeky git Zarrine, and no I have not found god it's much better than that." "You have got a Job in a brewery?" No, no, no, listen to me for a minute will you , I am in love at last." Zarrine looks at Jeff as if to say yes I have heard this before and says "Oh, right, nothing new then you are in love with half the college girls here, so what is new? But the new one has insomnia ay?" "Very good Zarrine you have been helping that dodgy Welshman for too long, you are almost funny, no I have found someone that feels the same as me. She really likes me to, do you know Jo from Gardner top floor? She has a dog named ah, ah, I forgot now she is a blonde very fit looking woman." Zarrine thinks for a minute and says "I can't think who you are on about Jeff but probably I know her, you must bring her in here one day so as I can meet her, but that's nice for you Jeff, I am so pleased, does Danny know? I think you should keep her from him until you are settled down together. Because you know what Danny is like and don't drink so much from now on, I like you like this." "I am not going to drink so much from now on and Danny already has met her he was with me over the student bar when I met her and he has enough trouble with Winnie at the moment so he is ok." Zarrine continues "Don't talk to me about that girl she is getting on my nerves also, she keeps snapping at me and telling me

238

not to talk to Danny and not to make his tea for him, it's none of her business and she is getting me down, she really is." Jeff looking around seen Danny come in and Danny said hearing Zarrine's conversation said "Zarrine tell me about it, she is a pain in the ass she really is. She thinks she is my girlfriend and she is not but she won't listen to me and I heard she is giving you trouble, I am sorry about that." Zarrine says "You don't have to be sorry, she is the trouble and I will make my boys tea and toast if I want to and she can go to hell first." Danny "Well said Zarrine, 2 pieces of toast and a mug of tea please, you really are wonderful." Zarrine giggles and slaps Danny and says "I knew you were going to say this you cheeky dodgy man you and did you hear about Winnie yesterday she had a lesson in the supermarket and bought a bag load of frozen food with sue just to learn how to do it and when she got back she emptied the bag of frozen food into the bin in the kitchen without even opening them." Danny said "Your Joking did she? What a stupid girl, she has no respect for anyone, so what happened to the food then?" Zarrine says "Well Carol and Lola seen her do this and they got it back out and split it between themselves, but what an attitude for Winnie to have, as if she is above anyone, it really annoyed me." Jeff said "Never, that's disgusting and I would have known that Carol was there to take advantage as she is so tight she really is, but Winnie is so stupid to herself, I told Danny she Is a trainee stalker, because that's what she is acting like, you know she has attacked Zarrine and Lidia, Danny next." Danny laughs and said "I am not putting up with her nonsense anymore, so don't worry about me mate you have your hands full now, did you hear about his new woman Zarrine?" "Yes I have but I don't know her but I am so happy for Jeff especially now he has stopped drinking ha, ha, ha." Danny "So you don't believe him neither then?" Jeff smiles and says "Ha, ha, I never said I was giving it up, I just said I was cutting it down that's all so get off my back." Danny "She is lovely Zarrine, a little young for Jeff but we will see, she has no eyesight mind so he stands a chance ay, she is only about 23 but a cracking body and very nice with it." Zarrine "Well Jeffrey you must look after her and keep her from Danny or she will be an alcoholic in a week ha, ha, ha." Jeff "Yes you have a point, I will do that." Danny "God Jeff, what are you wearing? You smell like a spare poof in a Bangkok brothel, phew she will be knocked out with that smell, it's your bone after shave isn't it? It attracts all the old dogs ha, ha, ha." Zarrine says "Danny, leave him alone he smells nice for a change." Jeff with eyes wide open says "What do you mean for a change Zarrine? Ha, ha, you are getting too cheeky now." Zarrine smiling "Ha, ha, I am only Joking Jeff ha, ha, but it's nice to see you so wide awake and this room smells good today with you boys sober." Danny looking puzzled "And what do you mean by that remark?" She replies "It usually smells of bad air and I have to open the windows because it makes me feel sick, but not today." Danny mumbles "Bad air, what is she on about?" Jeff burst out laughing and says "She means the smell of farts ha, ha, ha, ha." Danny smiling "Oh right, ha, ha, ha, ha." JEFF "That is Winnie and Carol not us, I went to his bedroom once and I was nearly sick I feel sorry for you Zarrine doing his room out." Zarrine says "Jeffrey your bedroom is just as bad, I go to all your rooms first and open all the windows to let the smell out, then have a cup of coffee before I start to allow the rooms to freshen up."

It was later at lunch time and Jeff and Jo was in the queue for lunch and Danny came up behind them along with Niel and said "Hello guys, fancy meeting you here." Jeff and Jo were kissing and canoodling and stopped for a second to answer, Jo said "Oh hello Danny, I am taking Jeff for some food, he looks as if he needs feeding up." Danny said with a chuckle "Funny you should say that he nearly had a feed last night, but his 4 brothers got him out of it didn't they Jeff?" Niel said smiling "Yes Jeff, Danny told me about that, very good, I laughed ha, ha, ha." Jo said to Jeff "What are they on about Jeff?" Jeff looking sheepish said "Oh I had trouble with that Adrian from the gym but I sorted him out no problem." Jo said "Adrian he is a really nice fella, he always talks to me, I am surprised, so what happened?" Jeff "Oh a silly mistake and a misunderstanding but no problem like I said it's sorted now, so Niel how did your hospital appointment go then matey?" Niel "Well the doctor said I am going to live but he wouldn't recommend it ha, ha, no, I am in tip top condition and if I don't drink with you 2 I will be ok ha, ha and how are you with this beautiful girl Jeff? She can't be all that fussy then." Danny laughs and Jeff said "I am infatuated with her and her with me and I can't wait to get away from you 2, you are making me nervous so shut up and give me a bit of peace and quiet, thanks." Jo said "Niel don't be a bully, Jeff is lovely and I am surprised at you, you are normally so nice Niel, stop it." Niel said "Sorry Jo I could not resist it, we are always like this, no offence intended girl, sorry." Danny said with a smirk "Yes Niel, you leave them alone you never see me make aspersions at Jeff and definitely not at Jo." Jeff butts in "You, you are the worst one matey." Danny defending himself said "Hey, hey, Jo did you hear that? Have I said anything about you 2 since I got here? I think I am being intimidated by Jeff this time." Jo speaks in Danny's defence and says "Jeff, that's true he has not said anything, so leave Danny alone please." Jeff stammered and said "But, but, but, it is usually him so don't be taken in by him." They get their food and Jeff rushes Jo off to a table on their own and Lidia guides Danny and Niel to another table and says to Danny "Hi Danny, I have had Winnie on to me today again, you will have to ask her to stay away from me, sorry." Danny "Good Lidia, I agree, I have told her not to bother with me and you do the same, she deserves not to be bothered with, I will speak to her again so don't get upset about this and if it continues I will speak to Anthea, so don't worry." Lidia "Ok Danny, I will see you later for my lesson ok? Bye." Danny says bye to her and says to Niel "Winnie is pissing me off now, she is giving Lidia trouble for talking to me and she has had a go at Zarrine twice now, I must sort this out." Niel said "She is becoming a nuisance, she keeps asking me where you are, I am going to fall out with her if this carries on, what is the Matter with the girl? Are you that good in bed?" "No Niel it's something to do with her culture, I have never seen a woman like her she insists I am her boyfriend and I am not and the more I tell her the more I tell her the more she disbelieves me. What else can I do?" "Well Dan, you will have to be more firm with her, I can see her giving you a lot of trouble soon mate." "Oh not you to, Jeff reckons she is stalking me, that makes me nervous, I have had that happen to me before so I must sort it out quickly. Tell me what do you think I should do?" "Me, well I think you should give her a wide birth and go and explain the problem to Anthea, that's what she is there for and maybe she will move WINNIE to another hall." "Do you think so?" "Well you got nothing to lose have you? And if Lidia is having the same trouble she should go and see her as well." "Yes you may be right, I think I will go and see her later, anyway hows that gorgeous wife of yours? Is she still asking about me all the time?" "Huh, Ceri sends her love again and she is still lovely as you can Imagine, it was nice to see her for a day but she is now picking me up at Bridgend station from now on as the Maesteg train has changed the time table and I would have to hang around in Bridgend for forty five minutes, but she won't mind, she is as good as gold Dan." "Yes you have a good one there and she is always happy isn't she? Well, she was in bed the other morning anyway, ha, ha, ha." Niel smiled and said "You keep on dreaming Dan, the boys were glad to see me too and they are doing allright for a change, no trouble from them for a real change. I am shocked." "Niel, you don't mean that, they are lads and you were worse than that when you were younger, I know I was, but they never have the police around do they.?" "No, your right, just little devils but I suppose I was just as bad and look how I turned out." Danny laughing said "Ha, ha, yes, look how you turned out, yeah." "What do you mean by that? Ha, ha, ha." "Nothing Niel I am only kidding, so are you going home on Friday?" "Yes I am leaving earlier from now on, I have changed my last lecture to the day before from now on." "So you can catch the same train as me then?" "I don't know what train are you catching? " "The 12 . 15 as usual." "Yes that's the same as me, we can share a taxi, we can meet outside the main entrance it will be nice to travel down at the same time, nice to have some company and I tell you what, I will tell Ceri to give you a lift up to Bettws as it is on the way home." "Awe, you don't have to do that mate, the taxi is paid for by the college" "Don't be silly Dan, she won't mind and maybe you can make a bit of money on the side ay." "Well if you are sure she won't mind I will except thank you." "No problem mate, I am happy to have some company for a change and I will feel safer with 2 of us travelling together." "So we are sorted then?" "And besides I can come in and see that beautiful wife of yours over a cup of tea, I bet she will be excited." "Yeh, ecstatic but not seeing me, you will get more out of her in that time than I will get all weekend huh." "Oh come on Dan it can't be that bad surely." "Oh yes it is and stop calling me Shirley ha, ha and I think that Jeff is coming on the train with us as far as Newport." "I wouldn't bet on that, I think he will be staying with Jo now, unless she is going home this weekend as well." " yes, I think she is the way Jeff was talking and perhaps she will take him home to meet her mum and dad, but there the shock for her parents would be too much for them ha, ha, I will ask him later if he comes out of that trance, I think we have lost him to love mate." "Do you think so? He won't give up his pint or two for a woman will he?" "I think maybe for a while until the novelty wears off and besides she will be leaving at xmas, we will just have to except Jeff is the type that will be by her side day and night and that will cut the relationship down to a few months as Jeff is like a kitten as far as a woman is concerned." Niel replied "Dan don't be awful we are as bad." "Speak for yourself Niel I did when Angie and me first met but it soon wore off and she spends most of her time in her sisters or her fathers and when her mother was alive all the time in her house, never at home ever." "Well that's not her mother's fault is it? She was ill." "Oh no, I loved her mother and father to bit's and done a lot of work on their house and I was one of the luckiest men on earth as they were the best and her granny Mrs James was a very lovely lady and I would get away with murder with her and she was in her eighties and a very good looking woman for her age, she was a little bit special, she really was, she used to think I was as she said a loveable rogue and we often laughed together. No I am not blaming her family for the reason she is, maybe I am boring ha, ha, ha." "Maybe your right, can I ask you a personel question Dan?" Danny's face turned serious and says "Oh dear, I don't like the sound of this... ok go ahead and I will decide if I want to answer it, fair enough?" "Ok, can I ask you what happened to your first son Nathan? I know he died and I am just curious why he did, I have never been told the truth and I hope I am not talking out of turn and if I am forget it and I will understand mate." Danny went silent for a minute or two and coughed and said "No that's ok Niel, it still hurts a hell of a lot but now I can talk about it. Well he was almost 7 months old when he died with no reason at all. We woke up normally one morning and I had slept late for work, I rushed down stairs to make a phone call to work to tell them I was on my way in and as I put the phone down I heard an incredible scream from upstairs the sent a shiver down my spine and a lot of commotion from my ex-wife and I rushed upstairs and she was screaming, he is not breathing, he is blue , do something, I picked Nathan out of his cot and I could feel he was stiff and cold, I started to panic badly and she went to phone an ambulance as I tried to

241

give him the kiss of life and anything I could but it was too late he was dead. I kept on trying for it seemed hours but it was too late, they had to literally tear him out of my arms to get him off me, it was the worst day of my life, it really was, nothing else in the world made any difference to me after that day, nothing. it changed my life forever and if there was a time I wanted to take my life, that was the day and many times after, they say time is a healer but not for me, that day is scratched in my heart and mind with a screwdriver. I still think of Nathan John Duckfield every day of my life and do you know what, I can't sleep with a baby in the house to this very day. I lay there listening to them breathing, I have done so with all my children for the first eighteen months of their lives and I am not kidding I am afraid in case the same thing happens again. It destroyed my life and punched a lot of love I can't give out of my life, it's like I am afraid to love anyone or anything too much in case they are taken away from me in the same way and I get hurt like this easily. No one could understand the terror and hurt you suffer when you lose a baby child, nothing, absolutely nothing, it destroys a huge part of you, I am not joking, you will never enjoy life the same way ever again." Niel almost crying by now said in a very quiet voice "I am so sorry Dan, I can't begin to understand how you must feel, I think I would have topped myself, I am sorry." Danny wiping a little tear away said "I nearly did several times Niel, I had to go on Vallium tablet's to keep me from going insane and my poor wife then was just as devastated and never talks about it even now she puts it to the back of her mind because I think she would have gone mad, we had a lovely daughter as soon as we could named Sarah Louise and then ginger little Shane Lee. We thought this would help our marriage but it was no good, the hurt was too much for both of us and we ended up parting and statistics say almost all cot death parents end up separating. Something like 90% split because of cot death." Niel said sadly "I could really understand that, so what kept you going then?" "Well I had been a DJ for most of my life and got back on the road for one of the biggest discotheques in Britain, Sam's Wax and we became the best of friends and had some real good times together in the music business and we still do to this day, he stopped me from killing myself, he really did and is my best friend to this day, Phil has stuck by me through thick and thin, I think he was one of the people responsible for the poem getting published a real good friend." "And I suppose if you could turn the clock back and change anything it would be that." "Oh yes and much more like Mary Davies, my mum, my brother Dennis an ex-girlfriend Angie Davies and I suppose even my father, but I would want him to put his family first instead of religion and his so called brother and sisters and concentrate on his real brothers and sisters and his close family, because he made our lives a misery he was like a dictator but that's bye the bye now, change the subject as my life is not worth talking about, it is full of sorrow, but if Nathan had not have died in a cot death I would be a different man and we would not be having this conversation as I would not be here. God Niel we are the only ones left here I must get off to lectures, see you later mate." "Ok Dan, I hope you find happiness someday, you deserve it mate, see you later and we will have a pint if you like." "Yes, why not mate see you." Danny left and Niel sat there for a few minutes with head bowed and looking sad.

Danny was in Student services and was in with Anthea and she sat down and said to Danny with a huff "Right Danny so what is wrong now? What can I help you with?" Danny replied "You would think I am here every day, it's about the trouble I am having with Winnie, she is following me everywhere and is making my life a misery and Lidia's and Zarrine the carer, she is rude to us and is threatening to us all of the time, she thinks she is my girlfriend and she is not." Anthea interrupts him and says "Well I thought you and Winnie were together, it looks like it from where I am sitting, so what give her that idea then?" "Well we got a little close but it was because I was helping her with her English that's all." "Right, so what do you want me to do about it then?" "I don't know maybe move her to another dorm, or at least speak to her or something and give her a warning." "I see, so every time someone disagrees with you we have to move them, you do seem to have a problem with women don't you?" "No, not really, I just want a bit of consideration that's all and to stop her threatening anyone else because they have talked to me." "Well this college does not revolve around you, I am afraid I will have a word with her but I shall not be moving her out of that dorm and if It continues I will have another word with her that's all I can do and I will speak to Zarrine and Lidia first is that ok with you?" "Fine I am happy with that I just want a bit of peace that's all, thank you." Anthea looking fed up said "I hope it will be, as it seems to go on and on with you, so please try and get on with her for all our sakes." "Fair enough, I will but she does not make it easy at all and before you say anything I am not after Lidia I just help her with her English and also Hose too and I am not gay I am a lesbian like all men ha, ha, ha." "Oh don't joke about it please." "Sorry, I am just trying to make light of the situation and I think if you have a little word with her things will settle down and that will be the end of it." "I hope so, I will do it later this afternoon and you must try and keep the peace as well mind." "Fair enough I promise I will and thank you, see you."

Danny later in the lounge and in walks Jeff looking happy and singing "Well hello Dodgy, hows you then? I am off to see Jo and we are having a night in her room, so don't wait up for me darling ok." Danny smiling for Jeff says "Ok sweetie, I won't so you will not be up for a pint later then?" "Not if I play my cards right I won't, are you going up? silly question, sorry I asked, I hope I will not be back till the morning, right I am almost ready, oh look out the other dodgy Welshman is here, hello Niel come in, plenty of room, a full couch for you to put that big ass of yours on here mate ha, ha, ha." Niel says "You cheeky sod I have not got a big ass ha, ha, ha." Jeff quickly says "Well there is someone on your back then ha, ha, ha." Niel "I can stay at home and get abuse mate, I don't have to come here, what do you think Dan?" Danny chuckling says "Someone on your back, nice one Jeff, sorry Niel yes I have lots of grief at home myself, Niel you won't get much sense out of that cockney git he is in love and is spruced up like a poof, so don't waste your breath he is deafly in love aren't you matey?" Jeff prancing about "You 2 can't upset me tonight so give it up, me and my darling are having a night in front of the telly watching coronation street and then play your cards right and I hope to be playing my cards right hey, hey, so don't wait up for me then, bye." Jeff skipped out and the lads said goodnight to him. Niel said to Danny "How's it Dan, ok now? I hope I didn't upset you lunch time, I felt awful after and should have not said anything it's none of my business" Danny "Don't worry about it mate I am ok, I must say one thing mind I didn't say earlier about the police and what happened directly after Nathan's death, the police arrived and Immediately they all but accused us of his death, the way they spoke to us and the questions they asked us, they all pointed to my wife and I, it felt like we were the cause of Nathan's death and that was that and I felt the neighbours were wondering the same for a few days, we felt like we were being looked at as murderers and I even began to think it was my fault I really did and even after the post mortem I felt this it was bloody awful but the worst was to come at his funeral." "How do you mean Dan?" Danny eyes welling up says "Well Niel it really hit home when I seen that tiny little white coffin being carried in, in the arms of just one person, it really hit me and the wife, I could not control myself anymore I went to pieces and almost collapsed and at the grave I can remember it as if it was only yesterday that tiny little white coffin being carried to the grave side and lowered in that hole, I just wanted to die there and then and be buried with him to keep him company, it was heart destroying and will stay with me forever. He would be 29 now and do you know what, we buried him a day before my 20ᵗʰ birthday and now even my birthday is not Important to me, as I always think about that day every year and there is one more weird thing, where he is buried directly across the little road that runs through the cemetery is my ex-girlfriend I met as my first serious girlfriend, we met at 14 and was in love, Mary Davies grave and you could almost read the words on her grave stone, she was my girlfriend when I was younger and we were together for a long time before she was killed by a car, she was run down in an accident, isn't that odd" Niel looking very distraught said "Oh my god mate, it must have been hell for you I am so sorry matey, but I expect god has got him safe for you and he is waiting up there for you." Danny butts in "Niel sorry man I know you and I are mates but I don't need that crap, I don't believe in god or anything to do with religion as far as I am concerned there is no god but you believe what you want but it is a load of rubbish to me, I can't live in faith sorry, it's man made rubbish I will never see Nathan or Mary again, so don't go there and if there is a god he has a very weird sense of humour mate and it's about time he picked on someone else." ." "I understand mate I do and I think we should go and have a pint or two in their memory ay?" "Why not and we shall have one or 2 for your lovely mam and dad when we are at it ay?" Niel "Oh yes, we really are a pair ay?" Danny wipes a little tear away and says "Yes and all these bastards in the world get away with a perfect life it seems the loving people who go first and suffer the most, if I was a murderer or a child molester or a drug dealer nothing happens to them, why? why? We will never know the answer to that question, c'mon mate my round, let's cheer up ay, honestly there are much more people in this world worse off than us even after the horrible things I have had to endure, some little kids in the world die after just a few years." Niel "And if you keep on thinking about it, it will eventually drive you mad mate so let's smile and have a pint, let's go." Off the lads went to the bar laughing as they went.

In the bar and Danny and Niel were sitting by the lovely Kezz and she was pleased to see them and said "Eek, eek, eek, the lovely Welshmen are here, where's Abby Niel?" Niel "She is sleeping in my room or chewing her bone." Kezz "And where is Barbara Dan?" Danny smiling said "Kezz, it's funny how you ask about Abby and Jeff in the same breath, both dogs I suppose ay ha, ha, he is out with Jo." Kezz "Eek, eek, so they are an item now then? Well I never ha, ha, ha, ha." Niel "He sounds happy too, she is a lovely girl, it's a pity she is leaving at xmas, it's nice and quiet without him and no chat up lines to contend with ay?" Danny says "It's funny without him, I am going to miss him, my drinking butty, but as long as he is happy ay?" Kezz "He will not give up drinking, not Jeff, I bet he will be in tonight knowing Jo." Danny looking confused says "Why do you think that Kezz?" Kezz "Jo likes her bed, she goes to bed sometimes at 9 o'clock and is up at between 6-7 to walk her dog, it's like a regime you can set your clock by her. She is boring like that, I couldn't be asked me." Niel "Oh dear, that won't suit Jeff and his life style will it?" Danny "No it won't will it? I can see trouble in heaven already maybe but knowing Jeff he will soft soap her into doing it his way, time will tell look out here is the big Brumby out on his own, maybe more trouble in paradise. Hello Tim, where's Mandy then?" Tim "Hi guys and you Kezz, she is having an early night and I was in need of a pint or 2 so here I am, so where is Jeff?" Danny "He is with his new girl, do you know Jo Lloyd from Gardner? She is his new conquest." Tim "Never, she is too young for him and too prim and proper, no way pull the other one." Danny "Niel am I lying?" Niel says "Tim he is telling the truth mate." Kezz chirps up "Yes eek she is seeing Jeff now." Tim "Well I never, don't you think she is a little young for him? And she is a pretty girl." Niel "So what are you trying to say Tim? Jeff is ugly or what?" Tim "Ha, ha, no I didn't mean that, you know what I mean she is just not his type it's like Princess Di and Les Dawson going out together ha, ha, ha." They all burst out laughing and Kezz said "Ha, ha, yes it is but Les Dawson after a slimming war ha, ha, ha." Tim "It's not a normal couple if you know what I mean, but if their happy fine, who am I to interfere, you have just surprised me that's all, well I never. Anyway how is John and Yoko then? Ha, ha, ha." Kezz laughing says "Who the hell is John and Yoko then?" Tim "Danny and Winnie of course." Niel and Kezz burst out laughing and Kezz said "Eek, John and Yoko, that's funny what a thing to call them ha, ha, ha." Danny looking serious and Niel said in laughter "Well I have heard it all now ha, ha, John and Yoko be buggered ha, ha, ha." Danny cracked a smile and said "Sorry Tim, that is not funny anymore, that woman is making my life a misery, she is threatening everyone not to speak to me except males and I have had a guts full of her, so drop the subject it's a sore subject now, pick on Niel or someone else ha, ha, ha." Tim says in reply "Imagine that, sorry mate just a pun. So it's all over then?" Danny looking serious says "to bloody right, I have moved on, I would rather go out with Lola." Niel "Winnie is not that bad is she?" Danny says "Oh yes, I would rather go gay it's easier ha, ha, well maybe not I could not stand the pain." Kezz laughed out loud and Tim said "Well I am happy with my Mandy no problems on that front." Niel "Yes I can honestly say that I have never had any trouble with Ceri in that respect, she is a wonderful wife and I would not swap her for anyone." Danny said "Shame I would swap you for Winnie." Niel said with a huff "Absolutely no chance mate, you can keep her ha, ha, ha." Kezz said "Eek, I have a new boyfriend now he is older than me mind, his name is Geordie Jim he is in piano tuning." Danny "Oh, I know, he is a lot older than you Kezz, he is my age." Niel said "So what? Age does not Matter if you are in love." Kezz let out a loud laugh and said "I don't know if we are in love it's early to say eek, ha, ha." Danny said "I didn't mean that, I was just saying that's all." Tim said in Jims defence "Well he is a nice man, I like him." Danny "I agree he is a nice fella but you know what they are like here, like Carol and Lola they would have a field day if they knew." Niel "Yes they would, they make it their business to make him feel like a pervert, so keep it quiet Kezz." Kezz "Oh bugger them, I don't care about them he is nice and he does not ask to borrow money off me." Tim "I should think not." Next thing in comes Jeff and it's only 9.30 and says "Hi guys everything allright then?" Danny said "Jeff it's only 9.30, I thought you were giving Jo one, I mean keeping her company and your first date, so where is she then?" Jeff cough's and says "Oh she has got a headache and is up early so I said I will let her get some sleep and I would see her lunch time tomorrow." Niel said "Yeah, allright I believe you too, you would be like a dog on heat and would never offer to go home, more like cuddle her up and make sure she is allright ,you would never offer to leave. So what really happened then?" Jeff snaps "I am telling the truth she needed to get a good night's sleep as she has a headache ha, ha, I am not lying." Kezz coming back from the bar said "Hi Jeff, no Jo, I knew she would go to bed early, she always does I told you Danny didn't I? Eek, eek, give me an eek Jeff." Jeff snapped "No Kezz, I am not speaking to you, you have got a big gob ha, ha." Kezz said "Oops, oops, I have upset Jeff, sorry mate but I know she always goes to bed early, she is boring like that ha, ha, ha." Danny said "So she has a headache has she? Ha, ha, ha." Niel said "Well Jeff she can't be that Impressed by you if she would rather go to bed instead of seeing you ha, ha, ha." Jeff looking sheepish says "Oh, shut up you lot, I don't know how she could resist me, she is just like that and that means I can have a couple of pints also, I get the best of both worlds, but I really needed some sex, shit just my luck ha, ha, never mind it's early days yet ha, ha, ha." Danny "I can see who wears the trousers in your relationship…. Her." Jeff "Look mate I am the boss in my house, she said I could be, ha, ha, ha." Niel "Well how is it going with her anyway Jeff?" Jeff "Ok I suppose, she is a woman very focused on her studies so I should be proud of her." Danny "Yes she must be like a daughter to you mate, are you giving her pocket money yet?" Jeff and Niel laugh and Jeff said "I will have you know she is besotted with me and I with her and she is very mature for her age so give it a rest." Niel said "Has she asked you to go home with her and meet her parents yet?" Jeff in a serious mood replies "Oh no not yet, give her time we have only just met." Niel said "Ok perhaps she is worried you and her dad went to school together at the same school ha, ha, ha." They all laugh even Jeff, then Tim said "Perhaps you are older than her dad you never know and her mother might try and get off with you ay?" They all laughed and Jeff went up to the bar and Kezz said "Awe stop picking on Jeff, he is getting upset." Niel added "No he isn't he likes it Kezz, he takes it all with a pinch of salt and anyway we have better things to talk about so don't worry it's probably my turn to have the piss taken out of now." Danny "Yes your turn or mine or we can all pick on Kezz for a change." Kezz says "Ha, ha, you don't know anything about me, so eek." Danny teased her "Oh don't we? What about you in that bar on the last karaoke night then? Flashing your ass on stage then Kezz?" Kezz went quiet and mumbled "I didn't did i?" She always gets a little drunk in these karaoke's and never remembers much about them afterwards but Danny knew this and made it up but Kezz never knew this. Niel said Right, is that so Kezz?" Kezz looking puzzled said "Huh, I don't remember doing that." Danny said teasingly "Ah, see you can't remember that can you?, I think you should stop getting pissed at the karaoke Kezz or put larger knickers on." Kezz laughs and said "Ha, ha, eek, eek, did I really flash my ass? I don't do things like that, your joking Danny aren't you?" Danny "Yes I am Kezz, so don't panic ha, ha, ha." Kezz "You bugger, eek, eek, I knew you were you bugger I am going home now eek, eek, bye, bye." They all said goodnight to her.

It was the next day and sitting in the common room was Jeff, Danny, Carol and Zarrine and Jeff says "I am meeting Jo in a few minutes so Zarrine can you smell beer on me?" Zarrine replies "Just a little Jeff, so it did not last long you were up the bar with Danny last night then?" Carol butted in "I expect so Zarrine him and Jo will not last long, she is too snobby for him, wait and see." Jeff looking amazed she said that says "Don't be like that Carol, I am in love and besides you have the big head looking after you now so move on with your life, I have." Danny says "Yes he has done that with you, he has had the t shirt so move on, he is in love with a real woman now." Zarrine snaps at Danny "Danny, that's enough, Jeff and Carol can still be friends also." Carol "Yes Daniel, he has got a new girlfriend and I was not his girlfriend anyway, I just worry about my uncle Jeffrey and don't want him to make a fool of himself that's all." Jeff "Awe, thank you Carol." Danny "That's right he was never your boyfriend but he nearly had his head kicked in and that didn't bother you it made you excited that 2 men were fighting over you, so let him alone if he makes a mistake and it all falls to pieces then he will have made his own mistakes so we must butt out." Carol "Ok, ok, I am not going to say anything from now on but I still think she is too young for him." Zarrine said "Awe Jeffrey, it's your business and not anyone else's so let them sort out their lives, you concern yourself with yours and look after Jo and no one else." Jeff replied "Yes I agree Zarrine it's Jo who is the one that I will make a fuss of from now on and she is all woman, even if she is a little younger than me." Danny smiling says "A little younger, she will still be a youngster when she is picking up your old age pension, ha, ha, she could kill you in bed by the time your in your sixties, so I think If I was you I would get in the gym and keep fit and give up the fags mate, she at her age needs someone who can perform more than once a week and I have seen you fall asleep watching the London marathon on telly." Zarrine laughing said "He is right Jeffrey you are like a Mr Muscle on telly, you need some meat on you and don't she say anything about the fags on your breath? " Jeff looking concerned said "Does my breath smell of cigarettes then? I try not to smoke near her at all and I don't have to worry about my performance matey, what I lost in height I made up for in length if you know what I mean." Zarrine stamps her foot and looks at Jeff said "Uncle Jeffrey that's enough of that talk ha, ha, and buy some mints to suck to hide your faggy breath, here I have some strong mints in my bag for now." She hands Jeff the mints and he hurries off to meet Jo. Carol also goes off and there was just Danny and Zarrine left Danny says "Well Zarrine it must be love with Jeff and I don't think Carol likes it, he is not at her beg and call but I think Carol will try to spoil it for Jeff if she has a chance." Zarrine "No she won't do that to Jeffrey, she has got her boyfriend Adrian." "Well she was happy for Jeff and Adi to fight over her in the kitchen and she seems jealous of Jo for not having Jeff at her beg and call, I hope I am wrong he is so happy and what about you Zarrine how are things with you and your family?" "Oh, my son starts back in university this week and Peter my husband is busy as usual and we are all ok thank you and what about you how are things in Bridgend?" "Well my brother is getting worse with his drinking and I will be going over to speak to him this weekend and as regards my wife she I think is having trouble telling me she wants a divorce, so I will suggest it and see her reaction, otherwise things are fantastic ha, ha, ha." "Oh dear, I am so sorry, your brother is worrying indeed I hope you can stop him getting worse and get some help and if anyone can, you can, you are so strong with other people's problems and as regards your wife maybe she will come around and give your marriage another chance Danny." "No Zarrine, I can tell by her voice it is something she is having a hard time speaking to me about so if it carries on I will suggest it to let her off the hook and then if she agrees I will know for definite but It will hurt very much, we have been together for sixteen years and with all the worry about Lyndon I need closure on it all. I have at least got my children and you could not ask for nicer children and I hope my oldest daughter will come around and speak to me one day as we have not spoken for about 20 years now." "Why is this Danny? I think you have not been a good man it is your daughter you must speak to her soon, what happened?" "Well my ex-wife met another man and they are married now and she wanted me out of the way to make room for him many years ago and so we just never met up anymore because my exx-wife was afraid of me telling her new husband the truth about her as he thinks the sun shines out of her ass but I know the truth and he would see her for what she really is and one day I met her on the way home from school and stopped to talk to her and I gave her a few pounds and her mother came up to my house and gave it back and told me If I wanted to be a father part time it was not good enough and slapped the money in my hand, she didn't want me near them in case I knackered up my ex-wife's relationship, so we never seen each other for all those years except when she had her accident in the car that nearly killed her and that was awful, she nearly died she was in intensive care in hospital and her mother never even contacted me, it was awful, I was in my local club and a friend asked how she was I said what do you mean? Well she said after her serious car crash it was in the local papers and I said I have not heard anything about this because in the paper it said not Sarah Duckfield but Sarah Keepings that was my ex-wife's new partner's name, she had adopted it So I rushed down the hospital and it was her and I had to stand my ground there as it was taken for granted she was a keepings and not Duckfield but I was not having any of it and I got back in her life for   a little while but it was an awkward feeling and her mother's husband kept saying things that made me feel she didn't need me in her life and so we drifted again until this day. But I would love dearly to have her back in my life, never mind let me sort out my blindness problems and I will endeavour to see her before long I assure you I will." "Good Danny, I believe you and she don't know what she is missing and you must insist in trying to sort things out it will make you both happier" "Yes I am looking forward to that day I really am, right I am off I have a mobility lesson with Ann, I am redoing the college routes just for today, see you later Zarrine." "Yes bye Danny."

It was around 10.30 in the morning in the college ground and Jeff was coming over to the main building and was amazed when he was walking along and there in front of him was a woman's backside facing him so he said "Oh hello can I help?" A voice came out he recognised it, it was Carol and she said "Is that Uncle Jeffrey?" Jeff now smiling looking at her rounded ass said "Yes it is and what a lovely view of your rear it is." Carol "ha, ha, ha, sorry I have lost my eye somewhere and I can't find it" "How the hell did you lose your eye?" "I was walking along and I sneezed and it popped out and I tried to catch it but failed ha, ha, ha." "So what does it look like ha, ha, ha." "It looks like a rabbit, what do you think it looks like if it is slimy and sticky it is a snail otherwise let me feel it, the eye I mean." Jeff got down on his hands and knees and laughing says "This is so funny I have never heard of anyone sneezing and their eye popping out ha, ha, ha." Carol also laughing said "I know and with all these bushes around and long grass it is Impossible to find it but I have to or I will look like long John silver , ha, ha,ha." Next thing a window opens and a man's voice said " Hello Carol, Jeff, what is wrong?" Jeff replies "Carol's eye has popped out and we are trying to find it." With that the man jumped out and got on his hands and knees to help then a few students climbed out of the window to help until there was about 14 people trying to find her eye then the gardeners gave a hand until the whole ground was covered with people looking for this eye and coming around the corner came Danny and Ann on their mobility lesson, they stopped with shock and Danny said to Ann "What the devil is going on here then?" Ann "I don't know, it's like a scene from the mummies film, I can see your mate Jeff on his hands and knees there." Danny laughed said "Oh that's what it is then, Jeff has dropped 50 pence and he has everyone looking for it." They both laughed and strolled up to the masses on the ground and Danny said to Jeff "Jeff what's going on? has something of yours fallen off and you are trying to find it? It is probably been eaten by a robin or some small bird it is not enough of a feed for anything bigger ha, ha, ha." Jeff smiling replied "Very funny, no, it's Carol she sneezed and her false eye shot out and we are looking for it, so give us a hand ha, ha." Ann and Danny got on their hands and knees and felt around after about ten minutes they all give up and stood up Carol looking worried said "What am I going to do now? I can't have a drink tonight now." Jeff said "What has that got to do with anything? You can't see anyway so why do you need your plastic eye to drink?" Carol said "Well that's the eye I put in my pint to stop anyone drinking it when I go to the toilet or have a dance, now someone can pinch my drink ha, ha, ha." They all laughed and being a hot day Carol opened another button on her blouse and Ann laughed out loud uncontrollably. Danny said "What's the Matter with you Ann? Ha, ha." She could not answer them because she was laughing so much and could not speak. Carol said "I think she is having a fit." Jeff "Whatever it is it must be very funny indeed ha, ha." Ann finally stopped laughing and got her breath back and said "Carol I can see your eye now and it looks so funny it really does." Carol said ha, ha, where is it then Ann? Ha, ha." Ann said in between laughter "Ha, ha, it is looking at me from in between, ha, your boobs, it is in your cleavage looking at us all ha, ha, ha." Carol felt the eye and burst out laughing and put it back in her head, they all laughed about 20 of them and Jeff said "I would have got that for you." Carol replied "I bet you would have but I only let Adrian down there these days, sorry Jeff ." Jeff "Oh, there we are then, see you all later bye." Jeff goes off in a huff and Danny and Ann carry on their lesson.

Things in the college were getting a little warm with many of the students getting on top of each other and the sun never helped as people rushed around. Well the lads went home for the weekend and travelled together, it was funny the way Niel travelled as he had such a large dog to contend with and he always carried a large holdall that made it difficult for him to get on and off the train without assistance from the station assistants and he would always as he got to the stop in Bridgend wait on the doorway of the train for Ceri his wife to grab the large bag so he can get off safely with his German shepherd dog Abby. He would stand there like a lord waiting for her or an assistant every time and would not move as he could not manage the dog and the bag at the same time. Danny however and others would have a haversack strapped over their shoulders so as their hands were free at all times and this problem made a great story later in this book and show Niel he must change with the times, a hard lesson was learnt, but back to the story and Niel and Ceri dropped Danny at his house and went in for a cuppa. Niel in the car said as they arrived "What is after s in the alphabet?" Danny said as he knew what was coming "It's t." Niel said "Oh yes please, no sugar for me ha,, ha, ha." Ceri said "Niel, you are so cheeky isn't he Dan?" Danny "Oh I don't take any notice of him anymore Ceri and I can show you my cherry tomatoes Ceri if you like?" She smiled and blushed a little and Niel said "And that's all you are showing her mate ha, ha, and I will sort out Angie for you ha, ha, ha." Danny replied "I wish someone would I have given up and don't take your dog in as my dog Murphy just does not like any other dog in there and he will go nuts, he will attack her, otherwise he is lovely with humans." They all go in and are met by Angie and Murphy by the door and Murphy was going crazy when he saw Danny and was bouncing around. Niel grabbed Angie and give her a huge kiss and said "I have a delivery for you, a booby prize from Herefordshire it's only fair we share such a horrible person." Angie said tutting "Oh god, he is a miserable bugger lately, I hope he is happier this time?" Ceri "Oh Angie they are all the same, he is a miserable bugger by Sunday and I am glad to see the back of him, he moans and groans for Wales he does." Niel "We are here you know don't talk as if we are still in Hereford, ay Dan?" Danny "I am not saying anything it will only be wrong and I have my little dog here, do you want to stroke him Niel? He is lovely and harmless." Niel "Yes ok, c'mon then Murphy, he is lovely, such a fusspot isn't he?" Niel plays with Murphy and Danny puts the kettle on and they sit and talk for a while and Angie says "Your sister in law was here last night, she is living with her sister now permanent as Lyndon is drinking more than ever now and is hiding drink all over the house, he is sitting in the house and only goes out when he needs more drink so you need to go and talk to him this weekend. It's getting out of control now." Danny replies "I know, I am trying to think of something to sort him out, has Melvyn rang?" Angie says "No he hasn't, he is sitting down there and only comes up when you have phoned him, he is too busy with religion and until something goes seriously wrong he will not do anything. So it's up to you by the looks of it." Danny "Yes I know, I will go over there later if you take me." Angie answers "Yes as long as it is before Josh gets home from school as I am not taking him over there." Danny "Yes ok." Niel says "So he is getting worse then Angie is he ?" Angie answers "Oh yes he is." Niel "It's a shame Dan it really is, he seems a nice lad so what are you going to do now then?" Danny looking upset says "I haven't got a clue I have tried everything I can, I will go and see how bad he is and speak to my brother and we will have to sort out something, it's a nightmare mate, but I will have to do something I will get him sectioned if nothing works. He will hate me for it, but as long as it cures him I don't care a damn." Niel "Well if that's all you can do so be it, better to do that than let him kill himself isn't it? Well thank you for the tea I am going to see the 2 little horrors and have some fun with them and then with you Ceri, don't worry I haven't forgotten you ha, ha, ha." Ceri "I am off to bingo so forget it ha, ha, unless you behave yourself then I will think about it." Niel "Don't beat around the bush just tell me straight ha, ha, ha." Danny "That's telling you mate, I will see you Sunday on the train." Niel "Yes mate the same time train, see you then." Niel and Ceri drove off and Danny and Angie set off around the corner to see Lyndon. They got to the front door and rang the doorbell and Lyndon called "Who is it?" Danny replies "It's me your brother Danny, open the door" Lyndon shouted back "What do you want Dan I am busy?" Danny says "Oh come on Lynd, open the door let's not be silly, please don't insult my intelligence please, if you don't I will call the police because of some feeble excuse or something so you might as well open it." Lyndon opened the door reluctantly and he looked like a vagabond, he was unshaven and scruffy and looked as if he had slept in his clothes. Angie said "Oh my god, Lyndon what are you doing to yourself?" Lyndon replies "Oh, get in, I don't want to speak in front of the neighbours for god's sake." They went in and the smell of booze nearly knocked them over. Danny said "My goodness Lynd what   is going on with you? I hear Debbie has left you and you have got booze all over the house mate." Lyndon "Don't be silly, don't listen to those idiots and yes she has left me and I don't need you telling me what to do, I have got enough problems without you telling me the obvious, so get on with what you want to say." Danny looking worried said "Allright, so you tell me what is going on then." Lyndon "Nothing, nothing at all, I am going through a bad time that's all, it will work itself out so don't worry yourself about it." Danny "And you are not drinking then?" "No more than usual." "I can smell the booze it's all over the house, it smells very strong mate so don't tell me otherwise" Lyndon with a look of sadness says "Yes I have been hitting it a little hard but I am feeling better now and I am going to have a shower in a bit, so don't make a big thing of it." Danny looking so sad says "So why has she left then?" "She is using my drinking as an excuse I think, I have been over and asked her to come back but she won't, so you must ask her not me." Danny "C'mon Lyn I am worried about you, please give it a try mate stop drinking like there is no tomorrow, I think I will have a word with her for you, what do you think Lyn?" He looks troubled and says to Danny "You can try but I won't hold my breath and don't phone Mel he has enough to cope with at home and by all means give her a call and see what she has to say and let me know because I don't know what is the Matter." Danny said "Ok mate I will do that and get back to you, ok?" "Right and I will come over and see you tomorrow and see if you have showered and stopped drinking, so please pull yourself together and let's get life back to normal." Angie comes in with a cup of tea for Lyndon, she gives it to him and says "Allright Lynd? drink this and I have left a little fresh milk in your fridge for another couple later and this house needs a good cleaning, so get on with it, I will come and see if you have done it tomorrow, ok?" Lyndon "Thanks Angie and I will clean up later after a shower." Danny puts his arms around lindens shoulders and says "C'mon Lynd pull it together for me mate, I am very worried about you please." He replied with a small tear in his eyes "Yes ok, I will and I will see you tomorrow." Danny says " I will get you something to eat if you like?" "No I will pop up the chippies later but thanks anyway, see you tomorrow."

Danny and Angie left and Danny looked concerned and so did Angie as they walked Angie said "Dan he looks awful and the house looks as if a bomb has hit it, I have never seen it in such a mess, it looks as if it has been burgled and there is booze everywhere wherever you look there is inches cider white lightening cider and you know what that does to you? He is a chronic alcoholic Dan you must face it." "Yes I know, but what can I do about it? I will speak to Debbie on the phone now at home." Angie "Huh, she has left the burning building, she can't see any money now that he is in this state and Dennis is not providing for her, you know that she is already planning her next conquest mark my words." "Yes I know she is like her mother the black widow, she has killed more men than Hitler and got the money after, I think Debbie is exactly the same, it's just a Matter of time and she will lie to everyone about it mark my words but I will try and get her to help him before she jumps." "I won't hold my breath, she got what she wanted and destroyed him in the process." They both get back to the house and he gives Debbie a ring and speaks to her and after putting the phone down he speaks to Angie "Well she will not go back unless he stops drinking and he won't I know, so what now she didn't give me enough to say otherwise, she is right, she is like you said a rat leaving the burning ship and she is getting Lyndon's supposed best friend to help her, he spoke to me and said that Lyndon is in a state, he was the person who helped him to become an alcoholic, he got him pissed as much as he could at all times and now he is married to Debbie's sister he is all for Debbie and stuff Lyndon, so he is not much of a friend is he? just a 2 faced bastard who as long as he is getting his end away will not rock the boat never mind if it is his mate, so even Lyndon has seen the real side of him the creep, she said mind she will come down to alcoholics anonymous if I can get him to go and we know what a waste of space they are, so I will have a word with Mel and see what he thinks because she don't seem to give a damn." Angie looking sad said "I thought you would not get any satisfaction with her or his so called best friend, it seems as if Lyndon has given up." Danny snaps "Oh don't say that please I am trying to have positive thoughts and negativity is not any good." Angie storms off to go and get Josh from school and Danny rings up his other brother Mel "Hi Mel it's me Danny, I am home in Bridgend and I have just been over to see Lyndon, he is in a bad state again and I have just spoken to Debbie and she is staying with her sister and is not going back unless we can get him to stop drinking and Angie says he is like a tramp living over there and there is booze all over the place there hidden everywhere, things are getting serious mate we need to act now." Mel on the other end of the phone said "Oh dear, things are getting worse I was hoping they were having the opposite effect, Flippin heck so he is not getting in trouble besides with bothering Debbie is he?" "Well he has been over there a few times to find out what is happening and she is not happy about it and his so called best friend is not lifting a finger to help things at all, so it's up to me and you Mel and I feel it is getting urgent now. So can you get up here sometime and we can see what we can do maybe tomorrow if you can." "Right I will have to leave here early in the morning and get up with you by about ten o'clock ok?" Danny replies "Right ok I will not say anything to him and we can pounce on him early, see you then." Danny looked a little happier after speaking to his brother Mel and he waited to see his little son Josh hoping he would cheer him up. Josh turns up and runs and gives his dad a big hug and plenty of kisses and was very excited to see him, Danny said to him "So Josh have you been a good boy then? I hope so and how is school?" "Yes I am always good and I am doing well in school, my teacher said and what are you learning in your school then dad?" "I am learning to use braile as I showed you before with all the dots in the right place and now without making mistakes for a change and I am doing my computer lessons when the thing is working properly and learning to get around with my cane and I am not boozing anymore." Josh laughed as if to say yeh, yeh and Danny tickled him for taking the Mickey out of him and said "I am not Josh, really." "Yeh, yeh, dad I bet you are in the pub every night and with that Jeff ha,ha, ha." "Well Jeff has a girlfriend now so I don't see him much anymore and my teacher told me not to go out with him too much anymore or I will have the slipper ha, ha, ha." Josh laughed and said "Have you seen uncle Lyndon he is not well, he keeps on drinking until he is ill and aunty Debbie is over with her sister, will uncle Lyndon die dad?" "No Josh, he has an illness but uncle Mel and I are going over there tomorrow to see him and see what we can do for him so don't worry too much I will fisk it as you used to say ha, ha." Yes I know I used to say lots of silly things when I was little didn't I?" "Yes you did but that was my favourite one, shall we have a Chinese for dinner mate?" Josh all excited says "Oh yes please, we always have a Chinese when you come home don't we? I like a Chinese I do, can I go up with mammy to get it?" "Of course you can and here is 50 pence for sweets for later if you eat your Chinese Josh, see you in a minute." Danny sat there wondering about Lyndon and looked very sad indeed.

It was the next day and Danny was up early waiting for Mel to arrive Impatient to go over and try and get something positive done. Well Mel arrived and had a cup of tea first and then they went over, even Angie went with them and Josh went over his big brothers for the morning. They arrived and knocked the door as the curtains were still closed, eventually Lyndon answered the door and Mel and Angie were shocked he had had a shave and showered as he promised, this was a pleasant shock and Danny was wondering if he knew Danny was going to phone Mel. However the house was in a mess still and they went in made a cup of tea and Danny sat and talked to Lyndon while Mel and Angie started to tidy the place up. Danny said to Lyndon "I bet you feel much better after having a shower and shave Lynd don't you?" "Yes I do, so did you get in touch with Debbie and what did she say?" "Yes I got in touch with her allright and that asshole you used to call your best friend." "Oh him he is in the past I only had one real best friend and that was Alwyn Jenkins, he was a true friend, so what did she say? C'mon tell me." "Allright take it easy, she is not coming home unless you make an effort to cool the drinking and she was serious Lynd, I could tell by her voice." "Nothing unusual there then, exactly what I expected." "Well there you are then, so what are you going to do about it then? And what can Mel and I do to help?" Lyndon with defeated look says "I suppose I will have to give it up Dan and I need to do it myself to try and get her back." At that Lyndon started crying and looking so dejected, this upset Danny and he was in tears as well and they hugged each other and Angie came in briefly and she burst into tears too and went back out of the room. After a while they separated and slapped each other on the back and Lyndon said "It's hard Dan it is, I want her back so much it's my fault I know it and I miss her and Wendy so much, I can't go without them, so I am prepared to do anything, anything." Next thing Mel came in after Angie went out crying and he was also visibly upset and said after putting his arms around the both of his brothers "Let's see what we can do is it? this can't go on Lynd, it's tearing us all apart and causing a lot of grief and if you want them back we must make a start on getting things back as they were." Lyndon said "I am trying Mel, I have had a good think and can do this, I love her and Wendy so much I have no choice mate." Mel "That's right Lynd, so let's sit down and see how to resolve it, I will back you up all the way and Danny will do his best also." Danny "That goes without saying, if only I still had my eyes this would not be happening, I can assure you, I mean that." Lyndon "I know that boys I am sorry I hardly had a drink last night." Mel "Well there is enough drink here to sink a battle ship Lynd and I have poured it down the drain, so it's only the drink, I have not found left if there is any, so give it a try Lynd please, do you need one of us to stay with you?" Lyndon "No I will be allright and hope it will not be long before she is back." Danny "Well you will have to earn that Lynd, I will speak to Debbie later again for you and tell her what you have decided and Gaffo is coming over later to see you also, it's time to get life back to normal, I know it is difficult I do but if I can do anything I am on the mobile at all times and Mel is staying with you for the day to help you get sorted and I will be back and for until I go back tomorrow, your my brother and I care a great deal Lynd so please for us all stop drinking, I can't lose another brother it would kill me it really would." Lyndon "I know, i know , I will do my best and I am sorry." He then started crying again and so did the other brothers and it was such a sad time for them all.

Later that day Danny spoke to Debbie again and told her what he had decided and she didn't seem that bothered as she said she had heard it all before and later when Danny phoned her she had gone out to the local club, that was a kick in the guts for Danny but he never said a thing about this to Lyndon.

Later Mel came over before he had to go back to Milford Haven, it was about eleven o'clock that evening, he was upbeat and said to Danny "Well Dan I think he is going to give it a really good go, he is much happier now and he was going to bed before I came from there, he had a good dinner and some tea and it looks a lot better than earlier but I don't know how it is going to go I really don't. What do you think?" "I don't know Mel he is in a bad way, I hope you are right he needs some luck to go with it, I am worried, if he could only get her out of his head because she don't give a damn, I phoned her and she has gone out to the club for a couple of drinks. She don't give a shit mate, she really doesn't." "Never, well there you are then, I am coming back a few times next week to keep an eye on him and do what I can to keep him on the straight and narrow and have you arranged for some of his mates to call as often as they can?" Yes I have, I can't do much, I can't even look after myself at the moment, I wish I was able to see again, I would sort this out in a few minutes it's frustrating it really is." "I know Dan, I will do all that I can do so don't worry ok? I am off now and I will phone you tomorrow before you go back to college about 10.30 in the morning ok?" Danny with worried look on his face replies "Allright Mel and take it easy driving back home, speak to you later." Melvyn and Danny hugged and slapped each other on the shoulders and looked visibly upset. Mel left and Angie came in and said "Don't worry Dan he will be allright if Gaffo and some of his real mates keep an eye on him and Mel will not take any messing you know, I am off to bed." Off she goes and Danny sat there wondering for a while.

The next morning he went up to see Lyndon before he went back on the train and he was very upbeat again and Danny felt a lot better and told Mel so when he phoned, he also blurted his soul out to Niel on the train and Niel made him feel a lot better with his good attitude to life. Niel was saying how his weekend went "I sat in a restaurant in Maesteg and the Irish chess champion was in there and I asked him to pass the salt and it took him forty minutes to pass it, ha, ha, ha." Danny laughing said "You idiot, that was funny, my neighbour phoned 999 and got 998 instead and said is this 999? she said no it's 998, he replied can you pop into next door and ask the police, i need to speak to them ha, ha, ha." Niel finished laughing and said to Danny "I am fed up of shouting over to you on the other side of the train, come and sit next to me for goodness sake." Danny said "No way mate, I sat by you before and that big ass is spread all over the seats and my seat was reduced so much one of my ass cheeks was permanently in the isle hanging off the seat and was so uncomfortable, no way am I sitting like that again, if you put the arm down between us I will sit by you." "Ok come on then I will put it down." Niel tried pushing it down but couldn't as his bulging stomach got in the way of his arm and so Danny grabbed it and pushed it down with great force and Niel let out a huge groan and screamed "Argh, my god that hurt that did, right you can sit next to me now." Danny sat next to him and they enjoyed the rest of the journey and as they got to the Hereford station Niel could not get the arm back up and he was stuck so Danny had a go he pulled and pulled and Niel screamed "Argh, argh, it's hurting me when you do that I am stuck solid, get the man to help me." Danny rushed to stop the doors shutting and got a guard to see Niel, he came and he could not move the arm either and Niel was screaming "Argh, it is solid and I must get off here so what are we going to do?" The guard said "My companion has gone to get some tools to free you, it was a stupid thing to do if I was your size I would have not done that." Niel "I didn't it was that idiot by you, he insisted I put the arm down, you dickhead Danny." Next a man came in with a tool box and everyone was looking on and Niel was not happy at all. Well it took 30 minutes and they had the 2 seats in bit's in order to free him and outside the station the boys were killing themselves laughing and Niel was holding his side and he was bruised, they jumped into a taxi and got back to the common room in Dowdell and were still laughing, they went in and there was Lola, Winnie Carol and Jeff wondering what all the commotion was about and they proceeded to tell them all about it in between laughs Danny said "I have had a horrible weekend with my brother upsetting me and Niel has pulled me out of it, it was on the train ha, ha, ha." Danny could not speak for laughing and Niel was just as bad but he tried to explain, Lola said giggling "Ha, ha, what is the Matter with you 2? Hee, hee." Niel explained "Hee, hee, we were on the train and Danny forced the arm rest down between us and I got jammed and at the Hereford station I couldn't heee, heee, ha, ha, get the arm rest up and I was stuck and the guard of the train had to take the whole seat apart to free me and the train was delayed by 30 minutes all because of that daft idiot by their ha, ha, hee, hee, he." Niel was crying with laughter and everyone else was laughing at him laughing. Jeff said "Your kidding, you had to take the seat apart, I bet that was embarrassing Niel." Niel still laughing says "Ha, ha, it was at first but it got funnier as the time went on ha, ha, ha." Danny "We didn't know what to do at first but I was panicking and as time went on the guard and the others found it funny and we got into the spirit of the thing ha, ha, ha." Lola "Oh my god, didn't they complain to you? It's time you went on a diet Niel." Jeff "It's too late now he is a chunky hunk and that's that, right Niel?" Niel "Dim problem, I am a happy and jolly person and what you see is what you get." Carol "We won't have you any other way Niel, we love you as you are." Niel "Thank you Carol, it's nice of you to say ha, ha, I am sore now mind and thought I was going to spend the rest of my time travelling up and down from Manchester to Milford Haven ha, ha, ha." Danny "It would have been cheaper for the train company matey ha, ha." All this time Winnie had not said a word, has she got the message time will tell and Jeff was a little subdued has anything gone wrong with Jo Niel said to him "So where is Jo Jeff? Has she come back yet? " Jeff " yes she has I think her father and mother have brought her back and are staying and going back tomorrow so I will meet up with her then." Danny "Aren't you going over to meet them?" Jeff seeming sheepish says "Oh no, I spoke to her on her mobile and think it's best if I give them time to get used to the idea first, so Jo agreed with me, so I will be coming up the bar tonight and I will see her tomorrow." Danny "Good idea mate, I need a drink after the weekend I have had, my brother mind is getting a little better so I need alcohol to cheer me up. Niel are you coming up mate?" Niel smiling says "As long as you don't sit too close to me, I will and if I can walk up there as my hip is killing me it's bruised badly, you idiot don't sit near me on a train again ha, ha, ha." Danny "It's lucky it happened in Hereford and not in Cardiff, you would still be there if it was, they are hopeless at Cardiff they see a blind man and they all disperse and hide not like Hereford and Bridgend for that Matter." Jeff "Newport is very good also and Swindon." Niel "Bridgend is very good and Swansea." Danny says "Yes Swansea is very good too and I think the old man on the platform here in Hereford is brilliant, he must be 70 and he is very good with the blind and groans a little but never about helping us and there is Tim he is good also there." Jeff "Yes they have got their hands full here too with the amount of blind people who go through the station, they deserve a medal each." Niel "Yes I agree, well I am off to have a Jacuzzi in my bath to sort out these bruises, see you." Lola chirped up hearing this and said to Niel "A Jacuzzi in your room, how come Niel?" Niel explains "Oh it's my own, I brought it in myself, it fits in a normal bath and has a motor on it and works exactly like a Jacuzzi." Lola "Really, can I have a look at it working Niel?" Niel "Of course you can and if you want I can let you use it sometime if you like?" Lola being really nice said "Really, you won't mind?" Niel "Oh no, I can come and watch telly while you use it or give you my room key and let you use it and if I can watch that's even better." Lola "Ok, I mean the bathrooms are too small here so I will manage on my own." Niel said "Lola how can I watch? I have glass eyes ha, ha, ha." Lola goes off to see Niel's Jacuzzi with him and Carol says "I might have a go too in his Jacuzzi and uncle Jeffrey can scrub my back, what do you think uncle Jeffrey?" Jeff looking shifty said "Has Adi come through the door or something? because I am not answering that question if he has." Carol said "No he is in Tradeger down his mother's for a visit." Jeff "In that case I will gladly scrub your back ha, ha, ha." Danny "Oh god." Jeff "Oh shut up dodgy, I will give her a good rub down if she wants." Carol "Mmmmmm, uncle Jeffrey, steady boy." Jeff goes and sit's next to Carol and starts to cuddle and canoodle again and Danny sits down then Winnie sets upon him in a gentle voice. She says "So Danny did you see your son in Bridgend?" Danny being cautious said "Yes he was happy to see me and I enjoyed his company for the weekend, so what did you do?" Winnie replies "I went shopping on Saturday and then I did some work in the FLC (computer library) and I went up to the bar with Alfonzo and he bought me a drink and we had a bit of fun there." Danny shocked said "Nice, I am glad you had a nice time as time is too short here to sit in your room all the time, you will soon be off back to China and so time is Important." Winnie smiling replies "No I have asked for an extension to my tutor and he said I should be ok to stay longer." Danny's face told it all he looked as if he had just lost all his money and said "Really, that's nice for you." Winnie smiling says "Do you think so really?" Danny "Well yes, it is and this Alfonso is he your boyfriend?" She looked daggers at Danny and snapped "Why do you say this? he is a friend and nothing else, I am not like your British girls and go with anyone, so don't be silly." Danny taken back by her reaction says "Steady Winnie, I was only asking that's all, I think you should find a nice man and someone your own age. There are a lot of them here." Winnie still looking nasty says "Stupid velshman, I don't need man no more." And she storms out to her room. Jeff said "I was just going to go for a ciggy ha, ha, ha." Carol chirps up "And I was going to smack her in the mouth saying things like that about British girls, the cheeky mare" Danny said "Why? She was right wasn't she." Danny and Jeff laugh and Carol said laughing "Yes I think she is ha, ha, ha." Next thing in comes Lola and is excited about the Jacuzzi and said "Carol it's good I am having it tomorrow night to try, it bubbles up and is very powerful, I will enjoy it." Danny "I will rub your back if you like no problem." Jeff said quickly "No I will be better for that I am smaller and will fit in the bathroom ha, ha." Lola "No that's allright I can manage thank you."

It was the next morning and all alone was Zarrine and Danny walks in and said "Good morning Zarrine ok?" "Yes fine thank you, I am a little tired but ok. And there is only you and me up so far." Danny said "You must tell Peter to go straight to sleep." Zarrine stamps her foot "Danny behave, Niel just limped through here to take Abby for the pen for her business, what happened to him?" "I jammed him in a seat on the train coming back yesterday, I pushed the arm rest down and he got stuck and the train people had to free him and it took 30 minutes to do this ha, ha, ha." "Oh Danny, trust you he must be badly bruised is he ?" "I am afraid so and yes it was my fault but we laughed our heads off all night last night. It always happens to me don't it? ha, ha, ha." "And why has Jeffrey gone so early this morning? he has not got lectures for another 2 hours yet?" "How do you know he has gone then?" "Trust me I know everything I do, he has left his cup here for me to wash again and he has had toast I can tell because it is his cup, it is huge, he could bath in it." "I bet he has gone off to see Jo before lectures as she went home and her father am mother came back with her last night and stayed until early this morning so he is standing behind a lamppost waiting for them to go," Zarrine laughs "Hiding behind a lamppost that's funny, he could hide behind one to he is so thin and all you would see is his beer belly sticking out ha, ha, well I bet he will bring her over for a cup of tea so I will make you a cup of tea before he and Jo and Niel get back." Zarrine and Danny sitting having a cup of tea and Niel, Jeff and Jo walk in with their guide dogs. Jeff introduces Jo to Zarrine and Zarrine says "Hello Jo, I know who you are now and you deserve a medal being with this man." Jeff smiling says "Zarrine you love me, you said I am your favourite here, I make you tea and toast every morning." Zarrine says after slapping Jeff on the back "Oh Jeffrey, you stop telling lies you only make yourself tea or I do most morning , so now you can make Jo a nice cup of tea and while you are there you can make Niel one." Jeff "I wish I had shut my mouth now, oh well dodgy do you want one?" Danny said kiddingly "Did I hear you offer to make me a cup of tea? well I'll be buggered, I never ever thought I would hear you offer to make me a drink, yes please Jeff and Jo you are welcome here anytime if this is the influence you have got on him." Jeff smiling says "Take it easy matey, this Is a one off offer and Zarrine do you want one my dear?" Zarrine thinks about it and says "No thank you my dear, I am fine." Jeff went off to make the tea and Niel said "Danny my leg is killing me this morning, I just told Jo and she found it funny too and I bet you told Zarrine did you? ha, ha, ha." Zarrine said "Yes he did, you two, I don't know I can't send you anywhere ha, ha, so Jo is this it? you and Jeffrey?" Danny "Zarrine don't be so nosey, so is it Jo?" She smiles and says "I think so I can't be sure but we are having a ball with each other at the moment, we will have to wait and see, it's early days yes but looking good." Danny "Why did Jeff not come over to meet the parents yesterday then?" Jo says "I think Jeff was too nervous really and I didn't want to push him so he decided to wait a few weeks that's all." Niel "Look out here is the tea boy, I bet there something wrong with it now." Zarrine "Niel don't be so ungrateful, this is hard work getting Jeff to do anything, this is going in the book of guinessess isn't it Jeffrey?" Niel laughs and says "The book of guinessess indeed, you mean the Guinness book of records Zarrine." Zarrine "Oh yes, that to." Jeff "Right I will never offer again and Zarrine call me Jeff pleas not Jeffrey." Zarrine "Ok Jeff, I can't help it, that's Carol calling you Uncle Jeffrey all the time." Jeff "I know she is a pain calling me that all the time." Danny "It's your own fault she calls you that and she will make trouble for you if you are not careful mate, she will mark my words." Jeff "Oh I can handle the likes of her, she is a pussy cat and she has got

256

her new boyfriend to keep her in check now." Jo looking worried said "Was Carol your girlfriend then Jeff?" Jeff stammering said "A, a, a, no, no, she is just a good friend that's all and she really thinks I am her uncle, she is a pest sometimes." Jo still looking suspicious and Niel said "No he would not have the guts to go out with her, he has had some fun convincing her new boyfriend mind, he is convinced there is something going on mind, but we all know she is not interested in Jeff, he is just a mug for anything in a skirt aren't you Jeff? ha, ha, ha." Jeff "Niel, stop shit stirring in front of Jo, don't listen to him Jo he is trying to wind you up, there is nothing going on with Carol honest." Jo "I believe you so don't keep on about it and I know Niel is a teaser." Danny "Like Carol she is a teaser, right I am off." Jeff "I thought I could smell something and good riddance mate, see you round like a doughnut." Danny leaves and Niel started laughing and said "Sorry, sorry, I was thinking about that train yesterday it was so funny, he don't know his own strength, it was so funny." Next thing Danny walks back in and said "I can't get out of the doors and I was informed that my lecture was cancelled, so here I am." Jeff "Why couldn't you get out then dodgy?" Danny replies "Because the workmen are putting new bulbs on the security lights and putting new ones up also." Zarrine butts in "Oh yes I forgot to tell you, a former student is coming back here next week and he is a very Important man. He is a prince from Bahrain and he has security men to keep an eye on him and he has 2 women servants who walk everywhere with him and so that's what is happening." Danny looking concerned says "What, do you mean a real prince Zarrine? or will he be singing purple rain ha, ha, ha." Zarrine being serious says "Yes he is very young and nice, he is a real prince indeed, his name is Calliffa and he has been here before, he will be in the same block as Jeff." Niel "Really, well that is a turn up for the books isn't it?" Jeff "And what's this about 2 servant girls?" Zarrine "Trust you to ask about his girl servants, he has them to do everything for him, do his food, dress him, bath him, everything and they will follow him wherever he goes in the college and his security boys are noisy people." Danny said "I'll give them noisy buggers if they keep me awake and so why is he coming here then?" Zarrine replies "He is coming to learn as he is partially sighted and he has a stammer also and so he is building his confidence up also, you will like him he is a nice chap, but very quiet indeed." Jo "So is he rich Zarrine? I remember him 2 years ago here for a while." Zarrine "If he is a prince from Bahrain he must be rich don't you think? and he will not bother with you lot of rabble, so don't worry ha, ha, ha." They all laugh and Danny said "Hey Zarrine don't hold back you just tell us straight ok? ha, ha, and so he will be segregated from us then will he?" Zarrine "Oh no, he is just a man who keeps himself to himself that's all, you will like him but won't see much of him, he stays in his room most of the time." Jeff with cunning smile says "I bet he does with 2 birds looking after him, wouldn't you?" Niel says "Oh, pervy Jeff is off, that's all he thinks of, now you can see what he is like Jo, your in for it tonight look out." Jo blushes and says "I don't think so, Jeff is not like that, he is and is always the gentleman, aren't you Jeff?" Jeff smiling says "Ha, ha, ha, yes dear, I am trying aren't I.? Ha, ha." Jo scalds Jeff and says "Jeff, I am sticking up for you so try and be sensible." They all laugh and Jeff says "Sorry dear, I was only kidding ha, ha, ha." Danny says "So when is he arriving then?" Zarrine "Sometime next week I think, I am not sure yet, why?" Danny looking worried "Because if I tell you this you must not say anything to the management here, promise?" Zarrine looking unsure said nervously "Ok so long as it does not compromise my job, so tell me." Danny "Well you know Billy sticks on B Floor he has his 18th birthday on Tuesday night and all the boys are invited." Jeff "I am not going so it won't affect me. " Zarrine says "Well I can't see any problem with that Danny, why do you think it will not be allright then?" Danny replies "Because it will be a big bash and besides that there is going to be a special thing happening there." Jeff "If there is going to be trouble there i am glad I am not going ha,ha, ha." Niel "So what is this special thing then Dan?" Danny looking worried said "Look if I tell you, you must not say anything to anyone it's secret and will spoil his party as Carol and Lola are trying to stop it now because they don't like him for some reason or other so you must swear not to say anything if I tell you." Everyone agreed not to say anything and Danny continued "Well there is a stripper booked for him because he is so shy, the lads on his floor thought it would be a good idea and they can't wait to see his face." There was a deadly silence and no one said anything for a minute and Zarrine then said "I know nothing, I know nothing." Niel said "Zarrine you sound like Manuel on fawlty towers, I know nothing, I know nothing, ha, ha, ha." Danny laughs and Jeff was looking shocked. Zarrine said "I never heard you say that, I think no one should say anymore after they leave this room please." Jeff said "Sorry, did you say Billy sticks, sorry I thought you meant someone else, I forgot about his birthday, what time is it on?" Niel said "Jeff you big shit you, a minute ago you was not going and now it's different, now a stripper is mentioned, you rat bag you." Jo said "Jeff, I thought you said we were going to have a meal in the winning post that night you creep." Jeff stuttering said "Well, well, I, I, forgot about that, he is my mate and is young, he needs all the support he can get for his 18th, he is far away from home so I thought I would make him feel wanted. I don't worry about strippers they don't bother me I would rather be in the room with you my darling." Jo smiling said "You liar you, I don't mind, I will get some washing done that night because that's what I normally do on a Tuesday, so no problem, have a nice time I don't mind." Danny chirps up "She don't care Jeff that's what she means ha, ha, and you are a shit and If I hadn't have to mention it you would not have gone would you?" Jeff defends himself while having a huge smile on his face "Don't be silly, it's Billy, I like a good booze up now and again and besides this was arranged before I met Jo and if she insists I will not go, I will take her for that meal. She is more Important than a stripper honestly." Jo said "Awe, it's ok Jeff I don't mind you go and enjoy yourself with the boys, I don't mind." Danny said "Ha, ha, hee, hee, look at his face you can see the relief on it ha, ha, ha." Jeff laughs and Zarrine says "Please don't say anymore in front of me about the arrangements, but why has Carol and Lola got it in for him then?" Danny "Only because his mates and Carol don't get on, they are the ones who play their music too loud and Carol bites every time and stamps on the floor and they turn it up even more to annoy her and Carol and Lola have become good friends and so Lola is backing up Carol and Billy is as you know Scottish and has crutches and cannot walk properly and I would have thought because she is Scottish she would be sticking up for him but she really hates him with a vengeance. She really does, so that's why I don't want them to know anything, so everyone keep it to yourself ok?" They all nod in agreement and Danny said "Well so do you agree, don't nod your head if you agree, we are all mostly blind and so I don't know what you think you dick heads ha, ha, ha." They all say a resounding yes and laugh then Niel speaks up again "So what has this got to do with the prince turning up before Tuesday then?" Danny replies "Well his security will be bouncing around for the first few days and they will put a stop to it and having a woman stripping on the premises is not a good idea with their religion and that will be it, so let's hope it is after Tuesday." Niel "Right I see now what you mean, I hope having a prince in the premises will not change anything, I had enough with Lola when she first turned up." Danny "Well that turned out allright, she is a pussy cat now and so will this turn out ok, so don't worry about that now." Zarrine says "Oh dear, I hope there is no problems here again." Danny said "If he is as nice as you say he is, there will be nothing to worry about" Jeff said to Danny "So what time does the party start Dan?" Danny "See what I mean Jo? he is so excited now, honestly, that's all he thinks about, I will let you know Jeff besides you always stick with me and Niel whenever we go to anything like this, so don't worry mate." Jeff "God, I was just asking that's all, good grief, right Jo let's go before they stir it anymore, see you all later." The love birds go off to lectures and Niel and Danny have another cuppa and next thing in walks Winnie and she was fuming and went straight to Danny and said "Why did you tell lies about me to Anthea? and I have not said anything to Lidia, so don't be silly, I want to stay here a little longer and now you have made me look bad to the college and I will never forgive you." She sit's and starts crying and Niel said "Well WINNIE you have been lying, a stalker to Danny and I have heard you having a go at Lidia too and Zarrine so you brought It on yourself" Winnie still fuming said to Niel "Right , you are another velshman who will stand up for him and so mind your own business, I am talking to Danny not you and I will do what I want." Niel said "Well Winnie that's where you are wrong, this is a free country and we have the choice to speak our mind and I just have and if you don't like it that's your problem and Danny I know has had a guts full of you making his life a misery and he doesn't need this at the moment and as a friend I have the right to say so and there is nothing you can do about it, sorry." Winnie mutters "Stupid velshman, I hate them." Danny said "Look Winnie, I am sorry it came to this but you will not leave me alone, I am not your boyfriend and so leave me alone and let's just be good friends. I don't want to have you thrown out of here and as regards Lidia, she is nothing to do with this, so leave her alone it's between me and you ok?" Winnie "So tell that velshman besides you to mind his own business and don't tell lies about me to the college again." Next in walks Carol and Winnie hearing her come in storms off to her room . Carol says "Oh dear, bad timing again ay, she is so up herself isn't she?" Danny with head in hands said "I give up with that girl, I wish she would just leave it there and get on with her life." Niel says "Don't worry about it mate she will come around sooner than later you'll see." Carol said cockily "I wouldn't bet on it, she is the type that does not forget it and get on with her life I assure you, she's funny like that." Danny sternly said to her "And I suppose you are, are you?" "Danny, it's not my fault I am just saying that's all so what have I done now?" Danny says "Well you say she don't forget about it and so why don't you forget the nonsense about you and the lads downstairs then? like Billy sticks, he has not got a bad bone in his body." Carol going red in the face replies "Oh him, he is just as bad as the rest of them on that floor, he is an ignorant pig so he gets what he deserves and if he thinks he is having a 18th birthday party here he is very much mistaken I can assure you and that's what this is all about isn't it?" Niel speaks up "That's not very nice is it Carol?" Carol "Neither is keeping me awake with the music most nights is it? so stuff them and Billy sticks because if I can spoil it, I will." Danny "You have surprised me Carol, I didn't think you were like that I really didn't, he is only 18 once in his life and you are going to ruin it for him, I didn't think you were like that, I didn't believe anyone who said it but I was wrong about you and I don't like being wrong." Carol smiling said "Well they are playing with the wrong girl and I don't forget things easily, so look out he will just have to have his party somewhere else that's all." Niel says "We know, we are going in to town for it now and you have done us a favour really as it will be more fun and we will be getting back about 2.30 so don't waste your sleeping tablet's you will need them that night." Carol replied "I will be waiting and the one in charge that night will have a busy night I promise you, so don't threaten me Niel." Danny in calm voice said "Oh c'mon Carol don't be like this, it's not his fault you don't get on with his mates is it ? give the boy a break please." Carol with huge smirk on her face says "Sorry Dan they never gave me a break

even after I reported them, they just went back to doing it again afterwards, so sorry I will not forget it, an eye for an eye, and a tooth for a tooth, sorry." She leaves and Niel said "It's not looking good Dan for Billy is it? I can't see what is gained from making a lads life a misery when he is nothing to do with her silly arguments, I think we had better get out of here now Dan before anyone else comes in and has a go at us." Danny "Yes your right mate it's not good to sit still too long." Next thing in walks Zarrine muttering to herself and looking worried. Danny said "Too late here's more trouble, why are you muttering Zarrine?" She replies "More problems heading our way, I am worried now." Niel says "No there won't, I think it will blow over and if it does blow up it will be in the evening when you are off and I don't think much will come of it and we must relax Zarrine and Danny is going up the chip shop and we can have a chip butty together today. have you ever had a chip butty Zarrine?" Zarrine looking puzzled says "No I have never had one of these, what is it?" Danny said "I will go up the fish and chip shop and you butter a load of bread and put them on a large plate and put some small plates and some salt and vinegar and I will show you, it's special in Wales isn't it Niel?" Niel smiling said "Oh yes and us Welsh only do this with anyone we love from other lands, so you are honoured and special. So what time Dan?" Danny "12.30 allright with you 2? you will enjoy this Zarrine." Zarrine looking very excited says "I will, I will do this and expect you at 12.30, this will be interesting."
The lads went off.
At 12.30 Danny turned up and Niel, Jeff and Zarrine were sitting in the kitchen waiting for him and next thing he comes in and had a huge bag of chips and put them in the middle of the table and said "Right tuck in, I will show you Zarrine, put as many chips in the middle of the bread some salt vinegar and squash it all together and sit back and eat it ha, ha, ha." Zarrine sat there and done this and she was like a cave woman eating it and they all ate and ate and Niel said "Zarrine did you enjoy that? wasn't it lovely?" Zarrine looking happy said "I really enjoyed that, I really did, I didn't think I would but they tasted lovely those butty chips mmmm." Danny chuckling says "No Zarrine, they were chip butties, they were nice weren't they?" She said again "Oh yes they were, we must have a chip butty day regular." Jeff said "Not for me I must watch my figure." They all laughed and Danny said "Your joking if you swallowed a malteeser I would think you were pregnant ha, ha, ha." Jeff replies "Oh matey I have feelings you know." Danny "Sorry mate and I think we have Impressed Zarrine with our chip butties." Jeff "Yes you have and she will have you running up the chippies every day now." Zarrine said "Yes Danny they were very nice indeed so buy new trainers you are going to be busy ha, ha, ha." Niel "I hope not I am too fat now and I love chip butties more than anything else, so don't go there please." Jeff "A nice cup of tea would go down a treat?" Zarrine said "Well you are the greatest tea maker we have got here so get on with it Jeff... oh look at that face I will make it." Jeff "I heard Carol speaking to Lola this morning about her talking to you about Billy sticks party, I think they are plotting his fate and she will not let it go mate." Danny said "I have a plan Jeff and it involves you matey." Jeff holds his head and says "Oh no, i am not doing anything you say I know it will end up a disaster if you are involved, no way man, sorry." Niel said "Jeff, don't be a big girls blouse you whimp, it's for a good cause." Danny "I'm glad you said that Niel because this involves you too." Niel said "Oh shit, not me I am a coward as regards them 2." Jeff snaps "But it's ok for me isn't it, right tell me first and I will decide." Danny "That's all I want to say is when you are about them 2 mention we are going to the rose and crown and we have asked some of his male friends to his party and they are all down for a bit of fun and keep on saying how brilliant it is going to be and they will bite you will see as she will believe anything you say Jeff, so what

do you think?" Jeff "I don't know mate I always get into a mess when you are involved, what do you think Niel?" Niel looking concerned said "Well, I don't know, I can't see us getting in trouble just saying things until they find out we are lying and we will be their next target, it's worth it I think." Danny "Great, it's a messy job but somebody's got to do it ha, ha and let's hope the lads down stairs don't foul it up, I will tell them the same it's worth a try ay?" Jeff looking unsure says "Yeh, if you say so." Niel "I am sure it will be ok Jeff and if it isn't we can drop Danny in it." Danny "No problem lads, I am used to it and they don't worry me in any way ha, ha, I like a good fight and it is for a good cause, Billy was the man who narrated my poem on a disc for me." Niel "Did he? I must hear that one day, I am off to my first lecture of the day, see you lads." Niel went off and the boys followed him later.

It was Tuesday early evening just before the party and Danny, Jeff and Niel were in the lounge waiting to leave and Danny said "So what do you think lads? do you think our plan has worked or what?" Niel "I don't know, they are a right pair those 2 and I don't think they will take it as gospel and by the end of the evening they will twig it." Jeff "I think you may be right Niel but it will be too late for them to do anything about it by then." Danny "That is what I was hoping too by the time they get themselves organised it will be too late, Billy will be in bed pissed." Jeff "We have to get the booze down there yet from our rooms, I hope they will not catch us as we take them down." Danny "No they won't, I will take it down my stairwell they can't go down there and I will have the replacements off you tomorrow ok Jeff?" Jeff "No problem matey, good thinking mate" Niel said "I am only taking a half bottle of whisky with me and a bottle of lemonade." The lads go off down the stairwell to the next floor and they start drinking hard and there was no sign of Carol and Lola but you could be sure they were not far away. So Danny decided to arrange a taxi to fetch some meals from the local Chinese and let the girls think they were off to the rose and crown pub.

They return from the Chinese and sit down and Billy said "It worked I seen Carol and Lola watching you go in the taxi and I think they got another taxi later, brilliant." Danny "There you go then it worked and hopefully they are gone for the night, let's dig into our Chinese, god Billy you are drinking too fast you will be pissed by 9 o'clock, slow down lad." Jeff "Yes Billy pace it out or you will miss most of your birthday ha, ha, ha." Billy said "I am only on shandies at the moment, after my Chinese I will have some decent beer so let's party." It was a little later and the lads were now on their way and the lounge was packed and with loud music and Clamper said "This is great, I am enjoying it, it's good and no Lola to spoil it for anyone, does Billy know he has a stripper coming in?" Jeff "Not to my knowledge, I think he is too pissed to worry about that at the moment, I can't wait to see her." Clamper "Neither can I, I have never seen one ever, is it going to be good for everyone? can we have a grope? Or is it only Billy?" Jeff laughing said "I wouldn't try and have a grope as you will probably get a smack in the mouth off her minder, I think Billy will be allowed to have a grope or 2 but you just watch and nothing else as it will be a little tense for a while and have a good ogle at her ok?" Clamper looking sad said "Yes, ok Jeff I will no problem, I need to get some beer off someone, I need to buy some cans , will you sell me some Jeff?" Jeff in a snappy voice "Clamper you knew there was a party here tonight and didn't get any lager, you are thick sometimes, I will give you a couple of cans and you get them back for me tomorrow ok?" "Oh thanks Jeff, you are a life saver I will ask Danny for a couple later and do the same with him." Next thing the doorbell rang and it went silent and Danny said " I hope it's not them bloody 2 Lola and Carol, answer the door and if it is get rid of them." Danny assumed it was the stripper and Billy had a face like thunder and thought it was Carol and Lola but he had a big shock when a police woman came in and said "Is there a Billy here? and if so can I have a word please?" Billy's face was a picture, he was about to start crying by the looks of him and he said in a timid voice "I am Billy it's my birthday and we were not doing any harm were we?" The police woman had Billy in front of her and she said "Well I have had a serious complaint that you are 18 today and it's your lucky day." She threw her hat off and took her jacket off and opened her blouse and took her breasts out and wiggled them in front of Billy's eyes, he was dumbfounded and looked as if his xmas's and birthdays had come at the same time, she then took off her skirt and stood there in stockings and suspenders, by now Billy didn't know where to look first, it was brilliant for him he had never seen anything like it before and was loving every minute of it, he was then beckoned to help her off with her suspenders, he was shaking like a leaf and did this and slipped the stockings off her legs and she then took her panties off and showed all and Billy was done for. She then squirted cream over her breasts and encouraged him to lick it all off and she pulled his face in between her breasts and he was covered in the cream, she then done a dance and Danny got a handful as her ass rubbed on his hand as it rested on the arm of the settee, that woke him up, she then laid Billy down on the floor and straddled him and teased him for a short time and everyone enjoyed it Immensely, she then left and Billy was like a schoolboy beaming from ear to ear. He got up and said "Brilliant lads, thank you I enjoyed that, I need the toilet now though" Jeff said "Ha, ha, I bet you do, we know where your going and we know what you are doing." Danny said "God I wish my eyesight was better but never mind I had a handful by accident, I will not wash that hand now for a fortnight, very nice ass etc." Clamper said "Yes you lucky bugger, I seen her sit on your hand, you jammy sod." Jeff "A cracking body too, really nice tit's and a gorgeous body, I am glad I came now." The beer was flowing by now and all were well oiled and they decided that Billy was not getting away with a easy night and the funniest thing happened and the lads in his floor decided to get out the ironing board and laid it down folded up on the floor top shiny side down and laid Billy on it and tied him down on it and took him to the top of the stair well and slid him off the top stair and watch him toboggan down the steps. They done this all the way from the top to the bottom and then picked him up like a king on their shoulders and took him to the top and did it again and he laughed all the way down. Later they untied him and went back into the lounge and they all sat listening to the music and all got very pissed and just when they thought they had got away with the night the warden came in and turned off the music and said in a loud voice "Right lads, I have had a complaint and the party has to stop now." Danny said "It's only quarter past ten, you got to be kidding? who is complaining then?" Simon the warden said "I can't tell you I have to stop it here and now though." Clamper "Awe, you are kidding it's a 18th birthday and there is no trouble so why?" Simon "Because we have had a complaint that's why." Jeff "From who then?" Danny said "Is it from Carol and Lola? I bet it is isn't it?" Simon did not answer and Danny said "I thought so and you are very friendly with them aren't you? so you can piss off and forget it we are partying and you can tell them to piss off too." Simon "I must insist you go home now and stop this party before there is trouble." Danny "The only trouble is me smacking you in the mouth so if I was you I would disappear now before I lose my temper, I mean it." Simon could see how serious Danny was and he left after saying "Ok I have warned you." He walked out and Danny said "Ok lads let's party and Billy forget it and let's enjoy ourselves until the person in charge comes and it will be a while yet so drink up and let's party." Billy's eyes lit up and they started drinking again, but it was not long before the person in charge came in that night and stopped the party. It was Ann Danny's mobility teacher, she was on call that night and she said "Right, turn the music down and listen to me . I am sorry but this will have to stop as we have had complaints." Danny said "Ann, we were expecting this party to be stopped by 2 vindictive women who said they would and they are friends of Simon the warden and that's why it is happening, so please don't do this it's the boys 18th birthday." Ann looking annoyed she has to do this said "I am sorry Billy and the rest of you but rules are rules and we have to abide by them and I can't comment on why or who but I must stop it and that's that." Jeff said "But that's not fair, we were not noisy and you know who is behind this and if we go now they will love it and I for one am staying." Clamper said "So we must live by their ways, so if they have a party next week we can do the same then, because I will, it's not fair." Ann "Well that's up to you and I must stop the party and so I want you all now to go back to your own floors." There was a deadly silence and Danny said "And Simon how do you feel now you are destroying his 18th birthday party? he is only going to have this opportunity to celebrate this today, after that it's too late." Simon looking smug said "I'm sorry Billy but that's the rules and I can't do nothing about it." At that Billy starts to cry and walks off to his room, this upset most of his friends and Danny said "Simon I think you are the lowest of the low and what you are doing to that boy is despicable and cruel, he has had a rotten start to his life being crippled and now he has a smack in the mouth from someone he supposed to look up to. I hope you can live with yourself and if it was up to me I would punch you out, but you are not worth it mate." Jeff said "Cool it Dan, he is not worth it and it will only get you in trouble so leave it now." Clamper said "Yes Dan leave it, I will never talk to him as long as I am here and I say we all should do the same." Ann snapped at Danny and said "I am sorry Danny I cannot let you threaten a member of staff and want you to apologise to him." Danny looking nasty said "I am sorry Ann I will not apology's to him, he is not worthy of anything sorry but you must do what you have to do, look at that lad he is inconsolable and I am nasty about this and I for one will make them pay for what they have done to that boy, excuse me I am going to see Billy before I go back to my floor." Danny, Clamper and Jeff leave and the other lads were having a go at Ann and Simon.

Later in Billy's room the boys reminisce how good the night was and had some drinks still on them and so had a little party in Billy's room very silently. Jeff feeling sad for Billy said "Never mind matey we will keep it quiet, I think they are leaving now and they think we have gone back to our rooms and look what I have found, good uncle Niel left us the last of his whisky and lemonade, he said we could have it, he went to bed rather drunk, any cups bill?" Billy seemed to cheer up somewhat and said "Yes there are some tumblers on my desk, let's party lads." Clamper said "I will never forgive them bitches I hate them especially that Lola, she is a cow and I ha, ha, ha, nothing." Danny and Jeff laughed and said "Well go on, finish what you was going to say." Clamper was by now laughing and so was Billy and Clamper said "No I can't tell you it's not very nice and you will tell her I know you, the last time you did remember." Danny "Who me? what do you mean Clamper?" Clamper replied "Do you remember when I told you I had never shagged a girl and would not mind shagging Lola and I was a little depressed and you went and told her about it and when I asked you about it you said to me, Clamper if you ever have a problem come and tell me and I will tell everyone else, no more problem. So I won't tell you ha, ha,ha." Jeff "Oh, c'mon Clamper tell us, please." Clamper "Danny if I tell you, you must first promise not to breathe a word on your granddaughters life." Danny replied "Sorry Clamper I can't do that I am sorry, I will not swear on anyone's life but I will give you my word and that is good enough for most, I give you my word, c'mon tell us." Clamper thinks about it and says "Ok, but you had better not tell anyone or that will be the last time I talk to you. Well you know she is having an affair with that married lad on the ground floor and she has got her own teapot in our kitchen and I hate her so much because she is always picking on me, so I rub my cock around the inside of the teapot every night after they have gone to bed, so she is having my cock in her mouth regular." With that they all started laughing and Billy was now much more cheerful and said "Fancy some music lads?" Danny said in urgency "No Billy, do you want to get all the trouble makers back here, let's just have a bloody good drink and be silent doing it. I will write a book about this place one day and this will be in it just to let Lola know what you just told me Clamper ha, ha, brilliant just brilliant." Clamper let one of his funny laughs out and Jeff said "I was thinking about the man on the building site ha, ha, ha." Billy said "So what about hymn Jeff? it's a joke right?" Jeff "Oh no he was a man who had a stutter and he was a very quiet man who just laboured all day without question and one day the owner sent his son to see how the building site was progressing and no one knew him there and he had to see if anyone was being harassed and to find out why if so. Well he stood up on the scaffolding and watched the men working and all of a sudden the foreman shouted down to this man and said "Oy you, you the donkey mixing the cement, hurry up with that mix we need it fast you bloody donkey." the man just looked up and started working a little faster moaning and groaning. Next thing the foreman shouted down at hymn again "Hey donkey, get some bricks up you bloody donkey." he rushed some bricks up and later after the day was over the son felt sorry for him and went to speak to the man and said "Tell me why does that horrible foreman keep on calling you a donkey? he is very bad mannered isn't he?" the man replied "Awe, e aw, e aw, e aw, e aw, e always says that about me." The lads fell about the room crying laughing at the joke and this was going to be a great night after all and the lads got absolutely legless that night .

It was the next day at around 11 o'clock when Jeff and Danny joined everyone in the common room as it was a quiet Wednesday and it was a good thing looking at Danny, Jeff and Niel. Niel started the conversation and said "Allright lads, I am still pissed so I expect you were worse than me? I just had to leave after that bloody Simon done what he did as I would have said something I would regret." Jeff holding his head in both hands "Niel you had the right idea, I wished I had come home the same time now, I am absolutely hammered and look at him he is the same aren't you Dan?" Danny head bowed said "Oh yes, I am still pissed, that whisky finished me thank you Niel, If I breathed on that door frame I would burn the paint off, it was a bloody good night mind, I think he had a brilliant night after all the fuss." Niel "How come? I thought the fun was stopped?" Danny "It was but we went back to Billy's room to console him, Jeff took the whisky you left us and thanks by the way and we drank it and had a good laugh with some jokes and some truths and we were in hysterics by the end of the night. We got back about 3 30 this morning, I hope Carol and Lola spoil some more parties it was brilliant." Talking about those pair they were here a while ago, did you know that Lola is moving to the ground floor this morning she has got a new room down there near her fancy man?" Jeff "Really, that was kept silent." Danny's face lit up "Oh thank god for that, only one to go now then, that's the best news I have had for ages, time to party Jeff, mind you I will miss that fabulous body of hers." Jeff "Oh not for me." Niel "Ha, ha, poor old Jeff, never mind mate she will probably be back for some help to move now, she was hinting about it as the S. S. W's are not here this weekend and she was looking for help earlier." Jeff "Huh, she has got no chance mate, not after what she done to Billy yesterday, I would not piss on her if she was on fire." Danny "Well I would help if it meant she wasn't coming back no problem." Niel "Would you?" Danny replies "Oh yes I bloody would anything to get rid of her, but I will miss that lovely body of hers especially in her pyjamas, she has got a cracking body, it's just the mouth that is too big ha, ha." Jeff "Yes your right, I will miss that lovely ass and the pyjamas caw and I wonder who is having her room then ? or will it stay empty till the new ones start?" Niel "Zarrine will tell us on Monday, I wonder why she didn't tell us about her leaving though? Strange." Niel "I wonder if Carol will follow her, they have become as thick as thieves and Adi doesn't like it I bet." Jeff "Good,, he is a bit of a creep anyway, I don't think Carol will leave her room at all she likes it here, I might see if I can get Jo to have Lola's room it will be handy." Danny "Do you think that is a good idea matey? look at the trouble I am having with Hong Kong fuey and it might come back and bite you the same way." Jeff smiling says "No, she is not a bit like her, she is madly in love with me and you deserve all you get with Winnie ha, ha, only joking matey." Danny smiling said "I hope you are mate, look out here comes Lola." She swans in and was very nice to the lads and they knew why, so played along with her, she said "Well are you going to miss me then?" Danny "No." Jeff "A bit." Niel "Of course." She replies "That's not very nice is it? I will miss you …..no honestly I will." Danny "Yeh, yeh, so what do you want then? you are never this nice unless you want something." Lola "Oh, don't be like that it's the end of an era." Niel "Yes, your right Dan, she does want something and I am off to my room for a sleep as I can't carry anything so it's up to you lads." Lola "I understand Niel can I have the use of your Jacuzzi later please?" Niel "Yes of course you can, I am going out at 6 shopping for something in the supermarket so I will leave my door open." Lola "Thank you Niel, so Jeff any chance you can do me a favour?" Jeff "Sorry I can't I have the hangover from hell, you will have to wait for the S. S. W's tonight after your Jacuzzi, sorry." Lola "Awe bloody hell, I was hoping to be in before then, well never mind see you all later and thanks for nothing." She storms off and the lads laugh. Danny "Even if I liked her after what she done to Billy she can forget it, let her sweat it's, nearly time for a pint." Jeff "Not for me mate I am bushed, I will sit here and watch some telly."

Later on in the lounge Lola passes through to Niel's room to use the Jacuzzi and Danny and Jeff were lounging around in the lounge and she said to Jeff "You still here then? you could have helped down stairs with my gear by now had you wanted to." Danny sleeping and Jeff said "After what you and Carol did to Billy I would not help you after that." Lola looking shocked said "It's nothing to do with me, Carol has got trouble with those lot on B floor not me and I won't get involved as my boyfriend is mates with them, you ask Carol when you see her." "Talking about her I haven't seen her all day she must be hiding?" "She is out with Adrian in town and I think you may be right she wasn't keen on bumping into you or Danny this morning and don't ask me what happened last night as i will tell you the same as I told Carol, I don't want to know I am not getting involved so leave it there Jeff please." Jeff says "Ok, I will, I am sorry for thinking you had something to do with it, have a nice Jacuzzi and if you want me to wash your back I will." "No that's ok thank you, I will see you later." She went off with some towels to Niel's room for her Jacuzzi and Jeff settled down and next thing in walks Winnie and sat down next to Danny who was still asleep. Winnie said to Jeff "Hello Jeff, there was lots of noise and shouting last night down stairs and I could hear Danny shouting." Jeff answered "Yes he was not happy because the warden stopped Billy's party and Danny nearly decked him." "What is decked?" "Oh sorry, he nearly hit him but I stopped him and we ended up in Billy's room instead and as you can see we had too much to drink." Winnie looking at Danny said "Yes he drinks too much, he will be dead in a few years if he continues drinking like this and you too." Jeff smirking says "No, we don't drink every day of the week." "Yes you do and even more on the weekends, it is not good for you Jeff." "I know but there is nothing to do as we don't like much of the activities here so we drink." "I wish I could get through to you pair but never mind I will keep on trying, I am off to see Alison she is taking me to the Cathedral for the afternoon, see you" "Yes have a nice afternoon and I will see you when you get back." She leaves and Danny was still sleeping and Jeff had a ciggy out of the window and as he went to sit down Lola came charging through the lounge and was in a panic and said to Jeff "Quick Jeff help me I have flooded Niel's bathroom." Jeff's eyes lit up as she was just holding a towel in front of her and nothing on her back as she went through you could see her bare back and a lovely ass in the raw, Jeff said nothing but charged after her to get a better view. He said "How did that happen?" Lola replies in a fluster "I left the water running a little and almost fell asleep and didn't realise it" She bent down to pick up some towels and Jeff realised she had dropped the towel around her and her boobs were just hanging in front of his face and he just froze and stared at them , she threw towels at him and said "Follow me Jeff." This he did and he was mesmerised at the view, she didn't give a damn and neither did Jeff, she went in Niel's room and just dropped her towels on the floor and got on her hands and knees and started wiping up the water and Jeff just stood there and was numb just looking at the incredible body in action. He was loving every minute of it, she stopped and looked at Jeff and said "Well, don't just stand there give me a hand please, this is not the time for window shopping." Jeff said "Oh yes, yes, of course, I'm sorry phew." And he got on his knees and helped her.

Later on he was sitting back in the lounge again with a can in his hands and looking pleased with himself and Danny awoke and heard him sitting there and said "Allright mate, sorry I fell asleep, I needed that, I thought you said you were not drinking today." Jeff just sat there and never said a word and Danny said to him again "Hello, earth to Jeff." Jeff shook his head and said "Sorry mate, I was miles away, you would never believe what just happened matey." "What happened mate?" "I don't believe it myself, I was just sitting here and there it was mate." "There was what?" "And as I followed her there was even more of it." Danny now looking very confused says "More of what?" Jeff still in a state of shock said "You know." Danny looked at Jeff and said in a confused state "Right Jeff, what the hell are you talking about? for goodness sake I can't get a decent answer out of you, what are you talking about?" Jeff snapped out of it and said "Sorry mate I will explain, it was Lola she came in and went to Niel's room for a Jacuzzi and after Winnie left Lola came running through with just a towel in the front of her and not another thing, her ass was bare and her back then I said what's the Matter and she said "Give me a hand I have flooded Niel's bathroom." So I followed her into her room to get some towels and I was right behind her watching her little ass just feet away from me, it was fantastic, then we got to her room and she dropped her towel to find some dry ones to wipe up the water in Niel's room and there they were perfect…. A lovely matching pair, the most lovely pair of tit's you have ever seen and with a nice pair of nipples pointing up in the air, mate it was like being in heaven it really was, I just froze and stared at them it seemed like hours and she did not bat an eyelid, then we run back to Niel's room and she got down on her hands and knees on the floor and started to wipe up the water not worrying about covering herself, I thought I had died and gone to heaven." Danny had sat there silently listening to Jeff and concentrating on what he said and then said "Oh dear I was getting a little excited myself there then for a moment, pull yourself together Dan phew, got another can there mate? I need one or a cold shower." "I know, Imagine how I felt mate I just wanted to jump on her and give her a damn good seeing to." "Why didn't you wake me up? I needed some cheering up and that would have done it for me ha, ha, ha." Jeff's brain starting to wander again said "Oh mate, you should have seen it, it was gorgeous, here a can for you, I will never look at that girl the same again and she is leaving for the ground floor, can't we do something to keep her here?" "I am not going that far mate she is going ha, ha, but I know what you mean, awe well, never mind it's a messy job but somebody's got to do it ay?" "Well it was lovely while it lasted, I wish you had seen it mate." "Yes and me, she reminds me of my second wife a little she had a cracking body too but was a very beautiful girl too mind." Jeff looking shocked said "Second wife, how many times have you been married then Dan?" "Four times." "Four times, bloody hell." Danny smiling said "I thought I told you I had been married four times." "I can't remember you telling me that." "Oh yes, I liked wedding cake ha, ha, no it's just how it was, but I wish I had done things different especially with my second wife she was gorgeous she really was and she broke my heart when she left me, I have not ever got over her, ever, she was a bit of a model she had a lovely body very pretty face and lovely hair she was very special to me." "She sounds nice so what was her name?" "Christine David she was from a place called get this Trerhyngyll near Cowbridge in Wales." "My god that's a mouthful mate." "Yes it is, I never ever loved any woman as much as her and the drink made me lose her, my own fault and I regret it to this very day." "So where is she now?" "I heard she moved to Australia but her one sister still lives near there, her brothers were piss heads and I got in with them, that was fateful and that's how it is mate, she came to mind as you were describing Lola's body." "You sound regretful mate, did she mean that much to you then?" "Oh my god yes I took a long time to get over her I mean years, it took me and some more, maybe not I still miss her to this very day I will never get over her, such a stunning woman she really was and a lot of fun if you know what I mean, the other wives as soon as that ring was on the finger they changed, that's it the fun stops here and it seemed as if life had changed but not her she loved life and if her mother had not met an asshole we might have made it together, he was a bastard of a man he took an instant dislike to me and that was it he made it his goal to get rid of me and her brothers he was a bastard he was and he took her mother for her money he had nothing and her mother had plenty and he moved in with her and the family and split them up, he did not like any competition he wanted her all to himself and he got it ." "Really, you get people like that." "And he was one of them, he lied to her family about me and they believed him, he made my life a misery and in the end it told and we split up because of the pressure he put us under and when we got married it was the biggest snow storm on record and he said it was an omen and the marriage would not last but it would have if he had not interfered, he was a bastard and probably dead now ha, ha, and good riddance to him." "Have you ever thought of trying to get in touch with her." "Every day of my life since mate, but she has her own life now and probably happy and she would not want me again now I am blind, so best left alone but I would like to have met her again just to say sorry and to see how she made out as I will always think about her as the only woman in my life I married and really loved to the end of our marriage, do you know I hardly ate any food for 18 months after we split, honestly, but it's nice to remember and wonder what could have been. Ok are we going up the bar for a couple as I think Niel is up there and I fancy a pint now after all that excitement" "Yes why not, the hair of the dog ay?" Off they went.

Up the bar and yes Niel was sitting there and Jeff went up Immediately to tell him about the event with Lola and he when Jeff mentioned his bathroom was flooded shouted at Jeff "What? I hope she cleaned it up after her, I had better get back and see the mess." Jeff tried to cool him down "Calm down Niel, calm down it is perfect we cleaned it up Immediately and it is as dry as Danny's jokes matey, honestly, it is ok no problem or as you bloody Welsh say dim problem, ha, ha, it is cleaner now than it ever has been ask Danny, look here he is." Danny sits down and says "I can hear you Niel from the bar and yes it is ok matey don't panic about nothing, Lola has done a good job cleaning it up and Jeff the lucky bugger had a show all to himself, I would have given anything to have seen that." Niel says "So would have I mate, so would have I." Jeff bragging said "I will never forget this day as long as I live, she has got a cracking body, perfect boobs and an ass to die for and she keeps her bikini line perfect ha, ha, ha." Niel "Right change the subject now I am having a movement in my trousers now and that does not happen very often so stop it now." Danny laughs and said "That's better, I am now at last getting over that party last night, we enjoyed the rest of your whisky in Billy's room and cheered him up after all that trouble, he was fine but not my head." Niel "I felt sorry for that boy, he didn't deserve that and Lola and Carol have got a lot to answer for." Jeff said "Lola had nothing to do with it, she promised that tonight it was only Carol who had anything to do with it and she said she didn't know that neither, she does not want to get involved with it at all and I believe her. Has Carol been in yet tonight?" Niel "No but she will be in any minute now as she is on the premises I heard her down stairs earlier." Danny looking lost said "Well there is nothing we can do about it anyway and she don't give a shit about it I bet." Niel "No I suppose not and Billy had a good night anyway so let it rest is the best don't mention it to her, that will hurt her more and she will be forever wondering." Jeff "Yes, that will kill her that would." Niel "So Jeff where is Jo then mate?" Jeff replies "Awe, she had to go home again to take a job interview and she will be back tomorrow and I think her dad is bringing her back so I may not see her tomorrow either." Danny "Awe, never mind mate, tell me is this a serious thing with you 2?" Jeff looking bewildered says shrugging his shoulders "I don't know mate, it's funny how her mind works, she is all over me most of the time and as soon as her parents phone I am in the background, she switches off and on like a tap, I am buggered if I know, like this weekend her mother phones and she goes running and she is definitely her dads girl . So I don't know where I stand so I will play it by ear, but I am sure she is besotted by me." Niel "Of course she is, you can hear it when she speaks to you and she defends you up to the hilt and as regards her mother and father she will always put them first that's obvious mate, so give it time and you will have a relationship like John and Yoko here, ha, ha, ha." Danny looked at Niel seriously and says "Don't go there mate, I think she has got the message now and don't wish anything like that on Jeff." Niel " C'mon Danny you don't hate her at all and she is madly in love with you, you should be flattered mate be honest." Danny "I don't hate her and she is a very pretty woman and I am flattered and if she was not the way she is I might think of getting together with her if my wife ever dumps me but she is more trouble than a old car, forget it" Niel says "And talking about old cars Carol and Adrian just walked in, I heard their voices, be careful what you say." Carol comes in very sheepish and sits on the table next to the boys and Adrian went for the drinks and Jeff talks out loud "Oh my head what a cracking party it was last night." Danny replies "I wish I had not gone now if I thought the beer would have been flowing that fast, I would have given it a miss and that stripper, what a body, she accidentally sat on my hand and a nice ass it was too and I felt sorry for Billy he had his head stuffed between her tit's and she rode him for all she was worth and to finish off with all that beer and whisky till the early hours was incredible, I didn't get to bed until 3 this morning." Niel added "Well I didn't last long I went to bed at 2 this morning and enjoyed myself very much, a good night for the men, Jeff was plastered I bet." Jeff continued "I was indeed and the warden kept trying to tell us something but we could not hear him over the music and Danny threatening him ha, ha, ha." Carol could take no more and said "Yeh, yeh, yeh, I know it was stopped so give it a rest, I know this is for my benefit and it is not working and so leave it there." Danny said to her "What's that then Carol? I don't understand we never had the party stopped, someone tried to but failed, so what do you know about it then?" Carol sounding not very happy says "Nothing, nothing, why would I know anything?" Danny "Because you were the one who reported the lad that's why because you don't like his mates so you stopped the party or at least tried to didn't you?" Carol with a smirk on her face "Nothing to do with me and you can't prove otherwise." Adrian said "Dan you need to get your facts right before you accuse anyone mate." Danny said "So you were with her last night then Adrian were you? because you were not in the party and some of your friends were, so where were you then?" Adrian stutters and says "No I was in Cardiff with the football and what has that got to do with it?" Jeff said "Plenty as you don't know what your own girlfriend was up to mate , ha, ha, ha." Adrian's voice rose up and he said "What's it got to do with you Jeff? I warned you to keep your nose out of my business before." Jeff said "Yeah, yeah." Danny jumped in and said "So if you were not here how do you know she didn't report him then? so Carol why did you do it? I thought it was an awful thing to do and don't deny it I know It was you, I was told categorically it was you so why did you do it?" She looked nasty and said "Because they are all giving me so much trouble and laughing in my face, I was determined to stop it, them bastards deserve it after what they do to me, so stuff them and that cripple." There was a deadly silence and Adrian looked as if he did not know what to think and said "Right there you are then, she had enough and it's her decision and that's that ." Niel "And I will never forgive you for what you just said about that young lad, that's an awful thing to say." Carol "Well, they should not mess with me." She stood up and said "I am off you can stay if you like but I am off." She put her coat on and left and Adrian went with her. Jeff said "And good riddance to bad rubbish, he is a total wanker, he gets on my nerves." Niel "Well it didn't take much for her to admit it did it?" Danny "Well she couldn't really could she, it was all around the college before the party and look out here comes the Clamper man." He comes in and he gets a pint and sits down like a rag doll falling off the bed onto the floor and says "Jeff " oh, what's the Matter with you? don't tell us let us guess, I can see you have got your shoes on the wrong feet, is that it?" Clamper answers "No." Niel "You have forgot to buy me a drink because I left you some whisky last night?" Clamper answers "No." Danny "You forgot to drop off the cans outside my and Jeff's door you owe us?" "No." Jeff you want a stripper for your birthday if you can remember how old you are." Clamper looking confused says "Ha, ha, no." Niel "Let me see, you are so excited about Lola moving in down stairs near your room permanently I bet?" Clamper looked up and said "Yes and the real reason is that none of you told me she was moving down there." Danny "Clamper I promise you we never knew either mate or we could not have resisted telling you, it was just as much as a shock to us mate" Clamper "You must have known and never said because you know I would have objected and you just wanted her out of there." Jeff "Not true matey, I had seen the other side of her and we all wanted her to stay after that so forget it if she wants to come back we will agree as she let slip her guard tonight and I seen it all and she didn't give a damn so please send her back." Clamper "Did she? I still think my life is about to end with her there now I will have a hell of a life now she is there." Niel said "You haven't got to take any nonsense from anyone mate, there is so many ways to skin a rabbit so let us know and we will help you, you big baby you." Clamper "Don't call me that and I will get your cans back on Monday if that's ok?" Danny "Yes we were only joking mate, that will be ok." Clamper now feeling braver said "So if that's allright can I ask if one of you will get me a pint until I get my money on Monday? ha, ha, ha." Danny "You cheeky little git you, here is a twenty get us all a drink in for your cheek." He smiles and said "Ok and one for me ha, ha, ha." Danny "Of course one for you, I said that didn't i?"

It was a few days later and Danny was sitting on his favourite bench when he put his hand down and found a bracelet and took it to the student services and was told he had found a Jesus bracelet belonging to a girl he met earlier in the year who had now become a Christian along with another girl who he knew and the girl who had lost the bracelet was very upset at losing this and Danny was glad to help out and he never heard anything about this bracelet for a day or two until one day he was in the bar with Jeff, Jo, Niel, Tim and Mandy, they were sitting there and all of a sudden the girl and her other Christian friend turned up and proceeded to thank Danny Sarah said "Hello Danny, I don't expect you remember me do you?" Danny "I could never forget you I remember the first day you arrived and I went to show you the way out of the refectory and you were facing the wrong way and I had one of your breasts in my hand by accident and nice it was too, thank you." She giggled at this and introduced him to Tracy and said "She is my friend and you were the one who found my Jesus bangle, thank you." Danny "No problem I found it on the bench outside the main entrance and as regards Tracey I know her very well although I have not seen you for a while now, please sit down and have a drink." Sarah "Oh no we couldn't thank you, we don't drink much anymore since we found Jesus, sorry." Danny smiling says "I didn't know he was missing, I am sure he won't mind you having a drink with me, I will get them, what do you want? it's nice seeing you I haven't seen you both for ages, we must catch up." Tracey butted in and said "C'mon Sarah we can have a drink or two it won't hurt." Sarah agreed and they both had a seat and Danny got them a lager each and they chatted and were both full up with religion and Danny tried to sway them away from the subject "I remember when you started here Sarah you had a bad time with your boyfriend, he was in the Navy I believe and are you still with him?" She replied "Oh no, I am married to Jesus now and we are his brides." Danny "What both of you? he is a greedy bugger isn't he? And no other boyfriend." Tracey chirped up and said "I have a boyfriend he is here as a student it is William and we have been together for a while now and he is very nice." Danny said "And Sarah what about you are you looking for a boyfriend?" Sarah taken back said "Oh no thanks I am all for Jesus and no other boy will do." Danny said "A pretty girl like you and you are not looking for a boy, I find that hard to except, really." Tracey tries to explain on behalf of Sarah who was getting a little tongue tied "She is happy as she is at the moment, we love our god and it means a lot to us." Danny "And how old are you both now?" Sarah "I am 18 and Tracey is 19 why?" Danny "Well I feel I am a good friend to you both and find the young girls here very unsure about things and grab the first thing they can an say this is it and go head first into it, for example I once went into my dormitory and found a new starter in there and I had had a little to drink and she had a boy with her and I thought she was with him like a boyfriend and I said innocently is this your boyfriend? and she said to me "No it bloody isn't I am a lesbian." this girl was 17 and she was a lesbian and I proceeded to say so what part of lesbania are you from? and myself and the boy started to laugh, but she took it to heart and got nasty and said to me " let me explain I prefer women and like to get their knickers off and do things to them sexually." and I said shit I think I am a lesbian too and this was funny but she took offence to it and now she is with a boy these days so what happened to her lesbianism then? and I think there is nothing wrong with being a Jesus lover but lighten up until you are a lot older as you are a teenager only once so take advice from an old fella who has been around the block a few times." Next thing Jeff arrived with new drinks and there was a couple for the girls who said "No please we don't want any more." Jeff said "Sorry it's too late now enjoy." The girls settled back and Danny continued and said "I remember you saying to me one day in here Tracey, correct me if I am wrong if you are going to have an orgasm don't wear black knickers and you were a Christian then and I think you are a lovely girl whether you are a Christian or a atheist, Muslim, catholic, protestant or whatever it does not make any difference to me at all, I think there is too much seriousness in this college and soon we are having new lads here and if they think you are stuck up you will still be on your own in ten years' time. Do you see what I mean?" Sarah "I told you I am in love with Jesus and can't think of anything else." Danny "Then Sarah why are you smiling when you say this? ha, ha, ha." Sarah smiling said "Because you don't take me seriously that's why." Danny "I do, but your so young and can't see the real side of life and it is far from what you are believing at the moment girl ha, ha, ha." Jeff interrupts and says "Is that dodgy Welshman given you some trouble girls? ha, ha, he is a pain when he gets stuck into a subject, Danny leave them alone matey." Danny "I am not picking on them at all just getting them to lighten up, they are ignoring their friends and it's a small world here and we need them here with us very much more often than they come over, we miss them and we need some lovely young girls here." Tracey by now was getting a little high on the drink and said "Well that's very nice of you to say something that nice to us isn't it Sarah?" By now Sarah was also getting the taste and enjoying it and says "Yes it is and we love coming over here and seeing you all, so don't think we don't it's nice to talk as they say." Next thing over comes Tracie's boyfriend and says "Good grief, what are you doing over here? you haven't been here for ages and it's nice to see you both here." Danny said "There we are he is glad to see you both here and so are we all." William said "Can I sit here trace?" Tracey said "Of course you can William no problem and we are enjoying it here." Next thing a friend of Williams joins them and says "Hi Sarah, my name is Andy and I have seen you about, do you mind if I join you?" Sarah looking a little coy said "No problem it's a free country Andy, help yourself." Danny said "Sarah please would you talk to Jesus like that, he is just being a gentleman." Sarah "Danny, I hope you are not taking the Mickey out of my god ?" Danny looking serious says "Lighten up Sarah, I told you not to be so negative, I am not taking anything out of anybody I respect your wishes and so be nice to Andy he is just trying to be friendly that's all." Next thing William turns up with a couple of drinks for the girls and they settle down and start to enjoy themselves and start to tell jokes and then a very surprising thing happened. Sarah comes out with a joke that astounded everyone, it went like this she said "A sign in a pet shop window says, clitoris licking frog's for sale, £5. You can try before buying." There was a deadly silence there and she continued "A woman who had been divorced for a few years thought this would be so exciting and went into the shop to enquire and said to the man behind the counter "The sign in the window the frogs." the man behind the counter replies "Yes madam I have 2 left, do you want one?" The woman replied "Well, can I try one first? to see it really works please." The shopkeeper said "Of course madam, you will have to go into the shed out the back of the shop through that door and take your clothes off and sit there with your legs open and I will bring one out for you to try ok?" The woman agreed and went out the back to the shed and stripped and sat on a comfortable arm chair and waited. Well it was not long and the man came in and put the frog on an upturned log in front of the woman with her legs open wide and he positioned the frog in front of her open legs. She said "Good grief he is a big frog isn't he?" The man replied "Yes madam he is from the rain forest in the Amazon jungle, are you ready for this?" She replied "Oh yes I am ready allright." The man aimed the frog straight at her

271

groin and said "Right frog lick." The frog just looked straight ahead and did nothing , the man made an excuse and said "Sorry madam these frogs have tongues some short some long and so we have to find the right distance." So he pulled the frog back about six inches and said "Right frog lick, c'mon you can do it, lick." The woman by now was over excited an disappointed nothing had happened and he said once again to the woman "I must take hymn a little further back madam, it's trial and error." He pulled the frog back again and said the same and nothing happened until the frog was at least six foot away and he said to the frog again "Right frog lick, I think he will do it now madam in my experience six foot is about right every time, right frog lick, c'mon lick." The man then got on his hands and knees and said to the frog "Right, I will show you one more time." The place erupted and they all fell about laughing and they had never heard this joke before and coming from a Christian girl was what it seem more funnier than ever. After a while they all gathered their selves together and Danny said "Brilliant and I never expected that from you tonight." Sarah was smiling from ear to ear and Andy by now was very affectionate towards her and she was enjoying this. Niel said "Sarah, I didn't expect that from you, I am shocked girl ha, ha, ha." Sarah now being brave from the drink said "Well there you go Niel, I have shocked myself too and hope this don't come back an bite me on the bum." Jo who had arrived as she was telling the joke said to her "Sarah, I didn't think you were like that telling dirty jokes, ha, ha, and to this lot too." Danny said "What do you mean this lot? and it's about time you turned up Jeff, has been fretting and almost crying because you have not bothered with him." Jo hung her head and looked worried and said to Jeff "Awe did you Jeff? I am sorry and I won't do that again, I was with my dad and we only got back an hour ago, I am sorry I am. " Jeff "Jo don't listen to that daft Welshman, he is only winding you up, I am ok about it so don't listen to him." Jo still looking sad "Really, you are not just saying that are you? I feel awful now." Jeff feeling sorry for Jo said to her "Don't be silly, I am not upset at all, I am glad to see you mind I have missed you, have you had a good time?" Jo replies "Yes I have, it was a waste of time, the job interview though but never mind." Jeff snaps at Danny "You idiot you, she thought you were serious ha, ha, and you keep winding her up." Sarah said "Yes Danny, you are a wind up merchant, look at me I have been telling dirty jokes and my credibility has gone down the drain now, but it was a good night ha, ha, and Tracy is pissed, look at her ha, ha, ha." Danny "See it's nice now and again to let your hair down isn't it? my turn to tell a joke now " Jeff "Oh look out the dodgy Welshman is off with his jokes again." Danny continues "My mate had a dog and this dog was a randy dog and kept disappearing who chased all the bitches on the site and not coming home for a few days at a time and he was fed up with this and so I told him how to stop his dog doing this. I said before letting him out in the evening if there is a bitch on heat nearby, just get a gallon of petrol and tip it all over your dog before letting him out and this will make any bitch run away from him and he won't smell her so easy. So my mate did this and a few days later he was telling me what happened. He said I poured the petrol over rover and let him out as you said and I thought he would be back at suppertime but he did not appear, he was gone all the night and for the next 3 days and my younger son was sat by the window every night waiting for him and getting sad all the time and after 3 days and nights the dog was seen by my son coming down the road, my son got very excited and came running up to me and he said "Dad it's rover he is coming down the road and I think he has run out of petrol." I said to him "Why do you say that son." He replied "Because there is another dog towing him." Everybody burst out laughing except Jo they were all falling about and after they stopped there was a small silence broken by Jo saying "Well I'm glad you think it is funny, because I don't, that

poor dog, really, pouring petrol over him and his friend having to help him home, you should be ashamed of yourselves." Jeff looked at Danny and then at Jo and said "No Jo it's only a joke." Jo snapped " well Jeff I can't see anything funny about it and Danny's friend should be reported to the R S P C A for what he did and if you think it is funny then we don't have a future together." Jeff tried to explain "No Jo it didn't really happen, it was not real, tell her dodgy." Danny took up the plight and said "C'mon Jo you didn't think it really happened, it's just a funny story honestly, it really is, let me explain." Jo in nasty way said "I don't like things done nastily to animals and neither do I find it funny." Danny "No, no, let me explain, it's a joke please Jo it never really happened and Jeff is not to blame for my joke please Jo" But it was too late she was off and Jeff with her still trying to explain. Niel said to Danny "I think there is something wrong with that girl, she believed it to be true, ha, ha, she has an innocent way about her and once she has made her mind up there is no changing it, I hope Jeff can get through to her." Danny looking bemused said "Did I just hear what I heard, she would not have it, it was a joke god she is more weird than Sarah." Sarah laughed and said "Steady Dan I heard that ha, ha, I know you were only kidding but she took it to heart didn't she?" Danny "Yes she did, I was surprised but she Is a lovely girl, strange, but lovely ha, ha, I am off to bed everyone, see you." They all said goodnight to Danny. Tim said "Niel so hows things going mate? hows your bruises after the train ride?" Niel replies "Oh much better now, but I will never insist that Danny sit's by me ever again, forget that, I will rather shout but it was funny mind and how is Mandy? she is quiet tonight isn't she?" Mandy chirps up "Hi Niel, I am fine thank you, it has been a good night and so funny and I haven't had a chance to get a word in edgeways so far but I enjoyed it all, even Tim has not said much for a change." Tim "Hey girl, don't be cheeky ha, ha, I will send you home early mind wench to make my supper ha, ha." Mandy "Yeah, yeah." Niel "Oh don't you 2 start, I thought Jo was a bit over the top mind she didn't really understand it did she?" Mandy said in Jo's defence "Well you see Niel I have known Jo for a number of years now and she went blind through a brain tumour when she was in her late teens and until then she was a normal lovely chatty girl and it was a tragedy believe me I have heard the story, she is lucky to be here really and she is so innocent in her ways she is lovely." Niel "Really, how sad and she is still very young isn't she and a very good looking girl I have been told." Mandy replies "Yes she is very attractive indeed and I wish I had a figure like hers." Tim said "You have got a lovely body Mandy, what are you talking about? just because you are short that's all you are complaining about, to me you are just right thank you." Mandy with huge smile says "Awe thank you my hunk, awe." Niel "Right what are you after? Mandy watch him tonight he has something in mind." Mandy looking wishful "Oh Niel I hope your right ha, ha, ha." Tim "Right Mandy, drink up we are off ha, ha, ha." Niel "And me on my own and my lovely Ceri at home, never mind 2 more days and home again and looks like Sarah is being chatted up too, love is in the air tonight. Right I am off for my bed, see you all, bye."
It was later as Niel walked in the lounge and Danny and Winnie was sitting there having a chat and for once very sensibly. Niel said "Well hello WINNIE how are you? and you 2 are not fighting is this a truce?" Winnie said "What is this truce Danny?" Danny "It's when 2 people who have not been seeing eye to eye forgetting their differences and becoming friends again and forgetting the past." Winnie "Oh I see so are we truce again?" Danny " we have always been friends, just because we don't agree with each other it does not mean I don't like you, so yes we are friends and that's it." Niel "All's well that ends well and look out here is Jeff. Looks as if he has been given his marching orders, is that so Jeff?" Jeff says "Ha, ha, I have just spent half an hour explaining that joke to her, she takes some things

literally and she is still not happy but forgives me that's the most Important thing. Dan don't tell jokes about dogs again please save me from that please ha, ha, ha." Danny smiling says "Sorry mate, it was an innocent joke." Niel said "Mandy told me that Jo was a normal teenager and she had a brain tumour and lost her sight, that's awful isn't it?" Danny looking serious says "Never, so that's how she lost her sight then and such a pretty girl." Jeff "Yes it was a real tragedy it really was." Danny "I have never heard so many tragic stories until I came here and it is very sad to hear them, look at us there is a story for each of us and all sad and until this happened I never knew anything like this was around, I just went along living my life without a care." Niel "I know what you mean, I have heard so many tragic things since I went blind it really hurts." Danny replies "Back in 1977 I had an accident and went to work in the Jane Hodge Holiday Home for mentally and disabled children and teenagers and that opened my eyes very much and the tragedy I came across was incredible and many loving kids it really made me think more about my life it really did and by the way Jeff that's where I met my second wife Christine David." Jeff "Her name has come up a lot lately with you, did you know Niel she is still the love of his life and she was a cracker and he is still in love with her to this day." At that Winnie stood up and left the room. Niel said "Yes I have heard this story too, she must have been someone special after all these years and it made Winnie leave for her room so she must be special." Danny looking sad said "Yes she was beautiful and I do miss her but she is happy I hope, she deserves it, never mind ay I just wish I could do it again and we would still be together, I would never make that mistake again, right the drink is making me silly now so I am off to bed. But I will say this, I have never loved anyone as much as I loved Christine David and would welcome her back into my arms anytime without hesitation and I would make her life a lovely one and that's a fact." Niel and Jeff said Goodnight and carried on talking. Niel "God he has a hell of a past mind, he used to tell me about his second wife all the time, she was a lovely and perfect girl as regards what Danny thinks about her, it's a pity it all went wrong he certainly would be happy now if they were still together I think." "Yes I agree he seems besotted with her even after all this time, I was astonished when he poured his heart out about her a tragic love story ay, never mind he will find happiness again one day just like me." "I was concerned about Jo she thought Danny was serious telling that joke mind, she is so innocent and a lovely girl Jeff, you must look after her she is one in a million you know?" Jeff replies "Yes I know, she is a sweet girl and not a bad bone in her body only sometimes ha, ha, I am only joking mate, mind you she is hard work sometimes, trying to explain things to her she believes anything you tell her, so much innocence ay?" Niel "So you have got over Carol now then? she was once your only love except Geraldine, mind I was expecting you to have a harem of women and Geraldine is a little jealous mind because you don't make such a fuss anymore." "Well I can't keep up with them all, I must disappoint one or two of them, they all can't have me." "As Danny says mate it's a messy job but somebody's got to do it ha, ha, I am off see you tomorrow."
It's the next day and they were in the bar for 11's and Jeff and Jo was sitting there and Danny said to Jeff "Is it safe to sit here now? I don't want to start world war 3, truce Jo?" Jo laughs and says "Ha, ha, ha, yes Danny, it's fine your safe, as long as we don't get into talking about animals." Danny "Fair enough we shall not mention Jeff or Niel then ha, ha, so what's happening guys?" Jeff "Not much, I seen Carol and she ignored me earlier and when she heard you come in she left, so she has got the message." Danny "Hmmmm, so have I, I am in front of the ayatollah later she wants to see me about Billy's party I expect, so look out I may not be here much longer matey." Jeff said "I don't know if that is good or bad ha,

274

ha, ha." Danny "Well thanks mate I love you to." Jo nearly crying said "Jeff don't you say that I hope they don't throw him out it would be awful and you will be the first to miss him so please don't say that." Jeff "Awe, I am sorry I was not serious." Niel "It won't come to that, it's probably just a warning mate." Danny looking serious and worried said "Well I don't know mate, she is looking for an excuse to get rid of me, think about it, first there was Bobby McLean then Lola, then it was patsy and now this, I don't fancy my chances mate they must be very slim." Jeff said "Your not serious? they wouldn't dare would they?" Niel said "Blinking heck I forgot all about those things, your right I don't fancy your chances now either, sorry mate." Jo "They won't send you home, I bet they will give you a row that's all." Danny said " Well we will see." Next thing Billy hobbled over on his sticks and says "Hi Dan, I am sorry you are in the shit because of me, I have just come out from there and I believe your next, she is not in a good mood mind I had a warning but I seen the warden you threatened go in just after me, good luck man." Danny replied to Billy "Don't worry about It , I knew what I was doing, even if I was sober it would have happened so it's nothing for you to worry about never mind what happens." Billy shook Danny's hand and said "They won't get rid of you because most of the students here will strike, you are well liked here, but not by the bullies mind ha, ha, ha." Niel "To right Dan, you'll be allright, good luck"

Danny goes off to his destiny and was called into Anthea's office almost Immediately and sat down and Anthea let out a loud sigh and said "You again, you spend more time in here than me, so what have you been up to now then mate?" Danny said "Well I have no defence at all, but I found it very unfair to spoil that teenagers 18th birthday, it was awful, he was so upset you should have seen him, all because of one person." Anthea looking at Danny said "It still doesn't give you the right to threaten the warden, that my friend was totally out of order and you know it so are you going to apologise? or are you going home today." Danny looking shocked said "So what do you mean by that then?" "Exactly what I say, I will send you home if you refuse to apologise and that's final. I don't care whose fault it was and that's final." Danny smiled and said "Well if that is how it is then …" Anthea "Then what, I am not messing at all here and I am very busy so c'mon tell me I am not in the mood for any stupidity today." Danny thought for a minute and said "Ok I will apologise as soon as I see him no problem" Anthea sternly says "Right sign this piece of paper, this is a written warning any more trouble from you and your out of here." Danny signed it and was about to say something and Anthea jumped in and said "Thank you , that's all, good morning." Danny looked at her and left sighing because he was staying.

It was the next day and Niel and Danny was off home for the weekend on the train and they were sitting opposite each other on a table seat and talking and Niel said "God, you were lucky mind she didn't expel you from the college." "I know I was not worried mind." Niel sarcastically said "Yeah, yeah, I could tell you were worried mate so don't deny it and Jo was very concerned to wasn't she? but she is a person who worries about animals so you are not in the top category are you? how is your brother now? Lyndon I mean?" "I don't know he has gone quiet lately and hopefully he has knocked the beer on the head a bit, I hope so. I will find out when I get home, I will ring him and see what the crack is, so how are we getting home? is Ceri picking us up at the station?" "Yes, my little darling will be there waiting for me, she always is. She is as good as gold you know." "Yes I know, she spoils you she does, you have got a good one there mate." "Yes I know I have and even Abby knows we are going home and she loves Ceri and the boys too, she seems to know , don't you girl?" Abby's ears pricked up and she whined a little. Niel continues "See you can tell." Danny "I should give you some petrol money for her taking me out of the way like this."

"Don't be silly Dan it's only 2 miles out of the way and a cup of tea will go down a treat and I can see that lovely Angie." "You can have her mate, take her with you." "No I can't handle the one I got thanks." The boys arrive at Bridgend station and as always Niel would stand by the doors after Danny had got off and Ceri would grab the large bag off Niel before he got off and he would then get off with the large guide dog Abby. This was the routine as always, but this didn't go to plan this time. The train was approaching the train station in Bridgend and the lads got up and stood by the doors and they waited for the double doors to open from the centre and slide each side until they were fully open, then Danny got off but Ceri was still coming down the platform and for some reason she was a little late, well picture Niel standing centre of the doors still in the train waiting for Ceri to grab the bag and the dog standing by his side waiting for him to pass the bag and then let the dog off. Well the doors all of a sudden shut with Niel still standing there and the doors closed either side of him and they closed on his neck either side, well it was like a huge karate chop his head was outside the train and the rest of him was still inside the train, well the doors jammed his head with a thud he let out a cry "Arrrrrrgggggghhhhh." and his eyes popped out of their sockets and there they were bouncing down the station platform like 2 ping pong balls. Ceri was trying to catch them but they were bouncing different ways it looked so funny then the platform attendant was helping her to try and catch them and by now Abby scampered as it frightened her. So there was Niel steam coming out of his ears and everyone else trying to retrieve his eyes and Ceri was laughing and so was Danny and a station steward, it was the funniest thing they had ever seen, then the doors opened up and Niel was in a rage and coughing and spluttering and said "What the bloody hell…. I nearly lost my head then, what a set of idiots, I haven't got off the train yet and the dog has gone somewhere too." The station master helped Niel off between fits of laughter and said "Ha, ha, ha, are you ok Niel? Ha, ha, ha, I am sorry it was the funniest thing I have ever seen ha, ha, and I will go and find your dog, she just ha, ha, ran off when you screamed ha, ha, sorry , ha, ha, sorry I will be back." Danny still laughing said "Ha, ha, are you allright mate? I am sorry it was so funny ha, ha, I didn't see what happened but by the sound I just knew I heard your eyes bouncing and the station master scream to open the doors ." Ceri was standing back laughing her head off and couldn't speak to Niel for a while, next thing the station master returned and he had Abby with him and said "Allright now Niel, ha, ha, ha, here is your dog, ha, ha, I can't help it sorry mate, she was at the very end of the train under a table hiding, she took some coaxing out she was so frightened." By now Niel had calmed down a bit and could see the funny side of it and said "Abby here girl are you allright, yes you are I can tell, ha, ha, all have a laugh at my expense ha, ha, so where is that bloody wife of mine to. Ha, ha,." At that they all started laughing again and Ceri couldn't speak for laughing then she composed herself and said "Sorry Niel I was chasing your eyes around the platform they don't half bounce don't they? ha, ha, ha, ha, sorry love but it was so funny ha, ha, ha." Niel said "Right ok so give me my eyes if they are clean so as I can pop them back in so I can go home ha, ha, ha." Ceri "You can't put them back in they are covered in grit, I can't wash them here I will have to use the solution at home." Niel said "Oh that's great so how am I going to get home now without them?" At that they all started laughing again and the station master said "Is that because you can't see where you are going Niel?" Niel "Well of course what else did you think I meant ? They all laughed again, well they all got in the car and still laughing when they arrived in Danny's house and there to meet him was Josh and he run up to Danny and gave him a huge hug and they went in for a cuppa. Josh said "Oh no, he has not got his eyes in again, I am going to tell my friend Josh Kendall ha, ha,ha." He ran to find his friend and then there was a huge sound of laughter as Niel finished telling Angie about the incident in the train station and he sipped his tea and said to Angie "Well you nearly had Danny home permanently this week, he threatened the warden and nearly got is red card and you could do with him home to give you a hand with the building work going on here, I know he is a good cleaner, ay mate." Angie looked worried and said "You haven't have you? got expelled I mean." Danny said "There we are then Niel, see what I mean? she is panicking in case I am home here permanently, she thinks I am never coming home aren't you?" Angie snarls "No I'm not, I am just asking that's all." Danny "Niel just heard you with his own ears didn't you Niel?" Niel sips his tea and said "Sorry mate, don't involve me in your marital arguments I am staying out of it and so is Ceri." Danny "In other words you did but I understand mate, I wish you would tell me what's happening with you? what is your intentions girl?" Angie "Oh Dan, don't keep on now's not the time for this ok? just leave it there." Niel finished off his tea and said "Sorry nice tea but we are off, I will see you on the train on Sunday Dan, bye Angie." Angie and Danny said goodbye and continued their conversation Danny went first "I am amazed you were worrying about me being home permanently, don't you want me back here or what?" Angie "Don't be silly Dan, you make a big thing out of everything, I was not serious ok and besides you have to go and sort out your brother again he is back on the drink and Mel has been over and is not happy with Lyndon. So give Mel a ring." "Ok I will now if it's not one thing it's another, I thought he was Improving now." Danny goes and rings Mel he answers the phone and Danny says "Hi Mel, so what's happening mate with Lyndon?" Mel replies "Oh Dan, he is back on it again and he is worse now than ever, I have been over to see Debbie and she don't want to know, Lyndon has been over there threatening her and making a nuisance of himself and he is now worse than ever and I don't know what to do, he keeps on about xmas and Wendy having xmas back home with him and I am worried now he is just laying on the settee and he is ill with it Dan, I am not able to get down this weekend but will be there on Tuesday next so pop over and see him and see if you can get him to sort himself out please." "I will Mel, I am going to see the doctor and get him sectioned if that's what it takes, I can't see no other way around it and I will have to do it now, it's getting close to xmas and they will all be on holiday soon and we will never get anything done otherwise." Mel sounding concerned said "Lyndon will go mad Dan, do you think that is necessary?" "What else can we try now? we have tried everything we can think of and if Lyndon falls out with me about this all well and good as long as I can get some help for him, I don't care, I want him to get better and if that's the only way then that's how it's going to be." "Yes I see what you mean, so how are you going to do it then?" Danny replies "I will not go back until Monday, I will go and see the doctor and make arrangements to do it and let you know the outcome ok?" "Yes ok mate, ring me on Monday and let me know how it is going." "Allright Mel I will speak to you then, bye." Danny puts the phone down and says to Angie "Will you take me over there later please? and ask Susan to have Josh for a while please, I must sort him out this can't go on any longer." Angie "Yes of course I will."

CHAPTER 12
THE HARDEST TIME OF ALL

It was a little later and Angie and Danny went across to see Lyndon. They knocked the door and Lyndon said from behind the door "Hello who is it?" Danny replies "It's me Danny, let me in and don't give me any crap, I need to see you now." Lyndon opened the door and let him in and he looked like a character off a desert island, a huge beard growing wild and he looked as if he was dying and his skin was yellow, he said "Yes what do you want now ?" Danny "God your slurring and I can smell the booze from here, why are you drinking again Lyn?" Lyndon replies "I don't know why I just am and if you are going to lecture me you can go, just leave me alone please." "Don't be like that Lyn I am your brother, I am concerned about you, this is breaking my heart, let me sort things out for you and you can go to a place that will help you." Lyndon snapped at Danny "Where? there is nowhere so don't tell me and alcoholics anonymous are useless as you bloody know, just leave me alone I will be allright." "But you won't Lyn and you know it, Mel and I are having a nervous breakdown over this and we don't know what to do, the system is useless and we know it." Angie said "Lyndon this is not doing anybody any good at all, you must try and help yourself and you know it, I will make you something to eat if you like." Lyndon answered "I have eaten and don't want nothing, I am going to have a sleep now for a while if you don't mind?" Danny in frustration says "Yes ok have it your own way mate I will be back tomorrow ok? to see you." Lyndon snaps at Danny "Ay, whatever, bye." Danny with sad answer "Oh don't be like that mate, we are only trying to help, I will see you in the morning." They leave and Danny was close to tears and said "I am worried now, he is in a state and he won't except help will he?" Angie "No he won't, Mel has tried and I have, he is like he has a death wish." "Oh great, that's all I need to hear, thanks." "Well if I told you a lie that would be wrong." "Yes I am sorry, I need to hear what you are thinking, no good hiding behind the truth." "I think only a serious word from Mel will help as Mel is a good listener, you lose your head to easy, let him have a word on Tuesday Dan, he will get further with him as there is something seriously wrong and he is not telling us." Danny says "Do you think so? he seemed as if he had had enough and he is not telling me so you might be right, I will go over with him in the morning and sit down and have a cuppa with him and try and find out what is wrong and if you go up the shop or home and come back up for me in an hour, what do you think?" "You can try but I think he is bottling it all up and that is what is making him drink."

It was the next morning and Danny was sitting with Lyndon on their own sipping a cup of tea and Danny said "She makes a lovely cup of tea don't she? fair do's, so tell me Lyn what is happening with you and Debbie then?" "Absolutely nothing, she is like a distant memory to me, she hates me and is making my daughter hate me, she is making out I am mad and she has gone to a solicitor already, she can't wait to divorce me and that's the truth. She has taken stuff from here and I am fed up and don't care anymore." "So what has she taken then?" "Everything of any value and left me with the rubbish, she also has left me in debt up to my ears. Did Mel tell you?" "No Mel has not said a word, well the envelopes keep coming she has got a load of letters from mail order clubs, loans from everywhere and just bills and more bills and I have been hiding them everywhere around the house and she don't give a damn, but it's got to me, now she is threatening to take my daughter away, she has told me this, she said I will never see my daughter again and that's a promise and she is seeing another man I have been told." Lyndon starts to cry uncontrollably and Danny comforts him and in a silent voice said to him "How do you know this Lyn?" Wiping the tears away he said "My friends have been telling me as there was a hell of an argument with her and her mother in the car park of the club and her mother was pleading with her not to go down the bottom site and not see this other man, it didn't take her long did it?" "Your joking, do you know who he is?" "Yes it's Jimmy Millwood." "Your kidding that weird wanker, surely not he is a whimp and his first wife left him because he was a pervert, instead of having sex with her he would rather masturbate while looking at her, she has caught him more than once doing it while she is asleep and that's why she divorced him, he is a total wanker, what do she see in him? I can't see her getting any better mind and if that is so Lyn she is not worth it anyway, I know that does not help mate but I never thought she was good enough for you, she is a money grabbing witch and her mother has seen off a few men too mind but at least she tried to stop Debbie." "I can't see anything for me in the future Dan, I have had her screaming at me with no thought for my feelings at all, it's as if she wants me to finish myself off, it really seems like it and I don't think she will ever let me see my daughter again, she said it to me in such a nasty way it is killing me." Danny almost crying for his brother says "Look Lynd Wendy will make her own mind up about you I am sure of that, she knows how much of a good father you are and she knows how much she loves you." Lyndon pulls out a letter from her solicitor and said while in tears "Read this." Danny says "I am blind Lynn as you know so you will have to read it please." Lyndon read it to Danny and it said that Lyndon was not a fit father and he used to threaten their daughter Wendy in her cot while she was a baby and was a bad father and this is one of the reasons she wanted a divorce and he had hit Debbie over the years. Danny could not believe his ears and said "The bloody liar, she is a bitch isn't she? I will give her a piece of my mind later." Lyndon said still crying "It's not true Dan, why is she doing this to me? I have never laid a finger on any of them, she is lying and I don't know why." Danny said in a temper "I know bloody why, she wants people to think you are the one in the wrong and not her, so she is making up stories to make people think you are a right bastard and everyone will think the same but one day Lyn I promise you the truth will come out and I need you with me as proof. So please snap out of it please, for me, we know the truth don't we?" "This is all destroying me and it never stops, she keeps on threatening me and talking about me that are lies, why? why? why? Because I don't know." He put his head in his hands and cried uncontrollably and Danny joined in feeling so sad, this woman and her new man had torn his heart out and left him a total wreck, he was such a gentle quiet man this was so hard to understand and Danny was totally shocked at what had gone on and felt helpless. Danny snaps "If I had my eyesight this would not be happening as he would shit himself and know I would kick his head in and he would have to go into hiding, the wanker, he is a shit he really is and your so called friend Adrian is just as bad, he is not a real friend, wait until I get on the phone I will give them what for." "No Dan you mustn't it will only make things worse it will, please promise me you will not do anything, please? and don't tell anyone about her and Jimmy Millwood as that man is an embarrassment." Danny says "Ok mate I will not do anything for now but I will never forget it, this is making my blood boil." Next thing in walks Angie and she sat there silent while they both pulled themselves together and Danny said to her "Read this." He passed her the letter for her to read, she read it and said "The cow, the lying cow, this is awful she is not going to get away with this surely?" Danny "Too bloody right she isn't after the xmas holidays Lyn when you are feeling better we will go down and see a solicitor, when you are better and sort this out ok?" Lyndon "To right we will, she is lying and she is not getting away with it." Angie said "And you won't have any problems as all you have to do is tell the truth and they will see straight away who is lying and believe me anyone who knows you here in Bettws will know this is all a load of lies, so don't worry about a thing." Danny "Anyone who knows you Lynd will know this is a load of crap." They had another cup of tea and later Danny was on the phone to Mel and told him about the letter and Mel's response was "Good grief, she didn't say that, that's not Lyndon he would never do anything like that, he is so gentle it's not him she is describing is it? no way, he must be devastated Dan?" "That's an understatement Mel, he is a mess it is destroying him and she is threatening him, he will never see Wendy again ever. He is in a terrible mess over there, she is being so cruel to him only since he started seeing that man and this is what they are trying to do, ruin him and try and make him look bad in front of everyone who knows him." "Well we will fight back as soon as he is fit to see a solicitor and the truth will come out, I will be down on Tuesday and stay with him for a while." "Ok and I will be back down on Friday if I can get him sectioned for his own good, he is drinking as if there is no future, it's urgent now Mel, I will go down the doctors first thing tomorrow and organise this." "Ok Dan I will speak to you on Tuesday on the mobile ok?" Danny rang off and said to Angie "So what do you think of all this with Debbie?" "Well she is lying through her teeth as we both know but she will maybe convince many of her friends he is the one in the wrong and as for her with Jimmy that's a joke it really is but don't worry the truth will come out soon enough, she is a liar anyway so people will see that, we need to concentrate on Lyndon now and get him better first."

It was the next morning and Danny went into the doctors room and lo and behold the new doctor was like a young girl just after her 11 plus and Danny was wondering if she was experienced enough but said "Hello doctor, I need to get some help for my brother Lyndon Duckfield, he has a drink problem and I want to get him sectioned for his own good." The doctor looks at Lyndon's record and says "Why do you want to do this? is he hurting himself or others?" "No, but he soon will be, he is getting worse and he will kill himself soon I know it, he is in a bad way." She looked at Danny as if to say so what do I do now Danny said "Is there a older doctor here, I would prefer to see an older one." "I beg your pardon?" "This is about some bodies life not something you can mess with and you don't seem to understand the problem, I bet you have never even met my brother have you?" She replied "As a Matter of fact I have seen him once and treated him, I will make some phone calls a minute I will be back now." "I am back home on Friday next if you can sort it out for then please, thank you." Angie said to Danny "God you have no patience have you? she might be young but she will do her best Dan." "Well I am making bloody sure she realises it as I think this is urgent and don't want any mistakes ok?" Next thing she comes back and said "Ok this will happen 11o'clock on Friday and you must get his care worker there at that time and I will attend also." Danny looking shocked says "Right thank you, I hope I didn't offend you? but this is a real urgent situation and I don't want any mistakes, thank you doctor." Danny and Angie left and went to the train station and told Mel and Angie not to say anything to Lyndon at all, just let it happen and Mel decided not to attend this meeting and a few hours later Danny was back in the college sitting in the lounge around dinner time having a cup of tea and in walks Jeff "Hello dodgy where have you been? I thought you would be back yesterday?" Danny replies "Yes I have had trouble with my brother again, things are worst now, worse than ever, he has had a letter off his wife's solicitor accusing him of hitting the baby in her cot when she was young and hitting his wife also and we know why she has done this as she has taken up with another man and she wants people to think this because they will think it is his fault all of this problem and that is why she took up with another man, so things were tense there this weekend it really was and I got my hands tied, I cannot do anything about it as she will make his life even worse. She has been screaming in his face that he will never see Wendy hiss daughter again as long as he lives and he is devastated, Jeff he is a gentle man and so quiet he would not harm a fly, he wouldn't, honestly mate." "Hey calm down Dan I believe you I do, she sounds like an animal, she is playing mind games with him, I have seen this before it's to throw the blame on to him and it's cruel." "Too right it is, he is breaking his heart. I think if the drink don't get him the heart attack will as he will break his heart, he is hurting so much." Danny puts his head in his hands and Jeff comforts him and says "C'mon Dan you are the strong one pick yourself up for his sake, he needs you so don't you crack up or he won't stand a chance mate, c'mon matey it will work out I know you she will not get the better of him as long as you have got a breath in your body, c'mon matey." Danny pulls himself together and says "If I had my eyesight this would not be happening, he would run a mile he is such a shit house, a slimy bastard, he really is he would never have gone out with her if I could 'see no problem, but some way I will have the last laugh, especially when it goes to court and they realise the lies she is telling them." "Well there you go the truth will shine through and she has not got a thing to back it up so she will be laughed out of court, anyway mate I am free tonight if you want me as Jo is going out with her friend tonight and I am at a loose end." "Awe have I got to go drinking again? bloody hell it's a nightmare this place." Jeff "It's a messy job mate but well you know the rest." "Yes it will help me get over the weekend mate and has Lola gone yet? and if so who is having her room?" "Well she has gone and she was allowed to do this so as the prince of Bahrain can have her old room, they have been doing work in there all weekend and they are still doing something there." Danny says "Wen is he coming then?" "He is arriving on Friday so look out we will be surrounded by his security men." "We had better make ourselves known to them Immediately, but there again I am off to Bridgend Thursday night as there is a meeting with some people at my brother's house on Friday morning and he don't know about it but I will be back on Sunday, he is Important and I must see this through, so you and Jo can have some fun." "Have you seen Niel has he come back allright? I told him I would meet him on the train, I bet he was wondering where I was?" "Yes he said he was looking for you on the train, but he thought it was something wrong with your brother." "And did he tell you about his eyes bouncing on the platform in Bridgend train station?" "Ha, ha, he did and we all laughed our heads off and he said they were like ping pong balls bouncing around and Ceri his wife had a job catching them ha, ha, I bet it was so funny being there ha, ha, ha." "Oh, yes it was I realised what had happened straight away I did not need to see it at all he had his hair off at first mind but then he seen the funny side of it and Abby ran to the end of the train inside and the station master had to go and find her ha, ha, it was so funny." "He is an idiot sometimes but great fun." "Awe yes, he makes me laugh all the time, he is so funny and down to earth he don't know sometimes he is so funny." "Carol has been at it again she won't leave it alone about Billy's party and is still having a go at the lads down stairs." "She should be careful she don't go too far as they will sort her out." "It's already been done and that excuse of a boyfriend has not done a thing about it." "Really, so what happened then?" "She was standing outside apparently on Saturday night all dressed up and standing outside the main entrance here with Lola and one of the lads upstairs stuck his head out of the window and seen Carol and Lola standing there waiting and he dragged up a huge gob full of phlegm and gobbed it at her and splat it hit her smack centre on the head, it was like a person smacking you across the head that's what it sounded like, she then started crying and stamping her foot on the floor and crying uncontrollably and had to get into Lola's shower to wash it off and ended up not going out at all and of course Simon was on as warden and tried to get to the bottom of it and ended up having the police out for assault as Simon grabbed one of the lads arms he accused and he fell down, so it is ongoing and Carol is not a happy bunny at all. So watch this page ." Danny then said "Well she asked for that, I knew something was going to happen, they will not forget what she done, well I missed it again damn, It always kicks off when I am at home." "Talking about home how did it go with your wife then?" "Oh, she kicked off when she thought I had been kicked out of the college and she smacked of panic, she is waiting to get a divorce mate." "It has not been your week has it mate?" "No, it hasn't mate, so it is up the bar tonight then, I will have to wait to give my big brother a call and see how my little brother is first, so it will be about 8 30 mate ok?" Jeff replies "Yes fine mate, are you going over for tea later or what?" "No I am knackered, I didn't sleep much last night so I am going to bed for a couple of hours." "I see, I thought it was not a good weekend you lying dog you." "Huh, huh, no chance of that mate I got more chance of becoming pope than getting a bit of nookie ha, ha." "Well I am off as I am meeting Jo for a late dinner as she is out with her mates later and I am stuck with an old codja or 2 tonight, see you later." Jeff goes off and Danny sat there thinking a long time about Lyndon and looked so sad and was so worried about everything.

Later on in the bar was Danny, Jeff, Niel, Tim, and Mandy sitting there having a nice pint and discussing Danny's brother and Tim continued "I feel for you Dan I really do, it is a cruel world we live in and I hope justice hit's that bloody wife of his and that bastard who is with her and your brother will see through her in the end. He sounds too nice for her anyway it's a pity he ever met her." Niel said "Yes I agree, I hope she gets pregnant and gives birth to a couple of hedgehogs, the bitch as what she is and as for him Danny should give him a good shagging with a four by two rough timber, this world is so unfair it really is. I knew there was something wrong when you were not on the train." Jeff trying to change the subject says "I told him about Carol and someone spitting on her head that was so funny but not for her." Next thing Danny's phone rang and it was Mel his brother, he answered it "Hello....Mel what's the Matter? never, your joking? when did you find that? well we know who sent that don't we? yes, it might be the both of them and has Lyndon read it? oh shit, is he allright? let me get my hands on them I would kill the both of them, how could anyone be so cruel and no one seen nothing I bet? it must have been there all day then, oh shit shall I come home? I can't concentrate anyway, are you sure? I can get back there tomorrow morning early if you like, ok I will phone you first thing and try to get him to settle down and not think about it, I will worry all night now, ok I will speak to you in the morning, bye." Danny turned his phone off and it was deadly silent on the table and Danny put his head in his hands and was visibly mad. Niel said "Is everything allright Dan?" Danny replies "Your not going to believe me when I tell you this, someone has put a note through my brothers door and the words and letters on the note has been cut out of a newspaper to hide their writing and it says, I am glad I fucked your marriage up and no signature, no prises for guessing who that was off, I think it might have been his wife and her new man, sorry he is no man to do something like that is he? well my brother found it sticking out of his letter box and is now so upset he is smashed out of his head and crying his eyes out and my other brother is panicking again now and staying the night with him. I will phone and go home in the morning if he does not Improve." Tim "What a pair of bastards, they must be cowards with it, I hope they rot in hell, I am so sorry Dan, I feel for you and your brothers." Jeff "They are no better than Hitler, how can they live with themselves?" Mandy looks at Danny and says "Are you ok Danny?" Danny answers quietly "Yes thank you Mandy, I will be allright, but you know what is hurting me the most is that I can't do anything about it, because I have lost my eyesight, that hurts me more than anything and this is killing my little brother." Niel says "Yes Dan, but as you have said if you had your eyesight it would not be happening would it? and that so called best friend married to her sister is not a man at all, I expect he is worried about not getting his nookie if he rocks the boat, so he is no friend at all, he is just a waster and after all your brother done for his mother and father as you told me I bet his mother and father are turning in their grave and are disgusted with him, he can rot in hell too." Danny "Awe well, I must be strong and help him as much as I can and get the message over to everyone that these are lies their saying about my brother but I think they will already know." Mandy "That's right Danny they will realise he was not to blame in time so don't you make yourself ill worrying about them, stay strong for your brother." Danny "I really wish I could get my hands on them just for a few minutes I really do, but they are cowards and that's obvious by their actions, I could always pay someone to sort them out and if there is any more I will, mark my words, I'll have the bastards, I will." Jeff "Oh Dan, that will only make you like them and that's not you, they will have no luck ever after doing that to him." Danny "I wonder if she has got anything to do with it? the note I mean, I wonder if she knows her new boyfriend is sending her husband who is ill these notes and what would she say If she knew, I don't suppose she would believe me as she is besotted by him, I will bide my time I will." Niel "Jeff get me a pint mate will you please? and get a double whisky for Dan please." Jeff replies "Sure mate no problem, I will get it now." He goes off and for a moment Danny sat there silent and then said "Right let's snap out of it, my brother if he was here now would tell me to pull myself together and enjoy life as it is not long enough and to treat every day like it's your last one on this earth because one day you will be right ha, ha, he is a lad ha, ha." Tim "That's the spirit Dan, keep your pecker up, he would not like you worrying all the time, he sounds too nice for that. So I heard about the Prince arriving at Dowdell on Friday, this should be fun, he has got 2 not 1 but 2 servants and their from the Philippines no less and they bath him and do everything for him Oooohh, Oooohh." Niel "I wonder how much of a bath they will give him, they will have to wash the royal penis and make sure they have him prim and proper for his lectures, I wonder what he is like and if he is brash or stern, I see the lights are being switched on before xmas on the Dowdell walls ha,, ha, do you remember last xmas? me and that bloody Clamper in town, it was a disaster but funny and I got some money for it, a consolation for our trouble ha, ha, ha." Danny laughing says "Yes that was funny and it made you ill Niel in the end didn't it? but so funny, one of the best xmas's I have ever had and Jeff with that mugger that was not so funny." Jeff handing Danny a whisky said "I just hope he has retired now he frightened the shit out of me, seeing Niel dressed up afterwards was not so frightening, we have had some fun here mind and it's going on for 2 years now, god it's gone quick hasn't it?" Tim "Yes it has mind and Mandy has been here a lot longer, she was waiting for me to come that is why." Danny "Yes she said something about that to me also." Tim "I don't understand?" Danny "About you a long time coming ha, ha." Tim smiling replies "Oh yes I see, very good Daniel ha, ha, well any good jokes matey?" Danny "I am not in the mood for any jokes really but here's one . The miracle of toilet paper, fresh from her shower, she stands in front of the mirror totally naked complaining to her husband that her breasts are too small. Instead of characteristically telling her it's not so, he uncharacteristically comes up with a suggestion. Rub a piece of toilet paper between your breasts, then every day take a piece of toilet paper and rub it between them for a few seconds." Willing to try anything, she fetches a piece of toilet paper and stands in front of the mirror rubbing it between her breasts. "How long will this take?" she asked." They will grow larger over a period of years." Her husband replies. she stopped and asked her husband "Do you really think rubbing a piece of toilet paper between my breasts every day will make my breasts larger over the years?" Without missing a beat he says "Worked for your arse didn't it?" He's still alive and with a great deal of therapy, he may even walk again, although he will probably continue to take his meals through a straw." They all laughed and it broke the ice that night as it had been a real bad weekend for Danny. But things were going to Improve somewhat just for a change.

He called his brother Mel just after dinner the next day and he asked how Lyndon was and got a shock "Well Dan he is up and about and is full of himself, he seems to have pulled himself together after that note he got, he was so upset last night and I felt so sorry for him but he has decided he is not going to let that waster beat him, he has had a shower a shave and has had some breakfast and he never had a drink later on after the initial shock. He is like a new man." Danny looking surprised says "Oh that's great news Mel but what do you think about that meeting I have arranged for Friday? I think I had better cancel it or I will look a fool otherwise." Mel answered "Well they will not section him as he is now, they would laugh at you." "I am glad, I will ring them as soon as I have finished talking to you, so have you seen any of the enemy at all?" "No and I don't want to either, I will only go off on one if I do so they are better off keeping away from here, I am hoping he is going to pull through now and he don't need her he is better off without her and as regards Wendy we can sort that out with a solicitor. I have spoken to him about a solicitor and he said he is going to leave it until mid-January as he don't fancy his chances at the moment the way he is." "Yes but Mel she has drove him to this and that idiot she she is living with, he is responsible too so keep that note as evidence, they will connect him and maybe her to that note one way or the other. She is not getting away with this I will pay his solicitors fees if I have to, he is the victim in this case as I have plenty of witnesses that she was arguing with her mother outside the club when she was carrying on with that nerd and the debt there is all in her name and the fact she took all the stuff from there and things from mam like the watch that you and Marice bought her, you witnessed her wearing it and the dolphin broach I seen her mother wearing and all the stuff that went missing from the house she has had it all, the cow." "Yes your right, I know, but Lyndon needs to settle down and sort himself out first and if they leave him alone he will be ok I am sure, I will be back and forth for a day or two to make sure he is ok, when will you be home again?" "Well I have a fortnight off and I am home until the first week of January, so I can keep an eye on him most of that time." "Right we will keep an eye on him but don't expect miracles mind, he has got a long way to go, so easy, easy, catch a monkey no hurry." "Yes I realise that Mel and I will take it easy with him." "I am helping him with tidying up the house and it's going ok and I am going to ask Angie to pop over from time to time and report on his progress and I will pop down as often as I can. So don't worry now just sort out yourself now ok?" "Right, will you tell him I was asking about him and I will see him over the xmas period ok? see you Mel." Danny put the phone down and a huge smile came over his face and he looked so pleased indeed.

Early evening and in the lounge was Jeff and Jo, Niel and Winnie and they were watching TV and chatting. Jeff said to Danny "How's your brother today Dan?" Danny replies "Good news he has had a shower a shave and is upbeat as he said to my other brother he is not taking that note lying down and he is going to fight it, he is in good humour and him and Mel have been tidying up his house, so I am happy now." Niel "That's great Dan, there's hope for him then at last, light at the end of the tunnel, brilliant." Jo says "Awe, that's good isn't it? Jeff told me about it, it's a shame and his wife is not very nice is she?" Danny answers her "No she is a cow to put it mildly, so I am not going home for the weekend now, I am here up to the xmas holidays now, so Winnie where are you staying for the xmas holidays then?" Winnie replies "I am staying with a family in London for two weeks, why do you ask?" Danny "Just curious that's all, do you celebrate xmas in China?" Winnie looking nervous replies "Oh yes we do but not like here, it's not as how you call it um, not as much British people spend too much money on it." Jeff "I don't." Niel says "You're a tight git but you have Jo to buy for this xmas, so get your hand in your pocket." Jeff laughs and Danny says to Winnie "Don't you spend too much money on me for xmas mind Winnie, ha, ha." They all chuckled and Winnie said "I am not buying you anything after you treated me lately, I am not buying no one anything so ha, ha, ha." Danny smiling says "Well thank you very much, I am buying you something but I have to put a plug on it first." Winnie's eyes lit up in a curious manner and said "Oh yes, so what is it?" Danny said "An electric chair ha, ha, only kidding." They all laugh except Jo and Winnie she says "So are you being horrible to me again, I will have to sort you out again." and she stands up and grabs Danny by the hands and wrestles with him light heartedly. He said "Don't hurt me again, I took a long time to get over that last time, I was only kidding so be careful." Jeff said "You big baby you, she is only a girl." Danny "Ok you wrestle with her then, she can put you in hospital instead." Winnie slips and falls on Danny's lap and stays there watching telly and he didn't move either. Niel says "My mates ex-wife called him last year to ask sarcastically what he had bought her for xmas and he replied, you haven't opened the one I bought you last year so I am not buying you another, she replied, I don't remember that what was it? he replied a plot in the graveyard." They all laughed and said it was not very nice. Jeff says "Well Jo I will settle with a massage or something, I am not afraid." Jo "Ha, ha, I don't think so Jeff, I will buy you a pint if you like." Jeff "Ok then, I am easy to please, I'll give you a massage instead then." Jo "Be careful matey I have got long nails so watch it." Danny smiles and says "I feel sorry for the turkeys I do, especially if Bernard Mathews is grinning at one, they must kill thousands over xmas, I used to help out on a turkey farm in Pembrokeshire in my school holidays and we used to kill thousands of them." Jo cringing says "Oh don't, that is not nice is it? you murderer you." Danny replies "Thank you Jo, my father and I used to kill tame lovely white bunny rabbit's for the plate, I remember one day my younger brother who had a huge breeding buck rabbit asking where he was one Sunday and I said your eating him ha, ha, ha." Jo starts again "Well I don't think that's funny Danny it's cruel and you should be reported to the RSPCA and I am the girl to do it. Those poor little defenceless rabbit's, I don't think it's funny, first it's a dogs you pour petrol over them and now it's rabbit's, I am not bringing my dog over here again to listen to this sorry, Jeff tell him off." Jeff says "Danny your a bad egg now stop it, upsetting my girlfriend with that loose talk about animals, she is not Impressed." Danny looking serious says "Sorry Jo, I won't say it again." Jo "I should think not either your a cruel man." Jeff said "Jo he laughed when they killed Bambi's mother." Jo in a nasty voice "Did you? that's awful you have not got any heart." Danny butts in "Now Jeffrey stop shit stirring Immediately, don't listen to him Jo he is lying." Jo turns to Jeff and says "Are you Jeff?" Jeff "Am I what?" Jo "Telling me lies." Jeff "I was only kidding." Jo "Well don't joke about things like that it's not funny at all, how would you like it if I threw all your cans out of the window then? you would be upset wouldn't you? so don't tease me about things that is close to my heart." Jeff stops her and says "Jo it was only a joke again so calm down dear ha, ha, ha." She stops and smiles. Winnie says "So what are you buying me for xmas Danny?" Danny thinks and says "Nothing now because you are not buying me anything." Winnie says "You are not a nice person to me, I will buy something if you like a cd or something and you can buy me something." Danny thinks and says "Ok I will think of something for you like some knuckle dusters a flick knife and iron maiden a cosh or even a gun ha, ha." Winnie laughs and say "Yes that is a good idea and I can shoot you first with it, mmmm a good idea and I can then shoot Patsy and Lola ha, ha, ha." Niel then says "Don't joke about that it is happening all over the world today, all these colleges in America it happens regular." Danny smiles and says "Right anyone for the bar tonight?" They all agreed it was a good idea and off they went.

Up the bar and Danny, Niel, Jeff, Winnie and Jo were sitting in their usual table and Niel was laughing his head off as he thought again about his eyes bouncing on the platform in Bridgend and Jeff said to him "Niel, are you all there? you have been laughing to yourself for ages now, what's the Matter?" Niel with tears of laughter running down his cheeks says "Ha, ha, ha, I was thinking about my eyes bouncing on the platform in the train station ha, ha, it must have looked so funny ha, ha, sorry lads I am allright now, I have a new joke are you ready?" They all said yes and he continued "My wife and I were sitting at a table at my high school reunion, and I kept staring at a drunken lady swigging her drink as she sat alone at a nearby table. My wife asked, Do you know her? Yes, I sighed, She's my old girlfriend. I understand she took to drinking right after we split up those many years ago and I hear she hasn't been sober since. my wife, 'Who would think a person could go on celebrating that long? They all laughed and Winnie said "Danny will you get me a drink of wodka please? if I give you the money when you go up to the bar next." Danny says "Certainly Winnie I will, are you celebrating then?" She replies "No I just fancy a drink and not whisky this time, I know I was drinking whisky last time, I am not stupid ha, ha." Danny said "Who me? I wouldn't do a thing like that." Winnie "Oh yes you would and you did, you thought you may take advantage of me but you were wrong, but you can try again one day." She smiled and looked at Danny in a seductive way and Danny looking shaken said "Really, I may take you up on that offer soon." Winnie "Really." Danny gulped and Jeff said "Right dodgy get up the bar and get the drinks in." Danny "On my way as you speak." Off he went and Jo said to Winnie "I could not help hearing you speak to Danny, so is he your boyfriend then?" Winnie says "I think so, he is very nice to me lately and he is the only man here for me, he is so kind but he has got a wife but he thinks she is going to divorce him. I wish she would hurry up, I have to go back to China soon and it may be too late for me and him." Jo "Oh there's nice you and Danny look good together I think, so will you come over here to live if you both get together then?" Winnie looking excited says "Yes, I will hope this will happen and I can teach Chinese medicine and Chinese massage and Danny can do his thing." Jo with love look says "That will be nice and maybe start a family to, what do you think?" Winnie face drops and she says "Oh dear, I don't know if I want any children, it would be hard to look after them and I need to work." "I understand, it would be difficult." Danny returns with the drinks and hand them out to everyone and Winnie thanked him and cuddled up to him and it all looked cosy. Jeff said "Is there a xmas party in our digs for xmas? did we have one last year? I can't remember." Niel said "Yes we had one last year, you and Danny were in the lounge with some of the S. S. W's plying them with drinks. Jacob was drunk and the others were dancing and you and Rhoda were sipping the punch she made and by 11 o'clock you were out of it and that dodgy Welshman over there paralytic the both of you and the music blasting, I don't think we will have one this year as the ones downstairs will try and spoil it after what Carol done the other week." Jeff "Yes there is that, I forgot about that." Danny chirped up "There is a simple answer to that, we don't invite Carol it's as simple as that." Jeff "We can't do that it is not nice." Danny "She was not nice to that poor boy on his 18th was she?" Jeff replies "No I suppose not, well I am not telling her Danny." Danny says "No problem, Niel will tell her won't you mate?" Niel replies "No I bloody won't, I am staying out of it, I suggest we go to the pretty pigs for a piss up." Danny "You shit house you , but you may be right the Pretty Pigs sounds a good idea, you could be father xmas or as my granddaughter says father missmus ha, ha, ha." Niel "Oh no bloody way, I am having a drink this year." Jo chirps up "Awe, we have got to have a father xmas or it will not be xmas will it?" Jeff "Don't worry babe I will be your father xmas." She laughed and said "But father xmas is fat and jolly like Niel and you are so thin you would look like a bulimic father xmas." Danny says "There is more meat in father xmas beard than Jeff has got ha, ha, and he is a perve so it will work out for him." Jeff "What do you mean by that?" Danny smiling replies "Well father xmas only comes once a year, think about it." Niel tutting says "Oh very good Danny a play on words." Winnie says "Your father xmas are so tall compared to the ones in China they are so small over there." Danny says "There we are then Jeff go to China ha, ha." Jo "I would love to go to China, I love Chinese food." Winnie "I am afraid if you love the Chinese food here you may not like it over there, as the Chinese food here is nothing like real Chinese food, too much salt and fat and it is made for the British pallet, real Chinese cuisine is much nicer if you really want real Chinese." Jo "Really I thought it was the same the world over, well I have learnt something tonight, right I am ready for my bed now so I am off now in a minute." Jeff said "Ok doll I will drink up and walk you over." Off they went and Tim and Mandy took their place and Tim said "God she goes to bed early don't she?" Niel "She is not the only one, I am off too, I am knackered and I have to take Abby to the pen for her to do her stuff, goodnight all." They all said goodnight and Mandy said "Yes Tim I won't be late tonight I feel tired also." Tim "So you fancy a bit then aye?" Mandy snapped and smiling "No, I am serious, I am tired." Tim "Sorry I thought you were hinting." Danny "Tim you were hoping really." Mandy "He thinks about that all the time ha, ha, I enjoy it Tim but I like some sleep sometimes too ha, ha, ha." Danny "Your lucky I never have that trouble, do I Winnie?" Winnie snaps at Danny "Why are you asking this Danny? huh, that's what men always think about, it is private between people dah." Danny "Steady girl I was only joking with you, flipping heck." Winnie smiled and said "Sorry, you tease me all the time ha, ha." Danny "I am the one being teased by you." She slaps him on the leg and Tim and Mandy leaves for home.

Later on back at the lounge Danny and Winnie were sitting on a settee and Winnie was cuddling up to Danny and in a very good mood and a little tipsy and she says "Danny this is nice isn't it? just me and you here." Danny "The way to say it is you and I, and it is nice and very warm in here not like outside it's freezing out there and it is warmer in your bed mind." "Danny, you must not say this it is not good." "What is not good about it then?" "We are not married and so must not do these things." "You are probably right, but we can sleep together can't we?" She thinks and looks unsure and says "Oh I don't know it is a temptation for you sleeping with a girl." "Yes it is but I will give you my word I just need some company at night." "Why do you need company at night? you have a wife at home." "She does not sleep with me, she sleeps in a different room and not with me." "Why does she do this then?" "She says it is because I snore loudly and sometimes I do but not all the time and if I snore I will go back to my room ok?" "Oh I don't know." Danny looking defeated stays "Ok, fair enough, forget it I won't keep on about it I will finish this drink and I am off to bed." Winnie's face drops and she says "Awe, don't go it is early and I am wide awake now." "Yes you might be right another ten minutes and Jeff will be back." Winnie thinks about this and said "Oh why not, let's go to my room and sleep together but you must be good, promise?" "I promise." Off they go to Winnies bedroom and in there Danny gets undressed down to his boxer shorts and gets into bed but Winnie sits on the side of the bed . Danny says "Well come on get into bed then, what's the Matter?" "I don't know what to do, I don't wear anything in bed normally, so what shall I do." Danny smiling to himself said "Well why change a habit of a lifetime ha, ha." Winnie said "I will leave my underwear on and you must be good you promised" Danny tutting said "Yes ok I will just get into this bed it's cold." She jumps in and they talk for a while and then both fell off to sleep.

The next morning and Danny woke up and didn't know where he was but realised he was wrapped up in a woman's body and was very comfortable, he then realised it was Winnie and slid his hand on to her stomach and was heading for no man's land and she woke up and grabbed his hand and said "Aha and you promised, Danny I knew I could not trust you, but I did not hear you snore much last night. Did you enjoy your sleep?" "Yes I slept like a baby and it's nice and warm and you had your cold feet on me all night." "It's time to get out of here now before Zarrine gets in or she will know." "Yes I suppose your right any chance of a bit of nookie before I go?" "What is nookie?" "Can we have sex like most people have?" "No this is not proper is it?" "It is in this country, you will enjoy it I promise and it will not hurt." "I don't think so, we do not do this in China." "Don't be silly how did your mother and father get you then? they didn't find you under a bush did they?" "I know but I am not ready for this to happen yet, I am too young, I am only 29." "Most women have got 3 children by this time and besides I cannot have any more children so it's perfectly safe, so don't worry." She gets out of bed and said "I am not getting pregnant as I am not doing nothing so forget it." She gets dressed and Danny gets up and sits on the side of the bed ready to get dressed. He says "Are you sure now? this is your last chance ha, ha." "Thank you I am fine as I am, so don't say this again thank you." "Fair enough I won't keep on about it I will go." Danny gets dressed and Winnie went into the bathroom and Danny left and that was that.

Well it came to the night of the party or at least a few pints at the Pretty Pigs pub and there was Danny, Jeff, Jo Niel, Tim and Mandy. It was half way through the evening and they were a little worse for wear with the drink and Jo started to tell a joke "Did you hear about the Indian who drank one hundred cups of tea?" All nodded no and she continued "He drowned in his tee pee ha, ha, I thought it was very funny when I was told." They all laughed to keep her happy and Danny said "Well it's the last night before we all split up for the xmas holidays, are you all looking forward to it?" Mandy said "I am, I am having some time home for xmas and then up to Tim's house for the rest of it, I will be meeting all his family now as I have only met some of them." Niel "Awe that's nice for you unless they are all like Tim ha, ha." Tim "You cheeky git ha, ha, I am meeting all her family also so look out, will I survive them?" Mandy "Don't be awful Tim they will like you." Jeff "We are having a few days together before xmas at my place and then she is going home for xmas and I will go to my mums for the rest of it, she spoils me no cooking, no washing, no cleaning and plenty of beer and you Niel?" Niel replies with a smile "I love xmas, we have a great time with all the trimmings and the boys enjoy it and so do Ceri and me? I love it, we will go out for a few drinks over the holidays and thoroughly enjoy it all." Danny says "Yes I am looking forward to xmas with my sons and daughters and my happy wife, I will have plenty to drink and enjoy hearing Josh opening his presents and I will pop over and support my brother a little, also he needs It. Let's hope xmas helps him as I am not a believer but like the idea." Niel "Yes I think I can say this for everyone here and more in the college we hope your brother gets well very, very soon, he deserves a bit of luck and we hope you keep your calm and help him out with some sympathy that he needs?" Danny said "Yes I will, I have never been so scared in my life with all the problems he is having but a little tact helps on occasions in the right place, anyway here's a merry xmas and a happy new year to all you heathens ha, ha." They all wish each other all the greetings and Jeff continues "Well this party is not as heavy as last year is it? we were all pissed by now and a huge party was going on." Niel said "Yes but I am glad I am not in Dowdell tonight as I have heard that Carol is having some of the girls over from her massage classes and the lads down stairs have found out and I am glad we are here, but I would like to be a fly on the wall when it kicks off and Simon is the warden so look out." Tim "Never? oh shit, I am not leaving until last thing tonight." Jeff "Why? it won't affect you as you don't live anywhere near us ha, ha." Tim "Oh no that's right sorry." Danny "And I am not getting involved in it at all, she deserves everything she gets after her performance in Billy's party." Niel "So what time are you getting a train tomorrow dodgy?" Danny answers "I am packed and will head for the one around eleven o'clock. What about you?" Niel says "In that case I will catch the normal one, because every time I go with you on a train something goes very wrong ha, ha, I am only kidding, I will share a taxi with you." Tim "I wonder what is going to go wrong tomorrow with you 2? there is always something." Jeff "I am going on a later train then ha, ha, no I will see you in the station." Danny "Yes ok, the train company will have us thrown off I can see it now." Well that was that for xmas and a new year was starting and was it going to be a good one for the lads? Will they find some sense in life? Time will tell.

At home in Bridgend and Danny was with his wife, Josh and his dog Murphy and having a good time out shopping for last minute xmas presents and sorting out the arrangements for decoration after all the work had been finished on their house, this was going well but he still had Lyndon on his mind all the time and tried not to poke his nose into Lyndon's business so as to let him get himself back to normal as he can to show he could do it almost by himself, but Danny went over a few days after he arrived home and he went in and could see Lyndon had Improved but was still a long way from getting better. Danny put his arm around Lyndon and said "Hello broth, how are you coping with things?" Lyndon replies "I am trying but it is not easy and Debbie has not returned as yet, but Gaffo and some others have been over to see me and I got to say Gaffo has been a godsend, he is here all the time." Danny "Good, he is a good friend to you and is concerned about you and as regards Debbie she is a waste of time, anyway she has not supported you in this problem much so don't worry about her she will be back when she runs out of money. Has your so called best mate been over?" "No he hasn't, he is not a good friend or he would have not taken sides because he is married to Debbie's sister, he is not a friend of mine anymore so don't mention his name in here." "Fair enough I know what you mean he is just good at shit stirring, he only comes here to go back and tell his wife and your missus what is happening to you so keep him away." "No problems, he is a real shit stirrer so forget him." Danny nervously asked "And hows the drinking going now? Tell me the truth it's no good hiding the truth is it? I am only your brother and will not start shouting, I am here to help not hinder." "I am still drinking every day but not so much now." "Well that's good mate, we can only hope it will get better in time, what do you think?" "Yes Dan your right I think I will, as long as people leave me alone and don't harass me I will pull out of it I am sure and I have Gaffo watching me." Angie "Well done Lyn, it is much tidier here at last and are you eating allright?" Lyndon's face lit up a little and he says "Yes I am but not a lot I need some things up the shop today and don't feel up to it, can you get me some stuff when you go later please?" Angie replies "Yes of course I will and do you fancy a cuppa now?" "Oh, yes please." Angie then said "Danny do you want one?" Danny replies "Yes please, tea please." Angie goes off to make it and Gaffo walks in and says "Oh, hello Dan is he behaving himself?" Danny "Yes I think so, what do you think? you are looking after him." Gaffo replies "Well he is doing ok, he is still drinking but not so much and as long as he is left alone he is ok aren't you Lyn ?" Lyndon answers in sarcastic voice "Yes Gaffo, I am aren't I ha, ha, and you are watching me like a hawk aren't you?" Gaffo smiling says "Well I am trying to but it's not easy, so be good or you will go to bed early, ha, ha." Danny "Ha, ha, so you have been told mate and what about that bloody car belonging to his mother in law? she still hasn't picked it up and she keeps on about the bloody thing, that she wants it back." Lyndon "Well she says that to everyone and then says to me or leave it there for a while, so what am I to think?" Danny "Well I think we should let Gaffo take it back or something as if you drive it at any time you will be over the limit and we don't want you arrested either, so give it back to her as she is a pain in the ass about it all the flaming time, so Gaffo will you drive it back and park it over by her house and drop the keys in her letter box and have done with it mate, will you?" Gaffo looking excited in doing this says "Yes I will do it later Dan no problem." Danny says "Thanks mate and don't let her tell you to leave it over here tell her I said no we don't want it over here any longer thank you." Next thing in walks Angie with tea for everyone and they sit as Angie goes up the shop for some stuff for Lyndon. Danny continues "So how is the family Gaffo?" Gaffo says "They are all fine thanks mate and keeping me on my toes, ha, ha." Lyndon "Is Mel coming down this week?" Danny "No, he is having a break as long as I am home from college, why?" Lyndon "Oh, just asking that's all no particular reason, he has been good coming down all this way regularly to help me fair do's." Danny "Yes I know and he will be back after xmas I expect, look out here comes Josh." Josh says "Hi dad, hi uncle Lyndon and Gaffo." They all say hello and Danny says to Josh "So what are you up to boy?" Josh says "I am outside playing with my friend, he lives over the other side of the street. Where's mammy?" Danny replies "She has gone up the shop for uncle Lyndon for a minute, she won't be long now." "Ok I am going back outside to play with my friend." Gaffo says "God he has grown hasn't he? it seems like it was only the other day he was being born, how old is he now?" Danny replies "He is 9 now and tall with it and chopsy with it." Lyndon says "Leave him alone he is a lovely lad." Danny "Yes I know, have you seen much of Wendy at all?" Lyndon filled up with tears "Not much, she keeps her away from me, I have seen her on the streets mind after school, I watch sometimes from a distance as she walks home and I have only approached her once and Debbie threatened to call the police, it's awful." He turns away filling up with and his eyes full of tears. Danny tried to cheer him up "Never mind Lynd she will come around as soon as you get better and even if she doesn't the law will make her let you see her and she will grow up one day and the truth will come out and see how Debbie likes it then, the cow." Gaffo tries to change the subject "Yes Lynd and we can do some more cars and get back to normal and we can get the tools back from Alan Richards and get on with our lives, I used to enjoy fixing up the cars with Lyndon and you remember it was a lot of fun?" Danny "Yes we had some fun in 51 Glannant didn't we? all those cars and the engines we replaced and out in the evenings for a couple and a dance and a laugh up the valleys , the Wexa club in Blaengarw, Aberkenfig Legion, the Prince down there The Vets The Halfway, Sarn Club and Bettws club what a lot of fun we had ay." Lyndon "Yes they were the days weren't they? not a care in the world then just fun, fun, and more fun and all through fixing cars." Gaffo smiling from ear to ear says "Do you remember that car we took the complicated brakes off and we could not put the thing back together again and we gave up after about 2 hours and said to Dennis watch this lot for us den while we go and have a cup of tea please." Dennis said "No problem, he just loved cars didn't he? then while we were in the house having a cuppa, after 20 minutes we went back out and he had worked it out and put it back together and we only had to put the circlip on, it was amazing." Lyndon "Yes, I remember that and he was supposed to be mentally retarded but he was really switched on sometimes." Danny "Yes he was, he was nowhere near as daft as he was thought to be was he? he made a lot of people look quite ordinary sometimes, bless him I miss him so much and so do we all he was a real gentleman wasn't he?" Lyndon "Yes he bloody was, he was a real ray of sunshine and we never saw it most of the time did we?" Danny almost crying says "No we didn't did we? at least you gave him a life after mam went and he loved you and Wendy, he would always ask after her if no one else he was a lovely man." Lyndon looking solemn says "Yes he was, I will never forget him till the day I die." Gaffo "I know what you mean he was a fantastic person and made me laugh many times taking the piss out of your father, Lyndon and you behind your backs, he was an original he was a real gentleman as you say and I think lots of people miss him here in Bettws." Lyndon says "Yes that's true he was one of the men that made Bettws what it is, they will be talking about him long after the rest of us are gone, a real character and I miss him so much." Danny "We are getting morbid again, we must remember him with a smile on our faces as he had all of the time, so what's for dinner Lyn?" Lyndon looking shocked says "I don't know what your having, I am having chips in some bread" Gaffo said snappy "Say it tidy,, a chip butty." Danny laughs and says "We have a woman in our college who looks after us who I love to pieces her name is Zarrine and I made her some chip butties and she loved them, she is Asian and she has never heard of them and never tried them so I gave her a try and now she loves them but she is now 20 stone ha, ha, ha." Gaffo "She's not is she?" Danny "No I am only kidding, she has a lovely body but she now loves chip butties. Right enjoy your dinner I am off as Angie is back, I will pop over and see you on Monday now Lyn ok?" Lyndon smiling says "Yes ok mate, I will see you then and thanks for your help Angie." Angie says "No problem Lyndon , see you all." They left and went back to the house with Josh.

Back in the house and Danny said to Angie "Well what do you think about Lyndon? he seemed a lot better now." "Yes there has been an Improvement but it's early days yet, if only he could get away from here for a long time to recover he will stand a better chance." "Yes, I know what you mean, he deserves a chance he has had no luck since he met that witch, the only thing good that came out of that marriage is Wendy, I hope he pulls through this I really do." Josh speaks up "So uncle lindens better now than is he?" Angie replies "No not yet, he is trying to get better though, so be good to him ok?" Josh "Ok, are we going Xmas shopping now mam?" Angie smiles and says "Yes if daddy is ok about it?" Danny says "Yes I will watch the football on the TV I think Liverpool are going to lose again." Josh snarls "Dad, don't say naughty things they are better than Man U, anyway." Danny "Ha, ha, your like Craig he bites every time I mention Liverpool ha, ha."

Later that day when Josh and Angie were xmas shopping Gaffo came over to see Danny and have a cuppa and says to Danny "Hi Dan, I am here for a cup of tea and to give you an update about Lyndon as you asked me to do, well. He is a lot better now, he is not being harassed by her and no threatening notes have come through the door lately as far as I know, he is more relaxed than he was but he is still very ill and on the point of breaking in my view." "Thank you gaff, I am glad of your help in this Matter , he is I know on the point of cracking, I could tell that this morning and I am still very worried about him that's why I wanted the car gone from there." "That's gone now and I did not say anything to the enemy ha, ha." "Thank you mate, I am helpless I can't do anything to help him, I feel useless I really do." "It's not your fault Dan he is ill and this has been coming for years, he has got worse mind since Dennis died." "Yes I know he has, it hit him hard and my attitude did not help taking him away in the way I did, accusing him of using Dennis for his money, I am sorry I said that now but it was directed at her not Lyndon, she only ever wanted to go drinking all the time and Lyndon didn't need encouraging, he was ready and waiting and I think his drink problem was a few peoples fault especially mine, I was drinking very hard when I lost my son Nathan and a long time after and I encouraged him to come with me as we have always been so close and Adrian used to get him plastered as often as he could the wanker, I am surprised at him the way he is treating Lyndon if he said he did not want to get involved to his wife and Debbie and he would have showed his friendship that way but there we are his cock rules his brain obviously." Gaffo looking sad says "There you are , anyway how are you then?" "Fine, I am not missing Bettws at all, it was nice to get some help in the college and things are not getting any better with my marriage, I wish I could turn the clock back to the old days me Wyndham Pit, Sam, Lyndon, you, and my first love Eileen Martinson." "God yes, what ever happened to her? I thought you and her were together for life if I seen you, there was Eileen and if I seen Eileen there was you, she was a lovely girl and a nice body, why did you and her split up?" "I think Wyndham had a lot to do with that, she was a lot younger than me and was not allowed in the pubs and Whyndam was always asking me to go to the pub, so we drifted apart and I ended up with more trouble than I could handle and wish it had been different there, I loved her family especially Eddie he was a real card and her mother was a real lady and so lovely and so quiet a real nice woman, I was mad about Eileen too at the time and still miss her very much , mind you there were some good friends and some characters here mind in them days like Toddy Andrews, Barry Banner, Jeff Davies, big Bryn, the pit family ANN, Decca, betty, Fred and the lovely Theresa and Maria, I lived in their house most of the time, George Parkin Mr. and Mrs Mathews Gino Morgan bless him, Alan Burfitt, Alan Pothecary the lovely Hoe girls Kathie Angela and Theresa a nice family the Kendall's, the Owens, all the football boys Terry Hiatt Dai Symons and all that lot, Len and Tubby Norris, and Mary she was a card Dewi and Ann wile and of course Viv who used to work for me and Barry Hiatt your family the Garfield's, the lovely Anne Webster and her family the Websters, my favourite English teacher and good friend Vernon Chilcotte and his family and god so many I could mention. This was a terrific place to live when we were young, now it is full of people we hardly know and most of the old ones have died young, what a bloody tragedy, this place brings out the best in people and then strangles it out of them when they are older and ready to retire and enjoy life, what a bloody tragedy and it keeps on repeating itself over and over. A dying village all the old characters have gone now it's a pity." "Yes your right there Dan, It was a fantastic place to live once, not anymore the kids have no character here now they all play video games now no tip tap the knocker, kick the tin or fox and hounds a good game of football, cricket on the weekends or no carnivals anymore, what happened to this village?" "Progress mate but I hope it will all come back one day but I can't see it can you?" "No not really Dan, I remember you and Lyndon doing the disco's in the club for a good bit of money and fighting the next time you were in there ha, ha, and your father not happy with you both and some of the cars you had, god and we used to laugh all the time, it's all gone Dan, look at us now." "Yes I know what you mean Bettws club has gone now because all the characters who made that club have all died now and the new ones replacing all those families I talked about have no idea how to enjoy themselves at all, we made our own fun in them days, you don't have to anymore here." "Yes I think you are right, it's not the same is it and I think Lyndon has the same dilemma." "So are you calling on him again today or do you want me to phone him?" "No I am popping in later if you like and then I am having a Chinese for me and mother." Danny smiles and says "And give her my love Gaffo and tell her to look after herself, she has not been well has she?" "No but she is much better now, she will outlast me ha, ha." "I think your probably right mate." "Right Danny see you later in the week." Gaffo left and Danny sat there and reminisced about the past.

It was later that day and Josh and his mother arrived home and Josh was hiding Danny's presents and taking them upstairs to hide them and when he came down he sat on Danny's lap and said "Dad." Danny said "Yes, what are you after?" "Are we having a Chinese tonight? I am starving." Danny smiled at this and says "Oh I don't know, I am not hungry really what about you mum?" Angie sensed Danny was teasing Josh and said "No, I am not hungry either ." Josh screws his face up and says "Awe, we always have a Chinese when you are home, I bet mammy is lying, she said she was hungry on the bus." Danny jumps up and says "Ok then, we will have some beans on toast is it?" Josh "No, c'mon dad you really want a Chinese I can tell, you love Chinese so can we?" Danny looks at Angie and says "What do you think mum shall we?" She replies teasingly "Oh, do we have to? we eat too many Chinese meals." Josh "Awe c'mon mum you know you want one like daddy." Angie says "Oh, allright then." Josh dances around and screams "Yes we are having a Chinese, were having a Chinese." Danny "Calm down Josh your like a nutter ha, ha, so are you going up with mum to get it then? or are you staying here with me?" Josh "Well dad, my legs are tired and need some rest see, I have been walking around Bridgend all day carrying those bags." Angie gave him a stern look and said "You little fibber, I carried those bags not you and he can stay with you, I will be quicker, he messes about too much." Angie has the money and goes off to the take away and Josh sit's by his father and says "So hows school then? "It's good, I have been a good boy lately and so I can stay there a little longer and are you doing allright in school?" "Yes I am top in my class in Maths and English and I do Welsh but don't like it much and my girlfriend thinks I am clever, my teacher used to teach Craig when he was there, she is nice." "Good, so what are you going to be when you leave school then?" "I want to be a vet." "So you still want to be a vet then? that's good and so you will have to work hard then to be a vet and I will be pleased if you make it." "Will I have to cut up dogs and cats because I will not like that much will i?" "Well Josh you will be older by then and if it makes the dogs and cats better it is the thing to do." "And so I won't mind then will I?" "No you won't. Have you seen your brother much since he moved up to Wolverhampton? has he spoke to you on the phone then?" "Yes I speak to him on the weekends and Lauren and Clare. He is working in a supermarket and other shops like the pines you know and he teases me on the phone all the time." "Never mind, I used to tease uncle Lyndon when he was little too, it's what you do to little brothers." "I know and he does it to Lauren and Clare, he is coming down in Easter, why don't he come down now for xmas?" Danny looks sympathetic and says "Because he has a family now and has to work hard to feed them and pay the rent and council tax, he has to work all day and night because he didn't do his exams in school and if you do your exams you will have a good job and make lots of money and never have to work your backside off." "I know, Craig is stupid, he used to Mitch school didn't he?" "No he is not stupid, he is lazy brained, he would rather work than study and I mitched school but I went back later in my life and got the grades and so could Craig, he is not stupid, he just takes the easy way out and if he went back to college and took a trade I have no doubt he would do well to, he has got it in him it needs someone to drag it out of him. Do you know I taught him to drive and he took to it like a duck to water, he was very good he really was, I did not take long to teach him, he can learn quickly but he sometimes can't be bothered but he can do almost anything he puts his mind to but he is young and kids these days don't like to be told what to do but one day he will realise he can be better than he is now." "It's a shame he stopped playing soccer he was good." "Yes I know I followed him in Europe and most other places, he won the European cup I mean he did alone in the end, he saved the goal in the final shoot out and won it for a little club called Brynna football club against clubs from Germany, Holland France all top clubs and beat them all and what a team of lads they were, that was in Holland and I bought a round to celebrate it cost me £32 but it was worth it. He then progressed to playing for the Welsh team and I used to take him up the valleys about 30 miles in the freezing cold for training after he played a season for Wales it seemed to collapse he found something that nearly destroys all us men and that's women, he never played top football again and he could have been somebody to Josh, I am not joking he was good." Josh excited says "He was silly giving it up then wasn't he dad?" "Yes he was but his loins ruled his head and that was the end of his football career." "I am going to be a football player." "Good for you Josh as long as it does not get in the way of your schooling mate, I don't care get to university and get your degrees and I will be proud of you as a vet or whatever you want to be." "So your not proud of Craig dad?" "Of course I am, he has chosen his way of life and it's his choice and I respect it as I did with my dad, I never did what he wanted me to do and the same with Craig he will manage and he will work his backside off and he loves life and it's up to him he will succeed but it will take him longer and I will always be proud of the both of you always, look out here is our dinner." In comes Angie and the lovely smell of Chinese food. They sat and ate and Josh continued talking "So you went to college dad?" "Oh no, not at first I left school at 15 and a half and went straight to the coal mine and trained and went underground to work that was all there was when I was a lad and it was dark and dangerous and no good for your health, I only lasted a few years there and got some more education and got the hell out of there and so did uncle Terry Hiatt, we both worked together down there and both got out and bettered ourselves, we had no choice but you have got a huge many choices today unless you want to go down in a huge hole in the ground and work in the dark all day in dirty smelly water and loads of dust and bugs and rats and always in danger." Josh "No thanks, I don't want to go down in a hole in the ground I am going to be a vet thank you."

It was several days after a reasonable Xmas break before the problems all irrupted over with Lyndon. It happened when Gaffo called Danny and said things had got worse over with Lyndon, he came over to see Danny and said "He has got himself in a real state over there, he is worse than ever and I know why, it was awful." Danny looking sad says "What do you mean? what's happened? he seemed ok yesterday, c'mon tell me." Gaffo says in urgency "Well I got over there this morning and he was crying in the chair with a bottle of white lightening cider in his hand and he was out of it, absolutely pissed, I asked him what was the Matter and he pointed at a piece of paper on the table and I read it as best as I could and it said "why don't you die you bastard" and it was done in funny writing, what a kid uses to print the letters out, , what do you call it now?" "A stencil set for children you mean?" "Yes that's right a stencil set something like the first letter pushed through that he got when Mel was down, why would anyone do that?" "Because they are sick in the head that's why and I think I know who it is and that's why they used a stencil set so as he and no one else would recognise their writing and I heard something I have hidden from him also." "Go on then, tell me I won't breathe a word about it." Danny continues "The other night Debbie and her mother were arguing in the car park of the club because Debbie was going down to Jimmy Millwood's house for some fun and games and her mother was pleading with her not to do this, she is carrying on with him and I bet he wrote this note and the other one the bastard, wait till I get my hands on him he will be very sorry, I just hope he comes near me sometime and I will kick his head in. He knows I can't see and that's why he is so brave but there is more than one way to skin a cat if you know what I mean." "Well Dan I heard something like that as well but was not sure, the bitch. She just don't care, I hope she burns in hell for what she is doing to that boy." "I will have to come over and see him and hope he has calmed down a little to listen to some sense, I am not going back until next weekend now and that's it, I will telephone Mel and tell him, I can't get over this, why did this happen, what a coward he is or even the both of them might be behind this. It can't be anyone else it has to be him or the both of them, how cruel can they be? the bastards, I will swing for them if I get the chance, they are destroying him between them and I hope they can tell Wendy when she is older because I certainly will, I have the proof and the witnesses, they have no conscience at all, just a pair of wasters." Gaffo looking concerned says "Calm down Dan I am worrying about you now, you will bust a blood vessel in a minute and it's not worth it, what comes around goes around. Time will tell, let's go and see Lyndon is it?" "Yes let's go and if you see any of them let me at them and I will tear their heads off."

They go over to see Lyndon. They enter and he was laying on the settee and was absolutely drunk and almost in a coma. Danny said to Gaffo "Any booze you can see pour it out please, I will try and talk to him." "And I will open some windows in here also, it smells like a brewery in here." Danny tried to wake Lyndon up and he got some murmuring out of him but that was all. Gaffo came back in and showed Danny the note and said "I can't understand it if she wanted rid of Lyndon she would just divorce him, she surely wouldn't send him a silly note, this is to childish." "Yes and your right he is childish the way he is he would do this I know, I know that he had a divorce from his last wife because he was said to be strange according to her and her sisters, he used to masturbate over her while she was lying in bed sleeping and was always masturbating and not having sex with her, that's why she divorced him, he is not the full shilling is he? he giggles like a little girl, it fit's these notes as he probably can't write all that good either so he did it this way because he knew he would be found out, yeah, yeah." "Yes I heard that too well, well, so it is true then, I am not surprised at all and I bet Adrian knew all about Debbie and him too, he must do as she say's down there and he and her sister had Wendy, it's a team effort." Danny "God I don't believe they could be so cruel after all he done for them in the past, do you think Lyndon knows anything? I know he does, and he has kept it all inside all to himself, he must be devastated, he is in a hell of a state and he was getting on top of it until this happened. What am I going to do? I will have to think this out today and do it quick." "Well have a seat it is going to be a long wait, he is out cold, I will make some tea." Danny sat there with his head in his hands and contemplated the future for Lyndon and he looked dejected. Gaffo hands him a cup of tea and said "I was out for an hour or two and lots of people here in the village were asking about Lyndon and you like, John Miles, Marilyn and her boyfriend Mike, Ernie and Miar, David Burtles, he is not too good with his chest to and big Bryn, loads of them, I told them he was Improving and now look at him they have sent him backwards with what they have done and the club is not the same anymore, it is empty compared to when we all went there with the Thursday and Sunday disco's, remember it was heaving and you and Sam started it all didn't you?" "Yes we did, but don't shout it out " " why not? " because it's my fault most of the girls and men met their husbands and wives because of those disco's, so it may come back and haunt me like big D and Denise Hodges most of her friends and their husbands Chris mason and his wife, Raynor came from Maesteg and married a Bettws girl and loads I can't remember their names but there were a good many, I am the godfather here, I am more to blame for marriages in Bettws than anyone and they don't know it ha, ha, so don't say a word for god's sake." Gaffo nodding his head says "No I don't think I will Dan." They sat there for a few hours waiting for Lyndon to come around.

Meanwhile in came Angie and Josh, she was told and shown the note and was disgusted with it all and left as Danny did not want Josh to witness the problems Lyndon was having and then Lyndon woke up. Lyndon went to the toilet and came back down and sat down Danny had a word "How do you feel now Lyn any better? Gaffo told me about the note that is so childish pushed through the door, are you concerned about it?" Lyndon with a stern face says "What do you bloody think? I know she is not coming back and it is her new boyfriend whoever he is that is doing this to get rid of me with her blessing I expect." Danny "She is with someone but I think he is the one doing the notes to get rid of you and when I get my hands on him he is dead I assure you, it is definitely Jimmy Millwood." Lyndon looked at Danny with a nasty look and says "Awe great, that's all I need that tit head with my wife and my daughter, god he is a pervert according to his ex-wife, where is my bottle of white lightening gone from here." Danny "I told Gaffo to pour it down the sink sorry but that is how it is mate this cannot make you a alcoholic and destroy yourself, they are not worth it." Lyndon "True they are not worth it, she has gone down in my books with that pervert and I think Ginger knew all about it too the bastard, he is no friend of mine I have finished with that twat for good. Gaffo will you get me a drink of water please? before I pass out again, thank you. Well my life has hit pit bottom now I have nothing left." Danny replies "Lyn that's not true, you have me." Lyndon smiles and says "Yes, haven't I just, I don't want you preaching at me about me drinking, I want you to stay away for most of the day and leave me get through this on my own ok? get off my back I have enough to put up with without your preaching and let Mel know I don't need visitors ok?" Danny snaps "Don't be like that Lyn we are your brothers, we care about you we have to do something we can't just sit back and do nothing." "Why not? I have managed for the past few years without any of you, I had no help with you or Mel with mum or Dennis, now I am drinking you won't leave me alone all of a sudden and besides what can you do now, you are blind, I know if you had your eyesight you would by now have kicked his head in but you can't now." Danny "No but I would drop someone a few pounds and they will do it for me, I know some boys who would kill their granny for a couple of quid." Gaffo "This is getting out of hand now, cool down boys you are brothers." Lynd "Well he is on my back all the time like a bloodsucker mun, leave me alone for goodness sake." Danny "Allright I will back off a little sorry." It went silent for a while and Lyndon said sarcastically "You can still give someone a few pounds to sort that waster out mind, I am not in a state to do much either." Danny "Don't joke, I am seriously thinking about it mate." Lyndon "Well a kid from the junior school could knock him out and what the bloody hell do she see in him i want to know? he is a whimp in drag, I feel sorry for her I do." Danny "He really is a wanker, he really is ha, ha, try and leave the drink alone a little Lyn, you were doing so well." Lyndon in sarcastic voice says "Yeh, yeh, I was trying for the sake of my marriage and my daughter but all along she was shagging half the village until someone stuck like a fool, I was wasting my time." His head falls into his hands and Danny nods and says "Well I am surprised you stuck her as long as you did, she was never the girl for you, you were so different I Imagined you with a quieter girl and a happier person and there is plenty of them about for you so pick yourself up, brush yourself down and start over again as I say it's a messy job but some body's got to do it ha, ha." Lyndon "No that's it for me, I will never want another woman again not after all this I ruined it and that's it never again, sorry there will be no more weddings Dan, I know you love weddings but no way Hose." Gaffo says "Be like me Lyn single and happy most of the time ha, ha." Danny "Well if it helps I think I will be with you soon as I am preparing for my divorce , I know she is going to do it soon enough, so we can get some fast cars again and have some fun like we used to, remember them days? we certainly had some fun in many places, we had some cracking times didn't we? and it always ended up just me and you, bloody brilliant." Lyndon "Yes we did and look at me now, this is the finished product mate." Danny says "Yes you might be right Lyn, we did used to drink a hell of a lot and I am sorry now it has come back and bit us on the ass, I am sorry." Lyndon "Don't be silly, you didn't hold a gun to my head, I was in control all the time but we did drink a lot, I used to laugh at Adrian he used to come out once a fortnight and I would get pissed before him but I was just topping up he was fresh but we would go home together both of us pissed not just me and I could drink that pleb under the table and I loved his mother and father like they were my own and I did a lot for them because I did love them and he repays me like this, well he can go to hell now, I never want to see him ever again and talking about time I think I am going to have a kip now shortly as I feel like shit." Danny "You need something to eat Lyn or it will make you very ill." Lyndon "Yes I have some pies and some sausage rolls out there, I am going to have them in a minute. Gaffo will walk you home, I am going to have 40 winks." Danny and Gaffo heads off home and leaves Lyndon warming up his food in the microwave.

Danny was very upset about this note Lyndon had and was reeling and talked to Mel on the phone and decided to go ahead with getting Lyndon put into some sort of hospital for his own safety. This was going to be hard and the following morning Danny went into the doctors surgery to make the necessary arrangements again. He said to the same doctor who looked about 17 years of age "I have come to speak to you about my brother Lyndon Duckfield, I hope you have his files in front of you? as you know he is having trouble with his drinking, he is not going to live much longer if something is not done, I want him sectioned again as soon as possible please as he has gone back the same again and I should have never have cancelled last time." The doctor said "Do you think this is the way forward, he was coming to terms with it as far as I knew, what makes you feel it's is urgent enough to try and get him sectioned?" Danny with concerned look says "Well you haven't seen him lately, he is laying on his settee and never moves from it, he sleeps on it and he is like a tramp, he is not eating, he is drunk 24 7 and he is not coping at all well, he drinks white lightening and anything that is cheap and he is killing himself. Do you think I need any other reasons?" "I don't think he will kill himself, you might be worrying a little too much but if you insist I will set it up." She gets on the phone to a psychiatric doctor and after speaking to him sat back down and said to Danny "I have arranged for hymn to see Lyndon on Friday morning next, I must inform his social worker also and we will all meet at his house at 11 o'clock prompt and see what we can do." "That's all I want and as soon as you all see him you will realise I am right and as regards his social worker, I never knew he had one, so where has she been all this time then?" "You will have to take this up with her, I have no power there and the psychiatrist will make the evaluation and he alone will decide, I will see you then." "Right thank you doctor, I will see you up there, bye." "Yes thank you Mr Duckfield, I will, bye."

Well the Friday came and Danny was not happy because Lyndon had been pissed all week and kept Danny standing at the door but he was in for a shock and Danny was a little nervous wondering how Lyndon was going to react. Well they all gathered outside Lyndon's house , Danny said "I have not knocked the door as I want you to see him just as he is ok? are we all here?" The doctor introduced him to the psychiatrist and the social worker and Danny knocked the door and Lyndon answered from behind the door "Hello, go away, I am not up yet, what do you want?" Danny replied "I am here with the doctor to let her see you, open the door." Lyndon opened the door and was not happy with Danny at all, he rushed back into the house and got back onto the settee and was very drunk indeed and he was sleeping in filth and faeces, it was smelling bad in there, they all came in and Angie found them seats to sit on and Lyndon snarled at Danny "What's this all about?" Danny said "I have asked the doctor to get you sectioned for your own safety and you know the social worker don't you and this is the psychiatrist doctor who has come to assess you." Lyndon slurred "You got to be bloody joking you nutter, you are the mental one mate not me I am fine." Danny in serious voice says "Well it's time for them to decide, look at the mess you are living in, this is not normal mate." The doctor speaks up and said to Lyndon "Now listen Lyndon this is Mr Khan he is here to determine your state of mind as you are not a well man, this drinking is out of control so let's see what he thinks." Lyndon "Fair enough." Dr Khan said "Hello Mr Duckfield how are you? " Lyndon slurred "Fine, fine, and you ha, ha." ""Yes I am fine, so what is the date of your birth?" Lyndon sat there for a minute and then said "The 19ᵗʰ June 61." Dr Khan "And can you tell me the name of the prime minister?" "Tony Blair." Dr Khan "Yes that's correct and what day is it tomorrow?" Lyndon "Saturday." Dr Khan "Yes very good, well I am sorry he is ok as far as I can see, I cannot see any reason for sectioning him, he has his faculties about him." Danny said in temper "Your joking aren't you? look at him he is dying with the amount of drink he is consuming, is that a professional view? to ask his date of birth and the prime ministers name and tomorrow's day, that's the basis for not section him what a bloody load of crap, if you don't do something today it will be a joke." Dr Khan "I am sorry he is of sound mind and nothing I can do about it." Danny "Your kidding me, tell me your joking? look at him, I am blind and I can see what a mess he is in." The doctor says "I am sorry Mr Duckfield I must go by what Dr Khan says and that is the end of the Matter." Danny turns to the social worker "And what about you? what do you think miss social worker?" She replies "I must go by the doctor and nothing I can say will make any difference, I am sorry." Danny "Yes you social workers are always sorry after doing nothing, I have never laid eyes on you until this day, where have you been to let him get into this state?" Doctor "I am sure she has been doing as much as the law will allow her do, there is no use picking on her we are leaving now sorry it didn't work out as you wanted but that's all we can do." Danny still raving "Well let it be on your head if you don't do something now he will be dead by the end of the month I assure you I am right, your all a bloody joke if it was one of your relatives it would be sorted." Doctor "I am sorry you feel that way but that's the end of it." They leave and Danny stood there shocked and Lyndon shouted at him "You are a prize dickhead aren't you? messing with my life not yours, mine now get the hell out of here and don't come back for any reason, I mean it I will not answer the door to you now piss off go on." "So you think you can look after yourself? I don't think so Lyndon picked up something on the table and Angie sees this and tells Danny to get out of it as he has picked something to throw at him so they leave. Lyndon slams the door behind them and Angie takes him home.

Back at the house Danny says to Angie "That's it, I have made a mess of it, I never believed that because he could tell him the name of the prime minister and his date of birth he will not help him. I should have become a psychiatrist if that's all it takes, a few simple questions and now it's worse I can't even talk to him now." Angie "I don't think he is going to forgive you now he was mad and I thought he was going to throw that ashtray at you for sure, I think you have cooked your goose there now, he won't let you in, I think you will just have to count on Gaffo now." "Yes I think your right, I have made a right mess of it but what else could I do, he needs help, but there is none if he carries on like this he will soon be dead for definite." "I don't think he is that bad, speak to Mel on the phone about it." "Yes you might be right there is nothing more I can do and being blind does not help, I feel useless."

Later that night Danny spoke to Mel and after Lyndon decided to tell him that he will not see him again so can Mel sort him out soon after, he agreed. Danny explains this to Angie "Well Mel is going to come down in a few days or so 2 see Lyndon and I think I will set off back up to college in the morning, so speak to Gaffo and let me know what is happening ok?" Angie smiled and says "Yes no problem and I hope things will turnout allright for him." Angie was showing a lot of delight that Danny was going back up to the college, was there a reason?

It was the next day and Danny had returned to the college and he walked into the lounge, sitting there was Jeff he was shocked to see Danny and perked up Immediately he said "Well dodgy how are you? I thought you were never coming back, how is your brother down there?" "Not good at all mate, he will not stop drinking and I tried to get him sectioned and failed, now he will not speak to me at all now and he will not have me in the house, so I was the one who lost out." "He took it bad then? if he is that bad why wouldn't they section him?" Danny looking sad replied "Because he could tell him his date of birth and the name of the prime minister." Jeff "Harold Wilson you mean, sorry, it's not funny." "No it's bloody ridiculous that's the only qualifications you need a chimp could do that, god and the doctor from my surgery was about 17, no experience with these Matters at all, she was too young." "Well you did your best mate, I am sure, so what next?" "My older brother Mel is taking over now and he will keep me informed, so what's been happening here then anything?" "No it's bloody boring, bloody boring and Winnie has been asking about you every day, she will be pleased to see you, she has gone on a trip to Cadbury world today so you are safe and Jo has left at xmas so I am on my own again so time to party if you feel like it, I mean." Danny "I could do with a bloody good drink to cool my nerves, so let's do it a few in the rose and crown is it? I am going to dump my bag in my room and we can eat there as well if you fancy it." Jeff "Yes why not, I am starving and I cannot take any more of the stuff they call food over there, I will get my coat and call a taxi, see you down stairs." The lads go off.

Later that evening in the rose and crown public house they sat at the table and ordered food and a pint. Jeff said "Well there are a few new ones in the college especially in our dorm. A woman old as the hills and has got bleached blonde hair and has got a guide dog and her partner is there also, he is a big chubby man good at quizzes but she is weird, she gets him to push her around in a wheelchair and the dog on his lead pulling her, she is a little on the large side and a real moaner, always complaining about her illnesses and believe me she has got it all, a real hypochondriac you will love her." Danny screwed his face up and said "Just like my brothers mother in law if you have had some illness she has had it or got it worse, she is the worst one I have ever seen, I can't wait to meet this one she sounds a real piece of work and he is good at quizzes, good for the barrels quiz then." "Good thinking, ah here's the food I am starving." The girl puts the food on the table and the lads get stuck into it. It was just then that Jeff started choking on his food and coughing badly. Danny said "Jeff are you allright? have a swig of beer mate quick. " Jeff kept on coughing and after a while said with eyes watering "My god, I thought my time had come, I only put a small packet of butter in my mouth and bit it and the butter exploded out and nearly choked me, it was more of a shock more than anything, god that was awful." Danny started laughing and said "How did you manage that? ha, ha, ha. " "Well it was on my dinner plate not on my plate with the roll and I stuck my fork in it and chewed it before I realised it was a slab of butter in tin foil, it just exploded in my mouth." "God that's dangerous it could have killed you, I shall complain if I was you." "Yes it was a bit silly wasn't it? awe forget it Dan I don't want to cause a fuss." "Ok up to you matey if it was me I would." "So what was I saying and there is another girl in our dorma also, she is a bit of a pain she loves herself and is another fat bird looking for a man too by the sounds of her, so look out mate." "Well you have got more chance than me you are single now." Jeff with serious face says "Not true I am still with miss Lloyd mate and hope it will carry on for a while until she comes back." "Oh, so she is coming back then is she how do you make that out? she told me she had finished her course." "Yes she has but she is applying for the job in the reception for next year, so she has been told she will probably get it by the woman who is running it and I will be back on the menu." "There we are then Jeff matey but don't stir it up with any of these old biddies for me, I don't need that now at the moment." next thing Ian the manager came over to see the lads and said "Was the food to your satisfaction lads?" Danny said "Well Ian it was lovely but it nearly killed my mate there, he nearly choked on a piece of butter in foil on the plate that should have never been there, as he is almost blind and didn't see it so I suggest that you tell your waiters to remove it off the main plate next time if they are serving any blind or partially sighted people, just a thought I hope you don't mind me saying but the food was excellent as usual." Jeff chirped up "I knew he would say something Ian he is always saying things to embarrass me." Ian "No he is right and I will sort it out with the kitchen staff and waitresses and the next 2 pints is on the house, I will get you one over here straight away lads." Ian goes off and Danny says "See it was worth saying something, 2 pints I was not expecting that mind, I was just making a statement to stop it happening again." "Good thinking batman, a couple of free beers." Ian comes back with 2 beers and sets them down on the table and says "There you go lads sorry again Jeff." Jeff "Not a problem mate and thanks for the beers, but you didn't have to, thanks. That was nice of him, so are we staying here tonight or do you want a wander." "No I fancy another here and a few in the student bar to catch up with the new ones, so Jo will be back to stamp your card then well, well." "So how were things with Angie over xmas?" "Nothing brilliant not much feeling from her I thought for one minute she was going to ask me for a divorce but never did, I can tell by her actions and the way she is with me she does not love me anymore and I am sure of that." Jeff with sympathetic voice says "No you don't mean that, I think it's all in your head Dan." Danny with head bowed replies "No mate I really can feel it she is beginning to hate me or maybe what's has happened to me I have changed so much and she has bared the brunt of it all, it has driven her away so really it's my fault I am nothing like the man she married and before you say in sickness and in health that's a load of crap and you know it, if I was blind when I met her she would not have married me, no way, I don't think she is happy and she is like a rabbit caught in the headlights of a car, but it is still going to hurt when it happens. I just hope it is a long way away." "Well you can only wait and see, I had the same thing when me and my wife split up and I wonder what she was thinking, maybe the same." Danny "I think she is having a big fight in her mind and it's not fair on her neither she needs to live her life too. I just

300

hope we can still be friends after it is all settled." "You mean you will forgive her?" "There is nothing to forgive her for, it's circumstance no one's fault it just happened and that's It life goes on and I am just as guilty. I was in a club in Bridgend with her not so long ago and I felt like a fish out of water after being here for a year, I don't belong in that world now, I just pop into it from time to time I will never hate her for anything but I loved the times we had." " Jeff looking sad now said "You are a funny man, I can't understand you sometimes, but you make sense, let's have another pint and go back to the college."

Back at the college bar and Danny and Jeff were by now a little worse for the drink and having a good laugh, just then the woman and her boyfriend that Jeff was talking about came in and spoke to Jeff. Sandy said "Hello Jeff and who is this?" Jeff replied "Danny this is Sandy and Mick her partner." Danny "Allright, nice to meet you." Danny shook Micks hand and Sandy said "Well hello Danny I am pleased to meet you." She was making eyes at Danny and Danny was trying to avert her gaze and Mick looked jealous as hell. Danny said "Well Mick I hear you are good at quizzes then?" Mick replied "Not bad, I have won a lot of them and you?" Danny says "Yes I love quizzes and go to a lot of them, we go to one in Hereford town on a Thursday sometimes in the barrels, it's a good one but all for charity but you get fed at the end of the night, you will like it." Sandy butts in "Yes we will, I can get used to enjoying quizzes." Mick said "You liar you hate quizzes." Sandy looking at Danny with a silly charmed look said "Well I like them now Mick ok?" Jeff "We never win mind." Danny "No you are a Inx, he is a doubting Thomas he always puts the spoke in, we decide on the answer and he puts doubt in our minds and we end up changing and the first answer was nearly always right." Mick "I hate that, you should stick to the first answer always." Sandy said to Danny "So what are you doing here? and why have I not seen you until now? are you in Dowdell then ?" Danny looking confused by all the questions said "Yes I am in Dowdell and I have had problems at home with my youngest brother, he is an alcoholic and is ill with it so I finished my holidays late, I am here learning to be blind and doing some music tech on the side and you?" "I am doing advice and guidance and any other enjoyable things that might come my way." Danny didn't know where to look and Mick got in between Sandy and Danny and said "I will get some drinks in Sandy, what do you want?" Sandy looking nasty said to him "Gin and tonic please." Sandy then asked Danny while Mick was out of ear-shot "So are you married Danny?" Danny answers in a hurry "Oh yes I am, we have been together for nearly 15 years now." Then Jeff butts in and said "Yes but you will soon be solo again as his wife is divorcing him." Sandy's eyes lit up and she said "Really, and why is that then have you been playing away then?" Danny said "No I haven't, I am a good boy." Sandy replied "Oh I hope not." Danny gulped and said to Jeff "Pint mate?" Jeff hands him his empty glass and he ran to the bar as fast as he could. Mick said to Sandy "So shall we go after this?" Sandy said "I might have another one but you go if you are tired." Mick "No I am not tired at all, I will wait for you." Sandy looking annoyed at his suggestion says "Yes I thought you might Mick." Mick said "I thought we could have a early night if you know what I mean?" Sandy said with a smile "Good god Mick, am I hearing things, I thought you said you fancied a bit then ha, ha, ha." Jeff laughed and turned away, Mick then said to Sandy quietly "No need to shout it out, we don't want the whole world to hear our business." Sandy snaps "It's normal at least with most couples, you only offer it to me when you think I am getting close to any other man, well we can have one more and head off, I could do with a bit now." Jeff smiles and Danny returns and strokes Sandy's dog and says "He's a lovely dog, what's his name?" Sandy sarcastically says "Mick, oh the four legged one, that's jester, he is 4 years old." Danny "Hello boy your a nice dog aren't you? yes you are aren't you, he loves beer he is licking my hand." Sandy "Yes he is like his master loves licking things ha, ha, ha." Danny smiling says "Really, I will keep that in mind, it's a nice pint in here for a change mind, it is not as good as this usually and being Welsh I only drink good beer and the lager up here is like piss, only for the lads up here not too strong." Mick butts in "Well I am drinking lager and it is ok." Danny "So where are you from then Mick?" Mick replies "I am from Redcar." Danny "I rest my case, another bloody English man." Mick "What do you mean?" His smirk turned serious and Jeff said "Mick don't listen to him he is not all there, he is Welsh, he can't help it and there will be another one here tomorrow night, Niel, he is huge and bald as a fish and when those two are together look out you can't get a word in edgeways." Mick "Right, I understand now a heathen up here in our country, can't get a decent education in little old Wales ha, ha, ha." Danny smiling says "Hereford is part of Wales, we are only leasing it out to the English for another 35 years and then we want it back." Mick "Do you still eat your young down there?" Danny "No we usually eat yours easier to get as they all love a Welshman." Jeff laughs and said "You have got an answer for everything haven't you?" Mick smiling still says "I don't know how you can live among all those anthills." Danny smiling replies "Do you know why we have all those hills and mountains in Wales?" Jeff excited "Oh, here we go, listen to this." Mick "Go on I will fall for it." Danny says "Because we won so much land off the English we had to pile it up and make mountains out of it ha, ha, ha." Mick laughs and so does Jeff and Sandy and she said "Ha, ha, very good, I think most Gallic men are very bouncy and funny, I think I would like living in Wales it sounds nice, which part of Wales do you live?." Danny says "At the moment I live near Bridgend, but I want to move back down to Narberth in Pembrokeshire again, it's lovely down there, as they say god's country." Sandy "I live in Lancashire it's nice there too, have you ever been there?" Danny "Of course I have been a few times to Blackpool and had some fun up there." Jeff "I live in Swindon." Mick "A very busy city and not much unemployment up there is there? that's where the train building place for the whole of Britain was until recently." Jeff "Yes that's right, it's huge now I live in Park South near the magic roundabout." Mick "Not far from the new hospital by the M4." Jeff "Yes that's right." Danny "Yes Jeff you look like Zebedee." Jeff "Yes Brian." Sandy "Mick are we having another or what?" Mick "Well I thought we would have an early one." Sandy "Mmm if you insist." Danny "Oh yes, can we watch?" Sandy "Watch, you can join in ha, ha, ha." Danny "Steady Jeff she is only kidding, calm down boy." Sandy "Am I? ha, ha, I am game." Danny said nothing and Mick gave Sandy a nasty look and off they went. Danny says to Jeff "Bloody hell mate, she is a randy bugger isn't she?" Jeff looking hot and bothered "Yeah, she was very forward considering she has only just met us, but she was all for you mate she is on your case mate." "No problem I will just tell Winnie she will sort her out no problem." Jeff said "Look out here comes Winnie as we speak." Winnie calls Danny, he said "Over here." She comes over and sit's by Danny and says "So hello, how are you? I was wondering when you were coming back." " Danny replies "I am fine thank you, I had some problems to sort out with my brother, so I never see you in this bar." Winnie "Oh we have been to Cadburys world and I have come here with the people who went on the trip, I have some free chocolate, do you want some?" Danny "No thanks I must not eat chocolate but thank you, Jeff might want some." Winnie then said "Oh sorry Jeff I didn't know you were there, do you want some?" Jeff "No thanks not on a belly full of beer." Winnie "I am going to have a drink with my friends, see you later in the lounge and velcome back velshman ha, ha, ha." She goes off and Danny pinches her bum she squeaks and says "Hey behave yourself." and storms off. Danny and Jeff laughs and Jeff said "Well she certainly missed you, maybe she is on the change." "Maybe, she can only get nicer she could not be more horrible to other people, it's a shame really such a pretty girl as well, ah well, never mind ay."

Later in the lounge as Danny and Jeff walked in, they were confronted by Sandy sitting on the settee with not much on. She seemed to be waiting for them but Danny was not interested but was polite to her, they had a sit and a chat. Danny knowing Winnie was going to come in soon and right on time she came in and Immediately sat by Danny and was so excited but Sandy was not Impressed and looked annoyed. Winnie said to Danny "So how have you been? did you have a nice xmas? and did you miss me?" Danny stopped her and said "Hey slow down, yes I did have a nice xmas, I have been fine and yes I missed you of course." Sandy spoke up "So you 2 are a item then?" Winnie said "Who is that?" Sandy replied "Hello Winnie it's me Sandy." Winnie said "Oh hello Sandy, I don't know you must ask Danny huh, I never know where I am with him." Danny stutters and said "Well, well, we are very close but not attached at the hip." Sandy "So the answer is no then?" Winnie looking serious said "Why do you want to know this?" Sandy "Just curious that's all, don't panic, just curious." Danny "I am a married man and will not do anything until I find out for definite she is going to divorce me so let's leave it at that." Next in walks Jeff and Danny asks him "Well there you are, where have you been?" Jeff smiling said "I have been on the big white telephone, phew." Winnie "What is this big white telephone Jeff?" Jeff "On the toilet having a dump, I have got the trots." Winnie "The trots." Sandy "He means the shit's, he has the runs, am I right?" Jeff laughing "Yes that's right I was trying to put it more politely though." Sandy "You don't have to beat around the bush with me." Winnie "We are not all common Sandy, I don't need to know all that information." Sandy "Oh, excuse me." Danny "It's probably that butter going through you, I hope it is not going to spread ha, ha, ha." Jeff "Ha, ha, ha, very good mate I will explain to the girls, I went for a meal and the waitress left a little slab of butter in foil on the dinner plate and I stuck the fork in it stuck it in my mouth and bit it and it exploded in my mouth and I nearly choked, it was so funny, I will check next time." Winnie "I would have told them." Jeff "We did and we had a free pint each, so no problem." Sandy looking interested said "Where was this Jeff?" Jeff "In the rose and crown, they do nice meals there and the lager is lovely there." Sandy said "I will have to remember that name, I can get a couple of free meals there now I know." Danny looking shocked said "You wouldn't do that would you?" Sandy with cunning look on her face says "Oh yes I would, anything for a cheap night out." Jeff "I could never do that see." Sandy "If you can get away with it, why not?" Danny "It's because of people like you, that makes the prices soar, that's awful." Sandy "Stick with me Danny and I will save you a lot of money, it's easy when you are partially sighted." Danny "No thanks, I am allright as I am thank you." Winnie looking discusted says "That's as good as stealing in my country, you would go to prison for this, it's not allowed. " Jeff "Well this is rip off Britain Winnie and there is a lot of this here and the honest person picks up the bill." Sandy smiling says "Yeah, whatever." Danny "Well that's what life is these days, look at this college there are some here that keep coming back here year after year and have no intention of getting a job." Sandy "This is my second time here I think it's ok, better than sitting in the house and not enjoying life I bet you will be back here in a few years." Danny "No I won't I will get everything I need and be gone." Sandy "Yeah, yeah, so why are you here now then ? and what course are you doing? and I bet you will not work after you leave here." Danny "To be honest I am not going to get a job after leaving here." Sandy snaps "See what I mean." Danny "No wait a minute let me explain, I am here to learn how to be blind and I cannot get here just for that I have to do a course or they won't let me in here but I need to learn braile, jaws, mobility and life in general as a blind man and it's working very well and after I leave here I will put it all to good use. I am too ill to work as I used to but I will put my new skills to something useful like writing as I have been successful already with that but I will be a happier man because this college is the finest in the world. I believe if you are blind I think so and it has saved my life as far as I am concerned but I will never use it and what I am doing as a course is of great interest to me and I assure you I will never come back after I have completed the course." Sandy "This place is not that great, full of people that cannot learn much and it keeps the unemployment figures down and makes the government look good." Danny "I disagree most here want to learn and it Is made easy here with some of the tutors who are dedicated to their jobs like for instance the braile babes, brilliant teachers and so dedicated. Jaws computer tutors love their jobs, massage teams the music tech and on and on and people use them and waste their time, I'm sorry your wrong I am getting my life back together thanks to those people and the only ones that I feel are a waste of time are the technical support team who can't keep and internet system running, absolutely useless as Niel will back me up on ha, ha, ha." Jeff "Yes they are dreadful aren't they? no idea at all and the best place here is the student bar ha, ha, ha." Winnie laughing to herself says "Yes you and Danny live up there." Danny "That's not a nice thing to say Winnie." Winnie "Ha, ha, it is true ha, ha, ha." Sandy "So Winnie what are you doing here?" Winnie snaps "I am here to learn English and I also teach a little head massage, I am here from China." Sandy sarcastically says "So it is a case of you wasting time here then just to learn English." Winnie snaps at Sandy again "Why do you say this? I am a Chinese doctor of herbal medicine and a professional masseur and the college is benefiting out of my skills as I am from them teaching me English so we all benefit." Sandy continued being sarcastic "So I am British and I am not entitled to get as much as a foreign student." Danny "Nobody is saying that but the British people do waste a lot of resources they don't need and Winnie forgot to tell you she is also a black belt ha, ha, ha." Sandy "There we are then, I am off to bed." Winnie laughs and says "Yes goodnight Sandy." Sandy replies "Yes goodnight." She goes off to bed and leaves the others sitting there and Winnie said "She Is not a nice person is she?" Jeff "On the fiddle, her boyfriend was saying to someone last week he has rented out his house for a few hundred each month while he is here." Danny "Never and I bet he has not owned up to it and is pocketing the money, see what I mean" Winnie "And I forgot to tell her that I paid half the airfare to get here and a local charity here paid the rest and not the college or the British government so she is wrong." Danny "Oh, don't worry about her she is the scum of the earth and will never amount to anything just like that drunk over there." Jeff "Ay, steady dodgy, I am getting on with my work here and will put it to good use when I finish here and I am also benefiting from braile and everything else, so don't go there ha, ha, ha." Danny "Ok, steady mate I was only kidding and I feel like a head massage now." This was a hint to Winnie and she smiled and said "I am off to bed get your wife to do it for you, goodnight." Danny "Oooohh, throwing your toys out of the pram now." Winnie "What is this?" Jeff smiling said "He means you are being nasty because of his wife." Winnie "It's his problem then, bye." Danny and Jeff say goodnight and she left Jeff says "I think you are going to have that Sandy chasing you also now mate, she is like a white witch and her boyfriend is not much better." Danny "I will not put up with her messing me about and I would not touch her with yours." "Thank god for that, I will be grateful for that, she has got her eye on you though mate." "I think she is dangerous and she is playing behind her boyfriend's back that is awful, he must be a mug hanging out with her, I have never been so horrified by her comments about using the system and blatantly saying it to." "I know she is and I don't think she had anything on under her nightie either." Danny curious says "Oh don't Jeff please, I will be sick that's all I need bloody Zig and Zag." "Ha, ha, ha, ha, Zig and Zag be buggered, what a name to give them ha, ha, ha." "Well I have to call them something and that fit's, does Zarrine get on with them?" "Oh I don't know, you will have to ask her in the morning, she has been worried about you and will be excited when she knows you are back, you can't do anything wrong in her eyes she adores you and spoils you rotten and don't deny it." Danny with huge smile says "Yes I agree and I adore her she is like a sister to me and makes me laugh a lot, she will not put up with any nonsense from them 2 I know it." Jeff holding his stomach said "Oh, here we go again my stomach is off again, I am off quickly see you in the morning." He runs for his room and Danny laughs and heads off to bed also.

It was the next morning and Zarrine was cleaning the worktops in the kitchen and Danny sneaked in and whispered "Hello, any room for a Welshman." Zarrine turned and smiled and ran across to Danny and threw her arms around him and said "Ha, ha, my Danny is back, how are you lovely, I have missed you, tell me all about it Danny after I make a cup of tea." They sit down later with tea and toast and Zarrine says "So how is everything at home with your brother and wife? I have been thinking about you all the time you were home." " Danny replied "Well my brother has got worse, I tried to get him sectioned you know taken in to a home for his own good and to get some help and he passed the exam so to speak and because he could tell the name of the prime minister and his date of birth they would not help him and now he hates me and does not want me around him. He was very nasty with me." Zarrine puts her hand over her mouth and says "Oh dear, I don't believe it and he will come around when he realises you were doing it for his own sake and if you didn't care you would not have done it, never mind Danny something will turn up and you will get help with him and how was your wife?" "She still has not said anything and does not want to bother with me much, so that is still the same, I don't know where I am." Zarrine "Well that might be a good thing, it may still work out in time, give it a chance Danny and don't worry." "I had a big shock last night, I met Zig and Zag." Zarrine looking puzzled said "Who is that?" "Sandy and her partner Mick." "Ha, ha, ha, why do you call them this?" "Because I have to give them a name and that seemed appropriate ha, ha, ha." "   They are strange, at least she is, she is lazy and she sits on her chair over there and Mick fetches and carries for her, she don't lift a finger to help him, he is stupid and she sits there like a big mamma ha, ha, ha." "And there is another girl here too her name is   Philippa, she likes the men too and she has a dog called Rosie, have you met her yet?" Danny "No I haven't yet." " "She is only here for six weeks though so you will be safe there. Has Winnie seen you? She has kept on asking when your back every day." Danny smiling says "Yes I seen her last night she was excited to see me and she kept herself between me and Sandy thank god." "Ha, ha, I think she will be a saviour to you there with Sandy and Jeff has been like a dog without a bone." "Well he accidentally ate a little pack of butter in the rose and crown and nearly choked and had the runs last night when we got back here, he is a hell of a boy." Zarrine "Yes he is so funny, so he will be late this morning if you 2 were both drinking last night then." "No we weren't too bad, I think Sandy sobered us both up last night, I think we were afraid of getting raped by her so we stayed sober ha, ha, I think you had better get him up yet again." "Yes I better had or he will be late again and they will blame you for it ha, ha, ha." In came Winnie and said "Hello Zarrine and the velshman, isn't Sandy here for Danny? She likes him Zarrine." Danny "Well I don't like her so let it be ha, ha, ha." Winnie "She follows him about and she was waiting for him last night ha, ha." Danny "Well she will have a long wait I might set her up with Jeff now miss Lloyd is not on the scene but she would kill him, talk of the devil and he appears." Jeff "Leave me out of this she fancies you not me thank god, Zarrine he always attracting the wrong women except Winnie I mean ha, ha, I nearly dropped myself in it then phew." Winnie "Yes Jeff you had better not say these things about me, she can have the dodgy velshman anyway." Danny "I think it's up to me who I see and she is not one of them, she has got Mick so leave it there." Zarrine said "Jeffrey so you want a cup of tea and what about Winnie?" They all say yes they want a cuppa and Jeff continues "Well my guts is much better now but it was a long time settling down, is Niel back?" Danny "Yes he has taken Abby for her slash, he will be here now, I have got a headache this morning, I never slept much thinking of my brother all the time." Winnie "Don't worry too much I know he is your brother but if you make yourself ill you will be no good to him will you?" Jeff "She is right mate, why don't you give him a ring before you start the day." Danny "He has only got the mobile now and he never answers it so it's useless, I will wait for my brother Mel to call there tomorrow." Zarrine brings in a tray of tea and they sit and have it. Zarrine says to them "I hope we won't have any trouble with those 2 new ones Zig and Zag as Danny calls them, I was hoping we would have some peace now Lola has gone down stairs , but I think we will be having trouble with them sooner or later." Danny "Well as long as they are not as bad as Lola I don't care and I am staying away from her so it will be quiet, look out here he is." Niel has walked in just as the tea had arrived and Zarrine had already made him one and said "Goodness Niel, you must have smelled the tea and how are you anyway?" Niel says "Oh, I am fine and I heard that Sandy is now on this floor? She is a bit of a girl you know, she don't take any prisoners as regard the men." Jeff "What do you mean? So you have seen her before have you?" Niel "Yes I have met them in Torquay and she was all over the men then, she was sex mad there, even though Mick was with her." Zarrine "Oh yes, c'mon tell me more ha, ha, ha." Niel continued "Well she was here also a few years ago and the young S.S.W. from somewhere or other was sleeping with her because she was giving him money to do so as you know they are almost always skint and she took advantage of this and offered him money for a bit of sex regularly, honestly." Danny and Winnie said it the same time "Your joking" Niel said "I am not kidding and this lad was about 20, no more than 21 and he was rubbing his hands and she is in her 50's he was a brave lad ha, ha, he always looked knackered ha, ha." Jeff "Well bloody hell, I have heard it all now ha, ha, I am locking my door from now on." Danny "You are not the only one, I bet that lad had to have his ankles tied to the posts of the bed to stop her swallowing him up the poor bugger." They all laughed and went to their lectures.

It was the following day and Danny was on the phone as his brother Mel had phoned him and the news was not good. Danny said "So what is the Matter Mel?" Mel replied "He is not well Dan I am getting an ambulance out, he is in a bad state, he is grey, he looks very ill mate, I am worried." Danny looking very concerned says "Is he that bad then?" "I am really worried, I am going straight to the hospital with him this can't go on he is killing himself, he was hardly moving when I got into the house, it's bad mate." "Right Mel I am on my way home and this time the doctors will have to bloody listen, no mister nice guy now, I will be there in about 3 hours Mel. I am leaving Immediately, my train is in 1 hour from here and is straight to Bridgend." He switches the phone off and put his head in his hands and looks upset, he then puts some things in a back pack and goes into the lounge to see Zarrine. Danny gets there and they were all there and he said to Zarrine "I am off home, my brother has taken a turn for the worse and my older brother is taking him into hospital Immediately

306

and so I am catching the next train in an hour, so can you tell everyone for me?" Zarrine "Oh Danny I am sorry about your brother I hope he will be ok, he must listen now I will sort out things here." Jeff said "Say hello to him and tell him we are thinking about him and get him to help himself now." Danny "No problem mate, I am going to give them hell until they put him away for his own sake before he kills himself, I have had enough now, no more Mr nice guy." They all wished him good luck and they could see he was so worried as he left for the train.

Danny is back home and is met by Angie and she says "Allright how are things?" "Fine except for what's happening to Lyndon, have you heard from Mel this morning?" "No he has not phoned here, he popped in before he went to the hospital with Lyndon though, he looked worried." Danny says "Yes I am worried also, he sounded upset on the phone." "I know, do you want a cup of tea before I go to Bridgend? I am off to get some things in." "Yes please I will and how is Josh?" "Fine, he is ok, listen I want to get this floor finished in the hall and new dining room and I was thinking I know somebody who wants a hobble cheap for cash, Gareth Chin, he is living around the corner in his aunties house, she died and left the house to him." Danny replies "I have not seen him for about 30 years, god what makes you think he can do it then?" "He was talking to me one day, I was with Susan outside and he said hello and said he was looking for work he used to work for my brother Terry." "Well tell him to call here for me to see him and tell him what I want and I will give terry a ring and see what he thinks." Angie eyes light up and she says "Fair enough, I am off here's your tea." Yes don't let me keep you I am here for a while as I am not going back before Lyndon is right never mind how long it takes." Angie's face dropped and she said "What do you mean?" "Well if the doctors are not doing anything I will have to stay, I can't go on like this all the time, stuff it." "But you are half way through your course you can't give it up." Danny says "Look I live here you think I am never coming back and that would suit you wouldn't it? What's the Matter with that?" "Nothing it's just…" Danny with serious look says "It's just what? I know you hate me coming home so don't try and hide it, you don't want me here do you?" "Oh god, you get on my nerves sometimes, it's nice not to have you telling me what to do all the time." "I don't tell you what to do, it's because you love to be anywhere except here, you are always up your sisters or down the other sisters and before that it was over your mothers or anywhere but your own home whether I was here or not so don't give me that crap." "Oh, there we are then I am off." She storms off. A little later Mel's wife phones and says "Hello Danny have you seen Mel yet?" Danny replies "No I haven't Mar ." Marice says "Well ask him to call me when you do, I was shocked when he called me about Lyndon, he sounded upset, I hope Lyndon uses his head now and pulls himself together, he is not having a good time of it with everything is he?" "No and I am also worried, I hope he will be ok too I will pass your message on, I am expecting him to call anytime." "Ok Dan speak later, bye." It was a little later when Mel knocked the door and came in and gave Dan a hug and said "Dan you should have seen him, he looked like death warmed up, he was laying in his own mess and was like an old man, he has frightened me it's upsetting." Danny looking worried says "I hope he will be ok, he is so stupid doing that, I tried to sort it out for his own sake but I failed." "I know he was chatting about that this morning after I arrived, he said he was not happy with you but I said he was not thinking and that if you did it for spite I could understand it, but I said that you did it because you were worried and because you loved him or you wouldn't care." "And what did he say?" "He sat there and thought about it for a while and then smiled and agreed. I will grab a cup of tea if you don't mind and we can get back down there." "Ok it will be quicker if you helped yourself Mel and make a sandwich for yourself." He did this and they sat back down and carried on the conversation about Lyndon, Danny said "I am not going back up the college until Lyndon is much better, never mind how long it takes." "What about your college work? It is Important don't give it up now." "Funny Angie said something similar but with a worried face, she does not want me back here and hopes I will never return and I am serious." Mell look of sadness says "No I don't think so." "I am deadly serious mate it's looking more like a divorce is on the way, she is panicking mate, it's over I am sure, besides Lyndon is more Important now." "Well I have talked to Lyndon about him coming down my house in Milford to live so as I can keep an eye on him and you know the pub in the village has closed down now and he can get himself back on the straight and narrow and he agrees with me. I think it is a cry for help I do." Danny smiles and says "That would be great and he can forget that bitch of a wife and that cretin of a boyfriend of hers too, he can make a new start." Mel "Wouldn't that be nice? I hope it works out." "Oh dear I forgot to tell you, can you phone Marice?" Mel phones her and after putting the phone down he says "Women always problems, she is panicking while sorting arrangements out for me but it looks as if I will have to drive home tonight and come back tomorrow, never mind." Well Angie and Josh walked in and Josh run up and gave a huge hug to Danny and a massive kiss and then done the same to Mel and said "Hello dad back again, is uncle Lyndon better?" Danny replied "No he is still ill." Josh then says "Can I come down and see him?" Danny "Not today he is not well and they are worried about germs so maybe another day this week ok? And you are only little." Josh smiles and says "What do you mean I am nearly twelve now I am big." Danny says "I know you are and I will tell uncle Lyndon you were asking about him so look after your mother and see she does not stay up her sisters all night." Angie said "Ha, ha, very funny aren't you?" Mel turns to Josh and says "Josh where's my hug them boy it's me your uncle Mel, I need another hug ha, ha, ha." Josh runs up to Mel and gives him a huge hug an kisses "Hi Uncle Mel I haven't seen you for a while, are you staying here tonight?" Mel smiling "I am afraid I can't Josh I have to go home to sort out some things but I will be back in the morning, I shall see you then so can I have another hug as you will be in bed later?" Josh hugs him and says "Of course you can I always give you hugs don't i?" Mel "You sure do and lots of nice hugs to, see you tomorrow, goodnight" Josh "Goodnight Uncle Mel." Mel gives Angie a hug and kiss and left. Danny and Mel head off to see Lyndon.

They arrive at Lyndon's bedside and he is struggling to breathe and is in pain, he sees Mel and Danny and gruffly said "Allright boys, I am having a terrible time here, I am suffering bad I feel awful, my guts is killing me, my throat feels like it has been cut and my tongue is stuck to my mouth." Mel fills up a cup with water and helps Lyndon to drink it Lyndon says "Ah that's better, I needed that." Danny smiling said "Allright Lynd how are you then?" Lyndon replies "Great mate, ha, ha, but I won't be going out tonight mate." Danny "I hope you never go out for a drink again and you start listening to us all, we are worried about you mate." Lyndon "I bet you will be out for a pint tonight ay if you had the chance." Danny looks upset and said "I would gladly give up the drink if you will, I mean that." Mel speaks up "I think Lyndon knows he has to pull himself together by the way he is feeling now." Lyndon "You had better believe it." Next thing a couple of nurses came in and asked Mel and Danny to wait outside for them to give Lyndon his medication and sort him out and make him more comfortable. The lads are sitting in the waiting room and Danny said "Oh my goodness, I never seen him this bad, he is dreadful, I hope he sticks to his word and comes down with you and live, otherwise I can't see no hope for him." "I will make sure he does Dan, I won't take no for an answer, he must as he will not live long otherwise I agree."

"I hope your right he needs a break he is a lovely man it's a pity and it breaks my heart to see him like this." "Yes he is, how did he ever come down to this? Such a loving lad that would not hurt a fly, this is very upsetting I am glad you cannot see him it would break your heart." "What do you mean Mel?" Mel says "Well he has a beard that is very scruffy he has long hair and looks like a maniac and he is grey and bloated it's awful." "Good grief, I didn't realise he was looking that bad, the poor man If only I wasn't blind this would be different I would dearly like to get my hands on that pair, I would rip them apart, a lot of this has been down to them." Mel "I know it has but he is more Important now as long as they stay away from him." A nurse pokes her head in and says "You can go back in now he is more comfortable now." The lads go back in and Danny sit's close to Lyndon's head and says "Is that better mate?" Lyndon says "Oh yes, yes much better and you?" Danny "I am fine, don't worry about me you have got the problem at the moment, we must look after you and I hear that you are going to go down to stay with Mel to get better, is that true?" Lyndon swallows deeply and says "Yes I am and I am going to get through this and make Wendy proud of me again, this is not good enough I must get back to normal." It went silent for a while and a small tear came from Lyndon's eyes and he grabbed Danny's hand and Danny smiled and grabbed his hand tight and said "What's this? Are you turning queer or what?" Lyndon shook his hand up and down calmly and said "Comfort Dan, comfort." And he held Danny's hand tight and Danny shed a small tier also and coughed to clear his throat and continued "It's nice to have you back Lyn, I have missed that little brother of mine, do you remember the fun we had together?" Lyndon with tears in his eyes replies "Yes do you remember that day driving behind Tubby Norris's car in the Capri?" Danny smiling says "Oh yes." Mel "What was that all about then?" Danny took up the story "Well we had that Lotus Capri car with the general grabber tyres and side exhausts etc. and it had a real police siren on it you know nee naw, nee new, nee naw, , and we were behind him in Braich-y-simmer and I put the siren on and he could not see it was me because of my headlights and thought it was the police and he pulled over and I passed him and waved, he was showing his fist and laughing. Then all of a sudden there was a real police siren behind us, I put my foot down and bombed off up the valley and he never caught us and we used to laugh about it all the time with tubby in the club." Mel's said "Ha, ha, ha, I remember you pair when me and Marice said to Lyndon after the big fight between you 2 after Lyndon had a big chunk of hair missing. Marice said "My friend had a vaticus vain on her leg and she rubbed some cider vinegar on it and it grew a huge piece of hair on the leg, you should try some on your head Lyn" and Lyndon said "Mar knowing my luck I will have a vaticus vain grow on my head ha, ha, ha, ha." That was so funny, Lyn you have always had a good sense of humour." Danny said "Yes we had some fun remember Lyn?" Lyndon shook his head and looked drowsy and said "Yeah, yeah, I do." Mel said "Are you allright Lynd." Still drowsy he replied "Yeah, just tired." Danny "Do you want us to leave and let you get some sleep?" Lyndon says "Oh no, I can still hear you and that's all that counts." Mel "Don't worry about us if you want to fall asleep just carry on, we will not mind it's Important you rest as much as you can mate." Danny squeezed his hand and said "Yes it's you who need sleep so don't worry about us we will just rabble on ok?" Lyndon "Yeah ok." Danny said to Mel "He is knackered, I remember a lot of fun we had me and him, he had that cat the grey one and that dog and he called them Smokey and the bandit ha, ha, and the cars we messed about with was incredible." Mel said "I think we had better leave him get some sleep, he looks all done in, Lyn we are going now for you to get some sleep ok?" Lyndon now very drowsy says "Aye ok." Mel grabbed hymn and gave him a huge hug and said "Get some sleep now boy and I will be back tomorrow afternoon ok?" Lyndon "Yeah ok see you Mel." Danny wrapped his arms around Lyndon and hugged him and said "We are always here Lyn don't forget and get plenty of sleep as we still have a lot to do in our lives, look after yourself, I need you just as much as I ever have and I will be back in the morning with Kelly ok?" Lyndon smiles and says "Ok Dan I will see you then, I am so tired." Danny "Ok matey get some sleep speak in the morning."

Danny and Mel left and in the car they spoke and Danny said "God Mel it's upsetting to see him like that, it is breaking my heart." Mel "I know it's affecting me also, he is such a lovely old boy." "I keep remembering the time when he was about 9 and it was bonfire night and I bought him some fireworks as dad didn't bother and I could only afford a cheap box and most of them didn't work and it upset me to see his little face as it was a disaster, I was crying that night, it was awful." "Well I hope it will all be ok from now on, he deserves a break." "Yes I agree, we had loads of fun before he met that bloody Debbie, he and I used to work on cars on a Saturday and make a fortune for the week and Gaffo, Terry Lambert was always up the house helping us and we had some laughs and many a good time with Wyndham and the lads from the pool team. He had so many friends he was loved and well-liked by everyone and look at him now. So you are going home straight away or are you coming in for a cuppa first and maybe a sandwich?" Mell says "I'll come in for a cuppa but I am not hungry, this has turned me off today." "Yes I know what you mean, we will have to keep the noise down Josh is in bed."

In Danny's house they were sitting down drinking tea and Mel said to Angie "He is in need of complete rest and so we came away from there, he looks like a man of 90 and it's upsetting but he has the right idea of getting better now, he is coming down to live with me so as I can keep an eye on him and get him out of this mess he is in." Angie "So he is not coming back here then? So what about the house?" Danny said "We will change the locks until we decide what he is going to do and yes you can smile now I am going back up to the college, that will cheer you up." Angie "Oh don't start, change the record or I am off to bed." Mel "Not now Dan, we have enough problems, I am off it's a long run home and I will be back up tomorrow ok." "Up to you Mel make it the next day if you like, I am about all day tomorrow for him." Mel "If you don't mind I can get everything sorted out by then and sat here for longer the rest of this week." "Yes I am going down with Kelly and she can come back to pick me up in the evening so we will do that." Mel "Great I don't have to rush tomorrow, I am off see you Wednesday." Mel left and Danny went to bed.

The next day and Kelly and Danny arrived at the hospital and ask the nurse how Lyndon's night was she replied "He had a restless night and he drank a lot of water and the doctors were here in the night, so we can only wait now, time is the healer here for him." Danny "Yes I understand, so he is Improving then?" Nurse replies "All I can say he has had a comfortable night but has a lot of drugs in him, he is not a well man and later the doctor will be around, you must speak to them ok?" Danny says "Yes ok, I will." Danny and Kelly enter Lyndon's room and he was sleeping and so they sat down and whispered not to wake him up and Kelly said "Oh god dad he looks so ill he is a mess, how can anyone do this to him? The bastards." "I know it's awful, I only wish I could give him a miracle injection and he will be back to normal and we will never touch the beer again and I will still probably be able to see too I bet and life would be better I wish, I just want him back as he was. This is killing me." "Don't upset yourself dad, he is in the best place and only he can help himself with this problem and you and the rest of us can back him up, I just hope he will get over that bitch of a wife of his but he dotes on Wendy and that will make it hard." "Well he can't

310

forget Wendy and never will, he said she has been taken from him and that it hurts a lot but she will grow up soon enough and learn the truth, I will make sure of that believe me if it's the last breath in my body I will. He is opening his eyes dad, allright uncle Lyn it's Kelly and dad?" He murmurs "Oh hello how long have you been here?" Kelly replies "Not long, I will pour you a drink of water you look dry." Lyndon "Thanks Kelly." Danny chirps up "Allright Lyn, did you have a good night's sleep." "I slept on and off all night Dan my mouth was so dry." Danny "And like when I was in hospital they kept on waking me up to give me a sleeping tablet ha, ha, well you need as much sleep as you can get Lyn it will take you a long time to get over this mate. I am seeing the doctor later." But it was too late he had gone back to sleep and Kelly said "Sorry dad he has gone back to sleep he seems drugged up to me and usually it is to help the recovery, so don't panic he is not going to say much but we will be here when he wakes up." Danny "How long are you staying here then?" Kelly says "I'll be off lunch time and back to pick you up when you want me too after 3 o'clock ok?" "That's fine so you will still be here when the doctor comes to see me? As you know I forget things." "Yes I will be here no problems." "It's hot in here isn't it? Is Lyndon allright in this heat?" "Yes he is, I will open his window just a tiny bit and put is flannel on his forehead to cool him off a little, it feels like summer in here. Why don't they turn it down a little? God." Well Lyndon kept on waking up and falling back off to sleep and not really getting into a conversation so it came time that the doctor came in and she said to Danny "Hello Mr Duckfield am I right that you are is brother and next of kin?" Danny said "Yes that's right and my name is Daniel Duckfield." Doctor then says "Could I see you in a private room? Can you follow me?" Danny replies "Yes certainly I will grab my daughters arm and follow you." They went off and Danny was expecting her to give him a run down and say he will take a long time to get back to normal and he sat down and she started the conversation "Your brother is very ill, he has abused his body badly for a long time and I am afraid all his vital organs are closing down, it's only a Matter of time before he dies here in this hospital. We cannot do anything for him it has gone too far, there is no hope at all I am sorry." Danny cried out "No, oh no, your wrong he will get better, he is only 41 he can't die please there must be something we can do." Danny starts crying and Kelly comforts him and the doctor continues "I am so sorry there is nothing anyone can do, are you allright Mr Duckfield?" By now Danny was inconsolable and crying fiercely in Kelly his daughter's shoulder, the doctor said to Kelly "Will you be allright with your dad?" Kelly with tears in her eyes said with emotion "Yes I will look after him." The Doctor stands up and says again "I am so sorry." And then she left. Danny sobbed for a while and then said to Kelly "I don't believe it there must be something we can do, there must be.? "Dad you heard her, he is too far gone let's go outside and phone Uncle Mel and see what he thinks." They stood up and lost no time and Danny phoned Mel on his mobile and said "Hi Mel are you sitting down? I have been speaking to the doctor and she says that there is nothing they can do for Lyndon and it's a Matter of time before he dies here in the hospital, all his organs are packing in, there must be something we have got to try something Mel, Mel are you still there?" Mel in a subdued voice "I don't believe it, flaming hell no, no, I will be down Immediately, I will tell Mar and will get in the car and be with you shortly." Dan "Why don't we try the same herbal medicine I used that took effect Immediately the devils claw ah, the milk thistle, it worked for me and very fast, at least let's give it a try Mel, bring some down with you, I am not giving up without a fight, I will give it to him I don't care. See you when you get here." Danny turned off his mobile and said to Kelly "Do you remember when I went on the wagon I was told by a herbal doctor to take milk thistle for my kidneys and it helped me get better quickly so we are going to try that, he is on his way down." They go back up to sit with Lyndon and Danny was still crying and Kelly stayed and after a while had to go back to work and then Mel arrived and came in and looked like the dog had dragged him through a hedge, he said "How is he, I have got the milk thistle, what shall we do with it?" "Put it in a glass of water and feed it to him so he can heal as fast as he can, I am not giving up yet, it is harmless and herbal it's worth a try." Mel poured some water and a few drops of milk thistle in a glass and fed it to Lyndon over a period of time but you could see Lyndon fading as the day went on. Danny and Mel kept holding his hand and rubbing his shoulder but there was no response, they kept on feeding him the milk thistle till late into the night. Later that night the lads went home and Danny just sat up all night and worried Mel had to drive home again and back the next morning as he had things to attend to at home.

The next day they sat with Lyndon all that day though he was sleeping all the time, they kept on feeding him the drops in hope of a miracle and Danny went home for the evening as he was so tired and his diabetes was playing him up and Mel continued to feed him the milk thistle as this was his last hope as far as the boys could see and Danny said he would sit with Lyndon all the next day, so as Mel could have a rest and they would sit together with him all the following evening.

Danny was sitting with Angie watching telly although Danny was dozing and Josh was in bed, just then the telephone rang and it was Mel. Danny said "Allright Mel how is he?" There was a deadly silence and Mel said "I'm afraid he passed away a few moments ago." Danny went hysterical and screamed out "No, oh no, no, it can't be true, no, no." Angie jumped off the chair and put her arms around Danny and said "Oh no, not Lyndon, steady Dan calm down please you will have a heart attack." Danny was crying his eyes out and could not speak and so Angie took the phone off him and said to Mel "He can't talk Mel he is in a real mess here." as she spoke she was crying too and Mel said "He passed away peaceful in the end, I will be up in half an hour." Angie turned to Danny and said "He died peacefully Dan Mel said." Danny was in a real mess for a long time and then he pulled himself together and said "Why, why, why him he was a lovely man and didn't deserve this, I will never be the same again, I am supposed to die first not him, he is my little brother, oh my god, why and it's Friday, this is the night we had most fun ever, oh my god, what am I going to do? I will miss him so much, this will destroy me, I can't take much more, I can't." Angie with tears says "Well Dan you will have to for his sake, you must phone around and tell people." "Yes your right, I will phone them now." Danny phoned Gaffo and some more of his friends and his aunties and uncles before Mel turned up. Mel arrived and the both of them wrapped their arms around each other crying and comforted each other and then Mel hugged Angie as she was sobbing badly, then they sat and talked, Mel explained the last moments "I was sitting there and he was sleeping and all of a sudden he sighed out and a trickle of clear water ran out of his nose and it was as pure and clear as a bell, then he stopped breathing, I knew he had gone. I grabbed his hand and said a prayer for him, then they came in and laid him out and that was it, it was all over I have got his personel belongings, it's a sad day indeed." They shed many more tears and Angie made a cup of tea for them both. Danny said "Why him Mel? this has ruined my life now it's worse than going blind, this hurts so much, oh god this is wrong, all the bastards in this world and they took him, he was one in a million he really was I don't think he was meant for this world, even Gaffo was crying on the phone, I will never forget what Debbie and that Jimmy have done to him and I will get them sorted out one day if it takes me the rest of my life I swear. They had better not turn up at his funeral I will kill them , Debbie or her mother they made his life a misery. I just hope

Wendy will be there Debbie's brother can fetch her ." Mel said "How can you stop them Dan?" "I already have, I made sure Gaffo and the other lads I phoned know this and they will let Debbie and her mother know as a Matter of conversation, I swear Mel I will kill them if they turn up, I swear it." "Yes I believe you and I don't want Debbie there mind, she has done enough to help his death." Angie said "They won't like that, they love being in something that they can be part of such as funerals, they won't like it at all and that will be punishment enough but they will spin a load of crap about you and Lyndon." Danny "Let them say what they want I know the truth and everyone else will one day, they are not liked much here in this village anyway as you know they make fools of themselves every day here so I don't care, this will be a big funeral as he was loved by so many and they won't be noticed anyway, so stuff them and I hope one of them come here for an explanation and I will certainly give it to them and if they think they are right in all this they will come over if they are guilty, they will avoid me, we will see." Mel "They won't come over here as they know what they have done, but we must concentrate on his funeral now and make the arrangements." Danny "Well Mel I will arrange the funeral director as a friend in this street is a relation to a good funeral directors in Bridgend. Who will sort out the talk for his funeral? I don't know." Mel buts in "Well I would like to do this if you have no objection? It will be more personel Dan." Danny with surprised look on his face says "I think that would be good Mel, rather than some old codger who never really knew him, but there is one thing Mel I don't want a religious affair as Lyndon and I were not religious at all as you know, so just a few words and 2 of his favourite songs and a prayer is in order from you, but just that I would like one of the songs one of his and my favourites, it's Let it be by the Beatles ." Mel looking sad "Another one I would like is Blackbird the Beatles." Danny "Yes I agree, I can't believe it he was here one minute and now we are arranging his funeral, this is not right Mel." Mel "I know this is such a sad day." Angie "It's one thing after another, we have had so much bad luck the last few years, we really have, it can't get worse." Danny "I know, we must be strong now for Lyndon and make his departure from this world a celebration of his life and show them bastards we are strong." Mel "I will have to sort out his house now, I will sort out his personel belongings and you and I will sort it out between us and what about the rest?" Danny "Well she took anything of any value and what is left is fit for the skip only so get a skip in I will arrange it, anything of hers that is personel I will get back to her, we don't want to be accused of keeping anything, it will not be of any value that's for sure and if you come across any bills pile them up and I will send them back also. I will cancel any bank accounts so she can't get him in more debt and get his birth certificate etc. and death certificate etc., just think that girl married Lyndon who had his parents house full of stuff and he left with nothing and she had everything, sad and I bet she will be over that house seeing what she can get. I must calm down I will have a heart attack in a minute, right Mel I will see you tomorrow." " Mel "Yes Dan and try and get some sleep, you are worrying me now." Danny "Don't worry about me this has made me stronger even though it has destroyed me inside, bless him Mel it's the saddest day of my life." Mel "I know Dan, I will see you tomorrow, bye." The 2 brothers hugged and Danny said "It's just the 2 of us now Mel, mam, dad, Dennis and now Lyndon, I can't believe it Mel I thought I was going to be the first brother to go with my life style, I am heartbroken now, it's like someone has shot me." Mel rubs the back of Danny's neck and says "I know Dan, I know it's not good, I am in a mess myself but we must look out for each other now ok? Get some sleep Dan I will see you tomorrow." Mel left and Danny and Angie sat there having the rest of the tea and Danny started sobbing again and Angie said "Oh dear, that poor man, he didn't deserve this." Danny wiping the tears away says "No he didn't, I will miss him so much, I was supposed to go before him, god, this has changed my life, it was only a short time ago he was screwing the sign on the front of the house and fixing things on the wall of the new bathroom for us, I just can't believe it." Angie said "I know, I can't believe it, I need some sleep I am off to bed Dan, see you later." "Yes ok I am not going to sleep much, so I will see you in the morning ok ?" "Yes ok goodnight." "Goodnight." Danny sat there for a while and was crying uncontrollably and got up and walked to the bathroom and stood there crying still and started feeling the items Lyndon had fixed to the wall and caressing them saying to himself "This is the last thing you touched, I am going to miss you." Danny crying sadly, this went on for a long time and he went outside then to feel the house sign he had put up for Danny and this looked so sad indeed. Danny never went to bed that night he just sat up plotting in his mind revenge on those who had done Lyndon down and thinking about the times he had with Lyndon when they were younger until he fell asleep in the arm chair.

The next morning up in the college and Zarrine was on the phone talking to Danny and all the students were sitting in the lounge Jeff, Winnie, Niel, Rhoda, etc. and Zarrine walked back in and said to them "I just got off the phone to Danny." Jeff interrupted "Is he allright? When is he coming home?" Zarrine looking so sad says "Let's have a little silence for a minute, Danny's brother died last night and he will not be coming back for a few weeks." There was total silence and Niel said "Oh no, that poor man, he had a bad time with his problem, he was such a brilliant man, he was so nice, there's a bloody shame I bet Danny is devastated?" Rhoda "Oh, god bless him Danny was so close to him, he is in a mess I bet." Zarrine said "The funeral is on Thursday and Danny sends his love to you all, he was so upset on the phone, I was almost crying for him, the poor man." Jeff "I know more than anyone how close he was to his brother and he must be ruined, I hope he is sensible and don't try and do something stupid to himself, I am worried now." Niel "He wouldn't do nothing stupid, he has got a good head on him." Jeff "Well he has gone through a lot lately, he went blind, his other brother died, his wife is carrying on with another man and about to divorce him and now this, how much can one man take?" Zarrine stamps her foot and says "No we must be positive for him and pray for him." Rhoda "I know Danny does not believe in god, but I shall pray for him, I think he needs our help now more than ever." Winnie says "He is a sensible man and he will be strong in his mind, but this will take him back a few steps and we must stand by him when he gets back, I will help him as he loves my head massages and they help with tension and makes you relax more, he will be fine I think." Jeff "I hope so, it's a pity we are all here and if we were there we could be more supportive." Zarrine "i told him we were with him all the time and not to worry we will be waiting for him with open arms." Niel "Steady Zarrine you are going a bit far now ha, ha, ha." Rhoda "Niel this is not a funny time." Niel "Rhoda as you know Danny would be the first to make light of the situation and smile that's how we are here and in Wales especially." Jeff "Yes Rhoda he is right, Danny looks at life exactly as it is." Zarrine "I am going to be thinking about him on Thursday and I hope you all will be also."

Back at Danny's house and Mel and Danny were having a sit down and something to eat. Mel says "Well the job of emptying that house will take a while, I have spoke to the council and they are sending men and a skip to put the rubbish in when I have finished so I won't be much longer." "Oh good, I have sorted out my records and his and any of hers I have put aside and a video of her and her mother so they can go back, nothing else worth keeping except some personel things of his, not a lot considering all that was over mums ay, not much to show for a life, I spoke to some of Lyndon's friends this morning they came over to see me and they said that the night Lyndon died the news got too Bettws club and his so called wife was sitting on a table with that bastard and enjoying themselves not a care in the world and when it was announced in the club from the stage as a Matter of respect he had died she did not know what to do and never went home mind in respect of Lyndon but got drunk instead and was crying crocodile tears at the end of the night and no one wanted to know. They were all disgusted with her, she didn't give a damn and it annoyed many people there." Mel with a disgusted look said "Never, well that goes to show just what type of person she really is, well we don't have to worry about her anymore she is history now." Angie spoke up and said "I wouldn't bet on it, she is a cow and will do something especially as soon as she finds out she is not welcome at the funeral." Danny "She already knows, the boys told her what I said and she had a face like a smacked ass, so we will Waite and see." Mel "I hope it does not affect the funeral at all, I expect something to happen before then mind." Danny "Yes I think so but I am prepared, I was shocked the people who have come to see me about Lyndon and was so upset, well not surprised I mean it was nice of them and I had a real good friend call this morning with a card and she was very emotional , it was Lyndon's best friend's mother Mrs Jenkins, Alwyn's mother, she was so upset and it was nice of her to call and made me think that wherever he is they were both together now playing tricks on everyone else and having a jolly time I bet, this has made me feel better, it really has." Mel "Yes I hope so he and Alwyn were very close, I remember." Dan "Yes they were, wherever you saw Lyndon there was Alwyn and vice versa and he loved Alwyn's father he was a teaser and you know I think when Alwyn died Lyndon totally changed forever and never was the same again, he really missed that boy and so did we all, it really upset me, I often wonder now how much better his life would have been if Alwyn was still alive for him, he was a terrific little chap and so honest with it and such a genuine lad." Mel "Yes I believe you, I never really knew him but Lyndon used to talk about him often, well I had better get back I am having some funny looks off one of his neighbours, I am sure I seen Debbie coming from there earlier." Dan "Do you want me to come over with you? I will fill her face in for her mate." Mel "No I can handle her and anyone else, don't worry I will see you later, let me know what the funeral director says." "Yes of course I will, look out it's the Gaffa, allright mate?" Gaffo replies "I don't know I am just wandering about and can't get Lyn out of my head Dan and I have heard something that makes me feel sick, Debbie is only going down the chapel of rest to view Lyndon's body." Danny "Never she's got a cheek, she never went to see him when he needed her, so why now? I know come to think of it, she wants to make people think she really cared for him, what a bullshiter she really is, if she did she would tell Jimmy to lay low for a while, but no she prances around with him all the time, so she can think again, I am waiting for the funeral director to call me and I will warn him to expect her and keep an eye on her, she is probably after his gold ring that my mother bought him for his 21st birthday, she don't give up." Angie "She is nothing but a gypo, she won't give up until she gets everything, you wait and see , I am off out for half an hour see you." Danny and Gaffo said goodbye and Gaffo says "It is my fault that Lyndon met her, I will never forgive myself now, he was happy before he met her." "Oh it's not your fault mate you were not to know how things would turn out, you used to go out with her sister didn't you? Mandy." "Yes until her mother kept putting her foot in and ruined it for me the same as she did for Lyndon and Debbie the cow." Danny smiling says "I seen Mandy without her make up once, god she is the ugliest thing I have ever seen without her makeup, my god she is ugly." Gaffo laughs "Ha, ha, ha, I used to put a bag over her head in the mornings until she had put the war paint on, I have seen better looking things in the bottom of a pond." "Well I hope she is taking Wendy to say goodbye to her dad, I feel sorry for that little girl, I do, she will never know how nice her father really was now he is not here anymore, oh god gaff, I miss him so much it's not real, it really is not I expect to find him over the house but no." Danny starts crying again and so does Gaffo they after a while pull themselves together again and Gaffo says "As you said he is probably up there with Alwyn looking down on us trying to tell us not to worry and they are having a great time and that's how I want to remember Lyndon Dan." "Yes gaff I hope your right mate I hope so I miss him." Just then the phone rang and Danny answered it and a few minutes later he puts the phone down and smirked and said to Gaffo "Well gaff that was the funeral director Clive, he had some bad news to tell me and yet good in a way, Debbie will not get to see Lyndon because this is the sad bit, they had to put Lyndon in his coffin Immediately and seal it urgently as his body is decomposing very quickly, because of the amount of alcohol that is in him, he is falling apart." Danny stops and starts crying again, he then composed himself and carried on "That tells me he committed suicide, he wanted to die to get away from it all, how sad, he is not supposed to die like that, he is my little brother, I am supposed to go first not him." Danny thumps the arm of the chair and cries again. Gaffo says "That poor man, I am not surprised he is that bad, as he drank that inches cider and that white lightening and it is lethal." "And that bloody Malik sold it to him from his shop without blinking an eyelid the bastard, I will wait until his children are about 14 and I will give them drugs free of charge and see how he likes it, the bastard and those bloody doctors are just as bad, I warned them he would not last a month if they didn't help him, but he knew his date of birth and so they did nothing, what a waste of time they really are and they didn't give a damn, useless bastards as they are." Next thing Mel walks back in and says "Allright, I have come back to borrow a Phillips screwdriver….what's the Matter now?" Danny says "I have just come off the phone with Clive the funeral man he told me they have had to put Lyndon straight into his coffin and seal it fast because he is decomposing so fast due to the alcohol in his body and so no one can go down and see him and guess who has gone to see him?" Mel "Debbie." Danny "Yes and she is in for a sucking isn't she? Good enough for her." Mel bowed head said "Oh, that poor old boy, he didn't deserve this." Danny said "I think he committed suicide really, the amount he put in himself an easy way to get away from it all, and it's suicide and all because he loved Wendy and her why? Why? Why? He was such a lovely man it's a tragedy." There was silence there for a while and Mel broke it and coughed and said "I am going back over to finish off." Gaffo said "Yes Dan I am going back over with Mel to give him a hand for a hour, see you." "Yes see you later gaff." They left and Danny got up and wandered back to the bathroom and was feeling the things Lyndon had put on the wall very gently and crying.

It was later that day when Mel left and returned the following day to meet up with the council workers to give them the keys for them to clean the house up for it to be rented out to another family, who they hoped would have a happier time there. Well it was later that day when Mel and Danny went over to see if they had finished to sign the house over as empty and Danny and Mel just wanted to be in the house that Lyndon had finished his days in, as they approached a workman approached them and said "We have had a hairy time here today." Mel "Why is that." council worker says "Well his ex-wife and her boyfriend and a mate came in and demanded the curtain poles and even the switches that they had put in and replaced them with plastic ones and they took half of what we put in the skip, they raped the place and most of it was rubbish." Danny looking nasty said "Was the other chap a ginger man?" "Yes, he was, they took everything and we just sat back laughing at them." Danny "I knew they would be over here and what is it to do with Jimmy and Adrian anyway the bastards, they are just grave robbers, well if that is how low they will stoop I feel sorry for them, what a load of pratts, no respect at all, I am glad Lyndon can't see this I think he would not be surprised mind he is not cold in his grave yet and they are like scavengers scrounging everything, the low life bastards, I hope they rot in hell I do." Mel "So have it all been sorted out now and finished?" Workman "Yes if you would like to just look around and I will ask you to sign the keys over to us." Danny and Mel stood in the house lounge and contemplated for a minute. Danny and Mel looked visibly upset by it all and so left the house and went back over Danny's house for a cup of tea and Josh was there.

Josh said "Ok dad and Uncle Mel? it is uncle Lyndon's funeral tomorrow, I am not sure if it will be hard for me, but I am glad I am coming to his funeral , I loved uncle Lyndon, I am going to play in the garden dad, see you later." Danny smiled at Josh and said "Ok kid, be good and stay away from the road ok?" Josh "Yeah." Angie said "Well I can't believe that they ransacked the house and that Jimmy the cause of most of the trouble and the reason Lyndon took his life, was interfering the waster as he is, none of his business and Adrian was supposed to be Lyndon's best friend, the tosser." Danny "I know, I was shocked I really was, he is not buried yet and they are grave robbing the wasters and to think I used to speak to those pair once upon a time and they treat a dead man like this, I am not happy." There was a knock on the door and Mel went to answer it and came back in and said to Danny "It's Debbie's brother , shall I ask him in?" Danny "Yeah, he has not done anything." Mel calls him in and Danny asks him to sit down. He speaks to Danny and says "I have come on behalf of my mother and Debbie to ask why they are not allowed in Lyndon's funeral and if you will change your mind, she was his wife after all." Danny said "She gave up that privilege when she shacked up and started shagging that wanker while she was still married, she is not welcome at all and your mother she sucked Lyndon dry and used him as much as she could, she only wants to be a moaner for a day in front of everyone to try and make a point, but not in Lyndon's funeral, he will have total respect tell her there is a few funerals after Lyndon's, go to one of them and you and Wendy are welcome but not your mother and Debbie, they are the main cause of his death so forget it." He replied "Is that your final word on it Dan?" Danny replied "Yes and I am not saying sorry either, I don't want them there and neither would Lyndon and if I could get a message to Adrian I would tell him to stay away as well, so you are wasting your time here with me mate, I have nothing against you, you have not done anything ." Debbie's brother says "Ok fair enough it's your decision, I am sorry it did not work out and I am sorry about Lyndon, I thought the world of him, he was a lovely chap Dan, I will take my leave goodbye all." They all said goodbye and Mel said to Danny "Well that's that then, I can't say anything, I agree with you, it will be hard enough tomorrow as it is Dan so don't worry about it." Angie smiling said "For what it is worth, I think you have done the right thing." Danny head in hands said "Tomorrow is going to be a hell of a day for me, I hope I can hold it together and not seeing the coffin will be awful for me, I am going to suffer I know I am but it's all about Lyndon not me or anyone else, I will remember January the 31st as long as I live. Well Mel how are you?" "I am numb and not looking forward to tomorrow myself, but we will always have his memory and that is what counts Dan, I am off I will see you in the morning and everyone else." Danny says "Ok Mel I will see you, I am going to have a stiff drink." Mell says jokingly "Don't you start Dan, please." Danny with a smile on his face says "Don't worry about me I am a person who can take it or leave it, mind you I never had the troubles Lyndon had, he never had much of a chance did he? Bless him." Mel leaves and Danny had a drink to calm his nerves and contemplated the funeral the next day. How will he cope with it? Time will tell.

Well the day had arrived and Danny was up very early as he was dreading the whole day. Josh was keeping his mind off things with his presence and that was good, his brother was due and all his aunts and uncles, they will also serve as some great comfort as Danny adored all his family with no exceptions, it would be a nice thing to see them all again. They all went off to the crematorium and was waiting for the coffin to be taken off the hearse and there was a vast crowd there showing Lyndon's popularity and show how loved he really was. Lyndon's coffin was taken off the hearse and placed on the trolley ready for his sons and nephews to be pallbearers and it was so quiet and sad in the end. Danny moved forward to his coffin and run his hands on the top of it as if to say, it's ok Lyn we are with you, Danny did this as his blindness made things unsure and so it was his way of coping with the tragedy of that day. As Danny ran his hands over the coffin he said "Goodbye Lyn, I am never going to forget you, I love you and hope for everything for you, you never had much of a chance on this earth, goodbye little brother." He then burst into tears as they walked on he grabbed Angie's arm and looked visibly ill. The actual ceremony was so personel to Lyndon, it was perfect. Mel kept his nerve and was so strong in his presentation to his little brother he loved so much and the music and all words spoken were apt, but when the music of the Beatles let it be came on many tears were shed and of course the song Blackbird had the same effect and truthful and it was all just perfect and more so because none of the people who were asked to stay away appeared.

Later in the wake in the club that Lyndon and Danny were members for many years and were very much at home in and where they done most of their drinking and dancing etc. All the family and friends were having a real good get together and enjoying the celebration of his life, Josh had survived the day very well indeed considering it was the first funeral he had been to and was determined to be at as he loved his uncle very much. The day was perfect and without any problems and that was that and Danny was happy about it all. A few days later he had Lyndon's ashes back and kept them in his house for a week as they were going to be put in a grave with his mother and his brother Dennis. This was going to be a personel burial with close family and in a beautiful cemetery, they all arrived there and Mel put his ashes in with his mother and brother and said a few words and a prayer and Danny felt Lyndon was home in the bosom of his mother and with his big brother Dennis. It seemed right. Well the day had came for Danny to go back to college and Angie seemed excited about this and the morning he was going they had a chat about the house and she insisted on the chap she wanted to do the work start as soon as possible and Danny agreed "Yes he can do the work but he had better do a good job of it or you will be responsible." Angie says "Right Dan he will, I will see to that and so I will call him tonight to start as soon as possible then and I will see you in 2 weeks then?" Danny left and was waiting for his taxi outside his house and he was yet again caressing the wall plaque on his wall that Lyndon had put up and thinking about his little brother and wondering how life was going to be now things had taken a tragic change and how his friends would treat him from now on, not realising Angie was having an affair with the very man who she was arranging to do the work in the house. Danny was a different person, this had affected him badly. Losing his little brother was something he will never get over at all as time will tell but he was determined not to let it bring him down and he knew he had a great amount of friends back at the college who would help him.

Back at the college and he walked in to his common room and it was empty and he made himself a cup of tea and sat down as he knew that Zarrine was there somewhere and would appear soon and like a breath of fresh air she did. She ran up to Danny and put her arms around him and nearly squeezed him to death and welcomed him as if he had just come back from war. "Oh my Danny, I have missed you and so has all the others, it seems like a year not a month since I seen you last. How are you my Danny? Sit down and tell me how you are." They sat and Danny said "Zarrine it was the worst thing that could have happened to anyone and it has almost destroyed me, it was all too much, I miss him so much it will take a long time to get over this, I mean it." Zarrine looking so sad says "Yes I believe you Danny, I can't Imagine how you must feel, but your brother would not like you to moan him for the rest of your life and he would want you to get on with your life, it is hard enough as it is you being blind, so you are so strong and will get back to normal I am sure." "I will I am sure, but it will take time, things have not gone well for me since the beginning of the 21st century, it has been awful, things are about to change I can feel it, so hows things been here then?" "Oh that bloody Sandy has been getting on my nerves, she had the cheek to complain one day but it was stupid, I came in and asked one day who had been using the cooker as it was stinking with grease and she said it was her and said she could not see the grease because of her eyesight, well a few days later she commented to me in a way that made me mad she said in a snappy voice "Zarrine, have you seen the dust on the telly screen?" I looked at her and said "Well you can see the fine dust on that screen and yet you could not see the thick black grease on the cooker the other day. She shut up Immediately and stormed off to her room and her boyfriend Mark didn't like It either, so she is a pain in the backside, then there is Niel, he stormed off home last week in the middle of the week because of his computer in the Queens building." Danny with a smile says "Don't tell me they are still not working properly?" "Yes and he lost it and stormed out of his lessons and packed a bag and left and never returned until this Monday, he is not happy mind." "The problem is that they don't know what the hell their doing with computers, they are hopeless they have never worked most of the time I have been here and they never will, as the people who are in charge are useless and it is off putting for a normal seeing person, so Imagine how frustrating it is for blind and partially sighted, I feel for him I suffer with the same problem, so is he happy now?" "Not really and he has caused a big fuss here about it all and the worst one here has been Jeff." "Why? What's been the Matter with him?" "He has missed you, he has been sitting around like a lost kitten, he has not been going over the bar till late and has hardly been drunk once, so he will be glad to see you, he knows you are back today so I expect he will be in soon." Danny says "I was expecting him to be here when I got back to be honest as he finishes early today and how has Winnie been?" "She has been silent most of the time, she knows you are back today so she will be happier and pestering you again and Rhoda has not been well she is under the doctor." "Oh, that poor doctor is he ok?" She slaps Danny and says "No you know what I mean she has got something wrong with her and she is having tests but it's not serious I don't think." "Well I hope your right, has Jeff brought any new women here lately or is he still with Jo?" "I don't know, he is so silent lately and I have not seen Jo here on the weekends, your guess is as good as mine. Clamper has been up asking If I have heard from you and Carol, mark, and even I heard Lola has been asking about you." "Well that is a turn up for the books then, she hates me, maybe she has got a heart after all, look out I can hear someone coming." Zarrine says "Look at who it is, it's Niel, how are you Niel? Danny is here? Niel comes up to Danny and holds his hand out for him to shake and says "How are you mate? I have been thinking about you, I am so sorry to hear about Lyndon, he was a nice guy he really was." Danny "Yes thanks mate, I have had a terrible time and it really was a tragedy and will take me some time to get over this, if it was not for my brother Mel I may have shot myself, he was a power of strength and he has got a heart of a lion, he did the ceremony for my brother, I thought it was just perfect and it made me feel a lot better. But how are you?" Niel replies "Me, I am fine now I have found a computer that bloody works but it's their last chance." Zarrine "Oh dear, I am off it's late, see you both tomorrow and be good." they say goodbye to Zarrine and Danny continues "Yes, Zarrine told me they still have not sorted out these computers, they are bloody hopeless aren't they? and I get my hair off with them too, why don't they sack the ones who have not got a clue and get someone in who knows what they are doing, I give up with the management here they don't consider the blind trying to work and can't because the computers are never working, so what happened after?" "Well I went home I had, had enough and stayed away for the week and phoned the principle here and she promised to get things fixed as she was probably panicking, when I got back they could not do enough for me and it is just barely working now, it won't last long you wait and see." "Your right it won't it never does, I know it will balls up again in a day or two so I am not putting up with it now not in the mood I am in." Niel with devilish smile says "So how is that gorgeous wife of yours? I expect she was all over you again." Danny looking serious says "Huh, you have got to be joking, you could see she was glad as hell when I came back up here today and all she kept on about is getting the floor laid in the house, she has found someone to do it cheap, so she is in a hurry to get it done, mind you she was very upset about Lyndon and so was Josh, he came to the funeral, he was as good as gold , I am more convinced now that Angie is going to divorce me, I don't doubt it now." Danny sighs and Niel says in a calm voice "Well Dan if it's true it may be for the best and you must get on with your life now and prove me right, I said that you have got a good head on your shoulders and was made of stern stuff and lo and behold Winnie backed me up. These things happen and the world does not stop and wait for it to get back to normal and besides you don't know for sure do you?" "No, I suppose not, I will just wait and see that's all I can do. I wonder where Jeff is he is finished a long time ago." "I think he is having a late lunch he went up the college green to get some cash, I think he is hoping you will go for a pint this afternoon." "Well I am thinking of just doing that, I feel like a pint with my mates just to get back into the rhythm, fancy a pint or 2 and some food in the rose and crown Niel?" "I have lectures Dan, I just can't leave them and go drinking." "Yes your right, I will go with Jeff he never has to be asked twice when it comes down to a pint, he never refuses, never mind mate are you here this weekend? If so we will have a pint then." "Oh stuff the lectures we need time together us 3, we haven't done it for ages and I think our friendship is more Important, I will phone in with some excuse. I am going to see to Abby and have a little nap, I can hear that Jeff outside, he is giving someone a hard time, I will see you in an hour, is that ok?" "Yes ok, I will meet you in here Niel, see you later." Danny sat there quiet and waited for Jeff to come in and here he comes and says out loud "Is there anyone in here? But Danny did not answer for a minute until Jeff got closer and could see someone sitting there and said "Ha, ha, I know it's you Danny, stop messing about you dodgy old git, say something then." "Hello you English git you , how are you then? And I hope you have taken out enough money to buy me drinks all day." Jeff with huge smile says "You have been talking to that other Welshman , how are you matey? I am so sorry about your brother it must have been awful, but hey I am here to cheer you up fancy a pint or what?" Danny answers "Or what? that's a stupid question Jeff, I never say no but I wish my little brother

320

had mind, sorry mate it still hurts a lot." "I know matey it must do, so I have decided to be your little brother ok." "No bloody way man I am pure Welsh and I don't drop my standards for anyone, sorry, it's good to be back matey I thought I was going to go off my head with all the sorrow I faced over this, I need to get back into the swing as soon as possible, so me you and Niel are off to the rose and crown for a couple and something to eat, fancy that in about an hour?" Jeff smiles and says "Do worms live underground? I will be here, fancy a cup of tea mate." "No mate I am going to my room and unpack as I have brought a lot back with me this time and want to sort them out for a minute and play some sounds before I go, see you in here in an hour ok?" "Right you are matey." Danny goes off to his room and sit's there for a while with his hands over his face and then he opens his bag and pulls out some cd's he had brought back with him and put them up to his heart, then he put one on and it was the greatest hits of the Electric Light Orchestra, this was Lyndon's favourite band and used to play it to death and it was Danny's favourite as well as Danny got Lyndon interested in them when he was very young and Danny turned it up and opened the window and let the world hear It and you could see Danny smile thinking about Lyndon.

Danny, Niel and Jeff were sitting in the Rose and Crown and looking happy with themselves and Niel said "I heard that music coming from your room it was so loud." Danny "Yes I needed to have a blow out and let everyone know I am back and besides it was one of my brothers cd's and I just want to remember him every day, so I give it a blast." Jeff said "Good idea mate, I wish I had got to know him he sounds a good laugh." Danny "Well he was when he was younger and before he met that bitch of a wife of his, but never mind I will have the last laugh." Niel "Oh let it go Dan, it will eat you up if you think like that for the rest of your life, your brother is out of it now and is enjoying himself up there somewhere I don't care if you don't believe in god, I do and I believe that so stop it now, anger is not good for you." Jeff said laughing "Listen to him he was like a raving loony last week, he threw his keyboard out of the window and stormed off home and didn't come back for a week." Niel laughed and said "Ha, ha, ha, I know , ha, ha, ha, it was funny now but your right I lost it completely but that does not make it right ha, ha, ha." Jeff still laughing said "The last time I was in here was when I swallowed that piece of butter and nearly choked, remember Dan?" Danny "Oh yes, I remember and we had a couple of pints free, order the same thing mate and we can have a few pints free again." A voice came from behind them and said "I don't think so Danny it won't work again ha, ha, how are you mate? I heard from someone in the college about your brother, sorry mate." Danny looking shocked said "Ian how are you mate? And thanks, I was only kidding I know you are not stupid It is nice to be back." Ian puts a glass of whisky in front of Danny and said "Here mate have a stiff one on me, it's a whisky your favourite and don't let the bastards grind you down mate." Danny with shock says "Well thanks mate you shouldn't have, but thanks, who told you about my brother from the college?" "A right old battle axe Sandra or something, she told me, she has bleach blonde hair and her boyfriend was tall and chubby, mick I think, they said they knew you and told me." Danny "Oh Sandy you mean, I don't regard her as my friend just an acquaintance, definitely not one I would like to be seen out with, tell me did they have a complaint and got some free food out of you or some drinks?" Ian looked at Danny in astonishment and said "Yes how did you know that? They told you did they?" Danny "No I guessed it as they heard Jeff telling everyone in our hall that he had a couple of free drinks because of the trouble with the butter and she asked where this was so she could try the same thing." Jeff "Sorry Ian." Ian says "That explains it I thought she was very forward, right I will watch out for them they won't catch me again don't worry." Niel laughing said "I don't like her, she is creepy, she is a real trouble maker, you should charge her a few bob more on her drinks to make up for it Ian." Ian "No I shall put it down to experience Niel don't worry, are you eating here later?" The lads say yes and get some drinks in and Ian said "I have a deal on the gammon tonight, so do you all want some later so I can book them?" The lads agree and sit down again. Niel "This is the way in a pub, instead of lectures, it's been a long time since we did this lads." Jeff "Yes it's nice and spring around the corner and my birthday soon." Danny "Yes you are getting on a bit now Jeff time to stop celebrating it now." Jeff smiling says Cheeky git I am only cough, cough, a, ha, ha." Danny "Yeah plus VAT." Jeff "Plus vat indeed, you cheeky git I am a lot younger than you matey." Niel "Yes but you look older ha, ha." Danny "That's true, so anything happened since I have been away." Niel "Winnie has not been around so much, but now you are back she will reappear, Sandy has tried to take over there and she is a lazy cow she will sit there and let Mark do everything for her, Rory has left semi-retired at least from here and Tim and Mandy are still in love, Kezz won the karaoke in the pubs competition and won £200 worth of vouchers for the Litton tree and Chris bail has been kicked out of the college alas a girl he talked to nastily committed suicide, she was such a nice girl too." Danny in serious voice says "Yes I was told about that the waster and such a quiet girl too." Jeff "It's been dull really I have not seen Jo at all since she seen me last holiday, Geraldine has got the hots for that bloody Shaun in technical support." Niel "Never I thought he was with Polly?" Danny looking shocked said "Yes so did I, how has Carol and Adi been?" Jeff "Arguing all the time and she is stuck to Lola like a second skin, Ginny has been asking about you, that's it really not much is it?" Danny "Not really, well no news is good news I suppose, I am dreading going home this Easter for 2 weeks. I may go somewhere for a while." Jeff "Why don't you come up my place for a couple of days to break it up for you?" Danny's face lit up and he said "Good idea if you don't mind mate?" Jeff "No problem mate as long as you know I live in a flat." Danny "Jeff I know this I have been there before." Jeff "Yeah, I forgot, I must have lost my memory for a while there." Niel "That's because you were both pissed all the time you spent there." Next thing 2 lovely young girls sat opposite and Jeff's eyes lit up and he said "Bloody hell, look at those beauties 2 crackers mate, they don't half breed them here in Hereford." Niel "Calm down Jeff you will be sitting on their laps next thing." Jeff "I hope your right Niel." Danny "Anyone ready for a pint yet?" Jeff "God mate what happened to the first one?" Niel "Too right mate I am still nearly full." Danny "Ok I will have one in between, I am thirsty." Jeff necked his down and said "II am finished now thanks mate." He went off to the bar and Niel said "Well he seems allright Jeff? I thought he would have been worse really." "Yes but I bet it is killing him when he is on his own and no one is around, that's when it hit's home, but it is nice to see him back just like old times, the 3 Amigo's." "Yes I suppose your right and it is good, I am enjoying this break." Danny comes back and puts 3 pints and says "There you are lads I got us one each in." Niel "Oh shit Dan, I will be wrecked if I drink too much so take it easy." Danny replies "Yes ok I will, I just felt thirsty and gulped the first one down." Jeff was ogling the girls opposite and Danny said to him "Oh god I hope you are not going to start up those silly chat up lines." Jeff "Ha, ha, oh shut up dodgy your back picking on little old me I am sober, wait until I have a drink first." Niel "I can't wait." A little later on in the day and the lads were slurring and laughing and it happened as the girls were laughing along with them Jeff started, he said "Do you know how much a polar bear weighs?" One of the girls said "No." Jeff with huge smile says "Neither do I but it broke the ice." Danny put his hand over his forehead and said as the girls laugh "Oh here we go Niel, time for a good belly laugh." Jeff continued and said "Girls are your trousers made out of space shuttle tiles? because your asses are out of this world ha, ha, I am like Dominoes pizza if you don't come in half an hour the second is free." The girls were now laughing their heads off and one of them said "He is so funny, where did you get him from ? Ha, ha, ha, ha." Danny said "He is only out for tonight, he will be locked back up by the morning." Jeff continued "My talking watch says you are not wearing any underwear." One girl snaps "We bloody are ." Jeff replies "Oh sorry it must be an hour fast ha, ha, ha, ha." They all were now laughing their heads off and Jeff said "Do you want to sit on my lap and we can talk about the first thing that comes up?" The girls got up to go to the toilet as it was urgent and they were peeing themselves laughing and Niel said "Jeff you are a daft bugger and this last week I haven't heard you, what happened tonight then?" Jeff "I think it's because things have got back to normal as it was and we 3 are out together at last again and those girls are a pair of crackers aren't they? And besides I have been dying to try my new chat up lines out for a while now." Danny said "And very good they are to Jeff, I haven't heard them before, very good ha, ha, ha." The girls come back and sit on the lads table and carried their drinks over and said "I have seen you lads here before and you always seem to be having a ball, how do you keep a brilliant sense of humour up considering you are blind?" Niel "Well girls there is nothing we can do about it, it's happened and so life has to go on and it's amazing not many seeing people like you ever bother to talk to the likes of me and these lads but we are exactly the same, we have feelings like you we love to laugh like you and we still love a couple   of girls just like anyone else, I still sit on the toilet and listen to rugby on the telly and have sad times and happy times. We are not any different, so don't you 2 change, it's been lovely tonight talking to you and hearing you laugh with us, but I have a feeling that dull bugger there has not finished yet." Danny said "I hope he has not I have not laughed so much since I kissed my mother-in-law with a lighted cigar in my mouth." Jeff laughs and said to the girls "So are you girls local?" One of the girls replies "Yes we live up the road and come here often for a drink, we see you here sometimes, you enter the quiz on a Sunday don't you? And have won it a few times." Danny "Yes but only if Jeff is not with us he is a doubting Thomas so next time you are here and he is call us and we will send him over to sit by you." One girl "Yes we would like that if he is as funny as tonight." Jeff "Well thanks girls, you can take me home with you tonight If you like." Girls reply "Sorry Jeff but our husbands wouldn't like it and my dog is not so friendly sorry." Jeff "Oh crashed and burned again." Danny smiles and said "Never mind Jeff, better luck next time the girls are fussy too mind and it's a messy job but somebody's got to do it ha, ha." Jeff "Tell me about it Dan, never mind I can but dream ha, ha, ha." Niel "He is hurt now and he will be like a little dog all night now, can you give him a kiss to shut him up girls please?" They both got up and gave him a huge kiss each and left, the lads said goodbye and Jeff went up to the bar and got some drinks in and when he got back he put them on the table and said "You would never believe it, those girls put 3 pints over the bar for us." Niel "Never, that was nice of them wasn't it." Danny "Yes it was, I think they really enjoyed themselves with this idiot by here." Jeff takes the Mickey "By ear see but isn't it and who's 2 jackets is this one ha, ha, ha." Danny smiled at Jeff Welsh accent and said "Are you sure you are not Welsh matey?" Jeff replies "No way mate, I am English all the way through and don't say well your mother is Welsh, I am English and that's that ha, ha, ha." Niel joined in "Watch I don't come over by there and sit on you mate." Jeff "See only a dodgy Welshman would say that, anyone for the last pint before they call time?" Niel "That's a silly question, we are Welsh and love our beer, so there's your answer." Jeff goes off to get the beer and Danny says "God, he's a bloody card isn't he? I missed you guys and am feeling a lot better now at last, it has been a hard time for me, I loved that boy as only a brother could and I only wish I had done more but I couldn't because of my eyes, but I will never forget him mate." Niel "I know you won't mate, I think if it was me I would have cracked up but you have handled it well, just don't keep on thinking about it when you are alone Dan it will make you go mad, just think of the good times you both had together, that's the way to remember him." "Yes that is what I try and do, look out the English git is back." Jeff puts the beer down and says "Bloody hell, you know those girls we were talking to, they are in the other bar with their husbands, they are huge, they must be rugby players, I was standing there and one of the girls shouted through to me and said hello sexy and her husband looked at me, so drink up were off." Niel laughing said "Dick head, their husbands are ok I met them here one day no worries about them being jealous of you, your safe I think." Jeff "Thanks matey, just burst my bubble go on, I love you to, this is my last one I feel a bit tipsy now and the taxi will be here now in a minute so as the Welsh say, take your time and hurry up." Danny said "You see Niel he has got to have the last word about us superior Welsh men, he can't resist it."

Later on as they arrived back in the taxi they pulled up outside Dowdell and got out and Danny just stood there and said "I will see you up there in a minute, I need to be alone for a minute." Danny walked off in the night, it was calm and cool and not a breeze about. He walked up to the bench half way up the road between dorm's and stood there looking into space and he started to cry and the tears were running down his cheeks, it was all too much for him and standing behind him quietly was Jeff and he stood there for a while and Danny turned and realised he was there and said to Jeff with tears running down his face "He was my little brother mate, he never hurt anyone so why? Why? mate,? He was such a lovely man he really was, I want him back by my side forever." Jeff calmly says "I know Dan, it's not fair, I wish I could do something for you, I don't like to see you suffer like this but you know he is probably looking down at you now and wishing you were not doing this to yourself, no one can hurt him now, he is safe and happy, he will never die as long as you are around mate and I know in my heart he never loved a person more than you after all I have heard said about him so let's just remember him as he was ok?" Danny still crying his heart out says "I don't know how I am going to manage to get over this Jeff it really hurts, I feel like my heart is going to explode it aches so much, do you know I will never see him again? Never mate, oh my god I wish I was dead sometimes." Jeff look of sadness says "Don't say that mate please, it's your round next thing tomorrow and besides Niel and I won't let you go, so let's get inside mate in the warm. Niel is waiting and is concerned, c'mon mate please I don't like seeing you like this." " Danny says "There's just me and Mel now out of six of us and I think Mel is hurting a lot and I know when I am gone he will be wondering why? he is such a lovely brother and I feel he has suffered most in all this seeing Dennis go then Lyndon this way and me blind as a bat waiting to die, if anything happens to Mel before me that will be the final for me I will not be able to cope as if anyone deserves to be here on this earth he does, but we have drifted so far apart because of religion and my bloody father, if he only done things the right way maybe we might have had a family with tons of love instead of fighting. A man who thought he could exploit us as he destroyed our family and I will never forgive him for that. A lovely family destroyed by one man who made our lives a misery by demanding full co-operation at all times and no questions asked without any feeling at all." I believe this is the cause of my 2 brothers dying so young, all because of his fanatic belief that at the end of the day is all based on faith no proof at all just a book written by men who are still killing each other to this very day." Jeff "I know Dan, I can see this all has destroyed you inside as we have spoke about this before so many times and I only wish that your father was more loving and easy going as you and your brothers and you would never have suffered like this, I know as I have a loving family and we were all loved by mum and dad and that makes a difference but I can only guess how it was, c'mon let's get in it's getting cold out here and you need to be with friends Dan." Danny wipes his face and goes in with Jeff and Niel and Winnie was sitting there silent and Niel said "Allright Dan mate?" Danny replies "Yes I'm fine now it's difficult mate." Niel "I know mate it must be hell, I know how I was when I lost my dad but life must go on Dan and the lovely Winnie is here to say hello." Winnie in soft voice said "Hello Danny, I wish you happiness after losing your little brother, it is a sad time and if I can do anything to help you over this sorrowful time I will, ok?" Danny "Thank you WINNIE I will keep it in mind, thank you maybe a head massage sometime as it relaxes me very much, but now I must say goodnight I am whacked I have not slept for a couple of weeks and this beer has made me knackered." he sadly walked off and they all say goodnight and after he had gone Niel said "Where did you find him Jeff?" Jeff looking flustered says "He was up by the seat crying his eyes out, he is hurting very much mate, it's killing him, it was so sad to see him like this it upset me." Winnie also looking so sad says "Well we must be strong for him now until he is better, I will try and take is mind off his problems and as you are his best friend I think you should do the same, it may take some time." Jeff "Yes I agree."

It was a few weeks later and Danny had settled down but was not ever going to be able to get back to normal. He and the lads were excited as spring was around the corner. Well Danny was in contact with his brother Mel and they often discussed how things were since the departure of Lyndon and reminisced on the past few years. Danny had lost interest in what was happening in his house until this week when he got home for a visit and nothing had been done to the floor downstairs. He asked Angie in a temper "What the hell is going on here? I thought you were having that idiot here to do this floor, where is he then?" Angie looking flustered said "Oh, he, he is busy for the moment he will be here next week." "Next week be buggered, you said he was desperate for the work, so where is he? I want to talk to him." "I don't know he has not been here for a few days." Danny looking nasty says "Right I will ask your brother terry about this idiot, see what he is all about." "Oh that's right cause a fuss, he will be here this week so leave it there." Danny was already on the phone and talking to terry his brother-in-law, after he put the phone down he said to Angie "Well he had nothing good to say about him, he used to work there for a while and he is not anymore so terry didn't say much, that tells me he does not want to get involved, that Gareth he is useless I am phoning bill from Aberkenfig he will sort it out for me and tell that useless asshole to get stuffed, he is a total wanker." Angie said "No he is not, don't be nasty about him." "What do you mean he has not done the work, what's the Matter do you fancy him? The way you are talking." Angie replied and this made Danny suspicious "Yes I have always fancied him." There was a deadly silence and Danny looked straight at Angie in a nasty mood and said "What did you say? You fancy him, is that why the work has not been finished you and him have been too busy shagging is it?" Angie did not answer and Danny took this as she is having an affair with him, he then said "Well what's your answer then?" "I am not answering you so there." Danny "Well is it true that you fancy him or what?" "Yes I do as a Matter of fact." Danny looked stunned and said "Are you having an affair with him?" Angie looking unsure as to what to say said "Don't be silly, leave it there now please." "You are, he is giving you one behind my back so where is his telephone number? If he is innocent you can give it to me." "I am not giving it to you, don't start now ." "I can get it off terry so give it to me now." Angie thinks and gives it to him and said "Right you carry on, I am off ." Danny shouted at her "You stand there until I get to the bottom of this" Danny dialled the number and he said to him "Gareth I want to know why you haven't done this work here for me it's Danny it is?" He answered "Oh, um, I have been too busy sorry mate." "Well don't bother now I am having someone else up to do it and I hope you are not having an affair with my missus mate?" "Hey mate I resent that accusation mate there is no need for accusations." Danny continues "Well you stay well away from here, I don't want to see your ugly face anywhere near here got it?" Danny slammed the phone down and said to Angie "I think you and him are having an affair, I hope for your sake I am wrong." Angie acted as if she didn't give a damn and Danny asked her outright "Are you having an affair with him or what?" Angie delayed her answer and Danny looked at her very suspicious as if he already knew she was, this was making him angry and she was just being arrogant to him, it was obvious and Danny did not know what to do so he sat there and Angie went off to get away from him. Danny phoned bill and he came up Immediately and sorted out the job which he would start Immediately and later Angie came back in and said to Danny "I am not staying here in this house tonight, I am off to my sisters to sleep." Danny looking puzzled said "Why would you want to do that then? If I am wrong tell me is it true you and him?" "I have nothing to say on the Matter, I am off." "Look wait a minute I will leave it at that , look I don't want any of this in front of Josh please it's not fair on him, we will sort it out when he is not here, I am off back up to the college tomorrow to get my head around what is happening, if there is anything." Angie said "See what I mean let it go now or I am off." Danny "Right fair enough, I will and I will go back tomorrow as I said instead of Sunday, I need to see Josh for a good day so let it go for now." Josh came in and they had a good night together and Danny returned on the train the very next day in a very upset state.

Back at the college he knew he would be mostly alone as Jeff was home for the weekend with his children and he would be back on Sunday late afternoon. Danny went up to the college green and picked up a bottle of vodka and some coke, he was not in a good frame of mind, he kept on phoning Angie to see if he could get more out of her on the telephone about what was happening with this other man but with no results and so he started on the bottle of vodka, it was going to be a long day indeed. Well he was now as drunk as a lord and still nasty, he then phoned Angie and said again "Hello Angie it's me again, I have got to know if there is anything going on with you and that prick?" Angie replied "Oh for god's sake Dan... no there is nothing going on at all." "Why don't I believe you?" Angie "I don't know why you don't believe me, you have already made your mind up before asking me." "So why did you say you fancy him then? Do you fancy him?" "I have always fancied him it does not mean I would jump into bed with him does it?" "Angie you have changed since I have gone blind, you know I can tell things have really changed and I think you are having an affair behind my back and I would rather you say so if it's true and not deceive me in any way as this is no life for me, I don't know what is happening, I am just existing and I have only just lost my brother that has crushed me so don't play games with me tell me the truth please." There was a deadly silence and Angie replied after about 30 seconds " am telling you the truth so get on with it you are getting on my nerves keeping on." "That is not good enough I want to know if you are having an affair with that prick? Yes or no? It's simple enough yes or no? Nothing else." No, ok now?" Danny "Right that's all I wanted to know so let me talk to Josh for five." Josh "Hi dad what's the Matter then?" "Oh nothing Josh, I am a little drunk here at the moment, sorry mate." "Not again dad, you are always drunk lately." "No I am not Josh you little fibber, so watch it sweet pea or I will stop your pocket money ha, ha, so what are you up to today?" "I am playing football with Josh Kendall and Murphy in the front garden, when are you coming home now dad?" "Awe, I will be back in two weeks for a game of football, I will be Man. U. and you Liverpool ok?" "Yeah dad we will always beat Man. U. always dad, I am going to a birthday party tomorrow, it's Josh's birthday in his house I will save you some cake dad." "Well thank you sweet pea but you will have to have it as It will go stale by the time I get home, but thanks anyway." Josh "Ok then dad I will eat it for you I am off to play with Josh Kendall now dad, I will speak to you tomorrow night." Danny with tear in his eye says "Ok I will, let me speak to your mother then." "She has gone into next door to see Jane." Dan's face dropped and he said to Josh "Oh, ok then I will speak to her tomorrow then ta, ta, sweet pea." Josh "Bye dad speak tomorrow, bye." Dan put the phone down and his head bowed down to the ground, he looked as if his world had come to an end, he started muttering to himself "Why me, I have only just lost my little brother, is that not enough? it's like I must suffer every year to please somebody, well Dan it looks as if it is over mate but I wish she would tell me straight not keep me hanging on and what about Josh? I can't see that pig looking after my boy, no way man it's not going to happen, she is a real cow to do this to me she just don't care about my

327

feeling at all. He had better not stay in my house I will kill the bastard, I don't know why I bother I would be better off dead, not many people would notice I had gone at all, it's the end Dan it is no doubt about it, your finished mate, I have lost my 2 brothers in the last two years and my eyesight now my wife is pissing off and leaving me and taking my youngest son with her away from me, I can't take much more and I just as well kill myself like I tried before because it's a hundred times worse now." He lay down on the bed and started to sob and he was in a terrible mess. He laid there for about half an hour and then he stood up shook his head and went and swilled his face with water, wiped his face while staggering and said to himself "Right Dan calm down and go and have a drink with any of your friends in the student bar." He went off and up in the bar it was deserted nearly except a few young lads who were giving Geordie Jim a bit of a ribbing. Danny went to sit by him and said "Hello there Jim, how are you then? I am a little pissed I am afraid." "I am going to be the same soon, I am fed up with people interfering with my life, do you know there is a rumour going around I am sleeping with Kezz and listen to those idiots over there making fun at me and Carol has taken Kezz to town with her to keep her away from me, I am just friends with her, god, it makes me seem like a pervert. I am fed up with it all." "Really she is a bit of a cow anyway, she loves making peoples life hell anyway but she is going too far now." Next thing a large young lad a little worse for drink came over to Jim stuck his face in his and said "Perve, missing the little girl then?" Next thing Jim stood up and smacked him in the face and he went down like a ton of shit, all the other youngsters stopped Immediately and went and sat down quietly, the lad was on the floor moaning and Jim stood up and said "Don't call me things I warned you it's your fault not mine you asked for it." Jim then stormed off and went to the toilet. Another lads came over to pick the large lad up and said "He is only one man let's go and give him a hiding in the bog." Danny on hearing this said to them "Cowards, I am a mate of his what if I give him a hand then? Look I am on my own lads come and have a go at me then." One lad says to Danny "We were only kidding Dan ha, ha, it's none of our business." Danny "Correct it's not so go and sit down as I am in a raving mad mood and won't mind giving a few lads a good smacking so piss off now." The lads looked at Dan and stayed there as they were and Dan said "What's the Matter lads? Don't you believe me or what?" Danny stood up and they dispersed and next thing Clamper came over to see Dan and said "Oh hard man, ha, ha, I thought you really were going to give someone a hammering then, I seen Jim in the toilet in a real temper." "Ah Clamper, how are you mate? Yes I was going to give them a hammering mate believe me." "Wow, what's the Matter mate? You look like a man possessed." Danny replied "I have had a bad weekend, I went home only to come back early and I am none too pleased so let's leave it at that mate." Clamper says "Ok Dan I understand, so why is Jim in such a mess then?" "A lad made a nasty remark at him and he kicked the shit out of him, serves his right ha, ha." "I heard some nasty rumours about him and Kezz, he is old enough to be her father the perve." Danny snaps at him "Oy, that's enough of that, it's just a rumour and not proved so keep your opinion to yourself mate before he attacks you if you know what's good for you, how would you like it if you were called a pervert for no proven reason? If he was guilty he would have walked away not give him a hammering." Clamper stunned says "Allright mate, I will back off it's none of my business anyway so I will not say another word." "Good idea Clamper, fancy a pint?" "Yes please." "Here go and get the beer in for me and you, I will have a Newcastle brown fore me thanks." Clamper goes off and gets the beer in and Jim returns from the toilet, he was looking over to the lads as if to say anyone else. Jim says to Danny "Hi Dan I am back." Danny replies "Well don't worry Jim I would have done the same and they won't bother you again now." Clamper came back and said to Jim "Looks as if you have made a few enemies Jim but it's not your fault is it?" Jim "No it's not, so don't you start either it's all lies mate." Clamper "Ok mate, it's none of my business anyway so leave it at that I am only here for the beer." Dan said slurring "Fancy getting out of this dump for the night lads?" Jim "So where do you fancy going then Dan?" Clamper said "Yeah I am fed up coming here all the time so where shall we go?" Danny "We could have a couple of beers in the barrels, they do some nice real ales there or the Pretty Pigs or the rose and crown for a laugh." Jim "I fancy the rose and crown, what about you Clamper?" Clamper says "Yes I am game I like it there let's finish the pint and we can get a taxi outside Gardener." Danny "Rose and crown it is then, I will call a taxi."

Later in the rose and crown Danny seemed to have cheered up and so did Jim and Clamper was joking around as per usual. Danny slurred "So why are you here this weekend Clamper? I thought you went home the same weekend as me?" "Yes I do most times, but my girlfriend was coming to stay with me this weekend but she never turned up." Jim "What happened to her?" "I don't know she left home on Friday and returned home as she could not get here and now she is not speaking to me." Danny "So it's your fault then?" Clamper laughs and says "No I have not got to the bottom of it, she won't speak to me at all, you know Lizzy it's her and she has dyspraxia and so she is probably embarrassed to tell me what happened but never mind I will make another date for her to come up and do it when you and Jeff are here for the weekend and we can all have a bit of fun." Jim smiling said "With Lizzy you got to be kidding, she never sit's still long enough and she will be bossing you about all weekend." Clamper "Yes she does tell me what to do it is a nuisance sometimes god, that's why I want her to come here when you are all about, I can send her to see her old friends here and come out with you lot for a pint ha, ha, ha." Danny "Good thinking mate, anyone for another one?" Jim "God Dan, slow down it's not a contest you know." Clamper "Flipping heck, I have only just started the first one." Danny "Ok I will have one in between then, no problem." The 2 lads gulped down their pints and said "Ok we are ready now cough, cough, I nearly choked then." Jim " Well take your time Clamper." Danny goes off to the bar and Clamper says to Jim "He's pissed isn't he?" Jim "Yes he is isn't he? that's why I suggested coming here to cool him off a little, I don't know what is wrong I am afraid to ask, but he is not himself at all." Clamper "Well it has not been so long since his little brother died and he has been having a hard time with that." "I don't know, I think it's more than that and by the way he is drinking he will kill himself if he don't slow down." Clamper "Look out he is coming back and Ian the manager is carrying our drinks." Danny sat down and Ian put the pints on the table and said "Allright fella's? All happy then?" They all said they were fine and Ian said "Anything you want just call me." Clamper not one to beat about the bush said to Danny "So Dan what's the Matter matey?" Danny thought for a minute and said it outright "I think my wife has got herself another man, in fact I am pretty sure really." Jim "So you have not got any proof then? So wait until you are sure Dan, don't beat yourself up about it mate." Dan "She told me she fancied a man up there and was feeling her way through my thoughts to try and tell me I think, well I am sure, he has been doing some work in my house, it's finally happened she used to fancy him when she was younger he is the same age as me as well, all because I have gone blind." Clamper "Well Dan , you have always said she is going to divorce you, so why all this, you were expecting it and now it is bothering you." Danny "Well mate I never in my mind really thought it was going to happen and losing her is not the worst of it, it is my son Josh, she is taking him away from me and that's what is hurting more, he is only a young lad and my youngest it is hurting man." Clamper "Yes I see mate but I have met Josh and he has got a good head on his shoulders, he loves you anyone can see that, he will stick by your side." Jim adds "He is right Dan I know he will be by your side all the time." Danny "I suppose, I need to rearrange my life now and sort out somewhere to live so as I can get him to stay with me as much as he can and there's Craig he is as good as my son , I brought him up from an early age and he will obviously stay by his mother's side and I think he will not bother with me again." Jim "If you brought him up he will be more than a man for her to dissuade he will stick with you as much as he can but I think he will lay low until the dust has settled." Danny "Maybe, he is a good lad, I don't need this now I am still getting over Lyndon my brother, that has cut me to the quick and also my life has changed so much in the past 4 years, I can't keep up with it lads and now I need a divorce like a hole in the head." Clamper "I think Dan if it is to be it will happen and you must be strong as I think you are for yourself for a change and let it happen as quickly as you can and as painlessly as you can and pick yourself up and dust yourself off and start again, you have no other choice, I have been in Josh's position and I love both my parents although they are living separate lives now." Danny "Separate lives, Phil Collins sings that very apt." Jim "I am divorced and it was messy, but I made it more messy than it needed to be, my wife fell for another man and did not want me anymore but I still wanted her to want me and so made everything difficult to divorce me thinking I would get her back and it caused me more hurt than it was worth and it caused a split with my children too. So get on with your life mate, I had a nervous breakdown because of my divorce." Danny head bowed looking at the floor said "Yes I know your right and I always told myself I would not fight it for the sake of the kids and that is what I will do for their sakes, I don't care what anyone thinks I am now realising it is all over and part of me thinks things are going to be allright, I will have to speak to her in a calm way and find out if she wants to divorce me." It went silent for a minute and Clamper said "And there are more fish in the sea." Danny "Huh, stuff that, I may turn queer as I have tried it 4 times now, maybe it will be better at least we can talk about football after sex and go to the pub together... no bloody way Hose I don't think so, things are not that bad ha, ha, your ok lads I am only joking but I will never find a woman that thinks like me, I have failed so far." Clamper "Anyone for a pint then?" Danny looking surprised said "God you must be feeling sorry for me Clamper, you never offer a pint usually." Clamper looking hurt says "You cheeky git ha, ha, I always buy my round." Danny "Yes after a few times of asking." Clamper went off to get the beer and Jim said "Dan I know it hurts, I thought I was going to die it destroyed me very much but life goes on." Danny smiling said "It has not hurt as much as when my second wife Christine from Cowbridge left me, that destroyed me, I wish I could find her again and try and get her back, my life would be complete it really would, I loved her more than any woman I have ever met, but life as you say goes on so I will need time to sort myself out and start again, but I think I will have to get over a massive hangover tomorrow yet and Jeff and Niel will be back by then, so look out." Danny picks his new pint up and says as a toast "Here's to new beginnings." The lads agreed with him and they sat and drank for a while and then got a taxi back to the dorma and went to bed.

It was the next day and Danny never got out of bed until late and he had the hangover from hell. He went into the lounge and in there was Winnie, she said to Danny "Oh dear, are you ill?" Danny replies with dry mouth "Oh no, I am still drunk and have got a hangover from hell, thank you for asking." "Silly velshman, still drinking and I thought you were home this weekend?" "I was but things went all to hell so I came back and went out drinking for a change." "What do you mean, you are always out drinking, so where is Jeff then?" "He is at home with his children but he will be back soon now." "And then you will be back in the pub won't you ? And then tomorrow you will still be drunk and I bet Zarrine will do your breakfast and look after you, won't she?" "Winnie, stop grilling me please." "What is this grilling?" "See another question, a grilling is when you keep asking me questions and not stopping when I only want to be left alone." "Fine I will not care and not speak to you then." "I don't mean that but stop the questions as my head is going to burst, instead give me a Chinese massage please will you?" "No, because you are being horrible to me." "Ok, I give up." He sat on the settee and blew his lips and made a funny noise and said nothing, after a few minutes he was falling asleep again and all of a sudden he felt hands on his head and it was Winnie she was starting to give him a massage. Danny smiles and says "Oh yes, that's lovely I need that Winnie thank you." "Your velcome, even though you are nasty to me." "I am sorry, I feel like shit this morning, I wish I had not had that bottle of vodka yesterday now and just stuck to the beer, so have you had a nice weekend then?" Winnie smiles and says "It's ok, I went to town shopping for some clothes and spent too much money and went to the cathedral, it is lovely there isn't it?" "Yes if you like that sort of thing and in that street there is a herbal shop a very old one that does old recipes and some Chinese things you know." "Oh dear, I thought I could smell some things that made me think of China, I will have to find this shop, maybe you could take me there one day?" "Yes, why not, I know exactly where it is and there is a nice pub there like a wine sort of place it's called the bunch of grapes, it's nice." Winnie was looking pleased with herself and she said "That would be nice Danny and we could have a lunch together if you wanted to?" "Yes, why not? I am as good as a single man now, so why not." Winnie kept on massaging his head and she was pressing up against him and Danny could sense this but didn't mind. She finished the head massage and sat by Danny and leaned up against him and he never moved for a change, she had a Denim mini skirt on and Danny felt as if she wanted him and tried not to show any desire for her as he was so hung-over. He said "That was very nice thank you Winnie I cannot think of anyone who can do that like you do it, it is so relaxing you know?" "Yes I used to do this for my father and he loved it too." "I bet he did, have you ever had a boyfriend then?" "Oh no, we never got involved with boys in my school, they don't allow that thing in China." "Don't they teach you about the birds and the bees?" "No, what is this birds and bees?" Danny thought about it for a minute and said "Sex education." Winnie looking disgusted says "Danny, why do you say this?" "That's what they mean about the birds and bees, in the schools here they teach children about having sex, like the sex organs and how they have sexual intercourse and have children and how it all works and how to prevent this happening until you are with a partner and want it to happen, how the male fertilises the females eggs and how they do it." Winnie interrupts and says "Why do you always talk about these things Danny? It's not proper you know." "No Winnie your wrong, if these things are not taught then there will be lots of little children everywhere and the children won't understand how to prevent it. That is why China is over populated." "Why is this Important then?" "Well people have urges for having sex with another person, man with woman and woman with man that's how it is women want sex as bad as a man does and vice versa, it's natural." "Right stop saying these things Danny it's not true I don't want to have sex why would I?" "Winnie it's human nature and you have not tried this and so you don't know how it feels and when you do you will like it and want to do it more and if you know all about it you can have it without the worry of getting pregnant, no problem." Winnie gets irritated and says "Right let's talk about something else or I am going to my room." "Fair enough , how is the time then?" Winnie presses her talking watch and it said

2.15 pm and she said "Jeff will be here soon after Niel, he is always back first with you, he will be wondering where you are and he will be shocked when he sees you already here so what happened at home then?" Danny "Oh my wife has got a boyfriend now I think anyway, but can't prove it." "Has she, I thought she was going to get a divorce with you?" "Yes I am sure she is now, so I came back so as not to upset my son, but she is definitely trying to tell me, so what are you doing later then ?" "Danny don't say this it's not nice, I am not going to fall for that one until you are not with your wife anymore." "Fair enough, I understand crashed and burned again" Next thing there was singing coming from the corridor, it was Niel and he said "Who is in here?" Danny replied "Danny and Winnie on the settee having rampant sex." Winnie said "Don't be silly Danny." And slapped Danny's leg, Niel laughed and said "When did you get back Dan? I was expecting you on the train, what happened man? You sound like shit." Danny "I feel like shit too, Angie has got a new man in her life mate, she said she fancied him and as soon as I wanted to discuss it she left the house to go up her sisters and said she was not coming in the house until i said no more on the subject." Niel said nothing for a minute and then said "Yes Dan I heard she was seeing another man from a mate of mine up there but said nothing until I could prove it." Danny looking shocked says "You mean you knew all the time?" Niel looking down says "Not really, I as I said I could not prove anything but my mate said she was with another man in a engagement party up there in the social club." There was silence for a long time and Niel said again "Sorry Dan, but that is not proof enough is it? But looks suspicious." Danny stayed silent and then said "Well there we go then it's true then or as good as, well, well, all this time and she has had another man behind my back." Niel said sympathetically "I'm sorry Dan, it's not nice is it?" Danny "It's a kick in the guts mate, I expected it, but it still hurts it feels as if I am not loved anymore by anyone, it's a lonely feeling and I don't know what to do now, god, what am I going to do? I can't go back there to live now it's over isn't it?" More silence and Niel said "Yes I think it is mate but wait and see how things turn out, that's all you can do Dan." Winnie said "She is a bitch then isn't she? and now it is going to upset a young boy and his brother, never mind Danny you are better off without her if she is cheating on you, so don't worry you are strong I know you will overcome this quickly." Danny "Yes, I hope you are right Winnie but this will take a long time to get over and so soon after I lost my brother, god, why me?" Niel "I am surprised at Angie mind, I didn't think she is that type of woman I am shocked." Danny holding the tears back said "I can understand it mind she married me because of the way I was and now I am blind she can't take it, I don't blame her really only the way she has done it, she could have been honest with me and waited, divorced me, then after a couple of months started a new life and the house is between us so we have to sort that out and so there will never be a cut off point for a long time will there?" Niel "No it will take a bit of time, I am off to put my stuff in my room and feed Abby, see you later, I expect you fancy a pint ay?" Danny "Don't I? I will see you about 7 in here if you see Jeff tell him as I am going for a nap before we go out." Niel goes off and Danny and Winnie sat together and Danny said "Fancy jumping in bed with me yes or no?" Winnie snapped "Danny, don't be horrible, no." Danny looking dejected said "Fair enough I will see you later, I am sorry." Danny left the room.

Later Danny was sleeping and a knock came on the door, it was Jeff and Danny realised he had slept late and shouted "I will be out in a minute ." He got up and went into the lounge . Danny walked into the lounge wiping his eyes and said "Sorry I slept late and that's not like me, especially if I am going out for a pint." Jeff said "Lightweight, call yourself a Welshman? I thought they could drink." Niel "Leave it now Jeff." Danny "I have been on it all day

yesterday and got totally pissed with it, I can't remember getting home last night at all."
Jeff "Yes I have heard and sorry you have had so much trouble at home, you always said it would happen though but I know it still hurts man, so let's go and have a drink and some laughs , Winnie is coming over too." Niel "So behave yourself Danny and show her some respect." Danny "I always do, what do you mean by that? She told you I asked her to jump in bed with me earlier did she?." Niel "No, she has not said anything she just fancied a drink with us or you probably, so treat her tidy if you get drunk that's all I am saying. She is not the one to take it out on it's your wife, that's all I am saying, ok?" Danny looked hurt says "Yes I know what you mean as long as Jeff don't start on his chat up lines , ok?" Jeff "I can't promise that matey." Up to the bar they headed.

In the bar and Clamper and Jim were already in there and they were also hung-over and spotted Danny coming into the bar and called him over, as the table was a huge one, enough room for all of them. Danny said "Allright lads? How did we get home last night then? I don't remember." Jim "Oh yes, we managed it you were blotto but gave me money for the Taxi, no problems, what a night, we were pissed and my knuckles are swollen after whacking that lad but he asked for it and thanks for sticking up for me, Clamper told me they would have killed me, so how are you now?" Danny "Great man I slept it off and am getting my head around the wife problems and time to party again, there are 4 of us tonight so can we sit by you lads?" Clamper "I don't know what do you think Jim?" Jim "I dunno, there 2 Welshman mind." Clamper and Jim agreed laughing it off so they stuck together . Jeff said "This is cosy isn't it?" Winnie said to Jeff "Yes but can you get off my skirt Jeff? I can't move." Jeff "Oh sorry Winnie, a mini skirt I hope?" She snarled "Jeffrey stop it." Danny said "She has got my favourite denim skirt on as I told her I liked a woman in one of them, I can't Imagine it, god let me at it." For a change Winnie laughed and said nothing as she finally thought she had a chance with Danny, time would tell. Niel said "I have been in touch with the helpline about this swine flu and all I got on the phone was some crackling ha, ha, ha." They laughed and Clamper said "By the way Dan I got hold of Lizzy and she told me what happened, she went out with her blouse on inside out and someone told her so she went home as she was embarrassed so I never had any nookie." Jim "Oh bless her she puts up with a lot with you lot. So you stayed here for nothing then mate, what a bummer, so you went drinking with the dodgy Welshman then, I can tell by your eyes." Clamper "Yes he was like a man possessed last night, he was drinking like a fish, bloody hell." Niel "And only a Welshman can do that and by the look of his face he needed that pint as he has gone to the bar to have one in between." Jim "I never seen him put that amount away as he did last night Niel, my god I thought he would have been dead this morning, he needs to cool it man or he will have lots of trouble with his diabetes." Niel "I know I will talk to him later and maybe Winnie can say something too." Winnie said "Why me?" Niel "Because he might listen to you and he needs all his friends now he is hurting but does not show it, but he will be fine as long as he gets over this." Jeff "Steady Niel he is coming back." Danny "Ah, that's better I needed that, the hair of the dog, you missed it in here last night, Jim gave the knockout blow to one of the young lads here and if he had said what he did to me he would be in hospital this morning." Jim butted in "Yes and my hand is twice it's size because of it." Jeff "I bet it's all over Kezz? So what happened?" Jim continued "A huge lad said to me I was a pervert and I got up and decked him no problem, they are over there now and not one of them said a word tonight, I was expecting trouble mind and that was that all over so no big deal." Jeff "It always happens when I go home for the weekend, I had an accident on the weekend I went to catch the bus from town and sat on the bench and leaned back and went ass over tip, some idiot broke the back off the bench, I looked a total ass and I burnt my chin with my cigarette at the same time ha, ha, so have a good laugh go on, I did." Winnie was laughing furiously and said "That was a shock I bet ha, ha, did anyone help you Jeff?" Jeff "Eventually after they stopped laughing ha, ha, ha." Niel "I would have loved to seen that, I would have laughed my head off ha, ha, ha." Clamper "I done that once and I ended up in a ditch of water at home, it's not funny it frightened me and once I missed a chair once and sat heavily on the arm and my nuts were bruised for a month, it really hurt." Danny "I have done that, it does hurt too, I needed a massage on them after Winnie where were you then when I needed you?" Winnie looked at Danny and said "I am not going to answer such a stupid question Danny so be good or else." Danny pulled back in his seat and said "Fair enough, well I feel like I am just topping up with this beer, god, I will be pissed again now." Niel "Well slow down it's not a race matey and you will be ill if you don't slow down." Danny "yes your right I will only have one more after this I think." Jeff "Well I never the Welshman is listening for a change." Winnie buts in "Jeffrey leave him alone he knows he should not drink like this." Jeff "Www, I feel a romance coming on." Winnie "Don't be silly." Jim "I think he has got to get over this one first ay Dan." Danny shaking his head says "Too bloody right mate and it will not take me long either." Niel "You don't mean that do you?" Danny "I don't know what I mean anymore, life is a bitch, then you die, nothing else can go wrong for me anymore but it can only get better, that's a fact." Well later on they all go home and in the lounge was Danny, Winnie, Niel and Jeff and Danny was wobbling like a jelly and he said "Well not a bad night ay? I won't be long going to bed either, god I feel pissed and I have not had that much to drink." Jeff "Well you should go and rest mate see you in the morning." Danny "Yes you may be right, see you all tomorrow." They all said goodnight and he went to bed . Niel chirped up "I feel sorry for him, he does not know what is going to happen next, if I tell you anything here and now promise you won't say a thing." Winnie and Jeff agreed and Niel continued "My mate lives near his wife and he tells me she is definitely having an affair with the man he was on about no doubt in my mind, so it's definite." Jeff "Never, well why don't you tell him then? Not let him keep thinking it might be ok." Niel "I can't tell him he will hate me for the rest of his life, would you tell him and break his heart?" Jeff pondered and said "Probably not." In the meantime Winnie was smiling on this news and said "Well she should tell him not mess him about like this, Niel can't you tell her to tell Danny and not keep him hanging on?" Niel "I really don't think it's my position to, I must stay out of it as it can only come back and bite me on the ass, so no I won't." Winnie "Well he will find out soon anyway if she is in love with another man she will want to finish it." Jeff "Well I hope she does it sooner than later so as he can get on with his life and have a happier life." Niel "And he can sort out his future, because as it is he has not got a clue what he is going to do next week and being blind he has not got much of a future." Jeff "Well we are damned if we do and damned if we don't, it's hard and he is our mate, I think he will find out soon and it will not come too soon as far as I am concerned and Winnie can't wait for that day either can you?" Winnie looking annoyed at the suggestion said "What do you mean Jeff? I don't want to see him unhappy, so why do you say this?" Jeff "Oh c'mon Winnie, I know and Niel knows that you like Danny very much and you are hoping it is the end for him and his wife, I am not picking on you I hope it works out for you and him at least he can get on with his life and hopefully be much happier." Niel butts in "C'mon Winnie, I know you are in love with him and if it wasn't for his wife you would be in there by now am I right?" Winnie snaps "Mind your own business and keep your noses out." Winnie storms off to her room and Jeff laughed and said to Niel "She is mad about him it's obvious, she kept trying to sit tight up to him in the bar." Niel also smiling says "I know she is like a fly around shit, she is after him and he is mad if he doesn't go out with her she has a great body, and she is very pretty isn't she? I remember you saying she was a model in China, you seen the pictures didn't you?" "Yes she is, the pictures are very good too, but I can't see it working out for her and Dodgy,, she is too demanding and he won't put up with her nonsense at all." "Who cares if it will help Dan get over his wife and get his end away at the same time there's no harm in that." Jeff "Niel, trust you, I think dodgy will be a gentleman in this case and not get into her knickers that easy, he will have to be coaxed by her…maybe not ha, ha,." "He will be there like a rat up a drainpipe, he will not have to be asked twice ha, ha, ha. " The lads go off to bed.

It was the next morning and Winnie was sitting eating some toast and Zarrine was fluttering about and Niel came in followed by Jeff and they said good morning to them and sat down, it was Monday morning a very busy day for all students and they always got up early so as to wake themselves up after the weekend of boozing. Niel said "I am knackered this morning, how are you Zarrine my darling?" Zarrine "Hello Niel, I am fine thank you and how are you?" Niel replies "I am fine thank you, has Danny been in this morning?" Zarrine "No he has not yet, he will be in soon enough, I heard he was drinking heavy this weekend and he came back from home early on Saturday, any idea why?" Jeff butts in "Yes, he has found out his wife has got another man or at least he thinks so and it looks as if he is right, so he has had a blast on the beer, I can't see us seeing him much before lunch he must have a head like a bucket this morning." Zarrine laughs at his statement and said "Oh dear, he always has a problem when he goes home and I can't understand his wife, he is such a nice man I can't understand her at all, well I will give him 15 minutes and go and wake him." Niel "I think it is all over Zarrine, I really do." Jeff looks at Niel and kicks his ankle under the table, he groans "Awe, what was that? Shit my ankle." Jeff "Oh sorry matey my fault, sorry." Zarrine goes in the kitchen and Jeff whispers to Niel "Don't tell her anything she is very close to Danny and will tell him," Niel "I wasn't going to say anything, no need to kick me that hard." Winnie was laughing at the boys and said "You 2 are so silly sometimes." Niel "Well thank you Winnie I love you too." Zarrine comes back in and says "Well I had better go and get him up." Off she goes. Jeff "I bet he has got the hangover from hell, he made a mess on Clamper and Jim on Saturday according to them, he must have had about ten or eleven pints and they were in a round." Winnie "Silly velshman, he drinks too much, he is silly." Niel "Yes Winnie, but he comes from the valleys and that's all there is to do most of the week, he can hold his beer mind." Jeff "He is a whimp mate all the Welshman should come up to Swindon if you Welshman want to know how to drink mate." Niel "Leave it there Jeff you won't stand a chance, especially with that dishwater you call beer up there." Next thing Zarrine rushed passed and went to the telephone and dialled, there was an answer and she spoke "Hello rosemary, can you come over to Dowdell as soon as possible, Danny is not very well at all, I think you should see him as soon as possible….. Right ok, see you then." She put the phone down and walked straight out of the door again and after several minutes came back. Niel said to Zarrine "What's wrong Zarrine is he ok?" Zarrine "No Niel, he is in a poor state in there, he is not well at all, the stupid man as he is and the smell of drink in there is very bad, he must have drunk them dry over the weekend." Jeff "Is he that bad? I said he should slow down." Winnie looking concerned said "Is he going to be allright Zarrine?" Zarrine "Yes I think so, Rosemary is on her way over, he won't be going to any lectures though. I will phone his tutor, do you know who his tutor is?" Niel "Yes it's Alison Carter, her number is on the list by the phone." Zarrine looks and phones and said "Oh hello, is this

335

Alison? Well I am phoning on behalf of Danny your student he will not be in lectures this morning as he is very ill with his diabetes, so can you let everyone know? Thank you." She puts the phone down and said "That man is going to kill himself if he is not careful, right you lot time you weren't here or you will be late." Zarrine ushered them out in a mood and off she went to see Danny.

Well 2 days passed before Danny got out of bed after being so ill because of his drinking and appeared on a lunchtime in the lounge talking to Zarrine and Jeff Danny says "I am much better now, I must learn to control my life as it has gone all to hell lately and it's not good but I am concerned about my future." Zarrine says "Well you must make your mind up what you want not your wife and soon before you drink yourself to death, Danny too many people are watching what you are going to do next especially your friends." Jeff "Yes Dan you can't go on like this you know." Danny "I know, but I have been speaking to my brother last night and I am afraid that it is true my wife is seeing this person and he said he went to my house after he was sorting things out for my younger brother and he knocked the door and a man answered and took my brother by surprise and he said to my brother, yes can I help you and as soon as my brother told him who he was he panicked and called Angie and left. My brother said that my wife was red in the face and did not know what to do with herself so she has got a new fella." It went quiet for a minute and Zarrine said in a soft voice "And what do you think about this Danny?" Danny "Well what can I do, nothing at all, but I am worried about my son Josh I don't want him in my house I will be demanding this and will be going home to sort this out Immediately without letting her know I am on my way." Jeff "Oh dear, it's going to be a bloodbath." Zarrine "Now Danny you had better think about this before you do something silly, your blind, he may not be a fighter but he can see." Danny looking calm said "I am not going to do anything if she wants someone else I can't stop her I can't force her to love me that's all over but I don't want that man near my son and that's that, he is not to live in my house or she will pay for it I promise you." Jeff "Well use your head then matey." Danny "No problem mate it's over, so I must get on with my life, it's hard to except and I feel like shit now but I will bounce back, I must sort this out before it goes any further or it will eat me away. I keep on thinking about it all the time and need closure on it and I don't mind saying this is going to be the hardest thing I have ever had to do, I love Josh and it's killing me, so see you all when I get back, I have squared it with the college and will see you in a few days." Jeff grabs Danny's hand and says "Well keep your temper mate and be careful ok?" Danny looking sad says "I will don't worry about me I can handle myself ." Zarrine "Come back in one piece please Danny, we want you back in this family as soon as possible and things this time next year will be so different, so be sensible for me." Danny "I will Zarrine don't worry see you babe and don't let my room out ok?" Zarrine slaps Danny "Don't be silly see you soon, bye." Danny leaves and Zarrine says to Jeff "I hope he will be allright and wish this was not happening to him." "He will be ok Zarrine, he is not stupid and I just hope his wife gives him some respect in this and make things easy for them both and I think Danny will be back before the weekend." "So do I and we need to get things back on track and have some fun again, remember the fun days? 2002 has not been so much fun since Danny lost his brother and now his wife, it's funny how things change and all within a month of each other, never mind it will return I bet, we must find a way of getting the fun back." Jeff "Yes, your right Zarrine I will talk to Niel and see what we can come up with."

Evening in the bar and the lads were sitting down having a pint or 2, there was Clamper, Niel, Jeff, Tim, and Mandy. They were all laughing and drinking and Jeff put the question to them "I was talking to Zarrine and she said it's about time we had some fun again here in the college as this year has not been a good start at all, I know there has been a lot of tragedy in Dowdell but we need to change things for the better." Tim "I don't think Danny is in the mood for a laugh is he?" Niel "Let me tell you now, Danny laughs if his ass was on fire mate, don't write him off lads he will be up for anything and I have got an idea, it's Saint David's day next week and Danny loves cooking so let's have a cowl day on that day, me and Danny will cook it." Jeff "I don't like the sound of that, it sounds like eating the inners of a cow or something, I know you Welsh people like eating odd things like sea weed." Niel "Oh shut up slapper, cowl is made of lamb carrots potatoes leeks Swede and parsnips and on onions." Jeff screws his face up and says "See what I mean, I don't do veg, it sounds awful Niel." Niel snaps "Jeff how do you know how it tastes? You have never tried it it's delicious." Clamper "I don't like the sound of it neither." Niel "Well don't bloody come then, I don't know I suggest something and you all kick it into touch without trying it, I give up." Jeff "Ok sorry, I will give it a try, so we just eat a meal and that's it." Niel "No we invite everyone in for a meal and put some music and get some booze in and have a good laugh, Danny would love that." Tim "Yes, at least it will get his mind off his problems for a while and a free meal sounds nice as the Welshman will be paying ." Mandy "Don't be awful Tim, we must all chip in." Niel "Don't worry Mandy I will get the meat and Danny and I will pay for the ingredients as it is a Welsh celebration, no problem." Tim "Danny is home now I wonder what's going on down there."

In Wales and Danny is sitting on his chair and Josh is out playing and this is the first time that they have had the chance to talk and Danny said "You sound nervous Angie, expecting anyone then like Gareth maybe?" "Oh here we go, is that why you sneaked home to see if you could catch me out is it? Well I bet you are shocked to find no one here then." "I spoke to Mel and I know he is staying here from time to time so don't deny it isn't he?" Angie paused to think and said nervously "No." "Mel told me he seen him in here last week and don't deny it, he described him to me and it's him, now I am telling you I will not have him here ever and I will sell this house if you do." Angie says "You can't sell this house without my permission so don't go there." "I don't want him here with my son here, do you understand? That's all I ask." "I don't know what you are on about, he doesn't come here." "Your a liar he does I know he does, he is a shit house, he is going to die if you do this behind my back I assure you and I mean it." "I haven't got to put up with this, I am off to my sisters until you have gone back up to college." Danny said "I will only come back here every week until it is sorted out so you just as well sort it out now." "There is nothing to sort out, nothing is going on, he has come here to find out about the work here and that's all, so drop it now. I am off up my sisters." Danny replies "Go on then I am not going back up until we have sorted this out, I mean it." Angie sit's back down and says in an uncaring way "So what do you want to sort out? C'mon then, we will only end up arguing again." "I won't want to argue I need to find out what is happening that's all." She snaps "There is nothing going on so leave it now, you are getting on my nerves now." "Please don't insult my intelligence, I know there is something going on, everyone is telling me so just stop all this crap and let me know that you won't have him in this house ever?" "I am off I can't put up with this crap I am taking Josh with me too." "Oh no your not, he lives in this house and I don't want him upset with all this, so you leave him alone, you keep your sordid life from him, he don't deserve this, just because you are a slut you are not getting him involved he stays , I can't see why you can't talk about this properly and if there is nothing going on then we can sort it out." "I can't stay here with you so forget it I am staying down my sisters." "Why are you

337

involving them? It's nothing to do with them and you running away tells me it's true. Why are you doing this to me?" Angie storms out and leaves Danny sitting there, he gets up and calls Josh and keeps an eye on him so he does not follow her. Josh comes in to see Danny and asks "Hi dad where is mammy going then?" "Oh she is going to Aunty Sue's for the evening to help her out, do you fancy a Chinese?" "Yeah, I will go and get it, I am starving dad, I knew we were going to have a Chinese I told Josh Kendall I was going to have one, right give me the money and what do you want then?" "I will have a special curry and fried rice and what are you having?" "Um, I will have a portion of spare ribs bag of chips, and a tub of barbecue sauce and" Danny butts in and said "And that's all, you will be sick and watch it is a £20 note so watch your change." "Ok dad can I have a can of coke to?" "Of course you can and straight back so it won't go cold ok?" "Yeah ok, see you later alligator." Josh left and Danny and Murphy sat there and Danny put his head in his hands and cried for a short while and the dog made a fuss of him.

It was the next morning and Danny was up very early as Josh had school and was hoping Angie would come home to speak to him before Josh got up and she did but she had her nephew with her who had been in the marines as if she needed protection from Danny, this shocked Danny and he said "Hello Simon, why are you here so early then? Or do I need to ask." Simon "Hi Uncle Danny, no I just come up for a walk." Danny in a mood said "C'mon Simon don't come up here trying to be the hard man because whatever she has told you lot she is wrong, so you can leave now I need to speak to her privately." Simon never answered or left. Danny repeated himself "Please leave, c'mon I want you out of my house please, I need to speak to Angie ok? I am not being nasty, what do you think I am going to do I am blind don't be so stupid will you?" He never answered again but stayed there Danny "I don't believe this is happening to me, ok listen then, so what's happening Angie? I know you are shagging Gareth Chin so don't deny it and I will say one thing don't have him in my house if you know what's good for you and him because if I hear he has stayed here your life will not be worth living I mean it and before Josh gets down here If I find out he has anything to do with Josh I promise you I will kill you and I am not joking and Simon don't think you will stop me I could get the police involved and get you thrown out of here just by clicking my fingers and if you think it is good to be hard with a blind man you should join the salvation army not the marines but it's not worth it and neither is she, he can have her as long as it does not affect Josh, so you both can please yourselves I am having a cup of tea and biscuit's and seeing Josh and see what I am going to do later, I will decide then." Angie "Well I won't be here today." Danny smiling "I will and I don't care if you are or not, I am here for my boy and nothing else, or except Murphy so piss off and be careful when crossing the street." Danny just got on with things and was laughing with Josh before he went to school and later as Angie was working all day in the school he got on the train and back to college as he was not getting anywhere.

He had a good think on his way back to college and thought why are the rest of the family getting involved? do they know what she is doing to the family or are they backing her and Gareth, I don't understand this, I have gone blind and they have all turned against me and Simon coming there like he did, I was the one who encouraged him to go to the Marines and I used to take him on holidays with us and much more and he has turned against me to support Angie who is doing all of this and all I done for Angie's mother and father-in-law when they needed support because of their bad illness and now they have turned against me now I am seriously ill. Why? Why? I can't understand it, if mother in-law was alive this would not be happening she adored me and all that I done for her and George, this is awful.

Well now I will have to change my whole life as I have not got anywhere to live now as I cannot go back there on my own, god knows what is going to become of me because I don't I really don't. I will have to get a guide dog and a new life some where I suppose, a new life is appropriate now just like this new life of darkness I have got to put up with. Not much to show for a life time is it? My god what is to become of me, this is a tragedy and I must do something as soon as I can. Danny put his head in his hands and looked very worried.

Back at the college that afternoon he met up with Niel and had a chat over coffee at 3PM. "Well Niel that was a waste of time she would not admit it but she was as guilty as hell, it is all over now for definite and she went down her sister's instead of answering any questions and she brought her young nephew who has been in the marines to protect her, what a joke and I was the one who coaxed him to join the marines instead of wasting his life and I used to take him on holidays with us and that's the way he repays me." Niel "Are you sure about Angie Dan?" "Positive mate, she is as guilty as hell, I just don't want him in my house or anywhere near my son, she can go to hell, she has shocked me, I talked to others and they confirmed she is seeing him. So it's over but why do I feel like hell inside? God and I didn't think life could kick me any further down." Niel looking sheepish "I am sorry Dan but I knew she was seeing someone but could not prove it and couldn't tell you as I am so close to you sorry mate, I feel awful but just couldn't." "Really, so I was the last to know then, oh don't worry about it mate I understand." "That other fella needs a good kicking, he must be the lowest of the low doing this to you after all you have been through." "Yes he must be a bastard, as long as he stays from my house and Josh that's all I care about, but there I can't stop him I must sell the house now." "If you get divorced you can't sell it from under her because of Josh, you can't do anything until he leaves school, that's the law Dan, nothing at all can you do." Danny looking down at the floor says "So I am got by the short and curlies? It just gets worse, I would rather Josh come an live with me." "Where Dan? In the college?" "Flaming hell it can't get much worse can it, I give up I don't know what I am going to do without him mate I can't stand it if I was not blind it would be better but I am stuffed." "The way I see it things will get better Dan, it may not seem like it now but you will see it will get better, you need to get stuck into some projects mate it will take your mind off things." "Well I am not going to kill myself or anything like that so don't worry, she won't beat me I must pull myself up and start over again that's all I can do but how? I can't see I can't drive anymore it's bloody hopeless." Jeff comes in and says "Yes dodgy you are hopeless." Niel grimaced and said "Trust you to say the wrong thing at the wrong time, he has just got back from home after finding out the truth about his wife and feeling down you say that." Jeff "Oh, sorry matey I didn't mean to make it worse." Danny "Oh don't worry about it mate I must sort this mess out, I am going to call her in my room, I will see you both later ok?" The lads say goodbye and Jeff asks Niel "So she admitted it then?" "No everyone told him and so did i so he definitely knows now and I think he is going to be allright the way he was with me, he will bounce back, watch this space." "I hope you are right he is not much fun at the moment and I miss the fun." "He has got through worse than this, he will come out the other end smelling of roses he always does, mark my words Jeff ."

Danny in his room speaking to Angie and he says "Well everyone is telling me you are seeing that bastard so I know now for sure, so where do we go from here?" Angie replies "What do you mean? This is all in your head." "I wish you would have the guts to tell me the truth for goodness sake, I know for god's sake, I know more than six people has confirmed I am right, so what do I do now? this is what you wanted for me to dump you but I will not because you want everyone to blame me, so I will tell you this I will not divorce you, the only way you will get a divorce is if you divorce me, so do you want a divorce?" There was a long silence and after a long while she said "Yes I do." Danny sat there looking as if his world had just collapsed as he never expected this answer at all and after getting himself together he said "Ok then, you will have to sort it out and I will not fight it in any way as I will not do anything to assist you in this, I will just agree with it, bye." Danny turned his phone off and sat there upset indeed . He after a long while pulled himself together and just sat there looking at his mobile phone and wondered why, is this the end of me? And how am I going to manage when I leave here? I can't even walk up the shops without anyone with me, I'm finished, I just as well die now this minute, this is what was going on in his head . He then got up and said out loud to himself "I don't think so Dan, you are going to live as normal a life as is possible, she thinks I can't live without her, well madam I will show you, I am not beaten yet." He went to the wash basin and swilled his face off and wiped it and set off to the lounge to see Jeff .

In the lounge was Jeff and Carol and he walked in whistling and Jeff said to him "Hello matey, look who is here Carol she has been left off her lead for the day." Carol "Hello Daniel how are you?" Danny "Ha, ha, ha, you wouldn't believe me Carol and hi it's nice to see you." Carol "Go on tell me Dan I am all ears." Danny "Well I am getting a divorce as from about 5 minutes ago, I called my wife to ask her if she is seeing a man behind my back she still denied that and I said do you want a divorce? And to my surprise she said yes." Jeff looking stunned said "Your kidding matey? She said that? Well, well, I never, welcome to my world man." Carol "Jeffrey, don't be horrible it's not funny." Jeff "Oh sorry." Danny "It's allright matey we knew it was going to happen but it shocked me when she said yes, at least I know where I stand now at last." Jeff "So you are allright with it?" Danny "Well it shocked me that she said yes but I have just entered a new world, I am on my own now and that is that, I need to make more of an effort and learn to get around myself now and chase up the guide dog people as I need a dog now and I am not afraid to say I am frightened." Carol "Daniel you will be ok, it's not as bad as you are thinking, I get around all the time and you will in time and I know a lot of people who get all over the world who are blind and once you get a dog look out." Jeff "So are you able to go home now?" Danny "Yes, I still own half the house and my son is there but I bet she will try and stop me, I will probably go there for a few days and somewhere else for the rest of the time." Jeff looking excited said "If you like you can come up my place in Swindon for a pub crawl, I have a flat of my own it's a little rough but it's home." Danny " I know that I have been there remember? But thanks mate I will take you up on that, we will hit the town hard ha, ha." Jeff "There we are then, sorted already matey." Carol "And there are lots of girls out there for you Dan and you are a free man now and can have fun again." Danny's eyes lit up "Yes, I am aren't I? Look out girls I am on the rampage, fancy going down town tonight Jeff? There's a karaoke in the Litton tree pub and we can see what the talent is like there." Jeff "Has Carol got big boobs? Matey of course I will be there. " Next in walks Niel and Jeff and Carol goes off to Jeff's room. Niel "Ok who's in here?" Danny replies "Only me and Jeff and Carol have gone to Jeff's room for a minute, how are you Niel?" "I am fine it's you have got the problems." "Not anymore, she wants a divorce so it's over mate and I am a free man, so look out." "Never, well you don't seem to unhappy." "I was at first but I have been expecting it as you know so I must get on with my life now so it's up and at it." "A good attitude to have mate but it will change your life now, so where are you going to live Dan? Have you thought about that?" "Well there's nothing stopping me living back at my home but not logical at all, so I will use some of the money coming to me to buy another house down in Pembrokeshire I suppose

340

and start all over again in my family's home town of Narberth and my oldest brother is living not far from there, well 19 miles just far enough. I will live alone I can't see me ever getting married again, no chance." "Well I am not being funny Dan but that's number 4 I think it's time to leave it there now." "Yes, I think I agree with you, I can always have a Chinese mind." "Winnie you mean, I don't see why not she is available and you are free now, good luck matey you will need it." "Mmm I know what you mean there, I am off to a Karaoke tonight with Jeff to see if I can still score, fancy it?" "No thanks mate I have got a good talking book on the go I am knackered as well so it's early to bed for me, but you be careful out there, see you later." "Yes mate see you."

Later that night and Jeff and Danny was in the karaoke and also in there was Clamper, m Mark and Kezz they sat by them and Danny said to Kezz "Eek, eek." Kezz looked around and said "Who is that? Ha, ha, I know that voice, let me think, it's that lovely Welshman named dodgy, isn't it?" Danny "Eek, eek." Kezz "Ha, ha, I know it's you Danny so say something." Danny "Hello Kezz fancy seeing you here, I am here with Uncle Jeff." Kezz in loud voice sounding so excited "Uncle Jeffrey and Danny, Danny and Barbara ha, ha, what are you doing here? I bet you heard I was singing here didn't you?" Jeff smiling "Well of course we did, why else would we come to a pub?" mark speaks up "O, o, o, I am worried now, I feel a piss up coming up j,j,j,jeff I am staying on my own and not with you 2 I,I,I, have lectures tomorrow so if you don't mind I will stay on my own?" Jeff "No problem mark." Clamper jumps in and said "I will come in a round with you guys." Danny "No it's alright mate we will stay as we are and there will be no arguing then." Clamper looking serious "What do you mean?" Danny "Well you and Jeff always end up arguing don't you? So it's best for all." Clamper "Ok fair enough." Kezz "Danny I am going up to sing now soon, you must listen and tell me what you think ok?" Danny "Of course I will, you are the best singer in here and before you ask I am not singing, I am on the pull." Kezz "Ha, ha, so your wife has gone now then ay? I know a girl in the college who likes you and I am not going to tell you who she is, so there, eek, eek." Danny "Don't be horrible." Kezz "I will tell you when we are on our own tomorrow." Jeff "I bet it is some old monster." Clamper "I expect so if Kezz knows her." Kezz warns him "Watch it Clamper or I will tell Lizzy things about you." Clamper shuts up and mark laughs at him and Kezz is called up to sing and the boys all cheer. Next thing a few women come and sit near Jeff and Danny and Jeff gets excited and says to Danny "2 cracking girls are sitting opposite in nice small skirts and they look fit matey and they are staring at me and smiling." Danny "Correction Jeff they are laughing at you ha, ha, sorry mate I am only joking, we will wait a while for them to settle in and have a few drinks before we do anything." Jeff "Good thinking mate, I don't care which one I get they are both crackers and nice bodies." Danny "Let's hope they are single then, forget them for now and wait , I need a drink mate and it's your round." Jeff goes up to get the pints and mark says to Danny "Are you drinking this Kronenberg? It's only one pound f,f,f,fifty pence a pint." Danny looking shocked says "Is it? I like that pint too I didn't know they had it here, I will get some after." Mark "I have had 4 pints already and feel pissed already so I had better take my time." Danny smiles and says "Don't worry about it mark enjoy it." Jeff returns and says "I got us some Kronenberg it's only one pound fifty a pint and I know you like it." Danny "It's amazing mark was just telling me all about that and it's like you heard him, good thinking mate." Kezz finished singing and the boys cheered out loud and Kezz returned and said "Eek, eek so what did you think?" Danny "Banging girl just banging." Kezz getting her breath back says "Ha, ha, I enjoyed that, so time for a pint." She goes off and Clamper said "Oh god, I bet she will go on and on about her singing all night ha, ha, I might sing if they have got my song up there." Jeff "I think they have the rocky horror theme." Clamper "Very funny Jeff, I am splitting my sides to." Danny "Oh here they go again, I will bang your heads together mind, you 2 are always arguing, honestly." Jeff "Well he picks on everything I say all the time." Danny snaps "Jeff he is a kid you are old enough to know better, you let him get to you, so don't, fancy going up there and giving a song then?" Jeff "Bugger off everyone will leave if I sang." Danny "What about you mark?" Mark nervously says H,h,h, who me s,s,s,ising sing ,n,n ,no fear." Danny "That reminds me of a mate of mine in Wales, he has a stutter and I took him and some friends to a karaoke one night, he got pissed and he enjoyed it so much he got up to sing and did a song from the rolling stones called fade away and he sang it and I killed myself laughing and he was smiling back this is him l,l,l,l,love is l,l,l,love and l,l,l, f,f,f,f,fade aw,aw,away." The boys laughed their heads off and mark was under the table he laughed so much and the women behind them were listening and laughing to , this was the break Danny was waiting for and he turned and smiled for a moment. This started the girls talking about him and Jeff and Danny could hear them talking, he turned to Jeff and said in a quiet voice "They have caught on that we fancy them they are talking about us mate so I will break the ice in a moment just follow me." Jeff "Are you sure Dan? I can't wait mate." Danny turned and told Jeff a joke and said so as the girls could hear him and at the end of the joke they laughed out loud and Danny said to them "Ah, someone who appreciates a good joke, that's rare to have a woman understand a good joke." The 2 girls smiled and the one girl said "You cheeky git, I will have you know we are not your average women ha, ha, ha." Danny "Yes I can see that, did you hear about the 2 Irish homosexuals? Michael Fitzpatrick and Patrick Fit's Michael." The girls laughed out loud again and Jeff said "So are you girls local?" Second girl replied "Yes we don't live far from here, it is in walking distance really, I am Dina and my friend is Janine and you are?" Jeff answered with huge smile on his face "I am Jeff and this is the dodgy Welshman, his name is Danny, pleased to meet you 2." Dina smiles back and says " likewise, I am Welsh too so be careful what you say about the Welsh." Jeff "Just my luck another bloody Welsh person, only joking, but such a nice Welsh person." Danny sighs and says "Just ignore him he is from Swindon or as I say swine down as it was originally named, it's our first time here what about you?" Janine "Well we have come here before, it's ok, but not brilliant. I bet you 2 are married to and looking for a bit of nookie." Danny "I am separated and in the middle of a divorce and Jeff has been divorced for a couple of years now but I am looking for a bit of nookie and you?" Dina "Both divorced from 2 right pratts and both brothers, so men are not the priority in our lives although you 2 seem a lot of fun." Jeff "Would you like a drink?" Dina "Yes please, we will have a half of Kronenberg please, thank you." Danny gives Jeff the money and turned to sit by the girls and said "I will give Jeff around 30 minutes and he will start telling you his chat up lines and they are terrible but funny, so humour him please he gets easily hurt." Janine "Awe, does he?" Danny "Ha, ha, no I am only kidding, he is funny though, so are any of you singing?" Janine "If I can get Dina drunk then we will go up together and sing but not sober, so what about you?" Danny "It takes guts I would not do it, I am a watcher." Dina in a giggly voice said "Oh yeah a watcher aye, right my kind of man." Danny "Whatever turns you on kid, either way is ok by me, so do you like women and men then?" Dina "Oh no, I am a one man woman at a time so don't get any ideas mate ha, ha." Janine "I am the same most of the time ha, ha, ha." Danny looking hot under the collar said "Right change the subject, I am getting excited now, cough, cough." Dina "Are you blushing Danny?" Danny replies gulping the same time "Well I think it's my blood pressure that's going wild, look out he is back." Jeff puts the beers down and gives Danny his change and sit's by the girls and Danny and says "There you go girls, this beer is strong it's hitting me right between the eyes." Janine "Yes it's strong and your mate is getting hot under the collar talking dirty to us." Jeff "Oh he is like that, I have to hose him down when we get home and he is dry in ten minutes ha, ha, so I missed some good conversation then?" Danny "Oh yes, these are a right pair of vixens and they have been telling me they like to be watched." Jeff getting excited said "What do you mean?" Dina "Don't listen to him Jeff he is teasing you, we are good little girls." Jeff "Oh god, I hope not ha, ha, ha." Danny "I feel a few chat up lines coming on, I have told them about them so when you are ready mate." Jeff "Don't listen to him he has not got any romance in him, not like me, I choose my time to get romantic ha, ha, ha." Danny "He is dying to say one or two, never mind I'll wait for it. So then girls do you live on your own then?" Dina "Yes I have a 3 bed house and Janine has a 3 bed house, but Janine has a little boy, he is 12, I have not got any children but like to practise ha, ha, ha." Danny "I have a lad who is 11 in a few weeks so we have something in common and I love them at that age, lots of fun and you don't know what is coming out of their lips next, brilliant." Janine "What about you Jeff any kids?" Jeff says "Yes I have 3 boys and 2 step daughters." Dina "God mate you are a busy boy for a little lad." Jeff "What I lost in height I made up in length ha, ha, and Danny has 6 children." Dina "Bloody hell Dan, no telly?" Danny smiling "I have been married more than once and one of my sons is my step son but he is just like he is one of my own and just as much loved by me, I have 3 daughters and 3 sons." Dina "So it's a sure thing you boys know what you are doing then?" Danny "I have a rough idea ha, ha, look out he is thinking here comes his chat up lines I think." Jeff "Well your wrong I just thought of a few jokes I was told today, what is black and hard? A crow with a flick knife. What goes peck, peck, peck, boom? A chicken in a mine field . A blonde calls her boyfriend on her phone and tells him she has bought a difficult puzzle with many pieces, what's it supposed to be? Asked the boyfriend, she replies a rooster. When he gets home he says I think you should sit still while I clean up the cornflakes, ha, ha, ha." Dina laughing said "Very good Jeff I haven't heard them before, so what are these chat up lines then?" Jeff "My way of breaking the ice, but the lads take the Mickey out of me when I say them, they are supposed to be funny and corny for instance, how would you like your eggs in the morning? Fried, scrambled, poached or fertilized." The 2 girls burst out laughing and Jeff continued "Do you sleep on your stomach? If not can I? And one of my favourites is, can you tell the difference between a burger and sex?" They both look at Jeff and then both say "No." Jeff "Fancy something to eat ha, ha,. Do you think they are corny then?" After a lot of laughter from the girls Janine says "Not at all Jeff, very good mate, I have never heard any of them before ha, ha, ha." Danny said "Your lucky, I hear them all the time, I must get him a regular girlfriend and then i wouldn't have to listen to them again." Jeff says "Shut up moaning dodgy, see what I mean, they are fun aren't they?" Dina "Very effective Jeff, you carry on the way you are it flips my lid." Jeff "Thank you Dina, I have proved a point then and thank you both, right ready for a drink then?" Jeff sets off to the bar. Danny "God this Kronenberg is going straight to my head." Dina "As long as it is not affecting anything else." Danny "No problem that is the last thing it effects girl, don't worry." Janine "Hey you 2 less of it I am getting very hot here with all that talking so calm down and your right Danny this is getting to me too and why does Jeff always go up to the bar for you both?" Danny "Because he has better eyesight than me, I am totally blind." There was a deadly silence and Danny felt this and Dina said "Are you really blind? Or are you joking me?" Danny replies "Yes, I thought you knew I was? I am totally blind, my eyes are perfect to look at but I can't see a bloody thing, does that make a difference then?" Dina stuttering "Oh no I, I, I just was shocked when you said you were blind that's all and is Jeff partially sighted then?" Danny "Yes he is but he gets around ok." Janine "I would never have believed it, I thought you were joking, so that's why you were sitting by the other ones from the college then? I see now, sorry it was not meant to be horrible, in fact that girl sings like an angel." Danny "Yes she does, she won the £200 last year on the karaoke, she is good." Jeff comes back all smiles and the girls smile back at him and say "Oh, thank you Jeff." Jeff "No problem, so what are you girls doing after? fancy a drink in your place?" Janine spoke unconvincingly "Well, well, why not, what do you think Dina?" Dina "I don't mind, we have to get some bottles from behind the bar, they sell flagons of cider" Jeff "I will get a few and Danny will get some too, what do you think dodgy?" Danny hesitates a while and said "Yeah, why not?" The girls finish their drinks after a while and say to the boys "You get the drink and we are going to the bog and book a taxi from outside by the rank and we will meet you out there ok?" Jeff "Right we will be there now." Danny seemed unconvinced and went up to the bar with Jeff and said "Don't buy too much matey, I have got a feeling they are gone, they didn't seem too happy to take us home with them." Jeff snapped at Danny "Wat are you on about? you heard them they were up for it and have been all night, why do you say that then?" "Because as soon as I told them I was blind and you were partially sighted they changed, they hadn't realised and changed their tones and sounded uncomfortable." "It's in your mind matey, I think they will be outside waiting so hurry up and get a couple of flagons matey and think positive for a change." "Ok I will, but don't say I didn't warn you, I will shut up now ok?" Jeff "I knew you were about to say that, c'mon let's go then." The lads go outside and there are no cabs left on the rank and no sign of the girls and Danny said "I knew it, they have gone mate and we have to wait for a taxi now as we were the last out of there." Jeff with nasty look on his face says "You always have to be right don't you ? I was sure they were genuine and meant what they were saying and look they have used us for their drinks and pissed off, charming." Jeff looked really fed up and his face told it all. Danny tried to humour him "I thought they were not Impressed that we are blind and you know what I mean, sorry Jeff I should have guessed they weren't genuine, so let's get a taxi and go home, cheer up mate I know how you feel matey I feel like a monster now that is how they treated us, let's forget it now." Next thing all the alarms went off in the Litton Tree and there was a lot of rushing about and a lot of arguing and apologising, it was mark outside the Litton tree and the lads went up to see what was wrong and Jeff said to mark "Are you allright mark? it's Danny and Jeff it is , are you allright? can we help?" mark "O, o, o, thank god you are here, I got lost in the toilet and everyone had left and I set the alarms off, I, I, I, couldn't help it I got I, I, I, lost, can I come home in your taxi?" Danny "Of course you can matey I hear some coming to the rank now so let's get back over there, we have had a dead loss of a night to, 2 girls used us for beer and then ran off and left us." Jeff "Wait until I see them again the bitches, huh and I thought I was going to get a bit tonight too ha, ha, ha." The lads go off to the college and off to bed.

It's Saturday and the boys were off again to the pretty pigs pub and in there was Tim an Mandy and they were sitting together and reminiscing over the night of the karaoke and Danny said "We were getting on very well with these two girls and as soon as they find out i was blind and Jeff was partially sighted they changed towards us, they said they were going to wait outside and when we got out there they had gone and we were standing there with a few flagons of cider and no one to share it with." Tim "It's like I said to you before it's hard to get a girl if you are blind, they think you are not all there and avoid you, but Dan you are not all there ha, ha, only joking but I think it is someone who has a eye problem we only stand a chance with and that's it." Mandy "So what are you saying then Tim? I am only going out with you because I could not get anyone else or what?" Tim looking nervous "Oh no, but most blind people go out with other blind people and the deaf are the same etc. but we are in love aren't we? I suppose I may be getting this totally wrong." Mandy snapped "In other words if you weren't blind you would not give me a second glance then?" Tim tuts and moves in his seat nervously "Well I don't think this situation would ever arisen because I would not have come to the college would i? so you can't say that, I am not being awful Mandy it's just a fact, people tend to stick with their own kind like, Chinese with Chinese and Arabs with Arabs and that's how it is, I am not being funny." Danny interrupts "I am sorry I said anything now, he is right Mandy and he was lucky to have met you, it's just how fate takes a hand in these Matters." Jeff "Anyway it's back to the facts it was annoying as I don't like cider that much ha, ha, and I bet we will never see them again, so it's back to the college girls then and as regards that I think that a certain Chinese woman would rather a Welshman rather than a Chinese man." Mandy smiles and says "Winnie you mean? yes she is always on about you Danny, she is very keen on you, I know for a fact and I think you have a bit of a thing about her also, don't you?" Danny "Yes I have but she is so old fashioned as regards a relationship and she would try and tie me down and before you say anything I don't mean that way, she is domineering but everything else is in the right place and I know she is a very beautiful girl." Jeff "And what a body matey, I wouldn't kick her out of bed, no way, you stand a good chance with her." Danny "I don't know, I will think about it, it would not hurt mind at least I will get my wicked way eventually." Tim "And you can't beat a Chinese every night hey?" Jeff "No your right there Tim and maybe she is a good cook as well." Mandy "Well I think she is lovely and a very brainy woman and she is good at massage and a doctor of medicine, I mean she cured you of some troubles once didn't she? A very handy person to have around, everything will fall into place in time surely and you don't know if you don't try it will you?" Danny thinking hard about what she is saying says "Yeah, yeah, I will think about it, I mean she may not be interested now anymore." Jeff "Tell me Dan, are we going down the karaoke next week then to see if those girls turn up?" Danny "Yes why not? I would like to give them a piece of my mind and I want to see if Mark gets locked in again." Tim "What was all that about?" Jeff "M, M, Mark Mathews had a skinner of that Kronenberg lager and went to the toilet at the end of the night and the owners locked him in the pub and he could not find his way out and was locked in and all of a sudden the alarms all went off. He had set them off and the owners had to run back and let him out, he was stuttering like a good one ha, ha, he gets in a state sometimes with the beer and I bet the only time he got in trouble and missed a lecture was when he drank with the dodgy Welshman that time." Tim "Yes I heard about that and I have heard from Niel that you and him are doing a Welsh meal in Dowdell for Saint David's day on March the 1st, is that right Dan?" Danny replies "Yes I forgot about that and I had better speak to him about it, it's on Monday next and he is going home for the weekend and he wants us to make enough for all to try and there is around 50-60 adults here that will take some doing I know, I will borrow a huge pan from the refectory and cook it on the 4 rings in the kitchen and it will take all day but you will enjoy it honestly it's nice." Mandy licking her lips "I have tasted it, it is lovely made with lamb and leeks and potatoes and other things, I loved it when I had it, so can you make it then?" Danny "Oh yes, when I cook it at home my kids eat it before it cools and come back for more, I have always been able to cook many things, cow pie, curries, cowl and bread, I have done a lot of cooking and my mother was a fabulous cook, she was something special mate and she taught me a lot and as a kid I would help her

345

and it's funny how much I remember considering I was so young and anything she made was so tasty, she was so good I miss her cooking I really do, she was so good at it, I hope you both come over and have a bowl full to try and see how nice it is." Tim "We'll be there won't we Mandy?" Mandy "Yes we will be there, I will make sure we are." Jeff "I don't do vegetables sorry so I won't be having any." Danny "You don't know what you are missing matey and you could do with some meat on those bones, you remind me of Mr Muscle your so skinny and I think you will like it because some of my boys don't like veg but it doesn't taste the same in cowl so give it a try." Jeff "I'll give it a try maybe and stop talking about my lovely physique, girls are chasing me all the time as you know ha, ha." Tim "Right anyone for a pint then? I have a taste tonight." All give their beer orders and Mandy says "Tim you always have the taste mate and these 2 don't need encouraging any time."

It was Saint David's day and in the kitchen Danny and Niel planning what they were going to do and Danny said "Have you brought the lamb then?" "Yes, is this enough do you think?" Danny grabbed a large carrier bag of meat off Niel and said "Good grief that's plenty and I will cut it up while you start the veg matey and I will give you a change later if you like." "Dim problem Dan, I love peeling veg, I will do it all, you are the cook I don't know how to cook it so you carry on, have you got a big enough pot?" Danny held the pot up for Niel to feel as he did so he said "Bloody hell mate it's big enough to bath in, will it fit on the cooker though?" "Yes it covers all 4 rings so I can put them all on and cook it all." It was a few hours later and Niel was sitting down knackered after standing for more than 2 hours peeling and Danny was still watching the pot boiling and stirring it from time to time and Niel said "I hope it will be cooked before tonight, I have a lot of people who said they were coming over to eat some. I have got some max Boyce to play to give it a Welsh theme, I hope they all turn up now." "If they don't mate we will be eating cowl for a few months ha, ha, and Jeff said he would tell everyone today to be sure." "You can depend on him to do that and I bet he is saying to them, and bring some extra cans to cover the cost for us lads ha, ha, he is a boy mind, my bloody hands are like a grannies backside they are all wrinkled up, I never have ever peeled so many vegetables before in my life, I hope it tastes ok Dan, how do you know how much salt to put in etc.?" "I am afraid I have had to guess and taste it from time to time but it's going as we planned, have a little taste to see what you think matey." Danny puts a little in a cup for Niel to taste and he says after the tasting "It's nice mate, I think there is enough salt now and the onions are giving it a pleasant taste, so how long do you think it will take to cook? it's nearly 4 o'clock now." "That's what I am worried about it will take another 2-3 hours yet." "Shit, it will be 7 before it is ready, mind you saying that they will not be over before then, as they will be letting their tea go down first, so it may work out good for us." "Well Jeff is due back in a minute and he will tell us the reaction he has had." "Yes I know the S.S.W's are all coming over so they will eat a lot of it, they love a freebee, I will get my machine out and put some Welsh cd's on, see you in a minute." He goes off and while he is gone in comes Jeff and Winnie. Jeff says "Aren't you ready yet? some of the people will be over soon as they are not having tea in the refectory." Danny "Well they will have to wait, it has taken ages for us to get it ready so tough, Niel has gone to get the Welsh music and I need to get the bowls out, hi Winnie, are you going to have some of my Welsh stew then? I made it with my own fair hands it's nice." Winnie "I will have a little try first when it is ready thank you, is Lola coming over and that patsy then?" Danny "I don't know but it doesn't Matter that is water under the bridge now." Winnie tuts and says "What is water under the bridge mean? stop trying to confuse me." Danny jokingly says "Confucius he say water under bridge mean it was the past and now

346

forget it and forget it happened, no good keeping on after it is all over." Winnie "Sorry I not forget Danny, they are bullies and I will not talk to them but I will not say anything to start a confrontation ok?" Danny "Ok and later I will take you for a drink up the bar if you like." Winnie smiling from ear to ear says "Yes I like very much, thank you, I will go and have a shower and change for your Velsh night ok? Bye." She walks off with a spring in her step after she had gone Jeff said "You little dragon, you decided to try your luck then with her." "Luck has nothing to do with it mate and if she plays her cards right, who knows." Jeff "I don't think patsy will come anywhere near here myself, but Lola will probably come up, she has no qualms about that and I want to see her in her mini skirt again, god , try not to think about it Jeff , sorry mate I had a funny moment then." "Yes I know what you mean Jeff, phew, it could be a good night." Meanwhile Niel had come back and put the cd player down and switched it on with some Welsh choir music on it and it certainly made the Welsh atmosphere, he said "There we go lads now it feels like Saint David's day and here Danny is your leek." Danny takes it and pins it on his jumper and says "It's a nice small one, thank you Niel." Niel "Don't say that in front of that heathen Jeff, you know how he will take it the wrong way." Jeff "Ha, ha, he will need a big one for tonight, he is taking WINNIE out to the student bar later Niel and she is one hard woman to Impress." Niel "Oh yes Dan, is this true? And if it is, about time too." Danny "Don't take it to heart you 2 I am feeling the ground before I decide so don't get excited, we will see." Jeff "Well if it makes any difference mate I think you 2 deserve each other and hope it works out, she is after a ticket to stay in Britain mind." Niel "Jeff you are a shit sometimes, ha, ha, but you might be right to." Danny "I am not biting lads, I know you are both trying to wind me up so forget it, this is Wales day so let's enjoy that first then." Jeff "Yes ok, I will go and change, I will be back soon, time for a ciggy." He trots off and Niel says to Danny "Do you know I have enjoyed this today, it has been bloody great doing this with you, it has been fun and we worked well together didn't we? I am knackered now mind but it has been worth it and nice to see you smiling again." "Niel, I am glad you said that it has been a release for me doing this, It took my mind off the divorce and the loss of my brother, I think about him every day you know, I can't help it and I feel he was helping us too, he was not much younger than you so thanks mate it has been fun." "No problem Dan I have enjoyed it Immensely, don't say anymore I just hope this cowl is nice for both our sakes." "If it's not I am blaming you ha, ha, I will deny anything to do with it, I am only joking mate. We both can blame Jeff ha, ha, ha." "I will tell him when he gets back, fancy a whisky Dan? I think we deserve one after all this." "It's a silly question to ask me now isn't it?" "Yes it was really but I have known you to say no." "I mean a double mind not half a pint, I know you." Danny smiled and says "As if I would." Niel goes off and Danny stood there stirring the pot and next thing Clamper comes in and says "Hi Dan, how is the stew going? I am starving." "Well go and have something to eat in the refectory as this won't be ready for a while at least 7 tonight." "I have already eaten in the refectory." "And you are still starving? well sorry mate later maybe ok?" Clamper says "Yes I will hang around for it." "Do you want to try a taste then?" All of a sudden Jeff had come back and said "No he does not want to he is a little shit, so don't give him none, he told everyone we were stood up in the Litton Tree so stuff him." Clamper in a panicky voice "I didn't say it nasty." Jeff "Your a little shit you are." Danny "Flaming hell you 2 are always arguing so give it a rest." Jeff "Don't you care what he said then about us?" Danny "Jeff we did get stood up at the Litton tree." Jeff "I know but he told everyone." Danny "And he told the truth." Clamper "Thank you " Danny." jeff "But I don't like people speaking about me behind my back, but I don't think you had malice in what you said." Well he had better stop it I mean it." Danny "Shut up Jeff and as you say to me change the record or have a drink to keep your mouth busy." Clamper laughed and Danny looked at him nasty and said "And if he gives you a good clip you deserve it, so be careful" Niel came back in and give Danny his scotch and said "These 2 are arguing again aye?" Danny "Yes again, they are like 2 gay boys in love ha, ha, I will not put up with this girls mind you will both go to bed early mind, ha, ha, ha." Jeff "Ha, ha, I'm sorry dad, it's him he gets on my nerves all the time." Clamper looking serious "See he never stops threatening me and saying things to annoy me." Niel "For god's sake the both of you give it a rest or get out it's our day today and if you are going to spoil it I want you to leave, I'm serious." Clamper "Your not serious Niel?" Niel "Oh yes I am, try me, I mean what I say I don't need this after a busy day I need silence to enjoy my scotch." In comes Winnie all dressed up and said "I can hear you lot out there, be quiet or you will frighten people away." Clamper got up and went off to his room and Jeff smiling said "Bye, bye." Niel "Jeff grow up." Jeff cowers down and sit's and watches the telly and Danny comes in and sit's near WINNIE and speaks "Hello Winnie would you like a visky, I mean a whisky?" Winnie "Oh no thank you Danny, you know it makes me drunk easy." Danny "Yes it does doesn't it? so would you like one?" She laughs "Danny, behave yourself please, is the stew nearly ready?" Danny "Yes it is nearly ready and me and Niel are going to try it first to make sure it is perfect and then my Chinese princess you can go next, so get your taste buds ready for a treat, are you ready Niel sir?" Niel "I certainly am mate, shall we retire to the nectar." The 2 lads go into the kitchen and shut the door and sit down and eat first. Jeff speaks to Winnie "Flipping heck, you would think it was a meal for the gods the way they are talking about it." Winnie "Well Jeffrey it is Important to them, they are passionate about tradition in their country and we must respect it, even if they are acting silly about it." "I think they are over the top about the Welsh, but never mind they are a pair of rogues and good mates. So you and Danny are going up the bar together tonight then?" "Yes, so, why do you say it like that Jeff? ha, ha." "I think he is making a move on you Winnie, do you know what I mean?" "I think so but you tell me." "Well he has just been served his papers by his wife and he is now after you to have a relationship." "Has he said this to you?" Jeff looking agitated says "Not in so many words but I can tell." "Well Jeff I would appreciate it if you kept your opinions to yourself, as gossip makes trouble and I would not like to put you right in front of everybody, do you understand Jeff? I am not one to mess with especially with my emotions." "Fair enough, I was just saying that's all, sorry, so you aren't interested in him then?" "That is my business not anything to do with you and if I was I would not tell you as it will end in tragedy for me as you can't keep your mouth shut." Jeff looking dumbfounded said "Fair enough I am sorry I spoke now, I am off for a ciggy." Next thing a few people came in including Lola and sat down in the lounge and Jeff came back in Immediately as Lola had a mini skirt on that revealed everything almost. Winnie sat there looking serious as she hated Lola for the trouble she caused her earlier in the year. Danny and Niel came in the lounge and Niel said "Well the cowl is ready, who's for who's first?" Lola stood up and Danny said "Winnie is first and then whoever came in after including Jeff." Winnie stood up and went into the kitchen as if to say to Lola, I am more Important than you, so back off, Lola tutted and said "So Niel what is it really like? and who made it?" Niel replies "We prepared it between us and it is very good even if I say so myself, so just enjoy it Lola and we can all have a little bit of fun ok?" Lola rolls her eyes and said "Ok calm down Niel, can I go in and get some now then?" Niel "Of course you can and Jeff you go and help people with the serving if you don't mind?" Jeff jumped up and walked behind Lola and she came up to Danny standing by the cooker and said "Allright Dan? I am looking forward to this bit of Welsh food." Danny "I am glad of that and it is ok I think you will like it and help yourself to the Welsh bread over on the table too and let Jeff help you with the skirt, I mean the cowl, sorry." She made a face and smiled and Jeff could not do enough for her, he says to her "I will get that Lola and you go and sit where you like." Lola "Thank you Jeff." Right behind her was Clamper and Jeff ignored him so he helped himself to a large portion , in next to no time the place was jammed packed with all the mature students and it was like a large party with plenty of food and beer flowing and Danny and Niel was beaming from ear to ear as it was such a success. Jeff in the meantime was staring at Lola as if he has not seen a woman before. Niel speaking to Danny "My god it's only 9 o'clock and the cowl has nearly gone and Clamper had about 5 bowls and it was tasty mind, even Lola never said anything nasty about it and Jeff has not taken his eyes off her legs since she got in here." Danny "I know he has he is almost panting out loud, I wish I could see them she is very raunchy." "I know she made me blush once and that is good for anyone to get me blushing, she was rubbing her crotch on my leg to tease me when we were friends and I was like putty, god she is a sexy woman mind but it's a pity she is so awful with her mouth, she would have been a good catch for you." Danny "Do you think so? I have had my arms around her a few times and she has a cracking body and she would be nice to me for about six months and then look out but I would not say no to her in my bed, don't worry about that now, she is   having a good time maybe she has given up trying to boss us about." Niel "I know what you mean but I would still prefer my Ceri thank you, I am surprised that Winnie is still here as she hates Lola, I think she is sticking around in case you forget to ask her to go up the bar tonight." Danny "I have already asked her earlier and she is coming with me I think but I am full now no room for a Chinese now." The lads laugh and Jeff comes and sit's by them and says "Hi guys, that Lola is really fit and she is driving me mad with that body of hers and she knows it, her boyfriend has gone out with the lads and left her alone dressed like that. So what time are we going up the bar? I am running out of tinnies now and all the food has gone now and we can wash up later." Niel "No we will wash up now before we go or we will have Zarrine beating us up, I will wash and you 2 can wipe." Jeff "I don't do washing or wiping sorry mates, I will catch you after you have finished." He slopes off and Danny said "That's typical mate, we are left to do it alone, well it is our night let's get to it." The lads stand up and head for the kitchen and Niel says out loud for all to hear "Are there any dishes left in here as we are going to wash them all if you have bring them into the kitchen please." Lola jumps up and says "I will do the washing up lads, that was a nice meal and I think we all agree?" Everyone claps for the lads and comment on the taste and how nice it was, Lola continues "Anyone volunteering to wipe for me?" Jeff as fast as he could said "I'll wipe no problem." Niel said "I thought you didn't do dishes?" Jeff interrupts "No I don't mind helping with the washing, what do you think I am heartless or what?" They go off and Jeff was right behind Lola and everyone went off to get ready for the bar and there was just Danny, Winnie and Niel left. Winnie said "I am ready to go, I liked the food Danny it was lovely, I never tasted anything like that before it was very nice, thank you." Danny "Your welcome Winnie, I am just going to change my t-shirt and I am ready, what about Niel?" Niel "I am ready just a wipe over on my face and I am ready, I will see you up there as I must take Abby out for the run for her to do her business and you can get a large table for us all, ok?" Danny replies "Yes ok, I will see you up there. Winnie you had just as well come to my room and we can go out that way if you like?" Winnie smiling says "Yes ok, I will and behave yourself ha, ha, ha.." Danny also smiling says "Spoil sport, I will just tell Jeff what I am doing." He went into the kitchen and Jeff was speaking quietly to Lola and Danny stopped and listened for a while. Jeff was saying "I think you are very beautiful you know and that bloke you are with don't know how to treat you at all, he must be mad not wanting to be with you I would never treat you like that, I think you are gorgeous you know." Danny coughed and Jeff shut up Immediately and Danny said "I am off to get a seat for us all up the student bar Jeff, thank you Lola for doing this for us it was very nice anything you want now before I go?" Lola "Yes take him with you he is making me feel tom and dick, he is half cut and he is talking a load of nonsense ha, ha, Jeff you haven't stopped talking since you got in this kitchen and you can't get any closer to me ha, ha, ha." Jeff smiling "Well I am not complaining am I ha, ha, I want to climb up those long legs of yours if you don't mind." Lola "You behave yourself mate or look out, right the dishes are all clean I am off ha, ha, you are a little bugger today Jeff you need some cooling off, see you." Lola leaves and Jeff's jaw drops and he says "I must sort myself out matey I need a woman I really do I am going for several ciggy's and stick my head down the bog to try and cool myself off. See you up the bar." "Yes and behave yourself in front of the girls as you sound as if you have already had enough to drink ha, ha." "Oh shut up, I am ok see you later." Jeff goes off to his room.

Later in the bar and Danny and Winnie was sitting holding the table for the others and he strikes up a conversation with Winnie "Here we are then, I think it is going to be a good night if Jeff behaves himself, he is playing around with Lola and she will eat him for breakfast." "She will and she is going to eat him all up and he will be in a mess again. He is always the same with the women, he is a silly man." "Yes and he never learns, so did you really like the cowl I made?" "Yes I did, it was unusual but tasty, so how are things now with your wife?" "That is dead in the water." "What is dead in the water mean?" "Sorry I forget you are Chinese, it means it is all over with us." Winnie smiles at the news and says "Really or are you just saying this for me to hear." "No I am telling you the truth she is going to divorce me so that is that and so it means I am a free man now so do your best Winnie" "Why do you say this? I am a woman who is not like these British women, I will get married one day and I will respect my husband and care for him for the rest of my life, not just throw them away when I get bored, you must make an effort at marriage, in my country this action of divorce is frowned on." "I am sorry, I don't need a sermon I agree with you, so have you ever had a boyfriend in your country?" "No never, I will wait until the right man comes along and then I will be his for the rest of my life not like the western world we have respect for ourselves in China." "Yes I can see that, this country has gone to the dogs, so what do you think about British men then?" "Stupid people most of you, too much drinking, smoking and messing around with women and having sex with anyone who comes along and fighting and arguing and too many lesbians and gay people here." "Wow, wow, I've had enough sorry I asked and I was hoping we were getting closer." "What do you mean Danny?" "I was wondering what you thought of me? not all British men but it's obvious you hate us all." "No I didn't say this at all, I am sorry if you are hurt by what I said but I am telling the truth and I don't really know you do I? so I must wait and see how you are." "Fair enough I can understand that, another drink?" "No thank you I am fine, I can't drink I am full of stew at the moment." Danny goes off to the bar and meets Niel there getting his pint "Hello Niel." Niel replies "Hi Dan, pint or what?" "Bottle of Newcastle please Niel, I have thee usual table Winnie is sitting there." "How's it going with her?" "I don't know really I say things to find out what she thinks about me and I get a sermon about the British here in this country, we are all sex maniacs, fighters, drug addicts and everything, so I can't say really I will let you know in a week or two, shall I carry your pint over?" Niel "Yes please Dan

I will follow you." They go over and sit and Niel said "Hello Winnie?" "Oh hello Niel are you ok?" Niel "Yes thank you, a little bloated after that meal so I will be sipping my beer for a while, are you enjoying yourself then?" Winnie "Yes thank you I am also bloated to if you mean full?" Niel "Yes I do and look out here comes Jeff mumbling to himself." Jeff sat down and said "That bloody Clamper is a total idiot, he borrowed some tobacco off me and he must have a pipe he has taken nearly all of it the idiot, god I don't believe him sometimes, wait till I see him, honestly." Danny smiling "Ha, ha, ha, I don't believe you 2, you are always arguing lately, what's the Matter with you both?" Jeff red in the face says "Well you know what he is like he don't care who he walks over does he? and he would have eaten all that stew stuff you made if I hadn't have stopped him, he just takes advantage all the time, a real dick head." Winnie was laughing out loud at Jeff and said "Ha, ha, ha, you make me laugh you are like a little boy who has had his chocolate taken away, it's silly." Niel "Here, here, he is, why don't you stay away from him then ? because it will end up in tears for somebody soon." Danny "Don't take it too serious mate I bet there is more to this than Clamper getting on your nerves isn't it Jeff?" Jeff "What do you mean Dan?" Danny "You have been like this since you was let down the other night in the Litton tree, is that the problem really mate?" Jeff looking down at the floor "Boys I haven't had a bit since last year." There was a deadly silence and they all broke out in laughter and Jeff butted in "I knew you would find it funny I knew it, I feel like no one wants me and seeing Lola in that mini dress was the last straw today. I need a woman." Danny "Steady Jeff you sound like a rapist, steady people will talk ha, ha, ha."   Niel was crying with laughter and said "I have got a blow up doll If you want to borrow it, I don't need it, it keeps on going down on me ha, ha, ha." They all laugh and he said "I bought an American one and I blew it up and it mugged me then I had one and her nose kept running I phoned the company and they told me to empty it ha, ha, ha, my brother who has asthma has got one he bought a Arabic one .....it blows itself up ha, ha, ha." They were all in fits of laughter and in walks Clamper and sits down and it all of a sudden went silent and they were waiting for Jeff to say something. He then exploded and said "You little twat you, I said you could have a little tobacco not a pouch full don't ask me ever for anymore." Clamper snapped back "I did I accidentally tipped some and it blew away sorry and you can stuff your tobacco from now on ha, ha, ha." Jeff really nasty by now replied "I ought to smack you in the mouth you ungrateful little git." Clamper "Oh shut up you asshole." Jeff jumped up and stood near Clamper and it was about to blow off and Danny shouted "Right that's enough we have had a good day and you 2 are not going to spoil it so sit down Jeff and Clamper, I agree with Jeff you are ungrateful and a spoilt little child so let it be now." Clamper pouted "I knew you would take his side." Danny "I am not taking sides but you did lose some of his tobacco and it is expensive and you instead of apologising and being humble as it was your mistake you give him abuse, so that is out of order in my book, so it might be nice to say sorry to him and mean it." Clamper after a few seconds "Ok I am sorry Jeff." Jeff sat there and said nothing, then Winnie said "You must be friends there is too much arguments here with good friends falling out all the time." Jeff "I suppose your right, I will forget it but don't let it happen again." Niel butted in "Right Jeff don't go on you are like a mother hen, let it go now, right we will now sing Welsh songs all night." Everyone moaned and Niel laughed and said "I am only kidding ha, ha." Danny laughing along with Niel says "Waste of time Niel these lot are all heathens and could not sing in their own language so us superior Welsh will have to put up with it." Winnie grabbed Danny's arm and playfully said to him "Hey don't you say this about me, I am the queen of China and you are my slave so be careful ha, ha, ha." Jeff "You tell him girl, oh dear look at that it's Christine that young girly with that beautiful body with next to nothing on, oh my god will you look at that, it's not worth putting on, Flippin hell." Christine heard him and came over to see him and tease him, she sat on his lap with a mini skirt on and said "Well hello big boy, so what have you got in your pocket? or are you glad to see me then? I had better take this jumper off." She lifted it over her shoulders and revealed just a bra over 2 huge breasts that were literally hanging out and Jeff's face was a picture and he was just lost in the moment. Jeff said "God I thought it was 2 bald headed men on my lap there for a minute." She grabbed his head and smothered him between her breasts and then stood up and walked away to leave him wondering. Jeff said "I am going to explode soon, I am, did you see that?" Niel "No but I think I know what just happened." Clamper "He had them in his hand and did not know what to do with them, what a plonker he really is." Jeff jumps up and says "Right that does it , I will teach you a lesson." The 2 boys started grappling with each other and the barman came running up to them and shouted "Right stop it or I will ban you both, stop it now." The lads stopped and he said to them "Sit down and if I have to get up to you again I will ban you for a long time, so don't let me see any more." The lads looked at each other and sat down and pulled themselves together and Jeff said to Clamper "Asshole, your lucky he stepped in I would have knocked your head off." Barman heard this and said "Right Jeff leave it now or I will ban you, I am not kidding, don't let me come over here again." The barman left and Clamper got his 2 penneth worth in "Whimp, think I am afraid of you, think again Jeff." Jeff was about to answer him and Danny said "Are you pair real? shut up now, there is a lot of bad feeling because you 2 are not agreeing with each other so if you want to continue this do it outside please." Niel laughing said "I wish I could see you 2 I can Imagine how it must look not one of you are big enough to fight ha, ha, I will have to ask the barman how he kept himself from laughing through that." Winnie "I was panicking then, I don't like things like that, I am going home if this continues" Jeff "Sorry Winnie I will be a good boy now sorry." Danny "So why don't you 2 shake hands and forget it now?" Jeff said "Yes ok, how about it Clamper?" Clamper smiles and says "Yes ok and let it be the last time." They shook hands and it was all over, or was it?"

It was later in the lounge of Dowdell and Danny and Winnie were sitting there, Niel had gone to bed and Jeff and Clamper were having a ciggy outside and Winnie was speaking to Danny "It was a nice night except that pair fighting all the time, are you drunk?" Danny replies "No I am not, I am sober, why?" "I thought you was not for a change." "No I have had a lot to drink lately and think it's time I stopped as it don't make things any better, look what it done to my brother." Winnie smiling says "That's right Danny, it is not good for you at your age." "You cheeky girl, how old do you thing I am?" "I know how old you are Niel told me before, you are nearly 48 ." "Yes that's right and how old are you then? I think I was told you were early thirties. " Winnie playfully punched Danny on the arm and says "You cheeky velshman, I am only 29, I am and that's the truth you cheeky man." "Is that all, I thought you were older, well, well, that has shocked me, you are a spring chicken and that is a nice compliment to give a woman." "Thank you and they say women are more mature than men." "I think you are probably right if I took you out I would be called a cradle snatcher, that is a man who is old enough to be your father." "Does that Matter? in our country it is a normal thing to marry a man older than yourself." "It does not make any difference to me." They put their arms around each other and kissed for a long time and while this was happening outside Jeff and Clamper were finishing their fags and got into the lift and Jeff had pushed the button to the second floor instead of the third floor on purpose to play a trick on Clamper and the lift stopped on the second floor and Clamper got out and headed for the lounge door and Jeff laughed and pressed the lift to go up to the third floor and left Clamper shouting abuse at him. Jeff got to the third floor and Clamper run up the stairs and as he got to the third floor he met Jeff outside the lift and they started fighting with each other wrestling and grappling each other on the top of the stairs and Jeff got Clamper in a hold and was trying to push him over the banister and on the next floor down there were a few residents returning from the bar and a large man named Les Wertly was holding his arms out and looking up at Clamper dangling over the banister and saying "Your allright Andy I will catch you, I will don't worry." Next thing another lad run up the stairs and helped Jeff pull Clamper back over the banister and Jeff fell down on the floor holding his chest. Les ran up and said to Jeff " are you having a heart attack or what?" Jeff "No I have pulled something in my chest trying to hold Clamper from dropping." Clamper said in a nasty mood "Stuff him let me at him, I will kill him." Les says "Right that's enough, Clamper get to bed now this minute I mean it, go on I am not joking , are you allright Jeff?" Jeff still clutching his chest said "I will be allright now." Another lad escorted Clamper to his room on the first floor trying to cool him down. Jeff got up to his feet and said to Les "Thanks mate I am going for a drink of water and off to bed." They shook hands and Jeff entered the lounge and walked in on Danny and Winnie canoodling. Jeff holding his chest said "Oh my god, my chest , my chest, it is bloody killing me." Danny let Winnie go and thought Jeff was having a heart attack and said "Are you allright Jeff? I will call an ambulance." Jeff "No, no, I am allright it's not a heart attack I hurt it fighting with Clamper." Winnie slapped her hands on her lap and said in a mood "Oh dear, I have had enough of this I am off to bed." She stormed out and Danny pleaded with her "No Winnie don't be like that." Danny turned to Jeff and said "Well thanks mate, I need you like a hole in the head." "Sorry Dan I didn't mean to do that, I have hurt my chest badly but I know it's not my heart." "I know you have not got any heart, just because you have not had a bit don't mean you can spoil it for me to have a bit , so what happened to you.? I played a trick on Clamper and done the press the button for floor 2 and when he got out I pressed it for this floor and he didn't like it and he ran up the stairs and we ended up fighting and in the end I had him hanging over the stairwell and pulled him back up with the help of one of the lads and I pulled a muscle or something, oh, oh, oh, I am in agony mate." "What about Clamper how is he? Is he allright?" "Yes he is ok, I managed to not drop him." "Well I am lost now, I stayed sober for Winnie and she has gone to bed, looks like I have stuffed it up for now anyway and your not a great deal of help, I don't know why I drink with you sometimes." "Because nobody else will drink with you." "Very funny Jeff, so how long is this bickering going on with you 2?" "I have had enough now Dan and he is just an idiot, I shall not bother with him any more ha, ha, ha, ha, ha." "What's so funny now?" "Ha, ha, ha, i was just thinking about Les Wertly down stairs, he was holding his arms out and saying I will catch you Andy, I will catch you. He would have caught him too and he is so large he would not feel anything if Clamper had landed on him, it was funny with is cockney accent and he sounded like Michael Barrymore ha, ha, it was so funny." Danny with sad look says "Well I had just as well go to bed now thanks again mate, no nookie for me either now again. So shall we go down the Litton tree again this week?" "Yeah, we can see if we can see those girls again and ask them what happened, there might be a perfectly good explanation and I can get my end away." "I don't think we shall see them again Jeff but there might be other nice girlies there." "What about Winnie then?" "She is going to London until Sunday and I don't know if we are an item after she stormed off, so I will play it by ear, I will see you in the morning mate." "Yes, goodnight."

It was the next morning and Danny, Niel and Zarrine were sitting having tea and toast and in walks Winnie and says to Danny "Hi Danny, what are you doing dinner time today Danny?" Danny replies "Besides eating, absolutely nothing, why do you ask?" Winnie says "I am going to London later this afternoon and I need things in town can you help me get them?" Danny "Certainly Winnie is it something for the weekend?" Niel giggles and she says "Why is that funny?" Danny "It's only his funny sense of humour, we here ask in the barbers shop someone who cuts hair for something for the weekend and it means you want a condom." She looks over to Niel and says "Don't be rude Niel, I want things that I don't know how to pronounce them so I need your skills with your tongue that's all." Niel laughs again. Winnie "Is he mad or what? now what have I said?" Niel "It's the way you say things, you said something that can be construed as a sexual invite, not your fault so don't worry Winnie." Zarrine stamps her foot on the floor and wags her finger and says "Niel, now stop it or I will send you back to your room you naughty boy ha, ha,ha." Winnie "And where is that stupid Jeff this morning? he was a fool last night he is always fighting with that Clamper." Danny "He will be here now and your right he is a fool and he had better cut it out." Zarrine "Yes I will be having words with him this morning, it was on the hand over notes this morning, so wait until I see him." Winnie "I will meet you in here dinner time then Danny." Danny "Ok Winnie, I will be here about 12.30, see you then and when you go to London don't spend too much money on me mind." Winnie smiles and says "Ok, I will see you then." She left and Jeff came in on queue "Awe, awe, awe." Zarrine "What's the Matter with you Jeffrey? as if I didn't know." Jeff holding his chest in pain every time he coughed says "Cough awe, cough awe, I am in agony every time I cough it's hurts like the devil." Niel "And you are always coughing with the smoking you do and serves your right, trying to kill our Clamper, I know he is a fool on times but no need to knock him off." Jeff "Cough ah, cough ah, don't make me laugh it hurts even worse then." Zarrine said in a harsh voice "Yes I read the report about the incident this morning, not your finest hour was it and I was told you were fighting in the bar too." Jeff "Your kidding it's in the book? did you hear that lads I am in the book ha, ha, ah, ah, bloody hell I am in the book." The lads were laughing at him and Zarrine slapped him on the arm. He continued "I bet that little brat reported me, I should have dropped him if Les was not in the way I would have, the little rat. I expect I will be in front of Anthea now, great that's all i need and I could do with a fag but I can't because if I cough it hurts too much, I am off to the nurses office cough ah, ah, oh dear." Danny "Ask her for some Bromide while you're there." Zarrine "What is bromide?" Danny smiling says "It's something you put in the tea to stop you getting the urge for sex." Zarrine "The urge for what?" Danny "The urge to have a bit, you know sex, they used to put it in the troops tea to stop them wanting a bit in the second world war." Zarrine hand over her mouth "Don't be silly." Niel butted in "It's true Zarrine as I am sitting here it's true and Jeff stated last night he has not had a bit for a couple of months now." Jeff "Don't listen to them Zarrine, they are Welsh and talk a load of crap ha, ha, cough awe, I am off." Zarrine said "Well I never, I have never heard about that before, I should get some and put in your tea the lot of you ha, ha, ha." Danny "It's Lola that started him like this with that mini skirt she had on and then that Christine sitting on his lap last night with hardly anything on and now he has pulled the wrong muscle ha, ha, ha." Zarrine asks "What do you mean?" Danny "Never mind Zarrine I am not explaining that to you I don't want a slap off you, I am off to my lectures."

354

It was Thursday night in the Litton tree again and sitting in there was exactly like the week before except no sign of the girls they met, Danny, Jeff, Kezz, M, M,Mark and Clamper. Kezz spoke first "Eek, eek, tickle, tickle, I think Danny is going out with Winnie, is that true?" Danny "No not yet anyway, why do you say this little miss Kezz?" Kezz "Because someone told me you were up the bar sitting next to each other and sitting very close to her and chatting nicely." Danny "And who was that then?" Kezz "It was the girl who told me she fancied you a lot." Danny smiling said "Oh yes, you was going to tell me about her, I forgot about that, so who is she Kezz? before I tickle you." Kezz "Ok don't tickle me, it is little Janet from Armitage the quiet one, she was watching you up there the other night, she fancies you eek, eek." Danny looking puzzled "But she is only 19, a little bit young to fancy a man of my age isn't she?" Kezz "Well she does, she told me a long time ago and she is very pretty but she does not like Miesha Paris though eek, eek." Danny "I am flattered, flipping heck I never knew but she is much too young for me, she should find someone her age even Winnie is border line, she is only 29." Clamper butts in "Is that how old she is, I thought she was mind." Jeff "Kezz tell Janet I will take her out ha, ha." Kezz "Ok." Clamper "She does not go out with bullies who try and push them over a cliff, so forget it Jeff ha, ha, she has more taste than that." Jeff "Oh here we go I am sorry mate but you couldn't take a joke that's why it all happened so let's forget it now." Danny "Yes please guys, I and the rest of us have had enough of this crap from you two, I have got enough on my mind with trying to sort this divorce out, I don't need this thanks so shut up or I will throw the both of you down the toilet, so let's here no more of it, I will give Kezz permission to clobber the both of you." Kezz "Eek, eek, I will if you don't shut up and I will tickle you both to death, tickle, tickle, tickle, ha, ha, and mark don't forget to go to the bog early before you leave, I heard the smell set the alarms off there last week ha, ha, eek, eek." They all had a good laugh and mark said "Y, y, y, y, you are probably right ha, ha, I won't make that mis, mis, mis, mistake again w, w, w, w, will I?" Jeff said "That's what set the alarms off then, you should stay off the heavy stuff mark." " Mark smiling says "I am in c, c, c, c, case I want to s, s, s, s, sing ha, ha." Kezz "Clamper is singing this week and he has got a good voice and if he wants I will sing one with him to." Clamper "I don't know if I will sing with you, you are too good for me but I will be singing." Danny "I have never heard you sing except last night doing the Romeo and Juliet with Les off the balcony, he was shouting I will catch you Clamper and you was saying I will fall into your arms Leslie, catch me, catch me Leslie." They had a good laugh and Danny said to Jeff "Well I told you mate they would not be here this week didn't I? it looks like it's Pam again tonight, it's not so full either and no Chinese for me tonight she is in London." Jeff "Oh dear I am going to cough, oh no, cough argh, argh, that hurt and my chest feels like it is going to explode." Danny laughs and says "Ha, ha, serves your right, maybe you will behave from now on, let's have a pint then I will give you the money and keep your eyes peeled for some birds." Jeff "My eyes are always peeled for birds, I may give the Oxford girl a ring tomorrow." Danny in serious voice says "You got no chance there mate she has done her time in the college now and that is that, time for some fresh ones now, go and get the drinks." Jeff "Alright I am on my way." Time went on that night and it was a boring night, hardly any talent there and Jeff was looking down with himself and it was time to go home. Jeff said "What a night Dan totally boring except for the lager, not a sign of any nice talent at all." Danny "I know well boring, Kezz are you and your gang having a taxi to the college? if so shall we share a London cab?" Kezz "Banging Dan, banging, will Jeff find a London type for us all?" Jeff "Of course I will squiggly Kezz." Kezz "Hey Jeff that is a good name I am now squiggly Kezz, I like it Jeff it suit's me ha, ha." Danny "Right it is then it's squiggly Kezz, are you all empty? so as we can get a taxi easier." All said yes and off to the rank they went.

Jeff got a London type cab and he helped everyone in the cab and there was just Clamper left and Jeff grabbed his elbow to try and help him in the cab just to let him know where his seat was and Clamper pulled his arm away and said "Get off me Jeff, I am ok doing this myself, leave me do it." Jeff in a temper Oh get in and stop pissing about, you little idiot." Clamper tugged his arm away from Jeff and thumped Jeff on the nose and ran away and Jeff's nose was bleeding. He got into the cab and said "Argh, Clamper just smacked me in the nose and he has ran off, the little bastard." Kezz "Did he? he has actually smacked you in the nose." Jeff "Yes and it is bleeding, wait till I get my hands on him." Danny "So where is he now?" Jeff "He ran down the street and disappeared and a few lads threatened me to leave him alone, so I got in here and let him go, I was just trying to help him into the cab and he attacked me." Kezz "Well I hope he will be allright, he is a bit pissed you know, I am worried now he might get into trouble." Danny "He should be allright, he will get another taxi I expect." M, Mark "H, h, h,h,h, he will be allright he's n, n,, n, not stupid." Jeff looking amazed "Well thanks guys, I am the one bleeding here and he gets all the worries cough argh, argh, this bloody chest." Danny laughing said "Well a little lad like that and he is ok and you are in a real mess, a bleeding nose and a set of pulled muscles in your chest, I think you had better stop messing with that boy or next time you will be in hospital at this rate." Jeff "Ha, ha, very funny man, dodgy I will beat him in the end." Danny "Well at this moment he is well in the lead, don't worry Jeff if he picks on you again tell the teacher." They all laugh and back at the college Kezz goes to her dorma and the lads go to theirs and waited to see if Clamper gets back allright.

They are sitting in the lounge talking and in there was Niel laughing at a comedy TV programme. He says "Ha, ha, hi guys, have a good night?" Danny "Well until Rocky Massiano and mike Tyson had a go outside the taxi rank and now Jeff has got a huge bleeding nose to go with his bad chest and Clamper ran off and we have not got a bloody clue what has happened to him and it is just getting too much now." Jeff "Awe shut up and don't keep on, I am the injured party here not him." Niel "You 2 are always at each other all the time, I can see you both getting expelled from this college soon enough as they will have had enough of the pair of you." Jeff "Oh don't you start on me as well, he was the one who clobbered me and ran off and before you ask I don't know why, I am just as confused." Niel "So he smacked you in the nose for nothing and then ran off is that what you are saying?" Jeff "Hooray, hold the front page he has got it at last, give the Welshman a banana he has got it, I am a bit worried also about the boy and why he did it." Danny "He did it probably because you didn't get a bit again tonight and had no patience with the lad, tell the truth Jeffrey." Jeff "Honest I don't know why he did it, I put squiggly Kezz in the taxi, helped you and M, Mark in and he was the last one to get in I showed him where the seat was and he pulled away smacked me in the face and legged it." Danny "Well he will be back soon and we can get to the bottom of it, got any cans in your room Jeff?" Jeff "No but I know a woman who has , they will be hanging on my door handle, I put them in Rhoda's room so they will not be discovered as she is a very religious woman and they won't search her room, so I tell her to put a half dozen in a carrier bag and hang them on my door every night before she goes to bed, I will fetch them." He goes off and gets them and they sit down and open one each and before you know it in walks Clamper and said very quietly "Hello all." Jeff shouts at him "So why did you smack me in the nose then mate?" Clamper standing there dripping wet and looking unhappy said in a tearful voice "Because you were pulling me about and bossing me into the taxi and it was not nice, you treated me like a rag doll and I hate you so I would do it again if you ever treat me the same ." Danny "I knew it was all about something your moody ways of late, so are you allright now Clamper? Is it all over?" Clamper came over to Danny and kneeled by him on the settee and rested his head on Danny's shoulder and started crying and Danny realised he was soaking wet and said "Hey what's this all about matey? what's the Matter? and why are you so wet?" Clamper sobbed quietly and said "He is always nasty to me and I think I fell in a pond or something and I am fed up here lately." Danny butted in and said "And your pissed?" Clamper with smile says "That as well, i am sorry I did it to him but he gets on my nerves, always treating me like I was an idiot." Danny said "Awe don't be stupid." They all laughed even Clamper, he sat down and Jeff said "Ok I am sorry if you think I am like that, it's time we stopped this, I didn't mean to upset you like this so do you want a can or what?" Clamper "I am sorry to Jeff an I will have a can please." Jeff "Well go and get those wet clothes off and put some dry pyjamas on and come back for your can." Clamper now smiling from ear to ear says "Ok I will be back now." He goes off and Niel says to Jeff "You big bully you, stop being so miserable with him, he is only a lad, bully." Danny "I knew something would have set him off you rat Jeff." Jeff laughing at the Welshmen "Ok fair enough, I didn't realise I was being so harsh on him, I have apologised so let's let it go now and I am giving him a can, so get off my back and let's watch fawlty towers in piece." Clamper came back and all seemed back to normal and they all had a good laugh over the sit com on the telly .

It was the next afternoon and Danny was on the telephone to Angie to see what was happening and he said "Is everything ok there? Is Josh allright?" Angie replies "It's fine here and Josh is in school and he is good and you?" "Well considering all that is happening to me I am fine and are you still seeing that asshole Chin?" "Don't start now or I am going." "I don't know why you are hiding it or is it you want your family to think it's my fault we are apart? Perhaps you want them to think I am carrying on not you? I tell you one thing If I ever find out he is in my house I will kill you and him somehow, I don't want that cretin near Josh, so don't even go there I warn you." "Right is that all you wanted to speak to me for? I am not seeing anyone so let it rest." "Your a liar I have been told by many a person so don't deny it, remember what I said I will keep my word as far as you and him are concerned, I mean it, I am off now and the money has gone through to your account now and from now on and I will sort out the mortgage until things are decided ok?" "Well you just as well sort it out now I am going to work in the school and by the way I have seen a solicitor and started the divorce." There was a silence for a minute and Danny said "Take your time what's the rush then?" "Well we just as well get it over with, no point in waiting is there?" " "You mean Graham has told you to get it done?" " Angie changes the subject and says "I am off now I need to go up the shop." "Right of course you do and we are not getting divorced because I have gone blind, bye." Danny put the phone down and sat there looking dejected and next he scanned a letter he had from his solicitors about his claim for his injury and it said as it read it to him the court has decided to pay you up to the year of your 64 birthday the compensation because you are not expected to live past that age due to you having diabetes. Danny shouted "Bloody hell they are so sure I am going to die before I am 65, how can they say this? bloody hell and she is divorcing me Immediately because I have gone blind , I just as well jump in the coffin and screw it down, everyone is after my blood, I give up I really do, I just as well go back to bed and sleep for the rest of my life." Danny sat down on his bed and just cried as this was such a bad day for him.

It was some time later when he pulled his self together and went for a cup of tea in the lounge. In there was Niel and Jeff, Danny told them about the letter and the divorce Angie told him about and he then said "Well that's it lads, I am single for definite, a free man, I had better make the most of it as I am not going to be around for long ha, ha, I don't believe that and I will do my best to prove them wrong, so Jeff I am coming home with you for Easter if you don't mind? I will go and see Josh for a while and then come up with you, we can hit all the pubs in Swindon." Jeff "Yes, no problem matey you will like it up there and as long as you try and hide that stupid accent of yours." Niel "Steady Jeff, you have not got Clamper here now, I am Welsh as well so be on your guard." Danny "Well a pint or 2 tonight to celebrate my freedom that I didn't want, so much for in sickness and in health, till death do us part, more like in blindness and in Hereford, till Gareth Chin do us part, why do i feel like he has just hovered on me like I was a toilet and he has just crapped on me." Niel "Thank god I am happily married because I don't know how that is but that's it Dan and I for one am sorry he has destroyed your marriage and it is a cruel thing to do to someone who has just gone blind, I bet." Jeff "Spot on Niel that man has destroyed a family really completely destroyed a family without blinking an eyelid, the bastard, it's a good thing you have got good friends matey." Danny "Yes I know, I must just get stuck into the way of blind life and make sure he does not destroy me and I will bloody well not let him win."

CHAPTER 14
A WILL TO WIN

Well it was a traumatic time ahead for Danny as he was wondering how he will manage his life now he was totally alone , but determination took over as he was not being beaten by a drunk and was determined to learn how to do everything alone without any help from any person who can see because in his mind he hated the attitude of people who could do it all because they could see. One of the reasons is that they did not understand what blindness was like, if for instance a blind man was looking to find a door to get through, a seeing person would grab his arm and drag him to the door not considering his feelings and they would treat him as if he was an idiot and if they asked some people a question the other person would reply and shout as if he was also deaf, some people would drag the children out of your way as if you are going to kill them, when serving you in a shop they would for instance a fruit shop and you asked for bananas they would get rid of the soft over ripe ones to you as you cannot see them and the potatoes they would give you all the small potatoes that no one else wanted, anything that was gone soft or ripe they would dump on you and the most hated is, they would dump false or foreign coins on the blind, leave things in your way and grab your arm and drag you around them. The same thing on a train or bus they would not help unless they would have to and then drag you on and many things like this. Park cars on the pavement, park by down kerbs , and generally make your life a misery because they think they knew exactly how a blind man sees the world. Danny was however determined no one would make him look a fool and this was the beginning of his battle to stop these things affecting his life. He was in the lounge one morning and in there was Jeff, Niel, Zarrine and Winnie and he walked with a skip, he said in good humour "Good morning everybody? what a beautiful morning it is then?" Niel "Your joking it's pissing down with rain and windy." Winnie laughed and said "Danny are you allright? I think you have got out of your bed the right side this morning, so cheerful." Danny "Not one of you can upset me this morning, today is the first day of the rest of my life and I am going to embrace it." Jeff "I am getting worried about you, I think you are batting for the other side." Zarrine "Jeffrey what does that mean? batting for someone else." Jeff "No batting for the other side, on the other bus , a bum chum, oh Zarrine I think he as turned queer, a poofta, no." Niel shouts at her nicely "A homosexual, a gaye, c'mon Zarrine wake up." Danny "And Zarrine I am not, no way Jose, I like women don't I Winnie?" Winnie looking puzzled says "Yes, I think so, why do you ask me?" Danny "If you don't know I am in trouble or was I kissing a Chinese man the other night?" Winnie chuckled "Oh yes I see what you mean." She went red in the face and Niel said "Woo, so there is something going on there then?" Winnie said nothing and just smiled and Danny continues "Maybe, maybe, I am starting my life as a blind man this morning, I am going to see Anne and ask her if I am ready to go into town on my own and discuss my future with everyone who I need to for me to get on with my life." Winnie chirps up "Well done Danny, I am totally blind and get on with life as if I am a seeing person and you will be able to do the same sooner than you think." Zarrine "Good for you Danny, that is what I like to hear, see Jeffrey you can be like him too ha, ha, ha." Jeff "Zarrine don't be cheeky I am far better than that dodgy Welshman, I am far superior I can do my shoe laces up now ha, ha, ha." Niel "Well good luck Dan I hope you make it but you won't be able to do everything for yourself, you wait and see." Danny snaps "We will see Niel, are you all going up the bar tonight? there is a karaoke up there." Everyone said yes except Zarrine and Winnie so Danny said to Winnie "Coming up Winnie? we can hear you sing." Winnie "Awe I can't sing, so I don't think so." Danny "Well come up with me I won't sing either and I would like your company if you don't mind?" She thought about it for a minute and said with a big smile "Ok then I will love to, what time Danny?" Danny "Meet you in here at about 7 o'clock if you like?" Winnie replies "Yes ok then." Jeff "Zarrine would you like to come up the bar with me tonight?" Zarrine "I would love to Jeffrey but I must go home and have dinner with peter my husband, sorry." Jeff "Crashed and burned again, the story of my life lately, I am off to my lectures, see you all later." He goes off and Niel was snoring in his seat and Zarrine shook him to wake him up and said to him "Niel wake up it's time you were gone to lectures ha, ha." Niel shook his head and says "Oh sorry, I nodded off then, so what day is it? never mind I remember." Danny "You need to leave them bloody sleeping tablet's alone matey, they are making you sleep all the time." Niel "I know what you mean, I have been very drowsy lately, maybe I will knock them on the head for a few weeks. Jeff has gone has he? I had better get a move on, see you." So just Winnie, Zarrine and Danny left and Zarrine was watching as Winnie nervously looked around as if to say why don't you go Zarrine so she makes an excuse to go and do some work. Winnie speaks up "So we are having a proper date then tonight then are we?" Danny smiling says "Yes why not and you sound very nervous there." "Oh sorry, I am a little, I have never been out with any man ever that's why." "Well I am not going to eat you, so don't worry I am a gentleman." "You? I don't think so or I have been missing something, I am looking forward to tonight but we must go somewhere else some time for a change instead of that bar." "Yes why not, I will take you to the Rose and Crown and the Pretty Pigs sometime, you will like it there, I have to go now so I will see you tonight, yes?" "Yes ok, I will be ready for you, see you then."

Later that evening and Danny and Winnie were sitting in the student bar and Winnie was certainly dressed to kill and Danny was making her laugh a lot and he said "Well this is nice and cosy isn't it?" Winnie replies happily "What is cosy mean?" "It means it is a nice warm feeling, nice and comfortable, it feels right , are you sure you don't want anything stronger to drink?" "No thank you, I may have a wodka and coke later, it is not good to drink too much and you will have to cut it down a little, it is not good at your age." "What do you mean my age? you talk as if I am old and decrepit, or something." "I did not say that, I mean anyone who drinks like you are in danger, you must look after yourself better and I will help to look after you now I am with you." Danny with worried look says "Yes I see, I am feeling better already. Did you ever have alcohol before you came here to Britain?" "No I never did and I think the British drink too much, lots of you die early because of it, I seen it on the TV and I just want to look after you now and you should not eat fatty things, you should eat fish more and give up curries, western people eat rubbish all the time, look how fit I am because I eat the right things ." "Well, yes, I know what you mean but you lack certain things British girls have." "Like what?" "Ha, ha, ha, I don't want you to take this the wrong way but you have very small boobs for a girl of your age." Thank goodness Winnie laughed nicely and said "I know but they have always been small, most women don't have larger boobs until they have their first child and when we are married and have our first child then they will be more to your liking." "Slow down, I am not yet divorced and I can't have any children anyway, I am afraid I have had the snip, well as good as I have got diabetes and my sperm has dried up so I have no seaman at all but it still works ok, sorry." "Are you telling me the truth Danny? this is awful I didn't know but never mind, I will have to find some other way to make them bigger for you." "I know a few ways we can try." "Oh yes I bet this is leading to sex again." "Well, yes." "I thought so ha, ha,, I don't know you and you are talking about sex, is that all you want me for? as I am not like the girls in this country, they

360

will do it any time and with anybody most of the time, I am not like this Danny, so get it out of your head please." "Right, I see this is all about you not getting carried away with your feelings and I must not want anything in this relationship , you are to easternized to, we are from different worlds, I don't know if this is going to work, I keep getting negative vibes from you." "Oh Danny, why do you say this to me?" "Well I mean, I must not touch you, I can't speak about any sex, must give up drinking give up eating I mean there's nothing left to live for. I can't change I am sorry, I can't live like a China man." "I am not asking you to, I am just saying." "And no sex until I marry you, it will be too late if I married and the sex is awful, now's the time to try, not wait until it is too late, I am not a robot and I am not waiting to satisfy you , This is a relationship between 2 people and we should both be happy and not be told what to do by the other, so forget it miss." Winnie looking serious says "Danny, why do you say this? this is not what I want, I must be like a lady, not a hoar, I think I am right." "And is that your final word on this Matter?" Winnie thinks a minute then says "Well no, I will think about this." "I should think so, I am off to get a pint, so do you want anything?" "No I am fine thank you ." Danny goes off to the bar and Winnie sat there in deep thought and when Danny returned he said "There is a folk night here next week, I might come and listen to it." Winnie in quiet voice said "Fair enough Danny I will seriously think about what you said." "That's all I ask, I am not making any demands but you have your culture and I have mine, we must meet in the middle somewhere." "Yes I agree, I must work it out in my mind, I promise I will." "So back to this folk night, do you fancy coming to listen to it?" "Oh yes of course I will have a listen, I don't know what it is mind butt I will give it a go." "It is usually someone singing with a guitar only, singing about local places etc. nice to listen to." "Yes I will try this and what are you doing for Easter then?" "I am going to stay with my son for a few days and then up to stay with Jeff for the rest of the time, so what about you?" "I am going back up to London to stay with some people, this has been arranged by the college, they are very nice people so I don't mind." "There we are then all sorted the both of us, I am going to enjoy it and I am not going to argue with Josh's mother, I hope she will go and stay with her sister and then I am up with that bloody English man, look out." "So you will be on the beer for the week then?" "Maybe, I don't think I will spend my time drinking tea, do you?" "No not really, I think you will do what you want to do anyway." "Well I will have a little blow out on the beer before I get back to college." "I wonder how many nights you will be ill again, well it's your body, I think you will abuse it again." Danny replies "Winnie, now let it drop, I don't smoke or eat rubbish very often so let me have some fun, I don't drink rubbish beers either so I think someone that looks like Jeff as just sat down." Jeff smiles and says "Well if it isn't John and Yoko, before you ask Winnie it is John Lennon and yoko Ono from the Beatles era, so how is things guys?" Winnie says "We were fine until you sat down trying to confuse me, I know who you mean, she is Japanese however, not Chinese, you silly Jeffrey ha, ha, ha." Danny "That put you in your place you ignoramus git ha, ha, I can't wait to come and see you in Swindon it will be a great week mate and I can see where you drink and tell them how thick you really are." Jeff "Ha, ha, they will not believe you matey. They have been told to expect you and the triads are waiting for your visit." Winnie "The triads are not in England Jeffrey, they are in China and will not worry about someone like Danny but you had better look out they would sort you out." Jeff "I am sorry to say there are 3 Welshman in the Polish club that will help you gang up on me, they are living on my estate where I live and I have not got any chance, I will take you to the   Spotted Cow for a meal and then the   Sun Inn for a good pint, they have a quiz there every week so we will have a go." Danny "That's nice of you to take me for a meal Jeff

" Jeff?" Jeff says "You know what I mean, not to pay for it, I am not that rich and you will meet my sons too they will be there to raid my money ha, ha, so what about Winnie what's happening to you over Easter?" Winnie replies "I am going up to London to stay with some people the college has sorted out for me, I stayed the other week for a few days, they seem allright so don't worry about me I will be ok." Jeff "At least you will be out of the way from Danny and you can enjoy yourself." Danny frowning at Jeff said "Steady mate." Winnie chirps up "I would rather be with Danny Jeff but it has been arranged for me so I will have some shopping trips and a look around the attractions there." Danny "Winnie if you came with me and Jeff we would be in the pub every day anyway so it would not be nice for you." Winnie hit's Danny on the shoulder and said "Don't make excuses Danny, I am not stupid ha, ha , ha." Danny "Fair enough I will be a good boy besides." Winnie "And no women." Jeff "Ha, ha, we will be too pissed most of the time and would never be able to handle any women, so don't worry I will keep an eye on him." Winnie "Is that supposed to make me feel better? I don't think so?" Danny "I will be ok I hope, I must be on guard for bandit's and robbers and pirates and muggers and killers and people with knives and all the nutters , so don't worry about me I am confident I will be allright." Winnie looking serious "Is it that bad up there?" Jeff "Na, it's worse than that but only between Thursday and Tuesday it's half day Wednesday." Danny "I drove up there once and I had to have insurance against Viking raids ha, ha,ha." Jeff "Your not kidding." Danny "Right fancy a wodka Winnie?" "Ok just the one, then I am off to bed." Danny "Jeff want a pint mate before I go?" Jeff "For a minute i thought I heard you say before you go, yes I will have a pint Dan but are you going this time of the night?" Danny "Yes I have to take Winnie home like, it's the gentleman thing Jeff, right i am off to the bar.." Jeff says to Winnie "So hows things going with Danny?" "Fine I think, it is early days yet and we nearly tried a few months ago remember and it was fine for the first few days and then it went funny, so I am not saying anything." "Yes but he was not ready for anyone then as he was under the idea he was still a happy married man, now he knows the truth it will be different you will see." Danny comes back with the beer and vodka and says "There you go Winnie and Jeff, merry xmas to you all." Winnie looking confused a what he had just said "A bit early Danny?" Danny "Yes it is but it will soon be with us, so when are you going back to China then?" Winnie replies with sad look "Next December, I fly back, why do you ask?" Jeff "Yeh, you have only just started out together, funny question to ask." Danny "Can't I ask I need to know also if I am going to woo you, get it?" Jeff rolls his eyes and says "Before you ask WINNIE it's the same as your last name but it means to court you or make love to you or make you feel more towards him but the same as your last name ha, ha, ha." Danny "Did you understand any of that Winnie? because I didn't and he is only on his 2nd pint, Jeffrey steady man I wonder where your boxing partner is?" Jeff "I don't know but things between us are ok now, although I still have not had a bit, I must be getting used to it and I see you are more cheerful looking, good mate Niel will be over now for the last 2 pints." Winnie "Well Jeff you won't be lonely will you as me and Danny are off now, I am finished Danny." Jeff "God you are in a hurry Winnie, is he that good? Ha, ha, ha." Winnie "I am not going to answer you Jeffrey because that's our business." Danny's eyes lit up and he thought this is it I am going to have a bit at last and firmly said "Yes Jeff, mind your own business, I keep things like this close to my heart and won't speak about it." Jeff was about to say different and Danny kicked him under the table and Jeff grunted and said "Argh, argh." Danny quickly said "Still got that bad chest Jeff, you know you should get that seen to before it gets any worse, I am off now see you in the morning, goodnight mate." Jeff "Yes goodnight mate and Winnie." Off they went and Jeff was holding his shin and moaning.

Back in Dowdell and Winnie and Danny went in and sat and had a cup of coffee and were arm in arm and Danny said to Winnie "Let's go to your room and have this coffee." Winnie "Why?" "Before anyone comes in and we can be alone and enjoy it." Winnie then shocked Danny by accepting, so off they went and in her room they sat on the bed and Danny was trying to drink his coffee as fast as he could and was sweating badly and so took off his jumper and Winnie said "Danny what are you doing?" "I am taking my jumper off it's so hot in here." "Oh right, do you want a Chinese biscuit with your coffee?" "Oh yes ok please, I like anything Chinese." "Yes I bet you do, here it is." Danny grabbed the biscuit and ate it as fast as he could and said "Right that was nice let's lay down on the bed and enjoy a bit of comfort is it? " Winnie looks a bit concerned at Danny's suggestion and then said "Oh I don't know, let's just sit here and talk." "We can talk laying down." "Well ok then, I will take my shoes off." "Is that all you are taking off?" "Well yes." "Oh right ok then but it will be even nicer if we took our clothes off." "Oh Danny, I don't know about that." "Right please yourself then and Danny put his arm around her and started heading for her breasts and she pulled his hand away and held it tight and Danny was like a rock he could not move, she had such a grip she then kissed him and lay on his shoulder. Danny said "Tell me are you a virgin then?" "Yes I am, I have never known what sex is all about. It is not done in China like here." "Yes it is you know,, you have had a sheltered life being blind and so it has never affected you and you think it is a bad thing don't you?" Winnie replies "Yes I am not wanting this so will you go to your room please?" She sat up and Danny said "You know all animals do it and they don't get married and it is human nature and if people like you were not so stuffed up about it then life on this planet would be much better for all and there would be less rape and people would still respect each other because if there was an Adam and eve they must have committed incest to make the population multiply and if religious people minded their own business and stopped trying to tell the population what to do life would be more pleasant and enjoyable. Adam and eve were naked according to their religion so why the fuss?" "I don't care about all that, I am not doing this until we are married." Danny looking very serious says "Well you have a long wait, I can't live like a monk so I am off." "Why are you off? because you can't get me to do rude things " "No everything I want is not your idea of courtship at all so it is not any good, Winnie we are not at all alike so let's not hurt each other, let's just let it go." Winnie with a tear in her eye says "Ok then go back to your stinking wife, go on I don't care go and have sex with her." Danny looked nasty at her and said "You haven't got a clue have you? I give up, it will always be like this and I don't like arguing, I will see you around." Danny walked through the door and shut it behind him and he could hear WINNIE through the door say "Yes go away you stupid velshman." Danny walked straight up to the student bar and got 2 bottles of Newcastle brown and sat by Jeff and Niel and Jeff said "What are you doing here? I thought you were in whinnies room giving her one." Niel "What's the Matter Dan? What happened?" Waddy puddy mate waddy puddy, I give up." Jeff "What the hell is waddy puddy Danny?" Danny replies "You ignorant English git tell him Niel." Niel looking bemused said shrugging his shoulders "I haven't got a bloody clue what it means, I never heard that before is it Welsh?" Danny smiling "Of course it's Welsh but I don't know what it means either, I just have had enough of Winnie and this is the first night I can't get on with her ways mate, she is different from us Britt's." Niel "Yes I bet she is, she has got a different look at life than us and I bet it's because you didn't get a bit." Jeff "Ah that's it he couldn't get his end away ha, ha, so don't say I am moody about this." Danny "No it's not just that I don't mind that it's everything she finds fault with, she wants me to be a monk and nothing else will do, she will have to meet me half way or it's off and that's final." Jeff "Don't beat about the bush matey you tell her straight." Danny "Well it is ridiculous, she does not want to compromise she wants it all her way no beer, no Chinese, no meat and no sex, stuff it I am not living like that and that's that and Jeff would you live like that? I would rather be dead." Niel "Even I wouldn't like to live like that, never mind who she is, I think you should give her a miss Dan, I would rather go out with mad max." Jeff "Niel, now you are going too far, there's no need for that, I think you should wait until you have got back from your Easter break before you decide matey." Danny "You maybe right mate, I just need a week on the binge after I have been home to see my children, good thinking, that's what I will do."

It was Easter and time for going home to their different destinations and Winnie was not a happy bunny as she has hardly seen Danny, he had been avoiding her. Danny got home early on the Friday that Josh was to break up for Easter and so was alone with Angie for an hour so he took the time to discuss their problems. Danny says "Well Angie how are you? and how are things going with the divorce?" "Don't start now." "I am not starting anything, I am just asking I am getting divorced by you mind for someone as I have been told who is alcoholic." "See what I mean, I knew you would start, I have not seen him and have not seen the solicitor yet either, I am too busy in work but I will get things sorted out eventually and don't go quizzing Josh he is only a boy and does not need to be interrogated about any of this, leave him out of it." "Why are you saying that? has that fat lump been here when Josh is here? I warned you he is not to come in my house if you want to be with him we will sell the house and Josh can come and live with me and he won't have to see you and him having a disgusting affair, he will be devastated by it all and like you said he is only a child." "Huh, you look after him, you can't look after yourself let alone look after a child." There was a brief silence and Danny looked visibly upset about what she said then he snarled "Well he would be safer with me than with an overgrown alcoholic and his own mother who has not got a care how that kid feels about her splitting up a happy family and let me tell you I can look after him and myself so be careful what you say." "Right I am off, I can't stand being in the same room as you when you are like this." "See what I mean it's allright for you to say things about me and when I give my input your running away" ." Angie says "I am not running away, I just can't stay here with you I am going to have a cup of tea with my sister Georgina and then I am going to fetch Josh, so how long before you go back? I am going to stay with my sister until you go back." "What do you mean?" "Well i am not staying here I will go and do my work in the boys club in the evenings and then I will sleep down Susan's or anywhere but here." "There's no need for that, there is 3 bedrooms here you know." "Forget it I am not staying here, so tell me when you are going back?" Danny in a calm voice replies "I am going up to stay with Jeff in Swindon for most of the holidays but I thought we could act normal for Josh's sake for the weekend but obviously not, i will leave early on Monday then." "Right I am off." Angie left without any thought for Danny and Danny was looking very dejected and almost crying, he then put his stereo on and blasted some music to take his mind off things. It was not long before Josh came in and he ran up to Danny and put his arms around him and hugged him, he said "Hi dad? how are you then? are you still at school? ha, ha, I have made a card for you for Easter look." Danny looked at the card and it said to mum and dad lots of love from Josh, Danny was fighting the tears back and said "That's lovely Josh, I am keeping this and taking it back to college so I can show my mates." "Can we go to Bridgend this week for my Easter present instead of eggs as

I will have enough eggs from my aunties won't I?" "I am sorry Josh I have to go back to college on Monday and I will give you money to get something for yourself with mammy ok? and we can have a Chinese tonight ok?" "Yes I knew we were having a Chinese." "We always have a Chinese don't we, so I am looking after you tonight as mammy is going to work or do you want to go with mammy?" "No silly you can't look after me I am staying with you and looking after you ok?" "Why can't I look after you?" "Because you can't see silly." Danny looked even more dejected and felt useless which annoyed him inside. Well the weekend was reasonably good but Danny found himself left out of everything as Angie in her wisdom again arranged for Josh to go to a birthday party on the Saturday and he only seen Josh for a whole day on the Sunday, this was an awful Easter for him and it soon came to Monday and up to Swindon to meet Jeff. Danny was up early as usual and he was saying goodbye to Josh before he went off to the train station and said to Josh "Well Josh you must be a good boy for your mother and no sweets with that money I have given you ok? and look after Murphy for me and I will phone you when I get back." Josh looking sad says to his dad "Ok dad and you be a good boy for the teachers up there ha, ha, he, he, I am doing good in school since you taught me maths and English you know." Danny holding the tears back says "Good boy, I am proud of you and do you love me?" "Of course dad and you love me don't you? I will tell you what I bought on the phone." "Right matey give me a kiss I will see you." Josh gave Danny a huge kiss and hug and Danny did the same back and left and got into his taxi for the station .

Danny was off on his trip, he had never been on his own going up to a city like Swindon since he had gone blind, this was not possible in Danny's mind before that day but he was now determined to start to live his life independently and it showed. Danny looked like a nervous wreck because it was also the Easter bank holiday Monday, he got to the train station in Bridgend and asked the ticket office to get hymn some help to get on the train and it proved to be so easy, a lovely man who had helped him before came to the ticket office and said "Allright there, it's Danny isn't it? my name is John and I will get you over to the other side and help you on the train and find you a nice seat, shall I have your bag for you?" From that moment on he felt a lot better and safer, he said "Hello John I am glad you are able to help me that's great, I am off to Swindon to see a friend for the Easter week." "Ok Dan, I will put you in a seat and phone Swindon and tell them exactly where you are on the train and they will come and get you off and take you to the taxi stand or to your friend and then it's up to you." "Brilliant John I can relax then for the journey." "You have 30 minutes to wait as the train is late and so If you want I can get you a cup of tea over there if you like?" Danny with huge smile replied "That's great John, thank you." "No problem Dan, you don't mind if I call you Dan do you?" "Some people call me worse." John takes him over to the other platform and put him in a seat and went off to get him a cup of tea and they sat and chatted for the time he was waiting for the train . On the train and Danny was feeling better on his journey but would get more panicky the closer he got to Swindon but there was no need as they got him off the train and into a taxi easily. The next problem was the taxi and he told the Taxi driver the address and district and said "Can you get as close as you can to the entrance?" Taxi driver says "No problem matey is someone meeting you?" "Yes I am going to give him a call now so he can meet me at the entrance." This he done and it was perfect as Jeff was right there waiting for him. He got out of the taxi and shook hands with Jeff as Jeff said "Hello dodgy, any problems getting here?" Danny shaking a little with nerves said "Not really, I am amazed it was so easy, so this is Park South then? shall I grab your elbow and go in?" They went in and Danny was amazed at the amount of stairs he had to climb, it was a small tower block, they got in and sat down Danny panting said "Bloody hell Jeff, that was a lot of stairs and being blind I would have thought they would put you on the ground floor, I am sweating cobs here, waddy puddy, waddy puddy, I had not better get drunk with all the stairs." "You will get used to it matey, this is my humble abode, let me take you around." "Good idea Jeff take me to the bog first I am busting mate." this he did and afterwards Jeff continued "This is my bedroom and there is only one and you have seen the bathroom so back into the lounge and through here is the kitchen and that is it, you will have the settee and it's easy to get to the bathroom from here, so there you are you will pick it up, fancy a cup of tea or a tinny?" "Give me a tinny mate for my nerves please." "I thought that's what you would say here's a cold one " "Cheers mate, I need this I was a bag of nerves, I can tell you." "Why? What went wrong?" Danny said "Absolutely nothing, that's the problem I was so nervous about coming up here on my own but it went smooth especially the station bloke in Bridgend, John he was superb and he phoned up Swindon station and someone was waiting for me and put me in a taxi and here I am, I don't know about the rest of the week mind but we will see." "Don't panic mate it will be a doddle and we will have a good couple of nights, so what do you fancy for tea? I suggest we should go over the Chinese chip shop and grab some chips, they are very nice." "Oh they do Chinese meals in there? because that's what I fancy and it will fill me up." "Yes they do and tomorrow we can go to the Spotted cow for lunch and a couple of pints we can walk up there and my uncle Sidney lives on the way so we can get a cup of tea, he is great you will like him, he is ex-army in his seventies and he can jump over mine and your head." " Danny says "Sounds good, so what now then? I suggest we sink a couple of cans and go for a chinky at about 6." "Right, so how was things in Bridgend then with Josh and Angie?" "It was great with Josh and Angie didn't want to know me at all, it was a little sad because of Josh I feel as if she is tearing him away from me and I could not take that Jeff." Jeff says "That's the only problem with divorce Dan, the children and the pets but in a year things will be much different." Danny says "We will see Jeff." "It will, well I think you are going to find it ruff here in park south but we are safe they all know me and are not all that bad, it's just the rioters on the weekend ha, ha, and the muggers so we will take a taxi home or as regards the Polish club it's not far we can go there tonight if you like?" "Yes fine mate, I am up for that." "Right, let's take a walk up the Chinese then is it? I will help you just grab my elbow."

It was later that evening and they went to the Polish club and Danny spent the night telling jokes and had all of them in there in stitches and they both got very drunk and enjoyed themselves and they walked home late that night. So things were going well for Danny in his new quest for freedom and independence.

The following day they took a walk with Jeff's young son Dean, this was the first time he had met Dean and they walked up to Jeff's uncle for a cuppa and had a nice chat with Sidney, this was half the walk they were doing to get to the Spotted Cow public house for lunch. They sat down and Jeff went to the bar for 2 pints of lager and a coke for Dean and as they sat there Danny sipped his drink and said "Well it is comfortable here isn't it, I don't think much of the beer here though." Jeff "It's ok, I have been drinking here for years, so what do you fancy to eat?" Dean "Pizza and chips please." Danny "I will have the fish chips and peas please, I will get these in as a thank you for having me." Jeff smiling said "Ok then." Danny "Look Jeff don't fight me on this I am paying ok?" Jeff "Ok then matey." Danny "No look Jeff I insist ha, ha." Jeff "Right I will have a T-bone steak and all the trimmings in that case ha, ha, ha." Danny "You have what you want mate, take advantage why don't you ha, ha,

Dean are you sure all you want is a pizza because it's not your tight father paying now it's a lovely Welshman." Dean "I do want a pizza anyway thanks." Jeff "I can't eat a T-bone I am only kidding, I will have the ham, eggs and chips Dan thank you matey. I will go and order Dan." Jeff goes off to the bar and Danny starts talking to Dean "So how old are you Dean?" "I am 12." "I have a son your age his name is Josh, so are you married?" Dean looks at Danny bemused and said "No I am too young." "Oh, ok then do you see your father often?" "Yes when he comes home and I go and raid his pennies jar and eat his chocolate biscuit's and he gets annoyed with me so he hides them in the wardrobe ha,, ha, ha, he gets real nasty when I eat them all ha, ha, ha." "I know he is like that when someone sips his beer, look out he is coming back." Jeff "Here is your change Dan, you should see that barmaid she is gorgeous matey and her boobs come in the room ten minutes before she does, I am sure she fancies me, she can't keep her eyes off me ha, ha,, ha." Dean "Yeh, yeh, dad, keep on dreaming." Jeff "Dean, you should stick up for your father boy ha, ha, ha, ha." Danny "He does live in a fantasy world don't he?" Dean "Yes he does don't he, I hear him trying to chat up girls all the time." Jeff "I can't help it if I am irresistible to women." Dean "I am off to Alton towers next week so I need money dad for the trip, so how much can you give me?" Jeff in a panic says "Well how much do you want? about a fiver?" Dean with shocked look says "A fiver, that is not going to go far is it? I need at least twenty five quid." Jeff pretended to choke on his drink "Twenty five quid, when I was a kid I had fifty pence and had a great day with it and still had change for chips when I got home." Dean mimics a violin playing sadly and said "Yes dad in the olden days that was ok but you were about five then about fifty years ago, times change mind dah, dah,." Danny "Yes you crabby old git this is the 21st century not the roaring thirties matey, keep up for goodness sake, tut, tut, honestly Dean he is so old fashioned isn't he?" Dean "Tell me about it, even this old Welshman is up with the times dad." Jeff "Ha, ha, ha, ok I will think about it Dean, here comes the food I am starving, right that is yours Dan and I will tell you where everything is now when we have got all the food." Danny "Yes ok Jeff no problem or dim problem." Dean "Daddy says that too." Jeff "Right Dan the fish is at twelve o'clock the peas are about 2 o'clock and the chips are to the left of them and some tartar sauce in a little dish on top of the fish." Danny "I don't want the tartar sauce so I will take it off, can you put some salt on everything and some vinegar on the chips only?" This is what Jeff done and they sat back and started to eat until half way through the meal and there was little left on the plates and Dean started on Danny helping him to find out what he was getting on his fork before he put it in his mouth and the same to Jeff. First it was Jeff he tried to annoy Jeff picked up his fork expecting something to be on it and Dean said "Nothing on it dad." Jeff put his fork into his food again and he put it up to his mouth and Dean said "Nothing on it dad." Jeff said "Dean I am going to smack you in the ear in a minute if you keep on ha, ha." Next thing Danny was chasing his peas all over the plate and Dean said as he put his fork up to his mouth "Nothing on it Dan ha, ha, ha., ha." Danny put his fork in his mouth and there was nothing on it so he dipped in again to get some peas and half way to his mouth Dean says "Ha, ha, nothing on it ha, ha." Danny put it in his mouth and laughed as there was nothing on his fork, he dipped in again and the same thing half way to his mouth Dean says "Nothing on it." Danny said after finding nothing on his fork again "Don't he get on your nerves Jeff? ha, ha, ha." All 3 burst out laughing and Danny got back into his peas and actually got a single pea on his fork and was putting it up to his mouth and Dean screams "Yes, yes, you got one." At that Danny started laughing and dropped the pea, they all laughed and Danny said "Jeff I am going to kill him in a minute ha, ha, can't you send him home ha, ha." Jeff "I know he is a pain in the ass, he does this all the time ha, ha." Danny was now laughing too much to eat so he grabbed the peas with a spoon and put them up to his mouth and Dean said "Now your getting there, try that with the chips though ha, ha." They all started laughing again . Jeff and Danny had another drink and Danny was screwing up his face as he was not a lover of the lager and said "So where's this other pub you mentioned Jeff? the sun, is it far?" Jeff replies "Yes it is, it is a bit of a walk mind so grab your cane and we shall take a stroll Dan, it's about a mile down the road towards Swindon town." Danny looked unsure and panicky says "Oh dear, do you think it is too far.? shall we get a taxi for safety sake?" Jeff "Now come on independence is the key as you said, think positive and let's walk it it's not that far and it will build our confidence up, so c'mon let's do it matey." Danny unsure still says "Fair enough let's do it then "

They all get up and take a walk to the sun public house and it took them at least half an hour before they reached the sun pub and Danny looked shattered with his nerves and he got in the pub and sighed and said "Well that main road was busy, I felt like I was walking on the hard shoulder of the motorway, nerve racking Jeff, didn't it bother you?" Jeff smiling says "No it was ok, I am used to the traffic, mind I have lived around it all my life. So what do you want to drink?" Danny replies "A triple whisky for my nerves, no I am only kidding, I need to stay sober for the walk home, do you know I am sweating like a pig I am so nervous, I will have the coldest pint of lager they have got please." Dean was smiling and said "Can I have J 2O please dad? I will look after the nutty Welshman, he looks as if he has just ran a marathon." Danny still puffing says "Your not kidding Dean I feel like that, I can't wait to have a pint and some Vallium ha, ha, i am not finding this easy at all." Jeff "Shut up moaning or you will never get it right, go with the flow and we are now nearer my place so not far to walk home and we will go down the Polish club tonight if you like?" Danny "Yes if you like, why not?" Well a couple of days went bye and Jeff decided to have a barbecue and it was him and Danny who were going to do the cooking, this was going to prove a damn good laugh as Danny was not prepared as to how difficult it was going to be. Jeff had set up the barbecue and was trying to light it and said "This bloody thing, I can't seem to light it, I need some more paper to light the fire lighters." Jeff goes in the house and gets some paper and Danny was sitting outside sipping a bottle of lager and Jeff comes back with a wad of paper and bends down with his head almost in the barbecue and he screamed and was dancing about slapping himself on the head "Argh, argh, I caught my hair on fire the bloody thing was alight all the time and I just put my head right in the flames, shit, argh, argh." Danny burst out laughing and said "Your a dickhead aren't you? didn't you realise it was alight? couldn't you feel the heat?" "Well no, I thought I failed to light it so was bending down to put the paper near the fire lighters and it was already alight now my eyebrows are gone ha, ha." "And we haven't started cooking yet, I can smell your hair burning ha, ha, I can't see how we can tell when things are cooked." "Don't worry we will know even if we have got to cremate it to be sure but we are having a barbecue, Argh, argh, argh my bloody hand the paper I am holding is alight too shit, another burn, right I think we will have to Waite for it to cool down a bit first or the flames will burn everything." " Good idea mate, have a bottle for a while until it is cool enough, have you prepared everything? I will help you so I can learn to do it." Jeff "Oh dear I think it is a good idea for you to learn but both of us could end up in the burns unit tonight ha, ha, ha." "If we do it together it will be allright and the neighbours will have a damn good laugh I bet they are all standing by the windows thinking this is going to be entertaining, 2 blind idiots having a barbecue ha, ha, ha, they will have the best laugh since Morecambe and wise." "Do you fancy a baked potato?

or had we better not push our luck? ha, ha, ha." "Why not? go for it, what can go wrong? if we can't get them out we will throw them at the neighbours after they have cooled down, I don't want to worry you but can you smell plastic burning mate?" Jeff stopped in his tracks looked serious and concerned and said "Now you come to mention it mate I can... shit it's my bloody plastic Gutter on the shed, the fire is too close to the shed, I will have to move it but how?" "Well we had better do it quick, is there any handles on the barbecue?" "I don't know, I can't remember I don't think so, shall i throw a bucket of water over the barbecue or what?" "No I know give me that cloth you had I will grab the leg and slide it over this way, you go and phone the fire brigade." Danny done this after he found the leg and he stopped and accidentally put his hand on the lid and jumped "Argh, argh, argh, I have put my hand on the bloody lid and it is red hot, shit, but the fire is away from the shed now." He sucks his hand and goes in and puts his hand under the cold tap, he returns and Jeff said "We are burnt in several places each and we have not cooked anything yet, god help us when we start cooking, I think we should get pissed before we start so we won't feel the pain." " I think you are right, right it is getting cooler" Jeff still holding his hand and rubbing it said "So how are we going to do this Dan?" "Well I suggest we cook one thing at a time like sausages then burgers and then steaks etc." Jeff looked up in astonishment "Steaks, steaks? i don't think so mate I have got some small stewing steaks like really small and that is it ha, right you stand on one side and I shall put 3 sausages on your side and 3 on my side, you look after yours and I will do mine, here's a fork Dan and good luck, ha, ha, can you hear people laughing somewhere? I can't wait to see how this works out." "Let me put my sausages on so I know where they are. Yes I can hear someone laughing too ha, ha, ha." Jeff hands Danny the sausages and he puts them on jumping with the heat. They both stand there and keep an ear on the cooking and the people laughing in the distance and Danny said "This is exciting but how the hell can we tell if they are cooked enough to turn them over?" "We will just have to take a chance they are done, I think we should turn them now." The boys both concentrate on their sausages and Danny was unable to find his and was jumping with the heat and so was Jeff, they both sounded like chimps "Ooh, ah, ooh, ah, ooh, ah, shit, shit, ow, ow, argh, argh." Danny said "I have turned one and now this, shit it has fallen through the bars into the fire, bloody hell, I have lost one how can I get it back Jeff?" "Well you can't how will you find it and besides we would have to take it apart so it is lost mate, shit it is hot here and the flames are leaping around my sausages with the fat dripping on the fire." "Oh bollocks, another sausage has gone in between the bars, these sausages are so small like chipolatas mate, I have only got one sausage left." Jeff was laughing and said "Ha, ha, don't worry we shall share anything left after we have cooked them and you have only got one sausage to look after now I have three, I am more professional than you shit, shit." Danny jumps and says "What's the Matter Jeff?" Jeff was sweating cobs and the sausages had caught fire and he was panicking "My sausages are on fire, and I can't get near them it's too hot, I need to get a glove from in the house so be careful Dan." Jeff ran off to get an oven glove and comes back and after a few minutes he gets the sausages off the flames onto a plate and Danny takes his sausage off as the flames were too much and they both put them on a plate and sat down sweating and moaning as they were full of small burns, they sighed and Jeff said "There that was easy ha, ha, ha, I am soaking with sweat matey and we have only cooked 4 sausages ha, ha,." "Shit, I know it was murder and I am sure I have burned my jumper as I can smell wool burning. Right let's try these sausages." Jeff put 2 on plates and handed Danny his 2 little pathetic sausages to him he sat and they looked like 2 orphans with these sausages in front of them with sweat running down their foreheads and Danny took a bite out of one and started spitting it out again and said "Jeff these are cremated, just ash, burnt to a cinder." Jeff also spitting out ash laughed "I know, like eating coke from the fire." "I will try the other one the one I cooked, well it is just about edible." "Yes the other one of mine is just edible but burnt on the ends." They sit silently eating this single sausage and enjoyed it and Danny finished and said "Do you know, I am bloody starving now so let's try these burgers before I starve to death." "Ha, ha, ha, I am getting hunger pangs myself and my hands are black either burnt or off the sausages, I will get the burgers from the kitchen, so 2 each you have yours and I will do mine if I can stand with weakness ha, ha." They both got their burgers and slapped them on the barbecue and they smelled beautiful as they cooked and they kept on turning them over and then Jeff turned one of his and it fell on the floor and he screamed "Bloody hell my burger is on the floor ha, ha, ha, and now I have trod on it." Danny laughed and Jeff was on his hands and knees and he found the burger and picked it up and put it back on the barbecue and Danny was shocked and said "Your not going to eat that now are you?" "Too bloody right, I am starving , ha, ha, I am not letting it get away, I need to eat, stuff it ha, ha, ha." " Danny laughed and said Ha, ha, ha, ha, I have seen it all now, this is like a comedy show ha, ha, and I am talking and one of mine has just gone on the floor, shit I will get it now." They were both laughing their heads off and Danny got his burger and slapped it back on the barbecue and got his other one off as it was burning and put it on this plate. After doing a juggling act with it in his hands they laughed so much that day it was good for the both of them and after they sat down with the 2 burgers like it was a gourmet meal and looked so funny, black burgers and a pint in their hands. Jeff said "I can't eat this if we don't stop laughing and my stomach is groaning with hunger pangs ha, ha, ha, I must eat now, shut up for five minutes because bye the time we eat this the fire will be out ha, ha, ha." "Ha, ha, ha, ha, I can't help it it's the funniest thing I have ever seen ha, ha, and the tears are running down my face from laughter and the bloody smoke of that fire ha, ha, ha, hows your burger? Ha, ha, ha." Jeff couldn't tell him for laughing and then he said "Ha, ha, I don't know I haven't been able to try it yet for laughing ha, ha, right I am biting it ….. it is not bad a little burnt but it tastes like a burger, I hope we don't get food poisoning that's all." "Probably as long as we don't get it before we cook those steaks I don't care ha, ha, ha." The lads crack up laughing again and Jeff said "I can't wait ha, ha, ha." "I am eating this and it's scolding hot but I am so hungry I can't help it, yum, yum ha, ha." The lads finish the burgers and they put the stakes on and at last they get it right and the steaks cook just right and they finish the food and they had, had so much to drink they were very tipsy and Jeff said "God I am getting a little cold now, I am going to warm my backside by the barbecue and look how long it has taken us to eat, all afternoon ha, ha,." Jeff in his drunken stupor drops his cigarette and bends down to pick it up and his backside pushed against the barbecue and he let out a cry "Argh, argh, argh, my ass, I have burnt my ass now I will have a huge blister on it and won't be able to sit down now and it has burnt a hole in the backside of my trainer bottoms, shit it hurts like hell." "Well don't look at me, I am not kissing it better ha, ha, ha." The lads fell about laughing again and that was that they had a shower each and went up to the Polish club for a drink.

They met the same Welsh boys they met earlier that week and had a good laugh. Jeff then suggested "I fancy a Polish lager that will knock my head off and yours dodgy." Danny "What is that then?" Jeff with his head wobbling from side to side said "It's called Sherbetsor something, it's Polish and very strong." Danny smiling says "I will have a jollop of that mate with you ." Well they drunk it all night and went home laughing and singing and they got to Jeff's stairway to his flat and half way up the stairs there was a young girl in her twenties walking down the stairs and she stopped Danny and Jeff and said "Hello, I was wondering if you can help me? I am locked out of my flat on the ground floor." Danny "Certainly we will try to see if we can help, we will follow you." She directed the lads to her flat and said "My partner has gone to work and I have locked myself out and the only way is to force the door, I have a bolt on the inside so I can lock it until he gets back tomorrow, if you can force it for me." Jeff walked up to the door and put his shoulder against it and hit it hard but it never moved and he said "Right Dan come here and put your shoulder into this door and get it open I still have got a bad muscle to do it on my own." Danny "Let me have a look at it Jeff." Danny put his arm against it and said "Look out mate I will have this open as quick as I can." Danny pushed his shoulder against it a few times and it opened and let them in. Jeff "There you go lovely girl, he is useful sometimes ha, ha, are you ok now?" She said "That's brilliant of you, have you got any rollies for me until the morning? I will pay you back in the morning." Jeff "I have got some in my flat, I will roll you a couple and bring them back down." She sounded so happy and said "Well that's very kind of you I will go inside and wait for you." She had a huge smile on her face and Jeff thought this was a come on and said "Ok then I won't be long now, I will be back in a Iffy." Jeff grabbed Danny and rushed him to his flat and they got in and Danny puffing said "Shit Jeff, what are you doing to me? I am knackered now, rushing me up those stairs." Jeff replies "Sorry Dan I must get these ciggy's to that girl and if I am not back by the morning make your own tea until I get back." Jeff sat on the carpet in front of the fire and put the telly on for Danny and crossed his legs in front of him like a red Indian and started rolling the fags and Danny said "Oh so you think your in there then do you?" "Well it looks good from my opinion Dan, she has asked me to take them to her so I think she wants a bit at last, I am going to get a bit, so if I am not back don't worry but lock the door and I will knock sometime in the morning ha, ha, yes my son." Danny looking sorry for himself said "Lucky git and I gave up smoking ha, ha, I will see you in the morning then, have fun." Jeff left and Danny sat watching telly and dozing and next thing the door had a knock and Danny shouted "Who is it?" Jeff outside said "It's me I am back." Danny let him in and said "That was a quick one, I didn't realise that you were that bad, did she remember it." "Ha, ha, bloody funny, there was 3 other men in there when I got there, she is a quick worker and they have not got very good furniture, they are deck chairs if that's fashion today, it's weird and she took the cigarettes anyway, then asked me in, I was so uncomfortable I left so I crashed and burnt again, my life story." "Never mind mate we have had a brilliant day and a good laugh, someone will turn up one day just when you least expect it, have a fag Jeff and we can go to bed." "Yeah I suppose so, I think those boys were American, they were smoking those Turkish fags, smelled awful." It was too late Danny was sleeping and Jeff was looking lost and went to bed.

It was the next morning and Danny and Jeff had planned a trip to town to do some shopping, they sat there finishing their breakfast of tea and toast and Danny said "How are you this morning? I can hardly touch my fingers as they are so sore with the little burns." "Tell me about it dodgy, I am the same and I feel as if I am bald as I have lost a lot of my hair ha, ha, and my hands are sore, I will get some cream out of the first aid kit for us now and my ass I have to sit on one cheek it's so sore, did you sleep ok?" "Like a baby mate, I was so pissed after that Sherbets I slept very well, what a pint so lovely." Jeff smiling says "Yes but I can't drink much of it and they have the cherry brandy you must try that, I did once and I was like a robot coming home it made me numb and I couldn't remember my name the next day and my mum had to come up to look after me I was so bad." "Does your mummy come over much?" "Yes, she cleans up for me once a week, she is marvellous and bill is very good too." "Bill he is her husband I guess? as you told me your father died when you were young, it must be nice to have a mother like that and what does bill do then?" "He is a Traffic warden." "Oh shit, a very popular man then? I must meet your mum and bill they sound nice." "Yes the next time you come down they will be about I expect, they are on holiday at present, I am hoping to move soon to a newly built bungalow over the road and it will be nicer than this." "Right and I bet you can't wait it is like Jurassic park here, lots of noise in the night, I don't like it here it can give anyone a nervous breakdown if it wasn't for the drink." "Yes it gets a little hairy here sometimes I can tell you." "I bet it can, so we had better get a move on, I ..." All of a sudden Jeff jumped up and grabbed a slipper and started bashing the floor with it and it was very aggressive and Danny jumped up and said "What's the Matter mate? what's going on ?" Jeff spoke in a nervous way "A bloody huge spider by my feet Dan." Danny ran to the kitchen and closed the door and all of a sudden it went quiet and Jeff was laughing and knocked the kitchen door and Danny wouldn't open it he said "Right Jeff don't mess about, I am petrified of spiders and you know it, I will not be responsible for what I do if you show it to me, I mean it mind." Jeff laughing on the other side of the door said "It's ok it's not a spider after all, my eyes were playing tricks with me come in and sit back down." "Jeff you had better not be messing about I will kill you I don't like spiders and so don't mess about." "There is no spider Dan, I will explain come and finish your tea, it's ok now." Danny comes back in the sitting room cautiously and sits down and says "Right, I am waiting tell me and no messing." Jeff started laughing "Ha, ha, ha, I feel an idiot, the spider was some tobacco I spilt last night and it looked exactly like a spider by my feet, I was beating up some tobacco ha, ha, ha." The both lads had a real good laugh and Danny told Jeff a true story "When I was going blind I went down my local club one night and came home a bit tipsy and as you know I will do anything to get away from a spider, well I got home and was busting for a crap and so was sitting on the toilet and all of a sudden a spider landed on my bare legs and it was a huge one I could tell, well I had my trousers around my ankles and got up and ran straight into the end of the bathroom door that was half open and knocked myself out. I woke up with a huge lump on my head and started shouting to get the spider, well I had a lump as big as the one on your head that time you missed the foot bar that didn't exist in the Barrels ha, ha, ha." The both lads were laughing profusely and got ready to go to town .

They locked the door as they were leaving and could hear a lot of noise down stairs and they were going down stairs and they could hear a bit of a fuss on the ground floor and there were police taking the boys and the girl from down stairs and arresting them. Next thing the girl said "There they are, they are the ones who broke in the door." Danny and Jeff looked as if they had seen a ghost and a policeman said to them "Is this true? did you break in here?" Jeff replies "You what? us break in there?" Danny took up the conversation and the policeman came over to the lads and he said "Do we look like burglars we are blind and partially sighted, this is ridiculous we couldn't have it's Impossible they would laugh you out of court, she is a druggy I bet by the smell vomiting out of the place." Policeman replies to the lads "Sorry, I didn't know you were blind, she must be mistaken and trying to blame anyone else but herself, sorry." Jeff says "So what have they done anyway?" Policeman "Well we got them out of there a few days ago and locked up the place as they were squatting and told them not to return and they did and I can't see how they broke that door down, so easy as the boys are so little and weak, I can't get over it so we have now charged them with squatting breaking and entering and taking drugs in there and if we find the person who broke in for them I will be charging them too, but sorry matey's I hope you have a nice day and take it easy." A man walked in and started to repair the lock on the door and Danny and Jeff left quickly. Just around the corner and out of sight from the police Danny burst out laughing followed by Jeff and Danny said "I can Imagine it now on the front of the papers, 2 blind men break in for squatters and were charged and yes they are really blind, the college would throw us out ha, ha, no wonder they got rid of you last night." "I am glad they did now that was close, right let's go to town on the bus now, I will get my pass out and you pretend you have left yours in the house and we will get you there for free, ok?" "Well we can give it a try." They get on the bus and it worked and they arrived in town and it was unbelievable, it was swarming with people and it was nerve racking for Danny who started to panic many times, as he was jostled around it was too much for him and so he stopped Jeff at one point and said "Right mate I have had enough, let's get into a chip shop and get some food then a pub for a pint, this is too much for me." This is what they do.

Danny and jeff sitting in the pub Danny looked shattered and said "How do you live like this Jeff? this place is like a ant hill, so many people and kids on skate boards and busker's people rushing all over the place, noise that drowns out any clue for a blind person, it's nerve racking, let's go home mate, I have had enough." "Don't worry mate I know what you mean it's busy." "Busy, that's an understatement, I can't ever see me getting use to this, people were kicking me, kicking my cane all over the place, knocking me, stepping on my feet, this is Impossible, I will have to rush the guide dogs people to get me a guide dog that's all." "Dan you must stick at it, you will get used to a cane soon enough, it takes time, it will be a time before you get a dog." Danny "I have been waiting a long time already, so it can't be long now, I just can't take the jostling matey it's getting to me now enough's, enough." "Oh well, you will have to depend on others helping you all the time and they won't be there at your beck and call, it's not so hard the cane." "Not for you Jeff, you can see a little, I am totally blind, you have at least got a clue, I haven't. I am waiting to walk into something or somebody and its cracking me up, it's like being in a car with a kid driving waiting to die." Jeff paused and thought a minute and said "Yes Dan your right, I never thought, I have got some help with a little sight and I should have taken this into account, I am sorry matey I will take my time now and think a bit more, I think we will stroll across town and get a bus to home and prepare to go out tonight for the last night before we go back and if I am going to fast tell me, do you want anything here in town?" "I would like to go to a good record shop if there is one?" "Yes there is a big one down the road, let's drink this have another one and we will go there." This is what they do and they take time and enjoy the stroll across town and stop a few times as people stop to speak to Jeff.

On the bus and Danny was much happier with the way they handled it.

Back up in the college and it was the first day back and Danny was sitting in the lounge the morning of his first lectures and in walked a tutor who had come over to speak to Danny "Hi Danny, I wonder if you have heard from Winnie?" Danny looking puzzled said in answer "Winnie, no I haven't, she is in London and is back I expect today, why?" Tutor replies "Well she has disappeared, she left her digs and went for a wander around London and no one has heard from her since, we are worried." "Don't worry about her she can certainly look after herself, no problem, I expect she will turn up, she is no idiot. If she can look after herself in China she will not blink an eyelid in London." Tutor looking unconvinced says "I hope your right, she should have been back last night." Danny looking a little worried says "I got back last night and I wished I had left it until today as on a Sunday it was horrific travelling it really was, I expect she found this out and stayed until today in a hotel somewhere but if I see her I will tell her to get in touch, ok?" " Tutor says "Yes please, I will appreciate that Dan, I have knocked her door and no answer." Next thing in walks Zarrine and says "I will check her room now as I have the master key." They go off and in walks Jeff " ok Dan? what's going on?" "Oh Winnie has not come back from London, she went AWOL from her digs and has not returned to college, probably gone underground in hiding to stay in this country." Jeff looking in discussed at Danny "Danny, that's not nice, aren't you worried at all?" Danny in deep thought "Yes I ought to be worried I suppose for those poor Londoners, she has probably got some of them by the throat threatening them, she has probably got a knuckle duster, flick knife, gun and a stiletto knife by now, I bet it will be on the news tonight ha, ha." Niel was listening by the door and Jeff and him laughed out loud. Niel then said "That's not a nice thing to say, is it?" Jeff "He is probably right though." Danny "I bet she will turn up dressed like the terminator with a Kalashnikov under her arm." The lads buckled up laughing and Zarrine comes back in and says "Well she is not in her room, what have you done with her Danny?" Danny looked bemused by her question and says "Ok I admit it, it was me, I took her to play hop scotch on the motorway, then I took her to sweep the road on the magic roundabout in Swindon, then spaghetti junction then took her to cut the grass in longleat safari park." Zarrine slapping him on the back laughed as they all did Zarrine then says "I wonder what she is up to and I hope she is ok." Danny "Yes I am only kidding, I would not like anything to happen to her, I bet she will turn up as if nothing has happened, she can handle herself believe me I know she would kill anyone who messed with her, I feel sorry for the mugger." Niel "So how did your week go Dan?" Danny replies "I am on vallium 40 fags a day, could burglar any property and leave no finger prints due to all my fingers burned through doing a barbecue and we almost got arrested for helping a damsel in distress to break down a door in a house that she was chucked out of by the police and we believed she had been locked out and so I broke the door in for her." Jeff "And the next morning we were walking past there and the police were arresting them and she identified us as the ones that opened the door, the policeman asked us if it was true, we denied it and told them we were blind and he let it go and Danny said Imagine it 2 blind men broke into house and were arrested in the papers, that was funny." Niel "A quiet week then?" Danny "then Jeff beat up a bit of tobacco he had dropped on his carpet that he thought was a spider and I locked myself in the kitchen until he had smoked it ha, ha, ha." they had a good laugh and Zarrine said "Of course you are afraid of spiders aren't you? that's why you were hiding in the kitchen, ha, ha, you silly sod." Niel "I had a lovely week, the boys had their motorbike out and I had to fix it first mind and we went down the caravan in Kidwelly then and had a great time and Ceri went to bingo and won a couple of hundred pounds, so that was handy." Zarrine "It's allright for some, I had to work most of my holidays here and peter was off so he was on his own sometimes." Danny "Right guys I am off." Jeff "I thought I could smell something." Niel "What have you got this morning Dan?" Danny replies "I am going to town on my own to try it and Anne is following me from a distance, this should be a good laugh and I may never see you all again, so wish me luck." Niel "You'll be alright mate just take a tip from me because in time your hearing and touch will take over and you will be expecting to get it right all the time, things will stick in your mind and it will all come together you will see but good luck." Danny goes off and the lads say "So how was he really Jeff? in Swindon I mean." Jeff said "He was a total mess really and the last day it showed he was in a state in the city centre until I slowed right down and he seemed better but he has got a long way to go, he should have a guide dog really."

Zarrine "Yes he should, he is a wreck, I can feel him grabbing my arm when I take him anywhere, he is so nervous, I can't understand why they are so slow getting him one." Niel "Well he has decided to wait until he finishes here as he feels it would not be fair to the dog here as they are mostly sat under a desk all day so he is waiting, so he has got a long way to go if he is using the cane only it is hard to get used to so god help him, but he will do it and if anyone wants a bet on it I will have a tenner on him winning with his cane." Jeff smiling "You pair of dodgy Welshmen have caught me too many times so forget it, mind you he is determined isn't he?" Zarrine with a serious look says "He has not got a choice, I am worried about when he leaves here he has told me he won't go and live with his children or any family, he is going to live by himself in a place where no one knows him and make a new start . I wonder what is going through his mind?" Niel "I am damned if I know I couldn't do that, I would rather be dead, stuff that." Jeff "So it's a case he has got to do it."

Danny and Anne sitting on a bench just before going out onto the main road going up to college green to catch the bus and Anne was going through the route "So you know how to get up to the college green and to the bus stop, so then just get on the bus and ask for Maylord Orchard and he will let you know when he gets outside and then stand there and I will speak to you again ok?" Danny looking puzzled says "Ok, I must do this Anne I really must, it's urgent now." "I still think it's too early to do the whole route, but we can give it a go, but don't expect too much to early." Danny starts off with his cane and was doing well until he got to the lights and he was supposed to feel the controls to get across and then face at about 11 o'clock and cross and he would come onto the path as he needed to but he turned but not enough and ended up behind the barriers and could not find the path and was stuck on the road . Anne grabbed him and got him onto the pavement and said "You didn't turn enough and so got stuck behind the barrier, never mind it will come with practise, don't worry, so you need now to turn right and find the path going up to the shops at college green." "Sorry I am an idiot, I will get on with it. I find it hard to concentrate that hard." Danny remembered what Niel said and concentrated very hard and he got up to the shops in college green without a problem, he missed finding the bus stop but not by much and he sat down and waited for the bus and Anne came up to speak to him and said "That was very good, I am Impressed, so now you have to get the door of the bus and get on and get your ticket and sit down, so how are you going to do this?" Danny answers "Well I will follow the bus side to the door use my cane to find the steps onto the bus and if I get a problem ask one of the passengers then ask for my ticket and ask him to tell me when I get to Maylord orchard and find a seat somehow." "Right and don't be worried to ask anyone." "Ok I just don't grab anything I am not supposed to ha, ha, ha." "Don't worry you are blind and they will understand." Next thing the bus turned up and Danny got up nervously and set off, this was the first time he is going to do this on his own and it showed, he felt his way along the bus and people let him go first and he found the steps and got into the bus and said to the driver "Hello can I have a single to Maylord Orchard please? and can you tell me when you get there please?" The driver replies "Certainly sir no problem." Danny smiles and says "Thank you very much." Danny then turned and walked up the bus and went to sit and sat on an old man's lap, he got up Immediately and said "Oh I am very sorry I am looking for a seat, is there one empty?" The old man ignored him and Danny said "Sorry I didn't know you were deaf." The man looked at Danny in a nasty way and a lady says to Danny "Here follow my voice here is a seat in front of me." And the woman grabbed his arm and guided him to the seat Danny says to her "Thank you very much, thank you." Danny sat visibly sweating with nerves and was wondering where Anne was and hoped she was on the bus, so he concentrated for his life but remembered it was at least seventeen minutes away so pressed his watch, it said ten fifteen so he counted it down with his watch and got his cane ready, then the driver said " Maylord Orchard and Danny got up quickly and stood even though the bus was still going and when it stopped he nearly fell to the ground as he was not expecting it and he got off and stood right in the way of everyone getting off and Anne grabbed him and pulled him out of the way and said "Right Danny sit here you are sweating very heavy indeed, are you allright?" They sat down and Danny answered "I am fine now." "Well that was good but take your time and ask someone if there is a seat and if they ignore you ask louder until someone helps and next time you get off the bus walk forward to let everyone get off ok?" Danny puffing said "Right I will remember that." " Danny looked totally rejected and was wondering if he really could do this as there was so much that could go wrong and so much to remember, then Anne says "Are you allright?" "Yes I am not too bad, it's just hard to do, it really is and I am wondering if I will be able to do this." "I would like a £1 for every time I have heard this from students. I would be a millionaire and they all now do it without thinking and you are no different. So don't beat yourself up, I have taught people in their sixties and they have got it eventually and you will not be any different, so trust me but it will take a lot longer than 3 or 4 lessons so now we are outside Maylord Orchard and if you sit and listen to noises on your right you will hear electric doors open and shut, can you hear them?" "Yes I can." "Well they are the doors into the Maylord Orchard shopping centre and I want you to head for them and go in and turn to your left and find the front of the shop and stand there for the next instruction." Danny done this then stopped and stood there like a rabbit with his eyes caught in a cars headlights and Anne said "Very good Daniel, now this is a set of shops that go around in a circle, so keep the shops on your left hand side and use your cane to follow around touching the shop fronts at all time and remember if there's nothing it is shop doors so keep going and count the doors there are six and then you come directly to a pair of doors that are manual and have 2 big handles on them, got that now?" Danny smiled and says "Yes I think so." "Right off you go then and wait outside the doors after walking away a few steps from them after you are through." Danny set off looking a bag of nerves and he done well and got to the doors he had to go through but someone was holding the door again it was exactly the same as happened before and Anne could see what was coming and it happened again, Danny put his hand out and grabbed the woman's breast and he said "Hello." The woman said "Oh I am holding the door and your not, it's my boob ha, ha, ha." Danny drew his hand away and said "Sorry." The woman says "That's ok no harm done, the door is open for you." "Thanks." Danny went through and walked a few steps and stood to one side and Anne came up to him and said "Right Danny very good, do you know where you are now?" "Ha, ha, yes I do I have done a little bit of walking from here before, I go straight forward to the shops opposite the square." Anne "But what must you do first?" Danny thought and didn't know so he said "I don't know, mirror, signal, manoeuvre, I don't know." Anne was giving him a chance to answer again and said "What about position of your body first before you set off? this is why you made a mistake at the lights at the college, because you had not positioned your body in the right direction, so tell me." "With my back to the doors and straight forward and if I hit a bench I must go right a little and continue straight , yes?" "Correct go ahead." Danny did this and found the bench and managed to keep his position right and found the shops some 100yds away, he was so pleased and looked so excited and Anne was too. Anne said "Brilliant Danny it's starting to stick, now we can go back and do it all again from where you get off the bus and do it how you would like it."

Off they went back to the entrance of Maylord and he stood as if he had just got off the bus and he stood there and thought "Forward and listen for the electric door and turn left after going through them find the shoreline and follow it in a circle and after six opening doors you will find the manual large handle doors go through and go straight and make sure your back is to the doors you have just come through and go straight forward and if a bench is in your way go to the left and after go straight to the shops the other side and stop." He got to the shops as if he had been doing this all his life and he looked so pleased with himself and Anne said "Brilliant Danny, very well done ,let's do it again, grab my arm I will take you back again until you do it without thinking." "So it can be done? I am so pleased, I could walk the marathon, so it can be done? I know now it can be done, I am going to be reasonably free again." It was like a ray of sunshine had landed on him and he looked a different man and was so excited. Then he got a little ahead of himself, he said to Anne "Right what's next Anne?" "I think that is enough for today, if you do too much it will be forgotten, well most of it, so we will now walk the route to the bus station with you holding my arm and get back to college green and you can take it from there back to college, do you need the bank or anything?" "Yes please I need the Halifax please and can you describe the way as we do it please?" "Yes no problem and we will stop for a cup of tea half way back to the bus station." "Ok that's fine and can we try and get in some more lessons to get me used to this as soon as possible?" "Yes I can only put another one a week though as I am so busy as I told you, you really are serious about learning everything quickly aren't you?" "Yes I have no choice now my wife is leaving me and I am alone now, so it's very Important." "I understand and will do my best, let's go." They do the walk to the bus station and at the bus station Anne leaves Danny to sort out the bus back to the college on his own again and so the bus came in and Danny got on and said "Ticket to college Green please and can you tell me when we get there please?" Driver "Yes of course." Danny starts to walk up the isle and says in a loud and precise voice "Is there a seat empty for me? can anyone tell me?" A lady said "To your left now." "Thank you very much." Lady says "Your welcome." He sits down and concentrates on the journey like clues, like sleeping policeman on the road, turns , traffic lights and any clue he can keep in his brain, he gets to the college green shops and the driver shouts "College green." Danny gets off and thanks the driver and sets off to find his way to the college and he walks forward and could hear the till making a noise in the mini supermarket and followed the sound and got to the front of the shop and put his cane against the shop frontage and followed it to the end and turned right and just took his time and followed the route he had been trying to learn for a few weeks and got it perfect but very slow, he however was sweating like a river and he said to Anne almost with a tear in his eye "Hows that? I did it very slow but I did it, phew, not easy mind." Anne says "Danny that was very good and I can see you are determined, that will make you pick it up very fast so I will see you tomorrow at the same time, so find your way to the refectory and have some lunch. See you tomorrow?" "Thanks very much Anne, see you, I am going to sit here for a minute to cool off, bye." Anne left and Danny sat there and contemplated how he done and he was beaming all over and looked so happy. Next thing someone sat by him and says "What's a little stinker like you doing here on the bench then?" Danny smiles and says "Hello Jeff, I know it's you, I have just finished my lesson to town and it went brilliantly mate. I am so pleased with It , I done really well." "I know I followed you from the college green and nearly fell asleep, you were so slow but that's the way to learn, well done matey I knew you would pick it up and I am glad I never had a bet with Niel that you would do it, coming to dinner?" "Yes ok, is Winnie back yet?" "No matey she has not turned up yet, I wonder what she is up to but as long as she is allright aye?" "I hope she is, right let's go." Sometime later and Danny went back to the lounge of Dowdell with Jeff for a cup of tea and they sat down and saw Zarrine and Danny said "Hello sexy, is Winnie back yet?" Zarrine looking serious "No she is not and everyone is panicking and phoning everywhere, can you tell me about anyone else she bothers with?" Danny thinks and replies "No I can't, she is a loner and far from home, she probably has had a tantrum and gone off to teach everyone a lesson, but I would have thought she would have turned up by now, I am getting worried now." Jeff "It's strange isn't it? has the police been contacted Zarrine?" Zarrine "They are going to contact them after dinner if she has not turned up, then she will be in trouble when she turns up, it's a puzzle" Danny "She will be back soon enough and I will give her a ballocking when I see her, I have just had a lesson on mobility and I was brilliant so I will take you out for a meal soon Zarrine." Zarrine smiles and says "I will look forward to that Danny, my choice of restaurant Danny?" Danny "Well of course Zarrine and I will guide you ok?" Zarrine "Yes of course as long as you pay the bill I don't care." Jeff "So your not taking me then? I took you home with me like a stray and no meal for me ha, ha, I am feeling hurt now." Danny "Ok don't cry, you can come to, bloody hell he is becoming Impossible Zarrine so jealous ha, ha, ha." Zarrine "Can I bring Peter?" Danny "As long as you don't say this is a foursome ha, ha, he is not my type." Jeff "Why not sweetie?" Danny looked at Jeff and said "I hope your joking, you know what I think." Jeff "Of course I am you idiot." Zarrine "You 2 worry me sometimes, I am off to see them in the office before I go home and worry about that silly girl. See you both tomorrow." The lads say goodbye and Jeff says "I wonder where she is?" "I don't know but she is silly and I am worried now, I haven't got her mobile number." "She will turn up smiling I expect." "Well I will be telling her off when I see her, anything could happen to her, she could have at least phoned the college, wait till I see her." Well she didn't return that day and all were worried and nothing the next day was seen of her until that evening and Danny walked into the lounge at around 6 pm and she was sitting on the settee and Danny walked in and said "Hello, who's in the room?" Winnie replied in a quiet voice "Winnie." Danny lost it and shouted at her and said "Where the hell have you been? your an idiot, everyone has been worried about you and wondering if you were dead or something. You should have phoned the college and stop thinking about yourself for a change." It went silent and Danny could hear her sobbing silently and said "Oh dear I am sorry Winnie, I didn't mean to upset you honestly I didn't, why are you crying?" She didn't answer and continued crying and Danny sat next to her and put his arm around her shoulders and comforted her and then she started crying even more, after a while she calmed down a little and Danny said "Ok now, I never meant to upset you, so stop crying Winnie it makes me feel awful, have you told anyone your back?" "Yes." "And what did they say?" "They told me I have to go back to China as soon as possible, now I am not happy as they put me up with those people in London and they were not very nice to me and told the college I was the one that was nasty, they expected me to stay in my room all the time and only go out when they take me to see the sites, it was not my fault so I left and stayed in a hotel and went looking around myself but the college believed them and not me. I had no lectures yesterday and this morning so I get back in time for my lectures, I am a grown woman and I am being treated like a little girl" She continued sobbing and Danny sympathetically said "Ok come on and stop this crying I am sure we can sort this out for you" She stopped crying and said "Do you think so? I want to stay until at least December and finish my course." "I am sure we can sort this out, just promise them you will not do this again and they will probably let it go this time, I'm sure I can get someone here to speak up for you, so wipe your eyes and tell me what you done over the holidays" Winnie got up and went and wiped her eyes with some cold water and sat down by Danny and says "Well I seen the tower of London, the palace and the houses of parliament and loads of things but I was bored after that and fed up with staying in my room so I had an argument with them and packed my things and left and had a great time on my own looking around, nothing wrong with that and they said I had to be back by Sunday but I had no lectures until today so what's the point, I got back in time, they were nasty to me in the office and told me off. Now they want me to go home and I don't want to so will you tell them for me?" "No I won't tell them I will back you up but you must tell them yourself and show them you are not afraid of them and explain it to them like you did me and they will understand I am sure, if I go there with all guns blazing they will not listen to me." "They will, they will, you know what to say." "If you tell them it looks better and besides they will have to pay extra to send you home now because they will have to change your ticket that you already have, I think they are bluffing so don't worry, it will be allright." "Ok I will go and see them, will you come over with me?" "Yes I will and be nice and calm to them, let them think you are sorry." "If it means I can stay I will." "Right so what did you buy me as a present from London then?" Winnie looked surprised and smiled and said "Nothing, what did you buy me?" "I forgot to bring it back with me ,never mind forget it." She hit Danny on the arm and laughed and Danny said "That's better I don't like to see a lovely girl crying." Next they embraced and WINNIE and Danny were off to her bedroom for the night.

It was the next morning and Jeff, Zarrine and Niel were in the lounge and Danny walked in and Jeff said "Well it's the dodgy Welshman, where were you last night? I knocked your door and no answer and you were not up the bar and why are you coming from that door? You haven't moved have you?" Niel chirped up "No he doesn't but Winnie does ha, ha, ha." There was silence for a minute and then Jeff said "You didn't did you? .... You lucky git, well I never, so did you?" Zarrine interrupted "Jeffrey spare us please and mind your own business." Jeff "I just want to know if." Zarrine stamps her foot and says "Jeffrey, shut up, so Danny is WINNIE allright?" Danny says "Very upset because the college gave her a real hard time over it and told her she must return to china as soon as possible and she was crying when I got here last night but she has calmed down now, I am going with her to see the principle to get her to explain what happened. Apparently she was confined to her room in London when they were not taking her out to see the sights and she got bored and fed up and so she left after a row and went to stay in a hotel and enjoyed herself and she didn't come back until yesterday because she had no lectures until then." Zarrine "Fair enough, but she should have called the college to tell them. Danny "I know I told her that and she was sorry she didn't now, I don't know I think she will be allright." Niel "They won't send her home I bet, this is the only time they have had any trouble with her and it's not really trouble is it?" Jeff "That's it she is not any trouble as a rule is she?" Danny "What do you think Zarrine?" Zarrine rubs her chin and says "Well I don't know, but I will have a word this morning as we have a meeting first thing so go over with her after dinner, I think she will be ok." Danny "Right, that's reassuring, I can't see them sending her home it wouldn't be a good idea and I know she is sorry." Jeff "You old dog taking advantage of the poor girl when she is vulnerable." Niel "Danny is that true? I didn't think you were like that Dan." Danny "Oh shut up you 2 ha, ha, I did comfort her and she is much happier for it and it's none of your business and don't tease her or she will probably belt you around the ear, so you have been warned but Zarrine there is no need to do my room today thank you ha, ha, ha." Jeff "Jammy git I am off to a brothel this weekend ha, ha, ha." Zarrine laughed and said "No don't do that Jeffrey you might come back with more than you went with." Niel "Yes Jeff, they can all see mind, so forget it." Jeff looked at Niel and said "What do you mean ? I don't like your attitude mate, remember what I lost in height I gained in length." Zarrine stamped her foot again and said to Jeff "Jeffrey I am not telling you again, behave." Danny laughing "Can you call me on my mobile when you know something Zarrine please?" Zarrine "Yes of course I will and I will put a word in for her if you like?" Danny "That would be great, thanks, right I am off to see her and tell her and then off for my first lecture." Jeff "I bet, Niel do you believe him?" Niel laughs and says "No I bloody don't but it's none of our business Jeff, I am off to I am late, see you all." They all disappear to their different things. Danny was in Winnie's room and he was telling her what Zarrine said "So she is going to put a good word in for you ok?" "Yes but I don't think it will make any difference Danny, I think I am going home by the looks of things." "Oh say you don't know WINNIE, it will be allright you'll see." Winnie just lay on her bed totally dejected and Danny said "Look I have to go to my lecture, don't you have to be somewhere?" "What's the point? it's all over here for me now." " Danny says to her "If I was you I would turn up and show willing to carry on and see what happens please, then it may look a lot better, don't be a defeatist, show them your not to be messed about with. C'mon I will walk over with you." Winnie got up and got dressed and washed and they went off to their different classes.

Zarrine spoke to Danny later and told him that Winnie was going to be given the benefit of the doubt and will get a warning and allowed to stay in the college. Danny was meeting Winnie that afternoon and going to town for a meal so he would tell her then.

It was in a Chinese restaurant they went and Danny said that he had good news "Well Winnie I heard from Zarrine today that you are not going home and that you will just get a warning from your tutor so that is good news hey?" Winnies eyes lit up and she says "Really are you telling me the truth Danny?" "I just told you the truth and that's it honestly now, so you can relax." Winnie smiled and cheered up Immediately and said "And you are buying me a meal, it's my lucky day." Danny looking amazed "I am? well it's not mine is it, never mind this is a real Chinese restaurant and I am sure you will like real Chinese food." "Well I will get the waiter to read me the menu and I will tell you what they are and we can order, it's about time I ate real food as I don't like the English food, much too much salt and loads of sugar, much too much it's awful how the British can eat that rubbish, I don't know argh, it's awful." They order the meals and Danny was enjoying himself and could not wait for the meal and hoped it would cheer WINNIE up if it reminded her of home, they had spring rolls for starters and they sat there and started to eat them and Danny said "Mmmm very nice." "Yes they are nice and fresh, I am enjoying this so far." Danny relieved says "Yes I have ate here before and it is nice, right now the main meal." They started to eat it and after a few minutes Winnie stopped eating and Danny said "What do you think nice aye?" "Not really, this is not traditional Chinese food, it's horrible compared to Chinese food, it has been made to the taste of the British pallet, I can't eat it." "But I was assured it was a traditional Chinese food restaurant, it says so on the brochure and menu." "Well it's not real Chinese food, it's horrible and wait until I see the waiter I will ask him." They waited for him to come up to the table and Winnie started on him in Chinese tongue. It sounded as if they were going at it hammer and tongs and next the manager came up to speak to Winnie, the manager also spoke in mandarin or some tongue and Danny shouted "Right can you both speak in English pleas as I can't understand a bloody thing you are saying?" Manager says "I am sorry you are unhappy with the meal, although sir have eaten it all but this is a traditional Chinese restaurant but with many European flavours as we can't sell the traditional as most people here don't like our cuisine. I understand why this lady who is from China would not like it as much but it is not the restaurants fault." Winnie "But you can call it a Chinese restaurant if it is not, it is British with a hint of Chinese cuisine, am I right.? Manager looking beaten says "As I said I am sorry it is not to your liking madam, I shall not then charge you for your meal however sir I will be charging you for yours as you have devoured it ok?" Danny spoke quickly "That's fine I am happy with that and we don't want any sweet thank you." Winnie said to Danny after the manager left "Why did you cut me off? I was ready to tell him." "Because he was right I think it is served for the British pallet, let's pay the bill and go." This they did and Danny took Winnie for a drink in his favourite pub. They walked in and WINNIE said "Is that a woman I can hear behind the bar?" "I expect so why?" Winnie looking serious says "You must not get served by her, you must not talk to women, I will get it." "You what? are you joking or what? I will talk to who I want, this is stupid." "I won't like you talking to any other women, I will not put up with it, you are my man and must not do these things." Danny looking shocked says "Winnie I will not listen to this thing, it is ridiculous, this is the most stupidest thing I have ever heard in my life, don't be silly I am British and we don't live like this ok? so leave it there now." Danny went up to the bar with WINNIE close to him. He said to the barmaid "Pint of the real guest beer please and what about you Winnie?" "I will have a coke please and hurry up this woman is not nice." Barmaid raised her voice to Winnie and says "I beg your pardon? are you speaking about me?" Winnie replies "I am and you must not speak long to him he is with me." Danny looking awkward said "Sorry she is a very jealous person from China and have a different culture to us Normal people." Winnie interrupts and says "Danny be careful, don't say these things please, I am just warning her to stay away." Danny "You don't have to do that, she is not doing anything just her job." Barmaid warns Winnie "You got a problem lovely girl? and I am not interested in him, I am a happily married woman and so you had better watch your mouth just because your blind does not cut it with me." Winnie was just going to say something and Danny said "Winnie just leave it there, you are embarrassing me and yourself, so shut up and let's sit down now, I mean it." They sat down and Winnie said "You are horrible, you did not speak up for me at all, I am Important to you not her." "Winnie I am not a type of chap who jumps into bed with any girl who just speaks to me, so don't be silly now." "You should not look at any other woman when you are with someone else, so don't do it please." "Which part of I will do exactly what I like don't you understand? I am a free man now and forever even if I married you I will still be a free man, so get that into your little head and remember it because if you want to live that way then I am not staying with you, I would rather be on my own and I mean that." "Danny you must not say this, I will never do this to you, I will not even speak to a single man and would never betray you ever, so why can't you commit to me the same way?" "Danny says I can't do that and that's that, so take it or leave it." "I will never except it but will obey your commands." "I am not demanding anything, just saying how it is, I am not in charge of your life, you are a free human being and your own person and can do exactly what you want, you don't have to answer to me ok?" Winnie sat there silent and it was a funny time and Danny then said "You have got to go and see your tutor later haven't you?" "Yes at 5 o'clock." When they finished their drinks they went back to the college and after Winnie seen the tutor she was much happier but she was not going to forget the pub situation and Danny was aware she would not leave it there and get on with the relationship.

It was later in the bar, they were sitting on a table by themselves when in came Niel and Jeff and they sat with Danny and were having a conversation and in walks Kezz and she approached the table and said Hello is that Jeffrey and Niel and who else?" Jeff "Danny and Winnie. "Kezz "Oh banging my favourite Welshman and of course you Niel ha, ha, can I sit with you lot?" Winnie chirps up "No why don't you sit with kids your own age for a change?" Danny and the lads looked astounded and Danny replied "Of course you can squiggly Kezz, ignore her she is just a bad mooded woman." Kezz "Eek, eek, are you sure? I don't want to spoil your night." Jeff "Come and sit between me and that dodgy Welshman squiggly." Kezz "Ha, ha, everyone is calling me squiggly now since Jeff named me it, eek, eek, can you do an eek Jeffrey for me please, go on just for me?" Jeff smiling "Eeeeeeeeeeeek, hows that a big one." Winnie "Oh god it's like a children's game on TV" Jeff says "Oops time for a ciggy." Kezz "What's a Matter with you Winnie? you don't sound happy today." Winnie replies "I don't like you sitting by Danny, so can you move please?" Danny snapped "No Kezz, you sit there, you are my friend so don't listen to her ok? I will decide who sit's by me and if she don't like it she can move." At that Winnie got up and turned on her heels and left the bar and Niel said "Woops, you have done it now Dan." Danny "Oh I don't care, she can't speak to people like that, it's rude, she has become too much, she was like that in the pub this afternoon, she won't except the fact I am a free man she wants me to do exactly what she wants and not talk to anyone so stuff her, I don't see this working." Kezz "She is rude, she must not be like that, I am not doing anything wrong am I?" Danny "No Kezz, she is jealous of you talking to me and sitting near me, she thinks we are having sex behind her back." Kezz "Does she? ha, ha, I will tickle you if you tried, tickle, tickle, tickle, she is not all there, there's no light on the landing and no carpet on the stairs with her." Jeff "I didn't think she was that bad matey, I thought you were bragging when you said she will not let you talk to another woman, but I see what you mean now, so what are you going to do now with her?" Danny "I am going to knock it on the head, I cannot put up with this for the rest of my life, it's over time for a couple of pints, I am in the chair." Danny goes up to the bar and gets everyone a drink. Jeff says "well another woman out of his life, he will be a miserable git again for a while." Niel " I don't think he will, he will be relieved more than anything, so we can have a laugh again "Kezz " I think he is better off without her she is not for him and she just wants to stay in Britain I think." Jeff "Kezz, don't say things like that it might be true, eek, eek ha, ha." Kezz "Jeffrey I will tickle you in a minute eek." Danny returns and the barman puts the drinks on the table for everyone and says "So Kezz are you still with Jim now? or has Carol put the knife in for him?." Kezz in nervous manner says "No I am not seeing him, I have been told he is not a good man for me and is too old." Niel "And I bet that was Carol and her gang saying that, so why? they don't know him from Adam, nosy git's." Kezz "Yes they did, they said he is a dirty old man so I am not going to see him again." Danny smiles and says "Right Kezz, will you answer me something and tell the truth, has Jim ever done anything rude to you? c'mon tell the truth." Kezz ponders and says "Well no not really but that don't mean he won't try will it?" Danny "I rest my case, you have taken the word of Carol and believed her, I don't think Jim is like that, it's just rumours that Carol and her pals have sent around the college because they don't like him isn't it? and you have believed her even that English idiot Jeff believes it he is just as bad as Carol." Jeff looking surprised said "Hey don't bring me into this it's nothing to do with me." Danny "Well you have said the same thing as her and Kezz has just told the truth and so Carol is lying isn't she?" Jeff "Not necessarily." Danny "Go on then Jeff tell me when this is supposed to have happened? he is rude to other students." Jeff stayed quiet and Danny continued "See I am right and she is a liar and you are a lemming if she goes off the cliff you will follow and if there is anyone rude it's you with Carol but no one said that about you do they?" Jeff "That's different." Niel speaks up and says "Hows that different then? It's just rumours going around just because of the age difference they assume he is a paedophile and for all you know they both might have been in love because it's not easy for someone with problems to find Mr right is it?" Danny "He is devoted to Kezz and he would look after her with the last breath in his body, so where will she find someone like him again?" Jeff "Allright perhaps your right I don't know anymore, I am not saying anymore so forget it, let it drop now." Kezz says "I am not getting involved with anyone now anyway, as it is too much trouble for me and I can't be asked, squiggle, squiggle." Danny says "Well Niel I am not having much luck with women am I, I will ask Kezz out I think." Kezz looking amazed said "I don't think I will, I have got enough trouble already, no thanks, I don't need the hassle ha, ha, ha, sorry Danny." Danny "Ha, ha, ha, I am only kidding Kezz, I knew you would not know what to say so don't worry, I am stuck with Jeff by the looks of it ha, ha, ha."

Later in the lounge in Dowdell Winnie was waiting and looking very upset and next thing in walks the lads. Jeff, Danny and Niel and she set about Danny Immediately "I think you should say sorry to me for not agreeing with me and letting Kezz sit by you earlier, I am not a happy woman Danny." Danny snaps "Wait a minute, I." Jeff butted in "Right I am off for a ciggy." Niel says "Well I am staying here, I am not missing this for the world." Danny continues "Thanks mate, listen now Winnie I am not putting up with you telling me who I can speak to and who I can't, so forget it I am not living like that so do as you please and I am not arguing every time about this, so I think we should not go out with each other anymore, so I am sorry I am finishing it as from now." You could hear a pin drop and then Winnie continued "Don't be silly, that is stupid, just over Kezz, I don't think so Danny ,you are being silly now." Danny "Oh here we go again, I knew you would not except it, I mean it Winnie I am not going out with you anymore, so that's it I am free and so are you, do you understand?" Winnie mumbled "Oh don't be silly, I am not excepting we are finished, so forget it." Danny "Please yourself I am not with you anymore and that's it, fancy a whiskey Niel?" Niel "Yes please Dan." Danny "Well go and fetch it out of your room then ha, ha, ha." Niel smiled "I might have bloody known you meant my whiskey, as you are out of whiskey and I am the only sucker here as far as you are concerned, I will be after your lager this week." Danny smiling says "Help yourself mate anytime you know that." Niel "I know mate I am only kidding Dan, I will be back now." He left to get it and Winnie came over to Danny and tried to put her arms around him and Danny pulled away and said "No Winnie it's over I mean it, so don't touch me, thank you." "Stupid man and I thought you were different to the others here." She stormed off to her room and Niel came back and just after him Jeff came in and said "Bloody hell she is in a mood, I guess you told her then?" Danny "I sure did mate, I am not being made a fool of by her again and I would rather be on my own if that is what it takes, so be it." Niel "There must be someone you fancy here besides her surely?" Danny "Well there's Ginny but she is already married and to a nice fella too but I really liked Winnie and stop calling me Shirley." Jeff "A student we mean." Danny "I can't think of anyone." Jeff " there's Sandy?" Danny "I am not that hard up thank you , it looks as if I am on my own for a long time now, might be forever by the looks of it." Jeff "Get the violins out Niel he's off again, how do you think I feel then? I haven't had a bit since they made the fawlty tower sit coms ha, ha, someone will turn up mate they always do, there is a lot more new students to come here after she has gone, so don't worry." Niel

"And maybe Winnie will change." Danny "I don't think so, she has done this twice now at different times, so I think I will knock it on the head, so anyone for the quiz on Thursday then?" Niel "Not for me, last time I went there I got pissed, the beer is too strong there, I expect Jeff will and John Haines will go with his friend mark, Mark is a nice chap, he really is." Jeff "Yes he is, I like him he is a breath of fresh air, I will be there Dan and I think Matt and Sandy are coming to." Danny looks heaven wood and says "So great that's all I need Zig and Zag to make my week, I don't mind Matt so much he is pretty good at quizzes and she is always right if she says anything as far as he is concerned, oh well nothing we can do about it is there? I am off to bed see you in the morning lads, thanks for the whiskey Niel." They all go off to bed.

It was the next morning and Danny was out in town with Anne and she was carrying on with his lesson through to town and he was getting very confused with it all and this was the third time he was going over it Danny said "I am sorry Anne, it is very hard and a long way to the bus station from here and a lot to remember, especially the banks as well, but I will get there." Anne replies "Danny we have got all the time in the world to learn this, take your time, right let's do it again and try and remember I will follow behind, keep touching the shore line Danny, now work your way across to the other side of the street and find the next left and I am going to shut up and let you find the bank." Danny is concentrating so much he is visibly sweating and not looking to sure but he finds the entrance to the bank and was so excited and said "Right I am going to find the bench outside and sit down on it for a minute or two ok?" Anne said "Yes ok, I need a sit for five to." Danny was walking around in circles and could not find the bench to sit down and he was getting angry with himself and Anne took over and said "Danny grab my arm and I will show you where it is and explain what you did wrong again." They sat down and Anne said "Your doing it again, when you get to the bank what must you do to find the bench? tell me as I have said it every time we get to the bank." "Put my back to the bank door and it is at ten to as it is on a clock face, sorry, I forgot again, I am always doing that, I will get it into my head in the end, sorry." "Well it is a lot to take in but that's why I want to do it in smaller stages, but you want to run before you can walk." "Sorry but I have been walking all my life and need desperately to know if I can do it or not and get to be a independent man again, because I am blind and look after myself and I have got a lot to do before I leave this college, including shopping, going to a pub, anywhere I want to eat, anywhere I want and not have people saying I can't do that or that, like my ex-wife said I can't have Josh with me as I will not be able to look after him, that hit home and now I am determined to prove her wrong in every respect." "Yes I can understand that, something like that would make me more determined also, so let's get on with it. Now can you remember what to do next? I will give you a chance to do it yourself if you like?" "Yes I like to, I will get us home so don't worry ha, ha, I will look after you Anne don't panic at all just let me have a go." Anne looking unsure says "Ok I will but take your time it is not too busy here today and remember the road you have to cross. Let's go over it from here, you get up and turn right at about ten past on the clock, find the shoreline and follow the shop fronts all the way to where you turn off to the right and remember that there is a huge gap from the shops to the other side off the road we just come down from Maylord Orchard and just try and keep going straight until you get into contact with the shops the other side and remember to listen to some of the clues we discussed ok? let's go." Danny got his cane out and off he went and found the bank again and followed it to the huge gap and went as straight as he could and found the shops the other side, he glowed with happiness at doing this and carried on very nervously and got to the road that he had to cross, that was only a single lane and you are only allowed to drive down it at 10 mph as it is a shared surface and it all went wrong and Danny just walked straight into the path of the cars if there had been any coming, but lucky there was not. He realised his cane had lost the shoreline he was following and he was in the middle of nowhere and then he could hear a car coming and turned around and try and retrace his footsteps and all the time Anne was right by him as his carer if he needed it, he got back to the shops and stopped and Anne said "You were going to fast Danny and launched yourself onto the road, if this had been a larger road then you would have been run over, so take your time and you even went down the kerb although it's only a shallow one but you need to concentrate and take your time, but well done you got yourself out of trouble by retracing your steps and now what are you going to do?" Danny looking in a mess and shattered with his nerves says with sad look "I am going to cross the road and then take your elbow until the next lesson and go home to the college, it's a lot to remember and your right, a bit at a time but at least I feel I am Improving all the time." Anne looking sympathetic says "Yes you are and will once you have learned most of this it will come naturally to you, you are a good learner and it won't be long before you will be doing this all by yourself, c'mon let's go." Off they went back to the college and Danny looked so unsure about things but time would tell.

Later Danny was laying on his bed listening to a bit of music and his door bell went, he pushed the button thinking it was Winnie again and lo and behold a lovely foreign voice speaking with a broken Spanish accent, it was Lidia. Danny said "Who is it? as if I didn't know." Lidia smiles and says "Hello Danny, it is Lidia can I come up to see you for a while please?" Danny said "Yes of course you can, I will push the button and you must push the door ok? come up." Danny went to let her in his outer door and she came in and they put their arms around each other and kissed and Danny said "I haven't seen you for a couple of weeks, so where have you been then?" "I have been sitting my English exams and other things before I go back to Peru and I came to tell you what I have done, I want to say thank you for helping me to learn English and now I have passed the English exams thanks to you and I had an A in that subject. Thank you very much I would not achieved this if it wasn't for you, but my teacher said this was unusual as I had took my subject as Paddington bear and that was normally for 11 year old kids but I had it perfect." "Wow, slow down Lidia you are very excited, you must take a breath, I am so pleased and so proud of you. You have done well but I have always said you are a very intelligent girl and you will go far, I know this for a fact." "Oh thank you Daniel, I am very happy and now the sad news, all the S.S.W's are finishing next month and we are all going back to our own countries and it is going to be a sad time and so we decided to go up to the student bar tonight to celebrate and i want you to celebrate with us please." Danny almost shedding a tear says "Well of course I will be very happy to join in, thank you and can I bring Jeff and Niel with me? they will make it a good night, what do you think?" "Oh yes please I know all the others will be happy if you did, I must go and get ready I will look forward to seeing you later my lovely Daniel, I am so happy I have done so well." "I am a very happy and proud man now I have been able to help in some way, I can't wait for tonight, I will see you up there and I am having the first dance with you." Lidia with huge smile on her face replies "Yes of course, see you up there, bye." Danny goes off to see Jeff and Niel.

In the lounge and there they were and so was Winnie and Danny said "Hello everyone and you Winnie." Winnie says "Silly velshman huh, have you come to apologise to me now?" Danny "No I haven't, I have nothing to apologise for." Winnie "Well don't speak to me then." Danny "Fine with me." Jeff says "Oh dear, I think it's time for a ciggy." Danny "No Jeff you don't have to do that I am not going to argue with anyone, so lads it's up the bar tonight for a celebration? the S.S.W's are leaving soon and they are getting together for a drink up the bar and they have all finished their exams and good old Lidia has passed her English thanks to me, even if it is only on Paddington bear that her tutor told her is normally for 11 year olds but she did the exam as you would anywhere so she has passed and now they are leaving and going back to their own lands soon." Niel "I am up for it, it will be a shame to see them go, they are a great bunch especially Joanna and Lidia and of course Jose, so funny and the rest of them really, Jacob and the others. So what time?" Danny says " I think it is fine if we go up at about 8 o'clock as they won't be up there early as they have not got much money and I am going to take the Mickey out of Joanna as she speaks so slow ha, ha, ha." Jeff "We should sort out a little party for them before they go home as a thank you." Danny "A good idea mate in here would be good." Winnie in a really bad mood says to Danny "So off with Lidia and Joanna is it?" Danny replies "Leave it there Winnie it's nothing like that but if it was it's nothing to do with you ok?" Winnie "Horrible velshman." She then turned on her heels and left. Niel "Sorted mate, I think we should buy them some drinks to say thank you." Danny "What if we club together and get a few slabs for them here in a week or two? and we can get some chips from the chip shop up the road if you like? what do you think Jeff? you are the tight ass here, is that ok with you?" Jeff in sarcastic voice says "Well, well as long as it isn't going to cost an arm and a leg you can count me in and what about music?" Niel "Well I got a player that I can bring in and Danny has got all the tunes anyone would need, sorted then." Jeff "There you go then just one of them women on each of our knees and that's sorted as you say let's party, I am off to get showered and put some nice brute on." Niel "I had a bath last week ha, ha, so I am ok." Danny "Well I have decided to change my pants as I threw them against the wall earlier and they stuck , ha, ha, ha, if they had not I could have worn them for at least another week ha, ha, ha." The lads laughed and went off and Danny had a cup of tea and in the meantime Winnie had came back in and was standing behind Danny with her mini skirt on that Danny liked and she spoke nicely to him and said "Oh Danny I don't like arguing all the time, so let's stop it and maybe we can have some fun hearer tonight instead of arguing?" Danny in stern voice "Sorry Winnie it will not work with us as you are different to me and your culture is like a religious fanatic. You won't change and neither will I, so let's just be friends and part as good friends when you leave here please." Winnie "No, I want us to be together and forever Danny, I can change a little as long as there are no other women to be talked to, it's not right." "No, see what I mean, I can't do that sorry and you should not ask me to do it either Winnie it's not right so let's just be friends from now on please." "But Danny." She cuddles up to Danny and Danny said "No Winnie I don't want to, so leave it now I am off." Winnie flew into a rage and shouted "You are a fool and stupid, I am a beautiful girl and could get any man if I wanted to but I don't talk to them, so why have you got to talk to other women? you should be proud having me on your arm, I am a beautiful girl I have been told and I am a model in China part time for my face, you are a fool." "Yes I have been told you are a very beautiful girl but looks are not everything Winnie, personality is needed to or it is not workable so let's agree to differ and go our own ways I am off." Danny turns on his heels and as he is leaving she shouts "Yes go on off with prostitutes, go on, see if I care , I won't be waiting for you tonight." "Good then you are getting the message then?" Danny walks out and Winnie was still shouting at him.

386

Later on in the bar the S.S.W's were sitting on a large table sipping coke and Danny said "Right time to get my friends a drink, my lovely S S W's." They all smiled and looked a lot happier and Danny got them a drink in each and then he sat by Lidia and said to Joanna who was from Poland and spoke very slowly "Hello Joanna and who says to me all the time she sees me hello Danny and it takes you about a minute to get that out?" Everyone of them started laughing and he next picked on Jose and did an Impression of him and at the same time waving his hands around as he does and they all killed themselves laughing. Next was Lidia, he took the Mickey out of her and her Spanish accent to a tee and then it was Jacob from Poland, he was laughing out loud as Danny did and they all settled down to a good night partying along with Jeff, Niel and Danny. Danny next said "Right drink up you lot, I am in the chair, what do you all want to drink then." Lidia had red wine and so they all followed her by having a red wine to start with and Jeff and Niel done the same for them for them to have a good night as they were not well off for money as they were voluntary students really. Well the night was a success and Danny then said "Right listen out you lot, Jeff, Niel and me have decided that we are going to throw you a party in Dowdell before you all go home to your different countries and we are paying for it all, so all decide this week which day and date and we shall get it sorted out and have some fun." Lidia "That's very kind Danny, Jeff and Niel and we don't deserve this." The rest of them thanked the lads and were excited about it all. Niel spoke up "Lidia you are wrong you all deserve it, you have all looked after us so very well without complaining once and we appreciate it all, thank you, all of you." The night ended up as a total success and the lads went home to bed and yes Winnie was waiting up for Danny and gave him a torrid time yet again and he snook off to bed when she was in the kitchen.

It was a few weeks after and the night of the party in Dowdell and Danny, Jeff and Niel kept it quiet from any of the other students in Dowdell and the S. S. W's turned up and the night was on Danny, Niel and Jeff. They got the beer and wine in and off the party went all laughing and dancing to the music and at one stage Jeff was dancing with Lidia to Saturday night fever and he punched a bulge in the ceiling while doing this, he was smiling from ear to ear and later they were all sitting there and looking very drunk indeed. Danny said in a slur "So how are you all? I am a little drunk and Jacob is pissed Jeff he looks like Clarence the cock eyed lion and Niel is pissed as he hasn't stopped laughing, Joanne is quiet so she is pissed and Lidia can't stop dancing so she is well on the way, I can tell and Jose is sleeping so he is pissed good that just leaves the happy Winnie when she comes in." Lidia says "What do you mean Danny? is she coming in here tonight?" Danny "Yes she always comes in here to wait for me to come in from the bar and then give me some gyp, that means to annoy me." Joanna "Oh dear, I hope there's not going to be trouble?" Jeff "No Danny will ignore her and I will go for a ciggy and Niel will sit there and listen to it all and that's exactly how it happens every time ha, ha, she wants a good." Danny interrupts "Jeffrey steady be careful what you say in front of our visitors please ha, ha, ha." Jeff sarcastically says "I was going to say a good spanking and I am the man to do it ha, ha, ha." Niel slurs "Well I am going to miss all of you when you leave for home, it will not be the same you know?" Jacob says "I am coming back to study music tech here in around four months so you will see me again. I have been offered a place here thanks to Danny putting a good word in for me to the music people." Danny "Well that's good Jacob I am so pleased for you no one told me and I think Jose is staying isn't he? Because his passport is Italian although he comes from brazil." Hose nods and says "I need you to help to fill in a work thing for the country chicken farm for me some time for me Danny please." Danny replies with a smile "No problem Jose I will do that any time and Joanna what are you doing?" In a very slow talking voice she answers "I am going to London with a job so I will still be in England and I will try and see you all sometime when I come to visit hose." Danny "There we are then and the lovely Lidia is going home to Peru aren't you? I am going to miss you very, very much, you have been a ray of sun to me." Lidia starts to cry and says "Yes I am going to miss everyone here tonight, you have become like a family to me I am sad at this time." Danny "Oh dear you are going to start me off if your not careful I will miss you all very much." Lidia "Well my nephew is coming over after the holidays and he is a nice lad, his name is Ricardo and he is funny and I have told him about you all especially Danny he is not good at English like I was when I came here and so I told him to come and see you and you will help him, he is only 21 and I am not worried about him coming here as you will all still be here." Danny "I will teach him in the ways of Paddington bear also and hope he draws the totty in for me, that's women I mean ha, ha, Jeff can teach him how not to behave and Niel can get him into the whisky and swear at computers." Niel "Your a right one to talk you swear at computers just as bad as me and drinking you are the master here so leave it there and Jeff well I hope he does not take after him and his silly chat up lines because Lidia he will come back as a smoking drunken lout that uses bad chat up lines." Jeff "You cheeky git, he will be a gentleman if I have to look after him, right Lidia I like this song let's dance I will make you look good ha, ha, ha." Lidia "I don't like what you say Jeff so dance with Jose." Jeff "I am joking with you c'mon let's dance." Off they went to dance and the others joined in and next thing in comes Lola and Carol they had heard the music from down stairs and come to join in. Lola smiling says "It's a party can we join in? we have got some booze." Danny smiling "Of course you can it's a going away party for the S. S. W's, they leave in a couple of weeks, so it's a goodbye night we will miss them." Carol says "Yes they have been a good bunch and very lovely people, I will miss them." Lola "Yes I will miss them making all the mistakes when they first come here and I wonder who is coming next?" Danny "Well Lidia's nephew is one of them so look out he can't speak good English and is 21 and single Lola so look out." Lola "If I can I will make a man of him no problem ha, ha, ha, I need a younger man." Danny "You women always say this but you can't beat experience like a man who has done it all, I would wear you out in one night and you would be begging for more." Lola smiling "Yeah, yeah, yeah, I don't think so, I have to go all night." Danny "That's right as they don't know how to please a woman, they get stuck in and get it over as quick as they can and that leaves a woman wanting, now me I will do the foreplay for a couple of hours until they are begging for it and then after the final assault they are knackered and pleasured." Carol huge smile on her face says "Daniel stop it, I am getting horny here and I am ready when you are let's go ha, ha, ha, I like a man that can go all night without much effort. I don't like that sweating and getting it over as soon as they can so as they can do it again later and it takes them all night, I agree." Lola "Calm down Carol, calm down at least put up a fight and besides tonight he is going to be pissed he is not far off now so another day what, tell me what he is really like I might give it a try." Carol "Yes no problem I will hold you to it Danny ha, ha, ha." Danny smiling replies "Ok Carol but what is it going to cost me, I mean you always want something back as your Scottish ha, ha, and Lola I think I would have to be locked in your room for you only, I have seen or rather felt your vibrator it is almost as big as me ha, ha, ha." Lola laughed out loud and said "Very good Danny I will keep it in mind, anyone for a glass of wine? I have brought up a few bottles." Danny "Look out Lidia loves wine so she will be singing by the end of the night and if you ply me with enough I will have heart burn all day tomorrow ha, ha, and Jacob is falling asleep trying to keep up with just cans of lager and Jeff is like a spider dancing, look at him." Just then in walks Winnie and she looks surprised and said in between the songs "Ah so what's going on here then?" Lola answers her "It's a party for the S. S. W's they are having a leaving party set up by the boys on this floor, isn't that nice ?" Winnie "What boys do you mean?" Carol "Jeff, Danny and Niel of course." Winnie's face turns to seriousness and she stamps on the floor and says "So is that Danny in here and Lidia and the other ones?" Niel "Yes we are, why? what is it to do with you? I can tell by your voice you are not happy, is that because of Danny or the S. S. W's Winnie?" Winnie snaps "Oh Niel is it I can't hears Danny has he lost his voice or afraid I will tell him off?" Danny chirps up "Oh god have we got to do this every time you are in here? I am having a good time and it's nothing to do with you and I am certainly not afraid of you, so get off my back." Winnie "You have got the cheek to say this and I am not happy with you not behaving yourself, I bet that Lidia is here also and I think you should go back with your ex-wife, you are not a very good man you lie to me all the time." Jeff "Time for a ciggy." Lidia snaps at Winnie "Winnie you must not say these things about Danny and me we are good friends and that's all, so don't say this again or I will report you to the principle, I mean it." Winnie "Go ahead I don't care, you have broken me and Danny up and now you are happy, so do what you like." Danny "Right Winnie there is no me and you, we are not an item and you know it and if I was with Lidia it's none of your business but Lidia is right we are good friends and she is leaving in a couple of weeks and this is goodbye so go away if you have come to cause trouble, I am not interested you know." Winnie "I am glad she is going home and I will be waving a flag when she goes, good riddance to bad rubbish, she is not worth it just like you Danny." Danny "Can I have that in writing? ha, ha, ha." Everyone laughs and Winnie storms out of the room and they laugh even more. Lola says "God she is a pain in the ass, she will not let you go Danny, it makes me wonder if you have got something she don't want to lose." Danny "I can't say anything I am sorry ha, ha , I can't wait for her to go back to China, she is getting me down and I need peace and quiet from her, sorry Lidia she is a pain, don't let it spoil the night for us get your glasses filled up and party." Lidia "Yeah, why not stuff her c'mon Danny your turn to dance, hey." Niel still laughing says "She is a nutter, she keeps on to Danny and he has told her many times she just ignores what he says, stupid girl." Jeff says to Carol "Well hello gorgeous hows you then?" Carol smiles and says "Look at the state on you, forget it Jeff your pissed and I am not going to be second best." Jeff "Aw my darling little scotch girl I am still in love with you and where is that idiot of a boyfriend of yours? Dumped him at last I hope." Carol "Wrong again, he has gone home to see his mother she has not been well so he has had parole but he is coming back tomorrow so I fancied a drink with my friend Lola so here we are and I am off to bed shortly and I mean by myself." Jeff looking sad says "Oh well, crashed and burned again, typical so Joanna fancy a dance?" Joanna "Sorry Jeff I can't dance." Jeff grabbed her hand and said "Well I will show you, I am like John Travolta you know." Niel "Well Dan it looks as if you are not going to get rid of her until she goes back to China mate she is determined to stay with you." Danny "I know, she is possessed by me, I am not bragging either Niel I just want to get her off my back and leave me alone, it's making a joke of things." Lidia "She has become a horrible person, she used to be nice when I first met her, never mind Danny it will all work out." Danny "Yes I am sure it will, only a month to go anyway then she is off home then and there is no way she can stay, I was talking to someone about her and they said she will never get an extension on her course as she is paid for by a charity fund and it cannot be extended so thank goodness for that." Niel "She might ask for political asylum or something of that ilk you never know, I will be surprised if she goes quietly Dan but we must just hope

389

ha, ha, ha." Danny "It will all be over soon enough you watch this space." Jeff comes back and says "I wouldn't put my house on it though." Danny "Right you pair stop trying to wind me up, let's enjoy the rest of the night." They partied on into the night and had a great time.

The next morning came around and no one was up on time and Zarrine had to get them up as they were still drunk from the night before except Winnie. The lads came in together holding their heads and Immediately Zarrine started on them "Right you three, are you responsible for this mess here?" Danny "Good morning Zarrine? I think it is not that bad just a few cans and bottles around the place and we shall sort this out Immediately, right Jeff grab a black bag and give it to Niel to hold open and we shall put the empties in and then he can take it out the skip while we go around wiping things off ok?" The lads agree and off they went but not in any speed they did it slowly as they had hangovers and Zarrine was laughing at them and in the end helped them out. They all sat after with a cup of tea and toast and told Zarrine all about the night and Danny was talking "I will miss them, they have been a lot of fun." Winnie butted in "You were having fun with all the women so they are prostitutes for Danny to play with." Danny flew into a temper and said to Winnie "Right now let's get this right Winnie it is none of your bloody business and they are not prostitutes just because you can't keep your man it's not their fault they are nice pleasant people and a lot nicer than you are and get this now I am nothing to do with you, I would rather go out with a prostitute than go out with you again, no problem, I am not your boyfriend so get that into your thick head ok?" There was a deadly silence for a minute and Winnie continued "You said you were my man and we are together and no other girl will have you it's me an you so stop it." Zarrine "Winnie you don't understand Danny wants to be on his own, so you must respect his wishes and leave him alone." Winnie snaps and says "Who is talking to you? you old bat, I am nothing to do with you so mind your own business ok?" Next it was Niel's turn to get involved "You just don't get it do you Winnie? you have no hold on Danny he is a free man and he can do what he wants and he doesn't want you so you have to by law leave him alone or he can get an injunction to keep you away and if this continues and he does you can get exported back to China, so be careful, it is called harassment, so be very careful." Jeff "Right time for a ciggy." Winnie snarled and mumbled something no one could understand and off she went in a temper. Zarrine says "What is it that girl don't understand? she Is a pain, I heard she tried to spoil the night last night didn't she?" Niel "She tried but failed and she only embarrassed herself in front of everyone so she made it worse for herself and I heard she wants to be known as Linda as from now on, she has put a notice on the student network asking that she is called Linda from now on." Danny "Has she? well I never did you hear that Jeff? Winnie wants to be called Linda from now on." Jeff "Really? I suppose she can do that but strange." Zarrine "I wonder why though it's a nice name but there we are, Niel have you brought that big plastic container back yet?" Niel "Oh sorry Zarrine I will go an fetch it in my room now in a minute, or I tell you what it is on the desk by the side of my bed go and get it if you are waiting for it ok?" Zarrine "Yes ok Niel is your door open?" "Yes it is, Abby is in there so give her a stroke." Zarrine "Ok I won't be long." She goes off to Niel's room and Danny smiling says "I think Winnie thinks she is a film star or something I bet, never mind it's her business I suppose so fancy a couple of pints tonight in the quiz lads?" Niel "Not for me I am getting ready for going home for the weekend." Danny "How about you Jeff?" Jeff says "Does a gorilla have pubic hairs? A silly question to ask me." Next thing in comes Zarrine shaking and sounding shocked says "Oh dear, oh dear, Niel Abby just went to bite me" Niel looking shocked says

"You what honestly did she? are you allright Zarrine?" Zarrine looking under the weather replies "Yes I just was shocked she didn't dig her teeth in just jumped at me when I went into the room and nipped me really, I jumped mind no blood or anything." Niel now fuming says "Right I will see to her now the bitch, I am not having this." Danny "Now calm down Niel she was probably guarding your room and possessions she is a German Shepard after all, I expect it was something like that." Niel "I'll give her now " Zarrine "Now Niel be sensible and don't go at her like a bull at a gate." Niel left the room and after a while he came back with the container and said "We will not have any more of that, she has been told I shouted at her that's all but it will have to be reported to the proper people here Zarrine so please do that and I will get someone from guide dogs to see her, that's not like her at all but she as was said earlier a German Shepard, sorry Zarrine." Zarrine "Don't worry about it Niel I think it would be a good idea to have guide dogs have a look at her mind, perhaps she is not so happy in the college Niel." Niel "I don't know but it is unusual for her, it has surprised me." Danny "Well don't let it worry you, I expect she has been sitting too near Winnie and got her bad moods off her ha, ha, just take it easy with her for a few days, I would be fed up under a desk all day to mind, not a good thing for such a big dog, she hasn't bitten Jeff has she and got rabies has she?" Jeff smiling says "I was waiting to get the blame for it, I was waiting, I wonder if she has been near Lola last night because whenever she is up here something happens that is nasty, not saying this is nasty but you know what I mean?" Niel "Maybe, you might have something there I will get her examined." Jeff "Who? Lola." Niel "No you dickhead, the dog you idiot, Lola has already got rabies ha, ha, ha." Danny "Right I am off to lectures see you all tonight for the quiz, I shall book a taxi Jeff." Jeff "Right dodgy one, see you later." Niel "Well Zarrine I will have the morning off and see the people for the dogs here and sort it out Immediately, so don't worry about It, I will probably take her home today instead of tomorrow, just to give her a break from here." Zarrine "Ok Niel I will see the ones about it later ok? see you later." Niel goes off to sort out poor old Abby and Jeff and Zarrine were left having a cup of tea and Jeff was holding his head. Zarrine said "You need to slow down Jeffrey or you will be ill, you and that Danny are always on the beer, so be careful. I hope Abby is going to be ok, I would not like to see anything happen to her she is a lovely dog isn't she?" "She is a lovely dog and very loving but I sometimes wonder if German shepherds are any good for guide dogs? I think she would rather be out catching burglars and the nasty people of this world and getting her teeth into someone that deserves it, not pansying about walking here and there and wasting her time under a desk all day, you can see she is excited when he takes her into town, a different dog altogether." "Well I think she is missing the children and his wife in Bridgend I do and they are always there for years every night and then all of a sudden she is not going home for a few weeks at a time and Niel says she adores Ceri his wife, he will be glad when his year is over and so will Abby." "Yeah, your right I bet that is what is wrong with her she is so excitable when Ceri comes up to see her and Niel. I think she is missing home, right I am off are you allright now?" "Yes I am allright, she did not touch me really I was just stunned that's all, see you later "

Later that night in the quiz and Jeff, Danny, John, Matt, Sandy and the quiet spoken mark were sitting around a table and waiting for the quiz to start. Jeff says "We are going to win this tonight now I am here with you." Matt laughs and says "I have seen more brains in a broad bean than you have got Jeff ha, ha, ha." Danny snaps "Matt don't insult a broad bean please." Matt "Oh yes sorry ha, ha, ha." John "We can win this easy I bet, we must give it a good go." Sandy "Why? you don't win anything anyway it all goes for charitable things and

391

more than not we all end up with the same scores, let's just enjoy it." Danny "Well yes that would be good so Matt are you going to do the writing?" Matt "I am the only one who can spell and the only one that can see enough so it might be a good idea." John snaps at Matt "Now wait a minute I can see allright and can spell so I can do it if you want Matt?" Matt smiles and realises that John is right and says "Oh yes I was only kidding ha ,ha, I don't mind doing it." Sandy "I heard that Niel's dog bit Zarrine today, she should be put down if she has gone that bad, she is a danger." Danny snaps "She didn't bite her at all she just warned Zarrine and she was shocked by it all so don't call her a nasty dog, I think she was just protecting his property that's all. I hate it when people who were not there assumes the worst." Matt "Well you said it she lunged at Zarrine, maybe the next time she will probably tear Zarrine's throat out." Jeff "Don't be silly she is not that bad, it was a one off and we were there, she made Zarrine jump more than anything and I knew you would stick up for the woman in your life and what about your dog then he is not the best guide dog is he?" Sandy in nasty voice "What do you mean? Duke is a marvellous dog he is well behaved." Jeff "You let him do what he likes , gets the left overs of your Chinese meals and then spews up all over the place, he is never on his lead in the common room and left to scrounge in the kitchen whenever he likes and when you can't be bothered to walk and get into your chariot I mean your wheelchair he is like a husky dog and Matt is pushing you and the poor dog is pulling you ha, ha, he is not a guide dog anymore he is fat and greasy from lack of exercise and grooming." Sandy "You cheeky bastard you, I never give him anything of the sort." Danny interrupts "I am sorry I must agree with Jeff he is always eating leftovers from your Chinese meals and many other meals so don't say any different I have witnessed that myself." Matt joins in "Now be fair Danny he is not that bad." Danny "See you don't like it when we say anything about your dog but it is allright for you to say it about a lovely animal like Abby." Sandy "Well it's true she did go for Zarrine and that's all I am saying, no need to be rude is there?" Jeff "Leave it there now let's concentrate on the quiz is it? because we can go on all night about this and it will get us nowhere." Matt "Right what shall we call ourselves?" John speaks up "The same we always call ourselves, the blinkies of course" Sandy chirps up " the quiz cats." Matt "There we are the quiz cats a nice name, we will call ourselves that." Danny "Excuse me Matt, this is a team and we always have called ourselves the blinkies so leave it at that as we have been here doing this before you joined us." Matt "Well I like the quiz cats so why not?" Jeff "Let's vote on it, right quiz cats " 2 of you Sandy and Matt, blinkies? 4 of us so the blinkies it is then." Matt and Sandy didn't like this but Matt crossed out quiz cats and put the usual blinkies down, then half way through the quiz a question arose. Quiz master asks "What is the longest river in Europe?" Danny "Oh dear I know this but am not sure, it is either the Danube the Rhine or another one I can't think of, let me think." Sandy "It's the Danube I am sure" Danny "I don't know but I don't think it is." Matt says "Yes it is, I am putting that down and it's the final answer." He wrote it down and John says "Don't write it down yet it might not be the answer, wait for us all to decide just because she said it does not mean it's true, I don't know but I don't think it is the Danube." Jeff "No good asking me I haven't got a clue Matt what do you think it is?" Matt with serious face says "I agree with Sandy I think it is right. Danny what is your final answer?" Danny concentrating hard says "Well I know it's not the Rhine but I doubt the Danube, I have a sneaky feeling it's the Volga or something like that but not the Danube try the Volga." Matt "Well 2 of us think it is the Danube and only you think it's the Volga so leave it at that." Danny "But how sure are you? I am almost sure I am right." Matt "Just as sure as that, Sandy what do you think?" Sandy "I am pretty sure to so leave it at that for goodness sake just because I said it leave it now, we have put it down." Danny "Well I will go by the rules of the team." Jeff "Bloody hell it is only a quiz." Danny "Ok then I will bow down to your answer and leave it at that, done now." Well that round came to an end and they swapped papers to get them marked and their paper that came from another table had the answer to the longest river as the Volga and Matt said "Well they've got one wrong and said that river as the Volga and it's wrong." Danny "Is it? I bet it is right I am pretty sure now that they have put it down as well." Sandy "Wait and we will see now I think you will eat your words." Well the quiz master read the question again and said "What is the longest river in Europe? the answer is the Volga." Danny sat there and smiled and Sandy shouted to the quiz master "Your wrong it's the Danube." Quiz master replies to Sandy "The Danube is the second longest the Volga is the longest and the Rhine is the third longest and that is a fact." Sandy "I was sure I was right, oh well." Matt didn't say a thing but Danny said "The Volga, I was right but outvoted because Matt will agree with anything Sandy says and not argue against her, so we lost a point." John "Yes Matt and you were so sure because Sandy said it. ha, ha, it's only a quiz so get over it we will get a good feed out of it at the end and we will all have the same points at the end anyway, Steve will see to that ha, ha, c'mon it's all for a bit of fun." Well the night was a good night except for Zig and Zag but they didn't pout so much as usual and at the end of the night they were all pretty drunk and went home.

Well the summer progressed much the same as ever and things were changing at the college and the older students were only getting 2 weeks off for summer not like the younger ones as they had 8 weeks off and the college was left to about 30 older students and Jeff was excited at the prospect of new older students starting in September but before that some sad news as many old friends were leaving including Winnie but first to go was one of Danny's many good mates and it was a big surprise indeed. Well the S. S. W's were the first to go and it was a sad day. They were all standing outside Gardner saying goodbye to Danny and Jeff etc. first was Lidia and this was indeed a sad day for Danny, they hugged and Danny said "This is it then Lidia? it's goodbye, please keep in touch with me and look after yourself and I am going to miss you very much." Lidia with tears running down her cheeks "Oh Danny, I am so sad for this day and I will miss you also so very much." Danny "Do you remember the first day I met you? I said about Paddington bear and you did not know who this was, now you have come a long way and learnt a lot, that proves that you are a very intelligent and beautiful lady and will go a long way and one day we will meet again I know it because you will be back in great Britain working and I will help you as much as I can, so keep in touch with me please." "You have become very Important to me and I will never forget you and what you have done for me, never." They hugged and kissed and she got into her taxi and Danny was brushing some tears from his eyes and she pulled off crying and waving to Danny although he could not see this. Next it was the lovely Joanna and she was speaking in her slow voice and they hugged and said their goodbyes. Joanna "Well it's goodbye Danny I will miss you and Jeff, it has been fun and I will come back here to see you before you leave, goodbye." Danny "Goodbye Joanna I will miss you very much, such a lovely lady." They all hugged and left Danny and Jeff standing there alone, they had all gone. Danny says to Jeff "It's a sad day Jeff and an end of another era, I feel we will never hear from them again, another part of my life over it's sad." Jeff looking very sad says "Yes your right Dan it is sad, I will miss them very much but there are more coming here soon, I can't wait a few lovely girlies, yahoo." "I wonder what we will have next. I know that one of them is Ricardo Lidia's nephew so we will have a pint for the ones who have left and six for the new ones tonight, I thought Niel was going to be here today to say goodbye?" "Yes he did say he was, didn't he? I wonder where he is?" Danny says "Yeah I wonder, so what are you supposed to be doing today?" "Well I have got lectures this afternoon but don't feel like going now, what about you?" Danny ponders and says "The same but I don't feel like it either, stuff it let's have the day off and go up the Bridge and sit in the garden with a few pints of cold lager in our hands is it?" Jeff with huge smile on his face says "I don't know what to do, stuff it I am up for it." The lads go off to the Bridge inn.

Well the lads were on their way to the bridge and bumped into Clamper and he asked if he could go up with them and as he did a girl named Emma came running out, she was a big girl who had many problems with her health and she was always wanting to help and she shouted to Clamper "Where are you going Andy?" Clamper says to her "We are going up the pub around the corner" Emma looking very excited says "Can I come with you?" Clamper "No your not allowed are you? so stay there." "Awe please can I? nobody ever let's me go with them." Danny "I don't think you are allowed are you Emma?" Emma smiling says "Yes I can, I will be good." The lads talk amongst themselves and Jeff says "I don't think it is a good idea to take her, she is hyper and loud and a bit of a handful Dan." Danny "The poor girl she is right no one takes her anywhere so I feel awful telling her no." Jeff says to Emma "Sorry Emma we can't take you we can't look after you." Emma with sad look on her face says "I can look after myself and help you and I will be good." Clamper "No you can't Emma sorry, see you later." The lads go to walk off and Emma starts sobbing out loud and Danny stopped and said "Ok Emma let's go and see your warder and ask them if we can take you with us." Off they go and Emma got excited, they found her warder Angela and Danny said "Hi Angela Jeff, Clamper and me are going up the bridge to have a pint in the garden and Emma is asking to come with us and we said we would ask you." Angela "If you want to go I will look after her." Danny "No what I mean is it ok for her to come with us ? I will be responsible for her." Angela "Well if your sure I can't see nothing wrong with that as long as she behaves herself." Emma was now bouncing on the spot and said "I will, I will and I will take some money with me so wait for me will you? I will get some money." Danny "We will wait right here." Angela "You must have a wash and change that jumper first." Emma looking stressed says "Will you wait for me Danny please?" Danny says "Of course I will and make sure you wash behind your ears ha, ha, ha." Emma laughed out loud and said "Wash behind my ear, ha, you are funny ha,ha, ha." The lads sat on the bench waiting for her and soon enough she turns up excited as she could be, she says to the boys "Ok I am ready and I have got some money to buy you guys a drink." Danny says to Angela "How much money has she got?" Angela replies "I have given her five pounds out of her money that's all." Danny "Good so I will sort her out with some cokes with it and have you told her to behave and hold my arm all the time, we are walking up to the pub?" Angela says to Emma "Did you hear that Emma?" Emma looking so excited said "I will help you Danny so you must take my arm and I will guide you ok? because I can see allright." Danny smiling says "That's a good idea Emma and I will not trip over anything with you. Right lads and Emma let's go." Emma "Bye bye Angela see you later I won't be drunk ok." Angela smiles and says "Ok Emma be good." Emma now beaming says "Ok . Off they went Danny holding Emma's arm and they had a good stroll to the pub and when they got there Emma insisted on buying the lads a drink even though she did not have enough money so Danny said "Look Emma I will get the drinks in for the first round ok and you can carry them out to the garden for us ok?" Emma standing to attention says "Yes I can do that no problem and I will get the last drink." After getting served they went out in the garden and sat in the nice sunshine and Emma was being a good girl and pretended to be a grown up and was very helpful. She said "I am a good girl aren't I? not like when I pulled off rivers wig and split it down the middle and he shouted at me and that was your fault Danny, I had a bollocking about that ha, ha, ha." Danny spit some of his drink out laughing and said "Ha, ha, yes remember that? that was so funny and river or Eric was mad and the tutors was trying to tell you off and I was making faces at you and you were laughing your head off and Barry said to me "Danny I am trying to correct this girl and you are making it Impossible, we laughed didn't we Emma?" Emma "Yes that was funny but I got £5 out of you for doing it for children in need didn't I?" Danny "Yes Emma but I never told you to rip it just take it and run off with it." Emma "I did but he grabbed it and when I went to run it split right down the middle and he said it cost a thousand pounds." The lads laughed hard and Jeff said "Remember he put it back on and the tare was right down the middle it looked like a parting like the M4, it looked so funny and I thought Niel was going to have a heart attack he laughed so much remember? his sides were in pain he laughed so loud, but that river was so mad ha, ha, ha." Clamper "Yes he was saying, oh look at what you have done Emma I will look as if the moths have had it you naughty girl you." Danny was laughing so much the tears were running down his cheeks and he says "Ha, ha, ha, I tried, ha, ha, ha, to get it off Emma to ha, ha, ha, give it back to him but I couldn't I was laughing so much ha, ha, ha." Emma was now laughing very hard and said "Shall I do it again sometime ?" All the boys said at the same time "No, no." Danny "Have you drunk your coke Emma?" Emma laughing says "Nearly I will get the next ones." Jeff says "No Emma I will and you can come and help me if you like ok? You must stay sober to help carry them back please." Emma very excited to be able to help says "Yes allright but it's mine next time." Off they went to the bar and Danny said to Clamper "Right matey here's a £1 for Emma's drink next time and say it came from you when you get your round and at the end I will let her buy a pint for me and she will be happy as she can't buy everyone a drink, she has not got enough money." "You have spent more on her coke than a pint?" "Oh it doesn't Matter I just want her to be happy, she has bought someone a drink I don't care about the money." Clamper "Your too soft you are, where's Niel today? I haven't seen him all week?" "I don't know he has gone home after all the trouble with Zarrine and Abby I expect just to give the dog a rest for a few weeks." "So is he coming back or not?" "Well I don't know it's all up in the air at the moment, I haven't spoke to him, I hope he will he is a good laugh and so funny and pleasant." Next thing back comes Emma smiling from ear to ear and she puts Danny's beer in front of him and Jeff's by his place and sat down and proceeded to play with the jack Russell dog belonging to the landlord with his ball. Emma started throwing it for the dog but she was very aggressive with it and Danny said "Emma don't throw it too hard if it hit's anyone it will knock them out and their pints off the table." Emma "Ha, ha, he is funny, I will be careful Danny, chill out man." Danny laughed and Jeff said "We got sorted out in the bar and I had to stop her running with the pints or there would not be anything beer left in the glasses, she is a handful ha, ha, ha." Clamper "I warned you what she is like didn't I?" Danny was just about to say something and Emma butted in Oh shut up Andy, I am not hurting you am I, leave me alone you are not so bloody clever yourself." Danny "So there, that told you, if everyone thought like you she would not go anywhere and as for anyone saying we are perverts for taking a girl like Emma out alone with us then tell them to come and say this to my face and I will sort them out, because there are too many narrow minded people here in this college and that is a big problem with this world, gone are the days when you can have a little fun because all the do gooders in this world would have her put in a home for her own good as far as they are concerned for her own safety and most perverts add up to a fifth of the population of this world so stuff them we know the truth and I can't be bothered with those kind of people." Jeff "I know what you mean, those type of people make other people's lives a misery, instead of helping they hinder." After a few more pints Danny said to Emma "Right Emma you can buy me a pint now if you want to it's your round and only you and me are in a round, so go and get them in please Jeff will come with you." Emma's eyes lit up and she felt very Important and stood tall going into the pub, she returned after a while and put the pint in front of Danny looking so proud and said "There you go me old mucker your pint, I hope you enjoy it Dan." Danny "Well thank you Emma and faster next time ha, ha, ha." Emma laughed out loud and threw the ball for the dog and said "Your welcome Mr rock and roll ha, ha, I am playing with the dog aren't I?" Danny "Why do you call me Mr rock and roll Emma? I have not been called that before." Emma says "It's Kezz and some of the others because you play a lot of rock music in your room and we can all hear it outside the Dowdell hall and sit there and listen to them." Danny "Oh right, that's a new one on me. Right I am off after this pint as I have to go and see the nurse tonight at 5 o'clock." Next thing Emma threw the ball and it bounced over the wall and the dog sailed over the wall after it and next thing you could hear glass breaking and Jeff said to Danny "Right drink up let's go." They left the pub and was laughing all the way back to the college. Emma's warden came out to take Emma over for tea and said "So Emma did you enjoy it?" Emma laughing replied "Yes I did, can we do it again Danny?" Danny "Of course Emma but not for a while as we don't often take a day off to go drinking, see you later kid." Emma bouncing says "Yes ok and thank you lads, see you." They all said "See you Emma." Danny went off to see the nurse.

It was by the nurse's office outside the Gardner hall and outcome Tim he said to Danny "Hello, who is that?" Danny replied "It's that handsome Welshman it is, how are you Tim?" "Well not so good Dan, I have got some news for you." "What's the Matter mate? you sound down." tim in sad voice says "I am matey, I am afraid I am leaving the college." Danny sounding devastated says "What do you mean leaving? you have got a long way to go yet." "I am afraid not they have said that I was not getting into the computers very well and suggested I should go home and think about what I was going to do and they are right, I just can't get used to computers as I am a man who is used to making things with my hands not messing with computers, I get bored to easy so I am leaving tomorrow mate." "Your joking?" Danny looked sad and so did Tim and Danny continued "Can't you make an effort to make it work? I don't want you to go, what does Mandy think about it all?" "She is not very happy but she has only got a few months here herself anyway so I have decided to leave mate and I will not change my mind, so it's goodbye until the wedding anyway in May next year. Anyway." The lads hugged and looked sad indeed and Danny then said "I give up it's all coming to an end, first the S. S. W's now you and Jeff is leaving next year after Easter or maybe sooner. I will be alone soon enough , I will miss you matey I really will, we have had a laugh and what has Niel and the others said about it?" "You're the first to know, I have only just decided this afternoon." Danny says "Well I don't know what to say Tim I really don't." "I know I will miss you, we have had a good time and so many laughs to go with it I will miss you very much but we will get together up my place and there is the stag night, I definitely want you there, I mean it." "I would not miss it for the world matey don't worry." The lads grab each other's arms and shook hands with a fury of friends that could not be beaten and Tim said "I am leaving at eleven o'clock tomorrow morning , will you come and see me off right by here for my taxi?" "You bet I will Tim and we must get together for a drink in the bar tonight ok?" "Definitely Dan, tell the others I will meet them up there, I am off now see you up the bar." They shook hands again and parted. Danny was shaken up by the news of Tim leaving and went and told Clamper, Jeff, Niel and all the others and they all went up to say their goodbye's to Tim.

In the bar they all sat around a large table and Tim looked like a man who was about to be executed. Mandy was almost crying as she was leaving her man go home alone and was worried Tim says to her "Don't worry Mandy I will be in touch at all times and you can come and stay with me at my house until you come home permanent, I will never leave you." Danny chirped in "Never mind Mandy looks like you are stuck with him sorry." Mandy "Oh well never mind aye." Tim "Yeah, yeah, I know you are kidding." Jeff "She is not, I can't wait until you have gone another woman free for the Adonis from Swindon ha, ha, ha." Tim "Jeff you don't stand a chance matey not after me, I know my girl she is all mine." Jeff "I know mate but I think Jo is coming back after the holidays, she is coming here next Thursday for an interview as the next receptionist here for the next year." Danny "Is she Jeff? she has got a nice ass to I love goosing her, a nice pert ass ha, ha, so he will be in love again." Tim "I know, I am glad I am leaving now ha, ha, ha." Danny "Can I come with you Tim I can't bare it again, he is like a little kitten with her." Clamper comes in and goes up to Tim and wraps his arms around him and says "I am sorry to see you go Tim it will not be the same, I am upset at the thought of you leaving, we have become very close matey." Tim "Steady Andy people will be talking about me and Mandy is getting jealous ha, ha, only kidding mate I will miss you to but I will see you in your 21st birthday party and in my wedding." Clamper "I know I am just being silly again, it won't be the same without you Tim and I will look after Mandy ok matey?" Tim "Thank you Andy, look out it's the other Welshman, Niel how are you?" Niel " hello Tim, what's going on here then?" Tim "You haven't heard I am leaving tomorrow?" Niel looking shocked said "Yeah your not leaving, go away with you." Tim looking serious replies "I am, I am sorry to say I leave tomorrow at 11 o'clock for ever, I cannot get on with computers and only get on with the braile isn't that right fanny ha, ha." Danny looks at Niel and says "Yes remember that Tim so funny, Niel he is leaving for definite, he is too dull to stay with us brilliant Welshmen you know." Tim laughs and Jeff says "Here they go again talking a load of rubbish, don't encourage them Tim because you can't get them saying anything sensible after ." Niel "Oh shut up you English git, I am going to miss you Tim I really will but I will look after Mandy if you like." Tim "She can look after herself thank you." Niel "Well the offer is there." Mandy "Ah that's very nice, thank you Niel, that's nice of you." Niel "Mandy your welcome girl you need a real man." Tim "Yeah, yeah, I am more than she ever needs but I will see you at the wedding won't i?" Niel smiling says "Yes I will be there mate, try and stop me." Danny "So where have you been then Niel? I could not get an answer on your door." Niel "I went home for a day or two, I was fed up about the situation with Abby, she is not happy here in my opinion, she went for Zarrine and it has upset me, I am thinking of leaving to and am back to see how things go for the next couple of weeks but I think I will be leaving if she does not settle down. So things are changing here and it has been fun mind, now Tim is leaving, the S. S. W's have left now him and I think I will be next after your favourite woman Dan." Danny looking puzzled "Who are you talking about?" Niel smiling "Well Winnie of course." Danny "Oh her, I will not be sad to see her go at all, she is a nutter." Jeff "Now c'mon Danny don't tell fibs." Danny "Jeff I will not be shedding any tears when she goes I assure you, so don't go there, you can have her if you like." Niel "Dan he has tried and got nowhere, he took her to his room to console her and it didn't work she told him to behave or else she was sitting on the bottom of his bed and she just ignored his advances." It went silent and Jeff said "I, I, i was just trying to stop her getting upset that's all." Danny "Jeff you big shit, trying to get off with her because I didn't want her your best friends old girlfriend you little shit you." Jeff was trying to convince Danny there was nothing in it and Danny kept pretending to be upset. Jeff by now was looking as if he was a dirty dog and Danny kept on teasing him "Well Jeff, I never thought you would do that to me you rat and I hope Jo never finds out or you will be blown out by her, I would not say anything mind as long as I don't get pissed any time she is around, oh dear." Jeff "Oh c'mon matey I wouldn't do anything like that ask her when you see her next and Jo would not believe you anyway." Niel butts in "No but she will believe me." Jeff "Look lads there was nothing in it honest, but if you want to persecute me go ahead I thought you were my mates." Tim "You never believed that Jeff did you?" Jeff "As a Matter of fact I did but I was wrong." Clamper "Serves your right it will teach you a lesson ha, ha, and I will tell her too for hanging me over the banister, I knew I would get my revenge." Jeff looking daggers at Clamper says "I knew you would stir the shit and I was not going to embarrass you but I will now, you have got your shorts on inside out and the netting is on the outside instead of the inside you idiot, you look a right div." Clamper felt his shorts and went bright red and says "Oh shit, I must look like a fool, sorry all, I am off to the toilet to put them right." Everyone was laughing and he rushed off to put himself right and as he went he said to Jeff "You could have whispered in my ear not blurt it out Jeff thanks." Jeff "No problem as Danny says it's a messy job but somebody's got to do it, yes that reminds me you haven't said that for a long time now, in fact it must be a good few months now." Danny looking sad said "Yes I think your right there, I must have said that before my brother's death it must have been knocked out of my brain because I haven't found much of anything funny and now Tim is leaving and Niel is thinking about it, times have got to change I suppose but it makes it even sadder." Tim looking sad by now says "Yes I don't know what I am going to do it will be strange for me next week not having Mandy there and all of you are not going to be about, it is another part of my life disappearing not to be repeated again, I will miss you all." All of a sudden Mandy started crying and it went all sad and then it happened, in walks Kezz as if she was walking into a saloon in the wild west, the door burst open and she screamed "Bloody banging man, bloody banging man.....eek, eek, right is that Welshman in here? he has missed the best programme on the radio about Miesha Paris, tickle, tickle, tickle I know you are in here c'mon own up I would buy you a pint but I am skint ha, ha, ha." Danny shouts "Over here squiggly Kezz, I thought you were already in here sitting over the other side of the table." Kezz says "I was in here earlier but went home to listen to the programme, is Tim still going home? If he is it is sad." Tim "Yes I am still going home Kezz but I will miss you, do you want a drink?" "Oh yes please I can't get you one back mind I am skint but I will have a pint of cider please." Kezz sits down an Mandy gets up to fetch some beer for everyone and Danny says to Kezz "So can I tickle you?" Kezz says "Eek, eek, eek, oh no you don't Danny I will tell Niel, I just nearly knocked out Clamper he was rushing so be careful I can be dangerous ha, ha, tickle, tickle." Danny "Well I hope you have knocked some sense into him and him into you and Jeff can stop fighting." Jeff "It's not me it's him, he always starts it." Danny. "Well look at Tim he is leaving and their mates now he will be looking at you for guidance because Tim won't be around to help him, he is only a lad, give him a chance Jeff it's not easy for him " Jeff "Yeah, yeah, I will try but he winds me up all the time as you know, and he will be hanging around now Tim is leaving, god help us " Kezz " oh Jeff Clamper is ok I went to school with him he has always been like that but he is harmless and can be a good friend even though he is like a old woman at times ha, ha, " Jeff " fair enough I will try and be a little more patient with him. So Tim when are you leaving did you say tomorrow?" Tim "Yes I am leaving at 11 o'clock, it will be funny not coming back here, I will be taking a few days to collect myself and then Mandy will be up with me so it will be next week before it really hit's home and Ginny was sad to hear I was leaving but we are going to keep in touch and I will be finishing my course of braile at home by telephone, I will miss those ladies up there." Danny "Yes I bet you will and it won't be the same there without you, we have had some good laughs there, it has been great and you are one of the nicest lads I have met here, it has been brilliant having your company Tim, I will miss you." Tim "And I will miss you, you have opened my eyes so to speak as regards having fun even if I have gone blind, it has been an experience meeting you and hope we will always be friends, I hope you will come and stay from time to time?" Danny "You try and stop me Tim I will be up for the stag night soon enough and then the wedding of course in May, I am looking forward to it and we will keep in touch for ever mate." Tim "I am glad to hear that and of course that goes for you Niel and Jeff , Clamper ... I will miss you all but let's stop this sad feeling and drink up it's Clamper's round ha, ha, ha." Clamper sit's up and looking shocked declares "Who me? I am not in a round and I have got no money ha, ha, but I will buy you a drink when I come up to visit." Tim "Well that's typical of you Andy I always get an excuse when it comes to you buying me a drink, your awful Andy, we all agree about that you never got money or fags you bugger but you are a good friend." Clamper "Come here matey let's have a hug." Clamper gets up to put his arms around Tim and Tim grabs his hand and shakes it and says "Calm down Clamper I am a man you know and it is not normal, is your name river or what? Steady man ha, ha, ha." Jeff "Yes sweetie, i do like you but you are awful." Kezz "I think river is strange and some girls here are the same, I stay away from them at all times and tie my knickers up tight when they are around as I can't see them coming ha, ha, and I have heard them talking about things rude and perverted, I always listen and laugh at them as they are so silly." Jeff "Oh don't start Danny off about them he goes on and on." Danny "I don't go on I just stop them talking about us normal people as if we were dirty and not normal, they call us straight and I don't think they should give us a label we are normal not straight, normal, they have the problem not us, but they say we have the problem that's all I am saying and they like to push it in our faces, not just get on with their lives, I don't go on and on about what my wife and me did to each other but they do." Niel butted in and laughing said "Wow, wow, slow down you will have a heart attack in a minute, Jeff is right ha, ha, we are not allowed to say things like that it's politically incorrect so be careful Dan ha, ha, ha." Danny smiling says "Bollocks to politically correct, are they going to jail everyone who thinks the same as me, I don't think so as most of us here think the same way but keep quiet because all the poofta's complained about it and some poofta's in parliament put the boot in for them, so I will say what I really think and that's that and before you say it I am not homophobic as the proper homosexuals don't publicize it they just get on with their lives and I am not saying any more about it." It went silent and Jeff then said "Well there are none of them in here tonight or they would have said something by now ha, ha, so what shall we talk about now?" Niel "Who's not here we don't like?" Danny "Sandy and Matt or as I say Zig and Zag." They all laughed and Niel says "A good topic, we were in here last week and Sandy as you know is always being pushed around by Matt and she uses the dog as a husky and she was in here and sitting in her wheelchair and the music was good and next thing she was dancing the rest of the night like ginger Rogers, there is nothing wrong with her and Matt is a mug pushing her around and doing everything

399

for her." Tim "Never, I heard she went mad one day as they used her wheel chair to get a few boxes of bottled water in the building and up the lift and she caught them and now someone has left the tyre down for spite, they are weird aren't they ?" Danny "They got on my nerves in the quiz last week, she can't do any wrong with Matt and she uses him something awful, she has tried to get off with me a few times and always got her tit's out for me, sorry not my type I was going to send her to see Jeff, he will shag a frog if you could stop it hopping but I thought even he don't deserve that." Jeff smiling says "You keep your opinions to yourself and next time send her to see me ha, ha, keep your nose out ha, ha, ha, ha." They all laughed and Kezz said "Why did she keep getting her tit's out then?" Danny "To try and get me excited and give her one that's why but I am not that brave." Kezz "Oh right I see ha, ha, ha." Jeff "I would have ha, ha, ha." Niel "I would have put money on that, he is a dirty old dog, I would watch your wives everyone if he is about ha, ha, I don't believe you sometimes Jeff." Clamper said "That's better I can walk easier now I have got the shorts the right way." Jeff laughing said "Well you had better go and try again, you have got them on back to front now." Clamper grunts "Oh bloody hell mun, I can't get it right today. Try again." Off he goes again. Jeff looked annoyingly and said "That boy is useless can't you take him home with you Tim?" Tim "Oh no thanks he is too much to manage thanks but no thanks, why don't you take him home with you Jeff and pretend he is your son who has been lost in the woods for 20 years. People would believe that just like bobby on Dallas." Jeff "Don't say things like that not even in jest." Danny "Right my round I think, I can't see me drinking any more after this one, I have lectures tomorrow afternoon, I will be over to see you off though Tim I will meet you outside gardener and no kissing and no tongues ha, ha, ha." They all have a few more drinks and go home to their digs.

In Dowdell and who was waiting for Danny was yes you guessed it Winnie sitting like sitting bull on the floor listening to the TV. She got up as soon as Danny got in and Danny was sitting on the sofa and Winnie got around the back of the settee and started giving Danny a Chinese head massage. She spoke gently "So it's the drinking velshman, I see you are drunk again not good Danny, I think you need some massage to help you sleep." Danny cheekily said "If you like you can come to my room and help me sleep? Not like you did to Jeff in his room." Winnie snapped and slapped Danny's head and said "What do you mean by saying this? What did Jeff say happened in his room then?" Jeff walks in just then said "Oops time for a ciggy." Winnie "No you stay by there Jeff. Danny tell me?" Danny smiling says "He had you in his room and he tried it on with you didn't he?" Winnie very nasty by now replies "Aha he was trying to get me to do rude things by asking me things but I never did any of it, I told him to stop it or I would use some kung Fu on him and he did nothing, I would not let him do these things to me I would not do that no -nonsense " Danny." Danny says "I know he told me, I was only teasing you ha, ha, ha." Jeff smiling from fear said "Right now can I go for a ciggy?" Winnie "Go away Jeffrey you make trouble for me and I will pull your ears off Danny, so behave yourself, silly velshman, huh . Danny being sarcastic says "So does that mean I am not getting any head? Ha, ha, I was only kidding you don't have to be so uptight Winnie." Winnie "I am not happy with you Danny and this is the last head massage I will ever give you if you say these things again, Is Tim leaving tomorrow? As Lola said he is." Danny says "Yes I am afraid he is and I will miss him, he is a nice guy, but we will see each other again from time to time, it's a pity I like him and Mandy and I think Mandy will not be here much longer now he is leaving and only a couple of weeks and you will be going back to China isn't it?" Winnie looking sad says "You sound as if you can't wait? I am trying to get an extension for a couple of months." "Is it looking good then?" "I don't know, you ask too many questions, how should I know all this? I will know shortly so I will tell you if you need to know ok?" "Oh dear, you are in a mood again tonight, right I don't want a head massage if you are going to pull my hair as that always happens when you get nasty." She let his head go and started shouting at him just then Jeff walked back turned on his heels and left the room saying "Oops, time for another ciggy." Danny and Winnie laughed and Jeff stopped and turned back around and sat down and said "That's better, you 2 are always arguing lately, what am I saying you have always argued." Winnie "It's not me, it's him, I am going to bed, he always tries to upset me so as I will go to bed." Danny "Go to bed Winnie, don't be stupid Winnie." Winnie "See what I mean? He always starts me off, I am going to bed goodnight." The lads wished her goodnight and sat there reminiscing. Danny says "Well Jeff it's an end of an era with Tim going an maybe Niel, Winnie is going and many more. It won't be long before you leave and I will be here alone again." "Yes it will soon come to that and we will be back home again except you. What are you going to do then Dan? Have you decided yet?" "Well I got a bit of money coming and would like to go down to Narberth in Pembrokeshire to live near my brother but not too near and I will start a new life and my children can come and stay with me from time to time and if Josh wants to he can live with me it will be ok and I can visit you up Swindon and Tim in Tamworth and you all can come and visit me and drink some decent beer for a change. I will have to make new friends all over again but will keep in touch with my old friends , I will be ok and you never know I might find myself a nice girl, mind you she will have to be nice after all I have gone through, I don't think I need a new woman now it's too much trouble I think I will be fine what about you?" "Well I have got my name down for a disabled bungalow and they are starting to build some near me so there's hope yet and it has been an adventure mind and hope it continues for the rest of my time here." "Yes it has been fun and I am glad I did it as I am almost there, I mean I can do most things I endeavoured to do and it has been mind blowing mind, but worth it, this place has saved my life no doubt about it . I think if I had not done this I would not be here now, I think I would have topped myself by now with all the trouble, I really mean that. I could not see any future. Now I can at last it is possible to live as Normal as any man within reason." "Yes it has had a benefiting effect on me also and I am a better man for it and it has helped me especially with the birds here, I will miss that, I wish I was taking a girlie home on my arm mind." "Don't worry about that matey it will happen one day when you least expect it, you wait and see and when it happens you can tell me I was right and I can say I told you so." "Yeah, yeah, I will believe that when it happens, I am still in love with Geraldine mind, I have not given up there yet I am still trying and what about you? You have been with a few girls here since you were told your wife was divorcing you? There must be someone you like." Danny thinks for a minute and says "There are some lovely girls here and some grottbags but none of them are for me. I was hoping Winnie was going to be different, she is gorgeous and I love her but her attitude to life stinks, I can't live like that so I am not bothering thanks but no thanks." "Never mind matey as you said there is someone out there for all of us   ." "Yes there is but we must party hard until you leave." "No change there then, but I will be in charge of the newcomers here for assessment in a few weeks as Mandy is stepping down to finish off her course here before she leaves to live with Tim, so I must be a little more responsible ha, ha, ha." "I agree it is funny so you will be breathing over the new girls here and frighten them away, I wonder who is coming here after some of them leave this floor?" "Well I know one of them a lovely girly I met in Torquay from bloody Wales mind you will like her she is in her later years not old but very nice her name is Lynne Morris she has been here before, a very Welsh accent but quiet and I think, Mandy is taking another room and C J from downstairs is coming up here." "C J, oh my god he will be singing all over the place again and this Lynne sounds very nice." "Down boy, down boy, she is a married woman." "Oh goodness me, I am getting your disease." "What disease?" "Crashing and burning, never mind I will have another Welsh person here and a pretty one for a change. Well I am off to bed matey I will see you in the morning, oh no I won't ha, ha, ha." The lads go their separate ways.

It was the next morning and Danny was sitting on the bench outside Gardner at nearly 11 o'clock waiting for Tim to appear as they arranged, he came out of the door with Laddie on his harness and a huge holdall on his shoulder. He came towards Danny and whispered "Hello Dan are you there?" "Danny replies "Yes Tim, come and sit by me on the bench, hello Laddie how are you pup?" Danny pats the dog and he makes a fuss of Danny as if he knew he was going home for good. Tim said "Well this is it mate, I am off, I will miss you mate give me your hand mate." They both shook hands firmly and passionately as they both felt a great loss and Danny says "Yes Tim, this is it, I will miss our fun and the laughs we have with Ginny Margaret and Christine very much and especially the mistakes we usually make." Tim laughs and coughs nervously then says "Yes it has been fun and I at least met the woman of my dreams, thanks to Rory, he introduced us and changed my life forever, I will never forget him or Clamper, Jeff, Niel and you. I don't know what I will do tomorrow now it's going to be funny and if you decide to marry Winnie let me know and I will be there in the wedding ha, ha, ha." "Well that will never happen, even if she was good for me I will never marry again ever mate, I will leave that up to you and let me know when the stag night is and I will get up there and of course the wedding in May, wild horses will not keep me away." "You have got to get to my stag night, the lads up home are dying to meet you with all your jokes, I have told them all about you and Jeff so I am looking forward to that." "I'll be there don't worry and of course Clamper is going to be there too, I hope he is sensible with the drink as he is only a youngster, we can't keep an eye on him but he should be allright." "He will be fine and he is sleeping in my house along with you and Mandy, so he will be ok, I don't know if Jeff will be there mind, I can't get a decent answer out of him." "I will do my best there but you know how tight he is with money, we will just have to wait and see, look out here is your taxi." The lads stood up and the taxi driver got out and took Tim's bag off him and it was solemn with the lads and Danny said "Well this is it mate, I will miss you, give me your hand." They shook hands firmly like 2 people who would not see each other again, Tim spoke "Look after yourself you old git and keep in touch and let's get together soon, promise me mate?" "Tim I will be there soon, I am not just saying that mate I mean it, we will be friends until I die, you look after that girl and yourself." They kept on shaking hands and then Tim let Danny's hand go and got into the taxi, as they parted they went silent then Tim shouted "Goodbye Dan." from the taxi as it sped away and Danny shouted back "Goodbye mate look after yourself and don't drink too much, goodbye Tim" In seconds the taxi was out of sight and Danny sat down on the bench silently in the sunshine contemplating his future, looking very sad and wondering if he would see any of his new friends in a few years' time. After a while someone sat by him and started to speak to him, It was Lennox. He said "Hello Daniel you look sad?" Danny replies "Oh hello Lennox how are you?" "I am fine thank you very much, are you ok?" "Yes I am fine it's just that Tim just left and I hate saying goodbye, you know what it is like ?" "That is why I need to talk to you, I am having some trouble getting anyone interested in coming up with me and Shirley marshal to Heathrow airport to take Winnie to get on her plane and say goodbye to her and I was wondering if you and Jeff would do the honour?" Danny looking surprised "So she is definitely going in a few weeks then? Because she thinks she will have an extension." "No, no, she can't get an extension, she is only allowed to stay here until the end of this month and then she has to go back I am afraid." "Well she will be unhappy and why me and Jeff? You know the trouble she has given me ever since I have known her?" Lennox looking nervous says "Yes but she is not that bad and you know her more than most, so what do you think?" Lennox was looking at Danny hopefully but was expecting the worst. Danny smiled and said "Yes why not? You can count me in." "Oh, I can? You have taken me back now, I expected you to say a definite no." "No I will be there and so will Jeff, I want to make bloody sure she gets on that plane and then I will be sure and Jeff can sit one side of her and me the other in the car so she can't escape." Lennox laughed to himself and grinned widely "Are you serious Daniel? She is not that bad, come on." "She is and I can't wait to see the back of her, no I mustn't say that she has been a ray of sunshine on times in my life, but I will be free and won't have to sneak about any more." "Daniel I am sure you are exaggerating." "No I am not Lennox, she has made my life here miserable sometimes, if she was a little more European and thought like western women not too much mind, then things might have been different, so yes we will be there just let us know when and I will be there so will Jeff." "Don't you want to ask Jeff first?" "No, he will jump at it to see her leave on the plane, it will bring a smile to his face also so leave him to me I will sort him out." "Right if you are sure Daniel I will leave it to you and you can tell her also but don't make it unpleasant for her please." "No I won't I will just tell her I am coming to see her off and say goodbye and I won't be lying will I?" "Well I will see you later Daniel." "Yes, ok Lennox I will see you." He leaves and Danny sat there thinking the end was coming too fast and he was afraid of being left alone again and looked sad sitting there.

Later in the refectory and Danny sat by Jeff and said "I have volunteered you for a job with me, Lennox and Shirley marshal." "Oh right, so what have you volunteered me for now? That sounds dangerous if you did it, what am I expected to do?" "Right keep your voice down this is top secret mind and if you tell anyone else I will have to kill you." "I am not betting with you if you are trying to get me to, I am not stupid and I am not falling for your tricks dodgy so tell me and then I will decide if I am going to do it." "It's bodyguard work and it's dangerous, very dangerous and I think you can handle it even if you are like Mr Muscle." Jeff looked at Danny as if he was trying to trick him and says "I don't think so mate, I am a lover not a fighter, forget it, it is bound to end up in tragedy if you are involved. Are you going to tell me what it is?" "Your going to like this and you will be a hero with many of the inmates and I will tell your family if anything happens untoward to you." "Right you are worrying me now, bloody tell me for god's sake, tell me will you?" "Right are you ready for this?" Jeff getting annoyed says "I am going to stab you in a minute because you are frightening me now, tell me or I am off, tell me will you." "We are required to escort Winnie in a car to Heathrow airport for her to catch her plane home at the end of the month and to say sayonara basically." There was a deadly silence then Jeff spoke "Your kidding? She is really going home? Who told you?" "Lennox did it's true and he has nominated us to see her off and it's worth it to make bloody sure she gets on that plane, what better way is there?" "Well, well, I never, she is actually going? I bet you are happy?" "I am not saying bugger all, one of her friends may be listening but in a way it is sad and I will never see her again and I suppose I will miss her." "Bullshit, I can hear it in your voice your ecstatic, well, well, things are changing now." "No I am serious I will miss her even though she has sometimes made my life hell here, I only wish she had been much nicer to me and I think things would have been different." "Yes your right she is such a good looking girl with a cracking body but as soon as she starts demanding that's it for me, so now you can get off with some of the other girls here now she is going to be out of the way." "No bloody fear mate I don't fancy any of the girls here, all the good looking ones are spoken for including Lola, I am afraid I will be on my own from now on until one day someone will turn up for me but she will have to be different. I can tell you." "Well I think you will have a long wait Dan especially now you are getting on a bit, I mean you will be a pensioner soon." Danny looking hurt says "You cheeky git, I am only in my forties, I am still a spring chicken and you are catching me up mind, so think before you speak." "I am only a kid compared to you matey your more like an old turkey waiting for xmas, well, well, she is actually going. How long did you say?" "Well I worked it out to 2 weeks as that is the end of term for the youngsters so that is it but she thinks she is going to get an extension to her term but I was assured by Lennox she isn't, so that's it I think it will be a week Thursday for definite, we must try and keep her sweet until then and give her a good time." Jeff smiling says "I tried to in my room but she was not having any of it ha, ha, ha." "Trust you, I mean a little party or something, you know?" "Winnie and parties, I don't think so, she is not really the queen of parties." "No, your right, well we will just be nice to her ok?" "Well we can give it a try." The lads went off to get changed for the bar.

Later that night after having a few drinks up the bar Jeff and Danny were sitting in the lounge in Dowdell talking and having a couple of cans and were very tipsy. Jeff tells Danny "It was dead up there tonight with Tim, Mandy, Niel and all the others who have left or leaving shortly, I felt strange up there." "Bloody right it was dead, I felt we had gone to a different bar tonight. I hope this is not the way it is going to be from now on, I couldn't stand that but there are more starting here soon so we will wait and see what we get and I believe you are taking them about for their first week to see if they want to come here?" "Yes I am, I am taking over from Mandy so we can look them over, I will be fetching them over here for a cuppa on breaks so make sure you are here." "No problem matey it's a messy job but some bodies got to do it and no Winnie." Just as he was saying that she was half way in the room and snapped "What do you mean? Why do you say this?" Jeff looked horrified and said "Oops time for a ciggy." He goes off and Danny said to Winnie "Well your leaving in 2 weeks aren't you?" "Who says this Danny?" "never mind that I and Jeff have been asked if we want to come to Heathrow airport to say goodbye and we excepted, I don't want to let you go and not see you off." Winnie looked as if she didn't trust Danny and replied "How do you know it is in 2 weeks? Because I don't even know this." "Well I am guessing as the term ends in 2 weeks today and you haven't been offered an extension have you?" "No but I am waiting for an answer, so don't try and get rid of me so quick." "Well Winnie if they were going to offer you an extension they would have done so by now and they will not leave it to the last minute, I think you should except it your leaving in 2 weeks, as you know I don't like any lies or deceit. I am telling you the truth I think I am right but I will tell you straight and not beat around the bush." There was a deadly silence and Jeff walked in and could feel the atmosphere in the room and said nothing then Winnie said in a sad voice "Do you really think so? Danny is that what you want?" More silence and Danny replied in a similar voice "I'm sorry Winnie, but you will have to face it it's going to happen and no I don't want that, I will miss you." Jeff speaks "We will all miss you Winnie, it will not be the same place without you but Danny is right we want to come and say goodbye to you, but only if you want us to?" Winnie starts crying which made the lads get upset also and Danny went and sat by Winnie and put his arm around her to comfort her and said in a quiet voice "C'mon Winnie, I know it's upsetting and you don't want to go back but life never gives us a good break much when your blind and we will miss you especially me, so don't cry I want to remember you as a smiling lovely girl, so c'mon let's be happy and enjoy the time left." Still in tears she says through them "I only wanted a few more weeks, I don't want to go Danny, i like it here and hoped to have more time here that's all." Danny in very sad mood says "I know, but you must have expected it to end at some time or another and so you can take all this experience back to China with you and maybe one day return here and we can all party. " Still crying Winnie replies "Do you really think so? Because I don't." Danny "Say you never know Winnie we may meet again all of us as we were but sadly life changes even though we don't want it to as Jeff and I were saying a minute ago how much it had changed up the bar, no Tim, Niel, Mandy and the S. S. W'S and soon you, it will not be the same here ever again and we just as well get the hell out of here now, all the fun has gone." Jeff "He's right Winnie it could not last forever sad though it is, all good things must come to an end and I will miss you I really will." Winnie speaks "This is so sad, I am going to my bed now, goodbye." Danny and Jeff says goodnight to her and the room was solemn. Danny says "Bloody hell mate, I was almost crying then, she is so upset." "Yes she is, I had to hold it together to matey, I have never seen her like that before." "Nor me, I wish she was not going now, in fact I wish things were back as they were a few weeks ago, why do they have to change? Can't we all just live here till we die together as one big happy family? God this hurts." "Yes I know, it is hurting me to and only another couple of months and I am off and there will just be you and a few others all the fun ones will be gone." "Oh thanks mate that's all I need is you telling me that, that makes me feel much better, thanks." "Well we got to face up to it Dan, life's a bitch and then you die." The lads sat there silent for a couple of minutes looking down at the floor and Danny then said "For god's sake Jeff let's pull ourselves out of this before I top myself, give me a can mate." "Only 2 left, I will go and see if Rhoda has left some on her door handle for us, be back now." The room now was empty and Danny started muttering to himself "What the hell am I going to do when they all go? I will be alone and have too much time to think about all the friends I have made here and they won't be around. Please don't let me become a lonely old man again, I would rather be dead." Jeff comes back in and had a bag of cans and said excitedly "Looking good dodgy, six cans, they will last us an hour and they are nice an cold." "Jeff promise me one thing?" "oh I don't know tell me what it is first before I say anything." "We will always be friends, never mind what, even if we fall out for something or someone, we will always be friends and will call each other once a month at least, can you promise me that mate?" "Don't be silly Dan of course I will and can you promise me the same? Because I have not had so much fun in all my life as we have had here." Danny almost crying said "Of course I will Jeff, you have been a good mate to me and we have had some fun haven't we?" Jeff looking at Danny looking upset said sniffingly "Right let's stop this now you would swear we were at the last supper, I think we have had too much to drink don't you? i think we should have a drink to all our friends who are not present here now and hope we all get together again soon, cheers." The lads clang their cans together and have a large swig of their beers. Danny then said "Yes I feel better now, we are a pair of silly sods aren't we?" Jeff "This has been an experience and it's a shame it is coming to an end, I don't know what is to become of you as everything is going to be different. What are you going to do? Besides moving to somewhere where no one knows you?" "Oh don't ask, I am petrified about that, I will manage I am resilient enough to get on with my life, I am only afraid of prejudice from seeing people that gets on my nerves that's all." "What do you mean?" " I have felt it since I have gone blind by many people who know me from when I was a kid, many friends and people who worked for me dodge me on the street and sometimes they pass me on the road and go silent until they pass and I know this as I have often heard them stop and talk to someone just after they have passed me and it's cruel and once I was on a bus and I knew someone was sitting near me all the way home and they used to drink with me in my local club and they have sat there all the way home and somebody gets on and talks to them and I think what a bastard they didn't speak to me and they have sat there all the way home not even a hello Dan how are you keeping, it's awful people parking on the pavements and not caring about us as long as they can get away with it. People parking on down kerbs in front of steps leading to the road in other words stuff the blind as long as I am allright and in my mind it's prejudice." "How do you work that out?" "Because if it was somebody referring to a black or gaye person it would not be tolerated and when you watch television and I like war stories from the second world war if it was a German man talking there would be subtitles for the deaf but nothing for the blind, in the adverts like the ones for music cd's they always say if you want to know more about this then phone the number on the bottom of the screen and let's face facts the blind buy more music cd's than any others you could mention and that bloody Dale Winton on that quiz for the lottery, he gives you a question and 3 options and if the person gets it wrong the real answer flashes on the screen I suppose but he never says what the answer is and on and on and on, it never ends and it makes a blind person look stupid even though they are a lot more clever than a seeing person as they have to overcome many problems to have a normal life. Look at us in the quiz in the Barrels and the Rose and Crown, look at how many times we have won the money compared to the others as they think Normal intelligent people are much less intelligent than them and a few times we have been the only ones that get an answer and no one else   does, it makes me sick and if we don't let them know it will stay like this forever, this is what I am dreading." "I know Dan I feel the same and so do many other blind people it's sickening." "It is very similar to the fight the blacks had in the south in America for their rights and one day one of them will become the president of America, watch what I am saying and so they have always been as good as any white man and the blind have a similar problem but not as bad as them. When are the people going to stop thinking they are better than anyone else?" Jeff now laughing at Danny says "Calm down Dan I can hear your voice getting louder and louder, you don't have to convince me, I understand and think your absolutely right matey and I hope things turn out ok for you as you have had a tough time here the last year but that's what I like about you, you find a way to overcome these problems." "Well Jeff that's what I think about you also but you have a way of saying something without all the arguing and fuss and you always laugh about it rather than get mad, well almost, most times, it's frightening mind for us all to leave the safety of this college and I for one will dread the day I leave but it is certain to happen and I wonder how far I get before it gets me?" "You, you , you will probably end up as prime minister one day but look out this country, you will bring back hanging heavy jail sentences and god knows what you will do with the gay community." "Oh be fair Jeff I am not that bad, I have always said I would bring back hanging for the ones that have murdered as long as it is proved without a shadow of a doubt they did the murder, like the Yorkshire ripper and Hindley and her boyfriend and that will make more room for many more people who are consistent law breakers, I would castrate all the child molesters and paedophile's, deport any person originating from other countries abroad who break the law, back to where their forefathers came from, even if they were born in this country and let them see how they live in their land and I would put a special force to pick up all absconders and send them back to where they came from and then legitimate people from European countries could come an work here, youngsters who consistently break the law conscript them into the army no questions, make the night club owners pay for all policing of their clubs and if they break the law in their places they will be shut down Immediately. These things will make this country a better place to live in and put the law back in the hands of the good population here, why should we have to put up with this crap?" "I agree Dan these governments are not working, about time we had someone there who actually does something for the innocent people here but they all live in their mansions in nice places and this don't affect them but they forget where they came from, they are absolutely useless." "I'll drink to that Jeff." The lads try and clang their cans together but they both miss as they were now drunk and they both start laughing and go off to bed.

Well a couple weeks go by and it is the day when Winnie is leaving to go back to China and they were about to leave at lunch time and the boys were in the lounge for breakfast with Zarrine. Zarrine said "Well it's going to be different here without Winnie and I don't know how to feel, she has been a nuisance sometimes but I will miss her, she is not that bad, mind you some of the girls won't miss her she didn't take any messing about." Jeff "No that's a fact, Lola and patsy will be glad to see her go and so will Danny ha, ha, ha." Danny snaps at Jeff "No I won't, she has been a pain sometimes but I will miss her a lot and that lovely body of hers ha, ha, ha." Zarrine slaps Danny and he continues "Aw, she is not that bad and I am dreading her last minutes in the airport, she will be crying I know and when I get back here then it will hit me especially when I get back from the bar as she is always here to greet me and give me a massage before she starts on me for drinking and talking to other women but it won't be the same without her it really won't but life goes on." Zarrine "Yes Danny it does and we will have more people here Immediately taking the rooms as they go and I heard Matt is moving up here to be nearer Sandy." Jeff looks bitter and says "Oh great, that's all we need, brilliant, brilliant." Danny "That's all we need now Sandy will not have to get out of bed even just open her mouth and Matt can shovel it in, so who else Is coming here?" Zarrine "Well C J will be having a room and a Welsh lady Lynn Morris, she is nice." Jeff "But she is Welsh." Danny So, from what I have heard she is very nice indeed but she is married but a looker and fit but just my luck she is married, never mind and who else?" Zarrine continues "Mandy is here for a few weeks and I am not sure what Niel is doing if he is coming back or not." Danny "I hope he does he is a good mate and lots of fun when he is not sleeping, oh hello Winnie come for breakfast for the last time? Come and have a drink, tea or coffee?" Winnie looking sheepish whispers "I will have some water if I may." Danny "God Deja vou, the same words you spoke when you arrived here a year ago, I had a shiver then, I hope you are not too hurt? We all want you to stay, it will not be the same without you here it won't you know ? Jeff "And you must keep in touch with us or at least Danny and he can tell us how you are getting on in China." Zarrine "Shall I make you some sandwiches for your journey Winnie?" Winnie by now is almost crying and replies "Oh no thanks, I will get something on the plane thank you, it is so strange leaving this country, I like it here but we have a different culture and I would have got used to it eventually and I will miss you all, especially you Danny and I am glad you are coming to see me off. I want some pictures in the airport with you if you won't mind?" Danny now looking visibly upset says "Of course you can I will be honoured Winnie and I have your mobile number and you have mine so keep in touch and maybe you will return someday I hope so anyway." Winnie "We will see, I am off to finish my packing now, see you all later." They all say goodbye to her and she goes off silently. Jeff says "This is awful, she is devastated the poor girl, it's terrible for her." Zarrine "Yes it is, I am going to go and help her and try and cheer her up, see you pair later." She goes off and Danny said to Jeff "She makes me feel guilty now, I wish life was much easier, she could be a good asset to Britain and she can't stay, she is so professional in her work she really is but she has to go back and she has no family there at all it's not fair, it really isn't, but I am sure she will make it whatever she does, she is so professional and will be in demand over there." "Yes I am sure your right and maybe she will now move her life on and get married to some nice China man out there?" "He would have to be deaf to put up with her matey and that's not being awful I am serious, so what are you taking with you to the airport? It is going to be a long run about 3 hours I guess." "Just my fags that's all, we can't have a pint or nothing and I have to sit there without a fag for three hours, shit just my luck." "Good enough for you, give it up it's bad for you." "Oh don't start matey." Danny smiles and says "It's a messy job but somebody's got to do it, I hope Winnie is going to be ok? she sounds seriously sad, I think we had better comfort her all the way and maybe she will get excited at the airport knowing she is going to see her home." "I wouldn't bet on it Dan." "No your right, I had better go and see her before anyone gets here for the trip." "Good luck matey." Danny goes off to see Winnie in her room.

In her room was Winnie still packing and Zarrine was just leaving. Zarrine said "Oh hello Danny what are you doing here?" Danny answers "I have come to see my very good friend Winnie and see if she needs anything?" Zarrine "Right I will get off then and start my cleaning, is there anything else Winnie you need?" Winnie looking so sad says "No thank you Zarrine I have everything I need, thank you for everything." Zarrine and Winnie hugged and kissed and said their goodbye's and left. Danny looking sad and not knowing what to say whispered "I will miss you, you know I have enjoyed your company even though we never always seen eye to eye and I do love you in my own way, we just will never make it together as we are so different." "I think I understand but you don't have to say you love me I know you don't." "Oh Winnie, your so wrong, I do love you and if things were different then it would have meant things would have worked out between us, so let's not end this time annoyed with each other please, just for the last day, please." Danny hugged her tightly and she hugged him back and cried and said after a while "Yes your right Danny, I will always love you until I die as you were the first man I have ever loved except my father but just as much and I will miss you forever, my heart is ready to burst it hurts so much, please speak to me on the telephone even if it is just for a while." "I will Winnie I promise but you must get on with your life as you are still young and such a beautiful woman you really are and too nice for any westerner and I will always love you too, I mean that with all my heart, I will never forget you and this is the last time I will have to tell you this." "And I will always love you Danny and I will always remember you till I die." Danny on the verge of crying says "This is hard Winnie I don't know if I will ever see you again and this is probably the last time we will have alone together, so let's get into bed for the last time is it?" Winnie says "Why not we are not going to get a chance like this again and this is for us after all no one else will ever understand so let's go out in a blaze of glory." They get into bed and make love for a long time and it came time for Winnie to leave and in the car they sat Winnie in the middle of Danny and Jeff and Lennox driving and by his side was Shirley Marshall, a lovely woman every student loved so on they travelled to the airport. Winnie held on to Danny's arm all the way and placed her head on his shoulder and Danny held her hand tightly all the way, it looked so fine and proper for these 2 to be like this and it just felt right and the atmosphere in the car was high and happy until they got to the airport and things took a turn as Winnie looked visibly shocked and she knew this was the end of her adventure and the end of her and Danny. They went into the foyer of the terminal, they were meant to be and Winnie was met by a man in his early 30's and he spoke very good Chinese and this shocked them all as he was English. He Immediately took Winnie's arm and led her off to check in and the others followed in amazement. Danny said to Jeff "Who is he? He sounds Important and maybe she is a princess in China." Jeff replies "I don't know but it is a shock to me, I wonder who he is he and Winnie are speaking nine to the dozen in mandarin or something and he is making her look very Important, look out they are coming back." The man spoke to them "Hello everyone I am taking Winnie away for a few minutes so maybe you can take a seat and have some tea while you are waiting and I will bring her back as soon as we have finished our business ok?" Everyone agreed and sat down at a table . Lennox said "I wonder who he is? I hope things are ok and there is no nonsense afoot." Danny "Like what? What do you mean?" Lennox "I hope she has not got in touch with anyone and asked for exile here or something like that as this is unusual to me, oh dear." Jeff "No I don't think so do you?" Shirley "Well I have heard of these things happening, Danny do you know anything about this? As you seem close as anyone can be to her." Danny looks stunned says "Who me? I don't have a clue what you are on about I really don't honestly, she wants to stay here but I have no knowledge of her doing anything about it, honestly now, I don't." Jeff looked at Danny and said "You haven't promised to marry her have you? Or got her pregnant have you?" Danny smiling says "Jeff don't be silly I shoot blanks you know that, I will never get anyone pregnant it's Impossible and no I have not promised to marry her, we are great friends and that's it but something is going on we may be in the police station for the rest of the day." Jeff "Oh dear time for a ciggy, I will be back, there is a room over there for me to have one." He goes off and Lennox looking nervous said "Oh dear, I hope things are ok, I will not rest until I see that plane take off and I am not going anywhere until I see it go." Shirley says "Oh don't worry Lennox she is not up to anything, I expect they do things different for those Asian visitors here, it will be ok here she comes now." Winnie returns with a camera in her hand and she was put to sit by the side of Lennox and she complains and said "I want to sit by my Danny before I go." Winnie pushed over and sat in Jeff's chair and said "That's better, ok Danny?" Danny smiles and says "Yes Winnie and you? I wondered where you had gone." Winnie says "I had to sort some things out in the office of the airway who are taking me home, oh dear, I said I am going home." Winnie started crying and sobbing badly and the man who spoke mandarin said to her in Chinese something and she smiled and wiped her face. Danny was full of tears himself but held it back. Lennox says "So is everything ok for your trip Winnie? No problems?" Winnie says "No everything is ok, I am to board in one hour so not much time and this man Richard is escorting me onto the plane and I need some pictures of me and Danny before we go please Danny?" Danny "Of course Winnie no problem, I will be delighted to have my picture of us together and you must send me a copy of one please, I will treasure it all my life." Winnie says "I think Richard will take them as I have asked him already." Richard says "Yes of course I will, let's do it." They all got up and went to a quiet end of the airport and Richard said "Who do you want to do this with? Everyone first or what?" Winnie "Oh no just Danny and me no one else." Richard then said "Don't you want any of your other friends in it?" Winnie shocked the others when she says "No just me and Danny." Danny said "Well Winnie just have one or two of them for memories." Winnie snapped "Oh ok then." Richard took a group photo and then it was the Winnie and Danny show, she wanted no one else to spoil her last minutes in Danny's company and she got her way, a picture of them holding hands facing each other, kissing and hugging and many more, it was so romantic for her and Danny and Danny and Winnie were visibly upset. They were not going to see each other ever again, it was a very tense moment for them both and the time came when they had to part and so they had a solemn moment alone and they put their arms around each other and Shirley started crying and said "Aren't they lovely together Lennox?" Lennox said "Yes as long as she is on that plane I don't care ha, ha, ha." Back to Danny and Winnie and they were alone for the last time ever. Winnie crying says "I will miss you forever Danny and will think of you every minute of the day and I will ask my father to point me to the North Star and wish for you to come back to me someday and will you do the same thing. I know we can't see anything and that we are so far away from each other but I love you very much." They kissed and Danny with tears in his eyes said "I will be looking at that star and think of you WINNIE and you will always be in my heart forever and I am sorry it was not to be but you will be very special to me until I die, please don't forget me because I will never forget you ever and I will always love you too, you have to go you are being paged on the tannoy, let's go." They walk to the entrance to the terminal gate and Danny was not allowed past this and Winnie burst out crying and Danny was very tearful also. Winnie screamed to Danny " goodbye Danny I will always think of you every day of my life, I love you." Danny now burst into tears said "And I will never forget you and will always love you, goodbye Winnie goodbye." Winnie "Goodbye Danny I love you." And she disappeared beyond the gate and Danny looked so alone for once, he pulled himself together and turned and grabbed Jeff's arm to go and Shirley still wiping her eyes with her handkerchief said "Are you ok Danny? Winnie will be missed by many in the college." Danny "I am ok, I will miss her it's the end of another friendship." Jeff "Ok matey? She is going to be ok I know this." Danny "I know but it is hard now I feel alone even more of my life is changing all the time, I will be ok in a while, let's go." They all turned and left for the car in the upper car park over the road.

On top of the car park and they went to the outer wall to see the plane that Winnie was on board to see her off and Lennox was keeping an eye on the tail of each plane to see if it was her plane, he was looking out for a German plane as she was going to Frankfurt to catch her connection, the first went up and Lennox said "No that's not her but this is about the time she had for take-off according to the monitor in the airport." Shirley says "Oh they never take off on time, don't worry." Danny looking very down said "Things in an airport are so final aren't they?" Jeff "What do you mean Dan?" Danny replies "Well you go in there to the TERMINAL, then you leave in the FINAL DEPARTURE LOUNGE, if that is not final what is and leaving Winnie there was not nice. Jeff with smile on his face says "Yes I see what you mean and I am worried that her plane has not taken off yet it is ten minutes overdue, I wonder if she has gone for political asylum or something. I have a funny feeling about this Dan." Lennox "Just what I was thinking Jeff she has got to the plane I know and said she Is not leaving and is in a room in the back of the airport somewhere, I know it, wait what is this taking off …. It's Australian and this one waiting is French something has happened I know it." Shirley "Ha, ha, calm down you lot, I bet there is a back log of planes waiting, calm down." They all waited for a while and all of a sudden Lennox cried out "Here it is, here it is, she has taken off now I can rest in peace." Shirley and Jeff sounded just as excited and Danny said "You rotten lot she is breaking her heart and you lot are cheering." Lennox composed himself and said "No we are not cheering just relieved she is going home to her homeland not that we wanted her gone Danny." Danny "No of course not." Jeff "Oh c'mon Danny you wanted her gone and don't say otherwise I heard you the other day, yes she is going." Danny "Yes your right, but when it came down to it I wanted her to stay and next week if she had I would be saying again I wanted her gone, I can't live without her and find it hard to live with her, never mind as long as she is ok that is all that Matters, I really do love her and never knew it, let's go home is it?" They all get in the car looking solemn and they drove back to the college and Danny hardly spoke all the way home and Jeff and Danny had tea in the refectory and went up to the bar for a few pints.

Standing by the bar and Jeff spoke first "Well that's another one of the original people who started here with us gone, she will be allright you wait and see, is she phoning you when she gets home?" "Yes she said she would but that will be day after tomorrow, she has got a long way to go, I hope she is happy from now on, I feel as if I let her down Jeff it's an awful feeling, I could have done things better for her matey." "Don't be daft how could you? She had her mind made up about anything before you suggested anything to her, no one could tell her what is to be done, she had a mind of her own and no one could change it she was a determined woman and you or no one else would get her to do anything she did not want to do. She was stubborn and that was that so don't think otherwise and you know it you did all you could for that girl and she threw it back in your face sometimes, well most of the time really so don't feel bad Dan." "Your right Jeff a hell of a girl and I will never forget her as long as she is ok from now on I will be happy." "Exactly Dan, she will be allright I know it, I feel sorry for anyone who crosses her I do, right drink up it's my round matey, I need a few after today what a trip and Lennox was worrying at the airport mind." "Yes he was, I was expecting her to walk back out of the door mind and still be here now, that would not have surprised me one bit." "Nor me, in fact I would have put money on it, maybe she is in a police station in London as we speak ha, ha, ha." "You could be right, so we have got 2 weeks off soon and look out Swindon I am coming up for a week and I am looking forward to seeing Josh for a while again, I miss him mind he is growing up fast and I will see that little one of yours who always picks on me when I am eating so look out and the Welsh boys will be in the Polish club waiting for some of my jokes and we can get on the sherbets for a night and look out the women of Swindon I am about to arrive, lock up your daughters." Jeff smirks and says "You don't stand a chance up there matey they are fussy and eat Welshmen for dinner." "They will not be able to resist me you wait and see, god it's dead in here isn't it? I think we should hit the town matey and try and find somewhere that is alive like a karaoke or something, I miss her, Winnie I mean." "Good idea Dan I will get my coat and finish this beer and go somewhere else, where shall we go?" "I don't know, where do you fancy going?" Jeff replies "Rose and Crown "." Danny looking serious says "I knew you were going to say that because it is where Geraldine lives and she drinks in there, I am not stupid mate." "Yes to both statements, yes Geraldine maybe there and yes you are stupid, I will get a taxi, let's go." They drink up and off they go.

At the Rose and crown and as you guessed it Geraldine was there and a little worse for wear. Jeff ran up to her and said "Well hello gorgeous hows you then? Fancy seeing you here? I thought I had died and gone to heaven." Geraldine slurred "Jeffrey hello how are things? And Danny the gorgeous Welshman hello." She grabbed the lads and gave them a huge kiss and said "I am a little bit drunk how are you? And my little Jeffrey is still here and Dan and I heard Winnie left this morning, I bet you are relieved Dan?" Danny "A bit of both really, I will miss her mind and I really did love her, what am I saying I still love her, you are lucky Jeff is still here for you." Geraldine sarcastically says "Don't I know it? He is like a love sick puppy isn't he ha, ha, ha." Jeff "I heard that gorgeous." Ger. "I know you did, not much gets passed you." Jeff "How are you so tipsy then Ger?" Ger. Smiling says "Because I may have a new man in my life, I don't know yet but it is looking promising if you know what I mean?" Jeff looking a little surprised said "Really, is it someone from the college? Do I know him?" Ger. "Yes you know him I think, he works there and no I am not telling you his name so don't ask." Jeff "So he is an older man then? You should stick with someone your own age like me, it will end up in tears Ger. Be careful." Ger. "Well you are wrong there he is the same age as me or maybe a little younger so stick that in your pipe and smoke it and I know he fancies me and I will not let it start if I think he is going to hurt me so don't worry." Danny says "Don't mind him Ger he has a soft spot for you and he will not like any other man who makes a move on you so don't listen to him." Jeff snaps "Oh shut up dodgy, I am serious he is just after one thing I expect just like most men." Ger. "I hope your bloody right…. I need some of that too so leave it Jeff he is a nice man and you don't know him so don't make aspersions until you know him, thank you but I expected you to be like this and you know I love you dearly but you are not my type and it is never going to happen with me an you so stop it now." Danny says "Yes Jeffrey you don't stand a chance so get over it ha, ha, she is not in love with you and she is in love with someone else, time for you to look elsewhere just like me matey and besides Jo is back soon so concentrate on that and leave Geraldine alone." Jeff "Dodgy you are a Pratt sometimes, so Ger. who is he then? It does not make a difference to me who he is." Ger. "Then you don't need to know then do you? I am keeping it in my hat until I know it is going to happen and I hope you will wish us luck if it happens and not be like a child over it?. Look Jeff I love you in my own way and don't need you trying to upset the apple cart so please be happy for me and let me get on with my life, things are bad enough struggling with my eyesight without anyone nagging at me from afar please be happy for me." Jeff looks at the ground and sighs "Sorry Ger. I have always had a soft spot for you and a hard one sometimes, ha, ha, but I would not hurt you for the world you know that so I hope you are going to be happy with what's his name when it happens and if it don't let me comfort you, so what's his name ?" Ger. smiling stares at Jeff and says "I am not going to tell you so forget it Jeff, I am not stupid ha, ha, ha, Danny take him home he is driving me nuts or take him to another pub and let me sit here happy as a march hare." Danny "Ok Ger, Jeff are you going to shut up or are we leaving? she is happy and nothing you can do is going to make it any different so get over it and stop asking questions please and get the beer in it's your round and I think we will be helping Geraldine up the road to her house later." Ger. "No you won't I will be allright to get home later I have been in worse states than this so don't worry." Jeff "Do you want a drink then Ger?" Ger replies "Yes please, a vodka please mate." Danny "Well I think he knows where he stands now but you were a bit hard on him, he is a good friend to you and I think he knows he don't stand a chance with you so go easy on him Ger, he is easily hurt by women." "Yes I was a little hard on him, I will make it up to him when he gets back, but he had to be told straight he will not listen to me if I am not nasty, now he knows ." "I know what you mean I had to be like that to Winnie she would not listen now I hate myself for it and I was so upset when she left, I didn't think I was going to be that bad, another page of my life is over now, i will find it strange just like when we all leave the college and are on our own again." "Yes I agree but I will have my new man with a bit of luck, do me a favour tell Jeff how it is when you get him alone." "Yes of course I will and he will be allright when Jo is back here if she gets the job and I can't see that going anywhere mind but it is a stop gap for him. He will find somebody someday and I hope I will too one day." "Oh you will you have got a lot going for you, you just need time to get used to everything, you will be allright I am sure of that if I am sure of anything that is It."

Later in the college lounge and Danny and Jeff walk in and there was no one there and Danny sat there while Jeff went to the toilet and get some cans and Danny was pondering on not having Winnie there as she usually is and he looked lost, then Jeff walked in and said "Right dodgy, only 4 tinnies left I am afraid it's not going to be a late night." "Jeff, sh, sh, sh, ..." "What is it? I can't hear anything." "I know no Winnie, it is so quiet she really has gone, it is not real I am so used to her picking on me or rather being sarcastic to me and I am going to miss that, it's not the same is it?" "Now you mention it your right it is not normal for us, I am usually going off for a ciggy now because you 2 are at each other's throat by now remember, oops, time for a ciggy, never mind Dan she will be happy for being here and will appreciate it one day but I will miss her too, your right she was one on her own." "She certainly was a gorgeous woman and so nimble and fit, I must be mad letting her get away but she was a problem woman and had strange ways and her culture was a permanent hard thing to get on with, bless her ha, ha, ha." "Do you think you will get used to not having her around?" "Who? Ha, ha, ha, ha." Jeff burst into laughter and says "Ha, ha, ha, I knew you were going to say that, I know what you mean mind I will miss Geraldine now she has got someone else, I never thought she would find someone mind but I will just have to get used to it." "Yes matey we will both have to get on with our lives and miss the ones we loved so much, I will always remember Winnie as long as I live, she was extraordinary indeed and a compliment to the Chinese nation and I will raise my can to that lovely lady, goodbye Winnie I love you so much and I will miss you." Danny starts crying and Jeff tries to comfort him as Danny really loves her and wants her back in his arms and it was not going to happen.

CHAPTER 15
ANOTHER LIFE BEGINS

Jeff and Danny had got back from the 2 weeks off and were recovering from a boozy fortnight and Jeff starts his job this very morning and he is sitting talking to Zarrine in the lounge as Danny comes in "Here is that bloody dodgy Welshman, he is a drunk Zarrine, he led me astray when he came up to Swindon, now I am suffering and start my new job here today and I am supposed to be aware as I have to take care of some new people visiting here to see if they would like to come here to do a course. It's his fault." Zarrine slaps Jeff's arm and says "Jeffrey don't be silly he does not have to make you drink, you can do that on your own, so be quiet." Danny "Yes you tell the English git Zarrine, he is always blaming me and if he can't handle the drink he should join the girl guides, he is hopeless he really is and I hope you are bringing the lovely girls here for me to inspect? I need a woman that fit's my lifestyle Jeff do your best." Jeff smiling says "I don't think there is any of them likes ratting but I will ask and you never know there might be one for me ha, ha, ha." Danny "She would have to be desperate. Zarrine "Right you pair let it go now and stop it, I had to have you pair left didn't I? Anyone but you pair." The lads laughed and Danny said "Zarrine you love us really." Zarrine "Do i? you pair give me a headache sometimes and my hair is going white because of you 2 but I am glad you are still here and Niel is back for a little while so there will be the 3 of you from next week and here is my favourite girl Mandy, are you allright Mandy?" Mandy with huge smile says "Yes thank you, still having trouble with these pair then I see?" Zarrine "Oh yes, still." Jeff "I am taking your job over this week Mandy, is it easy or what?" Mandy "Yes, it is and you will get used to it soon enough but they will make you run about a bit mind, that's why I have stopped to finish off my course and get up with Tim to live, I can't wait." Danny "How is Tim?" Mandy "Oh he is fine, getting back into work with his best friend who has got a company building barge boats for tourists to live in, he is enjoying it too." Danny "Good enough for him he needs something like that and he will enjoy it. It won't be long now for the wedding aye?" Mandy "No only a few months now It will be here before we know it, I am already panicking ha, ha, and Tim just takes it in his stride, you men are all the same." Danny "Oh don't say that in front of river we are not all men ha, ha, you will be alright you two were made for each other." Jeff "Yes he is right and Danny is the only one on the single seat now as Jo came back this morning and he is the odd one out now, I expect they all are staying away from the dodgy Welshman, they know what he is like." Zarrine "Hey Jeffrey don't say that about my Danny he is taking his time you wait and see, he will find someone one day soon." Jeff "Yeah and pigs will fly, I think he should give Winnie a ring and see if he can go over there and live with her." Mandy "Oh Jeffrey, don't be so nasty to him." Danny "I don't listen to that cockney git Mandy he talks rubbish all the time." Zarrine "Have you heard from her yet?" Danny "No I haven't but it is Imminent I expect, I just hope she is allright." Jeff "Right here comes another Welsh person, hi Lynne how are you babe?" A lovely quiet spoken Welsh voice came over and said "Oh hello Jeff, yes I am fine thank you. Hello Zarrine and Mandy and I am sorry I don't know your name but I am Lynne pleased to meet you." Danny sprang up in his seat and said "Well hello, I am Danny I heard we had a lovely Welsh lady here and I have been dying to meet you, hello." Lyn says "Hello Danny I have heard a lot about you, I hope it's not all true?" Danny with shocked look says "Well that depends what you heard, I hear I am not in luck anyway as your married aren't you?" Lyn replies "Yes I am thank you ha, ha, I am going to have a piece of toast, see you all later." She goes off to the kitchen and Danny sighs "She sounds lovely, just the type of girl to take home to meet your mother, so Zarrine what does she look like? I get the idea she is a stunner?" Zarrine smiles and says "Well she is petite and pretty and small with a divine body as you men would say but she is married Danny so behave." Danny's smile turns to being serious "I know just my luck, she sounds lovely, bloody hell I give up." Jeff "The only thing wrong with the girl is she is Welsh ha, ha, only kidding mate she is a stunner mind for her age and she is still younger than you, you dozy Welshman." Danny "Zarrine I am going to give him a clip if he don't stop calling me things, the English git as he is." Zarrine "Right you pair get to lectures and stop it before I start on the pair of you." Mandy says "You tell them Zarrine, they know who the boss is." Danny "What do you mean I am the boss here, Zarrine told me I could be." Jeff "Right I am off to my new job, I have been told there are 4 new ones coming to have a look at the place tomorrow and 3 of them are women Dan so keep your pecker up matey there may be a Welsh sheep in amongst them for you." Jeff leaves and Danny went into the kitchen to have a cup of tea and see this lovely Welsh girl, he speaks to her "So Lynn where in Wales do you arise from?" Lyn says "Oh I am from Mountain Ash and you?" "Bridgend, I have been in Mountain Ash, my son used to train up there on the astro pitch for the Welsh football team it's nice there now they have closed the coke ovens there and I used to go to Aberammon to the kings head pub years ago, they used to have heavy music nights there with the bands I mean." "I know the kings arms I have been there it has changed now mind not so noisy and I have not been there for years now, I hope this place has not changed much as I have been here before? I also went to the manor house Torquay, I seen Jeff there and Rhoda I never seen you there." "No I was not allowed to go there for some reason, I missed out there and do you know Niel David? He went there, he is in this hall too." "The name rings a bell I think so he has got a guide dog has he?" Danny "Yes Abby she is a lovely dog a German shepherd." Danny smiles and she smiles back and he says "So are you a happily married woman Lyn? Or do I stand a chance?" "Danny I wondered if I heard about you was right and I know it is now ha, ha, I am off to my lectures see you later, bye." See left and Danny looked dejected and went back into Mandy and Zarrine and they both said together "Awe never mind." Danny looking shocked said "What? What? Do you think I am trying too hard? Ha, ha, ha." Zarrine "Poor Danny, you are missing Winnie I am sure but it will happen one day." Danny "Awe , I am only kidding I am ok by myself for now, I don't need any woman complicating things, I need a woman who makes life easy to live with, no complications and they don't exist, so I am as happy as a Sam boy whatever that means?" Mandy "Never mind look at me and Tim it happened and I am not that young neither is Tim, it will happen one day as you have always said there is someone out there for everyone and it will be that way for you one day, I am off to lectures, see you both." She leaves and Danny sit's by Zarrine and he smiles and says " Can you have me for a while Zarrine? I won't be naughty I promise, you love me don't you?" Zarrine smiling "Yes Danny I love you as long as I don't have to take you home with me, I am with my peter and he would be upset I think ha, ha, it is a lovely day the sun is out and a crisp start good for September so off to your lecture, I have got to get Niel's room ready see you later." They both go their own ways.

That evening and Danny and Jeff in the student bar and it seemed puzzling as the new S. S. W's were there and it was noisy as they were all excited about the whole adventure and they were all from different lands and young and all drinking to get used to each other. Jeff looking daggers at one of them and said to Danny "My god Dodgy you should see this one she is gorgeous, she has a small skirt on, red lipstick on and high heels, she is stunning and very young. Flipping hell she is making me very excited, she has lovely legs and everything in the right place, god matey, phew." "Ha, ha, calm down Jeffrey you will have a coronary if your not careful, is she as nice as Lidia or Winnie or what?" "Younger and nicer mind you they had a body to dye for but this one is sexy, the way she dresses, I hope she dresses like that on the day when she is on duty, my god it will be brilliant I will not want to go home and they tell me there is another one here who is from Italy, she has got huge tit's apparently and is also a stunner, I can't wait." "Steady Jeff, steady matey I mean it, it is not good for a man your age." "Yeah, yeah, I am not as old as you matey so leave it there." "I wonder if we will get a piece of that action, I wouldn't bet on it, we will get to meet them eventually and you will be on all 3's for a while, I wonder how many more students have started? I heard a man called Arthur he had an awful Africana accent it was awful, he is here for a year and we will find out the rest maybe tonight, let's hope there are some decent ones." "It does not Matter to me I have got Jo starting here this week so I am spoken for." "The poor girl I feel sorry for her the poor mare, so where is she tonight then?" "Sorting her room out tonight, I will see her tomorrow night" Danny sniggers and says "No change there then, she would rather be working than be with you." "No , no , she would rather be with me but she needs the rest after being with me for an hour or two ha, ha, ha." "Right it's time for a pint mate go for it mate." Jeff went up to the bar and got the beer and returned and said "Bloody hell man she is so fit, she was rubbing her ass up against my leg she is hot and Lyn just walked in, she will be here for a drink now and Niel is back, she said he was and he is on the way over." "Oh good he is a lad mind." Lyn came and sat by the lads and her guide dog was sitting by her and she said "There is a lot of noise over by the bar with them students, they are very excited aren't they?" Jeff replies "Yes they are the new S. S. W's and they are having a good night before the serious work starts and how are you Lyn?" "I am fine thank you Jeff and how are you both?" Danny " I am fine now I have seen you Lyn but I am aware I am not Important to you ha, ha, I am only joking." "Lyn stunned says "I am sorry you feel like that Danny but I am always aware of men with your chat up lines." Jeff "See dodgy she knows you already and she has only just arrived." Danny "Well I can hear him the man from uncle it's Niel David, hello matey how are you?" Niel "I am fine, nice to see you all, I didn't think I was coming back but don't get excited I am not here for long just a few weeks." Jeff "Thank god for that, I was concerned that you were going to stay and 3 bloody Welsh people is too much for me, only kidding matey, it's nice to see you back and do you know Lyn?" Niel "Yes I met her earlier and don't remember her in the manor mind, I bet that place has seen some things? It was a den of iniquity." Lyn "Was it? I missed that damn, I have enjoyed it there mind shame it had to close down because I loved it there ." Danny "I was never offered to go there, I missed out by the looks of it." Niel "You, you would have shagged yourself to death up there It was a knocking shop." Lyn "It wasn't that bad Niel your exaggerating now Danny it was not any worse than here." Jeff "Do you think so, I liked it there but it was a lot of fun just like here, ah look out here comes my little swamp frog." Up comes Jo and Jeff kisses her and says "Hello hows you then?" Jo says to Jeff "I am fine thank you and I heard Danny and Niel, allright lads?" Both men said hello and then Jo asked "And who is this lady? Is it one of your wives or girlfriends?" Niel "No this is Lyn, she has started here this week." They both say hello and Danny said "She wants me but she is afraid of me ha, ha, ha." Lyn replies "Ha, ha, don't listen to him Jo he is in a fantasy world." Jo "Aren't they all?" Niel "Hey, there is no need for that ha, ha, you have upset Danny now and I have feelings you know." Jeff "The truth hurts, so hows my girl then? Out for the night aye?" Jo "Only for a glass of lager and then I am off to bed, I am tired tonight, sorry." Jeff looking dejected says "Oh right, so shall I come over to tuck you up in bed or what?" Jo smiling says "Or what? I am really tired and am having a bath and bed early so you just as well have a few pints with these trouble makers and of course Lyn." Jeff looking upset says "Allright then I will and I will come over after breakfast in the morning." Jo "Yes ok I will have had my beauty sleep by then and you can make me breakfast if you like." Jeff "Right." Danny "So Lyn do you want a drink?" Lyn "No I am fine thank you anyway." Danny "Jo what about you anything for you?" Jo "Nothing thank you." Danny asks Mandy and she also refused. Danny "Ok, just us 3 then I am off to the bar." He goes off to the bar and gets the drinks as he was there a funny little man in a foreign accent attacks him excitedly and says "You Danny I think?" Danny amazed said "Yes I am and you are?" "I am Ricardo, you know my aunty Lidia she told me to see you for help.." Danny "Well goodness me, how is she in Peru?" Ricardo says "She ok yes." Danny "Yes we can speak another day when the music is quieter ok?" Ricardo "Yes ok Danny I look for you ok?" He shakes Danny's hand and goes off back to his friends. Danny gets to the bar and the gorgeous girl is there and she says to Danny "Hello the man behind the bar says you live in Dowdell is this true? And if so what time do they get up there in the mornings?" Danny replies "Oh yes my name is Danny and what is your name??" "My name is Marge I come from Holland." "Well hello Marge It is nice to meet you and as regards the time to get up it is up to you depends what you are doing that day." "Oh right, I don't have nothing tomorrow so I can lay on in bed then?" Danny says "Yes of course you can, what room are you in?" "C16." "Oh you are on the same floor as me and my mate Jeff over there, actually you are next door to him, he will be thrilled and you will keep him on his toes, he likes a nice young girl next door." Madge "Oh I have a boyfriend back in Holland so he is too late and I love my boyfriend." "Don't panic he is a nice guy, he has a girlfriend anyway but he loves all women and is harmless an you will like him, nice to meet such a nice girl from Holland, well got to take my drinks back nice meeting you I hope to see more of you, bye." "Yes goodbye Danny, I will see you." Danny smiling all over his face said to Jeff as soon as he got back "Jeffrey I have great news for you, that beauty by the bar you keep on about is staying next door to you in Dowdell." There was a silence and Jeff says "Who me I am not asking about any girl what are you on about? I think you are stirring the shit for me in front of Jo so stop it." Danny "Oh right sorry." Jeff "Don't listen to that heathen dodgy he is always like that as you know." Jo "He is only teasing you Jeff don't take it so serious, I am off then see you all tomorrow. " She goes off and Jeff leans over the table and says to Danny "Is she really staying next door to me? Really is she?" Danny looking serious "No I was only kidding ha, ha, ha." Jeff's face drops and he let's out a huge sigh "Bastard." Danny "Jeff I am teasing she is staying next door to you honestly." Jeff excited says "I will go to the foot of our house, she is, I can't wait I will take her breakfast in the morning and get into her knickers as fast as I can, sorry Lyn and Mandy I forgot you were there." Lyn "That's allright don't mind me." Niel "And what about Jo?" Jeff "She won't mind sharing me around and I can handle a good couple of women no problem." Danny "Now for the bad bit." Jeff looking concerned "What? What? She is a lesbian or something, I don't mind." Danny "No she has got a boyfriend back in Holland, she is Dutch and she is very much in love with him." Jeff "Oh is that all, no problem she can share herself about between us both I won't tell him no problem, I will explain this to her." Niel "God Jeff you are so sure she will give in to you, I think you will be disappointed Jeff." Lyn "I know, listen to him it is as if it is a four-gone conclusion, she is his as he clicks his fingers." Danny "I know, he keeps saying he is the Adonis of Swindon maybe he really thinks he is ay Jeff?" Jeff "She will not be able to resist my charm you wait and see, she will be putty in my hand." Lyn "Nothing like confidence is there?" Danny "And I met Lidia's nephew over there also, he is nice and a lot of fun." Just then Niel said "Shit I forgot I have not had my insulin, I am off see you guys later I will be back." Lyn "Well, well, Niel you will be ill, we have got a full hall now with us on the third floor so it's nearly all girls except for you, Jeff, CJ, Matt and Niel, outnumbered so watch it." Jeff "I won't argue with you there I like being surrounded by women, send me more I say." Danny looking sad "It's ok being surrounded by them but it is better surrounding them in the bed." Lynn tutted " I was waiting for that I knew you were going to say that for some reason " Danny " I got it on the brain lately since WINNIE left and am alone, Lynn don't you feel sorry for me at all " Lynn going red " Danny now stop it please you are married too " Jeff " yes but she is divorcing him as we speak so it does not count, right Dan? " Jeff " this is the last one for me I have students to show around tomorrow so I must be aware " Danny " oh yes, I forgot all about them I wonder if there are any nice girls with them , you must bring them over to show me if there is mind you promised remember " Jeff " yes ok I will but I don't know who is coming " Lynn " I hope there are some nice fella's too mind we must not hog it all, I mean why not ha, ha, " Danny " you are happily married " Lynn " I can still look can't I " Danny " are you trying to make me jealous or what? " " " Danny don't be silly " Danny " yes Jeffrey it is all over we know that but no single woman in here does " Lynn " never mind there are a lot of new ones coming soon this week and there may be one for you " Jeff " she would have to have a guide dog to go out with him ha, ha, and very old to put up with his moaning " Danny " cheeky git, I am only miserable when I am waiting for you to get the beer in, so that is very often ha, ha, " Lynn " let me get these in please and get one in for Niel " Danny " no your allright Lynn you don't have to do that we have not got you a drink as you don't drink so we will stay alone as it is only fair but thanks anyway " " right I am off to the bar " Danny was sitting on his own and started muttering to himself " god I got to sort myself out I am so lonely but never mind she is out there somewhere I just haven't met you yet " in the meantime Jeff had returned and said " sorry, what was you saying? " Danny looking sad " awe nothing, I was talking to myself, as per usual " Jeff " oh dear are we feeling sorry for one's self " " " yes I suppose so, I am getting a little fed up on my own all of the time and don't think I am going to find anyone but never mind I will make it all on my own, no problem " Lyn " oh I think it will happen when you least expect It and I can't see you being alone for very long " Danny " well thanks Lynn so there's hope for me yet " Lynn " don't go there Danny ha, ha, ha, " " " fair enough I will let it go now and hope you are right in what you are saying, see you both tomorrow " Danny slugged his pint down and left as Niel was sitting down Niel said " your off are you? " Danny " yes I am having a early night as I will need my strength for tomorrow, as Jeff is bringing some nice new women over to see me so I must look my best " Jeff " he is going to iron his wrinkles out " Danny looked sideways at Jeff and said " goodnight all " Danny leaves and Lyn says " god he don't give up trying does he? " Jeff " he thinks he can snap his fingers and all the women will fall over him and he is a little down this year, he has had a terrible time of it lately, if it was me I think I would have topped myself by now but he will be ok " Lyn " what do you mean? he seems happy to me " Niel " well he has been married 4 times all have failed, he lost his first son at 7 months old, his first love was killed by a car, his father and mother died young, in December 1999 he went blind overnight then in 2 001his brother who was mentally retarded had a massive heart attack and died, then last year in January 2 years later his younger brother died of alcoholic problems and he was a massive wreck, he is now on his own as his wife is divorcing him and he Is one of 2 out of six left of his family and he has not had much to do with his brother who lives miles away from him so he is on his own,

418

so what do you think of that as a bit of luck? " Lynn " oh my god, he must be a mess in his head " Jeff " well I promised not to say anything but he is having counselling in this college and is getting better through it, I was so concerned about him when his brother died last year and kept an eye on him that's how serious I was concerned and I hope he meets somebody soon for his sake, or I fear the way he drinks he will not be long " Niel " serious, I didn't think things were that bad, but he is made of stern stuff " Lynn " maybe but you don't know what is going on in his head, he must be in torture in his head after all of that the poor man I hope he finds someone or something to distract him from all his tragedy and so why is his wife divorcing him then? " Niel " not clear he says it's because he has gone blind and he even forgives her as he thinks she would not have married him if he was blind, so it's ok if she leaves him but he has since found out she is carrying on with a man who came to do some work for them and he is an alcoholic and he is concerned about his young son not his divorce he must be in torment in his head " Lyn "she must be a real bitch then, the cow " Niel " no she is a real nice person really I can't understand It, she loved him to bit's until he became ill and then she changed and I think he is right it's because of what happened to him that caused it so I will not condemn her I get on with her and she is a lovely girl and he would not do anything to harm her " Jeff " it's a funny world and cruel with it and I know Danny will get passed this one way or the other and he will not want anyone feeling sorry for him, as he will admit that losing his so called friends in his village hurt him the most when he went blind so now he has made some good friends here who will stand by him always " Lyn " it's funny we all have stories to tell about how we all got into this situation and no one gets to hear it as we don't think they would care about it but we speak to each other, then we realise how sad it really is and this only happens with the blind people and when you think about it we feel silly if we are asked to tell our story so we don't " Niel " yes that's true I lost my dad and mum and that killed me I can't Imagine how he really feels so I can't complain and on that note I am heading home as I must be sensible for my lecture tomorrow goodnight, or are you coming back? " Jeff and Lyn said they would be going back with Niel and off to bed they went.

It was the next day and Danny and Jeff were in the refectory and Danny was holding a tape in his hand he had received through the post and an envelope covered in stamps from China. Jeff asked him what it was, Danny replied "A taped message from Winnie, I guess, I have not listened to it yet but I have also got my tape machine on me so when we go and sit on the bench over by Dowdell I will play it for us to listen to." Jeff "I might have to go to the toilet first as this curry is going to go straight through me I think, god it's rough, my ass is not going to like this I know." "That's why I had the fish because the last time I had that my ass went down in the toilet for a drink it was that hot, well never mind we are eating." "Yes thanks too much information thanks, I am sweating here and I feel like I am going to pass out, phew." "So the interns have not turned up yet then? I thought they would be here by now." "They are due as we speak, I will fetch them over for a cuppa at 3 o'clock." "Right, I will give them marks out of ten, Niel was laughing this morning at you and Jo he said to me where was Jo last night i thought she was going out with Jeff? I said she is in youth club, he found that hilarious and is still laughing now and when he chuckles he chuckles, he is so funny when he got a laugh on." Jeff laughs and says "Ha, ha, very funny, I am not seeing Jo for a few days as she is having a few nights in to swat up on her new job, as she is having some problems settling in so I have got to stay away until she is sorted but I must make sacrifices if I am to get my wicked way I suppose ha, ha, ha." Danny says "So we will be out on the razz again this week will we?" Jeff nodding his head "No, I will stay in like a good boy I am not going to go out without her sorry matey that's it." "Right I can go out with Niel and he will get his round in without any arguments at least so I will see you next week in the bar then." "Only kidding, can you see me staying in? C'mon it's me you are talking to, she does not drink much anyway and she goes to bed early anyway, so I will be there." "Ok then say what you mean, I am not one to keep waiting you know so speak up are you coming then?" Jeff looking sarcastically at Danny says "Yes I am coming and smile, take a joke." "Yeah, yeah, yeah." The lads go off to listen to the tape from Winnie in private. On the bench on a lovely autumns day in the sunshine and they sat waiting for the tape to start and Winnie's voice says "Hello Danny I am back here in Lang Chow province in China and I was very upset when we came over China on the airplane, I started crying it was very emotional for me to return without you , I am missing you very much, I started to get upset in Frankfurt Germany and had a horrific travel back here. I am now sitting in my house and don't know what to do next, I feel like my life is over and can't focus on anything as I miss you so very much. I can't wait to come back to England to see you and hope it will be soon, I love you Danny and will speak soon, here is my new number and mobile number, please send me yours so I can call you from time to time." The lads sat there in silence for a few minutes and Danny said "She is an amazing girl and can speak as if it is a movie, she really knows how to touch my heart strings and did you hear the peacocks in the background and the other birds singing it is like she is in a aviary, very touching." "So what are you going to do? Are you going to send her your number or what?" "Of course I am, I cannot desert her now, I am concerned about her even if I know it will never happen with her, I still love her in my own way and she is pretty and has a fantastic body why not? Sorry, that sounds callous, I love her as a good friend and will remain her friend and will speak to her until it dies out, she sounded very sad mind?" "Yes she sounds as if her life has come to an end, I hope she don't do anything silly." "She won't she is too level headed for that I am sure of that." The lads grabbed a can of lager out of Jeff's bag and sat there for a few minutes and Jeff said "It's a lovely day isn't it? I could sit here all day but I will only get pissed on this lager." "Go away with you, no one can get drunk with this rubbish only you." "Remember matey I kept up with you in the barrels last mother's day even though I spent 2 days in bed afterwards and I am less than half your size." "And your head was smashed up as if you had had a fight ha, ha, that was so funny I don't think I have laughed so much ha, ha, ha." "Yes it was a bit of a disaster as regards my head, head butting the bar was not a good thing, look out the squiggly girl is coming." Kezz walking bye said "Aha, it's Jeff and Danny or should I say Danny and Barbara? Ha, ha, I can smell lager can't i?" Jeff "You certainly can and we have only got one each so I am sorry but you can have a swig of mine if you like?" Danny "Here Kezz you can have mine, I don't want it I can't drink this afternoon, ugh." Kezz "Thank you Danny, I have not got any lectures for a hour so I will enjoy this can ha, ha, ha." Jeff "Well I must be off I think those new arrivals will be here by now and so I had better get over there." Kezz "They just arrived and gone into the refectory Jeff so you have got some time yet." Danny was about to ask Kezz something and then realised "I was going to ask you what they are like but you can't see them can you either?" Kezz "No I can't but they sound a lot of fun and there is a girl who is loud her voice carries through the building, I expect they will be up the bar tonight and there is a karaoke up there again so I will be singing, eek, eek, give me an eek Jeff." Jeff "No I am off sorry, see you both later." Jeff went off and there was a silence for a while and then Kezz spoke up "Danny can I ask you something?" "Of course you can little squiggle." "I Have always been blind and have asked this question many times and never got a good answer so tell me, what is water like? I mean what does it

420

look like? And why does it run through your hands? And what colour is it? It feels funny and there is a lot of it in the world so I am told." Danny looking puzzled and rubbing his chin says "Well, I, well, that is a hard question, well it is transparent like a window or glass you can see through it so no colour if you put your hand in it and looked at it you could still see your hand but you know the water is there and if you wash your hands it goes dirty so you can't see through it so easy, yet if you didn't have it you would die, it is a little magical like you." "What do you mean like me?" "Well you are different and special and not another like you, you are unique nothing else like you just like water." "Ha, ha, banging, banging, I am off now see you later Mr Welshman." "Bye Kezz I will listen to your singing tonight, sock it to me girl, bye."

Sometime later at 3 o'clock in the afternoon and Danny was in the lounge waiting for Jeff to bring the future interns in to see what they were like and in there with him was Niel and he was on the phone to his wife "Yes ok babe I will send it off when I get home, I am fine and Danny is in here with me so I will have to watch what I am saying to you, his ears are flapping as we speak." Danny spoke up "Is that, that lovely girl you are married to? I have a thing for her, it's in my pocket." "Did you hear that Ceri? He has got something in his pocket for you …. Ha, ha, she said that you can keep it in your pocket too I am the only man for her." Danny "She is only saying that." "Allright Ceri I will see you next weekend pick me up at 12.30, by love, bye." He puts the phone down and sat back in the arm chair. Danny enquires "How are they all down there?" "Fine, fine the boys are getting on with it and Ceri is missing me like a hole in the head ha, ha, ha." "That's why I stay out of the way when she comes up to give you a chance ha, ha, and you can have Angie now." "No thanks, any woman who does what she has done to you is not good to any man and you will never stand a chance with my woman so forget it and I bet you are waiting for those girls with Jeff to come over aren't you?" "Who me?" "Yes you, you bugger I am not daft they are late mind, perhaps Jeff has got them lost, he is not the brightest bulb in the box is he?" "You can say that again, he is late mind, I have got to go now or I will be in trouble, I am with Lennox this afternoon, stuff him he will have to wait I can hear them coming I think." "Yes that sounds like a load of women out there, they are taking the lift, I bet Jeff is knackered that's why, he is a lad isn't he, I bet he is trying to get into their knickers already." Danny smiles at the suggestion says "Without a doubt he is and if Jo finds out he will be on his ass with her, she will not take nonsense but I don't think she cares, I think she thinks it is a friendship nothing else, it's Jeff that takes it serious" ." "I know she laughs everything off and takes everything in her stride, look out they are coming in." They all pile in and Jeff introduces everyone "Right, this is Lucy, Anne, am I right?" They confirms this Jeff continues "Then this is another Jeff and last but by no means least is Inga, everyone these 2 degenerates are the 2 Welshman here Niel and Danny or dodgy." Everyone shakes hands and sits down and Danny says "Jeff don't make me any tea just do the others one." Jeff screws his face and says "Oh dear I can't make this amount of tea and coffee I need help." As he says this Inga jumps up and pushes her way to Jeff and says "I will help you Jeff, so what do everyone want to drink?" She takes their orders and grabs Jeff and he marches her into the kitchen. Niel says "God she is heavy with Jeff isn't she?" Danny looking shocked says "Just a little bit." Then Lucy chirps up "She has been like this all day with Jeff, I think she fancies him, he can't move for her." Other Jeff says "Yes she has, she is a nice girl mind but I think Jeff is in for a treat." Ann "Jeff, don't say that it's not nice." Danny "When it comes to Jeff it is fair he deserves everything he gets and is she pretty or what?" Jeff "Well gorgeous, I would not chuck her out of bed and a nice body to go with it, big boobs and firm." Lucy "Jeff we are still here you know ha, ha, sorry about Jeff." Niel "Good on you Jeff, just a lad like us and Jeff needs a woman he has been on his own for too long now, so let's hope he is lucky?" Danny "Yes I agree with you she is just right for him, so where do you all come from and are you all married?" Lucy "I am from Luton and I am engaged to be married to Jeff here." Anne "I am married and from Leeds." Danny looking dejected says "Right, crashed and burnt again , never mind, right I am finishing this coffee and I am off to my lectures." Niel "Right Dan never mind, out for a pint tonight or what?" Danny looking sad says "Has a centipede got 99 legs? I will be out with that daft cockney git out there if he is still free and by the sounds of it he is finished." Niel "You might be right there." Next thing Inga and Jeff comes in with the drinks and hands them about and Jeff says to Danny "Did I introduce you to Inga?" Danny "Yes you did, but I will shake your hand if you like Inga?" This she does and soon gets back to see what Jeff was doing and Danny says to Niel "Well no chance there, she is besotted by Jeff by the looks of it Dan, she will not leave him alone." Danny "Ha, ha, he is in for a treat by the looks of things, good for him." Anne "I think you are right he is in for something allright." Danny "Right I am off see you all tonight if you fancy it in the student bar? There is a karaoke up there." They all wish Danny goodbye and he went. Next thing Jeff sit's in Danny's seat and lo and behold Inga sit's next to him, so Niel says "So Inga where are you from then?" She replies "I am from Wolverhampton." Niel "h Nice and are you married or courting anyone?" Inga smiles and says "Well no I am not, why do you ask me that?" Niel almost chokes on his tea and replies fast "No, no, I am only asking I am happily married." Jeff chirps up "But there is Danny he is single and waiting for a woman to come along." Inga blanks this out and changes the subject "I am waiting for the right man and hope to find him here if I decide to come here." Jeff chirps up "As I said Danny is on his own and he can't help it he is Welsh." Niel "Steady Jeff I am here, I think you have got a thing for Jeff Inga haven't you?" Inga blushes and was about to say something and Jeff stepped in "It's no good I am going out with Jo." Niel smiling "In your dreams, she is not, she thinks you are her brother figure, so I repeat I think Inga has a thing for you, am i right Inga?" Inga giggles and said "Niel behave yourself and stop trying to embarrass me, I will put the cups in the kitchen." She gets up and gathers the cups and takes them in and washes them. Jeff snarling at Niel said "You are a shit stirrer aren't you? I don't know the girl." Niel says in reply "As if that has troubled you before, what's the Matter with you? You usually jump at the chance and don't tell me it's because of Jo because that's not the reason." Jeff "I just want to have a bit of peace and quiet for a while that's all." Lucy checks her watch and says "Look it's 1.30, aren't we supposed to be back in the room over the road Jeff?" Jeff presses his watch and replies "Yes we had better get back over there, are you all ready?" All answered except Inga who was still in the kitchen drying the cups so Jeff went in to get her and ended up helping with the drying and was a few minutes and when he came back into the lounge Lucy said "Right did you enjoy that Jeff and Inga?" Inga laughed and said "Oh Lucy stop it, your only jealous." They all laughed and Jeff looked sheepish and they left.

Later that evening in the lounge and Danny was sitting there and in crept Jeff and he whispered "Who's there?" Danny replied "Jeff, is that you? Why are you whispering?" "Has she left Dan?" "Has who left?" "Inga you idiot." "I have been in here for a while and I haven't seen her or heard her." "Good I have been avoiding her all night, if she comes in i am not here if I disappear all of a sudden ok?" "Fine, fine, I don't know what this is all about but I can guess, a real woman is actually interested in you and now with all the shock you don't know what to do." Jeff snapped "Oh shut up you don't know what you are talking about." Danny smiles and said "Let me guess, she is the one doing the chasing and you are worried and panicking about it as they usually refuse your advances, so am I right?" "You do talk a lot of crap sometimes don't you?" "So what's the Matter then with her? She seems a lovely girl nice boobs, nice figure not bad looking so what's the problem?" "Nothing I am spoken for as you rightly know." "Jo you mean, she is more like a sister to you, she thinks you are her father figure and her protector, she is too nice to have a little plonker like you as her long term boyfriend, she is much too young and you know as well as I do you will not be with her long, as soon as she finishes here you won't see her for dust." "Don't beat around the bush tell me straight why don't you, you don't know that for a fact." "I bloody well do and so do you and if her daddy said not to see you again she would drop you like a stone." "Shut up your getting on my nerves now." "Well I am going up for the karaoke later how about you?" "Don't you fancy going to the Pretty Pigs or the Rose and Crown for a change?" "Why because Inga will be up there is it? I am going up to listen to squiggly Kezz singing and have a pint up there." "Well do me a favour then?" "I don't know let's hear it first, I have a feeling I am not going to like this." "Will you get Inga off my back and ask her out if you think she has a nice body and nice boobs, you can have her I don't want to go out with her." "Then just tell her Jeff she can't kill you or anything, you have only known her for a day." "No, no, I can't I don't like hurting any girl so I will try and get you 2 together, please man." "I will entertain her and give her a good seeing to just for you as you are my friend, I might not like doing this mind but I will persevere", it's a messy job but somebody's got to do it." Jeff "Of course you will." "Only for you mind and if she never talks to you again that is not my fault." " Fair enough matey I will have to get on with it that's all." "Ok then I will do it so get some cans out I need a drink." "Right I will go and get some." Jeff toddles off and gets the cans and returns and Lyn was now with Danny in the lounge and Jeff thought it was Inga and stuttered "Oh hello do you want a can?" Lyn "No thank you Jeff I don't like cans." Jeff sighed with relief and said "Phew, I thought you were Inga." Danny "Don't ask Lyn it's a long story, Jeff has met a girl who loves him and he can't get used to it so he is panicking now." Lyn "Jeff you are a card and what does Jo think about this?" Jeff looking panicky says "Don't say nothing to her she does not know anything about this and besides it's all one sided so it's best not saying nothing." Lyn "Fair enough I will not say anything and leave other women alone ha, ha, ha." Jeff "I will don't you worry." Danny "Am I hearing things? You leave girls alone, are you turning queer or what?" Jeff snaps at Danny "No I'm bloody well not, I just don't want any trouble. Inga is lovely but not for me." Lyn "I don't understand you have a reputation for chasing any girl in a skirt and now you are telling me that the great Jeffrey is not interested in the female anymore? I don't believe that, there's something fishy about this Jeff so tell us what it is?" Jeff "It's nothing I just don't fancy her that's all, god can't I decide for myself." Lyn "Woo, throwing his toys out of the pram now." Danny smiling says "Yes your right Lyn he is, well I have seen you chasing girls who are ugly, huge in size and she is much better than most that you have been with." Jeff "Look it's just not right, I don't feel anything for her, I don't know why I just don't, c'mon let's go up the bar before I scream, see you Lyn." Lyn "Yes see you later and good luck." The lads go off to the bar, Jeff dreading what he will find up there and Danny smiling all over his face.

The lads walk into the student bar and in there was Inga and the other new students visiting the college and Jeff stands by the bar and yes you guessed it Inga was on him as fast as she could. She says "Hello Jeff I thought I was not going to see you tonight? I am sitting with the others over in the corner where you and Danny usually sit." Jeff replied "How do you know I sit there then?" Inga says "Because Niel is sitting over there and he said you sit there." Jeff mutters under his breath "Trust him." Inga "Pardon what did you say?" Jeff "Nothing, nothing, I don't suppose there is enough room now then for me and Danny, so we will stand here by the bar instead and I will see you later maybe" Inga "No there is 3 seats with your names on them so come on I will show you." Danny "Yes c'mon Jeffrey let's sit down." Jeff moves over to the seat and sits down and snarls at Niel, Niel says "What are you snarling at me for now?" Jeff smiles and said " Oh nothing Niel sorry, I was thinking out loud." Danny "Jeff don't be so grumpy, she is not doing nothing really just being nice to you, come on matey, cool it." Jeff "I know but I don't fancy my chances later she is going to hang on all night, look out she is back, allright Inga? Do you like the karaoke then?" Inga "Yes I do but I will not be singing, what about you?" Jeff "No I cannot sing no fear but here is a girl who can." Kezz "Eek, eek, hello all? I am up for it and Danny likes my singing don't you?" Danny "Yes she is the bestest singer here and the sexiest ha, ha, ha." Niel shouts "Yes your right Danny she is the best singer here, I don't know about sexy mind." Kezz "Ha, ha, ha, watch it Niel or I will get you to eek all night." Niel "Eek, eek." Kezz "Do a loud one Niel." Niel "No wait till I have a drink squiggle." Inga says "Who the hell is that?" Jeff "Oh that's our squiggly Kezz or Kerry, she is a nutter and loves singing and a good laugh." Inga "Nutter is the word I think, is she always like that?" Danny "Yes and that's why we love her and she can chuck a few pints down her too. She is amazing, wait until you hear her sing." Jeff "Here she goes now listen, her voice is very good, right ready for a pint dodgy?" Before Danny could say yes he grabbed his pint glass and left for the bar. Danny said to Inga "So what do you think of the college then?" "I love it here already and the people are nice too." "I know, I am having a drink at the lounge later in Dowdell do you fancy joining me?" "Will Jeff be there then?" Danny replies "No he will be over tucking his girlfriend in before he goes home if he gets back at all." Inga's face dropped and looked as if she could kill Danny, it was not what she wanted to hear. Inga snaps at Danny "I was told it was not serious between them just a friendly thing and why would he stay with her? She is staff and that is not allowed." Danny shrugging his shoulders said "I don't know I don't get involved with that sort of thing so what's the answer are you coming over for a drink with me later?" "No thanks, I have a early start in the morning." "Well thanks, you are supposed to have a good time as a student or you will fail the test as a student." "I will still give it a miss, no offence." Niel "Looks as if you crashed and burnt again Dan, oh dear I hope this never gets around as us Welshmen have a reputation to keep up." Inga "No offence Danny, I just don't fancy you at all, sorry." Danny sat back and had a face like thunder and says "No problem but if you are waiting for Jeff you will have a long wait." Inga "Why do you say that? Because I let you down, I am sorry I feel like that but no need to get offensive." Danny "Never mind forget it your loss, Niel I am coming to sit by you as it is not nice this side of the table." Inga frowned and Niel replied "No problem matey, dim problem, I have got a broad back, I can put up with you and there will be some more coming next week so don't worry about it mate, I didn't think Inga was your type anyway." Danny "Your not going to believe what I am going to say anyway, but here we go, Jeff asked me to get her off his back and ask her out and it has bounced back at me and smacked me in the mouth, serves my own right." Niel laughed and chuckled like he does replies "Well, well, I never, it has bit you on the bum that's what you get for helping a friend sometimes ha, ha, you know what it is like now and Jeff has not smiled since he got here, look out he is back and looking for you." Jeff "So where is he gone to now?" Inga "He has gone to sit by Niel over there." Jeff shouts "Dan, Dan, where are you? You dodgy Welshman." Danny calls him over, Jeff gave him his drink and said nastily "Why are you over here? You said you would ask her out and now you let me down." Danny interrupted and said "Wait a minute I just tried didn't I Niel?" Niel "Yes he certainly did and she blew him out without any reservation indeed, she made him look like a little tin soldier so he came and sat by me." Jeff looking annoyed says "Well you didn't try hard enough then did you?" Danny "I all but begged her, she has a thing about you I even told her you were going to see Jo later, that didn't faze her she just jumped down my throat, so that's it I can't do any more." Jeff "Oh great, what am I supposed to do now then?" Danny "That's your problem mate, I tried my best and if she refused me she must be hypnotised by you, why don't you come and sit by us and then she may get the message?" Jeff "I can't do that." Danny "Well sit by her and have a nice night, take her back to your room and give her a good seeing to and then marry her for goodness sake your getting on my tit's now, just do something get her pissed." Jeff "She is already half cut now I will finish that pint and sneak over here to sit, see you in a minute." He goes off and sits down by Inga and Niel talks to Danny "God he gets in a state, I can't understand this, he could give her one tonight she is only here for 3 days and Jo will never find out and then she is gone." Danny looking at the floor replies "I really don't care as long as I have not got to give her one, I don't want Inga the minga that's for sure." "Oh dear I sense a bit of bitterness, is this because she has blown you out? As you are now name calling, Inga the minga indeed ha, ha, I don't believe you sometimes and think of that poor sod he is stuck with her." Danny broke into a smile and says "I am annoyed because I nearly had a good shag with her and she has a nice body and I need one I really do so I feel let down and Jeff is refusing it. I can't believe my luck sometimes and that cockney git refuses it, well I am having a couple of pints and coming back with you and going to bed early." "I might stay till the end matey, so what makes you think I will go back early?" "Because you always do as you like your bed don't you? I can't hear Jeff he is drowned out by Inga and her mates, I bet he will be over in less than 15 minutes I just don't want us to cover for him all week, eek, eek ,come and sit on my lap Kezz and we can talk about the first thing that comes up. Kezz looking hot and bothered laughed and said "Don't be rude Danny eek, eek, I don't like that girl by Jeff she is miserable." Niel "Who? Inga the minga." Kezz "Ha, ha, ha, who is Inga the minga? Who gave her that name?" Niel "Keep it down Kezz, Danny did because she blew him out." Kezz "Awe did she Dan? Never mind, I am back now and you love me don't you?" Danny teased her "Yes I love you to bit's and all your bit's to, so are you singing any more tonight?" Kezz "If that dopey DJ gets his act together I will, it keeps breaking down, are you 2 going to sing tonight?" The lads nod a no and Niel says "I will sing if you want me to clear the place as that is what my singing does ha, ha, and Danny is not in a singing mood I don't think, he is upset." Danny laughs and replies "I am allright now Kezz is back and we can laugh all night long and I think I had better get her a drink, what do you think Kezz?" Kezz "Oh yes please I will have a pint of cider please and thank you I love you 2 Welshmen I do." Niel "I know Kezz we are like that and I will have a cider to Dan and don't forget Jeff." Danny sniggers and says "How can I forget him?" Danny goes off to the bar. No longer had Danny disappeared and Jeff comes over and sit's on Danny's seat and Inga follows Danny up to the bar. Jeff says "God a few minutes is all I need she goes on and on Niel." Niel "Well get in there my son." Kezz laughing says "Get in there Jeff she is in love with you and I think she wants to marry you already." Jeff looks at Kezz in a stern face and says "Haven't you got any songs that needs singing Kezz? Ha, ha, I am sorry that is not funny I don't need this." Kezz "Jeff don't be like that if she wasn't chasing you, you would be chasing her as per usual I think, she needs to be put right, I will tell her not to chase you and then she will wait for you to chase her, a good idea, yes?" Niel "That's it Kezz, well thought of." Jeff "It's too late for that now , I think it's too late for me, I will go home soon before she finishes drinking." Next thing Inga turns up and sit's by Jeff and smiling says "Hi guys, everyone enjoying themselves? I just seen Danny up by the bar he is chatting up that beautiful girl Marge the S.S.W. she is gorgeous isn't she? and I am going to sing in a while after Kezz I think, I seen your name just before me Kezz in about 3 more singers and that DJ has sorted his sound out now." Kezz "Eek, eek, I knew he would sort it out, I am ready for the song, everyone eek, eek." Inga looking at Kezz as if she was mad says "Right, ok then, I will be a bit nervous but will sing this song for Jeff my mate here, right Jeff?" Jeff "Well thank you Inga that's very kind of you." Niel smiling "Well Jeff that is a first for you, a girl singing for you especially for you and no one else, we will listen to it intensely Inga." Ann turns up David the barman puts the drinks on the table and Jeff says "Hope one of them is mine?" Danny "Yes there is one for you don't panic and can I have my chair back now please?" Jeff gets up and replies "There is no seat for me is there?" Danny "No your seat is over there by Inga so hop it sunshine ha, ha, back to your conquest boy, take him away Inga." They left and sat back over the other side of the table. Jeff frowning says "Well you know who your friends are, bloody Welshman." Kezz "Woo did you hear that he is nasty, eek, eek, I'm off to sing see you guys later." They said goodbye and she left. Niel "I don't think he is happy, let him sit by you when Inga goes up with Kezz to sing." Danny "He can sit there I just got him out of my seat." Niel shouts "Jeff you can sit here now Kezz has gone." Jeff "No he can stuff it now, he is a pain in the ass I don't want to sit by him now." Danny "Ok let him have a Paddy." Next thing Jeff sat by Danny and made him jump, Jeff laughed and said "Danny your still an idiot. " Danny jumps after Jeff startled him said "You idiot I jumped then, have you stopped whinging now?" Jeff "I am fine, I can't see her going off with anyone except me, I will have to disappear later, so if you can't find me I will be over the lounge in Dowdell ok?" Niel "Oh dear, she will not be happy about that." Jeff " Well that's tuff I can't do whatever she wants just because she fancies me can i?" Danny "I don't know why you don't just tell her she will understand man." Jeff "Do you really think so? I don't." Danny rubbing his chin says "No you are probably right, so you will have to put up with her chasing you for a couple of days , nothing wrong with that is there? I never thought I would be in this position of seeing you with 2 girls and me can't get a smile off 1." Niel "Trouble with you is you are fussy, there are loads of girls who try it on with you but you are fussy, so it's not that Jeff is that well off with women he just grabs what he can, greedy." Danny "Oh c'mon I know if you were not married and in the running you would refuse most of them here." Niel smiling "You cheeky git I would refuse them all just like you." Jeff "Now, now, fella's this is my problem and a little help would not go amiss, I can't hurt her so I will just let it play itself out and that will be that." Niel "Until she comes back permanently, then things will be worse so if it was me I would sort it out now and get it over with." Jeff looking at the floor says "I can't I really can't matey so I will play it by ear." Niel "Well one more pint and it's time for bed, my round, will you get them Jeff if I give you the money please?" Jeff "What did your last slave die of? Give me the money then, shall I get Kezz a pint of cider ?" Niel "You better had, has she finished the last one then?" Jeff "Ages ago." Niel "God that girl can drink for a little one , god, I am definitely off after this one" Danny "Yeh, yeah, I have heard that before, we will see Niel, right go on then Jeff we are thirsty." Jeff rushes his pint and went off to the bar. Niel "I am off soon Dan I mean it, because if Jeff goes first Inga will be hanging on to us to take her back with us to see Jeff." Danny "No she won't, I think Jeff is to certain of himself, it will all die down you will see." Inga sat by Danny and said "What's that Danny?" Danny sat up and said "The karaoke will die out once most of this year's lot leave at Xmas." Inga "Oh I don't, most people like Xmas

426

and karaoke, I am sitting in Jeff's seat aren't I?" Niel "Yes he is up by the bar, he won't be long now." As he said this Jeff turns up with the pints and puts them on the table and says "Oh jump in my seat why don't you ha, ha, I am having this pint and I am off." Kezz turns up and says to Inga "Can I have my seat back please?" She jumps up and says sarcastically "Sorry missus." Kezz "That's allright, Danny did   you hear me sing?" Danny "Oh yes I thought it was the radio it was so good." Kezz smiles and says "Ha, ha, banging, banging, you bugger is this my pint here?" Niel "Yes it is squiggly, I got it." Kezz "Oh thank you Niel that is very nice of you, banging, I needed a pint for my throat." Danny "That's allright it's your round next babe." There was a deadly silence and Kezz smiled and chuckled "I have not got any money, I am skint ha, ha, ha." Danny teased her and said "Well you will have to go and sell your body to the highest bidder and don't be long we will be empty soon and your not getting away with your round." Kezz looking worried "Your kidding you are, aren't you joking? I will get the first round on Friday when I get my money ok?" Niel "Awe never mind Kezz we are only joking so don't panic." Kezz "You Welsh buggers." Next thing Jeff comes up to Danny and Niel and says in a huff "Right I am off to bed or at least for a tinny in the digs, see you pair of tossers   later." He stormed off and left the lads wondering. Danny "You know for a minute I thought I heard Jeff saying he was going home and it's only quarter past ten." Niel said "Funny I thought I heard something to." Kezz looking serious said "It was Jeff he was going off home, I heard him." Danny "Never Kezz, I thought I heard something." Kezz "Your teasing me again aren't you? You pair of buggers, eek, eek, I bet Inga will be over now asking where he is?" Niel "I am not saying nothing." Danny "Me either, I am keeping out of it and then he can't blame me the little plonker." Sure enough Inga comes and stands by Danny and Niel and says "God it's hot in here, I wonder where Jeff is." Kezz not being able to resist telling her "Oh he has gone home for a couple of tinnies in Dowdell, he just told us." The lads rolled their eyes and Inga continued "Really, well I never he never said anything, does he normally go off like that??" Danny "Sometimes he does if he is knackered he does." Niel "Yes and I am off now after this pint." Inga jumps up at the chance and asks Niel "Can I come over for a night cap Niel?" Niel "Well not really I am going off to bed sorry Inga, maybe another night." Danny "Right Niel I am coming over with you." Inga "Can I come over with you Danny for a night cap? please, please, I will not be any trouble and I live near you." Danny pauses for a minute and then smiling says "Yes of course you can Inga, we will be leaving in a few minutes doll." Inga burst into smiles and says "Great, I will go and finish my drink and sort out my things, back in a minute." Kezz laughing says "Danny Jeff will not be happy." Niel "You are a bastard, he will go mad Dan, how could you do that to him?" Danny looking innocent says "What? What? I was asked by Jeff to try and get off with her to get her off his back and so I am." Niel "You bad bastard, you know what I mean, he will go ballistic with you I am going to bed... no I'm not I would not miss this for the world, ha, ha, ha." Kezz laughs and says "Oh my god, I bet you will not be alive tomorrow Danny, I am staying here to sing see you guys in the morning, you must tell me what happened ha, ha, ha." Inga returns and says "I am ready then." They all go off back to Dowdell.

Back at Dowdell and Jeff had invited Carol up for a chat as he passed her on his way back from the bar, they were sitting there with a can of lager in their hands and Carol cuddling up to Jeff as normal and talking like a little baby in her love talk "So uncle Jeffrey what have you been up to? I haven't seen you for a while, are you still my little uncle Jeffrey then?" "Of course, there is no other woman for me but you and I love only you and Jo of course." "Jeffrey, I don't like coming second to any woman, so don't be horrible, I have not seen Adi

427

this week he has gone home to see his family." "And tell me he is not coming back, make my day, please I need some good news." Carol slaps him on his arm and replied "Uncle Jeffrey that is not very nice, he is my cuddly little Welshman, I think you are not very nice to him. He is coming back next Monday so don't be nasty to him." "You know I don't like the man, he is a big shit and you can get better than him, like me for instance." "Awe uncle Jeffrey I love you too but not like Adi, he is my soul mate and you are spoken for, if it was not Jo it would be me and if not me Geraldine and if not her someone else etc. so don't give me all that crap Jeffrey." "Carol I would marry you tomorrow, I need someone like you to cuddle up to in the night so if Adi is not here what about it? I could sneak out of your room early and not wake you up." "Behave Uncle Jeffrey or I will tell Jo, so why are you home so early from the bar anyway?" "You would not believe me if I told you." "Well try me it must be serious if you are home from the bar this early." Jeff smiling says "Well you know I took over from Mandy with new students and looking after them and getting them where they need to go, well one of them has got a crush on me and I don't want to bother with her, she is not my type so I came back to get away from her." "Shut up, I don't believe you, you run away from a girl, this is Jeff who would shag a frog if it stopped hopping, I don't believe you, she must be the ugliest thing in the world for you to reject her." "Well that's where your wrong there, she is a very good looking woman and nice figure to go with it but she does not interest me." "Why? Because of Jo? She is not all that interested in you she is a user so go for it man." "You can't say that about Jo she is lovely." "And as daft as a brush, I bet she still has her Cindy doll in her room, she is so innocent and lovely but not man material, so get in with this girl." "Your rotten you are, Jo is not that bad and Inga is ok, but I can't seem to like her that way so I will lay low, I even got Danny to try and get out with her for me and she turned him down flat." "Christ she must have it bad then, I am surprised at you as you normally chase anything in a skirt and that's it I think you are ill or turning into a pouf." "Oh no, don't go there, I am not for turning ha, ha, I am a man's man, look out I can hear that rabble coming." In walks Danny followed by Niel and Inga quietly. Jeff says " "So you got rid of her then?" Danny coughs out loud to drown his voice out and said "Well is that Carol? Well long time no see, this is Inga she is here for a review to see if she is going to come back to do a course. Inga this is Carol Jeff's friend." Jeff goes red in the face and shuffles nervously away from Carol's caresses and his face turns serious and Carol says "Oh hello Inga, I have heard a lot about you from Jeff by here." Inga "Hello Carol, have you indeed, what has he been saying then?" Carol replies "Well he was telling me." Jeff butts in "I was telling her about all of the ones that came here today and that you might be over for a cuppa in a minute with Danny as I think Danny fancies you." Inga "Oh right, Danny and I are just good friends, we have discussed that and it is ok." Niel "Right I am making a cuppa anyone else?" Danny "No I am having a can." Inga "Thank you Niel I will have a cup of coffee please, I will help you if you like." Jeff and Carol said they would have a can of lager, so off Inga and Niel go. Jeff wait's for the door to shut and whispers at Danny "So why did you bring her here? I asked you not to and you did." Danny sarcastically replies "I could not do that to the poor girl she is madly in love with you and I can't be nasty just like you." Jeff "Bastard, you did this on purpose didn't you? I will remember this I will." Carol "Oh Jeffrey shut up and tell me what is wrong with her, she sounds delightful to me, don't be nasty." Jeff "There we are then, I am off to bed in a minute." Carol "Grow up Jeff, she is a woman and can take telling so do it but not in front of everyone, be a man ha, ha, I mean it or I will." Jeff pleads with Carol "No, no, don't, I will not forgive you, I will do the right thing in my own time please don't say nothing Carol or I will never forgive you." Back comes Niel and

Inga , Danny says "Allright Inga? Do you want to sit by here?" Danny gets up and gives Inga a seat opposite Jeff and he goes and sit's besides Niel. Carol "So this is nice isn't it? I didn't go to the Karaoke, was it any good?" Inga "Yes it was, except that strange girl who kept on going eek, eek, she is as nutty as a fruit cake but a good singer." Carol "Oh Kezz you mean, she is a hell of a girl isn't she? I like her I do although she can be strange sometimes and I bet these were buying her drinks all night? As per usual." Inga "Yes they were and I sang but Jeff left half way through it to come for a can or 2 and I sang it especially for him." Carol "Well that's men for you as you probably know, they think you do things for your own benefit ha, ha, ha." Niel "Hey steady Carol, that's not nice, we are not all like that cockney git over there he is a whimp." Carol "Oh no don't say this about my uncle Jeffrey." Carol put her arm around Jeff and you could see by Inga's face she was jealous and Carol cuddled Jeff and said "My poor little uncle Jeffrey, what are they saying about my Jeffrey then? I will look after you don't listen to them." Inga coughed and said "Uncle Jeffrey is it? The guys will love that tomorrow Uncle Jeffrey." Danny "It doesn't bother uncle Jeffrey does it Uncle Jeff? he loves it as long as he gets his head between the boobs he loves it, right I am off to bed enough is enough." Carol "Yes I must be off to, I have a lecture early tomorrow." Jeff "Dan I got some cans out now don't go I will walk Carol back to her room down stairs and be back now." Carol "I can find my own way back Jeff, I will use the lift, see you tomorrow goodnight all and nice meeting you Inga , take it easy on Jeff he is only little." Jeff "Carol now behave yourself." Carol goes off and Danny stands up ready for bed and Jeff thrusts a can in his hand and insists he drinks it. He says to Niel "Would you like a can Niel or Inga?" They both take one and Inga moves and sit's by Jeff and says "God you lot hang around with some strange people, are they all like this here?" Niel "Just the majority of them ha, ha, but it's the way to be in a college like this and they are all original and love a good laugh especially Jeff, he is a nutter when he is drunk and his chat up lines are the best in the world, have he used any on you yet?" Inga "No he hasn't." Danny "Don't worry he will sooner or later mark my words." Jeff throws Danny a nasty look and replies "I have not always used them but still get more results than you." Danny "Oooohh nasty, just because Inga turned me down flat for you no need to rub it in." Niel laughed out loud and Jeff tried to change the subject "Well Inga we must be up in the morning by 9 and meet in the main building in student services as we have a busy one tomorrow, so if you want me to walk you over the road to your digs I will." Inga "Oh trying to get rid of me aye? Thanks Jeff I was enjoying my drink." Jeff "No, no, I was worrying about if you were tired after a busy day today? I am used to it as you can tell so no rush I am not going to bed just yet." Danny "Well I am off, I am knackered." Danny nudges Niel as if to say let's go and leave him alone with Inga, just what Jeff did not want. Niel chirped up "Yes, I am off to I was falling asleep here then." Jeff "No lads I have got more cans here if you want one? Don't go yet the night is young, c'mon don't be spoil sports here have one." The lads declined and smiled and Jeff had a face like thunder and the lads said goodnight to them and they left for bed, within minutes Jeff was making excuses to go to bed and finally got Inga to go home.

It was the next morning and Danny and Niel was sitting having breakfast and Zarrine was pouring the tea and laughing at the story Danny had told her about Jeff and Inga. Danny continues speaking "Zarrine you will be laughing at that all day now won't you?" Zarrine with tears of laughter says "Yes that Jeff makes me laugh, he always moans he has not got a girlfriend and when one chases him he don't want to know." Niel "I know, I think he is afraid of this one, look out here he comes now." Danny "So how was Inga the minga last night then Jeff?" Jeff was walking and moaning as if he was hurt "Ooh ah ooh ah, I am in pain I really am." Niel "So what happened? She got you in her bed by the looks of it, she looked desperate last night." Jeff "Ha, ha, very funny, if you must know she nearly killed me last night I walked her back and she tried to kiss me and I tried to get out of it and fell in a ditch and lucky for me she pulled me out or I would still be there now, she saved my life." Danny burst out laughing and everyone looked at him as if he had gone mad. Niel said to him "What's the Matter with you Dan? It wasn't that funny." Danny stops laughing and explained "It reminded me of my bestest mate ever when I was younger I will tell you about it as soon as I stop choking, cough, cough as children we met in a place that had some houses here and there no roads no pavements just humps of earth everywhere , this was the beginning of a new village called Bettws and we became good friends from the day we met and we had some fun and I am going to tell you of just a few that made everyone laugh especially me as that's what we did. He was in the gazette one day for saving a lads life from our village from drowning, but it did not mention that he was the one who pushed him in in the first place. Another thing that happened was when him and I were out playing with Alan Pothecary and Alan was sent up to his bedroom for pushing other lads about by his mother, he was pretending to be Popeye and he was sent to bed so Wyndham and I sat by his wall and Alan was crying in his bedroom looking out at us. So Wyndham told Alan to open the window, that he did and Wyndham proceeded to tell Alan to get some of the grass in his pocket out and chew it and to pretend it was spinach and jump out of the window as he will not hurt himself as he is Popeye . To our amazement Alan chewed the grass and jumped out breaking his leg on his father's new rockery and as he was jumping we shouted, NO WERE ONLY KIDDING, but it was too late, so we legged it and hid from our parents. We had many days of fun. Another time we went picking cockles and it was at Penclywdd and the muddy beach had little muddy streams running down it and he just went to walk through one and disappeared and just his hat was floating on the water, it was about 8 foot deep, so I got him out and we decided that his clothes were smelly and I would not let him sit in my car with these smelly clothes on so he stripped and we tied his clothes on the roof rack to dry them out as we were going to the Gower to a friend's pub there. As we drove I decided to ask the way as I had got lost laughing at Wyndham sitting alongside me starkers and I stopped right in front of a bus queue of many people and he did not know what to do so just sat there with a huge grin on his face and hands covering his privates, he was a picture but did not give a damn. We both then as older men went to work in the FFaldau colliery at the end of our teens and he was not one to boast if he said something it was possible or he would not say it, but one day he I thought had gone too far he said he could put up a wood prop up in a coal face 5 foot high with a wooden prop that was 6 foot long, I watched him all shift put that prop up he beat them all as he put it up and the top was exactly above the bottom of the prop and he was about a stone lighter but he was determined to do it and he did and the wooden prop was like a banana. He never bet and shied out of it, what you seen is what you got with Wyndham. Another funny thing I seen him do was hilarious is when a gang of older men working underground did the initiation on him by greasing his nether parts and he did not like this and was determined to get his revenge and this was a treat to witness. A few days later he rushed up from underground and was washed and dressed before the older men from his work place had even had a fag, he waited and as they all got into the shower the first thing they always did was wash their hair several times and kept their eyes shut to stop the soap burning their eyes and as they were getting in the shower Wyndham went outside to get something he rolled his sleeve around his hand and grabbed a hand full of stingy nettles and snapped them off and went

430

into the shower and ran up behind the older men and touch each one of them all on the ass with these nettles and all you could hear is ah, ha, ow, ow, ouch, ouch, and they did not sit down after for a while and we were all in stitches laughing. Wyndham had a wicked sense of humour and was a very intelligent man to go with it, he was nobody's fool but a gentleman and I missed him when it was time to grow up, a hell of a boy, he has a son called Callum, I haven't seen him for a few years he was someone you should take a note from, he would have told Inga the score Immediately and not beat around the bush. Sorry I am wittering now, I get lost in conversation, sorry." Jeff "That was a nice story but what has it got to do with my accident?" Danny "Well you said she saved your life but she was the one who made you fall in the ditch in the beginning." Niel "Oh right I was wondering what the hell that had to do with Jeff's fall to, right I got it now." Danny chuckles and said "His name is Wyndham Pit and when we were training to go to the coal mines there was a local pit called the Wyndham western colliery and the first day there he was asked his name and he said Wyndham Pit and the trainer said no I want to know your name not where you are going to work so he said again Wyndham Pit . The trainer said are you trying to be funny? I will ask again your name boy not where you are going to work? well Wyndham rolled his eyes and shouted at the trainer, my name is bloody Wyndham Pit that is my name and the trainer looked stupid, it was a laugh a minute with him." Zarrine looked puzzled "So Jeff why don't you like Inga then?" Jeff answers her "I don't know I just don't fancy her but she is mad over me, but it is only 2 more days and she is gone so I will do my job and hide the rest of the time as I cannot rely on my friends to help me, that Dodgy Welshman brought her over and I was sitting by Carol here, what a mate and Niel was enjoying him doing these things to me I could tell so don't deny it Niel." Niel "Jeff you ask for it and I think you are a fool, just tell the girl for goodness sake mate, but no you are enjoying it all the attention you love it and we are laughing at you all the time." Jeff "Thanks matey, I love you to, right I am off I know who my friends are now." Danny "Shut up you, Niel is right, tell her straight and no more problem." Jeff "Yeah, yeah, your all jealous, I am off, see you all later." Zarrine "Hey Jeffrey don't shout here this time in the morning." Danny "To late he has gone, he is in a mood isn't he?" Zarrine "I can understand it with you 2 on his back all the time, he don't stand a chance with you pair, try and help him not drag him down all of the time, poor Jeff." Niel smiling says "Yes you might be right there 2 Welshmen on at the same time must be disconcerting." Danny "Steady Niel big words this time in the morning, flipping heck, steady, I think he brings it on himself by not just telling her how it is, she is a good looking girl and a lovely figure and I would loved to have her on my arm but for that cockney git." Zarrine "I don't think Jeff likes to hurt anyone not like you Danny, he won't hurt anyone's feelings at all that's how he is and that is not a bad thing, he is so sweet for a man." Danny "Yes your right I know he will not hurt a fly." Niel "Just wasps, he hates them with a vengeance, I think we should stay out of it Dan and there will be no argument then, let him sort it out." Danny "I agree , I think I will not come back to have a cuppa at lunch time, I will stay out of the way." Niel "Well I am coming back to listen in ha, ha, ha." Danny "Typical of you see what I mean Zarrine? He can't resist it, Niel you are a hell of a boy." Zarrine "See what I mean? Not one of you cannot resist it, that poor Jeff."

Well the day went without any interference from Danny or Niel and it was later that night and Danny had just had a nice bath and was coming out of his room to the stairwell to go through to the lounge and was startled by Jeff sitting silently on top of the stairs. He spoke in the deadliest silence and said "Allright matey?" Danny jumped and shouted at Jeff "Bloody hell, what are you doing hiding here? You frightened the shit out of me mate, bloody hell." Jeff "Ha, ha, ha, ha, sorry I didn't mean to frighten you, you jumped so high you frightened me also ha, ha, ha, I am hiding from the Inga girl, I heard her coming so came out this end of the lounge to get away from her, now I can't get back to my room." Danny rolling his eyes said "That again? I am staying out of it Jeff so why don't you go out of the building and go back in your side from the outside then?" Jeff looking surprised says "Of course, why didn't I think of that, nice one dodgy fancy meeting me outside later and go for a drink as I don't want to see her, so I will meet you up the bar about nine o'clock ok?" Danny "Yeah, yeah, I will see you up there." Jeff goes off and Danny goes through to the lounge and in there was Inga and Niel having a chat about Jeff. Niel "He is a private man and I think you should forget him he will not change, I think you are wasting your time with him." Danny walks in and says "Hello all it's only me, ignore me I am having a coffee, anyone else?" Both said they had a cup, Inga then said "I do like him mind but he is distant and a lovely man, I like him a lot, do you think he will be coming in here tonight?" Niel "Well I don't know, I never know what he is doing, Danny is the man to ask." Danny on hearing this replied "Don't involve me, I don't want to know, I am not Jeff's keeper, sorry." Inga "C'mon Danny you know I hope you are not still holding the thought that I did not want to go out with you affect our relationship? I need to know." Danny "Inga I have promised myself not to get involved and I am sticking to that, he may be coming in he may not be I don't know." Inga "Ok fair enough." Niel "Have you seen him tonight Dan?" Danny thought about it and replied "No I haven't." Danny's thought was that he was blind and was technically correct. Inga then goes on at Niel "What do you think I should do then Niel?" Niel blows his lips and says "Well I don't know really, he is a funny one is Jeff but he may come around in the end." Inga "I have never felt like this about any man ever, he is lovely and I am not giving up until he tells me anything different, I heard he has got children and he is divorced." Niel "Yes he has 3 children nice lads his wife left him for another man so I heard." Inga with serious face says "Well that is her loss and hopefully my good luck, I would look after him and love him with all I have got." Danny then says "If I was you I would not say anything else before you find out his intentions towards you." Inga's face told it all and she went into a mood, Niel said "I am off to my room to listen to the archers ." He stood up and Inga said "Oh I like the Archers can I come to your room and listen with you?" Niel "Yes of course you can." They went off to his room.

It was later and Danny met Jeff in the bar as planned. Danny walks in and says to Jeff. "Allright Jeff still ducking and diving then?" Jeff looking fed up says "To bloody right it's nuts, Rhoda told me she knocked my door a few times when I was in your stair well, she don't give up does she?" "No she is giving Niel earache over you as we speak, she is besotted by you and I can't figure out why." "Cheeky git, I am a charmer that's why but I can't wait for her to leave in 2 days and give me some peace, I hope Jo will come over here tonight and maybe she will get the message." "You can forget that mate she is waiting to pounce on you, she will be over here in a while bet your bippy she will and making a B line for you, so if I was you I would snog the face off Jo when she gets here." "No problem Dan I will, she must get it in the end, look out I can hear that squiggly Kezz can't I Kezz?" Kezz let out a scream "Eeeeeeeeeeeek, it sure is banging, Jeff, banging, so where is Inga the minga then? I thought you were attached at the hip." Jeff "Leave it there now she is nothing to do with me and if Jo comes in don't stir it for me Kezz." Kezz "Oh I won't but Jo has gone to the pictures with the others in the mini bus." Jeff looking stunned says "She hasn't, she said she might be up later." Kezz "Yes she has, I seen her getting in the bus or rather I heard her getting in the bus with rosemary and all the others , so na, na, na, I bet you any money you like." Jeff looking fed up says "Well bloody hell, she said she was coming up here, great." Danny "Like I always say she is not there some of the time, she is light headed and forgets things quickly and that's why you 2 will never amount to anything, she is a lovely girl and damn good looking but she is in a world of her own sometimes, bless her." Jeff "Oh shut up, that will not help my cause." Kezz "I don't know why you don't go out with Inga, at least she turns up ha, ha, she is in love with you Jeff I can tell and she pays more attention to you than Jo does." Danny "See I am not the only one who can see it." Jeff ignores them and says to the barman "With friends like these 2 who needs enemies? And here is another one coming, pint Niel?" Niel "Pint of cider please Jeffrey, thank you very much and before you ask she is gone back to her digs." Jeff sighs and says "Thank god for that." Niel "To change and come over to see you ha, ha, ha." Danny and Kezz join in the laughter. Jeff's face all serious says "Great, bloody great, that's all I need, fancy going to the pretty pigs?" Danny "No thanks, I will get bladdered if I go there on a Thursday, forget it." Kezz "I will if you are paying, there is a karaoke there tonight banging ." Jeff "Well let's at least sit down in the corner." They all go and sit down and in comes Inga who sit's as close as she can to Jeff and says "Hello Jeff I have been looking out for you all night, been hiding have you? Ha, ha, only kidding, it's a nice night but quiet here isn't it?" Danny "I have a feeling it will not last especially if his girlfriend comes in later , she has gone off to the pictures and let him down." Inga "Never that's not nice is it Jeff? Well never mind we can all have a nice night, Niel and I listened to the Archers in his room and he was a real gentleman." Niel "I am always a gentleman as you know?" Kezz "I can vouch for them lovely boys ha, ha, ha." Niel "Are you being nice so I will buy you a pint I wonder squiggly Kezz?" Kezz smiling says "Who me? Eek." Danny "I heard a good joke this morning, a woman was standing in front of the mirror in her bedroom without any clothes on and she said to her husband "I wish I could get these boobs bigger like Jordon's, I would look more sexy for you." the husband said "That's easy just rub a piece of toilet paper between them once every night before you go to bed for a month." she replied "Will that work then?" he replied "Well it worked for your ass." They all burst out laughing and Inga said "You daft bugger ha, ha, right it's my round anyone for one?" Inga took their orders and got them in.

Later after they had a lot to drink Inga was trying to cuddle up to Jeff without any joy. Jeff says "Looks as if Jo is not coming in then so I won't be long before I am off." Inga "Awe don't go it's early Jeff." Danny "God Inga you are like a love sick dog there, he is spoken for don't you understand it? He is spoken for." Inga "Ok I understand, sorry." That seemed to be the last straw as far as Inga was concerned and she finished her drink and stormed off. Jeff turned to Danny and said "There was no need for that was there?" Danny "Well, you didn't have the guts to put the poor girl out of her misery and it's not fair for her either Jeff, she has feelings too and she is a lovely woman." Niel "I am sorry Jeff he is right but he did it in the wrong way but he is right and I think we had better help Kezz home soon she is swaying like a pendulum here by the side of me." Jeff "I hope she will be allright, Inga I mean, I feel sorry for her now, typical of the loud mouthed Welshman." Danny "Oh allright I will apologise to her in the morning at elevenses ok? don't keep on now she was just getting on my nerves keeping on that's all, right I am off let's get squiggly home." the lads helped Kezz home.

It was the next morning at elevenses and Danny was sitting there with Niel and Kezz holding her head. Danny asked Kezz "So how's your head now? You had a lot of cider last night." Kezz replies "Ooh I know I am better now but this morning I was dry in my mouth ha, ha, eek, eek, but it was a good night and so funny even though it was dead in the student bar, did I behave myself?" Niel smiling "Yes except the time you stood on the chair and dropped your knickers and mooned at the barman, he liked it mind." Kezz looking shocked says "No I didn't did I? Your teasing me aren't you?" Danny "God you must have been drunk if you can't remember that." Kezz "Get off I didn't, did I? Be honest now I am feeling awful now, Niel tell the truth." Niel smiling says "No you didn't just pead in a pint glass because you couldn't be asked to walk to the toilet." Kezz "Now I know your lying Niel, I would never hit in a glass the state I was in ha,, ha, give me an eek Niel." Niel give her an eek and next in comes Jeff and his tribe. He rushed over to Danny and said "You prick, you have done it now, you'll never guess who the college is looking for? Inga, she has only disappeared out of sight and now I have to explain what I know after lunch if she is not found, all your fault." Danny "She is around somewhere and don't blame me it's your fault leading her on, they will look at that before they bother me just for telling her the truth." Jeff looking urgent says "And guess who they have got phoning around to try and find her?" Niel "Columbo, or what's the name of that man in awe Wexford am I right?" Jeff "Shut up Niel this is serious, Jo, only Jo and if she finds out anything I am dead all because of that dodgy Welshman, thanks matey." Danny "Shut up Jeff don't try and blame me I only told her what you had not got the guts to and besides she is probably gone home early this morning and never will she come back here anymore, so I have done you a favour, so don't thank me too fast, she has gone home matey I am telling you you'll see I am right I bet you." Niel "You had better hope she has Dan for all our sakes and as regards Jo she will not kill you it will take her a few weeks to work it all out so don't kid yourself Jeff." Kezz chirps up "She was strange mind and she would talk to any stranger perhaps she did last night and he has strangled her." Jeff "Oh great, thanks Kezz, I really need you like a hole in the head, well if she has been knocked off it will be Danny's fault and Niel's ha, ha, no it's not funny, I hope nothing toward has happened to her, I will never forgive myself I am bloody worried now." Danny "She will be allright you will see, surely they have got her mobile number somewhere?" Niel "She gave it to me last night but I don't know what I done with it, I probably threw it away as I could not read it Jeff ." Jeff looking down to the ground says "I am off to see them in the office now, I will be back in a minute." Jeff goes off and Danny looked worried and said "Well it's not my fault is it? I mean, I only told her to stop her making a fool of herself, I hope she is allright." Niel "She kept on asking me if she was doing anything wrong or what? She needed to do things different, I said perhaps your Fergal Sharky is all wrong. " Danny and Kezz looking puzzled said "What the hell is your Fergal Sharky Niel?" Niel scratching his head replied "You know, her Chinese layout." Kezz "What the hell are you on about Niel? I have never heard of a Fergal Sharky. Is it cockney rhyming slang?" Niel looking puzzled says "Oh you know mun, when the furniture has to be rearranged to get you Fergal Sharky in the right setting to the moon or something like that, it's a Chinese thing." Danny smiling "That's fen shewy you idiot, Fergal Sharky he is a singer you idiot, ha, ha, Fergal Sharky, your an idiot sometimes Niel." Kezz still laughing "Niel you are so funny sometimes you really are, you make me laugh." They all laughed out loud for a while then Jeff came back in smiling for a change and says to them all "Right I just read the wardens report with one of the staff and Inga was trying to leave last night but there was no trains at the time and so she left this morning at seven o'clock for home and she told the warden she does not like it here at all so will not return ever." Danny "Didn't I tell you that? So that's that then Jeff, things can get back to normal and Niel thought of Fergal Sharky was to blame." Kezz starts laughing out loud followed by Niel who was showing tears rolling down his cheeks through so much laughter, a puzzled Jeff said "What is Fergal Sharky? Sorry I am not with it." Danny laughing says to him "Ha, ha, Niel reckons her Fergal Sharky was not right, he meant her fen Shewy was not right." Jeff laughed and says to Niel "You idiot Niel, so I am in the clear thanks to Danny, no more ducking and diving thanks mate." Niel "Jeff your a false bugger, a minute ago Danny was to blame for everything now he is the hero you 2 faced git." Kezz "Eek, eek, I need a pee I am busting , please don't make me laugh any more I will pee myself, quick get out of the way I am busting." Jeff "Right I must get back to my job and by the way Danny there are a few more girlies in next week, maybe one for you." Danny "No thanks matey you can have them if they are all like Inga, thanks, but no thanks." The lads set off to their different departments for lectures.

It was the following week and the new recruits were due but Danny was not thinking about it, he had given up and was in a devilish mood. He had been home on the weekend with Josh and had bought some stink bombs to take back to college and gave some for Josh to use also. Danny was going to play tricks on all at the college. He firstly put a stink bomb under the leg of a bench careful not to break it and as soon as the smokers rushed into the undercover at the smoking corner it would break. This corner was also known as cancer corner and it was always packed with smokers and you could not breathe when passing. Well the people rushed in and off the bomb went and they were all gasping for air and the area cleared and many people were almost throwing up and Danny got pleasure out of this but was determined to be the phantom stink bomber. Well the following day the new recruits were due and Danny had the day off so continued his bombing campaign, he put one under the entrance carpet by the door of Dowdell so when someone stood on it, it would go off and it worked a treat as Jeff was the one who with his new recruit's stood on it first . Jeff heard the crushing sound of the glass bomb go off and wondered what it was and says to the possible new students "Oh dear I just stood on something." All the others were coming in behind him and the stink was unbearable and they were all holding their noses and ran for the stairs and shut the door. Jeff says to them "Oh my god it's not me someone has put a stink bomb under the mat and I stood on it, there are some childish people here in the college this week. This is the second one to go off this week and it is only Tuesday, sorry everyone." They all laughed and went into the lounge and in there was Paddy and Niel and Jeff introduced them all to the lads and Jeff complained to Niel "Another stink bomb has gone off at the bottom of the stairs, I would like to get the idiot who is responsible for it, it's not you is it Niel?" Niel "No it's bloody not, I am not that childish but I wish whoever it is would stop it they are real good ones and make me feel sick, I know one of these people here I knew them from the manor , Torquay." Paddy says "Yes I know this man to, hello Roy how are things? I haven't seen you since I was up there with you." They both wander off into the kitchen to talk out of the noise of the lounge and all the others sit down and had a cup of coffee each and Jeff said to Niel "So where is the dodgy Welshman then? I thought he would be here as he has the day off?" Niel "Listen can you hear that music? well then if you can you know where he is blasting his music for all to hear and as I say it he turns it off well, well he must have heard you." In walks Danny on queue and he was wondering what all the people were doing in the lounge, he says "Hello there are a lot of people in here today. Hello all I am Danny or as Jeff says the dodgy Welshman, I am a pussy cat really, nice to meet you all, I am off for a cup of tea back in a min." He goes off to the kitchen and Niel says "So I hope these are as bright as last week's group? It is nice to see more older ones this time, I felt old last week." Jeff "What do you mean? You are old." Niel "Cheeky git, so is anyone doing the advice and guidance?" One of the girls dawn spoke up "Yes I am, is it good or just a waste of time Niel?" Niel "No it's very enjoyable and I like it, it fascinates me, what about Karl?" Karl "I am doing the music technology, is it any good?" Jeff "Best to ask Danny about that he is in it in a big way." Danny came back in and asked a little quiet woman if the seat by her was taken? She replied in a French accent "Oh no there is no one sitting there." Danny's ears pricked up and Jeff said to Danny "Dan this is Karl he is doing the music tech and was wondering what it is like?" Danny replied "It is brilliant if you are into this sort of thing and the studios are Immense there is a few studios and workshops worth about 5-6 million and some Impressive facilities, you will be amazed and if you like I will take you along this evening as there is a session that is voluntary if you like?" Karl excited says "Can I? I will take you up on that Danny if I may, I will arrange it with Jeff when I find out what is happening thanks mate." Danny "No problem Karl I will be around and. So this little person here I spoke to, are you Hungarian? As the accent is familiar." French lady "No I am French from Paris." Danny intrigued says "You have come a long way." French lady replies "No I live in this country in Suffolk ha, ha, ha." Danny then says "So what course are you going to do here?" French lady "If I like it here I will be doing the business and administration course if I like it here." Danny "I just love that French accent it is lovely." French lady "Thank you." Danny "And are you married or what?" As he asked this Roy and Paddy came back into the room and Roy snapped at Danny "I am afraid she is with me, she is my girlfriend." Danny looked taken back by his response and the French girl seemed awkward. Danny responded "Oh right, never mind and can I ask your name?" She smiled and replied "My name is Malika and he is Roy." Roy looking annoyed said to Paddy "Well nice seeing you Paddy again, I will catch you up the bar tonight." Danny said "I will be up the bar tonight if you are coming up I and Jeff all sit in the corner on the left as you come in through the door and we have a damn good laugh." Roy "We will keep that in mind." Roy then proceeded to get in between Danny and Malika and Danny was moved to speak to Karl again as Karl asked him a question. "Will they let you use the mixing desk there in the first year? Or have you got to be coached for ever?" Danny "No you can get into it Immediately and there is never a shortage of students who want to sing but not so many musicians here." Karl "So how do they manage then?" Danny "We have choirs in and other artist who want to make a cd as it is cheap and to allow many students to practice with coaching." Danny now turned back to see if he could talk to Malika but Roy was all over her like a rash but Danny was determined to speak to her again before she left. Jeff then shouted "Right guys let's get back to it, it is getting late and Danny can you let us through your stair well? As some idiot has let off a stink bomb in ours ." Danny laughing said "Of course I will, nice to meet you all." Danny tried to say something to Malika but Roy got between them so he said out loud "Goodbye Malika and Roy nice to meet you both." They said goodbye and went off. After letting them through his stairwell he returned and Danny sat back down and said to Niel "My god she was lovely, her accent blew me away, she sounded nice." Paddy said "Her boyfriend was not Impressed with you and Roy is a big lad Dan." Danny "You know what they say the bigger they are the harder they fall." Niel "Oh he is allright, I remember him from Torquay but I thought he was married Paddy?" Paddy answers "Not any more he was caught with another woman in the manor, do you remember Gemma and he done the same to her so she dumped him now he is with Malika and he said he is living with her in her home in Suffolk so hard luck Dan." Danny looking serious says "Luck doesn't come into it Paddy, she is going to be mine one day if she comes back here, mark my words." Niel "Woo that is fighting talk Dan, old Roy is a big lad mind." Danny "We will see." Paddy smiling says "Well good luck Dan you will need it with Roy." Danny "Dim problem as we say in Wales Paddy, right I am off to play a bit of music and have a soak in the bath and get myself smelling nice for tonight just in case, see you later lads." Danny leaves and Paddy says to Niel "Damn he is so sure of himself isn't he?" Niel "Well I have not known him for many years but I realised early in our friendship he never says anything he doesn't mean or carry out, that's what I like about the man oops here his music again he has changed it soft music he means business Paddy ha, ha, I am off see you later." Danny was looking for Jeff later that afternoon in the refectory to sit with him hoping he was sitting by the others but no sign of him so he went to the counter and asked Marge the S.S.W. if he was in there and if she would sit him by him, this she did and he said. "Allright Jeff? Are the recruit's with you?" "No I am on my own, they are all sitting with some of the staff over there, why?" "I was just wondering that's all, did you hear that girl Malika? She was lovely and that accent it melted me, she is going to be mine if she comes back here I mean it, remember I said that matey." "Really and what are you going to do with Roy her boyfriend? As a Matter of interest." " Him, he will not last as soon as she is out of his grip I will see him off." "He might be coming here to with her." Danny looking serious says "Dim problem Jeff, he will be blown out mark my words." "God you are cock sure of yourself aren't you?" "Yep, so is she over there now?" "No her and Roy have gone to the town to eat for the evening and have a few pints." Danny looked annoyed and said "Shit, never mind I suggested they sit by us in the bar tonight, I hinted where we will be sitting." "And what did Roy think of that suggestion?" "Yeah I see what you mean as soon as he thought I was chatting Malika up he got between us and I think he will stay between us this week but you never know she might blow him out now this week." "I would not bet on it, you are just hoping that's all but we will see and here is Jo so be careful what you say now mind about Inga you know what I mean?" Jo " thank you Madge, hello Jeff I am starving." Danny "Hello Jo?" Jo replies "Hello Danny, how are you?" Danny "I am fine thank you and you are as gorgeous as always." Jo smiling says "Well thank you ha, ha, I need food it has been a hard morning on the phone." Danny "So did the college find out why that Inga left so sudden last week then?" Jeff chokes on his food and says hurriedly "It's all been settled she did not like it here and that's that." Jo "No nobody knows why, she seemed to like it until the last night, she is just strange that's all." Jeff trying to change the subject says "Guess what he just told me?" Jo "What did he tell you Jeff?" Jeff says "He is in love with one of the new recruit's that came here today, the French girl Malika but he forgot one little detail and do you know what that is?" Jo "No but I have a feeling you are going to tell me aren't you?" Jeff "I certainly am, she has got a boyfriend already." Jo looks at Danny says "Oh Danny, your silly she has got a boyfriend and you can't interfere with that it's not nice." Danny ashen faced says "I won't have to Jo she will get rid of him he is a tosser ha, ha, I can tell." Jo "You don't know that Danny, get a girl who has not got a boyfriend and leave the attached ones alone." Jeff "See it's not just me, you can't live on maybes, get someone for yourself Dan." Danny "We will wait and see, she is going to be mine you wait and see, I am off to speak to someone more friendly." Jo "Awe Danny we are only trying to help, don't be like that please." Danny laughs and says "I know I am only kidding so don't cry for me Jo and Jeffrey." Jo "You bugger, I am coming out for a drink tonight with you lads if that is allright?" Danny "Oh I don't know let me think." Jeff smiles at Jo then says "Don't listen to him Jo he is in a happy mood and I fear some tricks this weekend coming and do you know about these stink bombs here?" Jo deep in thought says "Oh yes there is a real stink over it in the office, if they catch the person he will be in real trouble, the smell is awful, did you smell it in the cancer corner this morning?" Jeff "I trod on one in Dowdell at coffee break. Whoever it is, is a nutter." Danny never said a thing and left for his lecture.

Later and Danny was sitting on a bench and Clamper joined him. Clamper says to Danny "Hello Danny, fancy seeing you here, I hear your in love is that true?" "You have been talking to Jeff haven't you?" "No I haven't seen Jeff, it was Niel, so is it love?" "No not yet, she don't know yet." Clamper starts laughing and says "Ha, ha, ha, she don't know, very funny matey, I am having more trouble with that bloody Lola, she makes my life a misery over that hall of residence, I wish I could get my own back on her." "Like what Andy?" "I don't know , anything as long as she don't catch me, any ideas then?" Danny ponders for a minute and then says "If I tell you something promise you won't tell anyone, because if you do it can only be you as I am the only one else who knows this." Clamper smiling said "I promise I won't tell a soul." "If I gave you a stink bomb to put off outside her room, I didn't give it to you ok?" Clamper started rubbing his hands together and proclaimed "It's you, it's you, I like it it's you, you bastard you, we have all been throwing up, it's you, brilliant yes give me one and I will have a flaming good laugh. How do you let them off?" "Right listen to me before I give you one? you must not walk around with it in your pocket or it may break and you will stink like a rotten fart for weeks, so put it in your room until your ready to use it and all you do is put it on the floor and crush it with your foot, make sure you have shoes on, then scarper and don't laugh or it will give the show away and make sure she is in her room first." "Ha, ha, brilliant, brilliant, give me one then." Danny gave him one still in the box and warned him "And if anyone finds out it's me I know who to look for and I will ha, ha, ha." "I won't say anything I will let this off tonight at six o'clock as she goes in for her nap ha, ha, I can't wait I will see you." He rushes off and Danny sat there for a while thinking of his life and wondered if he was ever going to get his life back together, as everything he touches lately goes wrong, this was a hard time for him, all his old friends now never even contacted him since he has gone blind and Jeff was leaving soon and he had seen most of his friends leave so soon and Winnie, Tim, Lidia, had gone and he feels alone, very alone, this was hitting home to him and causing him hard times. Well he was sitting there for a long time thinking and who should come past was Niel and Abby and Abby was wagging her tail and Niel said "Hello who is on the bench? I can tell it is someone we know well because Abby's tail is going mad." "It's me Niel Danny, come and sit for a while if you fancy it?" "So why are you sitting here all alone then matey?" "Awe just thinking." "Oh dear by the sounds of your voice it is a sad day for you? What's up Dan?" "Awe just reminiscing about times since I have gone blind and how they are turning out for me and it is not good Niel, I can tell you I am really down still after nearly 5 years now and I thought I was getting on with it, I still feel like shit and useless and now all are leaving here it is worse. I had a letter off my wife's solicitor telling me the divorce has been asked for from Angie and the terms of it all as if it was my fault. I am here alone far from my family, Lyndon has gone, Dennis has gone, mam has gone, dad is dead also, I can't get a girl, no future and to top it all I still feel like killing myself sometimes, I have even thought of walking in front of a lorry sometimes and get it all over with, otherwise allright, all hunky dory." "Well Dan I don't know what to say, I have felt this when I first went blind and since my father and mother died but it's the love of my children and Ceri who keep me going but I can see it's worse for you with the divorce but you must keep on going Dan it will pass one day when you find a lovely girl like this Malika. I thought you were set on her?" Danny looking down to the floor says "Let's be honest Niel she is with someone and she didn't show any interest in me, so I think I am only dreaming. I can't see me getting a woman ever again who will want a blind man, I am a bloody nuisance to anyone who wants a good life, why should they look after me, they will run a mile, it's over Niel I know it but won't admit it but don't worry I am not

438

going to do myself in, because of my children so there I just find life different than it ever was and it is making me feel so down that's all. I don't want you to feel sorry for me or anyone else for that Matter, just wish I could find something to feel happy about and something to look forward to more than once a month, you know what I mean Niel? Anything to hang onto, god that's not asking much, I spend too much time on my own and it is destroying me it really is." Niel now looking sad says "I know Dan it is awful for you at the moment but you will see it will get better I promise you and you have made so many friends here and some enemies mind but that is by the by, I don't like to see you like this Dan, come on we can go for a drink tomorrow night to the karaoke in town the Litton tree, we can take Kezz and her friend to hear them sing that will cheer you me and the girls up, we can be like parents and look after them, they will love that, what do you think? And we can ask Jeff and Jo and have a blast that's what you need matey." "Why not I am up for it I suppose, let's do it, I will leave you tell or rather ask Kezz and Amanda Mandy I will sort out the taxi's, sorry mate, I can't help the way I feel." "I know Dan forget it but let's not hear any more of suicide ok?" "Ok mate and this conversation never happened ok?" "Fine with me." "Well I had better get back to my lectures, I will see you later in the lounge and keep your chin up." "Your a good mate Niel." "Ditto, see you later." Niel left an Danny sat there for a while longer.

Later and Jeff and Jo were In the refectory for tea and Niel was looking for them and found them and sat to eat with them and said "Do you and Jo fancy coming to the Litton tree to the karaoke tomorrow night?" Jo replies "I am not all that fussed, who is going?" Jeff "Well I bet Danny has put you up to this, as the beer is cheap in there." Niel "Well Danny is coming and Kezz and Amanda Mandy and I found Danny sitting on his own on the bench outside Dowdell in a right state." Jo looking concerned says "What do you mean Niel?" Niel "Danny is still having a hard time with going blind and his wife's solicitor has sent him the letter asking him for a divorce and apparently is trying to put the blame on him and he told me he still feels like killing himself on times and now he can't get a girl has made him feel as if he will never have a happy life again, he was terrible Jeff." Jeff "Awe it's just because I made him feel bad about that Malika, because she has got a boyfriend and he has taken it to heart." Jo "But we were only teasing him Jeff wasn't we? Oh dear I feel awful now I didn't mean any of it." Jeff "Oh don't blame yourself Jo he is just attention seeking." Niel in serious voice "No I don't think so Jeff, the way he was it would not take much to push him over the edge, he can't see a way out of it honestly mate he is not with it at all, I don't think we should take this lying down and don't tell him I said anything I promised I wouldn't." Jeff "Fair enough I seen him when his brother died this year, I think things have got him down since Winnie left even though they were not getting on he misses her I think and losing his both brothers in such a short time has pushed him over the edge." Jo "And his wife leaving him, it is a lot to handle isn't it?" Niel "Yes I think so he needs to keep busy he has too much time to think that is the trouble, he will be allright but he must be hurting inside with all that going on in his head I know I would crack up. I am off to see him later to make sure so are you up for it at the karaoke? Can I book you both in for the taxi ?" Jeff "I think so Niel what do you think Jo?" Jo says "Oh yes of course I will come." Niel "Right then that's sorted then and remember don't tell him I have been talking to you about all of this." Jeff "Of course not Niel." Niel went off and went over to Dowdell to see Danny.

The following night in the Litton tree and there was Clamper, Danny, Jeff, Niel, Jo, M M M Mark, Kezz and Amanda Mandy, the girls were all excited to be there and were trying to get up to sing   and they were having a good drink and Danny said to the lads "The price of lager in here is reasonable isn't it?" Niel "Yes too reasonable I think, we will be pissed if we carry on like this." Mark "Well I won't be the last time I was in here with D,D,D, Danny I missed a lecture the next day and that is the only time I, I, I, have missed a lecture." Jeff "Never mind mark as long as we enjoy the evening I suppose." Clamper "I always like it here as long as Jeff don't start telling me what to do." Danny "Oh that won't happen tonight Andy as Jo is with him and she is the boss there and she loves you so you will be allright." Kezz "Eek, eek, eek, we are off to sing now lads see you later, keep our seats, bye, bye." Jeff "That's it we will not see them all night now they will take over the stage you watch what I am saying especially Kezz she is not shy at all." Niel "Well I am enjoying myself how about you Dan? Allright here isn't it?" Danny "Yes it's not bad and they serve a good pint to, it's going down well." Jeff "I thought that lot of recruit's may be here later as I told them about it, maybe the French girl will come and see you Danny you never know matey." Danny looking serious "I won't hold my breath, she is with that asshole Roy, I am having a good few tonight so if I get out of hand put me in a taxi and send me home, I wouldn't want to spoil anyone's night and besides she seem happy with him but mark my words she will be mine if she comes back to the college, I mean it, ha, ha, ha." Niel that's what I like positive thinking." Danny "Well we will see I need a woman like a hole in the head now as I am going to have a messy divorce I think as us men always do, I fancy something to eat now anyone else hungry?" Nobody said anything Danny continues "Fair enough I will have a burger then later, oh come on everyone let's crank it up a bit I am supposed to be the miserable bastard not you lot, what's the Matter with you all? C'mon get with it." Jeff "I am fine Dan happy enough and Niel is smiling ok? These youngsters are more interested in their mobile phones though." Niel "So you have cheered up then Danny boy? I was getting worried about you for a while there." Danny "I am fine now it comes and goes, I think being on my own a lot is not good for me and I am still even now not getting used to this bloody blindness, it's so restricting." Niel "Tell me about it." Jeff "You must not let it get to you Dan, I feel the same sometimes and think why me? Why me? but there is no answer so I just forget it as quick as I can and you have got more troubles in your head than most, all that has happened to you in the last 5 years, so don't beat yourself up about it life goes on Dan and as you always say to me we are lucky many kids don't live to see their 5th birthday do they?" Danny looking suspicious at Niel Ok, so you 2 have been talking haven't you? I knew it." Niel butted in "Oh c'mon mate I was worried about you, we are not gossiping behind your back honestly Dan we are just concerned." Jeff "You are a mate matey and a trouble shared, you know so how are you really feeling now?" Danny "Awful if the truth is told, I can't understand why all this is happening to me all of the time, if there is a god he has a funny sense of humour and he must hate my guts and soon all of us will depart to our different destinations and me where am I going to go all by myself? How am I going to manage my life on my own? And why the hell should I? I have not done anything to hurt anybody ever, why is this happening to me all the bloody time? What future do I have? these are the things that bother me and why go on anyway as I have one brother left he is too wrapped up in his religion and I never see him even before I went blind, all my other brothers are dead, mum is gone, why go on? I would be happier if I was dead, no more troubles all sorted and I am not saying this for you to feel sorry for me believe me I am not but can you see my predicament? really it is hopeless, if I had a running mate to have a reason to live I would not say so much but it's just me and who in their right mind wants a blind man as a partner from scratch?" Jeff "You got us as friends that counts for a lot." Danny "I know Jeff I am not saying that but it's not enough, you have got your own lives to live and sometimes I feel I don't want any friends at all." Niel looking shocked "What do you mean? Aren't we good enough for you then?" Danny "My point is if I had no friends or family then they could not hurt me like my 2 brothers did by dying and breaking my heart all of the time, I just can't handle any more heartache I am not condemning you or hating you I think the world of the both of you and all the rest of you but I can't stand any more dying around me. So maybe it's time I checked out for my own good." Jeff "Oh your being silly now, so you want to do the same to us then?" Danny "Sorry I am being cynical but that's how I have been feeling lately, I will come back to normal soon enough, it's just getting to me and it makes me mad whatever sorts out our destiny should go and pick on someone else for a change that's all I am saying, anyway who's round is it?" Jeff "It's yours." Danny smiling says "See what I mean, even the bloody round is me, stuff it here rip out my bloody throat while your at it ha, ha, it doesn't rain but it pours ha, ha, I am going to get bladdered so drink up." Danny goes up to the bar with Clamper to help him and Jeff says to Niel "God I see what you mean Niel he has just about given up the way he is talking, do you think he is going to be ok? He is worrying me." Niel "Yes he will be allright I think but I am leaving in a couple of weeks and I haven't told him yet so it will be up to you to keep him happy." Jeff answers "Well I leave soon also so I can see what he is on about now I just hope he finds someone that will make a difference, hello he is coming back." Danny hands the drinks over and says "I just met Madge by the bar and she left me have a feel of her mini skirt, what a pair of legs and that Italian girl was with her, god what a body I am having a dance with them later, shit I forgot my burger I will be back in a minute." He goes back up to the bar and Jeff says "Well there is a difference in a few minutes, I think he will pull himself together soon enough."

The following morning in the lounge and Jeff, Niel, Danny, Zarrine and Lyn sat having toast and tea Danny says "Well it was a good night last night in the Litton tree and I am aching from dancing with Madge, the lager is good there and cheap, have you ever been there Lyn?" Lyn "Yes I have been there it is good but when you have lectures the next day it is daunting with a hangover like Jeff." Jeff "Oh leave me alone, I am dying, it's these bloody Welshmen's fault." Niel "Don't blame me i dropped out after 5." Danny "And I didn't drink that much, Zarrine he was like a fish last night." Jeff "Well at least you have cheered up today feeling much better now Dan?" Danny "Ok I suppose." Zarrine "You need to relax a bit more and let your body catch up with your mind Danny, you need a woman to look after you." Danny "I don't need looking after I just need someone who is nice and fun to share my life with and I worry I will be left on the shelf, are you listening Lyn?" Lyn smiling says in a gentle voice "Oh here he goes again, I heard you were fancying a French girl is that true?" Jeff "Yes he was but she had her boyfriend with her, so that ruined it for him." Zarrine "Oh yes Danny, why was I not told then." Danny "There is nothing to tell Zarrine, so when are you going to tell me you are leaving then Niel?" Niel looking shocked "I don't need to tell you, you already know don't you by the sounds of it?" Lyn "So when are you leaving Niel?" Niel "3 weeks time, I will be finished, it should have been a few months ago so no big deal Dan is it?" Danny "No I was only kidding, I didn't want you to worry about telling us, I am allright you know just had a Paddy last night that's all, so are we having a party before you go ?" Jeff "Well we can have a drink to say goodbye can't we?" Niel "Well of course we can, I will miss you all but not this place but never mind." Zarrine "I am sad as it is all going to change here now Niel is leaving it will not be the same I will miss you and Abby." Niel "Why? You will still have these pair here and that's enough for anyone to put up with Zarrine. We have had some good times here haven't we? remember that summer day when Danny said we are going to have a chip butty day, Lyn you couldn't believe it, it was lovely we sat in here at the big table and I prepared a huge mound of bread and butter and placed them in the middle of the table and Danny got a huge bag of chips and placed them by the side of them and we sat down and scoffed it all up with a load of salt and vinegar, didn't we lads? It was a wonderful time, you should have been here Lyn you would have loved it." Lyn "I think it must have been lovely as it is a tradition in Wales, the Welsh butty I have had many in my time, I know what you mean." Danny "Well Lyn we also had a cawl day, Niel and me made a huge cawl in a borrowed pan from the canteen and it was that big it covered the cooker over by there all 4 rings, it was massive wasn't it Niel?" Niel "Yes it bloody was and guess who done all the peeling of the vegetables? yes me I was peeler and Danny was the chef and it was beautiful and the place had so many students it was unbelievable it really was and we had to stop Clamper, he had 5 bowls and there was none left after that day it was incredible." Zarrine "I know I never had a taste at all, I remember that day it was saint Welsh day." Niel smiling at what Zarrine said says "Saint Welsh day, Zarrine it was Saint David's day not Welsh day." Danny "We had some fun doing that, we have had some fun here mind." Jeff "We certainly have, I bet Zarrine will be glad to see the back of us next year?" Zarrine "To right I will, it has been a testing time with you 3, can't wait to see the back of you." Niel "Awe Zarrine you don't mean that do you?" Zarrine "Ha, ha, ha, I am only joking I will miss you very much, this has been the best time I have ever had here in this college and it will not be the same when you have all gone, I mean it, it will be a sad day for me I love you 3 to bit's as you all keep saying to me." Jeff "And Danny is your favourite, I know I have always said it." Zarrine "I love you all the same even though Danny has had more attention than the rest of you, he is a little special and you all know why he has had more than his fair share of problems not through his own fault so leave it now Jeffrey." Jeff "I was only kidding, shit look at the time I must be off I am late." Niel "Good god is that the time? Shit I must be gone to." They all leave except Danny and Zarrine who started to clear the breakfast things. Zarrine said "So how are you now Danny? Are you ok?" "Yes I am ok now I just get too much time to think sometimes, I just can't get used to being blind and wonder how and where I am going to end up, you know what I mean? Jeff and Niel are going back to family I have not got anyone to go back to." "What about your children then? your sons and daughters surely they would have you with them?" "I expect so but I would never throw myself on them, they have only just started their own lives they would make me sit down in certain places and do everything for me, no good, I am only young and my life is not over yet. I have decided to move away from Bridgend, there is no life there for me anymore, so off down west Wales for me thank you." "Well you know what you want and I just hope you find someone soon that you can settle down with." "I won't just grab anyone I need someone I love as well not just have them because they are there for my blindness, I must have someone I will love and that's hard when you are blind but I will manage if not I will come and live with you and peter ha, ha, ha." Zarrine "Ha, ha, I don't think so you are too much to handle, I hope you will come and see me from time to time mind?" "No problem Zarrine, you have become very special to me, I must run I have got to be in the FLC as soon as possible, see you later." "Yes and I will be in your room and if those stink bombs are still in there I will throw them in the bin and if not don't let anymore off here In Dowdell or else, see you later.

Well it finally came to the day when Niel was leaving but to Danny and Jeff's astonishment it was the evening before and his wife and her parents had come to pick him up that evening leaving no time for a party. Danny said "Well I am surprised you are going tonight Niel, I thought we were having a drink to say goodbye." Niel "I am sorry but my father in law could not make it tomorrow, so I must go when it suits him, he is good enough to come and get me." Danny "Ok fair enough, I understand." Niel "Can I ask you Mandy to hold the door for us to get these things out please?" Mandy "Of course I can Niel no problem." Jeff "Here I will give you a hand Niel." Niel "Thank you Jeff." After they had finished packing the car they sat down together in the lounge for the last time together. Niel, Jeff, Ceri, her parents, Jo, Mandy Clamper and Danny. Jeff said "Well Niel good luck with everything and look after yourself, I will be thinking of you." Niel "Well thank you Jeff but first can you get me a couple of glasses? As I have a bottle of whiskey that Danny missed in my room and we can have a goodbye drink." Danny "Well you kept that quiet, I always said you were a secret drinker." Niel "I am now going to tell you a story, my wife by their Ceri thought I was becoming an alcoholic because of the whiskey i was going through and it was him that was bloody drinking it with me, he is like a fish with whiskey." Ceri backs Niel up and said "Yes Danny I was very worried at one point and until I asked him I thought I was living with an alcoholic." Jeff "With whiskey they are as bad as each other and it was lovely to see mind, we would come back from the bar and sometimes Niel was sitting having a night cap for bed and him and Danny would finish the bottle off and they would be giggling like 2 little girls, it was so funny and the faces on them the next morning was a picture." Danny "If you should forget to put that bottle in the car I will fetch it down with me don't worry." Niel "No fear of that so don't come the raw prawn with me squire ha, ha, ha." Jeff "I am having a tinny Niel I don't like whiskey." Mandy "So will we see you in the stag night with Tim Niel?" Niel "Oh no, I will not be there for that I will let Danny, Clamper and Jeff do the honours there, I cannot travel the next day after booze I am hopeless so I will see you at the wedding, give Tim my regards and tell him I will phone him on the weekend." Mandy "Ok Niel I will and don't forget." Clamper "I will see you at the wedding then Niel." Niel "Yes ok Andy, I expect I will see you in Bridgend sometime Danny boy?" Danny "Not likely Niel I am off Bridgend but will come and see you at the Carmarthen bay caravan park at your caravan." Niel "Oh anytime mate and bring that English git with you." Jeff "Steady. " Niel stood up and said "Right we must be off sorry all, Clamper come here and shake my hand." He shook his hand then Andy put his head on Niel's chest and hugged Niel and said "Bye, bye, matey, I will be seeing you sometime." Niel "Yes Andy and get on with your own life and make a good go at things because your a good lad." Clamper "I will thanks matey." Niel "Mandy where are you ?" Mandy wrapped her arms around Niel and said "I am going to miss you a lot Niel be good and don't forget to call us and we look forward to seeing you at the wedding, love you." Niel "Love you to Mandy and look after that daft Tim for us." Mandy "I will, don't worry." Niel turned to Jeff "So long Jeff it has been fun hasn't it? I will miss you look after yourself and you Jo." He hugged Jo as she came through the door "Look after Jeff Jo I will miss you all." There was a pause and he finally turned to Danny and put his hand out and gave it a vigorous shake and said "So long Dan an good luck in the future, I have had some of the best times of my life and will miss you, so get on with your life and do it your way, look after yourself I will be seeing you." They hugged seemed like forever and then broke and slapped each other's backs. Danny then turned to Ceri and gave her a hug and she kissed him on the cheek and said "Look after yourself Dan and keep in touch, you have got our telephone number." Danny kissed her and said "Yes I certainly have and I will keep in touch, try and stop me and look after him he is worth his weight in gold, I will miss him." Danny then turned and got on one knee to say goodbye to Abby, Danny scratched her neck, she wagged her tail Danny said to her in a sad voice "Goodbye old girl, I will miss you very much look after your master and have a lovely life girl." Abby seemed to understand she pranced around a little as if she knew she was leaving, then they all went outside to see them off, it was a very tearful time for the lads and they got back to the lounge and in Danny seat was the remnants of the whiskey. Danny said "God bless you Niel, I will miss him he is a great man and I will keep this whiskey as a momentum of his friendship, c'mon Jeff let's go for a pint to celebrate good friends and see Mandy off." Mandy "I will be honoured lads." Off they went to the bar together.

Up in the bar and they were standing by the bar and Danny was smiling to himself and Mandy said to him "What's that cunning little smile you have got over your face Danny?" Danny replies "I was thinking about Niel and all the antics we got up to, especially when we went to town and he asked a old man the way to the vodophone shop and instead of showing him he pointed the way and when Niel got his hair off and said does this guide dog give you a clue I am blind the man got on his knees and pointed the way to Abby, it was so funny and the time he used Abby to empty the pub pretending he was the drug squad and Abby was a sniffer dog, god I will miss him and his temper with the computers, he is a hell of a man, just my sort of man and dependable and truthful and he cares about everyone and everything." Jeff "Yes he is a good one and I will miss him it feels like it was only yesterday we all got together here don't it?" Danny "I know, it has gone so fast but it has changed my life here for the good and now our Mandy is leaving tomorrow, she was the woman who first took me around and showed me the way and the same for Tim and now look at them getting married in May, I am so happy for you Mandy." Jeff "Yes all the best for the both of you a real nice couple." Mandy "Thanks lads it has been an experience and I am so happy with Tim and I will always think of my life here since you lot got here, I mean Danny, Jeff , Niel, Tim, and even Andy, Carol and Jo and of course gupta he is nice." Danny "Let's have a toast." Jeff "Look out the whiskey is kicking in." Danny "Ooh shut up, I want to say to the gang and especially Tim and Niel who have already gone all the best." They clang glasses and smile . Mandy "It feels funny it being my last night here I thought, I was destined to be here for the rest of my life until I met Tim" Danny "Well never mind Mandy you could always change your mind and marry me instead." Mandy "Sorry Danny it's Tim for me, Jeff where did Jo get to?" Jeff "She has got an early one tomorrow so gone to bed, look out here is Kezz, hello squiggly." Kezz "Hi guys eek, eek, who is here altogether?" Danny "Me Jeff and Mandy and your going to ask me when Niel is coming over aren't you?" Kezz "Yeah it is time to party if he is going." Danny "Sorry Kezz he has already gone, he had to go tonight, his father in law could not pick him up tomorrow but he said to say goodbye." Kezz "Awe that's not fair, he was supposed to have a proper drink and say goodbye, I wanted to see him before he went, awe bloody hell mun." Mandy "He had to go Kezz, he didn't want to go but he had no choice, but he said to say goodbye to you all before he went, just remember him as you have always done." Kezz "Yes I know but I wanted to buy him a pint, he is always buying me a drink it was my turn, oh dear it's not fair, well I will drink it for him, I will miss him." Jeff "Yes we all will but he will be back to see us all before we leave I am sure Kezz." Kezz "I remember him threatening a lad here for picking on me and the lad was petrified of me after, he has a heart of gold does Niel and you are leaving tomorrow to Mandy?" Mandy now nearly in tears says "Yes I am Kezz, you have been here as long as me I think, so when are you leaving?" Kezz "I think it is in Easter so not long. All the gang are leaving it is sad but we were a real cool gang, banging, banging." Danny "That's true it will never be the same again, it's been mad, I wonder who we will have next in Dowdell, I hope it's someone with a good sense of humour, my round drink up and you Kezz." Danny gets

444

the drinks in and they have a lovely farewell party in the student bar. And at the end of the night they were worse for drink.

Well Xmas came pretty quick in the college and things settled down a little for Danny and the lads had a few months of drinking and Danny decided to change his life one day while talking to Jeff in the lounge over breakfast. Danny says " well Jeff I have decided my life must Improve now I am still alone and looks like I am going to be living alone for the rest of my life." Jeff looks shocked says "What do you mean? And who said you will end up on your own for the rest of your life anyway?" "Well it looks that way so I had better do something about it, I mean I can do most things but now I am blind I need to find out the way a blind person would do it, I mean the easiest way for me I need to see Alison about personal care, cooking, cleaning, using things for the blind and doing bills etc. You know what I mean?" " Jeff being sarcastic says "You need personel hygiene I think." Danny "You cheeky git what do you mean by that?" "Ha, ha, I am only kidding Dan, do you think it is that bad for you then? Perhaps you can get a woman to come in on a daily basis, most people in your position does that." "Not for me, I would rather look after myself and get a woman once a week just to make sure it is done properly so I will go and see Alison in my tutorial this morning and get some help and I hope I will have a dog soon, you must be due for one now they don't rush do they?" Jeff "That's a point I need to phone them and see what is happening I suppose, good thinking batman." "I heard they give you a woman here to teach you how to use things safely, I mean I can already cook and do most everything but to do it safely now I am blind is another thing so I will find out, I don't know why you haven't tried that?" Jeff says cockily "No need I have got my mother to do that for me so I am ok." "Yes but you can't rely on your mother all of the time can you? it's not fair on your mother is it?" "She don't mind and neither do I ha,, ha, ha." "You never know I might be good at it and never need a woman again as long as i live except for a bit of nonsense I suppose, it's like a grandchild you can nurse them and always know when they start crying you can give them back, a bit sexist I know but I like it that way." "I will agree with you there I like my beer so that would suit me, have you heard from Niel lately?" "No I haven't, I will give him a ring later and Tim I will give him a call after xmas to, am I still alright for a couple of days after xmas up with you matey?" Jeff replies "Yes of course Dan I am looking forward to it and I bet you are?" Danny "Yes especially that Chinese chip shop in park south with you, the best Chinese in the world, we must eat every night there mate I love their food and can't wait." "Yes you do go over the top for that place don't you? and we can go to the quiz up the sun in by me and of course I have told the Welsh lads in the Polish club you are coming up." "Is Jo coming up to stay with you over Xmas then?" Jeff coughed and tried to change the subject but Danny kept on about it "Is she coming up to yours at Xmas Jeff? Yes or no?" " In a huff Jeff replies "No she is staying with her parents, nothing wrong with that is there? She has her family to think of." Danny smiles "Yeah, right, I am telling you she is not going to be around when you finish at this college mark my words, she has not got a clue what this is all about with you and her, so forget it." "Allright don't keep on now, I just want a good Xmas with plenty of booze." "I won't be touching the booze until I get to Swindon, I want to enjoy it with my kids and Josh before he grows up, so I will be fresh when I arrive with you." Jeff not convinced says "Yeah, yeah, I will believe that when I see it ." "Right Jeff I am off to see Alison and get my life sorted out see you later , we will have a pint tonight, yes?" " Jeff smiling says "Is there bark on trees? See you later."

Later in the college Danny in Alison's office for his tutorial and she asks him some questions "Well Danny how are things? Are you and Jeff still drinking heavy?" Danny looking shocked says "What do you mean?" "Well on the report this month from the hall at Dowdell it appears you and Jeff have come in around 25 out of 30 times worse for wear ha, ha, what do you have to say am I right?" Danny sniggering says "Yes I think maybe your right, but we have been a little lost since most of our friends have left and feel left out but it is cooling down now and that is another thing I wanted to say or rather ask." Alison says "What is that Danny?" "Well it looks more and more like I will be on my own when I leave here and need some sort of help with doing for myself, is there anything here for me?" Alison "You mean like cooking cleaning and things like that?" "Yes exactly I know how to cook and clean and do most things for myself but now I am blind and there must be easier ways of doing it and safely, . I wonder if there is anyone who can teach me before I leave." "Yes there is a lady called sue Bridgland who does it, called domestic science, but for the blind, she can show you many gadgets for the blind to make things simpler like cooking aids for the micro oven a talking microwave oven." Danny looking in amazement says "Your kidding, a talking microwave oven aye?" "Oh yes many things for the blind such as talking scales talking weighing scales talking measuring tapes talking levels and on and on. Do you want me to make a appointment to give you some lessons here? I can get you onto this Immediately as it is Important for you to get this right and anything else?" "Yes I need someone to help me to learn to shop for clothes, go to the supermarket and get goods and many general things, can we do this?" " of course we can, sue does all that I wish you had said something earlier, you would have been a ace at it by now, I will arrange it for you and you can start Immediately, Sue is very good." "Thank you Alison, that would be fantastic thank you again." Alison then said "Before you go have you heard from Niel lately?" "Funny enough I was talking to Jeff about that very thing and I am going to give him a ring after I finish with you." "Ok then give him my regards then, see you next week bye." "Thanks Alison, bye." Danny leaves with a huge smile on his face and goes off to speak to Niel in Dowdell on the phone.

Later up the bar and Danny and Jeff were sitting having a pint and Danny was telling him how Niel was "Well he seems ok, he was excited to hear from me and I thought he sounded a little bored but he also told me he has got plenty to do with himself and asked about you and all the others here and I told him about Kezz not seeing him before he left, he told me to say sorry to her but otherwise he sounded ok and guess what I forgot to tell you, Winnie called me this morning on the phone all the way from China, it was lovely to hear her voice, but she sounded a little sad, she is missing me and hopes one day to come back here. She has been in touch with Lennox to find out if she could come back and she sounded positive about that. I could hear the peacocks and other birds in the background it sounds lovely there, I felt like getting on a plane and joining her." Jeff's eyes lit up on this news and he said "Well that is not such a bad idea Dan, she would look after you like a king, those Chinese birds are so faithful to their men she would spoil you, you would never need for nothing you would be a king with her." "I often think about it mind Jeff, it would be nice I expect but she would only go back to the way she is with me and I am not that brave in someone else's country and she would have the Triads after my blood, but I wonder sometimes about it, would you go?" "I would go off like a shot especially with such a good looker as Winnie and that body and the weather where she lives It's fantastic, so I reckon you could not go wrong in my opinion and you could always come back if it didn't work out, what will you lose?" "My privates knowing her, mmmm, I know what you mean mind but not for me I got a feeling she will return here soon enough anyway, but a nice dream if only." "Well I think you are a fool, you complain you are on your own an so is she." Danny smiling says "Yes but you have seen it, we cannot sit in the same room without arguing if I won't do things her way, so that's why I am better off on my own and stop trying to get rid of me, change the subject." "So Niel is ok then? I am glad and how did your tutorial go with Alison then? Did you ask her about your living skills?" "That's it living skills I couldn't think of the name, yes it is all on, a lady named Sue Bridgeland is taking me to teach me, she is very good at it and did you know there are talking micro wave ovens, measuring tapes, weighing scales and small talking scales for measuring out food?" "Oh yes there is a lot of things like that but expensive as usual, everything for the blind costs an arm and a leg, it's ridiculous what they charge but you can get help with some of those things the micro oven is stupid mind it even tells you when the door is open as if you didn't know ha, ha, so when does this start?" "Immediately but I may ask her to leave it until xmas is over, there is only another week before we finish for xmas but I am looking forward to it." Jeff pondered and says "That Sue used to teach the JAWS on the computer, she must have changed her job and if I remember she is a fit young woman but I think she is married, never mind." "There we are then so she must be good at her job, I need this bad. Did you find out about the guide dog then?" "No they will phone when they are ready. God it's dead in here isn't it? I thought there were new students starting before xmas but they have left it until after xmas and that girl Malika is coming for definite and that dawn and Jeff and I forgot the other girls name." Danny smiling replies "Inga you mean." Jeff nearly choked on his beer then said "I hope not I don't need any trouble, mind you Jo stayed in again this lovely evening it's Friday and dead here, most of them have gone home by the looks of it except John Hood he was in the lecture room today and he brought his frock in for the girls to see, he is wearing it in the xmas ball next week and he looked really camp in it with his different coloured finger nails, it was obscene you would have not liked it. I was wishing you were there." Danny "Why was that?" Jeff "Because he would not have done it as he knows your views on it, homosexuality I mean." "I don't mind it as long as they don't keep pushing it in my face like he does, he didn't like it when I told him off for calling me straight and he got offended because I don't call him a homo, I wanted him to call me normal because that is what I am so don't give me a name, he did not like it but that's his problem ha, ha, I bet he looked a state in that frock? Be buggered, a frock, is he a preacher or what? I don't believe it ha, ha, so what are you wearing then?" "Ha, ha, I am wearing a diving suit ha, ha, ha." Danny laughed and says "Ha, ha, you would not be able to lift your legs up in those boots and what about Jo is she coming or staying in?" " Jeff still laughing says "No she is coming, her father is picking her up the following morning, I think he is staying in a hotel in Hereford and taking her home the next morning but I hope John don't sit by me I will die laughing." "Your not the only one I will ask Kezz to come with us that night jus to help her out nothing else, so don't make anything of it I love her to bit's but she is too young for me." "I think you would make a lovely pair." "If I was a lot younger, a lot younger and I could see you on John's arm mind he is your type I think ha, ha, ha." "Now that is not funny Dan, I feel sick now." Danny "I bet you do, I notice all the poofta's are the same not good looking at all, they don't stand a chance with most girls so they turn the other way with the exception of the likes of the odd one or 2, never mind, we all have a choice." "As long as I haven't got to join in. I think I will go back to Dowdell in a minute and open a couple of cans it's so boring here." "I think I will join you and finish off that whiskey Niel left me it is going to be quiet here until after xmas, so we just as well go home now." The lads go back to Dowdell.

Well xmas came and Danny went home to see Josh and the family and enjoyed it even though it was uncomfortable there with his wife not liking him home probably because she could not have her alcoholic boyfriend there while he was there but Josh made the most of his home coming and they both enjoyed never mind what. Then Danny joined Jeff up in Swindon and had a great time meeting the lads in the Polish club and seeing Jeff's family again and before you knew it, it was back to college and a chance to find out what all the new students were like. We join them back in the lounge in Dowdell early back at college and it was Jeff, Danny and Zarrine sitting there and Zarrine asked "Well lads how was your xmas?" Danny "Brilliant I seen all the children and had a great time with Josh, he was so excited." Zarrine "Well he would be seeing his dad for Xmas." Danny continued "Then I went up to stay with Jeff in Swindon and enjoyed every minute of what I could remember about it all, had a brilliant laugh isn't that right Jeff?" Jeff half asleep "Oh yes it was fun, I am still getting over last night, I am glad we have not got any lectures today. My god I feel drunk still ha, ha, I blame that dodgy Welshman by there." Zarrine snaps "No Jeffrey, nothing to do with Danny, you could say no he didn't have your arm behind your back at any time ha, ha, you are a stirrer that's what you are Jeffrey, go to bed and sleep it off, my poor Danny you always get the blame don't you?" Danny smiling says "Thank you Zarrine, he is always blaming me, at last someone else has noticed, mind you the longer the day goes on the worse I feel, I will be like you Jeff soon enough let's go for the hair of the dog in an hour up the bridge." Jeff "Oh I don't know I feel bad enough as it is, what time were you thinking of going?" Danny "In about an hour, what do you think?" Jeff "Fair enough I will come." Zarrine laughing says "You pair, I hope we are not going to have another season like the last one?" Danny "No I must get into it this term, I am in need of progress to, I am serious I am afraid so Jeff will have to entertain himself this term I am only going out twice a week from now on." Jeff "Yes I know Monday to Thursday and Friday to Sunday ha, ha, ha." Zarrine "Yes Jeff that's right I know what you mean ha, ha, ha, ha." Danny "So who has got Niel's room then?" Zarrine "Dawn somebody or other and there is another one Jeff by our Jeff and C J in Mandy's room and I don't know about anyone else yet." Jeff "What no girlies over by me except Madge? God I would." Zarrine "Jeffrey, I am watching you behave yourself and besides she is leaving next week." Jeff opened eyed says "Oh why is she leaving?" Zarrine "Because she is homesick, so she is finishing." Danny "Bloody hell the only girl here with sex appeal and by the way Jeff I would too, I mean except you Zarrine." Zarrine "I hope you are not being rude Danny?" Danny "Who me? No not me." Jeff laughing says "Well we just as well go now Dan it's terrible now." Just then in walks the S. S. W. Ricardo Lidia's nephew looking for Danny." Ricardo says to Danny "Hello Danny, glad to see you, I need help from you, I am having no luck, please can you do this for me?" Danny looking concerned says "What can I do for you Ricardo? Tell me." Ricardo "I need help with my British I need to speak better and my aunt Lidia told me to ask you." Danny "Well you mean speak English not British and the answer is yes of course I can help." Jeff butts in "Ricardo you are asking a bright one there, he can't speak English properly either ha, ha, ha." Danny "Don't listen to him Ricardo, I taught Lidia and she passed everything in Hereford college." Ricardo says "This I know already so what about tomorrow sae like 5 o'clock in your room Danny?" Danny "Um let me think, yes I will be finished by then, I will see you then?" Ricardo "Thank you my friend, I will see you then, adios." All wish him adios and in came a girl with loads of luggage it was dawn." Dawn says "Hello everyone, oh hello Jeff I am here I need to get to my room, who do I see?" Zarrine "I have got the key to your room come on I will take you." Off the pair of them went and Danny said "So what is she like Jeff?" "Not bad at all but she has got a boyfriend at home, I would mind." "Jeff that is no recommendation you would with anyone and there is only 2 men besides to come so let's go to the Bridge for a pint is it?" "Why not, are we going to wait for Clamper?" "No I can't afford it he has never got money or on time forget it, let's go before it gets manic here with people running around with suitcases, c'mon get out and then meet me down stairs." They meet and go off to the Bridge and stood by the bar talking. Jeff spoke first and says "Well matey a nice pint of lager, just what the doctor ordered." Danny "Right, I needed that I think the college is going to be boring now time to work a bit more." Jeff "Maybe your right but remember my bird is still here somewhere ha, ha, ha." "Well she Impressed the Welsh lads in the Polish club indeed and your head swelled up more than normal and you gave yourself some credit points there mind you, Jo has got a nice figure and a nice ass, I know I grabbed it in the karaoke in the Litton tree by accident and she never complained mind but you are a mate so I behaved myself." "Well that's very decent of you Danny I will remember that if you ever get a bird." "What do you mean? You tried all in your power to get Winnie in your bed behind my back, so don't come it Jeff ha, ha, ha." "Oh yes, sorry ha, ha, I was drunk." "At six o'clock in the evening, come on, your a dirty old man that's what you are." Jeff "Hey less of the old mate and besides she is a one woman man, I stood no chance and besides you didn't want her anyway, so shut up." "That's besides the point Jeff, I never dragged Jo in my bedroom did i?" "No I didn't but I will try if you like but I don't stand a chance just like you as I don't think you have ever done it with her either she just is not that type of girl, shall I ask her maybe?" "I know the truth go ahead ask her I don't care." Next thing a voice came over the room it was Carol and with her was Adi, she said "You 2 arguing again Uncle Jeffrey? You should know better." Jeff "Well hello gorgeous hows you then?" Carol "I am fine thank you, we just got back so felt like a pint or 2, didn't we darling?" Sat besides her was Adrian, he answered "Yes wing nut I needed a pint, how are you lads?" Danny "Fine thanks Adi how are you?" Adi "Great thanks and you Jeff? Allright or what?" Jeff smiling said "Fine thanks for asking." Adi "Well if you don't ask I won't know will I? I have shown Carol a good time over Xmas, we have had some fun haven't we love?" Carol "Yes we have had a great time and it's back now to the work at college, where did you 2 get to in the hols? Danny did I hear you went up Jeff's?" Danny "Yes we had a good piss up, up there so we came here for the hair of the dog and what did you 2 get up to?" Carol "We went down to Wales then up to mums to finish off it was brilliant wasn't it Adi ?" Adi "Yes, oh yes we didn't stop having fun I need the gym as soon as to get back to my fitness, what about you lads? I haven't seen you in there for a while now Dan?" Jeff answered first "I was in there just before Xmas on the Thursday, I popped in for a glass of water out of the large bottle in there ha, ha, ha." Adi "Yes Jeff very droll, so are you coming back Dan? I am looking for a case study, if you feel like it mate?" Danny thought for a minute and said "Why not, I should get back into it, I am getting lazy, I will Adi, I will let you have a copy of my schedule and you can work some days out ok?" Adi "Great I will, do you lads want a pint?" Danny "I will have a pint of lager pleas Adi." Adi "Jeff?" Jeff "Oh no thanks I am fine thank you." Adi "Oh come on I have forgotten it let bygones be bygones, what do you say? You are empty, go on?" Jeff "Ok I will have a lager to please." Adi "Fine, I won't ask Carol as the answer is always the same, yes." Carol "I heard that 2." Adi "I know that is why I call you wing nut ha, ha, the college is a pain today with all the new ones arriving and the student bar is not open tonight it's ridiculous." Danny "Yes it was manic when we left and there is nothing up here any night is there? It is just as boring here." Jeff "No there is nothing ever here, it is Monday nothing anywhere on a Monday." Carol "I thought I was leaving this week but have managed to con a extension out of the college but I will be gone definitely by Easter. How about you lads?" Danny "I have had an extension until august so am fine I think." Jeff "I am here for a couple of weeks that's all." Danny "I am here for another year or at least august I think, I had it because I have not got anywhere to go but I am grateful I can learn a little more for my benefit." Carol "Adi is here until Easter as well." Jeff grunted as if to say there we are then. Danny says "Oh he is grumpy because he don't like his girls with any other man, look at Geraldine she has just left and is living with Shaun now, he don't like Shaun now, for some reason I wonder what that is and he don't like Adi because he is with you and if he could have got all you girls at the same time he would be going out with each of you behind each other's backs and although he is with Jo he would get Madge in his bed behind her back, so he is two faced." Carol smiling says "It's like you with Winnie, I always laugh ha, ha, ha, ha, the time that you were going home early every night and I used to ask Jeff where you were going and he used to say for a Chinese and I thought it was a meal and thought you will be like a tank eating all those Chinese meals and then I realised that it was to give Winnie one, I felt so stupid awe. I can't get over how time has just gone, do you remember the day I sat on the bench outside Gardner the first day here and there was this English little man smoking and I took his fag off him and threw it away, it was my uncle Jeffrey, I will always remember that day as long as I live, you nearly stole my heart that day Jeff." Next thing back comes Adi with the beer and he was laughing and said "I remember Carol on about the amount of Chinese meals you were having and I was the one who worked it out and when I told her she was going no, no , your wrong he is having Chinese and then the penny dropped, we laughed for an hour, I took Carol to Cardiff the other day with mum and done some shopping with her and took her for a pint in the Yard pub on the brains brewery site for one of her tipple and I had a drink of a man's drink, brains S. A. A real man's drink." Jeff butts in "What a man's drink what are you trying to say then?" Adi "Nothing Jeff, I was referring to beer, I know you drink lager so it does not apply." Danny "It's my favourite drink that S A, I love it I am jealous now but we were in the Polish club in Swindon and one night we had a lager, what was it called Jeff?" Jeff takes over the story "Sherbets, a bottle lager that is so strong he thought he could handle but he was a jabbering idiot at the end of the night so was I, it made me numb and I am used to it, but he was finished and we had the hangover from hell the next day and I remember one day trying the Polish cherry brandy and I nearly died that night, I was sick all night." Adi "I bet, I remember drinking little bottles of barley wine when I was younger as it was said to be so potent and would save money and i was so ill after it I never touched it again." Danny "I done the exact same Adi I was pissed on about 3 little bottles but as soon as I hit the air outside I was ruined, I was so sick all night, never again." Carol "I have never heard of that I must try some." Danny "I wouldn't if I was you."

Next thing a little voice came across the room shouting "Danny Jeff is that you? If it is keep making a noise I can follow the noise and find you." Jeff "La la la la la . " Clamper arrived at the table and said "Thank you Jeff , thanks for waiting for me." Jeff "Danny said let him find his own way up, he is a pest so we came on up and he also said he could not afford for you to come up with us and that you are always late, I will split on him." Clamper looking hurt said "Well thank you Danny that is not very nice is it?" Danny "Don't listen to him Andy he is just shit stirring, so how did the holiday go then?" Clamper answered "Brilliant I went to my father's pub to help him out with my brother and then spent some time with mum and nick her new partner, it was great, how long have you been up here? Zarrine said you came up here." Jeff "About an hour, so is it still manic in the college?" Clamper "Yes and guess who I seen Dan? That girl the French one she is here so now then what do you think about that then?" Danny face lit up and he says "Not a lot she has got a boyfriend." Clamper "No, he was not with her, perhaps she dumped him." Carol laughing "Ha, ha, she is not going to bring him to college with her is she? You idiot." Clamper thought for a minute and smiled and says "Oh no I don't suppose so." Jeff "How is Lizzy did you see her over Xmas?" Clamper "Oh yes I did, she moaned all xmas but I got drunk most of the time and I was more interested in helping my dad as he has been ill and is going into hospital to have something done to his heart, so I will not be here much longer." Danny "Andy I am sorry to hear that about your dad, I hope he is going to get well soon and when are you leaving then?" Clamper "Just before Easter I think." Jeff as quick as a flash "Oh that long is it, oh well never mind ha, ha, ha." Clamper "You cheeky git Jeff." Danny "So let me see I am the only one left after Easter for sure, god I am going to be on my own. I am not looking forward to that at all I know." Jeff "I am having my new bungalow soon so will be busy, I can't wait for that to happen and I will be happier there." Danny "I bet you can't, it's like the Bronx where you are now at this moment, I am a bag of nerves in your place except for the Chinese there the best in Britain." Jeff "Here he goes again he loves the Chinese near my place he is nuts for it." Adi "I like Chinese food a lot." Danny "Well let me tell you Adi this Chinese shop is the best I have ever tasted honestly." Adi "Well you must invite me up Jeff for me to try." Jeff replies sarcastically "Yeah, right, well Clamper we have decided it's your round as a drink for us for xmas." Clamper looked nervous and looked down at the ground and says "Danny can you lend me some money then please?" Danny stared in amazement and says "See Jeff I told you I could not afford for him to come drinking with us didn't I?" Clamper laughs out loud and says "I knew you said something about me to Jeff like I can't afford him and he is never on time I bet." Jeff laughed Clamper continued "I thought so, do you know Danny says to me we are having a taxi outside Gardner at seven o'clock and that is when the big hand is on the 7 and the little hand Is on the... I got that wrong I mean the big hand is on the twelve and the little hand is on the seven, I got it right in the end and Danny i wish you would stop spreading rumours around about me." Danny "Andy their not rumours they are true." Carol "He is right Andy you do live as if there is no tomorrow, you think of yourself and think everyone must wait for you I noticed that." Adi "You have always been lazy and slow ha, ha, ha." Clamper "Yes I know, it's the way I am." Danny "And don't change it Clamper we love that about you, if you changed you wouldn't be Clamper." Adi "Why do you call him Clamper anyway?" Danny "Because every time he used to run over to Gardner slapping his flat feet on the ground it used to eco between the buildings and gave that distinctive sound like clamp, clamp, clamp, so I called him Clamper and he was always running over to make the taxi on time, I remember him slapping his feet so hard I had to put my fingers in my ears." Clamper laughing says "Ha, ha, ha, he is right and I wore worn out trainers on my feet and they used to make my feet very hot and burn." Jeff "The best thing I remember about Andy was coming back from lectures one day and he was sitting at the rear entrance on his own on a huge bench and I could hear him muttering wildly I asked him what was wrong and he while flapping his arms around wildly and kicking his legs about and wiggling his body and saying in a temper at the same time " this college is full of nutters " well I cracked up laughing as he was saying this and looked like a maniac ha, ha, ha." Clamper "Yes I remember that day, I was laughing at you laughing at me ha, ha, it must have looked funny I bet?" Carol laughing "And that Emma she is so funny the things she used to get up to, I will miss her even though I had to hide from her in my room sometimes as she wouldn't leave me alone." Danny "Awe she has gone has she, I remember her coming up here with me and Jeff and Andy in the summer in the beer garden, she loved it that day and the time she ripped off rivers wig and split it down the middle and it looked as if it had a parting like the m4, all because I told her if she got it off him I would give her a fiver for the children in need and she did it no problem and she laughed for days about that, a lovely girl." Jeff "God she was a handful that day in the beer garden mind but a heart of gold, she used to grab my arm sometimes and leave a bruise on it , she was very powerful, she will be missed here it's all changing isn't it?" Carol "Yes it is and there is more to come, we will all be gone by this time next year but it has been fun, many good memories especially you two." Clamper "Who?" Carol "Danny and Jeff and that Niel so funny and troublesome 2." Danny "Well thank you Carol, we are glad we entertained you." Jeff "Yes I will send you a bill, right Dan I am not staying here much longer I need some food at the refectory, one more pint and I am off." This they did and left for the college for tea.

The next day and Danny was sitting in his room watching telly and there was a ring on his doorbell and it was Ricardo come for his English lesson. Ricardo said "Hello Danny how are you I am fine and need help to ask girl question about love, yes?" Danny with serious face says "Sorry, come again? I not understand." Ricardo just as serious says "Need to talk English to women you know?" "Right no problem what do you want to ask them?" Ricardo smiling says "For to be friends you know?" "You don't need to speak English to have friends, just smile." "No I need to be lovers to them." "Yes I understand you don't need English language to have that just get on with it." Ricardo now looking puzzled even more says "Danny, I need to ask Marian the English S.S.W. to go to with me for love, yes?" "Right I understand Marion she is from Newcastle, I can't understand her never mind you understanding her so you want her to go out with you as lovers yes?" "Yes this is right." Danny "Well how do you do this? Just say do you fancy a date with me?" "I not understand?" Danny looking confused says "Nor me let me think." Danny puts his head in his hands and then he thought "Right I know just like Jeff would do it I think, with his chat up lines, right think of one Dan, oh no it's not going to work for Ricardo, it is too long and complicated for him, I need something short and to the point, let me think." Ricardo had a silly smile on his face as he waited for Danny then Danny had it "I got it, listen Ricardo repeat after me "." Ricardo concentrating hard says "Ok I will." "Hey " Danny acting out the gestures as he goes says "Hey babe, nice , nice ass " Ricardo says the sentence "Hey babe nice ass yes?" Danny looked Impressed with Ricardo and Ricardo looked frustrated and said "So what is this mean?" Danny sniggering says "It's telling the girl you are in love with her and want to be with her." Ricardo looking pleased with himself says "Yes this is it." Danny repeated it "Hey babe nice ass, short and to the point, now you say it ready?" "Nice baby ass." Danny "No, no, hey babe nice ass." "Hey babe nice ass." "Right Ricardo you have got it, keep on saying it." "Hey babe nice ass, nice, no it's hey babe nice ass." Ricardo kept on repeating it over and over it again. Danny "That's it, by the gods he has got it, now you must say this later in the evening not straight away ok?" "Sorry when?" " Danny rolled his eyes and said again "After a while ok?" "Hey babe nice ass, hey babe nice ass, hey babe nice ass,." Danny stops him and says "Ok it's enough it will drive me crazy, god so you keep on repeating this and try it out on Marion and let me know tomorrow how it goes ok?" Ricardo grabs Danny's hand and shook it and says "Oh thank you Danny, you are my friend, I will learn this and say it to Marion tonight, thank you, thank you." He left and Danny started laughing out loud and thought he had done a good job and could not wait to tell Jeff later.

It was later that night in the student bar and Jeff and Danny were standing by the bar as it was packed with the new students as well as the S.S.W's and Danny had just finished telling Jeff about the meeting with Ricardo. Jeff says to him "Ha, ha, ha, you didn't did you? He will get a smack in the face if he is not careful, she is a bit religious you know?" Danny looking surprised "She isn't is she? I didn't know that or I would have been a bit more sensitive, oh shit, I hope she has got a good sense of humour, perhaps I should go and stop him saying anything to her, what do you think?" Jeff pondered and replied "Nah, nah, let's see what happens ha, ha, you never know it may have the effect he is hoping for." "Jeff you are a swine just like me, your right let's see what happens first ha, ha, ha." Next thing a lad new to the college stood by the lads and said "You are a pair of buggers I like it ha, ha, ha." Danny said "Oh hello yes we like a bit of fun here, I am Danny this is Jeff and you are?" Stranger says "My name is Steve I started here yesterday, I am from Portsmouth, a Pompey." Danny "Never mind it's not your fault, I am from Wales and Jeff is a Swindon English git ha, ha, ha." Jeff "Don't listen to him he is an inferior sheep shagger." Steve "Yes that's all they do down there and I suppose Jeff supports Swindon and Danny is a Cardiff or Swansea supporter, am I right?" Jeff "I don't follow football at all sorry it's boring." Danny "And as regards me I am a Man U. supporter and they have sorted out Portsmouth many times, am I right?" Steve replies "Yes they have been lucky most of their lives mind and England has stumped you on the field lately not a good rugby nation as you used to be so it's swings and roundabouts." Danny "Oh fighting talk aye? well we are reorganising and look out from now on matey, they are coming back with a vengeance, you wait and see Wales are back, look out watch this space." Steve "You are a nation of dedicated rugby supporters I'll give you that but no match for England at the moment." Jeff "Yes he is right and there's no getting away from it sonny, we got you beat." Danny "Jeff I don't think you know the difference with the balls as you don't know anything about the subject." Jeff "Ha, ha, your probably right but I must support a fellow Englishman and i will support England from now on." Danny "Right I will bet you both a fiver each that Wales will stomp over England in the nations this year." Steve "Your on." The both shook hands on the bet and Jeff said "Oh no I am not betting on anything with you the dodgy Welshman and If I was you Steve I would count your fingers now he has shook hands with you." Danny "Typical of you Maxam, no guts, ha,ha,ha." Steve "So how long have you 2 got here before you leave?" Danny "Well I am here until next September and Jeff is leaving." Jeff butts in and says "Next week." Steve "Well Danny we must have a few pints together and hope we will see you back for a visit Jeff?" Danny looking stunned "Hang on a minute Steve, Jeff what do you mean next week? Since when?" Jeff looking solemn "I wanted to tell you tonight but I couldn't I only found out this afternoon, I should not have come back after xmas as there has been no acceptance of my extension and so I am leaving next Friday or at least Saturday morning and mum and bill are coming to fetch me matey, sorry." Danny "Jeff this can't be matey it's not on, you can't leave next week, you just can't, isn't there something we can do? This is disaster your kidding aren't you?" Jeff looking sad says "No it's genuine I am off and you are going to be the last of the gang left here, sorry man." Danny looks at the floor and Steve says "God that's a bit of a shock then, never mind you can keep in touch with each other." Danny still looking at the floor said "Well that's it then, it's all over, it won't be the same Jeff I shall miss you a great deal but it had to come to an end I suppose, but it has been fun hasn't it it?" Jeff looking as down as Danny says "Yes it has been fun Dan and we will keep in touch and come and visit each other all of the time don't worry about that and I need you here for me to come back every other weekend as Jo is still here, so I will come and see you both until September anyway before she leaves so it will only be the mid-week I won't be here and I am dreading telling Zarrine in the morning and everyone has gone so no party before I have to go." Danny smiled at last and says "Oh yes there will be a party even if it's just me and you matey no problem and Geraldine will come up to see you off and

Carol and we will have a jolly send-off." Jeff "We will see Dan, anyway let's have a pint." Steve "I have already got them ordered lads." Jeff "Well thank you Steve." Steve "No problem mate there is a row over there can you hear it?" Just then you could hear a girls voice saying "you cheeky git." And then a loud slapping sound and a girl storms out of the bar . Danny "Oops looks as if someone has fallen out ha, ha, ha." Jeff "Yes it's one of the S.S.W's and I think it was Marion hitting someone." There was a deadly silence and Danny said "Oh shit, Ricardo oh dear I hope he is ok ha, ha, ha." The both lads laughed and Steve asked "What's so funny lads? Do you know something about all of that? Ha, ha, ha." Jeff "It's a long story but Danny has been giving English lessons to a S.S.W. from Peru and he told him how to chat up girls and he told him to say Nice ass baby and she just got the chat up line by the looks of it and the reaction was a slap across the face and I think Ricardo is sore now." Steve "Got is it always like this here? Ha, ha, ha." Danny "Well until this big idiot leaves I can't get over that Jeff I really can't I won't sleep tonight now, I will need some extra drink now, it's a shame matey it breaks my heart, I will definitely be alone now." Jeff "No you won't, you will be allright and Steve will drink with you from time to time." Steve "No problem Danny, I am always in the bar and when I learn to get here without a S.S.W. it will be even better." Ricardo walked up to Danny holding his cheek an smiling says "Hey Danny it did not work what I said and it was Jacobs fault I think because I said to him I am going to say what you said to say and he said she has got a lovely big ass and I said it wrong I said hey babe nice big ass and she slapped me across the chops, I think I need to say something else as they were all laughing at me, what do you say Danny?" Danny says "Ricardo let me sleep on it and get back to you, so is it over with Marion then?" Ricardo "I think so, she does not want to see me ever again she said so I don't know." Danny "Ok mate leave it with me, see you later ok?" Ricardo "Yes, bye all." He leaves and Steve said "You are a pair of bastards doing that ha, ha, ha." Jeff "Don't look at me it's him that dodgy Welshman, not me, nothing to do with me." Steve "I can see I am going to enjoy it here." Danny "That reminds me of us saying that when we first arrived here remember Jeff?" Jeff "To right I do it sent shivers down my spine then." Danny "Yes and me so this is the last but 4 nights drinking with you then? So what about tomorrow have you got lectures then?" Jeff "Oh yes I have got to sort out a few bits and pieces, I don't stop until Thursday evening and I can't let you go out on your own can I?" Danny "So it's up here for a bye, bye, drink, I will tell everyone and no tears matey, now promise me?" Jeff "I won't matey I will be smiling all over my face to leave." Danny "Well thank you for that Steve will be my drinking butty from now on if I can find him?" Steve "If I am up here I will no worries." The lads have another pint and go home.

It was the next morning and Jeff and Danny were sitting there having a cup of tea and in walks Zarrine and said "Good morning." to them and it was Jeff's turn to spill the beans "Hello Zarrine I am afraid I have bad news for you, I am leaving on Friday or rather Saturday morning." Zarrine froze in her tracks and said "That is not bad news that is fantastic news Jeffrey." Jeff's face fell and he looked sad, Danny was laughing and said "That will teach you for being so sure of yourself won't it?" Jeff "Well fair enough I was hoping you would at least be sad." Zarrine "I am only joking, I am sad it is that time and I will miss you dearly I mean that, it has been a pleasure to have you and I will be lost with the both of you not together, it has been a experience, I thought there was something wrong when I went into your bedroom yesterday as there are not many cans there, I feel I should contribute some, I have never seen that room so empty of beer. I was worried for you, awe dear I am sad now first Niel now you and soon it will be Danny, I will not like it here after that I am sad it has been a lovely journey with you 2 here, I have had so much fun with you 2, I will miss you Jeffrey, come here." She grabs Jeff and hugs him. Jeff said "That's very nice of you to say these things Zarrine, I will miss you very much indeed, I will, you have been like a big sister to me and I will always remember you and look after this dodgy Welshman." Zarrine "That's my Danny and you are my Jeffrey, I will always think of you pair and Niel, it's not the same since he has left and now you it's not fair I hope you will be coming back to visit me from time to time?" Jeff "Of course I will and we can have some chip butties then." Danny "Yes remember that? Niel's face was a picture I bet all those chips and bread all over that huge table in there, he must have thought his prayers were all answered, we had some good times aye brilliant and it will be more sad now Niel and Jeff has gone, I might leave now also." Zarrine stamped her foot on the ground and said in a gruff voice "Danny don't say that you are staying here with me or I will be leaving also, so don't say that." Jeff "Yes I can remember when we came over here from Gardner and all the fights and fun it has been a fantastic time and I have benefited from the experience and I remember Danny could not even get to the front door here, now look at him, god you can't stop him, I will miss it here for a long time and poor Rhoda is not well in hospital I will have to go and see her this week, fancy that Dan?" Danny "Yes I was going anyway this week on Wednesday, it will be great to see her, I am surprised she has got that lupus it sounds bad but she will be smiling I bet, she is hell of a girl I can't see her coming back here now." Zarrine "Oh no, she is too ill to come back she will be off home to Slough soon I think." Jeff "Ok I will come with you Dan, she will be panicking when she sees us coming through that door and she will giggle like hell." Danny "Yes I know she will and she will be telling the nurses about us I expect but it will be nice to speak to her again, right I am off to lectures and organise a party for Friday night, see you both." They both said goodbye and Danny left. Zarrine speaks to Jeff "Oh Jeffrey he will miss you when you have gone, he will be walking round again wondering what is going to happen to him next, he wears his heart on his sleeve you know?" Jeff "I know he does and I hope he don't go back to the way he was not so long ago, keep an eye on him Zarrine will you? He is a nice guy and is a little lost at this moment in time." "Of course I will he is just a big daft sod and you and him have been damn good friends with each other and that is rare today, I bet you will miss him too?" " Yes I will be lost also for a long time, it will be so quiet without him, he can be so loud sometimes and a good friend." "And he will definitely miss you, he will put a brave face on but he will not know what to do next and you pair have made me so happy since you both arrived here in front of me, I will miss the both of you it will not be the same." "Right I must get to my lecture and finish off what I started before I go, I will say it now as we are alone, thank you Zarrine for putting up with me, it hasn't been easy for you but thanks for everything I mean it." They both hug and a tear came into her eyes. Zarrine "right Jeffrey go before you see me cry and I will see you later."

Not long after Jeff had left Zarrine was washing up in the kitchen and Danny strolled back in and Zarrine was surprised to see him and said to him "What are you doing back Danny?" "Oh my tutor is on the sick so I have got a free couple of hours, Jeff has gone has he?" "Yes he has and how are you feeling about him leaving then?" Danny looking sad and says "Gutted, I am gutted, he is going to be missed here by me it is not going to be the same but nothing can be done about it is there?" "No Danny nothing at all but you both will keep in touch won't you? So no worries." "Oh yes of course we will but I will miss him but don't tell him that mind ha, ha, he will love that." "Danny don't be horrible, he is just as gutted I think." "No I am only kidding, he is a good mate and I will be lost without him, it has all gone too fast for me but it has been nearly 3 years, what happened? Where has it all gone? so it's just me an you now and it will be strange but it goes on as you say and there are some new ones here, I will be allright and I am going up to Swindon when I can, so we will still be having some fun, it's been good Zarrine hasn't it?" Zarrine smiling says "Yes it has, it has been the best times I have ever had here with your lot, many times of fun and laughter and some sad times, we have been like a big family and it has come to an end, but it is a shame Danny, I remember you Jeff, Niel, Carol, Rhoda, Lola, Andy, Tim, Mandy, and many more at the same time, such a good lot together, it will never happen like that again I don't think so. Are you going to be allright then now he is leaving? I mean your not going back to depression are you? It was always going to happen Danny." "No, I am all over that I hope, no I knew it was going to happen, I will get on with it but I will miss him a great deal but it is not the end of the world, I will make friends with someone else in time and that's it." "I am happy to hear that, you have had a horrible time in the last few years, so look after yourself." "I will and besides he will be coming back here from time to time." Zarrine puts her hand on her head and says "Oh no, your joking I hope? You 2 together again? I don't know if I can take it ha, ha, I am only joking, I have told him he had better come and see us." "He will I will make sure of that no worries, I had better organise a little party for him in the student bar for Friday but who I am going to ask Is another thing as they have all left, huh, never mind it has always been him an me who enjoy themselves so that will do. Right I will see you later Zarrine, bye." Danny left and went to see Geraldine and some others to meet up the bar on the Friday to see Jeff off.

Well Friday came and it was up the student bar on the night and there was a karaoke there also, so that made it a bit better. Danny, Geraldine and Jeff sat on the usual table and Ger. was speaking to the lads "So it's goodbye then Jeff? I hope you are going to behave yourself tonight mind? No crying to me and falling over me when your drunk, I am a girl who is spoken for now and if he finds out he will not be happy." Jeff "He does not frighten me at all and I am only saying goodbye to you all, so take it easy, I have always been nice to you and still love you Ger." Ger. "Now stop it Jeff, I am going if you don't behave yourself." Danny butted in "Oh come on Ger. he is only playing with you, you know what he is like and besides he is going home tomorrow, he just wants to say goodbye to you, he will behave himself it's the drink kicking in that's all, you know he is harmless and no one here is afraid of Shaun, he is just as harmless so let's enjoy it." Kezz walks up to the table and says "Eek, eek, we are going to be sad Jeff when you leave, no more Danny and Barbara ha, ha, I am leaving soon also and I don't want to go, do you Jeff?" Jeff "No not really, I will miss you all especially Geraldine, she is my angel and all I want is a kiss before I go ok Ger? I will not shove my tongue down your throat, unless you want me to?" Ger. "See what I mean? Now you stop it, there is no chance that will happen." Kezz "Ha, ha, don't be horrible Geraldine he is leaving give me an eek." Ger. "No it's allright Kezz." Danny "Well I have heard it all now, don't be such a stick in the mud Ger. he is leaving let's enjoy it, he is upset he is leaving and Kezz will let him stick his tongue down her throat, won't you Kezz?" Kezz makes some noises "Argh, argh, don't be disgusting eek, eek, I need my throat to sing in a minute, no offence Jeff and besides you are getting drunk aren't you? I can tell shout an eek Jeff." Jeff "Eeeeek, eeeeek, hows that Kezz? I am leaving and will miss you all even that dodgy Welshman by there." Danny "Never mind Jeff it has been fun hasn't it ?" Jeff "Oh yes, it has been a ball, but it's all over now Dan or at least here it is as I am going in the morning and my fun stops here, god this beer is strong tonight, it's going to my head." Kezz "Ha, ha, he is getting drunk , he is funny when he is pissed, never mind Jeff we will all get together when you visit and have more fun so don't worry." Danny "Yes your right Kezz, it's not all over, he will be back and Ger. can't wait can you?" Ger. smiling "Don't you start, he is bad enough so don't encourage him Danny boy." Jeff swaying now from side to side laughs "Well i will never forget this place ever, I have had some fun here and met some lovely girls here, such as my first love Geraldine and my second Carol and of course my little Jo." Ger. "So where is Jo then Jeff?" Danny answers "She had already planned to go home for some reason or other so she could not change her mind, it was already arranged." Jeff slurring "But your here Ger. and I was hoping that Carol was here, everyone has left now only Danny left after today, so Ger. give me a kiss so long then, what do you think?" Ger looks serious and says "No it's allright Jeff I think you should stop drinking now your pissed ha, ha, ha." Jeff "Oh come on I am leaving tomorrow and might never see you again." Ger. laughing "Oh come on then and only once and no tongues mind." They kiss and Jeff sit's back down smiling and his smile turns to a sad expression as he speaks "I am going to miss you all, it's not fare, I can't handle it." He starts to cry and it went silent and everyone was holding back from joining him. Danny then said "Come on Jeff, it's not the end of the world." He puts his hand on Jeff's shoulder and continues "You will be back most of this year and it has been an experience for us all and what a bloody fantastic time we have had." Jeff still crying says "I know, I will miss you Dan and you Ger. It has been a ball I said I was going to be composed, but it has got to me, I can't help it sorry." Jeff grabs Danny's arm and Ger's and cries more. Kezz says "Oh dear Jeff I don't like to see anyone cry it makes me very sad, you will be allright Jeff, I know you will, so don't cry and I didn't get a kiss." Jeff hugs her and kisses her on the cheek and says "Little squiggly Kezz ,I will miss you also very much, you are a very special and unique girl, good luck little one, I hope you find what you want in life eek, eek, banging." Kezz "Ha, ha, that's my saying, banging, ha, ha, ha." Danny said "Right my round, who wants a drink? Besides Kezz, she never says no or Jeff for that Matter, I will just go up and get them I think." Off he goes and Jeff cuddles up to Ger. and whispers to her "It has been lovely getting to know you Ger. it really has and I wish you a great life in whatever you do, I love you and always will, so look after yourself and if ever you need me for anything give me a ring, promise?" Ger close to tears says "I promise Jeff, you are a good friend and it has been a pleasure having you as a good friend and I think one day you will find someone who will love you as much as you will love them, but do me a favour?" Jeff "Yes of course anything." Ger "Keep them chat up lines going, they are something special and it is you, that is what I will always remember about you, the fun you have in you and it is to be treasured so keep it up, the chat up lines I mean, before you make a rude thing out of what I said." Jeff laughs and says "Ha, ha, I will and maybe one day it will work and I have got a girlfriend Jo." Ger "You know as much as I do, that will not last, it is just a fling in college, it is not going anywhere and you and I know it." Jeff "Mmm, I think you may be right, I will have to wait and see, look out that dodgy Welshman is back with Kezz in tow, I can't drink much more Dan I am pissed now, but we will have another one after this I suppose ha, ha, ha." Danny "I am starting to feel the beer kicking in now and I have not had as much as you." Ger. "Well I am necking this and am off as Shaun will be wondering where I am, so down the hatch and I am off." She drinks it down and stands up and grabs Jeff gives him a big kiss and Danny and off she goes leaving Jeff near to tears again and he says "She has gone, I may never see her again, you know if she had only said yes my life would be perfect, I love her very much but she does not think the same as I do, what a shame, we would have been the perfect couple." Danny "Yes I was expecting something in the early days to happen with you two but I was surprised it never happened but that's in the past now Jeff, time to go forward and tomorrow you will not remember sobbing but I will remind you." Jeff "I am so sad Dan, it has been a brilliant time here for me it has made me a better man for the experience, me and you have had so much fun you should write a book about it, it will be a big seller." Danny "Who knows, I may do one day and little squiggly Kezz will be in it for definite, it will be fun writing it to as it will make me smile all the time I am writing it, I know." Kezz "I think I would buy it just to remember all the fun we have all had." An announcement from the stage "Right where's Kezz? It's her turn come on Kezz." She goes off to sing and left Danny and Jeff alone. Danny says to Jeff "Give me your hand Jeff, let me shake it for old times sake." The lads hug and shake hands Jeff says "It's been a blast Dan, i will never forget you, never." Danny "Nor I you Jeff, it has been a journey and I loved all of it, we have changed this college for the good, even the tutors smile when our names are mentioned, it's a partnership that will never be beaten here, I will miss you to Jeff." They hug again and tears come over them both, they sit down and compose themselves and Jeff swigs his lager down and says "Get it down you dodgy, let's have one for old times sake." Danny swigs his down and gives Jeff the glass and says "Thank you Jeff for being a friend, thank you." "It's been my pleasure, let's get legless." He goes off to the bar and the night carried on with plenty of beer being drunk.

Well it's the next morning and the lounge was empty, as Danny stumbled in still drunk for his coffee and toast, he looks at his watch and it said nine thirty and remembered that Jeff's mother and her partner were arriving around ten o'clock, so Danny went to get him up, he got to his door and knocked it and all he got was a groan, so he thumped the door and Jeff opened it looking like a tramp, hair all over the place and looking visibly ill Jeff says "Why are you getting me up this early?" "It's half past nine your mother is arriving soon, so get up and pull yourself together, argh, argh, I feel bloody awful how about you?" "I am the walking dead, what did we do last night? I feel as if we drank the place dry, I am still pissed ha, ha, ha." "My head is banging, I will make some tea for us, so get dressed and shower I will get the tea done, toast for you? Forget that question I will do some as you will be sick in bill's car otherwise, see you in the lounge." Danny goes off to the kitchen.

Later Jeff was in the lounge with Danny moaning together with massive hangovers. Jeff "What a night, I think, I can't remember, was I stupid or ok?" "Well you sobbed and pestered Ger but she forgave you and gave you a kiss before she went home and we were like 2 lovers saying goodbye, otherwise allright ha, ha, ha." "I wasn't crying was I? Oh now I hope your lying." Danny being serious says "Honestly, that's the truth, you were very emotional all night and very sad from time to time, but that's nothing to be ashamed of, it's natural, I can hear a car out there is it your mum and bill I wonder?" Jeff jumps up to the window and looks out and then opens the window and shouts "Mum is that you?" Mum shouts back to Jeff "Hello Jeff, can you let me in?" "Yes I will press the button and you push the door, I will be back now Dan." Jeff rushes off to let his mum and bill in. They come in and into the lounge and bill shakes hands with Danny and says "Hello Dan how are you then? What a trip here it was a little slippery on pieces of road, look out it's Sheila." She grabs Dan and gives him a kiss on the cheek and greets him and they sit down as Jeff makes them some coffee and tea. Bill "Well these few years have gone fast haven't they?" Danny replies "Oh yes they have and too fast for me and Jeff, we have had some fun here, we really have and he was crying because he is leaving last night in the bar, it's a sad time but we will keep in touch I know that for a fact and I will miss him too." Sheila "Well of course you will, you have been living in each other's pockets for 3 years now, it's going to be hard for a while and Jeff has got to move very soon as his bungalow is almost finished now, so things will change for the best for him with that and he is waiting for his first guide dog so he will keep himself busy for a while until you get up there in February for half term." Danny "Right it is all happening then for him? I will be on my own for a while now as there are all new ones here, so look out for me." Jeff comes in and says "Mother, don't listen to a word he says you know what he is like and it's a lie whatever he says." Sheila "Oh he has not said anything, nice cup of tea Jeff, at least you have learned something here." Jeff "Don't get used to it, I have got all my things in boxes and bags, but there is not a lot and no lager to worry about, we drank it all last week and just a can to drink later as the hair of the dog." Bill says "Ok Jeff I will make a start as soon as I have finished this coffee, as I am working this afternoon, so we can't hang about for long." Jeff "Yes ok bill, no problem." Danny "Yes get him out of here and I will save a fortune after he has gone." Jeff smiling says "You will miss me dodgy." Danny "Huh, do you think so? I think your right it's been fun Jeff." Jeff "Too bloody right it has, I bet there are going to be a lot of students etc. outside waiting to wave me goodbye." Danny "I don't think so, they have all left already, it's just me now." Sheila "Never mind Jeff you won't get a stiff arm waving now ha, ha, ha." Well they finish their tea and go off to pack the car. Danny cleaned the cups up and waited for them to finish packing and Jeff came back in the lounge and said tearfully "Well that's it matey, we are off, you look after yourself and don't do anything I wouldn't do ok?" They shake hands and Danny replies "I will and you look after yourself to matey and don't be long coming back to visit, it's been a ball mate and I will have a couple of pints to remember all the fun we have had here with a tear in my eye tonight and I will be seeing you, so long Jeff, it's been great." Jeff solemnly says "So long matey, I have enjoyed it, look after yourself, I will be seeing you." They hug and part and Danny sticks his head out of the window and wish them goodbye and sits on the settee thinking and put his head in his hands and cries for a minute thinking is this the last fun he will ever have and how alone he is going to be now his friend has gone.

It was the middle of the week and Danny had not been with anyone of the new people who were not settled themselves yet and so did not even see Steve the man he met the week before as Steve still needed to have help to get to the student bar. It was a whole week later that he met up with Steve at the bar on a Saturday night. Danny says to Steve "Hello is that Steve I can hear ordering a pint? I will get that." Steve says "Well hello Dan long time no see ha, ha, has Jeff left yet?" Danny replies "Yes he left a week ago, he was not a happy man either and it has been dead without him here." "I bet it has, he seemed a happy busy sort of person, I liked him very much he was so funny to go with it." "Yes he is a good mate and I miss him a lot, it's just not the same here now he has gone, but he will be back next weekend as his girlfriend is a secretary here in the main office, Jo, do you know her?" "No I don't think I do, oh Danny this is Malika, she started the same time as me and we are on the same course." Danny "Where have I heard that name before? Hello Malika." She spoke with her French accent "Hello, I met you in Dowdell with Jeff, you were in there and I spoke to you." Danny "Oh yes I remember that French voice now and you had your boyfriend with you Roy." Steve butted in and asked if Danny and Malika wanted a drink Danny "Oh I will have a Newcastle brown please." Malika "I will have a gin and tonic please Steve." Steve ordered the drinks and started talking to Malika "So did you understand that woman this afternoon in that lecture?" Malika said "No I bloody didn't, she was so boring, I wanted to get out of there." Steve explained to Danny "This tutor was so boring and not very clear, I was lost from the beginning Danny, she was not a good teacher." Danny "I know who you are talking about fluffy, but can't remember her real name, she is the vicars wife but can't remember her name." Malika "That's the one she is rubbish." Steve "Yes she certainly is and not very thoughtful regarding some bodies feelings." Danny "Yes that's her, talks as if she is above you and don't have any problems herself ever, a waste of time. So how are you settling down here then?" Steve "Allright I am going to enjoy it here I think and I just need help to get up here more often that's all, but I am having mobility lessons starting tomorrow." Danny "And how about you Malika?" Malika "Fine, fine, yes I like it except I am sharing a house in town with a girl I don't like much, she is new also her name is Sandra and a real slut I think." Steve "Wow, don't beat around the bush Malika tell us straight, you will be telling us that France will beat the English in rugby next ha, ha, ha." Malika takes the bait and says in a loud voice "Well they will Steve." Steve laughs and says "Not a chance, they are favourite to win the grand slam and the French don't stand a chance." Malika "Aha, so you think so do you? I don't know anything about rugby, but I will bet you they will beat England ok? £5." Steve looking sure of it and says "Right your on, shake hands on it and Danny you witness it ok?" They shake and Danny says "Yes I heard that, so look out it's on, I think the Welsh will win the grand slam myself, they have come on leaps and bounds lately." The other 2 both disagree. Steve continues "And I am not betting on the result of that one as they are getting much better as you say, some fast boys in that Welsh team and by the way Malika we are playing the French in the world cup qualifiers in a couple of months in football, so look out they don't stand a chance in football." Malika's eyes lit up and she stormed at Steve "So you think so do you? How about another fiver on that game also? Steve." Steve being very cocky says "No I can't take another fiver off you ha, ha, ha." Malika "Your not taking any money they have to beat us yet and so far you have talked a load of crap, so put your money where the mouth is." Danny "Oooohh, fighting talk Steve so back it up then Steve, go on my son." Steve smiling shook Malika's hand and the bets were on, Steve said "Don't cry Malika when I win mind." Malika "I won't it will be you who are crying you wait and see ha, ha, and I think they will even beat Wales to in rugby." Danny smiling cautiously says "Keep me out of this, I am not getting involved in your arguments thank you and by the way Steve we have already got a bet that Wales will beat England so don't forget, drink Steve and Malika?" Malika "Too late I have already got us a drink in here we are." Danny "Thank you Malika, it was my round though." Malika "I get my round in as well, so here it is you can get the next one before I go, I have got a taxi booked for ten o'clock." Danny "Fair enough thanks." Steve "I remember the bet now Dan, why are you going so early Malika?" Malika says "I have got a lot to do and I am up early tomorrow so I need some sleep especially with that noisy girl, she is a idiot." Danny "That's why I like Dowdell, it is not noisy there at all it's all older students." Steve "It's not funny when you can't get any sleep because of noisy people, I just make as much noise when they are sleeping on in the morning, that sorts them out." Danny "That's the exact thing to do I have done it a few times and it works every time." Steve "Malika you must be firm with her or she will walk all over you." Malika "Oh no she won't, I will not put up with their stupidity, I don't like the girl so she had better not start me up ha, ha, ha." Well they drank up and Malika was about to leave at ten o'clock and Steve went with her to use her to get him home leaving Danny alone in the bar and it was not much longer before Danny went home to bed also, he seemed lost for once in the student bar because Jeff was not there, this was new to Danny.

CHAPTER 16
LIFE BEGINS AGAIN.

Well the weekend came and on the Friday afternoon Danny was hanging around to see Jeff and sure enough he soon rang the bell on Danny's door. Danny opened up and let him in and said in a happy voice "Well hello matey how are you? I bet you have missed me ?" Jeff sarcastically "No, not really, ha, ha, ha." Danny stood back looking offended and says "Well don't beat around the bush matey just tell me straight ha, ha, ha." Jeff grabbed Danny's hand and shook it hard and said "Fair enough, I have been a little lost this last fortnight, it's not the same everything seemed to come to a stop, nothing happens, I have missed our fun I must admit. I have sobered up as well ha, ha, ha." "I know what you mean I have been bored, not the same fun as when you were here, so time to party if it's ok with Jo that is?" "Well yes we can go out together tonight if you like? I fancy going to that pub we went to around the corner, remember the one we went to with Andy and his mother and her friend, the food was really nice and the lager was beautiful, remember the place?" "Oh the swan you mean? Right is Jo ok with this?" "Yes she is ok with it, the fun will not start until after midnight will it?" "Ok there we are then, does she know about that? Ha, ha, ha." Jeff smiling says "If she don't she soon will, so what have you been up to and have you been good? C'mon tell the truth ." "Well I have been brilliant I drink sometimes with Steve from Pompey and that French girl Malika is here but she is living in town I think." "So have you been trying to get off with her ? As you said once when she comes back she is mine, remember?" "Yes I did say that didn't I? I don't know what the crack is with her, is she still with that Roy and I think sometimes she is after Steve as they are always together and so I will stay out of it and see what happens, if it happens it happens if it don't know harm done either way, no harm done it won't be long now before Tim and Mandy's wedding it is creeping up on us and by the way are you coming to the stag party? You said you will find out as so far it's only me and Clamper." "No I won't be at the stag night I have got a lot happening that weekend and I have got my mother keeping an eye on me to make sure I do it all, so no sorry but I will be at the wedding no problem, I would not miss that for the world and it will be like old times with Niel you me and Tim all together again." "Oh yes that will be great won't it? I miss old Niel too mind, he is a character, it's not the same here now Jeff and I would be happy to leave now if it was that easy." "Still worrying about leaving here are you? It will be ok once you get used to it mate don't worry." Danny visibly looking worried says "Easy to say that mate but not in your mind I will just have to have a bloody good go anyway, fancy a pint up the bridge before tea?" Jeff laughs and says "Does a dog wear a collar?" Off they went to the bridge for a pint and once in there decided it was dead and went to the pretty pigs instead and in there was Clamper and his girlfriend Lizzy. Clamper was excited to see them and they sat together and chatted. Clamper said "Hello Danny and Jeff it's fantastic to see you again, you remember Lizzy don't you?" Danny "Of course we do, hello again Lizzy how are you? Ok maybe but not with Andy I suppose ha, ha, ha, I am only joking." Lizzy "He is lovely my Andy so leave him alone, I am going to see Gloria soon Andy so we can't drink much more ok?" Andy looking annoyed said to her "Oh Lizzy, take it easy, we don't have to do anything and besides she is your friend not mine, so you don't need me there, I will get you a taxi if you like and see you up there later, ok with you?" Lizzy snaps at Andy "Well looks as if it will have to be but don't come back drunk, we are out tonight mind and I want a early night after, so stay sober, promise?" Danny and Jeff looked on and shook their heads as if to say to Andy I would tell her straight but Andy said nothing and took her out to get into her taxi. Danny turned to Jeff and said "Can't beat being in a happy relationship aye?" Jeff replies "I know what you mean, god isn't she a handful? If it was me she would have had the elbow by now, she is too much and Andy will put up with it." Danny "Well, he is not going to say much to her or he won't get his end away will he?" "No maybe not but after this weekend she would be gone." Clamper comes back in and explains "Oh dear mate's I am sorry about her, she likes to think she is the boss in this relationship and it gets on my nerves, so excuse her ha, ha, ha." Jeff "If it was me she would have had the elbow, so get in her knickers this weekend and dump her Andy she is not for you." Andy laughs out loud and proclaims "You got to be joking, she won't let me do anything with her, she is catholic and told me straight no way hose until I marry her." Danny "What your not getting your end away and she talks to you like a slave and you are still with her, sorry mate she would have been gone a long time ago, I would not put up with that nonsense." Jeff "He's right, it's not worth it, bloody hell Andy." Andy looking embarrassed "I know, I know, she is too much I have been thinking of finishing with her anyway, I know I can have more fun without her, she is too much of a bossy woman." Danny laughs says "Your not far wrong there Andy as I will be avoiding her, that's for sure." Andy looking hurt says "Well I hope you will not be avoiding me for goodness sake? We are friends and good friends Danny." Danny "Did I mention your name? No I didn't did i? But I don't want to be bored with her on a night out, she embarrassed you in a few minutes of us arriving here so she will do it again." Jeff "Well I am glad I am not having any trouble with my Jo like you Andy it's so easy with her and I can't wait to go out for that meal tonight with her." Clamper "Oh where are you going then Jeff?" Jeff "Jo, me and Danny are going up the swan for a meal tonight" Clamper "Are you? i would not mind having a meal up there with you?" Danny looking horrified "Oh Andy it's dear up there." Clamper "I have got money and I fancy a night out with my friends." Jeff "What just you? No Lizzy?" Clamper "Of course Lizzy, I can't leave her out, so what time are you going?" Danny "Well...well, about 7 o'clock what do you think Jeff?" Jeff says "Allright fair enough I don't mind her coming but no arguing or we will walk out on you I mean it, so tell her the same." Clamper rubbing his hands together excited says "Cool, cool, I will be ready when the little hand is on the seven and the large hand is on the twelve aye Dan?" Danny "At last you have got it Andy ha, ha, and as Jeff says I mean it also I don't want to be bored with Lizzy she must chill out like us ok?" Clamper smiling says "Ok I hear you, I will sort her out don't worry. It's a pity Tim Mandy and Niel was not here, there would be a great party, after I spoke to Tim yesterday he is looking forward to us going to the wedding and Danny and me at the stag night, I can't wait, have you heard from Niel?" Danny "Oh yes I have last week, he is good and the family but he has had trouble with Abby, she ran off and they were looking for her for a couple of hours, but she returned after that and he did not know what happened." Jeff "Never she has never done that before has she?" Danny continued "No he was surprised but she has become a little strange he said and is keeping an eye on her, I hope she is going to be fine, a lovely dog, I will give him a ring next week and let you know." Clamper "My god that's funny for her, she is so cool usually, I hope she will be allright and Tim never said anything as he phones Niel every week. Oh well I am having a pint, so do you want one?" There was a deadly silence and Danny and Jeff looked at each other and Danny said "Jeff did you hear something? I thought I heard Clamper asking us if we wanted a pint, no it can't be true." Jeff "Yes I thought the same, must be my ears failing me." Clamper laughed and sarcastically said "Ok I am not amused, I did ask if you wanted a pint so don't make a big thing about it ha, ha, ha." Danny "Sorry Andy I nearly fainted then, I usually got to tell you to get your round in, you must have got a lot of money? I however will have a pint and so will Jeff, then we must get back for tea in the refectory." Andy goes to the bar and Jeff said to Danny "That's strange about Abby I am shocked, perhaps she needs to retire now." "Yes she has been retired now so she can enjoy her last days without that harness on her and talking about dogs, any sign of your guide dog?" "Yes I am top of the list and it won't be long now and I am moving in march to the new bungalow so when you come down in February it will be in the old flat I am sorry but the last time there." "Well that's good news then, things are falling together for you, that's great, I am definitely leaving at August I have been informed and bad news Alison is leaving next week, retiring to go and whale watch in Canada, I am going to miss her she has been a god send to me, I will miss her a lot, it will not be the same, so things are coming to a head for me rapidly now, I will start my new life soon, I have also learned lots about cooking and clothing etc. from Sue Bridgland, she has been great to." "Never Alison leaving, she has been here for years she will be missed by all the staff to. She is very good at her job and as regards you, you will be ok I know it for sure." Danny says "Yes I have tried to persuade Alison to stay but no good she has made her mind up, it's a shame, but that's it I wonder what poor sod will look after my needs after her, I feel sorry for them." Clamper returns with the beers and says "Here we are lads your drinks, I heard about Alison to it is a shame she will be missed, she is lovely, I am leaving Easter." Danny "Thank god for that, I am only kidding Andy I will be the only one left as Kezz is leaving to and M,Mark that's it, just me left and as I was telling Jeff I am definitely leaving in august, but we will all keep in contact forever aye?" Clamper "of course we will Dan and so we should, we have had a great journey together and we will be getting together for Tim's wedding, that won't be long May." Jeff "Yes that will be here before we know it, I am looking forward to that." Danny "Well it's getting closer all the time, us leaving I mean but that's how it goes and I am not happy with Alison leaving, she has gone through this horrible hard journey of learning how to be blind with me but she has been a fantastic help to me, I will write a poem to let her know how I feel about her, I am off in a minute as I am starving and Jeff will be in trouble with Jo and Clamper with Lizzy so let's hop it."

Well the lads and girls went out for a meal and it went well but it was the next day Danny sat and wrote another poem about Alison to give it to her the next time they had a tutorial. Jeff returned home on the Monday and things got back to normal for a few weeks and it came the week that Alison was leaving. It was going to be a sad day for all but Danny had his tutorial cancelled and given a new tutor to look after him and was asked by Alison by e-mail to come and say goodbye at any time. So Danny plucked up courage and with a box of chocolates a farewell card and his poem in it he had wrote to a very special woman who had been by his side and helped him get his life back together, this poem reads.

THANK YOU FOR BEING A FRIEND
By Daniel Duckfield

In the beginning I could not see, this fearsome lady sat next to me.
At first I had often wondered why, I had come to her office high in the sky.
I Thought I had better get there quick, In case she has got a great big stick.
Hours, days and weeks they came to pass, then I realised, she is not such a bad lass.
Weeks turned to months and I wondered why, I was still going to her office, high in the sky.
Then things became so very clear, I was one of the reasons, she is here.
With all her work, toil and strife, she was trying to give me back, my life.

My eyes had gone she knew not where, but she let me know, that she did care.
She had many people here before me and made them realise, you don't have to see.
She will sort you out before she goes, but how she does it no one knows.
We are no problems for her you see, she loves us all that's clear to see.
Now she is leaving that office high in the sky, why she is going, we know not why.
We love her so, it will make us cry, that office will be empty, high in the sky.
Alison, is her name you knower really wish, she would not go.
And for many years after she is gone, she will be remembered by everyone.
Bless you Alison you have been so good, we will miss you in this neighbourhood.
And now your time has come to an end, Thank you Alison, for being a friend.

Danny walked into her office and she had someone with her from the college and Danny asked if he should come back later? Alison said "No don't be silly Danny I have always got time for my students and this gentleman will not mind will you?" The man replied "No problem at all." Alison reached up to Danny for the card and chocolates and opened the card and read the poem and after reading it she put her hand to her forehead and proceeded to cry and got up tears streaming down her face and put her arms around Danny and hugged him and kissed him and said in her tearful voice "This is so lovely, thank you Danny, you have made it all worth it with those kind words, I will always remember you, thank you and I will miss you very much." She said to the man in her office "You will have to excuse me this is very moving, I will have to stop everything for a while and cry thank you Danny I will see you before I leave, let me see you into the corridor." They left the room and outside in the hallway she was brushing tears from her eyes and said "This was a big shock thank you again I will treasure this forever, you get on with all the good work you have done here and you will be allright and one day I am sure I will read a book or 2 you have wrote and look after yourself, promise?" Danny moved by Alison's reaction says "I will Alison and you look after yourself and good luck for your future you deserve it and thanks, I mean it, thank you very much, remember the state I was in before I came here, well all this is due to your help and confidence in me, thank you again and good bye." They hugged and Danny left the lovely Alison wiping the tears away.

On his way up to his room he met Ricardo who was waiting for him on the bench, he called Danny and said "Danny hello, I have been trying to catch you in but you are never in, I need help I am not happy." Danny beckoned him in and they sat in Danny's room and chatted Danny says "I heard that you got a smack in the ear the other day, never mind she was a bit of an idiot anyway and I hear she has left now?" Ricardo looking at the floor says "Yes she has but not my fault I need to try again ha, ha, it was very funny I laughed a lot now I like a few girls here so what do I say to them?" Danny had a cunning smile on his face and said "Well Ricardo try this one, hey baby nice boobies." Ricardo looked at Danny and said "Hey baby nice ….ha, ha, I forgot." "Boobies." "What is this nice boobies Danny?" Danny trying not to laugh says "Nice body you know?" Danny makes shapely body shapes with is hands and Ricardo laughed understandingly and says "Yes, yes, I know now what is it. Boobies. Right, hey babe nice boobies." "That's it Ricardo you have got it by the way." "Hey babe nice boobies, hey babe nice boobies, hey babe nice boobies." "Right Ricardo you have got it now keep on saying it to yourself and when the time comes use it OK?" "Yes thank you Danny, I will remember this , hey boobies , no I said it wrong say it again Danny." "Hey babe nice boobies, got it? You go off and practise now." Ricardo says "Ok Danny, hey babe nice boobies." Ricardo left and you could hear him walking away practising this for ages and

Danny was laughing to himself. It was a few weeks later and Danny had found out that Ricardo had a few smacks in the face before he eventually got together with the Italian girl with the biggest boobs in the college and a very attractive girl to go with it. Danny had gone up to visit Jeff and he came down to see Jo and Danny regularly until just before Danny's birthday, not just any birthday but his 50th birthday and lo and behold none of his friends was left at the college to celebrate it with him. Jeff was not able to make it or anyone else for one reason or another so he was going to be on his own for his 50th birthday, not a good way to reach such a high point in his life. This was going to be a horrible time for him yet again.

It was the morning 2 days before his birthday in the lounge and it was Danny and Zarrine speaking about it all. Zarrine says "Good news I have sorted out your birthday, Sandy is arranging it all as there is no one left from your year and so it is sorted, she is getting in touch with students to arrange a meal." Danny looking concerned "Oh no, not Sandy, she will put everyone off her and bloody Matt, I think I will go home for the weekend, I know it will be a disaster, I know it." "Danny, I can't see any way it can be good as Jeff, Niel, Andy and the rest are not here anymore so just go for a meal and have a celebration when you are off in Easter it's only a week later, I can't see any other way so just try and make the best of it and besides I know Lynn is coming to your party." "Well that's something I suppose at least there will be a good looking woman there at least but it is not a party it is just a meal I will just have to grin and bare it that's all." "I have bought you a present and a cake for your birthday so just enjoy it, never mind it is your fiftieth ." "Yes I suppose so, I will try and enjoy it no problem, there's not much I can do about it is there?" Next thing in walks Lynn and she says "Well look who is here the birthday boy ha, ha, are you looking forward to it?" Danny ponders "Well yeh, I, well of course you will be there so it can't be that bad." Lynn "Oh dear, I feel it is not to your liking?" Danny "Well it's not that, it's my 50th and no friends are here anymore so it is not going to be the same and Sandy is arranging it all, can you see it being any good?" Zarrine "Oh Danny stop moaning and give it a chance, she might shock you." Lynn "Yes you never know and we will have a laugh anyway I think Naomi and Faye are coming and I think Paddy in the gym said he is coming, so there's a start let's see how it pans out before you make your mind up it is going to be rubbish. " Danny still looking serious "Yes you may be right I hope you are it's only once you get a 50th and only once can you celebrate it." Lynn "Well let's hope it is good and if it is not well you have the holidays at Easter a few days away to celebrate it at home and up with Jeff." Zarrine "There we are just as I said." Danny thinking said "I suppose so there's that I will try and enjoy it but I can't see it somehow and the best woman ,Lynn is spoken for, right I am off see you both later." Off Danny goes and a little while later in walks Sandy "He has gone has he? I will sort his party out later, I have got a few names but it's hard as his friends have all left and there are new ones here now but I will try." Zarrine "I know you will Sandy but it is an uphill task for you as you said no one knows him well now his mates have all left but he will be allright no worries." Sandy "As I say I will try, I have got six of us so far me Matt Lynn, Naomi, Faye, and Paddy so that is a start and I suggest we go to the Rose and Crown and the manager is a mate of Danny's and the food is good." Lynn "I like it there and it is a large place to eat so he will be happy, I think it will go off allright no worries as Zarrine says ha, ha, ha." Zarrine "It will be allright you will see."

Well it was the night of his 50th and they all arrived in the Rose and crown and Danny seemed happier as there were still only the six. He decided to pay for the meals and said to Ian "Can I have a tab over the bar Ian and pay with my card at the end of the night just for the meals and a drink for the others just one drink mind, is that ok?" Ian the manager "Of course it is Dan no problem, I have got a nice table for you all I will take you up to the table and take your orders for drinks and fetch them up and what do you want from me as a birthday drink? a double whisky ok?" "Well thank you Ian that will be nice, thank you." They all took their seats and ordered the drinks and meals and started to get into the swing of the night. Sandy "Right all got your drinks, I would like to whish Danny a happy 50th birthday, to Danny." They all toasted Danny and he said "Well thank you all for coming and have a nice night, I am glad to be here with such good friends and hope you enjoy the night it is nothing special as you all know all my mates have left, so it will be a little quiet for a birthday party so drink and enjoy yourselves." Danny felt it was a little plastic not having the likes of Niel, Jeff, Tim, Mandy, Carol, Lola, Clamper, M Mark and Zarrine there and never seemed as if he was celebrating. Well they had the meal and a little bit of banter and as the night went on Naomi and Faye made an excuse that they were off somewhere else and Sandy Matt and Lynn and Paddy got into a huddle and talked to each other most of the night so Danny looking fed up with it all decided to go back to the college for a few pints and made his excuses I am afraid I am off I think I would like a pint in the student bar, so I will love and leave you ok? see you all tomorrow and thanks for a good night." Danny left in a taxi so fast he forgot to pay Ian the manager the bill and went back to his room then over to the student bar and it was a Sunday so didn't expect many there as they mostly went home that weekend.

Up the bar and there were a couple of new students there and a pair of brothers Danny knew well, Jeff and his brother Les and standing by the bar was Malika and a few new students having a drink. Danny stood by the bar and asked for a pint and Jeff paid for it for his birthday and Danny said "Thanks Jeff very nice of you." Jeff "That's ok Dan happy birthday to you." Everyone asked him if it was his birthday and then wished him many happy returns. Danny "Well thanks, It has been the most boring 50th birthday on record I think but never mind." Jeff "Why is that?" Danny "Well those who started with me have all left and Sandy arranged a party, or rather a meal and it was a disaster, so I came back for a few here, that's how bad it was." Malika "God she is boring I think I would rather stayed in ha, ha, we are going to town to some nightclubs if you like you can come with us?" Danny replies "Well thanks but no thanks, I am not a night club man anymore as being blind in them places is bad enough but not being able to hear as well is even worse and I would not enjoy it, but thanks for asking me, I will stay here with the old Wertly brothers and waddle home later but I mean it thanks for asking me I appreciate it, maybe have a drink in the week to celebrate before I go home for the holidays." Malika "Ok no problem, I am going to enjoy a good dance, I love to dance but happy birthday anyway, see you again." Danny "Yes, see you Malika have a nice night, so long." She left and Danny sat with Jeff and his brother Les and had a few drinks until he was very tipsy. Jeff "Well fancy you not taking up Malika's offer to go dancing I would have gone if I was you, she seemed interested in you." Danny nods his head and says "No I don't think so, she has got a boyfriend his name is Roy." Jeff looked puzzled and says " I don't think so, she was telling me she dumped him a while ago, as he was a idiot." Danny then says "Think she is interested in Steve from Portsmouth, she is always with him." Jeff "Oh I don't know she is mostly on her own, I think she is just good friends with Steve." Danny smiled "Oh right she is free then, I never knew that, well, well, well time to party if your right mmm." Jeff "Well I am surprised at you, you always know everything about the girls here but I had to tell you about her." Danny "Ah yes but she is living in the town and is not here very much in the night so can't get any news from her." Jeff "Well she is in Armitage now for a week then she is coming to Dowdell as she can't get on with the girl Sandra so she has moved but is in with the kids and is only there until a room is available in Dowdell and there is one empty after Easter now you know." Danny's face lit up "Well, well, I never things are looking up I hope, thanks for the news mate I am having another pint, oh shit, o shit I have forgotten to pay for the meals in the Rose and Crown, I will have to call him in the morning, fancy me forgetting that, oh never mind." Les said "There is a pint for you Dan." Danny smiling says "Well thanks matey's time to party." Jeff "Well I have cheered you up now haven't I? ha, ha, ha, ha." Danny "Jeff you will never know how much, mind you I don't know if she fancies me ha, ha, ha." Jeff "She did ask you if you wanted to go to town and you refused." Danny "Yes I know that's what I was thinking what an idiot I really am sometimes." Danny sat there smiling all over his face and had a good night eventually but drank so much he was ill for a few days and stayed in his bed until Wednesday of that week and suffered for his indulgence in drink .

It was the Wednesday afternoon he went down the Rose and Crown to pay his dues he had forgotten about and he got in and Ian was at the bar and Danny said Immediately "I am sorry Ian I forgot all about it matey, here is my card." Ian "No problem Dan I knew I could trust you so don't worry about it matey it came to £62 altogether but mind you if it had been left to the bleach blonde chubby woman it would have cost you a lot more. The cheeky cow." "Sandy you mean that's the best description I have heard about her so what did she do?" "Well here is a pint from me first." Danny surprised says "Oh thank you Ian that's very nice of you." "No problem mate I wish others were as honest as you, well she came back to the bar after you went and her and her partner and 2 others were left and she asked me to put all their drinks on your bill, the cheeky bitch, I told her straight no chance, but what a cow." "Never, did she? Well I never and I am surprised at the couple she was with." Ian "Oh no the other girl said not to put hers on it and insisted on paying for the lot and she was only on coke." "Wait till I see that bitch I will give her a bit of my mind, and the lovely Lynn is gorgeous and I have always fancied her but thanks Ian." Ian "No problem, how did the night go for you in the end? I could see you were not enjoying yourself here as you could not get a word in edgeways, she kept on didn't she? God." " I went back to the student bar a little pissed off and went and got pissed with 2 mates and was chatted up and did not realise it but I am hoping to get in there tonight, I have been in bed until today as i was ill over the drink, right mate, I am not staying it's only 2 days and I am off on holiday and have got to pack my room up and get it into the attic as they rent out the rooms over the holidays to some large group." "Well that's fair enough, they have to make the college pay don't they? I will see you when you get back and thanks mate." "Your welcome Ian see you soon." Danny drank his pint up had another one and left by taxi to the college to pack his stuff up and get ready for the bar in the night hoping to see Malika and see if his thoughts were right.

Later up the bar and he stood by the bar and there was hardly anyone in and he soon heard a familiar voice and it was Steve and he said "Hello who is in here tonight?" Danny said "Only a dodgy Welshman." Steve smiled and says "Danny, hows things? let me buy you a pint for your birthday, I hear it did not go to well? never mind we will have a pint or two now." "Well thanks Steve a Newcastle brown please and how are you?" "I am fine and packed ready for the trip home, what a to do packing up all the things for them to let the rooms out over Easter." Danny "i know it's a pain in the ass but we have always done it and even at xmas time a bloody nuisance and as regards my birthday it was a dead loss except Malika asking me to go to town and I didn't go I stayed here and got pissed as a newt and was in bed up to today so not a good day and I learned my oldest daughter got married in Scotland on the 2nd and I was not told or invited or anything, that hurt a lot, so not a good 50th was enjoyed by me and I can't blame my daughter as she has not spoken to me for over 20 years all because of a divorce that got messy, so it's probably my fault but never mind as long as she is happy, but look out I am back to myself now. I was hoping Malika was going to be up here tonight." "No she is packing her room up as she finishes her lectures late on a Wednesday night, so she will not be up here tonight, I think she is coming up here on Thursday as she always does, why? are you after her?" "I don't know, I am keeping a low profile, I thought she was going out with you at one point." "Good god no, I am married and we are just good friends that's all, she is a bit of a girl though." "I hope she is all girl ha,, ha, I will bide my time and see what happens, so what time are you off Friday Steve?" "I am going early so as I can get to see Portsmouth play football Friday evening and my wife is off, so she can meet me at the station, I will be glad to get home this time it has been a hard winter and I feel the cold here a lot." "Yes I know what you mean the wind is cutting here, I am off to Bridgend for a few days with my son and his miserable mother who will want me gone as soon as possible and then I am up with Jeff for a boozy week or more, so I will be just as bad when   I come back but am I looking forward to it? To bloody right I am and when I get back it will be my last term here after nearly 4 years but I must say it has turned my life around and saved my life." Steve asks "What do you mean?" "Well it has, I think I was going crazy after I went blind and could not come to terms with it and if I hadn't come here I would still been just as useless and think I would have died of boredom or a hangman's noose, I was suicidal but this place has given me my life back and I feel like I could handle it now with a lot of difficulty mind but it will take time but I will get there." "I hope your right, that is what I want from this place more than anything to feel like I am of some use and not just a poor old blind man, it's hard to envisage that but I hope your right." "Let me tell you Steve you will be allright as you have got a good temperament just like me and you will handle it perfectly and get on with your life, this place will give you anything you ask for and more, I have been doing living skills with a woman sue Bridgland and I can look after myself now, no problem, I can't wait to see if I can do it I will mind, I am sure of that." "Well that's good Dan, I hope I will see it the same as you when I finish here. So it's dead in here tonight and I was hoping for a couple of laughs tonight with a good pint but the beer in the taps is awful isn't it? I drink the bottled lagers here and I see you drink the bottles here to, I can't drink that Newcastle brown, it is to potent for me I get pissed on a few of them." "Well that's the idea isn't it? I drink it and have about 5 or 6 a night and it makes me sleep like a baby and I am ok the next morning and I save a fortune as the kids etc. in here slap about 6 to 8 pints of lager, so I am getting the cheaper deal and not ill with my guts the next morning, so who is the dullest? them I think." Steve says "Yes I suppose so and it is a lovely drink besides, but I am a lager man I am afraid." "Well it's Newcastle for me all the time, keg beers today are shit full of sugar and chemicals, no thanks mate, I only drink the German lagers on tap as they will not allow any chemicals and tons of sugar in them and that's the difference today with crap British beers, that's why all these pubs are closing down because of the poor beers served in them, you can get that crap in the supermarkets in cans a third of the price , the British beer industry has gone to the dogs It certainly has. I remember it when beer was beer and a joy to drink but not anymore, even the CAMERA group miss the point of the amount of sugar that is in the beer never mind who brews it, so it is never real ale and the diabetes caused by the amount of sugar in the beers have lost them a lot of customers by given them the diabetes in the beginning ." "Steady

Dan, you sound like a vicar there, I know what you mean mind it's very poor quality nowadays, it is terribly made for the market and as cheap and as fast as they can make it." "On that point I am having another one and off to bed and I will be up here tomorrow for a couple." "Yes I am off now so I will say goodnight and see you when I get back Dan, have a good one." "Yes ok Steve and you have a nice holiday also, see you when we get back."

Well it was Thursday night and the last night before they all went home for the Easter holidays but some of the students went on that evening and so the bar was quiet again. Danny stood by the bar and had a bottle in his hand and was talking to the barman as he thought he was the only one there "God it's dead in here isn't it?" A little voice said in a French accent "Well most have gone home tonight instead of tomorrow." Danny's face lit up on hearing this voice and he says "Is that Malika?" Malika replied "Yes it is." "Well good grief how are you then?" "I am fine thank you, why have you not gone home yet?" "Oh it's a long story, I am not welcome at my house as my wife is divorcing me and can't see her boyfriend if I am there, so I leave it till the last minute to save arguments as I like to see my son who is 11 and have no nonsense with her and I am only there for a few days, then up with Jeff in Swindon for the rest of the time, I will be glad when I sell that bloody house down there and get her out of my hair." "So why is she divorcing you?" "Because I went blind that's all and she met someone who has also got bad eyesight and is now carrying on with him but I don't give a shit, she is not worth the trouble as long as I can see my son I don't care a damn, so where are you spending your holidays?" "I am going home to my house in Beccles in Suffolk all by myself for some peace and quiet." "What about Roy is he meeting you there?" "No bloody way I got rid of him a long time ago, he was so stupid I sent him back to his wife I even packed his bags for him, I am happy without him no problem." "I know what you mean, he was a little funny when I met you, getting heavy with me remember? he butted in and told me straight he was your boyfriend and got between us, he was a dick head." "Yes It was embarrassing he is a total idiot and his wife has got him back now, good riddance to bad rubbish." "So you are also single now then are you?" "Yes wild and free, I don't need a man to tell me what I can do with my life, I don't want a man like that so I can do what I want to when I want to." "I agree we are all born free as a bird and that's how it should always be, let me buy you a drink a gin and tonic is it?" "Oh yes please, I am going to your building after the holidays, I am having a girls room named Mandy do you know her?" "Yes it's on the same landing as I am in top floor, it's nice there and Zarrine will make a fuss of you, she is great you will like her and the rooms are nice there." "Yes I heard it's nice it has been renovated last year or so, I am looking forward to it, I am fed up with the youngsters there in Armitage I can't wait, so we will be neighbours then ?" Danny smiling from ear to ear says "Yes we will be, I am just around the corner and I think you will like it there but we have got Zig and Zag there do you know them? Sandy and Matt, they are a pain in the ass but the rest are ok and I will help you with anything you want up there and if you can't sleep I can smooth your forehead until you fall asleep no problem ha, ha, ha." "I bet you would ha, ha, I am going to sit over there my legs are aching after all that packing, are you coming over?" "Yes I will get the drinks in first." "No you will not it's my turn." "Oh don't worry about it you can get the next ones I will fetch them over now." They sit down and get chatting and they were getting closer and closer. Malika says "So it will be you and Jeff on the piss for the week then? I will be having a quiet time in my house all alone and getting on with some house work." "So have you always been alone?" Malika face turns serious and she says "Oh no I am a widow and have been for a year or so now, my husband was killed in a car crash." "Oh my god, I am so sorry to hear that , you have had a rough time then?" "Yes I was torn apart when he got killed, his name was Tony he was a chef and he was coming home one night from work and a man driving the other way swerved his van in front of Tony's car and he had to drive it off the road and straight into a tree and it killed him instantly, all because the man in the van was on his mobile phone." "Bloody hell that's awful, did they catch the bastard that done it?" "Yes they did and he lost his licence and that's all, he got away with murder, but his firm he was driving for has got a large bill to pay to me for his negligence I can tell you." "That's beside the point, I bet you were in a state?" "Yes I was for a long time and I still think and miss him to this day, it took a part of my life away." "I bet it did and the bastard has got away with it, I bet he is laughing that he did, I would throw him in a cell and throw the key away, but you are getting on with it now aren't you?" "Oh yes life goes on." "Well I am getting on with my life also as I am in the middle of a divorce but it's not a surprise to me anymore, she is a pain in the ass." "So what did you do wrong? it's usually the man ha, ha, ha." "Not always, this time it's not me, she left me because she could not put up with me going blind and I was a miserable git mind when I first went blind but that's not surprising is it it's not every day you go blind and to take it with a pinch of salt is not the human way and i am telling the truth, no one else involved on my part although she is now with a alcoholic so out of the frying pan and into the fire." "Really, she left you because you went blind?" "Yes I am not lying but in a way I understand her doing it, it was just as a shock to her as it was to me, but she never took any consideration into the children's feelings, that annoys me especially my youngest son Josh who is still only nearly 12 now but at the time he was only 8, it's hard for him I can take it at least I know where I stand." Malika with sympathetic look says "Yes but still it's death do us part and in sickness and in health." "Not these days it's not, a marriage is not a thing we take literally now it's a joke with the youngsters today, look at me I have been married 4 times, it's too easy to get a divorce but I have grown up now and if I never got married again it will be too soon, as I think a ring is not necessary these days and causes problems for couples these days." "Bloody hell, 4 times?" "I liked wedding cake but I am a diabetic now so I have as I say grown up now ha, ha, and yes some of those were my fault but I have matured, I am 50 now it's about time." "So how many children have you got then?" "3 girls and 3 boys although one of the boys is adopted by me, I brought him up with his mother but he is mine really I don't think of him as anything else." "Well, well, no telly ha, ha, ha." "Have you seen the cost of the licence ha, ha, well I love them all and would not change anything, it is the way I am but I can't have any more so I am lucky I had them when I did, you would like them all, so have you got any children?" "No but Tony had 2 daughters and we used to get together, but never see them now at all, but I have none of my own." "Right get them in then it's your round." "Wow, wow, I am on my way." She gets them in and she returns and says "Well it's dead in here isn't it? what time are you leaving tomorrow?" "I am leaving around 10.30 we have to be out by eleven o'clock, it's ridiculous isn't it and what time is your train?" Malika replies "My train leaves at 10.12 so I will be up and gone by the time you leave, I am not looking forward to going home as I have not been there for a month and I will have to clean all the way through and get my landlord to sort some things out, I live on a railway crossing it's nice there mind and a nice little town but a bastard to get to from here so many changes and waiting in train stations, a real pain in the backside, how far is your place?" "Oh about 2 hours and a half, it's in Wales and not a bad place but I will be glad to see the back of it now I am blind, then I have to get up to Swindon to Jeff's place on Tuesday and stay with him, that's about the same amount of hours and it's party all the way and he has got a fantastic Chinese take away there and cheap as chips, lovely, we drink every night and most days he is a nutter, oh I forget you have met him, I was talking to Steve last night he is a bit of a lad mind isn't he?" "Yes I like Steve a nice bloke and a lot of girls here think I and he are an item but it's a load of crap." "So you are single and free then are you?" Smiling she says "Yes I am, why do you ask?" Danny also smiling says "Oh nothing just asking that's all, I see you smoke the old rollies then? I used to smoke but had to give it up, shortage of breath." "Yes I do and I don't smoke a lot but it gets my chest going sometimes ha, ha, ha." Well the night came to an end and Danny asked Malika to his dorm for a coffee and she accepted, is this the woman he has been waiting for, for a while? Back in Dowdell Danny and Malika sitting having a coffee side by side and they were flirting with each other until they held hands and the talking got softer . Danny says "It's funny I knew this would happen." "Why do you say that?" "I just did, I will tell you if it goes any further so don't ask again until then, I only wish this was happening a week ago and then I would have enjoyed my 50th talking of which can I ask how old you are?" "Not a nice thing to ask a woman is it but I don't care I am 39." "God you are nearly 12 years younger than me." "So Tony was older than you it makes no difference and an older man is more mature I can't stand these young stupid males sorry." "Fair enough I am young for my age anyway, I don't feel 50 at all so are you looking forward to coming here to Dowdell?" "Yes I think it is much better in a place with people of your own age and I am fed up with being moved around and too many lesbians here for my liking, not that I mind them but they creep up on you ha, ha, I mean you don't know who is and who isn't." "Ooh tell me about it they are lesbians when they want to be and not when it suit's them, I give up with them. I met a girl here when I started here and she was a full blown lesbian and expected everyone to respect the fact, now she is engaged to a nice lad and is very much in love with him, I give up." "I know what you mean, I suppose that is how it is in college, right I had better let you get to bed and go home." "No rush, it's a pity to walk home in that cold wet weather, let's have a sit in my room and chat." "Oh I don't know, ok let's go, can I have a fag out of your window?" "Yes ok." Off they went and stayed there all night getting to know each other .

It was the next morning and Danny and Malika came into the lounge and there was Zarrine in there and she looked shocked to see Malika there and said "Well hello there? Danny introduce me then." Danny yawning says "Sorry, this is Malika she is moving in here after the holidays, she is having Mandy's room." Zarrine "Well hello Monica." Malika replies "Hello Zarrine, my name is Malika not Monica ha, ha, ha." Zarrine "Malika that's a lovely name and so why are you with him? he is trouble you know and it looks as if you have already moved in ha, ha, I am only kidding ha, ha, would you like tea or coffee?" Malika "Oh don't worry about me I will get one in my dorm." Danny "You just as well have one here as on your own over there, go on, I will put the toast on." Zarrine "Malika you will have to come again he never makes toast in the morning, he waits for me to do it ha, ha, ha." Malika "I bet he does, I will have coffee please and strong please, no sugar." Zarrine "Coming up no problem, you sit down and I will get it for you." Malika sit's and Zarrine goes in the kitchen where Danny was doing the toast, she hit's him on the arm and makes him pay attention and mimes to him with her thumbs up and realising he could not see she whispers "She is lovely you naughty man." and slaps him again, he makes the toast and they all sit in the lounge and enjoys the breakfast and Zarrine says "Your not English Malika are you? so where are you from?" "I am French from Paris originally and lived in Inverness in Scotland to do my degree they sent me up there to learn English." Danny "That's a joke I can't understand them in Scotland at all so not a good idea to send you there was it?" Malika "They told me if I could understand their English I can understand anyone's English."

471

Zarrine "I love Paris it's a beautiful city better there and here don't you miss it?" Malika "No I don't, it is horrible there now and my mum lives on the border of Italy it's beautiful there, I love it there I have to fly to Marseilles and my brother picks me up and we have a forty mile run to my mother's house and we pick wild leeks and wild lettuce there in the fields, it's lovely." Zarrine "I bet it is, so are you going there now for Easter?" Malika replies "Oh no I am living in Suffolk so I am going home there for Easter and that reminds me, I must make a move I have a taxi at ten o'clock so I must leave now." Danny "I will walk you over if you like?" They both left and Zarrine was smiling and gave a little shuffle to see Danny was looking so happy.

He came back after a while and Zarrine set upon him to find out everything "So what's going on Danny? is she the one?" "Zarrine I don't know, I think it may be mind, we don't see each other now for 2 weeks so I will see if I feel the same then but I hope so. I said to Jeff when she came here last year she will be mine when she comes back and she had her boyfriend with her when I said that and she is not with him anymore, so look out this may be it Zarrine, who knows?" "She is lovely and pretty with it, I think you make a lovely pair, you suit each other you looked good together this morning, it's perfect Danny I am so pleased I can't wait for next term I am so pleased for you." Zarrine hugs Danny and rubs her hands together excitedly and makes another cup of tea for Danny and chats to him about her for a while until Danny's taxi comes to pick him up.

Danny went home to see his little Josh and was like a new man he was bouncing and smiling all the time. He got home and was hugged by Josh and they had some fun that day and yes they had a Chinese meal and in the evening before Josh was going to bed he said to Danny "So dad is it ok up the college and can I come up sometime with you to see it up there?" "Yes of course you can Josh, I will arrange it now the summer is nearly here, no problem, I will come home and pick you up on a Friday ok?" Josh looking all excited says "Brilliant dad I will enjoy it up there I can play pool with the lads up there can I?" "Oh yes of course you can and we will go and do some shopping for some new clothes for you and have some fun ok?" "Yeah that's cool so why are you going up Jeff's then?" "To keep the peace Josh I don't think your mother is happy with me here now she is divorcing me so don't worry and I can have you up with me at any time, so let's take it easy so she don't pick on me again and start an argument just for the sake of trying to get me out, I want a nice weekend with my boy, so let's enjoy it aye?" "Yeah ok but I miss you not being here dad and Craig is not here anymore is he and I miss the holidays in the caravan in Chalaborough bay." "Well I will book it up for Whitson holidays if you like? we will ask Jeff if he fancies it with his son and we will have some fun, what do you think?" "Can we? is it ok?" "Yes it's ok and I will book it up for the summer if you like and we can ask Natasha to come to she will enjoy that and if you like you can ask a mate of yours to come if you like, as long as he pays for himself." "Allright I will." "Good I will get it sorted then and we will still have fun me and you, so don't worry about it ok?" "Ok I know we will I have got some new games on my computer I am going to play with one before I go to bed is that ok dad?" "Of course it is and then off to bed before it gets too late." They had a lot of fun while Danny was there but it came time to go up to stay with Jeff and Danny was sorry to go and leave Josh.

Up Jeff's and he got to his place and sat down with him in his flat and had a cup of tea and said to Jeff "Well Jeff it's nice to see you again and I am going to give you some news and maybe you will owe me some money if I am right, guess who I am seeing?" Jeff looked puzzled and thought and said "Sandy, she was always after you and you would make a good couple." "You cheeky git no it's not her I am not that desperate try someone who I said I would have." Jeff thought and his face then lit up "Oh the French girl is it? I can't remember her name now but she was with that Roy, is it her?" Danny with huge smile on his face says "Yes it is and I only had a few hours with her before I came on holiday as it was on the Thursday last week, so I don't know where it is going until I get back, just my luck it happened at the last knockings and it is not clear in my mind now, I hope she remembers but she spent the night in my room so she probably will, so what do you think?" "Brilliant Dan, so what happened to Roy then?" "She found him boring and kicked him out and told him to go back to his wife so he did and I thought she was seeing that Steve but it's no go with him they are very good friends so I am it ha, ha, ha." "So are you happy about it? is she the girl for you?" "Oh yes, I am over the moon, I am in love at last I hope she thinks the same, I think this is it matey, it's the one for me. I have been dying to tell someone as I couldn't tell Josh and I was dying to, it's a dream come true, so let's celebrate tonight is it?" "Why not it sounds that it's what you want is it?" "Definitely and that reminds me did I bet I would get her with you?" "No you bloody didn't it was not a bet you just said it and I didn't believe you , no money involved so don't go there ha, ha,, ha." "Ok I will believe you most wouldn't, this is it matey I mean it let's get the hell out of here and get a few pints is it up the red cow or the sun inn." "I don't mind we can walk up if you like it is a nice day and I am not getting pissed this time in the day, so forget it, just 2 and that's it I mean it." "Yeah, yeah, how many times have I heard you say that ? it's Easter time to party isn't it? you miserable git, ok I will only have 2 pints to join you ok?" "Oh allright I get it it's Impossible for you and me to have a few pints anytime so I should not say stupid things like that and on Wednesday we have got to go up to the Polish club I promised the taffies I would go up there and take you up to tell them a load of jokes and no I am not going on the Sherbets, no way Hose, I am staying away from that no questions asked, let's go." Up the red cow sitting having a meal and a few pints and Jeff asked "So what do you think is going to happen with you and Malika in the future if it works out any ideas?" "No matey I have not got a clue, I want to go back down to west Wales to live, it's just right for me down there I will if it goes ok to ask her to come an look at the place and see what she thinks but that is a long way away yet. I will have to play it by ear for now, I am still as far from knowing what I am going to do but at least I may not be doing it on my own now touch wood, maybe she wants to stay in Beccles in Suffolk, maybe she wants to go back to France, who knows? I would go to France no problem as long as it is not in a city and I don't know a bloody thing about Beccles so we will see, I haven't got any further than when I met you last time have i?" "I know, I think it will work out don't worry about it like me I don't know how things will be with me and Jo, but I think it will be fine however it goes between us and Carol phoned me the other day and wants to come down to visit but I am waiting for the bungalow to be finished that is next month , I can't wait it will be fantastic you wait and see, then I can enjoy life a bit more, I am not happy in that flat at all." "I bet your not it will be the making of you and you are soon getting the dog to it will be a new life for you, god it will be different then won't it ?" "Not arf, I will be in my oils then. A nice new bungalow fantastic, it will be here before we know it and I will have my mother there to help me and my sister so it will go smoothly I know then I will get Carol in my bed no problem ha, ha, ha." Danny says "Well you never know now she is not at the college she may be a different girl you never know." "Right another one ha, ha, ha." "See I knew you would not just have 2 I am sticking with my word I am ready to go back to your flat now ha, ha, ha." "Yeah I don't believe you either I will get them in, same again?" "Yes please."

Later that night Danny and Jeff were very drunk and Danny was keeping Jeff awake teasing him shouting "Malika I miss my Malika." Every few minutes, this got on Jeff's nerves and he kept on telling him to shut up.

The holiday with Jeff went well and a good time were had by Danny and Jeff and they were on the booze a lot that fortnight and it came time to get back to college and his thoughts came back to what will happen when he got back. Is she going to ignore him and act as if it never happened or will she be looking forward to carrying on their relationship? Time will tell. Back at the college Danny knew he would get back well before Malika as she had 3 different trains to catch and a long way to travel. Danny got back around dinner time and unpacked his stuff and got his stereo working and played some music and going back and forth to the lounge to see if there was any sign of Malika as he knew her stuff had been brought over from Armitage to her new room. Well it seemed a long time and it was around 5pm when she finally came back and Danny went into the lounge and she was sitting there with a cup of coffee and he said "Hello who is that in here?" "It's me Malika I have just got back from my home." "Oh hello did you have a nice Easter then?" "Oh yes I did it was quiet mind and the time went slow for me on my own and you?" "Well I saw my son and had some fun with him, then some fun with Jeff in Swindon and I am glad to get back and stop drinking." "Right, how is Jeff? has he moved yet?" "He is fine he is moving next month and his new dog is coming week or 2 later, so he is going to be busy." "Oh that's nice I am knackered and I have got to put my stuff away next, never mind ." Danny nervously asked "So what are you doing tonight fancy a drink up the student bar?" "Ok what time was you thinking about?" "9 o'clock give you time to get sorted in your room, what do you think meet in here is it?" "That will be fine for me I will be ready easy by then, see you later then? I must sort my room out now to be sure of being ready, see you later." She goes off to her room and Danny went back to his with a smile on his face and played some more music.

Well it was 8.45 and Danny had finished playing his favourite Phil Collins greatest hits album and set off to the lounge to wait for Malika and lo and behold he was so shocked as he passed her room as the cd she was playing on her music system was exactly the same Phil Collins album Danny was playing earlier, as he loved that album so he sat and waited for her in the lounge. Malika came in and off to the bar they went and got a beer in and sat down on a table alone in the corner and Danny said "I heard the Phil Collins cd you were playing in your room." Malika replies "Yes I love that album all his hit's, it's a fantastic album and I play it all of the time." "Well It's incredible guess what album I was playing before I met you in the lounge?" "I don't know, is it the Phil Collins cd?" "Yes it was Phil Collins not only that but the exact same album no difference, it is also one of my favourite albums and I am always playing it, what a coincidence, well I never out of all the millions of cd's in the world we were playing the exact same one at the exact same time, that is a million to one, we must have been made for each other." Malika smiled and turned her head not committing herself "I hope it is not going to be dead here tonight it's always dead here I hate coming up sometimes, I like a change, so where do you go in town?" "Well I go to the Pretty Pigs the Rose and crown it's nice there and nice food and I love the Barrels in the town a little old but a good pub for an atmosphere If you want to we could go for a meal in the rose and crown tomorrow night instead of the refectory? I don't like the food there much, all stodge for the youngsters really not my cup of tea, what do you think?" "I don't mind I don't like the food much in the refectory only the salad bar I use so yes we can go early and eat can we?" "Yes if you like we can get a taxi it is not expensive and I know the Manager Ian in the pub he will look after us and the beer is lovely there, so it's a date then about what time do you fancy going?" "I don't know about six o'clock I can't eat early." "Fine, fine, no problem that's suit's me fine, I will look forward to it I will have to pace myself with the lager there mind it's a little early to drink so I will take my time." "Ha, ha, you take your time I have seen you and Jeff drinking and when you are with Steve you are wobbling going home, talking of him I wonder if he is back, I should have called him as he might be stuck waiting to get over here he's hopeless he won't use a cane and has not got any sense of direction, never mind he will get here somehow." Next thing in walks a few of the new boys from b floor in Dowdell a few new ones and on old one Anthony he said "Hello Dan and Malika isn't it?" Malika replied she was Malika and he then said "It's nice to be back, I am going to have a few pints tonight I have been missing it here in the student bar." Malika "Have you, not a raver then?" Anthony "Sorry, what do you mean?" Malika smiling said "Well it's boring in here isn't it most of the time, I can't stand it here except on a Friday evening before I go to town." Anthony replies "I am not serious I only come in here if I am skint, I usually go to town with the lads, so where do you go Malika?" Malika "I go to the crystal rooms and many night clubs sometimes as I like to dance and sometimes we go to the what is it called Danny? the rose and crown for a meal and a few pints and a good laugh." Danny "Well that's where we are going tomorrow night isn't it Malika? and then a rave up the barrels maybe and dance the night away somewhere else, we will see." Anthony clicked that they were together and asked "So are you 2 together?" Both Malika and Danny hesitated to answer and Danny then said "Yes what is it to do with you is there a problem with that?" Malika smiled and waited for Anthony's reply, he stuttered and said "No, no I am just surprised that's all never mind." He moved nervously in his seat and then moved off to his place with his mates. Malika says "He was a bit up himself." Danny "Yes he seemed surprised as if I was an old monster, he was after you I think he seemed upset by it ha, ha, good enough for him." "No I don't think he was after me." "Why else would he be here asking all those questions? he was after you." Malika looked unsteady and says "I don't think so he was just being nosey that's all." "I am telling you he was, shall I leave and give him a chance? you seem interested"." Malika "No I am not interested he is so strange I would never entertain the likes of him." Next thing a voice came from the bar "Hello Malika is that you sitting over there? keep on talking so I can find you." "Over here Steve, keep coming, over here, that's it your going right now watch the seat on your left follow my voice here we are there is a seat to my left." He found the seat and sat down and said "Shit the trouble I had getting over here then a lovely big busted Italian girl led me over here, lovely, is that Danny you are talking to?" Danny "Yes Steve have you had a good holiday?" " Steve replies "Oh yes I did but a bad journey back, missed my connection in Newport and had to wait a hour and a half lost drinking time so how about you?" Danny says "Fine had a few days with my youngest son and then up with the Jeff man in Swindon and got pissed for a week or more." Steve "And you Malika what did you do?" Malika says "I went home to Beccles and did my house cleaning from top to bottom an went up the Buffs club a few times and my sister spoke to me a lot on the phone and enjoyed the time off really, did some cooking and chilled." "Well good enough I went to the footie and pissed my missus off most of the time ha, ha, had a few pints with my mates and generally lazed about, can't beat it Dan if you are going up the bar can you get me a bottle of coohrs pleas and whatever you are drinking?" Malika grabbed his money and said "I will get it if you like?" And off she went. Steve "So are you drinking the Newcastle brown tonight?" "Do bears crap in the woods ha, ha, I love my Newcastle brown the best beer here I can tell you, I also like the Budweiser to mind, I can't stand that coohrs it makes me have a bloated feeling." "Oh I

475

don't mind it, so how is Jeff up there? " "He is great he is moving next few weeks to his brand new built bungalow and he is then waiting for his guide dog." "Brilliant I am waiting for a guide dog." "Yeah, me to I am not having mine until I leave here, I don't think it's fair on the dog sitting under the desk most of the day, not nice for them." "No maybe not but I am only here for a year so it will not make any difference to me." Malika returns and gives the beer to the boys and the change to Steve and says "Well it's getting full here for a change and Anthony just ignored me by the bar, so he got the message." Steve "He is a nutter he is, watch him." Danny "He just come up to chat her up but he went off with a flea in his ear." Steve "Oh Malika you didn't hit him did you? ha, ha, ha." Malika "Steve I don't do things like that I am a nice girl." Danny "No he found he didn't stand a chance as she is going out with someone already." Steve sat there in silence for a minute and then said "Who ? you? she is with you?" Danny "Well who else is sitting here?" Steve "Well I never, when did this happen then?" Danny smiling says "The Thursday before we broke up for the holidays, so there we are." Steve "Well, well done, a good match I think, let's drink to that." They clanged their glasses together and smiled broadly and Steve says "I hope the pair of you stick together, a good couple, well I never, I bet Anthony disappeared fast when he found out, he is afraid of you Dan that I know." Malika "Yes he didn't stay long after that." The night went off as good as it possibly could have although Danny was still not sure of Malika's intensions and neither was she about Danny, they had not committed anything as yet. They spent another night together and went off the next day to their lectures but met at dinner and coffee breaks the next day.

Well the night came and off they went to the Rose and crown for a meal and they entered and behind the bar was Monica the bar manageress she greeted them "Well hello Danny, how are you? and who is this .lovely lady with you?" Danny smiles and says "This is Malika, Malika this is Monica." They said hello to each other and Danny continued "Can we have a nice table for us and somewhere quiet please?" Monica "Of course you can, here is a nice one near the bar for you to get to the bar easy." Danny "Lovely Monica you always look after me." Monica "It's a pleasure you are a good customer and we have come to know how you like things and by the way happy birthday for the beginning of the month, Ian told me, I was away I am afraid but I will get you the first 2 drinks on me, please enjoy yourselves and I will tell Ian you are in, he will read the Menu for you." Danny says "Thank you my darling I will have a pint of lager and Malika what would you like?" Malika replies "Just a cup of coffee please, thank you." Monica goes off to get the drinks and brings them back and puts them on the table and Danny says "There we go it's nice here." Malika "Yes it is and so helpful aren't they? it's a big pub too isn't it? I will come here again it's so nice." "Yes they look after you here and there is a quiz here on a Sunday it's brilliant we have won it a few times and you can win usually around £60 between you." "Never that sounds good, I will come next time I am not all that good but I will enjoy it." "Yes ok, I will tell the others, look out I can hear Ian coming." Ian says "Hello Dan and who is this lovely lady with you? another daughter?" Danny "Cheeky, this is Malika a lady from the college and she is French so behave." Ian says "Lovely to meet you, what is it again Monica?" Malika "No it's Malika." Ian "That's a lovely name and lovely to meet you, are you ready to eat? shall I read the menu?" Danny "I know what I want, I will have the cod and chips please and Malika what would you like?" She thinks and says "Do you do pasta?" Ian "Yes I do pasta with things like Tuna steaks." Malika stops him in his tracks "That's fine, my favourite, I love tuna that will be fine please." Ian "Well that was easy wasn't it? I will sort it out Immediately, enjoy the evening." They thank him and start drinking Malika chirps up "He is a lovely man, you are right Danny it's a real lovely place to come to, much better than the college." "Not much to beat there is there? I have been coming here since I started in the college and met Ian the first day I stepped in here he loved my sense of humour and we hit it off Immediately. He does the quiz here and helps a lot by that, I mean he describes the picture round without giving us the answer he is very good with us." "Well that's something you don't see much these days." "Your right there and it counts when you go out these days especially if you are blind like me, so what is wrong with your eyes then? can you see much?" "I have R. P. and I can see pretty good in the dark and in false light but the sun blazing down and I can't see anything it's just white and that's that. I can't see nothing." "Oh never I am sorry I am totally blind it was a medical mistake at the hospital and I went blind, human error, it's ok now I can handle it, I will not feel sorry for myself anymore." "I didn't think you would and your wife left you because of it, I have been told the story it's a shame but life goes on I suppose." "Well yes it's just a different world when it happens and I have got used to it nearly now so it don't bother me. So how long have you had RP ?" "I have had it all my life according to the doctor but it came out a few years ago I was working in Scotland and we moved down to Suffolk and it developed then and I had to give up work that's the story of it all but I get frustrated with it but as you say we get used to these things." "I can see you are like me no good keeping on about it just get on with it, well I hope you like the food here if you don't I will not pay ha, ha, ha." " Malika snaps "I will give you my half, I can't let you pay." "I will never live it down if Ian knows he will tell all the students in the college, I will get this one please, I am hungry now I am not eating well in the confectionery so I do half board now and cook so many meals myself in Dowdell." "Yes that is a good idea I may do that, it is much better than the food over there it's full of fat food and sweet stuff not to my liking." Danny says "I know what you mean I can't eat that crap all the time, mind you I and Zarrine, Jeff and Niel used to love having a chip butty, it's as it says it, Zarrine used to do a load of bread with butter and I used to go up the chip shop in college green and get a huge bag of chips put them on the table and we used to help ourselves, it used to be lovely." "I am not a lover of chips, look here is the meal." Ian "Here we are guys, enjoy." Danny "Thank you Ian we will." They eat their food and talk for a long time and drank a few beers and wine and carried on their conversation now with more confidence as they had some Dutch courage through the drink. Danny "I had a great time with Jeff but I have got to be honest with you I will admit it, I was missing you a lot." Malika replies "Really, I never, I also missed you I just wanted to get back to college to see you again." Danny had a huge smile on his face and says "Your kidding, I was the same I just wanted the holiday over with, I was missing you and just wanted to be with you, I was all but crying to Jeff about you and he told me I was getting on his nerves because I was wondering if you would be the same about me when we met again?" "And me, I was the same I just wanted it to be over it was the longest holiday I have ever had, I cleaned that house until my fingers were raw and I was thinking the same as you and wanted us to be together again." "I know I was the same I wished I had said to you to come to Jeff's for the holiday or I was going to ask you if I could come up with you but I had only been with you for a few hours that's all, I just wanted us to be together that's all, all of the time." "I was exactly the same it was murder on my own." "Well that's it then." Malika asks "What do you mean?" "Someone in the college told me I was going to find someone one day and it would all start to fall into place and I would be madly in love and it has happened I have found a new girl." "And me, a man I mean ha, ha, ha, well would you believe it we both thought the same about each other all of the time and that cd of Phil Collins both playing it the exact same time, it's unreal." "I know is that just uncanny , I was afraid to say anything in case you didn't feel the same and you did all the time, well, well." "There you go then, so let's just enjoy life from now on." "Right, get the beer in then ha, ha, only kidding it's my round I will get the same again is it?" Malika says "Yes but I will be taking it slower from that one on, I will be pissed otherwise." This was going to be it by the looks of it for Danny and Malika and what would the others think? Well it was going to be a real new opening for them both.

Later in the student bar and they were up there telling everyone that they were an item but that wasn't the ones who they cared what they thought about it, it was Jeff, Zarrine, Niel, Tim, Mandy, and Danny's children that counted. So they had a beer and sat in the corner they always sit and in comes Steve and he says "Hi both I was wondering where you were as you were not in the refectory for dinner were you?" Danny "No we went to the Rose and Crown for dinner and got intimate. " Steve says " Oh really, I had better not ask had i?" Danny "Oh it's no problem we somehow were thinking the same about each other on our holidays and we are now an item officially." Steve "Well congratulations to the both of you, so I will get the drinks in then, Malika what is it for you?" Malika replies "Just a diet coke for me I have had a lot of wine for now thanks." Steve "And a Newcastle brown for Danny is it?" Danny answers "Yes please Steve." Danny and Malika sat there like 2 teenagers in love and they had a lovely time at the bar with Steve, Steve then said "So Danny you are leaving in August aren't you? and Malika is still here for another year so what are you going to do?" Danny "Yes your right I will think of something, I will get a flat here in Hereford while I wait for her if we are still together I expect but I will sort that out in time for August and I have thought of something else to, it's Tim and Mandy's wedding in a few weeks I will ask him if I can take you with me to the wedding, I must sort that out also." Malika "Oh don't worry about that he has probably sorted everything out by now and gave a final figure so don't worry about it Danny." Danny "Well I understand but I will give him a quick ring tomorrow and ask him no problem and this weekend Jeff is coming here for the weekend so look out it's celebration time he will be pissed again I expect." Steve "And you will, you always are both the same as each other." Danny "I will have Malika to watch over us, so we will have to behave." Malika jokingly says "Yes your right I can keep an eye on the both of you ha, ha, ha." Steve smiling says "Oh yeah, they will listen to you to, I don't think so, but it will be funny you trying ha, ha, ha." Danny "We will have some fun with Jeff you will see he is a good laugh and we complement each other very well and it's a laugh a minute, so look out Hereford." Well they had a few more drinks and went off to bed.

The weekend came around and Jeff arrived on the Friday lunchtime and was sitting with Danny and Zarrine having a cup of tea and chatting. Zarrine says "Well Jeffrey he has been so quiet I have not heard him much since he has been with Malika, it must be love and he don't drink so much, but you are back so don't get him in trouble this weekend ok?" Jeff looking at Zarrine and says "Who me? he is the trouble maker and he starts me off drinking not the other way around but I am up for a couple of pints this weekend up the student bar tonight and down the town this weekend if the old man can still handle it?" Danny snaps "You won't be waiting for me matey I will be there and so will Malika and she likes to drink to." Zarrine "Now you pair take it easy on her, she is only little, be careful." Mandy the warden walked in and said "Be careful on who Zarrine? I expect you are warning these 2 aren't you again?" Zarrine "Yes they are on the town this weekend and Malika will be with them and I worry they will get her drunk and she is so little." Mandy "I think she will be to clever for them, she is a sensible girl I will warn her don't worry as I am on duty all this

478

weekend and there will be no nonsense I can tell you, I will sort these 2 out." Danny "I am not worried at all what do you think Jeff?" Jeff says "I am off home if she is going to spoil my holiday here ha, ha, only kidding we need watching I will respect Malika's wishes no problem, so Dan want a tinny? I have got some in my bag." Danny "Well thank you Jeffrey it's time to start, the weekend starts here." Mandy "Look at them they can't wait, I will be watching you pair like a hawk this weekend mind, I mean it, I will see you both later." They said goodbye and Zarrine then leaves and in walks Malika. Jeff greets her "Well hello Malika it's nice to meet you again, want a tinny of lager?" Malika smiling says "No thank you I can't stand cans of lager, I have just been warned by Mandy to keep an eye on you 2 this weekend so you had better behave yourselves If I am coming out with you ok?" Jeff "No problem at all it's this dodgy Welshman it is." Danny "You keep me out of it mate I don't get so pissed as you." Malika "I don't believe that I have seen you with Steve sometimes, both of you wobbling out of the bar, I don't watch what you are doing it's not anything to do with me I am only kidding." Jeff "Good I was about to go home so up the student bar tonight for a quiet one or 2 is it? come and tell me how things are going then, tell me all the gossip." They rambled on for a few hours and went to bed after going to the bar.

Saturday night came around and they had decided to go to the Rose and Crown for tea and that meant going early to eat so it was going to be a long night. They were walking down the stairs of Dowdell and there was Mandy waiting for them and she said to them with a smile on her face "Hello I am glad I have caught you." Danny and Jeff smiled at her and she continued "Malika don't let them get pissed again, it's up to you to look after them and keep them in trim ok?" Malika playing along with Mandy says "No problem Mandy I am in charge, they will be at their best behaviour no problem or else I will sort them out, don't worry about anything." Mandy "God a girl with some sense, you pair heard that, so look out she will sort you out I know that no problem, she is a no nonsense girl, I will see you all later and you pair enjoy yourself." Jeff "Oh yeah we will have a lot of fun now you have got us taped." Danny "Yeah, isn't it, we will have a blast now you have had your say." Mandy laughed and said "Well it's for your own good lads you get to pissed and don't know when to stop so she will be your guardian angel for tonight and Danny will not get expelled and Jeff will be able to visit again ok?" Malika teasingly says "Yes it's for your own good boys, don't worry Mandy I am on the case ha, ha." They got into the taxi and set off the lads with faces down to the ground as if to say the night is ruined but is it so.

In the Rose and crown and they are just getting over the meal and Jeff said "That was beautiful as usual, I will get the beer in, anything for you Malika?" Malika says "Yes please I am fed up with that coke it's to gassy I will have a small, I said a small red wine please Jeff, thank you and slow down the pair of you there's all night to go." Danny "So you are keeping an eye on us still are you ha, ha, ha?" Malika smiling says "Of course not I will just stay sober to keep an eye on the evening, I am not one to get drunk anyway, I was only kidding with Mandy but I think she was serious." Danny "Oh yes she was serious ok, she always warns us when we go out for a drink and has to report the state we come home in." Malika looking serious says "She don't, your kidding?" "No I am not she does honestly so don't ever get drunk as she will put it down in the book, I am not kidding she does." Jeff "He is right it is like big brother in that college I can tell you." Malika says "Bloody hell, that's ridiculous and none of their business is it?" Jeff "They don't worry about that, we have often been spoken to about how we come home on certain days I am not joking but we don't care ha, ha, so here is your wine Malika and Danny's your drink." Danny "So what's happening with the wedding Jeff? I have asked Tim if Malika can come and it's ok, what are you doing about the stag night etc." Jeff "I can't see me being at the stag night as I am about to move into my new bungalow, so it's up to you to hold our end up if you don't mind, but I will be at the wedding with Jo and will stay the night before and Tim is arranging the digs I mean for us all and that's it for me." Danny "I will be in the stag night no problem and so will Clamper but have not heard off Niel so I don't know about him." Jeff "I can't see him in the stag night either but he will surely be in the wedding, I can't see him missing that can you?" Danny "No but he has been having trouble with poor old Abbey she is not to well by all accounts, so he will have his plate full as he loves that dog as if it was his daughter so I don't know what's happening." Jeff "Oh dear I hope she is going to be allright, she is such a lovely dog and I hope he will be there, it will not be the same without him the big lump of lard ha, ha, only joking he is a lovely man I can understand why he is so soppy over that dog they make a funny pair and make me laugh." Danny "Yes I know what you mean I hope he will be there to and Tim has told me I am to have a Rolls Royce to take me back and fore to the church and reception and he and Mandy had got an old Ford car for themselves so look out and Ginny is going with her husband Phil, that will be nice, I am looking forward to it I really am." Malika "Well that will be nice for us I have never been in a rolls Royce before, I just hope the weather is good for them and I met Niel once didn't I? when I came over for coffee that day the stink bomb was let off." Jeff "Yes you did he was the large man always chuckling and he was sitting on the end of the couch you were sitting on, as bald as a fish a nice man." Malika "Yes I remember him I hope his dog is ok." Danny "Yes me to, she is such a lovely Alsatian and she loves me as I used to play with her. Right it's my round the same again?" Malika rushed her wine and they sat and had another one and Danny continued the conversation "So Jeff are you meeting Jo here on the wedding day? and travelling with us up there or what?" Jeff "Well that's the idea, I have not finalised it with Jo yet but I can ask her tomorrow, she will be back then but I think that's the best thing to do." Malika "I need to get some things to go to this wedding, I have not got anything yet I feel a shopping day on the cards." Jeff "Typical woman only needs the excuse to go and get a new cossi." Malika "Excuse me I don't need an excuse I am always buying clothes." They sat there all night and drank and drank and Malika got the taste for the wine and it came time to get a taxi home, it arrived and home they went and got outside Dowdell, paid the taxi and stood outside for a breath of fresh air for a minute and out came Mandy from her office to greet them half way up the stairs and she had a shock when she met them. There was Jeff on one side of Malika and Danny on the other side carrying her up the stairs her head drooped and she was as pissed as a lord. Mandy said OH my god, what have you pair done to her? the poor girl, what happened? she is supposed to be stopping you pair coming home like this not you 2 carrying her like this, let's get her to her room quick." Danny "She was ok in the pub it was when we got into the fresh air and that was it she went like a rag doll ha, ha, ha, ha." Jeff "Ha, ha, ha, he is right honestly, let's get her to her room and then Danny can get some tinnies out of his room and he can go and see her from time to time to see if she is allright." Mandy hand over her mouth says "You bloody pair, I am shocked she is like this and I told her to watch you 2, I never, ha, ha, that will teach me, wait till she is sober I will tease her something terrible." They marched her to her room and Mandy put her to bed.

Back in the lounge and Jeff and Danny was sitting having a few tins of lager. Jeff said "God I miss this it's not the same at home and it has brought a lot of good memories back to me they were good times Dan aye?" "Yes they were and still are we will always be good friends so don't worry it will always be the same and I am happy now I have got Malika, the bestest thing that has happened to me and you said I would meet someone one day some way or another." "And I was right, do you think she is the one Dan?" "I think so, but can't really be sure, they all start off ok but soon change don't they? but I think it will be good I am happy she is not a drinker though is she? Ha, ha, ha." "Your not wrong there, mind she is in a mess look out tomorrow she will have it in for us and did you see Mandy's face, she was gutted seeing Malika in such a mess , it was so funny." Danny smiling says "Yes she thought she had us taped and failed, I think Malika will be in the book tomorrow ha, ha, I don't worry about things like that and neither does Malika, no worries, well it is nearly time for Tim to sign off and get married, I just realised it's next week end that he has got his stag night, I will have to pull my socks up and get sorted it will be a fantastic night and I am dreading it trying to pace it out and we are staying at Tim's and that is Clamper also, look out, but Mandy will be there and will see us ok, she is lovely and Tim is a lucky man." "Yes he is, I wish I could make it for that night but can't Dan it's Impossible." "Don't worry mate I will be thinking about you as I am having some lovely beer up there it will be great and I am not coming back until the afternoon on the Saturday so no rush and off to bed when I come in with my Malika to sleep it off it will be nice." "You rub it in Dan why don't you? I will make up for it in the wedding, can't wait, it will be a huge wedding apparently in some theme park up there, his dad mind has got a bit of money, he had a builders diy place once, he is a nice man mind I have not met him but he is a diamond by all accounts." "Yes I heard that he will be around for the stag night I think I will meet him then, I am looking forward to it and I am so pleased for them both, they deserve each other and will be fine I know it, they are like shoes and socks, tea and coffee etc." Jeff says "Yes your right, god I feel pissed now so I am off in a minute I have got to go and meet Jo in the morning from the station, so I had better get some sleep now, see you in the morning?" "Ok I will have another one then check Malika is ok, then off to bed myself." Jeff looks sheepish at Danny and says "Oh go on then, I will join you, I don't want to leave you drinking alone ha, ha, ha." "I knew you was going to say that, I knew it, we will have another 3 at least so I am bringing six cans back." "Oh no Dan, ok then ha, ha, ha." "I know you like my own hand matey, be back now." Danny went to have a check on Malika and she was fast asleep, he done this from time to time, the lads stayed up until they could not stand and then retired to bed.

The next day and Danny was laughing at Malika as she was in such a state and hardly got out of her room for the day and Jeff met up with Jo and had some of the day with her until the night and yes you guessed it she went to bed early and so Jeff and Danny went out on the drink yet again without Malika as she also went to bed early.

Well it was the night of Tim's stag night and they all met in his house, there was Tim, Mandy, Danny and Clamper and some guessed arrived to meet Danny. It was Tim's sister Gainer and her husband and Tim's father who was a lovely man and so it was time to hit the town for Tim's night of remembrance before he lost his bachelor hood. In the first pub and Danny and Clamper did not know what to expect but got on well with Tim's mates who were some of the best drinkers Danny had ever been with, no longer had they had a couple of pints in one pub and they were off to the next one and Danny realised it was going to be the biggest drinking night of his life for some time and so he was worried about Clamper as he was such a young lad but he kept up with them all, well it was a brilliant night and they were all worse for ware and so the pinnacle of the night was to all go for a meal in the Dragon the finest Chinese restaurant in Tamworth and it had a bar in there. There was Danny telling jokes all night even the one about the eagle and he got an audience of a large group of women enjoying it all with them, in one case a young girl did not hear the punch line of one of the dirtiest jokes Danny has ever told and so came and sat on Danny's lap while he told her the joke again while all the others listened on again, the place irrupted with laughter and the girl never went red at all. They all enjoyed the night and it was early hours of the morning and Danny, Tim and Clamper went back to Tim's house where Mandy was waiting for them. She was in a state of panic when they got in as she was expecting them earlier, she gasped as they went through the door and said "Oh there you are Tim I have been worried sick, thank god your home, where have you all been?" Tim slurring replied "Stag night Mandy, who knows what time we were coming home it's a stag night, we are home now, anyone for a drink? can Dan? Andy?" Both lads said yes and then you could see Mandy settle down now Tim was home, they sat and reminisced about the night. Tim says "Mandy you should have heard this Welshman telling jokes in the Chinese it was hilarious and the whole restaurant was astonished by it all and the restaurant was 2 hours late closing, the owner just shut the doors and got on with it, it was brilliant and we were helping ourselves behind the bar and just putting the money in as the owner was sitting having some fun with us, so blame him for us being late but what a night I really enjoyed it and some of the lads are panicking about their wives as they were so late. So they are blaming Danny too ha, ha, ha." Clamper really slurring says "Yes Danny I am blaming you to because I am so drunk, god I have never ever drank so much in my whole life." Mandy "Your not going to be sick are you Andy?" Clamper like a nodding dog in the back of a car says "No I feel fine Mandy I can't understand how I drank so much and kept up with these old guys." Danny "Steady Clamper we may be getting on a bit but not old and I have had a great night it has been one of the best nights I have ever had and they liked my jokes didn't they ha, ha, ha." Tim "Ha, ha, ha, oh yes they had a great time allright and I can see some black eyes tomorrow, so look out and some of them are meeting us in the pub in the morning before dinner and we can all have a good laugh again and top up with the drink, as I will still be pissed in the morning and it's Mandy's hen night in a few days so she can have a good time as well with her friends isn't it Mandy?" Mandy "Yes it is my hen night and I will enjoy myself I am sure, I am having mine back in my home town so I am excited about it." Danny "Yes you go for it girl as it is not every day you get married is it?" Clamper "Yes enjoy it Mandy you have got a lot of guts marrying him ha, ha, I am only joking Mandy ha, ha." Danny "I think you will make a lovely pair I raise my can to you both, to Mandy and Tim" They all toasted the pair and decided to go to bed.

It was the next morning and up Danny got holding his head and he heard a bit of a rumpus in the living room, it was Tim and Andy having a little tiff, he entered and Tim was saying to Andy " Andy it is like a swimming pool in this blow up bed and I had it lent to me from a friend so we had better get it cleaned up, could you not make it to the toilet for god's sake?" Andy "Sorry Tim I don't remember doing it I was so drunk I think I will get into your bath and get myself cleaned up and then give you a hand, give me some tissue I will get the worst of it off before I get into the bath." Tim snapped "No Andy I will sort it out you go, go on." Mandy "Allright he could not help it calm down, calm down." Tim "Well Mandy it's not ours so what are we going to do now?" Mandy "We can put it into the washing machine and wash it, we will have to squeeze it up small and just put it in don't worry and then we can drape it over the line outside." Danny walks in and says "Everything allright Tim?" Tim in a mood replies "No Dan that bloody Clamper has pissed in the bed and it's not mine, I borrowed it I can't believe he did this I really can't it's like a swimming pool on the top of it, lucky it didn't get onto the carpet." Danny "Never that is all the drink he put away last night, it could have been worse I expected him to spew everywhere in the night, can I help? Silly thing to say I know being blind, it will make things worse I suppose, never mind, I can't wait to tell everyone when I get back ha, ha, ha." Tim "Sorry Dan I can't see the funny side yet, give me time, sorry." Mandy "Ok Tim it's not Danny's fault." Danny "Don't worry Mandy, I would be annoyed if it was my house I know but Tim it will seem funny in a few days especially when that hang over you have got subsides." Tim "Yes my head is ringing and yours Danny?" Danny "Yes it's the hair of the dog I am afraid this morning." Tim "To bloody right I am shaking from head to foot and this didn't help either, I could ring his neck, lucky the dog didn't lay in it with him, I have left him in the bedroom, right I will get over it, give me time." Danny "So what did Clamper say about the mess?" Tim in serious mood says "Oh he was ever so sorry and he told me he was thinking of leaving in the middle of the night and get a train off home to avoid me and disappear for good." Danny "Never did he?" Mandy "Yes he was afraid what Tim was going to say to him so he was going to do a runner, I don't blame him if it was me I would have ha, ha, wouldn't you?" Danny "Sorry no I wouldn't, I would have cleaned it all up before you got up somehow." Tim "At first he tried to say he tipped water over the bed but I could tell by the smell of urine, right Mandy open the door of the washing machine and I will force it in." They both go off to put it into the machine and Clamper comes in looking sheepish and said to Danny "Looks as if I have stuffed it up now, he is in a bad mood, I could not help it I didn't know I had done it until I felt the warmth of the pea on my legs and it was too late I have never done that before anywhere honest , have you ever done that?" Danny smiling says "Well not in the bed but I have got up and pead in the wardrobe and once went into someone's room and pissed on the bottom of their bed and they woke me up shouting at me, so don't worry he will come around and I can't wait to tell everyone in the college, they will laugh their socks off." Clamper looking horrified says "No don't you dare tell anyone up there please don't." Danny "I will think about it, so what have you done with the wet clothes?" Clamper "I have put them in a plastic bag." Danny "Right, I feel if Tim asks me to make a speech I will not be able to hold back from telling them all sorry Andy." Clamper laughing says "Don't you dare." Tim and Mandy came back in and Clamper was very quiet and Tim said "Is he here now?" Clamper said he was. Tim continued "Well Andy I am not amused sorry, so don't take it to heart if I am not myself for now, I will come around but I hope you are embarrassed?" Clamper head bowed says "Yes Tim, sorry Mandy and Tim I didn't realise i was doing it, sorry." Mandy "Right, let's forget it now and have some breakfast are you all ready?" They all agreed and went into the kitchen and Mandy made them a terrific breakfast and they enjoyed it.

Later they went to the local pub that was just 100yds from Tim and Mandy's house and they were all waiting there all holding their heads and moaning as the lads and Mandy walked in then there was a roar as they entered, one of the lads says "Here they are, the drunks and the comedian, allright you all?" Tim "Of course we are allright, a bloody good night wasn't it? I enjoyed it Immensely and that idiot of a Welshman was so funny wasn't he? even the boss was enjoying himself and Mandy was worried as to where I was all because of that daft Welshman." Mandy "Yes I was panicking, I was so worried, I was ready to call the police and then they walked in and he told me about the Chinese night I am glad you all enjoyed it." Tim's mate George "And some of the lads are not here, I hope it's not a case of a divorce as we were very late or they have got the hangovers from hell, I know I have, my god we drank some beer last night especially you Tim and Danny and this little fella Andy he kept up with us all, didn't you matey?" Clamper smirked and says "Well I done my best but it." Tim interrupted and said "Yes he was fine wasn't you Andy? no problems at all." Andy looked at Tim as if to say thanks mate for not telling anyone. Danny says "Did you hear the one about?" They all laughed and George said "Not anymore please I can't take anymore, so let's sit down before we fall down." The day went down a treat and Danny was off later to Hereford and Malika.

It was soon the day before the wedding and Danny, Malika, Jeff, and Jo were on the way to the great day and Danny was talking to Jeff on the train "Well Niel is not coming to the wedding he is not to well and he is still having some trouble with Abby she is not herself according to him, she is acting strange and she disappeared the other day just ran off and the police were looking for her all day but she either came back or they found her, not like her I hope she is allright I love that dog and so does he, he has taken her to the vets and he was telling me he is going to get a small Staffordshire terrier just like my little Murphy to keep Abby company, he fell in love with him when he visited me a few times, he is such a loving dog he really is, I miss him a lot." Jeff "It's a shame he is not going to be there mind I was hoping to see him again, it would have been like the old days again." "Yes I was looking forward to meeting up with him also but never mind we will be busy tomorrow and tonight I think as Tim and his father is meeting us at the pub later for a few whiskies." "I will be on the lager and that's it and you had better take your time it's going to be a long day tomorrow mind." "Yes your right I will, you and Jo and Ginny and Phil are staying in a bed and breakfast we are staying in the   hotel that will be nice for us." "Yes and Clamper is staying in the same bed and breakfast with us all, look out I hope he behaves himself, I heard about him pissing on the bed and Tim was not at all happy and I dread him doing that this weekend." Jo butted in and said "Oh leave him alone he has learnt his lesson now Jeff so I don't want to hear you saying anything to him ok?" Jeff looking innocent replies "Who me? as if I would." Jo "I know you would so don't Jeff please let's enjoy it as I am fed up with you 2 arguing all the time." Danny "Yes Jeffrey pick on someone your own size, he is too big for you now and you are getting on a bit now." Jeff laughed and says "He is a whimp but I will bow down to my girls wish I suppose." Malika then says "Why is that Jeff? because Jo will give you a hiding ha,, ha, ha." Jo "Ha, ha, yes that's it I will sort you out mate." Danny "So there we are then Jeff you have been told, I think this wedding is going to be something huge as far as I am concerned it is a huge wedding in a huge church and in the theme park for the receptions and 2 wedding cars I hope it all goes well and the weather is good for them." Jeff "Yes it is going to be massive and I hope none of the wives are out for your blood after the stag night." Danny looking serious "Oh yes I forgot about that, I will plead insanity ha, ha, they will believe me." Jeff "I just hope the meat in the wedding is not to tough or you will be picking it up again and slopping on it with the gravy on your face again and I will dye with embarrassment again." Jo "Your joking, Danny do you?" Danny smiling says "Yes I do I am not fighting with anything on that plate and I am not starving for no one so don't worry Jo you will not see it you might hear it mind ha, ha, ha." Jo "Danny I hope I am not sitting right beside you?" Jeff "Well we are all on the same table so who knows?" Jo "I will be listening for it now, Danny your awful." Malika "You can see what I have to put up with now Jo I carry a towel around with me." Jo "Do you?" Jeff "No she don't she is only kidding Jo."

Well it was the evening and they all met at the pub where they were all staying and sat all around the table talking and it was already late. Danny said to Tim "So are you nervous Tim? it's your last day of freedom, it's not too late to change your mind." Tim "No I won't be changing my mind, I love her Dan and I mean that, she is the best thing that has ever happened to me." Ginny "Oh Tim that's a lovely thing to say." Tim "No Ginny I mean it, I can't wait for tomorrow and Laddie will be there with his dicky bow on." Jo "That's lovely and Laddie will love that, are you nervous Tim?" Tim "Oh yes, I am already shaking that's my excuse for the whisky." Danny "As if you need an excuse it is to keep your dad company." Tim's dad "He knows it is my enjoyment of whisky that I love and I see you love it to Dan?" Danny "Oh yes too much I am afraid, I get on the whisky and there is no stopping me but I will be taking it easy tonight because of tomorrow but we will have one or two another day I promise." Tim "And Malika how are you managing putting up with this Welshman then?" Malika says "Well it's tough Tim but someone's got to, he needs looking after from what I heard in the stag party." Tim "He made the night and it was something we all did not want to end, the manager owner of the Chinese was sleeping at the early hours of the morning we had to wake him up to let us out it was a fantastic night, we never laughed so much in our lives, he was on form that night and made it for me." Tim's dad says "Yes I heard you were so funny that someone pissed himself laughing?" They all laughed and said no more on the subject as Clamper was not listening. Danny says " I hope he never let the college down as we always have a damn good laugh at the lectures in the braile dept." Tim burst out laughing and says "Especially that time with his name, I have told everyone about that it's so funny, I loved those classes with us lot there me Danny, Niel, you Christine and Margaret. She was nice and she is retiring now." Ginny "Yes it was a special time that year and yes she is retiring now, I will miss her." Danny "We used to turn out some good work and have a smile with it and a cup of tea or coffee to keep us interested, may it last forever as it makes that college does the braile babes." Tim "Too right Dan it does I have learned so much from the braile babes and it has given me a good outlook on life, I miss you girls very much and that dopey Niel and this dodgy Welshman as Jeff says." Jeff "Well I don't miss him, I have always got money in my pocket now and I don't drink so much." Danny smiling says "Yeah, yeah, we all believe you to Jeff, as if and now you have this new bungalow you will have to save some money so get your new dog and then I will see if you cut down on the drink but I don't think so." Malika was laughing and Jeff started laughing with her and asked her as Jeff says "What's wrong with you Malika? don't listen to him." Malika "I am going to tell everyone the truth Jeff as I was wrecked by you and Danny a few weeks ago and if you are like that every time you both go out then Danny is telling the truth, I was in a hell of a state and I was supposed to be looking after you 2 for Mandy the warden and they carried me to my room so I was told. I was absolutely smashed on the booze with these 2." Danny and Jeff was laughing. Danny then said "Oh yes, she was in a state ,we dumped her on her bed and went into the common room and had a few tins of lager and was laughing our heads off and Mandy was furious with us, it was so funny." Ginny "I seen Malika the next day and she was ill so I sent her back to her room to recover ha, ha, ha." Phil Ginny's husband continued "I have heard the stories of these two and I am amazed they have not been kicked out of college some of the things they get up to and Ginny is always laughing about them especially that Danny and Tim in lectures for braile and we are paying for them 2." Tim "I know but it's so funny and regards Niel I was disappointed when he said he was not coming to the wedding, he is a lovely man and that dog of his is a beautiful dog and hope she is going to be allright, her and Laddie used to hit it off ok so friendly." Well the night went off ok and they all retired early for the wedding the next day.

It came to the following day and in the church it was a huge affair and Tim came in so full of nerves he could hardly speak in the church yard his throat was so dry and they went in and Laddie looked so smart with his dicky bow on and the ceremony was underway and in comes Mandy and such a sigh was in the air when she appeared in her wedding dress. It was the wedding of weddings for 2 people who never met until a few months ago, a real happy end to a beautiful story that was going to last forever. Is this how Danny and Malika will end up as they were so very much in love with each other and everyone could see this in their eyes. The ceremony went off fantastically and the time came for photos in the front of the church and Danny and Jeff stood by the gate and all of a sudden there was a call for them all to get into a huge photo on the large green outside for a difficult photo. Danny, Malika, Jeff, Jo and the rest lined up and all of a sudden from the crowd came a whisper "There he is, he is the one who told all those jokes and kept us late that night of Tim's stag night." His wife replied "Is it now? I will be having a word with him in a minute." This reverberated around the crowd and Danny was starting to panic a little, well the photos were all done and Danny was set upon by several wives and their husbands and one spokeswoman said "So it's your fault we nearly had a divorce is it?" The husband backed her up "Yes that's him darling." Danny smiled gulped and said "I hold my hands up, it was my fault, so blame me I got carried away and they all behaved themselves, they were to pissed for anything else but yes it's my fault." The wives and husbands started laughing, one of the husbands said "We are only kidding Danny they are all allright about it and they have had a good laugh after we told them all about it." His wife said "I only wish we had been there to enjoy it, you are the talk of Tamworth since the stag night so don't panic your safe with us and we want a dance tonight mind.." Danny sighing and said "Phew, I thought I was a gonna then, I will love to have a dance with you all tonight." Danny ended up shaking hands with everyone there virtually and Jeff said "So you were your usual self then, I wish I had not missed it now." Danny "Well you get married now and we can do it all again no problem." Jeff "Hey steady now Dan." Jo hit Jeff on the arm and they got into the rolls Royce to the reception and followed Tim and Mandy in a very old Jaguar and there was also a very old ford also .

The huge hall in Drayton Manor was packed with guests and Tim and Mandy went off for more photographs on some of the rides at the theme park and eventually got back and the reception was on. It went very well and lots of laughter was had, it went straight through to the evening and dancing was on the menu and Danny and Malika danced the night away with Jeff dancing all night with Jo . The whole wedding was a great success and all enjoyed their time and returned back to the college the following day on the train and yes you guessed it Danny and Jeff had a massive hangover.

Well a few weeks went and Jeff had, had his new guide dog whose name was Scully a lovely Labrador so funny and mischievous and she loved Danny and Malika. Every time she seen them Jeff was dragged down the road by her until she was cuddled by them, they decided to have a short holiday with each other and their children Danny had Josh and Jeff had his 2 sons Tim and Dean and of course Malika. They decided to go to where Danny loved it in Chalaborough bay holiday camp in Devon that was very quiet for them to have some fun without worrying they had hired a caravan for a long weekend and there they were enjoying a good earned break. They had spent the afternoon in the caravan and it went well considering it was the first time with the new guide dog Scully who was a very bright dog but was young and was going to give Jeff his first taste of how a guide dogs mind works and this is not what he had expected. So it was starting to get dark and the caravan was a good walk from the pub and the concert hall on the site so off they went Jeff with his new guide dog on her harness and Danny was being guided by Malika. Danny says "So she will get you there no problem then Jeff and I will hold Malika's arm and we will follow you and the gorgeous dog good old Scully." The dog wagged her tail and off they went Jeff opened the caravan door and stepped out speaking to the dog all of the time as he was instructed on his training "Good girl Scully let's go then, forward then girl, good girl." Next thing off she went pulling him like as if she was in a race and Jeff struggling to hold her back and coughing and said "God take it easy girl there is no rush what's the Matter? take your time for god's sake, I don't know what is the Matter she is going nuts?" Danny "She is excited as she is going to the pub and she has already learnt that from you I expect." Danny and Malika was laughing and Jeff was holding her back and was sweating like a fool and trying to cool her down, he says to her "I can't understand it she is normally so gentle but she wants to go everywhere, bloody hell this is murder ha, ha, ha." Malika "Ha, ha, she is excited isn't she? shall we stop for a minute as we can't go on this pace?" Jeff tried to stop her pulling by being strict with her as taught "Right Scully sit and stay there, Scully sit now be a good girl , shit I am a ball of sweat, I don't know what is the Matter with her?" Next thing Josh Dean and Tim turned up laughing at Jeff. Jeff said "What the hell are you all laughing at? this is not funny I am covered in sweat, she won't stop pulling look at her she is still pulling, sit Scully sit." Dean then says "She is pulling because there are rabbit's everywhere and she wants to play with them I expect ha, ha, I was watching her she did not know which one to go after and she was pulling you all over the place ha, ha, it looked so funny ha, ha, ha." They all laughed furiously and then Jeff still laughing said "Right Scully no messing around, take me to the pub I need a drink to cool down." Danny "Rabbit's, rabbit's, find the rabbit's Scully I have not seen Jeff get so much exercise in all my life ha, ha, ha." Jeff "Don't encourage her Dan I am in a mess here trying to keep her in check ha, ha,." They get to the clubhouse and sit down Jeff with sweat running down his face and laughing and he drank the first pint of lager straight down he was so thirsty, Danny still laughing said "That was so funny and I bet she is just sitting there now looking innocent as hell ha, ha, ha." Tim says "Yes she is just sitting there wagging her tail ha, ha, look at her face ha, ha, ha." The lads were laughing and Jeff sat down and looked knackered. Jeff "I needed that pint I was so thirsty ha, ha, she gave me a song and dance on the way down I can't wait for the return journey ha, ha, bloody hell I am bushed." Malika "You did say she will be good for exercise and your right she is mad." Jeff "I was going to have a few pints tonight but I am worried now for later." Danny "Don't worry the lads will be with us to help with her ha, ha, sorry it was so funny." Next thing a few women came over to see the dog. First woman says "Oh hello, is it allright to stroke the dog?" Jeff's face lit up and he replies "Yes of course you can." Lady then says "Is it a girl or a boy?" Jeff "Ha, ha, how old are you? sorry I thought most women could tell the sex?" The woman laughed and blushed "Well I would have to get on my hands and knees to look." Jeff "Oh the dog you mean? she is a girl I understand now." The woman looked puzzled and smiled at Jeff and the other woman gave Scully a cuddle and said "Isn't he gorges?" Jeff with huge smile on his face says "Well thank you and what do you think of the dog though?" Woman "I was talking about the dog ha, ha, ha." Jeff talked to the women for ages and was smiling from ear to ear. Danny and Malika was cuddling in the corner and the first night went off allright until they got back to the caravan and Jeff decided to go for a ciggy and take the dog for a toilet break so off he went. Danny says "Jeff was so funny in the clubhouse tonight and he really thought that the women were trying to chat him up." Tim "Yes I know he did and he is now a little tipsy so he will keep on about it later when he gets back." Josh then said "Yes he was waiting for the women to leave but they had already left ha, ha, ha." Dean "I wonder where he is now? probably looking for them, I hope he don't get lost." Malika "The dog will find her way back no worries." Danny "I will light the fire and have a can before I go to bed." Danny did this after a few goes at lighting it and then says

"These bloody calor gas fires can be murder to light, so lads are you all settled in the right beds for tonight?" They all said yes and Malika made herself a cup of coffee and Danny put the telly on as they waited for Jeff but he was ages and they were beginning to worry now as there was no sign of him. Danny looking worried says "I wonder where he is now? he is a little pissed, I hope he has not done anything stupid." The lads went out to see if they could see him but there was no sign of him but after half an hour he turned up panting by the caravan entrance, he came in and said "Shit I just made a total fool of myself." Danny "There you are? where have you been?" Jeff still panting says "I went for a stroll a few steps from the caravan then walked back in here and found myself talking to some old woman who thought her luck was in, I had gone into the caravan just above us here by mistake and I could not get away from her, she even walked me back to here, I felt a real fool now she wants to meet me in the clubhouse tomorrow night and say hello properly, she is about sixty and thinks I am after her, I hope she gets that out of her mind? shit." The others were laughing and Jeff continued looking down at Scully "This bloody dog is useless aren't you Scully? you take me after the pensioners you silly dog." The dog just wagged her tail and looked happy . Danny says "Well you have pulled then? we must invite her to the bar-b-q tomorrow just for you Jeff ha, ha , ha." Jeff "Don't even joke about it matey." Malika smiling says "Now you have pulled the right one for you Jeff."

It was the next morning and they all sat around the living part of the caravan talking, all cuddled up to keep warm around the fire that was not on and drinking tea and coffee. Jeff commented "God it's cold in here." Danny "Well put the fire on, I can't get to it because all you kids and the dog is stretched out." Jeff "No it's ok and besides I can't work it so leave it for a while." Malika "So Jeff I bet you are excited about that woman you ensnared in her caravan last night? I think I saw her outside earlier hanging around waiting for you ha, ha, ha." Josh "I think I seen her to." Tim "That's who she is, dad I hope you get rid of her as fast as you can she must be 70 at least and thinking you can't see well so she is going to give it a go, good luck ha, ha, ha." Jeff not amused replies "Leave it there son, don't take the Mick out of your father, I have got the money mind not you so be careful." Dean "You tell him dad I would not say anything like that about you dad, I know you like the babes that are too young for you." Jeff smiling says "Steady." Danny "Ha, ha, Dean knows you to and I think you might as well get this granny as I don't fancy your chances with those 2 last night." Jeff "This Adonis of Swindon will show you all this weekend no problem, they will all be falling over me to get me into bed you watch." Malika "Expect they will if you get as pissed as last night." Jeff "Danny I don't like this new girl of yours, she keeps having a go at me ha, ha, I don't think she knows how I work with women?" Danny "No but I do and you are hopeless at it, so where is Jo now these days?" Jeff "She does not bother much now I have left the college and she is going to look at a flat in Oxford this week, I thought maybe she may come an stay with me in my new bungalow, strange girl." Danny "I told you this would happen if it came down to her dad or you are going to lose, she is a daddy's girl and that's it, what about Carol? she has left Mr Schnelgrove he has got a new woman living in Hereford." Jeff "I don't know she is off with Lola in stoke on Trent so she hardly calls or e-mails me anymore now I have gone up in the world with my brand new bungalow, talking of which you are leaving in a few weeks where are you going to live?" Danny "We are looking to rent in Hereford until Malika is finished in the college so we are going to see some estate agents who do that type of thing next week and get ready for the big move." Jeff "Well there are a lot of houses empty to rent in Hereford and are you going to stay living there or what ?" Malika "Oh no, we have not decided where yet but it will not be in Hereford no way, maybe in Wales, I don't know until we visit it for a break soon." Jeff "What, back in Bridgend?" Danny "Oh god no, I would not go back there as I need a break from the place, somewhere like Narberth or Tenby or Milford Haven, somewhere nice and quiet if Malika likes it there really." Malika "We are going to have a look down there soon to see what it is like, I have never been there." Jeff "And what about your house in Beccles Malika?" Malika "We have decided to leave our old lives behind and start a new one, including selling all my stuff and starting a new life totally and Danny is doing the same, we have already started we bought 2 Man Utd bean bags ha, ha, ha." Jeff "Well yes at least you will have some where to sit, you have got to start somewhere haven't you?" Danny "And we can always say as we get old we only had 2 bean bags to start our lives with and it will be true, everything else will be new except collectibles and personnel stuff and it will be fun doing it all." Jeff "Your not kidding there." Tim chirped up "God it's cold now, someone put this fire on I am freezing." Jeff looks at the fire and said "I don't know how to turn it on Tim only Danny is able to." Tim "Awe c'mon it's freezing." Danny "Right Jeff you do it I will tell you what to do right?" Jeff not looking confident at all says "Right go on then." Danny "Grab the dial and press it in and turn it clockwise still holding it in with your other hand on the button to ignite it." Jeff did this and you could hear the gas coming out of the fire. Danny said "Right Jeff hold it in until I tell you to press the button, hold it, hold it in, hold it in, hold it in, now press the button to ignite it." Jeff pressed the button and a massive ball of fire came out and engulfed Jeff's head and you could hear him gasp for air and the boys jumped off the floor and ran like the clappers, the dog was off like a bolt of lightning into the bedroom and Danny and Malika was doubled up laughing their heads off. Jeff gulped and said "Forget it I will get a duvet and as he went to get up you could see his eyebrows and his hair was all singed and you could smell hair burning, this sent the lads and Danny and Malika laughing their heads off for ages and so did Jeff see the funny side of it in the end, they all rolled about laughing and Malika said to Danny "That was not very nice was it? but I was expecting it, I knew what you were doing ha, ha, ha." They all laughed so much they were cuing up by the bathroom and Danny got up and lit the fire for them all and yet Jeff would not sit anywhere near it for the rest of the holiday, it was so funny.

The holiday was a great success and it was back to college for Danny and Malika and the others went home.

CHAPTER 17
THE BEGINNING OF THE END

All things have to come to an end and it was getting close to Danny finishing getting his life back together or as he says learning to be blind and he was looking anxious about it all as he had been 4 years doing this and was not at all sure but he had Malika now and felt more sure that what he was doing was right. But it did not feel good to him as he was stepping into the unknown. He was not going to have the reassurance of the college behind him much longer, he was going to be on his own now and putting into practice all he had learned, but was this enough? and could he do it? what if things go wrong? What if it does not work out with Malika? Is he going to end up all alone forever? These were all the questions going through his head and many more besides and things were not going to be easy as you will read.

It all started all wrong as we shall hear it is not easy if you are blind getting exactly what you want. There were only 3 weeks left in the college for Danny and Malika was adamant she wanted to live with him in a rented property for the rest of her course. This was not as easy as it sounds, they both went one day to a letting agent that specialised in this type of thing, renting out for six monthly periods for home owners and Danny and Malika had been to see many properties and decided on one near the college to rent, so easy for Malika to walk to lectures as it was just around the corner so they said they would take it and signed up for it and were waiting for a response from the agents which they got one morning by letter. Danny received it and went to see Malika and they read it and it said "We have as agents got in touch with the people who own the property you are interested in and they have informed us they are taking it off the agencies list as they are going to do it up and sell it after all." Danny looked at Malika and said "Well that's that then we will have to go and look at some more properties then." Malika not so happy said "Looks like we will but it was just right for us and the college, bloody hell I thought it was all sorted?" "Never mind it's the first one we looked at, there will be some more, fancy going this morning after your lecture? as we have a break until 2pm." Malika sad faced says "Yes if you like and we can have some fish in the chip shop in Hereford is it?" Danny smiles and says "Oh yes I love them pieces of cod in there, good idea."
Later they went into the agents and sat down but felt like fish out of water this time around and could not understand it, they were called in to speak to an agent. Danny said "Hello we received this letter about the house we wanted to rent but it has gone off the market, so we will like to go for the one that we also looked at a little further away from the college." Agent "Yes certainly I will get your files and look at it and get the one out for you and get into action." The girl leaves the office and Danny and Malika sat there for a while and she returned and abruptly said "Ok I have got the file out and will call them this afternoon after they return from work and get the ball rolling and we will get in touch with you as soon as we have it sorted." Danny "Oh right I will await your letter then, I must reinforce that I shall be leaving the college in 3 weeks so it is urgent." Agent "Ok I will rush it through for you." Danny and Malika left and on the way back into the town centre Danny said "I don't know about you but I felt so uncomfortable in there as if we were not wanted in there." "Really, I can't say I did it seemed allright to me it's in your Imagination Danny, let's go and eat, it will be allright don't worry your Imagining it." Danny shrugged his shoulders and they went for dinner.

Later on and Danny gave his mate Niel a call on the phone as he had not spoke to him for a long time. His wife Ceri answered and said "Hello." "Oh hello Ceri it's Danny how are you?" Ceri replies "Fine and I will hand you over to Niel." Danny looked astonished at that Ceri did not want to talk to him a little more as she usually did, then Niel came on the phone "Allright Dan?" "Yes fine Niel what have you done to that poor old wife of yours? she hardly said a word to me." Niel with cracked voice replied "Sorry Dan we had a bit of a tragedy here last night..., it's Abby she is dead." There was a long silence and Danny had a tear slide down his cheek as he pondered and said "Oh no, oh no, that lovely dog Abby, I don't believe it Niel, what happened?" "Don't start me off I have been crying all last night she collapsed in front of us last night and I got her into the car and rushed her to the vets but we were too late she was gone and the vet said she had had a huge heart attack and I am destroyed over this and so is Ceri and the boys Dan, I don't believe it." Niel started crying on the phone and so did Danny then Danny says "I am so sorry Niel, I am so sorry, a loving dog like her I will miss her so much, this has knocked me for six it really has." "Dan can I phone you on the weekend?, I am not up to talking now sorry mate." "Of course Niel I understand and give her a kiss for me and the family, speak soon matey and look after yourself, bye." Niel hanged up and Danny shed a few tears and said to himself "Oh god that lovely dog, bless her, she was so gorgeous it's not fair, I will miss her very much and the lovely times we had and so will everyone else here when I tell them." Danny sat there for a while and Malika came in to his room and said "Hello, allright? but what's the Matter? you look as if you have lost a lot of money." Danny said "I know you hardly knew them but you remember Niel and his dog Abby? well Abby dropped dead last night from a huge heart attack it has come as a big shock to me, I loved that dog, my god it always happens to the nice ones don't it?" Malika hugged Danny and said "I am so sorry she was always spoken about when you ever talked about Niel as if she was a part of him." "Yes I know she was such a lovely dog I since coming here feel like these guide dogs are so special like humans and it really feels like that they are so well trained and become as if they can tell what you are talking about so human and I have never cried over a dog this much before." Malika "I bet Niel is devastated as he has spent a long time with her and you said she was acting funny? was she still guide dogging? you know what I mean?" "No she was retired just after the problems with the time she went for Zarrine almost a year now, I can't believe she has gone such a lovely dog, bless you Abby I will miss you."

The following morning and Danny was sitting with Zarrine talking over breakfast and he told her about Abby "Niel was on the phone yesterday and gave me some bad news that Abby had died the night before." Zarrine covering her mouth with her hand in shock said with tears in her eyes "No what happened to her Danny? my god." "She had a heart attack at home and they rushed her to the vets but it was too late for her she had had a huge heart attack and that was the end of her I am afraid." "Oh no that lovely dog, I am stunned now, oh dear, such a lovely dog even though she once went for me I still loved that dog, she was always wagging her tail, that's so sad Danny, I bet Niel is in a state? he loved that dog and she was so comical, oh dear this has upset me now I am shaking." "I know I shed some tears when he told me and he was just numb and said he was calling me on the weekend when he will be able to talk as he was crying all of the time." Zarrine says "Oh bless him, tell him I am so sorry and most people here will be shocked when I tell them, oh that lovely dog gone forever, love her." Just then in walks Malika and she says "Oh Zarrine he has told you then about Niel's dog? I remember her she was a nice looking dog but had nothing to do with her at all but he has been upset so she must have been a lovely dog?" Zarrine "Oh yes she was

Malika even though she went for me I think she was so protective of Niel and his stuff, that's natural." Danny "I thought that also and she was getting on a bit to and I think she was fed up with being a guide dog and wanted some fun with Niel, Ceri and the boys and now it was not possible, she goes and has a heart attack." Malika "I have never seen 2 people so upset about a dog considering it was not theirs, so she must have been a lovely dog indeed." Zarrine "Yes she was a cracking dog with a lovely temperament I will always remember her." Danny "So will I and I can't see Niel without her it would be strange and not real to me but life goes on I suppose and it is a cruel life, I give up, there is some bad news every year of our lives." Malika "Yes and Zarrine that house around the corner fell through for us he is now doing it up and selling it so we have gone for the one further down the road so fingers crossed for this one as time is getting short now." Zarrine "Oh never mind, there are plenty of houses for rent in Hereford." Danny "If this one is not on I will change the agents as I don't think their hearts are in it, I felt it when I was there yesterday." Malika smiling says "I don't think so it is in your Imagination Danny I think." Zarrine "Typical of him Malika he has always been a doubting Thomas ha, ha, ha." Danny "I may be but I have got a horrible feeling about this and we have not got much time to get it sorted you know." Zarrine "Danny don't worry it will all work out in the end, I can't get Abby out of my head today, I am sorry it's so sad." Zarrine leaves leaving Danny and Malika talking. Danny says "She is upset considering that dog tried to bite her hand off, look I am not keeping on about this agent but If there is no response tomorrow I will phone them again to rush them up ok?" "Yes of course and don't forget it's the presentation night next week so get your clothes sorted out, no shorts this year just in case as it is your last one, let's be tidy and neat this year." "Someone has been talking again who is it?" "No one but it's the last time and you have got to pick up your certificates so look nice please." Danny looking suspicious says "Yeah ok I will, I must remember to call Niel this Saturday, can you remind me please?" "Yes ok, I am off I am late already, see you later bye." "Bye." They kiss and go separate to their lectures.

That day Danny made sure he told everyone the sad news about the lovely Abby and they all looked devastated by the news. Danny now was winding down as the end of his course was at an end so found himself often with nothing to do and with Jeff, Niel, Tim and Clamper not there he was bored. He wondered if this is how it would all end him bored, he was missing the company he had when he first got to the college and now had to find something to fill his day before he got so bored, he got into a regular rut and got into a system of doing the same thing the same time every day and he was determined to keep in touch with the ones that he was missing never mind what. He was starting a new life with Malika so he had to think of buying new furniture and setting up a new life with Malika that would take a lot of his time up and of course he had not even found anywhere to live yet and so set about getting himself and Malika ready to visit west Wales where his family originated from and getting her to meet his children, so he got stuck into it and arranged for 2 of his daughters to come up to stay for the weekend to meet Malika. He did this on the telephone, his youngest daughter was Natasha his other one was Kelly and her partner Andrew, he had arranged to go down to see Josh and come back with his 2 daughters by car and meet Malika.

Well the weekend arrived for this and on the way in the car they were talking. Danny says "Well I hope you will like her but don't be shocked when you meet her, I will tell you the truth now we are on the way." Kelly says "Oh dear dad, what is it? She is mad? mind you she must be to be with you ha, ha, only joking dad she has only got one leg or something?"

Danny smiling "No nothing like that." Natasha smiling says "She has an irritating twitch or something and you are worried I might laugh uncontrollably again ha, ha,." Danny made up a silly story about her as Malika is around 8 stone slim pretty and very fashionable but Danny's story went like this "Well do you know when you were kids and you used to watch tom and jerry on TV? well you remember the house keeper that rather large black woman about 22 stone and she used to shout at tom saying things like Thomas, Thomas, leave that chicken alone Thomas the big mama, well that is exactly what Malika is like identical in every way." The daughters tried to pass it off as if it don't Matter dad and Kelly said "Well that's allright dad nothing wrong with that." Natasha "No dad it's the person inside I think." Andrew was a quiet man who never made a comment about anyone so Danny said "So don't say I didn't warn you so give her a huge hug she will not crush you and I told you so you are not so surprised when you meet her ok?" The girls said "No problem dad don't worry." Well they got to the college and Malika was expecting them and was waiting in the foyer for them as they arrived but before that they were driving down the lane going into Dowdell and Cj who was around 22 stone scruffy and black was walking down the road and Kelly sitting in the front of the car said "Bloody hell look at the state of that." Her partner Andrew who was driving nudged Kelly and said whispering "Shhh, that might be Malika for all you know." Kelly sat quiet and said no more but felt embarrassed in case it was her, however Danny heard it and was sniggering under his breath. They arrived and parked the car around the back of Dowdell and the girls were dreading meeting Malika now they thought she was a huge black woman who would probably tell them what to do all of the time and so they went to the front of Dowdell to the foyer and Danny opened the door and yes you guessed it Malika was waiting inside for them. So she stepped forward and said "Hello." The girls and Andrew said hello back not realising it was Malika but someone who was just there and then Danny said "Oh let me introduce you this is Kelly and her partner Andrew and this is Natasha my daughters." They all said hello and Danny continued "This is Malika." The girls faces dropped and Kelly said "Hello Malika." and so did the rest looking at Danny as if to say you fooled us allright and then Kelly said "Dad your a big liar, I nearly dropped myself in it back there, I thought that large person walking down the road was Malika, sorry Malika let me explain, daddy said we were not to be shocked as you are a black woman about 22 stone and talked like the house keeper in the tom and Jerry cartoons and here you are totally nothing like that." Malika smiling says "Oh god you should know your father by now." Kelly "Yes I fell for it again so who was that person then?" Malika said "That was CJ he is overweight he was slim when he first came here but ballooned on the crap food here ha, ha, ha." Both girls slapped their father on the back as they started up the stairs and Andrew was laughing. They sat down and had coffee and a chat. Malika "I was nervous waiting to meet you all but I am ok now." Natasha "Oh don't worry about us we are down to earth being my father's daughters you should have known what to expect and you have got a nice French accent don't you?" Danny "Maybe that's because she comes from France ha, ha, ha." Natasha laughed and says "Ha, ha, you know what I mean?" Kelly "Yes tash we know what you mean." The conversation went well and the weekend also and so they were all good friends because of it and that was the first hurdle, it would be a long time before she met the other 2 children.

A few days later and no sign of the agency sorting out the accommodation, so Danny rang them and by the seriousness of his face when he came off the phone Malika could tell things were not going well. She asked "So what is it? What have they said? I can see you are not happy." Danny smiled and says "You would not believe it but the person who owns that apartment is also taking it off the renting register and is doing it up for selling, I am not stupid I know what's going on and so I have made an appointment for tomorrow to go and see the manager to see what is going on." Malika with serious face "I don't believe it the same thing again, they don't want to rent to us do they? because we are blind but cannot tell us that because it is illegal don't you think?" "Well of course it is that's why I am so annoyed they won't or can't tell us the reason so it's just an excuse, I bet the for rent boards are still on the properties but the landlords have said they don't want to rent to any blind students at all because they think we are going to burn the place down, it's not fare and illegal." "I think your right Dan I might have guessed it so there is nothing we can do is there?" "We are going to confront the manager and see what he has to say, then I am going to another agency to try again, this is not on." "I think we are banging our heads against the wall but we will find out won't we?" "To right I will and I am going to have to go and see Anthea and tell her of our trouble and hope she can get something through an agency and tell them we are competent enough to look after their precious property, the bastards, I feel like we are living in south Africa and we are black, I didn't realise this thing happened here? I have had my eyes opened since I went blind on what goes on here in this country." "Well that's how it is here disability discrimination is rife here and the government says it is not." "Well if I have got something to do with it I will stop it.".

Well it was the next day and Danny and Malika was sat waiting for the manager in the agency, he came in looking serious and sat down and said "Well hello there, what can I do for you?" Danny says "You must know what this is all about surely? we have enquired about renting two properties from your company and have had the same reaction on the both properties that they have decided to not rent anymore but sell their properties and we think it is because we are blind and it is an excuse." The manager looked astonished and said "I am sure you are wrong Mr Duckfield that is not something we would tolerate, I assure you and that there is a genuine reason for them to sell instead." Danny looking very serious says "So if I go up to see these houses next week they will no longer be up for rent and no signs will be on the properties mentioned and no leaflet's advertising them in your agency?" Manager "I am sure not and I resent you accusing us of underhanded ways but we may be able to help you with another property no problem." Danny "Sorry we have decided to go elsewhere and I am sure your glad we are, it let's you off the hook." Manager looking stunned says "By no means I assure you this is a serious accusation." Danny raises his voice for all to hear in the shop says "No accusation it's fact and I will not let you allow your company treat us as second class citizens so good day to you and I hope I don't see your signs outside those places because if I do I will slap you in a court of law before you can blink an eye, goodbye to you and your staff." Everyone was silent in the large room and the manager was shocked and Danny and Malika got up and walked out and that was that. They went to another agency along the road but you could see by the face on Danny he was expecting the same problems so he made an appointment with Anthea and see if she could put a word in the agency for him or he would be homeless.

The next day he went to see Anthea but was not holding his breath as Danny and Anthea had locked horns so many times, she probably would not want to know him but he had nothing to lose. Danny was beckoned in to her office, she sat down and said "Hello Daniel I thought you were leaving in a few weeks, is there a problem?" Danny smiled "Yes just a little one, I was hoping you could help Malika and myself? We are trying to rent a property here in Hereford while she finishes her course and then move back down to west Wales and buy a place to live but we have enquired about 2 different properties here with an agency

and they have let us down every time with the same silly excuses like the owner has now decided to sell their property and I know this is a load of rubbish, it's because we are blind and I have asked another agency about another property but think we will get the same reaction and was wondering if you would give them a ring or something to reassure them we are competent?" Anthea looked at Danny and said "Well Danny I am afraid I can't see how I can help you, they are not going to listen to me, but leave it with me, I will sort something out if I am able, come and see me on Monday, give me the weekend to think about it I promise I will but don't expect miracles from me mind." Danny "Of course not, I am just stumped and do not know what to do next." "You stumped, that's a new one, you usually have got a lot to say ha, ha, leave it with me I will think about this and see what if anything I can do ok?" "Well that's all I can ask, thank you Anthea." "No problem Danny." Danny leaves and meets up with Malika for a cup of tea and she asked him "So what did she say? not a lot I bet?" Danny pondered and says "Well I don't know she didn't make any sense to me, she said in one hand she can't make them listen then said leave it with me and come and see me Monday morning, leave it with her for the weekend, so I don't know really just as wise I suppose." Malika "So another waste of time, have you heard anything off the new agent?" "Not a word but it's only been 2 days, give them time ha, ha, they are a waste of time." "Well I am allright I have still got a room after august ha, ha, ha." "Oh thanks don't worry about me, mind I can look after myself, don't fret now." "Ha, ha, ha, if you were smaller I could sneak you in my room, only kidding come on it will sort itself out no worries." "I know it will, something will turn up, we can go and live with Jeff." "You will be an alcoholic within 2 months with Jeff ha, ha, don't forget it's the presentation night next Friday so sort yourself out go and buy some nice trousers for the day ok? no shorts please it only winds them up ." Danny smiled and says "I have arranged to do this with Sue Bridgland on Monday no worries." "Good boy and now I know you will be a smart boy ha, ha, ha." "On that note I am off to my lectures, it's Ginny and the braile babes so I had better not be late or I will miss a coffee, see you later." Danny left.
In the braile room and all questions were been thrown about to Danny by the braile girls Christine says "So where are you going to live when you leave here then?" Danny replies "Well we have been trying to rent a property here in Hereford but they don't want to know, they keep giving us excuses not to rent to us, so we will be on the streets I expect, ha, ha, ha, or at least I will." Ginny "If you told them you were a student you will, they don't like students from here." Danny "Of course they wouldn't I never thought of that, what a dick head, I have asked Anthea to help if she can but if it comes to the crunch I will go down Wales myself and Malika can come down when she has finished." Ginny "Things will turn out allright you will see, it always does, I hope you get more luck than Niel did with his dog Abby she has upset me this week." Christine "I know, it is on my mind all the time it's so sad." Danny "Life is a bitch then you die, she was such a loving dog like a human." Christine "Yes she was and a good friend to Niel, he must be out of his head, have you spoke to him Dan?" Danny looking sad says "Yes I have he is not in a good condition since the episode, he was all but crying and the boys were upset and of course so was Ceri she doted on that dog, it is like losing a family member." Ginny "A terrible tragedy, so I am not happy you are leaving we will miss you when you have gone only 2 weeks now and it will all be over." Danny "Yes it will and I will miss you all here, my own braile babes, a time of my life I will never forget to my dying days, honestly, I will miss you all very much." Christine looking very sad says "Oh don't you will start Ginny crying, then I will start, I will miss you, you have been an inspiration to us and a good laugh with it it's been a lot of fun with you here and

Tim, Jeff and of course Niel." Ginny "Oh dear I must keep it together but she is right Danny I will miss you so will this college, lots of fun here and remember to write that book." Danny "I will and I must do it quick before I forget it all but I will never forget you girls you have made my stay here a good one and I have learnt a lot from you both and of course Margaret I miss her also a lovely woman, the true braile babes." Ginny "Well we have finished the braile and I can't teach you any more as you have done it all but I will see you in the presentation day won't I?" Danny "Of course you will, I will make it a point of coming to see you before I leave no problem, never mind when it is." Ginny "Right you may as well go and have the rest of this lesson to yourself and I will see you soon." It was a sad time for all in that room that day, it was like leaving a place that had saved your life after terminal cancer, it just felt like that as Danny was now a person who could get on with his life again with many pitfalls to overcome but he would be able to get over them with confidence again.

The weekend went by and it was time to go and see Anthea and so it was Danny sitting outside the room he has frequently visited to have many a fight or something with Anthea and Danny was not expecting anything from Anthea so he had made his mind up to go back to stay in Bridgend with his family near at hand to help him sort his living arrangements out with some difficulty, then Anthea called him to her room and he sat down. Danny says "Hello Anthea I had no luck with the new agent, as much use as an ashtray on a motorbike, so I think I am homeless soon but it has been a experience here that's for sure." Anthea "So no luck at all then?" Danny looking a little sad nodded and says "No nothing, we are lepers here in Hereford as regards accommodation and I am resigned to sorting something else out on my own or sleep on the streets ha, ha, ha." Anthea smiles and says "Not necessary, I have got some good news maybe for you, I have got some property on the books of the college that is a little far out for the students here and it is empty and if you and Malika moved into it, it will be good for the college and you would have to pay a little rent for it but Malika will not as she is still a student and it's not that far but some students think it's the other end of the world, it's a sort of maisonette in a block that is behind security gates so it's quiet there and some shops and a pub near it, so what do you think? it is furnished I just ask you to look after the property ." Danny's face lit up and he almost jumped into Anthea's lap and then said "Really, so what's wrong with it honestly?" "Nothing it's nice there." "Anthea I am so grateful wait till i tell Malika she will be over the moon, thank you Anthea very much and how long can I have it for then?" "Well until Malika finishes her term here if you want?" "I want, thank you that will solve all my problems thank you, I am over the moon and when shall we move there?" "I suggest you do it before you finish here say a day or 2 ok?" Danny was smiling from one ear to the other "I can't get over it sorted and I was so worried thank you Anthea, thank you." Danny left to tell Malika all about it .

In the coffee room at the student bar and he sat there looking as if he had not sorted anything out and Malika sat down and said "So what happened?" Danny looking stern "Not a lot." Malika sat there numb and says "Well I am stumped, I still have the house in Beccles for a while longer so we will have to go up there to live that's all." Danny "Mmm I think you maybe right except I have got another idea…. Anthea has got a maisonette she needs someone to have to look after with me paying a little rent until you have finished next Easter so what do you think of that then?" Malika's face lit up and she says "What do you mean?" "Open them little ears of yours… we are saved, Anthea has saved us she has got a place we can have not far from here and we can stay there until you finished your course then I am saved I have to pay a nominal rent and she wants us to move in before the holidays and it is furnished." "Brilliant sorted then the agents can stick their houses up there asses." "Yes you could put it that way I suppose, but don't beat around the bush you tell them straight." "I am not telling them, you will have to but at least we can get ourselves sorted out and have you got those new trousers for the presentation ?" "Yes I have, we had a fun time getting this sorted and I got a new shirt and jumper for the occasion so I am sorted, just some smellies and that's it, only kidding I don't like these things they smell like dog crap." Malika smiling from ear to ear says "I know they do, people who wear this spray smell like atomic bombs there is nothing nice about them and it takes your breath away so don't you dare wear it." "I am allergic to them or at least the gas in the cans, I can't breathe if it is sprayed anywhere near me so no thanks I don't even wear after shave all you smell is man and nothing else ha, ha, ha." "Yes especially when you fart all of the time after a few pints and Jeff is worse than you, my god you both stink." Danny smiling from ear to ear "I don't think I like your attitude." Malika laughing "I don't care matey." "You will be saying boyo next like the Welsh." "I don't think so, right I am off to lectures see you later." They both leave for the lectures and Danny started to realise it was all coming to an end and was almost time to say goodbye to everyone and it showed as he started to be very quiet and a little solemn at times and things would get worse the last week of his college years that has gave him his life back. This was brought to the front on the Wednesday before he was to leave on the Friday. On that morning in the lounge as he got up to say his goodbye's to his long-time friend who had a huge Impact on his life and was his backbone for all those years he was at the college and that was of course Zarrine and this morning was very tearful. We join them in the lounge at breakfast and the mood was solemn there. In there was Malika, Danny, Zarrine and one or 2 students in the background. Danny was talking "Yes Malika I will get some chips for dinner for me and Zarrine and if no one else wants to join in then tough, it's the last time we will have a chip butty together isn't that right Zarrine?" Zarrine in a mild mood says "Yes my Danny it will be and I am not happy about it but it had to come to an end one day, first Niel, then Jeffrey and now you are leaving, it is a sad time for me." Malika jokingly says "I would have thought you would be glad to see the back of him Zarrine?" Zarrine "Oh I know I used to say that but only in fun not truthfully, no Malika I and Danny have been together for a long time here and I don't know what it will be like here after he has gone as I have never had such a lovely time here since he got here and made everyone smile all of the time and yes he has been a pain in the backside also but he is a man of truth and he is kind and a real gentleman." Danny laughing says "Wow Zarrine, you have never told me this that I am a gentleman before or any of this before? if I had known this I might of asked for an extension." Zarrine "No Danny they told me no more extensions he is going and that's that, ha, ha, ha, no more said Anthea and the people in the offices he is going they said, ha, ha, only joking but I will miss you very much. We often got together and had a laugh and a cup of tea and discussed the college and the idiots here haven't ?we and tried to put the world to right and now I am losing you and I am afraid you will be lost without me." Danny "We will still see each other from time to time no worries, I will come back and taunt you now and again." Zarrine with a little tear in her eye says "I hope you will I really do it will never be the same here after you leave, I mean it, Danny you have been a lovely wind here through this college and made many person take notice of the right way to live except for your drinking with that Jeffrey but no I hope you will be ok? I know you have this lovely woman to look after you but don't forget us will you?" Danny now looking solemn says "Zarrine I will be coming back to see you forever as I feel you are like a sister to me and have done more than just look after me you have been my inspiration and kept me sane and looking up in life so don't be silly I will always be around somewhere for you forever." She taps his cheek and smiles "And don't forget our chip butty dinner time and it will not be the last time either remember. " Malika "Right I am off to lectures see you all later and don't worry about him Zarrine he can look after himself and us girls." Zarrine "Yes I know." Malika goes off to her lectures and Zarrine asks Danny "Fancy another cup of tea Danny before you go?" Danny looking at Zarrine affectionately says "Yes why not, I will have a cuppa with my favourite woman and I am looking forward to my chip butty dinner time and it will just be you and I by the looks of it, Malika is not joining us she don't like chips from up there." Zarrine "Right no problem just us 2 then and are you all ready for the move tomorrow to your new home in Hereford town?" Danny "Yes I am and so is Malika and not very much did I come here with now I have loads and all my possessions are here." "What about the rest of your stuff in the house in Bridgend?" "I am not taking anything from there it is a new life and besides my son lives with his mother so he is entitled to anything of mine and will not break up the house ever, I will start again like getting blind this is my second life now and it must all change." "I see that might be a good thing and will your son Josh be coming up to see you in your new place?" "Oh yes and so will the other children and Jeff and Niel and Tim and Mandy etc. so you will see us all together again before it is all over no problem, so don't think this is goodbye yet." "Oh Danny, that will be nice I can't wait to see you all together again it will be nice, here drink this tea before it goes cold." "Thanks Zarrine I will miss this and you for all the right reasons, you are one of the best things that as ever happened to me and Peter is a lucky man to have a lovely lady like you to look after him and your son to have a lady like you to back him up through uni." "Well thank you Danny for saying this to me, look out the big boys are on the prowl I must get on with my work." "Right ok Zarrine, I will see you dinner time, do some butties ready for twelve thirty ok? see you then." "Right see you." Next thing Anthea walked in and said to Danny "Hello Danny how are you?" "I am fine and how about you is there something wrong?" "Oh no I am just doing a round up in the dorm's to see if anything is needed for the next term like dishes or cups etc. No problem and are you ready to move tomorrow?" Danny replies "Yes we are ready, I hope we can do it before 5 tomorrow night?" "Well see Barry today and he will sort it out." "Ok Anthea thanks I will see you tomorrow morning for the keys." Danny left and went to lectures.

Dinner time came and Danny turned up with the chips, more than enough for Zarrine and him . They sat down and started to enjoy this meal as Zarrine said "Well have you sorted things out for the last time?" "Yes I have and am not looking forward to leaving this hall without you, can you come with us? I would feel a lot better ha, ha, ha." "No I can't I have got my job here but look after yourself and that girl I will hope you will come and see me again from time to time?" "Of course I will, I will never forget you Zarrine I will miss you very much." Zarrine puts her arms around Danny and Danny puts his arms around her and they shed a tear and hug intensely. Danny emotionally says "I will miss you so much, this Is a new life for me and you have made it possible for me to live again and I mean it, I was a lost soul and thought it was all over for me, no way was I going to get through going blind, it was the end of me but you and many others here made me see that it made no difference if you don't let it. I can stand tall and stick my fingers up to the world and say I can put up with anything you throw at me, no problem." Zarrine wiping a tear from her cheek says "Yes you certainly can Danny, you have done it, I remember you read in the face and sweating trying to keep your nerves to do what seemed Impossible and you and Jeff did it together with a lot of encouragement from Niel the three guys who did it all together." "With a hell of a lot of help from someone as patient as you who put up with a hell of a lot with us all. I will never forget you Zarrine, I mean it you have helped me get my life back on track and I didn't know you from Adam a few years ago, so thank you Zarrine for being a friend, I could never have done it without you and many others here." Zarrine smiles and says "Oh don't be silly I only done what I always do." Danny smiling says "Well it worked for me and I will never forget you and when I get a house in west Wales you and peter must come and stay with us." "Yes it will be nice I will." "Right I must get on Zarrine before I burst into tears but I will say goodbye on Friday morning as I will be sleeping in my room, just moving the stuff tomorrow rather than putting it in the attic and I will say goodbye then, if I can bear to, then the presentation and off for good. It will be the hardest day of my life and I am not looking forward to it I can tell you, see you later." They hug and rub each other's backs and part and Danny went silently to his lectures.

It was the next day and Danny and Malika was up for the move and on the Friday they were both going up to Beccles at Malika's house for a break and meet up with Malika's sister and son Malik. This was the first time for Danny to meet anyone of her family her sister Louisa lived in Birmingham so it will be nice for them all to have a break together although it was only for 2 weeks before they had to return to Hereford. This day was the last full day at the college and it was winding down but the younger students had already gone to their rooms to pack their things and it was the day of the presentation and gala telling everyone that it was the end of term. Danny was not that fussed by it all and it was too soon for Malika as she was still sitting her course just a case of picking up their pass papers and scrolls and shaking hands with the mayoress of Hereford so they think, but was there a twist in the tail.

In the main hall and the proceedings were well on the way and Danny and Malika were sitting apart in their separate rows for the different presentations and Danny was looking very smart for a change, no shorts, this was a great Improvement and it came to Danny's presentation and then Malika a little later and so Danny was under the Impression that it was all over just a few Important presentations to go through with the local papers present to get the stories and it came around to the presentation for the distinction in the braile that was the most Important presentation there is in that degree. The principle was on the stage area speaking "This person is the person who the braile department decides the best and most Improved student in this category in the whole college, the student who has dedicated their time here to learn a difficult new way of reading for blind people and who was the most outstanding student in this field. This person even turned up out of lesson time and was not going to let these lessons go past without getting it perfectly right, his name Is Daniel Duckfield and." Danny sat up straight in his seat and was so shocked he nearly fell off it, the principle carried on "He has also found it almost Impossible as he is a diabetic with it being a bad form of diabetes and so it is almost twice the problem for him to feel the dots, this is the first time this certificate has been presented to someone with this problem such is the intense hard work this student has gone through to get this accomplishment result, no mean feat. The braile tutors have come to this conclusion without any hesitation at all, he was far beyond anyone else with is determination and graduated with full marks, I know of this person he has been with us for a few years now and is a determined man and gets done what he has in his mind without any diversion. So it is with great pleasure I present the braile award for outstanding achievement to Mr Daniel Duckfield." There was a massive round of applause and Danny stood up looking very sheepish, a person grabbed him and told him to grab his elbow and he would get him to the stage to accept this award and Danny was smiling from ear to ear, he got to the stage with lots of applause and the mayor shook his hand and gave him the award and a large bottle of

Champaign and a cheque for £50 and asked him a few questions and the cameras were flashing and then he left the stage to a huge applause from his fellow students and tutors. This was the pinnacle of his time at the college and it showed and he felt so proud as he sat down.

Well Malika was so proud of him and gave him a huge kiss and congratulated him and then it was the braile girls who was accompanied by the woman who was married to the man who created the format that was used in Britain to teach this complicated braile and make it easier to learn. Her name was Jill Berry and her late husband was Nigel Berry and was there to see Danny get this award and the cat was out of the bag, as Malika already knew he was up for this award but was sworn to secrecy and Ginny and Christine and Margaret were so proud of him. Ginny then said "It could have only been you as you struggled in the beginning and most of the way over the past few years but got there in the end, even with all the personal problems that you have been through since I have met you it was only going to be you and you thoroughly deserve it." Christine said "She is right Danny you worked hard to achieve this and well done." Danny "Well it was hard to learn but that's what kept me at it, I was determined to get there in the end." Margaret says "Danny you certainly were I remember a few times you turning up in my room out of the way of the other students on your time off lectures and getting stuck into the work and if it didn't work out you would start again and sit there for ages, well done and what did you get awarded? I forgot in all the excitement." Danny replied "A certificate and a bottle of Champagne and £50 cheque, so it's drinks on me." Malika "We must go to the refectory now Danny as the press are waiting for you and the other 2 award winners to have photographs taken for the paper, so let's go, we will see you all later up the bar for a celebrating drink." They all agreed and off they all went to their different places. The day went off well and was a little overwhelming for Danny and up the bar later he was having a drink with the braile babes and Malika and spoke to them "Well girls if it was not for you 3 I would not be here now enjoying the spoils of the day, so well done to all of you for being so good at your jobs, I mean it." Ginny "Well thank you Danny I am now wondering if we will ever see you again?" Danny "Oh yes you will I am not going far and Jeff was on about us getting together this summer for a meal, what do you think?" Ginny "Well yes why not, we always do this type of thing anyway so arrange it, what do you think girls?" Christine and Margaret agree and decided to have another drink for the road as Phil Ginny's husband had not turned up to pick them up as yet. Ginny "Well this is it Danny, your time here is all over, how do you feel about it now?" They all listened intensely at his answer "Well it is a part of my life that i will treasure forever and I will never forget this day for as long as I live and thank you girls for thinking I deserved it, I will miss you all, but will try and keep in touch and Ginny I will miss you a great deal as you have been a rock to me, I mean it and if it was not for the fact you were a happy married woman no one else in this world would have had a look in, I love you and will miss you, we have had some fun there in the braile classes fantastic times and if I do write a book I will have a lot to say about the time I spent in braile, I will miss Christine and Margaret to very much but it's time, it's time to see if I can make it on my own." Christine "Your not on your own you have got Malika now." Danny "Of course I know I have and will make a good go of things with her but you girls have got a special place in my heart and I won't forget you ever, right let's have a drink before we all start crying is it?" Ginny "Well I for one will miss you Danny, you have been a good man to get to know." Christine and Margaret agree. Malika "You girls will say anything to get rid of him ha, ha, ha." They all laugh and Margaret said "No I for one will agree with Ginny and Christine, he will be missed in the braile class." Malika says "I know I was only kidding." Danny "Well who knows I may come back one day." Christine "Oh no threats Danny." Margaret "Don't listen to her we will be glad to see you back except I have retired so I will not see you again here." Danny "Do you all fancy a get together after the holidays for a meal in the Rose and Crown? I mean me Malika, Jeff, Niel, Tim and Mandy and you girls just to say goodbye as I will be totally gone after xmas?" The girls talked for a minute and Ginny said "Yes what a good idea, we never had time to say goodbye to Niel so it would be nice, I will be here." Christine "So will I." Margaret "Count me in." Danny "Good that's settled then I will get the ball rolling, they can stay with us in the maisonette for one night, it will be brilliant and I can say so long to Niel also." Ginny "There we are then sorted as the Welsh say, I will look forward to it." The night ended shortly after that as Phil came to pick up the girls and Danny was starting to slur so an early night was on the cards.

The next day and Danny and Malika was informed they had to wait to move to the maisonette and so had a few hours to put their things in the loft of Dowdell hall and informed Zarrine they had done so and were off to Malika's house in Beccles Suffolk and off they went.

On arriving some 5 hours later Danny was amazed that she lived on a railway level crossing, a comfortable cottage with a small garden but cosy. They were there a few days before her sister and nephew arrived and when they did arrive they had a great time and Danny was Impressed with Beccles and soon the holiday was over and back to college for a few hours at least.

Back at the college and Zarrine was waiting for them all to get back and she looked sad as Danny was leaving this very day and Danny looked unsure about it all. This was a huge move for him as he has not been on his own outside the college ever and Malika in college all day. Danny was about to see if all he learned in college was going to make any difference to him, a nervous time was ahead for him, they all sat in the lounge surrounded by boxes of belongings of Danny and Malika it looked as if they were being evicted and it was silent until Zarrine in a quiet voice said "Cup of coffee?" Malika sat up and replied "Yes why not, I will have one, Danny how about you?" Danny looking as if he was somewhere else said "Oh, oh yes please, I was miles away then, I feel a little nervous if the truth be told." Zarrine "Oh Danny you will be ok I am sure of it, you must make the commitment to living on your own sooner or later and soon it will be like falling off a house." Danny smiling says "I know Zarrine it will be so strange mind I will have to make my own bed and tea and coffee and go to the chip shop by myself as there is one around the corner." Malika laughed "We won't be eating there every night, I won't eat there all of the time and you need to eat better than that with your diabetes to." Zarrine "You tell him Malika he needs to eat properly and I know you will watch him." Danny still smiling says "I know I am only joking time to sort my life out now from today as it's the first day of the rest of my life." Zarrine "This is hard for me to, I will miss you after today it's a sad day but you come and see me regularly." Danny "Zarrine of course I will, I haven't a key so be aware I will turn up all of a sudden so look out ha, ha, ha." Zarrine "That's ok as long as you come to see me." Danny "I will no worries and I will bring Jeff with me when he comes up to visit." Zarrine "Steady don't overdo it ha, ha, I am only joking I would love to see you Jeff and Niel sitting here soon as it is possible, that would be so good for me and will cheer me up a lot." Just then Barry and another man turned up to move Danny and Malika and he said "Hi guys we will have to make a move as I am on duty this morning, sorry to rush you, these boxes to go yes?" Malika answers them "Oh yes, these are all of them Barry I will sort myself out back soon Danny." Danny "Yes of course I will say goodbye to Zarrine." Malika went off and Danny and Zarrine was alone in the lounge, she got up so as not to start crying and went into the kitchen and Danny followed her grabbed her arm and they had a huge cuddle and Danny said "Well Zarrine this is it I will always remember you and all that you have done for me, I will always love you as a sister and I want to say thanks Zarrine for being a friend, I mean it I would not have done it without you, look after yourself and I will be seeing you from time to time I mean that too." Zarrine hugged Danny who was a lot larger than her and in a sad voice she said "And you look after yourself Danny I mean that, I will miss you, this hall will never be the same again it's a very sad day for me so you had better go now before you see me cry again and look after that girl and have a lovely life you deserve it, goodbye. " Danny and Zarrine kissed and parted as Danny met up with Malika outside the kitchen and left the hall for the last time and shouted to Zarrine "Goodbye" this was a real sad day for Danny and Zarrine and as Danny went to get into the car he looked back as if he could see everything and then he sat silent in the car to his new digs with Malika.

Well they arrived at the new house at 13 Radcliff Court and they went inside and Barry and his mate got the boxes inside amongst the furniture that was already there and the lads left and it was silent no music or anything and they sat there alone and Danny was wondering how he was going to manage all this new life and Malika said Immediately "Right a cup of coffee to celebrate the new place, a good idea, yes?" Danny sat up and pulled himself together and said "Why not let's celebrate the new gaff and get some music on, I will set up my stereo system as you make the coffee." Malika smiling says "Yes let's do that and hurry up I need a dance." Malika sorted the coffee out of the box and a pint of milk and went off to make the drink and Danny got hold of his stereo and placed it on the table and plugged it in and found a radio station Immediately and the house came to life and Malika returned with the coffee and put them down and started dancing and said "I think we will like it here it's not bad at all and the sun is shining so let's have this coffee and get these boxes sorted, what do you think?" "Yes why not and after we will go and have dinner in the rose and crown and a few pints to celebrate." "Yes why not, we need to get used to this place as soon as we can and don't worry about Zarrine she will be allright and so will you and me." "I know, but it's a strange thing that is happening to me and you of course but we will be fine, let's get this place sorted out." The both of them worked all day and finally got things sorted but no biscuit's or anything in the maisonette so they had to go shopping the next day and catch the bus which they have not done so far, this is all the start of a new life for them both, will Danny make it?

It was the first day back at the college for Malika and Danny looked worried a little and so it was he was left all alone at the new place and all he could hear was the traffic outside and so he set about sorting his vast CD collection out and other things like the television and the portable TV in the bedroom and before he knew it it was lunch time and he decided to walk with his cane around the corner to the chip shop for his first meal there and so it took him a little while and finally got there and walked into the shop and was called upon as to what he wanted and he was so far from the counter the lady in there told him where to go, like the golden shot programme on TV "A little to the left and come forward, right you are nearly by the counter, there you are so what can I do for you?" Danny "Thanks a lot I will have some fish and chips please and I recognise that accent it's Welsh isn't it?" The woman sounded shocked and says "Well yes we come from Pembrokeshire and so are you Welsh?" Danny answered "Oh come now I sound more Welsh than you, I am from Bridgend but I am going to live in Narberth soon, I am going to buy a house there with my partner if she likes it there." "Well, well, we are from Pembroke itself and what a coincidence, so where are you living now then?" "Just around the corner in Radcliff Court just until my partner finishes her course in the college here then we are off." She then says "Well it's nice to meet you and we will see you often in here I hope." "Depends on how nice your chips are ha, ha, only kidding if you are Welsh you know how to cook fish and chips so I will look forward to seeing you soon, bye." Danny left an found his way back with a little trouble but it was a success and this made him feel as if he was not useless and sat and enjoyed his chips and fish while listening to the news and felt good with himself, later that day he sorted out some more boxes and before he knew it Malika was home again. She asked "Ok, so how did your first day on your own go?" "Great, no problem it went well and the people who own the fish and chip shop are from Pembrokeshire in Wales so we hit it off Immediately and the fish and chips were gorgeous believe me they were, I ate them all and then got some boxes sorted out and the televisions all set up including the portable in the bedroom so we can have an early night if you like?" Malika smirked and agreed. From that day on Danny got used to living in Radcliff Court all except for a little dog at the end of his street who used to charge down his drive and stand at the gate and yap at Danny and make him jump and In a few weeks they went to drink in the local pub there called the White House and the people there were so nice and made them feel at home in there also.

Jeff , Tim and Mandy visited one weekend and had a fabulous time with the braile babes for a long dinner one day. It was working out perfect. Josh visited often and it was a great time there and so Danny and Malika were starting to build a home but no furniture except a new king sized bed was bought for their new life in Wales because they had nowhere to put anything as the Maisonette was full of the furniture that belonged to the college.

They both decided to go to Tenby and Narberth to let Malika see the place and see if she would like it there or if not find somewhere else, they arrived in Tenby and stayed in a bed and breakfast there and Malika fell in love with Tenby and west Wales and the very next time they went down they stayed in Narberth in the Plas-Hyffred hotel, very nice and went into the town shopping and Malika was bowled over with the shops, fresh food everywhere and a fruit shop called wise buys and they sold every sort of fruit and veg from all over the world, this shop was amazing , Malika and that shop alone made her mind up also the lovely people there and they went into some of the pubs like The Angel and they sold Brains beers in there Danny's favourite beer then the Farmers arms and they sat there with a good juke box and they got very hungry and asked the girl behind the counter if there was a Chinese take away there? she told them there was and then asked if they wanted her to go and get it and they could eat it in the bar there. Danny and Malika was amazed at this and agreed and did so. Malika and Danny were very happy with Narberth town and Danny talked to his brother Mel and asked him to sound out a house there for them as they decided to live there as they were so Impressed there .

Well xmas came and went and things were going along brilliantly, they visited Tim and Mandy and another time it was Jeff and Scully the dog, things were good and things could not get better, it was now January and not long for Malika to finish her course and leave Hereford for Wales and so Danny started to sort things out with his brother as regards to finding a house suitable for him and Malika to live in Narberth, Pembrokeshire, this would take a little time so he started in earnest and Mel his brother was a great help so Malika and Danny went down several times so as to try and find a place and Malika fell in love with Narberth especially the town shops that are on their own as regards shops that are original, a few coffee shops that are fantastic delicatessens that are original and full of goodies not

seen anywhere else in Britain, a fruit shop second to none that had fruit and vegetables etc. not ever seen in this country which Malika was determined to make her own when she goes to live there, 2 proper butcher shops not seen in many towns or villages these days, a load of unusual shops and gift shops, a Panini shop pubs that sell fantastic beers that made Danny's mind up straight away and many more things that could not be grasped all at once and the people were so nice, it was like a dream and Malika and Danny realised this is what they wanted, a shop specialising in health products and many fine healthy foods in fact this place he and Malika was in love with and was going to settle there as soon as possible.
Things were going along fantastically, nothing could spoil it now or so they thought.

CHAPTER 18
IS THIS THE END

Things were going along lovely for a while and Malika was enjoying the final days at the college and Danny was getting used to his new life away from the college but life kept smacking Danny in the face every so often and he got up one morning and went to the college to see if he had got any mail as he had not been for a week or two. He got in there and Barry was in there and greeted him Barry "Well goodness it's the Welshman or as Jeff used to say the dodgy Welshman, how are you and what do you want? ha, ha, ha." Danny with smile on his face says "Well it's nice to see you to Barry ha, ha, I need to see if there is any mail for me please?" Barry looks through a huge box and comes up with 2 letters for him and hands them over to him and said "Here we are just the 2." "Thanks Barry can you read them for me so as to save time?" "Here we are, the first one is from the agency for renting property saying that they still have not found any property for you." Danny says "Oh you can throw that away those idiots are useless, what about the other one Barry?" "Oh dear this one is an official one from the solicitor of your wife, it's a decree absolute and tells you that you are divorced as from the sixth of January, I am sorry to say." There was a silence and Danny shouted "Yes, yes my son, it's all over got rid of the 2 faced cow who tried to destroy me, I am rid of her for good, she can now settle down with that alcoholic and I can get my son to live with us if she does, it's not bad news believe me, it's the best thing I have heard, she went off with another man because I went blind and so she can now see what life is like without my money and the house she is living in because as soon as Josh is 18 I will sell that house and have done with her. I will frame that letter thank you Barry I mean it thanks, so I am off to meet Malika for lunch in the refectory, see you Barry." Barry looking bemused says "Yes ok Dan see you later and be careful out there."

Danny met up with Malika and went for something to eat and they sat down and Danny started to tell her about this divorce. "Well I had a letter from my wife's solicitor it's good news, i am now divorced as from the 6 of last month and so life is getting better all of the time, so what do you think then?" "I don't think nothing at all, it does not make any difference to me and so let's eat." "Ok then, the other letter is from that agency for the house here in Hereford to tell us they have not found a house for us as of yet, typical." Malika rolls her eyes and says "A waste of time as per usual so we need to get up to Beccles to sort out my place in a few weeks and I can put all my stuff up for the auction as I am not taking anything from my past with me just like you, I think it's for the best." "It's up to you, I agree with you mind, we must both start again a new life." "Yes I agree so what are you doing for the rest of the day?" "I am going to the Rose and Crown for a couple of pints to celebrate, you are finished at 2.30 fancy a pint with me? it's a nice day I am buying." "Yes why not? we can sit in the gardens there and I fancy a Chinese for tea and watch some telly tonight and maybe go for a pint in the White House." Danny smiling says "Yes batman, good thinking see you later then I will meet you by the bench outside Gardner." They had a good day as Danny felt as if a big weight had been taken off his shoulders and things were going along swimmingly.

A week went buy and he decided to give Tim a ring this particular afternoon to see how things were going. Tim answered and Danny replied "Hello Tim It's Danny so how are things?" Tim sounded out of breath and answered in a serious voice "I thought you were Niel's wife calling back, you haven't heard how he is have you?" Danny looked bemused and said "How who is?" "Niel of course." Danny still looking bewildered says "Sorry Tim I haven't got a clue what you are talking about, is there something wrong with Niel?" Tim in urgent voice says "Oh yes Dan I am sorry I presumed you knew he was not well earlier and was taken to the hospital with suspected Pneumonia, I was thinking you were calling to give me an update." Danny looked shocked and said "My god no I knew nothing." "Well I phoned him for a chat and there was panic on the phone and she told me Niel was being taken to hospital urgently." "Right Tim I will get off the telephone and call them to see how he is and call you back as soon as I know more." Tim "Right Dan speak later." Danny put the phone down and was like a ghost he went white and called Niel's home and says "Hello this is Danny is Ceri there please?" "I am sorry she is down the hospital I am her sister. " She was crying on the phone a little so Danny said "This is Danny Niel's friend from the college in Hereford can you tell me how he is now? as I have only just heard he has been taken to the hospital." There was a silence on the other end of the phone and then the words came "I am sorry Danny but Niel died a few minutes ago." Danny was stiff and stunned after a while he said "Oh no, oh no, please don't say that, oh no, he can't be that lovely man he can't be please, no." "I know it's so sad he has gone I am afraid it's so sad and I don't believe it either, are you allright I have been crying to, hello." Danny was wiping tears from his eyes and replies "I am sorry this is such a shock to me, I loved that man he was such a lovely man and a bloody good friend to me and many others here he was to young." "Yes I know he was only 44 so young, I will miss him so much and his boys and Ceri will." "This is not real I am sorry it's not sinking in I can't believe it he went so quick no warning." "Well he has not been well for a few days but it got serious this afternoon and now he has gone, I don't know how Ceri will cope with this?" Danny with tears streaming down his face says "I can't Imagine it either this has hit me for six, I can't Imagine what she must be like and the boys, oh my god how awful, I will call later to speak to Ceri if I can, please tell the boys I am so sorry and will speak later ok?" "Yes ok I understand, I am sorry to give you such bad news, speak later goodbye." "Goodbye my darling." Danny puts the phone down and puts his head in his hands and cries for a while then compose himself and calls Tim and said to him "Hello Tim it's Danny again." Tim says "Hi Dan so what's the crack? how is Niel?" There was a silence then Danny said "Tim I am sorry he died a short while ago." Tim stammers "Oh no, oh no, I must tell Mandy a minute Dan." He calls out to Mandy and he says to her "Niel died a short while ago." Mandy "Oh my god never, oh no." She starts crying and Tim comes back to the phone and says to Danny "It's unreal just not real, such a nice man, I can't believe it, did you speak to Ceri?" "No her sister told me on the phone, Ceri is still down the hospital and it was pneumonia that killed him, I can't believe it not him, what a waste of life, he is so young to, only 44 Tim" "I am stunned and Mandy is crying behind me I am numb Dan, oh my god I will sort things out now to go to his funeral, let me know when it is and let everyone know and I will call you tomorrow, I need to comfort Mandy, see you mate." "Yes I will call you tomorrow, by Tim" Danny put the phone down and explained to Malika all about it and later called Jeff to tell him all about it "Hello Jeff it's Danny." Jeff replies "Ah the dodgy Welshman, hows things?" "Not good Jeff I had some bad news." "Really can I do anything?" "No you will be just as devastated as me in about 5 seconds…. I am afraid that Niel David passed away earlier this afternoon." There was a deadly silence and then Jeff says "No, your wrong our Niel David you mean?" "Yes I am afraid our Niel David, he had caught pneumonia and died in hospital, I spoke to his sister in law and she confirmed it to me just not long after he died." "Oh no, I don't believe it not Niel, this is not real he was with us not long ago now he is dead, this is such a shock I can't believe it this is not real please tell me your joking Dan?" "I wish I could, Niel is gone matey, he is really gone, I am numb I don't know what to think, he was such a lovely man and a good mate, I will miss him badly." "Yes, so will I, he was a brilliant person, I will miss him and his lovely laugh, I am numb also, we will have to go to the funeral, we will meet in Newport and go together ok?" "Yes of course it's just like a dream I think someone is going to pinch me now and I will wake up." "it was only a few months ago we were all in the rose and crown together remember, this is unreal, this is not supposed to happen like this, I will call Rhoda and let her know, she has had a rough time losing her daughter and the illness I wonder if it is a good idea?" "Oh yes you will have to tell Rhoda, I will have to go and tell everyone in the college tomorrow, I am not looking forward to telling them but they need to know." "Of course you will have to tell them there will be a lot of tears there tomorrow and how is Ceri and the boys coping?" Danny says "I don't know I am phoning them later and I will let you know tomorrow but I am sorry to bring you such bad news." "It's a funny world Dan, not your fault, remember him losing his temper with the computers and the time he pretended to be the police squad with is dog as a sniffer dog, just to get a seat in the pub and it worked and the fun we had with him, he was a star man and I love him and will miss him." "The best time was when he took his phone back and that man who tried to tell Abby where to go, he lost it that day, so funny and his sharing with everything he had, no problem ever and never complained about it, this is not happening, he is messing about I hope, I can't Imagine life without him about can you?" "No he must come back we haven't finished our adventure yet, there is so much more to do, he can't go yet." "Sorry Jeff I feel the same he is going to be missed greatly by me and I suppose the gang is missing an Important man from our group, god this is not happening Jeff surely it's a dream?" " "If only mate, give me a ring if you hear any more and god bless Niel I will be thinking about him for months now it's a sad day Danny, speak tomorrow, bye mate." "Cheers Jeff." Danny put the phone down and looked so sad. Later when Malika had gone to bed Danny sat down and was a torn man, thinking he thought "Poor old Niel, I can't believe it here we go again, life has not been kind to me, I have lost so many people who was so close to me, first my childhood sweetheart Mary Davies, a lovely girl who would not harm a fly, then my first son when I was so young Nathan John and he was only 6 months old and I buried him on my 20th birthday and then a good friend who I went to school with Gino Morgan who died with multiple sclerosis, then my dad he was only 54, I was still young then. Them Mum who died through problems from the war, a loving woman and recently my older brother Dennis who was only 54 an a loving brother who had a torrid life and was mentally retarded and who also would not harm a fly, then little brother Lyndon, who was too young to die at 41 and he has left a mark on my life, and then my beautiful cousin Louisa only 30 and such a loving cousin, I miss them all so much and now Niel a man so young and was such a loving man and would not harm a fly and would give you his last pound, no problem, I can't go any more it's all too much, god." Danny broke down and cried for a while and was visibly shaking and looked as if he was about to have a breakdown and then kept on thinking nice thoughts to keep him sane "He was such a character he really was fun and a cracking laugh, bald as a fish, kept me in my place at times, all the lads loved him and all of the ladies in the college are going to be devastated when they hear about him, a special man indeed. If you are listening Niel, I love you and am missing you as a fantastic mate, I will always remember you and I am having a drink to you with a little whisky, I bought myself so here's to you matey, I will miss you forever and so will everyone else." Danny then picked up the telephone to speak to Ceri "Hi Ceri I am so sorry about Niel, I can't believe he has gone, please if there is anything at all I can do please don't hesitate to ask me, please." Ceri sounding as if her world had come to an end says "I know Danny and thanks, I can't believe it has happened he was allright yesterday and now he is dead, I don't know what I am going to do." Danny answered her trying to keep it together "Yes I can see life is going to be hard for you for a while but I mean it if I can help in any way don't forget to say, how are the lads?" "Devastated Dan, they are in a hell of a state." "Yes a silly question I suppose, sorry Ceri tell them to be strong for their dad sake he is still about somewhere looking down on them and you must be strong for them now, I will inform the college tomorrow so don't worry about that I know his friends there, what am I saying? everyone there was a good friend of his he was loved by everyone." Ceri gave a little chuckle and says "Yes he was so friendly with everyone, I am sorting the funeral out tomorrow so I will let you know as soon as I know Danny, he wanted to be cremated and I will sort that out for him and his favourite song will be played, he loved Bet Middler the wind beneath my wings, I will cry when it is played I will miss him Dan he was my rock and I don't know what I am going to do." Danny "Ceri, he will want you to carry on and bring up those boys the way you have been doing so far, he is around all of the time and will guide them boys I am sure of that so I know it's hard now but you must keep up your chin for those lads and for yourself ok?" "Yes I know I must and will try my best I will be much better after his funeral I am dreading that day it's going to be horrible for me." "Yes I know it will it is going to be a bad day for me too and Jeff and Tim are coming to the funeral I assure you, so let me know as soon as you know please Ceri." "Of course I will Danny no problem, I will say goodnight now as I have got people here." "Yes Ceri goodnight speak soon and don't worry things will be ok, I am sure Niel is standing with Abby by his side looking down on us at all times." Danny went to his seat and had some more of his whisky and bowed his head thinking how he is going to tell everyone in the college tomorrow as they remember Niel as a man with a smile on his face never mind what .

The next morning Danny shared the taxi to college with Malika and went straight to see Zarrine in Dowdell. He got out of the taxi and went to the door and rang the bell for the top floor and a student left him in, he got into the lounge and sat down and got himself a cup of tea as he waited for Zarrine to come back from the main building where she was taking a student. Danny stood by the sofa that Niel used to always sit and he stroked the back of the seat and remembered him sitting just there with Abby at his feet looking up at them both and was almost in tears again, he then said quietly "Poor Niel I am sorry mate it ended like this but I will always be your friend and I am missing you dreadfully, look after yourself mate and say hello to Abby for me, I know you are both together again, I just know this, love you mate. " Next thing in walks Zarrine with a huge smile on her face when she saw Danny and in excitement says "Hello my Danny? nice to see you so you can't stay away from Zarrine then and you have got some tea and where is mine then?" Danny smiled and beckoned her to sit by him on the sofa, she sat down and Danny proceeded to tell her as the lounge was empty "I have had some bad news Zarrine." Zarrine went serious and says "Oh Danny, what now? can I help? please tell me what is wrong." Danny went silent for a minute then said "Niel David died last night." There was a deadly silence and Zarrine put her hands up to her mouth and started to shake and then said "Oh Danny how? why? oh dear, oh dear, I don't believe it." Danny continues "He died of pneumonia and it happened so quick, it was all over in a Jiffy." Zarrine cried and was very upset and says "Oh that poor man he was such a lovely man, why? why? I remember he was always smiling when he was awake, the man I thought would outlive us all, he was such a happy man, how awful, it's not fair it's just not, I can't believe it, it was only a short time ago we were all laughing in this very room, I can't grasp this, oh my goodness he was sat all of the time exactly where you are sitting now." "I know that's why I am sitting here now, seeing if I can feel him here with us now although I don't believe in that type of thing, he is keeping me warm, I am absolutely devastated I can't believe he has gone, I still think he is coming in here in a minute for a moan and his breakfast of slim fast, he was a hell of a lad wasn't he? I can sense him here Zarrine and it feels good for me." "Danny I can always feel you three here since you all left but it is getting fainter and fainter but today I will feel him here I will clean his old room later and pray for him in there. Oh my dear this is a bad day for us all." "Yes it certainly is I will never forget him, never, he has been a man who was part of my life especially since he was the man who helped me so very much with my blindness, I will never forget him." "I know what you mean, have you told Jeffrey?" "Yes I have, he was the first one I told and also Tim and Mandy they were devastated and Jeff was so shocked and sounded lost on the phone, I am going to see the braile girls and then the Principle and then ask them in the FLC to put it on the E-MAIL system for students and staff as I promised Ceri his wife I would and before you ask she is in a hell of a state and I hope she can keep it together for those lads who Niel worshipped as you know, oh bless him Zarrine it's not fair is it?" "No it isn't Danny all the wasters in this world and he was taken from us so young, such a lovely man I will pray for him and you look after yourself as you have had a horrible time this past few years." "Yes I know and this I didn't need I was looking forward to us getting together when I got the house in west Wales, he was a man who would come down regularly to see us and have a good laugh, I was sure of that but it's all gone now, I am smashed about it all and he was only 44 it's a tragedy it really is." Danny stood up and gave his empty cup to Zarrine and she cuddled up to him and he cuddled her and they parted and Danny kissed her and said "If it was not for Niel I would never have come here, it was his suggestion, goodbye Zarrine, I will pop in to see you next week, bye." Danny went off to see Ginny, Christine and   Margaret.

He entered the Braile room before lessons were about to commence and sat down and Ginny and Christine were excited to see him and asked "So what are you doing here so early? nice to see you mind and you have made Ginny's day, Danny cup of tea or coffee?" Danny solemn said " No thanks Chris I think you had better sit down and listen for a minute." Ginny says "Look out another joke I know you, come on then let's have it." Danny just blurted it out "I am afraid Niel David died last night of pneumonia." Christine cried out loudly "Oh my god never?" Ginny "Don't be silly, I was talking to him last week on the phone." Danny repeated "I am sorry but it's true, he died last night, I was shocked myself and this is a tragedy, It will take a lot of time getting over this." Christine "Oh my god Ginny this is awful, poor Niel, a nice man who was such a character it's not real." Ginny "Had he been ill for long?" Danny "No not really, it happened so sudden, Tim told me when I phoned him for a chat yesterday afternoon that Niel was ill and I phoned Niel's house and his sister in law told me he had just died around about 4 o'clock and that was that so sudden, Tim, Mandy, Jeff, and Zarrine are devastated as I expect you are, I don't believe it." Ginny "Oh my god he was a lovely man, this is a tragedy indeed." Danny "Jeff, Tim and I are going to the funeral when it happens, this has set me back a few miles, I will miss him so very much ." Christine "We all will, a character in his own right, love him." In walks Margaret and realising something was wrong says "Hi guys, what's the Matter? oh dear what is it?" Ginny with sad look on her face says "Niel David died last night from pneumonia, it's awful." Margaret put her hand over her mouth and gasped "Oh no, oh no, not our Niel please don't say that, I give up, what a waste, he is so much of a kind man, well i don't believe it he will be missed by a lot of people, god bless him." Danny "Well he loved you girls, I remember coaxing him to come to braile classes and it took a lot to coax him but after only one lesson he was hooked and he loved it here and he always gave you girls the gossip didn't he? and more." Chris "Oh yes I loved it when he was here he could talk all day and made me feel at home in his presence." Margaret "Our Niel as we called him was so knowledgeable, there was not a lot he didn't know and was great with advice, a fabulous man I will miss him as I have since he left and his laugh more like a huge chuckle and all his body would move when he laughed, oh bless him." She was moved to tears. Ginny "Yes that's right he was such a nice human being, he will be on my mind forever bless him, Danny I hope this has not set you back in any way? I know he was a good friend to you and he used to tell us he and you used to share some whisky and brandy regularly and I know he was very fond of you, so keep your chin up for his sake." Danny "I was so fond of him too and his loss will be felt hugely by me and Tim, Mandy and Jeff, he was huge in my life as he was huge and I love him and miss him already and all his antics he used to get up to and the stories about him like him and Tommy the horse, why him? why him? I think he was needed elsewhere, so I will have a dram for him tonight, right I am off to sort out some more things. This is a sad time and we must remember him as he was a loving man with a heart of gold, I will see you all later in the week, bye." They all bid Danny goodbye and he went off to the FLC to put a notice on the college e-mail system.

In there was Jude a lovely girl who Danny got on well with, so she when seeing him smiled and said "God I thought they got rid of you?" "Well Jude, nice to see you to, let's get down to it. I have not got my shorts on today sorry." "Awe Danny why not it's only the end of winter and bloody freezing but you could have made an effort for little old me." "I will make more of an effort next time, I need a favour." "Is that all? depends on you, what is it now then? and be careful matey." "Can you put an e-mail to all staff and students for me on the system please?" "Depends what it is? no filth or any scams otherwise no problem if it's serious as you are a practical joker." "It is, can you jot this down for me?" Jude starts the computer and sit's waiting and then says "Right Dan tell me slowly." "I don't know how to put this right, a note to all students and staff. It is with sadness that I have to inform you that an old student that was at this college recently has passed away. Mr Niel David died last night at around 4pm after a short spell in hospital with pneumonia and as a man that was so lovely I have taken the initiative of sending his wife and 2 children all the best wishes from the college, more will be posted when I hear any new revelations on this Matter, god bless Niel from us all. That's it Jude." Jude looking sad said "Oh my god poor old Niel he was such a lovely fella, it's unbelievable , I am so sorry." She rubbed his arm and cuddled him and says "I know you and he were so close, look after yourself Dan." Yes Jude I will, It will take a time getting over this, he was a great man, I will see you around." Jude looking as if she was about to cry says "Yes bye Dan." Danny went off to be alone for a while. He decided to go to his favourite place where so many things used to happen and where him Jeff, Niel, Tim, Winnie woo sat so many times outside Gardner hall on the bench in the beginning of their time at the college. it was a lovely quiet place and you could watch the world go by from a distance. He sat on the very bench and was visibly moved muttering to himself "Hello Niel remember this bench? we had some fun here many times in the sun all of us, I hope you are happy now, not that you weren't when you was on this earth as I know you loved Ceri and the boys to bit's and of course Abby. I hope you are both together again, she was a lovely dog and you both deserve to be together forever, the lads and Mandy are missing you to bit's and I thought we were going to have much more fun than we have had although it was some of the best times of my life with you and the lads. Everyone is so shocked and hurt by you leaving us it's awful here now, I don't know why I am sitting here saying these things as I don't believe in god but this is different for us I think you can hear me and I know you will not be coming back, next time I see you it will bring tears to my eyes. I will think of you for the rest of my life you are and have always been a good friend to me, goodbye my friend." Just then a concerned voice interrupted Danny "Danny are you allright? it's rosemary, are you ok?" Danny pulled himself out of the trans and says "Oh rosemary, life has given me a slap across the head again." Rosemary sat by Danny and said "Danny move over let me sit by you, what's the Matter for goodness sake? you look awful." "Rosemary Niel David died last night from pneumonia." Rosemary sat upright and put her hand over her mouth and said with alarm "Oh my god never, oh my god no, it's not true Danny please?" "I am sorry it is, I am stunned and so upset." "I bet you are, you and him were good friends, I am so sorry Danny, poor old Niel but he was only 44 I think?" "Oh yes he was and you and him used to have a good talk from time to time, I remember it, he will be missed rosemary, everyone I talk to has been stunned, everyone." "Well he was a very loved man here, he will be missed greatly here, this is a sad day all around and a tragedy for all, I must be off Danny I am late as it is, are you going to be ok? if not come with me and have a coffee in the student bar." "No I am fine, I was just talking to him as we used to sit here a lot remember? I am going to say goodbye to him and off to meet Malika, I will be allright." "As long as you are sure? I will see you later" " Danny smiles and says "Yes bye Rose." She left and Danny sat there for a little while longer and just before he left he muttered "Well goodbye my old friend I will miss you and thank you for being a friend, goodbye." He stood up and walked off slowly to meet Malika.

Danny sat in the student bar with a tea for himself and a coffee for Malika, she arrived and sat by Danny and asked "How did it all go?" Danny "Well it was very sad and everyone I told was so upset, he was well loved here especially Zarrine she was devastated." "I expect she was, she had a lot to do with him, I wish I had got to know him he sounded a nice man." Next thing Mandy the warden came up to Danny distressed and says "Hi Danny and Malika it's Mandy from Dowdell, I heard about Niel, how awful, not fare he was such a loving man I am devastated by this, can you give Ceri and his family my love, I can't get over he has gone, my god life is so cruel isn't it?" Danny "Oh yes tell me about it? he is the talk of the college again but for all the wrong reasons, everyone is shocked and upset by all of this, I have put the information about him on the e-mail system here." Mandy "Good thing, he was well loved, I was asked by the principle Rashine, to ask you to call on her if you are still about, can you do this? she said anytime at all she will cancel her schedule at that time of the day." Danny "Yes I will go along after my tea Mandy." Mandy "Ok if I see her I will tell her but just go along anyway and look after yourself and don't let it get to you, you know Niel and you were good friends and he would not want you to do anything stupid, because I know you, no getting drunk and taking it out on someone else ok? tell Jeff and the rest of the gang we are all sorry about all of this with Niel and we will be thinking about him for ever ok Danny?" Danny "Yes of course Mandy he was someone special to us gang as you put it, he was one of the gang and still is no problem Jeff, Tim and I am going down to the funeral to say goodbye to our mate and celebrate his life as a man who made us all appreciate life as blind people, he enjoyed life and we will continue to do the same for his sake." Mandy left and Danny and Malika carried on with their tea break .

It was some time later that Danny went along to Rashine's office and as he approached he could hear music and singing it was coming from Rashine's room it was the Morriston Male voice choir who sing a lot of well-known Welsh songs that reminded Danny of Niel. Danny used to sing Welsh songs with Niel to taunt the English especially Jeff in Dowdell and in the bar, this stopped Danny in his tracks for a moment just to listen and as he did he thought "There we are Niel especially for you and me, you were a true Welshman and I bet you are singing on the top of your voice?" He knocked the door to Rashine's office and she turned the music down and beckoned Danny in and shut the door, he sat down and Rashine said. "Hello Danny I am sorry to hear about Niel it is a real loss to the college and the world, he was such a fine man indeed and I hope you don't mind me playing this music it seems appropriate now he is no more with us, it reminds me of him and helps me to remember such a lovely man." "I agree Rashine it is very appropriate, he would have loved it, I can see him singing on the top of his voice now and yes he will be missed, it's not real is it?" Rashine bows her head and says "No it is not and such a young man and he lost his dog Abby not so long ago, that was heart breaking enough, I Imagine his wife is besides herself? I can't Imagine how she feels and everyone loved Niel without question, a sad loss. Have you had any information about his funeral?" Danny says "No I haven't as of yet but will inform everyone on the e-mail system as soon as I know." "Thank you I believe his tutor is going to the funeral as she is devastated and had to go home, she is so upset and the college will be well represented to say goodbye to Niel. Look out there the sun is shining and our Niel has gone, such a shame, are you going down to his funeral as you used to live a few miles away from him didn't you?" "Yes of course I am, along with Jeff and Tim , I knew Niel for a few years before I came here, as a Matter of fact he advised me to come here to get my life back or as we used to say learn to be blind and that's why he came back because I was coming here and I remember the first day we arrived he was standing on the road outside the train station telling Abby off for doing a naughty on the platform and I surprised him with my ex-wife and we had a ball from then on. I can't believe he has gone it's a tragedy and yes we used to live about 8 miles from each other and he would come sometimes to my house and visit with Ceri and Abby, we became good friends and now he has gone bless him." "Yes I know, this world don't know when it is well off then this type of thing happens, it makes you wonder. I will wait for your e-mail Danny and hope things go well for his funeral, give his family our love please and If there is anything you want to see me about don't hesitate to come and see me." "Thank you Rashine I will, goodbye." "Goodbye Danny." Danny left and Rashine turned up the music a little in respect of Niel, this Danny was sure about .

Danny was having a hard time with the loss of Niel but felt he had to have a good drink to celebrate his life and did so most of that week. Well the day of his funeral was the following Thursday and not in the crematorium he had thought it would be in but further away from his village and a route Danny was not familiar with so he spoke to Jeff that was not a problem for him but he then called Tim "Hello Tim it's Danny, I have been told the day of the funeral it's next Thursday, but it is further from his home than I thought it would be, it's in Port Talbot crematorium and it's not easy to get to, it's a taxi job." Tim sounding upset "Dan I am sorry I will not be able to make it, it's Impossible to go, if I went I would have to leave here at around 4 in the morning and leave Immediately after his funeral it's Impossible so I have decided with Mandy to send flowers and apologise to Ceri, I will spend the whole day on the trains and not be able to give my regards reasonably sincerely to the family, can you see what I am saying?" Danny in deep thought says "Yes I see what you are saying Tim it's no good doing it if it's not sensible, I will explain to Ceri and family don't worry about it, I know if it was possible you would do it no reflection on you, I know how close you and Mandy was to Niel so don't feel bad about it I will represent all his friends who can't make it don't worry." "Well thanks mate as you can see it's Impossible but I will sit and think about him silently at eleven o'clock, he was so special to us." "I know mate you don't have to tell me, I know he will be missed by us all, I am meeting Jeff in Newport station and we will travel on together. I am dreading it, it will be so sad it really will be so sad and I hope we can go on to the club he used to go to for his wake and say a real good goodbye to him, lots of people will be there I have no doubt he was such a great fella and I will have a few pints for him." Tim "Yes I thought you would ha, ha, he will be up there looking down on it all smiling I bet and saying things like what the hell is he doing here he owes me money or he or she never liked me anyway, ha, ha, he was a lad, I have had visions of him these last few days standing up there with Abby standing besides him wagging her tail, a lovely thought I will treasure always." "Funny you should say that that's how I see him to and it would be nice if Tommy his horse was there to and his mum and dad, he will be made up if it is so he must be happy I think, bless him." "Yes I think so Dan, he was brutally honest about many things and will be missed by so many and if you do write this book of yours you must mention his antics and how we all loved each other's company and show how we met and enjoyed each other's lives." Danny smiling says "Yes we certainly did and I will miss him so much as I will miss all of you, the times in the college were so special it will never be repeated will it? It can't believe it is all over now that Niel has gone but we must remember him always he was one of the pieces of the puzzle and I will phone you after the funeral but not until the day after when I am sober ok?" "Yes ok Dan I will have a drink for him to that day, look after yourself and give my love to Malika and speak soon." "Ok Tim and my love to all up there, bye." Tim rang off and Danny smiled and went for a pint in the Whitehouse.

Well the day of the funeral came around so quick and Danny got on an early train to meet Jeff in Newport and a strange thing happened on the platform in Hereford, he was waiting for his train with one of the station attendants and another one came across to speak to Danny. It was another man who worked there named Tim, he spoke "Hello Dan it's Tim, I was wondering if you are on the way to Niel's funeral?" "Why yes Tim I am as a Matter of fact, did you know him then?" Tim with smile on his face says "Yes we all knew him he was a nice man and his dog Abby was a lovely Alsatian, can you give his family all of our sincere condolences and say how sorry we were to hear of his death, a great loss." Danny looked surprised and said "Well, yes of course, I didn't realise he had so many friends, but that's how he was our Niel." "He was well liked here Danny, he was helped by us all at one time or another just like you and he was a great conversationist and was a interesting man, this was such a shock to us all, one of the students told us, it was a real shock I and the old fella here was stunned, so our love to the family please if you don't mind and take care today and if you are having a pint, have one for us, I will speak to you soon." "Yes and thanks Tim" Danny looked amazed which showed how much loved Niel was.

In the station in Newport Danny was sitting in the café on the stand waiting for Jeff to arrive. Next thing he was coming in behind him speaking away "Well hello is that the dodgy Welshman I hear?" Danny smiled and replies "Yes it is, sit down and have a cup of tea and a cake." They grabbed each other's hands and shook them vigorously and Jeff says "Hello Dan are you allright matey?" "Still stunned I suppose and you?" "Likewise I am shocked it's unreal isn't it? one day we were all having a ball and the next thing he is gone, I can't get used to it, he can't be gone it's not true." "I am sorry mate it is and I hope this day will be a tribute to him, he was such a nice person, well we must celebrate his life today and smile as he will be there somewhere I know him ha, ha, so we had best be on the lookout for something tricky he owes me one or two." Jeff laughed and said "Oh yes I won't want to be you matey, no he loved you and the rest of us and had no bad bones In his body and I think he will bring a lot of smiles today to people that can't help but smile at his antics etc. I know I will and so will I have my sad moment for him." "And what about a few pints for him then?" Jeff rubbed his chin and said "Oh I dunno about that …. Why not he would like that, not too many we have got to get the train back tonight mind." "That's what I am worried about mate we will be pissed as parrots I know us ha, ha, or so we should stretch the pints out in case we make fools of ourselves." "They both looked at each other and together said "Naa stay on the beer ha, ha, ha." Danny "As soon as we start drinking we will get the taste that will be it, pissed again and why not if Niel was there he would be pissed to." "True enough, he loved to drink didn't he? especially the cider and the whisky with you in the lounge in Dowdell." "Too right, he used to get me pissed all of the time after the bar shut and he had not been out, those were great days, I will never forget them what about you?" Jeff smiled and says "Yes they were fine times I have missed it since I left and now it won't be long and you will be gone from there, are you looking forward to it?" "You know we used to say we can't wait to leave that college but I will miss it a hell of a lot it will be so strange when I am not there anymore." "Yes your right, I used to say I could not wait to leave but after being home a few days I was lost and wanted to get back there it was a great time of our lives wasn't it?" Danny smiled then said "and if it wasn't for Niel I would have never gone there and we would never have met and life would have been so different, so I have Niel to thank for my life changing for the best and I know he enjoyed it a great deal but he missed Ceri and the boys a hell of a lot or he might still be there now." "Yes he did didn't he, I will always remember the thing with the mobile phone and that old chap, that was so funny, I wish I had been there I still laugh about that now and again and people ask me what I am laughing about and when I tell them they are crippled up laughing, so funny." "Ha, ha, ha, ha, I know what you mean I was crying that day with laughter and so did he after cooling down, god I miss him a good fella." "Yes Dan there will never be another Niel David, never." Just then a porter said that he was ready to put them on the next train to Swansea so the lads stood up Danny grabbed Jeff's elbow and as he did Jeff said the words that he always remembers Jeff for "Elbow." Danny smiled grabbed his elbow and got on the train for Port Talbot.

They arrived at their destination and got off the train and found a taxi outside, got into it and went to the crematorium and stood outside the main entrance waiting for everyone to arrive. Jeff had a fag and Danny said "Still on the death sticks then?" "Yes I still have to have my fag an a cough regularly, we are early, no one here yet we must watch we don't go in with the wrong funeral." "I am worried about doing that to so I will ask when anyone arrives ." Jeff was shivering "It's always bloody cold at these places isn't it?" Danny "Yes I made sure I have got my heavy overcoat on or I would be chattering like you, when you have finished that fag we can stand more in the foyer it will be warmer for us." This they did and they could hear a funeral going on inside and Danny heard the person taking the service say the name Niel. Danny said "Oh dear Jeff I hope that is not our Niel , we can't knacker that up today it's definitely 11'clock I remember Ceri telling me, oh dear, or is it Niel playing tricks on me? you have put that in my head now, bloody hell Jeff, I wish you had not said that now ha,, ha, ha." "It's probably his name was Niel too, don't worry we will see soon enough." People started arriving and of course Danny and Jeff knew none of the family so just stood there until a few arrived. Danny was just about to ask someone if this

514

was the right funeral party when one of them spoke to him "Hello are you friends of Niel's ? I am sorry to ask but I can see you both have got canes and so I assumed you were." Danny replied "Yes we are good friends of his so we must be in the right place then? we came down by train from Hereford and Swindon and had to get a taxi from the train station but glad we got it right." Lady "So were you in the college with Niel?" Danny "Yes but I knew Niel long before that I am from Bettws and we became friends a few years ago when we first met and I know his wife and sons, this must be awful for them? tell me is there some where they are going for a drink later after the funeral?" Her husband answered "Oh yes in Nantyffylon club he went to, are you coming?" Danny "I can't see how we can get there so we may go on home or have a drink in Port Talbot for him." The man then said "If it's only 2 of you we can give you a lift up there if you want no problem." Danny then said to Jeff "I am for it what about you Jeff?" "I don't mind as long as you know what you are doing, I don't want to be stranded in Wales so I will leave it up to you." Danny "Then thank you sir we will take you up on your offer if you don't mind?" Husband and wife said together "No it's no problem i will come and fetch you at the end of the funeral." Danny thanked them and said to Jeff "Well that's ideal Jeff we can get a taxi into Bridgend and catch the train from there with the same tickets, perfect." "Ok matey we can do that then, great." "I may just warn you don't drink the beer here like you do in England, remember the time you visited us last time, pissed all the time you were here so take it easy I am used to it." "Yeah, yeah, take my time it's you that will go off like a train with the beer not me it's your fault if I don't get home tonight so remember that now." The place was very busy by this time and so many people were there and finally the hearse arrived and the family car and it went silent as the coffin was carried into the crematorium and people began to sob with the feeling about Niel was remembered. Danny and Jeff was visibly upset by it all and the amount of people was amazing but not surprising knowing how much people loved Niel. Many tributes were read out and the ceremony was very befitting Niel's memory and all of a sudden it became so sad when his favourite song was played, Bet Middler, The wind beneath my wings, a very sad loving song that Niel adored and this song left people wondering why he has gone and made them all realise they would never see him again, goodbye our loving friend father and husband.

Well Danny and Jeff was grabbed by the people they were getting a lift to the club for his wake and off they went.

In there they sat near the bar to make everything easier and many people came to talk to them, firstly there was neighbours "Hello we are living up by Niel's house, you must have been in college with him were you?" Jeff "Yes we were and became very good friends with him, a lovely man, we will miss him." Woman "Yes he was lovely and so funny with it, his wife will be lost without him and his lads are suffering without him already." Danny "I think he will be missed by many people, what a turn out for his funeral, unbelievable and so many lovely tributes to him." Woman "Yes he was loved by so many and his dog Abby was such a nice dog, now they are both gone, sad so very sad and all those bastards who are so bad never have anything like this happen it's not fair is it?" Jeff "I know what you mean not real is it?" Next thing Ceri came up to talk to the lads "Hello Danny and Jeff, thanks for coming all this way, he thought the world of you lads and he is probably watching you both now smiling at you having a few pints, betting with himself you won't leave sober ha, ha, he always used to laugh at you both and your antics, he loved it, sometimes he would just burst out laughing for nothing and he would then tell me what you have been up to." Danny smiling says "I bet he did and the amount of antics he got up to with us was just as funny, he was a scream a minute and sometimes so dry with it, he had a fantastic sense of humour, he was just as bad and I remember him and I doing the saint David's day Welsh night, we worked our asses off making the huge pan of cowl to eat for the college and it went off brilliantly, he laughed when he done all the vegetables and I was chef and did the cooking, he called me everything that day but we enjoyed it, he went to bed for 2 hours while I cooked as he was so knackered but he thoroughly enjoyed every minute and loads of people came over and ate with us. He felt as if his birthdays and xmas's came all at once he loved every minute of it, that you could tell and later we had a sit down and drank a bottle of whisky and laughed our heads off, remember that Jeff?" Jeff smiling says "Oh yes I do, he was very excited to see so many people in the lounge in Dowdell, he was like a child with all his xmas presents all around him, I got pissed listening to these 2 Welshmen talking and drinking the whisky and me keeping up with them on cans of lager, everyone talked about that day for months it was so nice seeing 2 convicted Welshmen enjoying it so much, a real pleasure to witness." Ceri with a loving smile on her face and a tear in her eye says "Yes that was my Niel he was so funny and excitable and loving husband and father I will never forget him or stop loving him, he was my soul mate lads." Ceri started crying and the lads bowed their heads for a minute and then Danny said "To Niel a man who loved the world and the world loved him, god bless him, I salute you matey where ever you are, he was a very special man and Ceri you must always remember that his sons must be very proud of him as he was of them that I know for certain and I as Jeff will say now he loved you to bits and pieces, he was always saying he was missing you so much, am I right Jeff?" "Oh yes he let us know almost every day how much he missed you, he loved you so very much, it was so obvious to all he met and that's the truth Ceri he was always telling everyone, god bless him he will never be replaced as a good friend to us and a true family man to you and the boys that's for sure." Ceri "I know he was so special, so have something to eat now lads don't go home on an empty stomach and just beer or you will be ill, I will see you both before you leave and thanks again for coming it means a lot to us." Jeff "Ceri it's a pleasure to be here and wild horses wouldn't have kept us away, see you later." She left the lads and Jeff said to Danny "She is gutted I felt sorry for her and the lads today it's not fair matey, she is such a lovely lady, so let's eat, I will get a plate of everything and if we need any more I will go up again ok?" " Yes ok a good idea I think we should eat or we will get drunk easy so go ahead Jeff I will get the beer in." Later on they were still sitting in the same place foddered and half cut with the beer and no sign of them leaving. Danny said "A nice pint here this was Niel's main place to drink and some good shows here to, he loved it here, I came here once when he was doing a thing for guide dogs a bloody good night it was to." "Yes the beer is good here, I can Imagine him after a few of these he would be gut laughing as per usual, he liked a good laugh." "Oh yes he did, I think we had better hit the road after this one don't you think and we can get the 5 30 train and get home before we are unable to walk, yes?" " ok just another pint then off." Jeff staggers to the bar and came back with the beers and they sat and drank them just as Ceri and her sister came to say goodbye. Ceri said "Allright lads everything ok with you?" Danny "Yes thank you." Jeff continued "This beer is very good I bet Niel got a bit worse for wear here a few times?" Ceri laughing says "Oh god yes, he loved it here I often helped him home from here and those stairs going down was a constant worry when he was in a state but he never fell down them amazingly." Ceri's sister says "Yes he used to get paralytic sometimes and I thought he was going to fall down them but he never did." Danny "Are you the sister I spoke to on the telephone the day Niel died?" her sister says "Yes it is, I will remember that day as long as I live it was awful, I am sorry to be the one who had to tell you I know how shocked you were." Danny "That's an understatement believe me I never expected that to come out of your mouth, I think I will always remember that day also and for a few days afterwards, it was as you say awful." Ceri "So what time train will you get, not that I am trying to get rid of you or anything." Jeff "The 5 30 in Bridgend, this is our last pint before we leave can you ask them by the bar to order us a taxi please Ceri?" Her sister offered to do this and Ceri continued to speak "Well it's all over now and I must try and get my life back on track it will not be easy on my own but Niel will not let me surrender to pity so I must get on with it and I hope I will see you all one day in the future." Danny "Ceri you never know, but serious he would want you to get on with your life, you are still young and got a lot to offer those lads of yours so knuckle down and go for it he would want that." Ceri with sad look says "Yes I know he would and I will, I have got to and you 2 look after yourselves, so Danny have you left yet?" Danny "The college you mean? yes I have but still living in Hereford and looking still for a house in Narberth in Pembrokeshire so I will never live in the Bridgend area again, I am now officially divorced she went ahead and done it so a free man now and I still see a lot of Josh and the rest of the children so it's not all bad, I will call you now and again so don't worry about a thing and if I can help in any way please don't hesitate to call me I mean it and look after yourself." Ceri "I will and I hope you get what you want in life, this would be good for you." Ceri says "I know this is a new start for me to, life don't stop for anyone always things to do." Jeff "As you say Danny it's a messy job but somebody's got to do it." Ceri laughs and says "You had Niel bloody saying that in the end, I am struggling with all of this." She bows her head. Danny tearfully says "I know Ceri it's so hard he was a great man but you must get on with it without him and always remember the good times his smiles, his wicked ways and most of all how much he loved you all especially you and that will make it allright, just remember him as he was and smile." Jeff "He is right Niel would be panicking if he seen you like this so keep your chin up and as Danny says remember Niel smiling and playing tricks on everyone. He still makes me smile even now and he has been gone for a while now but he still makes me smile." Ceri lifts her head and says "Yes i know I must and I will always remember you 2 lads with fondness, so look after yourselves." Danny "We will and we will be thinking about you for a long time to come so have a nice life you deserve it Ceri and you are so pretty so keep smiling, promise?" She smiles and puts her arm around her sister and says "Of course I will and thanks for everything." Her sister interrupts "Your taxi is down stairs." Danny "Ok thanks, we must make tracks then give me a hug Ceri." She did this and Danny offers her sister a hug but she hesitates and Ceri said "She had better not her husband is a jealous type ha, ha, look after yourself Danny." Danny "I will and you do likewise and look after those lovely lads, I will see you sometime, goodbye." Ceri with tears in her eyes says "Goodbye Danny and look after yourself, goodbye." She then hugs Jeff and repeats her words and the lads leave with everyone wishing them goodbye.

On the train and the lads had cheered up a little and were yes as you guessed it a little pissed for a change, as they sat there they started to reminisce Jeff said "Well what a tearful day it was, a sad one and bless Niel, it's all over and now I am off home pissed with the dodgy Welshman who is just as pissed as me. Are you allright Dan?" Danny smiling and swaying a little replies "Just about Jeff it's been a hard day trying to be upright and hard for everyone else but it's been so sad saying goodbye to one of the nicest men I have had the privilege to meet in my lifetime, he was so special as are you and Tim and Mandy and Clamper and a lot more who have gone out of my life for good now, but I have got my Malika now is this it, is it all over? I hope not, it's been a ball and we all need each other from time to time don't you think?" "Definitely, we must keep in touch with each other it's something we must do, I will always expect us to keep in touch and visit each other now and again, do you agree?" "Of course I do we must be friends till we die matey, I can't see any way it is ever going to stop, I have had 2 lives and this is the only one I have got left now, the world of darkness for the rest of my life, a new life that is miles behind the life I left behind and it's the same for you and so we became good friends because we understand this just like Niel understood it, you can't live as a seeing man if your blind it's so different and yet similar if you know what I mean like dogs play with dogs and cats play with cats we have become the same way because of our eyesight that can't be helped, that's why we get on so very well we understand what each other are going through, do you know what I mean Jeff?" "Funny enough I do Dan and your right it's up to us to show seeing people we are not different and it's up to them to understand that in the meantime it's you and me against the world and losing Niel has helped me understand that because he is not here anymore and people spoke about him as if he could see again, a person without any disabilities what so ever if you know what I mean he I hope is smiling down on us all and that's the picture I can see in my mind and that comforts me." Danny smiles "Yes I know what you mean but we have all come a long way since we started in the college and Improved Immensely, I was a nervous wreck and afraid to walk outside the house and now look at me I will go anywhere I please even with difficulty but I have got the knowhow and the guts to do it, I can read my mail and answer it with a computer, I can look after myself totally now thanks to that college. I have got fantastic friends who understand me and my problems and friends who I love and trust and yes I mean you to and you promise me we will always be friends?" "No bloody way, ha, ha, ha, only kidding I agree and soon you will have your own house in Pembrokeshire and your new guide dog and of course Malika to cherish and your friends on the end of the telephone, what more could you ask for? That is the spice of life." "Yes your right and I will be leaving you , you get off on the next stop so get yourself ready matey." Jeff gets his things together and Danny stands up to say goodbye to him as he is staying on the train all the way to Hereford, Jeff holds his hand out to shake Danny's hand and says "So long matey, I will miss these days so look after that girl and yourself, I will be seeing you soon." They shake hands and hug and Danny says "The same to you, give Scully a hug for me and look after yourself, I will be seeing you very soon." They separate and Jeff gets off the train and Danny goes off to Hereford.

Back in Hereford he meets up with Malika and they discuss the day and the funeral and go off to bed to sleep it off. The next day and Danny seemed upbeat and goes off to town to shop for some clothes and just too chill out and he bumps into some of his old friends Geraldine and Shaun. They find a bench and talk, Geraldine says "Hi Danny I was sorry to hear about Niel, I hear you went to the funeral, I was so upset about it all, not right, he was such a nice man, did you see Jeff?" Danny replies "Yes he was with me, a good friend and the funeral was good as we all said goodbye to Niel and laughed and cried for him, a lovely day for a lovely man and his wife was gutted and still had smiles for me and Jeff, a lovely woman and it so sad for her." Ger. "I bet it was, so why are you in town today?" Danny "I don't really know I needed to have something to do to keep me sane it was hard yesterday, my life has been full of death and it always gets harder so I take my mind off it as quick as I can, so it's a way of getting my life back to some sort of normality and Malika is in her lectures all day today, I was with Jeff yesterday and we both let ourselves say what we are thinking and it's hitting me as I am going to live in Narberth soon enough with Malika, she don't know anyone there neither do I it is worrying being blind and not know my future and starting again is like being born again it's getting me a little nervous and it will happen soon enough." Geraldine smiles and says "You, you will sort yourself out, I am worried about the people in Narberth they are in for a huge shock especially with your background and I think you will fit in anywhere and bore them with your jokes, only kidding you will be allright and soon you will have your guide dog and that will make a difference and it will work out. I never knew anyone here until I moved in here about ten years ago, it has been a culture trip and I have made a lot of friends here and love my life especially now I have got Shaun it's a dream come true and it will be like that for you to, I don't expect I will see you much anymore so here give me a hug and kiss and look after yourself and enjoy your life." "Yes I will and the same to you and good luck for the future after you get married, poor old Shaun." Geraldine slaps him and Shaun says "Thanks Dan and less of the old." They left and Danny sat on the bench outside his bank and started thinking about his life and his new life in Narberth and everything he had to do.

Well it all went on as good as it could Danny and Malika moved to Narberth and bought a house that was rather large for them and needed a lot of work doing to it but this is what Danny wanted something he could get his teeth into and Malika would enjoy as well and his brother Mel had that very much in mind when he found this house. It was in a perfect place for them near town but not too near and Danny trusted Mel's decisions at all times as Mel was such a loving brother and Danny trusted him Implicitly.

They arrived at this property with only 3 pieces of furniture and they were 2 Man. UTD. Bean bags and the new bed, that's really starting from fresh and they got on with their lives with tremendous difficulty for the first year, it was very hard starting again not knowing anyone but Danny soon befriended a fantastic man who made a difference to his life, his name was Ken Morris, the type of man that Danny linked with who was 20 years his senior but had a tremendous sense of humour, he and Danny became so close they were often seen together in the rugby club like 2 statues in the same place by the bar all of the time and they soon ended up doing many things together and ken was so helpful to him and Malika who he loved intensely as he often said he and Danny played many tricks on people, they became popular as a duo and for 2 years they kept this up and enjoyed their selves until yes you guessed it he became ill and died in less than 24 hours and this was another huge blow to Danny and Malika, Danny was blown away by losing ken and it took a long time for Danny to except he was not going to see ken again but Danny and Malika got their guide dogs at last. Danny had a lovely tall dog Aden and Malika had a dog from Scotland named Billie this helped change their lives and fill in the gaps left by so many in their lives and they live happy and Danny still goes up and has a pint in the crematorium with ken without fail and spends many times at different graves remembering.

Danny had a chance to turn his life around and did this in many hard times that many people would curl up and die but it's not in his nature and he has got good friends around him and loving family. His sons and daughters and his 5 grandchildren Lauren, Rhys and Lacy , Lottie and Alfie that keep him going but he is always trying to think positive, his health is a problem with his diabetes and blindness and a few aches and pains are something he excepts and uses to keep his mind positive and strives to be Normal as he can. Malika is getting on with things in the college.

Well things are swinging along some six years later and things are as simple as Danny and Malika wanted it to be, they often go off with the dogs and are enjoying their lives with the new guide dogs. Aden Danny's dog is a tall cross Labrador and retriever and so is Billie. Aden is soft as a brush and a loving dog as Billie is smaller 2 years younger and is a cheeky lad and so funny but a great guard dog as well as a brilliant guide dog and the 2 dogs love each other to bit's, they called them chunk and stretch. Life has got better and better for Danny and Malika all smiles after all the work of getting the house as they wanted it until one day in October in 2010 when Billie was taken ill and he was ill for around a week, even though the vet tried his very best to help him and then they decided to give him a scan in the vets surgery and it was not good news. One day the vet called and Danny answered the phone and it was devastating as Malika could not answer it and the bomb landed, the vet said "I am sorry but he has got cancer in his spleen and kidneys and I am afraid there is nothing we can do." there was deadly silence and Danny started crying and Malika put her hands to her mouth and said "Oh no what is it Danny ?tell me." Danny fighting the tears back said "I am afraid he has got cancer all through him and there is nothing they can do." Malika screamed out loud in grief "Oh no not Billie, I said there was something wrong, oh my god, oh my god." She ran into the other lounge and cried her eyes out as Danny tried to talk to the vet "I am sorry she is in a bad way and so am I, this is not happening to us, that lovely dog he is to young, he is only 4 years old for god's sake, I don't know what to do now I am devastated." Danny could not talk as he was so upset and the vet said "He is still alive on the operating table, do you both want to say goodbye to him before we turn the machines off? And put him to sleep." "I will ask Malika." Danny puts the phone down and went to see Malika who was still sobbing her heart out and said softly "Malika the vet wants to know if you want to say goodbye to him before they put him to sleep." Malika through the tears said "No, I said goodbye to him before they took him away because I knew I would never see him again." At that they both burst into tears and Danny went back to the phone and spoke to the vet "She has said her goodbyes when you came to pick him up the other day and so did I, so please just give him a pat for us thank you." The vet says "Ok I will make arrangements for his cremation and will keeping contact with you, I am so sorry." Danny still in tears "Ok thank you, I must go now and comfort Malika, she is very distraught, goodbye." Danny put the phone down and went into see Malika and she was so upset and nasty about this, she said "He is only 4 years old and he has got cancer, this is not fair he is too young and a lovely lad, I can't believe it, not Billie." "I know he was a fabulous lad he really was, I will miss him so much he was terrific and I will miss him in the garden all of the time with me, never mind the weather he was always out there with me, he loved that garden and he loved us to especially you and Aden and look Aden is silent he knows I think." Aden came up to Danny and put his head on his lap and that made them cry even more. Danny said "They are sending his body off for cremation and then we will have his ashes back for his burial ok?" Malika said sadly "Yes I will put them in the back garden as he loved being in there and we can see him every day." Danny comforts her and says "Yes I have got a good idea we have put that lovely new Japanese cherry tree out there we can put his ashes beneath it, that would be nice." Malika smiled sadly and replies "Yes that would be nice." They reminisced over that lovely dog all that week as they loved that dog with all of their hearts, this was the saddest day in their lives since they moved there and they would remember Billie like their own child that's how close they got to him especially Malika who went everywhere with him and had so many great times with him, he will never, never be forgotten ever, a loving and delightful dog if ever there was and this would take some getting over.

Well 2 weeks later and Billie's ashes arrived back home where he should be and this was going to be a tear jerking day as Danny had prepared a beautiful spot for Billie under the cherry tree and he had dug the hole for his ashes and put some rubber mats in front of his grave for them to kneel on. Danny suggested that Malika might want to put his dog collar in with him which she agreed with and it was a reasonable day weather wise and so they did it they knew it was going to be so sad and so Danny gave the urn to Malika and guided her to the grave and they knelt down to put his ashes in. Malika placed his lead in the grave followed by his ashes and they both broke their hearts as they did it and then a funny thing happened, Aden pushed his way between them as if to say I want to say goodbye to my pal Billie as well and he sat down between them and there they were all sitting by his grave looking so sad and then Danny covered his grave with earth nicely and they put some fresh flowers there in front of it and then Malika said "Goodbye Billie." Danny "Yes goodbye you lovely dog we will miss you." They cried together for a while and Malika said "I remember him seeing off the cats here in this garden and how funny he was chasing the birds and barking at the squirrels so funny, this was his garden and nothing else except him and Aden was staying here." "Yes I know and I was grateful no cat crap in this garden ha, ha, ha and he was in charge here in this house, so funny, I will miss him terribly." "I am glad I had him even though he died so young it was a pleasure to get to know him and if they had found out when he was a puppy I would not have had that chance, this has broken my heart and he died the day after the anniversary of my husband's road death, I don't believe it." "I know it's uncanny isn't it? he made a difference to my life in his short life, I will never forget him it is going to be hard for us to get used to him not being here now, I hope they are fast with a new dog for you, it will make it easier for us to get over things." Malika "I can wait for a while, it will not be the same as me and Billie, never ever." They tried to get on with their lives after Billie but found it Impossible without him. This time was very sad indeed but things with Danny and Malika took a huge turn in their relationship that would be crucial in their lives. Malika seemed to change after the loss of Billie and she turned very much against Danny, yes this was the beginning of the end of their relationship. Danny felt as if life had gone all to pot with Malika, she became unreasonable towards him and he did not help as he also retaliated when she spoke to him like she was talking to him like he was a common rat and this was to continue to breaking point.

A couple of months went by and on the 25 October he went down to Bridgend to meet his mate Phil to go to some concerts on that day and the 25 of October they went up to Saint David's hall in Cardiff to see Jeff Beck and stayed in Phil's that night then Danny went up his cousins for the day while Phil went to work and Danny and Mary his cousin was going to put some flowers on his son Nathan's grave and to his mums and brothers grave also to clean the grave stones up a little. They were sitting in his cousins house having a cup of tea and Danny's mobile phone rang and he answered it, it was his nephew Jarred calling and he had never called him before ever on his mobile, he said to Danny "Hi Uncle Danny I am afraid I have got some bad news.... Dad died this morning about forty minutes ago." It went silent then Danny screamed out "No, no, no, not Mel please, not Mel please, oh my god Jarred please tell me it's not true? Oh my god poor Mel how? Why? What happened Jarred??" "He has been ill for a day or 2 and he went up to the hospital with a bad stomach and this morning he was found dead by Abby and she tried to get him around and when the paramedics got here they tried for 30 minutes but it was too late he was gone, I am sorry Danny." Danny and Jarred were in tears on the phone to each other and Danny said "How is Abby? She must be devastated finding her father like that." "She is ok now but it has come as a huge shock to us all and the day before his mother's birthday, we are devastated Dan, I will have to go I can't keep talking it is so hard for me at this moment, I will speak tomorrow if you don't mind?" "Yes I understand Jarred I will speak to you then bye." Marry came into the room and said "Oh dear Danny what is it? it's Mel isn't it?" Danny wiping a tear away says "Yes he died this morning and he was so fit, never went to the doctor, I can't believe it, he never drank smoked or anything like that, he went up the doctors the other day and his doctor got his file out and there was one piece of paper in it with his name address and telephone number on it and the doctor never knew him, there will be an autopsy now to find out what killed him, what am I going to do he was the last of my Immediate family, I am the only one left out of six of us, why him? He was such a lovely man, not a bad bone in his body, a loving man and so trustworthy." Mary looking sad "Poor Mel he was a real credit to the human race, such a lovely man I can't believe it I really can't, so what are you going to do today Dan?" "Well I am not going to the concert of Robert Plant now I will phone Phil and tell him and head home I think, I must go and tell them down Pencoed if you don't mind taking me there, then I will get on the train and go home. This has devastated me I thought he would live forever at least he would out last me, I can't believe it Mary I feel awful now and the day before mums birthday, I must get a grip as Mel would not like me getting ill, I will miss him even though we did not agree about religion we were great mates and brothers and loved each other." Mary said "Yes I know Dan, I will take you to see everyone no problem."

Well Danny went home and he told Malika and she was so shocked and upset at the loss of Mel and Danny felt lost because he had no one of his Immediate family left and could not think how he was going to manage not having Mel to talk to ever again. Mel helped Danny with any problems he had like financial Matters insurances etc. and he would help Danny whenever he needed him no problem, now he had absolutely nobody from that day on this was going to have a profound effect on Danny. Danny went into a different world and was very troubled now this was a death too far for him and it effected his brain and Danny started to be very strange for months after including believing that if he stopped being friends with everyone he loved they would go away and never die if they did not have anything to do with him they could not hurt him by dying. And so eventually he insulted all the people he loved and thought now they would not hurt him so he fell out with them one by one not meaning to be as nasty as he did including Malika, his best friends Phil Evans, Alan Burfitt and even Jeff but jeff took no notice of his insults.

The next day Jarred phoned him "Hi Dan are you allright?" "Not really I can't get him out of my mind he was such a real nice man, there will be hundreds in his funeral, he was loved so much by many, how is everyone with you?" Jarred "Mum is ok, it hasn't hit her yet, Abby is ok and Seth is fine now, I am devastated and so sad he was always there for us all, now he is not going to be there ever again but he is asleep waiting to come back to us, he was a real fun dad, I used to say to him as you know he used to do many funerals and I always said he puts the fun in funeral ha, ha, that was dad. I must come down to you and have a chat this week if you don't mind, I need to talk to you about all of this is that ok with you?" Danny smiling says "Yes of course Jarred of course you can any time you want absolutely anytime I am here most of the time and you can have some biscuit's ha, ha, Mel used to come to see us and he would go through a packet of biscuit's and he didn't half drink some tea ha, ha, ha." Jarred laughing says "Yes I know he loved his biscuit's and mar used to stop him buying any unless you were coming down and she would send him to get one packet in the local shop." "I know I will look forward to you coming down and we can have a good chat on our own ok? And as soon as you know the result of the post mortem and the day of his funeral let me know ok?" "Yes ok Dan speaks soon." Danny sat and smiled thinking about his brother Mel as you couldn't help but do so, he was a practical joker and was always telling jokes.

Well a few days later and Jarred came to see Danny and he came through the door he and Danny hugged each other and cried a little tear. Danny affectionately says "How are you Jar? Hope things are getting better for the family?" They sat down and Jarred said "He died of a aneurism in his stomach that was the findings of the post mortem and the funeral will be known later today, I will phone you." "A simple thing did this to my big brother well, well, poor Mel he had a big part in my heart you know." "Yes I know he broke his heart when Dennis died, he was a lad mind he used to love it in Neyland and was always looking out for any one of us, so funny a loving man and dad broke his heart with what happened to uncle Lyndon and how he died because of that man, I really wanted to kill that man who ran off with his wife and daughter and sent threatening notes through the door to uncle Lyndon, I mean It I really wanted to kill that man for what he done, it broke dad it really did, I could see it in him. Dad used to tell us lots about his life as a boy and so many things that went on in Bettws, how granddad made him fight his battles even though he was going to get a hiding off the other bloke and how he became a witness at the age of 15 and not much later he moved down to Milford to be a pioneer with Dave Hopkins ." Danny smirked and said "Jarred the truth is he went to Milford to get away from his father, just like I did, I used to go and see Mel as much as I could to get away from my father's grip but Mel would never say so and it was the best thing he did, he loved Milford Haven he really did, he was always so happy there, he used to say if he went away that he was so happy as soon as he passed the sign welcome to Pembrokeshire he loved it and nothing would drag him away from there and he loved Marice and you children." Jarred replied "Do you know Dan he never ever said he loved us never, I wish he had you know." "Oh I can tell you he loved you all to bit's, he was always talking about you all but you must remember Mel was brought up in his father's shadow, he used to kill chickens and rabbit's for meat from the age of twelve and was expected to do this without blinking a eye, he was brought up hard just like me and there was a huge lack of love in my dad's life just hardness in everything he done and it rubbed off. We brothers never knew how to say I love you it was not the thing with us, Mel would kill a rabbit without batting a eyelid and thought it was normal to do this a way of life, I remember when Lyndon was young he had a rabbit he had to look after called thumper a huge breeding buck and Lyndon looked after this rabbit until one day he was gone and we were sitting by the table on a Sunday eating dinner and Lyndon asked "So what happened to thumper then dad?" Dad calmly replied "You have just been eating him boy." And carried on eating as if it was the norm and Lyndon started crying and dad sent him to bed , That's how it was in our house there was not a lot of love only from my mother and it oozed from her, so Mel thought that was the norm we were considered sissies if we didn't , but you must have seen it in Mel's eyes that he loved you all very much." "Yes I remembered being up there with mum and dad when we were little and I don't think granddad was talking to dad for some reason, that was funny." "Your granddad was more like Hitler and he made you believe what he did never mind what and I was glad to get away from him and I am afraid the witnesses altogether." "I know I remember dad being annoyed about you getting disfellowshipped from them he always said it was so unfair." "Well it was, I remember I was married and a few weeks before I had just lost Nathan my son in a cot death and a witness I considered a total fool Jim Kitchen called a meeting with the witnesses and me and my dad to answer the fact I was not married to my then wife when she conceived so wanted me kicked out, this he managed to do and even my dad was furious, I had just lost my son and he done this within a few days, that was such an awful thing to do don't you think so? I was suffering enough and he added to my sorrow by doing this , if that's what religion is all about then they can stuff it , sorry." "Yes I agree dad was not a happy man when that happened either, his name was Jim Kitchen I remember it to this day dad telling me his name will always stick in my mind, dad was everything to us kids and I never knew how much hurt you have when you lose someone so close, this has destroyed me, I can Imagine how you have felt with all the close people you have lost." "I am the only one left now, I have lost 3 brothers in 9 years and my mum and dad and my eyesight along with it, there's one thing for sure now I am definitely next ha, ha, ha." "If you put it like that ha, ha, I am looking at the picture of you and Dennis, Lyndon and dad, i wonder if you can get a copy of this for me please?" "Of course I can, I sent Mel a copy just like that a few months ago you know? that's the only picture we had together it was in Lyndon's wedding I was so ill I thought we should do this as I didn't think I was going to be around much longer and this was the only time we were together in a happy occasion since Mel got married some thirty years ago, that's how far apart we became." "Never, that's so sad isn't it? dad felt it too I think I wonder if some time we can get together and visit where dad was born and where he was brought up and where he grew up and a bit more about him? Where he went to school, because I don't know anything about my dad's life when he was young." "No problem Jarred I know I am blind but I can still take you there and show you where he lived and the schools he went to and where he spent his life, it would be a pleasure mate it will bring some memories back to me also, as children Mel and I were good friends we played practical jokes on everyone and he was then the same as he was always." "Dad used to get me involved with music, he loved music, he married mam only if she liked the Beatles and after the wedding she told him she didn't really, he always told me to listen to the lyrics and they all told a story, he was fascinated with it." "Well I know he was the person who got me interested in music especially the Beatles and buddy holly and the beach boys etc. We used to drive dad mad all of the time with it and many times was ordered not to play that music in the house, he loved music so do I as you can see by the collection I have got, Mel and I used to sometimes swap albums as he did not like that one and so we used to swap and when I came down Milford to stay with him and Dave Hopkins we used to always play music, in fact he got Dave into the Beatles as you know Dave was quiet and not much fun until he met Mel and Mel dragged him out of himself and Dave was a lovely man, have you got in touch with him yet?" "No I am trying to track him down." "Well he is living in Scotland now, he will be devastated when he finds out about Mel, they were so close for many years." "I will look forward to meeting up with Dave again we were together in Carmarthen for a long time in 1969 and we got on well, did you know us boys never called my father dad he insisted on being called Ray or Raymond not dad?" Jarred said "Never that's unusual Flippin heck I would never call dad Melvyn he would not have that ha, ha, ha." "We were brought up in unusual circumstances ,the only love there was from my mum, she was a lovely person and mum and dad were like chalk and cheese nothing alike at all, I can't understand why she married him, I really can't." "You don't have much nice to say about granddad do you? Ha, ha, ha." "Oh he had his good bit's but he was more for religion and his way of life it got me down, there was no real family life other than what mum tried to provide, sorry Jarred, that's how it was." "Oh that's ok I understand but we must go and see where he lived before he came to Milford and met mum." "No problem I will do that, I will look forward to it." "Uncle Dan we have had a chat in the family and we want you to come in the funeral cars as you are a big part of our family and we want you there and we have had the money from you through the post and will be getting something special with regards the flowers ok?" "I want to ask you something that is delicate now, I as you know am blind and I feel it is not real unless I can approach Mel's coffin and put my hands on it, then it will become real to me, can you understand that? I am not having any feelings it is not real until I have put my hand on the coffin, I did it in Lyndon's funeral but I did not do it in Dennis's funeral and wished I had because it did not feel real to me." "I understand Dan I really do and this is no problem at all we will sort this out between me and you on the day and we want you in the front with the family ok?" "Of course, thank you, I will miss Mel very much he was everything to me a great loss, I have shed a lot of tears this week over him he was such a loving man." They sat silent for a minute trying to compose themselves then Jarred said "Dan if you need anything doing just let me know, I mean that, I really do I would want you to call me promise?" "I do, thank you Jarred I will and if you need someone to talk to don't hesitate to come and see me or call me." "Thanks I will miss dads jokes very much and I will see you in the funeral ok? I am off now." "Yes ok, I remember cleaning up dirty jokes and telling Mel and he would clean them up a little more and by that time they were not funny anymore ha, ha, ha." "Yes I know he did that all of the time so funny, well I will see you Uncle Dan, bye." Jarred left and Danny sat there lost in thought.

The day of the funeral came and they all went down to Milford Haven to the Kingdom hall and there were hundreds of people there it was like as if Milford town all came there.

After they all went to Narberth crematorium where they read you a lot of things Mel got up to including playing tricks on everyone and the fun he was and of course his jokes and at the end they had organised that the curtain was not to shut because Abby his only daughter could not handle this happening and Danny stood up with his daughter Kelly and proceeded to approach the coffin draped with lilies from Danny and Mel's family, this was such a difficult thing for Danny and it showed he put his hand on the coffin and smiled then he put his other hand on the coffin and burst in to tears and so did his daughter and it was told that all the family and his many friends were torn to tears at that sight. Danny at this time thought his heart was going to explode and Danny felt something click in his head, this became a problem for him shortly after the loss of Mel.

Outside as he stood to pull himself together he was approached by a man speaking in a Indian accent he said "You must be Mel's brother, I can tell you look very much like him, I am a friend of Mel's I met him quite by accident some years ago and he has had a great influence in my life, he took me in as a friend without question and I love him for that he never condemned me, I was in the army for many years and a lot of trouble to many including the government and police but he never turned me away and treated me like a human being, he was an amazing man, he really was and a credit to the human race, I have come all the way down from Birmingham to be with him today and I got all the flowers cost price from the flower markets in Birmingham especially for him, he was my friend and my saviour he really was and I want to shake your hand and tell you , you were so lucky having Mel as your brother." They shook hands and Danny smiled and said " And I think you were so lucky meeting my brother he was some man he was a rock and a good friend to everyone and I am so proud of him always and I am so pleased to meet you an hope you have a great future now and remember all he stood for and if you are ever down here come and visit me sometime promise?" "I certainly will and look after yourself and god bless Mel." This turned out to be a very sad day and everything went off well and Mel had one hell of a send-off.

525

Well it was also Malika's birthday and Dan's best friend Phil was down for the funeral to support Dan and it was his birthday a few days earlier and so they decided to go off for a nice Chinese meal and it was on Dan a treat for them all .

Well time has gone by and Danny and Malika are missing little Billie very much and Malika is awaiting a new dog and has now got used to using the cane again although she feels it is going backwards and the loss of Billie has left a gap in their lives and Danny through loss of Mel felt so alone, it seems to have made him feel as if there is no one left on his side although he has got his children he is on his own at all times and is having trouble getting over his brothers and he cannot sleep at all in the nights. Danny will get over all of these problems in time just like he has always had to do and he hopes things will come back to as normal as it can with the new grandchild and 2 more on the way things are looking up for him.

He decided to go and visit his old friends Tim and Mandy this he did and had a fantastic time and on his return he found out that Malika was off to walk a new guide dog named Ziggy with a little bit of luck this is going to work and they will have their house back to normal, well almost as it will be a long time before they really get over Billie and Mel. The future looks bright for them even though they have got many obstacles to overcome.

Yes it happened Malika got her new dog Ziggy a beautiful black Labrador very bouncy and funny and his new granddaughter was born and was named Lottie Georgina and his new grandson Alfie Lee was next to be born.

Well things didn't Improve with Malika and Danny and they grew apart even more, different cultures set in and Danny had many issues to contend with in his head that made things worse for Malika as Danny was acting in a funny way, has he cracked up at last with all the death that surrounded him? and it became Impossible to carry on the relationship and this was killing them both so much love but no time for each other, yes, it happened they went their separate ways, Malika moved out into town and Danny was left alone in the house with Aden, this was devastating for Danny and he became very depressed even more now, he then cracked up and thought he was going mad and pushed everyone away so as not to suffer losing anyone he loved as he felt one more loss and he would top himself and so proceeded to insult everyone he loved because he thought in his head if he got rid of them even though he loved them they would not die and if they did he would not be so close to them as to suffer and probably commit suicide but this was not Danny and so he was getting help through his doctor and a private consultant about his mental state and he thought he was going to kill himself if his life did not change. This was a problem he should have shared with someone rather than try and solve it himself but it was now too late as his friends disowned him after the way he treated them and who could blame them. Danny now has got over this some 4 years later and has got himself back to normal but of course it is too late now and he regrets things and hopes one day he will gain their trust in him again as he was not himself after all the death he suffered and felt his life had been ruined for him and he is going to be alone for the rest of his life and this is still the same to this day. He loves Malika, they just can't live in the same house together.

Well at the other end of the country in Swindon Jeff was having the same problem, he had a lovely lady named Liz move in with him a good few years earlier and lo and behold the same thing happened to him, he was also now on his own and so Jeff and Danny decided to get together in Danny's place for a holiday and a piss up if the truth be known.

Jeff arrived and they shook hands vigorously and patted each other on the shoulder and Jeff said "Well hello matey, hows things then?" "I am fine really but depressed how things have ended up for me with Malika leaving me and if you are going to ask why, then I don't know so leave it there, so what happened with you and Liz I thought it was a match made in heaven." "That's exactly what I thought about you and Malika, you were so much in love, but as regards me and Liz I will say the same, don't ask as I don't know." Well the week was a huge drinking occasion and went too quick and on the last night Jeff and Danny were sitting feeling sorry for themselves and Jeff in quiet voice said "Can you tell me this record that is always going on in my head and find it in your collection, it goes like , da,d,d,d, it's just an empty space and you coming back to me is against all odds dee, dee, dee." Danny face lit up and he says "Gotcha , it's Phil Collins song why? I will find it now." Danny found it and put it on as Jeff stopped talking to Danny. Danny said "This is it How can I just let you walk away, let you leave without ...." Jeff "This is it ...your the only one who knew me at all, so take a look at me now, it's just an empty space ... this reminds me when I was sitting In my bungalow and she left taking her furniture and me sitting on a little stool I made in school and a small coffee table ha, ha, my fault, I gave my furniture to Mark as I never thought for one minute we were ever going to finish it all and we were both to blame and this bit kills me, just a memory of your face, this is so sad and reminds me of that awful time I lost Liz." Jeff and Danny went quiet for a long time while the song finished and Jeff said "Can you play this again?" Danny did this and said "It's amazing I am thinking the same about Malika while listening to this song, as a Matter of fact I was playing this album when I first met Malika when I got back from your place the first time we got together and she was playing the exact same album in her room, oh my god, this brings back some loving memories between me and Malika, if you ask me what happened I will answer I am damned if I know it just happened I cannot explain it so don't ask, but it was probably my fault." "And if you ask me the same question I will say the same I still love Liz with all my heart but we could not live under the same roof together and I am missing her very much, this is not real and it has happened to us at the same time, it's uncanny isn't it?" "Yes it is, I wonder if I or you for that Matter will ever meet another girl like we just lost again? The way we are now it seems Impossible." "Well I am having another can and off to bed before I get more depressed." "Yes I will have another bottle too, but it is nice to reminisce isn't it? I have lost a lovely woman and so have you, we are back together again the 2 amigo's and once it was the 3 amigo's, to Niel." They clanged their drinks together and Danny said "Bless our Niel I miss that man so much, he would probably start taking the Mickey out of us now and have us laughing our heads off, oh here is another song that kills me now Malika has gone Phil Collins other song, Separate Lives, this is a tear jerker I only wished Malika and me had worked it out for good, my god." Jeff says "Oh yes this is a tear jerker isn't it? my Lizzy has gone and left me and I still love her but I am lucky we are still very much good friends and see each other often." The boys toast again as they get more drunk "To the girls we have just lost and still love Malika and Liz." Danny said "I am lost now without her and must pull myself together and get on with my life, so much lost in the last few years and need some stability in my life that includes cutting down on my drink." "I can't believe how much you have already cut It down you have amazed me , no drinking in the day and only 4 pints in the evening, this is not good." "Well it is for me and this is carrying on I mean it, the drink is not in charge of me anymore and it is 4 good original beers in a bottle, I must look after myself now and try to live forever and enjoy life. I wasted so much of it with drink and before you ask that was not the fault of me and Malika drifting apart because this regime has been going on for a few years now and it is good for me.

The lads drank into the early hours in the morning they have not done this for many years as they felt this was not warranted since they were responsible people now they have got partners to think about, but not anymore. Jeff actually got up that morning and got on the train and could not wake Danny up but phoned him from the train, Danny answered it in his bed still Danny "Hello?" Jeff replied "Hello matey, hows you then?" Danny rubbing his eyes "Jeff where are you? I have slept late I think." "Yes you have I tried to wake you up but I could get nothing out of you so I am on the train going home and thought I would ring you to see if you are ok?" "Yes I am matey, sorry, I should have got up and got you some tea before you left but I am still pissed." "No problem mate I made myself a cuppa and made you one also but could not wake you up, I am still pissed also how I made it I don't know I feel like a nodding dog in the back of a car, how many did we drink yesterday? My god I can feel we drank too much." "Your not kidding Jeff we nearly hit the record yesterday and we ended up like 2 sad men reminiscing about the girls and it was so close to the heart and the truth came out didn't it? but we must get on with our lives now and pull ourselves together and start a new life or we will end up bitter and nasty with ourselves so I think we must find a new adventure like another college to go to, and go boldly where no man has gone before, I need some more I.T. and other things you need it very much as you are a clot on the computer and still use super nova, it's not in existence any more so let's search for another college to learn some more and maybe you never know, find some girlies as you say, what do you think?" Jeff paused for a while then answered in a excited voice "Why not?" Danny smiling all over his face said "Well it's a messy job but somebody's got to do it."

THE END

I would like to dedicate this book to some people that made a great deal to me and passed away in the first 9 years after I went blind. Some lovely people I will miss till the day I die Mr. Melvyn Duckfield died aged 63, Dennis Duckfield died aged 54, Lynden Duckfield died aged 41, three loving brothers so kind and warm who died so very young, my loving cousin Louisa died aged 30 I miss you all so very much and of course a fantastic friend to me Niel David died aged 44, a man who was my friend with no catches what you seen is what you got, thank you for being my friends and brothers. Also 2 beautiful guide dogs that made such a difference to my and Malika's lives Billie and Aden we will miss you both so much for the rest of our lives. Aden my beautiful guide dog died in 2015 aged 9 died of Limes disease caught by accident in Narberth and I am missing him so very much he was a wonderful guide dog and so handsome everyone who met him fell in love with him as I did. Goodbye my lovely dog and thanks to everyone in this country I had lots of fun and love with him as you helped me and many others to get our lives back to some normality by putting money into guide dogs for this reason, if I wrote what I and Aden done in our lives together this book would be a thousand pages long as I will remember him with such happiness and his love for me was unconditional.

I now have a new guide dog named Blakey who is so much like Aden and thanks to you all I can get on with my life with my new companion and friend, he is wonderful. And thanks to the guide dog association who work tirelessly to make my life worth living.

I also want to thank the staff and friends at the Royal National College for the blind in College road in Hereford who through their love and care for me and many others saved my life without a doubt.

Lots of thanks to Sue and staff of the Ivy Bush public house Narberth for the cover photo. To this day some 5 years after all his problems Danny still lives a single life and jeff something the same and life will always be enjoyed by the both of them and one day you never know they might end up back in some college again where they had so much fun and all the adventures will start again, watch this space.

Printed in Great Britain
by Amazon

35706485R00301